THE ENCYCLOPEDIA OF
TRAINS & LOCOMOTIVES

THE ENCYCLOPEDIA OF
TRAINS & LOCOMOTIVES

FROM 1804 TO THE PRESENT DAY

DAVID ROSS

THUNDER BAY
P · R · E · S · S
San Diego, California

Thunder Bay Press
An imprint of the Advantage Publishers Group
5880 Oberlin Drive, San Diego, CA 92121-4794
www.thunderbaybooks.com

THUNDER BAY
P · R · E · S · S

Copyright © Amber Books Ltd., 2007

All notations of errors or omissions should be addressed to Thunder Bay Press,
Editorial Department, at the above address. All other correspondence (author
inquiries, permissions) concerning the content of this book should be addressed to
Amber Books Ltd., Bradley's Close, 74–77 White Lion Street, London N1 9PF,
United Kingdom. www.amberbooks.co.uk.

Library of Congress Cataloging-in-Publication Data

The encyclopedia of trains : from 1804 to the present day / David Ross.
    p. cm.
  Includes index.
  ISBN 978-1-59223-783-8
  1. Railroads--Encyclopedias. 2. Locomotives--Encyclopedias. I. Ross, David (David
Southerland) II. Title.
  TF9.R65 2007
  625.1003--dc22
                        2007011569

Project Editor: Sarah Uttridge
Picture Research: Kate Green
Design: Zoë Mellors

Printed in China

1 2 3 4 5 11 10 09 08 07

CONTENTS

Introduction   6

CHAPTER ONE   **The Steam Days**   10
1804–1900

CHAPTER TWO   **Experimental Times**   66
1901–1924

CHAPTER THREE   **Investing in the Future**   128
1925–1935

CHAPTER FOUR   **The War Years**   190
1936–1949

CHAPTER FIVE   **The High-Speed Era**   252
1950–1961

CHAPTER SIX   **Technological Changes**   312
1962–1981

CHAPTER SEVEN   **The Modern Era**   368
1982–Present

Glossary   436

Index   442

INTRODUCTION

Railways go back a long way. Some historians consider their origins to lie in the rutted cart- or sledge-tracks of ancient cities. A more authentic and traceable use of railways is found in association with mining. Digging out minerals from under the ground produced heavy loads of ore or coal, whose haulage required desperately hard physical labour. Using wheeled trucks on rails made it possible for a pony, or a person, to move heavier loads at greater speed, and thus speed up production and improve efficiency. The first written mention of railways is in a Latin textbook on mining, *De Re Metallica,* published in Basel, Switzerland, in 1556. By then, up-to-date mines across Europe were using this technology. But the means of haulage was by animals, humans or gravity. Although a form of steam engine was devised before the end of the seventeenth century, and attempts to build 'steam

Preserved 'single-driver' 4-2-2 No. 1 of England's Great Northern Railway, built in 1870, makes a call at Hitchin in Hertfordshire with a special train, on a run from London to Doncaster, in August 1838.

The preserved Great Western 'King' class locomotives are a popular choice on steam-hauled excursions: this is No. 6024 King Edward I passing Henley-in-Arden, on its journey to Stratford on Avon.

carriages' were made in the second half of the eighteenth century, it was not until 1804 that a steam-powered engine ran successfully on rails.

This book reveals how, in the following two centuries, the range and pace of development accelerated with extraordinary speed. The 'push' of the railway defined our machine-based, technologically inventive society, not only through its epoch-making application of self-propelling machines but because it provided the opportunities and infrastructure for an ever-widening range of industry and commerce. Railways were the first big modern business corporations, pioneering many

aspects of commercial life, from accounting systems and record-keeping to advertising and public relations. Millions of private lives were transformed, as railways made it possible to travel to work, to go away on holiday, and to distribute products of all kinds on a far wider and cheaper basis than ever before.

In its first decades, the railway enjoyed a monopoly of powered land transport. But the wave of industrial and scientific progress that it had initiated swept on past it. Even as railway locomotives were becoming bigger and more powerful, capable of moving more people and

Canadian VIA Rail express – a Montreal Locomotive Works FPA-Y Bo-Bo diesel-electric with a train of tilting Talgo-type coaches at Montreal, in August 1984.

greater loads, the compact 'internal combustion' engine was developed. This could move only a handful of people or a lightweight load, but it was free-ranging, personal and private, while the train was confined to its rails, impersonal and public. At the end of the nineteenth century, some people were already prophesying the end of the railway. Many lines did go, killed off by road transport as well as increasingly fierce competition among rival railway companies. Rail transport was no longer at the leading edge of industrial progress, and with the advent of improved petrol engines and of air transport, the train seemed increasingly to be the dinosaur of technology. Constrained by their heavy investment in steam power and their strong links with the coal industry, the railways seemed old-fashioned, most of their equipment obsolescent if

not obsolete. Many companies experimented with electrical and internal combustion motive power, but steam remained overwhelmingly the main form of rail haulage until the late 1940s in the United States and the 1950s in other countries.

The second half of the twentieth century saw a renaissance of the railway. Among the factors behind this were the great growth of population in many countries, with the increase found in new conurbations and sprawling cities, and the increasing awareness of ecological factors and the need to use energy economically. But the railways' embrace of new technology was vital – after a spell as a sooty Cinderella, the train emerged as a fast, comfortable, clean and reliable alternative to travelling on ever-more congested roads and to waiting around in overcrowded and delay-prone airports. This was achieved by far more than a change of motive power – every aspect of operations was reinvented, from signalling and communications to catering and the transformation of city termini into shopping centres. For bulk freight transit, the train retained all its old advantages and was helped by computerized monitoring of loads and train movements. The part played by railways in the transport system of the world is vital and uncontestable, but as part of a more integrated pattern than before.

Today railways excel in urban mass transit, in medium-distance fast inter-city links, and in long-haul and bulk freight, but present success is no guarantee of future survival. In the earliest years of steam locomotion, the canal proprietors felt able to look coolly, even patronizingly, at the few snorting, ungainly, breakdown-prone steam engines that clanked along with a few wagons. Within two decades, the railway had superseded the canal. In terms of performance, some observers feel that

wheel-on-rail is close to the maximum of exploitation, though surprises are always possible. Meanwhile, work continues in some countries on friction-free means of transportation. But new railways are still being constructed, and, worldwide, more research and development work is being done on railways than ever before. We can be sure that there will be many interesting developments to add to the remarkable story recorded in these pages.

NOTE ON SPECIFICATIONS
The specification panels give key dimensions of locomotive types, in metric and Imperial measurements. In some cases, full information is not available. Unless otherwise indicated, the details refer to the original members of the class: later modifications often made large alterations.

The notations of wheel arrangements are explained under 'Wheel Arrangements' in the Glossary.

The sleek, polished lines of the German Railways' ICE-3 train set are intended to enhance its speed and minimize wind resistance, external air noise, as well as for appearance.

CHAPTER ONE

THE STEAM DAYS

1804–1900

When the world's first public railway, the Stockton and Darlington line in England, opened in September 1825, it had a single locomotive, the still preserved *Locomotion*. Its builders, Robert Stephenson & Co., of Newcastle, had set up the first purpose-built locomotive works in the same year. In October 1829 the Liverpool and Manchester Railway, due to open in 1830, organized trials to find a locomotive that could fulfil its conditions, which included pulling a 20-ton train at a steady 10 miles (16km) per hour, and completing a 70 mile (113km) course without breakdown. Only one contender passed the test, the Stephensons' newly built *Rocket,* but with such success that the future of the locomotive was assured.

By 1840, the basic design of the steam locomotive was established, and the railway industry was international. At first intended as short-distance coal-hauling lines (as feeders to canal or sea transport), railways were now the prime medium for long-distance passenger transport on land, and the first trans-continental lines were being planned. Locomotive designers and builders had to respond to the demand for more power and greater speed. Refinements to the basic machine still had to be made. Astonishingly, it was not until the 1860s that most locomotives began to be fitted with brakes. Improved technology brought driving wheel brakes from the mid-1860s, though even in 1889 about half of American locomotives had only tender brakes. By the end of the century, however, locomotive equipment and performance were steadily improving.

A Class 51 two-cylinder compound 4-4-0 of Indonesia's PNKA system stands on shed. The big low-pressure cylinder is conspicuous. This was a long-lived class, and some gave more than 70 years of service.

THE FIRST RAILWAY LOCOMOTIVE

Richard Trevithick (1771–1833), son of a Cornish mine captain, was the first man to successfully build relatively small, high-pressure steam engines. Before him, they had been large, fixed machines, used primarily for pumping water out of mine shafts, and dependent on atmospheric pressure rather than steam pressure. Trevithick had experimented with steam-powered road vehicles, and, as a man familiar with colliery tramroads, he formed the ambition to produce a

'travelling engine' – the word 'locomotive' did not come into use until the 1820s – to run on rails. His engines were adaptable enough to be fixed on a frame to drive pumps or winding engines, or to be put on wheels.

While Trevithick was installing fixed engines in Wales, he built the first steam locomotive as the result of a wager between two Welsh ironmasters, one of whom staked 500 guineas on the ability of a steam engine to pull 9.8 tonnes (10 tons) of pig iron

along his colliery tramroad. Trevithick responded eagerly to the challenge, and on 21 February 1804 the prototype of all locomotives duly performed the task and won the wager. It was a primitive and clumsy machine with a single cylinder and a piston of enormous length (137.2cm/54in), and a flywheel was needed to compensate for the lack of a second piston. Its designer walked in front of it, and stopped it when necessary to put more coal into the firebox. Its wheels broke the

brittle cast-iron track, and after one or two further displays, it was taken off its wheels, the cog-wheel drive mechanism was removed, and it was put to good work as a static engine.

Though Trevithick built further locomotives, none was a commercial proposition. Others would improve on his design, but his contribution of producing an efficient steam-pressure engine, and of showing what was possible with it, was fundamental. Detailed specifications are not known.

'PUFFING BILLY' WYLAM COLLIERY

War with Napoleonic France had dramatically pushed up the price of horses and horse-feed, and this encouraged Christopher Blackett, owner of Wylam Colliery in Northumberland, and his engineer William Hedley, to build three locomotives in 1813 to haul coal. Blackett had taken a close interest in Trevithick's pioneering efforts of almost 10 years before, and had carried out controlled experiments to establish that 'smooth' wheels on smooth rails could develop tractive power. This was the really important aspect of these engines, known as 'Puffing Billy', 'Wylam Dilly', and 'Lady

Mary' – all originally built with flangeless wheels to run on L-shaped tracks. Despite what Trevithick's locomotives had shown, many engineers believed that a cog-rail, or chain-hauling, was the only way to obtain load-hauling traction, especially on a gradient. Hedley's work had a strong influence on George Stephenson, engineman at the nearby Killingworth Colliery, who would start building 'smooth-wheeled' locomotives of his own design from 1814.

With primitive single-flue boilers and a cog-gear drive, the Wylam engines were not very efficient but marked a real step forward in locomotive design. Even at their very low operating speeds, they tended to break the brittle cast-iron tracks, and for a time each was mounted on two four-wheel trucks in order to spread their weight. In these trucks, some

writers have seen the first bogies, but the extent and method of their articulation is not clear.

One of the lessons that George Stephenson learned from the Wylam engines was that it was not enough to build an effective locomotive: the track also had to be right, and he worked on

developing strong rail joints and strengthening the rails. With further modifications, the colliery engines continued their slow but steady work until 1862, and, remarkably, 'Puffing Billy' and 'Wylam Dilly' are both preserved, in London and Edinburgh respectively.

BOILER PRESSURE: 3.5kg/cm² (50psi)
CYLINDERS: 250mm (10in) diameter;
500mm (20in) stroke
WHEELS: 90cm (36in)
TOTAL WEIGHT: 8.8 tonnes (8 tons)

The boiler and frame of 'Puffing Billy' are returned to the Science Museum, London, at the end of warfare in Europe, 20 June 1945.

NO. 1 *LOCOMOTION* 0-4-0 STOCKTON & DARLINGTON RAILWAY (S&D)

For the success of the steam locomotive, still a very new beast, it was vital that associated aspects of the railway kept pace in development. One of the most important features of the world's first public railway, the Stockton & Darlington (S&D), was that it used rails made of specially produced malleable wrought iron, which withstood the impact of a locomotive's wheels and weight much better than cast-iron rails. First produced by John Birkinshaw at the Bedlington ironworks in Northumberland, these rails were a vital part of the venture's success. *Locomotion* was the third engine to be ordered, and the first to be delivered, from the world's first

Locomotion had no springs, but a degree of cushioning was provided by the steam in the vertically mounted cylinders.

purpose-built locomotive works, Robert Stephenson & Co. of Newcastle on Tyne. This was a joint venture formed by the Stephensons with Michael Longridge of the Bedlington Ironworks and the wealthy Pease family of Darlington, who were also backers of the S&D Railway. Similar to the 14 or so colliery locomotives already built by George Stephenson, it had its 'works' mounted above the boiler, with vertical pistons and rods. The rod drive, with cranks and connecting rods, was among the Stephensons' most important contributions to locomotive development, replacing earlier attempts at chain and cog drives. The boiler was a single wrought-iron flue, lagged with wood, supplying steam to two cylinders and mounted on a cast-iron frame resting on four wheels. The wheels and axles were unsprung, but the action of the pistons in the vertical cylinders provided a primitive sort of suspension, though the motion must have been rather jerky. A four-wheel 'convoy cart' carried coal and water. *Locomotion*, driven by George Stephenson, pulled the world's first public train service on 27 September 1825 – a long train formed mostly of coal wagons but with the first ever passenger carriage, named 'Experiment', in the middle; and with anything

between 300 and 600 passengers (many uninvited) on board or clinging on. By 1828, the engine was already obsolescent, and following a boiler explosion it was substantially rebuilt in that year, and worked on until 1841. After that, it was used as a stationary pumping engine, and survived until its restoration in modern times and an honoured place as the first locomotive to pull a public passenger train. After that first run, steam haulage on the S&D was

normally restricted to coal trains, and passenger services were horse-drawn for several years. At that time, the concept of the public railway as operated by a single business was not yet established, and several horse-drawn passenger

services were operated, paying tolls to the railway company. When another train appeared, coming the other way on the single track, the train nearest to the next siding was supposed to enter the siding and give way.

BOILER PRESSURE: 3.5kg/cm² (50psi)
CYLINDERS: 241x609mm (9¹/₂ x24in)
DRIVING WHEELS: 1220mm (48in)
GRATE AREA: 0.74m² (8sq ft)

HEATING SURFACE: 5.6m² (60sq ft)
TRACTIVE EFFORT: 861kg (1900lb)
TOTAL WEIGHT: 6.9t (15,232lb)

ROYAL GEORGE 0-6-0 STOCKTON & DARLINGTON RAILWAY (S&D) 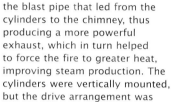 GREAT BRITAIN 1827

The Stockton & Darlington (S&D) Railway's engineer, Timothy Hackworth, had worked with Hedley and George Stephenson, and is perhaps not as well-known as he deserves to be as a pioneering locomotive engineer. This engine, known as the *Royal George*, was drastically rebuilt by Hackworth from a four-wheeler

built by Robert Wilson of Gateshead (an otherwise unknown builder), a poor steamer contemptuously known as 'Chittaprat' by the enginemen. The *Royal George* was the first really reliable revenue-earning locomotive.

Numerous novelties were incorporated, apart from the six-

wheel layout. It had the biggest boiler yet mounted on a locomotive, with a single U-shaped return flue; spring-loaded safety-valves, and self-lubricating bearings with built-in oil reservoirs. A leaf spring on each side linked the two front axles. Perhaps most importantly, a narrow aperture was made for

the blast pipe that led from the cylinders to the chimney, thus producing a more powerful exhaust, which in turn helped to force the fire to greater heat, improving steam production. The cylinders were vertically mounted, but the drive arrangement was neater than that of *Locomotion*. In its first year, *Royal George* moved 22,061 tonnes (22,422 tons) of coal at a cost reckoned to be £466, against an equivalent for horse-haulage of £998.

The success of *Royal George* helped to establish the 0-6-0 arrangement as the standard one for goods locomotives in Britain and many other countries. It worked on the S&D until 1840, and was then sold on for £550. But like all engines built in this still-experimental period, it was soon overtaken by new technical developments.

BOILER PRESSURE: 3.65kg/cm² (52psi)
CYLINDERS: 279x507mm (11x20in)
DRIVING WHEELS: 1218mm (48in)
GRATE AREA: not known
HEATING SURFACE: 13m² (141sq ft)
TRACTIVE EFFORT: 997kg (2200lb)
TOTAL WEIGHT: not known

Royal George was probably the first locomotive to be fitted with a warning bell. The early colliery railways were unfenced.

SEGUIN LOCOMOTIVE 0-4-0 FRANCE 1829

The first great name in French locomotive history, Marc Seguin was already a notable inventor when he became chief engineer of the St Etienne–Andrézieux Railway in 1826. He had visited the Stephenson works in Newcastle (a place of pilgrimage for all early mechanical engineers). He had already patented a multi-tubular boiler for a stationary engine, and was the first to apply this to a locomotive, though not to

this first design. Its boiler had return flues, bending back to exhaust through a chimney at the same end as the firebox. Externally its most obvious feature was the huge bellows mounted on the tender, which was pushed by the engine; driven from an axle, it provided a forced draught to maintain the fire. Early in 1828, Seguin imported two locomotives from the Stephenson works at Newcastle. His main criticism of

English engines was their inadequate steam production, and he established that under test, the English locomotives' boilers could supply only 300kg (660lb) of steam per hour – not enough to meet his haulage requirement. Seguin set about constructing his own locomotive, with his patent tubular boiler and incorporating many Stephenson features. Its heating surface was sufficient to produce 1800kg (3960lb) of steam

per hour, and a speed of 40km/h (25mph) was claimed for it. Twelve more were built to the same design. At this time, Seguin had not realized the potential efficacy of the blast pipe, not only in exhausting used steam from the cylinders, but in creating a draught that kept the fire hot, and his first locomotives incorporated a bellows, driven by a fan-belt from an axle, to provide this draught. He stands at the beginning of the

French tradition of applying science to produce the maximum possible amount of steam from the boiler, and to extract the maximum amount of work from it. A modern replica of his first engine has been constructed. Seguin did not start a 'school', however, and he withdrew from locomotive building after a dispute with his colleagues. French locomotive building would be based on further, and more effective, samples from the Stephenson works at Newcastle.

BOILER PRESSURE: 3.5kg/cm² (50psi)
CYLINDERS: 203x432mm (8x17in)
DRIVING WHEELS: 1435mm (56¹/₂in)
GRATE AREA: 0.74kg/cm² (8sq ft)
HEATING SURFACE: 10.9m² (117.75sq ft)
TRACTIVE EFFORT: 1089kg (2405lb)
TOTAL WEIGHT: 4.32t (9520lb)

The great size of the bellows for forcing a draught into the fire can be seen in this replica Seguin locomotive. Note the chock under the unbraked wheel.

ROCKET 0-2-2 LIVERPOOL & MANCHESTER RAILWAY (L&M)   GREAT BRITAIN 1829

The Liverpool & Manchester, opened in 1830, was to be the first public railway to rely exclusively on mechanical traction. This did not necessarily mean locomotives only; there were many at the time who believed that rope haulage by a stationary engine was the only way to get a train up a gradient. The celebrated trials held at Rainhill in October 1829 – the world's first contest of machines – were intended to establish whether any locomotive could actually fulfil the requirements set by the line. Each machine had to cost under £550, weigh no more than 6.2 tonnes (6 tons), pull a 20.3-tonne (20-ton) load at 16km/h (10mph), have a boiler pressure of no more than 3.5kg/cm² (50lb/in²), and 'consume its own smoke'. Built by George and Robert Stephenson, taken by cart across the country and shipped from Whitehaven to Liverpool, *Rocket* was the only contender to meet these demands, but it did so with considerable

ease. A number of new features helped in its success. In front of the boiler was a smokebox containing the exhaust blast-pipe. The boiler itself was not the old single or double flue kind, but a multi-tubular one containing 25 6.75cm (3in) copper tubes. The hot gases passing through these provided much greater heating surface than any previous locomotive, generating steam faster, and more of it. Development of this tubular boiler was almost simultaneous with Seguin's in France. The cylinders were set behind and alongside the boiler, at an angle of 45 degrees (later much reduced), driving the front wheels. It had a copper firebox, both axles were sprung, and the tender was the first vehicle to have outside bearings fitted to its axles. Huge crowds of local people, and many international observers, came to view the trials, and see the new technology in action. The course, of 2.4km (1.5 miles) had to be run 20 times, forwards and backwards, making a 96.5km (60-mile) journey, equivalent to the trip from Liverpool to

Manchester and back again. *Rocket* did this at an average speed of just under 22.5km/h (14mph), 6.4km/h (4mph) better than the speed stipulated for the test. Its performance established the case for locomotive power beyond doubt, and for its builders there was not only the winners' £500 prize, plus the locomotive contract for the new railway, but worldwide fame and a surge in demand from overseas.

After running on the L&M line for eight years, *Rocket* was sold for £300 as a colliery engine, and fortunately it managed to escape the fate of most redundant locomotives by being returned to Robert Stephenson & Co. in 1851. Though not in its original form, *Rocket* is still preserved in London, and is currently a very popular tourist attraction.

BOILER PRESSURE: 3.5kg/cm² (50psi)
CYLINDERS: 203x432mm (8x17in)
DRIVING WHEELS: 1435mm (56½in)
GRATE AREA: 0.74kg/cm² (8sq ft)
HEATING SURFACE: 10.9m² (117.75sq ft)
TRACTIVE EFFORT: 1089kg (2405lb)
TOTAL WEIGHT: 4.32t (9520lb)

Robert Stephenson was proud of the bright paintwork of *Rocket*, and the replica shown here is painted in the style used at the Rainhill trials.

'PLANET' CLASS 2-2-0 LIVERPOOL & MANCHESTER RAILWAY (L&MR)

*R*ocket was a one-off, though one or two similar models followed in the course of 1830 and the pace of improvement continued. The early products of the Newcastle factory were prone to breakdowns and loss of steam. Reliability and effective performance were demanded by customers, and already there were calls for standardization, so that spare parts could be stored and used. In October 1830, *Planet* was completed, and the 'Planets' were the first locomotives that could be said to form a class, with the same features replicated across a number of engines. Unlike previous Stephenson locomotives,

which had relied on the boiler to form the main structural member, the 'Planet' boiler was mounted on a solid frame, a 'sandwich' of ash or oak planking reinforced by iron plates, as some of the very earliest locomotives had also been. *Planet* was also the first Stephenson engine to have the cylinders placed inside the frame – 'the engine beneath the boiler' as Robert Stephenson himself put it – and set horizontally at the front. The inside placing of the cylinders under the smoke-box, which became a virtual British standard for decades, was considered to give better balance and weight distribution, though the fracture-

prone crank axles that were required as a result were troublesome, and abominated by American engineers in particular. In the 'Planets', however, the crank axles were well supported by the outside plate frame and inside bar frame members, so that the crank axle turned in no fewer than six bearings. This strength was in contrast to the lightweight 'American' bar frame introduced by Edward Bury (see 1837). Drive was now to the rear wheels, which carried more weight and had improved adhesion as a result. A small railed footplate was provided for the enginemen, but no effort was made to provide a cab. At that

time, keeping the weight low was an important consideration; also, the driver or fireman often had to jump down to apply lubrication or make some adjustment.

In 1831, Stephenson built two enlarged 'Planets' with coupled wheels, as 0-4-0s, to act as goods engines on the Liverpool & Manchester Railway, and they were named *Samson* and *Goliath*. Many further 0-4-0 types followed. By 1833, the 'Planet' type had developed into the larger 2-2-2 'Patentee' class, and these two types formed the original locomotive stock of many railways in continental Europe, Russia and the United States. By now, demand exceeded the Newcastle works's ability to supply, and Stephenson opened a second works, in the name of Charles Tayleur & Co., in Lancashire – later the Vulcan Foundry. His engines were also built under licence at other works.

With the 'Planets', the basics of the locomotive were established, though many adaptations and refinements were still to be made. Coupling gear, buffers, warning systems – first bells, then whistles from 1835; American locomotives soon had bells *and* whistles – were all necessary and a variety of inventive solutions was applied to these and other problems. Brakes, still in a rudimentary state hardly different to those of horse-drawn wagons, also needed attention. Railway workshops at this time were little more than superior blacksmiths' forges, and men like Hackworth and Robert Stephenson had to devise new tools and work systems to cope with repair and maintenance as well as with the building of new locomotives. At this time, there was no ironfounder in England who could make springs of the size and tensile strength required by railway locomotives, and this was only one example of how the coming of the locomotive stimulated growth and development in other fields of technology and industry.

Specifications are for the 'Planet' type
Boiler pressure: 3.5kg/cm² (50psi)
Cylinders: 279x406mm (11x16in)
Driving wheels: 1525mm (60in)
Grate area: 0.74m2 (8sq ft)
Heating surface: 46.8m² (504sq ft)
Tractive effort: 622kg (1371lb)
Total weight: 8.1t (17,920lb)

The modern replica of *Planet* shows how modest the boiler dimensions of these early locomotives were.

BEST FRIEND OF CHARLESTON 0-4-0T CHARLESTON & HAMBURG RAILROAD (C&H)   USA 1830

In 1825, John Stevens had built a small-scale steam locomotive to run on a cog-rail road in his garden, but the first American-designed and -built locomotive to operate a service on a public railroad was this vertical-boilered engine, designed by E.L. Miller and built at the West Point Foundry, New York. A precursor of the tank engine, it carried its water and coke within the frame, with two inside cylinders set at a slight angle. *Best Friend's* career lasted only six months before the boiler exploded on 17 June 1831. The fireman had tied down the safety valve, maybe because it was letting off steam prematurely – with a boiler pressure of only 3.5kg/cm² (50psi), any drop in pressure could make it almost impossible to move a train. It was rebuilt with a centrally mounted boiler, and returned to service with a new name, *Phoenix*.

BOILER PRESSURE: 3.5kg/cm² (50psi)
CYLINDERS: 152x406mm (6x16in)
DRIVING WHEELS: 1371mm (54in)
HEATING SURFACE: not known
GRATE AREA: 0.2m² (2.2sq ft)
TRACTIVE EFFORT: 206kg (452lb)
TOTAL WEIGHT: 4t (8820lb)

E. L. Miller had been an observer at the Rainhill locomotive trials in 1829 and this design owes a little to one of the competitors, *Novelty*, entered by Ericsson and Braithwaite, though it has a much bigger boiler.

JOHN BULL 0-4-0 CAMDEN & AMBOY RAILROAD (C&A)   USA 1831

Among several American observers at the Rainhill trials of 1829 was Horatio Allen, of the Delaware & Hudson Canal Co. With a brief from his chief, John B. Jervis, to order steam locomotives, he had already placed orders for four, similar to *Locomotion*, with vertical cylinders and rods. All proved unsuitable for the line and were ultimately adapted for use as stationary engines. But one, *Stourbridge Lion*, was the first full-size locomotive to work in the United States. Driven by Allen, it made a demonstration run on 8 August 1829 on the Delaware & Hudson's track before its axle-weight was judged to be too great for safe use. However, the demand for steam locomotives remained, and 'Planet' types were sent out from England in parts for assembly on US railroads. Built to the C&A line's original 1472mm (58in) gauge, *John Bull* was supplied by Robert Stephenson & Co. and set up at Bordentown, NJ, in 1831. On 12 November of that year, it worked a demonstration train carrying members of the state legislature, though it did not start regular service until 1833.

John Bull proved to be a great survivor, though not in its original form. US railroad men were quick to make their own adaptations to any imported locomotives, to suit the requirements of American operations, or their own ideas. In what would be a defining aspect of the US style, a leading truck and 'pilot' were fitted, and a wide chimney with a spark arrestor cap was added later, along with a cab and big headlight. The British engines were intended to burn coke, but in the United States coke was expensive and lumber abundant, and so for the first

BOILER PRESSURE: 3.5kg/cm² (50psi)
CYLINDERS: 228x508mm (9x20in)
DRIVING WHEELS: 1294mm (54in)
GRATE AREA: 0.93cm² (10.07sq ft)
HEATING SURFACE: 27.5cm² (296.5sq ft)
TRACTIVE EFFORT: 575kg (1270lb)
TOTAL WEIGHT: 10t (22,045lb)

The 'Americanized' *John Bull*, complete with wheelbarrow-like front bogie, lantern and a curious cab extended from the tender.

30 years of American railroad operation, wood was the basic fuel. Cordwood supply was a major ancillary industry until around 1865, and at the peak, US locomotives were consuming around half a million tons of wood each year. Being much more spark-prone than coke, wood fires prompted the development of another typical early American feature, the diamond or balloon stack, incorporating a spark arrestor. More than a thousand of these devices were patented in the course of the 19th century. In the early 1830s, the standard American rail track was not made of iron but of hardwood baulks, with an iron strip or 'strap-rail' fixed to the top, which engaged with the rail wheel. The tendency of the iron strips to break and curl up was one reason for the use of the pilot; another was the tight curves on many US lines.

In 1849, *John Bull* was taken off the road and used as a stationary steam plant for boiler testing. However, by 1876, when the C&A had become part of the Pennsylvania Railroad, it was fully restored and put on show at the Centennial Exhibition in Philadelphia as 'America's first locomotive'. This title was, of course, incorrect, though *John Bull* was the oldest surviving one. Its last run was from New York to Chicago in April 1893. Since 1940, the veteran has been a static exhibit at the Smithsonian Institute in Washington DC.

DE WITT CLINTON 0-4-0 MOHAWK & HUDSON RAILROAD (M&H)   USA 1831

John B. Jervis began his own career as a locomotive designer with this engine, built on the British model with horizontal boiler and inside cylinders, but with original features including all-iron wheels (previous locomotives had wooden wheel-centres). Its first journey in August 1831 was something of an ordeal for passengers. Like a stage-coach, its cars had no buffers and were at first joined by iron chains that yanked them violently into motion. Sparks emanating from the burning pitch-pine used as fuel dramatically set fire to the clothing of some passengers seated outside, but such things were accepted as routine hazards of early railroading. Dimensions unkown.

De Witt Clinton's first run was memorable for sparks setting fire to ladies' dresses and for its stage-coach type cars bumping into each other. But everyone had a good time.

EXPERIMENT 4-2-0 MOHAWK & HUDSON RAILROAD (M&H)   USA 1832

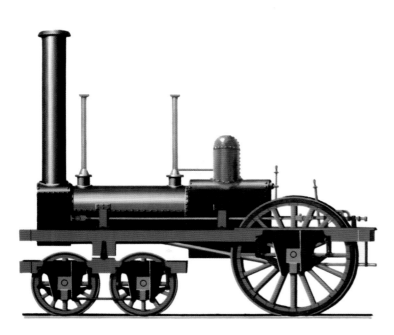

Jervis's *Experiment* was an altogether more epoch-making design, as it was the first locomotive to be fitted with a leading four-wheel truck, or bogie. Its wheels, with outside bearings and suspended springs, were set in a frame beneath the main frame of the locomotive. The crucial point was that this frame was pivoted, so providing a degree of articulation to the wheelbase, and helping to keep the engine on the road in places where the track curved sharply, as was often the case. Jervis did not patent this innovation and though Britain was very slow to take it up, the truck quickly became a standard American feature. For a decade or so, the 4-2-0 was the typical American locomotive. Another unusual aspect of *Experiment* was the placing of the driving wheels behind the firebox, foreshadowing the later (English) locomotives of Thomas Russell Crampton (see 1845). Converted from anthracite to wood burning in 1833, the engine was more thoroughly rebuilt as a 4-4-0 in 1846 and renamed *Brother Jonathan*.

BOILER PRESSURE: 3.5kg/cm² (50psi)	**HEATING SURFACE:** not known
CYLINDERS: 228x406mm (9x16in)	**TRACTIVE EFFORT:** 453kg (1000lb)
DRIVING WHEELS: 1524mm (60in)	**TOTAL WEIGHT:** 6.4t (14,175lb)
GRATE AREA: not known	

The first locomotive to have a swivelling bogie was built by William Chapman in England in 1812.

LANCASTER 4-2-0 PHILADELPHIA & COLUMBIA RAILROAD (P&C) — USA 1834

The year 1832 saw the beginnings of what was to be America's biggest locomotive-building company, Baldwin. In 1830, Matthias W. Baldwin, who had trained as a jeweller, built a small-scale steam locomotive for the Philadelphia Museum. His first full-size locomotive was built in 1832, for the Philadelphia, Germanstown & Norristown Railway. A four-wheeler that bore the name *Old Ironsides*, it closely resembled an English 'Planet' type. Its success created demand. In 1834 Baldwin turned out five, including *Lancaster*, which he sold to the Commonwealth of Pennsylvania for $5500. Most American railroads

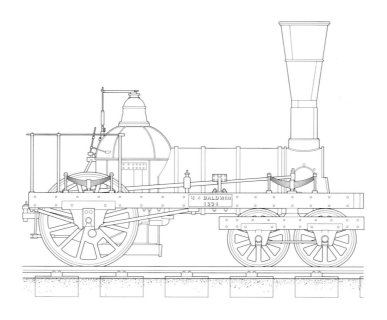

did not have their own drawing offices and were content to order suitable locomotives from the builder's range. At first, the 4-2-0 was the only type Baldwin offered, though with a choice of three sizes from 9090kg to 11,818kg (20,000lb to 26,000lb) weight. Baldwin was not the first American builder; William Norris had set up in 1831, also in Philadelphia, and Pennsylvania and New Jersey would remain the heartland of American steam locomotive buiilding for many years to come.

The 4-2-0 was the standard American locomotive type of the mid-1830s.

BOILER PRESSURE: 8.4kg/cm² (120psi)
CYLINDERS: 228x406mm (9x16in)
DRIVING WHEELS: 1370mm (54in)
GRATE AREA: not known
HEATING SURFACE: not known
TRACTIVE EFFORT: 1110kg (2448lb)
TOTAL WEIGHT: 7.7t (16,975lb)

ADLER 2-2-2 NÜREMBERG–FÜRTH RAILWAY — BAVARIA 1835

Back in 1815, two colliery locomotives had been built in Berlin, to British plans, for coalfield use, but without success. These were the first locomotives seen in Germany. Germany's first public railway, the Nuremberg–Fürth, opened on 7 December 1835 in

the kingdom of Bavaria. *Adler* ('Eagle') was a Stephenson 'Patentee' type, imported at short order when the intention to have a home-built locomotive fell through. While one engine was hardly enough to work a railroad, the distance was short, the service

infrequent, and it was always possible to bring in horses as a supplement. *Adler* remained in service until 1857, and two replicas have been built, in 1935 and 1950, to commemorate its primacy as Germany's first operational railway locomotive.

BOILER PRESSURE: 4.2kg/cm² (60psi)
CYLINDERS: 229x406mm (9x6in)
DRIVING WHEELS: 1371mm (54in)
GRATE AREA: 0.48m² (5.2sq ft)
HEATING SURFACE: 18.2m² (196sq ft)
TRACTIVE EFFORT: 550kg (1220lb)
TOTAL WEIGHT: 11.4t (25,245lb)

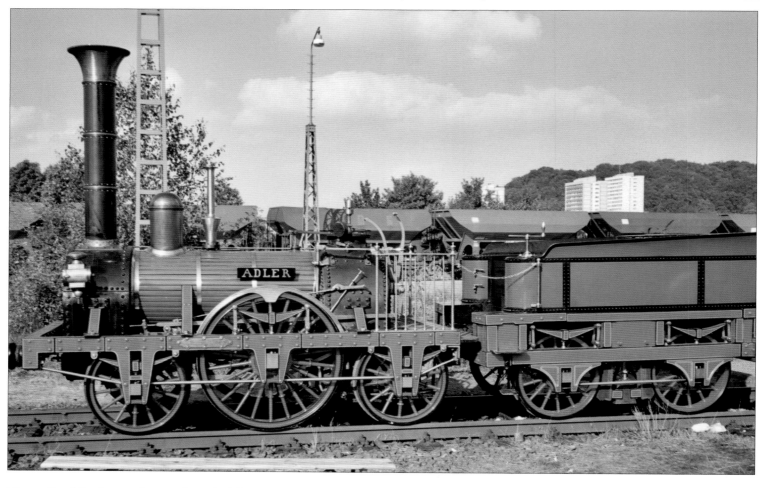

The replica *Adler* in a modern setting. The 'Planets' were fitted with proper tenders, with built-in water reservoirs and a coal space.

DORCHESTER 0-4-0 CHAMPLAIN & ST LAWRENCE RAILWAY (C&SL)

CANADA 1836

Based on Stephenson's 'Samson' type, effectively a more powerful version of the 'Planet' with coupled wheels, this was the first locomotive on Canada's first railway, and it was the expectation of good freight traffic to the St Lawrence harbours that led to the choice of the coupled-wheel formation. This locomotive is of interest to banknote-collectors, as it is the first known to be illustrated on a banknote, when the railway company issued its own notes in 1837. Canada would not remain wedded to English locomotive design, however; the influence, and similar operating conditions, of the neighbouring United States were too close.

BOILER PRESSURE: 3.5kg/cm² (50psi)
CYLINDERS: 228x355mm (9x14in)
DRIVING WHEELS: 1370mm (54in)
GRATE AREA: 0.74m² (8sq ft)

HEATING SURFACE: not known
TRACTIVE EFFORT: 413kg (910lb)
TOTAL WEIGHT: 5.7t (12,560lb)

BURY LOCOMOTIVE 2-2-0 LONDON & BIRMINGHAM RAILWAY (L&BR)

GREAT BRITAIN 1837

Edward Bury's foundry at Liverpool had begun building locomotives in 1830 with a design intended for the Liverpool & Manchester Railway. This was the first to have horizontal inside cylinders, anticipating the Stephenson 'Planets'. During the 1830s, Bury exported a number of locomotives to the United States and was responsible for the American adoption of bar-frames, giving the locomotive something of a 'see-through' look between boiler and wheels, as distinct from the more usual British plate-frames used by the Stephensons and most other builders. In 1838, he was appointed Chief Mechanical Engineer to the London & Birmingham and proceeded to supply a range of locomotives from his own works. They were lightweight, bar-framed engines with inside cylinders driving the rear wheels, and small boilers ending in circular fireboxes topped by a small 'haycock' dome. There were 58 in all, a substantial 'class' for those days, and they were cheap to build and reliable to operate. They were grossly under-powered for a trunk line, however, even for the lightweight rolling stock of the period; and up to four could be seen on the heavier trains, a serious waste of manpower and fuel. Bury lost his contract in 1847 and the company wasted no time in getting more powerful locomotives. Bury continued as an independent builder – his small engines were quite big enough for many local railways, and two of his later engines survive in preservation.

BOILER PRESSURE: 3.5kg/cm² (50psi)
CYLINDERS: 280x415mm (11x16.5in)
DRIVING WHEELS: 1546mm (60.75in)
GRATE AREA: 0.65m² (7sq ft)

HEATING SURFACE: 33.2m² (357sq ft)
TRACTIVE EFFORT: 629kg (1386lb)
TOTAL WEIGHT: 10t (22,045lb)

NORRIS LOCOMOTIVE 4-2-0 BALTIMORE & OHIO RAILROAD (B&O)

USA 1837

A businessman rather than a locomotive designer, William Norris was the first American builder to export locomotives. The success of an outside-cylinder 4-2-0, The Washington Country Farmer, for the Philadelphia & Columbia Railway in 1836 established the company's reputation, and eight 4-2-0s for the B&O, built between 1837 and 1839, were on very much the

Compared to the *Lancaster*, the inside bar frame and the outside cylinders may be noted: this would become standard American practice.

same plans. Bar-framed, with Bury-type fireboxes and a 4.2kg/cm² (60psi) power output that gave them a little more power than was delivered by most of their contemporaries, they gained a reputation as good hill climbers – enough for England's Birmingham & Gloucester (B&G) Railway to test one on its 1 in 37 Lickey Incline. The B&G ultimately owned 26 Norris locomotives, which were Britain's first locomotive imports; nine were also built in England under licence. Norris later opened a factory in Vienna, Austria, but other family members maintained the Philadelphia works.

BOILER PRESSURE: 4.2kg/cm² (60psi)
CYLINDERS: 266x457mm (10.5x18in)
DRIVING WHEELS: 1220mm (48in)
GRATE AREA: 0.8m² (8.6sq ft)
HEATING SURFACE: 36.6m² (394sq ft)
TRACTIVE EFFORT: 957kg (2162lb)
TOTAL WEIGHT: 20t (44,090lb)

4-4-0 PHILADELPHIA, GERMANSTOWN & NORRISTOWN RAILROAD (PG&NR) USA 1837

The power of the 4-2-0 was eclipsed by what became for a time the new 'American Type', the four-coupled locomotive. Although in a sense this was the obvious development at a time when demands for greater pulling power and running longer distances were increasing, certain technical problems had to be solved before the 4-4-0 became really effective. First man in the field was Henry R. Campbell of the Philadelphia, Germanstown & Norriston Railroad (PG&NR), who drew up a design for a 4-4-0 type in 1836 and obtained a patent for it. The prototype, built by James Brook of

Philadelphia, was claimed to be the largest locomotive yet. More significantly, it was also claimed to be capable of pulling a 458-tonne (450-ton) train over level track at 24km/h (15mph). This was a very respectable speed for a goods train in 1837; most scarcely exceeeded a fast walking pace. The Campbell design was reckoned to have a tractive effort 65% better than that of the typical 4-2-0. Unfortunately the design had its unsatisfactory aspects: the four big wheels, held in a rigid frame, tended to jump the tracks.

Campbell's claim to own the 4-4-0 arrangement was challenged

by the simultaneous appearance of another 4-4-0 from two Philadelphia engineers, Andrew Eastwick and Joseph Harrison, who designed and built for the Beaver Meadow Railroad. In their engine, *Hercules,* also a giant for the time, they had tried to tackle the suspension problem by fitting the four coupled wheels in a truck frame. But this was only partially successful and the difficulty was not overcome until Harrison devised the equalizing lever in 1838, enabling weight to be transferred from one axle to the other. Leaf springs and connecting levers ensured

that even in sudden dips and irregularities of the track, all the wheels – usually – stayed on the rails. Harrison patented his lever; Campbell failed in the claim that the 4-4-0 was his alone.

BOILER PRESSURE: 6kg/cm² (90psi)
CYLINDERS: 355x406mm (14x16in)
DRIVING WHEELS: 1370mm (54in)
GRATE AREA: 1.1m² (12sq ft)
HEATING SURFACE: 67m² (723sq ft)
TRACTIVE EFFORT: 1995kg (4400lb)
TOTAL WEIGHT: 12.2t (26,880lb)

LION 0-4-2 LIVERPOOL & MANCHESTER RAILWAY (L&M) GREAT BRITAIN 1838

By 1838, the Liverpool & Manchester (L&M) railway was firmly established, prosperous and beginning to diversify its locomotive stock. The oldest working locomotive in the world,

BOILER PRESSURE: 3.5kg/cm² (50psi)
CYLINDERS: 304.5x457mm (12x18in)
DRIVING WHEELS: 1523mm (60in)
GRATE AREA: not known
HEATING SURFACE: not known
TRACTIVE EFFORT: 888kg (1800lb)
TOTAL WEIGHT: 29.8t (65,880lb)

Lion, has appeared in numerous films. Built by Todd, Kitson & Laird of Leeds, it had a 0-4-2 wheel arrangement, used on only a handful of British locomotive classes. Its longevity is owed to the fact that it was used for many years as a stationary pumping engine at Liverpool docks before undergoing restoration to its original appearance.

Heavy cranks going round at high speed caused unsteadiness in locomotives weighing only a few tons. It was around this time that John Braithwaite, of the Eastern

Counties Railway in England, began to fit weights to the rims of driving wheels, in order to counterbalance the action of the cranks. His work was continued on the same line by William Fernihough, and the use of counterweights soon spread across all railways. The more balanced motion reduced the tendency of early locomotives to pitch up and down as they went along, and greater speeds could be maintained, with a valuable contribution to the efficiency of the locomotive as well as to the

Lion's boiler and firebox are lagged with wooden strips, secured by copper bands. It is a double 'sandwich' frame.

crew's comfort and safety. Step by step, inventions like Braithwaite's wheel weights and Harrison's equalizing lever were bringing the steam locomotive's development forward. Everything pointed towards greater weight, greater steam capacity, greater reliability and the ability to run longer distances at higher speeds.

2-2-2 NORTHERN RAILWAY (NORD)

Locomotive building in France was concentrated in the north-east at Lille, and the east at Belfort and Mulhouse, where the Société Alsacienne de Constructions Mécaniques was established by André Koechlin in 1838. Stephenson's English influence is strong in this first production of the company, with its inside cylinders and outside frames, but French design would soon establish its own forms. Locomotives of this type were built up to 1842 and used by a variety of other French railways as well as the *Nord*.

An early Koechlin 2-2-2 locomotive – compare with *De Arend*, below.

BOILER PRESSURE: 6kg/cm² (85psi)
CYLINDERS: 330x462mm (13x18.2in)
DRIVING WHEELS: 1370.5mm (54in)
GRATE AREA: 1.1m² (12sq ft)
HEATING SURFACE: 5.2m² (56.2sq ft)
TRACTIVE EFFORT: 1866kg (4115lb)
TOTAL WEIGHT: 15.6t (34,495lb)

DE AREND 2-2-2 HOLLAND IRON RAILWAY

Two engines were obtained from England to operate the first Dutch railway, between Amsterdam and Haarlem. *De Arend* ('Eagle') was the second, built by Longridge & Co. of Bedlington, originally an iron-founding company run by an associate of the Stephenson family, and which built 'Patentee' type locomotives under licence at a time when the Newcastle factory could not cope with the volume of orders. *De Arend* was scrapped in 1857, but in 1938 a full size replica was constructed for the line's centenary.

The replica *De Arend* on a visit to the USA in 1999 – it is a typical Stephenson 'Patentee' type of the late 1830s.

BOILER PRESSURE: 4kg/cm² (57psi)
CYLINDERS: 356x450mm (14x17.7in)
DRIVING WHEELS: 1810mm (71in)
GRATE AREA: 1.1m² (11.8sq ft)
HEATING SURFACE: not known
TRACTIVE EFFORT: 1074kg (2367lb)
TOTAL WEIGHT: 11.6t (25,640lb)

GOWAN & MARX 4-4-0 PHILADELPHIA & READING RAILROAD (P&RR) USA 1839

A product of Eastwick and Harrison of Philadelphia, this Philadelphia & Reading Railroad (P&RR) locomotive is a blend of old and new. It has the equalizing lever invented by Harrison in 1838 to link the coupled axles, but its firebox has an old-fashioned look, though it is oblong rather than circular in plan. At this time, designers were beginning to allow for higher boiler pressure, and the engine owes its pulling power to that fact, which gave it useful capacity to generate extra steam. It headed the first passenger train from Philadelphia to Reading on 5 December 1839, but its main purpose was freight, and it was famed for having drawn a train of 101 cars, weighing 481 tonnes (472 tons) on 20 February 1840. News of this feat was responsible for Eastwick and Harrison being

invited by the Tsar to set up a locomotive building plant in St Petersburg, Russia.

By the end of the 1830s, not

only had the locomotive developed with remarkable speed, but so had many ancillary aspects of the railway. The building of specialized

The lofty chimneys helped to increase draught and so keep the fire hot; *Gowan & Marx*'s **has a spark arresting device fitted at the top.**

vehicles like tank cars, mail vans, and cattle trucks began in this decade. The Cumberland Valley Railroad in the USA introduced 'bunk cars' in 1836, and the London & North Western Railway followed with 'bed carriages' in 1838. By the end of the decade, though, carriages remained unheated, and lighting was usually provided by means of dim oil-burning pot-lamps inserted into holes made for the purpose in the carriage roofs. Railway carriages, which had resembled sheds on wheels or stage coaches on rails, began to extend in length, and six wheels were often used, but corridors and on-board toilet facilities were not yet considered.

BOILER PRESSURE: 5.6kg/cm² (80psi)
CYLINDERS: 320x406mm (12.6x16in)
DRIVING WHEELS: 1066mm (42in)
GRATE AREA: 1.1m² (12sq ft)
HEATING SURFACE: not known
TRACTIVE EFFORT: 2331kg (5140lb)
TOTAL WEIGHT: 11t (24,250lb)

ST PIERRE 2-2-2 PARIS–ROUEN RAILWAY FRANCE 1843

An Englishman, William Buddicomb, was engineer to the Paris-Rouen railway, and this fact explains the thoroughly English pedigree of this particular locomotive, modelled on the 2-2-2s being built at the Grand Junction Railway's new works at Crewe. Forty of the class were built at Rouen, of which 22 were later converted into tank engines. *St Pierre*, which remained in service until 1916, is the oldest preserved locomotive in France today. The 'single-driver' type of locomotive, though well-known in France at this time, did not have the longevity it enjoyed in Great Britain, and was soon to be superseded by four-coupled engines.

BOILER PRESSURE: 5kg/cm² (70psi)
CYLINDERS: 335x535mm (13.2x21in)
DRIVING WHEELS: 1720mm (68in)
GRATE AREA: 0.97m² (10.5sq ft)
HEATING SURFACE: 65.8m² (709sq ft)
TRACTIVE EFFORT: 1460kg (3100lb)
TOTAL WEIGHT: 18t (39,690lb)

The restored *St Pierre* **sparkles in the sunlight. Locomotives in the early period were almost invariably maintained to a high standard of paintwork and polish: the railway companies were new and keen to show a good public image.**

BEUTH 2-2-2 BERLIN–ANHALT RAILWAY

The energetic William Norris was perhaps even more influential than Robert Stephenson in his influence on early locomotive designs and construction in Germany. One of the first German locomotive builders was August Borsig of Berlin, who began by using Norris designs from the United States, in 1841, before moving on to his own designs.

Such major locomotive builders as Esslingen (1847) and Henschel (1848) were also indebted to Norris' work in their first years, though Norris' own Vienna factory was actually a commercial failure and he returned to the United States to work in 1848. *Beuth* was typical of the early Borsig locomotives, and was American in its bar frames and Norris-type firebox, but used the English-type 2-2-2 wheel arrangement.

BOILER PRESSURE: 5.5kg/cm² (78psi)
CYLINDERS: 330x560mm (13.1x22.3in)
DRIVING WHEELS: 1543mm (60.75in)
GRATE AREA: 0.83m² (8.9sq ft)
HEATING SURFACE: 47m² (500sq ft)
TRACTIVE EFFORT: 1870kg (4120lb)
TOTAL WEIGHT: 18.5t (40,785lb)

2-6-0 MOSCOW & ST PETERSBURG RAILWAY

Russia's first locomotive was built for an industrial line in 1836 by E.A. Cherepanov, a serf-mechanic who had been sent to England to look at locomotives and locomotive works, and who modelled his engine on the English 'Planet' type. But domestic locomotive building did not really start until Eastwick and Harrison's St Petersburg factory of 1843, which stayed in production until 1862, building several hundred engines. One of its first products was an 0-6-0 freight locomotive. Since Russian operating conditions were very like American ones, it was not long before they equipped it with a two-wheel truck, making it the first of many engines of the 2-6-0 wheel configuration. The Russian rail gauge was 1500mm (5ft), not much greater than the British standard, but other clearances were much more generous, enabling Russia to build locomotives of imposing height and width.

PHILADELPHIA 0-6-0 PHILADELPHIA & READING RAILROAD (P&RR)

Originally named *Richmond*, this freight locomotive was built in Philadelphia by the Norris workshops but suffered a boiler blow-out and was comprehensively rebuilt as well as renamed in the same year. Coal was the Philadelphia & Reading (P&RR) Railroad's main freight traffic, and in the mid-1840s it was probably operating the heaviest trains anywhere, loading up to around 610 tonnes (600 tons) on its largely downhill grades from the coalfield to the port of Philadelphia. On such lines, brake power was as important as tractive power, but at that time powered or continuous brakes were unknown; engines had no brakes on the driving wheels at all, and the railroad relied on brakesmen to operate the hand-brakes on individual wagons.

BOILER PRESSURE: 8.4kg/cm² (120psi)
CYLINDERS: 365.5x508mm (14.4x20in)
DRIVING WHEELS: 1812mm (46in)
GRATE AREA: 1m² (11.4sq ft)
HEATING SURFACE: 78.8m² (848 sq ft)
TRACTIVE EFFORT: 4081kg (9000lb)
TOTAL WEIGHT: 18.5t (40,785lb)

CRAMPTON LOCOMOTIVE 4-2-0 LIÈGE & NAMUR RAILWAY

On the whole, the creators of odd or unusual locomotive designs fare better in their own countries than they do abroad. But Thomas Russell Crampton breaks this rule. In certain parts of France, at one time, *prendre le Crampton* might have been heard almost as much as *prendre le train*: to take the train was to take the Crampton. Reminiscent of John Jervis's *Experiment* in appearance, the Crampton locomotive was distinguished by large driving wheels set back in the rear of the firebox, and an otherwise somewhat low-slung appearance. Crampton, trained on the English Great Western Railway, subscribed to a view then common among engineers, though not tested out, that a locomotive's centre of gravity should be set as low as possible. He also wanted to produce engines that combined high speed with stable running. The result was 'Crampton's Patent Locomotive', of which little notice was taken in his own country, but which was taken up in France and Belgium. The Liège & Namur was the first to place an order, and two engines, named after each city, were built by Tulk & Ley in Whitehaven, England. Unlike later Cramptons, they had inside frames. A large and rather intrusive transverse laminate spring went

The Crampton look: by now, boilers were getting longer, with greatly increased heating surface enabling them to generate steam for sustained high speeds with light trains, or slower speed with a heavy load.

right across the footplate, bolted to the backhead of the boiler, linking the driving wheels. Perhaps the best feature of Crampton's design was his provision of unusually large steam ports, so that ample steam was available to the cylinders, and this undoubtedly contributed to their fast running. In 1852, 12 Crampton 4-2-0s were built for the Paris–Strasbourg Railway by J. F. Cail of Lille, with typical domeless boilers and outside steam pipes leading into a regulator box on the boiler top.

Others followed, and they ran the main-line services on this line, later the Est railway, into the late 1890s. By this time, the survivors presented a varied appearance, some with domes. On 20 June 1890, a Crampton type (by that time quite elderly and one of a dozen acquired by the Est from the Paris, Lyons & Mediterranean, and fitted with a Flaman double boiler with lower and upper barrels), reached a speed, on test, of 144km/h (89.5mph) with a train of 160 tonnes (157 tons). Around 350 Cramptons were built, including a handful for use in Britain and the United States; the vast majority ran in France and Germany. No. 80 of the Est, *Le Continent*, was retired in 1914 after 62 years of service, then reprieved for wartime work, and later preserved and restored (with one or two modifications) to working order.

BOILER PRESSURE: 6.3kg/cm² (90psi)
CYLINDERS: 406x507mm (16x20in)
DRIVING WHEELS: 2132mm (84in)
GRATE AREA: 1.3m² (14.5sq ft)
HEATING SURFACE: 91.8m² (989sq ft)
TRACTIVE EFFORT: 2113kg (4660lb)
TOTAL WEIGHT: not known

DERWENT 0-6-0 STOCKTON & DARLINGTON RAILWAY (S&D)

Early on, wheels were among the most often broken parts. Hackworth's wheel could withstand heavy jolting.

were also of Hackworth design. The work of the S&D was slow slogging with coal, and the engines clearly worked, but the persistence with an outmoded design suggests an entrenched conservatism that ignored useful progress. *Derwent* has been faithfully preserved, and ran under steam for the S&D centenary cavalcade of 1925.

With a certain doggedness, Timothy Hackworth on the Stockton & Darlington (S&D) continued to build engines with a single or double U-shaped return flue inside the boiler, despite the obvious success and superior efficiency and performance of the

Stephenson and Seguin multi-tube boiler. It was not a matter of avoiding patent, as Stephenson did not patent the *Rocket's* boiler design. His system required having the firebox at the front end, along with the chimney, which had to be set to one side, and the coal

tender was pushed along in front, while a water-cart was drawn behind, in a three-vehicle set. By 1845, Hackworth had retired, but his designs were perpetuated by W. and A. Kitching. The rear-set cylinders, at a steep angle, drove the front coupled wheels. These

BOILER PRESSURE: 5.25kg/cm² (75psi)
CYLINDERS: 362x609mm (14.5x24in)
DRIVING WHEELS: 1218mm (48in)
GRATE AREA: 0.92m² (10sq ft)
HEATING SURFACE: 127m² (1363sq ft)
TRACTIVE EFFORT: 3038kg (6700lb)
TOTAL WEIGHT: 22.7t (50,065lb)

ODIN CLASS 2-2-2 ZEALAND RAILWAY (ZR)

Sharps of Manchester were one of England's leading locomotive builders, and they supplied five of these compact engines to operate Denmark's first railway, between Copenhagen and Roskilde, on Zealand. The simple, almost austere design is normally credited to Charles Beyer, who emigrated from Saxony to Britain around this time and became a leading locomotive engineer. Internally they were less plain, with a crank axle of fiendish complexity to operate the connecting rods, valve gear and feedwater pumps for the boiler. Engines of this design, known as

'Sharpies' after the builders, were also used on other railways. *Odin* was scrapped in 1876, after three decades of service.

BOILER PRESSURE: 4.9kg/cm² (70psi)
CYLINDERS: 381x507.6mm (15x20in)
DRIVING WHEELS: 1523mm (60in)
GRATE AREA: 0.99m² (10.7sq ft)
HEATING SURFACE: 77m² (830sq ft)
TRACTIVE EFFORT: 1952kg (4305lb)
TOTAL WEIGHT: 22.1t (48,800lb)

The neat lines of *Odin* were typical of the British locomotives produced at this time.

'JENNY LIND' TYPE 2-2-2 LONDON & BRIGHTON RAILWAY (L&B)

Designed by David Joy, a fine engineer, and built by E.B. Wilson of Leeds, this was an unusual-looking single driver in as far as it had inside bearings for its driving wheels, which meant the usual axle-boxes were lacking. Otherwise it shows typical features for its time, including the carefully modelled chimney top, the fluted sides to the dome, and the perforated wheel splashers. With a touch of the public relations flair that the railways were sometimes good at showing, the first was named after a highly popular Swedish singer, and 'Jenny Linds' became well-known. Their fame was encouraged by the fact that they, too, were excellent performers, and Wilson's (who owned the design) went on to build more for British and other railways.

Part of the reason for their success was the high boiler pressure of 8.4kg/cm² (120 psi), which kept them well provided with steam and therefore power: the contemporary *Odin*, for example, ran at only 4.9kg/cm² (70psi), a significantly lower power output. British locomotives still had rigid frames with the wheels and axles fixed in position, but with their short wheelbase, this did not present a problem in running on curved track.

BOILER PRESSURE: 8.4kg/cm² (120psi)
CYLINDERS: 381x508mm (15x20in)
DRIVING WHEELS: 1827mm (72in)
GRATE AREA: 1.1m² (12sq ft)
HEATING SURFACE: 74.3m² (800sq ft)
TRACTIVE EFFORT: 2211kg (4876lb)
TOTAL WEIGHT: 40.3t (88,928lb)

Notable on Jenny Lind are the sandbox and sandpipe to spray sand under the big wheel and stop it from slipping when getting traction.

ATLAS 0-8-0 PHILADELPHIA & READING RAILROAD (P&RR)

Several innovative features appear on this Baldwin design for the Reading Railroad. One is the sandbox, set behind the smokestack and with a feed-pipe to the second set of driving wheels. Wheel-spin on wet or icy rails was a constant problem, particularly as trains got heavier, and a spray of fine sand helped to 'get the drag' and set the train in motion. Excessive wheel-spin also damaged the rail surface. Another novelty is the cab. Previously, any cab fitted was put on by the railway company, but from around this time, and long in advance of European and European-owned railways, American locomotives generally had cabs. It was said that some enginemen did not like them, because they made it more difficult to jump clear in the event of a coming collision, but the gain in working comfort, especially in

winter and wet weather, must have been very great. The third feature is less immediately apparent, though the clustering of the wheels is an indication. All four driving axles are

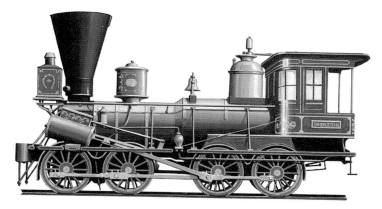

coupled and connected, but the front pair are mounted in a truck that allows a degree of lateral movement, helping to articulate the long wheelbase. The rod joining the

second and third sets of wheels is hinged to allow for this. Known as the 'flexible beam truck' system, it was introduced by Baldwin on a 4-2-0 converted to a 4-6-0, before being used on eight-wheelers. It was successful enough to remain in use for some 20 years, but its main disadvantage was that it was only suitable for low speed working. The introduction of the 4-6-0 locomotive, equally flexible and with far greater speed potential, killed off the flexible beam truck around 1866.

Atlas with its handsome cab. On this big engine, the outer skin of the boiler is no longer of wood, but polished 'Russia iron'.

BOILER PRESSURE: not known
CYLINDERS: 393x508mm (15.5x20in)
DRIVING WHEELS: 1167.5mm (46in)
GRATE AREA: not known
HEATING SURFACE: not known
TRACTIVE EFFORT: not known
TOTAL WEIGHT: 20.3t (44,800lb)

'IRON DUKE' CLASS 4-2-2 GREAT WESTERN RAILWAY (GWR)

The original engines of the Great Western Railway (GWR) in 1838–39 were among the weirdest mechanical contrivances of their time, built for the line by contractors who were trying to live up to the aura of genius surrounding Isambard Brunel, the company's engineer and presiding spirit. Fortunately, it also had a Newcastle-trained, practical locomotive engineer in Brunel's assistant, Daniel Gooch, who provided the company with a locomotive stock that was second to none. Brunel's contribution was the broad gauge track on which the locomotives ran. At 2138mm (84.17in), it was the widest in the

world. It was somewhat ironic that Brunel, who set himself against the Stephensons with his choice of gauge, should have ended up using standard Stephenson-type locomotives to operate the trains on his line. By 1847, Gooch had established the style and range of GWR engines, and in this year introduced the 'Iron Duke' class for the fastest expresses and mail trains. Twenty-two were built at the company's Swindon works between 1847 and 1851. Construction was very robust, with sandwich frames complemented by three sets of inside plate frames, running from the back of the two inside cylinders to the

front of the firebox. The cranked driving axle was supported by all five frames; the carrying wheels by the outer frames only. Despite the availability of American experience, Gooch did not provide a leading bogie, opting instead to fix the two front axles in the frame. The boiler was domeless and steam was taken from a perforated pipe that ran to a regulator box placed inside the smoke box. After 30 years or so of intensive service, they were replaced in the 1870s by locomotives of almost identical design, the only significant differences being higher steam pressure at 9.8kg/cm² (140psi)

and the introduction of cabs for the crew.

The GWR's choice of gauge brought difficulties as soon as railways began to extend across the country, and a Royal Commission was set up in 1845 to consider the future gauge of British railways. It decided in favour of the Stephenson gauge of 1435mm (56.5in), which accounted for many more miles than the broad gauge, and though the GWR retained its broad gauge until 1891, it ultimately had to come into line, just as happened with the US lines in the 1860s and 1870s. In the 1840s, however, the broad-gauge GWR was the fastest railway in Britain, if not the world. The Paddington (London)–Bristol mail train was allowed 56 minutes to run the 85km (53 miles) between London and Didcot, its first stop; and 29 minutes for the next 39km (24.25 miles) to Swindon. To maintain such a schedule, speeds of 112km/h (70mph) or more must have been commonplace.

BOILER PRESSURE: 7.05kg/cm² (100psi)
CYLINDERS: 457x609mm (18x24in)
DRIVING WHEELS: 2440mm (96in)
GRATE AREA: 2m² (21.5sq ft)
HEATING SURFACE: 166.2m² (1790.2sq ft)
TRACTIVE EFFORT: 3084kg (6800lb)
TOTAL WEIGHT: 24.4t (53,760lb)

A twentieth-century replica of 'Iron Duke', at the National Railway Museum, York.

LIMMAT 4-2-2 NORTHERN RAILWAY

SWITZERLAND 1847

Switzerland, today the hub of the European railway system, had no railway until 1847, when the Northern Railway was constructed from Zürich to Baden Baden in Germany. Opened on 19 August 1847, it was operated at first by two locomotives supplied by Emil Kessler of Karlsruhe, Germany. Like many other German engines of the time, *Limmat*, the first of the pair, has a Norris look. The firebox as well as the boiler is lagged with wood planking, and the engine has a bonnet-type chimney with a lid and inner spark baffles. The original boiler was replaced in 1866 and the engine then ran for a further 16 years before being scrapped in 1882. On the centenary of Swiss railways in 1947, a full-size replica was constructed, which is still preserved today.

BOILER PRESSURE: 5.5kg/cm² (78psi)
CYLINDERS: 340x500mm (14x20in)
DRIVING WHEELS: 1300mm (51.2in)
GRATE AREA: 1.1m² (11.8sq ft)
HEATING SURFACE: 63.1m² (679.4sq ft)
TRACTIVE EFFORT: 2302kg (5076lb)
TOTAL WEIGHT: 30t (66,150lb)

The replica *Limmat* poses under an electric power wire. Even the cylinders are lagged with wooden strips. The front four wheels are not in a bogie but are fixed to the frame.

STEINBRUCK 4-4-0 VIENNA–GLOGGNITZ RAILWAY

AUSTRIA 1848

If British designers balked at using the leading bogie at home, they were less constrained when designing engines abroad, and this engine had a radial truck developed by its designer, the emigré Scottish engineer John Haswell. Of course, in Austria, as in the United States, the tracks were often more lightly laid, as well as more sharply curved, than the proudly named 'permanent way' of the British railways. In other respects, *Steinbruck* was built very much on Norris lines, apart from a huge spark-arrestor chimney, which anticipated later Austrian practice. *Steinbruck* had a long and impressive career, ending with the Graz–Köflach Railway, a great home for veteran motive power, in 1910. It has been preserved and is displayed today in the Vienna Railway Museum.

BOILER PRESSURE: 5.5kg/cm² (78psi)
CYLINDERS: 369x790mm (14.5x31in)
DRIVING WHEELS: 1422mm (55.75in)
GRATE AREA: 1.0m² (10sq ft)
HEATING SURFACE: 70.6m² (760sq ft)
TRACTIVE EFFORT: 2610kg (5750lb)
TOTAL WEIGHT: 31.75t (70,000lb)

ELEPHANT 4-4-0 SACRAMENTO VALLEY RAILROAD (SVR)

Built to the one-time standard southern US gauge of 1524mm (5ft), by John Souther's Globe Works of Boston, Massachusetts, this 4-4-0 had the unusual arrangement of inside cylinders and external valve gear. Although almost certainly originally ordered by a Southern line, it was purchased by an engineering contractor and shipped to

California, where it was used in a land-clearing scheme on the San Francisco city waterfront before the civic authorities banned its use. California's first railway, the Sacramento Valley, bought it in 1850, renaming it *Garrison* after the company chairman. In 1865, it was regauged to the standard 1435mm (4ft 8.5in) gauge when the transcontinental line

reached California and the SVR became its western end. Rebuilt in 1869, fitted with link motion valve gear, and renamed *Pioneer*, it ran for a further 10 years and was then used as a reserve locomotive until 1886, when it was finally scrapped.

The re-gauged *Pioneer* locomotive shows its features. The big driving wheels suggest it was built as a passenger locomotive.

BOILER PRESSURE: not known
CYLINDERS: 381x508mm (15x20in)
DRIVING WHEELS: 1802mm (71in)
GRATE AREA: 0.9m² (9.63sq ft)
HEATING SURFACE: 66m² (710sq ft)
TRACTIVE EFFORT: not known
TOTAL WEIGHT: 25.4t (56,000lb)

'BLOOMER' CLASS 4-2-2 LONDON & NORTH WESTERN RAILWAY (LNWR)

Although still of single-driver type, like Edward Bury's small engines, these locomotives, replacing the Buries on the London–Birmingham line, were much more powerful, and gave good service on this trunk route, which was becoming increasingly busy as further lines were linked to it. The class ultimately numbered 40, plus a further 36 'Small Bloomers' with smaller driving wheels of 1980mm (78in) diameter, intended for secondary services. The designer was J. C. McConnell, who took an iconoclastic view of

the notion that boilers should be set low: in some way, the combination of high boiler and big driving wheels suggested the pioneering dress reforms of Mrs Amelia Bloomer, who recommended baggy cycling trousers for women – and the nickname became an enduring one. It is notable by now that the old wooden-lagged exterior of the locomotive boiler, almost universal in the 1840s, has given way to an iron skin, with lagging material packed inside to give better insulation. Later, asbestos would often be used for this purpose, with no awareness at the time of the health hazards being incurred. The 'Bloomers' would have looked very up-to-date compared with the older locomotives still running.

Gleaming in the LNWR's 'blackberry black' livery, the preserved 'Bloomer' No. 1009 on display in 1992.

BOILER PRESSURE: 10.6kg/cm² (150psi)
CYLINDERS: 406x558mm (16x22in)
DRIVING WHEELS: 2130mm (84in)
GRATE AREA: 1.33m² (14.5sq ft)
HEATING SURFACE: 106.6m² (1448.5sq ft)
TRACTIVE EFFORT: 3854lb (8500lb)
TOTAL WEIGHT: 30t (66,080lb)

'BOURBONNAIS' 0-6-0 PARIS–LYON–MEDITERRANEAN RAILWAY (PLM) FRANCE 1854

By the middle of the 19th century, railway freight traffic was increasing greatly with the rise of industry, the growth of population, and the increased output of coal mines and iron works. In industrial countries, freight locomotives began to outnumber passenger types, and to form classes of much greater number. Typical of this development was the 'Bourbonnais' type, first built by J. F. Cail of Lille, and reaching a total number of 1057 between 1854 and 1882. Comparable and almost contemporary was the British DX 0-6-0 of the London & North Western Railway, designed by J. F. Ramsbottom, of which 943 were built at Crewe between 1858 and 1874. Both classes were designed for heavy haulage at modest speed, and both went through modest evolution over the decades, including the provision of cabs. The French engines had outside cylinders, the British ones had inside cylinders. They were

relatively small locomotives, but much of their work was on short hauls and lightweight trains, and when the power of one was not enough, it was easy to add another. They had long careers: between 1907 and 1913, 215 of the Bourbonnais were converted to side-tank engines for shunting work in yards; and 500 of the DX class were rebuilt into 'Special DX', of which the last to remain in use was retired in 1930.

Both classes had valve gear operated by internal Stephenson link motion. For engines that might have to spend much time shunting or going backwards, an effective reversing gear was essential. This aspect of the locomotive was always very unsatisfactory in the early years. Some engines had to be started with the aid of a crowbar, and it was often extremely difficult to get an engine into reverse gear. The situation was much improved following the invention in 1842 of

the 'Stephenson link motion', so called because it was devised and perfected in Robert Stephenson's Newcastle workshops by two of his men, William Williams and William Howe. Instead of the old 'gab gear', which relied on hooking the mechanism into position, this gear used a curved slot that joined the ends of two connecting rods fixed to eccentrics on the driving axle. Raising or lowering the slot, by means of a lever in the cab, set the gear for forwards or backwards motion. Not only that, it could be set in intermediate positions that provided different cut-off points for the admission of steam to the cylinders, and so gave the driver far more control over the power at his disposal. Robert Stephenson & Co. did not seek a patent, though other engineers were not slow to design modified versions and obtain patents for them. However, the Stephenson link motion, which was usually fitted inside the frame,

remained the most frequently used form of valve gear right up to the twentieth century, in all countries.

A further refinement available from 1849 and fitted to these locomotives was the first efficient steam pressure gauge, invented by the French scientist Etienne Bourdon. Relatively crude mercury gauges had been available since the time of *Rocket*, but this was a great improvement. With its arrival, boiler explosions became much rarer, and drivers were much more willing to work their locomotives to the maximum safe capacity without going 'into the red'.

BOILER PRESSURE: 10kg/cm² (142.5psi)
CYLINDERS: 450x650mm (17.75x25.5in)
DRIVING WHEELS: 1300mm (51.2in)
GRATE AREA: 1.34m² (14.4sq ft)
HEATING SURFACE: 85.4m² (919.6sq ft)
TRACTIVE EFFORT: 8616kg (19,000lb)
TOTAL WEIGHT: 35.56t (78,400lb)
(engine only)

4-4-0 NORTH-EAST RAILWAY SWITZERLAND 1854

The 4-4-0 was usually considered as a wheel arrangement for a passenger train engine, but goods haulage was the primary purpose of this class of eight, constructed by Josef Anton Maffei's locomotive works in Munich. By this time,

Maffei had been in business for 17 years and was supplying locomotives to a growing number of railways in Germany and Central Europe. The Nord-Ost Bahn was centred at Zürich. Between 1876 and 1879, most of the 4-4-0s were given new boilers

at its own works, and some survived until 1889.

BOILER PRESSURE: 7kg/cm² (100psi)
CYLINDERS: 380x559mm (15x22in)
DRIVING WHEELS: 1676mm (66in)
GRATE AREA: 1.1m² (11.8sq ft)

HEATING SURFACE: 83m² (893.6sq ft)
TRACTIVE EFFORT: 2890kg (6375lb)
TOTAL WEIGHT: 43.7t (96,358lb)

SUSQUEHANNA 0-8-0 PHILADELPHIA & READING RAILROAD (P&RR) USA 1854

Camel was the name of the first of Ross Winans' distinctive locomotives in 1848, and 'Camel' became the designation of all of them, including this 0-8-0 type. All had a wide, sloping firebox, and the cab on top of the boiler, rather as if the engine had gathered up a signal cabin as it went along. Many had what looked like a double funnel, with a cylindrical ash-container set in front of the chimney.

Winans had been around railways since before 1829, when he was in England at the Rainhill trials. With the Camels, he set out to provide a locomotive that would burn coal effectively and economically. The first of the

BOILER PRESSURE: 6.3kg/cm² (90psi)
CYLINDERS: 482x558mm (19x22in)
DRIVING WHEELS: 1091mm (43in)
GRATE AREA: 2.2 m² (23.5sq ft)

HEATING SURFACE: c 93 m² (1000sq ft)
TRACTIVE EFFORT: 6970kg (14120lb)
TOTAL WEIGHT: 27.43t (60,480lb)
(engine only)

'Camels' had been intended for the Boston & Maine Railroad, which rejected it after road tests, and it was then sold to the Reading Railroad. From then on, Winans found his main customers in the Philadelphia & Reading (P&RR) and Baltimore & Ohio (B&O) railroads (he was quite a substantial shareholder in the latter), and around 300 Camels were built: the only type of locomotive his works would turn out.

The design was ingenious but had two structural drawbacks: the excessive weight of the unsupported firebox behind the wheels and frame, and the need for the tender drawgear to pass through the very hot area beneath the firebox. Though derided by some as 'mud-diggers', and loathed by firemen who had to stand on the open tender and shovel coal into the huge box, the Camels performed useful if slow service on

heavy coal trains. *Susquehanna* is recorded on one occasion as taking 110 four-wheeled coal waggons from Pottsville to Philadelphia, 153km (95 miles) at 13km/h (8mph), in the process consuming 4.57 tonnes (4.5 tons) of coal at a cost of $2.50 per ton. The fuel cost per mile, of 11.74 cents, compared favourably to the cost of cordwood, which could be as much as 25 cents per mile. In 1851, some Camels were built as wood-burners, however, for the Erie Railway, which had cheap timber supplies. The last of the breed was scrapped on the B&O in 1898, but elements of the design were perpetuated in 'Camelback' locomotives (see 1897).

THE GENERAL 4-4-0 WESTERN & ATLANTIC RAILROAD (W&A) USA 1855

A typical lightweight 4-4-0, of which hundreds were being built at the time, this locomotive would have no claim to fame had it not been caught up in a dramatic, though very minor,

action in the American Civil War. On 12 April 1862, it was hijacked at Big Shanty, Georgia, and the 'great locomotive chase' ensued before the *Texas* finally caught up with it. Built at Rogers Locomotive

Works, of Paterson, NJ, with its bar frames, big exposed wheels, wide stack, massive headlight, 'cow catcher', bell, and bright paintwork and polish, it stands for a whole generation of engines made

familiar through Western movies, but which could be found all over the spreading US railway system. Another feature more typical of American rather than European locomotive design at this time was the tapering 'wagon-top' boiler. Also typical of the period is the double-bogie tender. *The General* is still preserved at Chattanooga, and capable of running, though oil has replaced wood as its fuel.

BOILER PRESSURE: 9.8kg/cm² (140psi)
CYLINDERS: 381x558mm (15x22in)
DRIVING WHEELS: 1523mm (60in)
GRATE AREA: 1.15m² (12.5sq ft)
HEATING SURFACE: 72.8m² (784.4sq ft)
TRACTIVE EFFORT: 3123kg (6885lb)
TOTAL WEIGHT: 22.8t (50,300lb)

The *General*: American designers were very conscious of their engines' appearance.

CLASS Q34 2-4-0 GREAT INDIAN PENINSULA RAILWAY (GIPR)

INDIA 1856

India's first railway was the 1675mm (66in) gauge Bombay-Thana Railway of 1853, which by 1856 had expanded into the Great Indian Peninsula railway (GIPR). With colonial India administered by the British East India Company, British capital built the Indian railways, and Britain was the natural source of locomotives. This plain-looking inside-cylinder machine, supplied by Kitson & Co. of Leeds, was

typical of many that operated on the early Indian railway system. A canopied cab would normally be added on arrival to fend off the Indian sun and monsoon rain. One member of the class, *Sindh*, is preserved.

CYLINDERS: 381x533mm (15x21in)
DRIVING WHEELS: 1675mm (66in)
OTHER DETAILS NOT AVAILABLE

British austerity, as exported to India: the domeless Class Q34.

CLASS 030 0-6-0 MADRID–ZARAGOZA–ALICANTE RAILWAY (MZA)

SPAIN 1857

This was a very long-lived class of locomotives, their longevity partly due to their quality and partly to the facts that much of their work was light yard shunting, and that the MZA did not have the funds for replacing locomotives which, though technically obsolete,

were still capable of work. The inside-cylindered design was English, and Ritson, Wilson of Leeds, England, built the first 10, with others coming from Kitsons of Leeds and Cail of Lille. In the course of the years, wooden cabs were added, and the locomotives

were provided with air brakes. Some of the class were at work for a hundred years, and helped to make Spain a place of pilgrimage for veteran locomotive enthusiasts in the 1950s. One of the first batch, No. 030.213, has been preserved.

BOILER PRESSURE: 8kg/cm² (114psi)
CYLINDERS: 440x600mm (17.3x23.6in)
DRIVING WHEELS: 1430mm (56in)
GRATE AREA: 1.3m² (14sq ft)
HEATING SURFACE: not known
TRACTIVE EFFORT: 5532kg (12,200lb)
TOTAL WEIGHT: 49.2t (108,486lb)

'PROBLEM' CLASS 2-2-2 LONDON & NORTH WESTERN RAILWAY (LNWR)

GREAT BRITAIN 1859

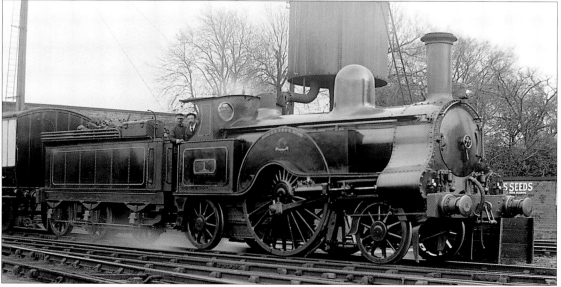

One can only suppose that the English Victorians liked problems, since this Crewe-built class was a popular and successful one, working passenger express trains on the London–Birmingham–Carlisle main line. Its official title was the 'Lady of the Lake' class, after the name of the first engine, but they were always known as 'Problems'. The designer was the company's Chief Mechanical Engineer, John Ramsbottom, who was also an inventor of great ability. One of his contributions was the water-trough, a long,

No.1, *Saracen*, at Lichfield (Trent Valley) station with a stopping train, around 1903. Note the davits for an alarm wire mounted on the tender.

shallow reservoir set between the rails, enabling engines to scoop up a supply for the tender tanks without having to stop. He also invented a safety-valve that could not be tampered with – to do so was still a temptation to engine crews frustrated by lack of steam. The Problems maintained the typical Crewe look, with the curve of the smokebox extended to embrace the outside cylinders.

Ramsbottom was also quick to seize on another invention that

was very important in terms of overall locomotive development – the injector, which had been invented in 1859 by the Frenchman Henri Giffard in connection with his lightweight steam engine for powered air flight. Apart from the first 10, all members of this class were equipped with injectors. Until the introduction of the injectors, locomotives could pump water into their boilers only when in motion, usually by means of a

pump worked from the crosshead crank, but the steam injector allowed water to be forced in when the engine was at a standstill. Some countries were slower than others to adopt the injector; it worked best with pure water, which was not always available for many operators. It worked only with a supply of cold water, and many railways were using feedwater heaters to pre-heat water in order to maintain a higher temperature inside the

boiler. The Problems were also the first engines to be fitted with a screw-operated reversing gear rather than the old heavy lever.

BOILER PRESSURE: 8.4kg/cm² (120psi)
CYLINDERS: 406x609mm (16x24in)
DRIVING WHEELS: 2322mm (91.5in)
GRATE AREA: 1.4m² (14.9sq ft)
HEATING SURFACE: 102m² (1098sq ft)
TRACTIVE EFFORT: 3102kg (6840lb)
TOTAL WEIGHT: 27.43t (60,480lb)

4-4-0 TARRAGONA–BARCELONA & FRANCE RAILWAY   SPAIN 1859

Although built for a Spanish railway, the two engines constructed by Slaughter, Gruning of Bristol, England, set the pattern for a whole generation of British 4-4-0 locomotives to come, with inside cylinders, low footplate at the same level for engine and

tender, and wheels part-concealed by splashers. Among the few differences between these and their later sisters is that they had outside-framed bogies, while most of the British 4-4-0s had bogies with inside frames and bearings. The Tarragona line, of 1567mm

(61.7in) gauge, later part of the Madrid Zaragoza & Alicante Railway, entrusted the design to the builders, who are otherwise best known for their tank engines for the North London Railway, and the two 4-4-0s were still running in the late 1890s.

BOILER PRESSURE: 9.8kg/cm² (140psi)
CYLINDERS: 393x558mm (15.5x22in)
DRIVING WHEELS: 1903mm (75in)
GRATE AREA: 1.3m² (14.5sq ft)
HEATING SURFACE: 92.4m² (995sq ft)
TRACTIVE EFFORT: 3803kg (8386lb)
TOTAL WEIGHT: 36.83t (81,200lb)

EXPRESS LOCOMOTIVE 2-2-2 EGYPTIAN GOVERNMENT RAILWAY (EGR)   EGYPT 1862

New locomotives were prominent at the London International Exhibition of 1862. One was this single-driver type, built at the Caledonian Railway's St Rollox Works in Glasgow, to a 1859 design by Benjamin Conner. Its curvaceous, Crewe-style lines, with smokebox and cylinders forming a single rounded shape, attracted the attention of Said Pasha, the Ottoman Viceroy of Egypt, who placed an order for it on the spot and later ordered two

more for passenger service between Cairo and Alexandria and in the Nile Valley. One of this locomotive's features, rapidly becoming standard on all locomotives, was steel tyres on the wheels. These had been developed by Krupps of Essen, Germany, in 1851, and were assiduously marketed to world railways. Custom was good, since the steel tyres could do five times the mileage of wrought-iron or cast-iron tyres, and were also more

suitable for fast running. The American historian John White Jr. noted that, 'the acceptance of steel tires is unparalleled for its speed and completeness' in an industry that was already showing signs of conservatism on both sides of the Atlantic.

BOILER PRESSURE: 8.4 kg/cm² (120psi)
CYLINDERS: 438x609mm (17.25x24in)
DRIVING WHEELS: 2487mm (98in)
GRATE AREA: 1.29m² (13.9sq ft)
HEATING SURFACE: 108.6m² (1169sq ft)
TRACTIVE EFFORT: 3370kg (7430lb)
TOTAL WEIGHT: 31.14t (68,656lb)

The Pasha's engine. Though outside cylinders are fitted, their presence is concealed as much as possible by the outer frame and the big 'paddle-wheel' splasher. A rudimentary cab is fitted, but the footplate space is very limited.

CLASS Y43 4-6-0T GREAT INDIAN PENINSULA RAILWAY (GIPR)

BOILER PRESSURE: 8.4kg/cm² (120psi)*
CYLINDERS: 508x609mm (20x24in)
DRIVING WHEELS: 1318mm (52in)
GRATE AREA: 2.4m² (25.9sq ft)

HEATING SURFACE: 133.5m² (1438sq ft)
TRACTIVE EFFORT: 8540kg (18,830lb)*
TOTAL WEIGHT: 49.79t (109,760lb)

Although Indian railways were first worked by standard British-type locomotives, there were aspects of the Indian system that needed more specialized attention. One of these was the Ghat Inclines of the Great Indian Peninsula Railway (GIPR) with their long stretches at 1 in 37. Five engines were built by Sharp, Stewart in Manchester for work on this section, to a design from J. Kershaw. Unusual in appearance, they had saddle tanks fitted over the front end of the boiler, supported by a very short four-wheel bogie, which could slide laterally. They had outside frames and inside cylinders – these being the largest yet fitted to a British locomotive – and sledge brakes, which worked by pressing down on the rails. Brakes of this kind were tricky to apply: too much force and they tended to lift the wheels off the tracks and derail the engine, and they were not widely used. By the 1860s, designers were beginning to apply brakes to locomotive driving wheels, though these were still much more the exception rather than the rule.

CLASS 250 2-6-0 ERIE RAILWAY (ERIE)

The era of the 4-4-0's dominance on US railroads was fading by the 1860s, and railroads were looking for greater freight-hauling power. Six driving wheels was the next step up, and the Erie ordered 10 2-6-0s from Danforth, Cook & Co., of Paterson, NJ, to work on its wide 1827mm (72in) line. Soon the company was ordering more. The '250' class were anthracite burners, equipped with a patent grate developed by James Millholland of the Philadelphia & Reading Railroad, a keen innovator. Formed of iron water tubes that linked the water spaces at each side of the firebox, this was only one of a range of more-or-less efficient patent designs on offer to US railroads. Spark-arrestor devices were the most frequent – more than 1000 patents were issued in the United States during the nineteenth century for different kinds of smokestack and spark-arrestor. Lineside fires caused by flying embers were not only a hazard but a drain on company finances, as compensation had to be paid to landowners.

BOILER PRESSURE: 8.4kg/cm² (120psi)
CYLINDERS: 431x558mm (17x22in)
DRIVING WHEELS: 1370mm (54in)
GRATE AREA: 1.95m² (21sq ft)
HEATING SURFACE: 116.5m² (1255sq ft)
TRACTIVE EFFORT: 4805kg (10,596lb)
TOTAL WEIGHT: 36.07t (79,520lb)
(engine only)

A later version of the 'Mogul' arrangement, No. 334 of the Central Vermont, built in 1884, with Westinghouse brake equipment.

NO. 1 4-4-0 GREAT NORTHERN RAILROAD (GN)

The first train in Minnesota was drawn by this engine, on the St Paul & Pacific Railroad, which was ultimately to form part of the Great Northern's coast-to-coast route, completed in 1893. Built in 1861 by Smith & Jackson of Paterson, NJ, it was shipped up the Missouri River by barge from the railhead at La Crosse in anticipation of the line's opening. Though beginning to be outmoded, 4-4-0s were the standard power of the St Paul & Pacific in its first years, hauling passenger and freight trains. No.1, bearing the name *William Crooks*, has been restored and preserved.

BOILER PRESSURE: 8.4kg/cm² (120psi)
CYLINDERS: 304x558mm (12x22in)
DRIVING WHEELS: 1599mm (63in)
GRATE AREA: not known

HEATING SURFACE: not known
TRACTIVE EFFORT: 2267kg (5000lb)
TOTAL WEIGHT: 46.27t (102,000lb)

Almost contemporary with No. 1, and very similar in design, this locomotive was built by William Mason in Massachusetts for the US Military Railroads in the Civil War.

0-6-6-0 FREIGHT LOCOMOTIVE NORTHERN RAILWAY (NORD)

FRANCE 1863

In its chief mechanical engineer, Jules Pétiet, the *Nord* had a man who was not afraid of innovation and risk. A variety of interesting locomotive types, some successful, some not, are attributed to him. Most of his experimental locomotives led to nothing, and almost all had short lives. This design, however, presaged the 'duplex' drive that would power some mighty locomotives in the twentieth century. In original form, it had two sets of six coupled wheels in a fixed frame, each driven by a pair of outside cylinders. Although the axles at each end had capacity for lateral movement, the engine was too rigid to be effective: the notion of the articulated locomotive had yet to be worked out. Pétiet, keen to maximize the use of steam, incorporated a long exhaust flue from the blast pipe, passing along the top of the boiler and ending in a chimney at the cab-end, and passing through a steam drier and feedwater heater on the way. Although the boiler's heating surface was more than double that of the basic 'Bourbonnais' 0-6-0 goods engine, its steam-raising capacity was more theoretical than actual, and it was always difficult for it to supply enough steam to make the four cylinders work well.

The engine, intended for heavy freight haulage, also suffered from lack of power. In the end, a remarkable piece of locomotive surgery converted the 20 0-6-6-0s into 40 shunting tank engines. Incidentally, in the previous year Pétiet had tried another 'duplex' experiment, a tank locomotive with a single driving axle at each end, and three independent carrying axles between them. The design, which defies the Whyte wheel-notation system, was even less successful than the 0-6-6-0. In the UIC notation, it is A-1-1-1-A.

BOILER PRESSURE: 9kg/cm² (128psi)
CYLINDERS: 440x440mm (17.3x17.3in)
DRIVING WHEELS: 1065mm (42in)
GRATE AREA: 3.3m² (35.5sq ft)
HEATING SURFACE: 197.3m² (2124sq ft)
TRACTIVE EFFORT: 10,798kg (21,866lb)
TOTAL WEIGHT: 59.71t (131,638lb)

0-6-0 GOODS ENGINE MIDLAND RAILWAY (MR)

GREAT BRITAIN 1863

By the 1860s, railways had largely abandoned coke as a fuel. It was expensive, and coal was much cheaper and readily available. The old requirement of the Rainhill test, that a locomotive should consume its own smoke, was forgotten or ignored, especially in industrial areas where a host of factories were filling the air with sooty fumes. But the locomotive firebox, as then designed, did not burn coal efficiently, and much work went on in Britain and the United States to find a means of getting the necessary degree of combustion, and to minimize smoke production. Many complicated systems were tested and patented, using double fireboxes and 'combustion chambers', but the ultimate solution had an elegant simplicity. Almost simultaneously, the US and British engineers found that an arch of flame-resistant bricks, built across the firebox, created a much hotter fire, capable of raising more steam, burning the coal more efficiently, and producing less smoke. George S. Griggs, an inventive engineer, and Master Mechanic of the Boston & Providence Railroad, patented a brick arch in 1857. Charles Markham, on the Midland Railway in England, developed a combination of the brick arch with a deflector plate attached to the firedoor, and these innovations swiftly became permanent features of the steam locomotive. Here was another milestone, opening the way to much bigger fireboxes.

BOILER PRESSURE: 9.8kg/cm² (140psi)
CYLINDERS: 431x609mm (17x24in)
DRIVING WHEELS: 1586mm (62.5in)
GRATE AREA: 1.56m² (16.8sq ft)
HEATING SURFACE: 101.5m² (1093sq ft)
TRACTIVE EFFORT: 5980kg (13,200lb)
TOTAL WEIGHT: 35.56t (78,400lb)

This Midland class of 0-6-0 outside-framed goods engines, of which 315 were built between 1863 and 1874, was the first to be equipped with modern fireboxes from the start. They proved to be long-lived, and the last was not withdrawn until 1951.

This engine, designed by Samuel Johnson, was built in the 1880s. The MR eventually had 1570 0-6-0 locos.

'THATCHER PERKINS' CLASS 4-6-0 BALTIMORE & OHIO RAILROAD (B&O)

For many decades, the 4-6-0 type was the ideal medium-size locomotive, capable of fast passenger work as well as freight hauling. The precursor was a Norris-built engine, *Chesapeake*, supplied to the Philadelphia & Reading Railroad in 1847, and Septimus Norris later tried unsuccessfully to enforce a patent on the 4-6-0 wheel arrangement. Relatively few were built in the 1850s, partly because it was seen as a 'big' engine and existing tracks were often too light, though

Baldwin included the 'ten-wheeler' in its catalogue after 1852. The length of the wheelbase was also seen as a problem, and in early 4-6-0 locomotives the front set of coupled wheels was almost always unflanged. With heavier trains in the 1860s, and heavier rails forming the tracks, the 4-6-0 came into its own.

The design here was the work of Thatcher Perkins. At one time the Baltimore & Ohio (B&O) Railroad's Master Mechanic, he became a partner in the Smith, Perkins

Locomotive Works of Alexandria, VA. The class was intended to work passenger trains across the Allegheny Mountains between Piedmont and Grafton, and all were built at the B&O's own workshops at Mount Clare. Both track and bridges had to be strengthened before the 4-6-0s were allowed on the line. No. 117 ran in service until 1890, but escaped the cutting torch. It ran in the B&O's centennial parade of 1927, and is now preserved at the B&O Museum in Baltimore, owing

its survival to chance rather than to any special distinction of design or performance. A handsome specimen of its time, it now bears the name of its designer, though originally it was actually nameless. By the mid-1860s, American railroads had largely forsaken giving names to locomotives, and only numbers were their sole identities.

Perkins designed other 4-6-0s, including a freight design for the Louisville & Nashville Railroad, which he joined as master mechanic in 1868, and other US railways also used them. It was in northern Europe, however, that they became a very widely used standard type. Adoption was slow, with the first one appearing in Italy (see 1884), but from the 1900s thousands of 4-6-0 types were built by British and European railways for passenger, freight and mixed-traffic service.

BOILER PRESSURE: 5.25kg/cm² (75psi)
CYLINDERS: 482x660mm (19x26in)
DRIVING WHEELS: 1472mm (58in)
GRATE AREA: 1.8m² (19.4sq ft)
HEATING SURFACE: 103.4m² (1114sq ft)
TRACTIVE EFFORT: 4670kg (10,300lb)
TOTAL WEIGHT: not known

'Thatcher Perkins', an exemplar of hundreds of workaday 4-6-0s, with the building date noted on the cylinder. Brakes on the driving wheels were not yet a standard item.

TYPE 1 2-4-2 BELGIAN STATE RAILWAYS (ETAT BELGE)

Unmistakable in appearance, the Type 1 was the first important design of a great engineer, Alfred Belpaire, and it shows the firebox that he designed: a high, round-edged box intended to maximize the use of space for combustion.

The Belpaire firebox was also widely used in Britain, though hardly at all in Germany or France, and by only a handful of US railways. These did, however, include the mighty Pennsylvania Railroad, which made extensive use of it across several locomotive classes,

including the famous K4 'Pacific' type. Cockerills of Seraing built the first Type 1, and other Belgian and French builders also contributed, with building going on until 1884. The class finally numbered 153. Originally they had narrow stovepipe chimneys, but as they were reboilered between 1889 and 1896, a huge, square funnel was put on (later these were

exchanged for equally imposing elliptical ones). Intended for express service, they ran fast passenger trains on most of the Etat Belge's main lines until replaced by 'Pacifics' after 1918, when they ran secondary passenger trains. The last examples of the type were scrapped in 1926.

BOILER PRESSURE: 12kg/cm² (171psi)
CYLINDERS: 430x560mm (17x22in)
DRIVING WHEELS: 2000mm (79in)
GRATE AREA: not known
HEATING SURFACE: not known
TRACTIVE EFFORT: 5306kg (11,700lb)
TOTAL WEIGHT: 33.5t (73,867lb)

The illustration shows the Type 1 as fitted with the unique square chimney. Despite its quaint appearance, it was an advanced locomotive for its time.

METROPOLITAN TANK 4-4-0T METROPOLITAN RAILWAY (METR) GREAT BRITAIN 1864

The Metropolitan in London was the world's first underground railway, and this locomotive was designed specifically for use on it. The line was partly a 'cut-and-cover' one, which made some direct ventilation possible, but the smoke-filled tunnels were unpleasant, especially for the locomotive men.

As originally built by Beyer Peacock of Manchester, the engines had no cabs. Their most striking feature was the condensing apparatus. On each side of the engine, exhaust steam was carried back in two wide tubes, condensing into water as it cooled, and being returned to the side water tanks. This saved on water consumption and reduced the emission of steam, but did nothing to reduce the amount of smoke that was produced. Using high-quality steam coal helped to

BOILER PRESSURE: 9.16kg/cm² (130psi)
CYLINDERS: 432x609mm (17x24in)
DRIVING WHEELS: 1753mm (69in)
GRATE AREA: 2.7m² (19sq ft)
HEATING SURFACE: 94m² (1013.8 sq ft)
TRACTIVE EFFORT: 5034kg (11,000lb)
TOTAL WEIGHT: 42.83t (94,416lb)

some extent. Numbering 120, this was a hard-worked and also efficient class, several of which ran more than 1.6 million km (1,000,000 miles) in their working lives on what was a relatively short line. In 1871, five were built to the same design for the Rhenish

The condensing gear is clearly shown in this photograph from the 1860s. Like many other locomotive classes, the Metropolitan tanks were later provided with cabs.

Railway in Germany. In 1905, the Metropolitan was electrified, and most of the tank engines were sold off. Some were converted to

tender locomotives by the Cambrian Railway in Wales. Today, one of the Metropolitan tank types remains preserved in London.

0-6-0 NO. 148 RUSE–VARNA RAILWAY BULGARIA 1865

Four typical English 0-6-0s with inside cylinders, tall thin chimneys and six-wheel tenders with outside frames were built by Sharp, Stewart of Manchester, England, for Bulgaria's first railway. The 224km (139-mile) line ran from the Black Sea port of Varna to

Bulgaria's oldest preserved locomotive, built in Manchester, No. 148 was sold to the Chemins de Fer Orientaux of Turkey in 1873, but returned to Bulgaria in 1888, and is still kept at Ruse.

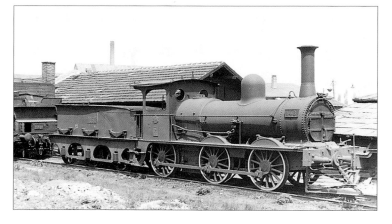

the Romanian frontier at Ruse, and the locomotives were shipped direct to Varna. In the first years of the line, they handled all traffic, goods and passenger. One of the engines, No. 148, is preserved.

BOILER PRESSURE: 8kg/cm² (114psi)
CYLINDERS: 432x610mm (17x24in)
DRIVING WHEELS: 1371mm (54in)
GRATE AREA: 1.3m² (13.9sq ft)
HEATING SURFACE: 92.6m² (997sq ft)
TRACTIVE EFFORT: 5347kg (11,790lb)
TOTAL WEIGHT: 30.6t (67,473lb)

CONSOLIDATION 2-8-0 LEHIGH & MAHANOY RAILROAD (L&M) USA 1866

The American locomotive builders, particularly Baldwins, always preferred to offer a catalogue of their own locomotive types for customers to choose from, making only minor adaptations or adding patent equipment as specified by the buyer. This usually worked very well, except when the customer had strong ideas of his own. Alexander Mitchell, Master Mechanic of the Lehigh & Mahanoy, was such a client: he

had drawn up a design for what he called a 'super-freight locomotive' for his hilly, coal-hauling road. It had eight coupled wheels, preceded by the single-axled 'safety truck', pivoted behind its axle, which had been patented by Levi Bissell in 1857. No locomotive of 2-8-0 formation had been built before, and Baldwins at first refused to take on the job, but then agreed, at a cost of $19,000 plus $950 war tax. It was built between April

and August 1866, and named *Consolidation* because the company had merged with the Lehigh Valley RR during its construction. The new engine was a triumphant success. In the end, its front truck was not the Bissell but a design by William Hudson of the Rogers Locomotive Works, using an equalizing lever to join the truck frame to the spring hangers of the front coupled wheels. Thus equipped, the 2-8-0 could make its way up

sinuous mountain tracks at speeds not considered possible before, and with unprecedented loads. Krupp steel tyres were fitted to the wheels and another still-new feature was the steam injector, backed up by feedwater pumps on each side, which worked off return cranks on the last set of coupled wheels. The long boiler, 4.5m (15ft) from firebox to smoke-box, could hold plenty of steam, and it was fired on high-quality anthracite. The

Lehigh Valley was extremely pleased, and ordered further examples.

Its high initial cost was quickly paid back in terms of work, and the 2-8-0, often called the 'Consolidation' type, became the standard 'big' freight locomotive for a time. From 1876, it became the Pennsylvania Railroad's basic road freight locomotive, and many more companies ordered it. On the Erie Railroad, it was calculated that 55 Consolidations were doing the work of 100 4-4-0 types. Although even larger types appeared, the 2-8-0 held its place and many thousands were built and worked all over the world, operating on narrow-gauge as well as standard and broad-gauge lines. In some regions, notably Latin America, its domination of freight traffic was not supplanted until the arrival of diesel-electrics, and modern versions were being built right up to the end of steam.

BOILER PRESSURE: 8.4 kg/m² (120psi)*
CYLINDERS: 507x609mm (20x24in)
DRIVING WHEELS: 1218mm (48in)
GRATE AREA: 2.3m² (25sq ft)

HEATING SURFACE: not known
TRACTIVE EFFORT: 10,070kg (20,400lb)
TOTAL WEIGHT: 38.88t (85,720lb)

Bereft of connecting rods, an extended-smokebox 2-8-0 awaits attention on a works road.

LANDWÜHRDEN 0-4-0 OLDENBURG STATE RAILWAYS   GERMANY 1867

German locomotive design was well-established by 1867, when Georg Krauss set up his new works in Munich (later merged with Maffei's). *Landwuhrden*, his first design, won a gold medal for design and workmanship at the Paris Exhibition of the same year. Among the little engine's features was a well-tank inside the frame, in which feed-water could be heated before transfer into the boiler. Used on lightweight passenger trains, it was withdrawn from service in 1900, but was preserved (without its tender) in the Nürnberg Transport Museum prior to the disastrous fire there.

BOILER PRESSURE: 10kg/cm² (142psi)
CYLINDERS: 355x560mm (14x22in)
DRIVING WHEELS: 1500mm (59in)
GRATE AREA: 0.98m² (10.5sq ft)

HEATING SURFACE: not known
TRACTIVE EFFORT: 4350kg (8820lb)
TOTAL WEIGHT: not known

CLASS G 0-6-0 SWEDISH RAILWAYS (SJ)   SWEDEN 1867

The first railway in Sweden was built from Nora to Ervalla in 1856, and by 1867 the country had a flourishing locomotive factory in Nydquist & Holm, of Trollhättan. These shared construction of the Class G, Sweden's most numerous locomotive so far, with Beyer Peacock of Manchester, England. Fifty-seven were built originally, and handled most main-line freight duties. As time progressed, some were fitted with new boilers and other modifications, forming subclasses Gb and Gc. Overall they were long-lived, with the last ones still active until 1921, and one member of Class Gc is preserved. Even for tough Nordic Sweden, it had a very open cab, with resultant discomfort for the crew. Makeshift shelters of tarpaulin were often rigged to mitigate the rigours of rain, wind and snow.

BOILER PRESSURE: 8.5kg/cm² (121psi)
CYLINDERS: 406x610mm (16x24in)
DRIVING WHEELS: 864mm (34ins)
GRATE AREA: 1.4m² (15sq ft)
HEATING SURFACE: not known
TRACTIVE EFFORT: 8425kg (18,580lb)
TOTAL WEIGHT: not known

CLASS 335 0-6-0 HUNGARIAN RAILWAYS (MÀV)

HUNGARY 1869

Two years old in 1869, MÀV was an amalgam of numerous mostly small or local lines, and it acquired as a result a great variety of essentially similar but unstandardized locomotive types. This new freight class was one of the first attempts to develop a coherent locomotive policy. In

appearance it was typically Central European of the period, with outside frames and outside cylinders, and an array of domes and boxes on the boiler-top, behind a stovepipe chimney fitted with a wide spark arrestor. Its 0-6-0 wheel arrangement was typical of European freight

locomotives of the time, and the class handled most of Hungary's freight trains, running on

independent company lines as well as those of the MÀV. One is preserved.

BOILER PRESSURE: 8.5kg/cm² (121psi)
CYLINDERS: 460x632mm (18x25in)
DRIVING WHEELS: 1220mm (48in)
GRATE AREA: 1.65m² (17.7sq ft)
HEATING SURFACE: 128.4m² (1382.4sq ft)
TRACTIVE EFFORT: 8570kg (17,355lb)
TOTAL WEIGHT: 39.6t (87,318lb)

'OUTRANCE' CLASS 2 4-4-0 NORTHERN RAILWAY (NORD)

FRANCE 1870

One of Jules Pétiet's most successful locomotives, this famous class was modelled on a 2-4-0 design of Archibald Sturrock's for England's Great Northern Railway, but with a four-wheel bogie and larger dimensions. Belpaire fireboxes were also fitted, to maximize steam production. Their prime task

was running heavy boat trains between Paris and the Channel ports over the rolling downs of northern France, a testing service for any locomotive, and which won the class its by-name of 'Outrance', 'utmost'. Much admired for their performance, Outrance-type locomotives were also built for the Madrid Caceres & Portugal

Railway in Spain, and for the Rosario & Puerto Belgrano Railway in Argentina, making them a truly international type, especially as the Spanish and Argentinian examples were built in Germany by Hartmann of Chemnitz and Schwarzkopff of Berlin respectively. The French later exchanged their original four-

wheel tenders for larger-capacity six-wheelers, and ran the boat trains until displaced by new de Glehn compounds from 1891.

BOILER PRESSURE: 10kg/cm² (145psi)
CYLINDERS: 462x609mm (18.2x24in)
DRIVING WHEELS: 2087.5mm (82.25in)
GRATE AREA: 1.95m² (21sq ft)
HEATING SURFACE: 99m² (1066sq ft)
TRACTIVE EFFORT: 5400kg (11,900lb)
TOTAL WEIGHT: 42.16t (92,960lb) (engine only)

Pétiet was among the first designers outside Belgium to appreciate the potential of the Belpaire-type firebox, which he used on the 'Outrance' class.

NO. 1 4-2-2 GREAT NORTHERN RAILWAY (GNR)

GREAT BRITAIN 1870

At a time when locomotive designers in most countries were trying to improve tractive performance by introducing more coupled wheels, there was something almost perverse about British railway engineers' continued preference for the single driving axle. In the case of this type, only one out of four axles is transmitting force to the rail. To American eyes especially, such engines seemed almost toylike. Factors in their favour included the relatively short journeys of British trains, the high quality of track – the 15.2-tonne (15-ton) maximum axle-load of No. 1 would have been unacceptable in many other places – and the fact that stabling and servicing equipment was built

for small engines. Single-drivers were cheaper to build than coupled engines. Trains, too, were relatively lightweight, though at 254 tonnes (250 tons) the Great Northern's tightly timed expresses to Leeds were by no means flyweights. Most of the larger British companies, including the GNR, designed and built their own locomotives, a process that insulated them to some degree from the wider world. Private British builders were producing much bigger engines for the export market. The Great Northern's chief mechanical engineer, Patrick Stirling, had strong views on locomotives' appearance, believing it should be as plain as possible. He was known

to dislike bogies and to abhor outside cylinders. But his most classic design, of which No. 1 was the class leader, embodies both these aspects. It had to have a four-wheel bogie to carry its weight, and only outside cylinders could drive a rod to turn the huge 2460mm (97in) wheels without pushing into the boiler space. But this engine was said to be Stirling's favourite among his designs. Certainly it excelled in terms of performance, though, like most British express engines of the period, it had to be 'thrashed' to achieve its potential, so much so that one observer compared its passage to an erupting volcano. Another of Stirling's prejudices was against 'double-heading' – his engines were

BOILER PRESSURE: 9.9kg/cm² (140psi)
CYLINDERS: 457x711mm (18x28in)
DRIVING WHEELS: 2460mm (97in)
GRATE AREA: 1.6m² (17.6sq ft)
HEATING SURFACE: 108m² (1165sq ft)
TRACTIVE EFFORT: 5034kg (11,000lb)
TOTAL WEIGHT: 39t (86,128lb)

meant to be able to pull their trains by themselves. In October 1875, No. 22 of this class ran from Kings Cross (London) to Peterborough, 122.7km (76.25 miles) in 92 minutes with an 18-carriage train, at an average speed of 80km/h (50mph), mostly against adverse gradients. In the 1890s, with steel tyres fitted on the driving wheels, they were still running high-speed

services. High performance was achieved by the driver and fireman producing the maximum amount of steam possible, which meant that a Stirling 4-2-2 at full speed trailed a shower of sparks and glowing coal

fragments as it roared along; but good design was evident in the generous steam passages and careful balance of moving parts. Scrapping began in 1899, and No. 1 ended its active service as

The preserved No. 1 demonstrates the 'volcanic' impression it gave to contemporary lineside observers. The coaches are modern.

station pilot at Doncaster, being retired in 1907. It is preserved at

the National Railway Museum in York.

ICHIGO 2-4-0T IMPERIAL JAPANESE RAILWAYS

Ten small tank engines were imported from England in 1871, in anticipation of the opening of Japan's first railway line, from Tokyo to Yokohama, on 14 October 1872. Five manufacturers supplied them, with No. 1, *Ichigo*, coming from the Vulcan Foundry at Newton le Willows, Lancashire. In British style, they had no driving cabs, which were added before they went into service. No. 1 was sold to the Shimabara Railway Company in Kyushu in 1911 and worked until 1936, when it was bought for the Tokyo Transport Museum as the first locomotive

to work in Japan. A famous coloured print of 1875 shows one of these engines with a train at the Tokyo waterfront.

BOILER PRESSURE: 8.4kg/cm² (120psi)
CYLINDERS: 304.5x456.8mm (12x18in)
DRIVING WHEELS: 1294mm (51in)
GRATE AREA: 97m² (9sq ft)
HEATING SURFACE: 52.5m² (565.2sq ft)
TRACTIVE EFFORT: 2350kg (5180lb)
TOTAL WEIGHT: 18.8t (41,440lb)

Japan's first locomotive. Initially British influence on Japanese railway development was strong.

FAIRLIE 0-4-4-0 FESTINIOG RAILWAY

Now a tourist line, the Ffestiniog Railway was built to carry slate from the hills to the coast, and, though of only 600mm (23.5in) gauge, needed effective motive power. As such, it was typical of hundreds of other small mineral-hauling lines throughout the world, and this was the market Robert Fairlie set out to tap with his articulated patent locomotive design of 1865. Though Fairlies were often double-ended, the 'single Fairlie' was also patented. The locomotive frame was rigid, and the two wheel sets were articulated independently, enabling it to traverse tight curves. Disadvantages of the Fairlie included the lack of coal space and

STEAM PRESSURE: 9.9kg/cm^2 (140psi)
CYLINDERS: 216x355mm (8.5x14in)
DRIVING WHEELS: 812mm (32in)
GRATE AREA: 1m^2 (11.2sq ft)
HEATING SURFACE: 66.2m^2 (713sq ft)
TRACTIVE EFFORT: 3400kg (7500lb)
TOTAL WEIGHT: 20.37t (44,912lb)

the difficulty of sealing the flexible steam connections between the boiler and the bogie-mounted driving wheels. Many were exported, however, mostly to narrow-gauge lines in Latin America and Russia, though they also flourished on the Welsh mineral lines. The Ffestiniog built an oil-fired Fairlie in 1979 to complement its veteran of 1872, and a replica 'single Fairlie' in 1999.

All the typical features of a double-ended Fairlie can be seen in the Festiniog Railway's veteran of 1872, *Merddyn Emrys*, with a train on the Dduallt Spiral, in July 1994.

'TERRIER' 0-6-0T LONDON, BRIGHTON & SOUTH COAST RAILWAY (LB&SCR)

The 'Terriers' were lightweight engines designed specifically for start-stop workings on the original lightweight rails of South London's suburban system (around 170 station stops in the course of a working day), and they placed a maximum axle weight of no more than 8.3 tonnes (8 tons) on the rails. Their smallness and resultant sense of dogged effort in action made them popular with the travelling public, but they were also well-suited to their work. Fifty of these inside-cylinder tanks were built between 1872 and 1880, originally given the names of stations on the routes they served, and most had long careers.

Stroudley had his locomotives painted in a striking yellow-green shade he called 'improved engine green', but this now lies beneath the liveries of the several successive owners of the two 'Terriers', which still survive in steaming condition.

BOILER PRESSURE: 9.9kg/cm^2 (140psi)
CYLINDERS: 330x508mm (13x20in)
DRIVING WHEELS: 122cm (48in)
GRATE AREA: 1.4m^2 (15sq ft)
HEATING SURFACE: 49m^2 (528sq ft)
TRACTIVE EFFORT: 3810kg (8400lb)
TOTAL WEIGHT: 25t (55,104lb)

The Bluebell Railway owns two preserved 'Terriers'; here is No. 672 *Fenchurch*, built 1872, leading a vintage train.

2-4-2 PASSENGER LOCOMOTIVE PARIS–ORLEANS RAILWAY (PO)

In the 1870s and 1880s, the 2-4-2 configuration was a typically French one for a tender engine, and little used in other countries, apart from a few in Belgium and Germany. This Paris–Orleans class was the first to operate express passenger services. With outside cylinders and outside-fitted valve gear (of the Allan 'straight-link' type, different to the Stephenson motion), they displayed a complicated arrangement of rods and links. In the early twentieth century, most were converted into 4-4-0s.

BOILER PRESSURE: 100kg/cm² (142psi)	**GRATE AREA:** 1.6m² (17.4sq ft)
CYLINDERS: 441.6x652.3mm (17.4x25.7in)	**HEATING SURFACE:** 142.7m² (1537sq ft)
DRIVING WHEELS: 1999mm (78.75in)	**TRACTIVE EFFORT:** 5408kg (11,925lb)
	TOTAL WEIGHT: 42.47t (93,630lb)

'PRECEDENT' CLASS 2-4-0 LONDON & NORTH WESTERN RAILWAY (LNWR)

In 1874, Crewe Works was one of the largest locomotive building plants in the world, producing engines only for the mighty LNWR: by 1876, it would produce its 2000th locomotive. The 'Precedent' class of express passenger locomotives, designed under the aegis of F. W. Webb, were among its best and most celebrated products, better known by the nickname of 'Jumbos'. Showing the usual British predilection for a 'no frills', stark but workmanlike appearance, the 'Jumbos' were nevertheless built with cabs rather than the scanty spectacle boards of earlier types, reflecting a greater consideration for the enginemen and also the growth of union activity, with its agitation for better working conditions.

These locomotives hauled express trains on the LNWR's main lines linking London with Birmingham, Manchester and Carlisle. Like other British express engines of the same period, they had to be worked at maximum capacity in order to maintain their schedules, but the robustness and simplicity of their construction meant that this could happen time and time again without ill effects, except for a great waste of fuel. The quality of the performance was assured by short and direct steam passages and a large steam chest between boiler and cylinders

One of the class, *Charles Dickens*, completed 3,218,500km (2 million miles) on the London–Manchester route between 1882 and 1902, and most of them clocked up very high mileages. Another, *Hardwicke* (now preserved), was a star performer on the 'mountain' section between Crewe and Carlisle in the east coast versus west coast 'Race to the North' of 1895. Retired from main line expresses, the 'Jumbos' ran secondary passenger trains well into the twentieth century.

Preserved LNWR racing 'Jumbo' No. 790 *Hardwicke* receives attention before setting off with a special train.

CLASS DIV 0-4-0T ROYAL BAVARIAN STATE RAILWAYS

GERMANY 1875

Shunting in yards and main-line station pilot duties were the daily activities of these small engines, of which 132 were built by Krauss and Maffei in Munich between 1875 and 1897 (the two companies were still separate commercial entities then). They

were well-tanks, with the water reservoir inside the frame. After World War I, on the formation of the *Deutsche Reichsbahn Gesellschaft*, the locomotives were numbered as Class 8871-72, the sub-class relating to some engines that had a higher axle-loading of

14.2 rather than 12.2 tonnes (14 and 12 tons). One particular member of a sister class originating on the Palatinate Railway (later DRG Class 8873) survived until 1961 as a works engine operating on the East German DRG.

BOILER PRESSURE: 10kg/cm² (142.5psi)
CYLINDERS: 330x508mm (13x20in)
DRIVING WHEELS: 1006mm (39.6in)
GRATE AREA: 1m² (10.8sq ft)
HEATING SURFACE: 64.3m² (692.3sq ft)
TRACTIVE EFFORT: 4671kg (10,300lb)
TOTAL WEIGHT: 21.3t (46,966lb)

CLASS F 0-6-0 INDIAN STATE RAILWAYS (ISR)

INDIA 1875

Built under a combination of state control and private capital investment, India's great railway system had developed on two separate gauges. Both on the 'broad' 1676mm (5ft 6in) and the 1000mm (3ft 3in) gauge, 0-6-0 locomotives dominated freight traffic in the late nineteenth century. More than 1500 were built by a great many suppliers. The first F-class locomotives, for the

1m (3ft 3in) gauge, came in 1875 from Dübs of Glasgow. Many of the metre-gauge engines were wood-burners, though the broad-gauge versions burned coal. Train loads of up to 609 tonnes (600 tons) were handled by the Fs, though speeds were generally very slow. F-class locomotives continued to be built until 1906, and by then many of the older ones were being given new

boilers, sometimes with Belpaire fireboxes. F-class locomotives were the first to be built at the Rajputana Malwa Railway's new works at Ajmer in 1902 – these had outside frames and outside cylinders. One of them is preserved. Specifications are for the F class of 1875.

BOILER PRESSURE: 9.8kg/cm² (140psi)
CYLINDERS: 343x508mm (13.5x20in)
DRIVING WHEELS: 1028mm (40.5in)
GRATE AREA: 1.1m² (12sq ft)
HEATING SURFACE: 60m² (648.2sq ft)
TRACTIVE EFFORT: 4858kg (10,700lb)
TOTAL WEIGHT: 21.54t (47,488lb)
(engine only)

A much-modified outside-framed Dübs F-class of the South Western Railway, with patent built-out cranks and a Belpaire firebox.

COMPOUND 0-4-2T BAYONNE–BIARRITZ RAILWAY

FRANCE 1876

Bayonne–Biarritz was a minor line linking these two cities in south-west France, but its small tank engines were the unlikely harbingers of a new phase of development for the steam locomotive. Designed by Anatole Mallet, an independent Swiss-French engineer, and built at Le Creusot, they operated on the

compound principle, long known and used in marine engines, but hitherto unsuccessful in application to steam locomotives, despite numerous efforts. Mallet was the first to make it work effectively. Steam from the boiler was passed first into a 'normal' high-pressure cylinder, but then instead of being expelled through

the blast pipe, it was passed to a low-pressure cylinder whose larger dimensions made up for its lack of pressure. This more efficient use of steam contributed to the vehicle's economy, and, once shown to be effective in use, compounding was taken up by other designers and used in many countries.

BOILER PRESSURE: 10kg/cm² (145psi)
CYLINDERS: hp 241x450mm (9.5x17.75in); lp 340x450mm (15.75x17.75in)
DRIVING WHEELS: 1199mm (47.25in)
GRATE AREA: 1m² (10.8sq ft)
HEATING SURFACE: 91m² (981sq ft)
TRACTIVE EFFORT: 1895kg (4180lb)
TOTAL WEIGHT: 33.78t (74,480lb)

FELL LOCOMOTIVE CLASS H 0-4-2 NEW ZEALAND RAILWAYS (NZR)

The Fell system, an engineering solution that comprised both rails and locomotive, was designed to cope with exceptional steep gradients beyond the capacity of the conventional locomotive, and without resorting to cable haulage. A double-headed central rail was set between the running rails, and gripper wheels, mounted horizontally beneath the locomotive frame, were pressed against this rail by powerful springs. The action of the gripper wheels in turn assisted the road wheels. A pressure equivalent to 30.3 tonnes (30 tons) was exerted by the horizontal wheels. To ensure safe downhill movement, sledge-type brakes could be applied on the central rail.

The most famous example of Fell working was on the 1 in 15 Rimutaka Incline on New Zealand's North Island main line between Wellington and Auckland. The system was invented by the Englishman J. B. Fell, and the first four locomotives for this section were built at the Avonside Works in England, to a design by H. W. Widmark; two more came from Neilson's of Glasgow 10 years later. All had outside cylinders driving the road wheels, with Joy's radial valve gear on the Glasgow engines and Allan's straight link gear on the earlier ones.

Normal practice on climbing the Rimutaka Incline was to cut a train into sections with three or four locomotives in use. Each one could pull 66 tonnes (65 tons) at 4.8km/h (3mph) up the grade. Remarshalling the train at the foot and the summit was a time-consuming business, as was the slow ascent or descent, and the fearsome incline was finally replaced in the 1950s by a tunnel. Thereafter the Fell locomotives, which had provided six decades of stout service, were retired.

BOILER PRESSURE: 11kg/cm² (160psi)
CYLINDERS: OUTSIDE 355x406mm (14x16in); inside 304.5x355mm (12x14in)
DRIVING WHEELS: 812mm (32in)
GRATE AREA: not known
HEATING SURFACE: not known
TRACTIVE EFFORT: 6044kg (13,328lb) (adhesion only)
TOTAL WEIGHT: 44t (97,112lb)

0-6-0 *CELESTIAL EMPIRE* SHANGHAI & WOOSUNG RAILWAY

On this short-lived railway, China's first, the first engine was a contractor's one, the tiny 0-4-0 *Pioneer,* built in Ipswich, England. Once opened, the line was worked by *Celestial Empire,* also an English import, its name chosen in the hope of placating the angry and suspicious locals, who resented the railway's presence. When a trespassing pedestrian was fatally injured, there were riots, and eventually the Chinese government bought up the railway, and closed it down in 1877. The engine and rolling stock were removed to Formosa (Taiwan), where they gradually rusted and rotted away.

Dimensions not known.

93 CLASS 0-6-0 NEW SOUTH WALES GOVERNMENT RAILWAY (NSWGR)

Some of this class almost achieved a century in service. Very much the standard British-type 0-6-0 in appearance, with inside-framed, inside-cylindered engine and outside-framed tender, 78 were built altogether. As with long-lived types, various modifications were made, and some were later fitted with Belpaire fireboxes. All had modernized cabs added. Fourteen were converted into 2-6-4 tank engines at the Eveleigh Works in the early 1900s. Reclassified as A93 in 1899, the last to survive, Nos. 1904 and 1923, worked in the yard at Newcastle, New South Wales, until 1972.

BOILER PRESSURE: 9.8kg/cm² (140psi)
CYLINDERS: 457x609mm (18x24in)
DRIVING WHEELS: 1218mm (48in)
GRATE AREA: 1.66m² (17.9sq ft)
HEATING SURFACE: 120.2m² (1294sq ft)
TRACTIVE EFFORT: 8960kg (18,144lb)
TOTAL WEIGHT: 57.5t (126,784lb)

No. 1904's last job was to push coal wagons up the ramp on the coaling platform at the Port Waratah yard, Newcastle. This was one of the engines later fitted with a Belpaire firebox. Photograph taken on 25 November 1871.

CLASS 97 0-6-0T KAISERIN ELISABETH RAILWAY (KEB)

AUSTRIA 1878

This tank locomotive class, with modifications of detail, was ubiquitous on several Austrian railways between 1878 and the 1930s, and examples were built at various works in the Austro-Hungarian Empire until 1913. From 1884, it was denoted by the newly formed Imperial State Railways as Class 97. Of simple-expansion, with outside cylinders and Stephenson link motion, they eventually numbered 225 on the State system. One of the 97s was the first locomotive to be built in the country that would become Czechoslovakia in 1918, at the PCM Works in Prague in 1900.

BOILER PRESSURE: 11kg/cm² (156psi)	**HEATING SURFACE:** 59.1m² (636sq ft)
CYLINDERS: 345x480mm (13.6x19in)	**TRACTIVE EFFORT:** 5770kg (12,730lb)
DRIVING WHEELS: 930mm (36.6in)	**TOTAL WEIGHT:** 30t (66,150lb)
GRATE AREA: 1m² (10.7sq ft)	

No. 97.209 has just run round its train at Eisenerz, in the Eisernerzer Alps, and is returning to couple up at the leading end. The date is May 1969.

CLASS 2131 0-8-0 NORTHERN RAILWAY (NORTE)

SPAIN 1879

While Spain's general dimensions were of normal European standards, its gauge of 1674mm (5ft 6in) was on a Russian scale.

From 1879 to 1891, 47 of these engines were built, and ran most of the *Norte's* main line freight services, through often mountainous country. Destined to be long-lived, most of the class worked into the 1960s. Thirty were named after rivers, but this was quite an unusual policy among Spanish railways. All were built outside Spain, in Britain, France or Germany, with consequent changes of detail in such matters as dome- and sandbox-placing, but all had simple-expansion outside cylinders, Stephenson link motion, and a low British-style footplate with splashers hiding the upper parts of the wheels. For main-line engines, they had small four-wheel tenders, perhaps reflecting short turntable lengths at certain depots.

BOILER PRESSURE: 9kg/cm² (128psi)	**HEATING SURFACE:** not known
CYLINDERS: 500x660mm (19.7x26in)	**TRACTIVE EFFORT:** 9762kg (21,500lb)
DRIVING WHEELS: 1300mm (51in)	**TOTAL WEIGHT:** 73.86t (162,839lb)
GRATE AREA: 1.72m² (19sq ft)	

'CAULIFLOWER' CLASS 0-6-0 LONDON & NORTH WESTERN RAILWAY (LNWR) — GREAT BRITAIN 1880

The existence of Stephenson's link motion did not deter others from trying to come up with a better valve gear, and one of the more successful efforts was by the English engineer David Joy, whose radical valve gear was first put to main-line use on this large class of goods locomotives designed by F. W. Webb. The valve gear was

hidden inside the frame, but the class showed some other aspects of modernity compared to earlier 0-6-0 types, including the high 'square' firebox designed by the Belgian engineer Alfred Belpaire. By now, steam brakes fitted to the locomotives' driving wheels, and steel tyres, were standard items. The LNWR specialized in

locomotive by-names, and for no very obvious reason these were nicknamed 'Cauliflowers'. More than 300 were built between 1880

and 1902, and they achieved a sound reputation as steady if unspectacular haulers of freight, mostly coal and mineral trains.

BOILER PRESSURE: 9.9kg/cm² (140psi)
CYLINDERS: 457x609mm (18x24in)
DRIVING WHEELS: 1560mm (61.5in)
GRATE AREA: 1.6 m² (17sq ft)
HEATING SURFACE: 112 m² (1208sq ft)
TRACTIVE EFFORT: 6800kg (15,000lb)
TOTAL WEIGHT: 33.88t (74,704lb)

Earlier 'Cauliflower' 0-6-0s had round-topped boilers; the Belpaire firebox was introduced on rebuilds.

L CLASS 4-6-0 INDUS VALLEY STATE RAILWAY (IVSR) — INDIA 1880

Built by Neilson's of Glasgow, this class included the first 4-6-0 tender locomotive to be built in Great Britain, and also the first of its kind to run in India. The Indus Valley Railway, built to 1677mm (5ft 6in) gauge, became part of the North Western Railway in 1886,

but the 149 members of the L class continued to operate on the same route, supplemented by a further 77 'Heavy L'. The Heavy L were distinguished by a slightly heavier maximum axle-loading of 12.4 tonnes (12.25 tons) compared to the L's 11.1 tonnes

(11 tons), and the driving wheels were 2.54cm (1in) greater in diameter. Otherwise the Heavy L and standard L classes were identical as two-cylinder, simple-expansion types. Both versions of the L class ran until the mid-1930s.

BOILER PRESSURE: 11.2kg/cm² (160psi)
CYLINDERS: 457x660mm (18x26in)
DRIVING WHEELS: 1269mm (50in)
GRATE AREA: 2m² (22sq ft)
HEATING SURFACE: 117.3m² (1263sq ft)
TRACTIVE EFFORT: 10,390kg (22,900lb)
TOTAL WEIGHT: 41.4t (91,280lb)

CLASS B 50 2-4-0 STATE RAILWAYS (SS) DUTCH EAST INDIES

No.14's tender has high rails for wood stacking. At the time of the photograph, the locomotive was approximately 90 years old.

Intended to operate stopping trains on the densely populated island of Java, this class of 17 wood-burning engines was built by Sharp, Stewart in Manchester between 1880 and 1885, and proved to be among the longest-lived of steam locomotives. With two simple-expansion outside cylinders, and no extraneous

BOILER PRESSURE: 10kg/cm² (140psi)
CYLINDERS: 381x457mm (15x18in)
DRIVING WHEELS: 1413mm (55.6in)
GRATE AREA: 1.1m² (11.8sq ft)

equipment, they had a simple design. This, as well as sturdy

HEATING SURFACE: 50m² (538.3sq ft)
TRACTIVE EFFORT: 3930kg (8668lb)
TOTAL WEIGHT: 22.47t (49,532lb)
(engine only)

construction, presumably helped their survival. All but three of the class (which had been shipped over to Sumatra) were still in service in the 1970s, and though withdrawals began, several reached a century in age before being scrapped in the course of the 1980s.

LOVETT EAMES 4-2-2 PHILADELPHIA & READING RAILROAD (P&RR)

Baldwin's 5000th engine was this unusual specimen for the United States, a single driver. A one-off, intended by the Philadelphia & Reading Railroad (P&RR) for running fast trains between Philadelphia and New York on the Bound Brook line, it was quickly sold on and acquired by an inventor, Lovett Eames, who gave it his name and used it to demonstrate a vacuum brake of his invention. It was shipped to England but little interest was shown, and the locomotive was broken up there in 1883. One feature that might have aroused interest in England (but did not) was an auxiliary steam cylinder

used to move an equalizing lever between the driving axle and the rear carrying axle, with the aim of transferring extra adhesive weight to the driving wheels when moving off. Incidentally, Eames' brake system, though overshadowed by Westinghouse's, appears to have been an effective one, and was used by the Manhattan elevated railroad.

BOILER PRESSURE: 9.5kg/cm² (135psi)
CYLINDERS: 457x609mm (18x24in)
DRIVING WHEELS: 1980mm (78in)
GRATE AREA: not known
HEATING SURFACE: 130m² (1400sq ft)
TRACTIVE EFFORT: 5187kg (11,439lb)
TOTAL WEIGHT: 21t (63,949lb)

The short-lived *Lovett Eames*. The cylinder under the cab is part of the patent brake equipment.

'SHAY' TYPE LOCOMOTIVE

USA 1880

Shays were not seen on main lines, or even branch lines. They were loggers' engines, designed for work on steep lightweight or temporary tracks on remote hillsides and in mountain valleys, pulling lumber cars. The first of the kind was sold by its inventor, Ephraim Shay, in 1880 and he took out a patent on his flexible-drive system in the following year. The drive system was quite unlike that of a conventional locomotive. To obtain maximum traction, every axle had to be powered; at the same time, in order to negotiate twisty routes, the engine had to be articulated. The Shay had a normal locomotive boiler and firebox, but the boiler had to be mounted off-centre to allow room for the cylinders that were mounted vertically alongside it, with the pistons working a crankshaft that ran the length of the engine, operating drive shafts through universal joints on each of the four-wheel trucks (two to four sets) on which the engine rode. Though very slow, a Shay needed only its own adhesion to climb a 1 in 10 gradient with a load behind it. Shay published a catalogue that set out his locomotives in various sizes, from the two-truck smallest to the 152-tonne (150-ton) four-truck Class D model.

BOILER PRESSURE: 14kg/cm² (200psi)
CYLINDERS: 330x381mm (13x15in)
DRIVING WHEELS: 914mm (36in)
GRATE AREA: 2.6m² (27.75sq ft)
HEATING SURFACE: 84m² (905sq ft)
SUPERHEATER: 17.5m² (189sq ft)
TRACTIVE EFFORT: 17,324kg (38,200lb)
TOTAL WEIGHT: 85.28t (188,000lb)

Manufacturing rights to the Shay locomotive were acquired in 1882 by the Lima Locomotive Company, which built nothing else until the early 1920s. Though other low-geared locomotives for forestry and mine work were developed, notably the Climax and Heisler types (see 1889), the Shay remained the most widely used. The last Shay to be built was in 1945, a three-truck locomotive for the Chaffee branch of the Western Maryland Railroad.

A lumber-hauling Shay in typical territory; note also the lightweight track. A spark arresting chimney was a very common feature of these locomotives.

CLASS 220 4-4-0 HUNGARIAN RAILWAYS (MÀV)

HUNGARY 1881

Though then part of the Austro-Hungarian Empire, Hungary retained many elements of national, political and commercial independence. The country's first locomotive works opened in the capital Budapest in 1880 and the 220 class of fast passenger locomotives was built there.

In the Danube valley and on the Great Hungarian Plain, the nature of the terrain meant that fast running was possible, and this was reflected in the design of the trains. Between 1881 and 1905, 201 of the 220 class locomotives were built, and they were dispersed widely over the MÀV

system. Simple-expansion, with outside cylinders, they had smokeboxes extended to the buffer beam in an effort to reduce smoke emission, always a problem with the sulphurous coal supplied from the mines in Bohemia. Most were scrapped before 1939, but one of the class is preserved.

BOILER PRESSURE: 12kg/cm² (171psi)
CYLINDERS: 450x650mm (17.75x25.6in)
DRIVING WHEELS: 1826mm (72in)
GRATE AREA: 2.1m² (22.6sq ft)
HEATING SURFACE: 135.6m² (1460sq ft)
TRACTIVE EFFORT: 7380kg (16,280lb)
TOTAL WEIGHT: 48.8t (107,604lb)
(engine only)

VOLK'S ELECTRIC RAILWAY RAILCAR

GREAT BRITAIN 1884

Though Volk's claims to be the world's oldest public electric railway, its existence was made possible only by Werner von Siemens' development of the electric traction motor in Germany. In 1879, he demonstrated a small two-axled electric locomotive that is still preserved in Munich, and it

was a Siemens motor that powered the enterprising Magnus Volk's tourist railway along the seafront at Brighton, on England's south coast. Its gauge was 610mm (2ft) and it first opened on 4 August 1882, with a single four-wheel railcar. In 1884, it was widened to standard gauge and extended in

TYPE: Seaside passenger tramcar
POWER: 160V two-rail, 4.5kW (6hp) Siemens D2 wound motor with transmission by belt drive via a countershaft to the axles
TRACTIVE EFFORT: N/A

MAX. OPERATING SPEED: 16.09km/h (10mph)
MAX. AXLE-LOAD: N/A
OVERALL LENGTH: 5.791m (19ft)
GAUGE: 1435mm (4ft 8.5in)

length to 1280m (4200ft). It still runs today, though none of the

nineteenth-century vehicles is preserved.

'VITTORIO-EMANUELE' CLASS 4-6-0 UPPER ITALIAN RAILWAYS ITALY 1884

The first 4-6-0 to run on a European railway, the Vittorio-Emanuele class leader was named after the first king of united Italy, and was built at the company's own Turin works. Later members of the class – 55 in all – were built by Ansaldo de Sampierdareno, by Miani & Silvestri of Milan, and also by Maffei in Munich. Two unusual features were a form of

BOILER PRESSURE: 11kg/cm² (156.75psi)	**GRATE AREA:** 2.25m² (24sq ft)
CYLINDERS: 470x620mm (18.5x24.4in)	**HEATING SURFACE:** 124m² (1720sq ft)
DRIVING WHEELS: 1675mm (66in)	**TRACTIVE EFFORT:** 6,960kg (15,335lb)
	TOTAL WEIGHT: 59.9t (132,079lb)

combustion chamber extending the firebox, and a very short wheelbase of 1200mm (47.3in) on the front bogie. The latter was made necessary by turntable length – the introduction of a

new, longer locomotive always had a knock-on effect on the stabling facilities. The route from Turin to Milan, over the Giovi Pass, was a busy but also formidable one, even after a relief

line had been constructed, which itself had a continuous gradient of 1 in 62 for 23.5km (14.6 miles) and an 8.3km (5.1-mile) tunnel. For the new 4-6-0s, the basic requirement was a capacity to climb this grade with a 130-tonne (128-ton) train at a steady 40km/h (25mph). From 1905, the class was designated 650 by the new State Railways (FS), and the locomotives were withdrawn by 1914.

CLASS 7 2-6-0 BUENOS AIRES GREAT SOUTHERN RAILWAY (BAGS) ARGENTINA 1885

Argentinian railways began in 1857 with a line from Parque to Floresta, on a 1676mm (5ft 6in) gauge, the same as that of India; its first locomotive, English-built, had been destined for India before the order was cancelled. European interests, mostly British, but also French and German, controlled most of the growing network of Argentinian railways, and the provenance of locomotives usually reflected the line's ownership. The BAGS company was British-

dominated and it was only to be expected that a new class would come from Britain, like this freight class of 28, all made by Beyer Peacock in Manchester. Interestingly, the 'colonial' lines were often more adventurous than the home ones in their choice of locomotive types: in Britain, a 2-6-0 would still have been seen as a 'foreign' American beast at that time. A wood-burner, with simple-expansion outside cylinders, its lines were typically restrained, the

main departure from British decorum being an extended smokebox in which it was hoped sparks from the wood fire would be caught. Although the class had a respectable 40-year career, with the last survivors withdrawn in 1926, it was showing itself to be underpowered by the turn of the century. A heavier 2-6-0 was introduced in 1901, but, as in almost all of South America, goods haulage was dominated by 2-8-0 locomotives from the mid-1900s

until the advent of diesels. On the BAGS, the Class 11 compound 2-8-0 of 1903 relieved the Class 7s of most of their more testing work.

BOILER PRESSURE: 10.5kg/cm² (150psi)
CYLINDERS: 431x609mm (17x24in)
DRIVING WHEELS: 1269mm (50in)
GRATE AREA: 1.9m² (20.1sq ft)
HEATING SURFACE: 100.8m² (1086sq ft)
TRACTIVE EFFORT: 6825kg (15,050lb)
TOTAL WEIGHT: 78.7t (173,484lb)

CLASS L-304 2-6-0 NEW SOUTH WALES GOVERNMENT RAILWAYS (NSWGR) AUSTRALIA 1885

With American hustle and well-honed sales technique – and early delivery dates – the US locomotive builders were always on the lookout for business in what the British liked to consider their own markets. Baldwin achieved a foothold in Australia

with this class of 10 2-6-0s intended for hauling passenger trains over the Blue Mountains, west of Sydney. American engines did not always have long lives, but these, albeit with two changes of boiler in some cases, lasted into the 1930s, by which

time they were working country routes in the west of New South

Wales. The final one was withdrawn in 1939.

BOILER PRESSURE: 9.8kg/cm² (140psi)	**HEATING SURFACE:** 120.9m² (1302sq ft)
CYLINDERS: 457x660mm (18x26in)	**TRACTIVE EFFORT:** 7014kg (15,467lb)
DRIVING WHEELS: 1548mm (61in)	**TOTAL WEIGHT:** 48.26t (106,400lb)
GRATE AREA: 1.5m² (16.9sq ft)	

FORNEY'S TANK LOCOMOTIVE 0-4-4 MANHATTAN RAILWAY USA 1885

Tank engines, appearing in their thousands in Britain and Europe, never enjoyed the same popularity in the United States (or in Russia). Carrying their own coal and water concentrated their weight and increased their axle-loading. Matthias Forney's patent tank locomotive of 1866 generated little interest until 1878, when the New York Elevated Railroad decided that it was the right engine for its elevated tracks that threaded the increasingly congested streets of Manhattan Island, as its original engines were too small to operate

A Manhattan 'Forney', with the cab built forward over the end of the Belpaire firebox, and destination plate on the platform side. It had a steam whistle but no bell.

BOILER PRESSURE: 8.4kg/cm² (120psi)
CYLINDERS: 304.5x456.8mm (12x18in)
DRIVING WHEELS: 1294mm (51in)
GRATE AREA: 97m² (9sq ft)
HEATING SURFACE: 52.5m² (565.2sq ft)
TRACTIVE EFFORT: 2350kg (5180lb)
TOTAL WEIGHT: 18.8t (41,440lb)

effectively. Forney's 0-4-4 design served them well, and more than 300 were in use by the time electrification replaced them in 1903. Many were then sold on to other lines. They were among the

first US engines to have brakes, using Lovett Eames' vacuum system rather than Westinghouse's air brake. In order to satisfy the clean-air demands of the civic authorities, they burned only the

best-quality steam coal. Painted bright red, they were specially fitted with ashpans and oil-holders to minimize the amount of debris and drips falling through the trackwork.

CLASS R 4-6-0 SOUTH AUSTRALIAN RAILWAYS (SAR)

Railways were a responsibility of individual state governments in Australia, and each chose its own gauge, which ended up causing numerous problems for interstate traffic. This class of 84 locomotives were classic 4-6-0s for the 1600mm (5ft 3in) South Australian Railways (SAR) gauge, designed for passenger or goods service, and proved very effective in such mixed-traffic work. A typical feature of the class, as with many other Australian locomotives, is the sun-cowl, intended to reduce glare and improve the crew's forward visibility. Some were home-built, by James Martin or the SAR's Islington works, and others were shipped in from Scotland. From 1925, at a point when withdrawal might have seemed the obvious option, a number were fitted with superheaters and continued to work up to the 1960s. Several of the class have been preserved.

STEAM PRESSURE: 10kg/cm² (145psi)
CYLINDERS: 457x609mm (18x24in)
DRIVING WHEELS: 1370mm (54in)
GRATE AREA: 1.9m² (20.3sq ft)
HEATING SURFACE: 120.2m² (1294sq ft)
TRACTIVE EFFORT: 7575kg (16,704lb)
TOTAL WEIGHT: 65t (143,360lb)

DECAPOD 2-10-0 DOM PEDRO SEGUNDO RAILWAY

Twenty years after constructing the first 2-8-0, Baldwin built the first engine with five coupled axles, the 2-10-0, and duly named it the 'Decapod'. Though the driving wheels were of small diameter, the second and third sets had no flanges, and the fifth set was given 6.3mm (0.25in) lateral movement, to help the engine round curves without derailing. Curves of 12.7m (42ft) radius could be negotiated at slow speed – which was, in any case, the norm in service. Although in time it would be a staple freight locomotive, and usually much larger than this rather modest ancestor, there was no great interest in the 2-10-0 at this time, and most narrow-gauge railways looking for a bigger engine would choose an articulated type.

BOILER PRESSURE: 11.3kg/cm² (160psi)
CYLINDERS: 558x660mm (22x26in)
DRIVING WHEELS: 1142mm (45in)
GRATE AREA: not known
HEATING SURFACE: not known
TRACTIVE EFFORT: not known
TOTAL WEIGHT: 64t (141,000lb)
(engine only)

FOUR-CYLINDER COMPOUND 2-4-0 NORTHERN RAILWAY (NORD)

In original form, this engine would have been most accurately described as an 0-2-2-0, as its driving wheels, each driven by a different set of cylinders, were not coupled, and it had no leading bogie. Coupling rods and the bogie were later additions. The two high-pressure cylinders, inside the frame, worked the leading drive axle, and the low-pressure cylinders, outside, drove the second. Designed by Gaston du Bousquet, this was the first 4-cylinder compound express locomotive, complicated for its size, but sufficiently successful in operation for the Nord to maintain an active interest in compounding.

A Webb-type 3 cylinder loco from Sharp Stewart in Manchester tried out unsuccessfully by the Ouest in 1884.

BOILER PRESSURE: 11kg/cm² (157psi)
CYLINDERS: hp 330x609mm (13x24in); lp 462x609mm (18.2x24in)
DRIVING WHEELS: 2113mm (83.25in)
GRATE AREA: 2.4m² (25.6sq ft)
HEATING SURFACE: 103m² (1109sq ft)
TRACTIVE EFFORT: N/A
TOTAL WEIGHT: 41.4t (91,280lb)
(engine only)

CLASS 56 0-6-0 IMPERIAL & ROYAL STATE RAILWAY (KKSTB)

To the eyes of observers, Austrian locomotives of this period had anything but a standard look. This was despite strenuous efforts, of which this class was one, to get a standardized fleet into being. Numbering 153 engines and spread across a large multinational system, the '56' simply became another locomotive in the varied plethora of types. It had no particular features to distinguish it from earlier 0-6-0 types, or to be passed on to others. With the end of the empire in 1918, like other Austrian locomotive types, they became part of the Polish, Hungarian, Czech and Yugoslav, as well as Austrian, locomotive stock, and a whole new set of varied modifications was implemented on the independent systems.

BOILER PRESSURE: 11kg/cm² (156psi)
CYLINDERS: 450x632mm (17.75x25in)
DRIVING WHEELS: 1258mm (49.5in)
GRATE AREA: 1.8m² (19.4sq ft)
HEATING SURFACE: 119.4m² (1285.5sq ft)
TRACTIVE EFFORT: 9524kg (21,000lb)
TOTAL WEIGHT: 41.5t (91,507lb)
(engine only)

LARTIGUE'S MONORAIL LISTOWEL & BALLYBUNION RAILWAY (L&B)

IRELAND 1888

The concept devised and patented by François Lartigue was for a lightweight railway that would be quick and cheap to instal, and which could provide effective service for a country district. Lartigue failed to get projects in Belgium and France off the ground, and his idea was finally put into working form in western Ireland. Its A-shaped gantry was not a true monorail, since it had guide-rails on each side about 30cm (12in) above the ground, helping to balance the train on the single top rail. The line, 14.9km (9.25 miles) long, was operated by three locomotives, designed by Anatole Mallet (but not as compounds) and built by the Hunslet Locomotive Co. of Leeds, England. They were twin units, with a tiny boiler and firebox on each side combining to supply steam to the cylinders that drove three double-flanged wheels running between the boilers on the top rail. Controls were fitted on either side but there was a single firebox, on the right. Unwieldy and quaint in appearance, it nevertheless provided a service for 36 years until 24 October 1924, when it was closed down and dismantled for scrap.

BOILER PRESSURE: 10.5kg/cm² (150psi)
CYLINDERS: 178x304.5mm (7x12in)
DRIVING WHEELS: 609mm (24in)
GRATE AREA: 0.46m² (5sq ft/two boxes)
HEATING SURFACE: 6.6m² (71.75sq ft)
TRACTIVE EFFORT: 998kg (2200lb)
TOTAL WEIGHT: 11.07t (24,4000lb)
(engine only)

Transporting weighty objects on the Lartigue monorail was always a problem. On one occasion, a cow was used as a counterweight to a piano being carried in one of the goods vehicles.

2-4-2T LANCASHIRE & YORKSHIRE RAILWAY (L&Y)

GREAT BRITAIN 1889

A real express tank engine, intended for fast outer suburban and commuter services to and from Manchester, this class was fitted with water scoops to enable it to replenish the tanks from line-set troughs without stopping. Sir John Aspinall, responsible for the design, had recently completed the establishment of the company's big new works at Horwich, in Lancashire, where these engines were built. He was one of a select band of locomotive engineers who progressed beyond the motive power side to become general manager of the whole company. On his high-speed tank design, the leading and trailing axles were pivoted radially, the pivots being behind and in front of the respective axles, and the engines ran well at speed. With a frame extending well beyond the wheelbase at each end, this was the largest 2-4-2T type produced in Britain. It was made in three versions, those of 1905 and 1912 having a Belpaire firebox and greater coal capacity.

BOILER PRESSURE: 11.3kg/cm² (160psi)
CYLINDERS: 457x660mm (18x26in)
DRIVING WHEELS: 1720mm (67.8in)
HEATING SURFACE: 113m² (1216.4sq ft)
GRATE AREA: 1.7m² (18.75sq ft)
TRACTIVE EFFORT: 7664kg (16,900lb)
TOTAL WEIGHT: 56.85t (125,328lb)

An Aspinall 2-4-2 of the 1905 batch, with extended bunker at the rear and smokebox at the front; and a Belpaire firebox, standing at Southport in 1961. This was the western terminal of its commuter expresses.

TEUTONIC 2-2-2-0 LONDON & NORTH WESTERN RAILWAY (LNWR)

Inspired by the work of Anatole Mallet, and with a natural wish to reduce the coal consumption of the LNWR's large locomotive fleet, F. W. Webb, its Chief Mechanical Engineer, began experimenting with compound expansion in 1879. His favoured system was a three-cylinder set, with two outer high-pressure cylinders and a large inside low-pressure one. Unfortunately, none of his compounds was really effective, a failure all the more embarrassing as Webb had publicized his intentions, and the LNWR was one of the world's largest railway companies. The 10 'Teutonics', named for the first engine in the class, were his last essay in compound express engines, and though more reliable than their predecessors, they were still problem-prone and heavy in fuel consumption and in repair and maintenance costs. The driving wheels, uncoupled, sometimes revolved in opposing directions

when the driver tried to start the engine. In addition, the Teutonics were much more expensive to build than simple-expansion engines like Webb's own earlier 'Jumbos'. At their best, they showed speed and power; No. 1304 *Jeanie Deans* was a famed performer on the Euston–Crewe leg of the 'Scotch Express' in the 1890s, taking a 305-tonne (300-ton) train northwards, against the grades, at an average speed of just under 80km/h (50mph). Another of the class, No. 1306 *Ionic*, achieved a mileage that totalled 1,140,240km (708,512 miles) up to 1904. But the defects of the compounds could not be hushed up, and after Webb's retirement in 1903 his successor acted rapidly to have the compounds scrapped or converted to simple expansion. By 1907, none were left.

The famous No. 1304, *Jeanie Deans*, one of the best performers among Webb's ill-fated compound classes.

BOILER PRESSURE: 12kg/cm² (175psi)
CYLINDERS: hp 355x609mm (14x24in); lp 761x609mm (30x24in)
DRIVING WHEELS: 2157mm (85in)
GRATE AREA: 1.9m² (20.5sq ft)
HEATING SURFACE: 126.5m² (1362sq ft)
TRACTIVE EFFORT:
TOTAL WEIGHT: 46.23t (101,920lb)

CLASS B 0-4-0ST DARJEELING HIMALAYAN RAILWAY (DHR)

This narrow-gauge 610mm (2ft) line climbs 2000m (6560ft) into the Himalayas, over a spectacular 87km (54-mile) route that includes many loops and zig-zags. These diminutive saddle-tanks, first built by Sharp, Stewart of Manchester, handled most of the services. Over four decades, 34 Class Bs were built, including three at the Darjeeling Himalayan Railway (DHR) workshops at Tindharia. Today the line, a 'World Heritage Site', is increasingly diesel-powered, although steam veterans still operate over it.

BOILER PRESSURE: 9.8kg/cm² (140psi)
CYLINDERS: 279x355mm (11x14in)
DRIVING WHEELS: 660mm (26in)
GRATE AREA: 0.8m² (9sq ft)
HEATING SURFACE: 29.3m² (316sq ft)
TRACTIVE EFFORT: 3515kg (7750lb)
TOTAL WEIGHT: 15.5t (34,160lb)

DHR saddle tank No. 782, Mountaineer, was built in 1872 by Sharp, Stewart of Manchester, England.

CLASS W 2-6-2T NEW ZEALAND RAILWAYS (NZR)

NZR's historic Class W 192 is now maintained by Rail Heritage Trust at Ferrymead and is still capable of being steamed.

Built to work on steeply graded routes, the two engines forming Class W were the first locomotives to be built at the NZR's own works at Addington. Though not fitted with a complete set of Fell traction equipment, they incorporated sledge brakes that worked on the central rail of a Fell track. Their

BOILER PRESSURE: 12kg/cm² (170psi)
CYLINDERS: 355x508mm (14x20in)
DRIVING WHEELS: 926mm (36.5in)
GRATE AREA: 1.1m² (12sq ft)

HEATING SURFACE: 63m² (683sq ft)
TRACTIVE EFFORT: 7040kg (15,500lb)
TOTAL WEIGHT: 37.5t (82,656lb)

original tasks were on the grades at Upper Hutt, outside Wellington, and on the Rimutaka Incline, where they assisted the Fell locomotives. Later they were transferred to South Island colliery branches, and both worked until the 1950s. The first of the pair, No. 192, is preserved.

BO ELECTRIC LOCOMOTIVE CITY & SOUTH LONDON RAILWAY (C&SLR)

GREAT BRITAIN 1890

History's first underground electric railway was also the first deep-level tube line in London and the world, 8km (5 miles) long. Indeed, only the possibility of electric traction made such a venture possible. Traction was provided by 14 small four-wheeled

electric locomotives, picking up current from a third rail. Mather & Platt of Salford built the engines, with parts also supplied by Beyer Peacock of nearby Manchester. One of the first engines, withdrawn in 1907, is still preserved; locomotives ran the line

until 1924, when it was enlarged to the same diameter as other

London tube lines, and operated by similar multiple-unit sets.

TYPE: Underground suburban services
POWER: Not known
MAX. OPERATING SPEED: 40.225km/h (25mph)
MAX. AXLE LOAD: Not known
WEIGHT: 10.3 tonnes (227,115lb)
GAUGE: 762mm (2ft 6in)

HEISLER GEARED LOCOMOTIVE

USA 1891

Charles Heisler developed his specialized locomotive design for the same purpose as Ephraim Shay's, to haul lumber trains over steep, twisting, lightly laid mountain tracks. His first locomotive was built in 1891 by the Dunkirk Engineering Co., NY, and he patented the design in the

following year. Running on trucks like the Shay, it had quite a different drive system. Its boiler was centrally mounted on the frame, with the cylinders set beneath it in a V-formation. The action of the pistons turned a crankshaft, which was linked by a universal joint to the driving axle

in each truck. An external connecting rod linked a crank on the drive wheel with the unpowered wheels, so that every axle supplied traction. Heislers continued to be built until 1941, and the specification given here is for the two-truck 'Arctic' model produced in 1908.

BOILER PRESSURE: 11.2kg/cm² (160psi)
CYLINDERS: 241x254mm (9.5x10in)
DRIVING WHEELS: 76mm (30in)
GRATE AREA: not known
HEATING SURFACE: not known
TRACTIVE EFFORT: 15,875kg (7200lb)
TOTAL WEIGHT: 16.33t (36,000lb)

MALLET 0-4-4-0T SWISS CENTRAL RAILWAY (SZE)

SWITZERLAND 1891

Successful compounding (see 1876) was not Anatole Mallet's only major achievement: in 1885 he obtained a patent for a design of an articulated locomotive, which was first used in a 1m (3ft 3in) gauge 0-4-4-0 tank engine for the Corsican Railways. Swiss railways, with their winding and precipitous mountain lines, took a close

interest, and a pioneer 0-6-6-0 locomotive ran on the Gotthard Railway in 1890. The SZE locomotives formed a class of 26. Mallet's design was 'semi-articulation', and also incorporated compound expansion. The front power unit, containing the low-pressure cylinders, pivoted under the main

frame and supplied (via a flexible steam pipe from the rear) high-pressure cylinders which, with their driving wheels, were fixed to the frame. Maffei of Munich built the first 16 of the class, and the others came from the SLM works at Winterthur in Switzerland. Withdrawal began as early as 1910 but the last survived to 1936.

BOILER PRESSURE: 12kg/cm² (171psi)
CYLINDERS: hp 355x640mm (14x25in); lp 550x640mm (21.6x25in)
DRIVING WHEELS: 1280mm (50.4in)
GRATE AREA: 1.8m² (19.4sq ft)
HEATING SURFACE: 113m² (1216.6sq ft)
TRACTIVE EFFORT: N/A
TOTAL WEIGHT: 60.41t (133,182lb)

CLASS P 4-6-0 NEW SOUTH WALES GOVERNMENT RAILWAYS (NSWGR)

AUSTRALIA 1892

A home design, though first built by Beyer Peacock in Manchester, the P class was intended to be the basic mixed-traffic locomotive of this increasingly busy network. Fifty were delivered in 1892, of which the last two were really a separate class: three-cylinder compounds with two high-pressure cylinders on one side and a single low-pressure one on the other, but they were converted by 1901 to the standard 'P' arrangement of two outside simple-expansion cylinders, with internal valve gear. All had Belpaire fireboxes. The P class was one of Australia's most

effective locomotive classes and the NSWGR ended up owning 191 of them, 106 from Beyer Peacock, 20 from Baldwin, 45 from Clyde Engineering in Sydney, and 20 from the NSWGR's works at Eveleigh. After 1911, they were progressively equipped with Schmidt-type superheaters and piston valves and in the re-classification of 1924 became class C-32. The design was chosen by the Commonwealth Railways for the new 1691km (1050-mile) railway across the Nullarbor Plain, and between 1914 and 1917 a further 26 were built as

Class G, with a supplementary water tank car behind the tenders. Clyde engineering built four, Baldwin provided 12, and 10 were built by Toowoomba Foundry in Queensland. G-class engines pulled the first Trans-Australia Express from Port Augusta to Kalgoorlie on 22 October 1917. Until gauges were standardized, passengers had to transfer to a 1065mm (3ft 6in) gauge Western Australian Railways train for the final section to Perth. The G-class locomotives were

withdrawn in 1938, but on the NSWGR, remarkably, all 191 of the P class were still in service in 1956, though many had been modified in various ways. By then, they were operating local passenger trains and fast mainline freights. Withdrawals began soon after, but it was a P class that hauled Australia's last scheduled steam passenger train service, between Newcastle and Singleton, in July 1971; and one member of the class, No. 3242, ran a total of 3,802,024km (2,362,468 miles) in its lifetime. Four of the P class, and G-1, have been preserved.

BOILER PRESSURE: 11.2kg/cm² (160psi)
CYLINDERS: 508x660mm (20x26in)
DRIVING WHEELS: 1523mm (60in)
GRATE AREA: 2.5m² (27sq ft)
HEATING SURFACE: 177.9m² (1916sq ft)
TRACTIVE EFFORT: 10,062kg (22,187lb)
TOTAL WEIGHT: 90.12t (198,688lb)

Workhorse of the NSWGR system, the P-Class was very British in style, though at the time Britain had no 4-6-0 locomotives in home service.

CLASS 7 4-8-0 CAPE GOVERNMENT RAILWAYS (CGR)

SOUTH AFRICA 1892

Though the South African rail gauge was a relatively modest 1065mm (3ft 6in), its overall loading gauge was generous, and its engineers were never inhibited from using big engines, which were necessary for the long hauls and heavy trains involved in running the lines. This was the CGR's first 4-8-0 locomotive, built by Neilson's of

Two views of Class C17; both updated examples with electric lighting but carrying the original round-topped boiler. The CGR locomotives and rolling stock had centrally mounted coupling-buffering fittings.

BOILER PRESSURE: 11kg/cm² (160psi)
CYLINDERS: 431.5x584mm (17x23in)
DRIVING WHEELS: 1079mm (42.5in)
GRATE AREA: 1.6m² (17.5sq ft)

HEATING SURFACE: 93.8m² (1010sq ft)
TRACTIVE EFFORT: 8462kg (18,660lb)
TOTAL WEIGHT: 46.23t (101,920lb)
(engine only)

Glasgow, and a number of other 4-8-0 types followed. Eventually the Class 7s were demoted from mainline freight to branch workings and yard shunting, and most received new boilers, with Belpaire fireboxes in some cases; and eight of the original engines were still working almost 80 years after their first arrival on the railway.

CLASS CC 4-6-0 SWEDISH RAILWAYS (SJ)

SWEDEN 1892

Like many other railways found throughout Europe in the late nineteenth century, the SJ was upgrading its passenger cars in the 1890s and 1900s, with bogie coaches replacing the old six- and four-wheelers from 1891. SJ also needed, therefore, bigger locomotives for heavier trains.

Nydquist & Holm were the builders of this numerous class, of which 79 were running by 1903. In characteristic Swedish style, a spark-arrestor collar was fitted to the chimney base. Some were wood-burners and one, as an experiment (not followed up), was fitted to burn powdered peat, in

an effort to use locally available fuel. Although intended for main-line service, this class was rather underpowered and spent most of its time on branch lines. Forty-eight were later re-boilered and given superheaters and reclassified CD. The last members of the class were withdrawn in 1956.

BOILER PRESSURE: 11kg/cm² (156psi)
CYLINDERS: 420x560mm (16.5x22in)
DRIVING WHEELS: 1880mm (74in)
GRATE AREA: 1.86m² (20sq ft)
HEATING SURFACE: 108m² (1162.8sq ft)
TRACTIVE EFFORT: 4860kg (10,730lb)
TOTAL WEIGHT: 41t (90,405lb)
(engine only)

CLASS K 2-8-4T WESTERN AUSTRALIAN GOVERNMENT RAILWAYS (WAGR)

AUSTRALIA 1893

Running on the WAGR's 1065mm (3ft 6in) gauge, these engines, 24 in all, were ordered from Neilsons of Glasgow to operate local trains around the city of Perth. Six of them were transferred across the Indian Ocean in 1899 to assist with

British war operations in South Africa. Most of the class spent its time on freight operations, and received new boilers during the 1930s. Centrally placed buffer-couplers, and kangaroo-catchers were the only alterations to a basically British look. Withdrawals

BOILER PRESSURE: 8.3kg/cm² (120psi)
CYLINDERS: 431x533mm (17x21in)
DRIVING WHEELS: 964mm (38in)
GRATE AREA: 1.55m² (16.7sq ft)

HEATING SURFACE: 90.4m² (973sq ft)
TRACTIVE EFFORT: 6953kg (15,332lb)
TOTAL WEIGHT: 53.85t (118,720lb)

began in the 1940s, but the longest survivors remained

working in light shunting employment until 1964.

CLASS S3 4-4-0 ROYAL PRUSSIAN UNION RAILWAYS (KPEV)

In the 1890s, unified Germany was in the middle of its swift rise to industrial and commercial power, and it was set to become a leader in steam locomotive development. August von Borries, Chief Mechanical Engineer of the Royal Prussian Union Railways (KPEV), took a particularly keen interest in what was happening on other railways and the S3 shows some of the results of a visit he made to the United States, including its bar-frame

construction and the general accessibility of its working parts. Much of the later look of German steam locomotives would devolve from this core design. The S3 was a compound engine: von Borries

BOILER PRESSURE: 12kg/cm² (171psi)
CYLINDERS: hp 480x600mm (18.9x23.6in); lp 680x600mm (26.6x23.6in)
DRIVING WHEELS: 1980mm (78in)

had devised his own system of compound working, with two outside cylinders, which was adapted by T. W. Worsdell on the Great Eastern and later the North Eastern Railway in England,

GRATE AREA: 2.3m² (25sq ft)
HEATING SURFACE: 117.7m² (1267sq ft)
TRACTIVE EFFORT: N/A
TOTAL WEIGHT: 50.8t (112,000lb) (engine only)

though with inside-fitted cylinders. On the S3, the valve gear was external, Heusinger's (almost identical to Walschaerts') using slide valves. The growing demands of German industrial development required large numbers of hard-working locomotives, and by 1904, when building ceased, the S3 class numbered 1027. Much of Wilhelm Schmidt's experimental work on superheating was carried out on this class (see 1902).

CLASS C12 2-6-0T STATE RAILWAYS (SS) DUTCH EAST INDIES

With a big system to run, and a range of haulage requirements, the Dutch-owned and managed, Java-based SS liked to keep up to date with mechanical developments elsewhere. They already had a simple-expansion 2-6-0T, Class C11, but the growing reputation of compound expansion led to the commissioning of a compound version, from Hartmann of Chemnitz, Germany. Class C12 eventually numbered 43, and was used mostly for pick-up freight and shunting duties, and running mixed trains on branch lines. Thirteen of them were still active up to the late 1970s.

BOILER PRESSURE: 12kg/cm² (171psi)
CYLINDERS: hp 380x509mm (15x20in); lp 580x509mm (22.8x20in)
DRIVING WHEELS: 1106mm (43.5in)
GRATE AREA: 1.1m² (11.8sq ft)
HEATING SURFACE: 61.1m² (658sq ft)
TRACTIVE EFFORT: N/A
TOTAL WEIGHT: 34.14t (75,264lb)

Beflagged ready for a locomotive parade, Class C12 No. 06 gets up steam on a depot road. The width of the side tanks is notable.

2-4-2T JAPANESE NATIONAL RAILWAYS (JNR)

Early Japanese locomotives were all imports from Europe or the United States, but there was a feeling that Japan should develop its own locomotive industry. Japanese National Railway's chief engineer at the time was Francis Trevithick, a grandson of the

builder of the first locomotive, and this one-off engine was built under his supervision at the Kobe workshops. In fact, it was an assembly job, as most of the parts had been prefabricated in Britain, but the two compound cylinders were cast in Japan, and this small

BOILER PRESSURE: 12kg/cm² (171 psi)
CYLINDERS: hp 381x508mm (15x20in); lp 572x508mm (22.5x20in)
DRIVING WHEELS: 1346mm (53in)

GRATE AREA: 1.1m² (11.8sq ft)
HEATING SURFACE: 71.5m² (769.8sq ft)
TRACTIVE EFFORT: N/A
TOTAL WEIGHT: not known

engine was the precursor of a large industry. From 1912, all

Japan's locomotive requirements were supplied by home builders.

CLASS 6 4-6-0 CAPE GOVERNMENT RAILWAYS (CGR)

SOUTH AFRICA 1893

Primarily intended for work on the long Cape Town–Johannesburg route, this was South Africa's first 4-6-0 locomotive class. The first batch came from North British Locomotive Co. of Glasgow (a large company formed by the amalgamation of Dübs, Neilsons and others), and a series of modified versions followed, up to 6L of 1904, from various suppliers, including Class 6K from Baldwin. All were two-cylinder, simple-expansion engines, with internal Stephenson link motion, and some of them worked into the 1970s.

BOILER PRESSURE: 12.6kg/cm² (180psi)
CYLINDERS: 431x660mm (17x26in)
DRIVING WHEELS: 1370mm (54in)
GRATE AREA: 1.6m² (17sq ft)
HEATING SURFACE: 96.7m² (1041sq ft)
TRACTIVE EFFORT: 8517kg (18,780lb)
TOTAL WEIGHT: 75.2t (165,760lb)

With the boiler evidently at full pressure, and a powerful blast sending hot gas, sparks and cinders high into the air, a Class 6 labours hard to get a long night freight on the move.

NO. 999 4-4-0 NEW YORK CENTRAL & HUDSON RIVER RAILROAD (NYC&HRR)

USA 1893

Several factors came together to make the 1890s a 'racing' decade for railways. On some inter-city routes, competition between rival lines was strong. Rail tracks, on main lines at least, were much more substantial and laid on stone ballast rather than earth or cinders. Signalling systems had become more sophisticated. Locomotives were capable of high speeds. Carriages were longer and more solidly built, and, mounted on bogies rather than rigid frames, could be run at

much higher speeds. And, far from least, trains could now be fitted with reliable automatic brake systems. After a shamefully slow start, and many shocking and unnecessary accidents, main line trains in most countries now had either compressed air or vacuum brakes, powered by a pump mounted on the locomotive. The best known is the Westinghouse air brake, invented by the American George Westinghouse and shown to be effective as early as 1869. By 1897, he had factories

in Pittsburgh, PA, London, Paris and Hannover, Germany.

Where all these conditions were met, racing followed naturally, as did advertising and sales promotion. To promote its New York–Chicago service, the NYC created the 'Empire State Express', and this one-off locomotive was built at the line's Albany works to run the eastern leg from and to New York. A handsome but typical 4-4-0 in most ways, its distinctive feature was extra-large coupled wheels, and, painted in a special

livery to match the train, it brought in the express in fine style. A world speed record of 180km/h (112mph) was claimed for it on 10 May 1893, running down a 1 in 350 grade with a four-car train. However, this was based only on the conductor's timing, and unfortunately remained unverified. No. 999, with reduced 1981mm (78in) driving wheels, is preserved at Chicago.

BOILER PRESSURE: 12.6kg/cm² (190psi)
CYLINDERS: 483x610mm (19x24in)
DRIVING WHEELS: 2184mm (86in)
GRATE AREA: 2.8m² (30.7sq ft)
HEATING SURFACE: 179m² (1927sq ft)
TRACTIVE EFFORT: 7378kg (16,270lb)
TOTAL WEIGHT: 92.53t (204,000lb)

The 'Empire State Express' was one of the first trains to have a distinctive livery applied to the locomotive as well as to the coaches: a step soon copied.

CLASS K 4-4-0 DANISH STATE RAILWAYS (DSB)

DENMARK 1894

With 100 built between 1894 and 1902, the K class was one of Denmark's most numerous locomotive classes, used on main-line passenger services. Its designer, the DSB's chief mechanical engineer Otto Busse, took the fairly unusual approach of

placing the valve gear – Allan's straight link motion in this case – externally, as well as the cylinders and connecting rods, so that a complex pattern of rod movements could be seen as the engine moved along. Between 1915 and 1925, superheaters were fitted, and half

BOILER PRESSURE: 12kg/cm² (171psi)
CYLINDERS: 430x610mm (17x24in)
DRIVING WHEELS: 1866mm (73.5in)
GRATE AREA: 1.8m² (19.3sq ft)

HEATING SURFACE: 87.9m² (947sq ft)
TRACTIVE EFFORT: 6220kg (13,716lb)
TOTAL WEIGHT: 42.67t (94,080lb)

the class received new boilers between 1925 and 1932.

'BIG GOODS' 4-6-0 HIGHLAND RAILWAY (HR)

Though British engines continued to seem small to most foreign observers, the arrival of the first 4-6-0 to run on a British railway indicates the start of a turning away from the small-engine policy that had prevailed for so long; by this time, one or two other companies also had 4-6-0s on the drawing board. The 'Big Goods' were simple-expansion engines, with two outside cylinders and internal Allan straight-link valve gear. Trademarks of their designer, David Jones, were the louvred chimney, to help raise the exhaust, and the hinged-back vacuum brake pipe. The class was also fitted with the Le Chatelier counter-pressure brake, which retarded the action of the cylinders by admitting water, helping to slow the train on the long downhill grades. Fifteen were built, by Sharp, Stewart of Glasgow, and went straight into service on the Perth–Inverness main line. Primarily intended for freight service, they also ran passenger

BOILER PRESSURE: 12.3kg/cm² (175psi)
CYLINDERS: 508x660mm (20x26in)
DRIVING WHEELS: 1600mm (63in)
GRATE AREA: 2m² (22.6sq ft)
HEATING SURFACE: 155m² (1672.5sq ft)
TRACTIVE EFFORT: 11,050kg (24,362lb)
TOTAL WEIGHT: 56.9t (125,440lb)

trains during the short peak season in summer. Fifty years later, they were still on the Highland

main line, though by then on pilot and banking duties. The original, No. 103, has been preserved.

The preserved No. 103, the first 4-6-0 to run on a British railway, on a special excursion train.

TYPE 5500 4-4-0 JAPANESE RAILWAYS (JR)

Until Japan ceased to import locomotives, American and British builders played box-and-cox in supplying motive power to the JR's developing system. Beyer Peacock of Manchester, England, supplied this engine for main-line

passenger services: a two-cylinder simple, with outside cylinders and internal valve gear, and its leading bogie outside-framed. With modest tractive effort, the Class 5500 was soon displaced on the main lines, but continued in branch line

BOILER PRESSURE: 12kg/cm² (171psi)
CYLINDERS: 406x559mm (16x22in)
DRIVING WHEELS: 1400mm (55in)
GRATE AREA: 1.33m² (14.3sq ft)

HEATING SURFACE: 73m² (786sq ft)
TRACTIVE EFFORT: 6750kg (14,880lb)
TOTAL WEIGHT: 55.81t (123,039lb)

operations into the 1960s.

CLASS F3 4-6-0 MEXICAN RAILWAYS (FCM)

At this time, Mexico was still importing many of its locomotives from Great Britain, though by the 1900s US influence would predominate. This was a small class of four powerful 4-6-0s, built by Neilson's in

Glasgow, with two simple-expansion outside-mounted cylinders, and internal Stephenson link motion. They had large American-style bogie tenders, and ran until 1927, when all were withdrawn.

BOILER PRESSURE: 12.3kg/cm² (175psi)
CYLINDERS: 469.5x660mm (18.5x26in)
DRIVING WHEELS: 1370mm (54in)
GRATE AREA: 2.2m² (24sq ft)

HEATING SURFACE: 123.3m² (1328sq ft)
TRACTIVE EFFORT: 11,116kg (24,512lb)
TOTAL WEIGHT: 58.16t (128,219lb)
(engine only)

0-6-6-0 JAROSLAV–VOLOGDA–ARCHANGEL RAILWAY

Operating in the Siberian far north of Russia, this was a 1065mm (3fft 6in) gauge line principally concerned, like most Russian railways, with freight haulage. They were Mallet compounds, the first to work in Russia, and were wood-burners.

All four cylinders were mounted outside, and the valves were operated by Walschaerts gear. This would later be very common, but even though it had been around since 1844, it was unusual in 1895. Another distinctive feature was that the rear set of

BOILER PRESSURE: 12kg/cm² (170psi)
CYLINDERS: hp 330x550mm (13x21.7in); lp 194x550mm (18x21.7in)
DRIVING WHEELS: 1091mm (43in)

GRATE AREA: 1.8m² (19.5sq ft)
HEATING SURFACE: 111.5m² (1200sq ft)
TRACTIVE EFFORT: 10,712kg (23,620lb)
TOTAL WEIGHT: 71.9t (158,480lb)

driving wheels were placed inside the locomotive's frame, in order

to make maximum space for the firebox.

'ATLANTIC' NO. 153 4-4-2 ATLANTIC COAST LINE (ACL)

As with many other railway events, locomotives of 4-4-2 formation appeared almost simultaneously on both sides of the Atlantic, on the Kaiser Ferdinand Bahn in Austria, and the Atlantic Coast Line in the United States. The American version made the biggest international impact, however, and the United States were much the most prominent user of the type. With this engine began the peculiar American fashion of calling a new wheel arrangement after the first company to use it, prompted in this case by the ACL's general manager, J. R. Kenly, and it did not take long for the 'Atlantic' to catch on both as locomotive type and also as a name.

The advantage of trailing wheels, rather than a third driving axle as in the 4-6-0, was that the lower-set axle enabled the firebox to be deeper than otherwise possible, while also allowing for the longer boiler necessary to produce the required amount of steam for a heavy passenger train. The Atlantic was *par excellence* a passenger locomotive, intended for high speeds. Baldwin built this first 4-4-2, though it did not take advantage of the possibility of a wider as well as deeper firebox, as subsequent models would do. Its designer, W. P. Henszey, took out a patent on it, though he was allowed to patent only his particular kind of 4-4-2 rather than the wheel arrangement itself.

The first ACL 'Atlantics' were substantial engines, with a wheelbase equivalent to a 4-6-0, and extended smokeboxes that provided space for a headlamp mounting on top, in front of the chimney. Further 4-4-2 types soon followed – competition made for intense rivalry on certain routes. . Perhaps none was more intense than the Philadelphia–Atlantic City route (see 1897) where Atlantics vied to provide the world's fastest train service.

Although 4-4-2 types would continue to be built up to 1939, they were always in small classes and often for specific services. As a standard express locomotive, the Atlantic was soon outflanked on one side by the greater power of the 'Pacific', and on the other by the superior tractive power and wider utility of the 4-6-0 locomotive. But on railways from the United States to France, Germany, Egypt, and India, they provided some of the most dashing and attractive-looking locomotives ever built.

BOILER PRESSURE: 12.6kg/cm² (180 psi)
CYLINDERS: 482x609mm (19x24in)
DRIVING WHEELS: 1827mm (72in)
GRATE AREA: 2.4m² (26.25sq ft)
HEATING SURFACE: 190m² (2047.2sq ft)
TRACTIVE EFFORT: 8344kg (18400lb)
TOTAL WEIGHT: not known

By 1895, most American locomotives were painted black, with the bright paint and polish of earlier decades forgotten; but the 'flyer' capability and status of the 'Atlantic' was emphasized by the colour scheme.

CLASS T-524 2-8-0 NEW SOUTH WALES GOVERNMENT RAILWAYS (NSWGR)

As was standard with the NSWGR at this time, this class was designed by the railway's own staff but built elsewhere, 15 from Beyer Peacock of Manchester, the other 129 by various Glasgow firms, in batches delivered up to 1916. As with the P class, the line was favoured with an excellent design, which gave long service on freight workings. Coal haulage in the Newcastle coalfield was their prime activity, but as the numbers grew, they were to be found all across the state. The design was

No. 5112 shunts at Goulburn, in September 1969. The high-capacity bogie tender is not the original.

also used for freight engines on the Commonwealth Railway's new transcontinental line in 1916. In 1924, they were reclassified D-50, and many were fitted with superheaters. More than 100 were still working in the 1960s, and the last, the un-superheated No. 5073, survived until 1973 and is preserved with two others.

BOILER PRESSURE: 11kg/cm² (160psi)
CYLINDERS: 533x660mm (21x26in)
DRIVING WHEELS: 1294mm (51in)
GRATE AREA: 2.7m² (29sq ft)

HEATING SURFACE: 204.1m² (2198sq ft)
TRACTIVE EFFORT: 13,050kg (28,777lb)
TOTAL WEIGHT: 113t (249,200lb)

BO-BO BALTIMORE & OHIO RAILROAD (B&O)

The first electrified section on a main-line railroad was installed by the B&O on its new Baltimore Belt line. Anticipating later controversies, the action was prompted by environmental and community considerations: the new line passed close to, and under, residential areas, and by the 1890s the proximity of a new railway line was no longer considered desirable. The short electrified section used a form of rigid overhead supply that was not used elsewhere (though rigid aluminium bar supply is now common in electrified depots), and the engines, built by General Electric, ran on twin bogies powered by gearless motors. Steam-hauled trains stopped at the beginning of the section; the electric locomotive was then attached to the train engine (whose steam was shut off), pulling it and the train the few miles to the other end, where it was detached, the train proceeded under steam again. In the early 1900s, the overhead supply was replaced by third-rail, and new locomotives were provided by 1912.

TYPE: Bo-Bo, electric
POWER: not known
TRACTIVE EFFORT: 200kN (45,000lbf)
MAX. OPERATING SPEED: 96km/h (60mph)
WEIGHT: 87 tonnes (192,000lb)
OVERALL LENGTH: 8.268m (27 ft 2in)
MAX. AXLE LOAD: 22 tonnes (48,488lb)
GUAGE: 1435mm (4ft 8.5in)

CLASS 170 2-8-0 IMPERIAL & ROYAL STATE RAILWAYS (KKSTB)

A Class 170 at Vienna Süd depot in May 1969. The prominent tail rods on the cylinders were intended to reduce wear on the pistons.

In the relatively short list of great locomotive designers, the name of Karl Gölsdorf stands high. He had been in charge of locomotive design on the KKSTB since 1891, and this class was his first major achievement. Although later used throughout the system, the Class 170 was originally planned for the new Arlberg route from Switzerland into Austria, as a powerful two-cylinder compound engine that would provide reliable traction on long mountain grades. Mechanically it was totally up-to-date, with a heating surface greater than that of any engine type in Europe. It used the Krauss-Helmholtz leading bogie, devised by Richard Helmholtz at the Krauss Works, which linked the single leading truck to the front driving axle and enabled the long engine to 'flow' into curves. Up to 1918, 908 of the Class 170 were built, and the last were not withdrawn until the 1970s.

BOILER PRESSURE: 13kg/cm² (185psi)
CYLINDERS: hp 540x632mm (21x25in); lp 800x632mm (31.5x25in)
DRIVING WHEELS: 1298mm (51in)
GRATE AREA: 3.9m² (42sq ft)
HEATING SURFACE: 240.7m² (2591sq ft)
TRACTIVE EFFORT: not known
TOTAL WEIGHT: 68.5t (151,042lb)

'DUNALASTAIR II' 4-4-0 CALEDONIAN RAILWAY (CR)

GREAT BRITAIN 1897

It was with the 'Dunalastair I' 4-4-0 of 1895 that the Caledonian's Chief Mechanical Engineer, J. F. McIntosh, took what was seen in conservatively minded Britain as a major step when he superseded small boilers and tall chimneys with fat boilers and a squat chimneys (to keep within the loading gauge). The big boiler of the Dunalastairs made a

significant difference to the power and performance of locomotives that were otherwise quite old-fashioned. Matched with a larger firebox, and slightly enlarged inside cylinders, it provided the basis of a sturdy and free-steaming engine. There were

several stages of expansion up to the 'Dunalastair IV' of 1904.

These engines were used for express services on the Caledonian main lines between Glasgow, Perth and Aberdeen, and Glasgow and Edinburgh.

BOILER PRESSURE: 12.3kg/cm² (175psi)
CYLINDERS: 482x660mm (19x26in)
DRIVING WHEELS: 1980mm (78in)
GRATE AREA: 1.9m² (20.6sq ft)
HEATING SURFACE: 139m² (1500sq ft)
TRACTIVE EFFORT: 8095kg (17,850lb)
TOTAL WEIGHT: 53.67t (118,328lb)

A 'Dunalastair II' locomotive with a stopping train from Perth to Crieff, on one of the Caledonian Railway's many cross-country single-track lines.

CLASS 321 4-6-0 HUNGARIAN RAILWAYS (MÀV)

HUNGARY 1897

Budapest Locomotive Works produced this class of 18 engines, all two-cylinder compounds, intended for main-line work in mountain districts. They were quite massive in appearance, with narrow running plates between the boiler and cylinders. Much work had been

put into their bogie design to allow for ease of downhill running on curving tracks: its pivoting pin was set well behind the centre-line, and it was also allowed a degree of lateral movement. Hungarian railways continued to favour the 4-6-0, perhaps to show an independent attitude to

Austria, where the 2-6-2 was preferred.

BOILER PRESSURE: 13kg/cm² (185psi)
CYLINDERS: hp 510x650mm (22.8x 25.6in); lp 750x650mm (29.5x25.6in)
DRIVING WHEELS: 1606mm (63.25in)
GRATE AREA: 2.6m² (28sq ft)

HEATING SURFACE: 163.6m² (1761.4sq ft)
TRACTIVE EFFORT: 8210kg (18,103lb)
TOTAL WEIGHT: 57.7t (127,228lb)
(engine only)

'MIKADO' 2-8-2 NIPPON RAILWAYS

Mikado was one of the styles of the Japanese emperor, and the name has clung to the 2-8-2 arrangement, which was first used in this locomotive built by Baldwin of Philadelphia for the Nippon Railways. Basic to the design was the need for a wide firebox to burn relatively low-grade coal. Since the Japanese gauge was 1065mm (42in) and the loading gauge was also quite restricted, a firebox placed behind the driving wheels, supported on a pony truck, was seen as the answer. Mikado was a simple-expansion engine, with two outside cylinders driving the third set of coupled wheels. First seen as a specialist locomotive for burning poor-quality coal, it was soon recognized that the Mikado had potential as a stretched 2-8-0 with greater boiler and firebox capacity, with the possibility of adding a booster engine to the trailing axle; Mikados were also built to run on

high-quality steam coal. The 2-8-2 remained a popular type on the Japanese railways. Always strongly identified with narrow-gauge working (see the 'McArthur' 2-8-2 of 1942), it also proved its worth on standard gauge tracks as an express passenger type as well as a freight-hauler.

2-8-2 locomotives ran freight trains like this mixed goods and mixed traffic services on Japanese railways right up to the end of steam.

BOILER PRESSURE: 12kg/cm² (171psi)
CYLINDERS: 469x609mm (18.5x24in)
DRIVING WHEELS: 1117mm (44in)
GRATE AREA: 4.2m² (45.1sq ft)

HEATING SURFACE: not known
TRACTIVE EFFORT: not known
TOTAL WEIGHT: 54.25t (119,600lb)
(engine only)

'CAMELBACK' 4-4-2 PHILADELPHIA & READING RAILROAD (P&RR)

Highly distinctive in appearance, this American-style locomotive owes something to Ross Winans' earlier 'Camels', but the two designs had little in common other than the boiler-mounted cab and the full-width firebox behind the driving wheels. Also known as 'Mother Hubbards', the 'Camelbacks' were mostly fast engines, built for express hustling, though some were also built as goods engines and yard switchers. Fundamental to the design was the wide firebox, patented by John H. Wootten in 1877 and usually called after him. It was meant to burn culm, the gritty anthracite waste that lay in mounds

around the anthracite mines, and was much cheaper than coal. The huge firebox required careful management, with enough draught to keep the fire hot but not so much as to blow it all out of the chimney.

The first 'Camelback' was built by Baldwin for the Atlantic City Railroad in 1896 just before it was taken over by the P&RR. It hauled the 'Atlantic City Flyer', for a time the fastest train in the world, covering the 90km (56 miles) from Atlantic City to Camden in 50 minutes. The P&RR version was a compound engine on the Vauclain system patented by Samuel M. Vauclain, who was to

A 'Camelback' 4-4-2, No. 804 of the Central Railroad of New Jersey, a prime commuter line, stands in the yard, around 1910.

become Chairman of the Baldwin company and a great innovative railwayman. Its four cylinders were all mounted outside the frame: high pressure above low on each side, and both driving a single crosshead. Both cylinders on each side were activated by a single piston valve. Though it had disadvantages, including the problem of balancing the work, the timing of the paired cylinders, and the tremendous mass of the combined piston thrust, it placed all the works on the

outside, removing the need for crank axles, for which the American engineers had by this time a hereditary dislike.

BOILER PRESSURE: 14kg/cm² (200psi)
CYLINDERS: hp 381x609mm (15x24in); lp 634x609mm (25x24in)
DRIVING WHEELS: 2134mm (84.25in)
GRATE AREA: 7.5m² (80.75sq ft)
HEATING SURFACE: 236m² (2541sq ft)
TRACTIVE EFFORT: 10,390kg (22,900lb)
TOTAL WEIGHT: 99t (218,000lb)

CLASS 384 2-6-0 EGYPTIAN RAILWAY ADMINISTRATION

EGYPT 1898

At this time, Egypt was in the British sphere of influence, but, as often happened, Baldwin picked up an order when the British builders were unable to meet a desired delivery date – in this case, for 18 mixed-traffic locomotives. The 2-6-0 type was a standard one for Egypt, where the trains were normally lightweight and the terrain of the Nile Valley and Delta almost level. In a way not currently possible, Egypt was linked to the wider international railway system by way of a line from Cairo to Aleppo and on through Turkey to Istanbul, enabling a Wagons-Lits service to run from Istanbul's Haydarpasa Station, on the east side of the Bosporus, to the Egyptian capital. With a train of two or three sleeping cars, the 2-6-0s could race along at a good speed.

BOILER PRESSURE: 12.6cm^2 (180psi)
CYLINDERS: 457x679mm (18x24in)
DRIVING WHEELS: 1529mm (60.25in)
GRATE AREA: 2.35m^2 (23.35sq ft)
HEATING SURFACE: 184.5m^2 (1990sq ft)
TRACTIVE EFFORT: 7900kg (17,423lb)
TOTAL WEIGHT: not known

'KLONDYKE' 4-4-2 GREAT NORTHERN RAILWAY (GNR)

GREAT BRITAIN 1898

The American gold rush had caught the public imagination when Britain's first 'Atlantic' design appeared, hence the nickname. The GNR needed more power to replace its obsolete single-driver engines, and its new Chief Mechanical Engineer, H. A. Ivatt, opted for the 4-4-2 design that was already very successful in the United States. Surprisingly, his design took no advantage of the 'Atlantic' locomotive's ability to provide a wide firebox and a

BOILER PRESSURE: 12.3kg/cm^2 (175psi)
CYLINDERS: 476x609mm (18.75x24in)
DRIVING WHEELS: 2020mm (79.5in)
GRATE AREA: 2.5m^2 (26.75sq ft)

HEATING SURFACE: 134m^2 (1442 sq ft)
TRACTIVE EFFORT: 8160kg (18,000lb)
TOTAL WEIGHT: 58.93t (129,920lb)

bigger boiler, and the 'Klondykes', though handsome in appearance and popular with the public, were underpowered compared with some contemporary 4-4-0s. The first to be delivered, from the GNR's Doncaster Works, No. 990 *Henry Oakley*, has been preserved.

Henry Oakley **piloting the saddle tank locomotive No. 118,** *Brussels*, **on the Keighley & Worth Valley Railway, on 11 September 1977.**

CLASS C 'COUPE-VENT' 4-4-0 PARIS–LYON–MEDITERRANEAN RAILWAY (PLM)

The 'streamlining' on this class, striking rather than handsome, was strictly utilitarian in its purpose. The PLM's main line runs northwards up the Rhône valley for many miles, facing the full blast of the south-blowing 'Mistral' wind, and its engineers had ample chance to experience the extent to which wind resistance can slow a train down and make the locomotives work harder. The pointed 'wind-cutter' look was devised by M. Ricour of

the PLM. The engines were four-cylinder compounds of a type developed by A. Henry from 1888, when he converted some old 2-4-2 simple-expansion engines into compounds, making them the first locomotives to have four cylinders driving two coupled axles. This worked well enough for Henry and his successor Charles Baudry to build 40 new 4-4-0s on similar lines but to larger dimensions, and

the streamlined casing was introduced on these.

Between 1899 and 1902, the Class C was introduced, with a further increase in boiler capacity and some modifications to the casing. In total, 120 were built by several workshops, including the PLM's own shops at Arles. As before, the high-pressure cylinders were inside, driving the leading coupled axle, and the low-pressure cylinders, outside, drove the rear axle. The low-pressure cylinders had a fixed cut-off of 63 per cent, and in some of the engines the driver could operate a steam valve to

admit 'live' steam to the low-pressure cylinders on starting his train. The earlier 40 locomotives were later modified to incorporate this feature. Whether greatly aided by their streamlining or not, the 'Windcutters' could run fast, and a maximum test speed of 150km/h (93mph) was recorded for the class. A typical service would be with a train of 200 tonnes (197 tons) on which a maintained speed of 100km/h (62mph) would be kept up. One is preserved, at Mulhouse.

BOILER PRESSURE: 15kg/cm² (213psi)
CYLINDERS: hp 340x620mm (13.6x24.6in); lp 540x620mm (21.25x24.6in)
DRIVING WHEELS: 2000mm (79in)
GRATE AREA: 2.48m² (26.7sq ft)
HEATING SURFACE: 190m² (2040sq ft)
TRACTIVE EFFORT: 10,990kg (24,256lb)
TOTAL WEIGHT: 101.38t (223,500lb)

The four-cylinder compound C-class in its original form was fast and sturdy and has a hint of the knight in armour about it.

CLASS T9 4-4-0 LONDON & SOUTH WESTERN RAILWAY (LSWR)

This class eventually numbered 66 in three series, all inside-cylindered simple-expansion engines. Thirty-five were built at the company's original works, Nine Elms in London, the others by Dübs in Glasgow. The later variants had fireboxes with water-filled cross-tubes, a notion of their designer Dugald Drummond, which did not add to their performance. But the performance of the class generally was very good (hence their nickname of 'Greyhounds') owing chiefly to an unusually large firebox and boiler set on the long wheelbase. Like the Caledonian 'Dunalastairs', this class took the traditional British inside-cylinder approach to its peak, but there was to be no development until modern US and European practice was studied and accepted. The T9s ran on express services and later on West Country locals for some fifty years. One has been preserved.

BOILER PRESSURE: 12.3kg/cm² (175psi)
CYLINDERS: 470x660mm (18.5x26in)
DRIVING WHEELS: 2000mm (79in)
GRATE AREA: 2.2m² (24sq ft)
HEATING SURFACE: 124m² (1335sq ft)
TRACTIVE EFFORT: 7574kg (16,700lb)
TOTAL WEIGHT: 51.2t (112,896lb)
(engine only)

A classic British 4-4-0 design, in the black livery of the former state-owned British Railways, and numbered 30120, the preserved T9 is on the heritage 'Watercress Line' between Alton and Alresford, in Hampshire.

CLASS G3 2-8-0 MEXICAN RAILWAYS (FCM)

MEXICO 1899

In Mexico, as in many other Central and South American countries, the 2-8-0 became the predominant locomotive type. High speed was of less concern than efficient pulling and braking power, and the ability to mount long curving grades at a steady speed. A variety of different versions and sizes was available from the US builders' catalogues, and the FCM made virtually all its purchases from the United States. Never a rich railway, FCM tended to buy in small numbers at any one time, and it took nine years for Baldwin to supply the 10 engines forming this class. All two-cylinder simples in standard US style, they worked for five or more decades, undergoing various modifications, some being fitted with the new Baker valve gear instead of their original Stephenson link gear; by 1960 only a couple were left, and they were scrapped soon after.

BOILER PRESSURE: 12.2kg/cm² (175psi)
CYLINDERS: 507.6x660mm (20x26in)
DRIVING WHEELS: 1117mm (44in)
GRATE AREA: 3m² (33.2sq ft)
HEATING SURFACE: 187.3m² (2047.2sq ft)
TRACTIVE EFFORT: 14,047kg (30,975lb)
TOTAL WEIGHT: 64.8t (142,884lb)
(engine only)

CLASS 180 0-10-0 IMPERIAL & ROYAL STATE RAILWAYS (KKSTB)

AUSTRIA 1900

Perhaps the most striking feature of this type, as in some other Austrian locomotives, was the wide tube fixed between the two domes, parallel to the boiler-top, containing a steam drier, whose function, anticipating the much more effective superheater, was to help supply the cylinders with steam that would expand as much as possible. A two-cylinder compound, it was Karl Gölsdorf's first 10-coupled design, built with coal haulage in mind. The connecting rods drove the fourth set of wheels, and the first, third and fifth axles were allowed a degree of lateral play to enable the engine to take curves of down to 200m (656ft) radius. Axle-loading was no greater than 13.7 tonnes (13.4 tons). Eventually numbering 239 locomotives, the '180s' were primarily used in the Bohemian coalfield region, though after 1918 they were distributed among Czech and Yugoslav railways as well as those of Austria. The first of the class is preserved.

A Yugoslav Class 180 with visible low-pressure cylinder and air-brake reservoir.

BOILER PRESSURE: 14.3kg/cm² (205psi)
CYLINDERS: hp 560x635mm (21.8x24.7in); lp 850x635mm (33.1x24.7in)
DRIVING WHEELS: 1258mm (49in)
GRATE AREA: 3.4m² (36.6sq ft)
HEATING SURFACE: 202.1m² (2176sq ft)
TRACTIVE EFFORT: not known
TOTAL WEIGHT: 65t (143,325lb)
(engine only)

CLASS 2.6 COMPOUND 4-4-2 NORTHERN RAILWAY (NORD)

Gaston du Bousquet had already introduced compound expansion on the Nord (see 1886), but with this type he produced the first really effective compound express engine. It was an 'Atlantic', a long engine with the outside cylinders set behind the outside-framed leading bogie, and big trailing wheels supporting the firebox. The compounding system, based on four cylinders, had been jointly developed by du Bousquet and Alfred de Glehn, the engineering director of the Société Alsacienne's shops at Mulhouse. On the outside, high pressure drove the rear axle; inside, low pressure drove the leading axle (this was the other way round from du Bousquet's first four-cylinder express locomotives).

A set of valve gear was provided for each cylinder, and two regulators governed the cut-off for high and low pressure respectively, and provided two sets of reversing gears. On starting, the low-pressure cylinders could be shut off, greatly sharpening the blast and increasing the initial tractive effort by a factor of as much as 50 per cent. It was an undeniably sophisticated machine, but, operated by trained men it worked magnificently. The long-standing French tradition of mechanically trained drivers was ideal for managing complex locomotives like these.

Two protoypes were built in 1900, and a further 33 followed; built both by the Société Alsacienne and by J. F. Cail of Lille.

In theory, it was not necessary to link the two sets of driving wheels, as they were each driven by separate 'engines', and the prototypes were of 2-2-2-2 configuration. But the production engines had the driving wheels linked by coupling rods, which did away with the compounds' occasional tendency, when incautiously managed, for the wheels to turn in contrary directions. Outside bearings were fitted on the front bogie frames. The long boiler barrel terminated in a Belpaire firebox.

The 2.6 class was put into service on the heavily loaded boat trains from Calais and Boulogne to Paris, where they established an immediate reputation both as hill-climbers and as fast engines. One experienced observer noted the speed on a 1 in 200 grade increasing from 83.5km/h (52.2mph) to 91.2km/h (57mph) with a 360-tonne (354.3-ton) train, when the driver admitted live steam to the low-pressure cylinders. A 400-tonne (394-ton) train could maintain a steady 120km/h (75mph) on level track, and their performance was soon a

Had it not been for the development of the superheater, the compounding system of the 2.6 class could been the basis of the express steam locomotive.

matter of interest and envy to other railways. Both the Great Western in England and the Pennsylvania Railroad of the United States bought examples and studied their mechanisms and working intensively. The Prussian Railways, another line that operated at the leading edge of technology, bought 79, and 10 went to the Egyptian Government Railways.

In 1912, superheating on the Schmidt system was fitted to the class, along with enlarged high-pressure cylinders worked by piston valves, and the increase in steam supply enabled them to reach new heights of performance. Later, some of them were fitted with Lemaître blast-pipes and wide-diameter chimneys, and the original six-wheel tenders were replaced by double-bogie tenders of increased capacity. They remained in high-speed main-line service into the 1930s. No. 2.670 is preserved, at Mulhouse.

BOILER PRESSURE: 16kg/cm² (228psi)
CYLINDERS: hp 390x640mm (13.5x 25.25in); lp 560x640mm (22x25.25in)
DRIVING WHEELS: 2040mm (80.25in)
GRATE AREA: 2.76m² (33.4sq ft)
HEATING SURFACE: 138m² (1485sq ft)
SUPERHEATER: 39m² (420sq ft)
TRACTIVE EFFORT: 7337kg (16,178lb)
TOTAL WEIGHT: 120t (264,500lb)

CLASS 1900 'CLAUD HAMILTON' GREAT EASTERN RAILWAY (GER)

The Great Eastern Railway (GER) combined an intensive London suburban traffic with a pattern of express services to the cities and towns of East Anglia, added to by summer holiday trains to coastal resorts. This handsome class was introduced to handle the fast trains as part of the 'big boiler' trend of the time. It was an enlarged version of the classic British 4-4-0, with two inside cylinders. Later 'Clauds' were given Belpaire fireboxes, and some were converted for a time to run on liquid tar fuel derived from gas-works waste, the first main-line British locomotives to do so. This was prompted by a short-term rise in the price of coal, and the locomotives were re-converted when coal prices fell again. Oil fuel was never used on British steam locomotives except in a handful of experimental cases.

BOILER PRESSURE: 12.7kg/cm² (180psi)
CYLINDERS: 483x660mm (19x26in)
DRIVING WHEELS: 2130mm (84in)
GRATE AREA: 1.9m² (21.3sq ft)
HEATING SURFACE: 151m² (1630sq ft)
TRACTIVE EFFORT: 7755kg (17,100lb)
TOTAL WEIGHT: 51t (112,448lb)

'Claud Hamilton' type No. 8787 of the LNER at Welwyn Garden City with a Kings Cross-Cambridge buffet car express in 1937. It is one of two 'Royal Clauds'.

COMPOUND 4-4-0 MIDLAND RAILWAY (MR)

W. F. Webb's failures with compounding on the London & North Western may have had a discouraging effect on some other British engineers, but not Walter Smith of the North Eastern, nor the Midland Railway's S.W. Johnson and his successor R. M. Deeley. Smith's first compound locomotive had a single high-pressure cylinder inside, and two low-pressure cylinders outside, and a boiler pressure of 14kg/cm² (200psi) –

the highest yet for a British engine, though soon to become common. It incorporated a valve that could switch the working from simple ('live' steam to all three cylinders), to semi-compound and full-compound working. Between 1900 and 1903, Smith's system was installed in five new express 4-4-0s built at the Midland's Derby Works. They had Belpaire fireboxes despite Johnson's qualms about their

'ugliness', and were the precursors of the celebrated 'Midland Compounds' as developed by Deeley from 1904. Deeley simplified Smith's system, removing the 'change valve' at some expense to flexibility of working, but making the engines more straightforward to drive: British enginemen were not taught the technical expertise of their French brethren. In the 1920s, the compounds were fitted with superheaters and further engines were also built, bringing the class to a total of 240. Critics had commented that they worked well

BOILER PRESSURE: 15.5kg/cm² (220psi)
CYLINDERS: hp 482x660mm (19x26in); lp 514x660mm (21x26in)
DRIVING WHEELS: 2134mm (84in)
GRATE AREA: 2.6m² (28.4sq ft)
HEATING SURFACE: 159.75m² (1720sq ft)
TRACTIVE EFFORT: 10,884kg (24,000lb)
TOTAL WEIGHT: 60.8t (134,176lb)

with lightweight trains, but the Midland Compounds were capable of sustained power output and gave smart service with express and, later, local trains on the hilly lines of northern England and southern Scotland.

Preserved Midland Compound No. 1000 pilots former LMS 'Jubilee' 4-6-0 No. 5690 Minotaur on a special charter train, at York on 28 October 1978.

'PRINCESS OF WALES' 4-2-2 MIDLAND RAILWAY (MR)

An artist in locomotive design, Samuel Johnson of the MR took a Janus-faced position at the start of the twentieth century. On the one hand, he backed compound expansion; on the other, he brought out this, one of the last and largest 'single-driver' engines, leader of a class of 10. The availability of steam-powered

sanding gear encouraged him, as the huge wheels' tendency to spin on starting could be checked by a high-velocity stream of fine sand to assist adhesion. Even so, it was virtually the last fling of the 'single-driver': the work of experienced locomotive performance recorders would show that its claimed free-steaming qualities and speed

BOILER PRESSURE: 12.6cm² (180psi)
CYLINDERS: 500x666mm (19.5x26in)
DRIVING WHEELS: 2397mm (93.5in)
GRATE AREA: 2.3m² (24.5sq ft)

HEATING SURFACE: 113m² (1217sq ft)
TRACTIVE EFFORT: 7337kg (16,178lb)
TOTAL WEIGHT: 51t (112,336lb)

potential were inferior to those of a coupled-wheel engine, and heavier coaches and longer trains were straining its powers too much.

The sandpipes to the driving wheel can be seen in this side view. Power sanding is fitted to locomotives even today.

CLASS B51 4-4-0 STATE RAILWAYS (SS) DUTCH EAST INDIES

A slightly later version of the B51, an oil-fired Hartmann-built Class B53 of 1912 vintage stands by a gushing water column.

The SS normally acquired its engines from Werkspoor in the Netherlands or from German builders, and the 40 engines of Class B51 came from Werkspoor, Hanomag of Hannover, and Hartmann of Chemnitz. Two-

BOILER PRESSURE: 12kg/cm² (171psi)
CYLINDERS: hp 380x510mm (15x20in); lp 580x510mm (22.8x20in)
DRIVING WHEELS: 1503mm (59in)
GRATE AREA: 1.3m² (14sq ft)

HEATING SURFACE: 85.5m² (920.5sq ft)
TRACTIVE EFFORT:
TOTAL WEIGHT: 35.4t (78080lb) (engine only)

cylinder 'cross-compounds', they worked main-line expresses from Djakarta, Bandung and Surabaja. Later they were demoted to local services, and 70 years on, about half the class were still on active service.

CLASS 500 4-6-0 ADRIATIC NETWORK (RA)

Affectionately known to the enginemen as *Mucca*, 'milch cow', this was an innovative design by Giuseppe Zara of the RA to greet the new century. In earlier decades, the small diameter of boilers had enabled enginemen to get a good forward view, but the growth of boiler width had made this increasingly restricted, often forcing drivers to lean far out of the cab side, with consequent danger to eyesight and, indeed, life. Zara's solution was the 'Cab-forward' locomotive, with the engine in effect running permanently backwards. Coal was

carried in bunkers on each side of the firebox, and a six-wheel water tender was attached at the smoke-box end, with flexible pipes feeding the injectors. A four-cylinder compound, the locomotive used the Plancher arrangement, with the high- and low-pressure cylinders on opposite sides. All cylinders drove the second coupled axle. Walschaerts valve gear was used, with a single piston valve on each side distributing steam to both cylinders.

Forty-three of this mixed-traffic type were built and they were

effective enough to work unmodified into the 1940s, used mainly on goods trains on the Po Valley lines, and capable of pulling up to 830 tonnes (817 tons) at low speed, or maintaining 90km/h (56mph) on passenger service. But they did not start a trend (though the idea was later picked up in the United States; see 1928), partly because their coal capacity was limited, partly because the Plancher compound system caused the engines to 'hunt', yawing from side to side rather than running straight. Consequently the Class 500s were suitable only for low-

speed working. On the inception of the state railway system in 1905, they became Class 670, and when some were fitted with superheaters they became the Class 671.

BOILER PRESSURE: 15kg/cm² (213psi)
CYLINDERS: hp 365x656mm (14.25x25.6in); lp 596x656mm (23.25x25.6in)
DRIVING WHEELS: 1938.5mm (75.6in)
GRATE AREA: 3m² (32.47sq ft)
HEATING SURFACE: 153.5m² (1653sq ft)
TRACTIVE EFFORT: 6698kg (14,770lb)
TOTAL WEIGHT: 100t (221,000lb)

CHAPTER TWO

EXPERIMENTAL TIMES

1901–1924

At the beginning of the twentieth century, just when it seemed that the steam locomotive had reached a plateau of development, the industry was galvanized by Wilhelm Schmidt's development in Germany of the superheater, which gave extra power to new and old machines alike. Railway companies remained aloof from the early developments of the internal combustion engine. This was not because they were hostile to new technologies but for practical reasons. The petroleum engine's small size and limited power seemed hardly relevant to an industry that by now was moving loads of 1000 tons as a matter of routine, and achieving high speeds. It was thought that it might, in time, replace the horse and cart on local deliveries from the railroad depot, but very few people saw any wider potential for it. Railways were too big and too busy to pursue untried technologies on anything but a tiny scale. Nevertheless, one of the first diesel-powered vehicles was a small railway locomotive built in Grantham, England in 1896, using a pump injection system patented by Herbert Akroyd-Stuart. More influential were the experiments carried out in Germany between 1901 and 1903, when electric railcars built by AEG and Siemens exceeded 200km/h (124mph) and set a world speed record of 210.2km/h (130.6mph). In 1902, high voltage current was employed on a public line for the first time, in a 15-period, three-phase system, on the new 106km (69-mile) Valtellina railway in northern Italy, where the electrification was undertaken by a brilliant Hungarian engineer, Kálmán Kandó.

With a very typical Eastern European chimney-mounted smoke lifter, this Class 324 2-6-2 of the Hungarian State Railways, dating from 1909, was still in service more than 60 years later.

CLASS 7B 2-6-0 BUENOS AIRES GREAT SOUTHERN RAILWAY (BAGS) ARGENTINA 1901

Beyer Peacock of Manchester built this 28-strong class of two-cylinder compounds, which were essentially enlarged versions of the simple-expansion Class 7 2-6-0 that had been running on the BAGS since 1885. They were operated on passenger and goods services into the 1930s. Being a long way from the centres of locomotive building, and also, from the late 1920s on, chronically short of available funds, the Argentinian railways tended to store, rather than scrap, older locomotives. This was done primarily so that spare parts could be taken from defunct engines and re-used to preserve the existence of live ones. In 1949, four engines of Class 7B were resurrected in

this way, using parts from other locomotives, and converted to oil burning. By 1967, the whole class had been scrapped.

BOILER PRESSURE: 12.25kg/cm² (175psi)
CYLINDERS: hp 457x660mm (18x26in); lp 660x660mm (26x26in)
DRIVING WHEELS: 1726mm (68in)
GRATE AREA: 1.9m² (20.1sq ft)
HEATING SURFACE: 48.8m² (1240sq ft)
TRACTIVE EFFORT: 6866kg (15,140lb)
TOTAL WEIGHT: 79.5t (175,280lb)

Argentinian Western Railway Class 10 2-6-0, No. 85. The 27 locomotives of this class were built by Kitson and Beyer, Peacock in 1902-3.

A1A - A1A TEST CARS 'A' AND 'S' ELECTRIC RAIL RESEARCH COMPANY (STES) GERMANY 1901

An unprecedented set of traction experiments took place in Germany between 1901 and 1903, unique in cost, thoroughness and in results. The aim was to test rigorously the potential of electric current for high-speed rail use. A new company, STES, was formed in 1899 by the two electrical companies, Siemens & Halske and AEG, with the Prussian government and certain banks as interested parties. It was allowed to use 23km (14.5 miles) of military railway between Zossen and Marienfeld, to the south-west of Berlin, to test three specially built vehicles, railcars 'A' by AEG and 'S' by Siemens; also a Bo-Bo steeple-cab locomotive from Siemens.

Direct current supply was rejected in favour of alternating current, provided by a three-wire catenary hung from poles alongside rather than above the track. Car A had three separate bow-type pantographs at each end of the vehicle to collect current from the wires, strung at different levels. Car B also had three current collectors at each end, but they were mounted

together on single poles. Both systems required modification during the tests. The current could be varied between 10,000V and 14,000V, 3-phase AC at 38–48Hz, transformed on the railcars to 435V on car A and 1150V on Car S. The cars were fully constructed and fitted, with passenger seats arranged in two compartments each seating 25 people. They were wooden-bodied, built on a steel framework, with driving cabs at each end, and all high-voltage equipment was mounted either beneath the floor or in the roof space. Clerestory roofs were fitted, both to provide light and ventilation and to hold air ducts to cool the transformers. The switch-gear was operated pneumatically. In the Siemens car, the motors were axle-mounted; in the AEG vehicle, they were placed on hollow shafts around the axles, and vertically sprung, with power transmission by spring drive from the hollow shafts to the wheels.

Walter Rathenau and Walter Reichel, directors of the tests, were breaking new ground: no-one

before had dealt with such a combination of voltage and high speed. In their way, the Marienfeld experiments were similar to the work begun later in the century on the Maglev test track. They found that the original track was too lightly laid, and one of the cars derailed while travelling at 160km/h (100mph). The car was rebuilt and the track relaid and realigned, with heavier rails and deep ballast. Braking tests were carried out in September–November 1903, and in the course of these both railcars exceeded 200km/h (124mph) – sensational speeds for that time. On October 28, car A reached 210.2km/h (130.6mph), a world land-speed record that was not broken until the Kruckenberg propeller vehicle of 1931, and not attained again by an electric train until the SNCF Co-Co 7121 reached 239.8km/h (149mph) in 1953. Hauling a trailer made little difference to speed or air resistance, although a heavy Prussian 12-wheel sleeping car left the rails behind one of the test cars at 174km/h (108mph). Much valuable data was

gathered from the experiments, though they did not lead to a sudden increase in electrification schemes. Many practical and operational problems had still to be solved, including that of simplified power supply (later resolved by single-phase AC current). But, as conclusive as Rainhill in their own way, the German tests established that electric traction was not just suitable for low speeds and specialized routes, but could be adapted to very high main-line speeds.

TYPE: experimental high-speed railcar
POWER: four gearless synchronous motors supplied with 10,000V three-phase AC at 50Hz collected from triple overhead wire and developing 186–560kW (250–750hp)
TRACTIVE EFFORT: not known
MAX. OPERATING SPEED: 210km/h (130.85mph)
TOTAL WEIGHT: 60t (132,250lb)
MAX. AXLE LOAD: 10t (22,050lb)
OVERALL LENGTH: 22,100mm (72ft 6in)
BUILDER: Van der Zypen Charlier, Cologne; electrical equipment by AEG

CLASS Q 4-6-2 NEW ZEALAND RAILWAYS (NZR) NEW ZEALAND 1901

The NZR ran a long-distance 1065mm (3ft 6in) gauge railway network in both main islands of New Zealand, often through difficult terrain. By this time, it had shaken off any automatic loyalties to British suppliers and had bought many of its engines from the United States, including some of the first 2-8-0s, from Baldwin. At this time, its chief engineer, A. L. Beattie, wanted a locomotive with a wide firebox, to burn low-grade lignite

coal mined on the west coast of South Island, to run main-line passenger services. He also required a low maximum axle-loading, because of lightweight rails and thinly ballasted road-bed.

Q-class No. 344, as new. The tender, though quite small, is mounted on two bogies, and its frame, unusually, extends forward beneath the cab's floor.

Such an engine was bound to be a long one, but another essential feature was flexibility in the wheelbase to cope with the often sinuous line followed by the tracks. The result was the world's first 4-6-2 or 'Pacific' class, built for NZR by Baldwin in Philadelphia.

The Q class, 13 in all, weighed 76.4 tonnes (75 tons), had a boiler pressure of 14kg/cm² (200psi), bar frames, and a Westinghouse air-brake pump. Walschaerts valve gear was fitted, actuated by outside-admission piston valves. Performance was very satisfactory, though the nature of the lines did not lend itself to the kind of high-speed running in which some later Pacific types excelled, and the last Q was not retired until 1957. At a time when bigger engines were being sought to haul new steel-bodied bogie coaches, the usefulness of the 'Pacific' arrangement was evident, and Baldwin began almost immediately to build 4-6-2 engines for other railways, beginning with the St Louis, Iron Mountain & Southern Railway, later part of the Missouri Pacific. Other manufacturers and other countries also began to build Pacifics. An important aspect of their success was the improvements made in signalling and trackwork. On many busy stretches of track, electric or pneumatic signalling and point systems were being installed, and flyover or dive-under junctions were put in at the busiest intersections.

BOILER PRESSURE: 14kg/cm² (200psi)
CYLINDERS: 406x559mm (16x22in)
DRIVING WHEELS: 1245mm (49in)
GRATE AREA: 3.72m² (40sq ft)
HEATING SURFACE: 155m² (1673sq ft)
TRACTIVE EFFORT: 8863kg (19,540lb)
TOTAL WEIGHT: 75t (165,000lb)

2-4-2 ROYAL SIAMESE RAILWAYS (RSR)
THAILAND 1901

With no coal reserves but ample forest, the RSR used wood burners on its new 1m (3ft 3in) gauge tracks, intended to make a through route from Burma to Malaya. For no very clear reason, this German-built (Krauss) class of seven passenger train locomotives was modelled on the Paris–Orleans 2-4-2 of 1873, though with modifications, including the Krauss-Helmholtz leading bogie. Krauss had built 2-4-2 narrow-gauge compounds for lines in Yugoslavia, but the Siamese engines were simple-expansion. The rear wheel was set back beneath the cab and the engines gave good service for many years.

BOILER PRESSURE: 12.4kg/m² (177psi)
CYLINDERS: 360x500mm (14x19.7in)
DRIVING WHEELS: 1350mm (53in)
GRATE AREA: not known
HEATING SURFACE: not known
TRACTIVE EFFORT: 3042kg (6707lb)
TOTAL WEIGHT: 28t (61,740lb)
(engine only)

CLASS K9 4-6-0 PLANT SYSTEM SAVANNAH FLORIDA & WESTERN RAILWAY (SF&W)
USA 1901

No. 111 of this class achieved a legendary – perhaps mythical – status when a speed of 193km/h (120mph) was claimed for it. The K9s were designed as express locomotives and built by Alco's (American Locomotive Company) Rhode Island Works. Alco had been formed by amalgamation of eight smaller builders in 1901. The occasion of the speed claim was a competition between the Plant System and the Seaboard Air Line to establish which would get the lucrative West Indies mail contract. No. 111 ran from Jesup to Jacksonville terminus, 186km (118 miles) at an average speed of 124km/h (77mph), a remarkable feat in itself, but the top speed was never verified. Despite its fame, it was scrapped in 1942.

BOILER PRESSURE: 12.6cm² (180psi)
CYLINDERS: 487x718mm (19x28in)
DRIVING WHEELS: 1846mm (72in)
GRATE AREA: 3m² (3sq ft)
HEATING SURFACE: not known
TRACTIVE EFFORT: 9633kg (21,240lb)
TOTAL WEIGHT: 114.7t (252,900lb)

CLASS 18 4-4-0 BELGIAN STATE RAILWAYS (EB)
BELGIUM 1902

An unexpected issue of the Caledonian Railway's 'big boiler' policy of the 1890s was a strong interest from the Belgian State Railways. Neilson, Reid & Co. of Glasgow built five 'Dunalastair II' engines for the EB in 1898, and this led to the building of no less than 719 locomotives of the Caledonian's 4-4-0 and 0-6-0 types, all by Belgian constructors, between then and 1906. Of these, 140 formed Class 18, which handled express passenger trains across the Flanders plain from Brussels. All were simple-expansion engines with two inside cylinders, and the last six were among the first engines to be equipped with Schmidt superheaters. The contrast between the Scottish designs and the Belgian Type 1 2-4-2s must have been a striking one. One of these Scoto-Belgian engines has been preserved.

A typical Belgian capuchon on the chimney and a windowed cab are the only non-Scottish aspects of this Caledonian design.

BOILER PRESSURE: 13.5kg/cm² (195psi)
CYLINDERS: 482x660mm (19x26in)
DRIVING WHEELS: 1980mm (79in)
GRATE AREA: 2.2m² (22sq ft)
HEATING SURFACE: 126.8m² (1365.5sq ft)
TRACTIVE EFFORT: 8930kg (19,690lb)
TOTAL WEIGHT: 50.3t (110,880lb)
(engine only)

CLASS D1 2-6-0 DANISH STATE RAILWAYS (DSB)

DENMARK 1902

Much of Denmark's goods traffic consisted of fairly light trains, carrying perishable items like milk and other farm produce, and the D class was intended to work this kind of traffic. From its beginnings with D1 in 1902, it became a class of 100, with several sub-classes as time went on. The pioneering D1s, were designed by Otto Busse, DS's chief mechanical engineer from the company's inception in 1892 until 1910. Numbering 41, they were two-cylinder simple-expansion engines, with a low boiler pressure for the period. The builders were Henschel and Hartmann in Germany, and Nydquist & Holm in Sweden. Between 1914 and 1925, the D1s received superheaters, and the original boilers were replaced between 1925 and 1940.

BOILER PRESSURE: 12kg/cm² (170psi)
CYLINDERS: 431.4x609mm (17x24in)
DRIVING WHEELS: 1383mm (54.5in)
GRATE AREA: 207.8m² (19.3sq ft)

HEATING SURFACE: 106.7m² (1149sq ft)
TRACTIVE EFFORT: 8340kg (18,390lb)
TOTAL WEIGHT: 44.7t (98,560lb)
(engine only)

CLASS G8 0-8-0 ROYAL PRUSSIAN UNION RAILWAYS (KPEV)

GERMANY 1902

With the appearance of this class, German locomotive engineering stepped into a leading position. An 0-8-0 in itself was not an innovation, and the G8 was based on an earlier design of 1893, the G7. But in terms of efficiency and performance, it had a 'secret weapon'. For seven years, Dr Wilhelm Schmidt had been working in the KPEV engineering shops to develop the concept of the superheater into a usable feature of the locomotive, and the fruit of his labours was built into the G8. Superheating, the reheating of steam to ultra-high temperatures, had long been a dream or ambition of locomotive engineers, even in Trevithick's day, and a number of unsuccessful or partial attempts had been made. Schmidt's aim was to get high superheat, boosting the temperature of saturated steam from 182ºC to 300ºC (360º–572ºF), or even more. The very hot, dry steam continued to expand in the cylinders, not only giving more work for every ounce of steam produced, but using less, with consequent economies in the use of fuel and water. In Schmidt's final system, completed in 1902, the main steam pipe of the engine led to a header, from which a set of narrow tubes were turned back and inserted in wider tubes in the upper part of the boiler, where they would be subjected to the fierce heat of gases streaming from the firebox. These superheater tubes, known as elements, terminated in a second header, from which the superheated steam was passed to the steam chest and thence to the cylinders. Schmidt's superheater added only 1 tonne (0.9 tons) or so to a locomotive's weight, and could be installed in existing engines. Once there, it needed little in the way of maintenance.

The importance of the superheater was very great. Previously it had seemed that the steam locomotive had reached a plateau of development. With the internal-combustion engine and the electric motor available, both offering a higher degree of efficiency and potential power, steam might have been abandoned several decades earlier. Instead, Schmidt's invention refocused attention on the power of steam, and most railway companies and locomotive builders relegated other forms of power to the sidelines. In locomotive design, the advent of the superheater brought about a decline in the use of compound expansion. Compounding had been regarded as 'difficult' – compound engines were more expensive to build and service, and the results did not always seem to justify the cost and effort. Superheating, by comparison was cheap, simple and delivered excellent results. It was not entirely without problems: the very high temperatures could make metal surfaces stick rather than slide over each other, and new internal lubrication systems were needed. Many designers opted for a lower level of superheat than the Schmidt system

allowed for. But by the later 1900s, almost all new locomotives incorporated superheating, though only the more ambitious locomotive engineers would seek to combine the effects of compounding and superheating.

The G8, designed by Dr Robert Garbe, was the first really modern steam locomotive. With a maximum axle-load of 14.4 tonnes (14 tons) and a compact wheelbase, it could go virtually anywhere on rails. The first examples were built at the Vulkan Works in Stettin, East Prussia. Unlike its G7 predecessor, which was built both in compound and simple-expansion versions, it was a simple-expansion engine, with two outside cylinders, external Walschaerts valve gear, and piston valves. This form of valve gear, devised both by Walschaerts and the German engineer Edmund Heusinger almost 60 years earlier, proved to be the most effective, combined with piston valves, for working superheated locomotives. Schmidt produced a broad-ring piston valve that was widely used until the 1920s, when the narrow-ring piston valve was developed, again in Germany, and passed into general use. Between 1902 and 1910, more than 1000 G8s were

built, and in 1913 a heavier version was introduced, as G81, first built by Hanomag at Hannover. The demands of war traffic pushed locomotive production to unprecedented heights and by 1921 a total of 5087 G8s and G81s had been built at 12 different workshops throughout Germany. Between 1933 and 1941, the Deutsche Reichsbahn Gesellschaft (DRG) rebuilt 608 of the class as 2-8-0s. By that time, as a result of post-war reparations, G8 locomotives had spread well beyond Germany and were working as far east as Turkey and Syria. Some were still at work on coal trains on the Turkish Railways in the 1970s. In the DRG's standard classification, the G8s, with their numerous modifications, became Series 5525-57. Several are preserved, in Germany and other countries.

BOILER PRESSURE: 14kg/cm² (200psi)
CYLINDERS: 600x660mm (23.4x25.75in)
DRIVING WHEELS: 1350mm (52.6in)
GRATE AREA: 2.66m² (28.6sq ft)
HEATING SURFACE: 139.5m² (1502.7sq ft)
SUPERHEATER: 40.4m² (435sq ft)
TRACTIVE EFFORT: 20,660kg (45,569lb)
TOTAL WEIGHT: 55.7t (122,752lb)
(engine only)

Some of the last G8 locomotives in service were those on the Turkish State Railways. Though usually employed on freight trains, they also worked local passenger services.

'SAINT' CLASS 4-6-0 GREAT WESTERN RAILWAY (GWR)

Unlike the KPEV, the GWR had no 'secret weapon', but this new class of express engine burst onto the British scene in a way hardly less revolutionary than the Prussian G8. The Locomotive Superintendent, George Jackson Churchward, who had begun his working life on a GWR subsidiary line as a 'gentleman apprentice', had been preparing for supreme office during a long period as deputy, and lost little time in launching a radical new range of locomotives.

Careful planning and meticulous engineering were Churchward's hallmarks, and despite his work experience being restricted to the conservative GWR, he studied overseas developments closely. The tapered 'wagon-top' style of boiler developed on US railroads was adopted and formed the basis of the design of GWR No. 1, the first of a series of tapered domeless boilers that would

incorporate flat-topped Belpaire fireboxes. Apart from the new boiler, many other improvements were included in Churchward's first 4-6-0, precursor of the 'Saint' class, which was tactfully named *Dean* after his predecessor. Among them was a 'top-feed' system, admitting feedwater at the top of the boiler and sending it through a series of trays so that it was heated to some extent before mingling with the steam and furiously boiling water around the firebox. Churchward did not rush matters, and rebuilt one of the prototypes as an 'Atlantic', having bought in a de Glehn compound 4-4-2 from the *Nord* railway in France, and making careful comparisons in performance, before deciding that the simple-expansion 4-6-0 was the right type for his purposes. Line production did not get under way until 1906, by which time further progress had been made. The most crucial

developments were those relating to the valve movements.

Today these locomotives look classically English, but when they first appeared there was something of an outcry among British locomotive observers, some of whom seemed to feel that a locomotive that showed off almost all of its driving wheels was, in some way, indecent. News of the new engines' performance effectively silenced the critics. The Saints, of which 77 were built up to 1911, had simple-expansion outside cylinders and inside Stephenson link motion, but with larger, longer-travel valves that allowed for a shorter cut-off of the piston stroke, to 20 per cent or less of the total. Churchward also adopted the Schmidt superheater,

though he later used a Swindon adaptation with a lower degree of superheat.

Though superseded by new classes, some Saints survived on the former Great Western lines until 1953, when the new British 'standard' classes then appearing clearly showed their descent from the veterans of 50 years earlier.

No. 98 was the second prototype 'Saint' and, like all the early examples, the cab sides came to footplate level, with a high-set buffer beam. It had a 'half-cone' boiler.

BOILER PRESSURE: 15.75cm² (225psi)
CYLINDERS: 461.5x769mm (18x30in)
DRIVING WHEELS: 2064mm (80.5in)
GRATE AREA: 2.5m² (27sq ft)
HEATING SURFACE: 199m² (2143sq ft)
SUPERHEATER: 24.4m² (263sq ft)
(from 1906)
TRACTIVE EFFORT: 11,066kg (24,395lb)
TOTAL WEIGHT: 71.3t (157,248lb)
(engine only)

CLASS B2 0-6-0 CENTRAL MEXICAN RAILWAY

This most common European type was not common in Mexico, which had no great need for specialized shunting or switching engines, and used 2-8-0s for road freights. Twenty-four Class B2s were produced, the first 14 being coal-fired, from the

Alco Rhode Island works; the others followed from Baldwin, being oil burners with Belpaire fireboxes. All were of classic American bar-framed construction, their tenders with downwards-sloping tops, intended to give the driver a

good view of the coupler or brakesman working behind.

BOILER PRESSURE: 12.6kg/cm² (180psi)
CYLINDERS: 482x609mm (19x24in)
DRIVING WHEELS: 1269mm (50in)
GRATE AREA: 3m² (32sq ft)

HEATING SURFACE: 154m² (1660sq ft)
TRACTIVE EFFORT: 9900kg (21,830lb)
TOTAL WEIGHT: 57t (126,000lb)
(engine only)

2-6-0 CORDOVA & HUATUSCO RAILWAY

Mexico, thinly populated and economically backwards in the early twentieth century, was not a rewarding territory for railways, but to exploit minerals or to 'open up' agricultural country, many branch lines were built, usually to a narrow

gauge. This line was of 609mm (2ft) gauge, accessing a hill district from the Mexico City–Vera Cruz main line. It was worked by three small 2-6-0 locomotives built by Baldwin as scaled-down versions of the standard US product.

BOILER PRESSURE: 11kg/m² (160psi)
CYLINDERS: 304x457mm (12x18in)
DRIVING WHEELS: 774mm-(30.5in)
GRATE AREA: 66m² (7.1sq ft)

HEATING SURFACE: 38.5m² (415sq ft)
TRACTIVE EFFORT: 4541kg (10,014lb)
TOTAL WEIGHT: 37.6t (82,906lb)

CLASS MA 2-8-0 SWEDISH RAILWAYS (SJ)

SWEDEN 1902

In the early 1900s, the iron ore trains running from Kiruna in Sweden to the Baltic coast, or to Narvik in Norway, were among the heaviest in the world (as they still are). This class was designed to handle 1016-tonne (1000-ton) loads across the tundra, and had enclosed and insulated cabs. Built

BOILER PRESSURE: 14kg/cm² (200psi)
CYLINDERS: hp 530x640mm (21x25in); lp 810x640mm (32x25in)
DRIVING WHEELS: 1296mm (50.5in)
GRATE AREA: 2.9m² (31.2sq ft)
HEATING SURFACE: 211.7m² (2280sq ft)
TRACTIVE EFFORT: 16,780kg (37,000lb)
TOTAL WEIGHT: 107.7t (237,440lb)

at Trollhättan by Nydquist & Holm, they were two-cylinder compounds that gave adequate but not great performance. The cylinders were

already quite large, but two of the class, provided with larger cylinders and piston valves, were superior to the rest.

Built for slow, heavy mineral trains, these were among the first big steam locomotives to be displaced by electric traction.

CLASS S 4-6-4T NEW SOUTH WALES GOVERNMENT RAILWAYS (NSWGR)

AUSTRALIA 1903

These big tank engines had a varied career. Many were built at the NSWGR's Eveleigh Works, the rest by Beyer Peacock of Manchester, to a total strength of 145. The last were delivered in 1917, by which time their original duty of suburban train haulage

was already being eroded by buses and tram-cars, but they ran local and commuter trains around Sydney, Newcastle and Wollongong. In the re-classification of 1924, they became Class C-30. Much of their purpose was lost with the

electrification of Sydney's suburban services, and 77 were turned into tender engines of Class C30T for use on rural branch lines, while the rest were mostly involved with shunting and freight. Several of both types are preserved.

BOILER PRESSURE: 11.2kg/cm² (160psi)
CYLINDERS: 474x615.4mm (18.5x24in)
DRIVING WHEELS: 1410mm (55in)
GRATE AREA: 2.3m² (24sq ft)
HEATING SURFACE: 144.2m² (1453sq ft)
TRACTIVE EFFORT: 9211kg (20,310lb)
TOTAL WEIGHT: 72.3t (159,421lb)

CLASS 206 4-4-0 IMPERIAL & ROYAL STATE RAILWAYS (KKSTB)

AUSTRIA 1903

Seventy-strong, this class of express engines was built at the Vienna works of Floridsdorf, Wiener Neustadt, and STEG (the state railway works) as well as at PCM in Prague, to the design of Karl Gölsdorf. These two-cylinder compounds marked the last of his four-coupled express engines, which had begun in 1894 with Class 6 and continued in 1898

with Class 106. Thereafter, the demands of heavier international trains, with diners and often loading sleeping cars, required more power, and the 4-4-0s were relegated to secondary services. Gölsdorf's series of 4-4-0s marks the evolution of his 'style' as a locomotive

designer, with a progression towards a plainer look with fewer external pipes and fittings. In this, he was influenced by a visit to Great Britain, where the fashion was still to hide as much of the

works as possible. Without going to extremes, Gölsdorf created a distinctive, almost sculptural look for his locomotives.

BOILER PRESSURE: 13kg/cm² (185psi)
CYLINDERS: hp 500x680mm (19.7x26.8in); lp 760x680mm (30x26.8in)
DRIVING WHEELS: 2100mm (82.75in)
GRATE AREA: 3m² (32.3sq ft)
HEATING SURFACE: 150m² (1615sq ft)
TRACTIVE EFFORT: not known
TOTAL WEIGHT: 54.2t (119,511lb)
(engine only)

Though to some eyes it seemed a quaint accessory, the steam-drier pipe was a useful means of producing hotter and more expansive steam in the period before the superheater was developed.

'CROSS-COMPOUND' 2-8-0 FRANCO-ETHIOPIAN RAILWAY (CFE)

ETHIOPIA 1903

Schweizerischer Lokomotiv- und Maschinenfabrik (SLM) of Winterthur, Switzerland built the first two of CFE's four 2-8-0s; the other pair came from the Société Alsacienne. These two-cylinder compounds were the most powerful engines on the line, which

at that point was still incomplete; it did not reach Addis Ababa from Djibouti on the Red Sea coast until 1917. French-designed, the locomotives were bar-framed. The tenders, running on two four-wheeled bogies, were fitted with supplementary water tanks.

BOILER PRESSURE: 13kg/cm² (185psi)
CYLINDERS: hp 420x550mm (16.5x21.6in); lp 630x550mm (24.8x21.6in)
DRIVING WHEELS: 1000mm (39.4in)

GRATE AREA: 1.3m² (13.8sq ft)
HEATING SURFACE: 91.5m² (985sq ft)
TRACTIVE EFFORT: not known
TOTAL WEIGHT: 34.5t (76,072lb)
(engine only)

CLASS TK2 2-8-0 FINNISH RAILWAYS

At this time, Finland was still a Grand Duchy of the Russian Empire, and its railways were laid to Russia's 1524mm (5ft) gauge. With wood as Finland's chief natural resource, its steam locomotives were mostly wood-burners, with high-railed tenders and balloon spark-arrestor chimneys. Finnish locomotives did not have the massive quality of Russian ones: they were more compact, reflecting German design influence. But the Tk 2-8-0s came from Baldwin in Philadelphia (Tk1) or were home-built at the Tampella Works (Tk2). Tk2 was a lightweight freight engine, with a maximum axle-load of only 8.3 tonnes (8.2 tons).

BOILER PRESSURE: 12.5kg/cm² (178psi)
CYLINDERS: hp 410x510mm (16x20in); lp 590x510mm (23.25x20in)
DRIVING WHEELS: 1120mm (43.7in)
GRATE AREA: 1.4m² (15sq ft)
HEATING SURFACE: 84.8m² (913sq ft)
TRACTIVE EFFORT: 4660kg (10,275lb)
TOTAL WEIGHT: 37.6t (82,900lb) (engine only)

CLASS 242.12 2-8-0 EASTERN RAILWAY (EST)

Powerful both in appearance and performance, this was France's first 2-8-0 design, a four-cylinder compound with high-pressure cylinders inside and low-pressure outside, driving the second and third sets of wheels respectively, and employing two different valve gears, Walschaerts on the outside and Stephenson's link motion inside. Two prototypes appeared from 1903 and production began in 1905. The total number was a 175, and these worked the great majority of the *Est's* main-line freights until the 1920s.

BOILER PRESSURE: 16kg/cm² (227psi)
CYLINDERS: hp 391x650mm (15.4x25.6in); lp 599x650mm (23.6x25.6in)
DRIVING WHEELS: 1396mm (55in)
GRATE AREA: 2.8m² (30.1sq ft)
HEATING SURFACE: 242m² (2282.5sq ft)
TRACTIVE EFFORT: 12,702kg (28,008lb)
TOTAL WEIGHT: 72.8t (160,720lb)

'CITY' CLASS 4-4-0 GREAT WESTERN RAILWAY (GWR)

Intended for fast, lightweight trains, this class was something of a hybrid in appearance. It was a short version of the GWR's new tapered boiler with Belpaire firebox, mounted on a rather traditional-looking double frame, with laminated springs above the running plate, outside cranks and two simple-expansion inside cylinders. But they were certainly very fast, and were used on Plymouth–London boat trains in competition with the London & South Western Railway's route via Salisbury. No. 3440 *City of Truro* was recorded on 9 May 1904 as having reached 164km/h (102mph) hauling the 'Ocean Mail' between Plymouth and Bristol. The train weighed 150.4 tonnes (148 tons) and was running downhill. Expert analysis has since thrown doubt on this achievement, setting the maximum at just under 160km/h (100mph), but this engine was long famed as the first to officially break the 'hundred'. It was saved from scrapping in 1931 and is still able to steam.

BOILER PRESSURE: 12.6kg/cm² (180psi)
CYLINDERS: 457x660mm (18x26in)
DRIVING WHEELS: 2045mm (80.5in)
GRATE AREA: 1.91m² (20.56sq ft)
HEATING SURFACE: 169m² (1818sq ft)
TRACTIVE EFFORT: 8070kg (17,790lb)
TOTAL WEIGHT: 94t (207,000lb)

In British Railways livery as No. 3717 of the Western Region, 'City of Truro' has been spruced up at this West Country depot, for a special run.

STEAM RAILCAR GREAT WESTERN RAILWAY (GWR)

The steam railcar or rail-motor was very much in vogue for branch-line working in Britain during the early decades of the twentieth century. The idea of a self-propelling rail carriage goes back to W. Bridges Adams on the Bristol & Exeter Railway in 1847–48, but was not really taken up until 1903, when there were many more branch lines. These were often short, sometimes only 1.6km (1 mile) long. Many had scanty traffic, and were beginning to lose business to the new motor lorry and bus. The railcar, cheaper to build and run than a locomotive and train, was intended to operate economically and to attract custom. Some versions left the locomotive part exposed, but the GWR built the coachwork round it. The small steam engines were temperamental, and many railcars were later de-engined and converted to 'driving trailers' for use in push-pull trains powered by tank locomotives. Specifications unknown.

A GWR steam railcar crosses Brunel's Royal Albert Bridge, completed in 1859, high above the Tamar estuary.

CLASS U 4-6-0 STATE RAILWAYS

As new lomotives, the Class Us were sent to the east of the Russian Empire, to the Ryasan–Ural and Tashkent railways, to operate passenger traffic. Engineer A.O. Delacroa designed it as a four-cylinder de Glehn-type compound, with the outside (high-pressure) cylinders driving the middle coupled wheels. Maximum service speed was 105km/h (65mph), but few Russian services attained that pace.

Built between 1903 and 1910, the Class Us played a part in Russian history. One headed the train that took Lenin on his fateful journey to the Finland Station in St Petersburg in 1917; another

pulled his funeral train from Gorki to Moscow in 1924. Both are preserved, in Finland and Russia respectively, and show the typical Russian feature of railings along the footplate, as on the deck of a ship.

BOILER PRESSURE: 14kg/cm² (199psi)
CYLINDERS: hp 370x650mm (14.5x25.6in); lp 580x650mm (22.8x25.6in)
DRIVING WHEELS: 1730mm (68in)
GRATE AREA: 2.8m² (30sq ft)
HEATING SURFACE: 182m² (1959.5sq ft)
TRACTIVE EFFORT: N/A
TOTAL WEIGHT: 72.1t (158.980lb)
(engine only)

Preserved at Moscow, this is locomotive U 127, the engine that drew Lenin's funeral train in 1924.

4-6-0 CAPE GOVERNMENT RAILWAYS (CGR)

With supplementary cylindrical water tanks mounted on the tender, these locomotives regularly traversed the arid Karoo Desert line with both passenger and freight trains. The large headlight was a necessity on the unfenced track.

The engineers on the bigger 'colonial' railways were often men of enterprise and innovation, who took care to stay in touch with new techniques and methods of operation. H.M. Beatty, Chief Locomotive Superintendent of the CGR, made his new 4-6-0 type the first British-built locomotive to have the still very new Schmidt superheater. It also had the Schmidt piston valves designed to function with superheated steam, but while many superheated types were fitted with Walschaerts valve gear, Beatty retained Stephenson's link motion. Locomotives on the South African railways were either for freight or, like this type, intended for undertaking mixed-

traffic work. Its large bogie tender was fitted with supplementary water tanks to assist operation in arid districts, where track-side water supplies might be scarce. After the formation of the South African Railways out of the various state systems, the CGR 4-6-0s were deployed quite widely through the country.

BOILER PRESSURE: 12.6kg/cm² (180psi)
CYLINDERS: 474x666mm (18.5x26in)
DRIVING WHEELS: 1384mm (54in)
GRATE AREA: 1.7m² (18.75sq ft)
HEATING SURFACE: 99m² (1068sq ft)
SUPERHEATER: 28.8m² (310sq ft)
TRACTIVE EFFORT: 7806kg (17,212lb)
TOTAL WEIGHT: 86.9t (194,811lb)

'SANTA FE' CLASS 900 2-10-2   ATCHISON, TOPEKA & SANTA FE RAILROAD (AT&SF)   USA 1903

Named for the Atchison, Topeka & Santa Fe Railroad, this was the first 2-10-2 to be built, developed from a 2-10-0 freight class of 1902, also for the Santa Fe. Samuel Vauclain designed its 'tandem compound' system, in which the four cylinders are mounted outside in pairs, low pressure behind high pressure, each pair sharing a common piston rod. The drive was to the middle coupled wheel, which was flangeless. Though used for a time in other countries as well as on other US locomotives, this was not a lasting solution because, like Vauclain's vertically paired cylinders, any inequalities of steam distribution set up stresses that affected the riding of the locomotive as well as reducing its efficiency. The powerful double thrust on the connecting rods,

though it provided a strong tractive effort, also created stresses.

In 1903–4, 76 of the class were built, all for freight service; the first 40 were coal burners, the rest were oil-fuelled. All were later converted to two-cylinder, simple-expansion types. After this time, compounding became rarer on American railroads, except on articulated locomotives. Especially once superheating was adopted (the American Superheater Company acquired Schmidt's patent around 1910), a big boiler and efficient simple-expansion cylinders could develop the

necessary tractive power, with far fewer operational and maintenance problems. The 'Santa Fe' type had its moment as 'biggest engine', but by now no-one thought it was the last word.

BOILER PRESSURE: 15.75kg/cm² (225psi)
CYLINDERS: hp 482x812mm (19x32in); lp 812x812mm (32x32in)
DRIVING WHEELS: 1461mm (57.5in)
GRATE AREA: 5.43m² (58.5sq ft)
HEATING SURFACE: 445.4m² (4796sq ft)
TRACTIVE EFFORT: 28,480kg (62,800lb)
TOTAL WEIGHT: 130.2t (287,240lb) (engine only)

Dismantling of withdrawn No. 1686, on the scrap road, has already begun, with the removal of brake pumps, cross-heads and connecting rods. The 1600 class was virtually identical to the original 900 class of 1903.

'PRAIRIE' TYPE 2-6-2   LAKE SHORE & MICHIGAN SOUTHERN RAILWAY (LS&MS)   USA 1903

New Zealand, first to use the 'Pacific' type, had already scored another first in the 1880s, when the Government Railways and the Wellington & Manawatu Railway both acquired locomotives

BOILER PRESSURE: 14kg/cm2 (200psi)
CYLINDERS: 525.6x718mm (20.5x28in)
DRIVING WHEELS: 2076mm (81in)
GRATE AREA: not known
HEATING SURFACE: not known
TRACTIVE EFFORT: 11,337kg (25,000lb)
TOTAL WEIGHT: 145t (320,000lb)

of 2-6-2 configuration from Baldwin. These were the first of the 'Prairie' type, though the by-name was not bestowed until the 1900s, when two Mid-West lines bought it simultaneously. Perhaps because of this, the Prairie was named after neither, but instead after the kind of territory they ran through. The Chicago, Burlington & Quincy and the Atchison, Topeka & Santa Fe Railroad both acquired locomotives of this configuration from Baldwin in 1901. It was the logical next step from the 2-6-0 for providing greater mid-range

power. The type was comparable in size and power to the 4-6-0 but, as with the 'Atlantic', the rear axle could support a deeper and wider firebox. In fact, for passenger trains, many lines continued to opt for the 4-4-2 Atlantic, whose front four-wheel bogie, as opposed to a two-wheel truck, was felt to be more secure at high speeds. Built by Alco for the Lake Shore, this example of the express 2-6-2 is generally considered to be among the most elegant American locomotives of its time. With its large-diameter driving wheels, it

was intended for tightly timed passenger trains, including the western laps of the 'Twentieth Century Limited' express, which was not a lightweight train. However, the design was not without defect, and the Bissell radial trucks fitted fore and aft more than once forced a Lake Shore 'Prairie' off the road. The Helmholtz truck, developed at the Krauss works in Munich, proved much more reliable for locomotives with a front truck and multiple coupled wheels. The Prairie was a versatile form and many lines used it as a mixed-traffic or freight locomotive. It was widely employed in Europe, especially by Italy and Austrian

railways, where it was used instead of the 4-6-0. Russia built many 2-6-2s. Prairies were also built in 'Camelback' versions in the

United States, and 2-6-2 tank locomotives were also frequently found in the mid-twentieth century in Britain and Western Europe.

The 'Prairie' design shows how a wider firebox is possible. The 2-6-2 was never as widely used as the similar-sized 4-6-0.

ELECTRIC MULTIPLE UNITS LANCASHIRE & YORKSHIRE RAILWAY (L&YR) GREAT BRITAIN 1904

Under the forward-looking Sir John Aspinall, the L&YR introduced electric multiple units in 1904 to work the busy suburban line between Liverpool Exchange and Southport. Electrical equipment was by Dick Kerr & Co., one of the forerunners of English Electric, and building was done at

the L&YR Horwich and Newton Heath works.

The units used 650V direct current third-rail collection – at first with a fourth rail bonded to the running rails for return current, though the fourth rail was later abandoned. The four-car sets could be extended to seven at

peak times. Three metres (10ft) wide, they were the widest railway

TYPE: suburban electric five car electric multiple units
POWER: 1200V DC conductor rail collection, four 112kW (150hp) DC traction motors on three power cars

coaches ever to operate in the UK. All had been withdrawn by 1942.

MAX. OPERATING SPEED: not known
MAX. AXLE LOAD: not known
OVERALL LENGTH: 18.29m (60ft)
GAUGE: 1435mm (4ft 8.5in)

TYPE S9 4-4-4 ROYAL PRUSSIAN UNION RAILWAYS (KPEV) GERMANY 1904

Around the turn of the nineteenth century, several attempts were made to produce a steam locomotive that could be driven from the front end. By the 1900s, Henschel & Sohn, of Kassel, had earned a reputation as an innovative builder of locomotives, and it produced this engine, which put the driver at the front end, as a one-off in the hope

of attracting orders. It was not the first cab-front locomotive (see the Adriatic Network's Class 500 of 1900), but in most other ways it was unique. A semi-streamlined design encased boiler and tender in one carriage-like body, with the chimney protruding from the roof. Driving controls were mounted in a vee-shaped cab, while the fireman sweated in an enclosed

compartment in the middle of the loco-tender unit. Anticipating the British A3 'Pacifics', the S9 also possesssed the world's first corridor-tender. The engine was a

BOILER PRESSURE: 14kg/cm² (200psi)
CYLINDERS: 526x636mm (20.6x24.8in)
DRIVING WHEELS: 2226mm (86.8in)
GRATE AREA: 4.4m² (47.3sq ft)

three-cylinder compound, intended for express passenger work, but no railway showed interest, and the S9 was eventually abandoned.

HEATING SURFACE: 258m² (2796.6sq ft)
TRACTIVE EFFORT: 9348kg (20,610lb)
TOTAL WEIGHT: 85.5t (188,496lb)

SERIES C4/5 2-8-0 SWISS FEDERAL RAILWAYS (SBB) SWITZERLAND 1904

When the Swiss railways required a new locomotive type, the standard practice was to set out the official work requirement that the locomotive needed to fulfil, so that there was no doubt in the minds of buyer or builder about what was wanted. In the case of this four-cylinder

compound locomotive, 10,000kg (22,046lb) of nominal tractive effort, or the ability to haul 200 tonnes (196.8 tons) up a 1 in 38 gradient at 20–25km/h (12–15mph), were required.

SLM at Winterthur built the class between 1904 and 1906. In the interest of standardization, it

shared a tender with the A3/5 of 1902. The cylinders were in line, high-pressure inside, with drive to two of the four axles. The class gave good and reliable service over a lengthy career. The last to be withdrawn, in 1959, was one of the oldest to be produced, No. 2701 of 1904.

BOILER PRESSURE: 14kg/cm² (200psi)
CYLINDERS: hp 370x600mm (14.5x23.6in); lp 600x640mm (23.6x25.2in)
DRIVING WHEELS: 1330mm (52.4in)
GRATE AREA: 2.8m² (30sq ft)
HEATING SURFACE: 174.2m² (1875.5sq ft)
TRACTIVE EFFORT: 10,000kg (22,050lb)
TOTAL WEIGHT: 109t (240,345)

S-MOTOR 1-DO-1 NEW YORK CENTRAL RAILROAD (NYC) USA 1904

Several key factors prompted the New York Central to electrify its Park Avenue tunnel line in New York City. It was extremely busy, with trains running in close

sequence, and as a result, the tunnel was always full of smoke. In January 1902, a packed train was hit by the train behind, whose driver had passed a red light

obscured by smoke. There was serious loss of life, and partly as a result, laws were passed prohibiting the use of steam locomotives in New York City,

where the NYC had been planning a huge new terminal, to be known as Grand Central. In 1904, a prototype electric locomotive was built by General Electric at

Schenectady, a compact unit with a 1-Do-1 wheel arrangement, and known as the T-Motor. It drew 660V DC from a third rail. A fleet of similar electrics was built. However, after a derailment with more fatalities in 1907, they were rebuilt with a 2-Do-2 wheel arrangement and reclassed as S-motors. In later years, the S-motors were largely relegated to switching duties. A few served until the early 1980s and several have been preserved, including the pioneering S-1 locomotive.

TYPE: 1-Do-1 (later modified to 2-Do-2) third-rail passenger electric
POWER: 660V DC at 1640kW (2200hp)
TRACTIVE EFFORT: 145kN (32,000lbf)
MAX. OPERATING SPEED: 128km/h (80mph)
WEIGHT: 90.9t (200,500lb)
OVERALL LENGTH: 11,278mm (37ft)
MAX. AXLE LOAD: 16t (35,500lb)
GAUGE: 1435mm (4ft 8.5in)

Journey's end – a redundant S-Motor stands on a siding in the shade of one of New York City's giant power stations.

0-6-6-0 MALLET BALTIMORE & OHIO RAILROAD (B&O)

USA 1904

Replacing the 'Santa Fe' as world's largest locomotive, and affectionately known amongst crew and customers as 'Old Maud' (after a mule in a strip cartoon), this was the United State's first Mallet-type locomotive. Big as it seemed at the time, it portended even greater things to come. Alco had acquired the American licence to build

Mallets, and the B&O were looking for something really powerful to help lift freight trains over the Western Pennsylvania mountains. As Anatole Mallet would have wished, it was a compound, with low-pressure cylinders driving the first, articulated set of wheels, and high-pressure cylinders driving the rear, fixed wheels. About 80 of this

type were built, of which some were later converted to 2-6-6-0. American Mallet users generally preferred the 2-6-6-2 configuration, allowing the use of a wide, deep firebox over the rear trailing wheels, and also providing a degree of rear articulation. 'Old Maud' survived until 1938, when she went to the scrapyard.

BOILER PRESSURE: 16.45kg/cm² (235lb)
CYLINDERS: hp 513x820mm (20x32in); lp 820x820mm (32x32in)
DRIVING WHEELS: 1436mm (56in)
GRATE AREA: 6.7m² (72.2sq ft)
HEATING SURFACE: 518.8m² (5586sq ft)
TRACTIVE EFFORT: 32,426kg (71,500lb)
TOTAL WEIGHT: 151.7t (334,500lb) (engine only)

'Old Maud' dwarfs an engineman. But almost every year was now producing a 'world's biggest' on the US railroads.

E69 BO LOKALBAHN AG (MÜNCHEN)

GERMANY 1905

Five individual electric locomotives were built between 1905 and 1930 for the steeply graded *Lokalbahn AG* (München) route between Murnau and Oberammergau in the Alps of southern Bavaria, powered at first by 5500V 16Hz AC, and later altered to 5000V 16.2/3Hz AC. On the DRG, they became Class E69, and later DB Class 169. In 1954, the locomotives were adapted to standard DB 15kV,

and E69.02 and E69.03 were redeployed on shunting work at Heidelberg. These two were virtually identical in external

appearance, while E69.01 and E69.05 are variations of the design, with a centrally placed 'steeple' cab. E69.04 featured a cab at one

end, but was rebuilt in steeple cab style in 1934. All five machines still survive, with 169002 and 169003 as museum locomotives.

TYPE: Bo local passenger and freight
POWER: E69.01 160kW (214hp); E69.02/03 306kW (410hp); E69.04 237kW (318hp); E69.05 565kW (758hp)
TRACTIVE EFFORT: E69.01 24kN (5400lbf); E69.02/03 33kN (7500lbf);

E69.04 30kN (6850lbf); E69.05 54kN (12300lbf)
MAX. OPERATING SPEED: E69.01 40km/h (25mph); E69.02–05 50km/h (31.3mph)
WEIGHT: 23.5 to 32t

(51,818 to 70,560lb)
MAX. AXLE LOAD: 11.8–16t (26,019 –35,280lb)
OVERALL LENGTH: 7.35–8.7m (24ft–28ft 4in)
GAUGE: 1435mm (4ft 8.5in)

BO-BO METROPOLITAN RAILWAY (METR)

GREAT BRITAIN 1905

The Metropolitan Railway's No. 1 poses for a promotional picture, just before the electrification went into service. A coach with a small compartment for the guard would be placed at each end of the train.

Though some misguided doctors claimed that the fumy atmosphere of the Metropolitan Railway, first opened on 10 January 1863, was beneficial to the lungs, it came as a great relief to the staff and the travelling public when electrification was introduced in 1906 and steam traction was removed from the tunnels. Ten electric locomotives had been ordered to run the services. With centrally mounted cabs and sloping front and back ends, they were technically steeple-cab locomotives but acquired the name of 'Camelbacks' (though quite different to American 'Camelbacks'). Current

was picked up by side-fitted shoes from a third rail, in what would be the standard London Underground fashion. The electrics originally ran from the City or Baker Street to Wembley Park before handing over to a steam locomotive. When electrification was eventually extended, locomotive changeovers switched to Harrow-on-the-Hill from 1908.

Although the electrical equipment came from the British

Westinghouse Company, the locomotives were built by the Metropolitan Amalgamated Railway Carriage & Wagon Company of Saltley, Birmingham. The electrics were originally fitted with enormous roller destination blinds, which were replaced by more modest-sized ones about 1911. In 1907, a further 10 locomotives, also Bo-Bo, were supplied by the same builder but with end cabs, and using British Thomson-

Houston electrical equipment. These were some 2.7 tonnes (3 tons) lighter than their predecessors, but in 1913 they were refitted with new bogies and Westinghouse 86M traction motors.

TYPE: suburban electric locomotives
POWER: 600V DC, four British Westinghouse Type 86M nose-suspended traction motors, 596.8kW (800hp)
TRACTIVE EFFORT: Not known
MAX. OPERATING SPEED: Not known
WEIGHT: 50.8t (112,000lb)
MAX. AXLE LOAD: not known
GAUGE: 1435mm (4ft 8.5in)

BESA 4-6-0 PASSENGER LOCOMOTIVE WESTERN RAILWAY (WR)

The 1m (3ft 3in) lines of India formed a vast network, across virtually every kind of terrain to be found on the sub-continent. The majority were rural lines, single-track, chiefly concerned with agricultural produce or mineral traffic, and serving passengers with mixed trains operating at low speeds, averaging around 19km/h (12mph). Some, however, offered long-distance services, like the 'Delhi Mail', running over a 965km (600-mile) route from Ahmadabad to the capital, which even in the 1970s took just under 24 hours, with 22 intermediate stops.

Oddly, only the gauge was metric; every other measurement was expressed in Imperial standards. The first metre-gauge line was opened in 1873, and the system quickly grew under a mixture of state and corporate enterprise. By 1969, the total route mileage stood at 25,845km (16,060 miles), and only Brazil possessed a larger metre-gauge network. At first, locomotive purchase was controlled by state governments, but from 1886 individual lines were allowed to order their own engines. This led to a wide variety of types and standards. At the beginning of the twentieth century, the Indian railway system was using as varied a range of locomotives as anywhere in the world, and an urgent need was felt in official

quarters for some standardization in the designs of steam locomotives. It was decided that a committee should be appointed for preparing designs of a limited number of standard classes in the hope that these would cater to the future requirements of all railways. The committee was to draw up standard plans based on the existing practice and experience with locomotives already in operation in India as well as in other systems in or outside the British Empire.

The first report of this committee in 1903 specified a 4-4-0 locomotive for passenger and a 0-6-0 for goods – both inside-cylinder designs with a 12.6kg/cm^2 (180psi) working pressure, a Belpaire firebox, balanced slide valves and Stephenson link motion. Most parts were common to both engines, and they had 1880mm (74in) and 1562mm (61.5in) coupled wheels respectively, reflecting the diameters already in use on the majority of working engines. The first were for the metre gauge, but a similar set for broad-gauge engines followed in 1905. Later, in 1910, an alternative larger boiler was also specified for lines requiring more power and capable of supporting a higher axle load. Superheating was also provided for, from 1912.

In 1905, following the revision

of permissible standard dimensions (and as a result of requests for more powerful locomotives by some railways), further designs were prepared, for 4-6-0s and 4-4-2s for mail trains, a 2-8-0 for heavy freight traffic and a passenger 2-6-4 tank version deriving from the 0-6-0 goods design. The Bengal Nagpur Railway (BNR) and the Great Indian Peninsula (GIP), the two most progressive railways of their time, had already introduced these types of locomotives in 1903 and 1904 respectively. The standard types were known as BESA classes (British Engineering Standards Association) and were built in large numbers. BESA's two 4-6-0 designs included one for a mixed-traffic type, and this one, sometimes known as the 'Heavy Mail' engine, for fast passenger and mail train services. The mail train was taken very seriously in India, which had a very efficient Post Office system, and railway mail contracts were as closely supervised as those in Britain.

Attempts to enforce a design standard were not always successful, but this one was applied with local knowledge and common sense, with accessibility of machinery, simplicity of operation, and a light maximum axle load of 10.16 tonnes (10 tons) as the keynotes. The tenders, Indian-style, had front

canopies. The designs were widely adopted and served the Indian railways well for many years, though individual locomotives were greatly adapted and modified at local depots as time went on. Large numbers of engines from the Indian metre-gauge lines were shipped out for war work in Mesopotamia and East Africa between 1914 and 1918. New engines were built to the BESA specifications (with the addition of superheaters and piston valves) as late as 1939, despite the formulation of new standard types (Indian Railway Standard; IRS) after World War I. BESA designs were constructed by many overseas builders – mostly but not exclusively British – as well as by Indian workshops like the Ajmer plant. The 'Heavy Mails', eventually numbering many hundreds, were finally supplanted by IRS or post-war 'Pacifics' on the most demanding long-distance duties, but some Indian lines, like the Rohilkund & Kumaon, retained 4-6-0s until the end of steam.

BOILER PRESSURE: 11.2kg/cm^2 (160psi)
CYLINDERS: 423x564mm (16.5x22in)
DRIVING WHEELS: 1461mm (57in)
GRATE AREA: 1.5m^2 (15.6sq ft)
HEATING SURFACE: 90.5m^2 (975sq ft)
TRACTIVE EFFORT: 6481kg (14,290lb)
TOTAL WEIGHT: 37.5t (82,880lb)

A 'Heavy Mail' and an F-class from Northern Railway in sheds at Lucknow. A strong wind gives the impression of movement.

CLASS 21 2-6-0 NORWEGIAN STATE RAILWAYS (NSB)

The production history of this class demonstrates the impact of superheating in the early twentieth century. The first of the class, later Class 21a, were two-cylinder compounds using the Prussian Railways' von Borries system and fitted with slide valves. The several sub-classes which followed, from 21b to 21e (1919), were equipped with superheaters, and compounding was dropped in favour of simple expansion and piston valves. Some were equipped for wood-burning, with spark-arrestor chimneys. The main function of the Class 21s, eventually 45 in number, was handling traffic on the longer branch lines, for which these lightweight locomotives, with a maximum axle load around the 10.16-tonne (10-ton mark), were well-suited.

BOILER PRESSURE: 12kg/cm² (171psi)
CYLINDERS: 432x610mm (17x24in)
DRIVING WHEELS: 1445mm (57in)
GRATE AREA: 1.8m² (19.4sq ft)
HEATING SURFACE: 78.1m² (841sq ft)
TRACTIVE EFFORT: 8020kg (17.680lb)
TOTAL WEIGHT: 58.9t (119,272lb)

CLASS 12B 4-6-0 BUENOS AIRES & GREAT SOUTHERN RAILWAY (BAGS)

In many parts of Argentina, it was difficult to find pure water for steam locomotive boilers, and so compounding, with its saving of water supply as well as of fuel, seemed a good thing to Argentinian railways in the pre-superheating years; later its mechanical complexity became something of a bugbear. Vulcan Foundry of Lancashire built this class of eight two-cylinder compounds as an express type, with a typically British appearance despite the larger dimensions possible on the 1676mm (5ft 6in) gauge, with low running plate and wheel splashers. Originally coal-fired, all were later converted to oil burning and superheaters were fitted from 1924. The maintenance difficulties of compound engines accelerated their withdrawal in 1937, though by then they already had 30 years of service behind them.

BOILER PRESSURE: 15kg/cm² (220psi)
CYLINDERS: hp 355x660mm (14x26in); lp 698x660mm (23x26in)
DRIVING WHEELS: 1827mm (72in)
GRATE AREA: 2.6m² (28sq ft)
HEATING SURFACE: 156.9m² (1690sq ft)
TRACTIVE EFFORT: N/A
TOTAL WEIGHT: 116.8t (257,600lb)

A work-worn but still active 12B has its motion inspected before another turn of service.

CLASS P8 4-6-0 ROYAL PRUSSIAN UNION RAILWAYS (KPEV)

What the Prussian G8 was to the *Güterzug* (goods train), the P8 was to the passenger train ('P' for *Passagierzug*). This was one of the most numerous and successful locomotive classes ever built: a mixed-traffic engine, with wide route availability, it ran every kind of service from main-line expresses to local goods trains. Its basic criteria of performance were to haul 700 tonnes (689 tons) on level track at 80km/h (50mph) and 300 tonnes (295 tons) up a 1 in 100 grade at 50km/h (31mph). Often it exceeded these requirements, but that was not the point. It broke no speed or haulage records, but it was that favourite type of the railway manager or accountant, a 'general user' or 'pool' engine that needed no specialist driver, used standard parts, and could undertake almost any task.

Thoroughly modern for its time, the G8 had the Schmidt superheater, by far the most effective device of its kind; and Walschaerts valve gear fitted externally, with piston valves set above the two simple-expansion outside cylinders. The maximum axle-load was 17.2 tonnes (16.9 tons) – relatively heavy, but these engines were not intended for minor branches. The boiler was straight-topped, with a dome and sandbox, and a round-topped

firebox with a long, narrow grate. Its mountings would vary later, with some engines receiving a second dome to house the top feed from a Knorr feed water pump and heater. The tender, on two four-wheel interior-sprung bogies, had a capacity of 4700 gals (5700 US gals), and 5 tonnes (4.92 tons) of coal. Schwartzkopff in Berlin built the first P8s, but almost every German builder was involved before long. Up to 1921 (when the KPEV was absorbed into the Deutsche Reichsbahn Gesellschaft), the total number built was 3370. The DRG built a further 101. Other railways in Germany and elsewhere bought it. Latvia, Lithuania, Romania and Turkey operated P8s, and the Polish State Railways bought 100, with larger grates. The grand total was little short of 4000. Many ended up in France, Belgium and some Eastern European countries as a result of war reparations both in 1918 and again in 1945.

During the lifetime of the class, many small adaptations but few significant changes were made. New boilers generally increased the heating surface available. The DRG fitted them with smoke deflectors, initially large ones fitted to the running plate, later replaced by smaller ones fitted to the smoke box sides. The stove-pipe style chimneys, relatively tall as allowed by the Prussian loading gauge, could be reduced in height when working on lines with lower clearance by removal of the top section. In the 1950s, some on the East German DR were fitted with Giesl ejector chimneys. As with other numerous classes, various engines were equipped with experimental valve gears in the 1920s and 30s. But essentially the

P8 remained as it had been first designed.

After World War II, the surviving usable P8s were divided, with the rest of the DRG assets, between the *Deutsche Bundesbahn* (DB) in the Federal Republic, and the *Deutsche*

Reichsbahn (DR) in the Democratic Republic, of Germany. By January 1975, the last to work in Germany (on the DB) was withdrawn, but P8s remained in service in other countries. At least eight have been preserved.

BOILER PRESSURE: 12kg/cm² (170.6psi)
CYLINDERS: 575x630mm (22.6x24.8in)
DRIVING WHEELS: 1750mm (68.9in)
GRATE AREA: 2.6m² (27.8sq ft)
HEATING SURFACE: 143.3m² (1542sq ft)
SUPERHEATER: 58.9m² (634sq ft)
TRACTIVE EFFORT: 12,140kg (26,769lb)
TOTAL WEIGHT: 78.5t (172,500lb)

A P8 with tall chimney and Witte-type smoke deflectors makes a brisk start with a passenger train.

CARDEAN 4-6-0 CALEDONIAN RAILWAY (CR)

This small class of five engines reached the limit to which J.F. McIntosh could take his 'big boiler' policy. Built at the CR's St Rollox works, to haul the Anglo-Scottish expresses over the Caledonian's main line, including the 314m (1032ft) Beattock

BOILER PRESSURE: 14kg/cm² (200psi)
CYLINDERS: 527x660mm (21x26in)
DRIVING WHEELS: 1981mm (78in)
GRATE AREA: 2.4m² (26sq ft)
HEATING SURFACE: 223m² (2400sq ft)
TRACTIVE EFFORT: 10,282kg (22,672lb)
TOTAL WEIGHT: 133.5t (294,000lb)

Cardean had a massive boiler by British standards, but otherwise was an old-fashioned design.

Summit between Carlisle and Glasgow, it was an expanded 'Dunalastair' with two simple-expansion inside cylinders and six coupled wheels. Compared to what was being built at that time

at Swindon, and also in its native Glasgow (though only for export), it was a distinctly old-fashioned machine. But No. 903 *Cardean* in particular had enormous prestige with the travelling public, as the

regular engine of the 'Corridor', the 2pm Glasgow Central–Euston express. Its big eight-wheel tender, holding 5000 gals (6000 US gals) enabled it to run over 161km (100 miles) non-stop

comfortably, without needing a re-fill. All were given superheaters in 1911–12. One of the class, No. 907, was wrecked in Britain's worst railway disaster, at Quintinshill on 22 May 1915.

CLASS 835 0-6-0T STATE RAILWAYS (FS)

ITALY 1906

A class of outside-cylinder side-tank engines built in 1903 by the Ernesto Breda works in Milan for the Mediterranean Railway formed the prototype for the FS' larger-cylindered 835s. This was as close as Italy came to a standard small shunting tank, the class

eventually numbering 370. Like similar engines elsewhere, they were apparently known as 'coffee pots'. In an unusual transformation, when the boilers of some eventually wore out, the locomotives were actually rebuilt with electric motors, with the

same frames and wheels as DC electric shunters of Group E321.

No. 835.106, built in 1910, has been preserved.

BOILER PRESSURE: 12kg/cm² (170psi)	**HEATING SURFACE:** 78m² (840sq ft)
CYLINDERS: 410x580mm (16x22.6in)	**TRACTIVE EFFORT:** 7434kg (16,390lb)
DRIVING WHEELS: 1310mm (51in)	**TOTAL WEIGHT:** 45t (99,225lb)
GRATE AREA: 1.4m² (15 sq ft)	

Under the electric catenary but still steamworthy, a Class 835 shunts stock in an FS freight yard.

'GAS ELECTRIC' MOTOR CARS VARIOUS RAILROADS

USA 1906

Use of the gasoline engine in trucks and buses led to its employment in these earliest internal-combustion railcars. In 1906, General Electric built a self-motored 'gas-electric' passenger and baggage car for the Delaware

& Hudson Railroad (D&H). Numbered as D&H 2000, it had an arched roof, rounded ends, a centre drop-step entrance door on each side, and seats for 91 passengers. Its power came from a 147kW (200hp) gasoline engine,

driving a generator that fed a 600V direct current to two traction motors, both mounted on the forward truck under the engine compartment. It was not the first such vehicle in the United States, but it was a refinement on earlier

versions. From around this year, American railroads began to employ them on light branch lines and secondary passenger services where steam-powered trains were not cost effective. As in Britain and other countries, branch-line traffic was being won away by road transport. Known to the travelling public as 'Doodlebugs', they were built to different plans by dozens of different manufacturers, though most followed the convention of end driving cabs. Around 700 were in action by the 1920s. Many were

unreliable, and more than a few caught fire, but both General Electric and (in the 1920s) Electro-Motive gained valuable experience in the production of these before moving on to bigger things. Some gas-electrics were powerful enough to pull a trailer or a few freight

cars, and ran all their branch's services with mixed trains. By the 1960s, the era of the gas-electric had passed. Some were converted to Sperry rail-defect detection cars, others became depot vehicles; numerous examples still operate on 'heritage' lines.

TYPE: gas-electric
POWER AND OUTPUT: various
TRACTIVE EFFORT: various
MAX. OPERATING SPEED: various
WEIGHT: various
OVERALL LENGTH: various
GAUGE: various

A gas-electric unit of the East Broad in a typical rural branch setting.

CLASS P1 4-4-2 DANISH STATE RAILWAYS (DSB)

DENMARK 1907

The DSB, though responsible for its own designs, generally turned to the large German manufacturers for locomotive construction, and 19 of this 'Atlantic', its first large express engine, designed by Otto Busse, were built in Hannover by Hanomag. It was a four-cylinder compound, the inner high-pressure cylinders driving the leading axle, and the outer low-pressure cylinders driving the second axle. Two sets of

inside Walschaerts gear, operating piston valves, were shared by the hp and lp cylinders on each side. With a high theoretical tractive effort, the P1s proved to be very effective on the road, and a further 14 with superheaters were built in Berlin by Schwartzkopff in 1910 and classed as P2. Their most regular services were on 'fast' trains – Denmark's speed limit was then 100km/h (62.5mph) – between Copenhagen and Korsør, Nyborg

and Ålborg, and Fredricia and Esbjerg. Some of the class were 'stretched' into 'Pacifics' in the late 1940s. As Atlantics, they were the last to be seen on public service in Europe, the last one surviving until

1963. Two 4-4-2s are preserved. A typical feature of DSB locomotives was the red-white-red national colour bands on the chimneys, which had an outer casing to prevent the colours from scorching.

BOILER PRESSURE: 15kg/cm² (214psi)
CYLINDERS: hp 360x640mm (14x25in); lp 620x640mm (24x25in)
DRIVING WHEELS: 1984mm (77.4in)

GRATE AREA: 3.2m² (34.5sq ft)
HEATING SURFACE: 192.5m² (2072sq ft)
TRACTIVE EFFORT: 18,140kg (40,000lb)
TOTAL WEIGHT: 119t (262,500lb)

CLASSES 4500 & 3500 4-6-2 PARIS–ORLEANS RAILWAY (PO)

FRANCE 1907

The first 'Pacific' design to run on a European railway, these locomotives were developed by the PO and the engineers of the Société Alsacienne at Belfort. They were large engines with relatively big driving wheels, intended for long inter-city runs through sparsely inhabited countryside. Four-cylinder compounds of de Glehn-du Bousquet type, the Class 4500 numbered 70 by 1908, and a further 30, with superheaters, were delivered in 1910. Thirty of the first set were built in the United States by Alco at Schenectady, NY, the rest in Belfort. A further 90, with coupled wheels of 1948mm (76.75in), designated class 3500, were built between 1909 and 1918. Piston valves, still

relatively new, worked the high-pressure cylinders, while more traditional slide valves worked the low-pressure ones. Their performance was considered perfectly satisfactory, but by 1926 the engines were showing signs of age, and the decision was taken to rebuild a Class 3500 locomotive on lines set out by André Chapelon, a brilliant and then unknown young PO engineer. A battery of changes – including the

provision of feed-water heating, a thermic syphon in the firebox, the enlarging and redesign of the superheater, improvement of the steam flow, refined valve control with poppet valves, greater draught from a new kind of double chimney, and smoke deflectors – combined to transform the engines inside and out.

Performance improved so dramatically as to startle the engineering world, and a new era

in the internal design of steam locomotives was inaugurated. Rebuilding of the other 3500s began immediately; eventually 102 were either rebuilt or built new. Specificatons are for the original non-superheated 4500 class.

BOILER PRESSURE: 16kg/cm² (232psi)
CYLINDERS: hp 390x650mm (15.3x25.6in); lp 640x650mm (25.2x25.6in)
DRIVING WHEELS: 1846mm (72.75in)
GRATE AREA: 4.33m² (36sq ft)
HEATING SURFACE: 195m² (2100sq ft)
TRACTIVE EFFORT: not known
TOTAL WEIGHT: 99.6t (219,600lb)

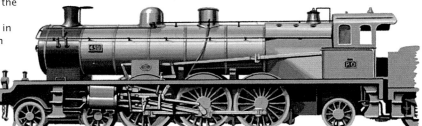

Class 4500 in its original form and paintwork as a Paris–Orleans express engine.

CLASS 640 2-6-0 STATE RAILWAYS (FS)

ITALY 1907

On Italy's railways, as in many other countries, the advent of superheating meant a sudden end of interest in compound expansion. The Class 600 of 1904, Italy's first 2-6-0, had been a compound, but in the Class 640 that followed it compounding was abandoned. No. 640.01 was Italy's first superheated locomotive. In a reversal of more conventional practice, the cylinders were inside, but operated by outside piston valves actuated by Walschaerts gear off the middle driving wheels. To assist with flexibility on tight curves, the leading axle was combined with the front coupled axle in a Helmholtz truck. The

2-6-0 became a popular type on the many long secondary lines in hilly country, hauling relatively lightweight trains, often of antique coaching stock; and Class 640 eventually comprised 173 engines.

The first 48 came from Schwartzkopff, Berlin, the rest from Breda and other Italian builders. No. 640.106 has been preserved.

The FS's first superheated locomotive class. The arrangement of cylinders and valve gear gave the Class 640 an unusual appearance below the footplate.

BOILER PRESSURE: 12kg/cm² (170psi)
CYLINDERS: 540x700mm (21x28in)
DRIVING WHEELS: 1850mm (73in)
GRATE AREA: 2.4m² (26sq ft)
HEATING SURFACE: 108.5m² (1168sq ft)
SUPERHEATER: 33.5m² (360sq ft)
TRACTIVE EFFORT: 10,830kg (23,890lb)
TOTAL WEIGHT: not known

0-10-0 CLASS 470 STATE RAILWAYS (FS)

ITALY 1907

The FS set out to standardize its steam locomotive stock into 12 basic types. For heavy freight trains, this Plancher-type four-cylinder compound was selected. Like the Class 500 cab-front 4-6-0 of 1900, it had high- and low-pressure cylinders on right and left sides respectively, one outside and one inside the frame. With only 143 engines in Class 470, the

effect of standardization in this area was not extensive. The first 12 were built by Maffei in Munich, the rest were from Italian shops. Their fuel arrangements were unusual. Four tonnes (3.6 tons) of coal were carried in a bunker built on the left-hand running plate and above the rear top of the boiler, while only water was carried in a short four-wheel tender. The

reason for this may have been to increase the weight at the rear end of the engine to balance the heavy compound cylinders, or because of short turntables, but in any case it was not a success, and 109 were rebuilt with conventional six-wheel tenders in the 1920s and 1930s. The last to be in service were withdrawn at Terni in 1970. No. 470.092 is preserved.

BOILER PRESSURE: 16kg/cm² (230psi)
CYLINDERS: hp 375x650mm (14.6x25.6in); lp 610x650mm (23.8x25.6in)
DRIVING WHEELS: 1360mm (53.5in)
GRATE AREA: 3.5m² (38sq ft)
HEATING SURFACE: not known
TRACTIVE EFFORT: not known
TOTAL WEIGHT: 67t (147,735lb)

0-6-0T CHUGOKU RAILWAY

Japanese industry was developing at a very rapid pace, and this small locomotive was typical of many that were ordered for work on industrial and colliery lines. Built by Kerr Stuart of Stoke on Trent, England, for the 1065mm (3ft 6in) gauge, it was shipped to Japan in 1907. A side-tank engine

with two outside cylinders, it was one of the manufacturer's standard catalogue types for export and for home industrial lines. Very similar engines also ran on 1m (3ft 3in) gauge lines in Argentina and Colombia, and standard-gauge colliery lines in England and Wales. A powerful

engine for its size, the 0-6-0T could move 606 tonnes (600 tons) on level track, though normally it could handle only a few wagons at a time. This engine was sold in 1952 to Kawasaki Iron & Steel Co. and worked there until it was finally condemned for scrap in 1966.

BOILER PRESSURE: 11.2kg/cm² (160psi)
CYLINDERS: 368x508mm (14.5x20in)
DRIVING WHEELS: 1067mm (42in)
GRATE AREA: 1.67m² (18sq ft)
HEATING SURFACE: 59.2m² (638sq ft)
TRACTIVE EFFORT: 6170kg (13,600lb)
TOTAL WEIGHT: not known

CLASS A 4-4-2 SWEDISH STATE RAILWAYS (SJ)

An inside-cylindered 'Atlantic' was relatively unusual, and the Class A, with its high-level foot-plate from buffer-beam to cab, looked as if it had lost its cylinders in some accident. The class was formed of 25 engines, built by the Swedish firms Motala and Nydquist & Holm for fast passenger services

BOILER PRESSURE: 12kg/cm² (170psi)
CYLINDERS: 500x600mm (19.5x23.4in)
DRIVING WHEELS: 1880mm (73in)
GRATE AREA: 2.6m² (28sq ft)
HEATING SURFACE: 133m² (1439sq ft)
TRACTIVE EFFORT: 7980kg (17,600lb)
TOTAL WEIGHT: not known

in the southern part of Sweden, in the hinterlands of Gothenburg and Malmø. Among its other distinctive features were an elongated dome (which also held the sandbox) and a wedge-fronted cab. The leading bogie had an outside frame and bearings, the pony wheel had inside bearings. The firebox was quite narrow, spurning one of the main advantages offered by the Atlantic format. In

1926–27, five were sold to the *Ostkustbanen* (East Coast Railway) and converted into 4-6-0s, and

three were also converted to 4-6-0 by the SJ. The rebuilding was largely prompted by the Class As' tendency to slip on starting. All the Atlantics were withdrawn by 1937, but one has been preserved.

These were the first 'Atlantics' built with superheaters, but though their steaming capacity was good, they were very prone to wheel slipping.

MALLET COMPOUND 2-6-6-0 EASTERN RAILWAY (EST)

The big Mallet articulated locomotive had acquired American nationality, and in a piquant form of re-import the *Est* ordered the two engines forming this class from Alco in Schenectady, NY, holders of the US building licence. They followed Anatole Mallet's standard form: the front truck, supported by the

carrying axle and first set of coupled wheels, was articulated. The second set of coupled wheels was attached to the main frame. Again as Mallet intended, they were compounds, with two outside high-pressure cylinders driving the rear axle of the rear set of coupled wheels, and the two low-pressure cylinders driving the

corresponding axle of the front set. At the time of delivery, these were the biggest engines in Europe, intended for use in short-distance freight haulage on steep grades in the industrialized but hilly country around Nancy and Mulhouse. Most of their time was spent on banking heavy freights up the grades.

BOILER PRESSURE: 15kg/cm² (213psi)
CYLINDERS: hp 444x660mm (17.5x26in); lp 802.3x660mm (28x26in)
DRIVING WHEELS: 1274mm (50.2in)
GRATE AREA: 3.8m² (40.9sq ft)
HEATING SURFACE: 124.9m² (1345sq ft)
TRACTIVE EFFORT: not known
TOTAL WEIGHT: 103t (227,165lb) (engine only)

CLASS S 3/6 4-6-2 ROYAL BAVARIAN STATE RAILWAYS (KBSTB)

The S 3/6 'Pacific' is one of the classic European locomotives, closely associated with the name of Maffei. In the early 1900s, the chiefs of that firm, Anton Hammel and H. Leppla, had purchased and explored Vauclain and de Glehn compounds from the United States and Germany before developing their own family of compound locomotives. The first Pacific of this type was built in 1907 for the Baden State Railways. The S 3/6 for the Bavarian Railways followed in 1908, and 159 of these were built between then and 1931, all at Maffei's Hirschau works except for the final 18, built by Henschel at Kassel. In the Maffei compounding system, all four cylinders drove the second coupled axle, with the inside (high-pressure) cylinders operated by the outside valve gear

by means of rocker shafts. The big low-pressure cylinders, forged in a single block with the steam pipes, combined with the conical smoke box door and a tallish, well-shaped chimney to give the front end a distinctive and powerful appearance, though the overall effect was of elegance rather than muscle. Ten were built for the Palatinate Railway in 1914. In 1912–13, 18 were built with driving wheels of a diamter of 2m (79in), and there were minor variations among the class in the fitting and placing of ancillary equipment like brake pumps (they had two, from Westinghouse and Knorr; also Knorr feedwater heaters). In the 1920s, the *Deutsche Reichsbahn Gesellschaft* fitted smoke deflectors to the class.

The Bavarian Railways had chosen compounding for its fuel economy, and the Class S 3/6 was exemplary in this respect, a testimony to the care with which the Maffei compounding system had been worked out. They worked expresses from Munich and other Bavarian cities to Berlin and Köln (Cologne) and on to the Dutch frontier. With heavy trains weighing up to 711 tonnes (700 tons) they could keep up a steady 112km/h (70mph) on level track and mount grades of 1 in 128 at 70km/h (43.5mph). Post-1945, 154 of the class were still available. Thirty were rebuilt with larger, all-welded boilers between 1952 and 1956. Always celebrated for their ability to maintain high speeds with heavy trains, they ran on prime services to the end, their final duties being

express trains on the Ulm–Friedrichshafen and Munich–Lindau lines, most famously the *Rheingold Express* between Hook of Holland and Basel. The last to run were withdrawn from Lindau in 1966. Thirteen have been preserved. Maffei also built Pacifics of similar type for Romania and the Madrid, Zaragoza and Alicante Railway in Spain.

BOILER PRESSURE: 16kg/cm² (228 psi)
CYLINDERS: hp 425x610mm (16.7x24in); lp 650x670mm (25.6x26.4in)
DRIVING WHEELS: 1870mm (73.6in)
GRATE AREA: 4.5m² (48.8sq ft)
HEATING SURFACE: 197.4m² (2125sq ft)
SUPERHEATER: 74.2m² (798sq ft)
TRACTIVE EFFORT: not known
TOTAL WEIGHT: 149t (328,500lb)

THE GREAT BEAR 4-6-2 GREAT WESTERN RAILWAY (GWR)

GREAT BRITAIN 1908

Britain's first 'Pacific' type, and the only one ever built by the GWR, was in effect a stretched version of G.J. Churchward's four-cylinder 4-6-0 'Star' class, with simple expansion, a long domeless boiler and a straight-sided Belpaire firebox. Its prestige was limited by its being a one-off engine, whose performance was not such an improvement over the GWR 4-6-0s as to justify the building of further examples, and it was too long (10.5m/34ft 6in) and heavy to operate on any route other than the London–Bristol main-line. In 1924, just as the British LNER company was developing its new Pacifics, the GWR rebuilt theirs as a 'Castle' Class 4-6-0.

BOILER PRESSURE: 15.75kg/cm² (225psi)
CYLINDERS: 381x660mm (15x26in)
DRIVING WHEELS: 2043mm (80.5in)
GRATE AREA: 3.9m² (41.8sq ft)
HEATING SURFACE: 263m² (2831.5sq ft)
SUPERHEATER: 50.5m² (545sq ft)
TRACTIVE EFFORT: 13,346kg (29,430lb)
TOTAL WEIGHT: 99t (218,400lb)
(engine only)

Four-cylinder 'Pacific' *The Great Bear* with a Bristol express at Paddington Station, London. For 15 years, this was Britain's sole 4-6-2 locomotive.

CLASS AP 4-4-2 EAST INDIAN RAILWAY (EIR)

INDIA 1908

AP was said to stand for 'Atlantic Passenger' and, like Atlantics elsewhere, was used as an express passenger engine. Though the BESA provided two Atlantic standard designs, of 15.2- and 17.2-tonne (15- and 17-ton) maximum axle loads respectively, they were fairly rare in India: in 1920 only 117 were at work, compared to 847 4-4-0s and 812 4-6-0s on the 1675mm (5ft 6in) gauge. The EIR, which proclaimed itself as 'India's premier line', linking Calcutta to Delhi, had the largest stock, at 45, though the Bengal–Nagpur had been first with the type, in 1907. The APs, to BESA design, with outside cylinders, Belpaire fireboxes, and raised front caps on the chimneys, were built in 1908–9 by the North British Locomotive Co. and the Vulcan Foundry. Most of the Indian Atlantics survived to the 1950s.

BOILER PRESSURE: 12.6kg/cm² (180psi)
CYLINDERS: 482x634.5mm (19x25in)
DRIVING WHEELS: 1218mm (48in)
GRATE AREA: 4.4m² (47.75sq ft)
HEATING SURFACE: 271.6m² (2924sq ft)
TRACTIVE EFFORT: 26,096kg (57,534lb)
TOTAL WEIGHT: 140.2t (309,120lb)

CLASS E550 E STATE RAILWAYS (FS)

ITALY 1908

In 1897, a government-financed initiative was launched for the *Societa Italiana delle Strade Ferrate Meridionali Esercente la Rete Adriatica*, part of the FS from 1907, to electrify their Valtellina line. Ganz of Hungary built the three-phase double-contact wire system from Lecco to Sondrio, and the government confirmed that as the standard national system in 1906. American Westinghouse set up a locomotive factory near Genoa and the engineer Kalmán Kandó from Ganz was installed there. The class E550 *'cinquanta'* 0-10-0 or 'E' wheel arrangement, was designed to work on the Giovi Incline. From 1908 to 1921, 186 were built, in four series, with cascade parallel control and two body-mounted motors driving through jackshaft and yoke. Despite their slow continuous speed of 50km/h (31.3mph), E550s survived almost to the end of the three-phase era. E550.025 was presented to the United States (now preserved in St Louis) while E550.030 survives in Milan.

TYPE: 0-10-0 three-phase electric freight
POWER: 1500kW (2011hp) from two body-mounted motors
SUPPLY: 3300V 16.2/3Hz AC from two-wire three-phase
TRACTIVE EFFORT: 139kN (30,800lbf) at 43.2km/h (27mph)
MAX. OPERATING SPEED: 50km/h (31.3mph)
WEIGHT: 60.1–64.0t (132,521–141,120lb)
MAX. AXLE LOAD: 15t (33,075lb)
OVERALL LENGTH: 9520mm (31ft)
GAUGE: 1435mm (4ft 8.5in)

0-4-4-0 MALLET TYPE MADAGASCAR RAILWAYS (CFM)

MADAGASCAR 1908

The 1m (3ft 3in) gauge Madagascar Railways had no less than 56 articulated compound Mallets, and they dominated all services on the island lines until the arrival of diesel *autorails*. Most were built in France by the Société Alsacienne of Mulhouse, whose engineering chief, Alfred George de Glehn, had a long-standing working relationship with Anatole Mallet, but Baldwin also supplied six in 1916. Around 18 were later superheated. They were tank-tender engines, with side tanks alongside the boiler but also a small four-wheel tender fitted with wood rails, as all were wood-burners equipped with tall spark-arrestor chimneys. A few remained active on shunting duties in the late 1950s.

BOILER PRESSURE: 12kg/cm² (171psi)
CYLINDERS: hp 280x500mm (11x19.7in); lp 425x500mm (16.7x19.7in)
DRIVING WHEELS: 1000mm (39.4in)
GRATE AREA: 1.2m² (12.9sq ft)
HEATING SURFACE: 71.4m² (768.7sq ft)
TRACTIVE EFFORT: N/A
TOTAL WEIGHT: 35.4t (78,080lb)

CLASS K 0-4-0+0-4-0 BEYER-GARRATT TASMANIAN RAILWAYS (TR)

Small precursor of many mighty locomotives, the restored original Garratt on display at the Festiniog Railway's Minffordd Yard, in May 1994.

By the early twentieth century the overall loading gauge, particularly of narrow-gauge railways, was a severe constraint on engineers who wanted to put bigger boilers on locomotive frames to cope with greater loads. Herbert W. Garratt, an English engineer who worked on colonial railways, was responsible for an imaginative solution. It consisted of two engines, each a complete mechanical unit, sharing a common boiler. The boiler, mounted on a low girder frame, was supported by pivoting links to the engine units. Ball-joint connections were used for the steam pipes. Such a boiler could be very large, sufficient to power both engines, and the entire machine, with its double joints, could negotiate tight curves. It also lent itself very well to narrow-gauge use.

Garratt eventually sold his patent to the Beyer Peacock locomotive works, of Manchester, and the type became known as the Beyer-Garratt. This pioneer, first of two built for the 610mm (2ft) gauge, was a pocket giant. At the purchasers' request, it was a compound, with the high-pressure cylinders driving the rear bogie and the low-pressure ones forward. The rear cylinders, under the cab, gave the enginemen very hot feet, and all subsequent Garratts had cylinders placed at the outer ends of the power bogies.

From 1910 to 1930, the K class worked nickel ore trains, but with the end of that traffic they were put into store. Beyer Peacock bought back K-1, with numerous parts cannibalized from K-2, and restored it. With the closure of Beyer Peacock in 1965, it was bought by the Ffestiniog Railway in Wales, where it has been restored for use.

BOILER PRESSURE: 13.6cm² (195psi)
CYLINDERS: hp 282x410mm (11x16in); lp 436x410mm (17x16in)
DRIVING WHEELS: 799mm (31.5ins)
GRATE AREA: 1.4m² (14.8sq ft)
HEATING SURFACE: 52.7m² (568sq ft)
TRACTIVE EFFORT: 6521kg (14,380lb)
TOTAL WEIGHT: 34t (75,040lb)

CLASS 429 2-6-2 IMPERIAL & ROYAL STATE RAILWAYS (KKSTB)

This class ran under several designations in different countries of the former Austrian empire after 1918. It began as a superheated two-cylinder compound, with slide valves to operate the low-pressure cylinder and piston valves for the high-pressure, and 57 were built in this form. From 1911, however, it was built only as a simple-expansion engine, denoted as Class 429.9, eventually numbering 197; many compounds were rebuilt as simples. In Poland, it became Class Ol.12; in Czechoslovakia, Class 354.7; and in Yugoslavia, Class 106. Modifications were made on the various national systems, and double domes connected by a steam-drier pipe were fitted on the Czechoslovak engines. Withdrawals began during the 1950s with the arrival of more up-to-date 2-6-2 and 4-6-0 locomotives, but it was into the 1970s before the last of the class disappeared; and one of the Czech engines has been preserved. Specifications are for the original compound form.

BOILER PRESSURE: 14kg/cm² (199psi)
CYLINDERS: hp 450x720mm (17.7x28.4in); lp 690x720mm (27x28.4in)
DRIVING WHEELS: 1574mm (62in)
GRATE AREA: 3m² (32.3sq ft)
HEATING SURFACE: 131.7m² (1418sq ft)
SUPERHEATER: 23.8m² (256sq ft)
TRACTIVE EFFORT: not known
TOTAL WEIGHT: 61.2t (engine only)

As No. 35.233 of the Austrian Federal Railways, a superheated Class 429 makes up its train at the Austrian junction station of Selzthal.

CLASS 324 2-6-2 HUNGARIAN STATE RAILWAYS (MÁV)

Budapest Locomotive Works built around 900 of this mixed-traffic class over a 34-year period, up to 1943. Some were also built for the Imperial & Royal State Railways as Austrian Class 329. As with the Austrian Class 429, the first examples were non-superheated two-cylinder compounds and the final products were superheated two-cylinder simples. Substantial rebuilding of older locomotives took place in addition to new construction. Many were fitted with Brotan boilers with water-tube firebox (see 1918), and Pecz-Rejto water-purifiers contributed to the maze of external pipework – Hungarian designers were never shy about add-ons. There was a fashion for conical smoke-box doors at the time, ostensibly to increase the air capacity of the smoke-box, and the Class 324 had these. The locomotives did excellent service and the last to run were withdrawn in 1970. Specifications are for superheated simple engines with the original boiler.

BOILER PRESSURE: 12kg/cm² (171psi)
CYLINDERS: 510x650mm (20x25.6in)
DRIVING WHEELS: 1440mm (56.75in)
GRATE AREA: 3.1m² (33.4sq ft)
HEATING SURFACE: 159.2m² (1714sq ft)
SUPERHEATER: 37.9m² (408sq ft)
TRACTIVE EFFORT: 11,895kg (26,228lb)
TOTAL WEIGHT: 60.1t (132,520lb)

CLASS B 4-6-0 SWEDISH STATE RAILWAYS (SJ) SWEDEN 1909

The trend-setting Prussian P8 was the model for this, Sweden's largest class of passenger steam locomotives, which by the end of its production run numbered 98. The main frames were of bar construction, but the bogie had plate frames outside the wheels. Superheated, working on simple expansion, the two cylinders were outside and worked by Walschaerts valve gear actuated by piston valves. Swedish features included the conical smoke box door, typical of Swedish new passenger engines at the time, and the vee-fronted cab, which had doors opening on to the running plate. A spark arrestor, essential on all Swedish engines, was fitted inside the chimney. Engines of this class were built up to 1944, and several have been preserved.

BOILER PRESSURE: 12kg/cm² (170psi)
CYLINDERS: 590x620mm (23x24in)
DRIVING WHEELS: 1750mm (68.25in)
GRATE AREA: 2.6m² (28sq ft)
HEATING SURFACE: 143.3m² (1542sq ft)
SUPERHEATER: 58.9m² (634sq ft)
TRACTIVE EFFORT: 12,190kg (26,880lb)
TOTAL WEIGHT: 8t (178,605lb) (engine)

In the 1920s, a 'B' class 4-6-0 pulls a passenger train out of Ockelbo station and over a lattice girder bridge. The first vehicle is a clerestoried baggage car.

CLASS 1500 4-6-2 BUENOS AIRES & PACIFIC RAILWAY (BAP) ARGENTINA 1910

By 1910, all new main-line locomotives were being built with superheaters, whether on the Schmidt system or one of the many variants now available. A typical example is this 'Pacific', running on the 1675mm (5ft 6in) gauge. Built by the North British Locomotive Co., Glasgow, it was a two-cylinder simple, with a Belpaire boiler and firebox, Walschaerts valve gear and a superheater. The BAP ran through flat cattle-rearing *pampas* country, and an unusual feature of these locomotives was front buffers that tilted back when out of use to minimize damage to animals (the cow-catcher was made of wood). Many Argentinian steam locomotives were converted to oil-burning, but this class was oil-fired from the beginning, from a tank fitted inside the bogie tender.

BOILER PRESSURE: 10.5kg/cm² (150psi)
CYLINDERS: 533x660mm (21x26in)
DRIVING WHEELS: 1701mm (67in)
GRATE AREA: 2.5m² (27sq ft)

HEATING SURFACE: 148m² (1597sq ft)
SUPERHEATER: 40.5m² (435sq ft)
TRACTIVE EFFORT: 11,995kg (26,450lb)
TOTAL WEIGHT: 53.5t (361,000lb)

CLASS 1099 C-C MARIAZELLERBAHN AUSTRIA 1910

Running from St Pölten to Mariazell, the severe gradients and 17 tunnels of this narrow-gauge 91km (56.9-mile) line, constructed between 1898 and 1907, made it an early candidate for electrification. It is still operated by the 'original' locomotives, though heavily rebuilt from 1959 with new bodywork. Eighteen were built by Krauss with Siemens electrical equipment between 1909 and 1912, and they are likely to see a century of regular traffic. Each of the two 1099 bogies has one traction motor each, driving three axles by jackshaft and coupling rod transmission. Despite the introduction of Class 4090 railcars in 1994, the 1099s continue in regular traffic with no signs of imminent replacement. Only one has so far been withdrawn (following an accident in 1991).

TYPE: C-C light branch narrow-gauge
POWER: 420kW (563hp)
SUPPLY: 6600V AC 25Hz
TRACTIVE EFFORT: 45kN (10125lbf) at 29km/h (18.1mph)
MAX. OPERATING SPEED: 50km/h (31.3mph)
WEIGHT: 50t (110,250lb)
MAX. AXLE LOAD: 8.3t (18,302lb)
OVERALL WEIGHT: 11,020mm (36ft 2in)
GAUGE: 760mm (2ft 6in)

The 'new' bodywork dating back to the 1950s belies the real age of the veteran Class 1099.

TYPE 10 4-6-2 BELGIAN STATE RAILWAYS (EB)

BELGIUM 1910

The massive effect of the Type 10 can be appreciated in this front-end shot of No. 10.018.

The Type 10 shared a boiler with the Type 36 2-10-0 freight locomotive, built at the same time. As the 'Pacific' type's frame was longer, its smokebox was, unusually, set to the rear of the cylinders, with a long extension of the frame stretching in front. Underneath this were the inside cylinders in J.B. Flamme's four cylinder simple-expansion design. In charge of the EB's motive power since 1904, Flamme had looked long and hard at compounding, but in the end he decided against it for his express engines. The inside cylinders drove the front coupled wheels; hence their far-forward placement. A round-topped firebox was used, rather than the squared-off design of Flamme's predecessor Belpaire. Twenty-eight of Type 10 were built between 1910 and 1912, and proved their worth on heavy boat trains from Ostend into central Europe, and to the French border. By 1914, there were 58 of them, though nine were lost in the course of World War I. After 1918, double chimneys, larger superheaters, ACFI-type feed water heaters, and smoke deflectors were fitted. German bogie tenders acquired as war reparations replaced the original small six-wheel tenders. Changes continued through the late 1930s, with a Kylchap double-blast chimney (still with the bright brass ring typical of Belgian locomotives since Belpaire's day) and further enlargement of the superheater. The modernized Type 10s hauled expresses on the Luxembourg line until electrification in 1956; they were finally withdrawn in 1959.

BOILER PRESSURE: 14kg/cm² (199psi)
CYLINDERS: 500x660mm (19.7x26in)
DRIVING WHEELS: 1980mm (78in)
GRATE AREA: 4.6m² (49.2sq ft)
HEATING SURFACE: 232m² (2500sq ft)
SUPERHEATER: 76m² (816sq ft)
TRACTIVE EFFORT: 19,800kg (43,800lb)
TOTAL WEIGHT: 160t (352,640lb)

TYPE 36 2-10-0 BELGIAN STATE RAILWAYS (EB)

BELGIUM 1910

On its appearance, this was hailed as 'the biggest, strongest locomotive in Europe'. Designed by J.B. Flamme, it was the freight-hauling brother of his Type 10 'Pacific', to which it had a more than superficial resemblance. It too was a four-cylinder simple, the inside cylinders driving the second coupled axle; the outside cylinders driving the third. It had the same boiler, which here was a better fit. The front carrying axle was linked to the leading coupled axle by a Bissell truck. The initial order was for 136, of which all but two were delivered by mid-1914.

In World War I, the Type 36's tractive power was a great asset to the German-Austrian alliance. Eighty were transferred to the Eastern Front in Galicia in north-east Austria. Some were captured by the Russians, who promptly designated them as Class F (for *Flamme*), converted them to the 1524mm (5ft) gauge, and used them on the Catherine Railway.

With some trouble, the Belgians eventually were paid for their engines by the post-war Soviet government. But 58 of the class had in one way or another disappeared, and in 1922–23 17 new members were delivered. From 1925, the whole class were fitted with double chimneys designed by M. Legein, and their superheating surface was increased to 75.8m² (816sq ft). Despite this, the Type 36s lacked the staying power of the Type 10s.

All were withdrawn by 1940. Though some were kept in store for a few more years, they were all scrapped by 1950.

BOILER PRESSURE: 14kg/cm² (199psi)
CYLINDERS: 500x660mm (19.7x26in)
DRIVING WHEELS: 1980mm (78in)
GRATE AREA: 4.6m² (49.2sq ft)
HEATING SURFACE: 232m² (2500sq ft)
SUPERHEATER: 76m² (816sq ft)
TRACTIVE EFFORT: 19,800kg (43,800lb)
TOTAL WEIGHT: 160t (352,640lb)

CLASS 375 2-6-2T HUNGARIAN STATE RAILWAYS (MÁV)

HUNGARY 1910

Built for compound working, and not superheated, this class was intended for hauling light trains over country branches, with a maximum axle-load kept down to 9.1 tonnes (9 tons). With 305 built, it was one of the more numerous MÁV classes. Despite their lack of superheat, they had piston valves and did useful work for many decades. When Croatia was ceded to Yugoslavia in 1945, 65 were transferred to the Yugoslav State Railways system, and a further 40 were built as superheated simple-expansion engines. All were designated as Class 51; some worked into the 1970s.

BOILER PRESSURE: 14kg/cm² (199psi)
CYLINDERS: hp 410x600mm (16x23.5in); lp 590x600mm (23.25x23.5in)
DRIVING WHEELS: 1180mm (46.5in)
GRATE AREA: 1.85m² (19.9sq ft)
HEATING SURFACE: 81.7m² (879.6sq ft)
TRACTIVE EFFORT: N/A
TOTAL WEIGHT: 52.1t (114,880lb)

With vast amounts of steam blowing off from various pipes and valves, a Class 375 – by then Class 51 of the Yugoslav State Railways – takes on water at its depot.

CLASS 27 4-6-0 NORWEGIAN STATE RAILWAYS (NSB)   NORWAY 1910

The NSB's own works at Hamar built this class of 15 two-cylinder simple-expansion engines, fitted with superheaters and piston valves. The NSB had been operating 4-6-0s since 1900, the first ones (Class 18) supplied by Hartmann of Chemnitz, Germany, being a mix of compound and

simple mixed-traffic engines. German-built 4-6-0s – in this case, from Borsig of Berlin – also ran on the independent Norwegian Trunk

Railway (incorporated into the NSB in 1926). Class 27, with bigger driving wheels, was intended as a passenger locomotive. They were

built between 1910 and 1921, and in 1927 two Class 18b compound 4-6-0s were rebuilt as Class 27s.

BOILER PRESSURE: 12kg/cm² (171psi)
CYLINDERS: 450x600mm (17.7x23.6in)
DRIVING WHEELS: 1600mm (63in)

GRATE AREA: 1.5m² (16sq ft)
HEATING SURFACE: 76.4m² (822sq ft)
SUPERHEATER: 22.7m² (244sq ft)

TRACTIVE EFFORT: 7730kg (17,060lb)
TOTAL WEIGHT: 72t (158,760lb)
(engine)

CLASS N1 2-6-0 CENTRAL RAILWAY OF URUGUAY (CUR)   URUGUAY 1910

This was a mixed-traffic type, for use on Uruguay's largest railway, with 1569km (975 miles) of standard-gauge track. The CUR was English-owned and English builders supplied most of its locomotives; the eight Class N1s came from Beyer Peacock in

Manchester. They had Belpaire fireboxes but no superheating, which suggests that price considerations outweighed those of efficiency, and they were used on cross-country services, both passenger and freight, and were claimed to be capable of hauling

15 wooden-bodied carriages, around 381 tonnes (375 tons), at 80km/h (50mph) on the level. From 1938, they were reboilered with superheaters, converted to oil-burning, and classed as N3. One is today preserved in working order.

BOILER PRESSURE: 12.6kg/cm² (180psi)
CYLINDERS: 457x609mm (18x24in)
DRIVING WHEELS: 1523mm (60in)
GRATE AREA: 1.8m² (20sq ft)
HEATING SURFACE: 101.5m² (1093sq ft)
TRACTIVE EFFORT: 8993kg (19,830lb)
TOTAL WEIGHT: not known

The preserved N-class of the CUR, No. 120 (formerly No. 119) gets up steam and clears its boiler tubes for a night run.

CLASS E6 4-4-2 PENNSYLVANIA RAILROAD (PRR)

In 1907, the PRR introduced all-steel coaches on its main-line trains. At 51.2-tonne (50.4-ton), these were 10.2 tonnes (10 tons) heavier than the old wood-bodied cars. The improvement was much-appreciated by the travelling public but put a heavy strain on the line's existing motive power. Its older 'Atlantic' classes, E2 and E3, were underpowered for trains weighing up to 508 tonnes (500 tons) and had to work double-headed. The PRR's chief mechanical engineer, Alfred Gibbs, conceived the E6 as the 'Super-

Atlantic', and it was planned with the company's usual close attention to detail. The prototype appeared in 1910, but production did not begin until 1914. Eighty-two were built, at the PRR Juniata works, the wide Belpaire firebox making the most of the space above the pony wheels. The prototype had no superheater, but superheaters were fitted to the others, with Walschaerts valve gear. Inside the chimney was the 'Goodfellow nozzle' devised by the Altoona test plant's foreman. These huge Atlantics had a long and

distinguished career in passenger service, at first on the old Philadelphia–Atlantic City racing ground, and as such trains as the *Broadway Limited*. Their hefty maximum axle-loading, at 29.5 tonnes (29 tons) helped to avoid the besetting problem of the Atlantic type: the propensity of the big driving wheels to slip on starting, or on a wet rail. A top speed of 165.7km/h (103mph) was claimed for an E6 hauling the 'Detroit Arrow' express. With the arrival of the K4 'Pacific', the E6s lost the heaviest expresses but

were still used on fast trains. The original engine was withdrawn in 1950 and the others followed by 1953. Until the Milwaukee 'Hiawathas' (see 1935), these were the world's biggest Atlantics.

BOILER PRESSURE: 14.4kg/cm² (205psi)
CYLINDERS: 558x660mm (22x26in)
DRIVING WHEELS: 2030mm (80in)
GRATE AREA: 5.8m² (62sq ft)
HEATING SURFACE: 266.3m² (2867sq ft)
TRACTIVE EFFORT: 14,186kg (31,275lb)
TOTAL WEIGHT: 105t (231,500lb)
(engine only)

DD1 2-BO-BO-2 PENNSYLVANIA RAILROAD (PRR)

Among the Pennsylvania Railroad's greatest undertakings in civil engineering were the construction of its New York Penn Station and the tunnels beneath the Hudson and East Rivers. A fleet of powerful siderod electrics was built to work trains through these long tunnels, drawing power from a 600V DC supply system. These engines were semi-permanently coupled pairs of locomotives based on the 4-4-0 steam locomotive arrangement. The PRR designated a 4-4-0 as Class D, so these 'double D' electrics were designated DD1s and used a 2-Bo-Bo-2 (or in steam terms, a 4-4-0+0-4-4) wheel arrangement. Using Westinghouse electrical equipment, PRR built 33 DD1 pairs at its Juniata Shops in Altoona, PA, in 1910 and 1911.

In later years, a few DD1s were retained for wire train service.

TYPE: 2-Bo-Bo-2, passenger electric
POWER: 600V DC from third rail
OUTPUT: 1587kW (2130hp)
TRACTIVE EFFORT: 220kW (49,400lbf)
MAX. OPERATING SPEED: 128km/h (80mph)
WEIGHT: 144t (313,000lb)
OVERALL LENGTH: 19.787m (64ft 11in)
MAX. AXLE LOAD: 23t (50,750lb)
GAUGE: 1435mm (4ft 8.5in)

Drawing power from the electrified third rail, this pair of DD1s appears to be propelling stock beneath the signal gantry. Pennsy and its Long Island subsidiary both used the tracks.

SERIES 310 2-6-4 IMPERIAL & ROYAL STATE RAILWAYS (KKSTB)

The four-cylinder compound design of this imposing class marks the peak of Austrian compounding practice. All cylinders were in line under the smoke box, with high-pressure inside, driving on to the second coupled axle. In full forward (for starting) or reverse gear, live steam was admitted to the low-pressure cylinders through ports that were not uncovered when valve travel was shortened as the driver notched up. The designer was Karl Gölsdorf, whose

locomotives, before 1911, had been characterized by a steam drier, often exposed above the boiler, placed between two domes. However, he abandoned this in favour of a superheater once its performance had been established. Ten 2-6-4s of Series 210 were built in 1908–10, followed by 111 of Series 310 between 1911 and 1916, the later version being fitted with a 24-element Schmidt superheater instead of a steam drier. Two things contributed to the logic of the 2-6-4 design,

rather than the conventional 4-6-2 now being built for many other countries: the stability provided by the Krauss-Helmholtz bogie linking the front truck with the leading coupled axle, and the ability of the rear bogie – anticipating American 'super-power' practice by about 17 years – to support the big broad firebox needed for Bohemian coal. Three Austrian and one Czech builders were involved, Floridsdorf, Staats Eisenbahn Gesellschaft (StEG) and Wiener Neustadt, of Vienna, and

PCM of Prague. The large-diameter driving wheels suggested high speeds, but their purpose was in fact to reduce piston speed and consequent wear in the single large piston valve that served both cylinders on each side: the maximum speed permitted in Austria was 100km/h (62mph). On test in 1911, one of the class recorded a speed of 117km/h (72.75mph) and an indicated horsepower of 1448kW (1970hp). The speed limit was dictated by the lightweight track and steep gradients that prevailed throughout much of the system, and the 310s had a maximum axle load of only 14.6 tonnes (14.4 tons). 'It is hard to save a ton in one place, but one can save two pounds in each of a thousand places', was one of Gölsdorf's dicta, and the stark but effective look of the Series 310 exemplifies the care that went into the design. These locomotives hauled the many trans-European expresses that passed through Austria or terminated at Vienna, including the 'Simplon-Orient Express' from Paris on its long journey to Istanbul; the 'Tauern Express' north-south to Ostend; the St Petersburg–Vienna–Nice–Cannes express; and the Berlin–Budapest express. They worked main-line services well into the 1930s, and after 1918 they ran on the Polish, Hungarian and Czech railways as well as on the post-war *Bundesbahn Österreichs.* The last to be in service were withdrawn on the Czech CSD in 1954. No. 310.23 has been preserved.

BOILER PRESSURE: 15kg/cm² (213psi)
CYLINDERS: hp 390x720mm (15.4x28.3in); lp 660x720mm (24.4x28.3in)
DRIVING WHEELS: 2100mm (82.7in)
GRATE AREA: 4.6m² (49.7sq ft)
HEATING SURFACE: 193m² (2077sq ft)
SUPERHEATER: 43m² (463sq ft)
TRACTIVE EFFORT: not known
TOTAL WEIGHT: 146t (322,000lb)

2-8-0 GREAT CENTRAL RAILWAY (GCR)

GREAT BRITAIN 1911

With its thousands of goods-hauling 0-6-0s, Britain was slow to take up the 2-8-0 type, which had been introduced in 1903 on the Great Western Railway. No other company took it up until this one appeared, to the design of J. G. Robinson. The Great Central Railway needed a heavy-duty engine for freight traffic in its Yorkshire–Nottinghamshire industrial heartland, where coal was the prime business. The engine had two simple-expansion outside cylinders driving the third pair of coupled wheels. Inside, admission piston valves were placed between the frames, worked by a version of the Stephenson's link motion. It was a workmanlike and sturdy but not particularly ambitious design, with a boiler pressure of only 11.2kg/cm² (160psi) and a modest grate area.

During World War I, when the urgent need for military trains and locomotives to support overseas campaigns arose, this was the type chosen for use by the government's Railway Operating Department (ROD). As 'war engines', 521 were built by several other engine works as well as the GCR's own Gorton works at Manchester. They were fitted with Westinghouse air brake pumps to work French and Belgian stock, and also with steam heating apparatus for use in troop trains. After 1918, a number of British railways acquired the ex-ROD engines, and others remained in foreign service, both in Europe and in Mesopotamia and Iran (Persia).

BOILER PRESSURE: 11.2kg/cm² (160psi)
CYLINDERS: 533x660mm (21x26in)
DRIVING WHEELS: 1436mm (56in)
GRATE AREA: 2.4m² (26.25sq ft)
HEATING SURFACE: 125m² (1348sq ft)
SUPERHEATER: 23.7m² (255sq ft)
TRACTIVE EFFORT: 12,630kg (27,840lb)
TOTAL WEIGHT: 75t (1625,424lb)

CLASS Z530 2-6-0T PIRAEUS–ATHENS–PELEPONNESUS RAILWAY (SPAP)

GREECE 1911

The length of the side tanks can be seen in this image of a skeletal Class Z standing on the scrap road.

The SPAP, with over 750km (466 miles) of 1m (3ft 3in) gauge railways, had acquired a variety of small tank locomotives over the years, but the 2-6-0T was the most common. Previous examples had often been compounds, but the arrival of these engines, from Krauss-Maffei in Munich, marked the advent of the superheater revolution – they were the first in Greece to be fitted with superheaters, with the accompaniment of two simple-expansion cylinders, Walschaerts valve gear and internal piston valves. They were very up-to-date engines in their time, and eventually the class, through acquisition of other lines and their locomotives, and rebuilds of the compounds into simples, numbered 25, operating a service in the hinterland of Athens.

BOILER PRESSURE: 12kg/cm² (171psi)
CYLINDERS: 420x500mm (16.5x19.7in)
DRIVING WHEELS: 1200mm (47.25in)
GRATE AREA: 1.2m² (12.9sq ft)
HEATING SURFACE: 56.1m² (604sq ft)
SUPERHEATER: 16.5m² (177.6sq ft)
TRACTIVE EFFORT: 7480kg (16,500lb)
TOTAL WEIGHT: 37.2t (82,026lb)

FAIRLIE LOCOMOTIVE 0-6-6-0 MEXICAN RAILWAYS

MEXICO 1911

Built by the Vulcan Foundry in Lancashire, England, this impressive double-ended locomotive was the largest Fairlie type, 4.42m (14ft 6in) high, and with a 10.81m (35ft 6in) wheelbase, to haul 304.8-tonne (300-ton) loads up gradients of

1 in 25, relying on adhesion only. Mexico, with steeply graded, curving lines in many parts, was one of the countries that took most strongly to the Fairlie type, even on standard-gauge lines. One displayed its road-holding qualities by running away after a brake

failure, back down a violently curved 1 in 25 gradient, for 11km

(7 miles), reaching 96km/h (60mph) without derailing.

BOILER PRESSURE: 12.6kg/cm² (180psi)
CYLINDERS: 482x634.5mm (19x25in)
DRIVING WHEELS: 1218mm (48in)
GRATE AREA: 4.4m² (47.75sq ft)

HEATING SURFACE: 271.6m² (2924sq ft)
TRACTIVE EFFORT: 26,096kg (57,534lb)
TOTAL WEIGHT: 140.2t (309,120lb)

EC 40 C+2Z JAPANESE GOVERNMENT RAILWAYS (JNR)

JAPAN 1911

The formidable rack section of the Shinetsu line over the Usui Pass in 1912 was Japan's second stretch of electric railway (the first was opened in 1906, a short line of 12.5km/7.6 miles from Nakano to Ochanumizo). The rack section, from Usui to Toge, was originally electrified at 600V DC using a third-rail supply.

Twelve locomotives, with six rail and two rack wheels, were

delivered from Esslingen, Germany, in 1911; a further 14, slightly

heavier, were built in the JNR's own workshops in 1919.

The two rack axles were placed between the second and third adhesion axles. All were replaced by more powerful Hitachi-built engines from 1934. This section of line is no longer in use. The '2z' in the wheel notation denotes the rack cogs.

TYPE: Rack-and-adhesion passenger locomotive
POWER: 470.1kW (630hp)
MAX. OPERATING SPEED: 20km/h (12.4mph)

TOTAL WEIGHT: 46t (101,430lb)
MAX. AXLE LOAD: 15.3t (33,736lb)
OVERALL LENGTH: 9.746m (32ft)
BUILDER: Esslingen, Germany; electrical equipment by AEG

CLASS PO3 4-6-0 STATE RAILWAYS (SS)

NETHERLANDS 1911

Dutch locomotives often had an English look, even in such minor aspects as copper-capped chimneys, as shown by this powerful but understated express design that originated with Beyer Peacock in Manchester, England. They built 36, the rest of the total of 120 coming from Werkspoor in the Netherlands and from German

builders. Four simple-expansion cylinders in line drove the leading coupled axle and two sets of Walschaerts gear drove the inside cylinder piston valves. Up until 1929, they handled the heaviest express traffic. Five were streamlined in 1936. No. 3737, now preserved, was the last steam locomotive to operate in scheduled

service on the Dutch railways. On State Railways and independent Dutch lines, like the North Brabant

BOILER PRESSURE: 12kg/cm² (170psi)
CYLINDERS: 400x660mm (15.6x26in)
DRIVING WHEELS: 1850mm (73in)
GRATE AREA: 2.8m² (30sq ft)
HEATING SURFACE: 145m² (1561sq ft)

German Railway, 4-6-0 locomotives handled all the major passenger services.

SUPERHEATER: 41m² (441sq ft)
TRACTIVE EFFORT: 8900kg (19,624lb)
TOTAL WEIGHT: 72t (158,760lb)
(engine only)

CLASS E 2-4-6-0T PORTUGUESE RAILWAYS (CP)

PORTUGAL 1911

Portugal had no domestic locomotive builders and all its engines were imported. A number of Mallet types were used from 1905 on 1m (3ft 3in) gauge lines through the winding valleys. Henschel of Kassel, Germany, built 18 of this articulated tank version between 1911 and 1923 to operate on the route from Regua to Vila, in the Douro Valley, and other branches. The uneven configuration of coupled wheels was unusual on a Mallet, but the class worked very efficiently. They had no superheating, but were fitted with piston valves. One was later fitted with a Giesl ejector, but no further modernization was carried out, though the engines worked on into the late 1970s.

BOILER PRESSURE: 14kg/cm² (199psi)
CYLINDERS: hp 350x550mm (14x21.6in); lp 500x550mm (20x21.6in)
DRIVING WHEELS: 1000mm (39.4in)
GRATE AREA: 2m² (21.5sq ft)
HEATING SURFACE: 137m² (1475sq ft)
TRACTIVE EFFORT: N/A
TOTAL WEIGHT: 59.5t (131,197lb)

A fine example of Henschel workmanship, down to the copper chimney cap, a well-kept Class E works a rural freight service in the 1970s.

CLASS S 2-6-2 RUSSIAN STATE RAILWAYS

RUSSIA 1911

The Class S was the staple Russian passenger locomotive for half a century. More than 3700 were built, and it could be seen in every part of the country on trunk lines up to the 1960s. Its inception can be traced back to an Imperial Ministry specification of 1908, setting out the requirement for a 2-6-2 with a Krauss-Helmholtz leading truck, a wide grate, Belpaire firebox, and a Notkin-type superheater (a modification of the Schmidt version). This was duly produced by the Sormovo Works in St Petersburg in 1910, and was used for services around that city. The design was seen to be highly

satisfactory, and became the basis of the S class. By 1918, around 900 had been built. After a pause during the revolutionary period, construction continued under the Soviet regime at various builders, including the Kolomna works, south of Moscow, which produced the Su in 1925, a longer-wheelbased version. Other sub-classes appeared as the basic S was tailored to fit different requirements, including Class Sv (CB) of 1915, to 1435mm (4ft 8in) gauge and lower clearance for the Warsaw–Vienna line. These were later widened to the normal Russian 1524mm (5ft) gauge,

restored to the height of 5.24m (17ft 2.5in) above the rails, and converted to oil burning for the Moscow–Kursk line. Though most Russian passenger services were slow, though reliable in timing, the S class' capacity for speed was shown on a test run in 1936, when a succession of them covered the 650km (404 miles) between Moscow and Leningrad with a light train in 6hrs 20mins, including stops for engine changing – an average of more than 96km/h (60mph).

Originally the Class S were provided with large petroleum front lanterns, but in the course of

the 1930s these were replaced by a smaller electric headlamp. Production continued, after an interruption in World War II, until 1951, and they ran until the final phasing-out of Soviet steam power.

BOILER PRESSURE: 13kg/cm² (185psi)
CYLINDERS: 575x700mm (22.6x27.5in)
DRIVING WHEELS: 1850mm (72.75in)
GRATE AREA: 4.7m² (50.9sq ft)
HEATING SURFACE: 198m² (2131sq ft)
SUPERHEATER: 89m² (958sq ft)
TRACTIVE EFFORT: 13,650kg (30,100lb)
TOTAL WEIGHT: 85.3t (188,160lb)
(engine only)

In the last years of Russian steam, a Class S stands under the electric catenary with a night train.

SERIES EB 3/5 2-6-2T SWISS FEDERAL RAILWAYS (SBB)

SWITZERLAND 1911

This was the SBB's first 2-6-2 tank locomotive, introduced to help with increased traffic on suburban and country routes, where short-section start-stop workings on steeply-graded lines were common. A Maffei-built 2-6-2T had been introduced successfully on the Bodensee-

Toggenburg Railway in 1910, and the SBB decided to adopt the same type. In the interest of standardization, the boiler and

motion of the B 3/4 2-6-0 engine were used, but the cylinder diameter was reduced to improve the tank loco's tractive effort.

Thirty-four were built, by SLM at Winterthur, between 1911 and 1916. Three have been preserved.

BOILER PRESSURE: 12kg/cm² (170psi)
CYLINDERS: 520x600mm (20x23.4in)
DRIVING WHEELS: 1520mm (59.25in)

GRATE AREA: 2.3m² (25.75sq ft)
HEATING SURFACE: 120m² (1294sq ft)
SUPERHEATER: 33.5m² (360sq ft)

TRACTIVE EFFORT: 10,350kg (22,820lb)
TOTAL WEIGHT: 57.8t (127,449lb)

1-E-1 CLASS BE 5/7 BERNE–LÖTSCHBERG–SIMPLON RAILWAY (BLS)

The Berne–Lötschberg–Simplon, with its new north–south route through and under the Alps, opened in 1912, and commissioned the most powerful electric locomotives yet built to work its lines. With a maximum gradient of 1 in 38, the line required real power, and the stipulation was for locomotives able to pull 310 tonnes (304 tons) up this grade at 42km/h (26mph). Twelve of these were constructed by Oerlikon and Brown-Boveri, in Switzerland, and as with most electric locomotives of the time, the influence of steam design can be seen in the layout of the wheels. They had two traction motors, which transmitted their drive via jackshafts on either side of the central coupled wheel, with heavy steel castings in the form of inverted triangles providing the link. Maximum speed was 75km/h (46.6mph). The single-phase AC electrical supply system became a standard for other mountain main lines; and the class remained in service into the mid-1950s.

TYPE: mixed-traffic locomotive
POWER: two 933kW (1250hp) motors fed by single-phase current at 15,000V 16.67Hz via overhead catenary, with jack-shaft drive via connecting rod
TRACTIVE EFFORT: 176kN (39,670lbf)
MAX. OPERATING SPEED: 75km/h (47mph)
TOTAL WEIGHT: 91.4t (201,537lb)
MAX. AXLE LOAD: 16.6t (36,586lb)
OVERALL LENGTH: 15.228m (50ft)
BUILDER: Oerlikon, Brown-Boveri

The steam wheel layout is still used on the Lötschberg locomotive, but electric locomotives with power on all axles were in development.

CLASS 34 2-6-(2)-0 OTTOMAN–ANATOLIAN RAILWAY (CFOA)

With its extra set of carrying wheels removed, a Class 34 of conventional 2-6-0 type works a freight on the Turkish Railways in the 1950s.

Twenty-two quite conventional 2-6-0s were built in Germany by Hanomag and Borsig for this line, then under German management (Germany played a substantial part in the devlopment of railways in the Ottoman empire). The unique wheel arrangement came about after their delivery. Some of the CFOA lines were lightly laid and the 15.5-tonne (15.25-ton) maximum axle load of the Class 34 locomotives was too great for them. An ingenious solution was reached: as there was sufficient space between the second and third coupled axles, an extra carrying axle, with wheels of similar dimensions to a pony wheel, was inserted there, reducing the maximum loading by 2.03 tonnes (2 ton)s. The CFOA later became the Turkish Railway's (TCDD) main Istanbul–Ankara line.

BOILER PRESSURE: 12kg/cm² (171psi)
CYLINDERS: 540x630mm (21.3x24.8in)
DRIVING WHEELS: 1500mm (59in)
GRATE AREA: 2.25m² (24.2sq ft)
HEATING SURFACE: 130.1m² (1401sq ft)
SUPERHEATER: 39.3m² (423sq ft)
TRACTIVE EFFORT: 12,570kg (27,717lb)
TOTAL WEIGHT: 59.6t (131,418lb)
(engine only)

CLASS 190 4-6-0 SOUTHERN RAILWAY (SÜDBAHN)

AUSTRIA-HUNGARY 1912

Hungary, into which the *Südbahn* extended, often had problems in finding pure water sources, free of lime and other minerals and chemicals. The Class 190 engines running in Hungary were fitted with two additional domes, not for steam collecting, but as part of a water purifying apparatus. Austria-based engines had a single dome.

Forty-four of this class were built between 1912 and 1914 to a two-cylinder simple design, with piston valves and superheaters. After 1918, the Hungarian Railways inherited 12 and built another four at Budapest Locomotive Works, as Class 302. Four went to Yugoslavia as Class 33 of the JDZ. One has been preserved in Austria.

Former Südbahn Class 109, No. 109, has been preserved and still makes appearances at steam days. The safety valves are mounted on the dome.

BOILER PRESSURE: 13kg/cm² (185psi)	**HEATING SURFACE:** 237m² (2552sq ft)
CYLINDERS: 550x660mm (21.6x26in)	**SUPERHEATER:** 52.8m² (568sq ft)
DRIVING WHEELS: 1700mm (67in)	**TRACTIVE EFFORT:** 12,910kg (28,470lb)
GRATE AREA: 3.6m² (38.8sq ft)	**TOTAL WEIGHT:** 66.9t (147,514lb)

CLASS H-6-G 4-6-0 CANADA NORTHERN RAILWAY (CNR)

CANADA 1912

In the twentieth century, new 4-6-0 locomotives were fairly rare in North America, but the Canada Northern relied strongly on this type, with more than 330, in several different classes. Sixty-six formed H-6-g, all built by the Montreal Locomotive Works during 1912–13, for the opening of the transcontinental through route to Vancouver. After World War I, the Canada Northern was absorbed into the Canadian National system.

The class operated mostly in the prairies, working passenger and freight services. Withdrawal began in 1954, but they survived to the end of steam working on the CN, with the last one withdrawn in 1961. One is preserved.

BOILER PRESSURE: 12.6kg/cm² (180psi)	**GRATE AREA:** not known	**TRACTIVE EFFORT:** 13,860kg (30,500lb)
CYLINDERS: 558x660mm (22x26in)	**HEATING SURFACE:** not known	**TOTAL WEIGHT:** 87.9t (193,760lb)
DRIVING WHEELS: 1599mm (63in)	**SUPERHEATER:** N/A	

CLASS 231C 4-6-2 PARIS, LYONS & MEDITERRANEAN RAILWAY (PLM)

The designation '231' is French notation for the Anglo-American 4-6-2, and this class is not to be confused with the later 231C 'Super Pacific' of the *Chemin de Fer du Nord*. Produced in large numbers (462 in total), the locomotive class was originally a mix of compound- and simple-expansion engines. All of them – with the exception of the first compound prototype – had four in-line cylinders. But from 1913 all were built as compounds, or converted to compound working.

BOILER PRESSURE: 16kg/cm² (228psi)
CYLINDERS: hp 440x660mm (3x25.6in); lp 25. 650x650mm (17.6x25.6in)
DRIVING WHEELS: 2000mm (78.7in)
GRATE AREA: 4.3m² (45.7sq ft)
HEATING SURFACE: 203m² (2185sq ft)
SUPERHEATER: 65m² (694sq ft)
TRACTIVE EFFORT: N/A
TOTAL WEIGHT: 145.5t (320,500lb)

By 1921, 177 had been built. In the wake of Chapelon's experimental work, about half the class were modified after 1928 on Chapelon lines, though not so extensively rebuilt. Thirty received new boilers and their steam passages were reconstructed. Some members of the class remained in service as late as 1969, and four have been preserved.

Through the 1930s and after 1945, modernization of the French Pacific fleet (now SNCF) continued, and many 'new' locomotives were actually rebuilds.

CLASS T18 4-6-4T ROYAL PRUSSIAN UNION RAILWAYS (KPEV)

Between 1912 and 1927, Vulkan of Stettin and Henschel of Kassel produced over 500 of these engines. In effect, they were tank versions of the P8 mixed-traffic 4-6-0, two-cylinder simples with high superheat. Their dimensions were not identical, but they had the same rugged appearance and showed similar characteristics of economy and reliability in handling suburban passenger services around Berlin and other Prussian cities. After World War I, building continued under Deutsche Reichsbahn Gesellschaft (DRG) auspices until 1927. The 4-6-4 was a notoriously unsteady side-tank type, but the T18s seem to have had no problems. Seven were bought by Turkey in 1925. Classed as 78D-5, the last were withdrawn from the East German *Deutsche Reichsbahn* (DR) in 1972. Two are preserved.

BOILER PRESSURE: 12kg/cm² (170psi)
CYLINDERS: 560x630mm (22x24.5in)
DRIVING WHEELS: 1650mm (64.3in)
GRATE AREA: 2.4m² (26sq ft)
HEATING SURFACE: 138.3m² (1489sq ft)
SUPERHEATER: 49.2m² (529.7sq ft)
TRACTIVE EFFORT: 12,085kg (26,648lb)
TOTAL WEIGHT: 105t (231,525lb)

One of the last of a once-numerous class, painted in the livery of the post-war *Deutsche Bundesbahn*, and numbered in its classification sequence, this T18 is still in brisk action on a passenger service.

4-6-2T LONDON, BRIGHTON & SOUTH COAST RAILWAY (LBSCR)

GREAT BRITAIN 1912

arge tank engines could match
the performance of tender
locomotives over distances up to
128km (80 miles), and might run
express services on such
stretches, about the distance from
London to the south coast towns.
D. Earle Marsh, the LBSCR's chief
mechanical engineer, brought out
two very successful express tank
classes. The company was the
second in Britain to use the
Schmidt superheater. In 1908, one
of its Class I 3 4-4-2T had
vanquished a tender engine of the
London & North Western Railway
(LNWR) in competitive fuel
economy trials. These 4-6-2Ts
were the second set, built at the
company's Brighton works. Water
capacity was 2000 gals (2400 US
gals), and with 3.04 tonnes (3
tons) of coal they carried little less
fuel than some tender engines.

**Two locomotives formed Class
J2: No 325 Abergavenny (1910)
and No. 326 Bessborough (1912).
This was a typical fast Pullman
service**

BOILER PRESSURE: 12kg/cm² (170psi)
CYLINDERS: 533x660mm (21x26in)
DRIVING WHEELS: 2038mm (79.5in)

GRATE AREA: 2.5m² (26.7sq ft)
HEATING SURFACE: 141m² (1523sq ft)
SUPERHEATER: 31.8m² (342sq ft)

TRACTIVE EFFORT: 9450kg (20,840lb)
TOTAL WEIGHT: 87.4t (192,640lb)

CLASS F10 2-12-2T STATE RAILWAYS (SS)

DUTCH EAST INDIES (INDONESIA) 1912

**No. F10 08 under steam in the
yard. A water tank wagon has
been attached behind the bunker
to provide additional supply.
Lack of water to feed the large
boiler must always have been
a problem.**

Nevertheless, jacks were carried
on the running plate, suggesting
that derailing was not unexpected.
The side tanks were set quite low,
but further tank capacity was
provided within the frame and
below the coal bunker.
    F10s hauled lengthy mixed
trains in the fertile and densely
populated but hilly districts of
eastern Java, around Malang and
Blitar. Several were also stationed
at Solok depot in western Sumatra
around 1970. Of fine appearance,
they were the only 12-coupled
engines on the Indonesian system,
and a sparklingly polished
No. F10.18 led the locomotive
parade at the Indonesian State
Railway (PNKA) 25th anniversary
parade in September 1970.

welve-coupled locomotives
were rare at the beginning of
the twentieth century, since their
long frame and wheelbase did not
lend themselves to tight curves,
and some engineers felt that much
of the energy of a two-cylinder six-
axled engine would be lost in
combating friction. But, with a big
boiler, and good steam passages,

they provided plenty of tractive
effort. For such a configuration,
this was a relatively large class of
25 locomotives. Superheated two-
cylinder simple-expansion types,
they were built up to 1920.
Eighteen, including the first one,
were from Hanomag of Hanover in
Germany, the others from
Werkspoor in the Netherlands. The

cylinders drove the third coupled
wheels, which were flangeless.
The coupled wheelbase was
inevitably a long one, 6250mm
(20ft 6in), and side-play was
allowed for in the first and sixth
axles – the same arrangement as
on a contemporary 0-12-0T
designed by Karl Gölsdorf for the
Vordenberg rack line in Austria.

BOILER PRESSURE: 12kg/cm² (171psi)
CYLINDERS: 540x510mm (21.3x20in)
DRIVING WHEELS: 1106mm (43.5in)
GRATE AREA: 2.6m² (28sq ft)
HEATING SURFACE: 122.2m² (1316sq ft)
SUPERHEATER: 40.7m2 (438sq ft)
TRACTIVE EFFORT: 14,970kg (30,320lb)
TOTAL WEIGHT: 80t (176,288lb)

CLASS 685 2-6-2 STATE RAILWAYS (FS)

ITALY 1912

Most 'Prairies' were handsome engines, helped by the symmetry of the 2-6-2 wheel arrangement, and this Italian class was a fine example of the kind. The Prairie in Italy was an express type. S. Plancher, of the Southern Adriatic Railway, first introduced it in 1906 as four-cylinder engines of his own compound design. These were later designated as FS Class 680, built in Italy by Breda and Ansaldo (except for 20 built by Schwarzkopff in Berlin). In 1912, compounding was dropped, however, and these new 2-6-2s were built as superheated four-cylinder simples and redesignated Class 685. The class eventually numbered 241. The four cylinders,

in line, drove the second coupled axle, each pair of cylinders operated by a common piston valve. On 'Atlantics', inside bearings on the rear truck often overheated due to their proximity to the firebox, but this does not seem to have been a problem with this class.

The Class 685 had a complex mechanical history. In 1924, four were rebuilt with rotary-cam Caprotti valve gear and classed as 686. In 1926, another 30 were built with Caprotti valve gear, and of these five were rebuilt in 1939–41 with streamlining and Franco-Crosti boilers, and classed s685. From 1918, a total of 119 of the pre-1912 compound 2-6-2s

BOILER PRESSURE: 12kg/cm² (170psi)	**HEATING SURFACE:** 178.6m² (1922sq ft)
CYLINDERS: 420x650mm (16.5x25.5in)	**SUPERHEATER:** 48.5m² (516sq ft)
DRIVING WHEELS: 1850mm (72.75in)	**TRACTIVE EFFORT:** 12,586kg (27,741lb)
GRATE AREA: 3.5m² (38sq ft)	**TOTAL WEIGHT:** 120.4t (265,362lb)

were rebuilt as 685s with superheaters; some were later fitted with Caprotti valve gear. One was even tried as a turbine locomotive in 1933–34. A few were given Friedmann injectors worked by exhaust steam. Italy was not building new steam locomotives, and the rebuilding programme continued into the late

1930s, by which time the older engines were being equipped not only with four higher pressure cylinders, but also triple blast-pipe chimneys, Knorr feed water pumps and pre-heating gear, and Caprotti valve gear. One of the veterans, s685.600, built in 1908 and the 1000th engine built by the Ernesto Breda works in Milan, is preserved.

Class 685 is generally regarded as the finest of Italy's steam locomotive designs. Altogether three have been preserved.

E SERIES E.50 E STATE RAILWAYS (FS)

ITALY 1912

This was an electric locomotive for heavy goods haulage, a 'ten-wheeler' with plenty of traction. The FS's predecessors had built special steam locomotives for the steep Giovi Pass lines between Genoa and Turin; now it was decided to electrify this route, on the pattern of the system installed

by Ganz of Budapest on the Valtellina line in 1902 – three-phase 3000/3300V 15/16.7HzAC cycles.

A compact, rugged-looking steeple-cab machine, the E50 was very reminiscent of Kandó's Ganz-built E 550 designs for the Valtellina line. Its five coupled

axles were driven by double jackshafts, and bow-type collectors

on extended arms collected the current from two wires.

TYPE: heavy goods locomotive	**MAX. OPERATING SPEED:** 44km/h (27mph)
POWER: two 746kW (1000hp) motors, driving five axles via jackshafts and triangular connecting rod	**TOTAL WEIGHT:** 60.2t (132,741lb)
TRACTIVE EFFORT: 131.4kN (29,547lbf)	**MAX. AXLE LOAD:** 12t (26,460lb)
	OVERALL LENGTH: 9.5m (31ft 2in)

CLASS E 0-10-0 RUSSIAN STATE RAILWAYS

RUSSIA 1912

This was by far the most numerous locomotive class ever produced. Over several decades, and through a variety of sub-classes, it numbered over 13,000 engines. Its genesis lay in the deliberations of early-twentieth century Russian railway bureaucrats, pondering on how to fulfil the need for more powerful freight engines as Russian industry grew in scale. The design that finally appeared in 1912 has been chiefly credited to V.I. Lopushinsky, and the first examples were built under his direction at the Lugansk works. They were massive engines, with two simple-expansion cylinders fitted outside, operated by piston valves that were actuated by Walschaerts gear. The first ones were oil burners, intended for the Far-Caucasus line. Coal burners, with larger cylinders, followed for

the Northern Donetz line. With a maximum axle load of 16.2 tonnes (15.9 tons), they were adaptable to a wide variety of track conditions. From 1915, following successful performance of the first engines, production of the E class really got under way at several different workshops, and by 1923 about 2800 had already been built.

The 1917 Revolution temporarily halted locomotive production and the Soviet government placed huge orders with builders in Sweden and Germany for E class engines: 500 from Nydquist & Holm of Trollhättan, Sweden; 700 from 19 assorted German builders. Built to the specification of Lugansk engines of 1917, they were said to have been paid for with gold bullion.

By 1926, an improved Class E had been brought out by the

Bryansk works, designated Eu, (*usilenny* = 'more powerful'). Between then and 1933, some 3350 were built there and at the re-named Lugansk, now Voroshilovgrad; also at Kolomna, Sormovo and Kharkov. Its boiler pressure was 12kg/cm² (171psi) and its maximum axle load was 16.7 tonnes (16.4 tons). A further version appeared in 1931, Em 710xx, with a higher power-to-weight ratio, boiler pressure at 14kg/cm² (199psi) and maximum axle load of 17 tonnes (16.7 tons) – about 2700 of these were built up to 1936. Many of these acquired a supplementary cylindrical water tank on the tender to increase their range; some E-types were also fitted as condensing engines.

In the early 1930s, the Murom repair works developed the Er as a

heavier version, and around 850 of these were built at Bryansk and Voroshilovgrad. After the end of World War II, with many locomotives destroyed or in dire need of reboilering or other major repair, Er types were built in great numbers, up to 1952. Most of these were built not in Russia but in Poland, Czechoslovakia, Hungary and Romania. Their total number is not certain, but may exceed 3000.

For travellers, the E class was the most frequently seen locomotive on Russian railways. Even in 1959, engines first built in 1912 were in use, and the class remained in service until the final abolition of steam power on the Soviet railways.

Specifications given are for the 1915 engines.

BOILER PRESSURE: 12kg/cm² (171psi)
CYLINDERS: 647x705mm (25.5x27.75in)
DRIVING WHEELS: 1333mm (52in)
GRATE AREA: 4.2m² (45.2sq ft)
HEATING SURFACE: 207m² (2231 sq ft)
SUPERHEATER: 50.8m² (547sq ft)
TRACTIVE EFFORT: 22,675kg (50,000lb)
TOTAL WEIGHT: 80t (176,400lb)
(engine only)

The locomotive as monument – an E-class on display in a public park; summing up a half-century of Russian railway history.

CLASS 20 2-6-0 SERBIAN STATE RAILWAYS (SDZ)

SERBIA 1912

The Borsig Works at Berlin went in for a distinctive uncluttered, linear, rather 'British' look, which can be detected in this class. The first five were built for the Ottoman Railway in Turkey, but taken by the Serbs in the Balkan War of 1912. The Serbian Railways decided that they liked it, and ordered another 40, of which 23 had arrived before World War I broke out, with Serbia and Germany on opposing sides. Another 200 were supplied by Germany in post-war reparations. It was a useful, modern design, on the now-typical pattern, with two simple-expansion cylinders, piston valves and superheater. It was also provided with a substantial bogie tender.

BOILER PRESSURE: 12kg/cm² (171psi)
CYLINDERS: 520x630mm (20.5x24.8in)
DRIVING WHEELS: 1350mm (53in)
GRATE AREA: 2.4m² (25.8sq ft)
HEATING SURFACE: 113.8m² (1225sq ft)
SUPERHEATER: 48.9m² (526.5sq ft)
TRACTIVE EFFORT: 12,960kg (28,580lb)
TOTAL WEIGHT: 55.2t (1217,716lb)
(engine only)

A Borsig-built Class 20 of the former Yugoslavian State Railways sets off from a wayside station.

ATLAS-ASEA RAILCAR SÖDERMANLAND MAINLAND RAILWAY

SWEDEN 1912

The first successful diesel-powered railcar, this engine was built by Atlas and ASEA engineering works in Sweden, pioneers of diesel-electric transmission. It ran on eight wheels, not in bogies but all fixed to the frame. A six-cylinder diesel engine developing 55.9kW (75hp) at 550 revolutions per minute was coupled to a direct current

TYPE: diesel-electric railcar
POWER: six-cylinder diesel engine developing 55.9kW (75hp) at 55rpm, coupled to a DC generator supplying current to two

axle-hung traction motors
TRACTIVE EFFORT: not known
MAXIMUM OPERATING SPEED: not known

TOTAL WEIGHT: not known
MAXIMUM AXLE LOAD: 10t (22,050lb)
OVERALL LENGTH: not known
GAUGE: not known

generator that supplied current to two traction motors applied to the two inner axles. Its tare (empty) weight was 29.5 tonnes (29 tons), and it seated 51 passengers.

The Södermanland line ran through well-populated countryside south-east of Stockholm, and the railcar operated a regular service. Later

models had more powerful engines fitted, and in this configuration they could haul up to four four-wheel trailer cars, a useful capability.

NO.101 2-8-0 SMYRNA–KASSABA & EXTENSION RAILWAY (SCP)

TURKEY 1912

During the German dominance of Anatolian railways, 12 of these two-cylinder superheated engines were supplied from Humboldt in Germany, and eventually they became Class 45.121 of the Turkish State Railways (TCDD). The design was a Maffei one, and very similar engines were also supplied to the Syrian Railways.

Compact and powerful, light on the rails with a maximum axle load of 12.5 tonnes (12.2 tons), the class provided useful mixed-traffic locomotives, and the Oriental Railway (CO), joining Istanbul to the European network, acquired 22 between 1924 and 1927, using French builders; these were absorbed, with the CO itself, into the TCDD in 1937.

BOILER PRESSURE: 12kg/cm² (171psi)
CYLINDERS: 530x660mm (20.8x26in)
DRIVING WHEELS: 1400mm (55in)
GRATE AREA: 2.4m² (25.8sq ft)
HEATING SURFACE: 173.9m² (1872.3sq ft)
SUPERHEATER: 32m² (344.5sq ft)
TRACTIVE EFFORT: 13,480kg (29,000lb)

A Turkish State Railways 2-8-0 with a passenger service climbs inland from Smyrna – a haven for old German-built locomotives.

CLASS 629 4-6-2T SOUTHERN RAILWAY (SÜDBAHN)

AUSTRIA 1913

The Class 629 was a large 'Pacific' tank engine with a typical, uncompromising Austrian front end with flat 'baker's oven' smokebox doors, built at the State Railway Engineering (StEG) works at Vienna. It worked not only on the *Südbahn* but also became a

standard class on the Imperial railways, and 45 were built up to 1918. Two simple-expansion cylinders, superheaters and piston valves were all features of the design. A further 55 were built in Austria by 1927; and 35, with modifications, were built in

Czechoslovakia for its independent state railway system. Many of the Austrian engines received Giesl ejectors in the 1950s, and several were still at work in 1970. Perhaps the least altered from the originals were those that ran as Class 18 in Yugoslavia.

BOILER PRESSURE: 13kg/cm² (185.25psi)
CYLINDERS: 475x720mm (18.7x28.4in)
DRIVING WHEELS: 1625mm (64in)

GRATE AREA: 2.7m² (29sq ft)
HEATING SURFACE: 142.7m² (1536.4sq ft)
SUPERHEATER: 29.1m² (313.3sq ft)

TRACTIVE EFFORT: 11,080kg (24,430lb)
TOTAL WEIGHT: 80.2t (176,841lb)

JDR (Yugoslav State Railways) No. 18.003 shows classic Austrian front-end design as it makes a noisy evening departure. The class members inherited by the JDR were the longest-lived of class 629.

0-6-6-0 ARICA–LA PAZ RAILWAY

BOLIVIA 1913

South American railways that had to traverse the Andes usually looked for something beyond the conventional steam locomotive types to cope with the gradients and extreme conditions, and the Mallet, developed in the high Alps, was a natural candidate for employment. On a gauge of 1005mm (3ft 3in), this line connects the capital of landlocked Bolivia, high in the Andes, with the sea at Arica in Chile. Mallet-type compound engines were supplied in 1913–18 by Hanomag in Germany and Baldwin in the United States to haul both passenger and freight traffic.

Though they had big boilers, neither was fitted with a superheater, though the US-built engines were more modern, with piston valves rather than slide valves, and power reversing gear.

BOILER PRESSURE: 14kg/cm² (200psi)
CYLINDERS: hp 406x558.5mm (16x22in); lp 634.5x558.5mm (25x22in)
DRIVING WHEELS: 1104mm (43.5in)
GRATE AREA: 2.9m² (31.3sq ft)
HEATING SURFACE: 136.4m² (1469sq ft)
TRACTIVE EFFORT: N/A
TOTAL WEIGHT: 69t (152,320lb)

CLASS 900 2-10-0 BULGARIAN STATE RAILWAYS (BDZ)

BULGARIA 1913

A four-cylinder compound, this class concealed quite sophisticated mechanics for its time inside a rugged exterior. The compounding system was the one developed by the Maffei Works, though the 70 locomotives in the class were manufactured between 1913 and 1917 by Hanomag in Hanover. The high-pressure cylinders were inside, and a common piston valve drove the high- and low-pressure cylinder on each side. All cylinders drove the third coupled wheels, which had no flanges. These were the most powerful Bulgarian engines before the modernization policy introduced in 1930. Many were fitted with chimney lids and a backwards-angled smoke deflecting semi-collar behind the chimney. In the renumbering programme of 1935, the class was redesignated as 19. By this time, more modern freight types had displaced them from main-line services, but some survived on remoter lines into the 1960s.

BOILER PRESSURE: 15kg/cm² (214psi)
CYLINDERS: hp 430x720mm (17x28.3in); lp 660x720mm (26x28.3in)
DRIVING WHEELS: 1450mm (57in)
GRATE AREA: 4.5m² (48.4sq ft)
HEATING SURFACE: 201.8m² (2172.7sq ft)
SUPERHEATER: 50m² (538.3sq ft)
TRACTIVE EFFORT: N/A
TOTAL WEIGHT: 83.8t (188,550lb)

CLASS 735 4-4-2 EGYPTIAN GOVERNMENT RAILWAYS (EGR)

EGYPT 1913

Egypt was good 'Atlantic' territory, with its arid climate and lack of gradients. Atlantics had worked there in small numbers since 1900, and 10 de Glehn compound 4-4-2s had been supplied from J.F. Cail in France in 1905, but this superheated class dominated main-line passenger traffic from Cairo to Alexandria and to Upper Egypt between the two world wars. Between 1913 and 1925, 30 were built in Germany and the United States and were of generally similar appearance and dimensions. However, after Nos. 1–5, from Schwartzkopff, the cylinder stroke went up to 711mm (28in). The two cylinders were outside, simple-expansion, driving the rear coupled axle, worked by Walschaerts gear with piston valves. A further 55, designated Class 760, later Class 26, were delivered in 1925–26 from the United States and Britain. Some were named after ancient pharaohs or modern governors. In the 1930s, two were experimentally converted into 4-6-0s, but this modification was not taken further.

CYLINDERS: 507.6x660mm (20x26in)
DRIVING WHEELS: 1980mm (78in)
OTHER DATA: not available

Predecessors of the 735s, Egypt's first 'Atlantic' class was introduced by F. H. Trevithick. Ten engines of De Glehn design were acquired from Cail in France, in 1905; and paid for by The International Commission for the Egyptian Public Debt.

BENZOL-ELECTRIC RAILCAR EGYPTIAN GOVERNMENT RAILWAYS (EGR)

EGYPT 1913

As in steam design, the engineers of colonial railways were sometimes at the forefront of internal combustion development. The power car of this two-car unit, commissioned by R. G. Peckitt, resembled a standard clerestory-roofed railway carriage with a long bonnet attached in front covering the petrol motor, and with a wide vertical exhaust pipe rising between the two front windows. Already in large-scale production for the motor industry, petrol engines offered a tempting method of traction to rail designers, though they could not be built on the scale of diesel engines. The motor bogie, at the leading end of the front vehicle, had an outside frame. Westinghouse air brakes were

TYPE: two-car petrol passenger set
POWER: AEG 74.6kW (100hp) petrol engine linked to dynamo of 350V and excitator of 100V, driving two bogie-mounted motors, one on each car
TRACTIVE EFFORT: not known
MAXIMUM OPERATING SPEED: not known
TOTAL WEIGHT: not known
MAXIMUM AXLE LOAD: not known
OVERALL LENGTH: 19.2m (63ft)
GAUGE: not known

fitted and toilet accommodation was provided in each car. This up-to-date set, with first, second and third-class seats, worked between Cairo and Alexandria, supplementing steam services.

CLASS VR1 0-6-0 STATE RAILWAYS (VR)

FINLAND 1913

Unusually for Finnish locomotives, these were coal, not wood, burners, but this reflected their size and function. As the first specifically designed shunting engine on the VR, they did not have enough storage capacity for logs. Between 1913 and 1927, 43 were built. Prior to 1925 they were not superheated,

BOILER PRESSURE: 12kg/cm² (171psi)	**HEATING SURFACE:** 52.9m² (566.3sq ft)
CYLINDERS: 430x550mm (17x21.6in)	**SUPERHEATER:** 15.4m² (162.5sq ft)
DRIVING WHEELS: 1270mm (50in)	**TRACTIVE EFFORT:** 8230kg (18,147lb)
GRATE AREA: 1.44m² (15.5sq ft)	**TOTAL WEIGHT:** 44.8t (98,784lb)

but from then on superheaters were fitted to the whole class. Six ended up in Russia after World War I, and four were bought back by the Finns in 1928. All the class were built at Tampere by Tampella, except for 10 built by Hanomag in 1921–23. Fitted with German Heusinger valve gear and piston valves, members of this very useful class worked up to 1970 and could be found at depots all over the country.

One of the second batch of five, No. 670 of Class VR1 was built in Germany in 1923 by the Hanomag works. For a small engine, it shows interesting complexities of design.

CLASS T161 0-10-0T ROYAL PRUSSIAN UNION RAILWAYS (KPEV)

GERMANY 1913

The Prussian railway system was a big one, extending over most of north Germany. It possessed several very substantial locomotive classes. This was one, numbering 1250 when construction ceased in 1924. In the classification applied by the *Deutsche Reichsbahn Gesellschaft* (DRG), it was Class 945-17, the sub-digits indicating the range of variants to the original class. Similar in dimensions to the G10 0-10-0, it had two outside simple-expansion cylinders, Walschaerts valve gear, a Schmidt superheater and a long, narrow grate. The leading and trailing coupled wheels were allowed a

BOILER PRESSURE: 12kg/cm² (171psi)	**HEATING SURFACE:** 129.4m² (1393.2sq ft)
CYLINDERS: 610x660mm (24x26in)	**SUPERHEATER:** 45.3m² (487.7sq ft)
DRIVING WHEELS: 1350mm (53in)	**TRACTIVE EFFORT:** 18,594kg (41,000lb)
GRATE AREA: 2.3m² (24.8sq ft)	**TOTAL WEIGHT:** 84.9t (187,204lb)

degree of side-play, and with all wheels contributing to the adhesive weight, it made a powerful and efficient heavy shunting engine. Several examples survived in use until 1973.

No. 094 538-6 of the *Deutsche Bundesbahn* was one of the last survivors of the class. One locomotive is preserved at Heiligenstadt.

DIESEL 2-B-2 ROYAL PRUSSIAN UNION RAILWAYS (KPEV)

GERMANY 1913

This was very much a test-bed locomotive, built by Borsig of Berlin to a design conceived by Rudolf Diesel himself. The traction power came from a four-cylinder two-stroke diesel Klose Sulzer engine, mounted in vee-configuration. A second 184kW (246hp) engine was installed to run auxiliary equipment. The prime mover used direct drive – the engine output was coupled to the wheels by jackshaft and side rods with no intervening transmission system. Test running started in autumn 1912 and many revisions were made before re-starting tests in spring 1913. Diesel died in that year, and a

year or so later the power unit itself suffered mechanical damage; further development was finally ended by the outbreak of war.

TYPE: 2-B-2 experimental prototype diesel
POWER: 883kW (1184hp) from Klose Sulzer engine
TRACTIVE EFFORT: 100kN (22680lbf)

MAX. OPERATING SPEED: 100km/h (62.1mph)
WEIGHT: 95t (209,475lb)
OVERALL LENGTH: 16.6m (54ft 5in)
GAUGE: 1435mm (4ft 8.5in)

CLASS 429 'DIRECTOR' 4-4-0 GREAT CENTRAL RAILWAY (GCR)

GREAT BRITAIN 1913

For its passenger services, as the newest major British railway, the GCR liked to do things with a bit of style, and this J.G. Robinson design was in classic British mode, with two inside cylinders and inside motion, low footplate and big double wheel-splashers hiding the upper halves of the driving wheels, but also a Belpaire firebox and superheating. The first batch consisted of 10 engines; 11 more, 'Improved Directors', were built in 1920–23, and a further 24 were put in service in 1924, after the GCR had been amalgamated into the London & North Eastern Railway. These last engines

worked in Scotland and were modified to fit a tighter loading gauge on the former North British Railway, with reduced boiler fittings. Only one member of the original class of locomotives has been preserved.

BOILER PRESSURE: 12.6kg/cm² (180psi)
CYLINDERS: 513x660mm (20x26in)
DRIVING WHEELS: 2077mm (81in)
GRATE AREA: 2.4m² (26sq ft)
HEATING SURFACE: 154m² (1659sq ft)
SUPERHEATER: 28.2m² (304sq ft)
TRACTIVE EFFORT: 8910kg (19,644lb)
TOTAL WEIGHT: 62t (136,640lb)
(engine only)

Working on a 'heritage' section of the former Great Central main line, preserved No. 506 *Butler-Henderson* approaches Swithland with the 10.20 Loughborough-Rothley service, on 11 July 1982.

TYPE 9600 2-8-0 JAPANESE RAILWAYS (JR)

JAPAN 1913

Japan had been importing a variety of British and American locomotive types, but in 1912 the JR announced that in future locomotives would be home-produced, except for specialized engines. Although the railways themselves were laid out according to British practice, it was the American form of design that prevailed in domestic locomotive building, as with this freight loco, built by Kawasaki Zosen Shipyard, Kisha Seizo Kaisha and JR's own shops at Kokura. The bar frames, high boiler, stubby chimney and exposed machinery all make the American influence plain. The design was a success and it was Japan's first 'mass-produced' engine, with a total of 770 built up to 1926, handling the bulk of the JR's rapidly growing main-line freight traffic.

BOILER PRESSURE: 13kg/cm² (185psi)
CYLINDERS: 508x610mm (20x24in)
DRIVING WHEELS: 1250mm (49.25in)
GRATE AREA: 2.32m² (25sq ft)
HEATING SURFACE: 154.5m² (1663sq ft)
SUPERHEATER: 35.2m² (350sq ft)
TRACTIVE EFFORT: 13,900kg (30,650lb)
TOTAL WEIGHT: 94.85t (209,144lb)

A Class 9600 is on the left in this visual symphony of steel and steam. A hint of residual British influence is detectable in the lipped chimney.

CLASS C 5/6 2-10-0 SWISS FEDERAL RAILWAYS (SBB)

In 1913, the Swiss railways' emphasis was increasingly on electric locomotives, and steam development was correspondingly restricted. The Class C 5/6 was to provide the heaviest and most powerful steam locomotives to operate there. Between 1913 and 1917, 30 were built to take passenger as well as goods trains over the Gotthard line. The class requirement was to work trains of 300 tonnes (295 tons) tare up a gradient of 1 in 40 at 25km/h (15mph). The first two were four-cylinder simples, later rebuilt as compounds; the rest were compounds from the start, with the high-pressure cylinders inside the frames, driving the second coupled axle; the low-pressure cylinders drove the third. To help with

stability on the track, and articulation, as often with Central European locomotive designs, the front carrying wheels formed a Krauss-Helmholtz bogie with the front coupled wheels. Several have been preserved.

BOILER PRESSURE: 15kg/cm² (215psi)
CYLINDERS: hp 470x640mm (18x23.5in); lp 690x640mm (27x23.5in)
DRIVING WHEELS: 1330mm (52in)
GRATE AREA: 3.7m² (40sq ft)
HEATING SURFACE: not known
SUPERHEATER: not known
TRACTIVE EFFORT: 20,408kg (45,000lb)
TOTAL WEIGHT: 128t (282,240lb)

The big low-pressure cylinders fitted outside can be seen in the picture. As on some other European locomotives, notably those of Sweden, the sandbox and dome are combined in a single housing.

CLASS MS 2-6-4T UGANDA RAILWAY (UR)

Formed in 1895, the Uganda Railway eventually became a constituent part of the 810mm (3ft) gauge East African Railways. It already used 2-6-2T engines for shunting and branch work (Class S) and this was intended as a larger (though still unsuperheated) version. Eight were built in England by Nasmyth Wilson. They had two outside simple-expansion cylinders and Belpaire fireboxes, and in branch service hauled 152.4-tonne (150-ton) trains at 48km/h (30mph). Some were fitted with supplementary tenders, partly because there were adhesion problems when the side tanks were less than full. Reclassed as EE in 1929, they survived in action to the mid-1960s.

BOILER PRESSURE: 11kg/cm² (160psi)
CYLINDERS: 381x558.5mm (15x22in)
DRIVING WHEELS: 1091mm (43in)
GRATE AREA: 1.18m² (12.8sq ft)
HEATING SURFACE: 95.1.5m² (1024sq ft)
TRACTIVE EFFORT: 7100kg (15,655lb)
TOTAL WEIGHT: 53.2t (117,376lb)

CLASS 11B 2-8-0 BUENOS AIRES GREAT SOUTHERN RAILWAY (BAGS)

Far away from the European manufacturers, and with limited repair facilities of their own, the Argentinian railways had embraced compound working for its cost-savings, but, like many others, abandoned it on new locomotive purchases when superheating became available. This large class of 100 locomotives, built up to 1932, had two simple-expansion outside cylinders. With fine impartiality for the time, the first order was divided between British and German builders.

The Class 11B ran freight services over most of the BAGS lines, and often worked branch passenger trains as well. After half a century of use, the ASTARSA company in Buenos Aires carried out a renovation programme on the class, which then ran until steam was finally phased out on Argentinian railways.

BOILER PRESSURE: 11.2kg/cm² (160psi)
CYLINDERS: 482x660mm (19x26in)
DRIVING WHEELS: 1409mm (55.5in)
GRATE AREA: 2.3m² (24.5sq ft)
HEATING SURFACE: 141.4m² (1522sq ft)
SUPERHEATER: not known
TRACTIVE EFFORT: 9818kg (21,650lb)
TOTAL WEIGHT: 106.4t (234,528lb)

A Class 11B, built by the North British Locomotive Company of Glasgow, sets off into the dusk with a freight train.

SERIES E.91 B+B+B ROYAL PRUSSIAN UNION RAILWAYS (KPEV)

The Series E.91 was a triple articulated locomotive with bodywork in three sections, and was one of the first big electric engines to dispense with carrying wheels and use all its weight for adhesion. It was one of numerous types built for the electrified line through the Silesian mountains between Berlin and Breslau. Twelve E.91s were built between 1915 and 1921 to handle heavy goods traffic. Transformers and switchgear equipment were in the front and rear parts, while the central section had a parcels compartment as well as two driving cabs. Only the cab sections were extended to the full frame width. These B+B+B locomotives, like the other Silesian locomotives (there were 89 in all, of six different types), had many maintenance problems and were expensive to run; but many valuable lessons were

learned from their operation, not least the superiority of the individually driven axle over rod-drive. After World War II, the entire electric installation, 274km (164.5 miles) long, was removed to Russia and installed on a Siberian railway line.

TYPE: articulated heavy freight locomotive
POWER: three motors with an hourly output of 873kW (1170hp), supplied by 15kV single-phase AC via overhead catenary
TRACTIVE EFFORT: not known

MAX. OPERATING SPEED: 50km/h (31mph)
TOTAL WEIGHT: 101.7t (224,248lb)
MAX. AXLE LOAD: 16.9t (37,374lb)
OVERALL LENGTH: 17.2m (56ft 6in)
BUILDER: Linke-Hoffman Werke, Breslau; electrical equipment by Siemens

BO-BO NORTH EASTERN RAILWAY (NER)

With much heavy coal traffic, the NER made a substantial experiment in electrification on its 29km (18-mile) Shildon to Newport line, using 10 centre-cab overhead-wire electric locomotives. Built at the NER Darlington works, they were fitted with twin pantographs to the cab roof. Electrification was never extended on the system, however, and electric working was abandoned in 1935 by the London & North Eastern Railway. The locomotives were kept in store until 1950, when all went for cutting up, except one, No. 11, which had been rebuilt in 1942 as a banking engine, and survived until 1960, having in its later years been used as Departmental Locomotive 100 in the Ilford car sheds of the London underground railways.

TYPE: Bo-Bo
POWER: 1500V DC overhead, four Siemens traction motors, each axle driven by a geared motor, 820.6kW (1100hp)
TRACTIVE EFFORT: 125kW (28,000lbf)

MAX. OPERATING SPEED: 72.4km/h (45mph)
WEIGHT: 75.7t (166,656lb)
MAX. AXLE LOAD: not known
OVERALL LENGTH: 11.99m (39ft 4in)
GAUGE: 1435mm (4ft 8.5in)

CLASS 601 2-6-6-0 HUNGARIAN RAILWAYS (MÁV)

Specifically designed for the steeply graded and sinuous Zagreb–Rijeka line in what are now Croatia and Slovenia, these were the biggest engines to run on the MÁV system. Built in the Budapest Locomotive Works, they were 'Hungarianized' Mallet-type articulated four-cylinder compounds, with Brotan boilers and Pecz-Rejto water-purifying equipment. Giving good results on the Rijeka line, they were also deployed to other mountain lines, in the Carpathians and other regions.

In all, 63 were built, including three built for the Turkish Oriental Railway. It was said that two firemen had to be carried to cope with their fuel demands, but some survived on the Yugoslavian JDZ until 1960, working as bankers on the line from Split on the Adriatic coast inland to Zagreb.

BOILER PRESSURE: 15kg/cm² (214psi)
CYLINDERS: hp 520x660mm (20.5x26in); lp 850x660mm (33.5x26in)
DRIVING WHEELS: 1440mm (56.75in)
GRATE AREA: 5.1m² (55sq ft)

HEATING SURFACE: 275.2m² (2963sq ft)
SUPERHEATER: 66m² (710.6sq ft)
TRACTIVE EFFORT: N/A
TOTAL WEIGHT: 106.5t (234,832lb) (engine only)

CLASS HS 2-8-0 BENGAL–NAGPUR RAILWAY (BNR)

The Bengal–Nagpur's tendency to do its 'own thing' resulted in some distinctive locomotives, often larger than the British Engineering Standards Association (BESA) standard designs. This class, however, was basically a BESA design. As part of the BESA programme (see 1905), a two-cylinder, heavy goods type (HG) had been introduced to the Indian railways in 1906. This was a superheated version of it, originally with the Schmidt superheater, later with J.G. Robinson's adaptation.

Between 1913 and 1920, large numbers were built by Kitson of Leeds, North British Locomotive, Vulcan Foundry and Robert Stephenson: the Bengal–Nagpur had 174, making it the most numerous class on the line. The North Western had 132, and it was also built for the Great Indian Peninsula Railway, the Madras & Southern Mahratta and the East India Railway. Their arrival was welcome, taking over long-distance freight from slower and less-powerful F-class 0-6-0 engines, and providing an improved service.

BOILER PRESSURE: 12.6kg/cm² (180psi)
CYLINDERS: 558.3x660mm (22x26in)
DRIVING WHEELS: 1434mm (56.5in)
GRATE AREA: 2.9m² (32sq ft)
HEATING SURFACE: 164.4m² (1770sq ft)
SUPERHEATER: 36.1m² (389sq ft)
TRACTIVE EFFORT: 15,419kg (34,000lb)
TOTAL WEIGHT: 74.4t (164,080lb) (engine only)

The No 26190. Timber and agriculture were important elements to this line's freight service.

1-C-1 E330 STATE RAILWAYS (FS)

ITALY 1914

Built by Ernesto Breda of Milan, with Westinghouse electrical equipment, this distinctive class – known to the railwaymen as *trentas* – first appeared in 1914. Intended for passenger work at 100km/h (62mph), they were compact in appearance, with three large coupled wheels bearing 51 tonnes (112,455lb) adhesive weight, and

TYPE: 1-C-1 three-phase electric
POWER: 2000kW (2717hp)
SUPPLY: 3300V 16.2/3Hz AC two-wire three-phase

TRACTIVE EFFORT: 93kN (20900lbf) at 104km.h (65mph)
MAX. OPERATING SPEED: 100km/h (62mph)

WEIGHT: 74t (163,170lb)
MAX. AXLE LOAD: 17t (37,485lb)
OVERALL LENGTH: 11.008m (35ft 11in)
GAUGE: 1435mm (4ft 8.5in)

two sets of double long-beam collectors mounted on the central roof to pick up the three-phase electric supply. At each end was an unusual tapered-in cab, terminating in a small, narrow 'nose' above the buffer-beam. The class comprised 16 machines in total, andwere numbered E330 001 to 016.

CLASS F 4-6-2 SWEDISH STATE RAILWAYS (SJ)

SWEDEN 1914

Nydquist & Holm of Trollhättan built the 11 Class F locomotives, the first 'Pacifics' to run in Scandinavia, between 1914 and 1916. They hauled the principal expresses from the Norwegian border and on the Gothenburg–Stockholm line. Imposing in appearance, their powerful-looking front ends were further enhanced by big headlights and snow deflectors.

They were four-cylinder in-line compounds on the Vauclain model, with the high-pressure cylinders inside the frame and the low-

pressure ones outside; each set worked by a single piston valve operated by Walschaerts outside valve gear. All cylinders drove the second pair of coupled wheels. Outside bearings were fitted to the leading bogie and the trailing wheels. On the boiler top, a large cover went over both regulator dome and sandbox. The cabs had wooden sides, a typically Swedish feature intended to provide better winter insulation than metal.

Main-line electrification made the Class Fs redundant on the SJ in 1937. Though almost a quarter

BOILER PRESSURE: 13kg/cm² (185psi)
CYLINDERS: hp 420x660mm (16.4x26in); lp 630x660mm (24.5x26in)
DRIVING WHEELS: 1880mm (73.3in)
GRATE AREA: 3.6m² (38.75sq ft)

HEATING SURFACE: 184.5m² (1987sq ft)
SUPERHEATER: 63.5m² (684sq ft)
TRACTIVE EFFORT: N/A
TOTAL WEIGHT: 86.8t (191,520lb) (engine only)

of a century old, they had plenty of working life left, however, and were sold to the Danish State Railways. There they were reconditioned, refitted for right-hand drive, and put into express train service as DSB Class E. Between 1942 and 1950, the Danish Frichs works at Aarhus

built a further 25 to the same basic design, but with steel cabs and an additional dome housing a steam drier. Fifteen of these later engines also had double chimneys with Lemaître blast pipes. The first of the original set, No. 1200, was returned to Sweden, where it is preserved.

1-C+C-1 SWEDISH RAILWAYS (SJ)

SWEDEN 1914

In 1910, the decision was taken to begin electrification of the Luleå–Kiruna–Narvik railway, beginning with the 120km (74.5- mile) section between Luleå and the Norwegian frontier at Riksgränsen. This line, north of the Arctic Circle, had been worked by 2-8-0 steam locomotives of Class Ma. To work the heavy iron ore trains, 14 1-C+C-1 articulated locomotives were supplied by ASEA and Siemens-Schukert, who were also responsible for all the electrification works. The new engines were intended to work in

pairs and required to draw a train of 1915 tonnes (1855 tons) up a gradient of 1 in 100 at a speed not less than 30km/h (18.6mph) and with a maximum running speed of 50km/h (31mph). This capability represented an 80 per cent increase in haulage capacity per train.

Each 'half' of the articulated units had a driving cab, and the motor drove the 1100mm (42in) wheels by means of cranks, jackshaft and coupling rods. Air brakes were fitted, worked by a 7.5kW (10hp) compressor that also operated the locomotives' whistle and sanding

TYPE: 1-C+C-1 heavy freight locomotive
POWER: 1800hp (1323kW)
SUPPLY: 15kV single phase AC
TRACTIVE EFFORT: not known

MAX. OPERATING SPEED: 50km/h (31mph)
WEIGHT: 140.2t (309,088lb)
MAX. AXLE LOAD: 17.7t (39,021lb)
OVERALL LENGTH: 18.6m (59ft 1in)
GAUGE: 1435mm (56.5in)

apparatus. The initial electrification was a great success, and extensions were authorized and a further four of the 1-C+C-1 engines ordered. By 1923, the full length of the Lapland line from the Baltic to the North Sea was electrified – 450km (279.5 miles) –

and three types of electric locomotives operated over it, with a new eight-wheeled 'D' freight type as well as further engines of the 1-C+C-1 freights and the B-B+B-B passenger locomotives that had worked from the first stage of electrification.

P1 2-8-8-8-2 'TRIPLEX' LOCOMOTIVE ERIE RAILROAD (ER)

USA 1914

No steam locomotive ever had more driving wheels than the P1 2-8-8-8-2 'Triplex' locomotives. Four engines of this configuration were built by Baldwin, three for the Erie and one for the Virginian Railroad, to a patent design by

George R. Henderson, consulting engineer to Baldwin. His aim was to maximize the adhesive weight, and therefore the total pulling power, of a big road engine, while spreading its total weight over a large number of axles, so

minimizing its impact on the tracks.

The Virginian locomotive differed from the Erie engines in having a four-wheel truck supporting the rear end of tender, making it a 2-8-8-8-4; its driving

wheels were also slightly smaller. Though the engines worked compound, the six cylinders were of identical size and cast from the same pattern. Steam was passed direct from the boiler to the middle pair, which acted as high-

Big as it was, that boiler found it too difficult to supply steam to three sets of cylinders. The rear exhaust stack can be seen at the back of the tender.

pressure cylinders; their exhaust was divided among the low-pressure cylinders at front and rear. The front cylinders then exhausted into the stack in order to create a draught for the fire; exhaust from the rear cylinders was sent through a feedwater heater and out through a pipe behind the tank. The total length

of these mammoths was 32m (105ft 1in).

The first Erie engine was given a name, *Matt H. Shay,* in honour of its oldest living engineman. It demonstrated its power on test by hauling a train of 250 loaded cars weighing 18,203 tonnes (17,912 tons) and 2.5km (1.6 miles) long. The Erie Triplexes were intended

as pushers, or banking engines, on the Gulf Summit grades. Unfortunately, the steam supply and distribution system proved to be inadequate and performance was far below expectations. The locomotives were dismantled between 1929 and 1933, and the Virginian engine was converted to a 2-8-8-0.

BOILER PRESSURE: 14.7kg/cm² (210psi)
CYLINDERS: 923x820mm (36x32in)
DRIVING WHEELS: 1615mm (63in)
GRATE AREA: 8.3m² (90sq ft)
HEATING SURFACE: 639.5m² (6886sq ft)
SUPERHEATER: 147m² (1584sq ft)
TRACTIVE EFFORT: 72,562kg (160,000lb)
TOTAL WEIGHT: 392t (864,400lb)

CLASS K4 4-6-2 PENNSYLVANIA RAILROAD (PRR) USA 1914

The K4 was one of the largest and most successful classes of 'Pacific' among the railways of the world. Even in 1914 it was a compact locomotive by American standards, but with a tractive effort rated at 20,163kg (44,460lb) it had ample power – some 33 per cent greater than the still-new E6 'Atlantic' that it would replace on the heaviest express services. It was superheated but, surprisingly perhaps, it was hand-fired, and a screw reverser was fitted. After thorough testing, line production began at Altoona in 1917. Eventually 425 K4s were built, all but 74 of them at the PRR's Juniata shops; the others were from Baldwin. A further 100 were ordered in 1927–28, at which time some critics said a more powerful 'Hudson' type 4-6-4 should have been brought in, but at that time the PRR was considering further electrification of the main line and was disinclined to embark on a new steam-powered express passenger type.

The K4 could maintain 96-120km/h (60–75mph) with a 1016-tonne (1000-ton) train over level or gently rolling terrain, and its top recorded speed was 92mph (148kph). By the mid-1930s, all were fitted with power reversers

and automatic stokers. A succession of larger tenders was fitted, the final version with almost double the capacity of the first. During the mid-1930s' streamlining vogue, five were streamlined, but the cladding was removed in the early 1940s.

K4s gave excellent main-line service through the 1920s and 1930s, on such demanding services as the 'Twentieth Century Limited', which they hauled in four stages, taking over from electrics at Manhattan Transfer and running

to Harrisburg (301km/187 miles), Harrisburg to Pittsburgh (394km/245 miles), Pittsburgh to Crestline (304km/189 miles), and Crestline to Chicago (449km/279 miles) – much of the latter a famous racing stretch. The PRR's confidence in timekeeping was such that in the 1920s it refunded a dollar to premium-fare passengers for every 15 minutes' delay on this train. As cars became heavier with the installation of air conditioning and other comforts, the K4s were often used in double-

headed formation. This did not inhibit their speed: in 1937 a pair hauling 'The General' , a 15-car express, ran the 95.75km (59.5 miles) in 50 minutes.

K4s lasted on secondary duties into the 1950s. The last of the K4s in passenger service, No. 5351, was finally retired in November 1957. The first of the class, No. 1737, was due to be preserved, but its condition was too bad, and in a polite deception, its identity and plates were assumed by No. 3750.

BOILER PRESSURE: 15kg/cm² (205psi)
CYLINDERS: 692x718mm (27x28in)
DRIVING WHEELS: 2051mm (80in)
GRATE AREA: 6.5m² (69.9sq ft)
HEATING SURFACE: 375m² (4041sq ft)
SUPERHEATER: 87.6m² (943sq ft)
TRACTIVE EFFORT: 20,163kg (44,460lb)
TOTAL WEIGHT: 140.5t (309,890lb)

A preserved K4, No. 1361, passes Tyrone, Pennsylvania with a vintage train on 21 June, 1987.

BOXCAB CLASS EF-1 CHICAGO, MILWAUKEE & ST PAUL RAILROAD (CM&SP) USA 1914

Milwaukee Road extended far from its parent cities, and in 1915 began electrification on its western mountain lines. By 1930, it had more than 1040km (650 miles) electrified in the Rocky and Bitter Root Mountains. General Electric supplied the 3000-volt direct current system and these 42 massive EF-1 boxcabs, each

consisting of two units semi-permanently coupled with a 2-Bo-Bo+Bo-Bo-2 wheel arrangement, were the first locomotives to work on the line. They were used to haul freight and passenger trains up and down mountain grades as steep as 2.2 percent, and were equipped with regenerative braking (which turned traction motors into

generators and fed electricity back into the system). Freight and passenger locomotives differed only in the gear ratio applied. The electric sections, though lengthy, were isolated on the system, and were dismantled after World War II, the exercise completed by 1974. One boxcab set is preserved in Duluth, Minnesota.

TYPE: 2-Bo-Bo+Bo-Bo-2, freight electric
POWER: 3000V DC from overhead wire
OUTPUT: 2235kW (3000hp)
TRACTIVE EFFORT: 501kN (112,750lbf)
MAX. OPERATING SPEED: N/A
WEIGHT: 261t (576,000lb)
MAX. AXLE LOAD: 26t (56,250lb)
OVERALL LENGTH: 34.138m (112ft)
GAUGE: 1435mm (4ft 8.5in)

MP54 ELECTRIC MULTIPLE UNIT PENNSYLVANIA RAILROAD (PRR) USA 1914

Despite its huge steam fleet, Pennsylvania Railroad saw scope for electrification on its intensive Philadelphia area suburban services, starting in 1915 with the main line from Broad Street to Paoli. An overhead wire system at 11kV AC was used. Rebuilt steel P54-type passenger cars were transformed into MP54 electric multiple units, using Westinghouse electrical components, at PRR's Altoona shops. Each car had a single pantograph and a single powered bogie driven by two AC traction motors. The ends of the cars were equipped with driving positions and a pair of circular port-hole style windows, which gave them

a characteristic 'owl eyed' look. Many hundreds of MP54s were built, and were also used on the New York–Washington DC route after its electrification

TYPE: suburban passenger electric EMU
POWER: 11,500V at 25Hz alternating current
OUTPUT: 298kW (400hp) per car
MAX. OPERATING SPEED: 104km/h (65mph) with some cars 128km/h (80mph)
WEIGHT: 59t (130,000lb) – varied among different classes
OVERALL LENGTH: 19.653m (64ft 6in)
MAX. AXLE LOAD: N/A
GAUGE: 1435mm (4ft 8.5in)

A well-known sight on the PRR lines for more than five decades: a three-car set of MP 54 stock heads for Newark, New Jersey, 1961.

4-6-2 FRANCO-ETHIOPIAN DJIBOUTI–ADDIS ABABA RAILWAY (CICFE) ETHIOPIA 1915

This was not a high-speed 'Pacific' type, but was built to deliver steady power from its big boiler throughout a long uphill slog. Its way to Ethiopia was far from direct. Built at Haine St-Pierre in Belgium as part of an order of six for a Spanish metre-gauge railway, its delivery was prevented

by the outbreak of war in 1914. Never supplied to the purchasers, it was kept in store, unused, for over 20 years, until it was sold in 1936 for passenger service on the Djibouti–Addis line, where it became Locomotive No. 231. The CICFE found it satisfactory, and ordered three identical examples

BOILER PRESSURE: 8.4kg/cm² (120psi)	**SUPERHEATER:** N/A
CYLINDERS: 400x560mm (15.6x22in)	**TRACTIVE EFFORT:** 5546kg (12,230lb)
DRIVING WHEELS: 1000mm (39.4in)	**TOTAL WEIGHT:** 48t (105,840lb)
GRATE AREA: not known	(engine only)
HEATING SURFACE: not known	

to be built; these were delivered in 1938. Operating speed was slow:

the Djibouti–Addis journey lasted two days, with an overnight stop.

CLASS Hv 1 4-6-0 FINNISH RAILWAYS (VR) FINLAND 1915

Until Finland's first 'Pacifics' in 1937, 4-6-0s ran all the express services. This class was not exclusively passenger but was designed for mixed-traffic work, which it handled with great efficiency. In Finland, the maximum operating speed was 95km/h (60mph). Hv 1 No. 575 was the first locomotive to be

BOILER PRESSURE: 12kg/cm² (170psi)	**GRATE AREA:** 1.9m² (21sq ft)	**TRACTIVE EFFORT:** 8985kg (19,800lb)
CYLINDERS: 510x600mm (20x23.4in)	**HEATING SURFACE:** 108.6m² (1169.2sq ft)	**TOTAL WEIGHT:** 55.2t (121,716lb)
DRIVING WHEELS: 1750mm (68.25in)	**SUPERHEATER:** 30.7m² (330.5sq ft)	(engine only)

built at the new Lokomo Works in Tampere; others of the class were also built by Tampella in the same city. Altogether there were 43, fitted with superheaters and

Heusinger valve gear (very similar to Walschaerts' and invented almost simultaneously in 1845). With minor variations, similar engines of classes Hv 2 and Hv 3

were built up to 1941. Most were coal burners, with stovepipe chimneys topped by mesh spark-arresters.

CLASS Ab 4-6-2 NEW ZEALAND RAILWAYS (NZR) NEW ZEALAND 1915

Said to be the first engine capable of developing one horse-power for every 45.3kg (100lb) of engine weight, the Ab, designed by H.H. Jackson, was New Zealand's most numerous 'Pacific' class, with 141 built from 1915 to 1926. Two outside cylinders were operated by Walschaerts valve gear. It had the spacious cab typical of NZ engines, and the other standard features of a cowcatcher and a large headlight. Slightly under half

were home-built, with 83 coming from the North British Locomotive Company of Glasgow (another two were lost in a shipwreck, joining the not-inconsiderable number of locomotives at the bottom of the sea). Between 1947 and 1957, another 11 were built at the NZR Hillside Works by converting Class Wab 4-6-4 tank engines. Vanderbilt-type tenders were fitted to the class, the first to be used in New Zealand. Disposals of the locomotives began in 1956.

The preserved AB, No. 778, with the 'Kingston Flyer' vintage train, at Fairlight, South Island, on 12 October 1991.

BOILER PRESSURE: 12.6kg/cm² (180psi)	**SUPERHEATER:** 17m² (183sq ft)
CYLINDERS: 431x660mm (17x26in)	**TRACTIVE EFFORT:** 9639kg (21,250lb)
DRIVING WHEELS: 1370mm (54in)	**TOTAL WEIGHT:** 54.3t (119,728lb)
GRATE AREA: 2.6m² (28.3sq ft)	(engine only)
HEATING SURFACE: 106.6m² (1148sq ft)	

CLASS 32A 2-6-2T NORWEGIAN STATE RAILWAYS (NSB)

NORWAY 1915

In Norway, only Oslo had anything approaching a system of suburban lines, and this class, Norwegian-built by Hamar, was used chiefly for local services on the lines that converged on the capital. A compact engine, it was typical of the NSB's fleet of suburban tank locomotives. It has

an American style, and engines of the sister 32c class were built by Baldwin and had bar frames. This class, however, is plate-framed. A substantial pair of outside simple-expansion cylinders were actuated by piston valves, driven by Walschaerts gear. As often in Scandinavian locomotives, a single

long housing on top of the boiler housed the sandbox and a dome

BOILER PRESSURE: 12kg/cm² (170psi)
CYLINDERS: 525x600mm (20.5x23.4in)
DRIVING WHEELS: 1600mm (62.5in)
GRATE AREA: 1.9m² (21sq ft)

that helped to keep the sand dry. No. 288 of the class is preserved.

HEATING SURFACE: 88m² (948sq ft)
SUPERHEATER: 27m² (290.7sq ft)
TRACTIVE EFFORT: 10,310kg (22,735lb)
TOTAL WEIGHT: 66.6t (146,853lb)

CLASS YE 2-10-0 RUSSIAN STATE RAILWAYS

RUSSIA 1915

On the Siberian *taiga*, its steam pipes are well-protected against frost, but this Ye locomotive looks as if it's not seen action for some time.

US locomotive sales to Russia in the twentieth century were always liable to be interfered with by politics. In 1914 and 1915, S.M. Vauclain, then vice-president of the Baldwin Locomotive Works, visited Russia, at that time a combatant on the Allied side in World War I. He was negotiating a large sale of locomotives, urgently needed to assist in the miltary and industrial efforts of Imperial Russia, and 1300 of these big locomotives were ordered. Alco at

Schenectady, and the Canadian Locomotive Company at Montreal, were involved with Baldwin in an intensive building programme, and between 1915 and 1917 881 locomotives were delivered before the Russian Revolution abruptly stopped trade between the two countries. One consignment is believed to have been lost at sea. Baldwin was left with 100 undelivered engines, which were bought by the US government, converted to standard gauge and

sold on to the Erie, the Seaboard Air, and other US lines. The rest were cancelled.

The YE class was employed on lines in Siberia and the Far East, and a large number were converted to standard gauge in 1935–36 and used in China. When Russia was again on the Allied side in World War II, arrangements under the Lease-Lend scheme were made to rebuild the same design, denoted as Class Yea. Between them, Alco and Baldwin built a

further 2120 between 1944 and 1947. With the onset of the 'Cold War', the last 20 were diverted to Finland. Some engines of the earliest vintage were still in operation in Siberia in the late 1950s.

BOILER PRESSURE: 12.6kg/cm² (180psi)
CYLINDERS: 634.5x710.6mm (25x28in)
DRIVING WHEELS: 1320mm (52in)
GRATE AREA: 6m² (64.5sq ft)
HEATING SURFACE: 210m² (2261sq ft)
SUPERHEATER: 63.6m² (684.75sq ft)
TRACTIVE EFFORT: 17,780kg (39,200lb)
TOTAL WEIGHT: 90t (201,600lb)

CLASS 140C 2-8-0 STATE RAILWAYS (ETAT)

FRANCE 1916

In the course of World War I, numerous deliveries of locomotives were made from Britain to France to assist with the war effort. This 2-8-0 class, built in Glasgow by the North British Locomotive Company, was intended to remedy a shortage of freight engines on the *Etat*. The design is typical of French engines of this period, with inside steam-pipes to the cylinders, and a long parallel-form boiler with a flower-pot chimney and round topped firebox. A Westinghouse air-brake pump was fitted to the right of the smoke-box. The cylinders were simple expansion, set in rear of the smokebox, driving the third set of coupled wheels.

BOILER PRESSURE: 12kg/cm² (171psi)
CYLINDERS: 590x650mm (23.25x25.6in)
DRIVING WHEELS: 1450mm (57in)
GRATE AREA: 3.1m² (34sq ft)

HEATING SURFACE: 170m² (1830.3sq ft)
SUPERHEATER: not known
TRACTIVE EFFORT: 16,000kg (35,280lb)
TOTAL WEIGHT: 74.9t (165,132lb)

CLASS DD50 2-8-8-0 MALLET STATE RAILWAYS (SS)

DUTCH EAST INDIES (INDONESIA) 1916

The success of big American Mallet types attracted attention in many other places, and resulted in a rare US order from the *Staats Spoorwegen*, who were looking for heavy-duty engines to haul freight trains on the 1065mm (3ft 6in) gauge. Eight of these great Mallets were built by Alco in 1916, with another 12 of the very similar Class DD51 following in 1919. By now, American Mallet buyers were opting for simple expansion, but these were superheated compounds. The high-pressure cylinders were operated by piston valves, with slide valves on the low-pressure ones.

Mallets did good work in Indonesia, and though all the DD50s were withdrawn and scrapped by the late 1960s, German and Dutch-built DD52 2-8-8-0s were still in use until the late 1970s.

BOILER PRESSURE: 14kg/cm² (199psi)
CYLINDERS: hp 445x610mm (17.4x24in); lp 711x610mm (28x24in)
DRIVING WHEELS: 1106mm (43.5in)
GRATE AREA: 4.2m² (45.2sq ft)
HEATING SURFACE: 213.4m² (2297sq ft)
SUPERHEATER: 64.4m² (693.4sq ft)
TRACTIVE EFFORT: N/A
TOTAL WEIGHT: 95.4t (210,375lb)

A buffer-beam joy-rider gets a good view as an oil-burning 'Mallet' crosses one of Java's many spectacular viaducts with a special working.

CLASS C27 4-6-4T STATE RAILWAYS (SS)

DUTCH EAST INDIES (INDONESIA) 1916

Thirty-nine C27s were delivered between 1916 and 1922. The Swiss SLM works at Winterthur built the first 14, another 20 came from Werkspoor in the Netherlands and five from Armstrong Whitworth in Newcastle, England. Employed on fast short-haul passenger service on the Javanese network, the C27 was unusual in appearance due to its minimal side tanks. Most of its water capacity was in a bunker tank, set beneath the coal-holder. Like the successor C28 class, the C27s were superheated two-cylinder simples, with piston valves operated by Walschaerts gear. Working on slow-speed mixed-train services typical of the Javanese country lines, numerous examples survived until the last days of steam on the Indonesian national PNKA system.

BOILER PRESSURE: 12kg/cm² (171psi)
CYLINDERS: 450x550mm (17.7x21.6in)
DRIVING WHEELS: 1350mm (53in)
GRATE AREA: 1.9m² (20.4sq ft)
HEATING SURFACE: 99.9m² (1075.5sq ft)
SUPERHEATER: 30.8m² (331.6sq ft)
TRACTIVE EFFORT: 8416kg (18,560lb)
TOTAL WEIGHT: 66t (145,530lb)

The side tanks of Class C27 were set very low but held only part of its water supply. The hinged chimney cowl was a typical feature of Indonesian steam locomotives.

CLASS TV1 2-8-0 STATE RAILWAYS (VR)

FINLAND 1917

For around half a century, this wood-burner was one of Finland's prime freight classes. Between 1917 and 1944, the VR acquired 144, mostly from Tampella and Lokomo in Finland, but some were built by Nohab (formerly Nydquist & Holm) in Sweden and Hanomag in Germany. With two simple-expansion cylinders, its modest 13-tonne (12.8-ton) axle load allowed it to operate on the lightly laid northern tracks. Various adaptations were made over the TV1's 27-year building period. Because of Finland's long sub-zero winters, the feedwater supplied from tender tanks could be just above freezing point, cooling the boiler temperature considerably, and the VR experimented with numerous different types of feedwater heaters on the Tv1. On post-1938 engines, the boiler pressure went up to 13kg/cm² (185psi). They were taken out of service between 1965 and 1969.

BOILER PRESSURE: 12kg/cm² (171psi)
CYLINDERS: 560x650mm (22x25.6in)
DRIVING WHEELS: 1400mm (55in)
GRATE AREA: 2.3m² (24.8sq ft)
HEATING SURFACE: 123.8m² (1332.9sq ft)
SUPERHEATER: 38.6m² (415.6sq ft)
TRACTIVE EFFORT: 11,350kg (25,026lb)
TOTAL WEIGHT: 61.5t (135,607lb)
(engine only)

For the engine crew, the footplate of the Tv1 in winter provided a mixture of freezing draughts and blasts of heat when the fire-doors were opened.

CLASS C53 4-6-2 STATE RAILWAYS (SS)

DUTCH EAST INDIES (INDONESIA) 1917

Though running on the 1065mm (3ft 6in) gauge, the C53 was not a slow-speed 'Pacific'. The design came from Werkspoor in the Netherlands, and 20 were built. An oil-fired four-cylinder compound, its outside cylinders, unusually for a six-coupled engine, drove the first coupled axle with very short connecting-rods. The C53's principal service was on the Javanese north-coast line between the major cities of Batavia (Djakarta) and Surabaya. These were fast trains, and the C53s were reputed to have reached 120.7km/h (75mph) on occasions. During World War II, 16 were removed to the Siamese and Malayan railways after the Japanese occupation of Java. The last two of the class were withdrawn at Surabaya in 1973; one is preserved.

A plume of oil-smoke rises and is caught by the wind as the 'blower' is turned on, a shovel or two of sand is tossed into the firebox, and the boiler tubes are cleared.

BOILER PRESSURE: 14kg/cm² (200psi)
CYLINDERS: hp 340x580mm (20.5x22.8in); lp 520x580mm (20.5x22.8in)
DRIVING WHEELS: 1600mm (62.5in)
GRATE AREA: 2.7m² (29sq ft)
HEATING SURFACE: 123m² (1324sq ft)
SUPERHEATER: 43m² (463sq ft)
TRACTIVE EFFORT: N/A
TOTAL WEIGHT: 66.5t (147,000lb)
(engine only)

CLASS 56 2-10-0 TURKISH STATE RAILWAYS (TCDD)

In 1917, Turkey was still the heart of the Ottoman Empire, and was the war ally of Germany, and these engines were German-built and based broadly on the Prussian Railways' G12 class. They were two-cylinder simples, with superheating, but with smaller wheels and cylinders, and round-topped firebox. These were Turkey's first 2-10-0s, a type that would become the most typical of modern Turkey's steam locomotives. Fifteen were built, of which 10 were requisitioned by the Ottoman army for war use. With the formation of the TCDD in 1927, under the new Turkish Republic, they were designated Class 56. They were scrapped in the early 1950s.

BOILER PRESSURE: 16kg/cm² (228psi)
CYLINDERS: 650x660mm (25.6x26in)
DRIVING WHEELS: 1450mm (57in)
GRATE AREA: 4m² (43sq ft)
HEATING SURFACE: 222.9m² (2400sq ft)
SUPERHEATER: 106m² (1141sq ft)
TRACTIVE EFFORT: 23,180kg (51,000lb)
TOTAL WEIGHT: 105.9t (233,509lb)
(engine only)

Apart from the TCDD insignia and plate on the cab side, the Class 56 were thoroughly German in aspect.

CLASS 328 4-6-0 HUNGARIAN RAILWAYS (MÁV)

Purists of locomotive design were apt to criticize the appearance of Hungarian engines, but there was sound logic in their pipe-hung look, and purpose behind every feature. Like the French, the Hungarian designers saw engines as workhorses, and their locomotives were designed to burn coal of low calorific value and to cope with water supplies that were often over-rich in salts and minerals. Henschel of Kassel, Germany, built 100 of the Class 328 up to 1920 and the Budapest Locomotive Works (known after 1945 as MÁVAG) built 58 in 1919–22. The design had been drafted in 1914, prior to Hungary's independence from Austria, but was not put into production until after the end of World War I. One of the features of this engine, as with many other Hungarian locomotives up to the mid-1920s, was a Brotan boiler, the 1906 invention of a Czech engineer. Originally it was a double boiler, consisting of a steam drum placed above a fire-tube drum, and with a firebox whose side walls (and sometimes also back wall) were lined with water tubes. On engines fitted with this double-barrelled boiler, the upper 'steam drum', of

smaller diameter than the 'fire drum', also bore the various domes, and created a remarkable appearance. This form was not wholly satisfactory in operation, and MÁV engineers adapted it into a single combined fire-tube and water-tube boiler, attached to a very wide firebox with its 60 water-pipes. Brotan's aim had been to minimize the corrosive effect of highly sulphurous coal on a copper-lined firebox, and as this was Hungary's prime type of fuel there was a good reason for employing his system. Outside Central Europe, the Brotan boiler was almost wholly ignored. It needed to be set above the fire-grate and was partly responsible for the lofty look of Hungarian locomotives. Normally only a proportion of engines in any class might be Brotan-boilered, but the 158 locomotives of Class 328 had it as standard. It was estimated that around a quarter of MÁV engines were so fitted in the 1920s, after which the proportion steadily declined. Another even more frequent Hungarian feature was a water purifier, fitted to reduce the amount of calcium salts and other impurities in the feed water.

The 328s were distinctive in other ways. A large dome was mounted on the first boiler ring, with safety valves protruding from its sides, and large steam pipes emerged from the superheater header and descended to the steam chests above the outside cylinders. The smokebox door was conical as in some other Hungarian classes, and some other Northern and Central European types; the chimney had a flared back; and the outer front edges of the cab were angled back – efforts to reduce wind resistance and raise the exhaust, but which also helped to accentuate the engines' 'express' status and appearance. In later years (some of the class survived into the mid-1960s), some were fitted with smoke deflectors and Ister-type exhausts, and often had the water purifiers removed. The cylinders were operated by piston valves, actuated by outside Walschaerts valve gear. MÁV provided good weatherproof cabs, and that of the 328 was roomy, with a built-up tender front to improve shelter.

With the resumption of peace, international passenger services were restored in 1919 and it was again possible to travel from

Western Europe through Austria to Budapest, and south from Hungary into the newly formed Yugoslavia. Class 328 locomotives hauled these trains on the Hungarian sectors. Although it was one of the first 'native' classes of independent Hungary, engines of Class 328 did run in other countries. Seventeen of the original 100 had been diverted to France as German war reparations; these turned out to exceed the loading gauge and the French sent them to Czechoslovakia, where they became Class 375.1. It was on Czech rails that their maximum recorded speed was noted, of 120km/h (74.5mph). Eight of these were returned to MÁV in 1939. Five of the class were sent to Yugoslavia in 1943.

BOILER PRESSURE: 12kg/cm² (171psi)
CYLINDERS: 570x650mm (22.4x25.6in)
DRIVING WHEELS: 1826mm (72in)
GRATE AREA: 3.25m² (35sq ft)
HEATING SURFACE: 164.7m² (1450.2sq ft)
SUPERHEATER: 45.2m² (486.6sq ft)
TRACTIVE EFFORT: 11,760kg (25,930lb)
TOTAL WEIGHT: 69t (152,145lb)
(engine only)

CLASS 740 2-8-0 STATE RAILWAYS (FS)

Italy's universal engine, this most numerous of all Italian locomotive classes could be seen everywhere on the mainland and also worked on lines in Sicily and Sardinia. Building went on until it was 470 strong in 1923. Along with its also numerous predecessor, the North American-built Class 735 of 1917–19, this superheated two outside-cylinder simple-expansion type ran most main-line freight services. Though goods traffic over much of Italy was lightweight and sporadic, or seasonal, there were heavy trains between the major cities and in the industrial areas of Piedmont and Lombardy. The FS' policy was to recondition and rebuild steam types rather than design new ones, and as with other large classes, many adaptations were made to the 740s, especially to the draughting system, which was poor in the original design. No. 740.324 was the first locomotive ever to be fitted with Caprotti rotary cam valve gear, in 1922. Five of the class were fitted with Franco-Crosti boilers in 1942. Around 80 were still at work in 1980.

BOILER PRESSURE: 12kg/cm^2 (171psi)
CYLINDERS: 540x700mm (21.25x27.6in)
DRIVING WHEELS: 1370mm (54in)
GRATE AREA: 2.8m^2 (30sq ft)
HEATING SURFACE: 152.9m^2 (1646sq ft)
SUPERHEATER: 41.2m^2 (443.6sq ft)
TRACTIVE EFFORT: 13,424kg (29,600lb)
TOTAL WEIGHT: 66t (145,505lb)

A preserved engine of Class 740 on a passenger excursion. Trenitalia has designated seventeen survivors as historic locomotives, so it is still Italy's most numerous steam class.

MIKA I CLASS 2-8-2 KOREAN GOVERNMENT RAILWAYS (KGR)

BOILER PRESSURE: 13.4kg/cm^2 (191psi)
CYLINDERS: 584x711mm (23x28in)
DRIVING WHEELS: 1370mm (54in)
GRATE AREA: 5m^2 (53.8sq ft)
HEATING SURFACE: 337.8m^2 (3637sq ft)
SUPERHEATER: 66m^2 (710.6sq ft)
TRACTIVE EFFORT: 20,195kg (44,530lb)
TOTAL WEIGHT: 98.7t (217,677lb)
(engine only)

As industrialization developed in Korea, larger and heavier steel-framed bogie wagons were increasingly used; and by this time the need for greater tractive power had become urgent. Alco's plant in Schenectady, NY, was the first builder of this powerful freight class, though later ones were built in Japan by Shakakou, Kisha Seizo Kaisha and Kawasaki as part of a growing Japanese export industry. In design and appearance, the MIKA I class was wholly American, with bar frames, two outside cylinders and simple expansion. The class proved effective, and over 400 of successive MIKA types were built, up to MIKA 7 in 1951–52. The 2-8-2 was a standard type, and South Korea's last engines of this configuration were Chinese Sys, built up to 1994.

CLASS BE 4/6 1-B-B-1 SWISS FEDERAL RAILWAYS (SBB)

Be 4/6s (the numbers indicate four powered axles out of six) were excellent locomotives that worked passenger and express freight trains for more than 50 years, and several still remain potentially active. Following the success of the Berne–Lötschberg–Simplon scheme, the Gotthard Line through the Alps from Lucerne in Switzerland to Chiasso in Italy was an obvious case for electrification. The catenary over the 219km (136-mile) route, with its 46km (28.6 miles) of tunnels was due to be completed in May 1921, and this locomotive triumphed over two competing designs to be become the passenger engine of choice. In all, 40 were built between 1918 and 1922. The body was mounted on two power bogies, each with two coupled axles whose steam-style big wheels were driven by jackshafts. Maximum power output per hour was 1641kW (2200hp) at 60km/h (37mph). Buffers and drawgear were fitted to the bogies and not to the long, rigid body frame. Substantial and solidly built, these locomotives had to be capable of hauling 230-tonne (218-ton) trains at 60km/h (37mph) up the gradients of 1 in 38.5 that led to the 14.8km (9.25-mile) summit tunnel. The train-weight was similar to that drawn by the Gotthard locomotives, but the average train-speed was much higher, enabling both a denser traffic pattern and greater utilization of the locomotives. On heavy international expresses, the engines frequently worked in pairs. Maximum speed was 75km/h (46.6mph).

TYPE: express passenger locomotive
POWER: four 380kW (510hp) motors, in pairs, supplied by single-phase current at 15,000V 16.67Hz via overhead catenary, each pair driving a four-wheel bogie via jackshafts
TRACTIVE EFFORT: 196kN (44,080lbf)
MAX. OPERATING SPEED: 75km/h (47mph)
TOTAL WEIGHT: 106.5t (234,730lb)
MAX. AXLE LOAD: 19.25t (42,427lb)
OVERALL LENGTH: 16.5m (54ft 1in)
BUILDER: SLM, Brown Boveri

'BI-POLAR' TYPE EP-2   1-BO-DO-DO-BO-1 CHICAGO, MILWAUKEE & ST PAUL RAILROAD (CM&SP) USA 1919

For passenger traffic on the Milwaukee Road's westernmost electrification over the Washington Cascades, General Electric built five massive three-piece articulated electrics of 1-Bo-Do-Do-Bo-1 wheel arrangement. Powered by state-of-the-art, gearless two pole, or 'Bi-Polar,' motors with armatures mounted directly on the driving axles, the EP-2s featured a distinctive exterior design with a centre-cab arrangement and rounded hood

sections at both ends. For maximum speed operation, the 12 motors were connected, three in series with 1000 volts per commutator. Control connections also provided for operating four, six or 12 motors in series.

These machines were the most powerful electric locomotives of the period, and Milwaukee Road demonstrated their strength by staging a well-publicized 'tug of war' between a single Bi-Polar electric and a pair of steam

Milwaukee Road's twelve-motored E-3 on downtown display. Bells were fitted on each hood section.

locomotives – the electric pulled the two steam locomotives (which were in full forward gear) backwards. In service, they pulled trains loaded up to 1016 tonnes (1000 tons) on gradients of 1 in 50 at a speed of 40km/h (25mph). The Bi-Polar form of electric traction did not become a standard one, but the Type EP-2 worked on into the 1950s.

TYPE: 1-Bo-Do-Do-Bo-1 passenger electric
POWER: 3000V DC from overhead
TRACTIVE EFFORT: 187kN (42,000lbf) at 43km/h (27mph)
MAX. OPERATING SPEED: 112km/h (70mph)
WEIGHT: 240.4t (530,000lb)
OVERALL LENGTH: 23.164m (76ft)
MAX. AXLE LOAD: 17.5t (38,500lb)
GAUGE: 1435mm (4ft 8.5in)

CLASS 434.2 2-8-0 CZECHOSLOVAK STATE RAILWAYS (CSD)   CZECHOSLOVAKIA 1920

This class originated on the Austrian Imperial Railways as the Class 170, a two-cylinder non-superheated compound design. The CSD inherited 368 of these rugged but by then somewhat obsolescent engines, and developed them into the 434.2 class. Rebuilding was extensive, involving new boilers, superheating and simple expansion, but the operation gave the engines a power boost of the

order of 25 per cent. The entire class was rebuilt, piecemeal, with further improvements being added at various times up to 1947. The steam drier, with its pipe between two domes, was retained. Three workshops were involved in the rebuilding, Louny, Plzen and Nymburk. After 1945, 127 were fitted with Giesl ejector chimneys and rocking grates. They were used primarily on freights, with the

BOILER PRESSURE: 13kg/cm² (185psi)
CYLINDERS: 570x632mm (22.4x25in)
DRIVING WHEELS: 1308mm (51.5in)
GRATE AREA: 3.9m² (42sq ft)
HEATING SURFACE: 163m² (1755sq ft)

SUPERHEATER: 77.3m² (832.2sq ft)
TRACTIVE EFFORT: 17,370kg (38,300lb)
TOTAL WEIGHT: 69.5t (153,247lb) (engine only)

ability to haul trains of up to 1400 tonnes (1380 tons), but saw occasional passenger service as well. Withdrawals began in the 1970s, but even in 1978 some

were still in use as station pilots and on local passenger trains. Several have been preserved. Dimensions given are for the small-bore superheater version, pre-1939.

CLASS K1 2-6-0 GREAT NORTHERN RAILWAY (GNR)

GREAT BRITAIN 1920

By 1920, a new era of development had begun on British railways, and up-to-date steam designs came in a stream. This class was the first in Britain to have a boiler of 1829mm (6ft) diameter, and the resultant squat chimney enhanced its portly appearance. Intended chiefly for fast freight traffic, it had three simple-expansion cylinders, all driving the second coupled axle. The K1s were also the first locomotives to use the conjugated valve gear, for three-cylinder locomotives, developed by H. N. (later Sir Nigel) Gresley. In this system, two outside sets of Walschaerts valve gear also drive the inside cylinder by means of cross-levers placed ahead of the cylinders and linking the valves. The restricted loading

Illustrated is a later K1 class, designed by Edward Peppercorn for the LNER and built by North British Locomotive Co. in 1949; now preserved on the North Yorkshire Moors Railway.

BOILER PRESSURE: 12.6kg/cm² (180psi)
CYLINDERS: 474x666mm (18.5x26in)
DRIVING WHEELS: 1744mm (68in)
GRATE AREA: 2.6m² (28sq ft)
HEATING SURFACE: 176.5m² (1901sq ft)
SUPERHEATER: 37.8m² (407sq ft)
TRACTIVE EFFORT: 12,018kg (26,500lb)
TOTAL WEIGHT: 117.4t (258,944lb)

gauge in Britain, allowing a maximum height of 3959mm (13ft), had a constricting effect on locomotive design, making it hard to place a big boiler on big wheels, so boiler-top mountings had to be reduced. The K1, compact and solid, was a very powerful engine for its size. From 1923, the Great Northern was amalgamated into the new London & North Eastern Railway (NER), with Gresley as Chief Mechanical Engineer. K1s were now built at the former NER Darlington Works as well as at the GNR Doncaster plant. A number of further 2-6-0 types stemmed from this design, the two-cylinder K2 and the three-cylinder K3 and K4. Gresley was an advocate of three-cylinder drive, though his conjugated gear, especially in its early stages on the K1, was a problem for maintenance crews. The first engines had tenders with a capacity of 3500gals (4200 US gals), and 7.6 tonnes (7.5 tons) of coal; bigger tenders were used on later members of the class.

CLASS AE3/6 2-CO-1 SWISS FEDERAL RAILWAYS (SBB)

SWITZERLAND 1920

Electric locomotives normally had symmetrical wheel arrangements, but this class, though provided with cabs at each end, was a 2-Co-1, the unusual configuration being used in the interest of weight distribution. The traction motors were locomotive body mounted. SLM of Winterthur were the constructors, and several Swiss companies supplied electrical parts for the class, including Brown Boveri, MFO and SAAS. Built for wide availability on middle-range passenger services, the class numbered 114, and was developed into the larger Ae 4/7, 2-Do-1, still with a bogie at one end and a pony truck at the other. Five of the Ae3/6 class are preserved.

TYPE: Mainline mixed-traffic electric locomotive
WHEEL ARRANGEMENT: 2-Co-1
POWER: 15,000V 16.67Hz AC overhead line collection; 1560kW (2090hp); three body-mounted single-phase AC traction motors with Büchli flexible drives
TRACTIVE EFFORT: 147kN (33,045lbf)
MAX. OPERATING SPEED: 110km/h (69mph)
WEIGHT: 94 and 96 tonnes (205,990 and 213,920lb)
MAX. AXLE LOAD: Not known
OVERALL LENGTH: 14.7m (48ft 3in)

CLASS 12M 4-6-2 STATE RAILWAY (FCS)

ARGENTINA 1921

The Class 12Ms were built to serve a new railway, the 1675mm (5ft 6in) gauge line constructed between 1921 and 1934 to open up the Rio Negro province from Patagones to Bariloche. The 18 'Pacifics' of this class worked most of the traffic over this long but lightly trafficked route. Thirteen were built by Maffei in Germany, four by Cockerill and one by Haine St Pierre, both of Belgium. Two-cylinder simples with bar frames and boiler-top sandboxes, they worked along this line for over 30 years. The best

BOILER PRESSURE: 12kg/cm² (170psi)
CYLINDERS: 500x629mm (19.7x24.8in)
DRIVING WHEELS: 1599mm (63in)
GRATE AREA: 3m² (32.3sq ft)
HEATING SURFACE: 215.3m² (2319sq ft)
SUPERHEATER: not known
TRACTIVE EFFORT: 9433kg (20,800lb)
TOTAL WEIGHT: 123.9t (273,280lb)

timing over the 827km (514-mile) route was 22 hours. They were withdrawn with the introduction of diesel traction in 1953.

CLASS 940 2-8-2T STATE RAILWAYS (FS)

ITALY 1921

A tank version of the 2-8-0 Class 740, and of the same specifications, this was a relatively small class, intended for short-range working in mountain areas. The long side tanks slope forwards to reduce water movement and to improve forward vision. Four of the locomotives were built by Officine Meccaniche, Milan, and 46 in Naples and Reggio Emilia, all for the FS. A further three were produced for the independent Santhia–Biella Railway. It is testament to their quality that some Class 940 engines remained

BOILER PRESSURE: 12kg/cm² (170psi)
CYLINDERS: 540x700mm (21.25x27.5in)
DRIVING WHEELS: 1370mm (54in)
GRATE AREA: 2.8m² (30.1sq ft)
HEATING SURFACE: 152.9m² (1646sq ft)
SUPERHEATER: 41.2m² (443sq ft)
TRACTIVE EFFORT: 15,065kg (33,220lb)
TOTAL WEIGHT: 87t (192,464lb)

in service around Como and Sulmona into the early 1980s. The first engine, No. 940.001, is preserved at Milan.

CLASS 31B 4-8-0 NORWEGIAN STATE RAILWAYS (NSB)

The 4-8-0 type, not a widely used one, seemed appropriate for Norwegian conditions, and the Swiss builders SLM of Winterthur had supplied Norway's first 4-8-0s in 1910 (Class 26). This four-cylinder compound class was the NSB's largest and heaviest 4-8-0, built primarily for passenger service on the trunk line between Oslo and Bergen. Despite the weight, the maximum axle load was 14 tonnes (13.8 tons). Twenty-seven were built between 1921 and 1926. The cylinders were in line, low-pressure outside, and all drove the second coupled axle. Piston valves were actuated by Walschaerts gear. Interestingly, four simple-expansion predecessors of this class had been built in 1915–21, but the combination of compounding plus superheating was chosen for the production run. The class remained in service until the phasing-out of Norwegian steam in the later 1960s.

BOILER PRESSURE: 16kg/cm² (228psi)
CYLINDERS: hp 420x600mm (16.5x23.6in); lp 630x600mm (24.8x23.6in)
DRIVING WHEELS: 1350mm (53in)
GRATE AREA: 3m² (32.29sq ft)
HEATING SURFACE: 166m² (1788sq ft)
SUPERHEATER: 45.5m² (489sq ft)
TRACTIVE EFFORT: not known
TOTAL WEIGHT: 118t (260,631lb)

CLASS S 2-8-0 CENTRAL RAILWAY OF URUGUAY (CUR)

As elsewhere in South America, the small-wheeled, powerful but flexible 2-8-0 was the standard freight locomotive of this line. This class, of British-style design with a Belpaire firebox, was unusual in possessing three cylinders, all simple expansion. Hawthorn Leslie of Newcastle on Tyne, England, were the builders. The early 1920s were the pre-Depression heyday of the Uruguayan railways, when freight traffic was substantial and still growing, and trains the chief means of conveyance, with cattle and agricultural products brought from the interior to the docks at Montevideo. One of the Class S is preserved at the Peñarol roundhouse.

No. 139 of Class S makes a display run with a freight train. Now preserved, the engine may be restored to working order.

BOILER PRESSURE: 12.6kg/cm² (180psi)
CYLINDERS: 431.5x660mm (17x26in)
DRIVING WHEELS: 1523mm (60in)
GRATE AREA: 1.8m² (19.5sq ft)
HEATING SURFACE: 133.7m² (1440sq ft)
SUPERHEATER: not known
TRACTIVE EFFORT: 8690kg (19,160lb)
TOTAL WEIGHT: not known

CLASS K 2-8-0 VICTORIAN RAILWAYS (VR)

A shortage of freight power in 1919 prompted the Victorian Railways to order a new light freight locomotive, but it was three years before the K class took to the rails. Often such delays in Australia were created by British builders, but the first 10 were built at the VR's own Newport shops. Traffic demands often seemed to take railway managements by surprise. However, since they had to rely on past statistics to project future trends, and also as it might take at least a year for a new locomotive type to progress from drawing board to actuality, they should not be blamed too harshly. Between 1940 and 1946, the class was enlarged with another 43 engines. The Ks were sturdy, reliable two-cylinder simple engines with Belpaire fireboxes, and though the boiler pressure was relatively low, they were very free steamers. They were Intended for freight, but they often ran in passenger service. Withdrawal of the class began in 1958, but nevertheless at least 12 remained in service in 1972, mostly on station pilot duty. Several are preserved.

BOILER PRESSURE: 12.25kg/cm² (175lb)
CYLINDERS: 508x660mm (20x26in)
DRIVING WHEELS: 1397mm (55in)
GRATE AREA: 2.4m² (25.75sq ft)
HEATING SURFACE: 134.4m² (1447sq ft)
SUPERHEATER: 26m² (281sq ft)
TRACTIVE EFFORT: 12,756kg (28,127lb)
TOTAL WEIGHT: 104.6t (230,643lb)

CLASS P10 2-8-2 ROYAL PRUSSIAN UNION RAILWAYS (KPEV)

GERMANY 1922

Coming into service just before the railways of the old German states were combined into the *Deutsche Reichsbahn Gesellschaft* (DRG), this three-cylinder express 'Mikado' locomotive ran on several provincial lines as well as the parent KPEV. All three cylinders drove the second coupled axle. On

the DRG it became Class 39. Eighty-five were built, and after 1945, all were inherited by the East German *Deutsche Reichsbahn*. From 1958 to 1962, they were among the classes rebuilt as Rekoloks ('reconstructed locos'); the renovation was on a substantial scale, with the engines ending up

longer and larger, and fitted with Russian Trofimov piston valves. In

this form (Class 22), they worked up to the early 1970s.

TYPE: 2-B-2 experimental prototype diesel
POWER: 883kW (1184hp) from Sulzer engine
TRACTIVE EFFORT: 100kN (22680lbf)

MAX. OPERATING SPEED: 100km/h (62.1mph)
WEIGHT: 95t (209,475lb)
OVERALL LENGTH: 16.6m (54ft 5in)
GAUGE: 1435mm (4ft 8.5in)

CLASS A1 4-6-2 GREAT NORTHERN RAILWAY (GNR)

GREAT BRITAIN 1922

At the end of 1922, the Chief Mechanical Engineer of the GNR, H. N. Gresley, found himself in charge of locomotives for four of the larger old companies and several smaller ones, all incorporated in the London & North Eastern Railway (LNER). His first 'Pacific' design, still very new, became the LNER's standard heavy express engine. Though it had numerous initial problems and flaws, it was essentially a fast, free-steaming locomotive, with a wide firebox that could make plenty of steam for the big boiler,

whose pressure was not particularly high for an express engine of the time. With double the power output of the 'Atlantics' that preceded it, it marked a great leap forward.

Built at the GNR's Doncaster Plant, it was a handsome, fluid-lined engine that set the basic look of LNER 'Pacifics' – except the A4 streamliners – for 25 years. It showed Gresley's qualities as a stylist as well as his limitations in failing to modify design defects. Using the conjugated valve gear first employed on the K1 2-6-0 of

1920, which gave frequent problems, three simple-expansion cylinders drove the second coupled wheels. Other details also gave trouble. The engines were prone to wheel-slipping on starting, and some working parts were very difficult or impossible to access without lifting the boiler off the frame. Comparisons made in 1925 with a Great Western 'Castle' 4-6-0 showed that the smaller and less expensive GWR engine could match the 'Pacific' and also use less fuel. Action was taken, resulting in a lengthening of valve travel and lap and substantial modification of the Walschaerts valve gear, and the provision of equalizing levers between the rear

driving axle and the pony wheel axle. By 1926, the valve gear problems were resolved and performance of the A1s improved dramatically. In 1928, an improved and slightly heavier version, the LNER's Class A3, with a boiler pressure of 225psi (15.75kg/cm²), was introduced and could be reasonably called Britain's 'Super-

BOILER PRESSURE: 12.6kg/cm² (180psi)
CYLINDERS: 508x660mm (20x26in)
DRIVING WHEELS: 2032mm (80in)
GRATE AREA: 3.8m² (41.25sq ft)
HEATING SURFACE: 272m² (2930sq ft)
SUPERHEATER: 49m² (525sq ft)
TRACTIVE EFFORT: 13,333kg (29,385lb)
TOTAL WEIGHT: 151t (332,000lb)

Preserved LNER 'Pacific' No. 4472 *Flying Scotsman* passes through the Oxfordshire countryside with a special charter train for Stratford on Avon, in 1993.

Pacific', capable of running non-stop between London and Edinburgh (632km/392.7 miles); in 1928, this was the longest non-stop run in the world. Some engines were fitted with a corridor-tender to enable a half-way crew change. On numerous occasions,

there was virtually nothing left in the 8.13-tonne (8-ton) coal bunker in the tender on arrival at the terminus. An A3 was the first British locomotive to definitively exceed the 162km/h (100mph) mark, with 174km/h (108mph) in 1935, and very fast running was

an everyday occurrence. The A4 streamliners took over some express services from 1935, but in practice the A3s and A4s were interchangeable.

Perhaps the most celebrated member of the original Class A1 – though like most others it was

later rebuilt as an A3 – was the still-preserved *Flying Scotsman*, No. 4472. All the Gresley 'Pacifics' bore names, mostly of famous racehorses, which suited them very well.

The last operating A3 was withdrawn at the end of 1965.

4-6-2 NORTH EASTERN RAILWAY (NER)

Produced simultaneously with Gresley's GNR 'Pacific', the two types became rivals when the NER and GNR merged with other railways to form the LNER. The NER Darlington-built version, designed under the auspices of Sir Vincent

Raven, was a three-cylinder simple, all cylinders driving the first coupled axle, and with a boiler so long that crewmen called it the 'skittle alley'. Five were built, but unfavourable comparisons with the A1s – and Gresley's position as

BOILER PRESSURE: 14kg/cm² (200psi)		**HEATING SURFACE:** 225m² (2422.2sq ft)	
CYLINDERS: 482x660mm (19x26in)		**SUPERHEATER:** 36.75m² (695.6sq ft)	
DRIVING WHEELS: 2032mm (80in)		**TRACTIVE EFFORT:** 9045kg (19,945lb)	
GRATE AREA: 3.8m² (41sq ft)		**TOTAL WEIGHT:** 98.5t (217,280lb)	

LNER Class A2 No. 2400 *City of Newcastle* was known as 'skittle alleys'.

chief mechanical engineer – meant that the NER design was taken no further. The Raven 'Pacifics' worked

on express trains, mostly to Leeds, but the class had a relatively short life in service.

BO-BO METROPOLITAN RAILWAY (METR)

The Metropolitan Railway extended well out of London, and this 20-strong class ran its 'main-line' outer commuter services for almost four decades. Two were conversions of the Metropolitan's 598.6kW (800hp) electrics Nos. 6 & 17; the rest were built new by Vickers of Barrow-in-Furness, with

electrical equipment from Metropolitan-Vickers, the first being delivered in 1922. Fifteen were extensively refurbished in the 1950s, when the Metrovick controllers and electrical equipment were replaced by British Thomson-Houston control equipment. After replacement by electric multiple-unit

TYPE: suburban passenger locomotive		**MAX. OPERATING SPEED:** 104.5km/h (65mph)	
POWER: 600V DC, four Metropolitan Vickers MV 339 self-ventilated traction motors, one per axle, 895.2 kW (1200hp)		**WEIGHT:** 62.18t (137,087lb)	
		OVERALL LENGTH: 12.04m (39ft 6in)	
TRACTIVE EFFORT: 100kN (22,600lbf)		**GAUGE:** 1435mm (4ft 8.5in)	

sets in 1961, some locomotives remained in departmental use and

for shunting work in the car sheds, and two survive in preservation.

2-CO-2 NORTH EASTERN RAILWAY (NER) GREAT BRITAIN 1922

The NER flirted more heavily with electric traction than any other British pre-grouping company, and in 1922 its Chief Mechanical Engineer, Sir Vincent Raven, oversaw the design and construction at the Darlington Works of a high-speed electric locomotive. Given the number 13, it was part of the preliminary trials and tests for the planned overhead-wire electrification of the York to Newcastle main line. Two motors of twin-armature type powered each driving axle through quill drives. Each developed 220kW (300hp) and could be connected in series, or in two or three parallel groups. Boxy and solid, with very poor front look-out, the engine worked on test on the Shildon to Newport electrified line, and satisfactorily started trains of 457.2 tonnes (450 tons) on a gradient of 1 in 78 and hauled it on level track at a steady 104.6km/h (65mph). Electrification of the main line did not take place (it had to wait 70 years until the 1990s), and No. 13 was put in store at Darlington, seeing the light of day for only occasional test trips and exhibitions. It was finally scrapped in August 1950.

POWER: 1500V DC overhead, six Metropolitan-Vickers traction motors, 1343kW (1800hp)
TRACTIVE EFFORT: 125kN (28,000lbf)
MAX. operating speed: 145km/h (90mph)
WEIGHT: 104t (228,480lb)
OVERALL LENGTH: 16.307m (53ft 6in)
GAUGE: 1435mm (4ft 8.5in)

CLASS E10 0-10-0T STATE RAILWAYS SUMATRA (SSS) DUTCH EAST INDIES (INDONESIA) 1922

Nineteen of the E10 class (later E101) built by Esslingen in Germany went to Sumatra to work the very steep, part-rack 1065mm (3ft 6in) gauge coal-hauling line from the port of Padang into the interior. They were four-cylinder compounds, superheated, with external valve gear. The inside cylinders drove the wheels that engaged on the central rack rail. Between 1964 and 1967, a further 16 were built, as Class E102: 10 from Esslingen and six from Nippon Sharyo in Japan. Mechanically the new engines were very similar to those of 1920s vintage, though with some significant modifications, including Giesl ejectors and chimneys. These were the last rack and adhesion steam locomotives to be built for regular service. Dimensions given are of the original engines.

TYPE: 1-C-1 three-phase electric
POWER: 2000kW (2717hp)
SUPPLY: 3300V 16.2/3Hz AC two-wire three-phase
TRACTIVE EFFORT: 93kN (20900lbf) at 104km.h (65mph)
MAX. OPERATING SPEED: 100km/h (62.1mph)
WEIGHT: 74t (163,170lb)
MAX. AXLE LOAD: 17t (37,485lb)
OVERALL LENGTH: 11.008m (35ft 11in)
GAUGE: 1435mm (4ft 8.5in)

With sandbox cap askew, No. E101.6 gives a good impression of the rugged build of these locomotives, designed for operating on one of the world's most challenging lines.

CLASS 741 2-8-0 STATE RAILWAYS (FS)

Class 741 originally comprised five members of Class 740 of 1918, fitted experimentally with Caprotti valve gear. Arturo Caprotti had trained as an automobile engineer, and brought his knowledge of the internal combustion engine to bear on the steam locomotive. In 1915, he produced a prototype of a valve gear in which vertically set poppet valves were operated by a rotating cam, which took its own motion from a gear set in a return crank on one of the coupled axles. Poppet valves were lighter, tighter, and controlled inlet and outlet ports separately: all useful benefits. They also promised more effective use of steam. But there were also problems in making the Caprotti system fully effective. The cam gear and the valve action did not always work properly, and the results were a mixture of promise and unreliability.

Ultimately the five Class 741 locomotives were restored to Class 740, but the FS did not give up interest in this Italian invention, and further work would go on to try to perfect the Caprotti gear. Other railways also showed interest, and Britain, France and Germany were among the countries that experimented with Caprotti gear, as well as other means of operating poppet valves. The Class 741 designation would be resurrected in the 1950s, for a different sort of modification (see 1955).

BOILER PRESSURE: 12kg/cm² (171psi)
CYLINDERS: 540x700mm (21.25x27.6in)
DRIVING WHEELS: 1370mm (54in)
GRATE AREA: 2.8m² (30sq ft)
HEATING SURFACE: 112.6m² (1212sq ft)
SUPERHEATER: 44m² (473sq ft)
TRACTIVE EFFORT: 14,700kg (29,767lb)
TOTAL WEIGHT: 68.3t (150,600lb)

No. 740 188 on a freight near Belluno in the Dolomites. More than 400 of this class were built, and more of it are preserved than of any other Italian locomotive type. The lead vehicle is a brake van.

CLASS OK-22 4-6-0 POLISH STATE RAILWAYS (PKP)

POLAND 1922

Polish railways ran on the European standard gauge, and Polish locomotive design was strongly influenced by Germany. The Prussian P-8 4-6-0 was the basic model for the PKP's first passenger type. Five were built by Hanomag in Hannover, with a larger and higher-set boiler than the P8 but riding on a P8-type frame and wheels. A further 185 were built by the Polish Chrzanov works between 1928 and 1934. Until the advent of the Po-29 4-8-2 and the Pt-31 2-8-2, in 1930 and 1932 respectively, the Ok-22s ran all types of passenger service, but from 1932 they were employed largely on secondary services and stopping trains. Some were still in active use up to the mid-1960s.

BOILER PRESSURE: 12kg/cm² (171psi)
CYLINDERS: 575x630mm (22.6x24.8in)
DRIVING WHEELS: 1750mm (69in)
GRATE AREA: 4m² (43sq ft)
HEATING SURFACE: 182.1m² (1960.6sq ft)
SUPERHEATER: 61.6m² (663.2sq ft)
TRACTIVE EFFORT: 12,100kg (26,680lb)
TOTAL WEIGHT: 78.9t (173,974lb)
(engine only)

Two of Class Ok22 are preserved, and No.31 is still operational. It ran until 1997, and after retirement was a static display loco until 2004, when it was restored.

CLASS 8E 2-6-4T BUENOS AIRES GREAT SOUTHERN RAILWAY (BAGS)

ARGENTINA 1923

The city of Buenos Aires had grown greatly in the early twentieh century, and population density along the Plate estuary grew at a similar rate. The demand for more intensive suburban services was catered for in the early 1920s, when the BAGS developed commuter traffic to the capital, remodelling and enlarging its terminus at Plaza Constitution, and quadruple-tracking the 1675mm (5ft 6in) gauge main line out for 18.5km (11.5 miles). The new motive power was supplied by 61 of this three-cylinder simple

expansion tank engine built at the Vulcan Foundry works, of Newton-le-Willows. The rear tank held 1953 gals (2343 US gals) of water, and the short side bunkers had a capacity for 4.1 tonnes (4 tons) of coal, though the whole class was also fitted for oil burning.

Built for quick acceleration and braking, the Class E turned in smart performances on the suburban lines. The illustration shows it in the livery of the Ferrocarril del Sud.

BOILER PRESSURE: 14kg/cm² (200psi)
CYLINDERS: 444x660mm (17.5x26in)
DRIVING WHEELS: 1726mm (68in)
GRATE AREA: 2.3m² (25sq ft)
HEATING SURFACE: 113.6m² (1223sq ft)
SUPERHEATER: 28m² (302sq ft)
TRACTIVE EFFORT: 29,859lb (kg)
TOTAL WEIGHT: 102.6t (226,240lb)

CLASS 231C 4-6-2 NORTHERN RAILWAY (NORD)

FRANCE 1923

Known for a time as the 'Super-Pacifics', the first 40 of these locomotives were built at the Blanc-Misseron shops at Lille. They had Belpaire boilers, but did not take advantage of the Pacific's ability to carry a wide firebox; theirs was narrow and entirely between the frames. Compound, semi-compound, or simple

working were all possible, depending on how the driver chose to admit steam to the cylinders. Two were built as two-cylinder simples in experiments with Caprotti and Dabeg valve gear. Later modifications to the class, eventually 86 strong, included the fitting of Lemaître blastpipes and chimneys, the

raising of the running plate, and the addition of smoke deflectors. Although a reliable class, its

'super' designation was lost with the arrival on the *Nord* of Chapelon Pacifics.

BOILER PRESSURE: 16kg/cm² (227psi)
CYLINDERS: hp 440x660mm (17.6x26in); lp 620x690mm (24.4x27.2in)
DRIVING WHEELS: 1700mm (74.9in)
GRATE AREA: 3.5m² (37.5sq ft)
HEATING SURFACE: 249m² (2680sq ft)
SUPERHEATER: 57m² (616sq ft)
TRACTIVE EFFORT: N/A
TOTAL WEIGHT: 160t (353,000lb)

'CASTLE' CLASS 4-6-0 GREAT WESTERN RAILWAY (GWR)

GREAT BRITAIN 1923

The first modern GWR express engine was the 'Star' class of 1907, with four cylinders, simple expansion, and internal Walschaerts valve gear, and which set the pattern for refinements to come. But the 'Castle', designed under G. J. Churchward's successor, J. B. Collett, was not just a bigger and better Star: it had a completely new taper boiler (No. 8). The detailed precision work continued in the Swindon works on the application of valves and valve gear paid off, too, as did the

combination of improved track and better understanding of the stress imposed by the 'hammer-blow' of reciprocating motion on the rails. The Castles ran smoothly, fast and economically, and with a short cut-off of steam entering the cylinders, the capacity for expansion was given full opportunity, thus conserving steam, water and coal. Collett was able to announce that the new engines consumed 1.25kg (2.83lb) of coal per drawbar-horsepower hour. At this time, the average for express locomotives

was in excess of 1.7kg (4lb). A saving of this order, plus the other abilities of the Castles, was remarkable, and they aroused intense interest among other British companies and set a benchmark for performance against which new engines of the LMS and LNER were tested during 1925–26.

The class eventually numbered 171, including 15 that were rebuilds of earlier 4-6-0 types, and it was the standard locomotive for fast passenger services throughout the GWR system. Castles pulled the 'Cheltenham Flyer', a lightweight express that was the world's

fastest scheduled steam service for a time in the early 1930s. But they also hauled such heavy trains as the 'Cornish Riviera Express', loading up to 15 coaches between Paddington (London) and Plymouth. The final member of the class was built at Swindon as late

BOILER PRESSURE: 15.75kg/cm² (225psi)
CYLINDERS: 406x660mm (16x26in)
DRIVING WHEELS: 2045mm (80.5in)
GRATE AREA: 2.8m² (30.3sq ft)
HEATING SURFACE: 190.4m² (2049.3sq ft)
SUPERHEATER: 30m² (324 sq ft)
TRACTIVE EFFORT: 14,285kg (31,500lb)
TOTAL WEIGHT: 81.1t (178,864lb)

Preserved No. 5053 *Drysllwyn Castle* on a special charter train, the 'Welsh Marches Pullman', at Newport, South Wales, on 16 April 1983.

as 1950, when the oldest ones were almost 30 years old – more in the case of those which were rebuilds, including the rebuild of the GWR's sole 'Pacific', *The Great Bear* of 1908. Between 1957 and

1960, a number of the class were given double chimneys and larger superheaters, which further enhanced their performance, but withdrawal began in 1962 and was complete by 1965.

Seven have been preserved, including the first one, No. 4073 *Caerphilly Castle*. As a general judgement on the class, one expert commentator wrote of them as, 'one of the major triumphs in

British locomotive history. In power-for-size, speed, and economy of fuel, they set standards that were unequalled for about 20 years and barely surpassed at all.

BO-BO CLASS EO NEW ZEALAND RAILWAYS (NZR) NEW ZEALAND 1923

New Zealand's first electric locomotives worked on the then newly electrified summit section of the steeply graded South Island Christchurch–Greymouth line between Arthur's Pass and Otira. English Electric supplied the five EOs. Train weights were limited to a maximum of 127 tonnes (125 tons) going uphill, and three forms of brake: Westinghouse

TYPE: heavy-duty mixed-traffic locomotive
POWER: four motors with a one-hour rating of 133.6kW (179hp) at 750V, sup-

plied by 1500V DC via overhead catenary
TRACTIVE EFFORT: 63kN (14,166lb)
MAX. OPERATING SPEED: 58km/h (36mph)

TOTAL WEIGHT: 55.3t (121,936lb)
MAX. AXLE LOAD: 13.8t (30,429lb)
OVERALL LENGTH: 11.7m (38ft 4in)
BUILDER: English Electric, Great Britain

automatic and air brakes and a locomotive hand-brake were fitted. From 1942, they were deployed as a multiple-unit set of three, with one acting as stand-by and another

undergoing servicing, and were partially rebuilt, with a driving cab at one end only. They were finally displaced in 1968 by the Toshiba-built EA class. Four were broken up

at Christchurch in 1969. The electrified line's catenary was dismantled in 1998, in favour of diesel working, but No. E.03 is preserved in running order.

CLASS O1 2-6-2 SERBIAN, CROATIAN & SLOVENIAN RAILWAYS (SHS) YUGOSLAVIA 1923

These German-built engines were designed in 1912 but delivered more than 10 years later, after World War I, to the SHS, which after 1928 became the main element of Yugoslav State Railways (JDZ). There were 126 in the class. Four-cylinder compound and simple versions of almost identical appearance had been built in 1912–13, both with outside Walschaerts gear and piston valves, operating both cylinders on each side. They were used for main-line passenger services between Belgrade and major provincial cities.

BOILER PRESSURE: 12kg/cm² (171psi)
CYLINDERS: 410x650mm (16x25.6in)
DRIVING WHEELS: 1850mm (73in)
GRATE AREA: 3m² (32.3sq ft)
HEATING SURFACE: 126.5m² (1362sq ft)
SUPERHEATER: 38.6m² (415.6sq ft)
TRACTIVE EFFORT: 6444kg (13,000lb)
TOTAL WEIGHT: 67t (147,735lb) (engine only)

The Serbian Railways shared the Central European enthusiasm for 2-6-2 locomotives, more common here than anywhere else. This is simple-expansion No. 75, of the Yugoslav State Railways.

1400 CLASS 2-8-2 MISSOURI PACIFIC RAILROAD (MOPAC) USA 1923

The 'Mikado' type had come some way from the fairly modest machine built by Baldwin for Japan in 1897. The first big 2-8-2s were constructed for the Northern Pacific by Alco in 1904. NP's motive power department wanted an engine with the same adhesion as a heavy 2-8-0, but

with more power. This required a bigger firebox than was possible with a Consolidation, and so eight coupled wheels with a rear truck were employed, with a big, wide firebox that sat behind the rear driving wheels. The firebox was supported by the two-wheel trailing truck, thereby creating the

2-8-2 wheel arrangement. The NP engines were put to work on the eastern end of the Yellowstone Division, between Mandan, ND, and Glendive, MT (later the stamping ground of the 2-8-8-4 Yellowstones'). This 348km (216-mile) section had a series of long 1.1 percent grades in both

BOILER PRESSURE: 14kg/cm² (200psi)
CYLINDERS: 685x812mm (27x32in)
DRIVING WHEELS: 1599mm (63in)
GRATE AREA: 6.2m² (66.7sq ft)
HEATING SURFACE: 369.6m² (3900sq ft)
SUPERHEATER: 97.6m² (1051sq ft)
TRACTIVE EFFORT: 28,548kg (62,950lb)
TOTAL WEIGHT: 138.4t (305,115lb)

directions, and frequently served as the proving ground for new motive power. Northern Pacific eventually owned 386 2-8-2s.

By 1920, the 'Mikado' had become the standard freight engine in America, and it was being continuously updated with new technology and modern appliances, including mechanical stokers,

superheaters, combustion chambers, thermic syphons, feedwater heaters, modern outside radial valve gear, and more. The MoPac 1400 class was typical, built by Alco, with the drive on the third set of coupled wheels, and a slightly tapered round-top boiler. About half of the class were fitted with steam boosters to the trailing

wheels, adding a tractive effort of 2029kg (4475lb) on starting. Originally invented in France as a booster to the tender wheels, the booster engine was a frequent add-on to American freight locomotives, to help them overcome the inertia of a huge load on starting, or at low speed on gradients. The 1400s, 171 in number, were a standard

freight type on the MoPac until the end of steam, working virtually every kind of freight service. Most were coal burners, though some were oil-fired. The bogie tenders had a brakeman's cabin built over the water tank. They survived in large numbers into the 1950s, by which time pick-up freights and yard duties were their main tasks.

CLASS M1 4-8-2 PENNSYLVANIA RAILROAD (PRR)　　　　　　USA 1923

The 'Mountain' was the type-name of the 4-8-2, and the first of the breed was built in 1911 by Alco, at Schenectady, NY, for the Chesapeake & Ohio Railway. At the time it was claimed as the most powerful non-articulated engine in the world, and the design was recognized as valuable where adhesion and tractive power were needed as well as speed. In 1918, it was one of eight standard types designated by the wartime US

Railroad Administration, and many were built for lines with mountain sections. The PRR built its first as a test engine, at its workshops in Altoona, and 200 others of Class M1 followed. Following typical US practice, it was a two-cylinder simple, with Walschaerts valve gear operating piston valves. The boiler tapered up from 2144mm (84.5in) behind the chimney to 2436mm (96in) and, Pennsylvania-style, there was a long Belpaire firebox,

supplied in this case by duplex automatic stokers. The running plate was stepped up to accommodate the air compressor equipment.

On these locomotives, braking power was as vital a feature as traction, as they negotiated the long descents with trains of 140 coal hopper cars loading up to 4776 tonnes (4700 tons). On the PRR test-bed, engine 6706 recorded a maximum power of 4662hp (3428kW) in 1931. The M1 was very much a freight engine, though also used on passenger trains between Pittsburgh and Altoona. On many other lines, the

4-82 was regularly used for express heavy passenger trains. Until the end of the 1920s, the 4-8-2 remained a popular type in the USA and Canada – after that most lines took up the 4-8-4, with its capacity for an even bigger firebox. The M1s were withdrawn in 1950.

BOILER PRESSURE: 17.5kg/cm² (250lb)
CYLINDERS: 685x761mm (27x30in)
DRIVING WHEELS: 1827mm (72in)
GRATE AREA: 6.2m² (66.8sq ft)
HEATING SURFACE: 379m² (4087sq ft)
SUPERHEATER: 97.6m² (1051sq ft)
TRACTIVE EFFORT: 29,274kg (64,550lb)
TOTAL WEIGHT: 254t (560,000lb)

The Pennsylvania Railroad did things in its own way, usually with good results. Careful testing before series construction was standard policy, and the PRR had its own test plant at Altoona.

CLASS 11C 4-8-0 BUENOS AIRES GREAT SOUTHERN RAILWAY (BAGS)　　　ARGENTINA 1924

Confidence was high on the various Argentinian railways in the 1920s, and many new locomotive types were ordered, including this, the country's first 4-8-0: a three-cylinder simple, it was one of the heaviest and most powerful engines to run on the country's 1675mm (5ft 6in) gauge. Seventy-five were built between

1924 and 1929, by Armstrong Whitworth in Newcastle and Beyer-Peacock in Manchester; all were oil-fired. Feed-water heaters and pumps were fitted to 40 of them, but later removed because of maintenance difficulties. These engines could handle 2032-tonne (2000-ton) trains over the level plains and their 16.2-tonne

BOILER PRESSURE: 14kg/cm² (200psi)
CYLINDERS: 444x660mm (17.5x26 in)
DRIVING WHEELS: 1434mm (56.5in)
GRATE AREA: 2.7m² (29.3sq ft)
HEATING SURFACE: 213.3m² (2297sq ft)

(16-ton) axle load gave good route availability. Worn out by the 1950s, they were overhauled by

SUPERHEATER: not known
TRACTIVE EFFORT: 15,600kg (34,400lb)
TOTAL WEIGHT: 85.3t (188,160lb)
(engine only)

the ASTARSA company in 1957, and were still in operation a decade later.

CLASS 1080/1180 E FEDERAL RAILWAYS OF AUSTRIA (BBÖ)

AUSTRIA 1924

Planning of Austria's programme of main-line electrification began in 1920, and the first to be converted was the Arlberg line, between 1925 and 1927, using local hydro-electric power for the Innsbruck–Bludenz–Bregenz to Buchen, St. Margrethen and Lindau route. Several designs of electric locomotive evolved, with Class 1080 dating from 1924/25, and the 1180s, of increased power output, from 1926/27. Intended to work on the mountain sections, all were built by Krauss-Maffei in Munich, with Siemens electrical equipment. They had a heavy, rigid five-axle layout based on steam locomotive designs, but proved to be great survivors, with some of the class lasting into the early 1990s on pilot and transfer work.

Electric ten-wheeler – a class 1080 still in service as a carriage shunter in the 1990s.

TYPE: E, freight	**MAX. OPERATING SPEED:** 50km/h (31.3mph)
POWER: 1080 – 1020kW (1386hp); 1180 – 1300kW (1766kW)	**WEIGHT:** 1080 – 77t (169,785lb); 1180 – 80.5t (177,503lb)
SUPPLY: 15kV 16.2/3Hz AC	**MAX. AXLE LOAD:** 20t (44,100lb)
TRACTIVE EFFORT: 1080 – 189kN (42,525lbf); 1180 – 197kN (44,325lbf)	**OVERALL LENGTH:** 12.75m (41ft 7in)
	GAUGE: 1435mm (4ft 8.5in)

CLASS S 2-6-4T DANISH STATE RAILWAYS (DSB)

DENMARK 1924

Though it was designed in Berlin by Borsig, they built only the first two of this big three-cylinder simple-expansion suburban tank engine; and the other 18 in the class were built in Denmark by Frichs of Aarhus. They worked the busy suburban lines in the Copenhagen area, and to conserve water supplies, and help maintain a steady boiler temperature, always a problem in frequent stop-start working, condensing apparatus was fitted, with exhaust steam passing into the side tanks, and a feedwater pump was attached on the left side. Smoke deflectors were fitted in the

BOILER PRESSURE: 12cm² (171psi)	**HEATING SURFACE:** 118.1m² (1272sq ft)
CYLINDERS: 431x672.5mm (17x26.5in)	**SUPERHEATER:** 45.9m² (495sq ft)
DRIVING WHEELS: 1726mm (68in)	**TRACTIVE EFFORT:** N/A
GRATE AREA: 2.4m² (25.8sq ft)	**TOTAL WEIGHT:** 100.1t (220,864)

1930s. After electrification of the busiest suburban lines, the class was re-deployed on longer-distance passenger trains until the early 1960s, with the coal capacity increased to 4.1 tonnes (4 tons).

CLASS EP5 2-B-B-2 GERMAN STATE RAILWAYS (DRG)

GERMANY 1924

While developing a standard steam range, the *Reichsbahn* engineers under Richard Wagner also identified certain lines for electrification, and Class EP5 was introduced for the Bavarian mountain lines. Four body-mounted traction motors were set in pairs driving jackshafts, a design that made it possible for smaller, more lightweight motors in comparison with the larger single machines of contemporary locomotives. Cabs were fitted at each end of the body, which was set on steam-size 1400mm (55in) diameter driving wheels. Constructed by Maffei and WASSEG (a joint venture by Siemens-Schukert and AEG) the class was

TYPE: 2B-B2 heavy passenger	**WEIGHT:** 140 tonnes (308,700lb)
POWER: 1660kW (2255hp)	**MAX. AXLE LOAD:** 19.6t (43,218lb)
SUPPLY: 15kV 16.2/3Hz AC	**OVERALL LENGTH:** 17.21m (56ft 2in)
TRACTIVE EFFORT: 78kN (17600lbf)	**GAUGE:** 1435mm (4ft 8.5in)
MAX. OPERATING SPEED: 90km/h (56.3mph)	

delivered as EP5 21 501 to 535, becoming E52 01 to 35 in 1927.

Twenty-eight examples surviving after 1945 became DB Class 152.

CLASS 424 4-8-0 HUNGARIAN STATE RAILWAYS (MÁV)

Construction of this class continued over 34 years, up to 1958. All came from the Budapest Locomotive Works. It had a slow start, with only 27 built up to 1929, and then a long pause until 1940, when building recommenced. Eventually it numbered around 365. The locomotives were two-cylinder compounds for mixed traffic working, with simple expansion and none of what one

commentator called 'exotic features'. As a result, they looked more German than Hungarian, especially the later examples carrying large smoke deflectors, and with Ister double blast pipes and chimneys (similar to the Giesl model). The base of the firegrate was above the coupled wheels, resulting in a high-set boiler. The

third dome contained water-purifying apparatus, not a frill as far as work in Hungary was concerned. Until the termination of steam on the MÁV, these were the most frequently seen engines, their work pattern involving passenger and freight work, handling both fast expresses and pick-up freights.

BOILER PRESSURE: 13kg/cm² (185psi)
CYLINDERS: 600x660mm (23.6x26in)
DRIVING WHEELS: 1606mm (63.25in)
GRATE AREA: 4.45m² (47.9sq ft)
HEATING SURFACE: 162.6m² (1750sq ft)
SUPERHEATER: 58m² (624.5sq ft)
TRACTIVE EFFORT: 16,325kg (36,000lb)
TOTAL WEIGHT: 83.2t (183,456lb)
(engine only)

Preserved Class 424 No. 247 leaves Budapest Nyugati station. Two members of the class are still kept in working order for steam specials.

DIESEL 1-E-1 SOVIET STATE RAILWAYS (SZD)

Russia's academically trained locomotive engineers, headed by G. V. Lomonosov (professor of railway engineering at Kiev and later St Petersburg, and for a time Director-General of the Russian Railways) took a close interest in the diesel engine and its potential for rail traction. In 1922, Lenin himself authorized the contemporary equivalent of £100,000 for the construction of three prototype diesel locomotives. Designs for four appeared in the course of the 1920s, of around 746kW (1000hp). Electrical, mechanical, hydraulic

and pneumatic transmissions were tried out, though only the diesel-electric and diesel-mechanical transmissions were successful. The intensive development of diesel engines for submarines in World War II had brought about a new generation of more compact power units, and this 1-E-1 diesel-electric was built in Germany by Esslingen, as Lomonosov design Yue-002 (later Eel-2), using a MAN 883kW (1200hp) submarine engine, and was quite successful, lasting until 1954. Regrettably it was not preserved, but Ge-1 (later Yue-002, then Shch-El-1), actually the first

diesel-electric to work in the Soviet Union, still exists today. Developed by Gakkel, it was powered by a 746kW (1000hp) Vickers engine (also from a submarine design) which drove 10 100kW (134hp) traction motors. Both the engine and the electric transmission proved unreliable, and Shch-El-1 was withdrawn from traffic in 1927 after running only 40,000km (25,000 miles). From then on, it was used as a mobile generating plant. This monster 1CoDoCo1 machine was 22.76m (74ft 7in) long and weighed some 180 tonnes (177 tons). Lomonosov

later moved to the United States and was an influential figure in diesel development there.

TYPE: 1-Eo-1 experimental prototype diesel electric
POWER: 883kW (1200hp) from MAN six-cylinder engine
TRACTIVE EFFORT: 220kN (49500lbf)
MAX. OPERATING SPEED: 50km/h (31.3mph)
WEIGHT: 124.8t (275,142lb); 98.2t (216,492lb) adhesive
OVERALL LENGTH: 13.822m (45ft 4in)
GAUGE: 1524mm (5ft)

CHAPTER THREE

INVESTING IN THE FUTURE

1925–1935

In this period, railway electrification really got under way. The electric motor was seen to have a number of advantages. It was quiet, it produced no smoke, it did not need to transport its own fuel, it could develop torque (turning power) even when stationary, and could deliver considerable power at low speeds. Against that, it was expensive to build, and required more capital investment in the form of overhead catenary or third-rail installation; and its power had to be purchased from an electric power company or supplied from a dedicated power station. It was also new, with numerous different ways of application, and locomotive engineers had become a conservative breed over the previous 70 years, mistrustful of novelty, and conscious of working for companies with a huge investment in steam power.

Electric operation was at first confined to specialized uses on steep grades and in urban tunnels, but by the mid-1930s it was being used on suburban networks as well as cross-country lines. With their huge investment in steam traction, railways were also experimenting with super-high pressure and other new ways of getting better performance and thermal efficiency out of their steam fleets. But though some ingenious designs were tried out, the best results were obtained by improving on what already existed. In France, work on internal streamlining produced steam locomotives whose power-to-weight performance was unrivalled anywhere. In the United States and other countries, external streamlining produced locomotives of unusual shape and sometimes of exceptional speed.

Seen here in British Railways livery, with a passenger train on the Keighley & Worth Valley heritage line on 21 July 1982, the Midland Railway's Class 4F 0-6-0 was more accustomed to freight haulage, especially of coal trains.

CLASS C 36 4-6-0 NEW SOUTH WALES GOVERNMENT RAILWAYS (NSWGR) AUSTRALIA 1925

Australia's biggest and busiest state system, the NSWGR had its own workshops at Eveleigh, where this famous class was designed; line production was shared between Eveleigh and Clyde Engineering Works, between 1925 and 1928. The 75 C 36s replaced the NN 4-6-0s, of 1914 vintage, on main-line workings, including the Brisbane, Wollongong and Werris Creek routes, and hauled Victoria interstate expresses to the state border at Albury. Very efficient free-steaming engines, with a good turn of speed, their by-name of 'pigs' seems to have been an affectionate one. In what was now by far the most common practice everywhere, they had two outside cylinders, piston valves and Walschaerts valve gear. From 1953, all but two had their original round-topped fireboxes replaced with higher-pressure boilers and Belpaire fireboxes, and with smoke-box mounted throttle valves as developed on the line's C 38 'Pacifics'. In 1958, No. 3616 was fitted with a Giesl ejector chimney and superheat booster. These modifications improved performance, but by

then the system was converting to diesel, and further modernization of steam locomotives was abandoned. In 1958, the two unrebuilt engines were withdrawn, and the numbers were gradually whittled down over the next decade. In 1968, the class was retired, but a

shortage of motive power meant that six were reprieved, fitted with power reversers and some other modifications demanded by the footplatemen's union. These

ran for a few months longer, the last being withdrawn in September 1969. Three of them have been preserved.

Ready for the road, preserved No. 3642 stands on the turntable at Goulburn, NSW, in November 1981 after renovation work, including the fitting of a new boiler, had been completed.

BOILER PRESSURE: 12.6kg/cm² (180psi)
CYLINDERS: 23x26in (584x660mm)
DRIVING WHEELS: 1751mm (69in)
GRATE AREA: 2.8m² (30.5sq ft)
HEATING SURFACE: 184.8m² (1990sq ft)
SUPERHEATER: 60.4m² (650sq ft)
TRACTIVE EFFORT: 15,060kg (30,498lb)
TOTAL WEIGHT: 159t (350,595lb)

1-C-C-1 CHILEAN TRANSANDINE RAILWAY (FCCT) CHILE 1925

An international line of extreme difficulty to work, the 1m (3ft 3in) gauge 254km (159-mile) Chilean *Transandino* linked Mendoza in Argentina, via the Uspallata Pass below Mt Aconcagua, to Los Andes in Chile. Its summit tunnel of La Cumbre is at a height of 3186m (10,450ft), and on each side the ruling gradients are of 1 in 12.5, where the rails are fitted with an Abt triple rack system. Between 1927 and 1942, 76km (47 miles) of the central section were electrified, using direct current at 3000V. To handle the line's relatively sparse traffic, three locomotives were ordered, all from Switzerland: Nos. 101–103, one from SLM and two from Brown-Boveri. They were, in effect, a pair of 1-Cs joined back-to-back rather than the articulated-bogie type, but very similar to other Swiss-built locomotives in appearance. Each

unit had three traction motors, one of which drove the rack wheels. With these engaged, tractive effort was 220kN (49,500lb).

Maximum trainloads of some 150 tonnes (147 tons) were taken up the rack section at a speed of 15km/h (9.5mph). Between 1934 and 1944, a long section was closed following a huge glacial washout, and the line was always very susceptible to landslide, floods and snow blockage. In 1961, Brown-Boveri supplied a further two locomotives, of higher power rating, which could take trains at 30km/h (18.6mph) over the rack section. With such high costs simply for maintaining the

permanent way, and the operating costs of two forms of traction, the finances of the *Transandino* were never healthy. In 1978, after the company had lost money for many years, services were suspended, with closure of the line in 1982. A renovation project remains under discussion.

TYPE: rack-and-adhesion mixed-traffic locomotive
POWER: four 239kW (320hp) motors supplied by 3000V DC via overhead catenary, driving the coupled wheels through jack-shafts; plus two 403kW (540hp) motors driving the rack wheels
TRACTIVE EFFORT: 98kN (22,000lbf)

A rare photograph of the compactly built Transandine 1-C-C-1, similar in appearance to Swiss electric units of the period, but with smaller coupled wheels.

CLASS 241-A 4-8-2 EASTERN RAILWAY (EST)

The *Est* acquired this class – Europe's first 'Mountain' type – for service on heavy passenger express trains in the hilly provinces of Lorraine and Alsace. In typical French express engine mode, they were de Glehn/du Bousquet type four-cylinder compounds. Four sets of Walschaerts valve gear actuated the cylinders. The long boiler had two domes: the one nearest the cab held a perforated steam-drier pipe. Fives-Lille works were the builders.

From 1928, larger-cylindered versions were also built for the *Etat* railway in western France, though they too eventually found their way to the old Eastern Railway (by then the SNCF's

Eastern Region). Extensive testing against other express locomotives in 1933 revealed that the class was an inadequate performer compared with 'Mountain' types of the PLM and 'Pacifics' of the *Nord* and Paris–Orleans railways. From 1933 onwards, 48 of the class were extensively rebuilt on Chapelon principles.

BOILER PRESSURE: 16kg/cm² (290psi)
CYLINDERS: hp 425x720mm (16.75x28.4in); lp 660x720mm (26x28.4in)
DRIVING WHEELS: 1950mm (77in)
GRATE AREA: 4.43m² (47.7sq ft)
HEATING SURFACE: 217m² (2342sq ft)
SUPERHEATER: 16m² (172sq ft)
TRACTIVE EFFORT: 11,205kg (24,707lb)
TOTAL WEIGHT: 123.5t (272,384lb)

The design of smoke deflectors fitted to French locomotives in the 1930s was aerodynamic, evolved in wind-tunnel tests to give best results.

CLASS 161.BE 1-A-B+B-A-1 PARIS, LYONS & MEDITERRANEAN RAILWAY (PLM)

These heavy twin back-to-back electrics were designed to work freight trains over the PLM's busy international route through the Alps, linking Milan and Turin with Lyons via Modane and Chambéry. The PLM wanted sufficient power to pull trains of 800 tonnes (787 tons) over the route. At this time, French railways were still committed to

working on a current supply system of 1500V DC, though Kandó's pioneering work using industrial-strength power was already in hand in Hungary and on the Höllenthal Railway in Germany. The PLM locomotives developed 3582kW (4803hp) but were superseded by the AE.2 class 2-Co-Co-2 locomotives of 1930, which had an output of

TYPE: heavy freight twin locomotive	**MAX. OPERATING SPEED:** 80km/h (50mph)
POWER: two 1791kW (2400hp) motors driving nose-suspended motors on three axles in each part	**TOTAL WEIGHT:** 122t (269,010lb)
TRACTIVE EFFORT: Not known	**MAX. AXLE LOAD:** not known
	OVERALL LENGTH: 20.58m (67ft 6in)
	BUILDER: MTE, Paris; Thomson-Houston, Belfort; Schneider, Le Creusot

2985kW (4000hp) per hour and could take the 800-tonne

(787-ton) trains up the grades at 85km/h (53mph).

CLASS 01 4-6-2 GERMAN STATE RAILWAYS (DRG)

Post-war rebuilds of the Class 01 'Pacifics' on the Deutsche Reichsbahn were classed as 0105. A Soviet-style fairing was applied to the boiler-top.

The ideal machine of the *Deutsche Reichsbahn Gesellschaft* (DRG), formed in 1920, was the *Einheitslok*, or standard locomotive. The new organization had inherited some some 212 different locomotive classes from the old state railways, but also had a serious shortage of engines, since many had been ceded to other countries as war reparations. A

Locomotive Committee was set up with the principal manufacturers to establish a set of standard types. The engineering chief was Dr R.P. Wagner, of the old Prussian Railways, an engineer of great distinction.

For express passenger work, the 'Pacific' type was chosen, with a brief to haul a train of 800 tonnes (787 tons) at 100km/h (62mph) on

level track, or 500 tonnes (492 tons) at 50km/h (31mph) on a rising grade of 1 in 100. Compound and simple were both tested in 1925–26, with 10 two-cylinder simple expansion engines and 10 four-cylinder compounds. Following comparative tests, the fuel economy of the compounds was shown to be outweighed by their greater maintenance costs,

and the decision was taken to proceed with the simple expansion type only. This became Series 01, with 231 built between 1925 and 1938 (the 10 compounds were also converted to simples in 1942).

The 01s were bar-framed, with a copper firebox, a flush-topped boiler and three low domes, the leading one being the boiler inlet for the Knorr feedwater supply system, the rear one holding a Wagner-designed regulator. Between them was a sandbox holding sand for application to all coupled wheels in the event of slipping. As these engines were intended to run on all main lines, they were given wider fireboxes than the Prussian standard, to allow for burning the lower grade coal available in Saxony and the South. Among many resemblances to American design was the transverse cylindrical feedwater heater partly built into the upper section of the smoke box. Walschaerts valve gear actuated the piston valves, with all the motion outside and easily accessible. The trailing wheels, with inside bearings, were set behind the firebox, under the cab.

The first 01s were built by Borsig and AEG, but Henschel and Krupp were also later involved. From 1930, they were supplemented by a light 'Pacific' type, Series 03. This was of very similar appearance, and 298 were built by 1937. With a maximum axle load of 17.5 tonnes (17.2 tons), they had a much wider route availability.

Among the useful, and soon-copied, innovations of the DRG's standard locomotive policy was

the introduction of the smoke deflector, sometimes known as a 'blinker'. Steam and smoke clinging around the smokebox and obscuring the driver's view was often a problem. It was resolved by fitting an upright steel plate on each side of the smokebox, arranged so that the air passing between it and the smokebox created a current that swept upwards, taking the exhaust with it. After wind-tunnel tests, large smoke deflectors were originally mounted on the 01s, later replaced by smaller wing-type deflectors designed by Wagner's successor, Friedrich Witte. Before long, blinkers were in use on express locomotives in many other countries.

The original maximum operating speed of the 01 'Pacifics' was set at 130km/h (81.25mph). Two of the 03s were streamlined in 1934–35, but it was decided that for really fast working, a three-cylinder engine was required, and so, between 1939 and 1941, 115 of this type were built and classed 0110 and 0310.

With the partitioning of Germany in 1945, the stock was divided: 171 of the 01s to the *Deutsche Bundesbahn* (DB), and 70 to the East German *Deutsche Reichsbahn* (DR). From 1951, some of the original two-cylinder engines and some of the three-cylinder engines working on the DB were rebuilt with larger boilers that also contained combustion chambers. Wide

chimneys were fitted to allow for ejection of steam from auxiliary equipment like the Knorr feed pump. Many of these rebuilds were converted to oil-burning. They ran express services until 1973 on the DB, and some of the DR engines were still operating in 1981. Several examples of both the two- and three-cylinder engines of Groups 01 and 03 are preserved.

BOILER PRESSURE: 16kg/cm² (228psi)
CYLINDERS: 600x660mm (25.6x26in)
DRIVING WHEELS: 2000mm (78.7in)
GRATE AREA: 4.3m² (46.3sq ft)
HEATING SURFACE: 23m² (2661sq ft)
SUPERHEATER: 85m² (915sq ft)
TRACTIVE EFFORT: 16,160kg (35,610lb)
TOTAL WEIGHT: 109t (240,000lb)
(engine only)

CLASS 4F 0-6-0 LONDON, MIDLAND & SCOTTISH RAILWAY (LMS) GREAT BRITAIN 1925

Ubiquitous on the LMS system, these engines were in fact scarcely altered from the Midland Railway's '3835' class of 1914, of which 191 had been built by 1923. Over 500 more were built by the LMS. Larger boilers with Belpaire fireboxes, piston valves and superheaters were their main differences from 0-6-0 types that were 50 years older. All the class were fitted with vacuum brake equipment. Their principal task was freight-hauling on main and secondary routes when speed was not essential, but, fitted with vacuum brake pumps, they were frequently seen on local passenger services and on piloting and banking duties.

BOILER PRESSURE: 12.2kg/cm² (175psi)
CYLINDERS: 507x660mm (20x26in)
DRIVING WHEELS: 1294mm (51in)
GRATE AREA: 1.95m² (21sq ft)
HEATING SURFACE: 107.4m² (1157sq ft)
SUPERHEATER: 23.5m² (253sq ft)
TRACTIVE EFFORT: 9796kg (21,600lb)
TOTAL WEIGHT: 91.4t (201,488lb)

In its final working livery as British Railways No. 43424, a preserved 4F approaches Oakworth, on the Keighley & Worth Valley Railway, on 10 August 1981.

2-8-2 NIGERIAN GOVERNMENT RAILWAYS (NGR) NIGERIA 1925

Under colonial rule, Britain was the Nigerian Railways' source of locomotives. The system, laid to 1065mm (3ft 6in) gauge, was primarily single-track, with lengthy sections between crossing points, as on other colonial African networks, and was operated by a pattern of

infrequent heavy trains. These in turn required powerful engines, though with a limited maximum axle load – in this case, some 16.75 tonnes (16.5 tons). This British-built 2-8-2 class answered the need in 1925. Designed as three-cylinder simples, they had the conjugated valve gear

developed by Gresley – whose own 2-8-2 freight locomotive for the LNER also appeared in the same year. In the Nigerian engines, combustion chambers extended the Belpaire fireboxes and reduced boiler-tube length: a consideration that much improved their steam-raising ability.

BOILER PRESSURE: 12.6kg/cm² (180psi)
CYLINDERS: 457x711mm (18x28in)
DRIVING WHEELS: 1370mm (54in)
GRATE AREA: 3.5m² (38sq ft)
HEATING SURFACE: 213m² (2290sq ft)
SUPERHEATER: 47m² (506sq ft)
TRACTIVE EFFORT: 17,487kg (38,560lb)
TOTAL WEIGHT: 127.8t (281,904lb)

CLASS 020 2-8-4T PORTUGUESE RAILWAYS (CFP)

PORTUGAL 1925

Much of Portugal's locomotive stock was actually supplied by Germany, and Henschel of Kassel built two 2-8-4T classes for the CFP's broad-gauge lines (1665mm/ 5ft 6in). In appearance, they resembled each other very closely. Class 018 was lighter and used for local services in the south of the country; the 24 020s were more powerful and used mainly in the heavier traffic around Lisbon and Oporto. They were of typical German bar-frame construction, with two outside simple-expansion cylinders.

Reliable performers on duties that did not run up high daily mileages, most 020s were still in service in the late 1960s.

BOILER PRESSURE: 13kg/cm² (185psi)
CYLINDERS: 610x660mm (24x26in)
DRIVING WHEELS: 1350mm (53in)
GRATE AREA: 3.6m² (38.75sq ft)
HEATING SURFACE: not known
SUPERHEATER: not known
TRACTIVE EFFORT: 11,072kg (24,414lb)
TOTAL WEIGHT: 103.7t (228,658lb)

Left to rust away, a derelict Class 020 stands forgotten. Many detachable parts would have been removed, leaving only an iron shell.

CLASS 16D 4-6-2 SOUTH AFRICAN RAILWAYS (SAR)

SOUTH AFRICA 1925

Considerations of efficiency, and also the demands of trade unions, loomed larger in the United States in the 1920s than they did in Britain. 'Labour-saving' was welcomed when it eased the enginemen's task, as with the power reverser. American practice was well ahead of British when it came to routine maintenance, and the turn-round times at depots were much brisker. These points did not go unnoticed, and even when ordering from Britain, colonial companies would often specify American features or wholly American designs. But this thoroughly British-looking 1065mm (3ft 6in) gauge 'Pacific' in fact came from Baldwin in Philadelphia. Various American features were built into the specification, including hard-grease lubrication, self-cleaning front ends, and shaking grates. Twelve of these engines were built, up to 1929. They clipped 101 minutes off the 'Union Limited' Cape Town–Johannesburg route, 1538km (956 miles), running at an average of 57km/h (35.5mph).

BOILER PRESSURE: 13.7kg/cm² (195psi)
CYLINDERS: 558x660mm (22x26in)
DRIVING WHEELS: 1523mm (60in)
GRATE AREA: 4.2m² (45sq ft)
HEATING SURFACE: 227.8m² (2453sq ft)
SUPERHEATER: 55m² (593sq ft)
TRACTIVE EFFORT: 15,206kg (33,530lb)
TOTAL WEIGHT: 87.4t (192,650lb)
(engine only)

CLASS D 1-C-1 STATE RAILWAYS (SJ)

SWEDEN 1925

The D classes of five-axle electric locomotives set the standard on the SJ for many years, their design coinciding with the adoption of 15kV alternating current with low frequency 16.2/3Hz for the national network. All had a 9400mm (30ft 8in) wheelbase under a 13m (42ft 5in) body-frame. The early D engines were wood-bodied, with double walls that provided insulation against wintry conditions. The design was of basic box-type, but alleviated by the rounded corners and by the ribbed pattern of the excellently carpentered varnished woodwork. Transmission was by jackshaft and connecting rod, with consequent low speeds: 70km/h (43.8mph) maximum for the goods, and 90km/h (56.3mph) for the passenger types. Both types were powered by two body-mounted ASEA 610kW (829hp) traction motors, though the power output was gradually uprated as time went by. All were home-built, by Nydquist & Holm, AB Motala, and Vagn & Maskinfabriken of Falun, with electrical equipment from ASEA of Västerås. The D classes have a complex history, with many having been rebuilt and re-motored in the course of long lives. The original classes were Dg, for freight haulage, and Ds, for passenger trains. With a total of 417 built between 1925 and 1955, they were by far the most common locomotive types in the country.

In 1954–55, 99 new engines were built, classed as Da and fitted with 930kW (1250hp) motors.

Originally intended for mixed traffic, their 100km/h (62mph) maximum speed later restricted their use on passenger trains, on which they were replaced by the new Class R locomotives, but they continued to operate on goods trains for many years to come, into the mid-1990s.

TYPE: mixed-traffic locomotive
POWER: two 930kW (1250hp) motors supplied by single-phase current at 15,000V 16.67Hz via overhead catenary, driving the wheels via gearing, jackshaft and connecting rods
TRACTIVE EFFORT: 154kN (34,600lb)
MAX. OPERATING SPEED: 100km/h (62mph)
TOTAL WEIGHT: 75t (165,300lb)
MAX. AXLE LOAD: 17t (37,468lb)
OVERALL LENGTH: 13m (42ft 6in)
BUILDER: Nydquist & Holm, AB Motala and Vagn & Maskin Fabriken

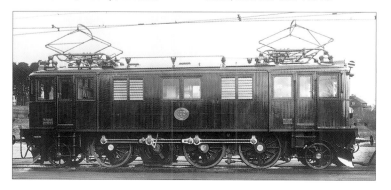

Newly delivered wooden-bodied No. D102 of the SJ, precursor of several generations of rod-driven electric motive power.

RHB CLASS GE6/6   C-C   RHAETIAN RAILWAY (RB)   SWITZERLAND 1925

At one time, there were as many as 15 'baby crocodile' articulated electric locomotives working on the *Rhätische Bahn* 1m (3ft 3in) gauge system. Five survived to more recent years, but all have been displaced from scheduled services on the much-modernized line. The design is articulated, with a central equipment section provided with cabs facing front and back, and two roof-mounted box-type pantographs. Each end of this central section rests on a powered bogie, a six-coupled unit carrying a large traction motor under the nose section. The motor drives a jackshaft that turns the wheels through side coupling rods.

Originally designed for mixed-traffic service, they worked pick-up freight trains between Chur

and Samedan in the last years of their scheduled operation. They are very popular among tourists and railway enthusiasts, and one or two are still maintained for charter work.

TYPE: mainline mixed-traffic electric locomotive
WHEEL ARRANGEMENT: C-C
POWER: 11,000V 16.7Hz AC overhead
LINE COLLECTION; 794kW (1065hp); one single-phase AC traction motor on each bogie driving through jackshaft and side coupling rods
TRACTIVE EFFORT: 172kN (38,665lbf)
MAX. OPERATING SPEED: 55km/h (34mph)
WEIGHT: 66t (144,940lb)
MAX. AXLE LOAD: not known
OVERALL LENGTH: 13.3m (43ft 8in)
GAUGE: 1000mm (3ft 3in)

The front end of No.407, with its snowplough, overhangs the narrow-gauge track and gives a sense of the power of the locomotives.

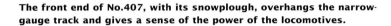

'BERKSHIRE' 2-8-4   ILLINOIS CENTRAL RAILROAD (IC)   USA 1925

In the early 1920s, locomotive construction in the United States was at a low ebb. The short post-war boom had passed, and few railroad companies were ordering new motive power. In addition, there was a sense that existing steam power could not be further improved now that superheating was standard. In a nation whose industries thrived on innovation, this was not encouraging for the steam builders. A new impetus was badly needed, and it came from an unexpected quarter. Lima Locomotive Company, previously a specialist builder of the 'Shay' locomotive type, found its market badly hit by the road truck, and sought to diversify by challenging Baldwin and Alco for the 'Class 1' market. Lima had a further motive, since its owners were also the proprietors of some major accessory companies, including the Franklin Accessory Co., the American Arch Co. and the Locomotive Superheater Co., all hungry for business. Domestic locomotive sales were in the doldrums, but Lima had a plan. William E. Woodard, the company's chief engineer, led the design of a new-style steam locomotive. Having tried his ideas in a rebuild of a New York Central Class H10 2-8-2 of 1912, he was ready to construct a new, and in crucial respects different, locomotive. Aware that boilers could not get much bigger, he sought other ways of getting more steam. With his focus very much on 'the combustion situation', Woodard revised the relative proportions of

firebox, boiler and superheater. To a large firebox, he added a combustion chamber, not a new feature in itself but with its shape scientifically worked out. His engine was a two-cylinder, simple-expansion locomotive, whose huge firebox was nearly a quarter the length of the boiler. Comparison of its heating surface and superheater area with those of the Pennsylvania Railroad's M1 4-8-2 of 1923 reveals the extent of change in these inner arrangements. The mighty firebox was supported on a four-wheel rear truck which was also an American first, though in a different design it had been used

in Austria for over a decade (see 1911). The truck was fitted with a steam booster, giving an additional 5986kg (13,200lb) of tractive effort at start-off or low speed.

The intention was to obtain high horsepower and economical use of fuel, and in this it was largely successful. In April 1925, the prototype 2-8-4 hauled a train of 2332.7 tonnes (2296 tons) through the Berkshire Mountains from Selkirk Yard to North Adams Junction in 10 minutes less time than the H10, which had been pulling only 1718 tonnes (1691 tons). Lima's publicists adroitly attached the label of 'Super-power' to this first 2-8-4, which in its

basic design was a model for all other 'super-power' engines to come from Lima and, very soon, from the other builders too. Known in the works as the A-1, the locomotive was built by Lima as an experiment and showpiece, but was later sold to the Illinois Central. The Boston & Albany was the first buyer of the type, and the name came from that company's main line through the Berkshire Mountains, though on the Chesapeake & Ohio Railroad it was known as the 'Kanawha' type. The importance of the 'super-power' concept was great. Railroads were prepared to invest in a new locomotive that combined power and economy, and sales began to rise, with Lima now established as a challenger to the big two. But also, the work done on the 'Berkshire' design could be readily applied to even bigger engines.

BOILER PRESSURE: 16.8kg/cm^2 (240psi)
CYLINDERS: 710x761mm (28x30in)
DRIVING WHEELS: 1599mm (63in)
GRATE AREA: 9.84m^2 (106sq ft)
HEATING SURFACE: 479m^2 (5157sq ft)
SUPERHEATER: 196m^2 (2111sq ft)
TRACTIVE EFFORT: 31,473kg (69,400lb)
TOTAL WEIGHT: 174.6t (385,000lb) (engine only)

One of the original 'Berkshires', No. 4005 of the Boston & Maine RR. The locomotive is fitted with a patent 'Coffin' type feedwater heater.

EL-3A BOXCAB 1-B-B-1+1-B-B-1+1-B-B-1 VIRGINIAN RAILWAY (VR)

USA 1925

Baldwin built these massive triple-unit electric locomotives, with electrical parts from Westinghouse, to haul long and heavy coal trains on the Appalachian mountain grades. In the mid-1920s, the VR electrified 216km (134 miles) of steeply graded main line between Mullens and Roanoke, Virginia. The 11kV alternating current overhead

TYPE: 1-B-B-1+1-B-B-1+1-B-B-1, siderod electric	
POWER: 11kV AC at 25Hz from overhead	
OUTPUT: 1 hour output at 44km/h (28.4mph) 5315kW (7125hp)	

TRACTIVE EFFORT: 420kN (94,500lbf) at 45km/h (28.3mph) continuous TE; 1233kN (277,500lbf) starting TE	
MAX. OPERATING SPEED: 61km/h (38mph)	

WEIGHT: 583t (1,285,160lb)	
OVERALL LENGTH: 46.406m (152ft 3in)	
GAUGE: 1435mm (4ft 8.5in)	

system was installed by Westinghouse. The coal traffic was worked by 12 Class EL-3A, whose tractive power came from

large body-mounted traction motors that transmitted the drive through jackshafts and siderods. The VR operated these machines

until the 1950s, when they were supplanted by more modern ignitron rectifier electric locomotives.

CNJ-1000 BO-BO CENTRAL RAILROAD OF NEW JERSEY (CNJ)

USA 1925

Complaints about the smoke from city freight yards sharpened interest in diesel-powered switchers during the mid-1920s, though sales were at a very modest level (only 196 diesel switchers were bought by US railroads in the period 1925–1936). A prototype slow-speed, low-output switcher was built by Alco in collaboration with Ingersoll-Rand, which supplied the motor, and General Electric, providers of the electrical components. It was demonstrated in 1923–25. Weighing 61 tonnes (60 tons), it ran on two swivel four-wheel trucks. The engine was an in-line, vertical type, six-cylinder Ingersoll-Rand diesel unit producing 220kW (300hp) at 600rpm and driving a 600V DC generator that supplied power to four 44.1kW (60hp) traction

motors geared directly to the four axles. Several railroads were interested, and after tests at the I-R factory in Phillipburg, NJ, it was tried out on the NYC's West Side yards and was then demonstrated on more than a dozen other lines. Carrying sufficient fuel for two days' work, it could operate on three crew-shifts a day. Running costs were less than for a steam locomotive. But for railroads there was also the consideration that its capital cost, at around $100,000, was double that of a large steam switcher.

The first commercially produced diesel, which became CNJ's No. 1000, was built on very similar lines to the prototype of 1923. Assigned to CNJ's isolated water front trackage in the Bronx district of New York City, it was the United State's first operational diesel-

electric locomotive. The manufacturers built a first batch of four, and the Baltimore & Ohio and Lehigh Valley railroads each bought one. After more than 30 years of regular service, CNJ-1000 was retired and its primacy was honoured by preservation at the Baltimore & Ohio Museum in Baltimore, Md.

TYPE: Bo-Bo, diesel-electric	
POWER AND OUTPUT: Ingersoll-Rand 6-cyl engine producing 220kW (300hp)	
TRACTIVE EFFORT: 133kN (30,000lbf) starting TE	
MAX. OPERATING SPEED: N/A	
WEIGHT: 61t (120,000lb)	
OVERALL LENGTH: 9.956m (32ft 8in)	
GAUGE: 1435mm (4ft. 8.5in)	

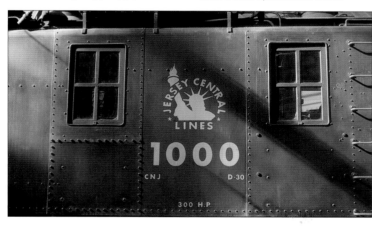

In body design and general appearance, the boxlike early diesels were hardly distinguishable from electric locomotives.

The driver stood on the right and had the aid of a windscreen wiper, then a very new feature on a locomotive.

CLASS 1170 BO-BO FEDERAL RAILWAYS OF AUSTRIA (BBÖ)

AUSTRIA 1926

Compact and sturdy, these four-axle, all-adhesion, electric locomotives were introduced as three basic classes by the pre-war Austrian railway administration *Bundesbahn Österreichs* (BBÖ) as classes 1170.0, 1170.1 and 1170.2. The post-1945 *Österreichische Bundesbahnen* (ÖBB) classed them as 1045, 1145 and 1245,

corresponding to successive increases in output power from 1140kW (1549hp) in 1926 to 1600kW (2283hp) in 1934. With the heavier machinery, adhesion weight rose from 60 tonnes (132,300lb) to 80 tonnes (176,400lb). The three types lasted in traffic through the late 1980s and into the mid-1990s, the last class 1245 not being

TYPE: Bo-Bo mixed-traffic	
POWER: 1140kW (1549hp)	
SUPPLY: 15kV 16.7Hz AC	
TRACTIVE EFFORT: up to 196kN (44,100lbf)	

MAX. OPERATING SPEED: 60km/h (37.5mph)	
WEIGHT: 61t (134,505lb)	
MAX. AXLE LOAD: 21t (46,305lb)	
OVERALL LENGTH: 12.89m (42ft)	
GAUGE: 1435mm (4ft 8.5in)	

displaced until the delivery of class 1163 from 1993 to 1995. Until that time, these locomotives

could still be found in action, including some triple-header workings on heavy freight trains.

CLASS 387 4-6-2 CZECHOSLOVAK STATE RAILWAYS (CSD)

CZECHOSLOVAKIA 1926

BOILER PRESSURE: 13kg/cm² (185psi)	**GRATE AREA:** 4.8m² (51.7sq ft)	**TRACTIVE EFFORT:** 11,030kg (24,320lb)
CYLINDERS: 525x680mm (20.7x27in)	**HEATING SURFACE:** 260m² (2799sq ft)	**TOTAL WEIGHT:** 89.6t (197,568lb)
DRIVING WHEELS: 1900mm (74.8in)	**SUPERHEATER:** 93m² (1001sq ft)	(engine only)

Up to 1937, the Skoda works at Plzen built a total of 43 of this 'Pacific' class, and were also responsible for the design, which owed more to current German practice than to the old Imperial Austrian tradition. It was a three-cylinder simple-expansion design, with Heusinger valve gear. The inside cylinder did not have a separate valve gear but was worked by a rocking lever driven from the third coupled axle on the left side. Later models, Nos. 387.022 to 387.043, had larger driving wheels, of 1950mm (76.8in) diameter and somewhat reduced heating surfaces. After 1945, 14 of the class were given Kylchap double blast-pipes and chimneys, replacing the original British-style lipped chimney. The class operated on express services and later on stopping trains until 1974, and the last one to be built, No. 387.043, is preserved.

One of the class, No. 387.043, was until recently operational but is now a static display locomotive in the National Railway Museum.

E.401 2-B-B-2 PARIS–ORLEANS RAILWAY (PO)

FRANCE 1926

TYPE: express passenger locomotive	**MAX. OPERATING SPEED:** 120km/h (75mph)	
POWER: four 895kW (1200hp) motors in the main frame, supplied by 1500V DC via overhead catenary or 600V via rail shoes, driving two sets of two coupled axles via connecting rods	**TOTAL WEIGHT:** 131.7t (290,330lb)	
	MAX. AXLE LOAD: 18t (39,670lb)	
	OVERALL LENGTH: 16.04m (52ft 7in)	
TRACTIVE EFFORT: 176kN (39,670lb)	**BUILDER:** Ganz, Budapest	

For its 204km (127 miles) of electrified track between Paris and Vierzon, the PO tried out three prototype locomotives, two of them, including this one, from Ganz of Budapest, pioneers in electric railway building. The electrical supply was direct current at 1500V, though Kalmán Kandó of Ganz, the designer, was a pioneer of three-phase supply – and, later, of alternating current supply. Of striking appearance, with a power rating of 3580kW (4800hp), the E.401 carried supports for third-rail pick-up shoes as well as its two pantographs, and the two traction motors were adapted to use a third rail's 600V (in the Paris area tunnels) at a reduced power output. With a jackshaft drive and complicated system of connecting rods, it was not reliable in service: rod drive, effective on slow trains, was not the future for main-line electrics. Failures were frequent, and the type was transferred from passenger services to freight work, and withdrawn in 1942.

CLASS 44 2-10-0 GERMAN STATE RAILWAYS (DRG)

GERMANY 1926

This very numerous class was the DRG's principal freight hauler, and, like the Class 01 'Pacific', was designed to be an *Einheitslok*, or 'standard engine', with consequent advantages of route availability, standardized spare parts, driving technique and assured performance standards.

For Wagner's team, it was another very successful design, with 1753 built between 1926 and 1944. It was a three-cylinder simple expansion engine, bar-framed, with a copper firebox (Germany normally favoured steel fireboxes). The maximum operating speed was 70km/h (43.5mph). Four-point suspension had been worked out, in order to make the ride easier. Its 20-tonne (19.7-ton) maximum axle load restricted it to main-line services, but as these were the lines on which the fast, heavy freights ran, this was not a problem.

BOILER PRESSURE: 16kg/cm² (228psi)
CYLINDERS: 600x660mm (23.6x26in)
DRIVING WHEELS: 1400mm (55in)
GRATE AREA: 4.5m² (48.4sq ft)
HEATING SURFACE: 237m² (2551.6sq ft)

SUPERHEATER: 100m² (1076sq ft)
TRACTIVE EFFORT: 23,140kg (51,000lb)
TOTAL WEIGHT: 114.1t (25,225lb)
(engine only)

For more than 30 years, this class was the standard heavy freight locomotive on the German railways, until displaced by diesel and electric traction.

'LORD NELSON' CLASS 4-6-0 SOUTHERN RAILWAY (SR)

GREAT BRITAIN 1926

All the new 'Big Four' British railways were bringing in new express engines in the 1920s, and in a publicity war each sought to claim its engine was 'most powerful'. The Southern's need for an engine able to cope with heavy boat trains from London to Dover and Folkestone, and pull holiday expresses to the south-west of England, were the principal reasons for the appearance of this 16-strong class. It enabled the company to boast – for a short time – an engine that had the highest tractive effort of any British express locomotive. Designed by R.E.L. Maunsell, it was a four-cylinder simple-expansion engine. They were effective locomotives but a poorly designed firebox made it hard to keep the fire hot enough. In the late 1930s, they were fitted with Lemaître multiple-jet chimneys, which helped considerably. The original Lord Nelson is preserved.

BOILER PRESSURE: 15.5kg/cm² (220psi)
CYLINDERS: 419x610mm (16.5x24in)
DRIVING WHEELS: 2007mm (79in)
GRATE AREA: 3.1m² (33sq ft)
HEATING SURFACE: 18.5m² (1989sq ft)
SUPERHEATER: 35m² (376sq ft)
TRACTIVE EFFORT: 15,196kg (33,500lb)
TOTAL WEIGHT: 142.5t (314,000lb)

Preserved SR No. 850 'Lord Nelson', first of the class, is still in operation on steam excursions.

CLASS 12 4-8-2 RHODESIAN RAILWAYS (RR)

No. 190 pauses with a freight at a wayside water stop. The RR permanent way is notably well-ballasted.

The Rhodesian (now Zimbabwean) Railways were, in effect, a northward extension of the South African system, on the same 1065mm (3ft 6in) gauge, and with similar long single-track lines through savannah country. Nineteen of this class were delivered from Britain in 1926 to the RR, and a further 11 in 1930. Some had Lentz-actuated piston valves, but these were later replaced by Walschaerts valve gear, which were already used by the rest of the class. Initially, they worked over the Salisbury–Gwelo line. In 1944, three were rebuilt as Class 12A with wider, shorter boilers and bigger tenders; two of these were sold to the Mozambique railways in 1964, by which time Garratt types had replaced them on the RR.

BOILER PRESSURE: 13.3kg/cm² (190psi)
CYLINDERS: 507.6x660mm (20x26in)
DRIVING WHEELS: 1294mm (51in)
GRATE AREA: not known
HEATING SURFACE: 187m² (2017sq ft)
SUPERHEATER: 33.6m² (362sq ft)
TRACTIVE EFFORT: 14,940kg (32,940lb)
TOTAL WEIGHT: 86.4t (190,560lb)

No. 181 of Class 12, no longer in service and with rods removed, stands with a Garratt on a siding.

CLASS AE 4/7   2-DO-1   SWISS FEDERAL RAILWAYS (SBB)

Work-horses of the Swiss railway system, the 127 engines of this class gave long and reliable service: the last to be withdrawn (in 1996) ran more than 8 million km (5 million miles). Four body-mounted Brown Boveri or SAAS single phase commutator traction motors powered the four driving axles using the Büchli drive system, whose asymmetric layout gave a different appearance to the two sides of the engine.

Responsible for working most front-line passenger services up to the 1960, they then transferred to secondary duties and parcels and mail work, contining to operate throughout Switzerland, except for mountain routes like the St Gotthard. Bern depot was deploying them as double- or triple-headers on heavy freight from the Lausanne yard until 1995.

TYPE: 2-Do-1 passenger
POWER: 2294kW (3075hp)
SUPPLY: 15kV 16.7Hz
TRACTIVE EFFORT: 196kN (44,100lbf)
MAX. OPERATING SPEED: 100km/h (62mph)

WEIGHT: 118 or 123t (260,190lb or 271,215lb)
MAX. AXLE LOAD: 18t (39,690lb)
OVERALL LENGTH: 16.76m or 17.1m (54ft 8in to 55ft 9in)
GAUGE: 1435mm (4ft 8.5in)

The uneven weight distribution of the Büchli drive system is responsible for the asymmetric wheel arrangement of this long-lived class, which for many years typified Swiss Railways for travellers.

CLASS 9000 'UNION PACIFIC' TYPE 4-12-2   UNION PACIFIC RAILROAD (UPR)

The Class 9000 was the most numerous of the world's small collection of locomotive classes with six coupled axles. Built by Alco's Brooks Works, these were until 1934 the longest and largest non-articulated locomotives in the world. The length of the coupled wheelbase was 9340mm (30ft 8in). Eighty-eight were built and a company statement said the aim was 'to haul mile-long freights at passenger train speeds.' Unusually for the United States, they were three-cylinder engines, though employing simple expansion. The inside cylinder, driving the second coupled axle, was not operated by separate valve gear but by the Gresley form of conjugated valve gear developed in England; this used a system of hinged levers connected to the external valve gear to operate the inner cylinder. Between 1934 and 1940, eight of the first 15 to be built had their conjugated valve gear replaced by a 'third link' system, using a double eccentric return crank on the right-hand side to work the inside cylinder valves. In the original design, the third and fourth sets of driving wheels were without flanges to assist negotiation of curves, but in the production engines, the first and last sets of coupled wheels were allowed lateral play, using a technique developed by Alco, and all wheels were flanged. The 4-12-2s ran on the UPR until 1956, and represented the maximum power to be got from a rigid-framed locomotive. Originally deployed on the main line through Wyoming, they later worked in Kansas and Nebraska. The first engine, No. 9000, is preserved.

BOILER PRESSURE: 15.5kg/cm² (220psi)
CYLINDERS: 685x812mm (27x32in); inside cyl 685x787mm (27x31in)
DRIVING WHEELS: 1700mm (67in)
GRATE AREA: 10m² (108.25sq ft)
HEATING SURFACE: 543.8m² (5853sq ft)
SUPERHEATER: 237.8m² (2560sq ft)
TRACTIVE EFFORT: 43,832kg (96,650lb)
TOTAL WEIGHT: 354.6t (782,000lb)

Running westwards with a train of 102 freight cars, the 4-12-2 maintains a steady speed of 25mph (40km/h) across the prairie. This shot of No. 9007 was taken at Archer, Wyoming, on 4 September 1955.

CLASS 2090 BO FEDERAL RAILWAYS OF AUSTRIA (BBÖ)   AUSTRIA 1927

The world's oldest working diesel locomotive, this was built as a one-off at the Floridsdorf works in Vienna. Numbered as 2090.001, it operates on one of the narrow-gauge systems operated by Austrian Federal Railways (BBÖ). Despite its age, it is in operational stock rather than preserved, doing light shunting work at Waidhofen an der Ybbs. Other elderly small shunting locomotives of classes 2190 (Bo of 1934), 2091(1Bo1 of 1936) and 2093 (Bo-Bo of 1930) still operate on the same 760mm (2ft 6in) gauge network.

TYPE: four-wheel narrow-gauge petrol-electric
POWER: 88kW (118hp) from Saurer BXD series engine
TRACTIVE EFFORT: 102kN (22950lbf)
MAX. OPERATING SPEED: 40km/h (25mph)
WEIGHT: 12t (26,460lb)
OVERALL LENGTH: 5.62mm (18ft 4in)
GAUGE: 760mm (2ft 6in)

Four-wheeler No. 2090.01, Austria's oldest working diesel, in ÖBB livery, doing shunting duty at Waidhofen an der Ybbs.

CLASS Tk3 2-8-0 FINNISH STATE RAILWAYS (VR)   FINLAND 1927

The most numerous steam class on the Finnish Railways, the Tk3 became immediately invaluable at a time when freight wagons and train loads were becoming heavier. A birch-log burner, with two outside simple-expansion cylinders like all VR locomotives, it had a light maximum axle load of 10.7 tonnes (10.5 tons), enabling it to run on track that was liable to undulate on soft, peaty soil outside the hard-frozen winter months. Within four years, 100 were built by Tampella and Lokomo, and building continued for 26 years until, by 1953, there were 158. Like some other Finnish locomotives of this period, including the passenger 4-6-0 Class Hv2, the cylinders were fitted with a by-pass valve, visible as an extension on the cylinder

BOILER PRESSURE: 14kg/cm² (199psi)
CYLINDERS: 460x630mm (18x24.8in)
DRIVING WHEELS: 1270mm (50in)
GRATE AREA: 1.6m² (17.2sq ft)
HEATING SURFACE: 84.8m² (913sq ft)
SUPERHEATER: 26m² (279.9sq ft)
TRACTIVE EFFORT: 9550kg (21,058lb)
TOTAL WEIGHT: 51.8t (114,219lb)
(engine only)

sides, which enabled the engines to 'coast' on downhill grades without putting stress on the piston valves. Electric headlamps and interior lights were fitted. After the horrors of the 'Winter

With its electric lights on, a Tk3 with fully stacked tender stands out against the snow in this evocative twilight shot.

War' of 1939–40, 24 were claimed by Soviet Russia and 70 were built after 1943, 50 in Finland and 20

by Frichs of Aarhus in Denmark. Withdrawals began in the 1960s, but several have been preserved.

CLASS V3201 2-C-2 GERMAN STATE RAILWAYS (DRG)

GERMANY 1927

A good deal of work on internal combustion was going on among engine designers in the 1920s, and a whole range of experiments took place, including direct and indirect mechanical drive systems, electric or hydraulic transmissions, and different thermodynamic cycle engines. The Class V3201 prototype locomotive was built by Esslingen in Germany, a company that was an early diesel traction pioneer as well as a specialized steam locomotive builder. The design relied on a modified air-diesel cycle using compressed hot gases at a temperature of 350°C (662°F) to expand in steam locomotive-style horizontal cylinders, and drive the three coupled axles through outside connecting rods. It seemed to have promise and was followed up in several countries before being finally abandoned as impractical.

TYPE: 2-C-2 prototype compressed-air diesel
POWER: 883kW (1200hp) from MAN engine
TRACTIVE EFFORT: 148kN (33250lbf)
MAX. OPERATING SPEED: 45km/h (28mph)
WEIGHT: 96t (211,680lb)
OVERALL LENGTH: 13.5m (44ft)
GAUGE: 1435mm (4ft 8.5in)

'KING' CLASS 4-6-0 GREAT WESTERN RAILWAY (GWR)

GREAT BRITAIN 1927

No. 6000 *King George V* on the Hereford–Shrewsbury line with a charter train on 31 August 1983.

Following the rebuilding of its lone 'Pacific,' the GWR's biggest passenger locomotives were the 'Kings', speedily dubbed as 'Britain's most powerful express passenger locomotives' when they debuted. The years 1926–27 were a time of significant locomotive development in Great Britain, stimulated by inter-company rivalry and a heightened sense of the value of good publicity. In effect, this engine was the culmination of the company's design policy that had begun in 1907 with the four-cylinder 'Stars', and this class was an enlarged version of the 'Castle' class. The Swindon-designed domeless tapered boiler reached a maximum diameter of 2837mm (6ft), and it was a four-cylinder simple with two sets of inside Walschaerts valve gear. The outside cylinders were operated from within by means of rocking shafts. A minor curiosity was its front bogie, whose lead axle had outside bearings (to make room for the inside cylinders) and whose rear axle had inside bearings. The heaviest 4-6-0s to run on British railways, the Kings hauled the main West of England and Birmingham expresses to and from London Paddington. A maximum axle load of 22.8 tonnes (22.5 tons) confined them to certain lines, but as they were main-line express engines this was not a handicap.

By 1930, the class numbered 30. Their great virtue was in maintaining consistent speeds in the order of 96–105km/h (60–65mph) with trains loading up to 508 tonnes (500 tons). In South Devon, there were numerous steeply graded sections (which originally Isambard Brunel had planned to operate by atmospheric traction), and the 'Kings' took trains of 365.7 tonnes (360 tons) unaided up banks as severe as 1 in 42. In 1927, the first of the class, No. 6000 *King George V*, made a 'state visit' to the United States, to appear at the Baltimore & Ohio Railroad's centenary celebrations. From 1948, double chimneys were fitted and a number of other technical refinements were made, with the result that their performance was further enhanced. The maximum recorded speed of a King was 174.6km/h (108.5mph), achieved by the modified *King Richard III* in September 1955. They operated on express services until their final withdrawal in 1963.

BOILER PRESSURE: 17.6kg/cm² (250psi)
CYLINDERS: 413x711mm (16.25x28in)
DRIVING WHEELS: 1980mm (78in)
GRATE AREA: 3m² (34.3sq ft)
HEATING SURFACE: 204.4m² (2201sq ft)
SUPERHEATER: 29m² (313sq ft)
TRACTIVE EFFORT: 18,140kg (40,000lb)
TOTAL WEIGHT: 90.4t (199,360lb) (engine only)

'ROYAL SCOT' CLASS 4-6-0 LONDON, MIDLAND & SCOTTISH RAILWAY (LMS) GREAT BRITAIN 1927

'Royal Scot' Mark 1, with original parallel boiler and minuscule single chimney (even so, a tiny capuchon rim was added).

The LMS had been planning to build a compound 'Pacific' class, until its design was shown to deliver inferior performance to a borrowed GWR simple-expansion 'Castle' 4-6-0. Instead, it came up with a simple expansion 4-6-0 design with a big boiler and driving wheels, and ordered 50 from the North British Locomotive Company of Glasgow. Prior to the LMS Pacific, this was its flagship engine, whose prime duty was pulling the new 'Royal Scot' London–Glasgow express on the 481.3km (299.1-mile) non-stop London–Carlisle stage. Masquerading as the class leader No. 6100, a later engine was sent on a display visit to the United States. The class did what it was asked, able to take a 457-tonne (450-ton) train unaided over the Shap summit, and a further 20 were built, incorporating detail variations. They were massive-looking engines, squeezed into the British loading gauge at 4022mm (13ft 2in) height, with a tiny chimney and low dome, and a straight-sided Belpaire firebox. One Royal Scot frame and set of wheels were used for an ultra-high pressure test locomotive, which was abandoned after failures on trial. After 13 years' intensive service, a programme of rebuilding the older engines of the class with new taper boilers and double chimneys was begun. The rebuilt 'Scots' were excellent engines and continued to work fast trains from London to Liverpool and Manchester until withdrawal during the 1960s.

'Royal Scot' Mark 2. The taper boiler allows for a taller (and double) chimney and outside top-feed. The loco's name is _Queen's Westminster Rifleman._

BOILER PRESSURE: 17.5kg/cm² (250psi)	**HEATING SURFACE:** 193m² (2081sq ft)
CYLINDERS: 457x660mm (18x26in)	**SUPERHEATER:** 41.3m² (445sq ft)
DRIVING WHEELS: 2056mm (81in)	**TRACTIVE EFFORT:** 13,242kg (29,200lb)
GRATE AREA: 2.9m² (31.2sq ft)	**TOTAL WEIGHT:** 86.2t (190,176lb)

CLASS ABMOT HUNGARIAN STATE RAILWAYS (MÁV)

HUNGARY 1927

The Ganz workshops of Budapest were specialists in modern traction, and the Hungarian State Railways turned to them for light railcars to compete with road traffic on branch lines. A total of 128 two- and three-axle railcars were built by Ganz from 1927 to serve branch and secondary lines. Small,

with a rigid wheelbase, the railcars proved a great deal cheaper to buy and run than steam trains, and their speed also improved services. The first examples actually had petrol engines, but these were replaced by Ganz diesel engines from 1934. Roof-mounted radiators were set vertically above the driving cabs. The railcars had

enough power to haul four-wheeled trailers, and eventually

they were in service across more than half of the MÁV network.

TYPE: local and branch passenger diesel railcar
POWER: 110kW (147bhp)
TRACTIVE EFFORT: N/A
DIESEL ENGINE (ONE PER CAR): Ganz VIJaR 135 underfloor diesel
GEARBOX: four-speed mechanical
MAX. OPERATING SPEED: 60km/h (37mph)
WEIGHT: 18t (39,530lb)
OVERALL LENGTH: 12.02m (39ft 5in)
GAUGE: 1435mm (4ft 8.5in)

The generous Hungarian loading gauge made it possible for the water tank and radiator for the water-cooled engine to be mounted on the roof.

CLASS XC 4-6-2 INDIAN RAILWAYS (IR)

INDIA 1927

Engines designed to the specifications of the Indian Railways Standards Committee (IRS) of 1924 did not enjoy a good reputation, in contrast to the designs of the British Engineering Standards Association (BESA) dating back to the 1900s. To supplement and replace the BESA 4-6-0 locomotives, the IRS provided for three levels of 'Pacific' power, XA, XB and XC, all two-cylinder simples, with the XC as the heavy express engine. Though locomotives were built in large numbers, the designs were of low quality, and the engines suffered from poor steaming as a result of such flaws as bad internal draughting, fractures of the plate frames, and, most seriously, insufficient built-in resistance to lateral movement of the leading bogie. This lack of side control led to several derailments and finally

one major accident, when an XB overturned in 1937 near Bihta on the East Indian Railway. Despite an inquiry, the cause of the disaster was not ascertained until an international panel of senior engineers was invited to India and conducted thorough tests. Although certain Indian railways, like the Bengal–Nagpur, developed their own express types (in their case, a huge four-cylinder compound Pacific), most followed the IRS line. The X classes numbered 284 locomotives in all, and continued in more reliable, if undistinguished, service into the post-Partition years. The Pakistan Railways acquired 60 and the remainder stayed in India. With the advent of the post-war WP Pacifics, the X classes were quickly relegated to minor duties and withdrawals began, but the last few survived until 1981.

BOILER PRESSURE: 12.6kg/cm² (180psi)
CYLINDERS: 584x711mm (23x28in)
DRIVING WHEELS: 1880mm (74in)
GRATE AREA: 4.75m² (51sq ft)
HEATING SURFACE: 226m² (2429sq ft)
SUPERHEATER: 59m² (636sq ft)
TRACTIVE EFFORT: 13,895kg (30,625lb)
TOTAL WEIGHT: 178t (392,500lb)

The XC classs were massive engines. In later years, they were relegated to freight train service.

0-6-0 SWITCHING ENGINE STATE BELT RAILROAD OF CALIFORNIA

USA 1927

Operating practice in the United States distinguished between the 'road engine' and the yard-based switcher, even if the latter might be a large 10-coupled engine, with boosters on the tender wheels. Train marshalling operations at termini, and in carriage and freight yards, could be heavy work, with passenger consists weighing as much as 1000 tonnes (907 tons) and freight trainloads often heavier still. Switchers also hauled local pick-up freights from factory sidings and local depots. Typically of 0-8-0 or 0-6-0 wheel arrangement, they were often modified 'Consolidation' or 'Mogul' types, with their front bogies removed; since they were not meant for use on the open road, and were restricted to low speeds, they were not considered to need front trucks. Their most important attribute was good adhesion, so the more weight on the driving wheels, the better; also desirable was a short wheelbase for tight curves on yard tracks. The frame length of these engines sometimes extended to more than double their coupled wheelbase.

With the American aversion to using tank engines, they usually had tenders, smaller than those of road engines, often sloped down towards the rear to give the driver a better view when reversing. By 1927, power-operated reversing gear, long pressed for by the labour unions, was almost always fitted in switchers. Being relatively straightforward engines in design, solid in build, and running up modest mileages, switchers often had long working lives. On industrial tracks in quarries and mines, steam switchers worked into the 1960s, well after the disappearance of main-line steam.

BOILER PRESSURE: 13.3kg/cm² (190lb)
CYLINDERS: 508x609mm (20x24in)
DRIVING WHEELS: 1294mm (51in)
GRATE AREA: 3m² (33.1sq ft)
HEATING SURFACE: 145.3m² (1564sq ft)
SUPERHEATER: 40.4m² (435sq ft)
TRACTIVE EFFORT: 15,000kg (30,400lb)
TOTAL WEIGHT: 67t (147,700lb)

Below: Yolo Shortline 0-6-0 No. 1233 crosses a creek whose wooden trestle has been partially replaced by a new girder span.

Above: Preserved 0-6-0 switcher No. 4466 of the Union Pacific. Balance of weighty elements was crucial to the design.

CLASS J1 'HUDSON' 4-6-4 NEW YORK CENTRAL RAILROAD (NYC)

USA 1927

First introduced by the NYC and built by Alco, the 4-6-4 quickly proved to be an excellent type for high-speed passenger express work, owing a lot to the 'super power' concept worked out by the Lima Locomotive Co. earlier in the decade. A single prototype was built and tested. With a substantial increase in power over the line's 'Pacifics', they took over NYC express services like the 'Twentieth Century Limited' and the 'Empire State'. The J1 class totalled 225. There was quite rapid development of the type, and by 1930, with the J1c, the boiler pressure had gone up to 19.3kg/cm² (275psi), the cylinders had been modified to 571x736mm (22.5x29in) to improve tractive effort, and larger tenders were attached, increasing the total weight by 48.3 tonnes (47.5 tons). All were booster-fitted on the rear bogie: a feature considered essential because the 'Hudsons', fine performers at speed, were of low efficiency in starting, even for steam locomotives. Water-scoops were fitted so that the tenders could be refilled from track-pans at speeds up to 121km/h (75mph). Such was the reliability and ease of maintenance that the J1s based at Albany depot averaged 185,000km (115,000 miles) a year.

Hudsons were built for long hauls over undulating terrain rather than mountain lines, and some worked right through from Harmon (New York) to Cleveland, 946.7km (588.3 miles), a trip necessitating a brief pause under a coal chute to replenish the tender. They sustained consistent high speed. On 20 July 1934, F6 Hudson No. 6402, built by Baldwin for the Chicago, Milwaukee, St Paul & Pacific Railroad in 1930, ran the 135km (84 miles) between Chicago and Milwaukee with the

A J1 and its train showing off the husky outline of a big passenger engine in the pre-streamlining era.

'Milwaukee Express', at an average 123.4km/h (76.7mph) speed, and with a maximum recorded figure on the locomotive's speedometer of 166.5km/h (103.5mph).

Among the driver's aids on the NYC Hudsons was a valve-pilot, based on the idea that for any given speed, there is a definite cut-off point for steam admission to the cylinders, to allow the locomotive to develop its maximum power. The valve-pilot was a gauge with two needles; a black one to show actual running speed, and a red one to show the

optimum speed relating to the cut-off used. It was up to the engineer to ensure that the two needles remained together, by opening or partly closing the regulator, but never letting the red needle occupy a position showing a longer cut-off than the optimum when working with full regulator. This was typical of American provision while main-line drivers elsewhere were lucky to have a mere speedometer.

Hudsons ran the NYC's main expresses for more than 15 years before the appearance of 4-8-2

'Mohawks' and then of 4-8-4 'Northerns' on the line relegated them to secondary passenger trains rather than the 'high varnish'.

BOILER PRESSURE: 15.75kg/cm² (225psi)
CYLINDERS: 634x711mm (25x28in)
DRIVING WHEELS: 2005mm (79in)
GRATE AREA: 7.6m² (81.5sq ft)
HEATING SURFACE: 389m² (4187sq ft)
SUPERHEATER: 162.1m² (1745sq ft)
TRACTIVE EFFORT: 19,183kg (42,300lb)
TOTAL WEIGHT: 256.3t (565,200lb)

CLASS 3000 2-8-2 BUENOS AIRES PACIFIC RAILWAY (BAP)

ARGENTINA 1928

Long-haul freights across the pampas towards the Andes and the Chilean border were the main

duties of this class, though they were mixed-traffic engines with vacuum brake equipment to handle passenger cars. British works were long accustomed to building engines

for export that were higher and wider than those the home railways ordered. This two-cylinder simple 'Mikado', built by Beyer Peacock for the 1675mm (5ft 6in) gauge, has a boiler of 2094mm (82.5in) outer diameter, greater than any built for a British locomotive.

The bogie tender was on a scale comparable with the engine, capable

of holding 15.24 tonnes (15 tons) of coal, and with one of the first steam-powered coal pushers fitted in Britain.

BOILER PRESSURE: 14kg/cm² (200psi)
CYLINDERS: 622x761mm (24.5x30in)
DRIVING WHEELS: 1700mm (67in)
GRATE AREA: 4.27m² (46sq ft)
HEATING SURFACE: 256m² (2760sq ft)
SUPERHEATER: 62.8m² (676sq ft)
TRACTIVE EFFORT: 18,272kg (40,290lb)
TOTAL WEIGHT: 208.25t (459,200lb)

The Class 3000 were among the biggest and heaviest locomotives ever built for an Argentinian railway, but, delivered just before the beginning of the Great Depression, their full capacity was rarely put to the test.

CLASS S 4-6-2 VICTORIAN RAILWAYS (VR)

AUSTRALIA 1928

A change of gauge between New South Wales and Victoria meant a change of train at Albury. The four engines of this class ran the 1600mm (5ft 3in) gauge Melbourne–Albury section of the 'Spirit of Progress' express. They were built at the VR Newport Railway Workshops as three-cylinder simple expansion engines, with cast-steel bar frames and outside Walschaerts valve gear, the inside cylinder operated by Gresley's conjugated lever arrangement. When an all-steel carriage set was introduced in 1937, the S class was given a streamlined casing, and larger tenders enabled them to make the 317km (197-mile) run to Albury non-stop with 10 cars weighing 508 tonnes (500 tons). Hand-firing

made this run a supreme task for the fireman, who shovelled 6.1 tonnes (6 tons) of coal in the course of 3hrs, 50 mins. In 1951–

52, the class was converted to oil-burning, but in the latter year it was displaced from the 'Blue' service by B-class diesel electrics.

All were eventually withdrawn and then scrapped between October 1953 and September 1954.

BOILER PRESSURE: 14kg/cm² (200psi)
CYLINDERS: 520x710mm (20.5x28in)
DRIVING WHEELS: 1852mm (73in)
GRATE AREA: 4.6m² (50sq ft)
HEATING SURFACE: 294m2 (3166sq ft)
SUPERHEATER: 57.7m² (622sq ft)
TRACTIVE EFFORT: 17,786kg (39,220lb)
TOTAL WEIGHT: 197.7t (436,016lb)

In streamlined form, S300 *Matthew Flinders* on a test run of the interstate 'Spirit of Progress' express at North Geelong in 1937.

NO. 9000 2-DO-1 CANADIAN NATIONAL RAILWAY (CN)

CANADA 1928

With a strong claim to be the first successful road diesel-electric, this large two-unit machine was built for the newly formed Canadian National Railway. The brain-child of Henry W. Thornton, it was built by the Canadian Locomotive Company with the electrical equipment supplied by Canadian-Westinghouse. Originally planned for both freight and passenger service, and intended to work as a pair, the two units carried the single number 9000, and worked as a 2-Do-1+1-Do-2 locomotive, producing 1984kW

(2660hp). Each was fitted with a William Beardmore V-12 diesel engine working at 800rpm. These engines, built in Glasgow, employed direct ignition, with the fuel being sprayed into the top of the cylinder through a number of fine orifices, a process that required high injection pressure. But it was a system economical on fuel and, importantly, easy to start from cold. The engines

drove generators that fed current to four traction motors geared to the axles of 1295.4mm (51in) wheels. Gear ratios could be altered for freight or passenger work, with the capacity to draw 3759 tonnes (3700 tons) of freight on level track at 56.3km/h (35mph). In passenger service, the No. 9000 hauled the 'International Limited' between Montreal and Toronto at a maximum

recorded speed of 117.5km/h (73mph), the train weight being 673.9 tonnes (663.25 tons). Later the two units were split up and one was numbered 9001. This latter machine survived until 1947. Though the onset of the Great Depression ensured that the 9000 remained a one-off, it served to demonstrate the high potential of diesel-electric power.

TYPE: 2-Do-1, diesel-electric
POWER AND OUTPUT: Beardmore diesels each producing 992kW (1330hp)

TRACTIVE EFFORT: 222kN (50,000lbf)
MAX. OPERATING SPEED: 120km/h (75mph)

WEIGHT: 170t (374,080lb)
OVERALL LENGTH: 14.34m (47ft 1in)
GAUGE: 1435mm (4ft 8.5in)

CLASS E466 1-DO-1 CZECHOSLOVAK STATE RAILWAYS (CSD)

CZECHOSLOVAKIA 1928

Five engines of this class were built to take passenger trains over the newly electrified tracks out of Prague's main station, to and from the meeting-point with steam traction. Three were built by Skoda, and two, of the same 1-Do-1 formation, were built by CKD in conjunction with the Czech

engineer F. Krizik and Brown-Boveri of Switzerland. The E466s were powerful locomotives with paired

motors driving gear wheels fixed to hollow shafts around the driving axles, with universal link couplings

to the wheels. The carrying axles and outer driving axles were joined in Krauss-Helmholtz bogies.

TYPE: express passenger locomotive
POWER: single-phase 15kV AC at 16.67Hz
TRACTIVE EFFORT: not known

MAX. OPERATING SPEED: 110km/h (68mph)
TOTAL WEIGHT: 86t (189,630lb)

MAX. AXLE LOAD: 17.5t (38,587lb)
OVERALL LENGTH: 14.5m (47ft 6in)
BUILDER: Skoda, CKD

CLASS CC50 2-6-6-0 STATE RAILWAYS (SS)

DUTCH EAST INDIES (INDONESIA) 1928

With winding mountain lines on a 1066mm (3ft 6in) gauge, the main Indonesian islands were natural territory for articulated locomotives, and Mallets operated here with great effectiveness for many years. A four-cylinder articulated compound like all true Mallets, the CC50 represents an intermediate stage in the State Railways' Mallet stock, between the earlier CC10s and the later BB class. Thirty were delivered in 1927–28, 16 from Werkspoor in the Netherlands and 14 from SLM of Winterthur in Switzerland. They were stationed at depots across Java to run mixed-traffic services.

BOILER PRESSURE: 14kg/cm² (199psi)
CYLINDERS: hp 340x510mm (13.4x20in); lp 540x510mm (21.25x20in)
DRIVING WHEELS: 1106mm (43.5in)
GRATE AREA: 3.4m² (36.6sq ft)
HEATING SURFACE: 150.8m² (1623.6sq ft)
SUPERHEATER: 50m² (538.3sq ft)
TRACTIVE EFFORT: N/A
TOTAL WEIGHT: 74.6t (164,640lb)
(engine only)

Belching oil smoke, a CC50 backs down on its freight train. The mountain background shows why the Indonesian railways found Mallets to be useful motive power.

CLASS 80 0-6-0T GERMAN STATE RAILWAYS (DRG)

GERMANY 1928

Although designed and built as one of the 'standard engine' types of the DRG, this always remained a small class, despite its excellent qualities – no doubt a reflection of the durability of the numerous older shunting tanks still in service. In many cases, elderly main-line engines were also used for this purpose, which though cheap on the capital account, was in reality expensive in maintenance and spares. The 39 examples of Class 80 built in 1928–29 were based at the major termini of Köln (Cologne) and Leipzig. This superheated shunter packed a great deal of power into a modest

Picture of compact power: Class 80.014. Now at Nördlingen, it ran on heritage lines in the 1990s.

3200mm (10ft 6in) wheelbase. It could move 900 tonnes (885 tons) at 45km/h (28mph) on the level. The type lasted on the DB up to 1965, and on the DR to 1977.

BOILER PRESSURE: 14kg/cm² (199psi)
CYLINDERS: 450x550mm (17.7x21.6in)
DRIVING WHEELS: 1100mm (43.3in)
GRATE AREA: 1.5m² (16.1sq ft)
HEATING SURFACE: 69.6m² (749sq ft)
SUPERHEATER: 25.5m² (274.5sq ft)
TRACTIVE EFFORT: 11,988kg (26,435lb)
TOTAL WEIGHT: 54.4t (119,952lb)

CLASS 86 2-8-2T GERMAN STATE RAILWAYS (DRG)

Most German builders had a share in building the 774 units of this *Einheitslok* type, in three main batches up to 1943. The original builders were Maschinenbau-Gesellschaft Karlsruhe. Meant for mixed-traffic local trains on lines with a 15-tonne (14.7-ton) maximum axle loading, the Class 86 ran in either direction with equal ease to a operating speed of 70km/h (44mph). The third coupled wheels were driven by two horizontal

outside cylinders, of simple-expansion and operated by Heusinger valve gear. Of its multiple domes, two held sand, and a compressed-air spray system assisted with sanding on slippery rails. The other two contained the feed-water valve and the steam regulator. A Knorr feedwater heater was fitted, with a Knorr-Tolkien feedwater pump. As with all DRG classes, electric lighting was fitted, driven by a steam-powered dynamo.

The hills of the Moselle and Swabia were their frst home, and the first 16 were fitted with counter-pressure brakes for downhill work. Around 20 were wrecked during the war years, and 184 were retained on Czech, Polish, Austrian and Russian railways after 1945, while the *Deutsche Bundesbahn* (DB) received 385 and the *Deutsche Reichsbahn* (DR) had around 175. They ran on the DR up to 1976, some on the causeway line from Heringsdorf to the Baltic island of

Usedom, for which they were fitted with smoke deflectors against the almost-permanent east wind, but most worked in the hills of Saxony.

BOILER PRESSURE: 14kg/cm² (199psi)
CYLINDERS: 570x660mm (22.4x26in)
DRIVING WHEELS: 1400mm (55in)
GRATE AREA: 2.3m² (24.8sq ft)
HEATING SURFACE: 117.3m² (1262.9sq ft)
SUPERHEATER: 47m² (506sq ft)
TRACTIVE EFFORT: 18,195kg (40,000lb)
TOTAL WEIGHT: 88.5t (195,142lb)

CLASS 22 2-4-2T HUNGARIAN STATE RAILWAYS (MÁV)

This was an almost-archaic wheel arrangement for 1928, but the little tank engine was created with a practical purpose in mind. In Hungary as elsewhere, competition from petrol-engined road transport was eating heavily into the railways' business from the mid-1920s. For the works and

repair shops whose investment was in steam power, there was also a threat of competition from the Abmot diesel railcars. The Class 22 was a small superheated tank class. It was introduced by the MÁV to speed up local services, and also compete with the opposition. With modern

features including large forward look-out windows and electric light, and equipped with the almost-invariable pair of simple-expansion outside cylinders, it numbered 136 by 1939, with 35 supplied to the Yugoslavian Railways. In 1948, the class was redesignated 275.

BOILER PRESSURE: 13kg/cm² (185psi)
CYLINDERS: 355x460mm (14x18in)
DRIVING WHEELS: 1220mm (48in)
GRATE AREA: 1.25m² (13.5sq ft)
HEATING SURFACE: 49.2m² (529.7sq ft)
SUPERHEATER: 16.7m² (180sq ft)
TRACTIVE EFFORT: 5240kg (11,550lb)
TOTAL WEIGHT: 34.4t (75,852lb)

CLASS EF-1 C-C GREAT INDIAN PENINSULA RAILWAY (GIPR)

Electrification in India began with work on the Bombay (Mumbai) suburban lines from 1922, but in the later 1920s the 1500V DC overhead catenary extended to the Bombay–Poona main line, with its difficult gradients mounting to the Deccan plateau. For more than three decades, these powerful electrics hauled heavy freight trains on the lines running inland from Bombay. With a strong resemblance to the Ce 6/8 'Krokodil' class for the SBB Gotthard line from 1918, and from the same builder, SLM at Winterthur, they were known on the Indian railways as *Khekda*, or

Crabs. As in Switzerland, they proved to be extremely reliable and durable, though the external rodding needed frequent lubrication. Eventually the class totalled 41, with later engines coming from the Vulcan Foundry of Newton-le-Willows, England, and with electrical equipment by Metropolitan-Vickers. The central body section, containing the main transformer, was pivoted on two power bogies. The bogies contained the motor units, wound for full line voltage of 1500V, each driving six wheels from connecting rods linked to a jackshaft placed

between the first and second axles; and with outside frames and bearings. The front ends of the bogie units were joined by concertina links to the closely fitted main body section. Electro-pneumatic control equipment gave nine running positions, and a regenerative braking system, by Newport-Shildon of Great Britain, was provided.

Reclassed as WCG-1 under Indian Railways, they worked mostly as banking engines on the steep gradient between Karjat and Lonavla, and some were still on these duties as late as 1992,

though withdrawals had begun in the mid-1970s. The first of the class is preserved at Delhi.

TYPE: heavy freight locomotive
POWER: four 485kW (650hp) motors in pairs driving two three-axle bogies through twin helical gears and jackshaft, supplied by 1500V DC via overhead catenary
TRACTIVE EFFORT: 135.5kN (30,480lb)
MAX. OPERATING SPEED: 80km/h (50mph)
TOTAL WEIGHT: 138.3t (305,000lb)
MAX. AXLE LOAD: 23t (50,825lb)
BUILDER: SLM, Winterthur, and Vulcan Foundry, Manchester

CLASS EA-1 2-CO-1 GREAT INDIAN PENINSULA RAILWAY (GIPR)

Long-distance services out of Bombay (Mumbai) were transformed with the arrival of this class, inaugurating what was referred to as a 'high-speed' era. In tests, they comfortably maintained an average speed of 96km/h (60mph) with trainloads around the 365-tonne (360-ton) mark. A single prototype was supplied in 1928, and 22 locomotives of this class were

subsequently ordered to specifications laid down by the GIPR's consulting engineers, Merz & Maclellan. Class EA-1 was of box-cab construction, with a central corridor linking the ends. Auxiliary equipment, including air reservoir, vacuum pump, blowers to cool the motors, and braking gear, was positioned over the single carrying axle. Control gear was situated centrally, and the

resistances, unit switches and certain other items of control equipment were housed in the space over the bogie. Reduction gearing transmitted the power from the six motors paired above each axle to hollow shafts surrounding the axles. The couplings between shaft and axle were designed to absorb movement of the wheels as they met bumps and irregularities in the tracks.

The motors could be run as all six in series, or as two parallel groups of three in series, or three parallel groups of two in series. Three field strengths were available for selection, giving a total of nine possible economic speeds without incurring circuit

resistances. Two driving axles were fixed in the frame and the third was linked in a form of Krauss-Helmholtz bogie with the single front truck. All wheels had inside bearings. Air-pumped sand was fed from the prominent sandboxes in case of need on a slippery rail. Though capable of running at 137km/h (85mph), their maximum operating speed was restricted to 112km/h (70mph).

Painted in the GIPR black, with red trim and with rounded rather than squared-off ends, they were more appealing to the eye than many box-body types, and with their freight-hauling companions of Class EF-1, the EA-1s provided an excellent advertisement for

TYPE: 2-Bo-A-1
POWER: 1656kW (2250hp)
SUPPLY: 1500V DC
TRACTIVE EFFORT: 95kN (21,500lbf) at 59.2km/h (37mph)

MAX. OPERATING SPEED: 136km/h (85mph)
WEIGHT: 100t (220,460lb)
MAX. AXLE LOAD: 20t (44,100lb)
OVERALL LENGTH: 17.214m (56ft 2in)
GAUGE: 1676mm (5ft 6in)

electric traction. In June 1930, they began hauling the 'Deccan Queen' express, running the 192km (119.3 miles) between Bombay and Poona in 2hrs 45mins – the fastest then achieved on a section that included the fearsome 1 in 37 Bhore Ghat incline and many others little less severe.

With the advent of the Indian Railways, Class EA became Class WCM/1. They had a long career, but with the conversion of the Deccan line to 25kV AC supply in 2000, all were finally withdrawn from service in 1999. Two are preserved.

An EA-1 in the late 1920s with a special train, perhaps the Viceroy's. The detail of the station design is very British, down to the fretwork trim of the roof.

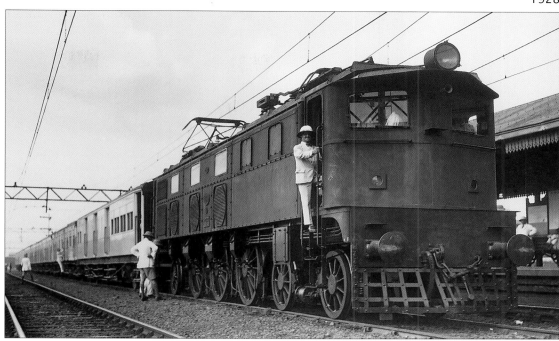

CLASS E432 1-D-1 STATE RAILWAYS (FS)

ITALY 1928

Unlike most contemporary Italian electric locomotives, which gave the driver a good forward look-out, the high-built nose of this rod-drive class offered only a restricted forward view. Forty were built by Ernesto Breda of Milan, and the E432s (001 to 040) operated over the 3300V three phase

alternating current network used by Italian railways. By the late 1920s, it was working across a 1900km

(1200-mile) network in north-west Italy. With a liquid rheostatic control system, Class E432 had 18 tonnes

(17.7 tons) over each of the four driving axles, and four running speeds up to 100km/h (62.1mph).

TYPE: 1-D-1 three-phase electric	**TRACTIVE EFFORT:** 161kN (36,225lbf)
POWER: 2200kW (2989hp)	**MAX. OPERATING SPEED:** 100km/h
SUPPLY: 3300V 16.7Hz AC two-wire	(62.1mph)
three-phase	**WEIGHT:** 94t (207,270lb)
MAX. AXLE LOAD: 18t (39,690lb)	
OVERALL LENGTH: 13.910m (45ft 4in)	
GAUGE: 1435mm (4ft 8.5in)	

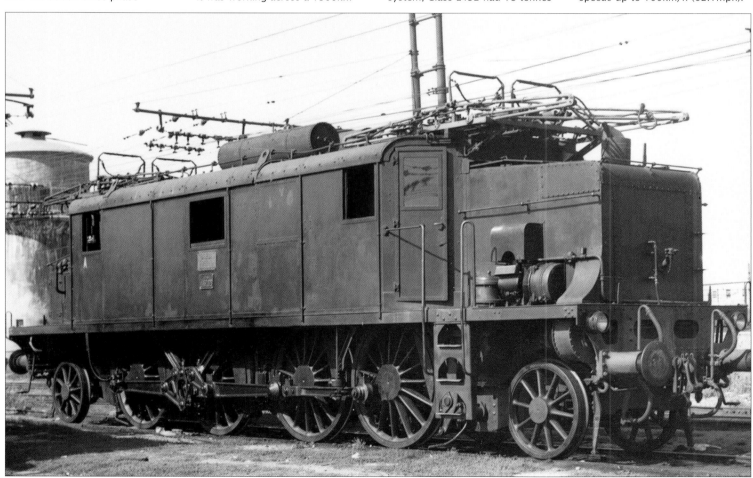

A complex blend of angles and curves shapes the ends of an E432, seen here in the yard at Alessandria, on 18 September 1947.

BO-BO HALMSTAD–NÄSSJÖ RAILWAY

The Halmstad–Nässjö Railway, running through thickly forested country, had been at the forefront of diesel pioneering in Sweden, and this locomotive, built specifically for it by the Atlas-ASEA combine in Stockholm as No. 5, was an early diesel-electric, brought out at a time when electric transmission was only

one of the apparent options to designers, and one of the more complicated and expensive. Diesel-pneumatic, and diesel-hydraulic transmissions were also being tried out.

The Bo-Bo's box-cab form followed the general shape and contours of Swedish diesel and electric locomotives set by the D

class in 1925, but its eight wheels, with outside roller bearings, were

mounted in a rigid frame, not on bogies.

TYPE: diesel-electric freight locomotive	**MAXIMUM OPERATING SPEED:** not known
POWER: eight-cylinder 149.25kW (200hp) engine working at 500rpm, driving two electric motors geared to the driving axles	**TOTAL WEIGHT:** not known
	MAXIMUM AXLE LOAD: not known
TRACTIVE EFFORT: not known	**OVERALL LENGTH:** not known
	GAUGE: not known

'CAB-FIRST' CLASS AC-5 4-8-8-2 SOUTHERN PACIFIC RAILROAD (SP)

Between Truckee and Blue Canyon, on the SP's Sierra Nevada line, 61km (38 miles) of snow-sheds were built to prevent immense drifts, which might be more than 15m (50ft) deep, from blocking the line. In these, as in the long tunnels of the line, smoke was a hazard. Here, as on other railways with lengthy tunnels, the engine crews often felt in danger of asphyxiation. Some took refuge by lying on the cab floor with damp cloths over their faces. Consequently, an engine whose cab was free from back-blown smoke was a great boon to the crew. In SP folklore, one bold engineer had his engine turned 'back to front' and ran it with the boiler behind, prompting the management to take action. SP's first cab-front locomotives had

been 2-8-8-2 Mallet compounds turned back-to-front in 1910; known as Class MC-2, these were rebuilt from 1927 as simple-expansion engines. The AC-5s were four-cylinder simples from the start, of greater mechanical dimensions than the AC-1s. Ten AC-5s were built by Baldwin in 1928, with a further 16 in the following year, and 25 more in 1930, when the boiler pressure was raised to 17.5kg/cm² (250psi). In all, the SP had 256 AC (articulated consolidation) locomotives, constructed up to 1944, of which only the coal-burning class AC-9 (built by Lima in 1939) was not cab-forward (AC-9 was later converted to oil but remained of conventional build). As the engines burned oil, the problem of access to the fuel

supply was easily dealt with: oil and water were towed in a huge 12-wheel double bogie tender, with the oil supplied at 2.2kg (5lb) pressure to the burners. The cab-firsts were also used on other divisions of the SP where their power and smoke-free driving position were of value. Class AC12 was the last set of steam locomotives to be ordered by Southern Pacific – 20 were delivered by Baldwin between 1943 and 1944.

The concept goes back to the Italian Class 500 (later 670/671) of 1900, still running in 1928; like these, the AC-5s ran permanently 'backwards', with driver and fireman occupying opposite sides from the usual positions. Hauling trains of 85 to 100 refrigerator cars on the Sierra grades, three ACs

might be employed, one at the head, one inserted after the fifteenth car, and the third inserted four cars in front of the caboose. Despite the train-marshalling involved, this was considered more effective than to have two locomotives pushing from the rear. The last in action was No. 4274 in December 1956; the last of the line, No. 4294, is preserved.

BOILER PRESSURE: 16.5kg/cm² (235psi)	
CYLINDERS: 609x812mm (24x32in)	
DRIVING WHEELS: 1612mm (63.5in)	
GRATE AREA: 12.9m² (139sq ft)	
HEATING SURFACE: 604.1m² (6505sq ft)	
SUPERHEATER: 277.5m² (2988sq ft)	
TRACTIVE EFFORT: 46,848kg (106,300lb)	
TOTAL WEIGHT: 278.4t (614,000lb) (engine only)	

CLASS X 2-8-2 VICTORIAN RAILWAYS (VR)

No. X27 in delivery condition. The steam feed pipe to the booster truck is clearly visible.

Although built for heavy mineral freight, the 1548mm (5ft) wheels of the X class could manage a fine turn of speed. Indeed, on one occasion X-32, fuelled by pulverized coal, hauled the 'Spirit of Progress' passenger Melbourne–Sydney express without losing time. The 29 members of the class were built at the line's own Newport shops between 1929 and 1947. All but two had a booster fitted to the pony truck, to aid in starting, contributing 4083kg (9000lb) of tractive effort when in operation (often they were cut off, or ignored by drivers as an extra complication). Some of the older engines were rebuilt with new Belpaire fireboxes and combustion chambers, and stovepipe chimneys – creating what in Australian parlance was known as a 'basher front end'. Smoke deflectors were also fitted. Scrapping of the class began in 1957 and was complete by 1961. Only one of the X class is preserved today.

BOILER PRESSURE: 14.3kg/cm² (205lb)	**HEATING SURFACE:** 242.8m² (2615sq ft)
CYLINDERS: 558x710mm (22x28in)	**SUPERHEATER:** 38.3m² (412sq ft)
DRIVING WHEELS: 1548mm (61in)	**TRACTIVE EFFORT:** 17,556kg (38,712lb)
GRATE AREA: 3.9m² (42sq ft)	**TOTAL WEIGHT:** 188.3t (415,184lb)

BEYER GARRATT 4-6-2+2-6-4 LEOPOLDINA RAILWAY (LR)   BRAZIL 1929

Brazil had the most extensive system of metre-gauge railways in the world, and the first two locomotives of this class were built by Beyer Peacock of Manchester, England, primarily for passenger service on the twisting metre-gauge tracks between Campos and Victoria, in Rio de Janeiro Province. A further 12 were supplied, from the same builders, in 1937 and 1943. They had Belpaire boilers, Walschaerts valve gear and piston valves.

Although the Garret was intended to burn low-grade coal, the built-up tender rails show that they often burned wood as fuel, and the capacious fireboxes and ashpans afforded by the Garratt design would have coped effectively with this. Good logs and poor coal provided much the same calorific value.

BOILER PRESSURE: 12.3kg/cm² (175psi)	**HEATING SURFACE:** 157.6m² (1697sq ft)
CYLINDERS: 393x558mm (15.5x22in)	**SUPERHEATER:** 31.1m² (335sq ft)
DRIVING WHEELS: 1015mm (40in)	**TRACTIVE EFFORT:** 13,300kg (29,330lb)
GRATE AREA: 3.1m² (34sq ft)	**TOTAL WEIGHT:** 113.3t (249,760lb)

CLASS T1 2-10-4 'SELKIRK' TYPE CANADIAN PACIFIC RAILWAY (CPR)   CANADA 1929

The Texas & Pacific Railway had 10 locomotives of this configuration built by the Lima Locomotive Works in 1925, and it was duly known as the 'Texas' type. As a 'super-power' locomotive, it proved an excellent heavy freight engine, like the 'Berkshire' type also built by Lima, but even more so. The CPR, however, wanted a Canadian name for its new giants, and they were known as 'Selkirks' following a staff competition, named for the mountain range through which they worked. Nos. 5900–5919 were built by the Montreal Locomotive Works in 1929, and were of conventional appearance.

The smooth-lined power of the 'Selkirks' – No. 5921 poses for the camera when still new. The off-centre placing of the bell is a distinctive feature.

Semi-streamlining of 'Selkirks' began in 1938 when Nos. 5920–5929 were built, the boiler pressure being raised to 20kg/cm² (285psi) from the original 19.3kg/cm2 (275psi). The final batch, 5930–5935, appeared in 1949 – the last steam locomotives built for the CPR. The final six had two large Westinghouse air compressors rather than the single air brake pumps fitted on the earlier locomotives. These oil-fired two-cylinder simple-expansion engines operated both passenger and freight services through the Rockies between Calgary and Revelstoke. On the spectacular climb from Banff to Beavermouth, through the twin spiral tunnels of the Kicking Horse Pass, they took 14-car trains on the trans-continental 'Dominion', of around 1016 tonnes (1000 tons), unaided. All the Selkirks' regular services were turned over to diesel haulage by 1954, and for a few years they were transferred to work on the Brooks and Maple Creek divisions between Calgary and Swift Current, Saskatchewan, and to haul freight trains between Alyth ands Edmonton. The class was all withdrawn by 1959. Two of the final set to be built have been preserved, No. 5935, and No. 5934 (originally 5931).

BOILER PRESSURE: 20kg/cm² (285psi)
CYLINDERS: 634x812mm (25x32in)
DRIVING WHEELS: 1599mm (63in)
GRATE AREA: 8.7m² (93.5sq ft)
HEATING SURFACE: 453.8m² (4886sq ft)
SUPERHEATER: 196.1m² (2112sq ft)
TRACTIVE EFFORT: 34877kg (76,905lb)
TOTAL WEIGHT: 202.7t (447,000lb)
(engine only)

CLASS 100 BO GERMAN STATE RAILWAYS (DRG)

GERMANY 1929

Looking for *Kleinlokomotiven*, two-axle rail tractors for factory sidings, the *Deutsche Reichsbahn Gesellschaft* (DRG) considered no less than 14 prototypes in 1929–30. V6004–V6006 were built by Berliner Maschinenbau (BMAG) with 31kW (42hp) Kamper engines; V6007–V6009 from BMAG with 29kW (40hp) Deutz; V6010–V6012 from Deutz with the same engine, V6013–V6015 from Rheiner

Maschinenfabrik Windhoff with 35kW (48hp) Hanseatischen engines; and V6016–V6017 from Fuerst Stollberg Huette with 26kW (36hp) engines.

In 1931, all these were renumbered 4000–4011 and 0001–0002, the lower numbers indicating less than 40hp, the higher numbers 40hp-plus. The two power ranges were grouped as I and II, and unified production

TYPE: four-wheel light shunting tractor	**MAX. OPERATING SPEED:** up to 30km/h (19mph)
POWER: type I to 29kW (40hp); type II from 29kW (40hp)	**WEIGHT:** 10 to 16t (22,050 to 35,280lb)
TRACTIVE EFFORT: various	**OVERALL LENGTH:** 6.45m (21ft)
	GAUGE: 1435mm (4ft 8.5in)

of group I was by Humboldt-Deutz, Gmeinder and Windhoff, with group II from BMAG, Deutz, Jung, Krauss-Maffei and Orenstein

& Koppel. By 1934, higher traction power requirements gave way to new 87/94kW (118/128hp) designs.

0-8-0T SOUTHERN RAILWAY (SR)

GREAT BRITAIN 1929

Numbering only eight, this was the only eight-coupled design built by the Southern. Intended for shunting in the company's newly laid out hump yards, it had a short wheelbase of only 8274mm (17ft 6in) against a total length of 11,999mm (39ft 3in). Power came from three simple-expansion cylinders, with the outside cylinders driving the third coupled axle via long

connecting rods, and the inside cylinder the second coupled axle. It had a relatively small grate and firebox to keep down fuel consumption during the long 'stand-by' periods typical with shunting engines, though this would also limit its ability to raise steam quickly. A steam-powered reverser was fitted. All were built at the company's Brighton works.

BOILER PRESSURE: 12.6kg/cm² (180psi)	
CYLINDERS: 406x711mm (16x28in)	
DRIVING WHEELS: 1421mm (56in)	
GRATE AREA: 1.72m² (18.6sq ft)	
HEATING SURFACE: 118.8m² (1279sq ft)	
TRACTIVE EFFORT: 14,568kg (29,500lb)	
TOTAL WEIGHT: 72.7t (160,384lb)	

Above: A no. 30956 approaching a junction.
Below: As British Railways No. 30951, an ex-Southern 0-8-0T stands near the coaling stage at Ashford, in the early 1950s.

CLASS PO4 4-6-0 DUTCH STATE RAILWAYS (NS)

NETHERLANDS 1929

With electrification and secondary diesels planned for the Dutch railway system, this was to be the last Dutch express steam locomotive. A total of 36 were built by Henschel of Kassel in 1929 and 1930, to handle trains made up of the NS' new steel carriages and *Wagons-Lits* stock, taking over from the Class 3700

4-6-0s. With an 18-tonne (17.7-ton) maximum axle load they originally suffered from route restrictions, being unable to use the Ijssel bridge between Utrecht and Groningen.

This class used the bogie tender design of the older 3700 of the SS and the 3600 of the NCS (State Railways and Central Railways

prior to the formation of the NS). The two outside cylinders drove the first set of coupled wheels, with internal Walschaerts valve gear. Maximum service speed was 110kph (68mph).

The class was a very effective one, and its boiler design was re-used in the class 6300 4-8-4Ts of 1930-31 (see 1930).

BOILER PRESSURE: 14kg/cm² (199psi)	
CYLINDERS: 420x660mm (16.5x26in)	
DRIVING WHEELS: 1850mm (73in)	
GRATE AREA: 3.2m² (34.4sq ft)	
HEATING SURFACE: 150m² (1615sq ft)	
SUPERHEATER: 53m² (570.6sq ft)	
TRACTIVE EFFORT: 13,575kg (29,940lb)	
TOTAL WEIGHT: 84t (185,220lb)	
(engine only)	

CLASS EC BO-BO NEW ZEALAND RAILWAYS (NZR)

The short line through the hills between Christchurch and its port of Lyttelton included the 2.57km (1.6-mile) Heathcoate tunnel, and an electric catenary was installed in 1929. Six Bo-Bo type engines were built as NZR Class EC by English Electric's Dick Kerr in 1929 to run all the trains, numbered EC7 to EC12. They were used exclusively on this section, and ran until it was turned over to diesel operation in 1970. EC7 is preserved at Ferrymead, where it may be found alongside another veteran, EO3 (see 1923).

TYPE: Bo-Bo
POWER: 885kW (1188hp)
SUPPLY: 1500V DC
TRACTIVE EFFORT: 112kN (25000lbf)
MAX. OPERATING SPEED: 85km/h (53.1mph)

WEIGHT: 50.8t (112,000lb)
MAX. AXLE LOAD: 12.5t (27,563lb)
OVERALL LENGTH: 12m (39ft 2in)
GAUGE: 1067mm (3ft 6in)

CLASS S 0-8-0 SOUTH AFRICAN RAILWAYS (SAR)

A powerful shunting engine, this class was involved in train marshalling in the SAR's major yards, Germiston (Johannesburg), Kimberley, Durban, Cape Town, Pietermaritzburg and others. Between 1929 and 1935, around 100 of classes S, S1 and S2 were built, all two-cylinder simple-expansion types of similar

An S2 shunts at Germiston, outside Johannesburg. Though primarily a shunting engine, its big tender enabled it to run considerable distances when required.

appearance but of varying power and axle load – the S1 being the strongest and the S2 the lightest. The original 11 engines of Class S were built in Germany by

Henschel; S1 was the first locomotive type built at the SAR's own Salt River Works, Cape Town, in 1947. Specifications are for Class S.

BOILER PRESSURE: 15kg/cm² (215psi)
CYLINDERS: 590x634.5mm (23.25x25in)
DRIVING WHEELS: 1218mm (48in)
GRATE AREA: 3.7m² (40sq ft)
HEATING SURFACE: 157m² (1690sq ft)
SUPERHEATER: 40.3m² (434sq ft)
TRACTIVE EFFORT: 20,590kg (45,400lb)
TOTAL WEIGHT: 62.9t (138,878lb)
(engine only)

BVZ CLASS HGE4/4 BO-BO SWISS FEDERAL RAILWAYS (SBB)

Similar in appearance to the Rhaetian Railway's 'baby crocodiles', these six locomotives were supplied by SLM when the rack-and-adhesion railway that links Brig and Visp in the upper Rhône Valley with Zermatt near the Matterhorn mountain was electrified in 1929. The BVZs are, however, of Bo-Bo wheel arrangement, though otherwise mechanically very similar to the RhB engines. For more than four decades, they worked on all services, and still survive in occasional special and peak period service.

TYPE: mixed-traffic rack-and-adhesion electric locomotive
WHEEL ARRANGEMENT: Bo-Bo
POWER: 11,000V 16.7Hz AC overhead line collection; 735kW (985hp); single-phase AC traction motors
TRACTIVE EFFORT: not known

MAX. OPERATING SPEED: 45km/h (69mph) off rack, 25km/h (16mph) on rack
WEIGHT: 47t (102,775lb)
MAX. AXLE LOAD: not known
OVERALL LENGTH: not known
GAUGE: 1000mm (3ft 3in)

'NORTHERN' CLASS S1 4-8-4 GREAT NORTHERN RAILWAY (GN) USA 1929

Class S1 was formed of six locomotives, oil-burners built by Baldwin at Philadelphia for heavy passenger service, particularly the line's flagship train, the *Empire Builder*. The 4-8-4 had been introduced on the Northern Pacific Railroad with its Class A, built by Alco at Schenectady in 1927, but other lines, including the Great Northern, were very close behind. Where the GNR line crossed the continental divide in Montana, the maximum westbound grade was 1.8 per cent and the Baldwin-built S1s took 14-car trains up without assistance. They replaced 'Mountain' 4-8-2s, which had seemed large and powerful only a few years before, but the 'Northerns' produced a tractive effort around 22 per cent greater. Since the advent of 'super-power', successive locomotive types had leap-frogged each other towards the ever-receding target of maximum speed and power. The S1s carried a boiler of 2487mm

(98in) diameter, matched with a Belpaire firebox. Both front and rear bogies ran in outside frames, and all axles had roller bearings. Two air compressor pumps were mounted on the smoke-box front, a common feature on US locomotives at this time. All were oil burners, apart from one, No. 2552, and had tank-tenders of the 'Vanderbilt' type, running on two six-wheel bogies, with a capacity of 4800 gals (5800 US gals) of oil and 18,300 gals (22,000 US gals) of water. Rugged and imposing in appearance, at 4.87m (16ft) high and 33.07m (108ft 7in) long, the Northerns were prominent in the company's advertising and promotions, with the promise of speed and big, comfortable trains. The arrival of the Northerns meant the Great Northern cut five hours from the schedule of its transcontinental *Empire Builder* train, with

speeding-up on all sectors as well as the Northerns' Montana territory. But the Class S1 too was soon to be surpassed by the GN's S2 4-8-4, with 2030mm (80in) driving wheels, which took over the long-haul passenger services, and the S1s were turned over to fast freight workings. In 1937, seven locomotives took the *Empire Builder* over its various stages between St Paul and Seattle: a P2 4-8-2 from St Paul to Breckenridge; then successive S2s on the sectors Breckenridge–Minot, Minot–Havre, and Havre–Whitefish. Another P2 took the train from Whitefish to Wenatchee, where an electric double 1-D-1+1-D-1 unit took over through the mountains between Wenatchee and Skykomish, with a P2 on the final leg from Skykomish into Seattle. The train, air-conditioned and with excellent catering facilities, took 56 hours 25

minutes to run the 3568km (2217 miles) between Chicago and Seattle.

Perhaps the most celebrated Northern was the *Four Aces*, No. 1111, built at Schenectady by Alco and purchased by Timken to demonstrate the virtues of roller bearings, which were fitted on all its axles. It toured US railroads, on one occasion showing its free-running quality by being pulled from a standing start by three young ladies at a Chicago publicity event. After running 162,000km (100,000 miles), it was bought by the Northern Pacific and then ran a further 3,258,225km (2,025,000 miles) over the next 23 years.

BOILER PRESSURE: 17.5kg/cm² (250psi)
CYLINDERS: 710x761mm (28x30in)
DRIVING WHEELS: 1853mm (73in)
GRATE AREA: 8.7m² (94sq ft)
HEATING SURFACE: 423m² (4560sq ft)
SUPERHEATER: 188.3m² (2028sq ft)
TRACTIVE EFFORT: 30,385kg (67,000lb)
TOTAL WEIGHT: 418.7t (847,900lb)

The *Four Aces* on its States-wide promotional tour in 1930. Apart from roller bearings, it featured fittings from 52 manufacturers.

'SCHOOLS' CLASS 4-4-0 SOUTHERN RAILWAY (SR)

A three-cylinder 4-4-0 was something unusual, and this express class, designed by R.W. Maunsell, was claimed as the most powerful of the type in Europe. It

was originally designed for the Southern's line to Hastings on the south coast, a curvaceous route with narrow tunnels and severe loading restrictions, and 10, all

named after well-known schools, were built at the Southern's Eastleigh works. In main-line performance they proved so successful that a further 30 were built, and they operated on a wider range of passenger services. The three cylinders were all simple expansion, each with its own set

of Walschaerts valve gear driving the first coupled wheels. The 'Schools' could compete with the 'Lord Nelson' 4-6-0s on express trains of 356–366 tonnes (350–360 tons). Wide-chimney exhausts with Lemaître blast pipes were later fitted to about 20 of the class: which represented perhaps

Southern Railway No. 928, *Stowe*, one of the preserved 'Schools' locomotives, approaches Freshfield Halt with a train for Horsted Keynes, on the heritage 'Bluebell Line' in Kent, on 14 June 1981.

the finest example of the British talent for getting maximum performance out of small dimensions. They were withdrawn by the end of 1962, but three have been preserved.

BOILER PRESSURE: 15.5kg/cm² (220psi)
CYLINDERS: 419x660mm (16.5x26in)
DRIVING WHEELS: 2005mm (79in)
GRATE AREA: 2.6m² (28.3sq ft)
HEATING SURFACE: 149m² (1604sq ft)
SUPERHEATER: 26m² (280 sq ft)
TRACTIVE EFFORT: 11,396kg (25,130lb)
TOTAL WEIGHT: 68t (150,080lb)

This time as British Railways No. 30926, the same engine runs on the restored Great Cerntral line in April 1992.

NO. 10000 4-6-4 LONDON & NORTH EASTERN RAILWAY (LNER) GREAT BRITAIN 1930

An ultra-high pressure marine-type water tube boiler was fitted to this experimental locomotive, designed by H.N. Nigel Gresley, CME of the LNER. A four-cylinder compound enveloped in a bulbous, streamlined casing, it was hoped that it would produce power comparable to the LNER 'Pacifics' but with greatly reduced fuel consumption achieved by the

super-high steam pressure. Built at the LNER's Darlington workshops, its boiler came from the shipbuilders Yarrow of Glasgow, a five-drum water-tube boiler pressed to almost double the conventional maximum for locomotives, consisting of a long upper steam drum connected to two pairs of lower water-drums via 694 narrow-diameter tubes. It worked a number

of scheduled services but was never in regular use, and, like other extra-high-pressure locomotives on other railways, proved expensive and troublesome to maintain. In 1937, it was rebuilt with a conventional A4-class locomotive boiler, though it retained its extra set of trailing wheels, making it the only example of a British 4-6-4. These wheels, incidentally, were not set in a truck; they ran on independent fixed axles. Another unusual feature was a turbo-generator for electric lighting; in

the 1937 rebuilding, this was adapted to floodlight the wheels and rods when the engine was in motion.

BOILER PRESSURE: 31.5kg/cm² (450psi)
CYLINDERS: hp 304.5x660mm (12x26in); lp 507.6x660mm (20x26in)
DRIVING WHEELS: 2030mm (80in)
GRATE AREA: 3.2m² (34.9sq ft)
HEATING SURFACE: 184.4m² (1986sq ft)
SUPERHEATER: 13m² (140sq ft)
TRACTIVE EFFORT: 14,510kg (32,000lb)
TOTAL WEIGHT: 168.6t (371,840lb)

To fit a marine-type boiler on a locomotive frame was a challenge for the designers, but they achieved a smooth and aerodynamic result, unlike any previous British locomotive.

CLASS GTO3 4-8-4T DUTCH STATE RAILWAYS (NS)

NETHERLANDS 1930

Later classed 6300, the GT03s, like many Dutch locomotives, had a part-British, part-German look – though they were German built. A heavyweight back-tank type, 22 were built by Henschel and Berliner Maschinenbau (the former Schwartzkopff) in 1930–31. Their role was to move bulk coal trains from the South Limburg coalfield to the cities in the west of the Netherlands. Sharing a boiler with the PO4 4-6-0, they had four simple-expansion cylinders all driving the first coupled axle, plus bar frames and Belpaire fireboxes. In order to pull passenger trains, when required, they had a maximum operating speed of 90km/h (56mph). The heaviest and most powerful tank type in Europe when new, it was also of

exceptional length at 17.39m (57ft). Coal capacity was 4.5 tonnes (4.4 tons); water capacity 3090gals (3780 US). One is preserved.

BOILER PRESSURE: 14kg/cm² (171psi)	**HEATING SURFACE:** 150m² (1615sq ft)
CYLINDERS: 420x660mm (16.5x26in)	**SUPERHEATER:** 50m² (538.3sq ft)
DRIVING WHEELS: 1550mm (61in)	**TRACTIVE EFFORT:** 14,720kg (32,457lb)
GRATE AREA: 3.2m² (34.4sq ft)	**TOTAL WEIGHT:** 127t (280,035lb)

No. 63211 at Dordrecht, around 1955. Unusually, all four cylinders drive the first coupled axle.

CLASS 15CA 4-8-2 SOUTH AFRICAN RAILWAYS (SAR)

SOUTH AFRICA 1930

On the South African railways, 4-8-2s had been in use since 1904, and newer, larger classes, like the '12' and its derivatives in the mid-1920s, produced a tractive effort of around 18,594kg (41,000lb) with a maximum axle load of 17.8 tonnes (17.5 tons). The 15CA class, known as the 'Big Bills', represented a further step forward. The first were built in the United States by Baldwin though Breda (Milan), and the North British Locomotive Company (Glasgow) also constructed them. The maximum axle load was 18.8 tonnes (18.5 tons), but the tractive effort was significantly higher than the '12'. Maximum height was 3.95m (13ft), and a width of 3.05m (10ft) gave a lateral overhang of 1.57m (3ft 4in) on each side. Two-cylinder simple expansion types, with piston valves actuated by Walschaerts gear, the 'Big Bills' in 1935 were then superseded by the 15E.

BOILER PRESSURE: 14kg/cm² (200psi)	
CYLINDERS: 609x710.6mm (24x28in)	
DRIVING WHEELS: 1447mm (57in)	
GRATE AREA: 4.5m² (48.3sq ft)	
HEATING SURFACE: 257.7m² (2775sq ft)	
SUPERHEATER: 64.6m² (696sq ft)	
TRACTIVE EFFORT: 21,809kg (48,090lb)	
TOTAL WEIGHT: 176.2t (388,528lb)	

Preserved 15CA 4-8-2 No. 2828 takes on water. De Aar was once a major steam depot on the South African Railways system.

4-6-2+2-6-4 GARRATT TYPE CENTRAL OF ARAGÓN RAILWAY SPAIN 1930

Spain apart, Garratts, and articulated engines generally (except on narrow-gauge lines), were not very common in Europe, and this was the only European Garratt class built specifically to haul passenger trains. As a result, its driving wheels were the largest yet used on a Garratt locomotive.

Six were built by Euskalduña at Bilbao to haul passenger trains between Valencia and Calatayud. On the long mountain sections, they were able to haul 305-tonne (300-ton) trains at 42km/h (25mph) up gradients of 1 in 46 and round curves of 300m (984ft) radius, and their reputation in

action was excellent. They had Walschaerts valve gear with piston valves, Belpaire fireboxes and ACFI feedwater heaters. Originally coal-fired, they were later converted to oil, and remained in service until 1970, long after the Central of Aragón Railway was incorporated into the RENFE. One is preserved.

BOILER PRESSURE: 14kg/cm² (200psi)
CYLINDERS: 482x660mm (19x26in)
DRIVING WHEELS: 1751mm (69in)
GRATE AREA: 4.9m² (53sq ft)
HEATING SURFACE: 298.9m² (3218sq ft)
SUPERHEATER: 68.9m² (742sq ft)
TRACTIVE EFFORT: 18,540kg (40,880lb)
TOTAL WEIGHT: 183.4t (404,320lb)

CLASS Z-5 2-8-8-4 NORTHERN PACIFIC RAILROAD (NP) USA 1930

Over the years, the United States had seen many 'biggest locomotives' appear and be superseded. But in certain respects, including grate area, evaporative heating surface and superheating surface, the Z-5 class and its sisters on other lines were never exceeded. Until the advent of the Union Pacific 'Big Boys' in 1941, these were undoubtedly the biggest locomotives in the world. American Locomotive Co. built the prototype for the NP in 1928, and in 1930 a further 11 were ordered, for some reason from Baldwin rather than Alco. Known as the 'Yellowstones', they were designed to haul 4064-tonne (4000-ton) freight trains on the 347.6km

(216-mile) sector of the transcontinental route through the 'Badlands' between Mandan, ND, and Glendive, MT, up grades of 1.1 per cent. Standing 5.23m (17ft 2in) from the rails to the chimney lip, they were engines of massive appearance. Though built Mallet-fashion, with the pilot and front coupled wheels forming an articulated truck, the rear coupled axles fixed to the frame and a pivoted four-wheel trailing truck. They did not work compound – the four cylinders were simple-expansion only. The very long firebox was intended to burn lignite, or 'Rosebud coal', from a NP-owned mine. A booster engine was fitted to the trailing truck to

assist with starting off, and delivering an additional 6077kg (13,400lb) of tractive effort. All were later fitted with roller bearings, something in which the NP was a pioneer.

Apart from the dozen NP Yellowstones, the Southern Pacific also had 12 (Class AC-9); the Duluth Missabe & Iron Mountain (DM&IR) had eight of Class M-3 and 10 of Class M-4, and the Baltimore & Ohio Railroad had 30 of Class EM-1.

The DM&IR road used its 2-8-8-4s to haul iron ore trains to the harbours on Lake Superior; some of them were also leased to the Denver & Rio Grande Railroad, where they were valuable as

helper engines pushing trains over the 3396m (10,359ft) Tennessee Pass on the continental divide.

The NP Yellowstone' worked their appointed route until the late 1940s, and the DM&IR locomotives survived longest, some working until 1963.

BOILER PRESSURE: 17.5kg/cm² (250psi)
CYLINDERS: 660x812mm (26x32in)
DRIVING WHEELS: 1599mm (63in)
GRATE AREA: 17m² (182sq ft)
HEATING SURFACE: 712.6m² (7673sq ft)
SUPERHEATER: 299m² (3219sq ft)
TRACTIVE EFFORT: 63,492kg (140,000lb)
TOTAL WEIGHT: 499t (1,010,475lb)

CLASS P5 2-CO-2 PENNSYLVANIA RAILROAD (PRR) USA 1930

Accustomed to designing and building its own locomotives, the PRR set out to produce a fleet of electrics for service on the New York–Washington DC route. It designed several types based upon its most successful steam locomotives, and the P5 Class was a boxcab unit using a 2-Co-2 wheel arrangement, making it effectively

TYPE: 2-Co-2, mixed-traffic electric
POWER: 11,500 V at 25Hz AC from overhead
OUTPUT: 2794kW (3750hp)

TRACTIVE EFFORT: 254kN (57,250lbf) starting TE
MAX. OPERATING SPEED: originally intended for 144km/h (90mph); later limited to 112km/h (70mph)

WEIGHT: 178t (392,000lb)
OVERALL LENGTH: 19.101m (62ft 8in)
MAX. AXLE LOAD: 35t (77,000lb)
GAUGE: 1435mm (4ft 8.5in)

an electric version of the K4 'Pacific' type. Although intended, like the K4, for fast passenger service, the

P5 was plagued by lateral swaying and cracked axles, so PRR relegated all 59 to slow freight service and

set out to develop more effective passenger power – resulting in the GG1 (see 1934).

CLASS 78 4-6-4T FEDERAL RAILWAYS OF AUSTRIA (BBÖ) AUSTRIA 1931

An express tank class, the 78s were normally employed on fast, short-range services, like the Vienna–Linz trains. Sixteen were

BOILER PRESSURE: 16kg/cm² (230psi)
CYLINDERS: 500x720mm (19.7x28.3in)
DRIVING WHEELS: 1619mm (63.8in)
GRATE AREA: 3.6m² (38.75sq ft)
HEATING SURFACE: 170m² (1830sq ft)
SUPERHEATER: 52m² (560sq ft)
TRACTIVE EFFORT: 15,260kg (33,650lb)
TOTAL WEIGHT: 109t (240,345lb)

Austrian 4-8-4 tanks – earlier (train engine) and later (pilot engine) versions speed along in winter sunshine with a special working.

originally built, with long side-tanks and capacious bunkers, at the Floridsdorf works, Vienna, between 1931 and 1936; and a further 10

were built in 1938–39 after the German occupation of Austria. These were built with German (DRG) style cabs and boiler fittings, and

they and the earlier models were given wing-type smoke deflectors. Two-cylinder simple-expansion engines, they had Austrian Lentz

oscillating cam poppet valves to operate the cylinders, and the whole class was fitted with Giesl ejector chimneys in the late 1950s.

SERIES 1082 1-E-1 FEDERAL RAILWAYS OF AUSTRIA (BBÖ)

Looking like a steam tank engine with pantographs, this was an intriguing one-off design, though it was kept in service for 10 years. Its frame supported a rotary converter, housed in a great cylindrical drum of steam boiler size, with the alternator in the place of the firebox, and a driving cab behind it. Coupling rods linked the five driving axles, though, as with inside cylinders, the actual drive mode was hidden. Three axle-hung nose-suspended

DC motors drove the three centre sets of wheels. For its electrified lines, the BBÖ had settled on single-phase AC current, at 15kV

and 16.7Hz cycles. The 1082 locomotive reduced the tension through a transformer and then altered it to three-phase AC in the

rotary converter. This was again changed through phase transformers into direct current and fed to the traction motors, which could be worked in series or in parallel. At front and rear, the carrying wheels were linked to the end set of coupled wheels in a Krauss-Helmholtz bogie, and to further help with flexibility on curves, the central wheels had flanges of reduced thickness. In 1941, it was removed from service and broken up.

TYPE: heavy-duty freight locomotive
POWER: three axle-hung motors, rated at 507.3kW (680hp) and supplied with single-phase current at 15kV, 16.7Hz, via overhead catenary
TRACTIVE EFFORT: not known

MAX. OPERATING SPEED: 50km/h (31mph)
TOTAL WEIGHT: not known
MAX. AXLE LOAD: not known
OVERALL LENGTH: not known
BUILDER: WIENER Lokomotivfabrik; Siemens-Schuckert

CLASS 46.01 2-12-4T BULGARIAN STATE RAILWAYS (BDZ)

With six coupled axles, these were the largest non-articulated tank engines in the world, a class of 12 built to German design by the Cegielski works in Poland. They were destined for heavy mineral traffic over mountain lines, particularly between the Pernik coalfield and the capital, Sofia. Two very large outside cylinders, actuated by Walschaerts gear and piston valves, drove the third coupled axle, which (like the fourth) had no

flanges on the wheels. The leading bogie and the first coupled axle formed a Krauss-Helmholtz truck, and the sixth coupled axle was allowed a lateral movement of 25mm (1in) either way. These refinements appear to have been enough to get the locomotive safely round curves at the low operating speeds maintained. The maximum axle load was 17 tonnes (16.7 tons).

The class represents the start of an era of modern and large-scale

design on the Bulgarian State Railways. On the long boiler top, the line of domes held a Wagner regulator, a Wagner top-feed system, sand (two domes) and the main regulator valve. A coal capacity of 10.16 tonnes (10 tons) and a water capacity, in side and back tanks, of 4000 gals (4800 US gals) were greater than those of many tender locomotives. The BDZ was sufficiently pleased with the locomotives to supplement Class 46.01 in 1943 with eight new mammoth tanks, also 2-12-4 but with three cylinders, of Class 46.13, built by Berliner

Maschinenbau. Their cylinders measured 550x700mm (21.6x 27.6in) and their calculated tractive effort, 29,922kg (65,980lb), was somewhat less than that of the two-cylinder engines.

BOILER PRESSURE: 16kg/cm² (228psi)
CYLINDERS: 700x700mm (27.6x27.6in)
DRIVING WHEELS: 1340mm (52.8in)
GRATE AREA: 4.9m² (52.7sq ft)
HEATING SURFACE: 224m² (2412sq ft)
SUPERHEATER: 83.9m² (903.3sq ft)
TRACTIVE EFFORT: 31,836kg (70,200lb)
TOTAL WEIGHT: 149.1t (328,765lb)

With injectors hissing, No. 46.12 hauls a long train of empty coal wagons on the Pernik loop, near Sofia.

CLASS 4.1200 2-8-2T NORTHERN RAILWAY (NORD)

The last steam trains out of the *Gare du Nord*, on 12 December 1970, were worked by this class, which had been at home in the terminus for almost 40 years. The 2-8-2 tank type had since 1910 been favoured by most of the main French companies for short-haul passenger and express suburban services. The Paris–Orleans line had an excellent version, Class 141.TA, with two sand domes, of which 37 went to the Moroccan Railways in 1924–26. In 1930 and 1931, the concept was updated on the *Est*, *Etat* and *Nord* lines with new designs. The *Nord* class, later 141.TC in SNCF coding, built at the line's La Chapelle shops, was a high-powered machine, which on one occasion in July 1932 took a 490-tonne (482-ton) train from Paris to Creil, a distance of 50km (31 miles), in 30mins start to stop.

BOILER PRESSURE: 18.3kg/cm² (261psi)
CYLINDERS: 641x700.5mm (25.25x27.6in)
DRIVING WHEELS: 1548mm (61in)
GRATE AREA: 3.1m² (33.4sq ft)
HEATING SURFACE: 166.4m² (1791.5sq ft)
SUPERHEATER: 45m² (484.5sq ft)
TRACTIVE EFFORT: 25,609kg (56,000lb)
TOTAL WEIGHT: 104.2t (229,783lb)

As its appearance suggests, this was very much an express locomotive, built for heavy, fast suburban traffic.

5-AXLE RAILCAR 'MICHELINE' EASTERN RAILWAY (EST)

The 'Micheline' type was the brain-child of the Michelin brothers, tyre makers who began in the late 1920s to develop pneumatic tyres with special profiles for rail use. In 1929, their first prototype was built and tried out on a test track at their factory in Clermont-Ferrand. Two more were built before No. 4 was produced, the first to be fitted with passenger seats. In 1931, demonstration services began using a Hispano-Suiza engine, and in September of that year, on the Paris–Deauville line, it maintained an average speed of 107km/h (66.5mph) with 10 passengers.

The purpose of the lightweight petrol-engined railcar was quite different from the slow-speed steam railcar. It was meant for cross-country work, carrying a small number of passengers willing to pay premium fares for a fast and prestigious service. Built on the lines of a contemporary road vehicle, its engine was beneath an extended bonnet in front of the cab, with the leading wheels on either side of it. Two more axles behind the cab helped bear the weight both of the traction unit and part of the carbody, which was articulated to the traction unit. Two further axles supported the rear of the car. Five axles were required because the pneumatic tyres were limited to a maximum axle-load of 14,000kg (30,800lb). Production began in 1932, using a Panhard engine rather than the Hispano-Suiza. The first purchaser was the French

An experimental Michelin seen here at work in Britain passing the Bentley Heath Crossing, near Birmingham in 1933.

Eastern Railway, and the example of the *Est* was followed by the *Nord*. 'Michelines' captured passengers' imagination and became both fashionable and popular. Railway companies elsewhere took note. The London, Midland & Scottish in Great Britain experimented with one in 1932. The SJ in Sweden did likewise. The Pennsylvania Railroad, always keen to be at the forefront of progress, tested one. Other motor manufacturers produced their own models, so that France in particular had a range including Renault vehicles and the high-

speed Bugatti cars, though the others all ran on conventional steel-tyred wheels.

It was to be in France, and in French colonies and dependencies, that the fast petrol railcar would establish itself most firmly. All railcars were withdrawn during World War II, when rationing of petrol and other fuel was introduced, but they were reinstated after 1945. High petrol consumption made it difficult to operate the Michelines economically. By 1953, the last of the type were being withdrawn. But their impact was hard to erase,

and the name lived on, attached by both railways and the public to single- or double-unit diesel railcars with neither petrol engines nor pneumatic tyres. The rubber tyres were not forgotten, either. In the mid-1950s, the *Est* was running steam-hauled expresses between Paris and Strasbourg, with locomotives of the 230 K class hauling rolling stock fitted with rubber tyres. The concept was revived again on the rebuilding of Line 1 of the Paris Métro around 1960, when its trains were fitted with pneumatic tyres. Michelines ran on the metre-

gauge Madagascar Railways into the early 1960s, and one of those was brought back to France for restoration and 'heritage' line service.

TYPE: articulated railcar
POWER: Panhard motor engine
TRACTIVE EFFORT: not known
MAXIMUM OPERATING SPEED: 100km/h (62mph)
WEIGHT: 72t (158,760lb)
MAXIMUM AXLE LOAD: 14t (30,864lb)
OVERALL LENGTH: 12.4m (40ft 7in)
GAUGE: not known

CLASS V40 1-D-1 HUNGARIAN STATE RAILWAYS (MÀV) HUNGARY 1931

In the early 1930s, the Hungarian State Railways was electrifying at the industrial voltage and frequency of 16,000V 50 cycles/sec, a frequency not used again on railways until the French mastered it (at 25kV) in the 1950s.

For the 29 locomotives of this class, used on the Budapest–Hegyeshalom route, Kalmàn Kandó developed a rotating phase converter that transformed the input voltage and current into

1000V three-phase AC. By switching the motor poles in different combinations, the locomotive speed could be locked into the electricity frequency at 25, 50, 75 and

100km/h (40, 80, 121 and 161mph). The motor, fixed in the locomotive body, drove a jackshaft with crank pins at the ends, attached to connecting rods that

were linked with the side coupling rods through a Kandó-patented triangular device that allowed for the vertical movement of the springs.

TYPE: mainline passenger electric loco-motive
WHEEL ARRANGEMENT: 1-D-1
POWER: 16,000V 50Hz AC overhead line collection; 1620kW (2170hp); one body

mounted three-phase AC traction motor with Kandó rod drive to side coupling rods
TRACTIVE EFFORT: 166kN (37,350lbf)
MAX. OPERATING SPEED: 100km/h (62mph)

WEIGHT: 94t (207,270lb)
MAX. AXLE LOAD: 18.5t (40,793lb)
OVERALL LENGTH: 13.83m (42ft 2in)
GAUGE: 1435mm (4ft 8.5in)

DIESEL RAIL CAR COUNTY DONEGAL RAILWAYS (CDR) IRELAND 1931

In the 1930s, narrow-gauge railways still were important in Ireland's transport system, though all were struggling financially. The County Donegal Railways Joint

Committee operated a network of narrow-gauge lines connecting Strabane, Letterkenny, Stranorlar, Donegal (town), Ballyshannon and Killybegs, in the northwest of the

country. Though it also used steam traction, its first railcar had been acquired as long ago as 1906 as a small four-wheel, 10-seat railbus powered by a 7.46kW

(10hp) petrol engine. With a cost of about a third of a new steam train, railcars had considerable appeal to the cash-strapped company. Perhaps the most significant cars were Nos. 7 and 8, built in 1931. Representing the first use of rail diesel engines in the British Isles, they were built locally by Doherty of Strabane, and the Great Northern Railways (GNR) shops at Dundalk. The power unit was a Gardner 6L2 diesel operating at 1300rpm, driving a power bogie. Each car carried 32 passengers and they were capable of operating together. While some later County Donegal cars have been preserved, these original diesel cars were scrapped.

TYPE: diesel mechanical railcar
POWER AND OUTPUT: Gardner 6L2 diesel producing 55kW (74hp)
TRACTIVE EFFORT: N/A
MAX. OPERATING SPEED: 64kph (40mph)
WEIGHT: 7t (15,680lb)
OVERALL LENGTH: 8.534m (28ft)
GAUGE: 914mm (36in)

Stranorlar station, in County Donegal. The CDR railcars had sufficient power to haul two or three goods wagons, giving a regular goods/parcels service.

CLASS FD 2-10-2 SOVIET RAILWAYS (SZD)

Class FD perpetuates the name of Felix Dzerzhinsky, the tough commissar who organized the state-run railway system. In 1931, the Soviet Union was facing a transport crisis due to a lack of motive power, but Dzerzhinsky-style rapid action upgraded a number of strategic main lines to take locomotives of 20.2-tonne (20-ton) axle load.

This two-cylinder simple-expansion class was designed to a tight deadline, to haul heavier and faster freight trains. American influence is very evident, including bar frames, a mechanical stoker, and thermic syphon in the firebox. Series production began at Voroshilovgrad in 1933, and over 3000 were built. In the late 1950s and early 1960s, around 1250 of these locomotives were transferred to China to become Chinese Class FD, and they were regauged to standard gauge.

BOILER PRESSURE: 15kg/cm² (215psi)
CYLINDERS: 672x761mm (26.5x30in)
DRIVING WHEELS: 1497mm (59in)
GRATE AREA: 7m² (76sq ft)
HEATING SURFACE: 294m² (3163.4sq ft)
SUPERHEATER: 148.1m² (1595sq ft)
TRACTIVE EFFORT: 29,251kg (64,500lb)
TOTAL WEIGHT: 137t (302,085lb)
(engine only)

The engine that rescued Stalin's 'Five-Year Plan' for Soviet industrial expansion: a preserved Class FD on a 'heritage' special service. The leading vehicle is a train heating car.

CLASS 551 2-DO-2 ROYAL SIAMESE RAILWAYS (RSR)

The RSR took a pioneering interest in developing diesel traction because of the low thermal efficiency of the wood burned by its steam locomotives. In 1931, it ordered both this class, with driving axles fixed in the frame, from Frichs of Aarhus, Denmark, and six bogie A1A-A1A locomotives from Sulzer in Switzerland. Driven by two six-cylinder Frichs 6285CL four-stroke engines and with an output of 746kW (1000hp), the 2-Do-2s were powerful engines and they were employed on main-line long-distance trains. A double version was supplied as a one-off in 1932, a 2-Do+Do-2, effectively two 551s back-to-back, for heavy freight work. The 551s were not wholly successful; their design had not taken the heat and dust and track conditions of Thailand into account, and there were problems with corrosion and effective lubrication. Also, the fixed driving wheels lacked the flexibility on the track of the A1A bogies of the RSR's Sulzer-built 335.8kW (450hp) diesels, driven by a Sulzer 8LV25 eight-cylinder engine. The less powerful bogie engines proved to be the more durable, with some still in service in the 1970s, while the 551 class was withdrawn in the mid-1950s. No. 556 is preserved, and the 2-Do+Do-2 also remains, in semi-derelict condition.

TYPE: heavy express diesel-electric locomotive
POWER: two Frichs 6285CL six-cylinder four-stroke engines each delivering 373.1kW (500hp) at 600rpm, driving four axle-mounted traction motors

TRACTIVE EFFORT: 64.5kN (14,500lbf)
MAXIMUM OPERATING SPEED: 60km/h (37mph)
TOTAL WEIGHT: 86.1t (189,850lb)
MAXIMUM AXLE LOAD: 10.9t (24,034lb)
OVERALL LENGTH: 15.38m (50ft 6in)

EP-3 2-CO-CO-2 NEW HAVEN RAILROAD (NHR)

New Haven Railroad, with its intensive traffic pattern through a heavily urbanized region, was keen on electrification, and General Electric built these 10 box-cab electrics for them. Designated EP-3, the electrics hauled long-distance and suburban passenger trains over the railroad's four-track main line between New Haven, Connecticut and two downtown New York terminals,

TYPE: 2-Co-Co-2, passenger electric
POWER: 11kV alternating current at 25Hz from overhead, or 660V DC from third rail
TRACTIVE EFFORT: 304kN (68,500lbf) starting TE
MAX. OPERATING SPEED: 128km/h (80mph) – one unit modified for 192km/h (120mph) running in tests
WEIGHT: APPROX. 183t (404,000lb)
OVERALL LENGTH: N/A
MAX. AXLE LOAD: 21t (46,000lb)
GAUGE: 1435mm (4ft 8.5in)

Grand Central and Penn Station, the latter reached by way of the line over New York's Hell Gate Bridge. They would also be used on electrified branches, such as the line to Danbury, Connecticut. In 1938, GE built six EP-4 electrics that were mechanically similar, but

Suburban lines were often served by relatively small engines, but the EP-3s were big locomotives, needed to haul heavyweight commuter trains on one of the world's most intensively used lines.

with a double-ended, streamlined carbody. During World War II, GE and Westinghouse divided an order for 10 additional streamlined freight electrics, designated EF-3. In the late 1950s, most of these electrics were displaced by new EMD FL9s.

240.P1 4-8-0 PARIS–ORLEANS RAILWAY (PO)

André Chapelon, then employed in the PO research department, had already established his reputation by transforming the PO 3500 class 'Pacifics'. Now, at his suggestion, the former PO four-cylinder compound Pacific No. 4521 was rebuilt as a 4-8-0 to his design. In an intensive effort at the Tours workshops between October 1931 and August 1932, radical alterations were made. The new boiler came from the *Nord* 'Super-Pacific', with a long narrow Belpaire firebox into which a Nicholson thermic syphon was incorporated. The handsome, racy lines of the original were transformed by an accumulation of pipes, domes, pumps and cylinders into a husky-looking double-chimneyed engine of very different appearance. Inside, the changes were equally drastic.

A significant test took place on 24 April 1933 on the Paris–Toulouse line, the locomotive pulling a 17-car train of 735 tonnes (723.4 tons) from Paris to Chateauroux, and a 654-tonne (644-ton) train from Chateauroux to Limoges. A

prototype 2-D-2 electric (see 1933) took the train from Paris to Vierzon, at speeds mostly around 120km/h (75mph) and a maximum of 132km/h (82mph), over fairly level track. No. 4521 came on at Vierzon for the 137.2km (85.3 miles) to Limoges, over much hiller country with a mostly rising grade. The train passed the summit at 95km/h (59mph), having increased its speed on several gradients. The average indicated power developed by the locomotive was 2426kW (3300hp) at an average speed of 85.3km/h (53mph) on a ruling grade of 1 in 100. The power produced was some 50 per cent above what had

been contemplated when the rebuilding was planned.

The PO, looking for more power to speed up the Paris–Toulouse line, found it in the 240.P1. Performance was increased by an astonishing degree. The free-steaming circuits, the draught and blast arrangements and the excellent boiler and firebox allowed the engine to develop 2984kW (4000hp) in the cylinders at a speed of 112.6km/h (70mph) with a train of 584 tonnes (575 tons). A further 11 were rebuilt in 1934, followed by 25 in 1940, fitted with mechanical stokers. The 240P.1 could run on grades or on the flat to the kind of

schedule that post-war planners devised for electric traction, and with heavier trains.

It is one of the mysteries of railway life that the SNCF, when established in 1938, did not choose to build more of these remarkable locomotives.

BOILER PRESSURE: 20.5kg/cm² (292psi)
CYLINDERS: hp 17.3x25.6 in (mm); lp 25.2x25.6in
DRIVING WHEELS: 1846mm (72.75in)
GRATE AREA: 3.75m² (40sq ft)
HEATING SURFACE: 213m² (2290sq ft)
SUPERHEATER: 68m² (733sq ft)
TRACTIVE EFFORT: 14,026kg (32,029lb)
TOTAL WEIGHT: 110.7t (244,160lb)

Comparison of this illustration with that of the Paris–Orleans 'Pacific' of 1907 shows the extent of alteration in the Chapelon 'rebuild'. In every way, it was a transformation.

CLASS 85 2-10-2T GERMAN STATE RAILWAYS (DRG)

Under the DRG's *Einheitslok* policy, this was to be a standard engine sharing numerous parts with other standard DRG classes. In German notation 1'E1'h3, it was a three-cylinder superheated 2-10-2. No more than 10 were built, all by Henschel of Kassel. They had the standard German Heusinger valve gear, with the inside cylinder that drove the second coupled wheels, worked from an eccentric on the third coupled wheels. At each end, a Krauss-Helmholtz bogie linked the pony wheels to the end coupled wheels, enabling the engine to run

BOILER PRESSURE: 14kg/cm² (200psi)
CYLINDERS: 600x660mm (23.6x26in)
DRIVING WHEELS: 1400mm (55in)
GRATE AREA: 3.5m² (37.7sq ft)
HEATING SURFACE: 195.8m² (2108sq ft)
SUPERHEATER: 72.5m² (780.5sq ft)
TRACTIVE EFFORT: 20,299kg (44,759lb)
TOTAL WEIGHT: 133.6t (294,588lb)

---

at 80km/h (50mph) in either direction. All were first based at Freiburg in the Black Forest, and proved a powerful type for use in

hilly country. They were cut up in 1961, except for one, preserved on static display at the Konstanz engineering school.

Though a 'standard' type, only ten were built. Some classes never got beyond the drawing stage, due to financial limits.

SVT 877 *FLIEGENDE HAMBURGER* GERMAN STATE RAILWAYS (DRG)   GERMANY 1932

Keen to develop the concept of the SVT, or *Schnellverkehrs-verbrennungtriebwagen* ('fast traffic internal combustion railcar'), engineers of the *Reichsbahn* had been experimenting for some time with very-high-speed vehicles using the internal combustion engine. One of these, the Kruckenberg four-wheel unit, powered by an aircraft engine and with a large four-bladed propeller mounted on the nose, reached a world record rail speed of 230km/h (143mph) on a 10km (6.2-mile) track between Karstadt and Dergenthin, in 1931. On test in

1932, the first two-car SVT reached a speed of 198.5km/h (124mph). The two cars were articulated, sharing a central bogie, with the engines mounted on the bogies at each end, each supplying current to traction motors on the near axle of the central bogie. The total weight of the two-car unit was less than that of all but the smallest steam locomotives.

The SVT was intended to provide high-speed rail links between Berlin and major provincial cities. Comfort rather than luxury was the keynote, and the 68 seats were all second-class.

In May 1933, the first service began to operate between Berlin and Hamburg. The route covered 286.6km (178.1 miles) and the timing from Berlin was 138 mins; from Hamburg 140 mins. The maximum permitted speed was 160km/h (100mph). A special brown and cream colour scheme was devised for the sets. The new service caused a sensation in railway circles. In 1934, a further 13 two-car sets were ordered, and in the course of 1935 they went into operation between Berlin and Frankfurt (the 'Flying Frankfurter'), Berlin–Cologne, Berlin–Munich, and Cologne–Hamburg. Among these were the world's first services to be scheduled at more than 128.7km/h (80mph) from terminus to terminus.

In 1936, a larger three-car articulated train was introduced with exhaust turbo-pressure chargers fitted to the engines, resulting in a power uprating to 448kW (600hp). Two of these three-car sets had Voith hydraulic transmissions, with a 10-tonne (9.8-ton) weight saving over electric transmission.

Until the outbreak of war in

1939, Germany had more of such high-speed services than any other country. During World War II, they were put in store, and after it they were found to be of little use on the truncated and divided German railway system, with its single access route to Berlin from West Germany via Helmstedt, and their limited accommodation was unsuitable for the needs of the time. Some of the power cars were adapted to hydraulic transmission, but by 1959 all were taken out of service. An original set has been recreated using a carbody and a power bogie from the first train.

TYPE: two-car articulated diesel-electric train
POWER: two Maybach 12-cylinder 305kW (410hp) engines supplying DC traction motors on the axles of the middle bogie
TRACTIVE EFFORT: not known
MAXIMUM OPERATING SPEED: 160km/h (100mph)
TOTAL WEIGHT: 78t (171,990lb)
MAXIMUM AXLE LOAD: 16.4t (36,150lb)
OVERALL LENGTH: 41.906m (137ft 6in)
GAUGE: not known

The only drawback of the original SVT format was the limited accommodation offered by the two-car unit. Advance reservation was usually essential to ensure a seat.

SCHIENENBUS (RAILBUS) A-A BREMEN–THEDINGHAUSEN RAILWAY   GERMANY 1932

Uerdingen works were the best-known of several German builders who specialized in the lightweight four-wheel railbus for rural lines. However, this railbus, which unusually had a petrol engine, came from the Wagenfabrik Wismar, which built similar models from 1932 to 1941 for a variety of gauges, from 750mm (29.6in) to standard.

An engine bonnet at each end earned the vehicle's the nickname *Schweineschnäutzchen*, meaning 'little pig-noses'. A roof-rack was provided for luggage and they could pack in up to 40 passengers at a time. Only one of the two Ford motors was operated at a time, and it was controlled like a car with mechanical gearbox, but with a

notched control handle instead of an accelerator. The Wismar car T2BTh ran for a total of 32 years

TYPE: petrol railbus
POWER: two Ford motor engines, driving via manual gearbox
TRACTIVE EFFORT: not known
MAXIMUM OPERATING SPEED: 60km/h (37mph)

(1936–68) between Bremen and Thedinghausen, and is now preserved.

TOTAL WEIGHT: not known
MAXIMUM AXLE LOAD: not known
OVERALL LENGTH: not known
GAUGE: not known

5BEL PULLMAN ELECTRIC MULTIPLE UNITS SOUTHERN RAILWAY (SR)   GREAT BRITAIN 1932

Having extended third-rail DC electrification in the south London suburban areas, the SR's first main-line electrification was from London Victoria and London Bridge stations to Brighton, followed by extensions to other south-coast towns. SR built a fleet of comfortable, corridor electric multiple units in its own workshops at Lancing and Eastleigh (some were also built by contractors). The top link sets were six-car units for the hourly Brighton express services ('On the hour, every hour'). These had a motor coach at each end, each with four powerful motors permitting the track speed

of 120km/h (75mph) to be maintained on the significant gradients on that route. Peak hour services had two of these sets in multiple forming a 12-coach train. One set had a pantry car, the other had a Pullman car for the more affluent passengers who wanted

TYPE: five-car electric multiple-unit Pullman trains
POWER: 660V DC conductor rail collection, two power cars, each with four BTH 168kW (225hp) axle-mounted traction motors, resistance control
TRACTIVE EFFORT: not known

breakfast on the way to the capital, and high tea on the way home.

To replace the former steam-hauled morning and evening 'Southern Belle' Pullman trains, the SR ordered three five-car all-Pullman electric multiple units from Metropolitan-Cammell. Two would

MAX. OPERATING SPEED: 120km/h (75mph)
WEIGHT: 40 to 63t (87,360 to 138,880lb) per vehicle
MAX. AXLE LOAD: not known
OVERALL LENGTH: 20.115m (66ft) per vehicle
GAUGE: 1435mm (4ft 8.5in)

form the morning up train, a return working to Brighton during the day, and the evening peak train back to Brighton. The third was held in reserve. In 1934, the train was named *The Brighton Belle*. As with the hourly trains on the Brighton main line, the 5BEL sets had a motor coach at each end, each with two power bogies carrying two axle-mounted 168kW (225hp) traction motors. When the 1932 main-line trains were replaced by British Railways' new 4CIG and 4BIG units from 1963, the 5BEL units continued to operate for another nine years before final withdrawal in 1972.

One of the most sumptuous of multiple-unit trains, painted in Pullman colours, the *Brighton Belle* speeds through the English countryside.

CLASS K 4-8-4 NEW ZEALAND RAILWAYS (NZR)

NEW ZEALAND 1932

A triumph of design, shoe-horning maximum power into a narrow space, the Class K was a rugged-looking locomotive in the American style, though of course considerably scaled down. Many up-to-date US features were incorporated, including power reversing gear, a mechanical lubricator and an air-operated fire-door. Apart from a 1065mm (3ft 6in) rail gauge, the New Zealand Railways were also restricted by a tight loading gauge, with a maximum height of 3502mm (11ft 6in) and width of 2589mm (8ft 6in), but trainloads and traffic

requirements needed something bigger than the Ab 'Pacifics' on certain trains, and the K class was designed for these services. A 4-8-2 had been first planned, but a four-wheel truck under the firebox was needed to keep the maximum axle loading to 14.2 tonnes (14 tons). Thirty were built at the NZR Hutt Workshops between 1932 and 1936, and put to work mostly on the Main Trunk Auckland–Wellington line. They ran both passenger and freight services, maintaining 80km/h (50mph) with 508-tonne (500-ton) trains, and 48km/h (30mph) with 1016-tonne

(1000-ton) trains on level track. The normal maximum service speed was 88.5km/h (55mph), which was often well exceeded, with a recorded maximum of 110km/h (69mph). Ka and Kb types followed, with modifications including roller bearings throughout. Kb, built at Hillside Workshops in Dunedin, South Island, had booster engines fitted to the rear bogies, delivering an additional 3640kg (8000lb) of tractive effort, and were intended to work the steep cross-country line on South Island. Ka types were built up Hutt Workshops to 1950

BOILER PRESSURE: 14kg/cm² (200psi)
CYLINDERS: 508x660mm (20x26in)
DRIVING WHEELS: 1370mm (54in)
GRATE AREA: 4.4m² (47.7sq ft)
HEATING SURFACE: 179.5m² (1933sq ft)
SUPERHEATER: 45m² (485sq ft)
TRACTIVE EFFORT: 14,850kg (32,740lb)
TOTAL WEIGHT: 88t (194,208lb)
(engine only)

and, in all, there were 71 assorted Ks. Originally coal burners, all except the Kbs were later converted to oil firing. Five of the Class K have been preserved.

K915 hauls the Rotorua–Auckland express up a 1 in 35 grade past Terukenga on 21 December 1955.

VL-19 SERIES C-C SOVIET RAILWAYS (SZD)

RUSSIA 1932

Russia's first main-line electric scheme was begun in 1928 and completed in 1932. It travelled over the Suram Pass on the Trans-Caucasus line, with gradients as steep as 1 in 34. Eight electric locomotives were ordered from General Electric in the United States (Type S) and seven from Brown-Boveri in Switzerland (Type Si), and the Dinamo Works in Moscow began production of electric motors based on the GE design, known as Type Ss. All the locomotives were of the C-C configuration. The

Russian-built VL (for *Vladimir Lenin*) 19 series was intended to become a standard class. Its 19-tonne (18.7-ton) axle load was considered to be the maximum possible without having to upgrade the tracks. The first was completed at the Dinamo Works in November 1932, and around 145 more were built between 1933 and 1938, when the larger VL-22 type was introduced. Rated at an hourly 2071kW (2775 hp), the VL-19s were fitted with rheostatic brakes, rather than the regenerative brakes of the GE

locomotives. Drawgear was fitted to the bogie, not the frame, and railed platforms fronted the cab ends. The VL-19s went into service on the newly electrified Donetz line from 1935, hauling trains of up to 2540 tonnes (2500 tons) at speeds 50–60km/h

(31–37mph). It was stated that the work of six electric locomotives replaced the work of between 35 and 40 steam engines of the 0-10-0 E-class, which may have been an exaggeration. VL19.01, the first Soviet-built electric locomotive, is preserved at Khashuri.

TYPE: mixed-traffic locomotive
POWER: six 340kW (455.6hp) traction motors, based on GE design, supplied with 3000V DC via overhead catenary
TRACTIVE EFFORT: 245kN (55,116lbf)

MAX. OPERATING SPEED: 75km/h (47mph)
TOTAL WEIGHT: 120t (264,600lb)
MAX. AXLE LOAD: 19t (41,895lb)
OVERALL LENGTH: not known
BUILDER: Dinamo Works, Moscow

CLASS EE 3/3 C SWISS FEDERAL RAILWAYS (SBB)

SWITZERLAND 1932

Design of these basic six-wheeled C-arrangement electric shunting locomotives began in 1928, and in the 1930s they were working on switching duties throughout the SBB network. They were all-adhesion machines, with their three axles connected by coupling rod and

jackshaft to a single commutator motor. Earlier designs featured end cabs and shunting personnel platforms, but the later series had a single centre cab. Production ran from 1932 until 1966, with many modifications and developments, hence the variations over time in weight and capacity.

TYPE: C shunter
POWER: 428 to 502kW (581 to 682hp)
SUPPLY: 15kV 16.2/3Hz AC
TRACTIVE EFFORT: 88 to 118kN (19800 to 26550lbf)
MAX. OPERATING SPEED: 40 to 50km/h (25 to 31.3mph)

WEIGHT: 39 to 45t (85,995 to 99,225lb)
MAX. AXLE LOAD: 13 to 15t (28,665 to 33,075lb)
OVERALL LENGTH: 9.51 to 9.75m (31ft to 31ft 10in)
GAUGE: 1435mm (4ft 8.5in)

A later derivative, No. 16.430 was built in 1956. Extra weight was built in to give it improved traction.

CLASS 464 4-8-4T CZECHOSLOVAK STATE RAILWAYS (CSD)

Evening sunlight reveals the worn paintwork of this Giesl-chimneyed Class 484 in Prague during the last years of steam on the CSD.

By 1933, Czechoslovakia had two substantial locomotive builders, with the PCM works at Prague dating back to 1900, and new locomotive works established by the Skoda industrial concern in Plzen during the early 1920s. PCM amalgamated with two smaller manufacturers, Breitfeld & Danek, and Emil Kolben, to form the CKD locomotive works. The CSD method of steady development through successive types is shown by this powerful tank class. In 1924, the Class 455.1 of 2-8-0 wheel arrangement was introduced, itself a development of a previous six-coupled design. In turn, it was made the basis of a large 2-8-4 tank locomotive, Class 456.0, dating from 1927. This proved very successful in service; some lasted into the 1970s. In 1933, a further enlarged version was produced, a heavier and more powerful engine, though with a smaller water and coal capacity than the 455. It was a two-cylinder, simple-expansion design, with Heusinger valve gear, and inside bearings on all axles. Like

all Czech designs, it had a wide firebox to burn the low-grade lignite 'brown coal' of the Bohemian coalfield. At first, only three were constructed, but by 1938 the class numbered 76, with larger superheaters and smoke deflectors added from the fourth onwards (deflectors were also fitted to Nos. 001-3). They were built by Skoda in Plzen and CKD in Prague.

At first dominated by Austrian influence, Czech locomotive building showed a more international flavour from the 1920s. German design was most influential, but the designers also took a keen interest in developments further afield, in France, Britain and the United States. This diversity of interest is evident in the Class 464, whose attention to neatness of detail has a British quality, as do the plain smokebox doors and the lipped chimneys. The last nine of the class were fitted with Russian

Trofimov piston valves, and Swedish SKF roller bearings on the front and rear bogie axles. Later, many of the class were fitted with steel fireboxes to replace the original copper ones, and also with larger superheaters. Other new equipment included pneumatically operated firedoors and Giesl double blast ejectors and chimneys. The Giesl ejector was as popular in Czechoslovakia as it was in its native Austria, perhaps because both railways used similar coal.

Tank engines are more commonly associated with shunting and branch work, but the Class 464, like some other large and powerful tank types in Europe and Britain, ran main-line express trains over relatively short distances. The line of development was continued when CKD built two engines of Class 464.1 in 1940, with a boiler pressure increased to 18kg/cm² (256psi), cylinders of 500mm

(19.7in) diameter and larger superheaters. Externally almost identical to Class 464.0, they were more powerful. In their final form, the Czech 4-8-4 express tank locomotives were also the last steam locomotives to be built for CSD: the 464.2 class of 1955. The tractive power of the 4-8-4 tanks on gradients was used on mountain routes like the main line between Chomutov and Cheb in the north-west of the country; others were based at Klatovy, south of Plzen, and at depots in Slovakia. Withdrawals began in the 1970s, and the last of the class in service was retired for preservation in 1981. The first of the class, 464.001, has also been preserved.

BOILER PRESSURE: 13kg/cm² (185psi)
CYLINDERS: 600x720mm (23.6x28.3in)
DRIVING WHEELS: 1624mm (64in)
GRATE AREA: 4.38m² (47.1sq ft)
HEATING SURFACE: 194m² (2088.7sq ft)
SUPERHEATER: 62.1m² (668.6sq ft)
TRACTIVE EFFORT: 17,560kg (38,720lb)
TOTAL WEIGHT: 114.5t (252,472lb)

MALLET TYPE R441 0-4-4-0T ERITREAN RAILWAYS (FE)

ERITREA 1933

From Massawa on the Red Sea coast to Asmara was a 10-hour trip, beginning in gruelling heat until the FE Mallet tank engines reached slightly cooler air as the line climbed 2175m (7143ft) over

An Eritrean 'Mallet' 0-4-4-0T runs with a flat-car attached, along an upland section of its line.

its 117.5km (73 miles) length. The track was 950mm (3ft 1in) gauge. The company's first Mallets were compounds built by Maffei in 1910. This later class of 15, built in Italy, were simple-expansion engines, 10 with Walschaerts valve gear and five with Caprotti poppet valve gear. In a further eight engines supplied by Ansaldo in

1938, compound expansion was again reverted to, probably as much to conserve water as to generate extra power, though the line was a very demanding one.

In 1954, five of the 1911 vintage were still in steam, but only one of the R441s, converted to compound expansion, was still a working engine.

BOILER PRESSURE: 12kg/cm² (171psi)
CYLINDERS: 330x500mm (13x19.7in)
DRIVING WHEELS: 900mm (35.5in)
GRATE AREA: not known
HEATING SURFACE: not known
TRACTIVE EFFORT: 11,636kg (25,660lb)
TOTAL WEIGHT: 46t (101,430lb)
(engine only)

CLASS E 503 2-D-2 PARIS–ORLEANS RAILWAY (PO)

FRANCE 1933

Resembling the Swiss Ae 3/6 design, this class was by-named 'pig's nose' in France, but proved successful and durable. It was introduced in 1933 by the Paris–Orleans, and two protoypes were built before the production series E503–E537 (later SNCF 5503–5537) was constructed by Fives-Lille, utilizing BBC and CEM electrical equipment. They were deployed initially on express

passenger work on the PO's 1500V DC network, and proved capable of handling heavy trains at high speed, easily reaching 132km/h (82mph) with a 735-tonne (723.4-ton) test train between Paris and Vierzon in April 1933. Two further series with differing styling (PO E538–545 and SNCF 2D2 5546–5550) appeared before World War II. Development after the war produced the 9100, which

adopted the same overall design and 2-D-2 arrangement. This class was to operate in service nearly 50 years – other 2-D-2 machines were less robust, lasting 20 years or less. At Toulouse depot from 1960 they served on parcels and freight traffic, with withdrawals from 1977 to the end of 1980. No. 5518 is in the Mulhouse railway museum and 5525 is privately preserved.

BOILER PRESSURE: 20.5kg/cm² (292psi)
CYLINDERS: hp 439x650mmm (17.3x25.6in); lp 648x650mm (25.2x25.6in)
DRIVING WHEELS: 1846mm (72.75in)
GRATE AREA: 3.75m² (40sq ft)
HEATING SURFACE: 213m² (2290sq ft)
SUPERHEATER: 68m² (733sq ft)
TRACTIVE EFFORT: 14,026kg (32,029lb)
TOTAL WEIGHT: 110.7t (244,160lb)

BUGATTI RAILCAR STATE RAILWAY (ETAT)

Like the contemporary French *Micheline* (see 1931), this was an innovative machine. A single two-way driving position was provided from a raised central cabin. Although this required a low height for the passenger compartments – only 2.69m (8ft 10in) – it enhanced the long, low, speedy look. Bugatti's wedge-shaped ends, tested in a wind-tunnel, and the circular windows of the toilet compartments also helped to give the whole unit something of a marine, or even submarine appearance. The car was

mounted on two four-wheel bogies, and four Bugatti 'Royale' benzol-alcohol engines were placed centrally, driving the two near axles on each bogie by means of cardan shafts, which were hydraulically-coupled to the engine, with no gearbox. The bogies had inside frames and bearings, with each axle suspended independently and given slight lateral movement to accommodate the curves.

Inside were two saloons each with 24 seats, separated by the engine and driving compartments.

A lever mechanism reversed the position of seats and seat-backs to allow passengers to sit facing the oncoming scene.

Appropriately for machines designed by Ettore Bugatti, the cars were very fast. On test, one reached 172km/h (107mph), though the service speed was at first restricted to the French Railways' maximum of 120km/h (75mph). Later this was raised for the railcars to 140km/h (87mph).

The Bugattis first went into service on the line from Paris to the Normandy resorts of Deauville-Trouville. Withdrawn in wartime, they were restored to use in the later 1940s, and the last one was

withdrawn in 1958. One car, restored to original condition, is preserved at Mulhouse.

TYPE: express and local passenger (36), parcels (2)
POWER: AEC 90/97kW (120/130bhp) six-cylinder
TRACTIVE EFFORT: N/A
GEARBOX: Wilson epicyclic, four/five-speed
MAX. OPERATING SPEED: 140km/h (87mph)
WEIGHT: 24 to 38 tonnes (53,760 to 84,225lb)
OVERALL LENGTH: 19.406m to 20.015m (63ft 8in to 65ft 8in)
GAUGE: 1435mm (4ft 8.5in)

The preserved Bugatti railcar, in Etat livery, at Mulhouse. The small buffers were intended only for yard movements.

CLASS E04 1-CO-1 GERMAN STATE RAILWAYS (DRG)

Fast passenger electric engines, the E04 class was developed by AEG for the relatively flat landscape and railway tracks of Saxony. It had three powered axles (by comparison with four in the contemporary E17 for more heavily graded routes). On the first eight, the maximum speed was set at 110km/h (68.3mph), but altered gearing in the next 15

TYPE: 1-Co-1 fast passenger
POWER: 2010kW (2731hp)
SUPPLY: 15kV 16.7Hz AC

TRACTIVE EFFORT: 83 or 63kN (18,590 or 14,190lbf)
MAX. OPERATING SPEED: 110 or 130km/h (68.7 or 81.2mph)

WEIGHT: 92t (202,860lb)
MAX. AXLE LOAD: 20.5t (45,203lb)
OVERALL LENGTH: 15.12m (49ft 4in)
GAUGE: 1435mm (4ft 8.5in)

increased this to 130km/h (81.3mph), trading off speed against a decrease in tractive effort. The final two locomotives, E04 22

and 23, were equipped with an early push-pull system for propelling passenger trains. On the post-war division of Germany, six

were passed to *Deutsche Bundesbahn* (DB) to become Class 104, and 16 stayed around Leipzig and Halle as DR Class 204.

'PRINCESS ROYAL' AND 'DUCHESS' CLASSES 4-6-2 LONDON, MIDLAND & SCOTTISH RAILWAY (LMS)

GREAT BRITAIN 1933

The first two 'Princess Royals', the first LMS 'Pacifics', were introduced in 1933 (Nos. 6200 and 6201). Experience with the prototypes brought about several modifications related to increased superheating and improved steam passages, and a further 10 were built in 1935, all at the LMS' Crewe works. All had a taper boiler, 1.90mm (6ft 3in) at its widest, with small wheel splashers needed to fit the big wheels and big boiler into the loading gauge. All were four-cylinder simple-expansion engines, the inner cylinders driving the first coupled wheels, the outer ones driving the second pair. Each cylinder had an independent set of Walschaerts valve gear. The bogie had inside bearings and the pony wheels had outside bearings. As in the 'Royal Scots', the boiler fittings were notably low, giving the engines a long, smooth but puissant profile. Like all progressive railwaymen, the LMS designers had observed with keen interest the work of André Chapelon in France, but the LMS had also developed its own considerable expertise in metallurgy, particularly special steels and alloys, which was of great value in producing high-performance locomotives while reducing the need for expensive maintenance and replacement of moving and sliding parts.

Competition on the main London–Scotland lines was fierce in the 1930s, and now there were also air services to contend with: the railway was no longer the speediest form of internal travel. In 1937, the LMS brought out a revised, streamlined Pacific design for the new 'Coronation' express; and this, slightly modified, was also the basis of the non-streamlined 'Duchess' class of 1938. The principal difference between these and the 1935 engines was a substantial increase in evaporative heating surface, from 215m² (2314sq ft) and in superheater area from 60.6m² (653sq ft); there was also a 76mm (3in) increase in driving wheel diameter and an additional 0.46 m² (5sq ft) of grate area. There were still four cylinders, but the outside valve gear now

In scarlet British Railways livery, preserved No. 46224 *Duchess of Hamilton* leaves York with the 'Limited Edition' charter express on 10 May 1980.

operated the inside cylinders through rocker arms. Due to the use of nickel steel, the weight increase compared with the earlier engines was only 748kg (1650lb). The cab fronts were angled to improve night vision, and the new engine had steam-operated coal pushers at the back of the tender to help in the fireman's arduous task (though no mechanical stoker), and some were fitted with Kylchap double chimneys.

The streamlining of the Coronation engines, always something of a public-relations exercise, was removed between 1945 and 1949. Altogether some 38 'Duchesses' were built, up to

1948. Formidable performers, their maximum speed recorded was 183.4km/h (114mph), by No. 6220 *Coronation*, hauling 274.3 tonnes (270 tons), on 29 June 1937, and the same engine on the return trip ran the 254km (158 miles) from Crewe to London Euston at an average speed of 128km/h (79.5mph) with 160km/h (100mph) again being exceeded. They regularly ran the 645km (401-mile) London–Glasgow journey at an average of 93km/h (58mph), including a crew-change stop. On a 614-tonne (604 ton) test train in February 1939, No. 6234 developed a maximum indicated power in the

cylinders of 2486kW (3333hp), probably a record for any British locomotive. They worked on main-line expresses until 1964. Three of the Duchesses have been preserved. Dimensions given are those of the non-streamlined engines of 1938.

BOILER PRESSURE: 17.5kg/cm² (250psi)
CYLINDERS: 419x711mm (4x16.5x28in)
DRIVING WHEELS: 2057.5mm (81in)
GRATE AREA: 4.6m² (50sq ft)
HEATING SURFACE: 260m² (2807sq ft)
SUPERHEATER: 79.5m² (856sq ft)
TRACTIVE EFFORT: 18,140kg (40,000lb)
TOTAL WEIGHT: 164t (362,000lb)

AEC DIESEL RAILCARS GREAT WESTERN RAILWAY (GWR)

GREAT BRITAIN 1933

The GWR acquired a total of 38 AEC diesel-mechanical railcars. The prototype had a single engine, but all others had two AEC vertically mounted engines on outrigger frames suspended

from the underframes. Each drove through a Wilson four- or five-speed epicyclic gearbox, cardan shafts and reversing gearbox at the outer end of one axle. The axle was joined to its neighbour

in the same bogie by a further shaft and gearbox. Nos. 2 to 8 were variants whose second engine had no gearbox, and direct drive to one axle. Nos. 18 upwards, with a more angular

appearance, could haul a van. The last four, Nos. 35 to 38, were single-ended and formed three-car sets with standard carriages between. Two cars were built as parcel vans.

TYPE: express and local passenger (36), parcels (2)
POWER: AEC 90/97kW (120/130bhp) six-cylinder
TRACTIVE EFFORT: N/A
GEARBOX: Wilson epicyclic, four/five-speed
MAX. OPERATING SPEED: 130km/h (80mph)
WEIGHT: 24 to 38t (53,760 to 84,225lb)
OVERALL LENGTH: 19.406m to 20.015m (63ft 8in to 65ft 8in)
GAUGE: 1435mm (4ft 8.5in)

Former GWR diesel railcar No. 22 is still running, preserved by the Great Western Railway Society at its depot at Didcot, Oxfordshire.

CLASS YA-01 4-8-2+2-8-4 SOVIET RAILWAYS (SZD)

RUSSIA 1933

Russia's only imported Garratt, built in Manchester, England, by Beyer Peacock, was also the largest steam locomotive ever built in Europe. The Russian railways had used articulated Fairlie and Mallet engines quite extensively in pre-Revolution times. In 1932, the Soviet Railways ordered a

4-8-2+2-8-4, for testing on 2540-tonne (2500-ton) coal trains. Despite its weight, 14 axles restricted the maximum loading to 20.3 tonnes (20 tons). Shipped to Leningrad, it was tried out on the Sverdlovsk–Chelyabinsk line in the South Urals. Allegedly because its maintenance requirements did not

BOILER PRESSURE: 14kg/cm² (220psi)	**HEATING SURFACE:** 337.1m² (3630sq ft)
CYLINDERS: 568.5x741mm (22.4x29.2in)	**SUPERHEATER:** 90m² (970sq ft)
DRIVING WHEELS: 1497mm (59in)	**TRACTIVE EFFORT:** 35,692kg (78,700lb)
GRATE AREA: 7.98m² (86sq ft)	**TOTAL WEIGHT:** 270.2t (595,840lb)

suit the Russian operating conditions, the Ya remained a

single-engine class, and the prototype was broken up in 1937.

1-B-1 GAS TURBINE LOCOMOTIVE HALMSTAD–NÄSSJÖ RAILWAY

SWEDEN 1933

The gas turbine appeared to offer several advantages, including the lack of reciprocating parts and an ability to run on low-grade fuel. Since 1908, the brothers Birger and Frederik Ljungstrøm had been working to exploit the double-action rotating steam turbine, developed by Birger. This was the pioneer application on rails, a relatively

TYPE: turbo-diesel locomotive	**TRACTIVE EFFORT:** 60kN (13,500lbf)
POWER: 485kW (650hp) diesel engine driving gas turbine. Drive to wheels via reduction gearing, jack shaft and side rods	**MAX. OPERATING SPEED:** 72km/h (45mph)
	TOTAL WEIGHT: 104t (229,320lb)

MAXIMUM AXLE LOAD: 15.5t (34,162lb)
OVERALL LENGTH: not known
GAUGE: not known

simple and small four-axle locomotive, with mechanical drive from the turbine shaft. A free-piston diesel compressor supplied the power gas. A reverse gear was

fitted, but there was no gearing for change of speed. Later turbo-diesel locomotives would use axial-flow compressors and electric transmission. Though

several countries took an interest in the Ljungstrøm system, it never became a commercial proposition, and the brothers finally withdrew from the business.

4-8-0 DELAWARE & HUDSON RAILROAD (D&H)

USA 1933

In the interests of thermal efficiency and fuel economy, railways in several countries experimented with very high-pressure boilers between the mid-1920s and the early 1930s. Wilhelm Schmidt, the father of superheating, was one of the chief proponents. A boiler pressure of about 17.5kg/cm² (250psi) was as much as could be sustained in the conventional 'Stephenson' locomotive. In 1926, Baldwin marked the building of its 60,000th locomotive by making it a 'special', a 4-10-2 with boiler pressure of 24.5kg/cm² (350psi). It was not a success and finished up in use as a stationary steam-raising plant. The New York Central essayed a high-pressure compound 4-8-4 in 1931, again

without success. The line to be most persistent in this form of experimentation was the Delaware & Hudson. Under its President, L.H. Loree, a steam locomotive enthusiast, the company had apursued a progressive design and maintenance policy. Its series began in 1924 with locomotive No. 1400, named *Horatio Allen*, a 2-8-0 of 24.5kg/cm² (350psi) with a Muhlfeld water-tube boiler. It was followed in 1927 by No. 1401 *John B. Jervis* (Jervis was a pioneer locomotive man of the D&H from the late 1820s), which was also a 2-8-0, with pressure raised to 28kg/cm² (400psi); a third 2-8-0, No. 1402 *James Archibald*, came in 1930 with a boiler pressure of 35kg/cm² (500psi). The fourth was No. 1403, a 4-8-0, named for

Loree, a four-cylinder triple-expansion compound with front and rear cylinders driving the same set of coupled wheels. The high-pressure cylinder on the right of the cab discharged to the intermediate-pressure cylinder on the left, and the steam was finally piped to the two front low-pressure cylinders. Dabeg rotary cam poppet valves were also fitted, and air jets were installed in the firebox to improve combustion. A six-wheel rear bogie on the tender was fitted with a booster engine. With so many innovative features, it unsurprisingly remained a one-off like its predecessors. This was said to be the only new locomotive built in the United States during 1933, at the depths of the Great

BOILER PRESSURE: 35kg/cm² (500psi)	
CYLINDERS: hp 507.6x812mm (20x32in); intermediate 698x812mm (27.5x32in); lp 837.5x812mm (33x32in)	
DRIVING WHEELS: 1599mm (63in)	
GRATE AREA: 7m² (75.8sq ft)	
HEATING SURFACE: 311m² (3351sq ft)	
SUPERHEATER: 99.9m² (1076sq ft)	
TRACTIVE EFFORT: 53412kg (108,000lb)	
TOTAL WEIGHT: 303.4 tonnes (669,000lb) (engine only)	

Depression. As in other countries, including Canada, Great Britain and Germany, the efforts of the American designers proved unable to combine ultra-high pressure with the reciprocal working of a steam railway locomotive in any sort of economic, reliable and easily maintainable form.

CLASS KF1 4-8-4 CHINESE GOVERNMENT RAILWAYS

CHINA 1934

In the 1930s, this was China's largest locomotive type, used on long-haul passenger expresses.

This was China's only 4-8-4 type, a class of 24 built by the Vulcan Foundry at Newton-le-Willows, England. They were two-cylinder simple-expansion engines, of great length – 30.8m (101ft 1in), including the large bogie tender – and built on bar frames, with the firebox supported by an outside-framed bogie. The original valve gear was an adaptation of Walschaerts', similar to the American Baker gear and more suitable for a long piston stroke, and operating large piston valves. Other modern fittings included a mechanical stoker, electric lighting and a valve-pilot similar to that used on American express locomotives, giving the driver guidance on what cut-off to apply to the steam. Some of the class had booster engines fitted to the leading bogie of the tender, driving two of its three axles and imparting an extra 3480kg (7670lb) of tractive effort. The class was used in express passenger service between Canton and Hankow, and Shanghai–Nanking, and was reputed to be effective in action, though despite its imposing appearance it was not particularly powerful for a 4-8-4.

Seventeen of the KF1 survived World War II and the revolutionary period that followed in China, and one of the class, No. 7, was returned by the Chinese Railways to Britain in 1981 and is today preserved at the National Railway Museum in York.

BOILER PRESSURE: 15.5kg/cm² (220psi)
CYLINDERS: 530x750mm (20.8x29.5in)
DRIVING WHEELS: 1751mm (69in)
GRATE AREA: 6.3m² (67.8sq ft)
HEATING SURFACE: 277.6m² (2988.8sq ft)
SUPERHEATER: 100m² (1076sq ft)
TRACTIVE EFFORT: 14,930kg (32,920lb)
TOTAL WEIGHT: 118.9t (engine only)

CLASS 05 4-6-4 GERMAN STATE RAILWAYS (DRG)

GERMANY 1934

Among the standard locomotive types planned by the DRG was the Class 05, intended for the haulage of light trains at very high speeds. Only three 05s were built (by Borsig) as prototypes. The requirement was for a locomotive to pull a 250-tonne (246-ton) train at 150km/h (93mph) in normal service on level track, and with a maximum operating speed of 175km/h (108mph). Such a train would match the performance of the diesel railcars operating between Berlin, Hamburg and Frankfurt, but with much greater passenger capacity and comfort. Three simple-expansion cylinders drove the first coupled wheels (inside) and the second pair (outside), and three sets of Walschaerts valve gear were provided. The boilers were of the same diameter as the 01 'Pacifics', but made of molybdenum steel plates, and the first two engines were bar-framed. The third was very different, built originally as a cab-front engine to run on pulverized coal fuel. All three were almost completely enclosed in a streamlined casing, which was painted in a red livery with a black, gold-lined band at footplate level. To help in slowing and stopping, double brake blocks were fitted to all wheels except the front wheels of the bogie, which had single blocks only, at the trailing end.

These engines were thoroughly planned and built to sustain high speeds over long distances. Surprisingly, perhaps, the copper-lined firebox was hand-fired; they were experimental engines, and careful measurement of coal input was a necessary part of the testing process. The tender was a large, seven-axle one, mounted on a four-wheel bogie with outside bearings, and three fixed axles with outside bearings set in the frame. Its capacity was 10 tonnes (9.8 tons) of coal and 8200gals (9840 US gals) of water. Germany had no water troughs.

On 11 May 1936, in the course of a test and demonstration run with many guests on board a 197-tonne (194 ton) train, including the Reich's Minister of Transport, No. 05.002 took the world record for steam with a speed of 200.4km/h (124.5mph). This was achieved on virtually level track. Many other very fast runs were credited to 05.001 and 002. One of the most remarkable was on 26 July 1935, when 05.002 kept up an average speed of 195.3km/h (121.4mph) for a distance of 39.2km (27.4 miles) on a train between Hamburg and Berlin. They were magnificent engines, but had a production run been made, it would have been difficult to adjust their full speed potential to the other, slower traffic on a busy main line like that between Berlin and Hamburg. This problem was not resolved until Japan and France began building dedicated high-speed lines. Nevertheless, from October 1936 until the outbreak of war in 1939, they operated Europe's fastest scheduled steam service – 2hrs, 24mins for the 285km (178.1 mile) Hamburg–Berlin route, requiring an average speed of 118.7km/h (74.2mph). To achieve this, substantially higher speeds had to be maintained over long stretches of track.

Krauss-Maffei rebuilt 05.001 and 002 for the *Deutsche Bundesbahn* (DB) in 1950, and the streamlining was removed, giving the locomotives a more conventional appearance. No. 003, which had not been a success and had been rebuilt in standard form in 1944–45, was again rebuilt at this time. All three then operated passenger express duties on the DB, until 1957, and 002 and 003 were scrapped in 1958.

No. 05.001 has been preserved, with its streamlined casing partly restored, but leaving the wheels and motion visible.

BOILER PRESSURE: 20kg/cm² (284psi)
CYLINDERS: 450x660mm (17.75x26in)
DRIVING WHEELS: 2300mm (90.5in)
GRATE AREA: 4.71m² (51sq ft)
HEATING SURFACE: 256m² (2750sq ft)
SUPERHEATER: 90m² (976sq ft)
TRACTIVE EFFORT: 14,870kg (32,788lb)
TOTAL WEIGHT: 213t (475,064lb)

CLASS 321-4 BO GERMAN STATE RAILWAYS (DRG)

GERMANY 1934

Hydraulic transmission proved very effective in small diesel shunting locomotives. This large class, over 1000-strong, was a development of the earlier Class 100 types (see 1929), with the same 850mm (33.4in) wheels, but with hydraulic transmission and power increased to 87/94kW (118/128hp). Deutz, Jung, BMAG, Krauss-Maffei and Krupp were the builders, using KHD or Kaeble engines, and construction went on until 1966.

Traffic changes, cessation of wagonload freight traffic, and increased use of passenger multiple unit operation eventually reduced their usefulness by the 1990s. A number were passed on to industry for further use in addition to many supplied direct. Under the DB computer system, they were numbered 321001 to 321626, 322001 to 322663, 323001 to 323999, and 324001 to 324060.

TYPE: B diesel-hydraulic light shunting tractor
POWER: 87 or 94kW (118 or 128hp)
TRACTIVE EFFORT: 47kN (10575lbf)
MAX. OPERATING SPEED: 30 or 45km/h (18.8 or 17.5mph)
WEIGHT: 15–17 tonnes (33,075–37,485lb)
OVERALL LENGTH: 6450mm (21ft)
GUAGE: 1435mm (4ft 8.5in)

2-6-4T LONDON, MIDLAND & SCOTTISH RAILWAY (LMS)

GREAT BRITAIN 1934

The LMS had built a three-cylinder 2-6-4 in 1934, but this two-cylinder engine, designed in that year and in production from 1935 with 15 per cent greater superheating surface, was to be the standard and a model for later developments. Built at the company's Derby works, it ran suburban services around all major cities in LMS territory. Intensive use was required, and it featured mechanical lubrication of the pistons, piston valves and piston rod packings, while hardened manganese-molybdenum steel was used for the coupling and connecting rods. It carried 3.56 tonnes (3.5 tons) of coal and 2000gals (2400 US gals) of water: water pick-up gear extended its operating range to some inter-city services.

BOILER PRESSURE: 14kg/cm² (200psi)
CYLINDERS: 497x660mm (19.6x26in)
DRIVING WHEELS: 1751mm (69in)
GRATE AREA: 2.5m² (26.7 sq ft)
HEATING SURFACE: 126.8m² (1366sq ft)
SUPERHEATER: 22.75m² (245sq ft)
TRACTIVE EFFORT: 9886kg (21,800lb)
TOTAL WEIGHT: 96.8t (196,000lb)

The illustration shows No. 42507 of the externally almost identical 3-cylinder 2-6-4T type of 1934, built at Derby Works to the design of W.A. Stanier.

CLASS P2 2-8-2 LONDON & NORTH EASTERN RAILWAY (LNER)

GREAT BRITAIN 1934

A shot of *Cock o' the North* on an Edinburgh–Aberdeen express. The impressive appearance of Britain's only express 'Mikado' class gave considerable prestige to the LNER.

The Gresley 'Mikados' were designed and built at Doncaster to work heavy express trains between Edinburgh and Aberdeen, a main line more steeply graded than the Edinburgh–London route. Two prototypes, both three-cylinder simples, explored different valve arrangements. The first, No. 2001 *Cock o' the North*, had camshaft-operated poppet valves. The second, *Earl Marischal*, had Gresley's

conjugated version of Walschaerts valve gear, which was used also on the other four members of the class, built in 1936. Two forms of streamlining were also tried, settling on one similar to that designed in 1935 for the A4 'Pacific'. Britain's only eight-coupled passenger express engines, the Mikados were

also the first British engines to have the Kylchap double-blast exhaust and chimney. The LNER designers were familiar with Chapelon's work in France, and through liaison between Gresley and Chapelon, No. 2001 was sent to France for testing at the Vitry plant and also on the Paris–Orleans main line.

BOILER PRESSURE: 15.5kg/cm² (220psi)
CYLINDERS: 533x660mm (21x26in)
DRIVING WHEELS: 1880mm (74in)
GRATE AREA: 4.6m² (50sq ft)
HEATING SURFACE: 324.m² (3490sq ft)
SUPERHEATER: 59m² (635sq ft)
TRACTIVE EFFORT: 19,955kg (44,000lb)
TOTAL WEIGHT: 111.7t (246,400lb)

Imposing though they were, the P2s showed none of the French compounds' economy, and substantially less power. Coal consumption per drawbar-horsepower hour at an average speed of 90km/h (56mph) was 1.38kg (3.1lb) compared to 1kg (2.45lb) on the Chapelon rebuild of the Paris–Orleans Class 3500 'Pacifics'. With a grate at the maximum size for hand-firing, they were very heavy coal users, requiring the fireman to shovel in about 36kg (80lb) per mile, or over 4.06 tonnes (4 tons) on a 161km

Side-on view of No. 2003 *Lord President*, showing the style of streamlined casing that was also used on the A4 'Pacifics'.

(100-mile) journey. The rigid set of driving wheels had a tendency to derail in engine-yards, and the engines also suffered from wear in the axle-boxes and hot bearings were common. During World War II, and following the death of Sir Nigel Gresley, all six were controversially rebuilt as rather ungainly-looking 4-6-2s, classified A2/2.

2-8-2T GREAT WESTERN RAILWAY (GWR)

GREAT BRITAIN 1934

Built primarily to pull coal trains from South Wales, the GWR 4200 and 5200 2-8-0T classes go back to 1910. But good steam locomotives are potentially long-lived, and all railway companies shared the urge to make the most of their potential, if necessary by rebuilding. In this case, when the 1930s slump caused a fall in coal exports from Wales, the engines were rebuilt with superheated boilers as 2-8-2Ts and transferred to slow main-line goods work. The boiler was a GWR standard used on other types also, and the wheels inserted beneath the extended bunker were also of standard type. Thus a company could acquire a 'new' class and charge it to repairs and maintenance, rather than to the capital account.

Neatly extended from a 2-8-0T, No. 7213 stands in the sidings behind an old-type coaling stage.

BOILER PRESSURE: 14kg/cm² (200psi)
CYLINDERS: 482x761mm (19x30in)
DRIVING WHEELS: 1408mm (55.5in)
GRATE AREA: 1.9m² (20.5sq ft)
HEATING SURFACE: 137m² (1479sq ft)
SUPERHEATER: 17.8m² (192sq ft)
TRACTIVE EFFORT: 13,288kg (29,300lb)
TOTAL WEIGHT: 94t (207,424lb)

CLASS 5P5F 4-6-0 LONDON, MIDLAND & SCOTTISH RAILWAY (LMS)

Engines given nicknames were either very bad or, more usually, very good. The 'Black Fives' belonged in the second category. Later designated 5MT (mixed traffic), this was the most numerous tender class to run on British rails, with 842 built by 1948. A general utility 'pool' engine, it could be worked by any driver over any part of the LMS system. Designed under the auspices of W. A. (later Sir William) Stanier, it had the coned boiler design with Belpaire firebox that he had brought from the Great Western, and two simple-expansion outside cylinders, operated by large piston valves of 254mm (10in) diameter with outside Walschaerts valve gear. The original version had a domeless boiler, with the regulator fitted to the superheater header in the smoke-box, and a top feed system mounted on the second ring; later examples retained the top feed but were normally built with domed boilers. From 1935, a larger number of superheating elements were fitted, 24 as opposed to 14, with an increase of almost 9.3m² (100sq ft) of heating surface; and from 1938 this was increased again to 28. The design was also intended for relative ease of maintenance, with the running plate above the wheels, and the cab was more spacious than in most British locomotives. But no attempt was made to install electric lighting, and only a manual screw reverser was fitted. The first order was for 70 – 50 from the Vulcan Foundry and 20 from the LMS' Crewe Works. Later they were also built at the Derby and Horwich works, and also by Armstrong Whitworth in Newcastle. It was a very popular engine with crews, and with its appearance the scrapping of older types began to accelerate.

The chief duties of the 'Black 5s' were on medium-distance passenger and freight trains, but they often ran express services. Their sturdy appearance managed to convey the reliability they undoubtedly possessed. Up to the end of 1939 ,they averaged some 233,340km (145,000 miles) between general repairs, and in the 1950s this increased to 257,500km (160,000 miles).

Despite a reputation for being rough riders at speed, they were capable of sustained speeds around 120km/h (75mph) and were 'clocked' on numerous occasions at speeds in excess of 145km/h (90mph). In 1947–48, 30 of the class were fitted experimentally with various permutations of Caprotti valve gear, double chimneys and roller

bearings. The first two features were not adopted on the British standard 4-6-0s of the early 1950s, which were in most respects a second-generation of the Class 5, but roller bearings became standard. All were fitted with a standard LMS six-wheel tender with high turned-in sides, with capacity for 9.15 tonnes (9 tons) of coal and 4000gals (4800 US gals) of water, and water pick-up apparatus.

The class operated until the final days of steam on British Railways, in 1968, and hauled the last scheduled steam passenger expresses in Britain. Fifteen are preserved.

STEAM PRESSURE: 15.75kg/cm² (225psi)
CYLINDERS: 470x711mm (18.5x28in)
DRIVING WHEELS: 1830mm (72in)
GRATE AREA: 2.6m² (28.7sq ft)
HEATING SURFACE: 135.6m² (1460sq ft)
SUPERHEATER: 33.3m² (359sq ft)
TRACTIVE EFFORT: 11,790kg (26,000lb)
TOTAL WEIGHT: 72.1t (159,040lb)

Approaching Glenfinnan on the West Highland line, preserved 'Black Five' No. 44767 heads a steam special in July 1985.

ÁRPÁD DIESEL RAILCARS HUNGARIAN STATE RAILWAYS (MAV)

HUNGARY 1934

MÁV commissioned the Ganz company, then in the forefront of diesel as well as electric railway development, to design a lightweight railcar with a powerful enough engine to accelerate well and to reach a useful maximum speed. With the first named 'Árpád' after a Magyar chieftain, seven were put into service from 1934. Good acceleration and a top speed of 110km/h (69mph) made them ideal for fast inter-city-type services. On the international Budapest to Wien (Vienna) service,

Árpád diesel railcars achieved a city-to-city timing of 2hrs, 58min, a record not achieved again until the end of the twentieth century.

A large Ganz VuaR 170 diesel engine was mounted on one bogie

and drove both axles of that bogie through a five-speed mechanical gearbox and propeller shafts. A capacious radiator for cooling water was fitted under the vehicle body behind the driven bogie. The

other bogie was not driven. Each railcar contained 64 seats as well as eight folding seats in the entrance vestibules. There was a toilet compartment and a wash room in the centre of the car, and a luggage compartment next to the cab at the non-powered end. The railcars were not intended to haul trailers, and thus had only small side buffers and a drawhook below each cab front. 'Árpád' railcar No. 23, named *Tas*, is preserved in working order and appears in public at special events.

TYPE: express passenger diesel railcar
POWER: Ganz VIJaR 170, 160kW (215bhp), bogie frame mounted
TRACTIVE EFFORT: N/A
GEARBOX: five-speed mechanical, driving two axles on one bogie

MAX. OPERATING SPEED: 110km/h (68mph)
WEIGHT: 33t (72,470lb)
OVERALL LENGTH: 22.00m (72ft 2in)
GAUGE: 1435 (4ft 8.5in)

CLASS E428 2-BO-BO-2 STATE RAILWAYS (FS)

ITALY 1934

Speeds up to 150km/h (94mph) were possible with some members of this express class, of which 241 were built up to 1940

by Breda, Ansaldo, TIBB, Fiat and Reggiane for the FS' rapidly expanding 3000V DC system. The two-part articulated underframe

supported a rigid body. Several external styling variants existed within the class. Up to E428 096, they had a boxy structure with

small squared-off noses, while later engines had variously raked-back or semi-streamlined designs. Eight DC frame-mounted motors in pairs drove the four main wheels through Bianchi or Nergri quill drive. Three gear ratios gave tractive effort ranges from 113kN at 72km/h (25,425lbf at 45mph) through 103kN at 78km/h (23100lbf at 48.8mph) to 93kN at 88km/h (20,900lbf at 55mph). Availability of different gear ratios was a feature of Italian electric locomotive development of that era, with higher traction pull traded off against speed depending on the duties required, and the original 150km/h (93.8mph) maximum speed of some members was later reduced to 100km/h (62mph).

TYPE: 2-Bo-Bo-2 fast passenger
POWER: 2800kW (3804hp)
SUPPLY: 3000V DC
TRACTIVE EFFORT: 93 to 113kN (20,925 to 25,425lbf)
MAX. OPERATING SPEED: 100km/h (62.1mph)
WEIGHT: E428 001–096 – 131t (288,855lb); E428 097–241 – 135t (297,675lb)
MAX. AXLE LOAD: 18t (39,690lb)
OVERALL LENGTH: 19m (62ft)
GAUGE: 1435mm (4ft 8.5in)

An E428 on a long-distance train enters a station south of Ancona on the picturesque Adriatic coastal line. The year is 1937.

SATA I CLASS 2-10-2T KOREAN GOVERNMENT RAILWAYS (KGR)

KOREA 1934

Japanese builders produced 24 of these powerful tank locomotives between 1934 and 1939, 14 from Nippon Sharyo and 10 from Keijo. They were two-cylinder simples, intended for heavy short-range freight work, chiefly in marshalling

BOILER PRESSURE: 14kg/cm² (199psi)
CYLINDERS: 560x710mm (22x28in)
DRIVING WHEELS: 1450mm (57in)

GRATE AREA: 4.75m² (51sq ft)
HEATING SURFACE: not known
SUPERHEATER: not known

TRACTIVE EFFORT: 19,860kg (40,200lb)
TOTAL WEIGHT: 110t (242,550lb) (engine only)

yards. Following the division of the country in 1947, eight were in South

Korea and 16 in the North. The fate of those locomotives in North Korea

is not known, but those in the South were all derelict by the early 1950s.

AA 20-1 4-14-4 SOVIET RAILWAYS (SZD)

In the varied history of the steam locomotive, only one single example has ever had seven driving axles. It was built in Stalinist Russia. Historically, Russian locomotive engineering was eminently practical, and though many experimental designs were tried over the years, this represented a serious attempt to obtain an effective operating type. But the one and only class AA 20, the largest non-articulated locomotive in Europe, and with the longest rigid wheelbase ever built, was something of an embarrassment. Named after its sponsor, Andrei Andreyev, it was intended more to demonstrate the modernity and grand scale of Soviet engineering than to exploit the maximum locomotive dimensions and performance possible within the generous Russian loading gauge, with its recently increased maximum axle loading of some 20.2 tonnes (20 tons). The original design was for a 2-14-4, to be built by Krupps in Germany, but a front bogie was substituted and it was built in Russia at the Voroshilovgrad works. A publicity visit to Moscow was made in January 1935, and it was duly hailed as a triumph of Soviet technology. Intended for use on coal trains from the Donbas region to Moscow, it never entered revenue-earning service, and nothing was ever published about its further activities. Three decades later, the Soviet technical press were able to admit that the AA 20 had been completely unusable. Even if capable of effective steaming, it spread the tracks, damaged points, and was excessively prone to derailment. It was scrapped, without publicity, at some unknown time.

BOILER PRESSURE: 17kg/cm² (242psi)
CYLINDERS: 741x807mm (29.2x31.8in)
DRIVING WHEELS: 1599mm (63in)
GRATE AREA: 12m² (129sq ft)
HEATING SURFACE: 448m² (4823sq ft)
SUPERHEATER: 174m² (1873.4sq ft)
TRACTIVE EFFORT: 40,286kg (88,830lb)
TOTAL WEIGHT: 211.3t (465,920lb)
(engine only)

CLASS S-3 2-8-4 NEW YORK, CHICAGO & ST LOUIS RAILROAD (NICKEL PLATE ROAD)

The S-3 'Berkshire' of the Nickel Plate Road was essentially similar to a range of others built during the 1930s for similar lines with heavy freight traffic. All were two-cylinder simples, fitted with the US standard Type E superheater, and with Walschaerts or Baker valve gear, and feedwater heaters and pumps of various patent manufacture, as specified by the railroad company to the builders. Differences in dimension and detail were relatively small. Some types had trailer boosters.

Engines of this configuration were the backbone of general long-distance freight. They normally ran with 12-wheel tenders with a capacity around 16,600gals (20,000 US gals) of water and 22.35 tonnes (22 tons) of coal. Lima Works built the 70 Nickel Plate S-3s, but all three main US builders built many examples.

BOILER PRESSURE: 17kg/cm² (245psi)
CYLINDERS: 634.5x863mm (25x34in)
DRIVING WHEELS: 69in (1751mm)

GRATE AREA: 8.4m² (90.3sq ft)
HEATING SURFACE: 443.2m² (4772sq ft)
SUPERHEATER: 179.4m² (1932sq ft)

TRACTIVE EFFORT: 29,070kg (64,100lb)
TOTAL WEIGHT: 201.5t (444,290lb)
(engine only)

GG1 2-CO-CO-2 PENNSYLVANIA RAILROAD (PRR)

Electric locomotives so far had made little impression on the travelling public in the United States, and it was the GG1 that first caught the general attention, due to its design, its numbers and its operation on one of the country's busiest routes, the New York–Philadelphia–Washington DC corridor. Electrification between New York and Philadelphia began operating in January 1933, and through electric working to Washington DC started on 10 February 1935, when the *Congressional Limited* inaugurated the service in both directions. The GG1's predecessor, the P5, had been unsatisfactory, and the motive power department was under pressure to get things right. PRR experimented with different wheel arrangements to select the best possible combination for high-speed service, borrowing a New Haven EP-3 electric of 2-Co-Co-2 arrangement, and in 1934 building two prototype machines, both streamlined centre-cab designs. One was of 2-Do-2 arrangement, patterned from the 4-8-4 type steam locomotive, and was classed R1; the other was on the EP-3 pattern and was classed GG1. After extensive testing, the GG1 type was picked, and over the following

Preserved and polished to gleaming point, one of the numerous preserved GG1 locos, No. 4935, stands on display at Strasburg, PA.

decade a fleet of 138 was built, the first ones at PRR's Juniata shops, but others were built by Baldwin and General Electric. The designer Raymond Loewy, also working on the look of new steam locomotives, was responsible for the final appearance. He created the famous 'cats whiskers' five-stripe livery, and most importantly gave it a smooth, welded carbody instead of the traditional riveted method used on the prototype No. 4800. From 1934 until the 1950s, the standard GG1 livery was PRR's 'Brunswick Green' with gold pin stripes and a crimson keystone – the state's symbol filched for PRR's corporate logo.

Current was supplied at high voltage from overhead wire, using 11,000V AC at 25Hz, and picked up by two high box-pantographs mounted on the 'noses' of the locomotive.

The GG1s had a 24–77 gear ratio and 1448mm (57in) driving wheels for 160km/h (100 mph) operation, and could easily accelerate a 18-car passenger train to top speed. Power was delivered by 12 287kW (385hp) traction motors, two on each powered axle, giving the locomotive a continuous 3447kW (4620 hp). But the GG1 could generate much greater power for short periods for rapid acceleration. In later years, some GG1s were re-geared for freight services.

With the GG1, the railroad company had an engine that performed extremely well in addition to looking ultra-modern, though still with a hint of steam-locomotive ruggedness. Initially they were mostly employed on passenger services, and remained the mainstay of the passenger electric fleet after the Pennsylvania–New York Central merger of 1968. The New Haven Railroad was absorbed into Penn-Central in 1969. The subsequent financial collapse of Penn-Central led to the creation of Amtrak as the national passenger operator. Amtrak assumed operation of most intercity passenger services and acquired a sizeable fleet of former PRR GG1s for its Northeast Corridor services.

Under Amtrak, GG1s were allowed to run over the former New Haven Railroad from New York Penn Station to New Haven, Connecticut. The last GG1s were operated by New Jersey Transit and made their final runs in October 1983. Sixteen are preserved in museums and on heritage lines.

TYPE: mixed-traffic high-speed electric
POWER: 11,500V at 25Hz AC
OUTPUT: 3442kW (4620hp) to 3680kW (4930hp)
TRACTIVE EFFORT: 314kN (70,700lbf) to 333kN (75,000lbf) – varied depending on weight – starting TE with 24:77 gear ratio
MAX. OPERATING SPEED: 160km/h (100mph)
WEIGHT: 208.6t (460,000lb) to 216.3t (477,000lb)
OVERALL LENGTH: 24.232m (79ft 6in)
MAX. AXLE LOAD: 22.9t (50,500lb)
GAUGE: 1435mm (4ft 8.5in)

M-10000 TRAIN   UNION PACIFIC RAILROAD (UP)

USA 1934

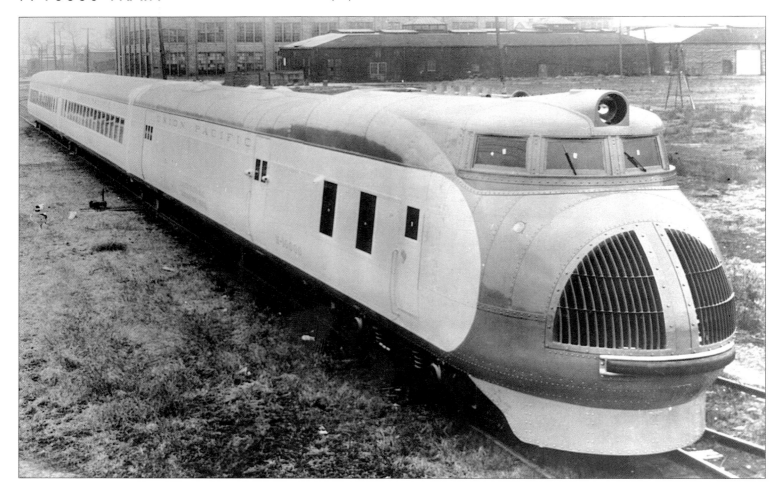

Strong hints of the automobile industry can be seen in the design of the M-1000, with its front grille and smoothed-out lines. In 1934, it was a dramatic change for rail travellers.

Road competition and economic depression hit US railroads in the early 1930s, and two lines, Union Pacific and Burlington, set out to combat the negative trend with the introduction of new-type passenger trains. Union Pacific worked with passenger car manufacturer Pullman to construct a three-car aluminium articulated train, America's first streamliner. To ensure aerodynamic efficiency, UP recruited help from specialists at Michigan State University. (For their *Zephyr*, Burlington would do likewise, but with MIT.) Completed in February 1934, it was powered by a Winton distillate engine with electric transmission. (A distillate engine required a spark plug for ignition, and is not a diesel.) Union Pacific painted the train in a flashy mustard and brown scheme and sent it on a nationwide publicity tour, where it was seen by over a million people. On test, it once achieved a speed of 178.6km/h (111mph). The set was too short for long haul service, and later the M-10000 was assigned to service as the City of Salina (Kansas). In 1942, it was scrapped and its valuable aluminium recycled.

TYPE: distillate-electric powered stream-lined articulated high-speed train
POWER: not known
TRACTIVE EFFORT: not known
MAX. OPERATING SPEED: 178km/h (111mph)
WEIGHT: 77t (170,000lb)
OVERALL LENGTH: 62.331m (204ft 6in)
GAUGE: 1435mm (4ft 8.5in)

BURLINGTON'S *ZEPHYR* BURLINGTON RAILROAD

The debut of Burlington's shining *Zephyr* only two months later than the Union Pacific's M-10000 dazzled the American public, and helped to confirm that a new era was at hand for both passenger travel and the future of motive power on American railways. In 1930, automotive manufacturer General Motors had purchased both Winton Engine and rail car manufacturer Electro-Motive. Formed as a corporation in 1922, the original EM, of Cleveland, Ohio, was a contractor rather than a builder, sub-contracting work to carbody, engine and electrical equipment manufacturers. (It would have its own works at La Grange, Illinois, from 1936, though dependence on subcontractors continued until 1938.) However, it had experience of building some 500 railcars through the 1920s, with engines from Winton. Hitherto, diesel engines had been heavy machines:

the challenge was to reduce the weight of around 36kg (80lb) per hp produced, to something much less. By the use of special alloys and a two-stroke cycle, the weight was dramatically reduced, to 9kg (20lb) per hp, in a state-of-the-art Winton 201-A diesel engine, with eight in-line cylinders, producing 441kW (600hp). *Zephyr* is credited as America's first diesel-electric powered passenger train. On its first outing, on 26 May 1934, it ran from Denver, Colorado non-stop to the site of the World Exposition in Chicago, 1633km (1015 miles) at an average speed of 124.8km/h (77.6mph). Capable of speeds well in excess of 160km/h (100mph), it could run for hundreds of miles without the need to stop for water or fuel. This allowed Burlington to substantially trim running times. Based on the success of the first *Zephyr* (later known as *Pioneer Zephyr*), Burlington ordered a whole fleet of

similar diesel streamliners. These trains were longer and had more passenger capacity than the *Pioneer Zephyr*. The streamlined trains were a spectacular success, and both Burlington and Union Pacific were rewarded by dramatic increases in passenger numbers. By the mid-1930s, many American lines were ordering streamlined passenger trains. Boston & Maine ordered a near copy of the *Zephyr* that was initially operated as the *Flying Yankee* between Boston, Massachusetts, Portland and Bangor, Maine. After World War II, the streamlined lightweight train enjoyed renewed interest and many conventionally coupled, locomotive hauled streamlined trains appeared.

These early diesel trains demonstrated the capabilities of high-output diesel engines and helped establish Electro-Motive's reputation as a source of up-to-date motive power. Electro-Motive

moved rapidly, developing a series of increasingly powerful and reliable diesel locomotive designs. Twenty-five years after the *Zephyr's* debut, the diesel-electric reigned as the premier motive power on American lines, and Electro-Motive had become America's largest locomotive manufacturer. After a long service life, the original *Zephyr* was preserved. In 1995, it underwent an extensive cosmetic restoration and now, looking much the way it did in April 1934, it can be seen at the Chicago Museum of Science and Industry.

TYPE: diesel-electric powered streamlined articulated high-speed train
POWER AND OUTPUT: Winton 201E diesel producing 44kW (600hp)
TRACTIVE EFFORT: N/A
MAX. OPERATING SPEED: 186km/h (116mph)
WEIGHT: 79t (175,000lb)
OVERALL LENGTH: 59.741m (196ft)
GAUGE: 1435mm (4ft 8.5in)

The *Pioneer Zephyr* was restored in the mid-1990s by Northern Railcar in Wisconsin, and is now on display in the Chicago Museum of Science and Industry.

CLASS 1 4-6-2 BELGIAN NATIONAL RAILWAYS (SNCB)

With a front end very similar to the British LNER's P2 2-8-2, and a generally 'air-smoothed' look, this was among the heaviest European 'Pacific' types, with a maximum axle load of 23.7 tonnes (23.3 tons). Designed by Raoul Notesse of the SNCB, it was built in Belgium by Cockerill of Seraing. Four simple-expansion cylinders were set in line, the inside ones driving the leading coupled

wheels; the outside ones the second pair. Kylchap double blast pipes discharged through a Legein-

type chimney, and ACFI feed water pumps and heaters were fitted. The class, totalling 35, was used

on the main line service between Brussels and Liège, and other heavy expresses. One is preserved.

BOILER PRESSURE: 18kg/cm² (260psi)
CYLINDERS: 420x720mm (16.5x28.4in)
DRIVING WHEELS: 1980mm (78in)
GRATE AREA: 4.9m² (52.75sq ft)
HEATING SURFACE: 234m² (2527sq ft)
SUPERHEATER: 111.6m² (1202sq ft)
TRACTIVE EFFORT: 9935kg (22,000lb)
TOTAL WEIGHT: 126t (277,760lb)

No. 1002 has been preserved and still makes public appearances at steam festivals.

CLASS JF 'STANDARD' 2-8-2 SOUTH MANCHURIA RAILWAY

JF represents the Chinese notation for a 2-8-2, and this numerous 'standard' type, later also named as the 'Liberation' class, was based on an Alco 'Mikado' supplied to the South Manchurian Railway in 1918.

By 1935, American locomotives had incorporated numerous refinements, many intended to improve ease of handling and maintenance, but this remained a very basic, though functional, type.

China had no locomotive-building industry until the establishment of Communist government in 1948, and Japanese builders dominated the market in the 1930s. More than 2500 of this very American-style

Most of China's last steam workings were on large steel works and mining sites, like this 1990s scene with a JF on a track-laying work train amid slag and sinter piles.

BOILER PRESSURE: 14kg/cm² (200psi)	**GRATE AREA:** 5.1m² (54.9sq ft)	**TRACTIVE EFFORT:** 20,737kg (45,725lb)
CYLINDERS: 580x710mm (22.8x28in)	**HEATING SURFACE:** 209.4m² (2254sq ft)	**TOTAL WEIGHT:** 103.8t (228,879lb)
DRIVING WHEELS: 1370mm (54in)	**SUPERHEATER:** 64.9m² (698.7sq ft)	(engine only)

class – two-cylinder simple-expansion engines, with Walschaerts valve gear actuated by piston valves – were built between 1935 and 1957, at first in Japan at several shops including Kawasaki,

Kisha Seizo Kaisha, Hitachi and Nippon Sharya. From around 1950, building was transferred to China at Dalian and Qingdao. Many of the JFs were adapted for shunting, with sloping-backed tenders.

In the 1930s, a variety of other 2-8-2s were imported by independent Chinese railway companies, all denoted as sub-classes of JF. In 1957, a modified standard version was built at

the Chinese works, of identical main dimensions but with longer piston valve travel – 161mm (6.3in) as against 152mm (6in). This was itself superseded from 1958 by the JS 2-8-2, built to a Russian design. Meanwhile, the 'standard' JF locomotives continued to work freight over most parts of the long-ranging Chinese railway network.

THREE-CAR *LYNTOG* DANISH STATE RAILWAYS (DSB) · DENMARK 1935

Danish railway operations had always been constricted by the seaways separating Jutland and the main islands, but this was partially eased by the opening on 14 May 1935 of the Little Belt bridge, linking the island of Fyn (Funen) to the Jutland peninsula and enabling trains to run from the mainland to the ferryport of Nyborg on the wider Great Belt between Funen and Zealand.

In the same year, the *Lyntog* ('lightning train') was introduced, first on the cross-country Esbjerg–Copenhagen service. The trains were built to fit the Nyborg-Korsør train ferry. The cars were articulated, with four two-axled bogies. The power bogies were at the ends, each with two diesel engines. Rounded ends suggested high speed, and this was justified by performance.

TYPE: diesel-electric articulated three-car train
POWER: four Frichs 205kW (275hp) diesel engines supplying current to eight nose-suspended traction motors in the end bogies
TRACTIVE EFFORT: not known
MAX. OPERATING SPEED: 144km/h (90mph)
TOTAL WEIGHT: 130t (286,650lb)
MAXIMUM AXLE LOAD: 16.5t (36,366lb)
OVERALL LENGTH: 63.703m (209ft)
GAUGE: not known

In this 1935 shot, a *Lyntog* set rolls off the train ferry on its run across Denmark from Esbjerg to Copenhagen.

SERIES 60 2-4-2T LÜBECK-BÜCHEN RAILWAY (LBE) · GERMANY 1935

Henschel built the two engines of this class to run the 84km (52-mile) Hamburg–Travemünde service in one hour, including an intermediate stop at Lübeck. The LBE was absorbed into the *Deutsche Reichsbahn Gesellschaft* (DRG) in January 1936, by which time the two Henschel-built streamlined

engines of this class were running these fast trains. Fast acceleration was essential, and they could go

BOILER PRESSURE: 16kg/cm² (228psi)
CYLINDERS: 400x660mm (15.8x26in)
DRIVING WHEELS: 1980mm (78in)
GRATE AREA: 1.4m² (15sq ft)

from 0 to 120km/h (75mph) in 5.5 minutes. The train was fitted for push-pull work to obviate the

HEATING SURFACE: 75.4m² (812sq ft)
SUPERHEATER: 26m² (280sq ft)
TRACTIVE EFFORT: 7310kg (16,120lb)
TOTAL WEIGHT: 69t (152,145lb)

need for changing the engines' position or turning them. On the return trip, the driver sat in a cab in the front coach, operating the controls by electrically powered links, and communicating with the fireman by telephone. A third engine, with some modifications, was also built.

CLASS E18 1-DO-1 GERMAN STATE RAILWAYS (DRG)

No. E 18.050 stands at Frankfurt am Main Hauptbahnhof, in May 1969. Shown at the 1937 World Exposition in Paris, the class was awarded a gold medal.

Most European electric locomotives had been of very functional-looking squared-off appearance up to now, but the E18 showed a new approach, with rounded ends on its integral body and cab structure, and a greater sense of applied design. Its genesis was in the desire to get through operations across the similar but separate 15kV systems in southern Germany around Munich and Stuttgart, in Saxony around Leipzig and Halle, and in Silesia around Breslau (today Wroclaw in Poland). Plans were drawn up in 1933 for a locomotive capable of through electric operation between Munich and Leipzig. A top speed of 150km/h (93.8mph) was specified for the new class E18. In May 1935, the prototype was delivered from AEG and put on high-speed testing the following month. E18 01 met all specified parameters between Munich and Stuttgart and attained 165km/h (103.1mph) between Munich and Augsburg. Line production was begun, and E18

053 was under construction before war production took priority, and building of the class came to a stop. The first series locomotives, delivered in 1936, ran between Munich and Stuttgart, Nürnberg and Regensburg. Eight others were used on the Breslau–Görlitz route. Compatibility of the Saxon and Bavarian electrified systems was achieved in November 1942, allowing through working between Munich and Leipzig, although there were difficulties with different contact wire and pantograph arrangements. The Saxon lines used a ±500mm (19.5in) wire zigzag and 2100mm (82.7in) pantograph head, but the E18 had only ±400mm (15.7in) zigzag and 1950mm (76.8in) head. Under war conditions, standardization was slow to take place.

At the end of hostilities in 1945, six of the total of 53 class E18

were completely destroyed by enemy action, six were in the Russian occupied zone, two in Austria and 39 in Allied-occupied western Germany. Around half the latter were in a seriously damaged condition, demanding major attention to return them to service. Two new E18s were built in 1954–55 by AEG and Krupp out of existing parts from machines cancelled at the outbreak of war. In 1977, main works overhauls were ceased on the class, which was reduced to 33 in *Deutsche Bundesbahn* (DB) traffic, being finally withdrawn in the early 1980s. In the eastern zone, five locomotives were taken by the Soviets for use on a projected 15kV line on the Vorkuta peninsula in Siberia. This never materialized, and the machines were returned to East Germany in 1952. When the *Deutsche Reichsbahn* (DR) restarted electric train working in 1955, it

rebuilt two E18s, using parts recovered from derelict E17s, and put them into service. In 1967, the DR investigated 180km/h (112.5mph) operation and altered the gear ratio accordingly, at the same time fitting new wheels and hollow drive shafts. E18 31 was set aside and preserved as a museum locomotive. The two machines in Austria became ÖBB Class 1118, along with eight locally assembled Class 1018 machines. These outlived the locomotives remaining in Germany by several years, working into the 1990s.

TYPE: 1-Do-1 express passenger
POWER: 2840kW (3859hp)
SUPPLY: 15kV 16.7Hz AC
TRACTIVE EFFORT: 84kN (18,800lbf)
MAX. OPERATING SPEED: 150km/h (93.8mph)
WEIGHT: 108.5t (239,243lb)
MAX. AXLE LOAD: 19.6t (43,218lb)
OVERALL LENGTH: 16.92m (55ft 2in)
GAUGE: 1435mm (4ft 8.5in)

CLASS E19 01/02 1-DO-1 GERMAN STATE RAILWAYS (DRG)

The E19 was essentially a higher-speed – 180km/h (112.5mph) – version of the E18, of similar design and layout. E19.01 and E19.02 were built by AEG in 1939 with four single armature motors and 20-step control, while E19.11 and E19.12 were built by Siemens with four

TYPE: 1-Do-1 express passenger	**MAX. OPERATING SPEED:** 180km/h (112.5mph)	**OVERALL LENGTH:** 16.92m (55ft 2in)
POWER: 3720kW (5054hp)	**WEIGHT:** 113 tonnes (249,165lb)	**GAUGE:** 1435mm (4ft 8.5in)
SUPPLY: 15kV 16.7Hz AC	**MAX. AXLE LOAD:** 20.2t (44,541lb)	
TRACTIVE EFFORT: 77kN (17270lbf		

double armature motors and a 15-step control system. The latter were intended as test engines for

operation at 225km/h (140.6mph), but all testing was halted at the outbreak of war. One

E19 is preserved in the national railway museum in Nürnberg in its original Third Reich livery.

CLASS V16 (LATER V140) 1-C-1 GERMAN STATE RAILWAYS (DRG)

Diesel-hydraulic transmission, though used far less widely than diesel-electric (except in multiple unit trains and small shunting locomotives), has always been a viable alternative, and remains so today. Germany in particular has been a source of main-line diesel-hydraulic locomotives – right up to contemporary units like the Vossloh G2000BB. The V16 prototype, built by Krauss Maffei

TYPE: 1-C-1 diesel-hydraulic prototype	**MAX. OPERATING SPEED:** 100km/h (62mph)
POWER: 1030kW (1400hp) from MAN W8V 30/38 series engine	**WEIGHT:** 83t (183,015lb)
TRACTIVE EFFORT: 137kN (30,800lbf)	**OVERALL LENGTH:** 14.4m (47ft)
	GAUGE: 1435mm (4ft 8.5in)

in Munich with MAN power unit and Voith transmission, is the direct ancestor of modern German diesel-hydraulic locomotives. The brief was for a locomotive equally capable of

medium-weight freight duties on secondary routes, and of hauling local passenger trains on main lines. The eight-cylinder MAN engine developed 1030kW (1400hp), with transmission

through jackshaft and coupling rods to the three driving axles. The 1400mm (55in) driving wheels took 52 tonnes (51 tons) of adhesive weight. World War II interrupted further development and the prototype, re-classed V 140, passed to the *Deutsche Bundesbahn* (DB) test department in 1953. From 1957, it was in a technical school in Karlsruhe, and from 1970 has been on display in the Deutsche Museum in Munich.

CLASS 8F 2-8-0 LONDON, MIDLAND & SCOTTISH RAILWAY (LMS)

The 'scrap and build' motto was LMS policy in order to achieve a modern standardized locomotive stock, and this was the company's standard main-line heavy freight locomotive, of similar design style to the 'Class 5' of the previous year. Like the mixed-traffic engines, it proved a reliable and efficient type, handling main-line freight. The first batch was classified 7F on the company's power scale, but later ones were uprated to 8F.

Early in World War II, the 8F was selected as the standard engine for military use at home and abroad, until the design of 'Austerity' 2-8-0 and 2-10-0 types. These were fitted with Westinghouse brake pumps to the right of the smokebox, to work air-braked stock. By 1945, over 700 had been built, and virtually every locomotive works in the country had contributed some. Many remained in the Middle East after the war, and some were still working in Turkey in the mid-1980s, 20 years after the last of the class had been withdrawn in Britain.

BOILER PRESSURE: 15.75kg/cm² (225psi)
CYLINDERS: 470x711mm (18.5x28in)
DRIVING WHEELS: 1435mm (56.5in)
GRATE AREA: 2.6m² (28.7sq ft)
HEATING SURFACE: 136m² (1463sq ft)
SUPERHEATER: 21.8m² (235.25sq ft)
TRACTIVE EFFORT: 14,965kg (33,000lb)
TOTAL WEIGHT: 72.1t (159,040lb)

Preserved LMS No. 8233 leaves Highley with a freight train for Bewdley, in an enthusiasts' run on the Severn Valley Railway on 24 September 1989.

CLASS A4 4-6-2 LONDON & NORTH EASTERN RAILWAY (LNER)

GREAT BRITAIN 1935

Unmistakable with its wedge front, the A4 is one of the most celebrated of all locomotive classes.

It was designed for a new train, to be called the *Silver Jubilee* in honour of George V's 25 years on the throne. Only six months elapsed between approval of the project and the delivery of the first A4, No. 2509 *Silver Link*, on 5 September 1935. The LNER's locomotive chief, H.N. Gresley, enlisted the aid of Ettore Bugatti to streamline the A4s on a scientific basis, with a significant claimed reduction in air resistance. The angle-fronted cab also gave better vision to the driver. But undoubtedly the most significant streamlining was inside, where the casing concealed a 17.5kg/cm² (250psi) taper boiler with very carefully designed steam passages feeding three simple-expansion cylinders slightly smaller than those of the LNER's A3 'Pacifics'. Here the LNER designers put into effect what

they had learned from their work with André Chapelon in connection with the P2 2-8-2s of 1934.

The new train, with streamlined articulated coaches was a sensation in itself, and *Silver Link* broke the British speed record with two maxima of 181km/h (112.5mph) on the demonstration run, and exceeding 160.9km/h (100mph) for 40km (25 miles) at a stretch. Between 1936 and 1938, a further 31 A4s were built at the LNER's Doncaster plant, mainly for use on other extra-special services like the six-hour London–Edinburgh 'Coronation' train of 1937. This train, of 312 tonnes (307 tons) tare, had Britain's fastest-ever steam timing, requiring an average 116km/h (71.9mph) for the non-stop London–York section. In early 1938, a number of new A4s were fitted with Kylchap double chimneys. One of these was No. 4468 *Mallard*. On 4 July that year, this engine was authorized to

try for a maximum speed. In Gresley's mind, the *Mallard* would certainly break not only the British record, but the world steam record, held since May 1936 by the German State Railway (DRG) 4-6-4 No. 05.002 with 200.4km/h (124.5mph). With six 'Coronation' articulated coaches, and a dynamometer car, the train weight totalled 243.9 tonnes (240 tons). On the East Coast main line south of Grantham, the engine, at full regulator and initially 40 per cent, then 45 per cent cut-off in the cylinders, accelerated down the 1 in 200 gradient until a maximum sustained speed of 201.1km/h (125mph) was reached. The German record was – just – beaten. Since that day, debate has gone on. The Germans pointed out that their record was reached on level track, with no assistance from gravity. The suggestion that Mallard actually touched 202.7km/h (126mph) has in recent years been discounted, but computer-aided reviews of the dynamometer car records leave no doubt that the A4 attained the fastest fully

verified speed of any steam locomotive.

The class hauled express trains on the East Coast Main Line until the early 1960s. During the war years of 1939–45, they often took trains of more than three times the weight of the pre-war 'Coronation' express. From 1957, all the single-chimney A4s were fitted with double Kylchap chimneys, and even in the twilight years of steam power, the class was attaining speeds in excess of 160km/h (100mph). In 1961, the 2462kW (3300hp) 'Deltic' diesel-electrics began to relieve the A4s on East Coast main-line services, but for several years they worked lightweight Glasgow–Aberdeen expresses. Six A4s, including *Mallard*, are preserved.

BOILER PRESSURE: 17.5kg/cm² (250psi)
CYLINDERS: 470x660mm (18.5x26in)
DRIVING WHEELS: 2030mm (80in)
GRATE AREA: 3.8m² (41.3sq ft)
HEATING SURFACE: 239m² (2576sq ft)
SUPERHEATER: 70m² (751.6sq ft)
TRACTIVE EFFORT: 16,326kg (36,000lb)
TOTAL WEIGHT: 104.6t (230,720lb)

On 8 July 1980, preserved A4 No. 4498 *Sir Nigel Gresley* is turned at Carnforth depot before working the 'Cumbrian Coast Express' special excursion train to Whitehaven and Carlisle.

TURBOMOTIVE 4-6-2 LONDON, MIDLAND & SCOTTISH RAILWAY (LMS)

Swedish-designed Ljungstrøm non-condensing turbines, with the frames and boiler of a 'Princess Royal' 4-6-2, formed this experimental locomotive, built by the LMS at Crewe in collaboration with Metropolitan Vickers. The turbines were at the front, forward or main drive on the left, and backward on the right. Main drive delivered its maximum hp output at around 99km/h (62mph), appropriate for hauling heavy trains at moderately fast speeds. A double blast-pipe chimney was fitted from the start, and three different boilers were used up to 1939. Test results, both in tractive power on gradients and in coal and water consumption, were favourable, and if war had not intervened, more might have been done with turbine traction in some practical designs.

The engine was normally employed on the London–Liverpool expresses, and up to 1939 its annual distance in service was just over 87,200km (54,200 miles), compared with about 128,740km (80,000 miles) for its non-turbine 'Princess Royal' sisters. Delays in spare-part production, inevitable with a single-model engine, were partly responsible. In 1951, it was rebuilt as a conventional reciprocating locomotive, but in that same year was destroyed in a disastrous crash at Harrow, in north London.

BOILER PRESSURE: 17.5kg/cm² (250psi)
CYLINDERS: None
DRIVING WHEELS: 1981mm (78in)
GRATE AREA: 4.2m² (45sq ft)
HEATING SURFACE: 215m² (2314sq ft)
SUPERHEATER: 61m² (653sq ft)
TRACTIVE EFFORT: 18,150kg (40,000lb)
TOTAL WEIGHT: 166.5t (367,000lb)

The 'turbomotive' climbs from Euston Station, London, towards Camden Town with a Liverpool express in the late 1930s, a regular turn that it shared with conventional LMS 'Pacifics'.

LMS DIESEL C (0-6-0) LONDON MIDLAND AND SCOTTISH RAILWAY

For a successor-type to its large range of 0-6-0 steam shunting tanks, the LMS sought a standardized diesel-electric shunting engine, also of 0-6-0, or 'C' formation. From 1932, nine prototypes were tried before the first production units began to appear in 1935, LMS 7059–7068, built by Armstrong Whitworth using a Armstrong-Sulzer 6LTD22 engine and Crompton Parkinson

electrical transmission equipment. These locomotives looked unusual due to the positioning of the traction motor between the centre and rear coupled wheels, with an unequal wheelbase as a result.

The second batch of nine, Nos. 7069–7078, featured two axle-hung traction motors. Hawthorn Leslie of Newcastle-upon-Tyne supplied the axles, frame, superstructure and wheels of these

outside-frame locomotives, with English Electric supplying the engines, control gear, transmission system and wiring. This design was based upon a EE prototype 0-6-0 diesel-electric shunter built in 1934, which had been loaned to the LMS, and which became very much the precursor of the standard British diesel shunters. It was purchased by the LMS in 1936, being numbered 7079.

While some alterations were made to make 7079 look more like the production locomotives, including the fitting of larger side fuel tanks, it weighed some 4.06 tonnes (4 tons) less than the others. Originally rated at 223.8kW (300hp), its engine was uprated to 261.1kW (350hp).

In comparison with the Armstrong Whitworth locomotives, the EE shunters showed a weakness in their transmission system, where the higher maximum speed ruled out the inclusion of double reduction gearing. A further problem lay with the traction motor ventilation, whose armature-mounted fans were ineffective in the low speed and big-current conditions that prevailed in hump shunting yards.

In 1940, No. 7074 was re-geared to double reduction gearing with forced ventilation and a maximum speed of 32.18km/h (20mph). The other members of the class were not modified.

The 19 diesel shunters were originally allocated to Crewe South, Willesden in London, and Carlisle Kingmoor. In LMS

ownership, they carried a plain black livery with red buffer beams. Cab doors were mainly of wooden construction. The only survivors into British Railways ownership in 1948 were 7074 (renumbered 12000) and 7076 (12001), and the prototype 7079 (renumbered 12002 by BR). These three continued to be based at Crewe

South depot until withdrawal and cutting up between 1956 and1962.

Eight class members were taken over by the War Department and sent to France in 1940. Abandoned in the Dunkirk evacuation, some were destroyed, but Nos. 7069 and 7075 were used by the Germans. No. 7069 was later salvaged and finally repatriated to the Swanage Railway, Dorset, in December 1987. It is currently based at the Gloucestershire–Warwickshire Railway.

Type: shunting locomotive
Power: English Electric 6K, self-ventilating four-pole traction motors, 261.1kW (350hp)
Tractive effort: 133.44kN (30,000 lb)
Max. operating speed: 48.27km/h (30mph)
Weight: 5t (114,660lb)
Overall length: 8.84m (29ft)
Gauge: 1435mm (4ft 8.5in)

First of the next generation, LMS diesel shunter No. 7120 was built in 1944 and showed the body design that would be continued in British Railways' Class 08.

CLASS 49 'DOVREGUBBEN' 2-8-4 NORWEGIAN STATE RAILWAYS (NSB)   NORWAY 1935

The first European 2-8-4, or 'Berkshire' type, was built for the NSB, to work through the Dovrefjell mountains between Oslo and Trondheim. The first three, built by Thunes Mekaniske Vaerksted of Oslo, were classed 49a, and a fourth with detail differences, including a Dabeg feed water heater, was 49b. The first was named *Dovregubben*, 'Dovre Giant'. They were four-cylinder compounds, with the high-pressure cylinders inside. Walschaerts valve gear, positioned outside, served both cylinders on each side. Double blast pipes and chimneys, and thermic syphons in the fireboxes, were fitted. The maximum axle loading was no more than 15.5 tonnes (15.25 tons). Despite the large grate, firing was done manually. The tenders were of Vanderbilt type, frameless, and mounted on outside-framed double bogies, with a covered coal bunker set on top of the water tank. A booster was fitted to

No. 465, but later removed. From the first, the class was put into intensive use and operated very satisfactorily. High speed was not a requirement and the maximum running speed was 100km/h (62mph), but they climbed the Dovre grades with heavy trains at a maintained 60km/h (37mph).

During the German occupation of Norway in 1940 four more were delivered, two from

Krupp in Essen and two from Thune, classed 49c. These had single chimneys and smaller-diameter cylinders, and German-type smoke deflectors attached to the smoke-box sides. They worked on until the mid-1950s, when Class Di3 diesel-electrics replaced them in service, and six were scrapped in 1958. One of the Krupp-built engines is preserved, though the number and name-plates of the very first, No. 463,

have been transferred to it. Specifications refer to the original 49a models.

Boiler pressure: 17kg/cm² (240psi)
Cylinders: hp 440x650mm (17.5x25.5in); lp 650x700mm (25.5x27.5in)
Driving wheels: 1530mm (60in)
Grate area: 5m² (55.5sq ft)
Heating surface: 255m² (2742sq ft)
Superheater: 101m² (1092sq ft)
Tractive effort: N/A
Total weight: 151.5t (334,000lb)

The original form of the 'Dovregubben', with double chimney. This is the booster-fitted engine, with a steam-pipe to the power unit on the trailing bogie.

'ANDES' CLASS 2-8-0 CENTRAL RAILWAY (FCC)

The ascent of the mountain line between Lima and Huancayo, from virtually sea level to a maximum height of 4783m (15,693ft), was one of the hardest tasks presented to a steam locomotive relying only on wheel-to-rail adhesion, with a ferocious maximum grade of 1 in 22 (4.5 per cent). Tight curves and ice-covered rails added to the difficulties. The FCC and its neighbours used mostly American engines, apart from a couple of Garratts, but this 'Consolidation' type, though primarily American in design, was built by Beyer Peacock in England. There were

29 locomotives of this class, built in eight batches between 1935 and 1951. They were oil-fired two-cylinder simples, solidly built on bar frames and with short boilers to avoid exposing the crown sheet when the line was steeply inclined. The fireboxes were of Belpaire type, and Walschaerts valve gear was fitted. Braking was of prime importance and a double set of air brakes was fitted, so that pressure was maintained at all times. To help in the vital business of maintaining traction, sand from the boiler-mounted container was also air-blasted to the coupled wheels. In all respects, the

construction was extremely sturdy, to permit hard usage in extreme conditions. In one respect, the high altitude was an advantage since steam locomotives, unlike those powered by internal-combustion engines, perform more efficiently as the atmospheric pressure drops. Apart from the FCC, five of the 'Andes' type were also used on the Cerro de Pasco Railway, which meets the FCC at Oroya; and the Southern of Peru, whose 20 locomotives had driving wheels of slightly greater diameter.

The Andes class were mixed-traffic engines, hauling passenger trains and also the mineral freights

for which the line had been built. Although ore trains were largely downhill, large amounts of oil and other industrial supplies had to be hauled up into the mountains.

No. 206 has been preserved and is still capable of being steamed.

BOILER PRESSURE: 14kg/cm² (200psi)
CYLINDERS: 508x711mm (20x28in)
DRIVING WHEELS: 1321mm (52in)
GRATE AREA: 2.6m² (28sq ft)
HEATING SURFACE: 160m² (1717sq ft)
SUPERHEATER: 32m² (341sq ft)
TRACTIVE EFFORT: 16,600kg (35,600lb)
TOTAL WEIGHT: 113t (250,000lb)

CLASS 16E 4-6-2 SOUTH AFRICAN RAILWAYS (SAR)

Generally on the SAR, locomotives were either freight or mixed-traffic haulers, and the six engines of this class were its only exclusively passenger locomotives. Designed by A.G. Watson of the SAR, and built for the 1065mm (3ft 6in) gauge by Henschel of Kassel, they were delivered in parts and assembled at the Salt River works, outside Cape Town. Two-cylinder simples, they had rotary cam gear operating poppet valves; though admittedly a very small class, it

A 16E locomotive heads the royal train during the visit of King George VI and Queen Elizabeth to South Africa in 1947.

was one of the very few in which all the locomotives were so equipped. Although the gear seemes to have worked well on the 'Pacifics', it was not taken into wider use on SAR locomotives. Their 1830mm (6ft) driving wheels required the boiler to be mounted quite high, compressing the chimney and other fittings but enhancing the speedy and powerful look. In performance,

they did turn out to be fast runners, as far as the track and operating rules would allow: the SAR had no competition and did not encourage waste or superfluous fuel consumption. On a test run in 1935, No. 854 reached 112.6km/h (70mph) but the class is said to have often exceeded this speed in service on the Kimberley-Bloemfontein *Orange Express*. Two firemen were needed

to keep the big grate fed. All 16Es had been withdrawn from service by the end of the 1970s, but one of the class has been preserved.

BOILER PRESSURE: 14.7kg/cm² (210psi)
CYLINDERS: 609x710.6mm (24x28in)
DRIVING WHEELS: 1827mm (72in)
GRATE AREA: 5.8m² (63sq ft)
HEATING SURFACE: 249m² (2682sq ft)
SUPERHEATER: 55m² (592sq ft)
TRACTIVE EFFORT: 16000kg (35,280lb)
TOTAL WEIGHT: 169.8t (374,416lb)

RAE 2/4 RAILCAR 'ROTE PFEIL' SWISS FEDERAL RAILWAYS (SBB)   SWITZERLAND 1935

When new, these were the fastest machines running on the SBB, and were awarded the name Rote Pfeil ('Red Arrow'). They were also the first on that system to provide the driver with a chair rather than have him standing at a control pedestal.

Looking more like a diesel than an electric, with a bulbous bonnet protruding before the driving cab at each end, each was a single-unit bogie railcar, with capacity for 60 passengers in single-class accommodation. Six were built, and two others were rebuilds of class RCm 2/4 cars. They were lightweight units, with tubular steel seat frames and wide-view windows, built to compete with car or coach traffic. Other up-to-date features included automatic

doors. Their popularity led to the building of an extended fast railcar, the Rce 2/4, in 1936. After World War II, the 'Red Arrows' were mostly used for hire and for special services. One is preserved today in the Lucerne *Verkehrshaus* museum.

TYPE: single railcar
POWER: two 200kW (268hp) motors driving the outer axles, supplied with current at 15kV, 16.7Hz, via overhead catenary
TRACTIVE EFFORT: 25kN (5621lbf)
MAX. OPERATING SPEED: 125km/h (78mph)
TOTAL WEIGHT: not known
MAX. AXLE LOAD: not known
OVERALL LENGTH: not known
BUILDER: not known

Preserved 'Rote Pfeil' unit No. 1001 at Biel, on a special run on 18 July 1997. The low body-height needed a tall pantograph.

CLASS A 4-4-2 CHICAGO, MILWAUKEE, ST PAUL & PACIFIC RAILROAD (CMSTP&PRR)   USA 1935

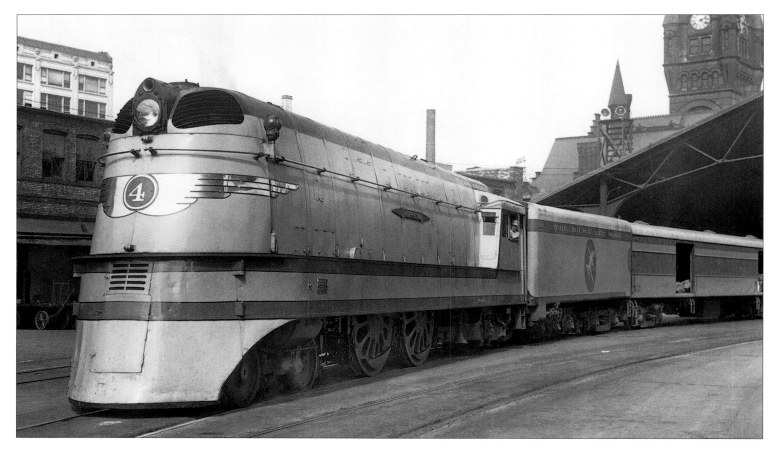

The fastest, as well as biggest and heaviest 'Atlantics' ever built, these were the 'Hiawathas'. Between Chicago and Minneapolis–St Paul, travellers had a choice of three routes, all competing fiercely to provide the highest standards of speed and service. With no serious grades to climb, high speeds were possible, and Alco built four specialized oil-burning

locomotives with streamlined casings to pull the Hiawatha flyer. They had cast-steel frames with integral cylinders. 'Goodfellow tips', as developed on the Pennsylvania Railroad's works, were fitted in the blast pipe. The trains ran on a timing of 6hrs, 30 mins for the 663km (412-mile) route, giving an average running speed of 106km/h (66mph). The

No. 4 of the Class A 'Atlantics', *Chippewa*, awaits departure from Milwaukee as a 'Hiawatha' express is loaded. The lead car is a baggage van.

journey had to incorporate six stops, at some of which water had to be taken on, and no less than 58 service slacks, whose maximum permitted speed ranged from 48.3km/h to 145km/h

(30–90mph). On a test outing, one of the Atlantics made one of the fastest-ever steam runs, 227km (141 miles) from Milwaukee to New Lisbon in 113 minutes. The Hiawatha timing was later cut to

6hrs, 15mins, despite five intermediate stops. Sustained speeds in excess of 160km/h (100mph) were necessary to maintain time, and it is likely that the trains frequently attained a speed of 193km/h (120mph) or more. Such speeds, day after day, were possible only because of the quality of the track as well as of the engines and rolling stock. Most of the rails on the route were of 58.2kg (131lb) weight to the yard (0.915m), laid on gravel ballast 610mm (2ft) deep under the sleepers, and with the rails canted on the curves.

Engines and trains were painted in a striking livery of yellow, orange, maroon and brown. It was not a lightweight train: with nine cars it weighed 419.1 tonnes (412.5 tons), and the locomotives' own weight was later increased by larger tenders. Despite the fierce competition from the Burlington (with its new *Zephyr*), and Chicago North Western routes, the Hiawathas were immensely popular – three trains a day each way, with an average of 380 passengers per train. The result was that demand began to outreach supply, and the four

great Atlantics needed to be supplemented. After three exhilarating years, new streamlined F7 4-6-4s, able to maintain the schedule with a 12-car train, took over the route. These 'Hudsons' were also more versatile than the Atlantics, able to haul the Hiawatha one way, and return with a heavy sleeping car train, at more conventional speed, in the other direction.

From 1940, the Atlantics were diverted to operate a new 'Mid-West Hiawatha' operating between Chicago, Omaha and Sioux Falls. By 1948, diesel locomotives had taken

over these services and the 4-4-2s, not adaptable to other kinds of use, were retired by 1951. By then, their prestige and superb performance were forgotten, and none of the superb quartet was preserved.

BOILER PRESSURE: 21kg/cm² (300psi)
CYLINDERS: 483x711mm (19x28in)
DRIVING WHEELS: 2134mm (84in)
GRATE AREA: 6.4m² (69sq ft)
HEATING SURFACE: 301.5m² (3245sq ft)
SUPERHEATER: 96m² (1029sq ft)
TRACTIVE EFFORT: 13,900kg (30,600lb)
TOTAL WEIGHT: 265.18t (537,000lb)

CLASS J3 4-8-4 CHESAPEAKE & OHIO RAILROAD (C&O) USA 1935

The C&O called its 4-8-4 types 'Greenbriers' rather than 'Northerns', but in other respects they were express locomotives of typical design, though at the upper end of the dimension scale. In terms of height, length, weight and boiler diameter, its J3 class was the biggest two-cylinder locomotive ever to serve on the C&O, apart from some very large 2-10-4s of 1930. Fifteen-strong, the class was built by Lima between 1935 and 1948; the later ones, classed as J3a, had roller bearings and other improvements but the same dimensions. The last five were ordered in 1947 and all were delivered by 1948 – a proclamation of the C&O's faith in coal and steam at a time when other roads were converting to diesel electrics on a wholesale

basis, especially for the kind of long-haul passenger service for which the 'Greenbriers' were intended.

Among the features provided on the final batch were an electro-pneumatically controlled braking system intended for use with new passenger cars, but these were never produced in quantity and the J3a locomotives hauled the old-style heavyweight coaches. Apart from ancillary equipment, one significant dimensional change was made in the 1947–48 engines, with the extension of the combustion chamber in front of the firebox by 30.5cm (12in) with corresponding shortening of the boiler tubes, which was generally agreed to improve steam production. Before long, all the J3s were turned over to freight

service. For the railroads that derived large revenues from coal haulage, the transfer from coal-burning to diesel locomotives was something of an embarrassment, and lines like the C&O, the Virginia Railroad, and the Norfolk & Western were among the last to convert. In 1947, the Chairman of the C&O was reported as saying, 'I do not think it is in the public interest to operate diesels at all', but in 1952 a rapid phasing-out of C&O steam began. Even in 1957, the N&W had 408 steam locomotives in service, by which time many other Class One railroads had none at all.

The last of the J3s to be built, No. 614, which had been preserved for special excursion work, gained some notoriety when it was hastily overhauled and used for the ill-judged ACE (American Coal Enterprises) display runs in the winter of 1984–85. Set up at a time when the price of oil had risen to

very high levels, ACE was intended to promote the use of coal for a 'second generation' of efficient and pollution-free steam locomotives. Nothing about the J3a made it a 'clean coal' locomotive; it was essentially a design that went back to the 1930s, and this was abundantly obvious on its demonstration runs. The ACE scheme, though initially backed by the Chessie System and US coal interests, expired in 1985. No. 614 survives, however, and is still used as a special excursion locomotive.

BOILER PRESSURE: 17.2kg/cm² (245psi)
CYLINDERS: 699x762mm (27.5x30in)
DRIVING WHEELS: 1829mm (72in)
GRATE AREA: 9.3m² (100sq ft)
HEATING SURFACE: 514m² (5534sq ft)
SUPERHEATER: 218m² (2347sq ft)
TRACTIVE EFFORT: 33,179kg (67,187lb)
TOTAL WEIGHT: 216t (476,280lb)
(engine only)

Resplendent in C&O paintwork, the last survivor of the Chesapeake & Ohio 'Greenbriers' and one of Lima's last steam locomotives for a US railroad, No. 614 stands at Port Jervis, NY.

CHAPTER FOUR

THE WAR YEARS
1936–1949

From early days, it was appreciated that the most effective way to utilize diesel power in locomotives was through electric motors that drove the wheels or axles. The engine drove a generator, from which electric power was fed to the motors. Such a machine was expensive to build, much more so than a steam locomotive. But there were several factors in favour of the diesel-electric: its higher thermal efficiency saved on fuel costs, and diesel fuel was relatively cheap; unlike the pure electric locomotive, it needed no external supply; it was seen as 'clean' compared to a steam locomotive; it could be operated from either end and offered much better working conditions to the driver. As the technical features were developed and improved, it also became possible to operate two or more locomotives in 'multiple-unit' format from a single control panel; now one person could be employed where four or more were needed before. Lightweight, high-speed express trains in several countries, including the German 'Fliegende Hamburger' and the United States's 'Burlington Zephyr', showed a new and appealing face of railway transport to travellers. In 1935, General Motors set up its Electro-Motive Division (EMD) plant at La Grange, Illinois, applying production techniques learned on the automobile assembly lines to the construction of a standardized range of locomotives, backed up by a powerful sales operation. The advent of the World War II slowed but did not stop the spread of dieselization in the United States, and it resumed with new vigour in 1945.

A class WP 'Pacific' of India's Northern Railway displays its 'bullet' front. The decorative ironwork in front of chimney is an individual feature, applied to the locomotive at its home depot.

CLASS F-2A 4-4-4 CANADIAN PACIFIC RAILWAY (CPR)

Like the US 'Hiawathas', the F-2A was a special design to haul high-speed inter-city expresses. Many North American railways, with road transport growing ever more popular in the 1930s, were developing 'super-trains' to protect their traffic. The CPR was well to the fore in this, and introduced four fast inter-city services in 1936 on its more vulnerable routes. These were Toronto–Detroit, Edmonton–Calgary, and two services between Montreal and Quebec. The four-car

trains weighed about 203 tonnes (200 tons), lightweight in North American terms, and a 'lightweight' locomotive was designed to help run them. These were referred to in company publicity as the 'Jubilees', in celebration of 50 years of CPR transcontinental service, but the name did not catch on with the public. A 4-4-4 was an unusual wheel formation, for a tender engine at least, though the Philadelphia & Reading in the United States had briefly had some

in 1915. They were built at Montreal Locomotive Works, and had the kind of features normally associated with much larger engines. The two simple-expansion cylinders drove the leading coupled axle. The firebox, larger than that of most European large 'Pacifics', was fed by a mechanical stoker. All axles ran on roller bearings.

The F-2A probably brought more weight and power to its task than was really needed, and a second batch, classed F-1A, were slightly

smaller, and the cylinders drove on the rear coupled axle. Twenty-eight of those were built in 1938. By 1958, both classes had been scrapped, but one of F-1A is preserved.

BOILER PRESSURE: 21kg/cm² (300psi)
CYLINDERS: 438x711mm (17.25x28)
DRIVING WHEELS: 2032mm (80in)
GRATE AREA: 5.2m² (55.6sq ft)
HEATING SURFACE: 263m² (2833sq ft)
SUPERHEATER: 102m² (1100sq ft)
TRACTIVE EFFORT: 12,000kg (26,500lb)
TOTAL WEIGHT: 209t (461,000lb)

Preserved Class F-1A No. 2928 at the Canadian Railway Museum, Delson, Quebec. Though it is sometimes referred to as a streamlined locomotive, 'air-smoothed' might be a better description.

CLASS ET6 0-8-0 CHINESE GOVERNMENT RAILWAYS

Like most Chinese locomotives of this period, this class was an American design, though the first four were built by Armstrong Whitworth of Newcastle, England, and further engines were supplied by the North British Locomotive Company of Glasgow in 1949–50. Designed for shunting and

banking, the ET6 was a good deal lighter than an American 0-8-0, with a maximum axle load of 13.7 tonnes (13.5 tons) enabling it to run on light track and trestles. The first batch had sloping tenders; the later ones had back-sloping tanks but built-up coal bunkers set in from the

BOILER PRESSURE: 15.5kg/cm² (221psi)
CYLINDERS: 420x600mm (16.5x23.6in)
DRIVING WHEELS: 1200mm (47in)
GRATE AREA: 3m² (32.3sq ft)
HEATING SURFACE: 104m² (1119.7sq ft)

SUPERHEATER: 40.8m² (439.3sq ft)
TRACTIVE EFFORT: 11,646kg (25,680lb)
TOTAL WEIGHT: 51.8t (114,219lb)
(engine only)

tender sides. All were also equipped with a bell set in front of

the chimney, not a standard fitting on Chinese locomotives.

CLASS V2 2-6-2 LONDON & NORTH EASTERN RAILWAY (LNER)

Intended as a mixed-traffic type, this Doncaster-built 'Prairie' did its best work on fast freight trains. Four were built for testing in 1936, and eventually it became a class of 188. Three-cylindered, with simple expansion, it closely

resembled the Gresley A3 'Pacifics', with the same conjugated valve gear and the same extensions behind the chimney to accommodate the superheater header. But its cylinders, smokebox saddle, steam and exhaust

passages were all a single casting, with the outside steam pipes. The 'banjo dome' accommodated a steam collector rather than a regulator. A useful feature was the angled cab front, taken from the A4 design, and avoiding night-time

reflections from inside the cab. Engines with a front truck could sometimes be rough riders, unless fitted with the Helmholtz-type linking of front truck and leading coupled wheels. This, though common elsewhere, was rarely used in Britain, but the V2s had a good reputation for smooth running. The first of the class had a name, *Green Arrow*, given in connection with a new fast freight service. From the first, the V2s did regular passenger turns, notably on the Kings Cross to Doncaster section of the Leeds and Harrogate 'Yorkshire Pullman', typically loading to around 406 tonnes (400 tons) and timed to average 96.5kph (60mph) over the 251km (156 miles).

BOILER PRESSURE: 15.5kg/cm² (220psi)
CYLINDERS: 470x660mm (18.5x26in)
DRIVING WHEELS: 1880mm (74in)
GRATE AREA: 3.8m² (41.2sq ft)
HEATING SURFACE: 226m² (2431sq ft)
SUPERHEATER: 63m² (680sq ft)
TRACTIVE EFFORT: 13,514kg (29,800lb)
TOTAL WEIGHT: 94.5t (208,544lb)

The class leader, preserved No. 4771 *Green Arrow* heads a rail-tour special on the Settle & Carlisle line in northern England.

CLASS 42.01 2-8-2 TRANS-IRANIAN RAILWAY

Built by Nohab of Sweden (the former Nydquist & Holm), this class of 11 engines was designed to operate long-distance passenger trains over this long cross-country route through desert and mountain, from the Persian Gulf to the Caspian Sea, via Tehran. The Class 42.01 were three-cylinder

BOILER PRESSURE: 12.5kg/cm² (178psi)
CYLINDERS: 497.5x660mm (19.6x26in)
DRIVING WHEELS: 1350mm (53.2in)
GRATE AREA: 4.2m² (45sq ft)

HEATING SURFACE: 216m² (2325sq ft) (including superheater)
SUPERHEATER: not known
TRACTIVE EFFORT: 12,882kg (28,406)

TOTAL WEIGHT: 87.3t (192,640lb) (engine only)

simple-expansion engines. During World War II, the line was of immense strategic importance, and the demands of intense wartime traffic were probably responsible for the early demise of a class that needed too-careful maintenance for emergency conditions.

CLASS D51 2-8-2 JAPANESE RAILWAYS (JR)

A robust and workmanlike engine, not of refined appearance but a solid performer, this was one of Japan's most numerous locomotive classes. Between 1936 and 1945, 1115 were built. Twelve plants were involved, including Kawasaki Sharyo, Kisha Seizo Kaisha, Nippon

BOILER PRESSURE: 14kg/cm² (213psi)
CYLINDERS: 550x660mm (21.6x26in)
DRIVING WHEELS: 1400mm (55in)
GRATE AREA: 3.3m² (35.5sq ft)
HEATING SURFACE: m²)
SUPERHEATER: m²)
TRACTIVE EFFORT: 18,110kg (39,930lb)
TOTAL WEIGHT: 76.8t (169,344lb)

A preserved D51 is turned at the Kyoto roundhouse in 1997, its appearance a contrast to the last years of service, when most were in a neglected state.

Sharyo Seisakusho, and Hitachi Seisakusho, as well as JR workshops. Lighter and shorter but with greater tractive power than its immediate predecessor the D50, it had a long boiler-top housing typical of Japanese locomotives, and a flowerpot chimney. In North American style, a feedwater heater cylinder was fixed crosswise in front of the chimney, and various other pumps for brakes and lubrication were fixed on the sides. Two outside simple-expansion cylinders were operated by piston valves actuated by Walschaerts gear. This was the first Japanese locomotive to have Canadian-developed Boxpok-type wheels. After the first 96 had been built, some modifications were made, making the later ones 0.9 tonnes (0.88 tons) heavier. A large number were built during World War II, and engines built in 1943–46, when steel was in short supply due to the war, had wooden smoke deflectors and running plates, and were often weighed down with concrete to compensate for the weight loss. All of these were rebuilt after 1945. Also after 1945, a number were fitted with smoke collection devices, and others were adapted to burn oil as well as coal. Although belonging to the 'let it all hang out' school of design, the D51, aptly a 'Mikado' type, was the classic Japanese goods locomotive.

CLASS 142 2-8-4 ROMANIAN RAILWAYS (CFR) ROMANIA 1936

Around this time, bigger Eastern European locomotives often acquired a 'skyline' casing that concealed the array of domes and devices on the boiler tops. This feature, together with long smoke deflectors set high on the smoke-box sides, is distinctive on the Class 142. The general design was originally Austrian, but whereas the ÖBB built only 13, as Class 214, the CFR built 79 at the two workshops of Malaxa and Resita between 1936 and 1940. Romania's largest passenger engines, with two simple-expansion cylinders, they worked most principal passenger trains until the mid-1960s.

The rear four-wheel truck had inside bearings. Most of the class had Lentz overhead cam poppet valves to work the cylinders, though some were for a time fitted with Caprotti gear. No mechanical stoker was fitted, but, as with most other Romanian large locomotive types, both tank and tender, the 142 class was equipped to burn a coal-oil mixture when working hard. Through this system, invented by Romanian engineer H. Cosmovici, heavy oil could be sprayed into the firebox above the firebed, where it ignited to provide an immediate supplementary source of heat. It was also used extensively in Bulgaria, and was tried out on some large German engines. The oil tanks were fitted in the tender, or located above the side water tanks in the tank locomotives.

BOILER PRESSURE: 15kg/cm² (213.75psi)
CYLINDERS: 650x720mm (25.6x28.4in)
DRIVING WHEELS: 1940mm (76.5in)
GRATE AREA: 4.72m² (50.8sq ft)
HEATING SURFACE: 262m² (2820sq ft)
SUPERHEATER: 77.8m² (837.6sq ft)
TRACTIVE EFFORT: 20,040kg (44,190lb)
TOTAL WEIGHT: 123.5t (272,317lb) (engine only)

The long connecting rod and valve-gear links of the Class 142 are clearly seen in this side-view, with the driver in classic pose. No. 044 of the class is preserved.

'UNION' CLASS 0-10-2 UNION RAILROAD (URR) USA 1936

The Union Railroad was short but strategically placed, providing links between six trunk-line railroads in the Pittsburgh industrial complex. It had less than 72.4km (45 miles) of track, but usage was extremely intensive. This class, though only three in number, is interesting partly because its specifications can be readily compared to European and other 10-coupled types. It was commissioned from Baldwin, as the first 0-10-2. Since the locomotive would only ever operate at low speeds, a leading truck was dispensed with, though the end product, like many American switchers, looked oddly like an engine that had managed to mislay its front carrying wheels. To assist moving heavy trains up the grades, a booster was fitted to the leading tender truck, whose wheels were coupled. It added a tractive force of 7770kg (17,150lb) to the locomotive's effort. The tender was a relatively small one by US standards, holding 14.2 tonnes (14 tons) of coal and 10,000gals (12,000 US gals) of water, but the 'Union' class locomotives were never very far away from a coaling or watering point.

Short lines like the Union Railroad and many others tended to have a high proportion of switchers in their locomotive stock, because of the nature of their traffic and the short transits normally involved. The 0-10-2s were later sold to the Duluth Missabe & Iron Range RR, which needed big switchers to move lines of heavy ore cars in its Lake Superior Dockside yards, and they worked there until 1958.

BOILER PRESSURE: 18.25kg/cm² (260lb)
CYLINDERS: 711x812mm (28x32in)
DRIVING WHEELS: 1548mm (61in)
GRATE AREA: 7.9m2 (85sq ft)

HEATING SURFACE: 445.9 m2 (4800sq ft)
SUPERHEATER: 129.1 m2 (1390sq ft)
TRACTIVE EFFORT: 41,220kg (90,900lb)
TOTAL WEIGHT: 292.3t (644,510lb)

'CHALLENGER' CLASS 4-6-6-4 UNION PACIFIC RAILROAD (UP)

'Challenger' No. 3985, built by Alco in 1943, in action at Green River, Wyoming, on 29 June 1982.

Based on the Mallet principle, these locomotives were two-in-one articulated engines, with a single huge boiler supplying steam to two power units, but with simple-expansion cylinders only. Union Pacific and Northern Pacific (NP) both put locomotives of this configuration on the road in 1936. Arthur H. Fetter, the UP's General Mechanical Engineer, had a long-standing working relationship with Alco, and the design of the 4-6-6-4 was evolved between the railroad and the manufacturer. UP was already operating the 9000-class 4-12-2 (see 1926) and it was clear that little more could be achieved with a rigid frame. Articulation and four cylinders were decided on, with a larger-diameter boiler and increased pressure. The articulated form also enabled the provision of a larger firebox, its weight supported by the four-wheel rear

truck. Walschaerts valve gear actuated the piston valves, and the cylinders drove the third pair of coupled wheels in each set. On both the UP and NP engines, the front cylinders were positioned further ahead of the coupled wheels than the rear ones, with an extra-long piston rod taking up the space. The UP named their class 'Challengers', and designated them as mixed-traffic engines, though most of their work was on fast freights. Until now, articulation had been associated with high power but low speed slogging, but the 'Challengers' could and did run at 130km/h (80mph). Their prime route was from Ogden to Wasatch and on to Green River, which for an unaided locomotive with a heavyweight train was certainly a challenging

one. Considered as passenger engines, they were the largest and most powerful ever to run. Forty were ordered from Alco in 1936, and a further 65, incorporating some modifications, were built between 1942 and 1945.

The type proved excellent for high-speed freight trains, and other lines quickly followed. Baldwin built 4-6-6-4s for the Denver & Rio Grande Western in 1938, and for the Western Maryland in 1939. But Alco were the prime builders of the type, producing it for the Carolina Clinchfield & Ohio (12), the Delaware & Hudson (40), and seven for the Western Pacific. All these were fast freight haulers: the UP's 'Challengers' were the only engines of this configuration to operate regular passenger

services, notably between Salt Lake City, Las Vegas and Los Angeles.

Some were converted to oil burning, but the great majority were coal burners, the huge grates fed by automatic stokers. They remained in service until 1958, by which time the UP's diesel programme had advanced far enough to deprive them of any suitable duties.

UP No. 3985 is preserved in working order: the biggest operational steam locomotive in the world.

BOILER PRESSURE: 17.9kg/cm² (255psi)
CYLINDERS: 533x813mm (21x32in)
DRIVING WHEELS: 1753mm (69in)
GRATE AREA: 10m² (108sq ft)
HEATING SURFACE: 431m² (4642sq ft)
SUPERHEATER: 162m² (1741sq ft)
TRACTIVE EFFORT: 44,100kg (97,400lb)
TOTAL WEIGHT: 486t (1,071,000lb)

ELECTRO MOTIVE E TYPES A1A-A1A BALTIMORE & OHIO RAILROAD (B&O)

Steam locomotive builders had been building the occasional diesel-engined locomotive since the 1920s at the request of customers. However, their history, their plant and tools conditioned them to think in terms of steam power, even though Baldwin had bought up a diesel-engine builder, the De La Vergne Engine Co., and Alco had acquired McIntosh & Seymour, also builders of internal combustion engines, and had its partnership with General Electric. Most railroad mechanical engineers thought in similar terms: their training and experience was also in steam. The Electro Motive Division (EMD) of General Motors, wholly dedicated to internal combustion, had to work hard to create a market for its products. But when that work was successfully done, it reaped the benefits.

At this time, EMD was anxious to move away from articulated streamlined unit trains, and to produce a 'platform' for the Winton 201A diesel engine that could operate 'real' trains. Two prototype units were built in 1935 under contract by General Electric's Erie works, and equipped with GE generators and carbodies. Each had two 12-cylinder V-type 201A engines, producing 671kW (900hp) apiece. The pair could be operated as a single unit of 2686kW (3600hp), comparable power to a 4-6-2 or 4-6-4 passenger locomotive. EMD publicity proclaimed that the new diesels could haul trains of 12 to 14 cars – i.e. up to 1016 tonnes (1000 tons) for 1000 miles (1609km) at current steam schedules, but at a running cost 40–60 per cent less than that of a steam locomotive.

The first buyer was Baltimore & Ohio (B&O), with a single unit; Santa Fe was also an early buyer, with a double unit. In 1936, Santa Fe inaugurated the weekly 'Super Chief' diesel-hauled service of Pullman cars between Chicago and Los Angeles, in the shortest-yet timing between these cities, of 39hrs, 45mins. The same engines did the entire run of 3584km (2227 miles). In 1937 with the E-1 type, first built for the B&O, Electro-Motive created a look that was to set the pattern for express diesel locomotives. It had a

practical aim: to give the driver a good look-out and a degree of collision protection. In some of the streamlined multiple-unit trains, the lower-set look-out led to drivers being virtually hypnotized by the pattern of converging rails and endless sleepers, and collision protection had been poor. The body was designed as structurally integral framework with a smooth external finish. B&O's first example is still preserved in shell-form at the B&O Museum. A cabless 'booster' unit was also available. But internal design was even more important. This engine was the spear-head of a massive sales drive, and it had to be right. Many problems had to be resolved in order to put an effective and reliable large diesel-electric on the road, and not all were fully dealt with at this time. The lightweight 201A engine was still suffering from teething troubles. By 1938, the concept was refined with the E6, the first volume-production road diesel to be produced, of 1470kW (2000hp). By now, EMD was doing its own building and producing its own ancillary

equipment, and the E6 had EMD generators and traction motors, while the engines were uprated to produce 735kW (1000hp) each. A set of three, working multiple-unit under one man's control, now gave 4410kW (6000hp).

Seaboard Air Line was first to acquire E6 locomotives, to run the Washington–Miami 'Orange Blossom Special', a winter-season tourist train using heavy Pullman cars, working triple with a 'B' booster unit between two 'A' cab units. Other lines soon began to show active interest, and the sales graph was rising steadily until wartime legislation put a temporary halt on the building of passenger diesels.

TYPE: A1A-A1A, passenger diesel-electric
POWER AND OUTPUT: A pair of Winton 12-cylinder 201-A diesels producing 1343kW (1800hp)
TRACTIVE EFFORT: 216kN (48,600lbs) starting TE
MAX. OPERATING SPEED: N/A
WEIGHT: 129t (285,000lbs)
OVERALL LENGTH: N/A
GAUGE: 1435mm (4ft 8.5in)

The preserved shell of an EA locomotive shows the prominent nose section, which was strengthened to provide crew protection in a collision.

CLASS H1C 4-6-4 'ROYAL HUDSON' CANADIAN PACIFIC RAILWAY (CPR)

Built at Montreal Locomotive Works to haul transcontinental trains, and to specifications set by CPR, these 'Hudsons' gained the 'Royal' appellation by pulling the royal train during the visit of King George VI and Queen Elizabeth to Canada in 1939. Class H1, building of which began in 1931, was intended as a replacement for the G3 'Pacifics', which were underpowered for heavy modern trains. The arrival of 20 Hudsons made it possible to reduce the number of locomotive changes on the CPR's long transcontinental haul from 14 to nine. All were mechanically stoked, and capable of running the longest section of the trans-Canada line, across the prairie from Fort William (Ont.) to Winnipeg (Man.), a distance of 1320km (820 miles). The first 20 were of conventional North American appearance, although the 30 1937 locomotives of Class H1c were not exactly streamlined but carefully styled to give a smooth and rounded look, with a big chimney, whose housing curved back into the boiler top.

On the standard North American model, they were two-cylinder simple expansion engines. Combustion chambers were incorporated, extending the firebox at the expense of some boiler length, and with arch tubes in the firebox. The boiler was round-topped, with no dome, but a safety-valve housing was set just in front of the firebox. From the 1937 batch on, the Hudsons were built with a one-piece cast-steel frame, and certain modern conveniences like power reversers were fitted. Between 1938 and 1945, a further 15 were built. Boosters were fitted to 20 of the class, driving the rear trailing axle, whose wheels were larger than the front pair, and these were stationed at points where the additional power enabled them to take trains up grades without a helper engine being needed. The last five, built to operate in British Columbia, were oil-fired; and others based in the prairie provinces were later converted to oil burning. The Royal Hudsons worked on express

Preserved CPR 4-6-4 No. 2816 at Portage, Wisconsin, USA, in the course of a special run.

duties into the mid-1950s, when the class began to be scrapped. By 1965, all had left the regular

scene, but five have been preserved, and two run heritage services from Vancouver.

BOILER PRESSURE: 19.3kg/cm² (275psi)	**HEATING SURFACE:** 352m² (3791sq ft)
CYLINDERS: 559x762mm (22x30in)	**SUPERHEATER:** 143m² (1542sq ft)
DRIVING WHEELS: 1905mm (75in)	**TRACTIVE EFFORT:** 20,548kg (45,300lb)
GRATE AREA: 7.5m² (81sq ft)	**TOTAL WEIGHT:** 299t (659,000lb)

CLASS HR1 4-6-2 STATE RAILWAYS (VR)

Despite using the Russian 1524mm (5ft) gauge, Finnish engines did not have the lofty height of Russian ones, and

BOILER PRESSURE: 15kg/cm² (214psi)	**GRATE AREA:** 3.5m² (37.7sq ft)	**TRACTIVE EFFORT:** 15220kg (33,562lb)
CYLINDERS: 590x650mm (23.25x25.6in)	**HEATING SURFACE:** 195.4m² (2103.8sq ft)	**TOTAL WEIGHT:** 93t (205,065lb)
DRIVING WHEELS: 1900mm (75in)	**SUPERHEATER:** 68m² (732.1sq ft)	(engine only)

Finland's only 'Pacific' type has a more European sense of scale. Twenty-one were built between 1937 and 1957, the work shared between the Tampella and Lokomo works in Tampere. It was a very successful, free-steaming engine and only detail modifications were made over two decades, with the final version having roller bearings, but essentially it was a two-cylinder simple design showing considerable German influence, as did most Finnish engines. Until 1963, they worked on passenger expresses in the south, then were displaced by diesels to run fast freight on central Finnish lines, which they did into the 1970s. Two are preserved.

Lokomo-built No. 1008, with a chimney-top spark arrestor as fitted to most of the class. They were known by the nickname _Ukko-Pekka_, after Finnish President Pehr Evind Svinhufvud.

CLASS 5400 2-DO-2 STATE RAILWAY (ÉTAT)

FRANCE 1937

The French railway companies built numerous 2-Do-2 electric types in the 1930s – 105 locomotives in all, of which this was the most successful. Comprising 22 locomotives, all were fitted with the Büchli drive developed by Brown Boveri in Switzerland. This system employed a driven gear wheel fixed to the frame. Inside the wheel, two levers bear gear segments that mesh with each other; at the other end are universal joints connected to tension bars. These bars in turn are linked via universal joints to pins fixed on the rail wheel. Each axle was driven individually, with the tension bars and universal joints allowing the wheels to move both horizontally and vertically without inhibiting the transmission of drive from the motor. Despite the apparent complication, this system had an excellent record for long life and low cost, and was used on numerous electric locomotive classes, especially in Switzerland. The Class 5400s developed 3694kW (4950hp) at 96.5km/h (60mph), and gave many years of heavy express duty. In the 1960s, they were still handling express work on the Le Mans–Paris route.

TYPE: Express passenger locomotive
POWER: 3780kW (5065hp) 1500V DC from overhead catenary
TRACTIVE EFFORT: 225.5kN (50,700lbf)
MAX. OP SPEED: 130km/h (81mph)
TOTAL WEIGHT: 130 tonnes (286,650lb)
MAX AXLE LOAD 18t (39,690lb)
OVERALL LENGTH: 17,780mm (58ft 4in)
BUILDER: Fives-Lille-Cail; electrical equipment Cie. Electro-Mécanique

The 2-Do-2 in France was pioneered by the Paris-Orleans Railway, followed by the État; from 1938, they were absorbed into the SNCF as Class 5400.

262 BD1 2-CO-2+2-CO-2 PARIS, LYONS & MEDITERRANEAN RAILWAY (PLM)

FRANCE 1937

This was still very much an experimental era as far as big diesel-electric locomotives were concerned. The PLM was looking for engines of comparable power to its most modern steam express engines, but able to run an annual 275,000km (171,000 miles), with better turn-round times and longer intervals between routine services. Two experimental locomotives of

TYPE: twin unit express diesel-electric locomotive
POWER: four 765kW (1025hp) MAN six-cylinder four-stroke diesel engines each driving a generator mounted on the main frame and supplying power to six traction motors via a Kleinow quill drive
TRACTIVE EFFORT: 314kN (70,500lb)
MAX. OPERATING SPEED: 130km/h (81mph)
TOTAL WEIGHT: 224t (493,700lb)
MAXIMUM AXLE LOAD: 18t (39,670lb)
OVERALL LENGTH: not known
GAUGE: not known

this 2-Co-2+2-Co-2 type were built in 1937–38: the BD1 with a MAN engine, and AD1 with Sulzer engine, both developing 3060kW (4100hp). These air-smoothed engines were not an articulated unit but were joined by a semi-permanent corridor link.

Mothballed during the years of World War II, they were returned to service in 1945 and ran until 1955, though no others were built.

SR 4COR ELECTRIC MULTIPLE UNITS SOUTHERN RAILWAY (SR)

GREAT BRITAIN 1937

Among the four British railway companies, only the SR opted for large-scale electrification, using its already proved third-rail system at 660V DC, and ultimately possessing 720 route miles (1158km) and 1796 track-miles (2890km) of third-rail track. A series of sub-stations along the way converted three-phase AC at 11kV and 25 cycles (50 cycles from 1948) to feed direct current to the third rail. Current was returned through the running rails. SR also opted for multiple-units, formed of motor coaches with trailer cars, which suited its rapid-interval timetable, rather than locomotive-hauled trains. For the 1937 electrification of the London Waterloo to

A 12-car formation, the maximum. The corridor connections between units did not improve appearance.

Portsmouth via Guildford line, the Southern ordered a fleet of four-car express EMUs with gangways throughout, including the cab ends, enabling walk-through multiple-unit trains of up to 12 carriages. A total of 87 were built, including some with buffets and restaurant

facilities, coded 4BUF and 4RES, which covered services from London Victoria to Littlehampton and Bognor Regis. They were liveried in Southern green, later in BR blue. After intensive working, their replacement by more modern EMU stock was completed in 1972.

TYPE: four-car electric multiple-unit express trains
POWER: 660V DC conductor rail collection, two power cars, each with two English Electric 168kW (225hp) axle-mounted DC traction motors, resistance control
TRACTIVE EFFORT: not known

MAX. OPERATING SPEED: 120km/h (75mph)
WEIGHT: 33 to 47t (72,350 to 104,160lb) per vehicle
MAX. AXLE LOAD: not known
OVERALL LENGTH: 19.355m (63ft 6in)

CLASS PM-36 4-6-2 POLISH STATE RAILWAYS (PKP)

POLAND 1937

Poland's first 'Pacific' shows the German design influence shared by most Polish locomotives. In Poland in the 1930s, express services were both internal, between the major cities, and international, linking Germany and Czechoslovakia to the Russian frontier and its change of gauge. Heavy expresses were mostly hauled by the Class Pt-31 2-8-2, a powerful and efficient locomotive dating from 1932, but in 1937, at the height of the international

enthusiasm for streamlining, the decision was taken to begin a two-cylinder Pacific class for high-speed express work.

Two prototypes were built at the Chrzanov works in Warsaw, Pm-36.1 as a streamliner, the second as a conventional engine whose lines closely resembled those of the *Deutsche Reichsbahn's* Class 03 light Pacific. They were built in German fashion, with bar frames, as two-cylinder simples. Both were planned to run at speeds up to

140km/h (87mph) and had the largest-diameter driving wheels of any Polish engine. As a typical feature of modern Polish locomotives, the flat-roofed, clerestory-ventilated driving cab was fully enclosed, but unusually its entrance was built into the tender frame. Electric headlamps and cab lighting were installed.

The German invasion and occupation of Poland in 1939 put a stop to any further development of the class, and during the war

period the first engine had its streamlined casing removed. No. Pm-36.2 is preserved.

BOILER PRESSURE: 18kg/cm² (256.5psi)
CYLINDERS: 530x700mm (21x27.6in)
DRIVING WHEELS: 2000mm (79in)
GRATE AREA: 3.9m² (42sq ft)
HEATING SURFACE: 198m² (2132sq ft)
SUPERHEATER: 71.2m² (766.5sq ft)
TRACTIVE EFFORT: 16,227kg (32,860lb)
TOTAL WEIGHT: 94t (207,270lb) (engine only)

The preserved PM-36, No. 2, on a steam excursion near Glogow, in July 1995.

CLASS 46 2-8-2 TURKISH STATE RAILWAYS (TCDD)

TURKEY 1937

Of standard German style and equipment, Turkey's first modern express locomotive was this two-cylinder 'Mikado' built by Henschel of Kassel, Germany. Simultaneously, from the same builder, came a mixed traffic 2-10-0 with which it shared a boiler and a number of other parts. Eleven of the 2-8-2 were

Also numbered in the 46 series were six 2-8-2 locomotives built in 1929–32 by Robert Stephenson & Hawthorn of Darlington, England, with Belpaire fireboxes, for the Ottoman Railway.

delivered in 1937, and a further 10 were ordered in 1940 but never delivered. As with the vast majority of Turkish engines, they worked on the Asiatic side of the Bosporus. Excellent engines, they

performed well on the Turkish section of trains like the 'Taurus Express', Istanbul–Ankara–Baghdad, into the mid-1960s, often rostered with the incoming diesel-electrics. in the later years.

BOILER PRESSURE: 16kg/cm² (228psi)
CYLINDERS: 650x660mm (25.6x26in)
DRIVING WHEELS: 1751mm (69in)
GRATE AREA: 4m² (43sq ft)
HEATING SURFACE: 222.9m2 (2340sq ft)
SUPERHEATER: 106m² (1141.2sq ft)
TRACTIVE EFFORT: 21,700kg (47,850lb)
TOTAL WEIGHT: 104.5t (230,422lb)
(engine only)

CLASS F7 4-6-4 CHICAGO, MILWAUKEE, ST PAUL & PACIFIC RAILROAD (CMSTP&PRR)

USA 1937

Successors to the 4-4-2 'Hiawathas', these locomotives were introduced to enable heavier trains to be hauled on the Chicago–Minneapolis–St Paul expresses, while keeping the exceptionally fast schedule on this most competitive of routes. Given a streamlined front and boiler casing that also covered the cylinders, they showed the tendency of American designers at this time to play down the 'steamy' aspect of their passenger engines, but the wheels and running gear were left uncovered for easy access. The F7 boiler was made of silico-manganese steel, and it had a welded-construction firebox fitted with two thermic syphons and three arch tubes. The frame was a single cast-steel piece, as was by now standard with large American locomotives, and all axles ran on roller bearings. At this time, other lines

Only partially streamlined compared to their 'Atlantic' predecessors, the 4-6-4s were more powerful, and equally fast.

were using larger 4-8-4s for similar purposes, like the Union Pacific's semi-streamlined GS type operating the San Francisco-Los Angeles 'Daylight' streamlined train. But it is unlikely that any 4-8-4 has exceeded the speeds attained by the F7. Unlike their 4-4-2 predecessors, they were

coal-burning. They ran trains of up to 12 cars, 559 tonnes (550 tons) at an average of 106km/h (66mph), including five stops. Although there are accounts of these engines exceeding 193km/h (120mph), none are authenticated. In 1940 they did, however, operate the fastest scheduled

steam service anywhere, on the Hiawatha's Sparta–Portage sector, 126.3km (78.5 miles) run at an average of 130.75km/h (81.25mph). These locomotives typically averaged 18,506km (11,500 miles) a month, an indication of high reliability as well as of intensive utilization.

BOILER PRESSURE: 300psi (21kg/cm²)
CYLINDERS: 597x762mm (23.5x30in)
DRIVING WHEELS: 2134mm (84in)
GRATE AREA: 8.9m² (96.5sq ft)
HEATING SURFACE: 387m² (4166sq ft)
SUPERHEATER: 157m² (1695sq ft)
TRACTIVE EFFORT: 22,820kg (50,295lb)
TOTAL WEIGHT: 359t (791,000lb)

GS2 CLASS 4-8-4 SOUTHERN PACIFIC RAILROAD (SP) USA 1937

For decades, American locomotives had been in a class by themselves, with only the Soviet Russians making attempts to match their capitalist rivals in size and power. The power and efficiency of the big American locomotives by now were awesome. The 'Daylight' name of the San Francisco–Los Angeles streamlined train referred to its ability to do the 756km (470-mile) run within daylight hours, and the four Lima-built GS2 locomotives supplied the power. Like the 'Hiawatha' expresses of the Milwaukee Road, locomotive and train were both painted in a distinctive livery, in this case black, silver and gold. The design had been introduced in 1930, first built by Baldwin; GS2, built by Lima, was the first to be

streamlined. Altogether, 74 GS types were built, up to 1943. They were all oil burners, and booster-fitted to help tackle the heavy 1 in 45 (2.2 per cent) grade of Santa Margarita Hill, up which they commonly hauled their 577-tonne (568-ton) trains unaided. Spring-loaded side-play was allowed for on the leading coupled axle to assist flexibility on curves, of which there were many. Among

their other numerous up-to-date features was electro-pneumatic braking, which, actuated by electric current, applied brakes throughout the train simultaneously. Three turbo-generators were carried, a feed-water heater and pump to supplement the injectors. The normal air-brake system took a few seconds to become fully effective, as the pressure-change

had to pass along the piping system of a lengthy train. A further 63 4-8-4s followed of sub-classes GS 4 to 6 between 1937 and 1943; with GS2 and the original 14 GS1 locomotives built by Baldwin in 1930, the SP had a fleet of 81 GS 4-8-4s. Withdrawals began in 1954 and no GS1 or GS2 survives, but a GS4 and GS6 have been preserved, the former in working order.

BOILER PRESSURE: 21.1kg/cm² (300psi)
CYLINDERS: 648x813mm (25.5x32in)
DRIVING WHEELS: 2032mm (80in)
GRATE AREA: 8.4m² (90.4sq ft)
HEATING SURFACE: 454m² (4887sq ft)
SUPERHEATER: 194m² (2086sq ft)
TRACTIVE EFFORT: 32,285kg (71,173lb)
TOTAL WEIGHT: 400.5t (883,000lb)

The Daylight Limited – its replica hauled by preserved GS-4 No. 4449 with double tender, stops at Brock, California, USA.

231-132 BT GARRATT 4-6-2+2-6-4 PARIS, LYONS & MEDITERRANEAN RAILWAY (PLM) ALGERIA 1938

One of the most striking and remarkable Garratts ever built, it was also one of the very few intended for express passenger service. A pleasing blend of the Beyer-Garratt format with French design, managing to be both elegant and muscular-looking, its cylindrical tank and tender were of the same diameter as the boiler, giving it a more unified appearance than most Garratts. A prototype was built in 1932 by Franco-Belge of Raismes, France. Technically it was very advanced, with a variety of refinements built in, including electrically operated,

Painted in Algerian Railways (CFA) livery, No. 4 rolls into the main station of Algiers on 4 May 1939, to be coupled to its train.

cam-worked Cossart valve gear, which enabled steam to be worked at very short-offs. Dual controls were installed to help with driving in either direction, and there was fan ventilation for the enclosed cab. A steam coal-pusher brought coal forward in the tender (surprisingly, perhaps, hand-firing was employed) and a unique feature was the double chimney, whose two pipes were placed side by side rather than fore-and-aft. The PLM operated lines in Algeria until amalgamation with the state system created Algerian Railways (CFA) in 1938, and the new organization ordered first 10, then 29 of the Garratts.

In scheduled service, the Garratt ran the 422km (262 miles) between Algiers and Oran in 7hrs. The North African lines ran other fast expresses, some with *Wagon-Lits* stock, linking cities in Tunisia, Algiers and Morocco, and the Garratts ran the full length of the Algerian main line, 1368km (850 miles) from Ghardimaou on the Tunisian border to Oudja on the border with Morocco.

This engine was the fastest Garratt type on record, achieving a maximum speed of 132km/h (82mph) on test in France. But like all engines with complex details, it required skilled maintenance, and in the wartime conditions prevailing in North Africa between 1940 and 1945 their state deteriorated. By the mid-40s, they were in quite a decrepit condition, and the CFA, pressing ahead with the purchase of diesel-electric units, did not attempt to restore them. By 1951, all had gone.

BOILER PRESSURE: 20kg/cm² (248psi)
CYLINDERS: 490×660mm (19.25x26in)
DRIVING WHEELS: 1800mm (71in)
GRATE AREA: 5.4m² (58sq ft)
HEATING SURFACE: 260m² (2794sq ft)
SUPERHEATER: 91m² (975sq ft)
TRACTIVE EFFORT: 24,950kg (55,010lb)
TOTAL WEIGHT: 216t (476,280lb)

3-CAR ARTICULATED DIESEL SET   LONDON, MIDLAND & SCOTTISH RAILWAY (LMS)   GREAT BRITAIN 1938

In concept not unlike the Danish *Lyntog* of 1935, and also with the centre car sharing bogies with the end-vehicles, this streamlined diesel-electric was built at Derby in 1938 under the supervision of William Stanier. All three cars had two 93.25kW (125hp) Leyland engines with all but the two outermost axles being powered. Many forward-looking features were incorporated, including air-operated sliding doors and SKF roller bearing axleboxes. The train was finished in an attractive livery of red and cream with a silver roof, and black lining bands at the cantrail and waist. The unit ran regular services until put in storage during World War II. It was withdrawn in February 1945, its underframe and bogies becoming parts of departmental vehicles for overhead electric work.

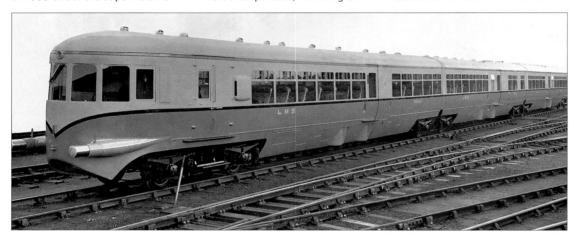

TYPE: lightweight diesel unit for stopping services
POWER: six Leyland diesel engines each developing 93.25kW (125hp) at 2200rpm
MAX. OPERATING SPEED: 120.675km/h (75mph)
WEIGHT: 74t (163,520lb)
OVERALL LENGTH: 56.24m (184ft 6in)
GAUGE: 1435mm (4ft 8.5in)

The potential of this advanced and good-looking design for cross-country services was ruined by the outbreak of war in 1939.

CLASS 56   4-6-2   MALAYAN RAILWAYS (MR)   MALAYA 1938

A small-wheeled 'Pacific' rather than the racing sort, this metre-gauge class dealt efficiently with the mail trains between Singapore and Kuala Lumpur, and Kuala Lumpur–Butterworth. The rails were light and the track not heavily ballasted, and it had a maximum axle load of not more than 12.95 tonnes (12.75 tons). To keep the weight as low as possible, bar frames were used, and the boiler shell and inner firebox were of nickel steel. Three simple-expansion cylinders were operated by poppet valves through a rotary camshaft system. It was very unusual – perhaps unique – to have a whole class of locomotives using rotary-cam operated poppety valves. Usually these were regarded as an experimental feature, to be tried out on one or two selected locomotives, but in the Class 56 they seem to have worked well.

A class 56 with a freight. The station has typically British equipment.

The bogie tender held 10.16 tonnes (10 tons) of coal and 3500gals (4200 US gals) of water. Fifteen Class 56s were delivered in 1938–39, and a further 51 in 1940 and 1945–46, all from North British Locomotive in Glasgow. In the mid-1950s, all were converted to oil-burning. Displaced by diesel units on to secondary passenger and freight services, they continued in active use until the late 1960s. Smoke deflectors, hardly necessary with the tall chimney and an overall speed limit on the single track of 72.5km/h (45mph), denote its express status. Two are preserved.

BOILER PRESSURE: 17.5kg/cm² (250psi)
CYLINDERS: 317x609mm (12.5x24in)
DRIVING WHEELS: 1370.5mm (54in)
GRATE AREA: 2.5m² (27 sq ft)
HEATING SURFACE: 123.25m² (1327sq ft)
SUPERHEATER: 20.2m² (218sq ft)
TRACTIVE EFFORT: 10,928kg (22,130lb)
TOTAL WEIGHT: 58.9t (129,920lb)
(engine only)

CLASS 232 4-6-4 SOVIET RAILWAYS (SZD)

Despite the Russian railways' preoccupation with freight, there were prestige passenger services, the prime one being the *Krasnaya Strela* ('Red Arrow') express between Moscow and Leningrad (650km/404 miles). This was to be a small class of 10 streamlined engines, specially built to work the express on an eight-hour schedule with two engine changes on the way. Details of American locomotives were readily available to Soviet engineers, though little about their own work was released, and American 'Hudson' design is reflected in these locomotives. In the end, only three were built, two at Kolomna, one at Voroshilovgrad, the former Lugansk. The first, 232 No. 1, attained the maximum recorded speed of any Russian steam locomotive, 170.5km/h (106mph) near Kalinin on 29 June 1938. War and the German invasion put a stop to development, and work on the class was not resumed afterwards. Nos. 2 and 3 remained in active service on the 'Red Arrow' until diesels ousted them in 1958.

BOILER PRESSURE: 15kg/cm^2 (213psi)
CYLINDERS: 579x700.5mm (22.8x27.6in)
DRIVING WHEELS: 1995mm (78.6in)
GRATE AREA: 6.5m^2 (70sq ft)
HEATING SURFACE: 239m^2 (2573.2sq ft)
SUPERHEATER: 124.5m^2 (1340.4sq ft)
TRACTIVE EFFORT: 14,960kg (33,000lb)
TOTAL WEIGHT: 148.8t (301,340lb)
(engine only)

CLASS 15F 4-8-2 SOUTH AFRICAN RAILWAYS (SAR)

The 4-8-2's combination of power and route availability suited SAR very well; it had been operating the type since 1910 and this design reflected the results of long experience. One of the largest South African classes, it eventually numbered 225. The first came from Henschel and Berliner Maschinenbau; 30 were delivered by Beyer Peacock in 1944, and others followed from North British Locomotive Co. The boiler, slightly tapered, had a maximum diameter of 2.02m (6ft 7.5in). At 3.95m (12ft 11.5in) high and 3.05m (10ft) wide, they just squeezed into the loading gauge.

The bogie and truck wheels, and the two four-wheel bogies of the tender, were all fitted with roller bearings. Most had automatic stokers; crews also liked their smoke boxes with self-cleaning screens, power shakers to clear ash from the grates, and steam-operated fire-doors.

BOILER PRESSURE: 14.7kg/cm^2 (210psi)
CYLINDERS: 609x711mm (24x28in)
DRIVING WHEELS: 1523mm (60in)
GRATE AREA: 5.8m^2 (62.5sq ft)
HEATING SURFACE: 317m^2 (3415sq ft)
SUPERHEATER: 61.3m^2 (660sq ft)
TRACTIVE EFFORT: 19,202kg (42,340lb)
TOTAL WEIGHT: 180.3t (397,600lb)

CLASS E-4 4-6-4 CHICAGO & NORTH WESTERN RAILROAD (CNW)

This line vied with Milwaukee Road and Burlington's *Zephyr* for the Chicago–Milwaukee traffic, and so had to come up with some very effective motive power. In this case, competition bred similarity, and the nine streamlined 'Hudsons' built by Alco for the C&NW were in a style not at all dissimilar to the Milwaukee Road's F7 4-6-4 locomotives, also from Alco. The E-4's styling exposed the cylinders as well as the motion. A hard-coal burner, it had a smaller grate than the rival, and larger-diameter cylinders gave it a higher nominal tractive effort (good for publicity), but the dimensions of the two were otherwise almost the same, and both turned in high-quality performance on a tight timetable. However, the CNW did not match the top speeds of the Milwaukee Road 4-6-4s; the highest recorded was 151.3km/h (94mph). One of the Class E-4 participated in a set of tests run by the Association of American Railroads in 1938, primarily to establish the drawbar horsepower needed to haul a train of 1000 US tons (907 tons/921 tonnes) at a constant 160km/h (100mph) on level track. E4 No. 4003 with a test train of 912 US tons (827 tons/840 tonnes) maintained 120.7km/h (75mph) up a grade of 1 in 480, and 103km/h (64mph) on 1 in 200.

BOILER PRESSURE: 21kg/cm^2 (300psi)
CYLINDERS: 634.5x736mm (25x29in)
DRIVING WHEELS: 2132mm (84in)
GRATE AREA: 8.4m^2 (90.7sq ft)
HEATING SURFACE: 369.5m^2 (3979sq ft)
SUPERHEATER: 175m^2 (1884sq ft)
TRACTIVE EFFORT: 24,940kg (55,000lb)
TOTAL WEIGHT: 186.8t (412,000lb)
(engine only)

CLASS J-3A 4-6-4 NEW YORK CENTRAL RAILROAD (NYC)

There could be no doubt that in the late 1930s, the 4-6-4 was the express locomotive of choice (few people were taking note of what was even then being hatched at Electro-Motive's new La Grange factory). Thirty-nine of the Class J3 were built by Alco, with another nine in streamlined form, tailored for the 'Twentieth Century Limited', bringing the NYC's stock of the

BOILER PRESSURE: 19.3kg/cm^2 (275psi)
CYLINDERS: 571x736mm (22.5x29in)
DRIVING WHEELS: 2005mm (79in)
GRATE AREA: 81.9m^2 (82sq ft)
HEATING SURFACE: 388.9m^2 (4187sq ft)
SUPERHEATER: 162m^2 (1745sq ft)
TRACTIVE EFFORT: 19,700kg (43,440lb)
TOTAL WEIGHT: 163.2t (360,000lb)
(engine only)

Behind a J-3A 4-6-4, the 'Twentieth Century Limited' sweeps under the Bear Mountain Bridge in New York State, in 1939.

type to 275, and taking the NYC's racing 'Hudsons' to their peak development. Five of the streamliners also had roller bearings fitted to the connecting and coupling rod cranks. In 1941,

another two were streamlined to run the 'Empire State Express'. The streamliners' casing added only 2494kg (5500lb) to the engine weight. A booster engine fitted to the trailing bogie could supply a

further 5487kg (12,100lb) of tractive effort in starting. The J-3 locomotives had cast-steel frames, nickel-steel boilers, lightweight reciprocating parts and roller bearings on all axles. While of

similar weight to the NYC's Class J-1 4-6-4s, they developed 3456kW (4700hp) at 124km/h (77mph) compared with the earlier locomotives' 2868kW (3900hp) at 106.2km/h (66mph).

CLASS GS-6 4-8-4 SOUTHERN PACIFIC RAILROAD (SP) USA 1938

As a result of higher train speeds, improved refrigeration and market growth in the Mid-West and East of the United States, the traffic of fresh fruit and vegetables increased dramatically in the later 1930s. A chief task of the GS-6 was hustling perishable Californian

GS in Southern Pacific parlance originally stood for 'Golden State', a reference to California; but during World War II, the reference was changed to mean 'General Service'.

farm produce eastwards across the prairies in 12.2m (40ft) insulated and ice-packed refrigerator cars, each weighing up to 76.2 tonnes (75 tons) fully loaded, and with up

to 30 in a trainload. Although the 4-8-4 is mainly associated with passenger trains, a number of other lines also acquired freight or mixed-traffic versions, usually with high-speed freight in mind. For the SP, 23 were built, all by Lima, and the dimensions of this locomotive compare interestingly with those of its express passenger sister of 1937. The nominal tractive force as stated by the builders was marginally less than the 1937 vehicle, and in most respects the engine was just slightly smaller. Notably the driving wheels were smaller and the steam pressure considerably lowered, reflecting a lower running speed. The freight model had more weight borne by the coupled wheels, 128.4 tonnes (126.4 tons) compared to the passenger engine's 125 tonnes (123 tons), a modest extra amount of adhesion in getting the drag

on a lengthy train. Both were oil burners and were fitted with the same standard 'Type E' superheater.

Though the tenders, on two six-wheel bogies, were identical in appearance, the GS-6's carried slightly less water and slightly more oil. The GS-6 was also subjected to semi-streamlined styling, though its paint finish, befitting a freight type, was a glossy black.

BOILER PRESSURE: 18.2kg/cm² (260psi)
CYLINDERS: 685x761.4mm (27x30in)
DRIVING WHEELS: 1865.5mm (73.5in)
GRATE AREA: 8.4m² (90.2sq ft)
HEATING SURFACE: 450.6m² (4852sq ft)
SUPERHEATER: 193.75m² (2086sq ft)
TRACTIVE EFFORT: 29,115kg (64,200lb)
TOTAL WEIGHT: 212.4t (468,400lb)
(engine only)

Apart from the boiler-top fairing, all attempts at streamlining were abandoned in the wartime production batches of GS locomotives.

CLASS 1018 1-DO-1 FEDERAL RAILWAYS OF AUSTRIA (ÖBB)

AUSTRIA 1939

This Austrian electric class was based on the design of the *Deutsche Reichsbahn* Class E-18 1-Do-1, and eight were built during the German annexation of Austria at the Floridsdorf Works in Vienna. Removed to Germany during World War II, they were returned to Austria at the end of hostilities. Modified cabs were fitted in the 1970s in common with the ÖBB's two Class 1118s, and they ran in traffic, based at the Linz depot, until the 1990s.

TYPE: 1-Do-1 express passenger
POWER: 2840kW (3859hp)
SUPPLY: 15kV 16.7Hz AC
TRACTIVE EFFORT (ON STARTING): 196kN (44,100lbf)
MAX. OP. SPEED: 130km/h (81.2mph)
WEIGHT: 110t (242,550lb)
MAX. AXLE LOAD: 19.6t (43,218lb)
OVERALL LENGTH: 16.92m (55ft 2in)
GAUGE: 1435mm (4ft 8.5in)

Though numerically a very small class, the 1018s were powerful and reliable, and survived in traffic for more than half a century.

CLASS 12 4-4-2 BELGIAN NATIONAL RAILWAYS (SNCB)

BELGIUM 1939

Here was the last fling of the 'Atlantic' express locomotive: no more would be built after this. On a more modest European scale, the Class 12 replicated the aim of engines like the CPR 4-4-4 in Canada: to operate lightly loaded high-speed inter-city services. It was designed by Raoul Notesse, locomotive chief of the SNCB, and its outer shell provided effective streamlining while leaving working parts accessible. Yellow speed-stripes on its green paintwork helped to give it the look of a

One of only a handful of surviving members of the 'Atlantic' locomotive type, No. 004 of Class 12.

flyer. Six were supplied in 1939, from Cockerill's shops at Seraing. All had bar frames and inside cylinders, and four had piston valves and Walschaerts valve gear with outside return cranks to the leading coupled wheels; the others had rotary cam valve gear, one Caprotti, the other Dabeg. The six-wheel tenders were cannibalized from redundant stock, and given a streamlined casing. The Atlantics

operated a one-hour service with 250-tonne (246 ton) trains between Ostend, Ghent and Brussels, 115km (71.5miles), with a maximum operating speed of 140km/h (87mph), though at high speed their ride was reputedly uncomfortable.

World War II brought the service to an end. Post-war, when the Ostend line was electrified, they worked similar trains on the

Brussels–Lille route, up to 1960. One member of the class has been preserved.

BOILER PRESSURE: 18kg/cm² (256psi)
CYLINDERS: 480x720mm (18.8x28.4in)
DRIVING WHEELS: 2100mm (82.75in)
GRATE AREA: 3.7m² (39.8sq ft)
HEATING SURFACE: 161m² (1729sq ft)
SUPERHEATER: 63m² (678sq ft)
TRACTIVE EFFORT: 12,079kg (26,620lb)
TOTAL WEIGHT: 89.5t (188,500lb)
(engine only)

SERIES 61 4-6-6T GERMAN STATE RAILWAYS (DRG)

GERMANY 1939

A development of the Series 60 express tank of 1935, this locomotive took Germany's streamlined tank operations to a peak. A partnership between the Kassel firms of Henschel and Wagenfabrik Wegmann had produced its immediate prototype, a 4-6-4T, No. 61 001, in 1935. Their aim was to design a steam train that would match the performance of the new diesel-powered lightweight expresses, and be as convenient in operation.

Streamlining was applied to the locomotive and the four-car train. A driving cab was installed in the end coach, so that on a return journey it became the front of the train. The engine was a big one, a three-cylinder simple, though its shrouding was so complete that it was only with difficulty recognized as a steam locomotive.

In 1936, the solitary 61 001 ran a twice-daily express with the *Henschel-Wegmann Zug,* as it was known, between Berlin and

Dresden, doing the 176km (109-mile) journey in 100 minutes. It was clear, however, that its water and fuel capacity were limited, and the 4-6-6T was produced, with an outside-frame six-wheel truck at the rear to carry 5 tonnes (4.9 tons) of coal and 1010gals (1210 US gals) of water. The advent of war ended the service. The stock of the train was used, with an additional coach, for the post-war V-200-hauled *Blauer Enzian* express. No. 61 001 was taken out of service in 1952;

while the 4-6-6T was rebuilt by the *Deutsche Reichsbahn* in 1961 as a 4-6-2 tender locomotive for testing new rolling stock.

BOILER PRESSURE: 20kg/cm² (285psi)
CYLINDERS: 390x660mm (15.3x26in)
DRIVING WHEELS: 2300mm (90.6in)
GRATE AREA: 2.8m² (30sq ft)
HEATING SURFACE: 150m² (1615sq ft)
SUPERHEATER: 69.2m² (745sq ft)
TRACTIVE EFFORT: 7380kg (16,270lb)
TOTAL WEIGHT: 146.3t (296,257lb)

CLASS WM 2-6-4T EAST INDIAN RAILWAY (EIR)

INDIA 1939

An IRS (Indian Railways Standard) locomotive design, this British-built class was designed to replace older locomotives on the ever-busier suburban networks of the great Indian cities. The 2-6-4 was a familiar configuration: in the 1900s, a standard 2-6-4

passenger tank type was designed. The Bengal–Nagpur Railway had 34 2-6-4Ts of class FT dating from 1906; the East Bengal Railway had 53 Class K or KS (superheated) from 1907 to 1927, and the EIR had 15 of Class BT from 1912 to 1914. The WM class, with two simple-

BOILER PRESSURE: 14.7kg/cm² (210psi)
CYLINDERS: 406x710.6mm (16x28in)
DRIVING WHEELS: 1700mm (67in)
GRATE AREA: 2.3m² (24sq ft)

HEATING SURFACE: 88.7m² (955sq ft)
SUPERHEATER: 22.3m² (240sq ft)
TRACTIVE EFFORT: 8660kg (19,000lb)
TOTAL WEIGHT: 105.9t (233,630lb)

expansion outside cylinders, superheater and other modern equipment, enabled longer and

faster trains to be run, and the more elderly locomotives were retired for scrapping.

A small boy takes a free ride on the roomy buffer beam of Class WM 13002 as it trundles along with what appears to be a well-filled commuter train.

CLASS 800 4-6-0 GREAT SOUTHERN RAILWAY (GSR)

The three engines of this class were the largest and most powerful locomotives ever built in Ireland. Historically, locomotive design on the 1524mm (5ft) gauge Irish railways was closely identified with the British tradition, and the economic difficulties of the Irish Free State had allowed for little new building. Consequently, by 1939 the main Dublin–Cork line was chronically short of adequate motive power, and the '800s' were designed and built at the GSR Inchicore shops in Dublin to provide express services on this route. Named *Maeve, Macha* and *Tailte* after legendary Irish queens, they were three-cylinder simples, with three sets of Walschaerts valve gear, and double chimneys. Dimensions were comparable with those of the English 'Royal Scots'. They handled the traffic with ease, though their performance was to be constrained by the 'Emergency' years of 1939–45 and the fuel

The 800 class, though similar to the British 'Royal Scots' in size and power, had their large boilers placed on a shorter wheelbase.

shortages in post-war Ireland. In 1950, the Belfast–Dublin express became for a time through train to Cork, reversing at the capital's Amiens Street terminus, from where it was hauled by an 800 via the link line under Phoenix Park on

to the GSR main line. The 800s could run fast, though rumours of speeds of up to 160km/h (100mph) were fanciful. *Tailte* was withdrawn in 1957, the two others in 1964. *Maeve* is preserved at the Ulster Transport Museum.

BOILER PRESSURE: 15.75kg/cm² (225psi)
CYLINDERS: 470x711mm (18.5x28in)
DRIVING WHEELS: 2007mm (79in)
GRATE AREA: 3.10m² (33.5sq ft)
HEATING SURFACE: 174m² (1870sq ft)
SUPERHEATER: 43.5m² (468sq ft)
TRACTIVE EFFORT: 14,970kg (33,000lb)
TOTAL WEIGHT: 137t (302,500lb)

ETR-200 THREE-CAR TRAIN STATE RAILWAYS (FS)

The first *diretissima* route between Florence and Bologna, was begun in 1913 and completed in 1934 (a second, even more direct, is under construction). The line, with a ruling grade of 1 in 106, still had some quite tight curving sections, and was electrified from the first. Encouraged by the government of the time, the FS built a luxury high-

speed train that would fully exploit its possibilities. The ETR (*elettrotreno*) 200 was an articulated three-car set with streamlining developed in the wind-tunnel of the Turin Polytechnic. All three cars were powered, driving both axles of the front bogie of the front and rear cars, and the outer axles of the inner bogies. At speeds over 130km/h (80mph), the behaviour

of the pantograph caused concern (the one on the rear was always raised in Italian practice), and in addition to the two drivers positioned at the front a third was stationed in the rear compartment to observe and operate it. The Italian practice of using direct current line at 3000Vs enabled the designers to dispense with the heavy transformers needed to convert alternating current, and was directly responsible for the light weight and consequent high speed of the train.

On a special run made on 20 July 1939 from Florence to Milan, the ETR covered the distance of 315km (195.8 miles) in the remarkable time of 115.2 minutes – an average speed of 163.8km/h (101.8mph). On the racing stretch just before Piacenza, the train reached a maximum speed of 202.8km/h (126mph). Two factors helped this achievement: most normal speed restrictions were raised, and the voltage strength was increased to 4000V, making a considerable amount of extra power available.

No train in the world had ever gone so far, so fast, and the record remained unbroken until 1964. The outbreak of war in 1939 put an end to such gestures, and it was August 1946 before the ETR 200 re-inaugurated a new high-speed Milan–Florence service. Between 1960 and 1966, ETR 200 sets were converted by the addition of a fourth car and other alterations and refurbishments, and redesignated ETR 220. This train was the direct precursor of the later Italian high-speed sets like the *Settebello*.

TYPE: three-car express train set
POWER: six axle-hung motors of Type 62 (derived from FS class E624) with hourly rated power output of 1100kW (1474hp), supplied by current at 3000V DC via overhead catenary
TRACTIVE EFFORT: not known
MAX. OPERATING SPEED: 210km/h (130mph)
TOTAL WEIGHT: 103t (227,115lb)
MAX. AXLE LOAD: 10t (22,050lb)
OVERALL LENGTH: 62.8m (206ft 2in)
BUILDER: Breda, Milan

The Breda Works plate can be seen to the right of the driver's door in this shot of the ETR 200 at carriage sidings in Rome.

CLASS 131 2-6-2T ROMANIAN STATE RAILWAYS (CFR)

Romania had two locomotive works, but most Romanian-built locomotives were actually based on German or Hungarian designs. Though mechanically similar to the Hungarian Class 375 2-6-2T, which it replaced in service, this was one of the few

classes to be designed within Romania. The Resita works built 65 between 1939 and 1942, and they were used in suburban and local passenger services. They were two-cylinder simple-expansion types, and their main variation from the European norm

was the fitting of the Cosmovici dual oil and coal burning system,

with oil tanks placed above the side water tanks.

BOILER PRESSURE: 12kg/cm² (171psi)
CYLINDERS: 510x650mm (20x25.6in)
DRIVING WHEELS: 1440mm (56.75in)
GRATE AREA: 3.6m² (38.7sq ft)

HEATING SURFACE: not known
SUPERHEATER: not known
TRACTIVE EFFORT: 11,900kg (26,250lb)
TOTAL WEIGHT: not known

2-8-2 STEAM-DIESEL LOCOMOTIVE SOVIET RAILWAYS (SZD)   RUSSIA 1939

The concept of the 'hybrid' dual-power locomotive is not a new one. However, in the 1930s, the marriage of the steam and the internal combustion engines turned out to be a forlorn hope, despite numerous efforts and much intensive research work.

In 1924, the British Kitson company built a 2-6-2 'diesel-steam' prototype. Known as the Kitson-Still, it had double-acting pistons moved by diesel combustion at the inner end and by steam expansion at the outer end. Without a firebox, it started on steam raised via a burner placed in the boiler, and the acceleration eventually produced a compression rate at which the diesel fuel ignited and drove the cylinders, while the waste heat thus generated was used to heat water into steam to operate the 'steam end'. Ansaldo in Italy made a similar experiment. Kitsons went bankrupt in the post-1929 slump, and their work was not followed up in Britain, but the concept was revived in Soviet Russia in the late 1930s, where it was known as the *Teploparovoz* type. The Kitson locomotive had eight inside cylinders, arranged in banks of four on opposite sides of a crankshaft set parallel to the axles. The much bigger Russian engines were a 2-8-2 and a 2-10-4, from the Voroshilovgrad works, and a 2-10-2 from Kolomna. These, for good measure, were also designed as opposed-piston locomotives, in which a centrally mounted set of outside cylinders on each side drove the pistons in opposing directions, thereby obtaining (in principle at least) a balance of revolving forces that resulted in less hammer-blow effect on the track and less wear and tear on the moving parts of the engine. The 2-10-4 burned gas rather than diesel, generating it from pulverized anthracite. It had an anthracite pulverizer for steam fuel, and a tender condenser. Expensive and complex, these designs were abandoned by 1948.

Detailed specifications are not available.

CLASS 19D 4-8-2 SOUTH AFRICAN RAILWAYS (SAR)   SOUTH AFRICA 1939

On the SAR, successive 'Mountain' classes showed the march of technical progress. The Class 19, mostly German-built and first delivered in 1928, were designed to haul branch traffic, goods, passenger and mixed, and did so until the final phasing-out of steam, by which time many were in very poor condition. Class 19D, built by Krupps of Essen and Borsig of Berlin, was identical in most respects to the preceding 19C of

BOILER PRESSURE: 14kg/cm² (200psi)
CYLINDERS: 533x660mm (21x26in)
DRIVING WHEELS: 1370mm (54in)
GRATE AREA: 3.3m² (36sq ft)
HEATING SURFACE: 171.5m² (1847sq ft)
SUPERHEATER: 36.2m² (390sq ft)
TRACTIVE EFFORT: 16,370kg (36,096lb)
TOTAL WEIGHT: 81.2t (179,088lb)

1933, except for having Walschaerts valve gear and piston valves, instead of rotary cam gear with poppet valves. A further delivery was made in 1948, and Vanderbilt 12-wheel tenders were

A coal-burning 19D with a Vanderbilt-type tender works a train of mineral wagons across the level veld.

fitted to these. One of the class, known as a poor steamer, was modernized using L.D. Porta's gas-producer firebox in 1979, with dramatically improved performance.

AE 8/14 1A-A1A-A1 + 1A-A1A-A1 SWISS FEDERAL RAILWAYS (SBB)   SWITZERLAND 1939

In 1931, the Swiss Federal Railways was considering the use of large articulated electric locomotives on its busiest and most profitable mountain routes, particularly the St Gotthard line. The class Ae8/14 machine was one of the results: effectively two Ae4/7 Büchli drive locomotives permanently attached back to back. They were 'A' units, with cabs at the outer ends only, and the wheel configuration was altered to a symmetrical 1-AA-1-AA-1 in each half.

Two other prototype designs were evaluated, but operational experience demonstrated that such large locomotives were not actually essential, and smaller ones were more effective. Although it never went into series production, Ae8/14 11801 remains today as an operational museum locomotive at the SBB Erstfeld depot.

TYPE: 1A-A1A-A1 + 1A-A1A-A1 heavy freight double unit
POWER: 4650kW (6320hp)
SUPPLY: 15kV 16.7Hz AC
TRACTIVE EFFORT: 490kN (110,250lbf)
MAX. OPERATING SPEED: 100km/h (62mph)
WEIGHT: 240t (529,200lb)
MAX. AXLE LOAD: 19.5t (42,998lb)
OVERALL LENGTH: 34m (110ft 11in)
GAUGE: 1435mm (4ft 8.5in)

The third AE 8/14 prototype, known as the *Landi-Lok*, was the most powerful locomotive in the world when built in 1939. It is also preserved.

CLASS FEF-2 4-8-4 UNION PACIFIC RAILROAD (UP)

The abbreviation 'FEF' stood for 'four-eight-four', and the period from 1939 to 1944 marked the real heyday of this type as a passenger engine. Most long-haul passenger railroads invested in 4-8-4 locomotives. A Norfolk & Western Class J was recorded at 177km/h (110mph) with a 1041-tonne (1025-ton) train on level track, and similar feats have been ascribed to the UP FEF. Forty-five of these were built, with variations of design, between 1938 and 1944, all by Alco. Ironically, these engines were demonstrating their power and efficiency just as the General Motors Electro-Motive Division

One of the last of the FEF-2 to be built, No. 8444 on Sherman Hill, Wyoming, on 22 April 1981.

diesels were starting to eat seriously into the domain of steam. Later fitted with long smoke deflectors but not streamlined – that fashion was largely played out by then – and free both of cosmetics and gadgets, the FEFs were merely superb two-cylinder simple-expansion steam locomotives. The principal variation with comparable locomotives was in the design of the connecting rods by a form of sleeve bearing that embraced the forked ends of each rod in a single joint. With

FEF-1 No. 815, the UP participated in the comparative runs set up by the Association of American Railroads in 1938, in which the Pennsylvania Railroad and the Chicago North Western also took part. With its 840-tonne (827-ton) test train, the FEF achieved a top speed of 143.2km/h (89mph) on a rising grade of 1 in 660; and of 164.8km/h (102.4mph) on a downhill grade levelling out from 1 in 500 to 1 in 100. On the uphill run, a maximum horsepower of 3708kW (5043hp) was developed.

Post-1945, the FEF-2 class was converted to oil burning, and continued to operate fast express services. Their final road service was in autumn 1958. Four or five of these mighty engines have been preserved.

BOILER PRESSURE: 21kg/cm² (300psi)
CYLINDERS: 635x813mm (25x32in)
DRIVING WHEELS: 2032mm (80in)
GRATE AREA: 9.3m² (100sq ft)
HEATING SURFACE: 393m² (4225sq ft)
SUPERHEATER: 130m² (1400sq ft)
TRACTIVE EFFORT: 28,950kg (63,800lb)
TOTAL WEIGHT: 412t (908,000lb)

CLASS S1 6-4-4-6 PENNSYLVANIA RAILROAD (PRR)

Looking rather like a rocket on its transporter, this monster engine showed that at the apogee of steam power even the PRR, with all its design and building experience, could get things wrong. Though claimed to be the world's largest and fastest coal-burning passenger engine, this remained a one-off locomotive,

A sleek but ineffective monster: seen at Chicago on 24 June 1941, No. 6100 is ready to depart with *The General*, a PRR luxury train bound for New York.

despite making a test run at 162.5km/h (101mph) with a 1363-tonne (1342-ton) train. Its heavy maximum axle load limited its use, and since its adhesive weight was only 26.5 per cent of the total, both sets of driving wheels had a tendency to slip at the same time on starting.

Because of its length and axle weight of 34 tonnes (33.5 tons), it was restricted to the Crestline–Chicago division of the line. On this famously fast section, it turned in notable performances, and was said to have exceeded 160km/h (100mph) and even 193km/h (120mph) on occasions,

but sustained bouts of wheel slipping, with adhesion on only four of its 10 axles, greatly reduced its effectiveness.

Built at the PRR's Juniata shops, the Class S1 was exhibited at the New York World's fair in 1939–40, but little used, and was broken up in 1949.

BOILER PRESSURE: 21kg/cm² (300psi)
CYLINDERS: 558x660mm (22x26in)
DRIVING WHEELS: 2132mm (84in)
GRATE AREA: 12.26m² (132sq ft)
HEATING SURFACE: 525.2m² (5660sq ft)
SUPERHEATER: 193.6m² (2085sq ft)
TRACTIVE EFFORT: 35,456kg (71,800lb)
TOTAL WEIGHT: 523.4t (1,060,000lb)

ELECTRO-MOTIVE SW1 VARIOUS RAILROADS

USA 1939

A switching engine of 101.6 tonnes (100 tons) and 441kW (600hp) was the first locomotive to emerge from the new erecting shops of Electro-Motive Division (EMD) at La Grange in May 1936. In Electro-Motive's original designation, the initials SW indicated 'six hundred horsepower, welded frame'. But 'SW' also suggested 'Switcher', and later more powerful switchers retained the SW prefix in their designations. The Alco-General Electric partnership had been pioneers in building yard

locomotives, but overall numbers were small. They were seen as even more expensive per unit of horsepower than the bigger diesels. By refusing to customize, and building in batches of up to 50, EMD cut the capital costs down, and sales began to build. US railroads bought 176 switching engines in 1939; in 1941, the number was 583. The SW1 was soon available as a 662kW (900hp) and then 735kW (1000hp) unit (from 1938). They were built up to 1953 and operated on many lines. One or two may still be

found working on American short lines. Its single exhaust stack, the large platform behind the cab, and

the exterior sandbox located below the radiator on the hood end are the prime identifiers.

TYPE: diesel-electric
POWER AND OUTPUT: six-cylinder 567 engine producing 450kW (600hp)
TRACTIVE EFFORT: 107kN (24,000lbf) at 16km/h (10mph)
MAX. OPERATING SPEED: 80km/h (50mph)
WEIGHT: 90.8t (200,000lb)
OVERALL LENGTH: 13.538m (44ft 5in)
GAUGE: 1435mm (4ft 8.5in)

100-ton switcher No. 1126 of the Boston & Maine Railroad, photographed at Lowell, Massachusetts, in April 1987.

ELECTRO-MOTIVE FT FOUR-UNIT SET VARIOUS RAILROADS

USA 1939

In the 1930s, a new diesel locomotive cost around $100 per unit of horsepower, while a steam locomotive cost around $35 on the same scale. Railroad men were also still generally sceptical about the heavy pulling-power of diesels. Having begun to make significant inroads into the passenger

locomotive market, and developed its line of switchers, Electro-Motive now turned its attention to the road freight locomotive, with the first real attempt to design such a type for volume production. The prime essential was the engine, which was a new and much improved design, the 567-series,

16-cylinder, V-type, two-stroke cycle, rated at 993kW (1350hp). Freight was the US railroads' prime source of revenue, and any savings made in this area went straight to profit. Electro-Motive's FT freight diesel was promoted as the ideal way of achieving this. A four-unit 3974kW (5400hp)

TYPE: four unit diesel-electric in 'A-B-B-A' configuration, all units using Bo-Bo wheel arrangement
POWER AND OUTPUT: each unit powered by an EMC 16-567 diesel rated at 993kW (1350hp), for a total output of 3974kW (5400hp)
TRACTIVE EFFORT: 978kN (220,000lbf) starting TE
MAX. OPERATING SPEED: N/A
WEIGHT: 400t (900,000lb)
OVERALL LENGTH: 58.826m (193ft)
GAUGE: 1435mm (4ft 8.5in)

demonstrator, No. 103, toured the country in 1939 and 1940, running 133,000km (83,000 miles), and demonstrating on line after line that a diesel-electric could move heavy tonnage in demanding circumstances. One of the more spectacular examples of performance was made on the Northern Pacific's line between Livingston and Missoula, MT, a

'A' and 'B' units of the Boston & Maine Railroad. A full set would consist of a further 'B' and 'A' unit, but operational flexibility made it desirable to split the pairs if necessary.

mountain section of 386km (240 miles). Hauling the 'North Coast Limited', a 4-6-6-4 articulated steam locomotive could take a 10-car train westbound over the section in 6hrs, 30mins, unaided; a helper engine was provided for a heavier load. No. 103 took the train loaded to 17 cars, unaided, in 6hrs, 19mins. As reports of such feats accumulated, buyers were soon lining up.

As would become a standard practice, No. 103 was formed of two A-B units, semi-permanently coupled, and designed to form an A-B-B-A set. The 'A' units had an end cab, the 'B' units were cabless 'slave' engines. Initially the entire four-unit set was treated as a single locomotive because of concerns that labour unions would otherwise insist on putting a driver on each 'unit' as if they were

individual locomotives. With later F unit types, the semi-permanent coupling arrangement was discontinued and normal couplers became standard. Considered as a single locomotive (which is how it operated), it was the largest ever seen, weighing 408 tonnes (401.75 tons). But this weight was carried on 32 axles, all of them driving, so that maximum axle load was less than that of the big

steam locomotives, and adhesion for traction was much greater. Although 'F' was intended to designate freight locomotives in the Electro-Motive catalogue, post-war F units were often geared to provide passenger haulage, and provided with steam-heating boilers. No. 103 was sold to the Southern Railway, and Santa Fe was the first to purchase production models, in 1940.

CLASS 1020 CO+CO FEDERAL RAILWAYS OF AUSTRIA (ÖBB)

Seen at Villach, one of the surviving Class 1020 locomotives is the train engine of a freight waiting for a clear road.

Supported on a girder frame on two long, big-wheeled, three-axle powered bogies, this engine had a long central cab section with low nose ends, a typical 'Alpine' electric shape. Though its longest survivals were as ÖBB Class 1020, it was originally designed and built as E94 of the German *Deutsche Reichsbahn* (DR). In the normal way of development, it was itself a more powerful version of the earlier Class E93, and the first 11 were converted from orders for E93. On the annexation of Austria by Germany in 1938, a further 87 were ordered for service there, and delivery of these began in 1940.

Further orders through to 1941 took the planned total to 285, mostly sent to German depots, but some also to Innsbruck in Austria. Designed for heavy freight work, the Class E94s worked on virtually all the electrified German and Austrian mountain routes. Many were decrepit, and some destroyed, by the end of World War II. At the end of hostilities, 44 German class E94s were taken into the ÖBB as Class 1020, and supplemented by three further units built in Vienna. Others of the

class were to be found in East and West Germany and also Russia (returned to East Germany in 1952, where some worked on the East German DR until 1990). The Austrian locomotives were refurbished between 1967 and 1980 with new cabs and 675kW (917hp) electric brakes. In this form, some continued working into the 1990s, based at Villach on the Tauern line. No less than 36 of E94 and 1020 are believed to be still in existence, many of them restored as museum items.

Interestingly, as late as 2002 two E94s were restored (ex DR E94 052 and DB E94 051) for revenue-earning freight service by private operator PEG as their E94.01 and E94.02.

TYPE: Co+Co heavy freight
POWER: 3000kW (4076hp)
SUPPLY: 15kV 16.7Hz AC
TRACTIVE EFFORT: 314kN (70,650lbf)
MAX. OPERATING SPEED: 90km/h (56.3mph)
WEIGHT: 118.5t (261,293lb)
MAX. AXLE LOAD: 20t (44,100lb)
OVERALL LENGTH: 18.6m (60ft 8in)
GAUGE: 1435mm (4ft 8.5in)

CLASS TR1 2-8-2 STATE RAILWAYS (VR)

The demands of heavy freight haulage and a relatively high boiler pressure made this one of the VR's coal-burning classes. A need for greater power to move heavier trains was the reason for this design in the later 1930s. Its boiler and tender were shared with

No. 1086 of the class, built by Lokomo in 1955, at Kouvola, on the Helsinki–Leningrad line, in the winter of 1970.

those of the Hr1 'Pacific' class of 1937, and a number of other parts were interchangeable between these two classes. The front carrying and coupled axles formed a Krauss-Helmholtz bogie and the trailing axle was an Adams radial one. Sixty-seven Tr1s were built between 1940 and 1957, mostly in Finland by Tampella and Lokomo in Tampere, but also 20 were built by the German firm of Jung. Over the 17 years, various minor alterations were made to the design, and the final four engines had roller bearings on all axles. During the World War II years, some of the class were adapted to burn wood as a measure to cope with coal shortages.

BOILER PRESSURE: 15kg/cm² (214psi)
CYLINDERS: 610x700mm (24x27.5in)
DRIVING WHEELS: 1600mm (63in)
GRATE AREA: 3.5m² (37.7sq ft)

While the backbone of Finnish railway freight operation was the Tk and Tv 2-8-0 types, which were seen everywhere, the Tr1 operating ground was in the centre and south of the country, working the heaviest main-line goods

HEATING SURFACE: 195.4m² (2103sq ft)
SUPERHEATER: 68m² (732.1sq ft)
TRACTIVE EFFORT: 20,740kg (45,730lb)
TOTAL WEIGHT: 95t (engine only)

trains. With a maximum operating speed of 80km/h (50mph), they were also used quite often on long-distance passenger trains in summer-time. After 1945, they were supplemented by the more powerful 2-10-0s of class Tr2, imported from Alco and Baldwin, and by the late 1960s, their use had declined, although some were employed into the early 1970s. Several of the class have been preserved.

160.A.1 2-12-0 FRENCH NATIONAL RAILWAYS (SNCF)

FRANCE 1940

André Chapelon, the greatest of all steam locomotive designers, was lucky and unlucky in his employers. The SNCF allowed him to produce two of the most remarkable steam designs (among many other excellent ones) but did not put either into line production. This six-cylinder steam locomotive was a fundamental rebuild of a 6000-class 2-10-0, from a class of four-cylinder compounds that had been running freight trains on the Paris–Orleans system since 1909. The aim was to produce a big freight engine that would perform economically at low speeds – something steam locomotives were historically very bad at doing. They could not be geared down like internal combustion-powered vehicles or even like the humble human-worked bicycle (in fact, starting off pedalling a fixed-wheel bicycle is a good parallel to setting a steam engine in motion). In the rebuilding, every effort was made to generate, to conserve, and to make the most effective use of steam. Six coupled axles were needed to give the long boiler and firebox adequate support with a sufficiently low maximum axle loading. Six

cylinders were considered necessary to provide the power and traction required, as a single pair of low-pressure cylinders would have had to be so large as to break the loading gauge. Four in-line low-pressure cylinders were set ahead of the first coupled axle, with the inside pair driving the second axle and the outside pair the third. The high-pressure cylinders, also inside, towards the middle of the locomotive, and receiving steam via a Houlet superheater, drove the fourth coupled axle. They had steam 'jackets' to retain maximum heat. The boiler was divided into two parts, an adaptation of the Italian Franco system, the front end being a pre-heating drum, from which almost-boiling water was fed by an overflow system into the main boiler. A Nicholson-type thermic syphon was fitted in the firebox. Exhaust steam drove the ACFI feed pump that supplied the pre-heater. Steam was re-superheated in a Schmidt superheater between the high-pressure and low-pressure cylinders. Lentz poppet valves were used to work the pistons, actuated by oscillating cams driven by Walschaerts gear, all of it outside the frames, with the hp

cylinders worked from the fourth coupled axle. Kylchap double exhaust pipes were fitted. The original frame was substantially reinforced as well as lengthened. The three driving axles were fixed, and the others had a degree of lateral movement to enable the long wheelbase to traverse curves.

Rebuilding began in 1936, but was not considered a high priority. It was not completed until June 1940, just before the German invasion, when the engine was stored away until after the war. Tests began in 1948, both on the Vitry static plant, and on the track, at the same time as Chapelon's other masterpiece, the 242 A1 4-8-4, was undergoing trials. The aim of the design was fully met. At low speeds, the locomotive showed no decline in thermal efficiency. Its fuel consumption went down, not up, as had been the norm hitherto. A valuable result, not anticipated, was that the steam jackets on the high-pressure cylinders, combined with moderate superheat in the low-pressure cylinders, removed the need for super-hot superheating, whose extremely high temperatures were a constant source of expensive damage to

castings, joints and lubricated surfaces.

Although speed was not a part of the brief, the engine recorded 95km/h (59mph) on test. The maximum actual tractive effort recorded on the move was of the order of 22,200kg (49,000lb). On one occasion, starting a 1686-tonne (1660-ton) train on a curving 1 in 125 gradient, the dynamometer car registered a tractive effort of 39,836kg (87,840lb). The 2-12-0 was inevitably a test engine, referred to by its designer as a laboratory. But no further conversions were authorized, and it remained a single-engine class until, two years after Chapelon had retired from the SNCF, it was scrapped in November 1955.

BOILER PRESSURE: 18.3kg/cm² (261psi)
CYLINDERS: hp and inside lp 520x540.6mm (20.5x21.3in); lp outside 640x649.75mm (25.2x25.6in)
DRIVING WHEELS: 1396mm (55in)
GRATE AREA: 4.4m² (47.4sq ft)
HEATING SURFACE: 218m² (2347sq ft)
SUPERHEATER: 174m² (1873sq ft)
TRACTIVE EFFORT: 25,167kg (55,490lb)
TOTAL WEIGHT: 152.1t (335,500lb) (engine only)

CLASS PC 4-6-2 IRAQ STATE RAILWAYS (ISR)

IRAQ 1940

Iraq was by the 1930s a British protectorate, and in 1939 four streamlined two-cylinder simple-expansion 'Pacifics' were ordered from Robert Stephenson & Hawthorns of Darlington, England. Despite war conditions, three reached Iraq in 1940; the fourth was lost *en route*. Handsome

engines, reminiscent both of the British 'Coronation' and A4 classes, they were intended for the completion of the line from Baghdad

BOILER PRESSURE: 15.4kg/cm² (220psi)
CYLINDERS: 533x660mm (21x26in)
DRIVING WHEELS: 1751mm (69in)

via Tel Kotchek into Turkey, the route of the 'Taurus Express' from Istanbul, and the engines were still operating the service in the 1950s.

GRATE AREA: 2.9m² (31.2sq ft)
HEATING SURFACE: 251.3m² (2706sq ft) (including supeheater)

The schedule was a distinctly slow one, taking altogether three days and nights to make the 2603km (1617-mile) journey.

SUPERHEATER: not known
TRACTIVE EFFORT: 14,092kg (31,074lb)
TOTAL WEIGHT: 100.2t (221,088lb)

CLASS E636 BO-BO-BO STATE RAILWAYS (FS)

ITALY 1940

Standardization of electric locomotive types and equipment was taken seriously in Italy, and manufacturers were required to work to designs supplied or approved by the Locomotive

Development Bureau. Four types of axle, one type of bogie and three types of axle-box were admitted for use. All locomotives used the same design of pantograph to pick up the 3000V DC system, which

became the national standard from 1934. There was one type of motor, with a one-hour rating of 350kW (476hp) at 700rpm, and a continuous rating of 315kW (428hp) at 730rpm. The two-

section articulated body mounted on three four-wheel bogies became a typical Italian design, and this form was continued in the subsequent E646/645 and E656 classes. A set of levers and springs rested the weight of the two parts on the central bogie, and the entire locomotive formed a statically controlled unit. Buffers and coupling gear were fixed to the locomotive frame, not to the outer bogies as in the preceding Class E626. The E626 was very much the prototype of the far more numerous Class E636, which amounted to almost 500 locomotives constructed in two phases, first from 1940 to 1942, then from 1952 until 1963. Most had frame-mounted flexible quill drive motors for 120km/h (75mph) work, but 49 were geared for 105km/h (65.6mph), with axle-hung nose-suspended motors.

In 2002, 300 E636 were still in service, largely employed on cargo business. However, until the late 1990s they were regularly used on passenger work, including heavy international expresses over mountain routes. In addition to the 469 built for the FS, 50 locomotives of the same design were delivered

to Yugoslavian Railways from 1960, as JZ Class 362. These were adapted for 120km/h (75mph) operation, with rheostatic braking, 2640kW (3587hp) continuous power and 18-tonne (17.7-ton) axle load. Though many detail improvements, like air-conditioned cabs and the removal of asbestos packing, were made up to 1996, the class had been completely phased out by 2006.

TYPE: Bo-Bo-Bo mixed-traffic
POWER: 2100kW (2853hp)
SUPPLY: 3000V DC
TRACTIVE EFFORT: low gear 113kN at 54km/h (25400lbf at 33.8mph); high gear 84kN at 45km/h (19000lbf at 45mph)
MAX. OPERATING SPEED: low gear 105km/h (65.6mph) or high gear 120km/h (75mph)
WEIGHT: 101t (222,705lb)
MAX. AXLE LOAD: 17 tonnes (37,485lb)
OVERALL LENGTH: 18.25m (59ft 6in)
GAUGE: 1435mm (4ft 8.5in)

Though no longer engaged in express passenger work, as here, locomotives of Class E636 are still in use on Italian railways.

DL109 V A1A-A1A VARIOUS RAILROADS

Like the other 'steam' builders, Alco had been building occasional diesels since the 1920s, with General Electric providing the electrical equipment. Having acquired the McIntosh & Seymour marine diesel corporation in 1929, Alco could build its own engines. Facing the challenge of the Electro-Motive 'E' range, it developed this high-speed road diesel-electric, with both 'A' units (with cab) and 'B' (without), and styled in a somewhat art-deco manner by Otto Kuhler.

Known by their specification numbers, the locomotives were designated DL103b to DL110, the most numerous being the DL109, of which 69 were built. The various DL locomotives had only minor differences. All were powered by two turbocharged six-cylinder in-line diesels with 317.5 x330.2mm (12.5x13in) bore, and stroke operating at 740rpm. With the advent of stringent wartime regulations, Alco had to cease production of the DL range and concentrated instead on making yard switchers and steam locomotives.

TYPE: A1A-A1A, diesel-electric
POWER AND OUTPUT: a pair of Alco 6-539T diesels producing 1492kW (2000hp)
TRACTIVE EFFORT: 136kN (30,500lbf) continuous TE at 32.2 km/h (20mph); 250kN (56,250lbf) starting TE
MAX. OPERATING SPEED: 192km/h (120mph) with 58:20 gear ratio
WEIGHT: 153t (337,365lb)
OVERALL LENGTH: 22.758m (74ft 6in)
GAUGE: 1435mm (4ft 8.5in)

A diesel-electric from a home better known for steam locomotives – a DL 109 of the New Haven Railroad.

S-2 TYPE BO-BO VARIOUS RAILROADS

USA 1940

In the 1940s, Alco had success with its S-type diesel switchers, and in the decade between 1940 and 1950 more than 1500 of the 746kW (1000hp) S-2 were put in service in North America. There was also the less powerful S-1s, of 448kW (600hp), which were superseded by the S-3. In 1950, S-2 was eventually superseded by the S-4 model.

South Buffalo RR Alco S2 locomotives Nos. 104 and 105 move a transfer freight of container wagons at Buffalo, NY, on 4 May, 1989.

All were powered by Alco's successful 539 engine and many had long careers. Like all Alco diesels of the period, they employed General Electric electrical components. The generator was a GE GT-533, while the traction motors were GE-731-D. Both the S-1 and S-2 models used the unusual Blunt trucks, while S-3, S-4 and later switcher models used variations of the more common Association of American Railroads truck design.

TYPE: diesel-electric
POWER: Alco six-cylinder 539 diesel producing 746kW (1000hp)
TRACTIVE EFFORT: 151kN (34,000lbf) at 12.9km/h (8mph) continuous TE; 307kN (69,000lbf) starting TE
MAX. OPERATING SPEED: N/A
WEIGHT: 104t (230,000lb)
OVERALL LENGTH: 13.862m (45ft 6in)
GAUGE: 1435mm (4ft 8.5in)

GENERAL ELECTRIC '44-TON' BO-BO VARIOUS RAILROADS

USA 1940

The diesel revolution had repercussions in unexpected ways. The weight of this engine was a prime selling point because of an industry agreement that all locomotives exceeding 40,909kg (90,000lb) must have a fireman. One-man operation was a huge cost-saving, and General Electric was one of several manufacturers offering a lightweight centre-cab diesel-electric switcher. Its 44-tonner was among the more popular models. Power came from two small eight-cylinder diesel engines, one at each end of the locomotive. Large railroads bought them for light branch line work and they were also used by short lines and industrial lines. More than 350 were built for domestic lines from 1940 to 1956.

TYPE: Bo-Bo, diesel-electric
POWER AND OUTPUT: a pair of Caterpillar D17000 eight-cylinder diesels rated between 207kW (350hp) and 305kW (410hp)
TRACTIVE EFFORT: 99 kW (22,280 lbf) starting TE
MAX. OPERATING SPEED: 56km/h (35mph)
WEIGHT: 40t (89,112lb)
OVERALL LENGTH: N/A
GAUGE: 1435mm (4ft 8.5in)

GE built a series of centre-cab Bo-Bo switchers in the 1940s. Here a Housatonic Railroad unit moves stock at Canaan, Connecticut, on the former Central New England line.

H-CLASS 4-8-4 'HEAVY HARRY' VICTORIAN RAILWAYS (VR)

No. 220 on the VR, this was the largest locomotive on the system, and also Australia's first 4-8-4. Three were planned, but only this one was built, at the Newport workshops. With American-style bar frames, and a Belpaire firebox, it was intended to haul the 'Overland' interstate express between Melbourne and Adelaide, but it almost always ran on freight service. Unusually for the time, it was a three-cylinder, though simple expansion, engine – most 4-8-4s were two cylinder locomotives. Another unusual feature was the separated double chimneys. 'Heavy Harry' had a hard-working career from 1941 to 1958 on fast goods trains between Melbourne and Wodonga, running 1,314,976km (817,126 miles in total). The tender was appropriately massive, running on two six-wheel bogies, and feeding into a mechanical stoker. 'Heavy Harry' is preserved at the Newport Railway Museum.

BOILER PRESSURE: 15.4kg/cm² (220psi)	**HEATING SURFACE:** 369.6m² (3980sq ft)
CYLINDERS: 546x711mm (21.5x28in)	**SUPERHEATER:** 72.4m² (780sq ft)
DRIVING WHEELS: 1624mm (67in)	**TRACTIVE EFFORT:** 24,946kg (55,008lb)
GRATE AREA: 6.3m² (68sq ft)	**TOTAL WEIGHT:** 264.2t (582,512lb)

'Heavy Harry' heads one of the locomotive line-ups at the Australian Railway History Society's North Williamstown Museum on 7 February 1979.

TYPE 97 2-12-2T GERMAN STATE RAILWAYS (DRG)

Powerful rack-rail crawlers, the two engines forming this class were built to haul ore trains. During the period of Austria's annexation by Germany, and the amalgamation of its railways into the DRG, Floridsdorf works built them and fitted them for rack and adhesion, working on the mineral line between Vordenberg and Eisenerz in the province of Styria. In the post-war revived ÖBB, they became Class 297. Two outside simple-expansion cylinders drove the rail wheels and two on the inside, of welded construction, drove the two rack wheels. These were governed by a separate regulator, so that they could come into action only over the rack sections of the track. The line was very steeply graded, climbing 440m (1338ft) in 8km (5 miles) from Vordenberg to the summit. Maximum speed on the rack section was 25km/h (15.5mph). Unusually for such a railway, it was laid to standard gauge, so that iron-ore wagons could be worked straight on to the Vienna-Villach main line. The engines were intended to work trains of 400 tonnes (393.6 tons) unaided up the grades, more than double the tonnage taken by the previous Class 197, designed by Karl Gölsdorf, which were also six-coupled but without front and rear carrying axles. But in daily operation the older engines were more reliable, and the 297s spent a lot of time in the repair shops. They were later fitted with Giesl ejectors. One has been preserved.

BOILER PRESSURE: 16kg/cm² (228psi)	**GRATE AREA:** 3.9m² (42sq ft)
CYLINDERS: outer 610x520mm (24x20.5in); inner 400x500mm (15.75x19.7in)	**HEATING SURFACE:** not known
	SUPERHEATER: not known
	TRACTIVE EFFORT: 25,620kg (56,500lb)
DRIVING WHEELS: 1030mm (40.5in)	**TOTAL WEIGHT:** 98 tonnes (216,090lb)

NOS. 153–7 2-8-2 DONNA TERESA CHRISTINA RAILWAY

BRAZIL 1941

Like many of Brazil's railways, this predominantly freight-carrying line was laid to metre-gauge in order to traverse difficult terrain, and 2-8-2s were well-suited to running on sinuous tracks. Alco works at Schenectady built these five 'Mikados', which were of relatively moderate power. They

were standard US-style locomotives, scaled down to the narrow gauge, with bar frames and two outside simple-expansion cylinders. By the later 1950s, they were definitely underpowered for the traffic requirements, but were not officially withdrawn until 1984, though little used in their latter years.

BOILER PRESSURE: 12.6kg/m² (180psi)
CYLINDERS: 406x558mm (16x22in)
DRIVING WHEELS: 1066mm (42in)
GRATE AREA: 4.42m² (47.6sq ft)
HEATING SURFACE: 92.9m² (1000.5sq ft)

SUPERHEATER: 19.8m² (213sq ft)
TRACTIVE EFFORT: 9305kg (20,517lb)
TOTAL WEIGHT: 57.8t (127,500lb)
(engine only)

The No. 153 of the Donna Teresa Christina's Schenectady-built 'Mikados' shunts a line of coal trucks in the sidings at Tubarao.

CLASS 11 4-10-0 BULGARIAN STATE RAILWAYS (BDZ)

BULGARIA 1941

Not many 4-10-0s were built, and the engines of this class were a Bulgarian design, incorporating the three-cylinder simple-expansion pattern established by the BDZ in 1935 as standard for its big engines. Most came from German builders, 10

from Henschel in 1941 and 12 more in 1943 from Borsig and Skoda (then under German control). Intended for heavy trains of either passengers or freight, the Class 11's primary route was the steeply graded international main line from Sofia to Belgrade, over

the Dragoman Pass. German-style smoke deflectors were fitted, but

BOILER PRESSURE: 16kg/cm² (228psi)
CYLINDERS: 520x700mm (20.5x27.5in)
DRIVING WHEELS: 1450mm (45in)
GRATE AREA: 4.9m² (52.75sq ft)

also a Bulgarian flared semi-collar chimney cap.

HEATING SURFACE: 224m² (2411.7sq ft)
SUPERHEATER: 83.9m² (903.3sq ft)
TRACTIVE EFFORT: 22,570kg (49,770lb)
TOTAL WEIGHT: 109.6t (241,668lb)

19-1001 2-8-2 GERMAN STATE RAILWAYS (DRG)

Henschel, who prided themselves on being at the cutting edge of steam technology, were developing this experimental type at their works in Kassel in the early stages of World War II, but it was set aside in the drive to build war engines. It was an eight-cylinder locomotive, each driving axle being turned by a two-cylinder V-format driving unit suspended from the main frame, outside the wheels. Piston valves operated the cylinders by means of eccentrics, the eccentric shaft being chain-driven from a main crankshaft. It was never completed to the point where testing could be carried out. After 1945, American forces removed the locomotive to Fort Monroe, USA, where little attention was paid to it, and it was broken up in 1952.

BOILER PRESSURE: 20kg/cm² (2284psi)	(2580.75sq ft)
CYLINDERS: 300x300mm (11.8x11.8in)	**SUPERHEATER:** 100m² (1076.6sq ft)
DRIVING WHEELS: 1244mm (49in)	**TRACTIVE EFFORT:** N/A
GRATE AREA: 4.5m² (49sq ft)	**TOTAL WEIGHT:** 96.5t (212,782lb)
HEATING SURFACE: 239.7m²	(engine only)

'MERCHANT NAVY' CLASS 4-6-2 SOUTHERN RAILWAY (SR)

Superbly restored to 'original' rebuilt condition, 'Merchant Navy' No. 35028 Clan Line approaches Sherborne from Salisbury with a special charter, 'The Blackmore Vale Express', on 11 October 1986.

The SR's locomotive chief, Oliver Bulleid, was a determined innovator of steam power on a largely electrified system. He saw this 'Pacific' type as a new-generation locomotive to work in an era when trains loading up to 610 tonnes (600 tons) would be hauled at average speeds of 113km/h (70mph). It was a bold but prescient vision.

Bulleid was an authority on welding, and much weight was saved by welded construction of an all-steel firebox and boiler. The three simple-expansion cylinders were operated by piston valves, actuated in turn by a unique chain-driven valve gear devised by Bulleid, enclosed within an oil-tight casing that also enclosed the middle connecting-road, crosshead and crank. This feature was to present many repair and maintenance problems; it was extraordinary that in a time of war,

some 200 new engines could be built with an untried and inaccessible system for such a crucial part of the works. Lemaître multiple-blast chimneys were fitted, and disc-type balanced wheels rather than the traditional spoked sort. Many useful minor features new to British operation were also included: power-operated fire-doors and reverser,

luminous gauge-dials, electric light, even windscreen wipers. The 'Merchant Navies' were followed by a lighter-weight 'West Country' class, 110 strong, of the same design (including the Canadian-developed Boxpok wheels) and intended for cross-country passenger services. Both types were heavy coal and oil users, and frequent breakdowns through

unreliability of the valve gear had to be balanced against the steam-raising capacity of the excellent boiler, and their undoubted ability to run fast.

Eventually, after Bulleid's departure, all the Merchant Navy and many of the West Country classes were rebuilt without the outer casing and with three sets of conventional Walschaerts gear, in which form they proved more reliable and easier to maintain, and turned in many excellent performances. Unconverted and converted examples have been preserved.

BOILER PRESSURE: 19.75kg/cm² (280psi)
CYLINDERS: 457x609mm (18x24in)

DRIVING WHEELS: 1880mm (74in)
GRATE AREA: 4.5m² (48.5sq ft)
HEATING SURFACE: 236m² (2451sq ft)

SUPERHEATER: 76.3m² (822sq ft)
TRACTIVE EFFORT: 17,233kg (38,000lb)
TOTAL WEIGHT: 96.25t (212,240lb)

CLASS CC CO-CO SOUTHERN RAILWAY (SR)

GREAT BRITAIN 1941

For the few locomotive-hauled services on its electrified lines, the SR built three electric locomotives, the first emerging in 1941. They were numbered CC1 and CC2 (later BR Nos. 20001 and 20002). A third, No. 20003, came from Brighton works in 1949. A motor-generator set, with a flywheel to maintain smooth output, was used to convert the 660V DC conductor-rail current into the lower voltages required at

the traction motors in the acceleration phase. By varying the excitation of the motor field windings through the action of the driver's controller, the generator could be driven at slower speeds, thus producing lower voltage. The flywheel had a secondary advantage in that it kept the motor-generator set spinning as the locomotive traversed gaps in the third rail. The last of the trio was withdrawn in 1968.

TYPE: Co-Co mixed-traffic mainline electric locomotive
POWER: 660V DC conductor rail collection; 1095kW (1470hp); motor-generator control; six axle-hung DC traction motors
TRACTIVE EFFORT: 178 and 200kN* (40,000 and 45,000lbf*)
MAX. OPERATING SPEED: 120km/h

(75mph)
WEIGHT: 102 and 107t* (223,440 and 234,640lb*)
MAX AXLE LOAD: 17.8 tonnes (39,249lb)
OVERALL LENGTH: 17,295mm (56ft 9in)
GAUGE: 1435mm (4ft 8.5in)
* Second figure for 20003

Under the ironwork and glass of London's Victoria Station, No. 2002 stands at the head of a boat train for Newhaven Harbour, one of the regular duties of this class.

USATC SWITCHER 0-6-0T UNITED STATES ARMY TRANSPORTATION CORPS (USATC)   USA 1941

The demands of wartime use brought this small locomotive on to the tracks of many different countries. The USATC had always had a small stock of locomotives, both steam and diesel, but this increased dramatically in the course of World War II. This side-tank design was one of the USATC's standards. Three US

BOILER PRESSURE: 14.7kg/cm² (210psi)
CYLINDERS: 419x609mm (16.5x24in)
DRIVING WHEELS: 1370mm (54in)
GRATE AREA: 1.8m² (19.4sq ft)

HEATING SURFACE: 81.3m² (876sq ft)
TRACTIVE EFFORT: 9810kg (21,630lb)
TOTAL WEIGHT: 45.6t (100,650lb)

builders – Davenport, Vulcan and Porter – built 382 for military use, and they became a familiar sight, especially in Greek and Yugoslavian station yards after the end of the war. Built for service in Britain, Europe and the Middle East, they conformed to the British loading gauge, but with two sand-boxes and a dome on one short boiler, plus a stovepipe chimney, they had a characteristically American look. The two outside cylinders were operated by Walschaerts gear.

The first ones arrived in England in July 1942. During 1943, 30 oil-fired engines were sent for work in the Middle East, operating in Iraq, Palestine and Egypt, and some of them remained in civilian service after 1945. Four were supplied to the Jamaican Government Railways in 1943–45. After the war, 13 were acquired by the Southern Railway, for working in Southampton Docks, and some of these remained active until 1967. The USATC Switcher also appears to have influenced the outside-cylinder design of the Great Western's 1948 Class 1500 0-6-0T. Seventy-seven were bought by the French SNCF, where some lasted until 1971. Yugoslavia received 120, and added another 23 to the same plans in 1956–57. Twenty went to Greece, where some were converted to tender 0-6-0s. Several examples are preserved, in Britain and other countries.

The short wheelbase of the 0-6-0T made it a popular locomotive for use in dockyards in countries from Great Britain to Greece.

CLASS J 4-8-4 NORFOLK & WESTERN RAILWAY (N&W)   USA 1941

Of all the American railroads, the N&W worked hardest to modernize and retain its steam fleet, striving to match the levels of availability and use promised by the diesel-electric builders. It was, after all, a coal-hauling line. Its stud of express engines was not large, but their quality was first class. Eleven of Class J were built between 1941 and 1943 to handle the line's principal passenger trains, and a further two were built in 1950, North America's last passenger express engines to be constructed. By 1950, the first example had run well over 1,609,000km (1,000,000 miles) in service.

Designed and built in the raiload's own workshops, these engines were designed to travel about 386,000km (240,000 miles) before major overhaul. To many operators of steam locomotives, such figures would have seemed like science fiction. But intensive, detailed planning went into this design. It was a two-cylinder simple-expansion engine with no mechanical frills or oddities, but with probably the most effective lubrication system of any steam locomotive. Automatic lubrication took care of over two hundred bearing surfaces, supplied from a 24-gallon tank that needed refilling every 2414km (1500

miles) – hardly more than three days' running. Other aspects of the design, like internal steam passages and valve events, had been scientifically worked out. High standards of shed maintenance and preparation matched those of design and build, and paid off for the N&W in terms of efficient and cost-effective service.

In the end, N&W could not buck the trend, but its steam services were all the more distinguished because of the hilly terrain in which they operated. The Class J was recorded as having reached 177km/h (110mph) on a test run with 1041 tonnes (1025 tons) on

the Pennsylvania Railroad near Crestline, and speeds of up to 145km/h (90mph) in regular service with 14- or 15-car trains were also recorded. By the time the Js were taken out of service in 1959, two had exceeded 3,218,000km (2,000,000 miles). No. 611 is preserved.

BOILER PRESSURE: 21kg/cm² (300psi)
CYLINDERS: 685x812mm (27x32in)
DRIVING WHEELS: 1776mm (70in)
GRATE AREA: 10m² (107.7sq ft)
HEATING SURFACE: 489.6m² (5271sq ft)
SUPERHEATER: 202.2m² (2177sq ft)
TRACTIVE EFFORT: 39,506kg (80,000lb)
TOTAL WEIGHT: 431t (872,600lb)

CLASS 4000 4-8-8-4 UNION PACIFIC RAILROAD (UP)

USA 1941

Some engines had more wheels, some had bigger firegrates, but for most people the Class 4000 were the 'Big Boys' – the name was chalked by an unknown employee of Alco on a smokebox door during construction, and it stuck. They were the largest and most powerful steam locomotives ever built. Although Union Pacific was an early user of diesel locomotives for its passenger express trains, it did not begin to use diesels for freight until 1947. In this department, steam was still unchallenged. The requirements were severe, however. The design was worked out by the company's Research & Standards department in close association with Alco, which built the 25 engines of the class. The moving spirit was Otto Jabelmann, the UP's head of motive power and machinery since 1936, and vice-president in charge of research and mechanical standards since 1939. He had also overseen the design of other giant locomotives, including the 'Challenger' 4-6-6-4s of 1936, which preceded the 'Big Boys'. Although it continued to order 'Challengers', UP did not feel it had yet reached the ultimate point of steam power, and the 4-8-8-4 was conceived as an enlarged 'Challenger', longer and heavier, with a vast firebox extending forward over the two rear coupled

Class leader of the 'Big Boys' – Union Pacific's 4000. Its driver gives an idea of the scale of this giant.

axles. The frame was a huge single cast steel piece. Welding was extensively used in the building, notably in the construction of the boiler, pressed to a higher level than the 'Challenger's' 19.7kg/cm^2 (280psi). Multiple-jet exhausts fed out through a double chimney. All axles were fitted with roller bearings. A very significant new feature was the redesign of the joint between the front truck and the frame to allow lateral movement only. Any changes in gradient or unevenness in the track were absorbed by a highly effective suspension system. This solved the problem that all 'Mallet' types had tended to suffer from, of sudden transfer of weight from one set of driving wheels to the other, and a final batch of 'Challengers' incorporated the same feature. The 4000's operating requirements were defined by the UP's mountainous Sherman Hill main line through the Wasatch Mountains between Ogden, Utah, and Green River, Wyoming, a 283km (176-mile) stretch rising from 596m (1933ft) to 2444m (8013ft) with a ruling grade of 1 in 83. Turntables of 135ft (41m) length, the world's longest, were installed at Green River and Ogden, and later at other depots, to turn

the giants. The 'Big Boys' hauled trains of up to 70 refrigerated fruit cars, weighing some 3251 tonnes (3200 tons), over the road without assistance. On one observed trip, No. 4015 with 70 loaded fruit cars totalling 2910 tons (2956 tonnes) covered the 122.3km (76 miles) between Ogden and Evanston, with an average rising grade of 1 in 167, in 3hr, 55min, including a 23-minute refuelling halt. Its fuel consumption, through two mechanical stokers, was between 10.2 tonnes and 11.2 tonnes (10–11 tons) per hour, and it used between 50.8 and 55.9 tonnes (50–55 tons) of water in the same period.

The 'Big Boys' developed full power output at 112km/h (70mph), though they could operate at up to 130km/h (80mph). This maximum equated to around 7460kW (10,000hp) developed in the cylinders, an output beyond that of any other steam locomotive and far beyond that of contemporary diesel units. But at low speeds, they were unable to exert their full power potential. This was the perennial problem of the steam locomotive: at the crucial phases of starting off and accelerating with a heavy train, the 4000s were unable to

put more than half their tractive potential to use. Steam designers might have shrugged this off in previous years, but now it was a serious disadvantage in comparisons with the competing diesel-electrics, which though individually much less powerful, could be worked multiple-unit, and could deploy full power over a much wider spectrum of speeds. Despite this, the Big Boys were effective in service and the first batch, built in 1941, all achieved more than 1,609,000km (1 million miles) of running. Wartime traffic gave them much heavier loads, and they often worked double-headed, a stirring sight and sound, as they swung up the grade. Their last revenue-earning duties were completed in July 1959, and withdrawal began from 1961. Four survived at Green River depot until July 1962. Eight are preserved as static museum and display items.

BOILER PRESSURE: 21kg/cm^2 (300psi)
CYLINDERS: 603x812mm (23.75x32in)
DRIVING WHEELS: 1726mm (68in)
GRATE AREA: 14m^2 (150.3sq ft)
HEATING SURFACE: 547m^2 (5889sq ft)
SUPERHEATER: 229m^2 (2466sq ft)
TRACTIVE EFFORT: 61,394kg (135,375lb)
TOTAL WEIGHT: 350t (772,000lb) (engine only)

NORTH SHORE 'ELECTRO-LINER' CHICAGO, NORTH SHORE & MILWAUKEE RAILROAD

USA 1941

Long a familiar part of the US city scene, inter-urban lines were eventually killed off by the bus and motor car. North Shore was one of the last to go, finally ending operations in 1963. It linked its namesake cities on a direct route running parallel to the Chicago & North Western and Milwaukee Road steam railroad lines. The North Shore line tied into Chicago's famous 'Loop' – a third rail electrified rapid transit line operated in later years by the

Chicago Transit authority. In Milwaukee, it reached downtown by way of street trackage. Competition on the 145km (90-mile) run was intense, and to push up its traffic share the North Shore followed the lead of other railways and bought bright, streamlined trains to attract

passengers. Two four-car streamlined articulated trains were constructed for it by St Louis Car Company using Westinghouse electrical components. Named the 'Electro-Liners' and painted in a distinctive aqua and salmon livery, they made multiple round trips

daily over the route, supplementing the line's intensive Chicago–Milwaukee service. In 1963, the Electro-Liners were sold to Philadelphia's Red Arrow Lines, where they were known as 'Liberty-Liners', and worked into the 1980s. Both trains have been preserved.

TYPE: high-speed articulated four-car electric train
POWER: 650V DC via trolley wire or third rail

TRACTIVE EFFORT: N/A
MAX. OPERATING SPEED: 136km/h (85mph)
WEIGHT: 95.5t (210,500lb)

OVERALL LENGTH: 47.346m (155ft 4in)
MAX. AXLE LOAD: 9.7t (21,380lb)
GAUGE: 1435mm (4ft 8.5in)

RS-1 BO-BO ROCK ISLAND RAILROAD

USA 1941

Until the early 1940s, diesels, like steam locomotives, had been seen as either road engines or yard switchers. It fell to Alco to show that both functions could be combined in a single diesel-electric type. Confined to building yard diesels with a maximum power of 746kW (1000hp), it made a virtue of necessity with its immensely influential RS-1 design. First built for the Rock Island, it was the first road-switcher – working equally well as a road diesel or yard switcher. Over almost two decades

more than 400 RS-1s were built for North American railroads, but very many more of similar design and power were sold by other manufacturers. Versatility was the key to its success. By 1949, all the major builders were offering road switcher types, and by the 1950s it had become the dominant type bought by American railroads. Today, still, nearly all freight diesels are variations on the same

theme. A variation of the type known as an RSD-1 used a Co-Co wheel arrangement. During World War II, Alco built a fleet of these for the Soviet railways. As a result, post-war Russian diesel development was a direct outgrowth of the RS-1. The RS-1 was powered by a development of the reliable 539 diesel engine and had a maximum road speed of 96.6km/h (60mph).

TYPE: Bo-Bo, diesel-electric
POWER AND OUTPUT: Alco 6-539 diesel producing 746kW (1000hp)
TRACTIVE EFFORT: 151kN (34,000lbf) continuous TE at 12.9km/h (8mph); 264kN (59,500lbf) starting TE.
MAX. OPERATING SPEED: 96.6km/h (60mph) with 75:16 gear ratio
WEIGHT: 108 tonnes (238,000lb)
OVERALL LENGTH: N/A
GAUGE: 1435mm (4ft 8.5in)

As No. 405 of the Green Mountain Railroad, a preserved RS-1 pauses with a period passenger train at Chester, Vermont, on 7 October 1992.

CLASS 52 2-10-0 GERMAN STATE RAILWAYS (DRG)

There is very little that can be done to a steam locomotive to turn it into a military machine, but the value of railways and trains in supporting military campaigns was realized in very early days. In the major wars of the twentieth century, with whole nations mobilized in a high concentration of effort, the contribution of railways was vital. *Kriegslokomotive* is German for 'war engine', and the Class 52 is the classic example of the kind. Its genesis was in the *Deutsche Reichsbahn Gesellschaft* (DRG) Class 50 2-10-0 heavy freight locomotive of 1938, very much in the DRG tradition, with bar frames, round-top boiler, and wide firebox. In late 1939, production of this line was stepped up, with a modified design to speed up building. It was classed as 50ÜK ('transitional war locomotive'), and a total of 3164 were built. In 1941, with a severe shortage of motive power, a massive increase in locomotive production was demanded. The only way to achieve this was to produce a new design that could be built much faster. The details of Class 52 were worked out by a technical group from the DRG and

the principal manufacturers. The prototype was built by Borsig: a two-cylinder engine, with simple expansion and Walschaerts gear operating piston valves. Speed of construction, and the minimum use of materials consistent with durability were essential. Welding was used to a greater extent than in any previous locomotive; they had completely welded boilers and welding was used wherever possible to join parts that would once have been riveted or bolted together. Emphasizing the 'no extras, no frills' approach that typified the whole design, the steam-pipes and steam chest above the cylinders were square-shaped. From 1943, lightweight small smoke deflectors of the type developed by Friedrich Witte were fitted to the smokebox sides and made the engines look less gaunt. All German manufacturers except the bomb-damaged Krupps built the Class 52, as did the German-occupied Skoda works at Plzen in Czechoslovakia, Graffenstaden in France, and the Polish Chrzanov and Cegielski works. It was never a totally homogeneous class. The different makers, and a stream of revised detail instructions, ensured

considerable variety, apart from the major amendments for specific purposes that formed effective sub-classes. Most of the 52s had plate frames, of steel 30mm (1.2in) thick, much thinner than the 80mm (3.1in) bar frames of the Class 50. Between 1942 and 1945, about 6700 were built.

For the Russian front, a number of special features, including a chimney cowl, insulation of outside-mounted pumps, fully enclosed cab and, in some cases, insulated tender tanks, were fitted to some of the first *Kriegsloks*. Feedwater heaters, standard on the Class 50, were not, however, fitted to the Class 52s. Another variant was fitted with a condensing tender to run supply trains to the German armies fighting on the Russian front, as the retreating Soviets had razed all their engine sheds and refuelling facilities, and sufficient water supplies were hard to come by. Armour plating was fitted to some of these engines. Some Russian lines were re-gauged to standard by the Germans, but around 1500 of the Class 52s were fitted with axles for the Russian 1524mm (5ft) gauge.

The original version was coal-fired, but an oil-burner later appeared. This had a tank fitted

in and around the coal bunker space on the tender. From 1943, the standard tender for the class was the welded Type 914, known as the *Wanne*, or 'bath-tub', from its rounded sides. A remarkable piece of design in itself, riding on two four-wheel bogies, it could be built in one-third of the time of a conventional tender, held more coal and water, and used less metal in construction. Its capacity was 10 tonnes (9.8 tons) of coal and 7000gals (8400 US) of water. The Class 52s had a maximum speed of 80km/h (50mph), running either forwards or backwards. They were involved in an intensive network of conventional freight trains running normal goods services, in addition to rostered or special supply trains carrying military equipment. They were also among the locomotives involved in the dark, secret and hideous business of hauling trainloads of human beings over new lines laid right into the concentration and death camps. Over a thousand operated under military direction in the eastern occupied territories; and some hundreds of others were sold or sent on loan to Croatia, Hungary, Romania, Serbia and Turkey. The *Kriegsloks* were used in all German-controlled regions before May

More of the *Kriegsloks* have been preserved than of any other class of locomotive – this is an example from the Deutsche Reichsbahn.

1945, including Norway. After the defeat of Germany, large numbers were taken over by the liberated nations, and 2130 were held in Russia. Construction on a limited scale went on until 1951, including around 150 built in Poland, 100 in Belgium and 84 in West Germany.

Though the *Kriegsloks* were built in the anticipation of a short if busy life, their construction proved robust enough to ensure many years of service. In Germany itself, the stock was divided between the Federal and Democratic Republics, operating the *Deutsche Bundesbahn* (DB) and *Deutsche Reichsbahn* (DR) systems respectively. The DB phased its Class 52s out rapidly

after 1954. Their life on the DR was much longer; the 52s formed the DR's most numerous steam class, and 20 were rebuilt between 1960 and 1967 in the DR *Rekolok*, 'rebuilt loco' programme, with new all-welded standard boilers, Heinl feedwater heaters and such refinements of detail as rotating spectacle glasses in the front lookout windows. Some also received double Giesl blast pipes and chimneys. Twenty-five were adapted to burn pulverized brown coal – a hopeful experimental treatment also carried out in other countries, including Australia, that never yielded satisfactory results. The last unmodified Class 52s remained in service until the

1980s, and some of the rebuilds were only retired with the final abandonment of steam traction in the DDR.

On most Eastern European systems, the Class 52s ran into the 1970s or even later. They were widely deployed in the western Soviet Union and its satellite states until the late 1950s, with many converted to oil firing. On the Yugoslavian system they were designated Class 33 and were the largest single class on the JDZ. After the collapse of Yugoslavia, some were brought from storage into active use in Bosnia during the mid-1990s.

The furthest-flung were 12 from Russia and Poland, supplied to

North Vietnam around 1984. Some of the longest-lived specimens were in Turkey, until 1990. In the late 1990s, large numbers were still in several East European countries, and perhaps as many as 200 have been selected or bought for preservation in numerous countries.

BOILER PRESSURE: 16kg/cm² (228psi)
CYLINDERS: 600x660mm (23.6x26in)
DRIVING WHEELS: 1400mm (55in)
GRATE AREA: 3.9m² (42sq ft)
HEATING SURFACE: 177.6m² (1912sq ft)
SUPERHEATER: 63.7m² (685.8sq ft)
TRACTIVE EFFORT: 23,140kg (51,000lb)
TOTAL WEIGHT: 84t (185,220lb)
(engine only)

Q1 0-6-0 SOUTHERN RAILWAY (SR)

GREAT BRITAIN 1942

Replicating a once-familiar scene: a preserved Southern Q1 with a traditional-style freight train, photographed in June 1994.

Distinctive, like all of Oliver Bulleid's designs, this wartime engine was Britain's most powerful 0-6-0 type, produced as a 'general utility' locomotive. The main reason for the lack of running plate and other features, was that the boiler and firebox were large and proportionally heavy. As with his 'Merchant

Navy' Pacifics, Bulleid made use of welding techniques to save on weight and building time. It also had cast steel Boxpok wheels of the same type as the larger engines. With its 18.8-tonne (18.5-ton) maximum axle loading, the Q1 had 93 per cent availability over the entire Southern system. The two

cylinders, set inside, had piston valves actuated by Stephenson's link motion. The inward tapering dog-bowl chimney crowned a five-jet blast-pipe nozzle. Although chiefly intended for freight work, train heating equipment was fitted, and the Q1, though used only on local services, could reach 120km/h (75mph).

BOILER PRESSURE: 16.1kg/cm² (230psi)
CYLINDERS: 482x660mm (19x26in)
DRIVING WHEELS: 1548mm (61in)
GRATE AREA: 2.5m² (27sq ft)
HEATING SURFACE: 152.5m² (1642sq ft)
SUPERHEATER: 20.2m² (218sq ft)
TRACTIVE EFFORT: 13,086kg (26,500lb)
TOTAL WEIGHT: 89.8t (182,000lb)

CLASS V4   2-6-2 LONDON & NORTH EASTERN RAILWAY (LNER)

Production of this three-cylinder mixed-traffic class, intended for wide usage and route availability, was abruptly halted on the death of its designer, Sir Nigel Gresley. His successor as chief mechanical engineer replaced it with his own

design: the two-cylinder B1 4-6-0, also of 1942, which was built in large numbers. Only two V4s were built. It was a simple-expansion design, with Gresley's conjugated valve gear working the inside cylinder. It incorporated such other

late-Gresleyan features as a steam collector behind the dome. The first two engines, as prototypes, had different fireboxes, the first of

copper, the second of welded steel. They ran mostly in Scotland, and were withdrawn for scrapping in 1957 and 1958.

The second of the pair, numbered 61701, at Ferryhill locomotive depot, Aberdeen, in the 1950s. The first was officially named *Bantam Cock*; this one was known as 'Bantam Hen'.

BOILER PRESSURE: 17.5kg/cm² (250psi)	**HEATING SURFACE:** 134m² (1444sq ft)
CYLINDERS: 380x660mm (15x26in)	**SUPERHEATER:** 33m² (356sq ft)
DRIVING WHEELS: 1725mm (68in)	**TRACTIVE EFFORT:** 11,950kg (24,200lb)
GRATE AREA: 2.6m² (28.5sq ft)	**TOTAL WEIGHT:** 114.9t (253,456lb)

CLASS 151.3101   2-10-2 SPANISH NATIONAL RAILWAYS (RENFE)

Spain in the later 1930s, racked and impoverished by civil war, built relatively few new locomotive types, and conserved its veterans. But there was need for heavy freight engines, and the Spanish firm La Maquinista built 22 of this class between 1942 and 1945. Originally numbered 5001–5022, they were soon afterwards renumbered as 151.3101–3122. It is hard to define a Spanish look in locomotives, though they tended towards a massive appearance, with large boilers on small wheels.

French, British, American and German influence all played a part in Spanish locomotive design, and in this one, perhaps, a French air predominated. It was a three-cylinder simple, all three in line, the inside cylinder driving the second coupled axle and the outside ones driving the third. Walschaerts valve gear was fitted, operating Lentz oscillating cam poppet valves. Kylchap blast pipes exhausted into a double chimney. A degree of flexibility was given to the long wheelbase by a Krauss

truck, linking the front carrying axle and the leading coupled axle. ACFI feed water pumps and heaters were fitted, most of the equipment being on the running plate – on the Spanish gauge of 1676mm (5ft 6in), and with generous clearances, there was

room to spare. Two of the class had mechanical stokers, and seven were oil burners. First deployed on coal trains from the mining area of Ponferrada to the coast at La Coruña, they were later were transferred to work between León and Venta de Banos.

BOILER PRESSURE: 16kg/cm² (228psi)	**HEATING SURFACE:** 267.6m² (2880sq ft)
CYLINDERS: 570x750mm (22.4x29.5in)	**SUPERHEATER:** 140.9m² (1516.6sq ft)
DRIVING WHEELS: 1560mm (61.5in)	**TRACTIVE EFFORT:** 21,150kg (46,640lb)
GRATE AREA: 5.3m² (57sq ft)	**TOTAL WEIGHT:** 213.1t (470,000lb)

4-6-2   ROYAL SIAMESE RAILWAYS (RSR)

Baldwin and Hanomag had both supplied 'Pacifics' to Thailand following the RSR's first 4-6-2s for the metre gauge, which came from

North British in Glasgow in 1917. In 1942, during the Japanese occupation of Thailand, 10 new 4-6-2s were supplied, from Hitachi

and Nippon Sharyo. Standardized as much as possible with the railway's Japanese-built 2-8-2s (supplied 1936–42), they were

finely finished compared with Japanese engines built for home use at this time, boasting copper chimney caps. In the post-war era,

Nippon Sharyo built a further 30 of this wood-burning class between 1949–50. Two-cylindered, simple expansion, with Walschaerts valve gear, they were robust engines that served well in express services until steam was ended on the Thai railways in 1982.

BOILER PRESSURE: 13kg/cm² (185psi)
CYLINDERS: 450x610mm (17.7x24in)
DRIVING WHEELS: 1372mm (54in)
GRATE AREA: N/A
HEATING SURFACE: 134.5m² (1448sq ft)
SUPERHEATER: 40.7m² (438.2sq ft)
TRACTIVE EFFORT: 8780kg (19,360lb)
TOTAL WEIGHT: 58t (127,890lb)
(engine only)

Last of the post-war batch of Japanese-built 'Pacifics', No. 850 was built in 1950, and was converted on delivery from wood to oil-firing. It normally ran between Haat Yai and Bangkok.

CLASS H8 2-6-6-6 CHESAPEAKE & OHIO RAILWAY (C&O)　　　　　　　　USA 1942

The cold wind of diesel competition was wafting round the US steam builders, but big new steam types were still appearing. The Chesapeake & Ohio were contemplating the purchase of further 'Texas' type 2-10-4 locomotives for coal-hauling on its Allegheny Division, which had long steep grades both ways between Hinton, West Virginia, and Clifton Forge, Virginia, when Lima proposed something both newer and more powerful.

The Class H8 was an articulated four-cylinder simple-expansion 2-6-6-6, with 12 driving wheels and a big six-wheel bogie that

supported a huge firebox 4568mm (15ft) long. Outside bearings were fitted on all the carrying wheels. Ten were ordered from Lima and delivered in December 1941, gaining the 'Allegheny' name from the mountains through which they worked.

In operation, one 'Allegheny' leading and one pushing could move a 140-car loaded coal train, of almost 10,160 tonnes (10,000 tons) up the mountain from the Hinton terminal. At the top, the pusher would be taken off, turned around and sent back to Hinton. The leading locomotive could handle the descent to Clifton

Forge, where it would be turned around for a return trip with a train of empty coal cars. The Class H8s were also known to take trains of up to 5200 tonnes (5130 tons) unaided, and Lima publicity claimed 5888kW (8000hp) for them. Twenty-three were fitted witth steam heating for passenger service, since their big driving wheels gave them a good turn of speed, but uses in passenger service were rare.

Somewhat overshadowed by the appearance of the Union Pacific's 'Big Boys' at much the same time, the 2-6-6-6s were also among the supreme examples of steam power.

Altogether 68 locomotives were built up to 1949, including eight for the Virginian Railroad in 1944, but the last examples had a short life, all being withdrawn by mid-1956. Two C&O Alleghenies are preserved.

BOILER PRESSURE: kg/cm² (260psi)
CYLINDERS: 571x837.5mm (22.5x33in)
DRIVING WHEELS: 1700mm (67in)
GRATE AREA: 12.4m² (133.3sq ft)
HEATING SURFACE: 631m² (6794sq ft)
SUPERHEATER: 115m² (2922sq ft)
TRACTIVE EFFORT: 49,970kg (110,200lb)
TOTAL WEIGHT: 498.3t (1,098,840lb)

CLASS TC S160 2-8-0 US ARMY TRANSPORTATION CORPS (USATC)　　　　USA 1942

Coming to grips with the fact that a vast logistical operation was needed to underpin the country's war effort, the USATC concentrated on four basic locomotive types, of which this was one. Between 1942 and 1945, 2120 of the TC S160 class and its variants were built to standard gauge by the three major US builders: Alco, Baldwin and Lima. By American standards, it was a small engine, built to fit within the tight British loading gauge, but a wholly American design: bar frames, two outside simple-expansion cylinders, operated by piston valves, actuated by Walschaerts gear, a high-set boiler and a wide, round-topped steel firebox. Steam brakes plus a Westinghouse air brake pump were fitted, with air cylinders placed

under the running plate on each side. The compressor pump was fitted to the left of a narrowed smokebox door. On the engines used in Britain, dual air/vacuum brake equipment was fitted. Fireboxes were fitted with rocking grates and hopper ashpans. On the boiler top, dome and sandbox were in a single housing. The standard American three-point suspension system gave them a stable ride even over ill-maintained and bomb-blasted tracks.

Several American 'convenience' fittings made the locomotives popular with British and European crews, though there was no power reverser. The great majority were coal burners, though some oil-burners were built or converted, including 106 for the south-west region of France, which had oil-

fuelling facilities. The design was a very sound one, with only one significant defect that emerged with time – a weakness in the screw fixing of the firebox roof stays, that caused a number of firebox collapses.

Britain was the first overseas destination, partly to provide extra motive power under the Lease-Lend scheme, partly as a holding base for the invasion of Europe. A total of 139 went to Oran by mid-July 1943. By late 1944, they were being shipped to the continent in large numbers to operate in liberated and Allied territory. Two Military Railway Services (MRS) control departments kept track of their locations and allocated their functions, together with those of other military locomotives. Apart from military use, they were

loaned to supplement deficiencies in available power on civilian services. Usage was at a peak in 1945; then, as hostilities ceased in Europe, many were gathered together in a 'dump' at Louvain, Belgium and also at other depots. A vast redistribution took place. Almost the only country not to take some into permanent service was France. Thirty went to the ÖBB in Austria, 244 to Italy, 27 to Greece, 65 to Yugoslavia, 40 to the DB in Germany, 50 to the TCDD in Turkey, 80 to Czechoslovakia, about 500 to MÁV in Hungary and a similar quantity to PKP in Poland, 101 to South Korea, and 25 to China. Around 30 remained at work on the Tunisian and Algerian railways. The remainder probably ended up in Russia, joining the 200 that had been sent directly there in the course of 1943 (wheeled to fit the 1524mm/5ft gauge). Another 60 had been built to Indian broad gauge (1675mm/ 5ft 6in), shipped out in parts, and assembled at works near Bombay and Calcutta, going into service with the Indian Government Railways from August 1944. Most were given fittings or adaptations normal to their new owners, most often taller chimneys, and in time some were more substantially rebuilt. Small numbers were sent to Jamaica and Peru (1943) and Mexico (1946). In Poland and Hungary, many were still in regular service in the early 1970s. Examples have been preserved in several different countries.

BOILER PRESSURE: 15.75kg/cm² (225psi)
CYLINDERS: 482x660mm (19x26in)
DRIVING WHEELS: 1447mm (57in)
GRATE AREA: 3.8m² (41sq ft)
HEATING SURFACE: 164m² (1765sq ft)
SUPERHEATER: 43.7m² (471sq ft)
TRACTIVE EFFORT: 14,280kg (31,490lb)
TOTAL WEIGHT: 73.6t (162,400lb) (engine only)

An S160 working in China. Classed as KD6 by the Chinese Railways, they were used exclusively on industrial work, mostly on mining sites.

CLASS TC S118 'MACARTHUR' 2-8-2 US ARMY TRANSPORTATION CORPS (USATC)   USA 1942

Again a USATC standard type, this immensely versatile class saw service on a world-wide basis. Long after 1945, it remained a staple engine on many systems. Designed by Alco for working on the metre or 1065mm (3ft 6in) gauges, 859 were built between 1942 and 1945, with Baldwin, Davenport, Porter and Vulcan also involved in building. Its unofficial name of 'MacArthur' was in honour of US General Douglas MacArthur, whose star was high at the time. Maximum route availability was required, so its maximum axle loading was only 9.1 tonnes (9 tons) and it was built to clear even restricted loading gauges. Various kinds of drawgear and braking equipment could be fitted, and it could easily be switched from coal to oil firing. Both in construction and in operation, it was intended to be as economical and simple as possible.

A 'MacArthur' at work with a passenger train on the 1065m (3ft 6in) gauge in India, in the post-war period.

The majority of the MacArthurs were sent to the Indian metre-gauge lines, delivered in crates for assembly on arrival. In the later stages of the war, and after it, some were dispersed to Burma, Malaya and Siam (Thailand). Others were in service – in some cases into the 1970s – in Iraq, Algeria, Tunisia, Nigeria, the Gold Coast (Ghana), the East African Railways system, the French Cameroons, the Manila railroad in the Philippines, the Queensland Government Railways in Australia, the United Fruit Co. lines in Honduras and the White Pass & Yukon Railroad in Alaska. After the war, some were built for the Peloponnesus Railway in Greece and the Djibouti–Addis line in Ethiopia. MacArthurs ran on every inhabited continent of the world, probably the only single steam class to do so.

BOILER PRESSURE: 13kg/cm² (185psi)
CYLINDERS: 406x609mm (16x24in)
DRIVING WHEELS: 1218mm (48in)

GRATE AREA: 2.6m² (27.7sq ft)
HEATING SURFACE: 127.3m² (1371sq ft)
SUPERHEATER: 34.7m² (374sq ft)

TRACTIVE EFFORT: 9900kg (20,100lb)
TOTAL WEIGHT: 54t (119,000lb)
(engine only)

T 1 DUPLEX-DRIVER 4-4-4-4 PENNSYLVANIA RAILROAD (PRR)   USA 1942

With its 'shark-front' styling by Raymond Loewy conveying a sense of modernity, the T 1 showed steam designers fighting back against the diesel-electric threat. For some years, Baldwin had been promoting the concept of duplex, or divided, drive to produce power beyond that of a 4-8-4. The PRR had built for itself a locomotive of this type, with two sets of cylinders and driving wheels set within a rigid frame. This was the bullet-fronted 6-4-4-6 Class S1, completed in 1939, and numbered 6100. The advantages of this non-articulated form were that the operating machinery could be lighter, the cylinders could be smaller and the stroke shorter, the stress on moving parts significantly less than in a two-cylinder 4-8-4, and the piston

thrust could be lower. In addition, the rigid frame promised more stable running at high speeds when compared with an articulated locomotive. Although the S1's performance was questionable, the PRR maintained its faith in the duplex drive, and went to Baldwin for two prototypes of the T 1, Nos. 6110 and 6111, each with two sets of outside cylinders each driving four big wheels. In addition, No. 6111 had a booster engine fitted to the rear bogie.

In all respects, they were thoroughly up to date. Franklin poppet valves, tested successfully on some K4 'Pacifics', worked the cylinders. All axles had Timken roller bearings. They were fitted with big 180-P-84 tenders. The trials of the prototypes brought in

good reports. Both could achieve 160km/h (100mph) in service with 1036-tonne (1020-ton) trains. To the PRR, looking for a replacement for the now ageing K4 class, they seemed to fit the bill. Once upon a time, the Pennsy had spent a year and more thoroughly testing a new locomotive type, but while the T 1s were still on test, 50 more were ordered, 27 from Baldwin, the others from Juniata. But as the new engines came into service in 1945–46, problems began to mount.

Operating over the whole Harrisburg–Chicago line (1147.4km/713 miles), they began by monopolizing the express services, and once again accounts of 160km/h (100mph) and more became common. When they were good, they were very good, but

very often they were far from good. Lack of adhesion bedevilled these engines, with wheel-slip endemic. Other mechanical and operating problems also arose. For all its robust appearance, the T 1 was not a successful design, and by 1950 most were out of service while the old K4s soldiered on. By 1953, they had all gone, most of them with less than 10 years of service. The PRR would have been better served by a more conventional design of engine, like the NYC 'Niagara' 4-8-4.

BOILER PRESSURE: 21kg/cm² (300psi)
CYLINDERS: 501x660mm (19.75x26in)
DRIVING WHEELS: 2032mm (80in)
GRATE AREA: 8.5m² (92sq ft)
HEATING SURFACE: 391m² (4218sq ft)
SUPERHEATER: 132.8m² (1430sq ft)
TRACTIVE EFFORT: 31,925kg (64,650lb)
TOTAL WEIGHT: 432.6t (4,000lb)

Sole precursor of the T1 in 4-4-4-4 format was the Baltimore & Ohio Railroad's No. 5600, *George H. Emerson*. The B&O did not go into series production with the type.

CLASS C-38 4-6-2 NEW SOUTH WALES GOVERNMENT RAILWAY (NSWGR)   AUSTRALIA 1943

Australian designers by now were more likely to study American than British models, seeing parallels in operating distances and train weights. The C-38 class, which marked a massive leap in power from the C-36 4-6-0 that it supplanted on express services, clearly showed American influence, especially in its semi-streamlined form.

Designed by Harold Young, Chief Mechanical Engineer of the NSWGR, the first five – partially streamlined – were built by Clyde Engineering works, and the next 25 at the line's own Eveleigh and Cardiff shops. These were not streamlined, though all had a deep running plate valance. All had American-type cast-steel frames, and roller bearings on all axles,

and Canadian-type 'Boxpok' unspoked wheels. Power reversers were fitted. All were in service by 1949, painted in a distinctive green livery, with buff and red lining out (replaced by standard black in the 1950s).

The 'Pacifics' ran many express trains, but their crack service was the Sydney–Albury leg of the 'Melbourne Limited' sleeping car

train, usually loaded to about 500 tonnes (492 tons), and facing grades of up to 1 in 40 (20 per cent) along the 643km (399-mile) route. The locomotives were manually fired, a stiff test for the fireman. When diesel-electrics took over the 'Limited' in 1955, many C-38s were transferred to fast goods work, though they continued to run Sydney–

Newcastle expresses until 1970. The last to be in regular service was 3820, withdrawn in December 1970. Examples have been preserved in both streamlined and unstreamlined forms.

BOILER PRESSURE: 17.1kg/cm² (245psi)
CYLINDERS: 546x660mm (21.5x26in)
DRIVING WHEELS: 1751mm (69in)
GRATE AREA: 4.4m² (47sq ft)
HEATING SURFACE: 243m² (2614sq ft)
SUPERHEATER: 70.2m² (755sq ft)
TRACTIVE EFFORT: 17,912kg (36,273lb)
TOTAL WEIGHT: 222.5t (450,688lb)

An admiring crowd gathers to see three C-38s head a special excursion train at Moss Vale, NSW, in 1988.

CLASS 520 4-8-4 SOUTH AUSTRALIAN RAILWAYS (SAR)   AUSTRALIA 1943

Even more than the C-38 'Pacific', Australia's second 4-8-4 type reveals a strong American influence – in this case, the Pennsylvania Railroad's 'shark-nose' design. Operating on the 1600mm (5ft 3in gauge), and able to run on light 29.7kg (60lb) rails, it was the SAR's last new steam design. Twelve were built at the SAR's own Islington shops, and used for passenger and freight trains between Adelaide and Port Pirie and Terowie and Tailem Bend, but they also appeared on most other lines in the state. In 1948 all were converted to burn oil fuel, and ran until the early 1960s. Two have been preserved.

Australian shark-nosed 'Hudson', No. 520 of the SAR, *Sir Malcolm Barclay-Harvey* shows off its lines.

BOILER PRESSURE: 14kg/cm² (200psi)
CYLINDERS: 521x711mm (20.5x28in)
DRIVING WHEELS: 1676mm (66in)
GRATE AREA: 4.2m² (45sq ft)
HEATING SURFACE: 228m² (2454sq ft)
SUPERHEATER: 60.5m² (651sq ft)
TRACTIVE EFFORT: 14,800kg (32,600lb)
TOTAL WEIGHT: 221.8t (449,120lb)

CLASS 2000/2050 1-CO-1+1-CO-1 SOROCABANA RAILWAY (EFS)   BRAZIL 1943

One of the few Brazilian metre-gauge lines to be modernized was the *Estrada de Ferro Sorocabana* in Sao Paulo province. Its electrification was interrupted by the war effort in the United States – 46 locomotives ordered from General Electric and Westinghouse in 1943 did not arrive until 1948. There were some differences between the 25 nominally GE-built (Class 2000), and the 21

TYPE: 1-Co-Co-1 freight and passenger
POWER: 1350kW (1840hp)
SUPPLY: 3000V DC
TRACTIVE EFFORT: 137kN (30800lbf)

MAX. OPERATING SPEED: 90km/h (56.3mph)
WEIGHT: 130t (286,720lb); 108.7t (239,680lb)

MAX. AXLE LOAD: 18.29t (40,320lb)
OVERALL LENGTH: 18.59m (61ft)
GAUGE: 1000mm (3ft 3in)

Westinghouse machines (Class 2050). The heavily constructed inter-connected bogies ran on 1117mm (44in) drivers and 838mm (33in) idlers. Deployed solo on passenger services and in multiples at the head and tail of freight trains, they dominated traffic from Sao Paulo westwards. Some were taken out of service in 1995, but the end came suddenly in 2000, when private operator Ferroban took over from state-controlled FEPASA and ceased electric operation. A few 2000s are retained on works trains in the inner Sao Paulo suburban area.

AM 4/6 1A-BO-A1 SWISS FEDERAL RAILWAYS (SBB)

Interest in turbine drive had not disappeared among railway engineers, and this locomotive, built by SLM of Winterthur, may be considered the world's first successful gas turbine-electric. Brown Boveri had considerable experience of static turbine motors, but progress with the locomotive was slow; it was commissioned by SBB in 1939 and did not run on test until 1943. The aim was for a locomotive suitable for working relatively lightweight, fast trains on

routes whose traffic did not justify electrification. Brown Boveri produced the seven-stage axial flow 5800rpm turbine and 18-stage compressor, which (via reduction gearing stepping down to 876rpm) drove a generator that in turn powered four traction motors. Eleven running notches corresponded with turbine speed from 3529 to 5257rpm. With an air intake temperature of 20°C (68°F) turbine efficiency was reckoned at 17.7 per cent at 1620kW (2200hp)

shaft output. An auxiliary diesel engine was provided for turbine starting and for movement of the locomotive only. Though only of moderate power, the Am 4/6 demonstrated the practicality of

locomotive turbines. It was accepted into SBB stock, and also tested in France and Germany, but was not the start of a production run, and in 1952 it was rebuilt in conventional electric Ae4/6 form.

TYPE: 1ABoA1 gas turbine electric prototype
POWER: 1620kW (2200hp) from Brown Boveri industrial turbine
TRACTIVE EFFORT: not known

MAX. OPERATING SPEED: 110km/h (68.8mph)
WEIGHT: 92t (34,170lb)
OVERALL LENGTH: 16.34m (53ft 4in)
GAUGE: 1435mm (4ft 8.5in)

CLASS L4-A 4-8-2 NEW YORK CENTRAL RAILROAD (NYC)

On all other lines, a 4-8-2 might be a 'Mountain', but on the NYC they were always referred to as the 'Mohawk' type, recalling the name of one of its earliest constituent railroads, the Mohawk & Hudson. With the first supplied in 1916, the NYC had over 350 of its 'Mohawks' in service. The 50 members of Class

Early in 1952, L4-A No. 3113 wheels a freight past Dunkirk, NY. By this time, the class was employed almost exclusively on freight services.

L4-a were built between 1942 and 1944 by Lima, by then a division of Lima-Hamilton (the steam firm of Lima had merged with the diesel-engine Hamilton company). It comprised 25 of Class L4-a and

25 of the almost identical L4-b. This was a versatile mixed-traffic locomotive, capable of running at 130km/h (80mph), and able to deputize for 'Hudsons' in express service.

BOILER PRESSURE: 17.5kg/cm² (250psi)
CYLINDERS: 660x761.4mm (26x30in)
DRIVING WHEELS: 1827mm (72in)
GRATE AREA: 6.9m² (75sq ft)
HEATING SURFACE: 434.2m² (4675sq ft)
SUPERHEATER: 195.3m² (2103sq ft)
TRACTIVE EFFORT: 27,165kg (59,900lb)
TOTAL WEIGHT: 181.9t (401,100lb) (engine only)

CLASS U1-F 4-8-2 CANADIAN NATIONAL RAILWAYS (CN)

The Toronto–Montreal route was a key one for the CN, operated in competition with the Canadian Pacific, and consequently always provided with the latest in motive power. U1 was the CN designation for 'Mountain' 4-8-2s, a design it had used since 1923. The 'f' was their ultimate example, 20 in number, constructed at the Montreal Locomotive Works. They had one-piece cast steel frames, Boxpok-type balanced coupled wheels (a feature developed in Canada), and a combined injector and feed water heater of novel design, mounted under the running plate. All were given Vanderbilt tenders, mounted on two six-wheel bogies. Until the

advent of diesels, they ran the CN's fast Toronto–Montreal services. Six members of the class are in preservation.

BOILER PRESSURE: 18.3kg/cm² (260psi)
CYLINDERS: 610x762mm (24x30in)
DRIVING WHEELS: 1854mm (73in)
GRATE AREA: 6.6m² (70.2sq ft)
HEATING SURFACE: 333m² (3584sq ft)
SUPERHEATER: 146m² (1570sq ft)
TRACTIVE EFFORT: 23,814kg (52,500lb)
TOTAL WEIGHT: 290t (638,000lb)

Known as 'Bulletnose Betty', CN 4-8-2 No. 6060 photographed at Quebec on 15 September 1973.

2-10-0 MINISTRY OF SUPPLY

One of two preserved WD 2-10-0s, as British Railways No. 90775, on the North Yorkshire Moors Railway. This loco is 'Dame Vera Lynn'.

A 'war engine', this and a similar 2-8-0 design of 1943 were the first volume-production locomotives to be designed in Britain under the auspices of a government agency rather than a railway company or locomotive builder. The only previous 10-coupled engines to run in Britain had been two exceptional one-offs, but British builders had sent many hundreds abroad. This engine too was primarily intended for use abroad in the support of military campaigns, and the general brief was for an engine combining a light maximum axle weight of 13.5 tonnes (13.3 tons), low enough to run on lightweight or improvised track, but with a good tractive effort. Another requirement was a tight turning circle, achieved here despite a wheelbase of 6.39m (21ft) by making the third driving wheels flangeless, and allowing a 127mm (0.5in) degree of lateral play to the front and rear coupled axles. The North British Locomotive Company abandoned battle-tank production to build it, and its 'Austerity' background is shown by many features: the round-topped parallel boiler and firebox lent themselves to quantity production; fabricated parts were used instead of heavy forgings and castings; some wheels and wheel parts were of cast iron, rather than steel. The boiler pressure, cylinders, motion and wheel diameter were identical to those of the 2-8-0, giving the same theoretical tractive power, but the actual capacity for making steam was much greater, as was the adhesive weight, and so performance was significantly better. In the design of the firebox, provision was made for easy conversion to oil firing. Efforts were made to keep the controls as simple as possible, for inexperienced and non-English drivers; even so, both vacuum and air brake equipment had to be fitted, for hauling British and continental rolling stock; and the engine also had its own steam brake. An eight-fixed-wheel tender carried 9.15 tonnes (9 tons) of coal and 5000gals (6000 US gals) of water.

The class provided a valuable basis for the British standard 2-10-0 of the 1950s, and, many of them were taken into British Railways stock in the post-war period and ran on freight duties into the 1960s, sharing duties with its much more short-lived successor.

BOILER PRESSURE: 15.75kg/cm² (225psi)
CYLINDERS: 482x711mm (19x28in)
DRIVING WHEELS: 1434mm (56.5in)
GRATE AREA: 3.7m² (40sq ft)
HEATING SURFACE: 181m² (1951sq ft)
SUPERHEATER: 39.3m² (423sq ft)
TRACTIVE EFFORT: 14,913kg (30,200lb)
TOTAL WEIGHT: 148t (299,712lb)

CLASS AE4/4 BO-BO BERN–LÖTSCHBERG–SIMPLON RAILWAY (BLS)

The form of things to come was shown by this class: the Ae4/4 was the world's first electric locomotive with 736kW (1000hp) motors on each axle. Built by SLM and Brown Boveri, its all-adhesion bogie layout broke with previous Swiss electric practice, using fully suspended spring borne traction

motors and a flexible drive system. Eight were built between 1944 and 1955. In 1959, a permanently coupled back-to-back twin unit, classed Ae8/8, entered service for heavy freight and international sleeping car trains between Bern, Brig and Domodossola. Ae4/4s were used

on a wide range of duties, lastly on car-carrying tunnel shuttle trains, but both types were put in store from 1995 onwards.

BLS No. 186 on home ground at Brig. The locomotive frame is built out to make a short mounting platform at each end.

TYPE: Bo-Bo heavy passenger and freight
POWER: 3238kW (4400hp)
SUPPLY: 15kV 16.7Hz AC
TRACTIVE EFFORT: 235kN (52,875lbf)
MAX. OP SPEED: 125km/h (78.1mph)
WEIGHT: 80 tonnes (176,400lb)
MAX. AXLE LOAD: 20t (44,100lb)
OVERALL LENGTH: 15.6m (50ft 11in)
GAUGE: 1435mm (4ft 8.5in)

CLASS Q2 4-4-6-4 PENNSYLVANIA RAILROAD (PRR)

Despite the problems of the T1 class, the Pennsylvania still had faith in the potential of the 'duplex drive': two sets of wheels and cylinders in a rigid frame. A 4-6-4-4, Class Q1, was built in

1942 but found unsatisfactory. The prototype Q2 followed, and trial results were successful enough for the War Production Board (assured that it was a mixed-traffic locomotive) to allow

a production run of 25, built in 1944–45. Five out of nine axles had adhesion, and to help further, a booster engine was fitted to the rear bogie. A heavy maximum axle-load of 35.5 tons (36 tonnes)

put serious restriction on their route availability.

Although the least problematic of the duplex drivers, the Q2s had short careers, most being put into store in 1949, by which time the PRR diesel fleet was growing rapidly; all were scrapped between 1953 and 1956, most having done little in the way of revenue service.

BOILER PRESSURE: 21kg/cm² (300psi)
CYLINDERS: front 502x711mm (19.75x28in); rear 603x73mm (23.75x29in)
DRIVING WHEELS: 1751mm (69in)
GRATE AREA: 113m² (1216.6sq ft)
HEATING SURFACE: 573m² (6169.25sq ft)
SUPERHEATER: 337m² (3628.3sq ft)
TRACTIVE EFFORT: 45,722kg (100,800lb)
TOTAL WEIGHT: 280.7t (619,000lb)
GAUGE: 1435mm (4ft 8.5in)

PRR No. 6131. On the test plant, the Q2 developed about 8000bhp at 83km/h (57mph) with steam cut off at 40 per cent – believed to be a record for a locomotive with reciprocating motion.

CLASS 2900 4-8-4 ATCHISON, TOPEKA & SANTA FE RAILROAD (ATSF)

USA 1944

A classic 'standard' design of a well-proven and effective locomotive type, like the great majority of American 4-8-4s of the late 1930s and early 40s, the Class 2900s were simple two-cylinder engines relying on a proven basic design and a range of established patent ancillaries like compressors and feed-water heaters to give consistent high-level performance. The Santa Fe had operated 4-8-4s since 1927, with only the Northern Pacific beating them by a short margin, and this class of 30 oil-burners, built by Baldwin, were to be its last order for express steam. Fitted with roller bearings on all axles, these, like some other 4-8-4s, were said to have operated at speeds of more than 160km/h (100mph). One of their racing grounds was between Los Angeles and San Diego, though they also ran the long haul between LA and Kansas City without change of engine. These 34-hour runs, of 2880km (1790 miles) via Amarillo, or 2830km (1760 miles) by the

Raton Pass, were by a considerable margin the longest-distance steam services to be run without change of locomotive. As with other 'Northerns', the 2900s and their predecessors on the Santa Fe were capable of high speeds, and ran at 145km/h (90mph) and more on long stretches of level or undulating single track, as well as hauling 10 passenger cars unaided

up the grades of the Cajon Pass. Some of them had the curious and unique Santa Fe special feature of an extensible chimney that could be raised on the long stretches of open road across the desert to improve draughting. The tenders were very large and long, mounted on two four-wheel bogies, and the combined length of locomotive and tender was unmatched by any

other passenger locomotive. Later the 2900s were used to assist their diesel-electric replacements up the grades with the 'Super Chief' and 'El Capitan' trains, and then they were transferred to run freight trains in Texas and Oklahoma. Still with much useful life ahead of them, they were all taken off in 1959–60. Several are preserved.

BOILER PRESSURE: 21kg/cm2 (300psi)
CYLINDERS: 710x812mm (28x32in)
DRIVING WHEELS: 2030mm (80in)
GRATE AREA: 10m² (107sq ft)
HEATING SURFACE: 493m² (5306sq ft)
SUPERHEATER: 219m² (2357sq ft)
TRACTIVE EFFORT: 29,932kg (66,000lb)
TOTAL WEIGHT: 231.4t (510,150lb)

With smoke-stack fully hoisted, No. 2928 of the Santa Fe pilots a diesel-electric A-B-A unit up to the Cajon Pass in California, with the 'Super-Chief' train.

FAIRBANKS-MORSE H10-44 BO-BO VARIOUS RAILROADS

USA 1944

With every sign of the diesel market expanding enormously, engine-makers and railroad equipment suppliers Fairbanks-Morse decided to

TYPE: Bo-Bo, diesel-electric
POWER AND OUTPUT: Fairbanks-Morse six-cylinder opposed piston diesel producing 746kW (1000hp)
TRACTIVE EFFORT: 275kN (61,775lbf)
MAX. OPERATING SPEED: N/A
WEIGHT: 112t (247,100lb)
OVERALL LENGTH: N/A
GAUGE: 1435mm (4ft 8.5in)

Loewy styling on a diesel – a preserved H10-44 attached to passenger stock at Green Bay, Wisconsin, on 21 June 2004.

expand into locomotive-building. During World War II, its opposed-piston diesel engines were well regarded in marine applications, especially in US Navy submarines. In 1939, five 551kW (750hp)

versions of these engines had been installed in diesel motor trains for the Southern Railway, and F-M felt these O-P engines could be effectively adapted to further railroad uses. Its first mass-

produced type was the H10-44, a 746kW (1000 hp) switcher, very similar to Baldwin's successful VO1000. The industrial designer Raymond Loewy, already well-known to the Pennsylvania RR,

was commissioned to style the H10-44, giving the otherwise utilitarian machine a bit of flair. Nearly 200 were built up to 1950, when the more powerful H12-44 was introduced.

CLASS 534.03 2-10-0 CZECHOSLOVAK STATE RAILWAYS (CSD)   CZECHOSLOVAKIA 1945

War-torn and run-down like almost all European systems, the CSD picked on what was essentially a pre-war design, hurriedly put into production in 1945 to provide badly needed new motive power. By the end of 1947, 200 had been built by the Skoda and CKD works. Class 534.1 goes back to 1923, based on an Austrian Gölsdorf design, complete with steam-drier pipe between the domes. Very capable and versatile, it was updated in many respects in 1937 as 534.02 and this version, again updated, was the basis of the 534.03. Roller bearings and a power reverser were among the new fittings. Though overtaken in power by later classes, it remained valuable on secondary services until the end of steam in Czechoslovakia.

BOILER PRESSURE: 16kg/cm² (185psi)
CYLINDERS: 580x630mm (22.8x24.8in)
DRIVING WHEELS: 1310mm (51.6in)
GRATE AREA: 4.1m² (44.1sq ft)
HEATING SURFACE: 190.8m² (2054sq ft)
SUPERHEATER: 65.8m² (708.4sq ft)
TRACTIVE EFFORT: 17,810kg (39,280lb)
TOTAL WEIGHT: 82.7t (182,353lb)

Fitted with a Giesl blast pipe and chimney, Class 534 0323 has been preserved and is still in use on steam excursions.

CLASS 47 0-8-0 NETHERLANDS RAILWAYS (NS)   NETHERLANDS 1945

Electrification was the aim in the post-war Netherlands, but in the short term, locomotive capacity had to be renewed. Anticipating the outcome of World War II, Nohab in neutral Sweden accepted the order for this three-cylinder simple-expansion freight class from the Dutch government in exile in London during 1944, and the first two were shipped to Rotterdam in August 1945. A further 33 were in service by the end of 1946. They were modern machines with SKF roller bearings, electric generators and feedwater heating. The shortage of motive power saw them first put in passenger service, before being transferred to the South Limburg

coalfield for the mineral freight work for which they were originally intended.

BOILER PRESSURE: 13kg/cm² (185psi)
CYLINDERS: 500x660mm (19.7x26in)
DRIVING WHEELS: 1350mm (53.2in)
GRATE AREA: 3m² (32.3sq ft)
HEATING SURFACE: 135.8m² (1462sq ft)
SUPERHEATER: 48.5m² (522sq ft)
TRACTIVE EFFORT: 16,680kg (36,780lb)
TOTAL WEIGHT: 74.8t (164,934lb)

Seen here shunting at Eindhoven in 1947, the Class 47 was the NS's first three-cylinder locomotive, and quite unlike previous Dutch engines.

CLASS 4001 4-6-0 NETHERLANDS RAILWAYS (NS)

NETHERLANDS 1945

The provident Dutch ordered this passenger class simultaneously with the Class 47 0-8-0s, also from Nohab. A total of 15 were built, which were then ferried over to Denmark and delivered from there by rail in 1945 and 1946. The Class 4001s were three-cylinder simples, their coned smokebox doors and vee-form cabs giving them a distinctly Swedish appearance. Though they were equipped with modern features such as electric lighting, their boiler pressure was relatively low. The tenders were modelled on Gölsdorf's Austrian design. These engines hauled main-line expresses until the early 1960s, by which time the inexorable take-over by electrics and diesels was complete.

BOILER PRESSURE: 12kg/cm² (171psi)
CYLINDERS: 500x660mm (19.7x26in)
DRIVING WHEELS: 1890mm (74.5in)
GRATE AREA: 3.25m² (35sq ft)
HEATING SURFACE: 147m² (1582.7sq ft)
SUPERHEATER: 50m² (538.3sq ft)
TRACTIVE EFFORT: 11,000kg (24,255lb)
TOTAL WEIGHT: 83.6t (engine only)

CLASS L 2-10-0 SOVIET RAILWAYS (SZD)

RUSSIA 1945

Though Russia had gained many German 'trophy' locomotives, a powerful new main-line goods engine was badly needed. L. C. Lebedyanski was responsible for the Class L (originally P for *Pobyeda*, or victory), designed at the Kolomna works as a straightforward two-cylinder simple-expansion design. Adopted as a standard, it went into production at several factories, and some 5200 were built over the next 10 years, up to the end of steam construction in Russia. The locomotive stood 4873mm (16ft) high, and there was a large airy space between frame and boiler. The casing between chimney and dome covered a steam drier pipe. This was the first Russian locomotive to have balanced Boxpok-type wheels, which became a post-war standard. The L class remained in service until 1975.

BOILER PRESSURE: 14kg/cm² (199psi)
CYLINDERS: 650x800mm (25.6x31.5in)
DRIVING WHEELS: 1150mm (59in)
GRATE AREA: 6m² (64.5sq ft)
HEATING SURFACE: 222m² (2390sq ft)
SUPERHEATER: 113m² (1216sq ft)
TRACTIVE EFFORT: 27,690kg (61,000lb)
TOTAL WEIGHT: 103.8t (228,879lb)
(engine only)

The great height of the Class L is evident by comparison with the passenger cars. A klaxon horn is mounted above the headlight.

S1 'NIAGARA' CLASS 4-8-4 NEW YORK CENTRAL RAILROAD (NYC)

USA 1945

Surviving a major early flaw, when the nickel-steel boilers developed hairline cracks and had to be replaced, this class became star performers in the United States' last years of express steam. Ostensibly planned for mixed-traffic work, but in practice purely express passenger engines, the design of the S1s – or 'Niagaras', as they were better known –was drawn up at a time when air competition scarcely existed, and the fast way from New York to Chicago was still by express train. Ten years later, a great deal had changed. But these engines showed that the railroad's era of monopoly had not led to complacency. Massive as they were, they were built for consistent high speed and performance, to a degree that was probably never equalled with steam. A prototype, classed as S1a, was built, followed by 25 more between 1945 and 46, all by Alco at Schenectady and to the specifications of Paul Kiefer, the NYC's head of motive power. One of the class was fitted with poppet valves rather than piston valves, and was denoted as S1c. The 1493km (928-mile) Harmon (New York)–Chicago run, once requiring up to four locomotive changes, was now to be run by the same engine, with a pause for a rapid top-up of the tender coal. Water could be picked up from troughs ('pans' in the United States) laid between the tracks. To achieve this, the locomotive had to be capable of a power output of 4412kW (6000hp) in the cylinders, not as a peak but as a regular operational necessity. For each locomotive, an annual distance run

Class S1 No. 6016 on the outskirts of New York City at Oscawanna, around 1947, with a nine-car consist of clerestoried stock: a baggage van is behind the locomotive.

in excess of 442,000km (275,000 miles) could be expected and average speeds were very high. Large-diameter driving wheels and a large boiler meant that even within the US loading gauge there was little space for boiler-top fittings, and the chimney and other boiler-top fittings were compressed to a very low height (the NYC was more confined in this respect than some lines, with a maximum height above the rail of 4.62m/15ft 2in). Cast steel frames supported the great weight of boiler and firebox, and not only all axles but also the coupling and connecting rods had roller bearings. Baker valve gear was fitted, and the cross-head, on a single slide-bar, drove a connecting rod to the second set of coupled wheels. Mechanical stoking was essential

for a grate whose area was 9.3m² (100sq ft). The whole structure was built for continuous hard pounding. The Niagara's tender was of the 'centipede' type, with a four wheel outside framed bogie followed by five axles fixed in the tender main frame.

The prime train was the 'Twentieth Century Limited' and its timing was 16 hours, requiring an average of 93km/h (58mph) including stops. Steam engines were not permitted within New York City limits, so electric locos hauled the fliers out to Harmon, where the Niagaras took over and relinquished their trains. To and from there, mile after mile at 128km/h (80mph) plus was

needed to maintain the schedule. Sophisticated and swift work in the depots at each end kept the engines serviced to a peak of efficiency in the short time between duty turns. For consistent heavy-duty performance, this class was almost unrivalled by any other locomotive in the world.

Through October 1946, Niagaras were tested against an EMD E7 set of twin diesel-electrics capable of developing 2941kW (4000hp) on the Chicago run. Cost, as much as performance, was at issue, and over the month the Niagaras averaged 43,807km (27,221 miles) each and the diesels 46,596km (28,954 miles). Average operating costs per mile were $1.22 for the

steam locomotives and $1.11 for the diesels. It was a narrow margin, with the additional considerations that diesels were much more expensive to build, and were expected to have shorter working lives. But only a handful of other steam classes could have emulated the S1's performance.

BOILER PRESSURE: 19.3kg/cm² (275psi)
CYLINDERS: 648x813mm (25.5x32in)
DRIVING WHEELS: 2007mm (79in)
GRATE AREA: 9.3m² (100sq ft)
HEATING SURFACE: 4.48m² (48.27sq ft)
SUPERHEATER: 191m² (2060sq ft)
TRACTIVE EFFORT: 27,936kg (61,570lb)
TOTAL WEIGHT: 405t (891,000lb)

FAIRBANKS-MORSE 'ERIE BUILT' A1A-A1A MILWAUKEE RAILROAD (MILW)   USA 1945

Having put its H10-44 switcher into production, Fairbanks-Morse moved on to a design for a large road locomotive. Lacking the factory space and equipment at its own Beloit works to build such sizeable machines, it contracted with General Electric to assemble its large A1A-A1A cab types.

Built at GE's Erie, Pennsylvania, facilities, they came to be known

as 'Erie-builts', and in total 111 were constructed. With 1492kW (2000 hp) per locomotive, these streamlined diesels were intended to compete with Electro-Motive's

latest E-units, as well as models from Alco and Baldwin. Milwaukee Road employed them, with elaborate stainless steel styling on the front ends, for the prestigious

high-speed *Hiawatha* service in succession to the F7 4-6-4s. However, only a few other railroads operated them.

TYPE: A1A-A1A, diesel-electric
POWER AND OUTPUT: Fairbanks-Morse model 38D81/8 (eight-cylinder opposed piston diesel) producing 1492kW (2000hp)

TRACTIVE EFFORT: 117kN (26,400lbf) continuous TE at 38.6km/h (24mph); 265kN (59,600lbf) starting TE
MAX. OPERATING SPEED: N/A

WEIGHT: 155t (341,500lb)
OVERALL LENGTH: 19.761m (64ft 10in)
GAUGE: 1435mm (4 ft 8.5in)

DR-12-8-1500/2 2-DO+DO-2 PENNSYLVANIA RAILROAD

USA 1945

The multiplicity of wheels earned this engine the name of 'Centipede'. This was Baldwin's bid for the high-power, high-speed diesel market, with its origins in a wartime project for a multi-engine high-speed diesel based largely on electric locomotive practice. Intended for speeds up to 187km/h (117mph), the ambitious 4470kW (6000hp) machine never entered production. Baldwin did

build a scaled-back version with two engines producing 2235kW (3000hp) per unit using an articulated frame with a 2-Do+Do-

2 wheel arrangement. Seaboard Air Line was the first to order the type, and Pennsylvania Railroad (PRR) and National Railways of

Mexico (NdeM) also bought them. PRR had the largest fleet, used initially in passenger service, but later re-geared for freight work.

TYPE: 2-Do+Do-2, diesel-electric
POWER AND OUTPUT: a pair of Baldwin eight-cylinder 608SC engines producing 2235kW (3000hp)
TRACTIVE EFFORT: 235kN (52,800lbf) continuous TE at 28.7km/h (17.8mph); 454kN (102,205lbf) starting TE
MAX. OPERATING SPEED: 150km/h (93.5mph) with 21:58 gear ratio
WEIGHT: 269t (593,700lb)
OVERALL LENGTH: 27.889m (91ft 6in)
GAUGE: 1435mm (4ft 8.5in)

A pair of 'Centipedes' acting as helpers to push a freight train up and round the Horseshoe Curve near Altoona, PA.

CLASS WP 4-6-2 INDIAN RAILWAYS (IR)

INDIA 1946

This was the world's most numerous 'Pacific' class, working hundreds of express services all over India. Designed for the Indian 1675mm (5ft 6in) broad gauge, its production marked a significant change of locomotive policy on the IR. Sixteen prototypes were built by Baldwin in Philadelphia and had no relation to the 'Indian Railways

Standard' designs that had produced such indifferent performers in the 1930s.

The Class WP were American-style engines, and nearly half of the class, 320 altogether, were built in the United States or Canada. Chrzanov in Poland and Vienna Lokomotivfabrik of Austria each built 30. In all, 755 were built between 1947 and 1967, the last

435 at the new Chittaranjan works set up with British support in India in 1950.

Free-steaming, reliable and designed for ease of maintenance, the WPs were received with great relief by locomotive crews. Built in the classic American manner, with bar frames, two simple-expansion cylinders, and Walschaerts valve gear actuating piston valves, their

forward-set bulbous smoke-boxes and big boilers gave them a massive appearance. The parallel-design boiler was topped by a long casing concealing all fittings except the just-protruding chimney. Most of the class had Boxpok-type balanced wheels, with a three-point suspension system well-adapted to Indian tracks.

The WPs served well for over 30 years, and were one of the most familiar sights to the foreign traveller in India, hauling such trains as the 'Punjab Express' and the Agra-bound 'Taj Mahal' from Delhi. Class withdrawal was not completed until the 1990s, and some are still in special service.

BOILER PRESSURE: 14.7kg/cm² (210psi)
CYLINDERS: 514x711mm (20.25x28in)
DRIVING WHEELS: 1705mm (67in)
GRATE AREA: 4.3m² (46sq ft)
HEATING SURFACE: 286.3m² (2257sq ft)
SUPERHEATER: 67m² (725sq ft)
TRACTIVE EFFORT: 13,884kg (30,600lb)
TOTAL WEIGHT: 172.5t (380,000lb)
(engine only)

These bullet fronts with their stars were familiar all over Indian Railways. Many received additional decorative features at their local depots.

CLASS QR-1 4-8-4 MEXICAN NATIONAL RAILWAYS (NDEM)

Perhaps influenced by the NYC's fliers of the previous year, these 'Northerns' on the NdeM were referred to as *Niagras*. US influence had been dominant on the Mexican railways for decades, and these

two-cylinder simples were very much US-style engines. Thirty-two QR-1s were built, half each by Alco and Baldwin. Among the lightest in weight of North American 4-8-4s and intended primarily for freight

train haulage, they were the last steam locomotives ordered for Mexico, and the last to work regular duties. The last ones were taken out of service in 1965. Even after diesels had taken over practically all services, a few of the *Niagras* remained as banking engines and on standby duty.

Built in 1946 by Baldwin, No. 3034 of the Nacionales de Mexico, on a freight in the Valle de Mexico, in 1964.

BOILER PRESSURE: 17.5kg/cm² (250psi)
CYLINDERS: 634.5x761mm (25x30in)
DRIVING WHEELS: 1777mm (70in)
GRATE AREA: 7.1m² (77sq ft)
HEATING SURFACE: 388.8m² (4186sq ft)
SUPERHEATER: 154.8m² (1667sq ft)
TRACTIVE EFFORT: 25,814kg (56,920lb)
TOTAL WEIGHT: 175.5t (387,00lb)

FA/FB BO-BO VARIOUS RAILROADS

Another product of the Alco-General Electric partnership, the FA/FB had an Alco/GE standard cab unit and was of the same basic configuration as the EMD F-unit, which far outsold it. Like the F-unit, it was intended for heavy road freight service. The FA was intended to operate in sets of three or four and often ran in multiple with other Alco types, especially RS-2 and RS-3 road switchers.

The FA/FB type was produced between 1946 and 1956. In 1950, Alco boosted the output of the 12-cylinder 244 engine from 1119kW to 1194kW (1500 to 1600hp), but mechanical problems with this engine type doomed many FA/FBs

Two FA and three FB units with a New Haven RR freight, on the Maybrook line, in 1960.

to shorter careers than the rival EMD F-units built in the same period.

TYPE: Bo-Bo, diesel-electric
POWER AND OUTPUT: Alco 12-cylinder 244 diesel producing 1119 to 1194kW (1500 to 1600hp)
TRACTIVE EFFORT: 167kN (37,500lbf) continuous TE at 20.1km/h (12.5 mph); 256kN (57,500lbf) starting TE (depending on weight)
MAX. OPERATING SPEED: 105km/h (65mph) with 74:18 gear ratio
WEIGHT: 104t (230,000lb)
OVERALL LENGTH: 15.697m (51ft 6in)
GAUGE: 1435mm (4ft 8.5in)

RS-2/RS-3 VARIOUS RAILROADS

With RS-2 and 3, Alco built on the success of the RS-1 road switcher. Increased power at 1119kW (1500hp) and a hint of streamlining made RS-2 one of its better-selling designs. New York Central used them in local passenger service, on local freights that needed to switch en route, branch-line freights, and in multiple-units on heavy road freights. As with the FA/FB diesels, Alco installed a more powerful 1194kW version of its 244 engine in some later RS-2s, though mostly to the RS-3 of the mid-1950s. With more than 1350 RS-3s built for North American service, it became one of the

In New York Central paintwork, an RS-3 heads a line of passenger cars at Otter Lake, NY, on 22 July 2004.

most numerous Alco designs. It was superseded in 1956 by the RS-11, powered by the newer 251 diesel. However, despite greater reliability fewer RS-11s were sold because by that time most railroads had largely completed their transfer to diesel fleets. A few RS-3s had very long service lives, some surviving on short lines past the year 2000.

TYPE: Bo-Bo, diesel-electric
POWER AND OUTPUT: 12-cylinder Alco 244 producing 1119kW (1500hp)
TRACTIVE EFFORT: 271kN (61,000lbf) starting TE
MAX. OPERATING SPEED: 105km/h (65mph) with 74:18 gear ratio
WEIGHT: 111t (244,000lb)
OVERALL LENGTH: 16.91m (55ft 6in)
GAUGE: 1435mm (4ft 8.5in)

EMD E-UNITS MODEL E7 A1A-A1A VARIOUS RAILROADS

Electro-Motive's E-units went back to the pioneer EA of 1936. All used a pair of high-output two-cycle diesel engines in a streamlined body riding on A1A trucks. From mid-1938 onward, they were powered by the highly successful Electro-Motive 567 diesel in 12-cylinder configurations. ('E' allegedly stems from the initial output of 'eighteen-hundred' horsepower per unit). With the introduction of the 12-567 engine, the per unit output was boosted to 1472kW (2000hp), but the 'E' designation continued. Models E3 to E6, built from 1938 until 1942, featured a steeper sloping nose than the post-war E7, E8 and E9s, which used the standard 'Bull dog' nose first seen on the FT freight diesel in 1939. The two most numerous E-unit models were the E7 and E8, built from 1946 to 1949, and 1949 to 1953 respectively. The E7 stood 4.55m (14ft 11in) tall, and was 21.67m (71ft 1.25in) long. It held a pair of GM Model D-4 generators, and four GM Model D-7 traction motors. With a 55-22 gear ratio, the B&O's locomotives could reach a maximum permitted 158km/h (98mph). By contrast, Burlington's E7s, with a 57-20 gear ratio, were capable of speeds up to 187km/h (117mph).

The final E-unit type was the 1790kW (2400hp) E9, which remained in production until 1963. All were built in both 'A' and 'B' configurations, the latter type being a cab-less 'booster' engine. Most railroads ran E units in multiples to haul heavy passenger trains, among them New York Central's Twentieth Century Limited, Pennsylvania's

Wisconsin Southern E8A No. 801, at Horicon, Wisconsin, in 1995.

Broadway Limited; Southern Pacific's 'Daylight' trains; Southern Railway's *Crescent;* and Illinois Central's *City of New Orleans.* Amtrak inherited a sizeable fleet of E-units, some of which it operated until the mid-1980s. As passenger services declined in the 1960s, a few lines, such as Erie–Lackawanna, assigned E's to freight services, often using them on priority intermodal trains. In more recent times, American

freight haulers such as Illinois Central and Conrail used E-units for company 'Executive trains', deluxe passenger consists reserved for officers' inspection trips and customer relations jaunts. The last large fleet of E-units in regular service was Burlington Northern's, used to haul its 'Dinkys' – Chicago area suburban trains that operated from Union Station to Aurora over its triple track mainline.

TYPE: A1A-A1A, passenger diesel-electric
POWER AND OUTPUT: a pair of EMD 12-567-A diesel producing 2681kW (2000hp)
TRACTIVE EFFORT: 84kN (18,800lbf) continuous TE at 53.1km/h (33 mph); 236kN (53,075lbf) starting TE
MAX. OPERATING SPEED: 157.7km/h (98mph) with 55:22 gear ratio
WEIGHT: 143t (315,000lb)
OVERALL LENGTH: 21.673m (71ft 1in)
GAUGE: 1435mm (4ft 8.5in)

EMD F-UNITS, MODEL F7 BO-BO VARIOUS RAILROADS

By 1946, General Motors' Electro-Motive Division (EMD) was beginning to power ahead as the United State's prime supplier of diesel-electric locomotives. The success of the FT type in World War II period helped set up its reputation, and after the war ended and restrictions on implementing new designs were lifted, EMD improved its F unit line and introduced the F3 (an interim F2 model was built for a short period). The F3 was slightly more powerful than the FT, with each unit rated at 1119kW (1500hp), instead of 1007kW (1350hp). Other mechanical improvements enhancing performance and reliability were incorporated in the F7 that replaced the F3, although output remained the same. In 1954 the F9, rated at 1306kW (1750hp), superseded the F7. EMD's streamlined F units were a ubiquitous symbol of American dieselization and could be seen on most railroads.

TYPE: Bo-Bo, diesel-electric
POWER AND OUTPUT: EMD 16-567B producing 1119kW (1500hp)
TRACTIVE EFFORT: various
MAX. OPERATING SPEED: various
WEIGHT: various
OVERALL LENGTH: 15.443m (50ft 8in) (A-unit)
GAUGE: 1435m (4ft 8.5in)

Above: No. 1508, beautifully restored, on the Adirondack Scenic Railroad, at Thendara, NY, on 22 July 2004.

Left: F7A model No. 1508 on the Alaska Railroad in December 1996. The loco put in long service on this line.

CLASS PT-47 2-8-2 POLISH STATE RAILWAYS (PKP)

By 1947, Poland's devastated railway network was largely restored, and a new generation of steam locomotives was emerging. The Pt (passenger 2-8-2) type had been introduced on the PKP in 1932, and this was a post-war version, fitted with a welded firebox and with mechanical stoking. Some 180 were built by the Cegielski and Chrzanov works, and used on express services. Large cylinders and coupled wheels of mixed-traffic diameter gave it a powerful tractive effort. The Polish railways had a high clearance, and this engine stood 4.67m (15ft 4in) above the rails. On the standard gauge, international services linked Poland with Germany, Czechoslovakia and Hungary, and the Pt-47s hauled international expresses on all non-electrified lines. Some of the class have been preserved.

BOILER PRESSURE: 15kg/cm² (214psi)
CYLINDERS: 630x700mm (24.75x27.5in)
DRIVING WHEELS: 1850mm (72.75in)
GRATE AREA: 4.5m² (48.5sq ft)
HEATING SURFACE: 230m² (2476sq ft)
SUPERHEATER: 101m² (1087sq ft)
TRACTIVE EFFORT: 19,110kg (42,120lb)
TOTAL WEIGHT: 173t (381,500lb)

Polish steam still in action – a PT 47 ready for the road at Wolsztyn, Poland, on 25 August, 2006.

ALCO PA/PB A1A-A1A VARIOUS RAILROADS

USA 1947

By 1947, Alco was building steam locomotives only for export, and the diesel-electric P-type was its competition, with GE electric parts, to the EMD E-units in the US express passenger sector. This market would soon evaporate with the decline of long-distance rail transport, but while railroads were hurrying to divest themselves of steam locomotives, it was still a buoyant one. Railway enthusiasts liked the handsome streamlined car body with its long pronounced nose section, and the throaty sound of the 244 diesel engine. Santa Fe and Southern Pacific had the largest fleets of PA/PB diesels. Those that are best remembered are four former Santa Fe PAs operated by Delaware & Hudson through the late 1970s. They later went to Mexico and have since been preserved.

Photographed in the early 1950s, Southern Pacific's high-snouted Alco PA unit No. 27 at a desert depot in the Far West.

TYPE: A1A-A1A, passenger diesel-electric
POWER AND OUTPUT: 16-cylinder Alco 244 diesel engine producing 1492kW (2000hp); boosted to 1676kW (2250hp) on PA-2/PB-2 models
TRACTIVE EFFORT: 227kN (51,000lb)

for PA-1/PB-1
MAX. OPERATING SPEED: various
WEIGHT: 139t (306,000lb)
OVERALL LENGTH: 20.015m (65ft 8in) (PA only)
GAUGE: 1435mm (4ft 8.5in)

BALDWIN RF16 'SHARK NOSE' BO-BO VARIOUS RAILROADS

USA 1947

Seeking a distinctive identity for its road diesels, Baldwin borrowed the look of the PRR's T1 steam locomotive to give some of them, including the RF16, the so-called 'sharknose' body style. Baldwin also continued to use the 'Babyface' style of the 'Centipede' of 1945, with its big front windows. Some of its diesel types, including the DR-6-4-20 high-speed passenger locomotives, were styled in both ways – as 'sharks' for the Pennsylvania Railroad and 'Babyfaces' for other customers. The RF16 class was the most numerous of the 'sharks', built up to the early 1950s for the Pennsylvania Railroad, New York Central, and Baltimore & Ohio. The RF16 was essentially an upgraded DR-4-4-15. The Baldwin eight-cylinder 608A diesel engine was good for low-speed heavy freight service, and many 'sharks' worked, with low-geared drive, on coal and iron ore trains. The last to be at work were a pair of former New York Central RF16s, passed on successively to Monongahela, then Delaware & Hudson, and later short lines in Michigan.

TYPE: Bo-Bo, diesel-electric
POWER: Baldwin eight-cylinder 608A producing 1194kW (1600hp)
TRACTIVE EFFORT: 328kN (73,750lbf)
MAX. OPERATING SPEED: 112km/h (70mph)
WEIGHT: 113t (248,000lb)
OVERALL LENGTH: 16.739 m (54ft 11in)
GAUGE: 1435mm (4ft 8.5in)

The Pennsylvania was the only railroad to order 'shark nose' locomotives for passenger train.

DD17 CLASS 4-6-4T QUEENSLAND GOVERNMENT RAILWAYS (QGR)

Though its wheels, at 1294mm (51in), were more of freight-engine diameter, this was a passenger train engine. It was built to work around Brisbane, which had the only suburban network in Queensland, on 1050mm (3ft 6in) gauge. The last tank class built in Australia, numbering 12 engines, it was introduced to replace older engines. Modern features included

roller bearings, mechanical lubrication and self-cleaning smoke boxes. In looks, it is American, and though built at the QGR's own Ipswich shops, it owes much to Baldwin's USATC-16 tender engines. Diesels took over local passenger traffic in the later 1950s, and the DD17s were transferred to shunting duties. The last to be taken out of service was No. 1046 in October 1969.

Three of the DD 17 locos were acquired by the Zig-Zag tourist railway at Lithgow, NSW. No. 1046 is seen here with vintage carriages.

BOILER PRESSURE: 12.6kg/cm² (180psi)
CYLINDERS: 431x609mm (17x24in)
DRIVING WHEELS: 1294mm (51in)
GRATE AREA: 1.7m² (18.5sq ft)
HEATING SURFACE: 98.8m² (1064sq ft)
SUPERHEATER: 13.9m² (150sq ft)
TRACTIVE EFFORT: 10,275kg (20.808lb)
TOTAL WEIGHT: 68.5t (138,88lb)

CLASS 423/433 2-8-2T CZECHOSLOVAK STATE RAILWAYS (CSD)

This class of 60 was essentially a modernized form of the earlier Class 423, numbering 231 and built up to 1946. Twenty were equipped with roller bearings, and some also received Giesl ejectors. Apart from an increase in boiler pressure from the original 13kg/cm² (185psi), the alterations to the Class 423 were largely cosmetic. A shorter, wider chimney was substituted for the original tall one, and the combined sandbox and dome were separated into two domes and a sandbox. Other changes included the clerestory-type roof to the cab, extension of the tanks over the cylinders, and a rearward and

upward extension of the bunker. Larger superheaters were also fitted.
All in all, it was a highly successful class, with the 433s as the final development. Several examples of both 423 and 433 are preserved.

BOILER PRESSURE: 15kg/cm² (180psi)
CYLINDERS: 480x570mm (19x22.5in)
DRIVING WHEELS: 1150mm (45.2in)
GRATE AREA: 2.1m² (22.6sq ft)
HEATING SURFACE: 97.6m² (1051sq ft)
SUPERHEATER: 33.8m² (364sq ft)
TRACTIVE EFFORT: 12,956kg (28,568lb)
TOTAL WEIGHT: 70.6t (155,673lb)

A modified Class 423, with Giesl ejector, on a train of short-wheelbase Prague suburban stock.

CLASS 241.P 4-8-2 FRENCH NATIONAL RAILWAYS (SNCF)

A 241.P, one of the last remaining in active service, runs past the marshalling yards at Nevers with a lightweight train in April 1968.

After 1945, the SNCF resumed its pre-war policy of main-line electrification, but France, like other countries, had an immediate locomotive shortage that could be answered only by new steam power. For a new express engine

to work in the south-east, the chosen prototype was an ex-Paris, Lyons & Méditerranée (PLM) 4-8-2 type, 241.C, designed in 1931 and not famous for performance or efficiency. André Chapelon was given the task of converting it into

an effective locomotive before series construction began. New cylinders, fed by an improved steam circuit, were made, and the frames were strengthened by fitting transverse steel members. Double blast pipes and chimneys were installed. In externals too, the design closely followed Chapelon's established pattern. But it was impossible to incorporate the range of radical changes that marked his earlier rebuilds, and though much improved they were moderate rather than exceptional performers in service. Between 1948 and 1952, 35 were built by the Le Creusot Company, replacing 40 2-8-2s of the 141.P class.
First based at Marseille, the 241.Ps hauled heavy expresses up and down the Rhône Valley between there and Lyon. By 1952, the Paris–Dijon section of the old PLM main line was electrified, and

as the catenary was extended further south the 241.Ps were dispersed among a number of depots in the North, East and West regions. Staying active until 1970, they were the last of France's big four-cylinder compounds in regular service. The last three were taken out of service at Le Mans depot in May 1970, after running trains between there and Nantes, but have been preserved.

BOILER PRESSURE: 20.5kg/cm² (292psi)
CYLINDERS: hp 447x650mm (17.6x25.6in); lp 675x700.5mm (26.6x27.6in)
DRIVING WHEELS: 2018mm (79.5in)
GRATE AREA: 5m² (53.8sq ft)
HEATING SURFACE: 244.6m² (2632.5sq ft)
SUPERHEATER: 108.4m² (1116.5sq ft)
TRACTIVE EFFORT: N/A
TOTAL WEIGHT: 145.7t (321,348lb)

CLASS 242 A.1 4-8-4 FRENCH NATIONAL RAILWAYS (SNCF)

FRANCE 1948

A unique steam locomotive in many ways, Chapelon's lone Class A1 outperformed its electric-powered contemporaries.

Among claimants for the elusive title of supreme steam locomotive type, this engine has a strong case, weakened only by the fact that it was to remain a solitary example of excellence and was never replicated in a class. Like so many of André Chapelon's designs, it was based on the conversion of an existing engine: a prototype 4-8-2 express passenger type with poppet valves for the *Etat* Railway, built at the Fives-Lille works in 1932, but found unsatisfactory. In the late 1930s, permission was given for it to be rebuilt under Chapelon's direction as a three-cylinder compound. Wartime delays meant that the work did not begin until 1942, at the *Forges et Aciéries de la Marine et d'Homecourt,* at St Chamond. Reconstruction was radical. Though Chapelon's preference was a single-piece steel chassis, as standard in the United States for big locomotives, he was obliged in this case to strengthen the frame by a combination of transverse steel stays and welded steel plates along the sides. This increased the weight to a point where an additional carrying axle was needed in order to keep the

maximum axle load at 21 tonnes (20.6 tons), and the engine became a 4-8-4. The high-pressure cylinder, driving the first coupled axle, was placed inside, in line with the external low-pressure cylinders, each operated independently by Walschaerts valve gear, with that for the inside cylinder worked off the third left-hand coupled axle. The low-pressure cylinders drove the second coupled axle. The original poppet valves were replaced by double piston valves. Particular attention was paid to the size and positioning of steam passages and to the draughting and exhaust system. A triple Kylchap ejector and chimney were fitted, a large Houlet superheater installed, and two Nicholson thermic syphons fitted in the firebox, which was made of steel and mechanically stoked. Roller bearings were fitted to the front and rear bogies. Timken roller bearings were fitted on the front bogie, with SKF bearings on the rear truck. Franklin automatic wedges were applied to the axle-boxes of the coupled wheels. The original engine's tendency to rough riding was attended to by means of an Alco geared roller-centring device

– Chapelon was happy to adopt American improvements. Many minor details were also attended to, and the effect of the rebuild was to increase the weight by 20.3 tonnes (20 tons), but to virtually double the locomotive's potential power output.

Exhaustive tests between 1946 and 1949 showed that there was nothing theoretical about this power. Measuring output in horsepower, this was the first European locomotive to sustain a continuous 2984kW (4000hp) or more at the tender drawbar, corresponding to more than 3730kW (5000hp) developed in the cylinders, while running at speeds of up to 120.7km/h (75mph). It achieved these results without excessive use of fuel or water: its fuel economy was as great as that of the French four-cylinder compounds, and considerably greater than that of, for example, the British 'Pacifics' of the 'Coronation' class or any large American locomotive. A further important consideration was its ability to start off heavy trains on rising gradients without suffering that bugbear of so many steam locomotives, slipping of the coupled wheels. In such situations,

a calculated tractive effort of 25,400kg (56,000lb) was produced. The 242 A.1 had no trouble in mantaining steady speeds of 121km/h (75mph) with trains of 711–813 tonnes (700-800 tons).

Though a large engine in European terms, it was only of moderate size compared to American express locomotives. But any former notion of correlation between dimensions and power output had to be set aside. The Southern Pacific's GS-4 class 4-8-4 weighed 215.4 tonnes (211 tons), more than half as much again as the French engine. The New York Central's Class S-1a 4-8-4 had 44 per cent more evaporative heating surface, 40 per cent more superheating surface and almost double the grate area. These were regarded as first-rate express passenger locomotives, but the A.1 could at least match them in performance, and leave them far behind in economy. At this time, the delayed tests of Chapelon's 2-12-0 were further reinforcing the steam case. The fuel economy displayed by his engines also negated the argument that the capital costs of electrification would be balanced by lower running costs.

Here, in the words of one expert observer, was 'a steam locomotive with a 2-ton axle load which was not only at least as powerful as the most powerful high-speed electric locomotive but which could repeatedly develop its maximum power without any mechanical trouble.' The SNCF, however, was embarked on electrification, and no further A.1 types were to be built. Placed at the Le Mans depot, the lone A.1 took its turns with 'Pacifics' at running Paris expresses, which were easily within its power, its capacity revealed only when having to make up time after delays. In 1960, it was withdrawn from service and broken up.

BOILER PRESSURE: 20.4kg/cm² (292psi)	**GRATE AREA:** 5m² (54sq ft)	**TOTAL WEIGHT:** 150.3t (331,520lb)
CYLINDERS: hp 600x720mm	**HEATING SURFACE:** 253m² (2720sq ft)	(engine only)
(23.6x28.3in); lp 680x760mm (27x29.9in)	**SUPERHEATER:** 120m² (1249sq ft)	
DRIVING WHEELS: 1950mm (76.75in)	**TRACTIVE EFFORT:** 25,400kg (56,000lb)	

CLASS 1500 0-6-0T BRITISH RAILWAYS (BR), WESTERN REGION

GREAT BRITAIN 1948

The four British railway companies were taken into state control as British Railways in 1948, and this was one of the last locomotives built by the Great Western Railway. In 1948, it was still building inside-cylinder 0-6-0 tanks on a pattern that had hardly changed since the 1920s, but these 10 pannier tanks were of more up-

to-date design. They were of largely welded construction, with Belpaire boiler and Walschaerts valve gear, no running plate and a minimal buffer beam. These omissions were intended partly to reduce weight and cost, and partly to improve access for maintenance.

The traditional GWR-style copper chimney band was kept, however. They worked as carriage shunters at London Paddington, until 1960.

BOILER PRESSURE: 14kg/cm² (200psi)	**GRATE AREA:** 1.6m² (17.4sq ft)	**SUPERHEATER:** 6.9m² (74sq ft)
CYLINDERS: 444x609mm (17.5x24in)	**HEATING SURFACE:** 108.9m2	**TRACTIVE EFFORT:** 10,204kg (22,500lb)
DRIVING WHEELS: 1408mm (55.5in)	(1172sq ft) t)	**TOTAL WEIGHT:** 59.1t (130,368lb)

CLASS A1 4-6-2 BRITISH RAILWAYS (BR), EASTERN REGION

Designs for a standardized locomotive range were quickly put in hand by the state-owned British Railways, but in the first years the designs of the former companies, often very recent, were continued. All the old companies had continued to design and build locomotives, as was indeed essential after the intensive usage of the war years.

The A1 class, designed by A.H. Peppercorn for the London &

North Eastern Railway (LNER), took over the designation A1 from the first LNER 'Pacifics', many of which had been rebuilt as Class A3. Though there was some family resemblance in appearance, and the company remained faithful to three cylinders, there were many changes from the earlier types. The conjugated valve gear was replaced by three sets of Walschaerts gear. A larger, though still manually fired, grate

was installed. A stubby, stovepipe-style double chimney and Kylchap blast exhaust were fitted, and they were among the first British locomotives to have electric lighting. The boiler, with a steam collector in its 'banjo dome' was of the same dimensions as that designed for the previous class, A2. This had been something of a mixed bag, consisting of the rebuilt Gresley 'Mikados' (designated A2/2), a

1944 Pacific, A2/1, and a 1946 development of that, A2/3, later versions of which were heavily remodelled at the front end when Peppercorn took charge at Doncaster in mid-1946. The new Class A1 was much more homogeneous. Compared with the A4 boiler, it had a reduced heating surface despite the bigger firebox. The Peppercorn A1, of which 49 were built at the Doncaster Plant, was an effective engine in service, free-steaming, fast and relatively fault-free. Kylchap double blast-pipes were fitted and, at first, they had stubby stovepipe chimneys, later replaced by more elegant lipped versions. The last five had roller bearings on all axles, and four of these ran over 1,609,000km (1,000,000 miles) in their relatively short careers. The last was withdrawn in June 1966, by which time the arrival of new diesel-electrics had left no suitable duties for them.

Class A1 60157 *Great Eastern* restarts a northbound express from Grantham, on the East Coast Main Line. This engine was withdrawn from service in 1965: none of the Peppercorn A1s was preserved.

BOILER PRESSURE: 17.5kg/cm² (250psi)
CYLINDERS: 482x660mm (19x26in)
DRIVING WHEELS: 2030mm (80in)
GRATE AREA: 4.6m² (50sq ft)
HEATING SURFACE: 228.6m² (2461.3sq ft)
SUPERHEATER: 64.8m² (679.7sq ft)
TRACTIVE EFFORT: 11,306kg (24,930lb)
TOTAL WEIGHT: 105.6t (232,960lb)

NO. 10000 CO-CO LONDON, MIDLAND & SCOTTISH RAILWAY (LMS)

With No. 10000 and its companion 10001, the British railways made the same kind of discoveries that were already familiar to American operators. The LMS was determined to get its first main-line diesel-electric locomotive into service before the company dissolved into a region of British Railways. No. 10000 emerged from Derby works in December 1947, just in time to carry legitimately the initials 'LMS' on its bodysides. This first British essay into serious use of diesel power on main-line express trains used an English Electric 16-cylinder V-form supercharged low-speed diesel engine coupled to a large EE823A DC generator. The cylinders were 254mm (10in) bore and 305mm (12in) stroke. This supplied power for six EE519 traction motors, one coupled to each axle and suspended directly on it through a nose suspension bearing. Each locomotive was carried on two three-axle bogies in Co-Co formation. The engine also drove an EE909A auxiliary generator providing power for battery charging, control circuits, lighting, drives to compressors and vacuum exhausters. At 1194kW (1600hp),

the power was about that obtainable from a good Class 5 or 6 steam locomotive, but the diesel locomotive's tractive effort – that is, the force it could exert on the rails – was equivalent to a much larger Class 8P steam locomotive. The six powered axles enabled this tractive effort to be produced by a diesel locomotive without wheel slip. Thus the starting and initial acceleration performance of these new locomotives was outstanding for

their time. The locomotives needed no sanding apparatus because of this inherent better adhesion factor.

These two locomotives were initially used singly on express trains on the Midland main line. Later, they were run in multiple on the Royal Scot express over the difficult West Coast main line between London and Glasgow, their combined 2387kW (3200bhp) producing unprecedented performances. Flush doors in the

nose fronts of each locomotive could be opened to release a concertina corridor connection so that the train crew could move about between the locomotives – for example, to attend to the train heating steam boiler.

Nos. 10000 and 10001 were later transferred to British Railways' southern region, and ran their last years again on the West Coast main line on freight and passenger trains. No. 10001 was withdrawn in 1963 and No. 10000 was out of action also about the same time, though not officially withdrawn until three years later.

Nos. 10000 and 10001 most often worked in tandem, but they also operated singly, as on this express northbound from London in the 1950s.

TYPE: mixed-traffic main-line diesel-electric
WHEEL ARRANGEMENT: Co-Co
POWER UNIT: English Electric 16SVT 16-cylinder V-form diesel, 1194kW (1600bhp); DC generator; six axle-hung DC traction motors
TRACTIVE EFFORT: 184kN (41,400lbf)
MAX. OPERATING SPEED: 145km/h (90mph)
WEIGHT: 124t (272,160lb)
OVERALL LENGTH: 18.644m (61ft 2in)
GAUGE: not known

CLASS C62 4-6-4 JAPANESE RAILWAYS (JR)

JAPAN 1948

Before World War II, the Japanese Railways had been running express trains with 'Pacific' classes, and 'Hudsons' were seen as the natural follow-on to the C59 heavy 'Pacific'. Development began with the C61s, of which 33 were built in 1947. Class C62, of which 49 were built by the Hitachi Seisakusho, Kawasaki Zosenjo and Kisha Seizo Kaisha workshops, was in fact a rebuild of D52 2-8-2 locomotives. The rebuilds were

new locomotives to all intents and purposes. Articulation of engine and tender was unusual, with the tender's leading bogie set well forward, partly under the cab, and with no footplate extension on the tender front. Japan had inaugurated its 'super-expresses' with the *Tsubame* ('Swallow') in 1930, running the 601.4km (373.7 miles) between Tokyo and Kobe in 9hrs, and *Tsubame* was picked up as a byname for the

C62s, which took over the train and had a swallow device on the smoke deflectors. Following electrification, they were transferred to work express trains on Hokkaido. Two are preserved, including the first of the series, which is in working order.

Postwar Japanese design continued to follow American styles, though the smoke deflectors give a European touch. Note the *Tsubame* emblem, indicating express work.

BOILER PRESSURE: 16kg/cm² (228psi)
CYLINDERS: 520x660mm (20.5x26in)
DRIVING WHEELS: 1750mm (69in)
GRATE AREA: 3.8m² (41.5sq ft)
HEATING SURFACE: 244.5m² (2632sq ft)
SUPERHEATER: 77.4m² (833sq ft)
TRACTIVE EFFORT: 13,925kg (30,690lb)
TOTAL WEIGHT: 145.2t (320,166lb)

CLASS 1001 1-DO-1 STATE RAILWAYS (SS)

NETHERLANDS 1948

A 'universal locomotive' was what the Dutch Railways, with limited resources, wanted – a type capable of heavy and high-speed freight haulage, and also of express passenger work. The resulting class of 10 Swiss-built locomotives owed much to the SBB Ae 4/6 and 8/14 classes. Eight traction motors were the key to its adaptability, with SLM individual

axle drive. They could be operated in series-parallel grouping at low speed, or in parallel grouping at speeds in excess of 100km/h (62mph). Driving wheels were of 1550mm (61in) diameter, and the pantographs were mounted on an unusual clerestory-style roofline. In service, they hauled 2000-tonne (1968-ton) coal trains at 60km/h (37mph), mixed freight of 850

tonnes (836 tons) at 80km/h (50mph), and 250-tonne (246-ton) passenger expresses at 160km/h

TYPE: universal locomotive
POWER: eight traction motors developing a maximum of 3343kW (4480hp) hourly, or 2836kW (3800hp) continuous, supplied by 1500V DC via overhead catenary
TRACTIVE EFFORT: 176.5kN (39,690lb)

(100mph), though schedules at the time rarely required the latter speed.

MAX. OPERATING SPEED: 160km/h (100mph)
TOTAL WEIGHT: 99.6t (219,618lb)
MAX. AXLE LOAD: 20t (44,100lb)
OVERALL LENGTH: 16.22m (53ft 3in)

'RIVER' CLASS 2-8-2 NIGERIAN RAILWAYS (NR)

NIGERIA 1948

Several railway systems in former British colonies used this type, once again underlining the suitability of the 2-8-2 to narrow gauge. In the post-war years, the British Crown Agents, responsible for supplies to colonial governments, commissioned them as 1065mm (3ft 6in) gauge freight locomotives for Nigeria, each locomotive named after rivers of the country. Virtually identical locomotives were built for the Tanganyika Railway and the East

African Railways (EAR) from 1948 to 1954. The original order was supplied by the Vulcan Foundry and the North British Locomotive Company. It was a medium-power freight engine, with a 13.2-tonne (13-ton) axle loading and able to work over lightweight rails and poorly kept track. The Nigerian and Tanganyikan engines were intended to burn low-grade locally-mined coal; the EAR followed its usual policy of that time in having oil-burning engines that could

readily be converted to coal firing if the need arose. The engines were bar-framed, two-cylinder simples, with outside Walschaerts valve gear. The boilers were of the parallel type, with straight-sided Belpaire fireboxes. Both the front

and rear trucks were fitted with outside bearings; the EAR engines (Class 29) with roller bearings on all axles including those of the tender. They were fitted with Giesl ejectors, with debatable benefits, in the 1960s.

BOILER PRESSURE: 14kg/cm² (200psi)
CYLINDERS: 533x660mm (21x26in)
DRIVING WHEELS: 1218mm (48in)
GRATE AREA: 3.3m² (36sq ft)

HEATING SURFACE: 174.4m² (1878sq ft)
SUPERHEATER: 45.4m² (489sq ft)
TRACTIVE EFFORT: 14,716kg (29,800lb)
TOTAL WEIGHT: 74.9t (165,312lb)

CLASS CP 1500 A1A-A1A PORTUGUESE STATE RAILWAYS (CP)

PORTUGAL 1948

Portugal was the first European country to import diesel-electrics from the United States. They were Alco-GEC 'hood units',

essentially the same machines as the RS-2 road switchers. Employed on main-line passenger and freight trains throughout the country, they

gave excellent service for many years, ending up up in the south on overnight passenger trains between Barreiro and Faro, and in

the Barreiro suburban area. During the 1970s, CP re-engined them to raise their power from 1230kW (1650hp) to 1600kW (2150hp). As

Portugal's oldest main-line diesel locomotives they survived, just, into the 21st century.

TYPE: mixed-traffic main-line diesel-electric
WHEEL ARRANGEMENT: A1A-A1A
POWER UNIT: Alco 244 12-cylinder V-form diesel, 1230kW (1650bhp), changed to Alco 251-C 12-cylinder V-form diesel, 1600kW (2150bhp); General Electric DC generator; four axle-hung DC traction motors
TRACTIVE EFFORT: 153kN (37,400lbf)
MAX. OPERATING SPEED: 120km/h (75mph)
WEIGHT: 111 to 114t (243,765 to 250,355lb)
OVERALL LENGTH: 16.99m (55ft 9in)
GAUGE: 1668mm (5ft 6in)

In all essentials, this was an Alco RS-3 built for the Portuguese loading gauge. It was a useful mixed-traffic engine.

ALCO-GE GAS TURBINE LOCOMOTIVE UNION PACIFIC RAILROAD (UP)

USA 1948

Union Pacific was the only railroad to run anything like a 'fleet' of gas turbine locomotives. Starting point was an experimental

TYPE: gas-turbine electric
POWER: 3357kW (4500hp)
TRACTIVE EFFORT: 467kN (105,000lbf)

MAX. OPERATING SPEED: 104km/h (65mph)
WEIGHT: 250t (551,000lb)

OVERALL LENGTH: 25.45m (83ft 6in)
GAUGE: 1435mm (4ft 8.5in)

double-ended gas-turbine electric built in 1948 by General Electric. Its gas turbine turned a generator that powered eight DC traction motors. The advantage of the turbine was that it produced very high power output and burned a low-grade 'Bunker C' oil that was much cheaper than diesel. It was preheated to 93ºC (200ºF) in the tender before being piped to the engine. On the downside, the turbine locomotive had significantly higher fuel consumption because the turbine operated at a constant high rate of speed. Union Pacific operated three varieties of GT locomotives. Nine were delivered up to 1952 – they were similar to the prototype, 3357kW (4500hp) machines on a Bo-Bo+Bo-Bo wheel arrangement; 15 between 1952 and 1954 with 'verandah' side walkways and overhang roofs; and 30 of Co-Co wheel arrangement between 1958 and 1961, which delivered 6341kW (8500hp). All were out of service by 1970. One is preserved at Ogden, and one in Illinois Railroad Museum.

Specifications are based on Union Pacific Nos. 51–60.

The size and length of Union Pacific's gas turbine type GT-EL No. 18 can be appreciated at the Illinois Railroad Museum, where it is now a static display locomotive.

CLASS 350 BO-BO SOUTH AUSTRALIAN RAILWAYS (SAR)

AUSTRALIA 1949

SAR's own works brought out the first Australian-built diesel-electrics. Engine and electric parts were supplied from the UK by the English Electric company, establishing a long association with SAR, and in time English Electric set up its own plant at Rocklea for local construction. Only two of Class 350 were built, as four-axle Bo-Bo machines, the EE 6KT engine driving an EE801 traction generator and four EE506 traction motors. They were deployed on shunting (switching) work in the Adelaide area for their entire working lives until the late 1970s, and both are preserved, No. 350 still in full working order.

TYPE: Bo-Bo diesel-electric shunting
POWER: EE 6KT series engine producing 250kW (335hp)
TRACTIVE EFFORT: 39kN (8775lbf) at 28km/h (17.5mph)

MAX. OPERATING SPEED: 40km/h (25mph)
WEIGHT: 50t (110,250lb)
OVERALL LENGTH: 5.44m (17ft 7in)
GAUGE: 1600mm (5ft 3in)

Retired Nos. 350 and 351 at Islington locomotive workshops awaiting preservation work, on 31 January 1980.

CLASS 101 BO+BO BELGIAN NATIONAL RAILWAYS (SNCB)

BELGIUM 1949

Like the Netherlands, the SNCB embarked on an intensive electrification scheme in the later 1940s. As part of this, 20 Bo+Bo locomotives were ordered to run under the SNCB standard 3000V DC overhead line system. These were mixed-traffic engines, able to cope with fast passenger services or moderately heavy freight. Four traction motors powered the axles, acceleration being achieved by diverting traction current through body-mounted resistances. With more modern locomotives on stream from 1953, the Class 101s were diverted almost wholly to freight, and worked on into the 1980s. Belgium was unusual in that its locomotive numbering changed in the 1970s from a 'class + serial' number scheme to a straightforward four-digit scheme, under which No. 101.001 became 2901. One Class 29 locomotive is preserved.

TYPE: Bo+Bo mixed-traffic electric locomotive
POWER: 3000V DC overhead line collection; 1620kW (2170hp); resistance control; four axle-hung DC traction motors
TRACTIVE EFFORT: not known

MAX. OPERATING SPEED: 100km/h (62mph)
WEIGHT: 81t (17,790lb)
MAX. AXLE LOAD: not known
OVERALL LENGTH: not known
GAUGE: 1435mm (4ft 8.5in)

4-8-4 NATIONAL RAILWAYS DEPARTMENT (DNEF)

BRAZIL 1949

The DNEF had responsibility for Brazil's vast metre-gauge network – over 35,200km (22,000 miles), much of it in poor condition and with out-of-date equipment. An order for new locomotives, both 4-8-4s and 2-8-4s, was won by the French consortium GELSA, which appointed André Chapelon as designer. Two-cylinder simple-expansion engines, they make an interesting comparison with the Indian Railways' YP and YG locomotives, built at the same time. They had Kylchap double exhausts and mechanical stokers, and Belpaire fireboxes fitted with two thermic syphons. Some were still at work in the 1970s, not only in Brazil but also in Bolivia, but even though they were less complex mechanically than French locomotives, servicing standards of the time meant that they did not produce exceptional performance.

BOILER PRESSURE: 19.6kg/cm² (280psi)
CYLINDERS: 431x639mm (17x25.2in)
DRIVING WHEELS: 1523mm (60in)
GRATE AREA: 5.4m² (58sq ft)
HEATING SURFACE: 167m² (1797sq ft)
SUPERHEATER: 732m² (7879sq ft)
TRACTIVE EFFORT: 15,894kg (35,056lb)
TOTAL WEIGHT: 93t (205,030lb)

CLASS 476.0 4-8-2 CZECHOSLOVAK NATIONAL RAILWAYS (CSD)

In the brief post-war revival of steam design, some of the most interesting engines were built in Czechoslovakia. The Czech loading gauge allowed engines of a height of 4.62m (15ft 2in) and a width of 3.1m (10ft 2in), which gave designers useful scope. This class of three three-cylinder engines was a development of a two-cylinder 475 Class 4-8-2 of 1947, which borrowed numerous features from André Chapelon's work in France. The high-pressure cylinder was set inside the frame. Class 476 was originally intended to be a compound design, but the compounding system was not a success. After the first three, the remaining 12 of the class were built as three-cylinder simples, in which form they gave good service on long-distance east–west express trains.

BOILER PRESSURE: 20kg/cm² (285psi)
CYLINDERS: hp 500x600mm (19.7x23.6in); lp 580x680mm (22.8x26.8in)
DRIVING WHEELS: 1624mm (64in)

GRATE AREA: 4.3m² (46.3sq ft)
HEATING SURFACE: 201m² (2164sq ft)
SUPERHEATER: 63.3m² (681sq ft)
TRACTIVE EFFORT: N/A
TOTAL WEIGHT: 108.4t (239,020lb)

CLASS 232.U.1 4-6-4 FRENCH NATIONAL RAILWAYS (SNCF)

For the haulage of international and long-distance expresses, often with heavy sleeping cars, the *Nord* railway had been looking in the late 1930s for a new generation of steam power to take over from its 'Pacifics'. This was the genesis of the 232.U.1. A 4-6-4 design by the *Nord* engineering chief Marc de Caso was favoured because of the wide grate it offered. Although compounding was well established in France, SNCF decided to build both compound and simple examples, for comparison purposes. Both types of course benefited from the principles of internal streamlining laid down by Chapelon. Four streamlined versions of each type were ordered from the Société Alsacienne of Mulhouse in 1938 – three simples, Class 232.R, were delivered by April 1940, and the four compounds, 232.S, were completed in late 1940. Plans to build the uncompleted simple with turbine drive were dropped, and it was completed as a four-cylinder compound by the Corpet-Louvet works in 1949. A number of distinctive features ensured its

separate classification as U.1, including a Houlet 33-element superheater, long-travel piston valves driven by Walschaerts gear and SKF roller bearings on all axles. Unlike its seven predecessors it was semi-streamlined, with strong, sweeping lines and ready access to the working parts. But although they all turned in impressive performances, and 232.U.1 could comfortably handle a Paris–Lille express of 576 tonnes (567 tons) at an average 114.25km/h (71mph) for the round trip, they were neither as powerful nor as economic in running as Chapelon's 4-8-4 242A.1, whose design had a considerable influence on the U.1. For any locomotive other than a French one, this might be an unfair comparison. Although a tentative move was made to order cylinders for a further 20 of the same type, this was quashed by high authority and it remained a one-off. 242.U.1 is preserved at Mulhouse.

BOILER PRESSURE: 20.5kg/cm² (292psi)
CYLINDERS: hp 447x700.5mm (17.6x27.6in); lp 680x700.5mm (26.8x27.6in)
DRIVING WHEELS: 1999mm (78.75in)
GRATE AREA: 5.2m² (55.7sq ft)
HEATING SURFACE: 195m² (2099sq ft)
SUPERHEATER: 87.4m² (941sq ft)
TRACTIVE EFFORT: N/A

France's last steam-powered passenger express locomotive, the unique part-streamlined 232-U.1 can still be seen at the Mulhouse railway museum.

Class 232.U.1 at La Chapelle depot, outside the Gare du Nord, Paris, when working on the Paris–Lille expresses.

'LEADER' 0-6-6-0T BRITISH RAILWAYS (BR), SOUTHERN REGION

The quest for a 'new generation' of steam locomotives that could match the operating characteristics of a diesel lay behind this design, Oliver Bulleid's last for a British railway. The project was dogged by design troubles and the single prototype was little used. It was mounted on two articulated six-wheel bogies, each driven by a three-cylinder engine on the centre axle, with steam distribution by sleeve valves. The motion and cranks

BOILER PRESSURE: 14.7kg/cm² (210psi)
CYLINDERS: 387x609mm (15.25x24in)
DRIVING WHEELS: 2128mm (54in)
GRATE AREA: 2.6m² (28sq ft)
HEATING SURFACE: 102.25m² (1101sq ft)
SUPERHEATER: 30.7m² (331sq ft)
TRACTIVE EFFORT: 8367kg (18,450lb)
TOTAL WEIGHT: 58t (127,680lb)
(engine only)

were encased and automatically lubricated. Each end had a driving cab, with a hot space for the fireman in the middle. Four thermic syphons were fitted in the firebox. The class was

'Leader' prototype No. 36001 outside Brighton Locomotive Works in 1949, facing a veteran Stroudley 'Terrier' (see 1872).

provisionally rated 5MT, for mixed traffic haulage. Work on three part-built examples was

abandoned at Brighton Works after 1949, and by 1951 all four were dismantled.

NO. 18000 A1A-A1A BRITISH RAILWAYS (BR)

Commissioned by the old Great Western Railway from Brown Boveri of Switzerland, this gas turbine electric locomotive arrived in 1949 after the company had become BR's Western Region. Like the Union Pacific/GEC gas turbine locomotives in the United States, though with much smaller dimensions and a single unit only,

it used a gas turbine engine coupled to a DC electric generator, supplying power to four traction motors that drove the outer axles on the two three-axle bogies. The motors drove through spring drives to reduce the unsprung weight on each driving axle.

The engine was used intermittently on premier express

trains between London, Bristol and the southwest until 1960, but

remained a one-off class. It is now preserved.

TYPE: main-line gas turbine electric
WHEEL ARRANGEMENT: A1A-A1A
POWER UNIT: Brown Boveri gas turbine 1865kW (2500bhp); DC generator; four DC traction motors
TRACTIVE EFFORT: 267kN (60,000lbf)

MAX. OPERATING SPEED: 145km/h (90mph)
WEIGHT: 117t (257,600lb)
OVERALL LENGTH: 19.22m (63ft 1in)
GAUGE: 1435mm (4ft 8.5in)

CLASS YP 4-6-2 INDIAN RAILWAYS (IR)

The 'Y' in the Indian Railway code indicated narrow gauge, and 'P' was 'Pacific'. Modern Indian locomotive design in the post-war

and early independence years was provided for the metre-gauge as well as the broad gauge. Designed to be a standard express type, the

YP became a very numerous class, totalling 871. Baldwin built 20 prototypes in Philadelphia, and the first main production runs came

from North British Locomotive Co. in Glasgow and Krauss-Maffei in Munich; from 1956 on, they were built by the Telco works at

Indian locomotives often had individual decorations applied at their depots, like the 'express' symbol on the smoke deflectors of this well-worked YP.

Jamshedpur and by Chittaranjan, where the final batch was built between 1969–72.

These were the last express steam engines to be constructed in India. The class shared a boiler with the simultaneous new 2-8-2 standard Class YG. Harmoniously proportioned, the engines were only 3.15m (10ft 4in) high, with a maximum axle loading of 10.7 tonnes (10.5 tons). Their construction was of similar specification to the new standard broad gauge Pacifics of Class WP, and showed a strong American influence: two cylinders, simple expansion; bar frames, with one-piece steel castings at each end; a substantial firebox incorporating

combustion chamber, thermic syphon and arch tubes. Roller-bearing axle boxes were fitted to the pony and tender wheels. By this time, steam designers everywhere fully appreciated the value of large-diameter long-travel piston valves in ensuring the free passage of steam to the cylinders, and those fitted to the YPs, actuated by the ubiquitous Walschaerts gear, were of 228mm (9in) diameter. Smoke deflectors were fitted, though the trains were rarely very fast. Over 750 YP locomotives were still in service during 1974–75, widely distributed across the system, and many were still at work in the 1990s. Several have been preserved.

BOILER PRESSURE: 14.7kg/cm² (210psi)
CYLINDERS: 387x609mm (15.25x24in)
DRIVING WHEELS: 2128mm (54in)
GRATE AREA: 2.6m² (28sq ft)
HEATING SURFACE: 102.25m² (1101sq ft)
SUPERHEATER: 30.7m² (331sq ft)
TRACTIVE EFFORT: 8367kg (18,450lb)
TOTAL WEIGHT: 58t (127,680lb)
(engine only)

Compact but strong performer on the metre gauge, a YP hauls a passenger train. Speeds rarely exceeded 40kph (mph).

CLASS 15A 4-6-4+4-6-4 RHODESIA RAILWAYS (RR)

The later 1940s and the 1950s saw a range of new or modified Garratt designs, especially in Africa. Based on the RR's Class 15 Garratt of the same wheel arrangement, which dated from 1930, the 15A was altered in various ways, of which the most apparent was the down-curved ends of the tank and tender, an aesthetic rather than a practical

BOILER PRESSURE: 14kg/cm² (200psi)
CYLINDERS: 445x660mm (17.5x26in)
DRIVING WHEELS: 1448mm (57in)
GRATE AREA: 4.6m² (49.6sq ft)
HEATING SURFACE: 216m² (2322sq ft)
SUPERHEATER: 46m² (494sq ft)
TRACTIVE EFFORT: 21,546kg (47,500lb)
TOTAL WEIGHT: 189.5t (418,000lb)

change that considerably improved the look of these and later Garratts. Forty were delivered between 1949 and 1952, and ran both freight and passenger services on the 1065mm (3ft 6in) gauge route between Bulawayo

and Mafeking. A number of these locomotives still survive in Zambia.

A Class 15A running across the veld between Wankie and Bulawayo.

Despite its weight of almost 190 tons, the 14 axles of the Class 15A meant that the maximum axle load was less than 17 tons, making it quite a light-footed monster.

GE 'LITTLE JOE' 2-DO-2 VARIOUS RAILROADS

USA 1949

The 'Little Joe' name was a reference to Josef Stalin. When in 1948 hostility between the United States and Soviet Russia prevented General Electric from fulfilling a Russian order for 20 completed, powerful modern streamlined electrics, it had to look around for other buyers. With some encouragement from the US government, Milwaukee Road took 12 of the 'Little Joes' for use on the eastern electrified segment of its Pacific Extension between Harlowton, MT, and Avery, ID. Chicago-area interurban electric line Chicago, South Shore & South Bend took three of the locomotives, which continued to run freight

services up to the early 1980s. Brazil's Paulista Railway bought the remaining five. All the 'Little Joes' were re-gauged to fit the standard 1435mm (4 ft 8.5in) gauge.

TYPE: 2-Do-Do-2, electric
POWER: 3000V DC on Milwaukee/1500V DC on South Shore
TRACTIVE EFFORT: 492kN (110,750lbf)
MAX. OPERATING SPEED: 112km/h (70mph)
WEIGHT: 243t (535,572lb)
OVERALL LENGTH: 27.076m (88ft 10in)
MAX. AXLE LOAD: 25t (55,100lb)
GAUGE: 1435mm (4ft 8.5in) – originally built for 1524mm (5ft)

The Chicago, South Shore & South Bend Railroad used three 'Little Joes' to run freight trains until they were replaced by diesels in the early 1980s.

EMD GP7/GP9 BO-BO VARIOUS US AND CANADIAN RAILROADS

USA/CANADA 1949

Once a ubiquitous sight on US railroads – GP9 locomotive No. 1758 of the New Hampshire North Coast Railroad, at Dover, NH, in March 2002.

TYPE: Bo-Bo, diesel-electric
POWER AND OUTPUT (BASED ON GP9): EMD 16-567C producing 1306kW (1750hp)
TRACTIVE EFFORT: 196kN (44,000lbf) at 19.3km/h (12mph)
MAX. OPERATING SPEED: 104km/h (65mph)
WEIGHT (BASED ON BURLINGTON NORTHERN GP9): 115t (254,000lb)
OVERALL LENGTH: 17.12m (56ft 2in)
GAUGE: 1435mm (4ft 8.5in)

This was the boom time for diesels in the United States; in 1948, demand for new units had run around 40 per cent ahead of manufacturers' ability to supply. GP, standing for 'general purpose', designated Electro-Motive Division's first 'proper' road switcher, a type pioneered by Alco and already on offer from all the other major diesel locomotive builders. Prior to the GP7, EMD had produced a form of road switcher with its BL2 'Branch Line' locomotive without much success, and had also constructed a few hybrid switcher types such as the NW3 and NW5. Internally, the GP7 was effectively the same as EMD's successful F7. It used a 16-cylinder 567-series engine and

was rated at 1119kW (1500 hp). In 1954, EMD upgraded its locomotive line, introducing a host of small improvements that resulted in substantially better performance and reliability. Its improved road switcher model was the GP9, which used the 16-567C engine rated at 1306kW (1750 hp). Despite EMD's relatively late and slow entry into the market, this became the classic road switcher, a ubiquitous symbol of modern American railroading and one of EMD's best-selling locomotive types. Built at La Grange and Montreal Locomotive Works, more than 4000 of these locomotives were sold to railroads in the United States and Canada, aside from export markets.

Heading a freight at Palmer, Massachusetts, in August 1987, GP9 No. 4923 of the Central Vermont Railway.

BUDD RAIL DIESEL CAR (RDC) VARIOUS RAILROADS

The self-propelled gasoline-engined railcar had a long history, as motored machines go. Edward Budd had worked for the McKeen Company, which produced self-propelled gasoline-engine railcars in the early 1900s. His Philadelphia-based Budd Company entered the limelight with the introduction of Burlington's *Zephyr* which used Budd's lightweight stainless steel cars. By the late 1930s, Budd was producing streamlined passenger cars for many American railroads, and its fluted stainless-steel cars were assigned to some of America's best known trains including Santa Fe's *Super Chief*. Edward Budd died in 1946, three years before his company made a successful diesel-powered railcar. The first Budd Rail Diesel Car (commonly known as an

RDC) was built in 1949. The lightweight construction techniques learned with the passenger cars were used, and the Budd RDC had a distinctive appearance, with stainless-steel bodywork and the typical fluted sides. It was powered by two General Motors in-line six-cylinder 205kW (275hp) engines, later uprated to 224kW (300hp), driving through torque converters to the inside axles of the four-wheel bogies. Engines and transmission were entirely beneath the car body floor, and a distinctive structure on the roof held the radiators, cooling fans, air intake, exhaust pipe and bell, leaving the interior space entirely for passengers and baggage. Disc brakes were standard, and the cars were heated and air conditioned.

A driving compartment was provided at each end. RDCs were designed to operate singly or in multiples. In the 1950s, hundreds of Budd cars were ordered by North American railways for use on secondary passenger services. While many RDCs ran on branch-line or suburban commuter services, others were equipped for long-distance runs.

There were several standard types of cars. The RDC-1 was a basic coach, while the RDC-2 had a baggage compartment, and RDC-3 had baggage and Railway Post Office sections in addition to coach seats. They played an important part in the railroad companies' struggle to keep secondary routes and rural branch lines economically viable for passenger transport. They gained a reputation for reliability,

and within 10 years of purchase two RDCs on the Western Pacific had exceeded a 1.69 million km (1 million miles) of running. Some also ran on main-line services: in the 1950s, the Baltimore & Ohio ran a three-car set with dining facilities between Philadelphia and Pittsburgh, 690km (428.7 miles), improving by 1hr, 30mins on the locomotive-hauled schedule.

TYPE: self-propelled diesel-hyraulic passenger rail car

POWER AND OUTPUT: a pair of GM 6-110 diesel engines producing 205kW (275hp) to 224kw (300hp)

TRACTIVE EFFORT: N/A

MAX. OPERATING SPEED: 136km/h (85mph)

WEIGHT: 58t (126,730lb)

OVERALL LENGTH: 25.908m (85ft)

GAUGE: 1435mm (4ft 8.5in)

A Budd RDC refuels at the Communipaw, NJ, depot of the Central of New Jersey Railroad, on 25 August 1959.

CHAPTER FIVE

THE HIGH-SPEED ERA

1950–1961

By 1950, the steam locomotive was disappearing from all but a few US railroads, and the same process was about to get under way elsewhere. Rebuilding after wartime damage, most European countries, as well as Japan, opted for electric traction on main networks, with diesel on subsidiary lines – in some cases, diesel-hydraulic rather than diesel-electric, especially on the renovated West German railways. In other continents, diesel-electric was the preferred mode, with electric haulage generally reserved for urban rapid transit and specialized mineral lines. During the phasing-out period between steam and new forms of traction, some countries built new steam locomotives of remarkable efficiency, but most of these were destined for short working lives. The profitability of

railways was threatened in almost every country by the vast increase in road transportation and in domestic and international air traffic. Many railways were closed and the tracks lifted. But signs of future promise could be seen, in the rise of diesel-hydraulic and diesel-electric multiple-unit sets. In combination, these can generate as much power as a big locomotive. In some countries, including Britain, they have ousted locomotives from almost all passenger duties except a handful of overnight sleeper trains. Beginning in Japan in the late 1950s, and later taken up in France, Spain and Italy, another development has been the construction of high-speed lines linking major cities. The services they provide have been popular and have won traffic back from internal airlines.

The Italian State Railways' Class 741 2-8-0, with its double Crosti boiler, and apparent lack of a chimney, was one of the most distinctive locomotive designs of the twentieth century.

CLASS 12L 4-6-2 CENTRAL ARGENTINE RAILWAY (CAR)

ARGENTINA 1950

No Argentinian railway had ever placed such a large single order – 90 locomotives, and 'Pacifics' at that. It was placed with the British Vulcan Foundry in 1948, just before Argentinian railways were nationalized. Only 40 were delivered, however, the rest of the order being cancelled in favour of 21m/69ft-gauge diesel-electrics. This was Argentina's last steam type, running from 1950. Most worked on the Central Railway, though five went to the former Great Southern. The design, a three-cylinder simple, was said to be based on the Class 12 Armstrong-Whitworth Pacifics of 1930, but the new engines had Caprotti cam-operated valve gear and parallel boilers with wide round-topped fireboxes. The big tenders, on two six-wheel bogies, weighed more than the locomotives when full, but the capacity allowed the locomotives to run between Buenos Aires and Rosario, 303km (188 miles), without taking on water. The class was withdrawn in the late 1960s.

BOILER PRESSURE: 15.8cm² (225psi)
CYLINDERS: 507.6x660mm (20x26in)
DRIVING WHEELS: 1903mm (75in)
GRATE AREA: 4m² (43sq ft)
HEATING SURFACE: 232.8m² (2507sq ft)
SUPERHEATER: not known
TRACTIVE EFFORT: 11,460kg (25,270lb)
TOTAL WEIGHT: 101.5t (224,000lb)
(engine only)

CLASS 2D2-9100 2-DO-2 FRENCH NATIONAL RAILWAYS (SNCF)

FRANCE 1950

Built for mixed-traffic haulage, this was the last of the long line of 2-Do-2 electric designs that worked on the 1500V DC railways in France before the SNCF made the move to bogie-motored locomotives, whose superior performance and reliability was now clear. The 35 Class 2D2-9100 locomotives were impressive in appearance and reliable in action. Constructed for the electrification of the former Paris–Lyon–Méditerranée (PLM) main line, with its heavy loads and long inclines, they were liveried in pale green, with a single 'cat's whisker' stripe on each end. They lasted more than 30 years, and were still in use with PLM in the early 1980s.

TYPE: 2-Do-2 mixed-traffic mainline electric locomotive
POWER: 1500V DC overhead line collection; 3690kW (4950hp); resistance control; four body frame mounted, axle-hung DC traction motors; four carrying axles
TRACTIVE EFFORT: unknown

MAX. OPERATING SPEED: 140km/h (87mph)
WEIGHT: 144t (316,235lb)
MAX. AXLE LOAD: 22.35t (49,280lb)
OVERALL LENGTH: 18.08m (59ft 4in)
GAUGE: 1435mm (4ft 8.5in)

Class 2-D-2 No. 9110 swings into its platform road at the Gare de Lyon, Paris, with one of the first electrified express services on the Paris–Lyon–Méditerranée main line.

X-3800 DIESEL RAILCARS FRENCH RAILWAYS (SNCF)

FRANCE 1950

Distinctive in appearance – hence their nickname of 'Picasso' – these were designed as single railcars that could haul trailers at times of extra traffic. The driving cab projected above the low roof of the vehicle. Thus, though the carriage was relatively low slung, the driver (who sat sideways to the direction of travel) had a good view in either direction. The cars were also unusual in having access doors at two levels, one suitable for high platforms and one for low ones. Over 100 were built by four manufacturers, ANF, de Dietrich, Renault and Saurer.

TYPE: diesel mechanical railcar for local and branch-line services
POWER: Renault 517G or 575 or Saurer BZDS of 250 to 265kW (335 to 355bhp); mechanical transmission
TRACTIVE EFFORT: N/A

MAX. OPERATING SPEED: 120km/h (75mph)
WEIGHT: 33t (71,680lb)
OVERALL LENGTH: 21.85m (71ft 8in)
GAUGE: 1435mm (4ft 8.5in)

Pablo Picasso's revolutionary artistic style was responsible for the nickname of this railcar, with its distinctive 'lop-sided' driving cab.

The Picassos were first painted in standard SNCF red livery, with cream above waist level. They operated on secondary routes and branch lines in most areas of France. The whole class had gone by the end of the 1980s. Several are preserved.

SERIES E.10 BO-BO GERMAN FEDERAL RAILWAYS (DB)

To the managers of West Germany's extensive but war-racked railway system, all forms of motive power – steam, diesel and electric – needed to be renewed and developed. Less than a quarter of the pre-war stock of 880 electric locomotives was in a usable state. In the renewal plan, five Bo-Bo electric prototypes were initially produced, with various forms of drive and other differences, though in many dimensions they were very similar. By this time, it was clear that rod drive was not a viable option for a modern, fast main-line electric

locomotive. Wheel- or axle-drive were the choices, and the prototypes had, variously, Alsthom universal link drive, Siemens rubber ring transmission and two forms of disc drive, Brown Boveri's and Sécheron's. Another aim was to ensure that the ultimate production runs would share as many standard parts as possible. The manufacturers Henschel, Krauss-Maffei and Krupp participated, with the electrical companies Brown Boveri, Siemens-Schuckert and AEG. There was a great deal at stake, and extensive and searching trials were

organized before the first production run of 200 E10 locomotives was ordered. These had the Siemens rubber ring transmission, four nose-suspended motors and twin transformers for HT regulation. Wheel diameter was 1250mm (49in). The DB engineers

consulted the experience of electric traction in Switzerland, Italy and France, as well as Germany, and the intensive research and development work put in on Class E10 played a vital part in the further development of German electric motive power.

TYPE: Bo-Bo express passenger electric locomotive
POWER: 15,000V 16.7Hz AC overhead line collection; 3620kW (4855hp); mechanical notching-up control; rheostatic brakes; four frame mounted DC traction motors

TRACTIVE EFFORT: 275kN (61,820lbf)
MAX. OPERATING SPEED: 150km/h (93mph)
WEIGHT: 85t (185,790lb)
OVERALL LENGTH: 16,490mm (54ft 1in)
GAUGE: 1435mm (4ft 8.5in)

CLASS V55 BO-CO HUNGARIAN STATE RAILWAYS (MÁV)

Hungary had been an early pioneer in electric locomotive development, but by 1950 work elsewhere had overtaken what was being done in Budapest. The V55,

Hungary's first post-war electric locomotives, still used synchronous motors with phase converters and fluid resistor control. The relatively unusual

asymmetric five-axle layout was an attempt to achieve adhesion on all wheels while supporting the very heavy phase-splitting equipment. Ten production examples were

built. Five synchronous speeds were possible in the prototypes, but the later 10 had a blanket upper speed limit of 100km/h (62mph). Low-quality construction and materials made the class unreliable, and the bulk of Hungary's electric traffic remained in charge of the pre-war class V40. V55 014 survives in the Budapest railway museum.

TYPE: Bo-Co synchronous electric
POWER: 2354kW (3198hp)
SUPPLY: 16kV 50Hz AC
TRACTIVE EFFORT: 208kN (46800lbf)
MAX. OPERATING SPEED: 100km/h (62mph)
WEIGHT: 92.5t (203,963lb)
MAX. AXLE LOAD: 18.5t (40,793lb)
OVERALL LENGTH: 14.6m (47ft 8in)
GAUGE: 1435mm (4ft 8.5in)

Now retired, the last of the V55 class stands as a display locomotive at Budapest.

CLASS 1200 CO-CO NETHERLANDS RAILWAYS (NS)

The NS's prime aim by 1950 was almost complete electrification of its main lines, using a range of locomotives and multiple units. The 35 Class 1200 locomotives were intended for freight haulage and had Dutch-built electrical equipment. Bogies with prominent compensating beams for the primary springing came from Baldwin in the United States, and

final assembly was by Werkspoor in the Netherlands. The design, with its broad, flat-nosed front, was a distinctive one. Initially in blue livery, which made them look smart, the class received the later standard NS grey-and-yellow style in the late 1970s. They lasted until the late 1990s on NS. A small number are now operated by the private company ACTS.

TYPE: Co-Co mixed-traffic electric locomotive
POWER: 1500V DC overhead line collection; 2360kW (3165hp); resistance control; six axle-hung DC traction motors
TRACTIVE EFFORT: 194kN (43,615lbf)

MAX. OPERATING SPEED: 135km/h (85mph)
WEIGHT: 108t (237,175lb)
MAX AXLE LOAD: not known
OVERALL LENGTH: 18.085m (59ft 4in)
GAUGE: 1435m (4ft 8.5in)

An NS class 1200 shows off its angular 1950s styling on a local service at Amsterdam Central.

CLASS TKT 48 2-8-2T POLISH STATE RAILWAYS (PKP)

POLAND 1950

Though intended for freight haulage, this class of big tank engines actually spent more time in passenger service. Its extra power and adhesion weight and its lighter axle-loading gave it the edge over the heavyweight earlier Ok1-27 2-6-2T. Up to 1958, the Polish works of Cegielski and Chrzanov built around 195, and they ran Warsaw's last steam-powered

suburban trains. Originally without smoke deflectors, they later had the high-mounted kind fitted.

The use of forward-pointing cylinder tail-rods, intended to ease wear on the piston and cylinder lining but an obsolete practice in

most other places by 1950, was perpetuated on this class. In the 1970s, with steam in Poland being phased out, and since they had a useful service life left, 20 of these engines were sold to the Albanian State Railways.

BOILER PRESSURE: 15kg/cm² (213.75psi)
CYLINDERS: 500x700mm (19.7x27.6in)
DRIVING WHEELS: 1450mm (57in)
GRATE AREA: 3m² (32.3sq ft)
HEATING SURFACE: 123.1m² (1325.3sq ft)
SUPERHEATER: 48.6m² (523.2sq ft)
TRACTIVE EFFORT: 15,420kg (34,000lb)
TOTAL WEIGHT: 95t (209,475lb)

Goods hauler turned passenger loco, a Class TkT shows its power with a long train as it climbs a grade through rural countryside.

CLASS TM11 B SWISS FEDERAL RAILWAYS (SBB)

SWITZERLAND 1950

Lightweight diesel tractors, these four-wheelers were primarily intended for moving single wagons or short trains about in stations and yards and on industrial spur lines, but a use was also found for them in transporting personnel and

equipment in their roomy platform cabs. They are still in use, as Class Tm 233. Some are equipped to carry snowploughs for track clearance in yards; others have hydraulic cranes for assisting in track-laying and overhead-wire work.

TYPE: diesel mechanical shunting tractor
WHEEL ARRANGEMENT: B (0-4-0)
POWER UNIT: Saurer C615D diesel, 70kW (94hp); mechanical transmission driving axles through cardan shafts and bevel gears

TRACTIVE EFFORT: N/A
MAX. OPERATING SPEED: 45km/h (28mph)
WEIGHT: 10t (21,960lb)
OVERALL LENGTH: 5.24m (17ft 2in)
GAUGE: 1435mm (4ft 8.5in)

FAIRBANKS-MORSE C-LINER VARIOUS RAILROADS

In 1950, Fairbanks-Morse moved all production to their own Beloit plant. 'C-liner' indicated the Fairbanks-Morse Consolidated Line, introduced in that year, which enabled customers to choose from a variety of machinery options: 8-, 10- and 12-cylinder engines and power outputs, housed in a standard-length streamlined carbody. General Electric supplied the electrical equipment. The styling of the C-liner car body was a more refined version of F-M's 'Erie-built' locomotives of the 1940s, with a shorter nose section. Between 1950 and 1956, six different models of C-Liner 'A-units' were produced, the most common being the CFA-16-4, with an eight-cylinder F-M opposed piston engine producing 1194kW (1600hp). C-Liners came as both 'A' and 'B' units, and some had an asymmetric Bo-A1A wheel arrangement, rather than Bo-Bo. Coming at a time when hood units were growing in popularity among customers as road engines, the C-Liners were not as popular as their EMD and Alco-GEC counterparts, but were used on numerous US lines as well as the CPR in Canada.

Canadian Pacific F-M C-liner No. 4104 at the motive power depot in Nelson, British Columbia. Behind it is a F-M XXXX, No. 8728.

TYPE: diesel-electric
POWER AND OUTPUT: various
TRACTIVE EFFORT: various
MAX. OPERATING SPEED: various
WEIGHT: various
OVERALL LENGTH: various
GAUGE: 1435mm (4ft 8.5in)

CLASS 11 4-8-2 BENGUELA RAILWAY (CFB)

Eucalyptus wood, quick-burning and producing good heat, was the fuel of the CFB, and was grown in long forest strips parallel to the tracks, chopped down and split into 609x253mm (24x10in) chunks for hand firing. This sophisticated wood-burner for the 1066mm (3ft 6in) gauge was built by the North British Locomotive Company of Glasgow. The design was modelled on the South African Railways 24-8-2 of the 19C/19D class. Modifications to the firebox included ashpan ventilation and a dust protection plate, and a spark arrestor was fitted inside the smoke-box. The chimney looks classically British, but beneath it is a Kylchap blast pipe. Other features of the class included electric lighting, power reversing gear and steam-operated firedoors.

Rising from the coast to a height of over 1500m (5000ft), the line is steeply graded and sharply curved, like the East African Railway on the other side of the continent. Mineral haulage by Garratts was the line's main business, carrying copper ore, and the 4-8-2s were largely used on passenger services, taking the hefty 508-tonne (500-ton) trains over sections with a ruling gradient of 1 in 80.

BOILER PRESSURE: 14kg/cm² (200psi)
CYLINDERS: 533x660mm (21x26in)
DRIVING WHEELS: 1372mm (54in)
GRATE AREA: 3.7m² (40sq ft)
HEATING SURFACE: 165m² (1777sq ft)
SUPERHEATER: 39m² (420sq ft)
TRACTIVE EFFORT: 16,375kg (36,100lb)
TOTAL WEIGHT: 133.5t (295,000lb)

A Class 11 sets off from the coast with two perishable goods vans and a brake placed in front of a long line of passenger coaches.

CLASS R 4-6-4 VICTORIAN GOVERNMENT RAILWAYS (VGR)

Built by North British Locomotive Co. in Glasgow to VGR specifications, this up-to-date 'Hudson' type was part of 'Operation Phoenix', a programme for modernization of the somewhat run-down system. Existing main passenger motive power was the A2 class 4-6-0 dating back to 1907. Seventy of the Hudsons were ordered to run all express services. They were two-cylinder simples, of very solid bar-frame construction 127mm (5in) thick. A 'Pacific' had been the first intention, but the addition of mechanical stokers to the design – since it was hard to recruit shovelling firemen in the 1950s – necessitated the four-wheel bogies. Considerable care was put into cylinder, valve and steam circulation design in order to make the locomotives free-steaming. Belpaire fireboxes were fitted, and large 279.5mm (11in) diameter piston valves were set above the cylinders. Provision was made for later conversion from the 1600mm (5ft 3in) gauge to standard gauge. For visual effect, the running plate was deepened and curved at each end, and with the smoke deflectors and buffer beam it was painted scarlet, though otherwise the engines were finished in unlined plain black.

The Rs performed excellently on express duty, but full use of the

class's potential was much restricted by the simultaneous introduction of B-class diesel-electrics, and the Hudsons were

mostly deployed on secondary and freight work. At one time, they were all to be fitted with 'Stug' apparatus for burning pulverized

coal, but this plan was cancelled. Withdrawals began in 1961 and all were out of service by the 70s. Four have been preserved.

BOILER PRESSURE: 14.7kg/cm² (210psi)
CYLINDERS: 546x711mm (21.5x28in)
DRIVING WHEELS: 1827mm (72in)
GRATE AREA: 3.9m² (42sq ft)
HEATING SURFACE: 88.3m² (2243sq ft)
SUPERHEATER: 42.9m² (462sq ft)
TRACTIVE EFFORT: 16,197kg (32,800lb)
TOTAL WEIGHT: 190t (418,880lb)

Two of the preserved Rs, R707 and R761, double-head a centenary special away from Barnawatha on 24 November 1973.

CLASS W 4-8-2 WESTERN AUSTRALIAN GOVERNMENT RAILWAYS (WAGR)

AUSTRALIA 1951

In 1950, the WAGR clearly felt that steam had a long future. Sixty of these locomotives, designed at the WAGR headquarters in Perth, were ordered from Beyer Peacock in Manchester, England, for the 1066mm (3ft 6in) gauge, and were delivered in 1951–52. It was a compact-looking locomotive, with a single extended boiler housing

for steam dome and sand-box, and the usual central buffer-coupler and cow-catcher of WAGR locomotives. They were chiefly intended for branch freight work, but were versatile enough to operate main line passenger trains and all but the heaviest freight workings. Ease of operation and maintenance was by now increasingly important, and

the class had self-cleaning smoke boxes, self-emptying ashpans, power reversers and roller bearings on all axles.

Despite all these features, the Class Ws were short-lived; withdrawals began in the 1960s, and the last 11 of the class were taken out of service in December 1973. Several are preserved.

BOILER PRESSURE: 14kg/cm² (200psi)
CYLINDERS: 406x609mm (16x24in)
DRIVING WHEELS: 1218mm (48in)
GRATE AREA: 2.5m² (27sq ft)
HEATING SURFACE: 103.7m² (1117sq ft)
SUPERHEATER: 28.3m² (305sq ft)
TRACTIVE EFFORT: 10,701kg (21,670lb)
TOTAL WEIGHT: 102.7t (226,464lb)

CLASS 40 A1A-A1A NEW SOUTH WALES GOVERNMENT RAILWAYS (NSGWR)

AUSTRALIA 1951

NSWGR introduced main-line diesel traction on its system with this large engine. Twenty were supplied by Alco in the United States, based on its RSC3 road-switcher model, but with

bogies of A1A-A1A rather than Bo-Bo layout to keep the maximum axle weight down. The wheel layout gave problems, with high wheel wear through the Class 40s' working lives.

Originally used on freight, they also hauled passenger trains. Withdrawn from traffic between 1968 and 1971, all were broken up except for No. 4001, which is preserved.

Alco was later to supply many locomotives to various Australian railway systems through licensing arrangements and local construction by Goodwin, competing against similar international joint ventures between Electro-Motive Division and Clyde, GE and Goninan, and English Electric and Rocklea.

TYPE: A1A-A1A diesel electric
POWER: 1305kW (1750hp) from Alco 12-244 series engine
TRACTIVE EFFORT: 205kN (46,125lbf) at 18km/h (11.3mph)
MAX. OPERATING SPEED: 120km/h (75mph)
WEIGHT: 113t (249,165lb)
OVERALL LENGTH: 17.26m (56ft 4in)
GAUGE: 1435mm (4ft 8.5in)

No. 4015 was the last of the Class 40 in service; seen here near Exeter, NSW, with a Junee-bound mixed freight on 5 October 1971.

CLASS 477.0 4-8-4T CZECHOSLOVAK STATE RAILWAYS (CSD)

CZECHOSLOVAKIA 1951

Despite being closed off by the Iron Curtain from 1948, Czechoslovakia's post-war locomotive development was greatly influenced by the work of André Chapelon. The effects of this were seen in the two-cylinder 4-8-2 Class 475.1 of 1947, and reproduced in this remarkable tank design. It was of three cylinders, all simple expansion, the inside valve gear driven off the left-hand third coupled wheel in typical Czech style. The boiler, already

lofty, was covered by a 'skyline' casing holding the steam pipe, as in contemporary Russian engines. Originally designated 476.1, the class was redesignated following the addition of extra side-fitted water tanks (the third digit, plus 10, indicated maximum axle loading, which increased from 16 to 17 tonnes (15.7 to 16.7 tons). The last 22 of this 60-strong class had false side-tanks between these tanks and the cab-front. Uniquely for a tank engine, the 477s were

all fitted with mechanical stoking apparatus.

Czech engines were invariably well turned-out, with a variety of colour schemes for the most prestigious classes , and these were nicknamed *Papousek* ('Parrots')

after their colourful red, white and blue livery. The first of the class, originally numbered 476.101, was the 3000th engine built by CKD, and also the last steam type to be built by this works for CSD. Three are preserved.

BOILER PRESSURE: 16kg/cm² (228psi)
CYLINDERS: 450x680mm (17.75x27in)
DRIVING WHEELS: 1624mm (64in)
GRATE AREA: 4.3m² (46.3sq ft)

HEATING SURFACE: 201m² (2164sq ft)
SUPERHEATER: 75.5m² (813sq ft)
TRACTIVE EFFORT: 11,680kg (25,760lb)
TOTAL WEIGHT: 130.7t (288,193lb)

CLASS 556 2-10-0 CZECHOSLOVAK STATE RAILWAYS (CSD)

CZECHOSLOVAKIA 1951

This was one of a range of big engines that made a worthy finale to half a century of Czech-built steam power, and was a large class in itself. Between 1950 and May 1958, Skoda built 510. Intensive and gruelling wartime experience had given this works special expertise in welding, and the welded boiler and firebox with thermic syphon, arch tubes and combustion chamber were all standard items, as were mechanical stokers and Kylchap double blast pipe chimneys. These superb two-cylinder engines could haul 1200-tonne (1180-ton) trains at 80km/h (50mph) on the level and frequently took much heavier loads, up to 4000 tonnes (3930 tons). On 1 April 1981, with the electric catenary in place, No. 556.0506 worked the last scheduled steam service on the CSD. Numerous examples remain in preservation.

BOILER PRESSURE: 18kg/cm² (256psi)
CYLINDERS: 550x660mm (21.7x26in)
DRIVING WHEELS: 1400mm (55in)
GRATE AREA: 4.3m² (46.3sq ft)
HEATING SURFACE: 187.2m² (2015.5sq ft)
SUPERHEATER: 72.2m² (777sq ft)
TRACTIVE EFFORT: 23,920kg (48,440lb)
TOTAL WEIGHT: 95t (209,475lb)

A sense of presence is exuded by Class 556 No. 0298 as it rolls into a station in the days when Czech locomotives wore red stars on their smokebox doors.

FIVE-CAR DIESEL TRAIN EGYPTIAN STATE RAILWAYS (ESR)

EGYPT 1951

Egypt had had early motor railcars (see 1913), and this modernistic air-smoothed five-car articulated train revived the tradition with a new generation of power and styling. British-built, with two power coaches and three trailers, it provided high-speed transport on the level Nile Valley routes north and south of Cairo. The engines supplied

TYPE: articulated diesel-electric train
POWER: two English-Electric 4 SRKT engines developing 298.5kW (400hp), driving two power bogies via electric transmission

TRACTIVE EFFORT: 80kN (18,000lbf)
MAX. OPERATING SPEED: 120km/h (75mph)
TOTAL WEIGHT: 154.4t (340,452lb)
MAX. AXLE LOAD: 11t (24,255lb)

OVERALL LENGTH: 83.14m (255ft 3in) Electric
GAUGE: not known

power to a single motorized bogie on each power car. Sixty first-class and 112 second-class passengers were carried in air-

conditioned saloons. It was intended to be a self-contained unit and the ends had buffers but no coupling gear. A very similar

two-car unit was supplied by the same manufacturers, English Electric, to the Argentine Central Railway.

CLASS 65 2-8-4T GERMAN FEDERAL RAILWAYS (DB)

The history of this class shows the pitfalls that can await the locomotive designer. Intended to be a standard type, it had an all-welded boiler and firebox, the latter with combustion chamber.

Basic equipment included a Knorr feedwater heater, compressed air sanding gear operative either in forward or reverse gear (boxes not on the boiler-top but built into the side tanks), pressure lubrication

and electric turbo-generator. Built by Krauss-Maffei, it was a mixed-traffic engine, designed for frequent stops, rapid acceleration, and a top speed of 85km/h (53mph) in either direction.

Yet in several respects the design proved defective. A maximum axle load of 17.5 tonnes (17 tons) restricted its use on minor lines. Water spilled from the tanks on braking. Its fuel bunker and tanks were on the small side for freight work, and it developed an increasingly strong hunting motion at speeds in excess of 50km/h (31mph), caused by an imbalance in the reciprocating and revolving masses of the machinery. While 87 of the 'rival' Class 6510 of the *Deutsche Reichsbahn* (DR) were built, Class 65 numbered only 18. Withdrawals began in 1966 and all were gone by 1972.

BOILER PRESSURE: 14kg/cm² (199psi)
CYLINDERS: 570x660mm (22.4x26in)
DRIVING WHEELS: 1500mm (59in)
GRATE AREA: 2.7m² (29sq ft)
HEATING SURFACE: 139.9m² (1506.2sq ft)
SUPERHEATER: 62.9m² (677.2sq ft)
TRACTIVE EFFORT: 16,960kg (37,400lb)
TOTAL WEIGHT: 107.6t (237,258lb)

A class 65, No. 014, waits for duty at the country station of Bad Schwalbach, on the Taunus Mountain line between Wiesbaden and Limburg.

CLASS 7MT 'BRITANNIA' 4-6-2 BRITISH RAILWAYS (BR)

On the formation of the nationalized British Railways in 1948, a Locomotive Standards Committee began to set policy for future motive power. Despite, or because of, the great variety of existing locomotive types, some of them very recent, it was decided to design a completely new set of standard locomotives that could cope with all traffic requirements. Several of the committee had been involved in the design of the wartime 'Austerity' locomotives, and hoped for a similarly successful outcome. Though classed for mixed traffic, the 'Britannia' was really a medium-size express passenger locomotive, and for an engine designed by a committee and at several different locations it was a

distinct success. The first, No. 70000, was built at Crewe. Unlike any previous British 'Pacific' for home use, it had only two cylinders. Fifty-five were built, and after some initial problems with self-detaching driving wheels and tenders, they performed reliably in an era when maximum power output was rarely required. Many component parts were taken from, or modelled on, existing equipment, but the range of 'modern' features was greater than on any predecessor. Many of these were labour-saving, like self-cleaning smokeboxes, rocker grates, self-emptying ashpans, mechanical lubricators and roller bearings – all long familiar in some other countries. The cabs were mounted on the boiler, not on the

frame as in previous British practice. Some features of proved effectiveness, like the double blast-pipe and thermic syphon, were not employed: these engines were not intended for high performance. A more advanced and powerful

standard express 'Pacific' was also planned, but only the prototype of this was built. The best service of the 'Britannias' was on express trains from London to East Anglia, where they greatly improved on the old scheduled times.

BOILER PRESSURE: 17.6kg/cm² (250psi)
CYLINDERS: 508x711mm (20x28in)
DRIVING WHEELS: 1880mm (74in)
GRATE AREA: 3.9m² (42sq ft)
HEATING SURFACE: 229.8m2 (2474sq ft)
SUPERHEATER: 65.4m² (704sq ft)
TRACTIVE EFFORT: 14,512kg (32,000lb)
TOTAL WEIGHT: 95.5t (210,560lb)

'Britannia' class No. 70001 *Lord Hurcomb,* in the green express livery of British Railways. These locomotives had relatively short working lives because of the elimination of steam traction.

CLASS 4 2-6-4T BRITISH RAILWAYS (BR)

One of the first of Britain's post-war standard classes to come on stream, this new 2-6-4T, despite its more fluid lines and such features as an angled cab front, was quite recognizably a smoothed-out version of the LMS two-cylinder class of 1935, and its dimensions were very similar, though the cylinders were smaller and the piston-stroke longer. It operated interchangeably with the older types in handling the same suburban and local passenger traffic; some were also used as

banking engines on steep grades. The bunker coal capacity was 3.55 tonnes (3.5 tons) and the side tanks held 2000gals (2400 US gals). The class numbered 155.

BOILER PRESSURE: 15.8kg/cm² (225psi)
CYLINDERS: 457x711mm (18x28in)
DRIVING WHEELS: 1599mm (63in)
GRATE AREA: 2.5m² (26.7sq ft)
HEATING SURFACE: 126.8m² (1366sq ft)
SUPERHEATER: 33m² (248sq ft)
TRACTIVE EFFORT: 11,936kg (24,170lb)
TOTAL WEIGHT: 88.4t (194,880lb)

A 2-6-4T shunts insulated meat vans at a goods depot in Manchester, in the 1950s. Perishables traffic was once an important part of the freight service, with fast overnight connections to city centres.

10201 TO 10203 1-CO-CO-1 BRITISH RAILWAYS (BR)

The management of BR's Southern Region maintained the former Southern Railway policy of developing technically advanced locomotives. Its first large main line diesel was No. 10201, built at its Ashford Works, and entering

traffic early in 1951. After display at the Festival of Britain exhibition, it joined its sister locomotive No. 10202 on fast trains beyond the electrified area, from London Waterloo to Bournemouth/Weymouth and Exeter.

As in the pioneer post-war British main-line diesels 10000 and 10001, the prime mover of the 10201–10202 was the English Electric 16SVT, upgraded to 1305kW (1750hp). The unusual bogie design had no centre pivot, with the locomotive body resting on lubricated segmental side bearers, a feature that reappeared

in the BR Class 40 locomotives and which was also used, in varying forms, on various French and other diesel and electric locomotives. In 1954, Brighton Works produced the more powerful No. 10203, an upgraded EE 16SVT. In 1955 all three were transferred to the London Midland Region, until they were taken off in 1963.

TYPE: main-line diesel-electric
WHEEL ARRANGEMENT: 1-Co-Co1
POWER: English Electric 16SVT 16-cylinder V-form diesel, 1194kW (1600bhp)/1492kW (2000bhp)*; DC generator; six axle-hung DC traction motors
TRACTIVE EFFORT: 214kN (48,000lbf)/222kN (50,000lbf)*
MAX. OPERATING SPEED: 145km/h (90mph)
WEIGHT: 138t (302,400lb)/ 136t (279,920lb)*
OVERALL LENGTH: 19.43m (63ft 9in)
GAUGE: 1435mm (4ft 8.5in)
* Details for No. 10203

The most powerful of the eight-axled trio, No. 10203 at Stewarts Lane depot, London. The sidewall shape and styling reflected that of passenger coaches.

2-8-2 RAILWAYS OF THE HASHEMITE KINGDOM OF JORDAN (JR)

Built originally to transport pilgrims to the holy site of Mecca, the 1050mm (41.4in) gauge Hedjaz Railway, which from 1908 to 1924 linked Turkey, Syria, Lebanon, Jordan and Saudi Arabia, now currently operates only on isolated sections in Syria and Jordan. 'Mikados' had always been the staple Hedjaz engine, and

between 1951 and 1955 the JR bought nine 2-8-2s from three different makers – Robert Stephenson & Hawthorns in England, Jung in Germany and Haine St Pierre in Belgium, all of standard two-cylinder simple-expansion design. Though not in regular service, some are still maintained to do 'heritage' runs.

BOILER PRESSURE: 12.6kg/cm² (180psi)
CYLINDERS: 431.4x609mm (17x24in)
DRIVING WHEELS: 1218mm (48in)
GRATE AREA: 2.4m² (26sq ft)
HEATING SURFACE: 129.2m² (1391sq ft)
SUPERHEATER: 28.8m² (310sq ft)
TRACTIVE EFFORT: 10,026kg (22,108lb)
TOTAL WEIGHT: 57.9t (127,680lb)

A number of the Jordanian locomotives still run steam excursion trips. Here 2-8-2 No. 51 leaves Amman on a run in July 1992.

CLASS 01.49 2-6-2 POLISH STATE RAILWAYS (PKP)

POLAND 1951

Hauling modern close-coupled stock, a Class 01.49 passes the city water tower and enters the station at Zaban, Poland.

Polish locomotive design was now in the Russian sphere of influence. Modelled on the Russian Class Su 2-6-2, which ceased production in the same year, this was a modernized version, both in building methods and in aspects of the design. Planned for mixed-traffic use, it was employed mostly on passenger trains.

Between 1951 and 1954, Chrzanov Works built 112, using welding techniques extensively in the construction of boiler and firebox. They were two-cylinder simple expansion engines, and were the first to be fitted with the PKP standard 'elephant's ear' smoke deflectors, mounted high up alongside the chimney. Like the Russian 'S' class, they were free-steaming engines, capable of high speeds.

BOILER PRESSURE: 14kg/cm² (199.5psi)
CYLINDERS: 500x630mm (19.7x25in)
DRIVING WHEELS: 1750mm (69in)
GRATE AREA: 3.7m² (40sq ft)
HEATING SURFACE: 159.4m² (1716sq ft)
SUPERHEATER: 68.3m² (735.3sq ft)
TRACTIVE EFFORT: 10,810kg (23,840lb)
TOTAL WEIGHT: 83.5t (184,117lb)
(engine only)

CLASS AD60 4-8-4+4-8-4 NEW SOUTH WALES GOVERNMENT RAILWAY (NSWGR)

AUSTRALIA 1952

Surprisingly perhaps, the NSWGR had not used Garratts before, as its standard gauge tracks had generous loading gauge limits that suited this type of locomotive. The AD60 was the largest and heaviest steam locomotive to run in Australia. Another claim for it as 'the most powerful locomotive in the southern hemisphere' ignored the superior power of some African Garratts. But in any case, it was a success, working for 20 years on up to 1524-tonne

(1500-ton) trainloads, usually bulk loads of wheat or coal, but also operating general city-to-city goods trains. The maximum axle loading did not exceed 16.2 tonnes (16 tons), enabling it to work over most of the system, including branch lines if they generated heavy freight traffic. In the west of the state, beyond Dubbo, they ran on lightweight 29.7kg (60lb) rails, and could reach such remote parts on the southern division as Captain's Flat,

Temora and Narrandera. They were not allowed to pass through single-line tunnels, as the clearance was so tight that the crews would not be able to get out of the cab in an emergency.

The original order placed with Beyer Peacock of Manchester was reduced from 60 to 50, though in the end only 42 were built, the last of them entering service in January

1957. Five were delivered in pieces as 'spare parts' and the final three were cancelled.

Handsome and imposing engines, they had the curved-front water tank first used on post-war African Garratts. The boiler was supported on a one-piece 'Commonwealth' cast steel frame with integral cylinders, and all axles and the main crank pins had roller bearings. The bogie

No. 6042 rolls tender-first into Parkes Motive Power Depot, May 1975. Details of its frame construction can be seen behind the buffer beam.

wheels were not spoked, but solid with perforations. Twenty-five of the class had two thermic syphons fitted in the firebox, plus two arch tubes; the others had two arch tubes only.

Modifications were made to the original design in the course of usage. On some, the tender unit was built up, the coal capacity increasing from 14.2 tonnes (14 tons) to 18.3 tonnes (18 tons); 29 locomotives also had their cylinder diameter increased, raising their tractive effort to

28,570kg (63,000lb). In addition, 30 were fitted with dual controls, enabling them to be easily driven in either direction, a particularly useful facility on branch lines.

The AD60 was an effective engine, though its overall power in relation to its great weight has been criticized as less than it could have been. At 85 per cent of maximum boiler pressure, its tractive effort was calculated as 28,843kg (63,600lb), compared to the South African Railways' GL Garratt at 40,421kg (89,130lb)

but weighing only 214 tonnes (21 tons). The class worked until the 1970s, losing only two members, and one, No. 6042, was assembled from the 'spare parts' in 1969, replacing the original 6042 which needed major repair. Their last years were spent working north of Sydney, stabled at Broadmeadow shed, Newcastle, mostly hauling coal trains to the docks at Port Waratah. No. 6042, withdrawn on 18 March 1973, was the last steam locomotive in regular government service in

Australia. It remains in working order, and another three of the class have also been preserved.

BOILER PRESSURE: 14kg/cm² (200psi)
CYLINDERS: 488.5x660mm (19.25 x26in)
DRIVING WHEELS: 1396mm (55in)
GRATE AREA: 5.8m² (63.3sq ft)
HEATING SURFACE: 282m² (3041sq ft)
SUPERHEATER: 69.5m² (748sq ft)
TRACTIVE EFFORT: 28,843kg (63,600lb)
TOTAL WEIGHT: 264t (582,400lb)

RS-3 BO-BO ESTRADA DE FERRO CENTRAL DO BRAZIL (EFCB)

BRAZIL 1952

By 1952, the export of American diesel locomotives was well under way. Fifty-eight of the Alco-GEC RS3 road switchers were bought by the EFCB, originally for freight haulage until cascaded to lighter local passenger duties by newer types. Several survive today, as both Sao Paulo and Rio de

Janeiro suburban train operators use refurbished RS-3s as works engines. In Rio de Janeiro, some

FLUMITRENS machines now have GE 7FDL-12 engines, while others retain the original Alco 244. CPTM

units in Sao Paulo have similar GE engines recovered from U20C locomotives.

TYPE: Bo-Bo diesel-electric freight
POWER: 1193kW (1620hp) from Alco 244 or 251 series engine

TRACTIVE EFFORT: 245kN (55,000lbf)
MAX. OPERATING SPEED: 100km/h (62.1mph)

WEIGHT: 109t (240,345lb)
OVERALL LENGTH: 16.988m (55ft 5in)
GAUGE: 1600mm (5ft 3in)

CLASS CC-7100 CO-CO FRENCH NATIONAL RAILWAYS (SNCF)

FRANCE 1952

With this classic design of electric locomotive, the SNCF took a great step forward. Built by Alsthom, the all-adhesion Co-Co layout was specified to be 25 per cent lighter than preceding 2-D-2 types, and every aspect of the locomotive in structure, mechanics and motor equipment was re-assesssed and adapted or changed for high-speed, heavy-duty service. Alsthom used new, lightweight traction motors and the body structure was fabricated from steel tubing using electric welding techniques. The side sheets, jointed to rigid upright members, helped to absorb the longitudinal and vertical stresses of high-speed motion with a heavy load. With a smooth external finish and rounded-off ends and angles, they were neat and efficient-looking locomotives, with four 'port-hole' shape windows to let daylight in on the equipment compartment. Paint style was the SNCF standard pale turquoise, in two tones separated by a pair of stainless steel bars with a blue stripe between them. CC-7001 was the first all-adhesion locomotive designed to run at speeds greater than 125km/h (78mph): until now, it had been standard to provide truck wheels on high-speed engines. Alsthom and SNCF devised a new body suspension design for these locomotives, dispensing with the usual bolster and pivot arrangement, and attaching the body-frame to the bogie by means of two swinging pivots articulated at top and

bottom on conical tough rubber pads. Resting on cross-members fixed between the traction motors, the pivots moved in opposite directions to allow the bogie to turn relative to the body on curves, or for both to tilt the same way to permit a small degree of lateral displacement of the body from the bogie centre-line. Two transverse spring rods restored the link to the vertical position. The six DC traction motors were fixed to the bogie frames and drove each axle through bilateral gearing mounted on a hollow shaft. Flexible coupling between hollow shaft and axle was provided by a floating ring and connecting rods fitted with 'Silentbloc' rubber cushioning. DC-wound traction motors were, for a century, considered the best means of electric rail traction. Such motors have a high starting torque, enabling them to get a heavy train readily under way, and this reduces as speed increases, to a level sufficient to keep the train moving at its designated maximum speed.

Prototypes CC-7001 and 7002 appeared in 1949, immediately proving themselves to be a satisfactory design. CC-7001 hauled a 22-coach train of 1016 tonnes (1000 tons) over the 335km (208 miles) from Paris to Poitiers in 3hrs, 9mins at an average speed of 106km/h (66mph) without exceeding the upper speed limit of 120km/h (75mph), and proved capable of starting a 1219-tonne (1200-ton)

freight on a 1 in 100 grade without assistance. The prototypes went into regular service, but series production did not start for three years. The initial batch consisted of 43 machines numbered from CC-7101, with a further 15 taking the fleet up to CC-7158. The first two were rated at 2770kW (3764hp) increasing to 3490kW (4742hp) in the others, through improvements in traction motor design. The improved motors were later retro-fitted to the prototypes. The last 15 (CC-7144 to CC-7158) were equipped with a revised motor design, reducing overall locomotive weight, but of slightly lower output at 3240kW (4406hp). Electrification of the main line south from Paris to Lyon was completed by 1952, and through the 1950s and 1960s class CC-7100 was always associated with this route.

In a series of tests in early 1955, two electric locomotive designs were credited with jointly holding the same new world record speed of 331km/h (206.9mph). On 28 March, CC-7121 was reported as having achieved this speed between Lamothe and Morcenx on the Bordeaux–Dax section. A rival four-axle machine from Jeumont Schneider, BB-9004 was credited with the same 331km/h (206.9mph) speed the following day. In more recent times, it has been admitted that CC-7121 reached only 326km/h (203.8mph), holding the record for only a day. The resultant prestige

helped gain orders for CC-7100 derivatives from Spain, the Netherlands and Morocco. In France, the arrival of newer higher-speed designs were to cascade CC-7100s on to fast freight duties. CC-7100s were authorized for 160km/h (100mph) from 1969, but were later limited to 140km/h (87.5mph) after drivers complained of unstable riding. Twenty-nine of the class were given new bodywork, including reinforced cabs of altered appearance, adding 5 tonnes (4.9 tons) to overall weight; the remainder received a less extensive treatment. In 1958, six 7100s were equipped for 750V third-rail operation over the Mauriennne section of the Chambéry–Modane line (converted to standard 1500V overhead in 1976). Overhauls ceased in 1985, and gradual elimination of the class went on until 2001, when just five remained operational at Avignon depot.

TYPE: Co-Co mixed-traffic mainline electric locomotive
POWER: 1500V DC overhead line collection; 3240 and 3490kW (4406 and 4742hp); six bogie frame mounted DC traction motors
TRACTIVE EFFORT: 225kN (50,580lbf)
MAX. OPERATING SPEED: 140km/h (87mph)
WEIGHT: 107 tonnes (234,980lb)
MAX. AXLE LOAD: not known
OVERALL LENGTH: 18.922m (62ft 1in)
GAUGE: 1435mm (4ft 8.5in)

CLASS V80 B-B GERMAN FEDERAL RAILWAYS (DB)

GERMANY 1952

German enthusiasm for main-line diesel-hydraulics produced this set of 10 prototype central-cab locomotives, built by Krauss-Maffei in Munich and MaK in Kiel. Each had a single medium speed engine driving all axles via hydraulic transmission through cardan shafts and right angle gearboxes. The layout was

asymmetric, the main engine compartment being considerably longer than the equipment compartment set behind the cab.

Smoothly styled and painted red, the design led to the standard diesel-hydraulic classes in the DB's dieselization programme.

V80s ran in passenger service as late as the mid-1970s. At least one is preserved.

TYPE: mixed-traffic diesel-hydraulic
WHEEL ARRANGEMENT: B-B
POWER: medium-speed 12-cylinder 821kW (1100bhp) diesel; hydraulic transmission

TRACTIVE EFFORT: 180kN (40,000lbf)
MAX. OPERATING SPEED: 100km/h (62mph)
WEIGHT: 58t (127,370lb)

OVERALL LENGTH: 12.8m (42ft)
GAUGE: 1435mm (4ft 8.5in)

CLASS VT95 DIESEL RAILBUSES GERMAN FEDERAL RAILWAYS (DB)

GERMANY 1952

Uerdingen were the prime German manufacturers of light powered railcars, and they built a large fleet of four-wheeled railbuses for the DB's many rural branch lines, at low operating cost. Each car had two Bussing automotive diesel engines underneath, each driving one axle through mechanical transmission. Underframes were welded, and the body carried on

four coil springs, suspended from the underframe. The interior was open with a clear view forward for passengers, and furnishing was basic, with bench seats trimmed in wipeable leather-like material. Either 104 or 180 passengers could be seated, depending on the length (later versions had a 5.78m/ 19ft 8in wheelbase). The ride was uncomfortable because these were

the days before long link suspensions. For busy times, or to provide a goods-parcel service, each railbus could haul a non-powered trailer of similar design, and trains of up to four vehicles were possible. Apart from disc brakes on the wheels, magnetic track brakes were fitted, suspended from the underframe on vehicles that ran on unfenced track.

TYPE: secondary and branch-line passenger
POWER: 112kW (150bhp) six-cylinder, two per power car
TRACTIVE EFFORT: N/A
TRANSMISSION: mechanical
MAX. OPERATING SPEED: 90km/h (56mph)
WEIGHT: 27t (59,295lb)
OVERALL LENGTH: 13.95m (45ft 9in)
GAUGE: 1435mm (4ft 8.5in)

CLASS 04 C BRITISH RAILWAYS (BR)

GREAT BRITAIN 1952

This tractor-type light diesel-engined shunter, built by the Drewry Car Company, was intended to be a standard 'C', or 0-6-0 type for British Railways, but its mechanical transmission proved to be difficult to control in shunting movements. Jerky operation of the mechanical gearbox tended to cause

snatching of wagon couplings, and crashing of buffers, comparing unfavourably with the continuous torque curve of diesel-electric and hydraulic shunting locomotives. The Class 04s, numbering 133, and the similar 192 BR-built '03' class, were also made increasingly redundant by the closure of local goods yards.

Scrapping was put in hand from the late 1960s, but a large

number are preserved and often still in use on 'heritage' lines.

TYPE: C (0-6-0) diesel mechanical shunting
POWER: Gardner 8L3 eight-cylinder diesel engine, 150kW (204hp); four-speed epicyclic gearbox, cardan and jack shafts and external coupling rods
TRACTIVE EFFORT: 75kN (16,850lbf)

MAX. OPERATING SPEED: 32km/h (20mph)
WEIGHT: 30t (66,640lb)
OVERALL LENGTH: 7.93m (26ft 2in)
GAUGE: 1435mm (4ft 8.5in)

CLASS EW BO-BO-BO NEW ZEALAND RAILWAYS (NZR)

NEW ZEALAND 1952

Built by Robert Stephenson & Hawthorn of Darlington, England, with electrical components from English Electric, these locomotives had articulated bodies, with Bo-Bo-Bo wheel arrangement hinging on the central bogie. Their tasks were passenger and freight haulage on the steep grades around Wellington, with 1500V DC overhead wire current supply. An EW could move a 610-tonne (600-ton) freight train between Wellington and Upper Hutt at 48.3km/h (30mph) and could restart a 508-tonne (500-ton) train

A locomotive class that outlived its intended purpose – NZR's powerful articulated EW ended up on commuter trains.

TYPE: Bo-Bo-Bo
POWER: 1340kW (1800hp)
SUPPLY: 1500V DC
TRACTIVE EFFORT: 187kN (42075lbf)
MAX. OPERATING SPEED: 96km/h (60mph)
WEIGHT: 76t (167,580lb)
MAX. AXLE LOAD: 13 tonnes (28,665lb)
OVERALL LENGTH: 18.90m (61ft 8in)
GAUGE: 1067mm (3ft 6in)

on a 1 in 57 grade. It could handle a 400-ton (406-tonne) train at a steady 88.5km/h (55mph) on level track. Six axle-hung, nose-suspended, force-ventilated traction motors drove the axles

through spur gearing, and a compressor was fitted in each section to provide air for braking, controls and auxiliaries. Class EWs were effective locomotives, but after the lowering of tunnel floors

between Wellington and Paekakariki in 1967 allowed through working by diesels, they gradually found less work, being used finally to haul peak hour commuter services on lines into Wellington, a duty for which they were more than somewhat over-endowed with power, but which lasted into the 1980s.

CLASS 277 CO-CO SPANISH RAILWAYS (RENFE)

Intended for mixed-traffic work in the Cantabrian Mountains area, the hinterland of Bilbao and Santander, the 75 locomotives of this class came from English Electric and looked rather like nose-front diesels with pantographs – very different to the French-style Alsthom-built Class 276 ordered by RENFE at

much the same time. They were withdrawn from service in the 1990s, although several are preserved by enthusiasts today.

English Electric actually supplied machines that were almost identical both electrically and in appearance to Indian Railways (Class WCM-1) and the Brazilian EF *Santos e Jundai* Railway.

TYPE: Co-Co heavy passenger and freight
POWER: 2208kW (2960hp)
SUPPLY: 3000V DC
TRACTIVE EFFORT: 136kN (30500lbf) at 58km/h (36.3mph)

MAX. OPERATING SPEED: 110km/h (68.8mph)
WEIGHT: 120t (264,600lb)
MAX. AXLE LOAD: 20t (44,100lb)
OVERALL LENGTH: 20.657m (67ft 5in)
GAUGE: 1676mm (5ft 6in)

RENFE No. 7765. Though built by English Electric, this was an export-only model as far as British railways were concerned.

CLASS AE6/6 CO-CO SWISS FEDERAL RAILWAYS (SBB)

The excellent performance of the Lötschberg Ae4/4/ Bo-Bo locomotives of 1944 prompted the SBB engineers in 1949 to develop a six-axle all-adhesion type, capable of hauling heavy trains on the Gotthard line without assistance, and this was the origin of the Ae6/6. Good electric locomotives often have long lives, as many Swiss types have proved, and this one was no exception. SLM and Brown Boveri built the first two, Nos. 11401 and 11402. The demanding specification required capacity to haul a 650-tonne (640-ton) train up a 1 in 38.5 grade – the steepest on the Gotthard line – at 75km/h (46.5mph), or a 750-tonne (735 ton) load up a 1 in 48 grade. At the maximum speed on 125km/h (78mph) and with a voltage of 15kV on the overhead line, a minimum tractive effort of 8000kg (17,600lb) was required. On

starting and at low speeds, of course, the tractive effort was vastly greater.

Although electric locomotives had run on six axles before, there was no previous experience of power-bogie design producing such an output as 4300kW (6437hp) on a one-hour rating, and with a 19.6-tonne (20-ton) axle load. Immense care went into the design of the Co-Co bogies with their 1260mm (49.5in) diameter wheels, part of the aim being to ensure weight transfer between the bogies to even out the tractive effort. The first 15 of the class had rods between the bogies transmitting both vertical and transverse forces, but from No. 11415 on this was altered to transverse only. The single-phase AC traction motors, cooled by forced draught ventilation, were secured to the bogie frames, and welding

was used in their construction to keep them as light as possible. The body was a self-supporting, stress-free construction, of welded steel plate. Power equipment was similar to the BLS Ae4/4, with a 27-notch high-tension tap changer and permanent parallel connected motors, which makes for the best possible utilization of the locomotive's adhesion weight when making difficult starts. Like the French CC-7100 DC locomotives, the Class Ae6/6 were state-of-the-art types using alternating current supply.

The prototypes were followed between 1954 and 1966 by production machines of slightly greater weight, from SLM, Brown Boveri and Oerlikon. The first order, in 1954, was for 14, but eventually the class numbered 120. The production engines also had an improved tractive effort.

Fifty were allocated to Erstfeld and 70 to Bellinzona (north and south of the St Gotthard tunnel) displacing Ae4/7s from passenger services and Ce6/8 1C+C1s from freight. Later, the Ae6/6s in turn were cascaded onto freight service, hauling loads up to 1600 tonnes (1574 tons). Some are still in action. All the class were named, after Swiss cantons and towns.

TYPE: Co-Co heavy passenger and freight
POWER: 4300kW (6437hp)
SUPPLY: 15kV 16.7Hz AC
TRACTIVE EFFORT: 11403–11520 – 392kN (88200lbf)
MAX. OPERATING SPEED: 125km/h (78.1mph)
WEIGHT: (11403–11520) 128t (282,240lb)
MAX. AXLE LOAD: 21.5t (47,408lb)
OVERALL LENGTH: 18.4m (60ft)
GAUGE: 1435mm (4ft 8.5in)

CLASS LV 2-10-2 SOVIET RAILWAYS (SZD)

RUSSIA 1952

The Class Lv was a development of the very successful Class L, first introduced in 1945. It had a larger boiler and a feedwater heater was also fitted. Its extra weight required the additional rear truck to spread the load. The Lv was also intended to be easier to run tender-first, which big Russian engines often had to do. Voroshilovgrad

works built the prototype, and series production began in 1954. Several hundred were built up to 1956, and undoubtedly many more would have followed but for the abrupt decision made that year to cease all building of steam locomotives. However, the plans for this type were passed on to China, and production continued there of a

BOILER PRESSURE: 14kg/cm² (199psi)
CYLINDERS: 650x799mm (25.6x31.5in)
DRIVING WHEELS: 1497mm (59in)
GRATE AREA: 45m² (669.5sq ft)
HEATING SURFACE: 256.6m² (2762.6sq ft)

SUPERHEATER: 149m² (1605sq ft)
TRACTIVE EFFORT: 26,750kg (59,000lb)
TOTAL WEIGHT: 123.4t (272,160lb)
(engine only)

very similar engine, the QJ class, from 1956. In Russia, most of the Lv class worked on routes in

Siberia, including the 'Gulag peninsula' line to Vorkuta, of grim reputation.

CLASS TE3 CO-CO SOVIET RAILWAYS (SZD)

RUSSIA 1952

Though dating from 1952 and in production from 1953, the numbers of the double-unit TE3 *troiyak* began to rise dramatically with the termination of steam building in 1956. Its history began under the post-war Lend Lease scheme, by which 100 engines, 30 from Baldwin (Soviet Railways class Db) and 70 from Alco (Da) were imported. Class Da were modified RS1s, which were then copied by Soviet engineers to produce the 1947 TE1 Co-Co. Twin unit Bo-Bo TE2 followed, with a lighter maximum axle load, giving much wider route availability over the lighter Soviet track. Between 1950 and 1955, some 527 TE2 locomotives were built with 746kW (1000hp) engines in each unit. From then until 1973, production was intensive. Actual units are: TE3 001 to 598, built at Kharkov, TE3 1001 to 1406 at Kolomna, and TE3 2001 to 7805 at Lugansk, plus Nos. 7807 to 7809 put together in 1983 from spare parts. To these must be added triple units 3TE3 001 to 073 built up to 1962, and

the higher-geared TE7 001 to 113, built from 1956 to 1964.

Soviet production of main-line diesels started at the Kharkov factory in 1948 with the TE1 and TE2, based on the US models. The Co-Co TE3 was the next step. Keeping to a ruling 20-tonne (44,100lb) axle load, power was doubled to 1492kW (2000hp). Engines were two-stroke opposed piston 2D100, copied from the Fairbanks Morse 38D1/8 marine engine, with identical 210mm (8.25in) bore and 254mm (10in) stroke. The TE3 bogie was also copied from imported Alco DA units.

TE3 was essentially a freight design geared for 100km/h (62mph), but its huge availability meant that it was also used for slower passenger services. The triple set 3TE3 variant, with cabless middle section, appeared at the period when Soviet engineers were looking ahead to 4416kW (6000hp) twin units. It was not initially intended for production, but a small series

were built since delays to the TE10 had created an urgent need for higher-powered units. TE7 was simply a TE3 modified for passenger use by altering the traction motor gear ratio – increasing service speed from 120 to 140km/h (75 to 87.5mph) at the expense of tractive effort. This version also had a new cab design: earlier TE3s built at Karkhov used the TE2 cab design but switched to the revised design first introduced on the TE7 as production went on.

Under the Soviet numbering system, a multi-section unit was considered a single entity with both cab units of a twin suffixed 'A' and 'B'. The middle section of a triple unit was suffixed 'V', and, the second middle in a four-piece unit 'G'. The system was complicated by single and twin units having no prefix, but triple units were always prefixed '3' and quads '4'. Later this was revised with twin units prefixed '2', but this change did not affect the TE3.

Top line passenger work for the

TE7 included principal expresses between Moscow and Leningrad (St Petersburg) until the early 1960s, and Moscow to Minsk and Kiev. By the beginning of the 1990s, the TE3 fleet had diminished by two thirds, and by 2000 use had all but ceased, though many could be found as spare units at depots and in strategic reserve dumps.

The Chinese DF is a TE3 copy based on a 1958 prototype *Ju Long* ('Great Dragon'). Between 1964 and 1974, 706 DF and 226 DF3 were built, being slightly lower powered at 1325kW (1800hp) and heavier at 126 tonnes (124 tons) than the TE3.

TYPE: Co-Co diesel electric freight twin unit
POWER: 1492kW (2000hp) from Kolomna 2D100 series engine
TRACTIVE EFFORT: 198kN (44,550lbf) at 21km/h (13.1mph)
MAX. OPERATING SPEED: 100km/h (62.1mph)
WEIGHT: 120.6t (265,923lb)
OVERALL LENGTH: 16.974m (55ft 5in)
GAUGE: 1524mm (5ft)

This TE3 twin unit shows the cab and body styling as applied to the majority of the class. Bogie design, as on the TE1, is a direct copy of the US imports of the 1940s.

EMD SD7/SD9 SOUTHERN PACIFIC RAILROAD (SP)

Slow at first to bring its own version of the road switcher, Electro-Motive Division (EMD) was by now setting out to take a lead. Its 'SD' designation meant 'Special Duty', and this six-motor machine offered a combination of greater tractive effort with lower axle loading. It was a 'hood unit', the hood being the metal sheet covering the engine, generator and other mechanical equipment rather in the way a car bonnet covers the engine, but with no attempt at streamlining. Normally the hood is narrow enough to allow access from walkways at either side, making the machinery easily accessible. There was little take-up among the railroads for this new EMD line at first. Then, in 1954, EMD upped the power output of its 16-567 engine, replacing SD7 with the SD9, and sales began to rise. Southern Pacific was the largest user of these early SDs, and many of them, known as 'Cadillacs', operated for more than 40 years, their lives extended by rebuilding at the Sacramento (California) Shops. The first of the 118 built is preserved in working order.

TYPE: Co-Co, diesel-electric
POWER: EMD 15-567C (on SD9) producing 1303kW (1750hp)
Tractive effort: continuous TE 67, 300kN (500lbf) at 12.8km/h (8mph)
MAX. OPERATING SPEED: 105km/h (65mph)
WEIGHT: 147t (324,000lb)
OVERALL LENGTH: 18,491mm (60ft 8in)
GAUGE: 1435mm (4ft 8.5in)

CLASS 122 BO-BO BELGIAN NATIONAL RAILWAYS (SNCB)

Modern electric haulage arrived in Belgium with the Class 122 (later Class 22), and almost 50 years later they were still to be found in action on the SNCB. Fast passenger service like the Ostend-Brussels boat trains were their first duties, though later they were displaced to run on freight and suburban passenger services. Painted dark green originally, they later appeared in the lighter mid-blue/green. Though nearly 50 years old, almost all the class is still in use. Potential replacements in the form of the new Class 13 locomotives are already in position.

TYPE: Bo-Bo mixed-traffic mainline electric locomotive
POWER: 3000V DC overhead line collection; 1880kW (2520hp); four axle-hung DC traction motors
TRACTIVE EFFORT: 196kN (44,060lbf)

MAX. OPERATING SPEED: 130km/h (80mph)
WEIGHT: 87t (191,060lb)
MAX. AXLE LOAD: not known
OVERALL LENGTH: 18m (59ft 1in)
GAUGE: 1435mm (4ft 8.5in)

No. 2204, one of the SNCB's long-lived mixed-traffic electric locomotives.

CLASS BB-12000 BO-BO FRENCH NATIONAL RAILWAYS (SNCF)

With two pantographs squeezed on to roof extensions of the centre cab, and mounted on a heavy external frame, this was one of four electric types designed for the Paris–Lille 25kV AC electrification, a class of 150 mixed-traffic locomotives especially intended to work on the busy Valenciennes–Thionville lines. The builders of the BB-12000 were Matériel de Traction Electrique, of Paris, and Schneider of Le Creusot. In those early days of high-voltage AC electrification, various kinds of current rectification were tried between this and three other classes, the lower-powered class BB-13000 and the heavier Co-Cos of classes CC-14000 and 14100, also ordered for this section. In the BB-12000 locomotives, eight single anodes supplied four six-pole DC motors, housed in the bogies. Drive was made through cardan shafts and 'Silentbloc' joins. The BB-12000s were later used almost entirely for freight work, as the faster boxcab BB-16000 and 16500 classes which followed soon after, displaced them on passenger service. All have been withdrawn, but a few have been preserved.

TYPE: Bo-Bo mixed-traffic mainline electric locomotive
POWER: 25,000V 50Hz AC overhead line collection; 2477kW (3320hp); four axle-hung DC traction motors
TRACTIVE EFFORT: 353kN (39,360lbf)

MAX. OPERATING SPEED: 120km/h (75mph)
WEIGHT: 82 to 86t (180,080 to 190,060lb)
MAX. AXLE LOAD: not known
OVERALL LENGTH: 15.2m (49ft 10in)
GAUGE: 1435mm (4ft 8.5in)

CLASS V200 B-B GERMAN FEDERAL RAILWAYS (DB)

GERMANY 1953

A classic post-war design, though not a large class – 86 locomotives plus 50 of the sub-class V200.1 from 1960 – the V-200 diesel hydraulic earned a huge reputation. It was very much a *Deutsche Bundesbahn* (DB) project, with collaboration from manufacturers Maybach, MTU, Voith and Mekydro. Five prototypes appeared in 1953, and series production began in 1955.

In terms of tractive effort per tonne of weight, it was unique in its day. Its two engines were much smaller and lighter than the well-tried but cumbersome marine-based diesel electric engines used elsewhere, and rotated under maximum load at around 1500rpm. They were coupled to hydraulic converter units, each of which transmitted its drive to the wheelsets of the adjacent bogie through cardan shafts and permanently engaged bevel gears. Body design and construction were

also innovative in reducing weight: the body was built as a box, with sides of stressed steel sheeting, and all members contributing to carrying the combination of load, traction, buffing and braking forces.

To promote standard-ization and with the aim of making maintenance easier, DB persuaded the relevant manufacturers to adapt their engines and transmissions so that different designs could be fitted on to the same mountings and couplings. Thus a Maybach engine could be interchanged with a MTU or MAN engine, and a Voith transmission became interchangeable with a Mekydro. The bogie design was also unusual in that the wheel bearings were fitted to inside axleboxes, and the bogie frames were single strong structures, not of riveted plate construction as had previously been the norm.

Smoothly finished, the V200s looked impressive in their red

livery with black roof and body base lines, set off by stainless-steel lining, stainless-steel numberplates and raised lettering on the bodysides. As the pride of the non-electrified railway, which in the early 1950s was most trackage north of Heidelberg, the V200s held their place for years. They performed reliably on heavy passenger express trains as far north as Hamburg to as far south as Munich. They were equally at home on freight, to which they drifted more in later years.

The V200.1s, later reclassified 221 (by which time the original locomotives were Class 220), had 1000kW (1350bhp) diesel engines in pairs, which put 2000kW (2700bhp) on one B-B chassis. As electrification spread, the V200 duties changed to secondary passenger and freight work, the class being finally withdrawn from the DB in the 1980s. Many were then exported to countries such as

Greece and Albania, particularly the more powerful Class 221. Later, sold-off examples ended up in Switzerland and Italy on infrastructure trains. In the twenty-first century, some of these expatriates have been brought back to Germany for possible use by open access railway operators. And, of course, several are preserved in working order and see occasional use on special trains. British Railways adapted the V200 design for their diesel hydraulic 'Warship' class locomotives.

TYPE: mixed-traffic main-line diesel hydraulic
WHEEL ARRANGEMENT: B-B
POWER: Maybach, MAN, MTU 745, 820 and 1000kW (1000, 1100 and 1350bhp)
TRACTIVE EFFORT: 220kN (50,000lbf)
MAX. OPERATING SPEED: 120 and 140km/h (75 and 87mph)
WEIGHT: 79t (173,490lb)
OVERALL LENGTH: 18.53m (60ft 10in)
GAUGE: 1435mm (4ft 8.5in)

The V200s were compact locomotives with a high power-to-weight ratio. No. 116 displays the high quality of design and finish that helped to make it such a successful class.

CLASS 2MT 2-6-0 BRITISH RAILWAYS (BR)

Built at Darlington Works in 1954, British Railways 2MT No. 78019 has been preserved and can be seen on the restored Great Central Railway between Leicester and Loughborough.

This was the smallest and lightest of the tender engines in the British Standard range, and two more powerful 2-6-0 types were also included. All were mixed-traffic engines designed to work light trains on main lines and most services on cross-country secondary routes like the Shrewsbury–Aberystwyth line across Wales, the lines from the English Midlands into East Anglia, and in south-west Scotland. The

BOILER PRESSURE: 14kg/cm² (200psi)	**GRATE AREA:** 1.6m² (17.5sq ft)	**TRACTIVE EFFORT:** 8396kg (18,513lb)
CYLINDERS: 419x609mm (16.5x24in)	**HEATING SURFACE:** 95.2m² (1025sq ft)	**TOTAL WEIGHT:** 50t (110,320lb)
DRIVING WHEELS: 1294mm (51in)	**SUPERHEATER:** 11.5m² (124sq ft)	(engine only)

small diameter of the boiler enabled it to have a more prominent chimney and dome than most post-war British locomotives. The lines on which the 2-6-0s

operated were lightly used, and in the severe cutting back of the British network that took place in the early 1960s many of them were closed down. This, plus the

onset of the 'modernization' (i.e. dieselization) programme of British Railways, gave these engines rather brief careers before they were sent to the scrapyard.

CLASS EM2 CO-CO BRITISH RAILWAYS (BR)

For the electrified former 'Great Central' route between Manchester and Sheffield, BR's Gorton Works built the seven of this class to work an hourly passenger train service. Electrical equipment was from Metropolitan-

Vickers of Manchester. Nose-suspended motors drove the axles, supported by links from the bogie cross-stays, with Silentbloc bearings that absorbed movements of the motors. Two of three motors in each bogie were

permanently connected in series, with three different combinations enabling any of three speed ranges to be selected by the driver. Two motor generator sets were mounted in the body, one for independent excitation of the

motors and to power the cooling blower; the other to power the machinery cooler and also supply 50V current for battery-charging, control gear, lighting and heating. The Brunswick green EM2s hauled standard BR vacuum-braked carriages and, like all the early BR electrics and diesel-electrics, had engine-mounted electric steam boilers to provide carriages with steam heating. They had short lives on BR because the passenger trains were found not to lose much time if hauled by the 95km/h (60mph) EM1s that were becoming available as freight workings diminished. The EM2s were sold to the Netherlands Railways, where six of them worked InterCity trains between Amsterdam and Heerlen, Maastricht and Venlo for over two decades. Three are preserved today.

TYPE: Co-Co mainline passenger electric locomotive
POWER: 1500V DC overhead line collection; 1716kW (2300hp); six axle-hung DC traction motors; regenerative braking
TRACTIVE EFFORT: 200kN (45,000lbf)
MAX. OPERATING SPEED: 145km/h (90mph)
WEIGHT: 104t (228,480lb)
MAX. AXLE LOAD: not known
OVERALL LENGTH: 17.985m (59ft)

Class EM2 were Britain's first post-war electric passenger locomotives, and the first of the series was even named as *Electra*. But they had short working lives on British metals.

CLASS 08 C BRITISH RAILWAYS (BR)

The LMS diesel shunter of the 1930s was the ancestor of this type, which became the standard shunting engine on BR. Its power unit was the English Electric EE6KT naturally aspirated in-line engine, with six 254mm (10in) by 305mm (12in) cylinders. Two traction motors drove through double reduction gears to the front and rear wheelsets, which were connected externally by coupling rods on fly cranks. In a design strongly reminiscent of the typical steam shunting tank, the single cab was placed at the rear.

The Class 08 was ubiquitous in Great Britain, and a total of 1010 were built. It could be seen in every large station, where it replaced steam tanks as pilots in the mid-1960s, and few goods yards of any size did not have at least one. More than 200 still survive, with many still in use as yard shunters.

TYPE: C (0-6-0) diesel-electric shunting
POWER UNIT: EE6KT diesel engine, 260kW (350bhp), DC generator, two axle-hung traction motors, double-reduction gears
TRACTIVE EFFORT: 156kN (35,000lbf)
MAX. OPERATING SPEED: 32km/h (20mph)
WEIGHT: 50t (109,760lb)
OVERALL LENGTH: 8.92m (29ft 3in)
GAUGE: 1435mm (4ft 8.5in)

Seen here at the Freightliner terminal at Mossend, Scotland, in August 1901, the Class 08.

CLASS MA 2-10-2 HELLENIC STATE RAILWAYS (SEK)

GREECE 1953

Part of the war reparations made by Italy to Greece after 1945 consisted of this class of 20 new locomotives, built by Ansaldo of Sampierdarena. Joining the Hellenic Railways' stock of mostly German- and Austrian-built locomotives, it was intended for express freight work, but the design – the first new Italian steam design for 30 years – was a failure. The plate frames were too lightweight to support the huge boiler, and the firebox too small to generate the requisite amount of steam for the two big cylinders.

Despite many modifications, the Class MA locomotives remained unreliable, and spent much time in repair shops. A number of Austrian 2-10-0s were borrowed between 1957 and 1961 to supplement them. They were scrapped in the late 1960s.

BOILER PRESSURE: 18kg/cm² (256.5psi)
CYLINDERS: 660x750mm (26x29.5in)
DRIVING WHEELS: 1600mm (63in)
GRATE AREA: 5.6m² (60.3sq ft)
HEATING SURFACE: not known
SUPERHEATER: not known
TRACTIVE EFFORT: 31,290kg (69,000lb)
TOTAL WEIGHT: 135t (297,675lb) (engine only)

CLASS CC200 CO-2-CO INDONESIAN STATE RAILWAYS (PNKA)

INDONESIA 1953

The old State Railways became the PNKA after Indonesia ceased to be a Dutch colony, and a dieselization programme was launched in the early 1950s. Although PNKA and its SS predecessor had bought few steam locomotives from the United States, American designs monopolized its early diesel fleet. Twenty-seven of these road engines were supplied by General Electric, the first main-line diesels in Indonesia and precursors of many more. Their Co-2-Co wheel arrangement was unusual, caused by the requirement for a maximum axle loading that did not exceed 12.2 tonnes (12 tons). The carrying wheels were set in a truck that could be detached from the locomotive frame, converting it into a Co-Co type if the axle-weight restrictions should be relaxed. The convertible format was not repeated in further orders, which were all for Co-Co locomotives.

The class went into service on the 1066mm (3ft 6in) gauge main lines in Java, but despite being designed with the heat and humidity of Indonesia in mind, they were not very successful in operation. By the 1960s, several were out of service, being cannibalized for spare parts to keep the others going. One was completely rebuilt into a switching engine. By the end of the twentieth century, three remained in store, and in 2001 No. 200 15 was selected for repair and restoration to running condition as a historic locomotive.

TYPE: diesel-electric mixed-traffic locomotive
POWER: Alco 12-cylinder 244E engine developing 888kW (1190hp) at 1000rpm
TRACTIVE EFFORT: 211kN (47,500lb)
MAX. OPERATING SPEED: 100km/h (62mph)
TOTAL WEIGHT: 96t (234,420lb)
MAXIMUM AXLE LOAD: 12t (26,455lb)
OVERALL LENGTH: 13.147m (43ft 2in) (wheelbase)
GAUGE: not known

ETR-300 *SETTEBELLO* FAST ELECTRIC TRAIN STATE RAILWAYS (FS)

ITALY 1953

The FS had acquired valuable experience in running very fast electric multiple-unit trains with the ETR-200 in the late 1930s (see 1939), and the concept was taken further in the seven-car *Settebello*. 'Beautiful seven' is a lucky hand in cards, and a seven-card motif was used for the logo of this service. There were three trains, two in service, one as a reserve, all composed of two articulated end-units and a central three-car articulated set. As Europe's first post-war luxury train, with all first-class accommodation, at first for only 160, later 190, passengers, it quickly became famous. The driving positions were in raised cupolas towards the rear of each of the end cars, allowing for observation lounges – hence the sun-blinds of the end windows. The central set was entirely formed of service vehicles, with separate restaurant-bar car, kitchen, baggage and mail compartments and spacious crew quarters. The design, in green and grey livery, was a streamlined one, and features like the streamlined fairings between the articulated units showed the way forward for the high-speed inter-city trains of the later twentieth century, though these

The driver's canopy can be seen above the *Settebello*'s viewing windows. The once futuristic styling now looks rather dumpy.

would improve on its ratio of more than 2 tonnes (1.9 tons) of train-weight per passenger. The train was sound-proofed, double-glazed and air-conditioned. Among the amenities were shower compartments, a shop and a radio/telephone office. Pantographs were fitted to the second car of each end-unit, and the six bogies of these were all motored, with a traction unit for each axle.

The four-wheeled bogies were supported on laminated springs, supplemented by hydraulic shock-absorbers, with rubber pads between the bogie frame and the centre pivot and also at the side bearers. The riding quality of the

bogies was first-class. A crew of three qualified drivers worked the train, two in the front cupola-cab and a third in the rear, whose job was to watch over the auxiliary equipment. The two driving cabs were linked by telephone.

The *Settebello* ran on the Milan–Bologna–Florence–Rome route, (633.25km/393.5 miles). Until the completion of the first section of the Rome–Florence *direttissima* line in 1977, the speed was limited to a 112km/h (70mph) maximum for the first 145km (90 miles), because of the severe curvature of the old main line. The 314km (195.1-mile) section from Rome to Florence, where the train reversed

direction, was the longest non-stop run on the FS system. Speeds of 160km/h (100mph) were regularly achieved on open stretches of track between Arezzo and Florence, and in the Lombardy plain.

Later alterations to the *Settebello* sets included the fitting of more powerful motor units, giving an increase in rated output of 28 per cent. Rheostatic or regenerative braking, in addition to the original air brakes, was installed, and cab signalling was fitted.

In 1968, the *Settebello* was incorporated into the Trans-Europ Express (TEE) network. In 1976, it was renamed as *Colosseum*, and ran

under this name until 1987, when the train was discontinued as a special service. Though not a 'bullet train' on a dedicated line, its success pointed the way forwards.

TYPE: articulated electric express train
POWER: 12 187kW (250hp) motors fed by overhead catenary at 3000V, driving 12 axles via gearing and hollow-axle flexible drive
TRACTIVE EFFORT: not known
MAX. OPERATING SPEED: 160km/h (100mph)
TOTAL WEIGHT: 325t (716,300lb)
MAX. AXLE LOAD: 17t (37,468lb)
OVERALL LENGTH: 165.202m (542ft)

DEII DIESEL MULTIPLE UNITS NETHERLANDS RAILWAYS (NS)   NETHERLANDS 1953

For 1953, this was a very modern-looking DMU, though the sliding windows show that air conditioning was not yet standard on Dutch trains. Twenty-three two-car units were supplied in 1953–54 by the Dutch firm of Allan. They were articulated, with a central bogie carrying the inner ends of both cars. Each outer bogie was provided with a DC motor mounted on each axle. The bogies themselves were of

unusual design, with the axleboxes carried on two long links hinged to the bogie frame near the centre. Primary coil springs located at the outer ends were damped by vertical hydraulic dampers angled at about 40°. Power was supplied by an under-floor Cummins diesel engine in each car. The DEII units, later classified Plan X-v in NS' standard system, have all been withdrawn from NS, but several

are still working for private operators on routes near the German border.

TYPE: local passenger diesel-electric two-car multiple unit
POWER: Cummins NT895R2 180kW (240bhp) six-cylinder, under each car
POWER TRAIN: DC generator; two traction motors on each outer bogie
TRACTIVE EFFORT: not known

In 1953, this was a very advanced DMU design. The yellow livery was introduced in the 1960s.

MAX. OPERATING SPEED: 120km/h (75mph)
WEIGHT: 45t (98,824lb) per half-unit
OVERALL LENGTH: 22.7m (74ft 6in) per half-unit
GAUGE: 1435mm (4ft 8.5in)

CLASS TY 51 2-10-0 POLISH STATE RAILWAYS (PKP)

Poland's last steam locomotive class was a large one, and quite numerous, with 232 built at the Cegielski works in Poznan between 1953 and 1957. In almost all respects, they were American-syle, closely based on the American-built Ty 246, acquired in the pre-Cold War year of 1947. They had slightly bigger fireboxes, and a range of American features including Laird crossheads working on a single slide-bar, and mechanical stokers. Polish touches included the small smoke deflectors fitted high up alongside the chimney, and the all-enclosed cabs. A longer form of the typical box-like eight-wheel tender was attached. One of the class is preserved.

BOILER PRESSURE: 16kg/cm² (228psi)
CYLINDERS: 630x700mm (24.8x27.6in)
DRIVING WHEELS: 1450mm (57in)
GRATE AREA: 6.3m² (67.8sq ft)
HEATING SURFACE: 242m² (2605sq ft)
SUPERHEATER: 85.6m² (921.6sq ft)
TRACTIVE EFFORT: 26,175kg (57,715lb)
TOTAL WEIGHT: 112t (246,960lb)
(engine only)

TY 51 No. 223 is preserved at the Wolzstyn museum depot. A number of others are preserved in plinthed form. Coal haulage was the main task of these locomotives when in service.

CLASS P36 4-8-4 SOVIET RAILWAYS (SZD)

The engineer I.S. Lebedyanskii, with several excellent locomotive designs to his credit, was responsible for the first 4-8-4 to be built in Russia. The prototype, P36.001, appeared in March 1950, from the Kolomna Works. Throughout the Soviet period until 1960, passenger traffic was the poor relation of freight, and in 1953 the P36 went into production as Russia's first modern express locomotive, and the first Russian locomotive to have roller bearings on all axles. In some respects, it was a development of a 1930s class, the JS (Josef Stalin) 2-8-4 of 1934 (a passenger version of the FD 2-10-2), but design detail and building

Despite the official denigration of steam power in the late 1950s, Soviet Russia preserved a large number of steam locomotives in various depots and museums, and many, like this P36, still work excursions.

techniques had changed a great deal in the intervening 20 years. Kolomna built 250 of the class up to 1956, and the last one, P36.0251, was also the last main-line steam locomotive constructed for the Soviet Railways. Like the Lv class, more would have been built if government policy had not stopped steam construction.

It was, typically, a two-cylinder simple, mechanically on conventional lines but with distinctive external styling: the upper part of the cab was

backward-slanted, and large smoke deflectors extended from the buffer beam back alongside the smoke box and formed a unit with a deep running-plate. As with some North American and German locomotives, a heat exchanger for feedwater heating was situated transversely on the smoke-box top, in front of the chimney. A more typically Russian feature was the insulated 'skyline' casing that was continued back to the cab, and which held the boiler fittings and carried the main

steam pipe from the dome to just behind the chimney. Coal-fired versions were equipped with mechanical stokers, but the majority were oil burners.

The P36 locomotives replaced earlier types on most of the Soviet Railways' prestige trains, including the Leningrad–Moscow expresses, those from Moscow to Minsk and the Polish frontier, and the eastern, not yet electrified, sectors of the 'Trans-Siberian Express'. A few were painted blue, but most were painted light green, with red wheel

centres and white rims – an attractive livery that suited them well.

BOILER PRESSURE: 15kg/cm² (213psi)
CYLINDERS: 574x799mm (22.6x31.5in)
DRIVING WHEELS: 1846mm (72.75in)
GRATE AREA: 6.7m² (72.6sq ft)
HEATING SURFACE: 294m² (3163.4sq ft)
SUPERHEATER: 132m² (1420sq ft)
TRACTIVE EFFORT: 18,160kg (40,040lb)
TOTAL WEIGHT: 149.3t (302,400lb)
(engine only)

CLASS 25 4-8-4 SOUTH AFRICAN RAILWAYS (SAR)

SOUTH AFRICA 1953

For the South African Railways, the quality and conservation of water supplies was a prime consideration, and the idea of a locomotive that could recirculate and reuse its own water was an

appealing one. The condensation concept was not new (see 1864), but much development work had been done by Henschel in Germany from 1933 onwards to make it effective. The condenser

did not detract from the locomotive's power output, but recycled the exhaust steam that is otherwise lost through the chimney and other vents. Having passed through the cylinders, the

steam was transferred via a flexible pipe to the tender, in which a grease separator and turbine fans were mounted. The latter were used to cool the steam back to water, assisted by air-vents

A non-condensing Class 25 rolls its freight out of the yard past a handsome set of latticed semaphore signals.

in the tender sides, and the still-hot water was then reused to make new steam. The exhaust steam also drove a smaller turbine fan that provided draught in the smoke box to draw heat through the boiler tubes and maintain the fire. With no blast up the chimney, these engines did not 'puff'; instead, the whine of the fan was heard. To hold the condensing equipment as well as fuel, the tenders of the Class 25s were longer than the locomotives.

An effective condenser system offered a 90 per cent saving on water use, and around 10 per cent on fuel. For working the Cape

Town–Johannesburg trunk line across the Karoo Desert, particularly the sector between De Aar and Beaufort West where water is inaccessible, this was an attractive proposition, and after a successful single-engine experiment carried out by Henschel on a Class 20 2-10-2 and the building of a single 4-8-4 protoype in 1948, the Class 25 was developed. Between 1953 and 1955, 89 were built by North British Locomotive Co., Glasgow, with the tenders coming from Henschel. In addition, 50 non-condensing engines of identical dimensions were built, designated

Class 25NC, of which 10 were from NBL and 40 from Henschel. To maximize heating surface, the boilers were pushed out to the maximum extent the loading gauge would allow, though the steam pressure was not particularly high for a 1950s locomotive. Their weight was supported on an American-type cast steel frame, with the cylinders as an integral part. Roller bearings were fitted on the coupling- and connecting-rod joints as well as to all the axles. As locomotives, they were excellent, and hauled most trains across the 'dry' section, but unfortunately, the condensing apparatus was often

problematic, and this made the Class 25 more prone to failure than conventional locomotives. Class 25NC grew larger, and Class 25 smaller as, from 1974 onwards, the condenser locomotives were rebuilt with conventional tenders.

BOILER PRESSURE: 15.5kg/cm² (220psi)
CYLINDERS: 610x711mm (24x28in)
DRIVING WHEELS: 1524mm (60in)
GRATE AREA: 6.4m² (68.9sq ft)
HEATING SURFACE: 284.1m² (3059sq ft)
SUPERHEATER: 58.5m² (630sq ft)
TRACTIVE EFFORT: 23,353kg (51,492lb)
TOTAL WEIGHT: 238t (525,000lb)

CLASS 141F 2-8-2 SPANISH NATIONAL RAILWAYS (RENFE)

SPAIN 1953

Spain built few large steam classes in the mid-twentieth century, and this 'Mikado', with 241 engines, is the major exception. From its formation in

BOILER PRESSURE: 15kg/cm² (214psi)
CYLINDERS: 570x710mm (22.4x28in)
DRIVING WHEELS: 1560mm (61.5in)
GRATE AREA: 4.8m² (51.5sq ft)
HEATING SURFACE: 239m² (2578sq ft)
SUPERHEATER: 74.5m² (802sq ft)
TRACTIVE EFFORT: 20,520kg (41,553lb)
TOTAL WEIGHT: 166.5t (367,132lb)

1943, RENFE continued to operate a huge range of older locomotive types, most of which continued to work until steam was phased out in the late 1960s and the 1970s. Constructed between 1953 and 1960, the 141F gave a powerful fillip to passenger train and fast freight work. The first 25 came from the North British Locomotive Co. in Glasgow; the rest mostly from Spanish works, Euskalduña, Babcock & Wilcox, Maquinista Terrestre y Maritima and Macosa. All were two-cylinder simples, with Walschaerts valve gear and fitted

with varying types of feedwater heaters. The final 116 were oil burning, with double chimneys.

RENFE operated the Spanish sectors of international expresses to Portugal and France. The 'Lusitania Express' ran between Madrid and Lisbon from 1943, while the 'Sud Express' from Paris had been running since 1887, both trains under the auspices of the International Wagon-Lits Company.

The 2-8-2s took their turn on these prestige trains as well as on internal services between Madrid and major Spanish cities, until electrification of the trunk routes. Long single-track sections and steep grades meant that Spain was not a country of high speeds, and a general maximum of 110km/h (68mph) was imposed. The drivers' task was to maintain consistent speeds within the limit.

Two members of Class 141F stand on shed, one with steam up and ready to go, the other with smoke box door open, still undergoing cleaning-out operations.

CLASS DA 1-C-1 STATE RAILWAYS (SJ)

By now, new electric locomotives on most railways were running on powered bogies, but the SJ still held to the rigid-frame design established with the first D types 30 years before. And they worked reliably all over the country on all types of traffic. But this was to be the last of the D types, and when SJ acquired more powerful locomotives, the class was downgraded to secondary duties.

They lasted into the 1980s, and one or two still survive with private infrastructure support companies.

TYPE: 1-C-1 mixed-traffic light electric locomotive
POWER: 15,000V 16.67Hz AC overhead line collection; 1840kW (2500hp); one large body mounted AC traction motor driving the wheels through a jackshaft and side coupling rods
TRACTIVE EFFORT: 205kN (46,085lbf)
MAX. OPERATING SPEED: 100km/h (62mph)
WEIGHT: 75t (164,705lb)
MAX. AXLE LOAD: not known
OVERALL LENGTH: 13m (42ft 8in)
GAUGE: 1435mm (4ft 8.5in)

Ninety of Class Da were built between 1953 and 1957, the last rod-driven passenger electrics.

BO-BO TURKISH STATE RAILWAYS (TCDD)

Improved suburban services from Istanbul's west-side terminus, Sirkeçi, to Halkali was the reason for an electrification, at single-phase 25kV AC, at 50 cycles – the first use of this voltage and frequency on suburban tracks. In addition to 18 French-built three-coach emu trains, three Alsthom-built Bo-Bo locomotives, with transformers and gradation equipment from Matériel de Traction Electrique (MTE) of Paris, were provided to haul heavy passenger and freight trains over the 27km (16.8-mile) electrified section.

Train loads of up to 700 tonnes (686 tons) could be hauled by a single locomotive. For more than 10 years, the Bo-Bos remained Turkey's only electric locomotives, until electrification of the Istanbul–Ankara main line. New TCDD diesels speeded up their withdrawal in the late 1960s.

TYPE: mixed-traffic locomotive
POWER: four 300V (500hp) traction motors of 14-pole commutator type, supplied by 25kV AC at 50Hz via overhead catenary
TRACTIVE EFFORT: 156.8kN (35,280lbf)

MAX. OPERATING SPEED: 90km/h (56mph)
TOTAL WEIGHT: 77.5t (170,887lb)
MAX. AXLE LOAD: 19.4t (42,722lb)
OVERALL LENGTH: 16.138m (53ft)
BUILDER: Alsthom, France

H-24-66 'TRAIN MASTER' CO-CO VARIOUS RAILROADS

Late-comers to the market, Fairbanks-Morse worked hard to establish a position and gain share, but found the going was tough. Nevertheless by 1953 they were selling more locomotives than Baldwin, which had merged with Lima-Hamilton in 1951 to form Baldwin-Hamilton-Lima. The H-24-66 was the most powerful of F-M's diesel-electric road switcher types, promoted by the manufacturer as the 'Train Master'. F-M continued to use engines of their successful opposed-piston arrangement, and the six-axle, six-motor model H-24-66 was powered by a 12-cylinder F-M opposed piston engine developing 1790kW (2400 hp). The company concentrated on the high-power end of the market (its 1764kW/ 2400hp C-Liners set a record in its day of 31.6kW/42.5hp per 30cm/ 12in of length), and in its time the Train Master was by far the most powerful single-engine road switcher. The machine proved versatile. The Virginian used its H-24-66 in heavy coal service, while Southern Pacific employed its fleet on weekday San Francisco–San Jose suburban services and on heavy freight work at weekends. Despite its capability and versatility, the Train Master production totalled just 127 locomotives, tiny compared to the number of road switchers built in the same period by market leaders Electro-Motive.

TYPE: Co-Co, diesel-electric
POWER AND OUTPUT: 12-cylinder Fairbanks-Morse opposed piston diesel producing 1790kW (2400hp)
TRACTIVE EFFORT: 500kN (112,500lbf)

MAX. OPERATING SPEED: various depending on gear ratio
WEIGHT: 170t (375,850lb)
OVERALL LENGTH: 20.117m (66ft)
GAUGE: 1435mm (4ft 8.5in)

CLASS X 2-DO-2 WESTERN AUSTRALIA GOVERNMENT RAILWAYS (WAGR)

These 32 boot-ended locomotives, built in England by Metropolitan Vickers for light passenger and freight were not a commercial or practical success story. The 2-Do-2 arrangement was needed to stay within a maximum 9.8-tonne (10-ton) axle loading specified by the Western Australia Government Railways. All were fitted with Crossley aluminium-piston two-stroke engines, whose excessive vibration, cracked heads, belching smoky exhaust, ring scuffing and oil flow problems kept the class shut in the repair shops for much of the time. Some of the class, designated XA, were fitted from new for multiple working, the rest were adapted later and then classed XB. Despite their problems, several remain in preservation following withdrawal in the 1980s.

TYPE: 2-Do-2 light axle diesel-electric
POWER: 825kW (1105hp) from Crossley HSTV8 series engine
TRACTIVE EFFORT: 116kN (26,100lbf) maximum; 53kN at 39km/h (11,925lbf at 24.4mph) continuous

MAX. OPERATING SPEED: 89km/h (55.6mph)
WEIGHT: 80t (176,400lb)
OVERALL LENGTH: 14.63m (47ft 9in)
GAUGE: 1067mm (3ft 6in)

CLASS D70 CO-CO VARIOUS RAILWAYS

CHILE/URUGUAY 1954

In 1952, General Electric's long-standing alliance with Alco came to an end, and GEC began to build its own range of diesel-electric locomotives and to look beyond the United States for world markets. In the course of the 1950s, they supplied the railways of Latin America with many different designs. Amongst the most distinctive are the single-ended 'shovelnose' units, of which 17 were supplied to Chile in two batches delivered in 1954 and 1956/1957. *Ferrocarril del Pacifico SA* (FEPASA) continues to operate five today as its Class D1600 on freight traffic from La Paz. Forty-seven less powerful engines were built for the Uruguay Railways, again in two batches with 20 units in 1952 and 27 in 1954. About 10 are believed to survive today. In 2003 they were still operating four daily commuter services between Montevideo and 25 de Agosto.

TYPE: Co-Co diesel-electric
POWER: Chile 1288kW (1750hp); Uruguay 1030kW (1400hp) from Alco 12-244 series engine
TRACTIVE EFFORT: 245kN (55000lbf)
MAX. OPERATING SPEED: 120km/h (75mph)

WEIGHT: 106 to 112t (233,730lb to 246,960lb)
OVERALL LENGTH: 17m (55ft 6in)
GAUGE: Chile 1676mm (5ft 6in); Uruguay 1435mm (4ft 8.5in)

CLASS 498.1 4-8-2 CZECHOSLOVAK STATE RAILWAYS (CSD)

CZECHOSLOVAKIA 1954

The CSD was unusual among post-1945 railway operators in continuing to build three-cylinder locomotives, while two cylinders were almost universal on other systems. Three cylinders were more expensive to build and maintain, but they made more efficient use of available steam, provided greater power and made for a smooth-running engine. Among the last steam locomotives designed and built at the Skoda Works was this impressive simple-expansion express passenger type, an improved version of the 1947 Class 498.0. As typical in modern three-cylinder Czech steam locomotives, the Walschaerts valve gear for the inside cylinder was operated by a long rod off a return crank from the crank-pin of the third coupled axle on the left side. The firebox, of welded construction, had a combustion chamber, a thermic syphon and two tubular arches, and was fed by a mechanical stoker. Roller bearings were fitted to all axles,

The high point of steam traction came later in Czechoslovakia than in most countries: a preserved Class 498.1 heads a steam special in the late 1990s.

BOILER PRESSURE: 16kg/cm² (228psi)
CYLINDERS: 500x680mm (19.75x26.75in)
DRIVING WHEELS: 1830mm (72in)
GRATE AREA: 4.9m² (52sq ft)
HEATING SURFACE: 228m² (2454sq ft)
SUPERHEATER: 74m² (797sq ft)
TRACTIVE EFFORT: 19,018kg (41,920lb)
TOTAL WEIGHT: 194t (428,500lb)

including those of the large five-axled tender, and to the rods. In anticipation of eventual displacement from main-line services, there was a provision for adjusting the maximum axle load between coupled and supporting wheels, applying more to the latter and reducing it on the former from 18.8 tonnes (18.5 tons) to 17 tonnes (16.8 tons) to allow it to run on secondary lines. The cab was integral, with no footplate extension to the tender, which was, unusually, mounted on four and six-wheel bogies.

The CSD had a maximum operating speed limit of 120km/h (75mph) but No. 498.106, on a test run on 27 August 1964, achieved the maximum speed on Czechoslovakian rails, of 162km/h (100.6mph). As electrification of the network advanced, the express engines of the CSD were required to run certain routes, like that from Prague to Kolín, to schedules devised for electric traction. Both 498 classes rose splendidly to this demand. No. 498.106, and one other of the class, are preserved.

ETA515 BATTERY RAILCAR GERMAN FEDERAL RAILWAYS (DB)

GERMANY 1954

Requiring no catenary but with the other advantages of electric power, the battery railcar's main problem was always its limited operating range. In this respect, the wartime development of large batteries for submarines proved useful, and with the VARTA company, DB developed the technology further. Only lead acid accumulators were suitable, making up one-third of the vehicle weight, with 11 20-cell battery troughs suspended from the car's underframe. VARTA manufactured batteries in ever-increasing capacities ranging from 1038 Ah in the earlier class 515.0 and 515.1 to 1344 Ah in the 515.6 version. Batteries of less weight but higher capacity at 1071 and 1479 Ah later allowed effective operating ranges of 200 and 300km (124 and 186 miles), and the 86-seat cars could also pull a Class 815 trailer.

ETAs entered service from 1954 in Munich, and in the following year they began wider operation, initially in the south, then all over the DB. Even international cross-border services such as Aachen to Maastricht were worked by Class 515 railcars. Tighter and faster schedules made possible by new electric and diesel trains began to make them obsolescent, however. Their last regular work, in the Ruhr metropolitan area, ended in 1995. Overall production of the Class 515 numbered over 200 engines.

TYPE: single battery railcar
POWER: 200kW (268hp)
TRACTIVE EFFORT: N/A
MAX. OPERATING SPEED: 100km/h (62mph)

WEIGHT: up to 56t (123,480hp)
MAX. AXLE LOAD: 14t (30,870lb)
OVERALL LENGTH: 23.5m (76ft 8in)
GAUGE: 1435mm (4ft 8.5in)

CLASS 9F 2-10-0 BRITISH RAILWAYS (BR)

GREAT BRITAIN 1954

More of this class were built than any of the other standard British locomotive types – 251 in total – but a big engine for main-line bulk freight was badly needed. The success of the wartime 'Austerity' 2-10-0 was decisive in making this the adopted wheel arrangement. The boiler was similar to that of the 'Britannia' 4-6-2 class, but 533mm (21in) shorter and set high in order to provide the widest possible space for the ashpan. The resultant space between boiler and frame earned the class the nickname of 'spaceships'. Nevertheless, the compromise necessary between a wide, deep ashpan and 1525mm (60in) wheels was perhaps the weakest point in a generally excellent design. As in the 'Austerity' engines, the central drivers were flangeless in order to improve turning. Many were provided with a concrete arch in the firebox instead of the

conventional brick arch. All were two-cylinder engines, of conventional build, apart from 10 built at Crewe Works in 1955 with the Franco-Crosti boiler. Feedwater heaters were a normal sight on American, French and German locomotives, among others, but had never been widespread in Britain. British engineers' distaste for external fittings may have played a part in this. The Class 9F was by far their most serious attempt to provide such an aid to efficient steam generation, in which exhaust steam is channelled back through a pre-heater fitted beneath the main boiler. The injectors fed water into the pre-heater, and from there it passed through top-mounted clack valves into the boiler. Unlike Italian Crosti-boilered engines, the 2-10-0 retained its front chimney in addition to the exhaust vent fitted on the right-hand side of the boiler, though it was used only for

lighting-up. Sulphur dioxide corrosion of the tubes was a problem, and the Crosti variation was not particularly successful. The 9Fs were fitted with smoke deflectors, unusual in a freight engine, possibly in anticipation of a low-pressure exhaust that would not rise clear of the boiler. The British designers were reluctant to use double blast-pipe chimneys, partly because they believed these were best employed at full-power output, not a common occurrence. However, later engines of this class were so equipped. Other variants included a Giesl ejector, experimentally fitted on one engine. Three of the class were fitted with mechanical stokers in 1958.

The 9Fs were employed chiefly on vacuum-brake fitted mineral trains. Although not fitted with train-heating apparatus, they did run passenger trains on occasions. One of these was to deputize on

an express between Grantham and London King's Cross, at an average 93km/h (58mph) start to stop, and including a maximum of 145km/h (90mph). The operating authorities later placed a maximum of 96.5kph (60mph) on the class.

This was the last steam design for British Railways, and No. 92220, built at Swindon in 1960 and named *Evening Star*, was the last steam locomotive built for regular service in Britain. Eight years later, no steam locomotives were running on British Railways. *Evening Star* has been preserved, with some others of the class.

BOILER PRESSURE: 15.8kg/cm² (225psi)
CYLINDERS: 508x711mm (20x28in)
DRIVING WHEELS: 1525mm (60in)
GRATE AREA: 3.73m² (40.2sq ft)
HEATING SURFACE: 181m² (1950sq ft)
SUPERHEATER: 49.3m² (530.6sq ft)
TRACTIVE EFFORT: 18,140kg (40,000lb)
TOTAL WEIGHT: 88.4t (194,880lb)
(engine only)

The preserved No. 92220, in British Railways' green express livery, at York Station with the charter 'Scarborough Spa Express', on 14 August 1983. Volunteers shovel coal down to the coal door.

CLASS WCM1 CO-CO INDIAN RAILWAYS (IR)

The worker in overalls seems to be pulling No. 20071 along, at Bombay Victoria depot, on 14 November 1991. These locomotives had a single, off-centre, access door on each side. One is preserved at Chennai Rail Museum.

Almost identical in body styling to the Spanish Class 277 of 1952, the Indian WCM1 and WCM2 classes were also built by by English Electric and Vulcan Foundry. The seven larger class WCM1s of 1954 were 1500V DC for use in the Bombay (Mumbai) area, while the 12 smaller class WCM2, delivered in 1957, were originally 3000V DC for the Calcutta area. These were modified for 1500V operation on conversion of the Calcutta electrified lines to 25kV AC. Both

were passenger engines, and marked a considerable advance over pre-war Indian electrics. Underframe and body were of welded steel construction, and the bogies were also all-welded, not on pivots but supporting a bolster, with the locomotive weight passed down to the axle-boxes via four pairs of coil springs, each pair resting on the equalizing beam of each bogie. Slots in the tops of the roller-bearing axle-boxes held the equalizing beams in position, and

manganese-steel liners were fitted to the rubbing surfaces between the bolster and the bogie and body frames.

Three traction motors were mounted in each bogie, one to each axle, driving through single-reduction resilient spur-gears. Waterproofed against monsoon flooding, they were force-ventilated. All electrical equipment was installed in such a way so that in the case of a failure of the control or ancillary equipment, half could be isolated and the

locomotive could proceed on the other half. Class WCM1s kept up fast express work into the 1990s. No Class WCM1 locomotive is in service today, but two class WCM2s were still operational in 2002, based at Kalyan depot.

TYPE: Co-Co electric mixed-traffic
POWER: 2365kW (3170hp)
SUPPLY: WCM1 1500 V DC
TRACTIVE EFFORT: 306kN (68860lbf)
MAX. OPERATING SPEED: 120km/h (75mph)
WEIGHT: 124t (251,100lb)
MAX. AXLE LOAD: 21t (46,305lb)
GAUGE: 1676mm (5ft 6in)

CLASS 2400 BO-BO NETHERLANDS RAILWAYS (NS)

Alsthom were the amalgamation of the Société Alsacienne, famous steam locomotive builders, and

Thomson-Houston, specialists in electrical technology. The Class 2400 compact diesel-electric hood units were a typical

Alsthom product of the 1950s, intended by NS for short-distance freight and heavy shunting duties. Totalling 130 in the class,

they were used all over the Netherlands, sometimes hauling main-line freights in multiples of up to four locomotives under control of one driver. They were withdrawn by the end of the 1990s, but some saw further use in Belgium and elsewhere, working for infrastructure companies on projects like new high-speed lines.

TYPE: freight main-line diesel-electric
WHEEL ARRANGEMENT: Bo-Bo
OWER UNIT: SACM V12 SHR 12-cylinder V-form diesel, 625kW (840bhp); DC generator; four axle-hung DC traction motors
TRACTIVE EFFORT: 161kN (36,195lbf)
MAX. OPERATING SPEED: 80km/h (50mph)
WEIGHT: 134t (293,440lb)
OVERALL LENGTH: 18.64m (61ft 2in)
GAUGE: 1435mm (4ft 8.5in)

Three Class 2400 units wait in the carriage sidings for their rostered turn. Freight haulage was, however, by far the main task of this class.

DF CLASS 2CO-CO2 NEW ZEALAND RAILWAYS (NZR)   NEW ZEALAND 1954

Immensely long-looking, these 10-axled locomotives built by English Electric were the first main-line diesels for NZR. Thirty-one were initially ordered, but second thoughts reduced their number to 10, with the balance converted to 42 smaller locomotives of Class DG. English Electric fitted the same Mk.II 16SVT engine that British Railways used in their Class 40, but although this engine was to evolve into a reliable and robust power unit, the early versions were beset with problems and Class DF units were not noted for their reliability at first. Many modifications were required. Beginning with main-line freight on the North Island, the DFs' own problems plus newer diesels moved them on to secondary work where their relatively light axle load remained useful over light track. Withdrawal began in 1972, and all were gone by 1975.

TYPE: 2Co-Co2 diesel-electric
POWER: 1119kW (1500hp) from EE 16SVT series engine
TRACTIVE EFFORT: 180kN (40,500lbf)
MAX. OPERATING SPEED: 96km/h (60mph)
WEIGHT: 110t (242,550lb)
OVERALL LENGTH: 18.7m (61ft)
GAUGE: 1067mm (3ft 6in)

CLASS P-38 2-8-8-4 SOVIET RAILWAYS (SZD)   RUSSIA 1954

Russia's last steam locomotive class also contained the biggest and heaviest engines actually built in Russia – only the imported Ya-01 Beyer Garratt of 1932 exceeded them. Heavy freight haulage of trains of 3556 tonnes (3500 tons) was the intention, and two prototype locomotives were built. To provide the necessary adhesive weight, and yet stay within the 16.25-tonne (16-ton) limitation of the maximum permitted axle load, required eight coupled axles, and so the Mallet type, with simple expansion, was chosen. The two P-38s emerged from Kolomna Works in December 1954 and January 1955, with two cylinders driving each set of big wheels.

At this time, steam power still seemed to have a vigorous future in Russia. Lazar Kaganovich, the Commissar of Transport, had announced: 'I am for the steam locomotive and against those who imagine we will not have any steam locomotives in the future.' On test, P-38.001 pulled a 3556-tonne (3500-ton) train at 24km/h (15mph) up an incline of 1 in 110. The new engines were tried out in southern Siberia on lines between Krasnoyarsk and Ulan Ude. Further details of their performance were not published, but it was later stated that they had not functioned well in conditions of extreme cold.

After a brief working life, both P-38s were withdrawn. Before that, by 1957, steam power had been officially denounced as 'uneconomic and out of date', and all building stopped. Kaganovich was disgraced, part of the case against him being that: '. . . he stubbornly insisted on developing steam traction', an acute failure under the Soviet regime.

BOILER PRESSURE: 15kg/cm² (213psi)
CYLINDERS: 574x799mm (22.6x31.5in)
DRIVING WHEELS: 1497mm (59in)
GRATE AREA: 10.7m² (115sq ft)
HEATING SURFACE: 396.3m² (4266.8sq ft)
SUPERHEATER: 236.7m² (2548.4sq ft)
TRACTIVE EFFORT: N/A
TOTAL WEIGHT: 218.3t (481,376lb)

CLASSES GMA AND GMAM 4-8-2+2-8-4 SOUTH AFRICAN RAILWAYS (SAR)   SOUTH AFRICA 1954

On the SAR in the mid-1950s, steam power was not only vibrant but fully up-to-date in technology. Here the Garratt type reached its peak of effectiveness, and the SAR had more of them than any other railway. It was back in 1919 that the first Garratts for the South African 1065mm (3ft 6in) gauge, Class GA, were delivered, and a variety of Garratts and other articulated types followed. In the late 1920s, the original Garratt patents expired, and the way was open for other manufacturers to use the principle. The Germans were foremost in this effort, and from 1927 Hanomag, Maffei, Krupp and Henschel feature among the Garratt suppliers, as well as Beyer Peacock. The North British Locomotive Co. of Glasgow also contributed from 1924, though its 'Modified Fairlies' were not true Garratts. In the mountainous districts of South Africa, Garratts were an established part of the railway scene, and hauled all kinds of traffic.

No less less than three new classes were introduced in 1954:

BOILER PRESSURE: 14kg/cm² (200psi)
CYLINDERS: 520x660mm (20.5x26in)
DRIVING WHEELS: 1370mm (54in)
GRATE AREA: 5.9m² (63.5sq ft)
HEATING SURFACE: 298.6m² (3215sq ft)
SUPERHEATER: 69.4m² (747sq ft)
TRACTIVE EFFORT: 27,528kg (60.700lb)
TOTAL WEIGHT: 190.3t (419,776lb)

GMA, GMAM and GO. The first two were identical in their main dimensions and power rating, the difference being that GMAM carried 14.2 tonnes (14 tons) of coal and 2160gals (2952 US gals) of water and GMA 11.8 tonnes (11.6 tons) and 1650gals (1980 US gals). Both had a maximum axle load of 15.2 tonnes (15 tons), enabling them to work on lightweight 29.6kg (60lb) rails, but GMAM weighed an extra 13.3 tonnes (13.1 tons). Both had a water-cart tender in addition to the front-end tank, and the latter had the curved-front style of most post-war Garratts. It was treated as a reserve supply, the engine normally taking its water from the detachable tender, and this helped to maintain the total adhesive weight. The 'Commonwealth' cast steel bedframes were made in the United States. Welding was extensively used in the boiler and firebox, and all axles had roller bearings, with Franklin spring-loaded wedge horns fitted in the hornblocks. All were equipped with a mechanical stoker, and mechanically rocked firebars in the grate. Some GMAs were altered to GMAM, and vice versa; the combined total number built between 1953 and 1958 was 120, making it by some way the most numerous Garratt class ever built. Henschel, Beyer Peacock and North British were the builders. However, they were not the most powerful South African Garratts. That distinction belonged to the Class GL, also a 4-8-2+2-8-4, built by Beyer Peacock in 1929, which had a nominal tractive effort of 35,669kg (78,650lb) at 75 per cent of maximum boiler pressure.

The SAR was also pushing ahead with electrification and dieselization plans, and the Garratts were moved around the country as the tide of modernization caught up with them. Their last stronghold was in Natal, increasingly used on GMA/Ms were still very much in use, chiefly on industrial branches, but some had been put into storage, and in 1979 the SAR was able to hire 21 to the National Railways of Zimbabwe; others were hired out to Mozambique. In these countries, combined steam and diesel working went on until the mid-1990s, when the GMA/Ms were finally phased out.

Specifications are for Class GMA.

An SAR 4-8-2+2-8-4 sends a plume of coal smoke high into the air as it pushes its wagons past a water tower at the entrance to a freight yard.

CLASS 4E 1-CO-CO-1 SOUTH AFRICAN RAILWAYS (SAR)

SOUTH AFRICA 1954

Among the first of the heavy-duty electrics that gradually displaced the SAR steam classes, the Class 4E was built by the North British Locomotive Co., Glasgow, using electrical parts from the (British) General Electric Company. Forty units were supplied, designed with bogie articulation like the previous Class 3E. Intended for mixed-traffic work, they were required to be capable of starting a train of 1087 tonnes (1070 tons) on a 1 in 66 gradient, or a 508-tonne (500-ton) train on 1 in 50.

These gradients reflected reality on the route between Hex River and New Kleinstraat. Each of the two bogies had four axles, but the outer ones were 'idlers' without motors. On the driving axles, the

DC motors were axle-hung, of the four-pole series type, arranged for forced ventilation. Drawgear was mounted directly on the bogies, which were linked to take the strain. Due to the variety of

haulage tasks, the motors could be worked in series, series parallel and parallel combinations. A particular feature of this and other SAR electrics was its extra lightning proofing; apart from the standard double spark-gap on the roof, it carried a roof-mounted Ferranti surge absorber, and auxiliary spark gaps with blowouts were fitted to power and auxiliary circuits. This was the last SAR class of this wheel arrangement; subsequent electrics would be all-adhesion types.

TYPE: 1-Co-Co-1	**WEIGHT:** 157.49t (347,200lb)
POWER: 1878kW (2518hp)	**MAX. AXLE LOAD:** 22t (48,510lb)
SUPPLY: 3000V DC	**OVERALL LENGTH:** 21.844m (71ft 3in)
TRACTIVE EFFORT: 141kN (31,725lbf)	**GAUGE:** 1067mm (3ft 6in)
MAX. OPERATING SPEED: 96km/h (60mph)	

CLASS M2 A1A-A1A CEYLON GOVERNMENT RAILWAY (CGR)

SRI LANKA 1954

In the mid-1950s, Sri Lanka began to supplement its steam locomotive fleet with diesels, and purchased two contrasting main-line A1A-A1A classes. M1 came from the British suppliers Brush Bagnall, with Mirrlees engines. M2 was American, an export version of EMD model G12. The G12 was usually produced in Bo-Bo form, but the three-axle bogies were specified by Ceylon Railways to run on its light track. Built in several small batches from 1954 onwards, the majority were still at work at the start of the twenty-first century, having outlasted the rival Class M1 which was withdrawn during the 1990s.

TYPE: A1A-A1A or Bo-Bo diesel electric
POWER: 1065kW (1425hp) from EMD 12-567 series engine

TRACTIVE EFFORT: 201kN (45000lbf)
MAX. OPERATING SPEED: 80km/h (50mph)

WEIGHT: 90t (198,450lb)
OVERALL LENGTH: 14.507m (47ft 4in)
GAUGE: 1676mm (5ft 6in)

CLASS 1010 CO-CO AUSTRIAN FEDERAL RAILWAYS (ÖBB)

AUSTRIA 1955

Designated as 'mixed-traffic' types, the 20 electric locomotives of this class were mainly used on express passenger trains. Their acquisition coincided with the final stage of electrification of the 'spinal' main line from Vienna to Salzburg, Innsbruck and Bregenz. They began life in ÖBB's standard dark green livery, but emerged after subsequent overhauls carrying the later standard light red. The Class 1010s were durable machines – they lasted 45 years in service, with their final duties on trains carrying heavy trucks through and under the Alps. A variant was Class 1110, geared for heavy freight; 30 were built. In the Austrian numbering system, the first digit indicates locomotive type ('1' is electric), the second digit indicates variants within the general class ('0' being the first version), and the third and fourth numbers represent the general class number. The locomotive's identifying number follows afterwards (e.g. 1010.015).

TYPE: Co-Co mixed-traffic mainline electric locomotive
POWER: 15,000V 16.67Hz AC overhead line collection; 4000kW (5360hp); six axle-hung SC traction motors
TRACTIVE EFFORT: 275kN (61,820lbf)

MAX. OPERATING SPEED: 130km/h (80mph)
WEIGHT: 106t (232,785lb)
MAX. AXLE LOAD: not known
OVERALL LENGTH: 17.86m (58ft 7in)
GAUGE: 1435mm (4ft 8.5in)

The 'heavy' version, Class 1110, is shown here, ready to bank a heavy freight train at Landeck, in the Austrian Alps.

CLASSES 202 TO 204 CO-CO BELGIAN RAILWAYS (SNCB)

More so than with steam locomotives, the design and construction of diesels was a supra-national industry, heavily influenced by the United States. But narrower national considerations might also apply: SNCB was careful to balance its orders between builders in the Flemish and Walloon parts of the country. Anglo-Franco-Belge was licensed to build Nohab/General Motors diesel locomotives, these 39 Co-Co types being the first to

appear. They had American-style streamlining, heavy GM two-stroke diesel engines, DC generators and six axle-hung traction motors. In the 1970s, they became classes 52 to 54.

The class number differences were that Class 53 locomotives had no train heating boilers and 54 had no rheostatic braking. Changes in use resulted in

locomotives being transferred both ways between classes 52 and 53. Later survivors were rebuilt with new cabs. They were used on mixed traffic services, including paired heading on heavy block freight trains through the Ardennes. Local passenger trains between Namur and Dinant in the mid-1990s were their last duty before withdrawal.

In all, AFB built 48 of these locomotives, including four for CFL, Luxembourg. This one is on a local service in the Ardennes in the 1990s.

TYPE: mixed-traffic main-line diesel-electric
WHEEL ARRANGEMENT: Co-Co
POWER UNIT: GM 16-567C 16-cylinder V-form two-stroke diesel, 1265kW (1700bhp); DC generator; six axle-hung DC traction motors
TRACTIVE EFFORT: 245kN (55,080lbf)
MAX. OPERATING SPEED: 120km/h (75mph)
WEIGHT: 108t (237,176lb)
OVERALL LENGTH: 18.85m (61ft 10in)
GAUGE: 1435mm (4ft 8.5in)

CLASS 464.2 4-8-4T CZECHOSLOVAK STATE RAILWAYS (CSD)

The government decision of 1955 to speed up railway electrification put an end to new steam design in Czechoslovakia. This was the last class of steam locomotives to be ordered by the CSD. Built at the Skoda Works in Plzen, it numbered only two. Lighter but more powerful than the

Class 477.0 4-8-4T of 1951, they too were modelled on the very successful two-cylinder Class 475.1 4-8-2 of 1947. They were intended for short-haul fast passenger service, and with their very high running plates, wing-type smoke deflectors and an overall height of 4.65m (15ft 4in), they were

imposing machines. As on the 476.1 class, the side water tanks

were small, with the main supply carried below the coal bunker.

BOILER PRESSURE: 18kg/cm² (256psi)
CYLINDERS: 500x720mm (19.7x28.4in)
DRIVING WHEELS: 1624mm (64in)
GRATE AREA: 3.8m² (41sq ft)

HEATING SURFACE: 166m² (1787.2sq ft)
SUPERHEATER: 67.1m² (399.4sq ft)
TRACTIVE EFFORT: 16,990kg (37,470lb)
TOTAL WEIGHT: 112t (246,960lb)

CLASS 8310 2-8-4T GERMAN STATE RAILWAYS (DR)

Although the two Germanies were politically separate until 1990, striking parallels can be seen in many of their post-war railway operations. (In fact, the two railway authorities maintained a relationship). In 1955, both the *Deutsche Bundesbahn* (DB) and the *Deutsche Reichsbahn* (DR) introduced their last new tank types. The DB's was a 2-6-4T, Class 66; the DR's a 2-8-4T, a slightly smaller version of the Class 6510, built in the previous year. Twenty-seven were built, by Lokomotivbau 'Karl Marx'

at Babelsberg. Water was carried in side tanks and beneath the bunker. Two cylinders, operated by outside Heusinger valve gear, drove the third set of coupled wheels via long connecting rods. The boilers and fireboxes were of all-welded construction. Even in this late model, there were problems with the prototype, and various alterations were made, including the repositioning of a sandbox from running plate to boiler top, and the removal of a second regulator in the

superheater header, leaving a single regulator in the dome. A feedwater heater and pumps were installed, as was an electric turbo-generator.

Heavy mixed-traffic services were the function of the class, with a brief to haul a 1000-tonne (984-ton) passenger train at 60km/h (37mph) on level track, and a 1500-tonne (1476-ton) goods train at 45km/h (28mph) The advent of diesel traction in the form of railbuses and the V60 and V100 locomotives curtailed both

the production and the working lives of the class; withdrawals began from 1970, and by 1973 all had been scrapped at the Brandenburg Steelworks.

BOILER PRESSURE: 14kg/cm² (199psi)
CYLINDERS: 500x660mm (19.7x26in)
DRIVING WHEELS: 1250mm (49.25in)
GRATE AREA: 2.5m² (26.9sq ft)
HEATING SURFACE: 106.6m² (1147.7sq ft)
SUPERHEATER: 39.25m² (422.6sq ft)
TRACTIVE EFFORT: 15,716kg (34,655lb)
TOTAL WEIGHT: 99.7t (219,838lb)

DY CLASS B-B INDIAN RAILWAYS (IR)

A diesel-hydraulic type designed and built by the North British Locomotive Co. in Glasgow, and originally classed DY, later Class YDM1, this was the first metre-gauge diesel locomotive for Indian railways. Specifically built for use on freight traffic over the Kandhla–Palanpur section of the Ahmedabad to Delhi main line, where maintaining adequate water supplies for steam locomotives proved difficult, they were later redeployed at other places. In the mid-1970s, Chittaranjan Works replaced the original Paxman 12RPHXL 12-cylinder vee-type engine with the simpler MaK 6M282 series 515kW (700hp) in-line six cylinder unit. The Voith hydraulic transmission remained unchanged. Not all the NBL diesel-hydraulic types were good performers, but a few YDM1 are still in service – they are particularly valued for their relatively light 11-tonne (10.8-ton) maximum axle weight.

TYPE: B-B diesel-hydraulic lightweight
POWER: 460kW (625hp) from Paxman 12RPH
TRACTIVE EFFORT: 80kN (18,000lbf) at 12km/h (7.45mph)
MAX. OPERATING SPEED: 96km/h (60mph)
WEIGHT: 44t (97,020lb)
OVERALL LENGTH: 16.63m (54ft 3in)
GAUGE: 1000mm (3ft 3in)

CLASS 741 2-8-0 STATE RAILWAYS (FS)

This was not so much a new class as a radical transformation of an older one. The original build of FS Class 740 went back to 1918, and for a time there had been a Class 741 consisting of five 740s fitted with Caprotti valve gear. Later they were restored to Class 740 and the designation 741 was revived in 1955 for 81 engines, rebuilds from Class 740, fitted with Franco-Crosti boilers between 1955 and 1960.

The system was devised by the Italian engineer Attilio Franco, and first tried out in Belgium in 1932, though its real development was carried out in association with Dr Piero Crosti on the FS in the late 1930s. Hot exhaust steam was channelled back through a large drum or drums set parallel with the boiler, before being ejected from a rearward chimney or vent at the right-hand side of the firebox. These drums were virtually secondary boilers, through which feedwater from the tender was passed and converted into steam at sufficient pressure to make its way into the main boiler. The effect was to maintain the boiler steam at a more consistent and also higher temperature than when cold or partly warmed feedwater was sporadically admitted. A fuel saving of up to 25 per cent was claimed. The first Italian experiment was made with a cab-front Class 670, with the auxiliary boiler mounted on the water-cart tender. Some of Class 743 had been modified from 1951. The final form, as used with the 741s, had the pre-heater as a single drum placed beneath the main boiler, inside the locomotive's frame. The smokebox was placed behind the pre-heater drum, and the chimney was attached to the right-hand side of the boiler, just in front of the firebox.

Mechanically the engines were unchanged, and there was no difference in the power output. The Crosti-boilered engines ran on the same schedules as the 740s. It was suggested that the improvements owed almost as much to better boiler proportions and internal draughting as they did to the pre-heating system. Nevertheless, the potential of the system attracted interest and numerous state railways built one or two prototypes. British Railways built 10 of the BR standard 9F 2-10-0s with Crosti boilers at Crewe works, also in 1955. It was also used in Germany. Like all other post-1945 technical improvements to steam traction, however, it came too late to be seriously developed. The last of the Class 741s survived until 1980.

BOILER PRESSURE: 12kg/cm² (171psi)
CYLINDERS: 540x700mm (21.25x27.6in)
DRIVING WHEELS: 1370mm (54in)
GRATE AREA: 2.8m² (30sq ft)
HEATING SURFACE: 112.6m² (1212 sq ft)
SUPERHEATER: 44m² (473sq ft)
TRACTIVE EFFORT: 14,700kg (29,767lb)
TOTAL WEIGHT: 68.3t (150,600lb)

CLASS 30 2-8-4 EAST AFRICAN RAILWAYS (EAR)

East African Railways introduced two new 2-8-4 classes in 1955-56. Class 30 was the heavier and more powerful, comprising 25 oil-fired engines built by the North British Locomotive Co., of Glasgow. The outside-framed four-wheel bogie allowed for a bigger Belpaire firebox than on the Class 29 2-8-2, with which it shared a boiler. Some adhesive weight was lost as a result, but the bogie was not booster-fitted. A large-capacity 12-wheel tender holding 7000gals (8400 US gals) of water and 1950gals (2340 US gals) of oil was supplied to allow the engines to work over long distances where water supplies were uncertain. During the 1960s, the original blast-pipes and chimneys were replaced by double-blast Giesl ejectors.

BOILER PRESSURE: 14kg/cm² (200psi)
CYLINDERS: 457x660mm (18x26in)
DRIVING WHEELS: 1218mm (48in)
GRATE AREA: 3.5m² (38sq ft)
HEATING SURFACE: 169.6m² (1826sq ft)
SUPERHEATER: 41.4m² (446sq ft)
TRACTIVE EFFORT: 13,531kg (29,835lb)
TOTAL WEIGHT: 85.9t (189,588lb)

Detail of the motion of No. 3016, *Mwera*, showing the size of the rods that turned those four-foot driving wheels.

'59TH' CLASS 4-8-2+2-8-4 EAST AFRICAN RAILWAYS (EAR)

Also in 1955, the EAR brought into service the most powerful steam locomotives ever to run on metre-gauge tracks anywhere in the world. When the American 'Big Boys' were retired from the Union Pacific Railroad in the late 1950s, they became the largest steam locomotives in regular service anywhere, their 2284mm (7ft 6in) boilers being more than twice the width of the rail gauge. The line from Mombasa on the coast to the Kenyan capital, Nairobi, climbed from sea level to 1705m (5600ft) over a distance of 531km (330 miles), at a ruling gradient of 1 in 66. In the late 1940s, traffic was increasing rapidly and congestion in yards and at crossing points was causing serious delays. Since 1926, the EAR had made good use of Garrat-type locomotives; with articulated frames and low axle loading, they were ideal for the slow, heavy hauling it required, and there was a tradition of expertise in handling them. The 59th Class was ordered in 1950, with detailed design entrusted to the manufacturers, Beyer Peacock of Manchester. The

A 59th class mounts one of the long grades between Mombasa and Nairobi, with a 1000-tonne train of boxcars stretched out behind.

original order for nine was increased to 34 before deliveries began in 1955; all were in service by the end of 1956.

Some technical uncertainties hung over the railway at this time. Oil was the fuel of preference, but coal might become cheaper. The metre gauge might be widened out to 1065mm (3ft 6in), linking with the South African and Rhodesian systems. New engines had to be built so that their axles could be readily widened; and also be convertible to coal firing. In the 59th Class, that meant providing for the installation of a mechanical stoker if necessary, though these were never installed, and also the

piping for a vacuum brake system (EAR used air brakes).

The 59th Class locomotives were simple-expansion types, the four cylinders operated by piston valves actuated by outside Walschaerts valve gear. Long connecting rods, tapering towards the crosshead, drove the third sets of coupled wheels. Roller bearings were fitted to all axles and to the big ends of the connecting rods. The maximum axle loading at 21.3 tonnes (21 tons) was not particularly light, reflecting improvements to the track and strengthening of embankments and bridges. For the long runs made by these locomotives, the

deep ash-pan of the Garratt type much reduced the danger of a fire choked by its own ash and clinker, something of a problem with coal-fired engines over long distances.

With the introduction of this class, schedules between Mombasa and Nairobi were improved by up to a third. The 59ths could take a 1219-tonne (1200 ton) train unaided up the gradients of 1.5 per cent at 22.5km/h (14mph). The 'caboose' system was used, whereby a relief crew slept in the van and took over its shift at one of the many crossing loops. Development work continued after delivery and the class was fitted with Giesl ejectors in the early 1960s.

Pride in the engines was reflected by the policy of giving them names

after the great East African mountains. Potential enlargements of the Garratt design were drawn up by the EAR during the later 1950s, including a condensing tender type, but none were built. When diesel-electrics took over the mail trains, the Garratts continued to work on some of the longer branches. Withdrawals began in 1973 and by 1980 all were out of service.

BOILER PRESSURE: 15.7kg/cm² (225psi)
CYLINDERS: 521x711mm (20.5x28in)
DRIVING WHEELS: 1372mm (54in)
GRATE AREA: 69.4m² (72sq ft)
HEATING SURFACE: 331m² (3560sq ft)
SUPERHEATER: 69.4m² (747sq ft)
TRACTIVE EFFORT: 38,034kg (83,350lb)
TOTAL WEIGHT: 256t (564,000lb)

CLASS DA A1A-A1A NEW ZEALAND RAILWAYS (NZR)

The US market for diesel locomotives had settled down after the boom years, and American manufacturers were increasingly looking for business overseas, with a range of export models based on their standard lines but able to be shrunk to fit narrow gauges and tight clearances.

NZR's Class DA was EMD export model G12, mounted on two three-axle bogies as usual for larger diesel-electrics on this system. From 1955 until 1967, 146 were supplied in eight batches, variously from EMD's La Grange plant, GMD, Canada, and EMD's Australian licensee Clyde Engineering. Most were deployed on mainline passenger and freight work, but the first 30 were soon restricted after delivery to freight work due to excessive rolling on curves. Later deliveries were fitted

with revised bogie and suspension arrangements to overcome this problem.

In 1970, five locomotives were modified with slow speed hump shunting controls and designated Class DAA. Clyde rebuilt 80 units to Class DC between 1977 and 1983. The DA class was finally withdrawn by 1990 but five are preserved.

TYPE: A1A-A1A diesel-electric
POWER: 1060kW (1425hp) from EMD 12-567 series engine
TRACTIVE EFFORT: continuous 140kN (31500lbf)
MAX. OPERATING SPEED: 100km/h (62mph)
WEIGHT: 81t (178,605lb) (GMD and EMD built); 79t (174,195lb) (Clyde)
OVERALL LENGTH: GM-built 14.1m (46ft); Clyde-built 14.6m (47ft 8in)
GAUGE: 1067mm (3ft 6in)

Preserved DA No. 1410 at Fernleigh on 13 March 2002 shows its American 'export' styling for limited clearance tracks.

CLASS DG/DH A1A-A1A NEW ZEALAND RAILWAYS (NZR)

NEW ZEALAND 1955

A change of mind by NZR resulted in the conversion of an order for 21 large engines from English Electric into one for 42 smaller engines. The originally planned DF was of 1120kW (1500hp); in Class DG and DH, this output was reduced by half. Thirty-one DGs and 11 DHs were built, all of them weighing 70 tonnes (68.8 tons), but the DH's suspension arrangements placed a greater load on the powered axles of the A1A-A1A bogies. Some worked around Auckland and Wellington on secondary traffic, but all 42 were gradually moved to South Island between 1962 and 1976. All DHs were converted to DGs in 1968. Other modifications included new driving cabs for 10, with a further 10 modified as slaves to operate with the rebuilt units. The DG was extinct from revenue-earning service in 1983, but four are preserved, including two in full working order.

TYPE: A1A-A1A diesel-electric
POWER: 560kW (750hp) from EE 6SRKT series engine
TRACTIVE EFFORT: DG: 114kN (25,650lbf) DH: 130kN (29,250lbf)
MAX. OPERATING SPEED: 96km/h (60mph)
WEIGHT: 70t (154,350lb)
OVERALL LENGTH: 14.7m (48ft)
GAUGE: 1067mm (3ft 6in)

CLASS 5E BO-BO SOUTH AFRICAN RAILWAYS (SAR)

SOUTH AFRICA 1955

Rather than build ever-bigger electrics, the SAR resolved on Bo-Bo machines, to be used in multiple when high-power output was required on its 300V DC system. It followed that large numbers of Bo-Bos would be needed, and 850 of Class 5E and 5E.1 were ultimately built.

All 160 Class 5E were built by English Electric in the UK. The body forms an integral unit with the underframe, and is attached to the bogies through a cross-transom having downwards projections rigidly bolted to a cast-steel bolster. Two semi-spherical, grease-lubricated, side bearing pads support the bolster and form the upper part of two manganese-steel sliding surfaces, whose lower parts are integral with a cast-steel tie beam that joins a set of leaf springs at their centres at either side of the bogie. Each spring is fitted with rubber dampers, and the cast-steel bogie frame itself is carried on the axle-boxes by laminated springs with auxiliary coil springs and rubber dampers. The detail description serves to indicate how vital bogie design and construction was on a locomotive with directly driven axles. On the Class 5E, a spring-loaded link between the bogies keeps weight balanced between them on uneven track. Electrically Class 5Es are conventional series parallel resistance control machines with regenerative braking. Class 5E.1s were first built from 1959, in Birmingham by Metropolitan Cammell with Associated Electrical Industries (AEI) electrical parts, and 135 locomotives were completed before production moved to Union Carriage & Wagon in South Africa. By 2002, heavy withdrawals were taking place under Spoornet and of the total build of 850, less than 200 remain.

TYPE: Bo-Bo universal
POWER: 5E 1300kW (1743hp)
SUPPLY: 3000V DC
TRACTIVE EFFORT: 122kN (27400lbf) at 43km/h (26.9mph)
MAX. OPERATING SPEED: 96km/h (60mph)
WEIGHT: 86t (189,630lb)
MAX. AXLE LOAD: 21.5t (47,408lb)
OVERALL LENGTH: 15.495m (50ft 10in)
GAUGE: 1067mm (3ft 6in)

Bogie design and suspension can be clearly seen on this smartly turned-out 5E locomotive, ready to work the Johannesburg–Cape Town 'Blue Train'.

CLASS 500 4-8-2 SUDAN RAILWAYS (SR)

SUDAN 1955

The railway network in Sudan, sparse but with long-distance lines laid to the 1065mm (3ft 6in) gauge, was developed and run by the British, and Britain was its prime source of locomotives, mostly of 2-8-0 or 2-8-2 type. The 500 class, oil burners, were shipped in fully erected condition from North British Locomotive Co. in Glasgow direct to Port Sudan. With the necessary light maximum axle-load of 15.2 tonnes (15 tons), they were intended to run both passenger and freight services, based mostly at the central depot at Atbara. Steam in independent Sudan was phased out in the 1970s but revived for a time in the 1980s, using reconditioned 2-8-2s.

BOILER PRESSURE: 13kg/cm² (190psi)
CYLINDERS: 546x660mm (21.5x26in)
DRIVING WHEELS: 1370mm (54in)
GRATE AREA: 3.7m² (40sq ft)
HEATING SURFACE: 207m² (2230sq ft)
SUPERHEATER: 50.3m² (542sq ft)
TRACTIVE EFFORT: 16,299kg (35,940lb)
TOTAL WEIGHT: 96.3t (212,280lb)

Derelict in the desert – a 500-class 4-8-2, stripped of rods and everything transportable, stands forlorn against the sunset.

CLASS E8000 EMU TURKISH STATE RAILWAYS (TCDD)

French contractors installed Turkey's first electrification on the lines leading in to Istanbul and Ankara. As part of this significant undertaking, French makers Alsthom, Jeumont and De Dietrich supplied 28 three-car multiple-unit sets in 1955. These locomotives were among the earliest built for

TYPE: EMU three-car
POWER: 1100kW (1495hp) per unit
SUPPLY: 25kV 50Hz AC
TRACTIVE EFFORT: N/A

MAX. OPERATING SPEED: 90km/h (56.3mph)
WEIGHT: 120t (264,600lb)
MAX. AXLE LOAD: 17.5t (38,588lb)

OVERALL LENGTH: 68m (221ft 10in) per unit
GAUGE: 1435mm (4ft 8.5in)
BUILDER: Alsthom, Jeumont and De Dietrich

25kVAC operation, using the then-conventional transformer and camshaft-driven tap changer.

Turkish State Railways' Class E8000 units had a second locally built intermediate trailer added,

and ran in this form for several years, but the extra vehicles were later removed.

CLASS EP-5 DUAL CURRENT CO-CO NEW HAVEN RAILROAD (NHR)

Among US railroads, the New Haven had been a pioneer of overhead-wire electric traction. In order to run into new York City's main termini, Penn Central and Grand Central, however, its locomotives had to run on the third-rail electric system installed by the Pennsylvania Railroad, which supplied current at 660V DC. Just as its Fl-9 was a hybrid electric diesel type (see 1956), the New Haven had to provide for dual-current electric locomotives to avoid time-consuming and costly engine changes. This class of 10 double-ended Co-Co locomotives, built by General Electric in 1954–56, were New Haven's first all-adhesion

locomotive type, and also its last electric before it was amalgamated into the Penn-Central in 1969. State-of-the-art ignitron rectifier tubes, an alternative to mercury arc technology, were used to convert 11,000V AC from the overhead catenary to low voltage for the DC traction motors, in a manner identical to that of the Virginia Railroad's EL-C/EF-4 class (see 1956). DC current was picked up from the third rail by collecting shoes located on the side of both bogies. Connections were made from fuses through two line breakers and a change-over switch to the accelerating resistors and traction motors.

Arrangement of the traction motor circuit provided for different motor combinations: two in series, three in parallel for starting and low-speed working, and full parallel for operating at high speed. The end-body design of the EP-5s was very reminiscent of that used on Alco-GE built FA diesel-electrics; with a length of 20.73m (68ft), it was quite compact for a six-axle locomotive. The class was employed on fast passenger trains between New Haven, Connecticut, and both New York City passenger terminals. In 1969, the EP-5s were absorbed into Penn-Central's fleet, but had a short life after that, being scrapped in the mid-1970s.

Picking up current from the third rail, an EP-5 passes through Woodlawn, in the Bronx district of New York City, with a train for Boston, in the summer of 1961.

TYPE: Co-Co, passenger electric
POWER: 11kV AC at 25Hz from overhead
OUTPUT: 2980kW (4000hp) at 70km/h (44mph)
TRACTIVE EFFORT: 387kN (87,000lbf) starting TE; 151kN (34,000lbf) continuous TE
MAX. OPERATING SPEED: N/A
WEIGHT: 157t (348,000lb)
OVERALL LENGTH: 20.73 (68ft)
MAX. AXLE LOAD: 30t (65,000lb)
GAUGE: 1435mm (4ft 8.5in)

MLW RS-18 BO-BO VARIOUS RAILROADS

Montreal Locomotive Works (MLW) had been Alco's affiliate since steam days, and its diesel-electric products were essentially Alco designs. The RS-18, produced from 1956 to 1968, was the same as Alco's RS-11, but featured a slightly higher hood style. Rated at 1341kW (1800hp), the RS-18 was comparable to EMD's GP9 road-switcher type, and was used in a variety of services. Canadian

Pacific (CPR) and Canadian National both bought RS-18s, and they were common on lines in eastern Canada. CPR chopped the nose of most of its engines to improve visibility. RS-18 was among the last types of MLW power on CPR, with some locomotives surviving in regular service until the late 1990s. Some shortlines in Canada and the United States still operate the type.

TYPE: Bo-Bo, diesel-electric
POWER AND OUTPUT: Alco 12-cylinder 251B engine producing 1341kW (1800hp)
TRACTIVE EFFORT: not known

MAX. OPERATING SPEED: 120 km/h (75mph)
WEIGHT: N/A
OVERALL LENGTH: 16.91m (55ft 6in)
GAUGE: 1435mm (4ft 8.5in)

Resting from their labours on ore trains are two RS-18 locomotives from the fleet of the Quebec-Cartier Mining Company.

CLASS QJ 2-10-2 RAILWAYS OF THE PEOPLE'S REPUBLIC

CHINA 1956

Intensive industrialization programmes in China during the 1950s created enormous demand for motive power on the state-run railways, made even more intensive by the fact that the railways themselves were being extended with multiple tracking and new lines, some of them long-distance. A locomotive standardization scheme had been developed in 1948, in which the 2-10-2 was the largest freight type. QJ, meaning *Qian Jing* ('March Forward') was the most numerous class in China and one of the world's largest, with more than 4500 built from 1957 until the late 1980s. The basis of the type was the Russian Lv class, whose specifications and detailed drawings had been sold or given to the Chinese around the time the Russians ceased production, but subsequent modifications included the provision of a combustion chamber with a shorter boiler. Most of the QJs came from the giant Datong works that were set

up to build them, but construction went on at five other locomotive works in China.

The attractions of the steam locomotive for the Chinese authorities were that it could be built quicker and more cheaply than a diesel or electric (of which large numbers were also under construction) and construction required fewer skilled workers. In response to the imperative demand for more motive power, the engines were being built at maximum speed, with intensive use of fabricated parts and wholly welded boilers. Meeting the ambitious production targets was vital, and a certain degree of 'clapping together' of parts was apparent in the end products, with problems of vibration, 'hunting', and self-detaching fittings. These were common in service, but could be promptly dealt with by maintenance and repair shops. In the basics it was a solidly built class, capable of handling 3000-tonne (2953-ton)

trains while burning low-quality coal, mostly dust and slack. Built-up bar frames were used, with bolted-on cast-steel cylinders. Mechanical stokers, feed water heaters, power-operated firedoors, power reversers, Franklin type grate shakers and mechanical lubricators were the main ancillary equipment fitted. There was also an adhesion booster for use on starting or at speeds of less than 30km/h (18.6mph): not an auxiliary engine, but a system of air cylinders attached to the spring equalizing system between the various axles. Application of this transferred a combined weight of 6.1 tonnes (6 tons) from the leading and trailing axles to the coupled wheels.

The standard tender was an eight-wheeler, with capacity for 14.5 tonnes (14.2 tons) of coal and 8700gals (10,400 US gals) of water, but engines operating in the semi-desert western provinces were provided with 12-wheel tenders of greater water capacity.

Hot-water and cold-water pumps were incorporated with the feedwater heater, and there were also two injectors.

In action, they were to be seen in almost every part of the country hauling freight trains, usually loaded between 1016 and 2032 tonnes (1000 and 2000 tons). On grades, they were double-headed or banked. Until the elimination of steam on the main lines in the 1990s this class, originally considered a stop-gap, was one of the mainstays of the Chinese railway system.

BOILER PRESSURE: 15kg/cm² (214psi)
CYLINDERS: 650x799mm (25.6x31.5in)
DRIVING WHEELS: 1497mm (59in)
GRATE AREA: 6.4m² (69.5sq ft)
HEATING SURFACE: 265.6m²
(2859.6sq ft)
SUPERHEATER: 141.2m² (1520.2sq ft)
TRACTIVE EFFORT: 28,725kg (63,340lb)
TOTAL WEIGHT: 123.4t (272,160lb)
(engine only)

Speed-built but tough and sturdy, a well-maintained QJ pounds along with a main-line freight train.

CLASS 10 4-6-2 GERMAN FEDERAL RAILWAYS (DB)

GERMANY 1956

Coming from a thoroughbred tradition, Nos. 10.001 and 10.002 of the DB were the last high-speed express steam locomotives to be built – Krupps of Essen were the constructors. The main difference between the two was that 001 began as a coal burner, with a Cosmovici-type coal-oil supply available as a supplementary fuel; 002 burned oil only, and 001 was converted to this form also. In all other major respects, they were indentical; both were three-cylinder simple-expansion types, with the inside cylinder driving the leading coupled axle, and the outside cylinders driving the second. Three sets of Walschaerts valve gear operated long-travel piston valves. The frames were of I-

No. 10.002 – the epitome of German steam locomotive design and production, though it did not break the German speed record set by the Class 05 (see 1934).

section, prefabricated and welded to cross-members and the cast-steel cylinder block (it might have been expected that a US-type cast-steel integral frame would have been used, but this form was lighter while still of more than sufficient strength and resilience). Welding was used wherever possible in the construction. Double blast-pipes and double chimneys were fitted. All axles and main bearings were of the roller type. The front look-out windows had revolving clear-

vision screens. The locomotives had air-assisted reversers, dual-pressure air brakes and a range of instrumentation that would have amazed drivers of an earlier generation. Even a foot-warmer was provided to shield the enginemen against draughts. Below boiler level, they were partially streamlined, with a deep valance covering the cylinders, partly obscuring the wheels and motion, and terminating in a rounded casing covering the front end between smoke box and buffer-beam, with inset electric headlights. The tenders were also of welded construction, with a curved bottom section, and a sliding roof over the coal bunker. Like the last American express types, these were steam

locomotives designed to compete with diesels on the diesels' own terms, with comparable economies of maintenance and similar levels of availability. They were capable of an average monthly running of 20,000km (12,400 miles) and a fuel consumption of about 11 tonnes (10.8 tons) per 1000km (620 miles). Only two were built.

BOILER PRESSURE: 18kg/cm² (256psi)
CYLINDERS: 480x720mm (19x28in)
DRIVING WHEELS: 2000mm (79in)
GRATE AREA: 3.96sq² (42.6sq ft)
HEATING SURFACE: 205.3m² (2211sq ft)
SUPERHEATER: 105.6m² (1137sq ft)
TRACTIVE EFFORT: 16,797kg (37,037lb)
TOTAL WEIGHT: 119.5t (263,424lb)
(engine only)

CLASS E10 BO-BO GERMAN FEDERAL RAILWAYS (DB)

GERMANY 1956

DB introduced a trio of Bo-Bo classes in 1956. Class E10 locomotives (later Class 110) were for main-line express trains. Eventually the Class 110 fleet totalled over 400 examples, with more streamlined cab fronts on later versions. They hauled heavy, fast trains on routes such as Köln to Munich, and were DB's top

electric passenger locomotives until the advent of Class 103 from 1969. In 1962, 23 of the E10s were uprated for operation at 160km/h (100mph) and painted blue-and-cream to match the luxury stock on such services as the *Rheingold* and *Rheinpfeil* expresses. These locomotives' top speeds have since been down-

TYPE: Bo-Bo express passenger electric locomotive
POWER: 3620kW (4855hp); four frame-mounted DC traction motors
SUPPLY: 15,000V 16.7HzAC overhead line collection

rated and the locomotives reclassified '113' and '114'. Many

TRACTIVE EFFORT: 275kN (61,820lbf)
MAX. OPERATING SPEED: 150km/h (93mph)
WEIGHT: 85t (185,790lb)
OVERALL LENGTH: 16.49m (54ft 1in)
GAUGE: 1435mm (4ft 8.5in)

110s are still in use on local and S-Bahn (suburban) trains.

CLASS M44 SWITCHER BO-BO HUNGARIAN STATE RAILWAYS (MAV)

HUNGARY 1956

This was the standard diesel-electric shunter on the Hungarian system, used by industrial organizations as well as by MÁV. Ganz-MÁVAG were the builders, and it was in production for a relatively long period from 1956 until 1971. Total production was well over 200 units. M44s may be found distributed throughout Hungary on shunting, station pilot and light freight trip and transfer duties. A sub-class, M44.5, works on 1524mm (5ft) gauge for exchange traffic on the border with Ukraine. From 2002, MÁV has been replacing the original Ganz Jendrassik engines with Caterpillar series 3508 power units, at the same 440kW (598hp) rating.

Around 50, designated Class M44.4, are expected to see service to beyond 2010 in this form. The GySEV railway system has acquired several second-hand M44 and A25 to supplement its original five and also has a re-engining programme, but with Deutz 626kW (850hp) engines. Between 1958 and 1982 the Soviet Union, Bulgaria, Poland, Yugoslavia and China (ND1) all imported engines of M44 type.

TYPE: Bo-Bo diesel-electric shunter
POWER: 440kW (598hp) – Ganz-Jessendrik 16JV17/24 series engine
TRACTIVE EFFORT: 97kN (21825lbf) at 10.7km/h (6.9mph)

MAX. OPERATING SPEED: 80km/h (50mph)
WEIGHT: 66t (145,530lb)
OVERALL LENGTH: 11.24m (36ft 8in)
GAUGE: 1435mm (4ft 8.5in) or 1524mm (5ft)

Carriage shunter No. 427 shows the compactness of this Bo-Bo switcher type.

CLASS DL500 BO-BO SOUTHERN RAILWAY OF PERU (FCS)

PERU 1956

Unlike steam locomotives, diesels do not perform well at high altitudes. When the British-financed *Ferrocarril del Sur* took Alco's export-design 'World Series' road-switcher units for mountain work, they were derated from the standard power setting to take account of oxygen starvation in high-altitude mountain operation. The FCS operates from sea level at the Pacific coast to one of the world's highest railway summits, Crucero Alto, at 4474m (14,668ft). The DL500 engines usually worked as back to back pairs with dynamic braking on mineral trains. In later versions, full power could

TYPE: Bo-Bo diesel-electric
POWER: 1324kW (1800hp) from Alco 251 series engine
TRACTIVE EFFORT: 273kN (61,380lbf)

MAX. OPERATING SPEED: 96km/h (60mph)
WEIGHT: 104t (229,320lb)
OVERALL LENGTH: 17.958m (58ft 7in)
GAUGE: 1435mm (4ft 8.5in)

be developed at lower altitudes by barometric governors. The class survived into the 1990s, but were all withdrawn by 2000.

4-8-4 SPANISH NATIONAL RAILWAYS (RENFE)

SPAIN 1956

Spain was the last European country to build main-line steam locomotives, and though this was perhaps the finest and most advanced Spanish steam class, it was not the last. Ten of these engines were built by Maquinista Terrestre y Maritima in Barcelona. Spain had a long history of using eight-coupled engines, which suited both the hilly terrain and the often lightly-laid tracks. The 4-8-4s were used to haul international expresses to and from France on the not-yet electrified main line section between Avila and Miranda del Ebro. These sleeping car trains could weigh more than 762 tonnes (750 tons), but this was well within the compass of the 4-8-4s.

Spain had formerly been a compounding country, but these, like all its post-1943 locomotives, were simple-expansion, two-cylinder types. Stretched and enlarged forms of the RENFE 4-8-2s, built to the Spanish 1676mm (5ft 6in) gauge, all were

BOILER PRESSURE: 16kg/cm² (228psi)
CYLINDERS: 640x710mm (25.25x28in)
DRIVING WHEELS: 1900mm (74.75in)
GRATE AREA: 5.3m² (57sq ft)
HEATING SURFACE: 293m² (3161sq ft)
SUPERHEATER: 104.5m² (1125sq ft)
TRACTIVE EFFORT: 21,000kg (46,305lb)
TOTAL WEIGHT: 213t (469,500lb)

oil burners with Kylchap double blast pipes and double chimneys. The ubiquitous Walschaerts motion was used, but the valves themselves were Lentz-type poppet valves, actuated by oscillating camshafts. Auxiliary equipment included a French TIA (*Traitement Intégrale Armand*) water treatment system to reduce boiler scale, a feed water heater and pump, and a turbo generator that provided train lighting. Roller bearings were fitted on all of the axles. As on some US oil burners, a spot-light was directed just above the chimney so that at night the fireman could judge the exhaust colour and the need for replenishing or adjusting the oil supply.

Spain's overall speed restriction to a maximum of 110km/h (68mph) cramped the style of these locomotives somewhat: on test, one had run at 134km/h (84mph) with a 480-tonne (472.4-ton) train, but they maintained a consistent speed just within the limit on heavyweight trains like the Paris–Madrid 'Sud-Express'. To fit existing turntables, the 4-8-4s were fitted with oddly short tenders for such large locomotives. One of the class has been preserved.

CLASS 276 CO-CO SPANISH RAILWAYS (RENFE)

SPAIN 1956

Very much a French design with adaptations for the Spanish 1676mm (5ft 6in) gauge and 3000-volt supply system, Class 276 closely resembled the SNCF's Class CC-7100. Supplied originally for newly electrified lines in Catalonia in the 1950s, the class totalled 136 locomotives. Alsthom built the first 20 in 1952, though they did not enter traffic until 1956. Further locomotives were built under licence by Spanish builders until 1965. Withdrawals began in the 1990s and the class has been virtually eliminated, except a few held back for special duties.

TYPE: Co-Co heavy passenger and freight
POWER: 2355kW (3155hp)
SUPPLY: 3000V DC
TRACTIVE EFFORT: 162kN (36,400lbf) at 49.5km/h (31mph)
MAX. OPERATING SPEED: 110km/h (68.3mph)
WEIGHT: 120t (264,600lb)
MAX. AXLE LOAD: 20t (44,100lb)
OVERALL LENGTH: 18.83m (61ft 9in)
GAUGE: 1676mm (5ft 6in)

Some of the Class 276 were painted in special livery for passenger service but this freight hauler is in rthr drab RENFE green. The French origin of the design is apparent.

EL-C/EF-4 CO-CO VIRGINIAN RAILWAY (VR)

USA 1956

Ignitron rectifier technology, to convert high-voltage AC current from the wire to low-voltage DC current for the motors, then very new, was applied in this class of 12 heavy-haulage electrics built by General Electric for use on bulk coal trains on the VR main line between Mullens and Roanoke, Virginia. As well as being heavy haulers on the road, these engines were required to do switching work as well, and in design they resembled diesel hood units, witha full-width cab close to the No. 1 end, on which the single pantograph was mounted. A high-tension link enabled two locomotives to operate together, drawing power from one pantograph. The body was of fabricated steel construction, with access to the equipment compartments from the open side walkways. Inside one of these compartments was housed what was at the time state-of-art current rectifier technology, very similar in form and layout to the New Haven Class EP-5 Co-Co of 1945–55, also

Virginian No. 130 heads a pair of EL/C locomotives on a long coal train. The high clearance power wire required tall pantographs.

a General Electric product. Twelve 304.8mm (12in) ignitron rectifier tubes and their associated firing circuit apparatus, with six tubes in each of two cabinets, were arranged in groups of three and bridge-connected, with four iron-core reactors between the cabinets. A water pump and thermostat system kept the temperature of the rectifier tubes within optimum values. In the

bogies, the six series-wound DC motors were axle-hung and permanently connected in three parallel groups, each group consisting of two motors in series. Rated at a 2459kW (3300hp) power output, the class had twice the muscle of single-unit diesel road freight engines of the period. Normally they worked in pairs, taking trains of 9144 tonnes (9000 tons) up the grade of 1

in 172 that prevails between Clark's Gap and Roanoke. After Virginian's old competitor, Norfolk & Western, acquired the line in the early 1960s, electrified operations were ended. New Haven Railroad bought the Virginian rectifiers in 1964 and they became its EF-4 class. They later served New Haven's successors, Penn Central and Conrail.

TYPE: Co-Co, heavy freight electric
POWER: 11kV AC at 25Hz from overhead
OUTPUT: 2459kW (3300hp)
TRACTIVE EFFORT: 353kN (79,500lbf) continuous TE at 25.35km/h (15.75mph)
MAX. OPERATING SPEED: 104km/h (65mph)
WEIGHT: 177t (389,760lb)
MAX. AXLE LOAD: 29t (64,960lb)
OVERALL LENGTH: 21.184m (69ft 6in)
GAUGE: 1435mm (4ft 8.5in)

CLASS RS-11 BO-BO VARIOUS RAILROADS

USA 1956

Flaws in the design of the Alco 244-series diesel engine affected the performance and reputation of the company's post-1945 road locomotives. In the end, Alco developed a new and better engine design, the 251 series, which was first used in six-cylinder configuration on the S-5 and S-6

switcher models built in 1954 and 1955. In 1956, the 1341kW (1800 hp) RS-11 road switcher was introduced. Powered by a 12-cylinder 251B engine, this locomotive featured a taller hood and a more boxy appearance than the previous RS-2/RS-3 road switcher types. It was well received,

TYPE: Bo-Bo, diesel-electric
POWER AND OUTPUT: Alco 12-cylinder 251B engine producing 1341kW (1800hp)
TRACTIVE EFFORT: N/A

MAX. OPERATING SPEED: N/A
WEIGHT: N/A
OVERALL LENGTH: N/A
GAUGE: 1435mm (4ft 8.5in)

and more than 425 RS-11s were built over the next five years for North American service. Central

Vermont, Delaware & Hudson, Lehigh Valley, and the Pennsylvania Railroad were among the user lines.

Still at work after almost 50 years, an RS-11 of the Falls Road RR seen at Lockport, NY, in July 2006.

CLASS FL9 B-A1A NEW HAVEN RAILROAD (NHR)

USA 1956

A streamlined 'A' unit (cab at the nose end only), this EMD product was a dual-mode locomotive capable of running under its own diesel power or of picking up electric current by means of a shoe from a third rail.

This was in order to allow New Haven to run the FL9s directly into New York's Grand Central Terminal and Penn Station, both of which required long journeys through tunnels laid with electrified track, on which diesel-engine emissions

were prohibited. In this way, through passenger trains could run from Boston to New York (the main line not yet electrified) without changing locomotives.

Placement of the additional machinery required the use of

an asymmetric bogie arrangement. In later years, the FL9s were used by suburban passenger railroad Metro-North, and also by Amtrak for passenger services travelling along the Hudson River to Grand Central.

TYPE: B-A1A diesel-electric/electric
POWER AND OUTPUT: EMD 16-567C producing 1305kW (1750hp) and powered by a 660V DC third rail.
TRACTIVE EFFORT: 258kN (58,000lbf)
MAX. OPERATING SPEED: 145km/h (90mph)
WEIGHT: 130t (286,614 lb)
OVERALL LENGTH: 17.882m (58 ft 8in)
GAUGE: 1435mm (4ft 8.5in)

On a typical service, a New Haven FL9 pauses at a wayside station on the main line, 1989.

CLASS E40 BO-BO GERMAN FEDERAL RAILWAYS (DB)

Universal work-horses of the DB's electric fleet, the E40 (later Class 140: the '1' denoting electric), came to number almost 900 examples. By 1957, electrification was being rapidly extended on the DB. Essentially, the E40s were mixed-traffic versions of the express Class E10, with a lower maximum speed. Originally they were painted in a dark-green livery. Though numbers have reduced greatly, they can still be seen, mostly on lines in western Germany, sometimes hauling freight trains in pairs, also on works trains and performing carriage shunting.

TYPE: Bo-Bo mixed-traffic mainline electric locomotive
POWER: 15,000V 16.67Hz AC overhead line collection; 3620kW (4855hp); mechanical notching up control; rheostatic brakes; four DC traction motors
TRACTIVE EFFORT: 275kN (61,820lbf)
MAX. OPERATING SPEED: 110km/h (69mph)
WEIGHT: 83t (182,275lb)
OVERALL LENGTH: 16.49m (54ft 1in)
GAUGE: 1435mm (4ft 8.5in)

A rugged and durable design, the E40s ran all kinds of trains on the DB for half a century.

CLASS 31 A1A-A1A BRITISH RAILWAYS (BR)

Among the last tasks of Class 31 locomotives before most were withdrawn was to run holiday trains to seaside resorts in the summer months.

The Brush Works at Loughborough normally used Mirrlees diesel engines, and Mirrlees 933kW (1250hp) engines were first fitted to this 263-strong diesel-electric class. These engines developed early fatigue cracks in service, and were replaced by more robust and powerful English Electric engines, using the original Brush electrical equipment.

The locomotives worked on the Eastern Region lines, and later more widely across England. Most were scrapped in the 1980s and 1990s, but a few re-conditioned survivors were still hauling coal trains for FM Rail in 2006, and others are at work on 'heritage' railways.

TYPE: mixed-traffic main-line diesel-electric
WHEEL ARRANGEMENT: A1A-A1A
POWER: Mirrlees JVS12T 933kW (1250bhp), then EE12SVT 12-cylinder 1095kW (1470bhp); Brush DC generator, four axle-hung traction motors
TRACTIVE EFFORT: 176 to 190kN (39,500 to 42,800lbf)
MAX. OPERATING SPEED: 120 to 145km/h (75 to 90mph)
WEIGHT: 106t (232,960lb)
OVERALL LENGTH: 17.3m (56ft 9in)
GAUGE: 1435mm (4ft 8.5in)

'TRANS EUROP EXPRESS' DUTCH RAILWAYS/SWISS NATIONAL RAILWAYS (NS/SBB)

Here leaving Hamburg, Germany, and once a familiar but glamorous sight in European major stations, the Trans-Europ Express heralded a new age of international rail connections.

International rail travel in 1950s' Europe was perceived as slow, and unable to provide fast connections between capital cities and major business centres across country borders. The great majority of express services were still worked by steam locomotives, which were changed over at frontier stations, and though some steam-hauled services were very fast, others were not. Delays were also created by customs examinations and by the very common practice of attaching and detaching carriages for different destinations at major junctions. By the mid-1950s, short-haul air services were also drawing away many premium-price fare-payers, and the international motorway network was beginning to expand. Faced with a pattern of decline that threatened to intensify, the railways of five nations decided to launch an attack on the business market, and the Dutch-Swiss 'Trans Europ Express' (TEE) diesel-electric sets were part of this cooperative attempt to promote high-quality international business travel.

Germany, France, Switzerland, Italy and the Netherlands each contributed trains for the operation. Destinations ranged from Hamburg, Brussels, Paris and Amsterdam in the north to Munich, Zürich, Bern and Milan in the south. NS and SBB collaborated in producing luxury sets that were jointly owned by the two railways. Unusually, one vehicle in each four-car set was totally given over to power equipment and services. The power cars were designed by Werkspoor in the Netherlands, and the cab fronts, as with the driving trailer cars at the other end of the units, were distinctly Dutch with their rounded noses, giving the trains a somewhat heavy appearance. Traction equipment on the Dutch-Swiss sets was diesel electric, designed for high performance. Diesel traction was chosen for all the original TEE trains, since electric technology could not then reliably enable electric trains to operate under four different voltages and systems, and in any case long stretches of European main lines were not yet electrified.

All vehicles were first class only, double-glazed and fully air-conditioned – the first general use of air conditioning in standard trains in Europe. The layout ensured that all seats had ample space and legroom, and tables at which meals and refreshments could be served. With no locomotive changes, and passport and customs checks usually undertaken on board, journey times were substantially reduced, aided by the better performance possible with high-performance, dedicated, fixed-formation unit trains. The trains were deservedly popular, and as with some other pioneer services like the American *Zephyr*, demand for seats often exceeded supply; the service becoming a victim of its own 'exclusive' quality.

Other participating systems followed with their own TEE sets, mostly, apart from those for Germany, based on existing DMU designs. The West German TEE trains were eight-car fixed-formation units with power cars at each end that had a small seating section in each. These were diesel hydraulics using similar proven equipment to that used in the V200 B-B locomotives, 820kW (1100bhp) in each power car (i.e. half a V200 at each end). They were particularly prominent because of their bulbous front ends and strikingly streamlined appearance. When, eventually, the TEE concept began to be abandoned in favour of international trains like the EuroCity brand, these units took over some internal *Deutsche Bundesbahn* (DB) InterCity services. In France, the SNCF upgraded its two-car diesel hydraulic RGP set with air conditioning and new seats for TEE use, but they could not cope with the demand, and instead SNCF introduced special steel-clad, air-conditioned and locomotive-hauled stock on its original TEE route to Brussels. The SBB provided five-car electric multiple-unit trains on the TEE 'Cisalpin' route between Milan, Lyons and Paris, but the Italian FS had to revert to locomotive hauling between Milan and Munich. The great contribution of the TEE concept was as forerunner of international railway collaboration in Europe, and in showing that there was an eager market to be tapped if the railways could provide a convenient and fast service between the capitals and major cities. Some systems not involved in the original scheme, like the East German *Deutsche Reichsbahn* (DR), operated their own version of the TEE – in this case, on the Berlin–Vienna route. All original TEE trains ran in a common livery of red and cream, but the whole concept gradually became outmoded during the 1970s and 1980s, when regular-interval InterCity and Eurocity trains spread across Europe. These longer locomotive-hauled or multiple-unit formations had more accommodation, and separate restaurant cars catering for both first- and second-class passengers. The Dutch-Swiss TEE sets were sold to the Ontario Northland Railway in Canada, where they provided services around Toronto, with standard diesel locomotives replacing the Werkspoor power cars. One set has since returned to Europe for possible preservation.

TYPE: 'Trans Europ Express', first class only diesel-electric units
POWER: Werkspoor 16-cylinder diesels (two per power car), each of 746kW (1000hp)
TRANSMISSION: Electric DC generator and four traction motors, two per three-axle bogie
MAX. OPERATING SPEED: 140km/h (87mph)
WEIGHT PER FOUR-CAR SET: 253t (555,610lb)
OVERALL LENGTH: 96.926m (318ft)
GAUGE: 1435mm (4ft 8.5in)

'TURF BURNER' 0-6-6-0T IRISH TRANSPORT COMPANY (CIE)

IRELAND 1957

For some years, CIE had been experimenting with dried peat as a locomotive fuel. Ireland had very little coal but billions of cubic tons of peat. Oliver Bulleid (see the 'Leader' locomotive of 1949) was consulting engineer, and in 1952 an elderly 2-6-0 engine had been converted to oil or powdered peat

fuel. Now a new prototype was built at Dublin's Inchicore Works in 1957 to continue the tests. It was in many ways a version of the Leader with two cylinders driving each of two six-wheeled chain-drive power bogies. Crushed peat was fed to the firebox by two mechanical stokers. There were

many problems, not all resolved, and its use was confined mainly to

short freight transfer trips. In 1965, it was withdrawn.

BOILER PRESSURE: 17.5kg/cm² (250psi)
CYLINDERS: 304.5x355mm (12x14in)
DRIVING WHEELS: 1091mm (43in)
GRATE AREA: not known

HEATING SURFACE: not known
SUPERHEATER: not known
TRACTIVE EFFORT: not known
TOTAL WEIGHT: 130.5t (287,920lb)

FPA-4 BO-BO CANADIAN NATIONAL RAILWAYS (CNR)

CANADA 1958

Alco's Canadian affiliate Montreal Locomotive Works continued to build carbody diesels after Alco ceased construction of the FA/FB and PA/PB types. Canadian National bought FPA-

4/FPB-4s between 1958 and 1959 for passenger service (the letter 'B' in the designation indicating a cabless 'B-unit'). The most significant difference between it and earlier Alco/MLW cab models

was the use of the newer and more reliable Alco 12-251B engine in place of the troubled 244 engine. In the late 1970s, when VIA Rail took over Canadian intercity passenger operations, it

took over the FPA-4/FPB-4 fleet, and sold some to American railways in the late 1980s and early 1990s. California's Napa Valley Wine Train uses FPA-4s on its vintage train.

A long way from its original cross-Canada route, an ex CNR and VIA-Rail FPA-4 stands at the head of the Napa Valley Wine Train in California on 30 March 1990.

TYPE: Bo-Bo, passenger diesel-electric
POWER AND OUTPUT: Alco 12-251-B diesel producing 1341kW (1800hp)

TRACTIVE EFFORT: 169kN (38,000lbf) continuous TE
MAX. OPERATING SPEED: 147km/h (92 mph)

WEIGHT: 117t (258,000lb)
MAX AXLE LOAD: 29.5t (65,000lb)
OVERALL LENGTH: 16.205m (53ft 2in)
GAUGE: 1435mm (4ft 8.5in)

CLASS RM 4-6-2 RAILWAYS OF THE PEOPLE'S REPUBLIC

Passenger services were the intended purpose of the last 'Pacific' class to be built, appropriately designated *Ren Ming* ('People') class. The Chinese railways had had 4-6-2s before, of the SL class, provided by the Japanese when they occupied Manchuria in the 1930s, but this class also owed much to Russian tradition and modern Chinese practice. They were tall engines (4.87m/16ft), their massively built-up front ends making them seem even taller, with fairings to each side of the chimney, a feed water heater cylinder fixed in front of it, and a long Russian-style casing above the boiler, enclosing the main steam pipe on

its way from dome to cylinders. They were, almost inevitably, two-cylinder simple-expansion engines, with external Walschaerts valve gear operating piston valves with long travel, ample superheating space and mechanical stoking. First built at

the Szufang (Tsingtao) works, the class was constructed from 1958 until 1964, and the total number is estimated at around 250. They worked on main-line passenger services, typically hauling trains of around the 609.6-tonne (600-ton) mark, at a consistent 105km/h

(65mph). Diesel and electric locomotives began to replace them after the 1980s, and all were taken out of service in the 1990s, though some have been preserved, along with one of the preceding SL class 4-6-2 in streamlined form.

BOILER PRESSURE: 15kg/cm² (213psi)
CYLINDERS: 570x660mm (22.5x26in)
DRIVING WHEELS: 1750mm (69in)
GRATE AREA: 5.75m² (62sq ft)
HEATING SURFACE: 210m² (2260sq ft)
SUPERHEATER: 65m² (700sq ft)
TRACTIVE EFFORT: 15,698kg (34,597lb)
TOTAL WEIGHT: 174t (380,349lb)

No. 1228 at Changchun Depot. Prefabricated parts were used as much as possible in the building of latter-day Chinese steam locomotives.

CLASS BB-16000 BO-BO FRENCH NATIONAL RAILWAYS (SNCF)

Designed in a simpler and more unified style than earlier DC classes like the CC-7100, this was a trailblazer as France's first modern express passenger AC electric locomotive. Electrically similar to the Class BB-12000, its motors were of higher power, using current transformed to DC at 920V 1040 Amp rather than the mixed-traffic type's 675V 1000 Amps. The body was boxcab style with driving compartments at each end. Two pantographs of simplified, elbow form were fitted. Ignitron rectifier technology was used, with 25.4cm (10in) rectifier tubes. Their early duties included the fastest passenger trains

TYPE: Bo-Bo passenger main-line electric locomotive
POWER: 25,000V 50Hz AC overhead line collection; 4130kW (5538hp); four DC traction motors
TRACTIVE EFFORT: 309kN (69,465lbf)
MAX. OPERATING SPEED: 160km/h (100mph)
WEIGHT: 88t (193,250lb)
MAX. AXLE LOAD: not known
OVERALL LENGTH: 16.68m (54ft 9in)
GAUGE: 1435mm (4ft 8.5in)

between Paris and Lille, Aulnoye (the Belgian frontier station) and to Amiens on the route to Boulogne and Calais, until displaced by more modern locomotives and TGVs. It was a very successful class, and

In its prime as a long-distance express locomotive, No. 16049 awaits departure from the Gare du Nord in Paris with a Lille train.

some were modified to work outer suburban push-pull commuter trains on lines running north from

Paris, but all were withdrawn by 2006. There was also a 1500V DC version known as Class BB-9200.

CLASS BB-16500 BO-BO FRENCH NATIONAL RAILWAYS (SNCF)

Less fluid in its lines than the BB-16000, this Alsthom-built electric class was also a pioneer type. Previous electric and diesel-electric types normally had traction motors for each axle in a Bo-Bo formation. Its two bogies each carried only a single traction motor, a form that came to be known as *monomoteur* (monomotor), and which was so often used in later French locomotives as to be a national type. As the class – numbering almost 300 – was intended for mixed-traffic service, the motors were geared for two speeds, passenger and freight.

TYPE: B-B mixed-traffic mainline electric locomotive
POWER: 25,000V 50 Hz AC overhead line collection; 2580kW (3460hp); two frame mounted DC traction motors; alternate gears for passenger or freight work
TRACTIVE EFFORT: (passenger or freight ratios) 192 or 324kN (43,165 or 72,840lbf)

MAX. OPERATING SPEED: 140km/h (87mph) or 100km/h (62mph)
WEIGHT: 71 to 81t (155,920 to 177,880lb)
MAX AXLE LOAD: not known
OVERALL LENGTH: 14.4m (47ft 3in)
GAUGE: 1435mm (4ft 8.5in)

The *monomoteur* electric class BB1 6500 was a large one, and examples could be seen over most of the French electrified network.

CLASS V100 B-B GERMAN FEDERAL RAILWAYS (DB)

Around 700 of these compact diesel-hydraulic engines were built for DB, which used them for a range of light mixed-traffic services on secondary routes. The V100 was, in effect, half a V200 in power. Later classed as 211 and the slightly more powerful 212, it had a short operating life, as the reduction of branch lines and light freights, and also the introduction of electric and diesel multiple units for passenger service, all combined to erode its spheres of activity and profitability. A few remain active.

TYPE: mixed traffic secondary service diesel-hydraulic
WHEEL ARRANGEMENT: B-B
POWER: medium-speed MTU 12-cylinder 820kW (1100hp) diesel; Voith L216rs hydraulic transmission

TRACTIVE EFFORT: 183kN (41,140lbf)
MAX. OPERATING SPEED: 100km/h (62mph)
WEIGHT: 62t (136,160lb)
OVERALL LENGTH: 12.1m (39ft 8in)
GAUGE: 1435mm (4ft 8.5in)

Like some other classes in other countries, the V100 was a good locomotive whose traffic withered away and which consequently left the scene earlier than would otherwise have been the case.

CLASS 4CEP ELECTRIC MULTIPLE UNITS BRITISH RAILWAYS (BR)

In the course of the 1950s, new third-rail electrification in Britain was installed at 750V rather than the previous standard of 600V, and already electrified track was gradually upgraded. The reason was primarily to help overcome problems caused by icing-up of the power rail in cold weather. Able to form trains of up to 12 coaches, these four-car units were ordered by BR's Southern Region for the 750V electrification of its main lines from London to the North Kent coast. Two motor coaches were in each set, each with a single powered

A 4CEP in 'Network Southeast' livery approaches London Victoria Station. The neat end corridor connection can be noted.

bogie driven by two axle-hung self-ventilating traction motors. Electro-pneumatic control equipment was mounted under the floors. Intended to work at express speed, they had inter-unit corridor connections, and internally were decorated in more modern style than the BR Mark 1

carriages on which they were based. The 102 4CEP units, supplemented by 20 buffet-fitted 4BEPs, provided a more intensive and faster service that saw passenger traffic on the lines rise by over 30 per cent. All have now been replaced by modern stock.

TYPE: four-car electric multiple unit express trains
POWER: 750V DC conductor rail collection, two power cars, each with two English Electric 187kW (250hp) axle-hung DC traction motors, resistance control
TRACTIVE EFFORT: not known

MAX. OPERATING SPEED: 145km/h (90mph)
WEIGHT: 33 to 42t (71,680 to 91,840lb) per vehicle
OVERALL LENGTH: 19.66m (64ft 6in)
GAUGE: 1435mm (4ft 8.5in)

TYPE 2 CO-BO BRITISH RAILWAYS (BR)   GREAT BRITAIN 1958

Metropolitan Vickers' preference for the two-stroke Crossley engine had already had unfortunate effects on the West Australian Class X of 1954, and its use on the 20 'Type 2' locomotives also resulted in problems. The engine used a patented 'exhaust pulse pressure charging' system. In theory,

TYPE: mixed-traffic main-line diesel-electric
WHEEL ARRANGEMENT: Co-Bo
POWER: Crossley HSTV8 two-stroke V-form

diesel 895kW (1200bhp); Metro-Vick DC generator and five axle-hung traction motors
TRACTIVE EFFORT: 220kN (50,000lbf)
MAX. OPERATING SPEED: 120km/h (75mph)

WEIGHT: 97t (213,020lb)
OVERALL LENGTH: 17.27m (56ft 8in)
GAUGE: 1435mm (4ft 8.5in)

contact with the high-pressure exhaust gases pushed the intake air pressure up, but in practice this did not always work properly.

The weight distribution of the mechanical layout led to the asymmetrical bogie design. The 'Type 2' fleet operated from

Barrow-on-Furness for most of their lives, but all were withdrawn within 10 years. D5705 is preserved.

CLASS 40 1-CO-CO-1 BRITISH RAILWAYS (BR)   GREAT BRITAIN 1958

Preserved Class 40 D345 passes Touch Hall Cutting with a train from Rawtenstall to Bury on the restored East Lancashire Railway, on 11 August 1998.

British express 4-6-0 and light 'Pacific' steam types were due to be displaced by the 200 Type 4 – later Class 40 – locomotives, built by English Electric and Robert Stephenson & Hawthorns. In mechanical and electrical design, they followed closely that of the 1951 Southern Region

diesel No. 10203: bogies, power unit and traction equipment were virtually identical. Body styling was different, with vertical side-sheets, and cabs set back behind nose compartments containing auxiliary equipment.

The Class 40s performed well and reliably, with a top speed of

TYPE: mixed-traffic main-line diesel-electric
WHEEL ARRANGEMENT: 1Co-Co1
POWER: English Electric 16SVT 16-cylinder 1490kW (2000bhp); DC generator; six DC axle-hung traction motors

145kph (90mph). Initially allocated to BR's Eastern, North Eastern and London Midland regions, they hauled principal expresses like *The Royal Scot* and

TRACTIVE EFFORT: 230kN (52,000lbf)
MAX. OPERATING SPEED: 145km/h (90mph)
WEIGHT: 136t (297,920lb)
OVERALL LENGTH: 21.19m (69ft 6in)
GAUGE: 1435mm (4ft 8.5in)

The Flying Scotsman. The advent of the BR high-speed trains caused them finally to be displaced and all were eventually withdrawn by 1984.

CLASS WT 2-8-4T INDIAN RAILWAYS (IR)

Steam power had a long, slow demise on the Indian Railways, and some of the first members of this class ran for almost 40 years until steam working finally ended in 1995. Thirty were built at Chittaranjan Works between 1959 and 1965.

In appearance, they looked as if an American boiler had been put on a British tank-engine frame, which was essentially the case. The Class WTs were designed to use standard parts, and the boiler was that of the WL 'Pacific', while it shared cylinders and wheels with the WP class. City line electrification displaced them from suburban to cross-country services in the last great years of Indian steam.

BOILER PRESSURE: 14.7kg/cm² (210psi)
CYLINDERS: 514x710.6mm (20.25x28in)
DRIVING WHEELS: 1700mm (67in)
GRATE AREA: 3.5m² (38sq ft)
HEATING SURFACE: 121.9m² (1613sq ft)
SUPERHEATER: 41.8m² (450sq ft)
TRACTIVE EFFORT: 14,520kg (32,000lb)
TOTAL WEIGHT: 136t (300,120lb)

A Class WT 2-8-4T coasts slowly past a gang of track workers clearing ash with the aid of a steam-powered bucket-crane, in a quintessential Indian Railways scene from the Mumbai locomotive yards.

CLASS WCM-3 & 4 CO-CO INDIAN RAILWAYS (IR)

Japan supplied these two similar-looking electric classes. WCM-4 was the more high-powered, with six Hitachi 497kW (675hp) axle hung nose suspended motors, and was intended for express passenger and fast freight service. With lower-rated 442kW (600hp) motors, the WCM-3 ran stopping trains. Both were built by Hitachi originally for the Calcutta area

3000V direct current system. Along with the British-supplied class WCM-2, the three WCM-3s of 1958 and seven WCM-4s of 1960 were later modified to accept 1500V DC on conversion of the Calcutta direct current system to 25kV AC. Both used conventional three series and parallel traction motor combinations and weak fielding. These were the last Indian electrics of bonnet-end design, all subsequent models being of flat-front box cab layout. Displaced from passenger service in the 1980s, both classes ran freight traffic before withdrawal.

TYPE: Co-Co
POWER: WCM3 1835kW (2460hp); WCM4 2454kW (3290hp)
Supply: 3000 V DC later 1500 V DC
TRACTIVE EFFORT: WCM3 – 276kN (62040lbf); WCM4 – 306kN (68860lbf)
MAX. OPERATING SPEED: 120km/h (75mph)
WEIGHT: WCM-3 – 113t (249,165lb); WCM-4 – 125t (275,625lb)
MAX. AXLE LOAD: up to 21t (46,305lb)
OVERALL LENGTH: NOT KNOWN
GAUGE: 1676mm (5ft 6in)

In its latter years, a WCM-5 of Indian Railways heads the Bombay–Hyderabad express. All WCM types have now been withdrawn from service.

KODAMA TRAIN JAPANESE NATIONAL RAILWAYS (JNR)

JAPAN 1958

Precursor of very much faster things to come, the *Kodama* ('Echo') was designed to run on the newly electrified 1065mm (3ft 6in) gauge main line between Tokyo and Osaka. The 553km (344-mile) route was covered in 6hrs, 50min, at an average speed of 80km/h (50mph). Originally the trains were made up of eight cars, all air-conditioned, with a passenger capacity of 425. Cupola-style raised driving cabs were fitted in each end car. The motors, with an hourly rated output of 1550kW (2077hp), were fitted in the second and seventh cars, which had dynamic and clasp brakes; the trailer cars had disc brakes. The service was an immediate success and the sets were soon extended to 12 cars to cope with demand.

TYPE: electric passenger train
POWER: 16 100kW (134hp) motors supplied by 1500V DC via overhead catenary, geared to axles of two power cars and of the two adjacent inner cars
TRACTIVE EFFORT: 48.9kN (11,000lbf)
MAX. OPERATING SPEED: 125km/h (75mph)
TOTAL WEIGHT: 276.3t (609,242lb)
MAX. AXLE LOAD: 9.6t (21,168lb)
OVERALL LENGTH: 166.42m (546ft)
BUILDER: Kawasaki, Kinki Sharyo, Kisha Seizo Kaisha; electrical equipment supplied by Toshiba

A '*Kodama*' eight-car set from Osaka runs on the elevated tracks towards Tokyo Central. The carriage design still has external equipment casing mounted on the roofs.

SEVEN-CAR TRAIN MOROCCAN RAILWAYS (CFM)

MOROCCO 1958

Long inter-city distances in Morocco gave scope for some fast running, and this air-conditioned, high-speed seven-car diesel-electric set, built in France, was comparable to the Dutch-Swiss TEE trains. The intention was to attract custom back to the railways at a time of falling passenger numbers. It had two power cars,

TYPE: seven-car diesel-electric multiple-unit train
POWER: two MGO engines with an output of 746kW (1000hp) at 1500rpm, driving two

with engines mounted in the car frames. Two auxiliary diesel generators for train lighting, air conditioning, etc. allowed the full

power bogies via Alsthom electric transmission
TRACTIVE EFFORT: not known
MAXIMUM OPERATING SPEED: 121km/h (75mph)

power of the engines to be applied to traction. There were driving positions at each end, and it accommodated 288 passengers.

TOTAL WEIGHT: 251.2t (553,896lb)
MAXIMUM AXLE LOAD: 12t (26,460lb)
OVERALL LENGTH: not known
GAUGE: not known

Tested on the SNCF Paris–Strasbourg line, it maintained an average speed of 117.5km/h (73mph) over the 503.7km (313-mile) route.

CLASS TE10 CO-CO SOVIET RAILWAYS (SZD)

RUSSIA 1958

With the TE10 diesel-electric, Soviet railway engineers sought a significant power increase on the TE3 of 1952 but with a minimal weight increase – and when the prototype TE10 001 was completed at the Lugansk factory in November 1958, it was the first Russian 2208kW (3000hp) diesel-electric. New diesel engines made the difference, the final version being the 10-cylinder 10D100, still using the opposed-piston system 'borrowed' from the Fairbanks-Morse engines of the 1940s. Initial limited numbers of the single-unit TE10L were quickly replaced by the

mass production twin-unit 2TE10L, running to over 3000 from 1961. These locomotives were of the original Kharkov cab design. Production and development went on into the 1990s, resulting in a wide range of sub-classes.

From 1974, the 2TE10V version featured a new body and increased axle load. The negative-rake cab front windows and new bogies both came from the contemporary TE116. The TE10 'V' suffix denotes *Voroshilovgradskii* (the name of the Lugansk factory at that time) with units built up to 2TE10V 5090, and one triple 3TE10V in 1978. Next

came the double and triple unit TE10M ('M' for *modernizirovannyi*) built as 3TE10M and numbered 0002–0200, then the 2TE10M numbered 0201–1000, the 3TE10M numbered 1001–1440 and the 2TE10M numbered 2001–3664. For service on the BAM (*Baikalo Amurskaya Magistrale*) trans-Siberian route then under construction, 25 4TE10S quadruple units with suffix 'S' for *severnyi* (north) operation were built by 1983. Two further production versions were introduced in 1989/1990: 2TE10U, with 50 built; 3TE10U *universalnyi* (80 built); and 100 of 2TE10UT,

with electropneumatic train braking for passenger work and 120km/h (75mph) maximum speed.

An interesting technical diversification was the experimental 2TE10G of 1988, for dual fuelling on diesel and natural gas. Despite the '2' classification, both units were actually triple section with an unpowered central cryogenic tender carrying liquefied gas at -162°C (324°F). No more was heard of this type after the initial publicity. Another limited production version was 2TE10MK from 1981 with the same Kolomna 5D49 engine as installed in the 2TE116.

All the TE10 locomotives, apart from the 100 2TE10UT, were freight haulers. A passenger version was originally to have been model TE11, then altered to TEP10. First built in the city of Kharkov from 1960, it was later also built at Lugansk, and more than 550 were constructed, 335 of TEP10 and 218 of 2TEP10L.

TYPE: Co-Co diesel electric freight
POWER: 2208kW (3000hp) per unit from Kolomna 10D100 series engine
TRACTIVE EFFORT: various

MAX. OPERATING SPEED: 100km/h (62mph)
WEIGHT: TE10L 130t (286,650lb); TE10V 138t (304,290lb)

OVERALL LENGTH: 16.969m (55ft 5in)
GAUGE: 1524mm (5ft)

Their maximum operating speed of 140km/h (87mph) was through 20:63 gearing (replacing 15:68 in the freight version), and reduction of continuous tractive effort to 175kN (393,75lbf) at 35km/h (21.9mph). The TEP10 was a two-cab single unit design; the 2TEP10Ls were double units.

CLASS CHS2 CO-CO SOVIET RAILWAYS (SZD)

With Russian locomotive works heavily engaged in the construction of electric and diesel-electric freight locomotives, the Soviet Railways ordered this large class of passenger electrics from Skoda in Plzen, Czechoslovakia. The prototypes built in 1958 were considered to be under-powered for heavy express work at 3516kW (4715hp), and eventually motors uprated by 700kW (938hp) were supplied for the production run. Between 1964 and 1973, series production totalled 942 locomotives. Units 875/876 were prototypes for a new class – ChS2T, which was 117 strong with different body and improved systems. Both versions remain in passenger traffic.

TYPE: Co-Co electric passenger
POWER: 4200kW (5632hp)
SUPPLY: 3000V DC
TRACTIVE EFFORT: 162kN (36,450lbf) at 91.5km/h (57.2mph)
MAX. OPERATING SPEED: 140km/h (87.5mph)
WEIGHT: 125t (275,625lb)
MAX. AXLE LOAD: 21t (46,305lb)
OVERALL LENGTH: 18.92m (61ft 9in)
GAUGE: 1524mm (5ft)

Power to haul Russia's very long and heavy long-distance passenger trains, rather than high speed, was required of the Class CHS2.

EMD SD24 CO-CO VARIOUS RAILROADS

A distinctive bulge behind the cab of this big hood unit revealed the fact that it was EMD's first turbocharged high-horsepower diesel-electric. Otherwise, it externally resembled the SD9. Built until 1963, this six-motored 1788kW (2400 hp) machine foreshadowed the type of motive power that would become the standard on most American freight railroads. Santa Fe and Union Pacific both ordered SD24s with the better-visibility 'low nose' option that was just becoming popular, and which would be a standard option in the late 1960s. Burlington and Southern Railway had high-hood examples. When Santa Fe rebuilt its SD24 fleet with EMD 16-645 engines to boost output and improve reliability, these were re-designated as SD26s.

TYPE: Co-Co, diesel-electric
POWER: EMD 16-567D3 producing 1788kW (2400hp)
TRACTIVE EFFORT: 425kN (95,700lbf)
MAX. OPERATING SPEED: N/A
WEIGHT: 174t (382,800lb)
OVERALL LENGTH: N/A
GAUGE: 1435mm (4ft 8.5in)

A 'high hood' SD 24, No. 2402 of the Wisconsin Central Railroad. Compared to later diesel-electrics, it's slender and spare, but it was not short of power.

CLASS VB 0-4-0 VICTORIAN RAILWAYS (VR)

AUSTRALIA 1959

This tiny locomotive, possibly the smallest ever to operate for any main-line Australian railway system, was a four-wheel diesel shunter with hydraulic transmission. It was built at the VR's own works and was fitted with a tractor engine. It remained a one-off, used in shunting passenger cars for all its working life and is now preserved.

TYPE: 0-4-0 diesel-hydraulic light shunter
POWER: 30kW (40hp) from Fordson Major engine
TRACTIVE EFFORT: 48kN (10800lbf)
MAX. OPERATING SPEED: 16km/h (10mph)
WEIGHT: 22t (48510lb)
OVERALL LENGTH: 6.32m (20ft 7in)
GAUGE: 1600MM (5FT 3IN)

The V56's last job was pushing cars and multiple-units through the washing plant at Jollimont.

CLASS 48 CO-CO NEW SOUTH WALES GOVERNMENT RAILWAYS (NSWGR)

AUSTRALIA 1959

Over the 10-plus years from 1959 to 1970, 165 of these locomotives were delivered, and they became dominant in main-line freight haulage in New South Wales. All were Alco-engined, but different electrical manufacturers were involved at different times: the first 45 had all General Electric (GE) electrical parts, the next 40 had GE generators but British-designed Associated Electrical Industries (AEI) motors; the last 80 had wholly AEI electrics. The switch from GE to AEI was due to GE competing directly against Alco where previously the two had worked together. In 2002, over 100 remained operational, deployed largely on NSW grain and coal as well as most branch freight traffic. Some refurbished examples are likely to work for some years yet.

TYPE: Co-Co freight
POWER: 780kW (1050hp) from Alco 6-251 series engine
TRACTIVE EFFORT: (serials 4801-4885): 151kN (33975lbf) at 10km/h (6.2mph)
MAX. OPERATING SPEED: 120km/h (75mph)
WEIGHT: 75t (165,375lb)
OVERALL LENGTH: 14.76m (48ft 2in)
GAUGE: 1435mm (4ft 8.5in)

No. 4827 in Rail Infrastructure Corporation colours, for train workings in connection with new rail projects. Following privatization, many Australian locos have passed through several ownerships.

CLASS 44 1-CO-CO-1 BRITISH RAILWAYS (BR)

Closely related to the BR Class 40, but a more powerful variant on the British Railways 'Type 4' theme, the Class 44 diesel-electrics were built at British Railways workshops. The power unit was a Sulzer twin-bank engine, the 12LDA28 type, coupled to robust Crompton Parkinson electric traction equipment. The four-axle 1-Co bogies were of the type designed for the BR Southern Region 10201 locomotive (see 1951).

Ten class 44s were built, and they were the prototypes for the 183 locomotives of classes 45 and 46 that followed. The '44s' began operating on main-line passenger work, particularly on the Midland division of the LM Region, but graduated to freight work as the '45s' and '46s' became more numerous. Known as the 'Peak' class, and named after English and

Welsh mountains, they ended their days working on heavy freight trains from Toton depot in the East Midlands.

Like some other British diesels of this period, early members of the class were fitted with end-doors to enable crew to pass between locomotives working in a multiple-unit configuration.

TYPE: mixed-traffic main-line diesel-electric
WHEEL ARRANGEMENT: 1Co-Co1
POWER: Sulzer 12LDA28 12-cylinder twin-bank diesel 1715kW (2300bhp); Crompton Parkinson DC generator and six DC axle-hung traction motors
TRACTIVE EFFORT: 310kN (70,000lbf)
MAX. OPERATING SPEED: 145km/h (90mph)
WEIGHT: 141t (309,345lb)
OVERALL LENGTH: 20.7m (67ft 11in)
GAUGE: 1435mm (4ft 8.5in)

No. 81007 pulls out of Lancaster station with a London-bound relief express during the holiday peak on 12 August 1989.

CLASS AL1 BO-BO BRITISH RAILWAYS (BR)

In the 1960s, when lineside telegraph wires and poles were still a feature of railways, a Class 44 fronts a train of assorted mineral wagons on the Midland main line.

By the time British Railways came to electrify its busy West Coast main line, certain matters relating to electric traction had been generally accepted. One was that 25,000V 50Hz AC was the right supply system. Another was that the Bo-Bo format was the right one for the locomotives. Initially 100 locomotives were ordered, all specified to have a power output of 2240kW (3000hp) and all Bo-Bos, from five different British manufacturers. The intention was to gain experience of several types, classified as AL1 to AL5 (later 81 to 85).

The 25 Class AL1 locomotives were built by the Birmingham Railway Carriage & Wagon company with electric equipment by Associated Electrical Industries (AEI). The others came from Beyer

Peacock/Metropolitan Vickers, English Electric, the North British Locomotive Company/GEC, and British Railways/AEI. The AL1 locomotives were built to run at 160km/h (100mph), apart from two which were geared for mixed-traffic use with a top speed of 130km/h (80mph).

Initially the rectification of alternating current to direct current for the traction equipment was by means of mercury arc rectifiers, using three-phase cathodes to strike arcs to the liquid mercury. Later, advances in solid-state rectification enabled the relatively unreliable mercury arc rectifiers to be replaced by silicon rectifiers. Traction motor voltage was adjusted by means of mechanical tap changers, which were tapped into different stages

of the transformer windings. When built, the locomotives had two pantographs of the Faiveley single arm type, but one was later removed. To keep track stresses low, the traction motors were not axle-hung but were fully suspended in the bogie frames. The axles were turned by spring drives that could take up the vertical movement of the wheelsets. This bogie design was not always totally reliable, but the layout was not changed in the life of these locomotives.

When new, the class was painted in BR's new 'electric blue', with white cab roofs and red buffer beams, stainless steel cab side numerals and aluminium crest in the middle of the bodysides. From the early 1960s, they acquired small yellow warning panels, later

all-over yellow cab fronts, and then, from 1965 onwards, the standard BR corporate rail blue livery, which most retained through to their withdrawal at the end of the 1980s.

With the gradual changeover to air brakes on BR, the electrics were modified to handle air-braked stock in addition to the earlier vacuum-braked vehicles that they had hauled since new. The Class 81s, as the 'AL1s' had become, were downgraded in 1986 to 130km/h (80mph) and ran parcels and freight trains and trip workings of empty stock into and out of terminal stations. With the other four 'prototype' classes, they were superseded by later Class 86, 87 and 90 locomotives.

TYPE: Bo-Bo passenger mainline electric locomotive (two mixed-traffic locomotives)
POWER: 25,000V 50Hz AC overhead line collection; 2385kW (3200hp); mercury arc rectification with tap changer control; four DC traction motors
TRACTIVE EFFORT: 222kN (50,000lbf)
MAX. OPERATING SPEED: 160km/h (100mph); two locomotives 130km/h (80mph)
WEIGHT: 81t (178,305lb)
MAX AXLE LOAD: not known
OVERALL LENGTH: 17.22m (56ft 6in)
GAUGE: 1435mm (4ft 8.5in)

CLASS WAG1 B-B INDIAN RAILWAYS (IR)

Geared for haulage power rather than speed, the Class WAG1 was the first 25kV industrial frequency alternating-current locomotives to be put to work on the Indian sub-continent. The class was drawn up and built for Indian Railways by the European 50Hz Consortium. Mechanical and electrical parts came from several members of the consortium, with the two Belgian companies La Brugeoise et Nivelles and Société des Forges et Ateliers assembling 30, and the remaining 92 built in India by Chittaranjan Locomotive Works (CLW).

All of the class were equipped with regenerative braking and links for multiple working on heavy trains. Traction motors were of Siemens origin, fitted in monomotor bogies designed by Alsthom. Control was by transformer tap changing through ignitron rectifiers, with traction motors connected in permanent parallel. Equipped for regenerative braking and multiple-unit working, they were wholly comparable to European electric locomotives of the period.

TYPE: B-B freight
POWER: 2900kW (3940hp)
SUPPLY: 25kV 50Hz AC
TRACTIVE EFFORT: 293kN (66,000lbf)
MAX. OPERATING SPEED: 80km/h (50mph)
WEIGHT: 85t (187,425lb)
MAX. AXLE LOAD: 21.3t (46,967lb)
OVERALL LENGTH: 20.66m (67ft 5in)
GAUGE: 1676mm (5ft 6in)

WAG 1 freight locomotive 20782. No members of Classes WAG 1 to WAG 5 remain in action on Indian Railways.

CLASS 165 ELECTRIC MULTIPLE UNIT TRAIN JAPANESE NATIONAL RAILWAYS (JNR)

At peak periods, Class 165 units would run in ten-car sets and with only a two-minute headway, requiring very tight timing in station stops.

The rate of electrification of suburban networks in Japan speeded up dramatically as the post-war economic recovery made capital available. A great variety of electric multiple units were built for local and suburban traffic between 1959 and 1971, with the major Japanese builders sharing in the work, including Nippon Sharyo Seizo, Kinki Nihon Sharyo, and Hitachi, with Mitsubishi and Tokyo Shibaura Electric Co. contributing electrical equipment.

This class is typical in design and specification, a basic three-car set with two power cars, but configurations went up to 10-car sets.

TYPE: three-car electric suburban train
POWER: Eight traction motors supplied by 1500V DC via overhead catenary, driving all axles of two power cars
TRACTIVE EFFORT: 31.3kN (7050lbf)
MAX. OPERATING SPEED: 110km/h (68mph)
TOTAL WEIGHT: 108t (238,140lb)
MAX. AXLE LOAD: 9t (19,845lb)
OVERALL LENGTH: 59.923m (196ft 9in)
BUILDER: Nippon Sharyo Seizo, Kinki Nihon Sharyo and Tokyo Shibaura Elecric co.

CLASS 060-DA CO-CO ROMANIAN RAILWAYS (CFR)

The sturdy and reliable Sulzer diesel engine fitted to the British Class 44 was also used in this CFR locomotive, which became a numerous and effective class. Romania has tended to buy-in technical designs from other countries, mainly in Western Europe – in this case, Switzerland. The Brown Boveri Company (BBC) provided the design for a compact

TYPE: mixed-traffic main-line diesel-electric
WHEEL ARRANGEMENT: Co-Co
POWER: Sulzer 12LDA28 12-cylinder twin-bank diesel 1544kW (2070hp); Brown Boveri DC generator and six axle-hung traction motors
TRACTIVE EFFORT: 314kN (70,590lbf)
MAX. OPERATING SPEED: 120km/h (75mph)
WEIGHT: 118t (259,840lb)
OVERALL LENGTH: 17m (55ft 9in)
GAUGE: 1435mm (4ft 8.5in)

A CFR Class 060-DA passes a fine array of semaphore signals as it leaves a station with a local passenger service.

main-line Co-Co locomotive, with the Sulzer engine and BBC electric traction equipment. A total of 1407 Class 060-DA locomotives (later reclassified '60' to '62') were built for CFR, most of them by the Electroputere workshops in the southern Romanian city of Craiova. They are extremely successful locomotives, being suitable for both heavy passenger and freight trains. Electroputere has also supplied many examples for the railways of Poland and Bulgaria.

In the early 2000s, CFR refurbished several locomotives for further service. Two have been updated with Caterpillar engines and more up-to-date electrical equipment. The type still operates in Romania and Poland, and many surplus locomotives have been sold to private operators in Germany, Italy and elsewhere.

EMD GP20 BO-BO VARIOUS RAILROADS

EMD had introduced turbo-charging on the SD24: now it was the turn of the GP ('General Purpose') road switchers. One of the strengths of Electro-Motive early diesel locomotives was the powerful, compact and reliable 567 engine (a contrast with Alco's 244 series), which powered thousands of Fs, GPs, Es and switcher types in several variant forms. Hitherto, it had been supercharged, normally using a Roots scavenger blower. In the late 1950s, Union Pacific modified some of its EMD GP9s with turbochargers to obtain greater output, and EMD followed up with the turbocharged 1492kW (2000hp) GP20. Like the SD24, it used the 16-cylinder 567 (model D3 in this case) and was offered

with either a traditional high short-hood (nose-section), or a low short-hood for better forward visibility. Well suited to fast intermodal services, GP20 was produced from 1959 only until 1962, when GP30 arrived on the scene.

TYPE: Bo-Bo, diesel-electric
POWER AND OUTPUT: EMD 16-567D2 producing 1492kW (2000hp)
TRACTIVE EFFORT: 200kN (45,000 lbf) at 22.4 km/h (14 mph)
MAX. OPERATING SPEED: 104 km/h (65mph)
WEIGHT: 116 tonnes (256,000 lbs)
OVERALL LENGTH: 17.12m (56ft 2in)
GAUGE: 1435m (4ft 8.5in)

As Kyle Railroad's No. 2035, a GP 20 powers a freight train in the Midwest. Kyle traffic was primarily agricultural produce.

CLASS MX A1A-A1A DANISH STATE RAILWAYS (DSB)

Good Europeans as the Dutch might seem, the MX was in origin an American class that came to Europe by way of Australia. It began with EMD's F unit, which was adapted by Clyde Engineering of Granville, NSW, for Australian use as type ML1 (single cab) and ML2 (two cabs). Nohab of Trollhättan, Sweden, another EMD affiliate, adapted the ML2 to fit European

TYPE: mixed-traffic main-line diesel-electric
WHEEL ARRANGEMENT: A1A-A1A
POWER: GM 12-567C 12-cylinder V-form diesel, 1050kW (1405bhp), DC generator, four traction motors
TRACTIVE EFFORT: 176kN (395,665lbf)
MAX. OPERATING SPEED: 133km/h (83mph)
WEIGHT: 89t (195,450lb)
OVERALL LENGTH: 18.3m (60ft)
GAUGE: 1435mm (4ft 8.5in)

clearances and other standards, giving it a more arched roof, lowering the nose slightly, and modifying the shape of the double windscreen. DSB were the first customers, and four were delivered to them in 1954 as Class MY 1101–4; and Nohab also built a fifth as a demonstrator loco that was sent round numerous railways in Europe in the hope of attracting sales (this was a very American selling technique). In Norway, NSB eventually bought 35, with a Co-Co wheel arrangement. MÁV in Hungary also bought 20 in Co-Co form in 1963–64 (see 1963).

In Denmark, the MY class, later enlarged to 55 engines, ran mainline services, and were later downgraded to secondary working when more powerful diesels arrived. The MXs from 1960 were a slightly smaller version, with lighter axle load, intended for branch working from the start, and in this

DSB's MX, a variant of one of Europe's most successful locomotive types, with a pedigree going back to EMD's F-unit (see 1946).

form, very similar in appearance to the MY class, were unique to DSB. Both types were very highly regarded by their owners, and in later years worked on freight and infrastructure trains until retired by

DSB at the end of the 1990s. After class withdrawal, several locomotives have been sold to private operators in Denmark and elsewhere, and to infrastructure companies, and continue to run.

'BLUE PULLMAN' TRAIN BRITISH RAILWAYS (BR)

Influence of the 'Trans-Europ Express' can be detected in the 'Blue Pullmans', though Pullman luxury trains had been running in Britain since the nineteenth century. In Britain as in continental Europe, however, motorways were being built, and the long-distance coach and increased use of private cars, as well as internal air services, were obvious threats to long-distance rail services. Britain's first air-conditioned trains, these locos introduced new, higher

TYPE: Pullman diesel unit
POWER (EACH OF TWO POWER CARS): MAN L12V18/21S 12-cylinder V-form diesel, 746kW (1000bhp); GEC DC generator; four fully suspended DC traction motors
MAX. OPERATING SPEED: 145km/h (90mph)
WEIGHT: 305t (669,760lb) six-car sets; 371t (815,360lb) eight-car sets
OVERALL LENGTH: 20.9m (68ft 7in) power cars; 20.725m (68ft) trailer cars
GAUGE: 1435mm (4ft 8.5in)

London Paddington in the 1960s – a 'Blue Pullman' arrives from the West of England. The Pullman format and price level restricted their use to 'business' and wealthier travellers.

standards of sound insulation for a quiet passenger environment. They were fixed formation diesel-electric units, and the Manchester to London service had six all first-class cars, aimed at the top business market. The Birmingham to London route had eight-car sets with first- and second-class seats.

Able to sustain a maximum speed of 145km/h (90mph) where traffic and route conditions allowed, they ran to faster schedules than steam-hauled expresses.

Each of the two power cars contained a MAN 12-cylinder engine with a GEC generator. Two traction motors were under the

rear bogie of the power cars and two on the leading bogie of the adjacent trailer coach. Later, all sets went to the Western Region and worked on Bristol to London and Swansea to London peak business services. The original blue-and-white livery was replaced after 1965 by BR blue-and-grey in

reverse application. They ran until 1973, their restricted routes and accommodation meaning that they had only a limited impact on the travelling public. To the railway managers, however, they indicated the way forward, though it would be another 14 years from 1960 before the '125s' came into service.

CLASS 02 B BRITISH RAILWAYS (BR) GREAT BRITAIN 1960

Though never as numerous as equivalent types in Germany, BR introduced a variety of small B (0-4-0) diesel-powered shunting locomotives for use in locations with tight curves and light loads, as Class 02. Hydraulic transmission worked very well in such tasks, and this was a group of 20 locomotives from the Yorkshire Engine Company, powered by a Rolls-Royce high-

speed diesel engine coupled to a three-stage hydraulic torque converter. The final drive was a Yorkshire Engine Co. double-reduction reversing bevel gearbox. Abandonment of 'wagon-load' freight consignments, and the closure of many factory spur lines and small goods yards in the 1960s, limited their utility almost as soon as they were introduced. One at least is preserved.

TYPE: B (0-4-0) diesel-hydraulic shunting
POWER: Rolls-Royce C6NFL diesel 125kW (170hp); RR series 10,000 three-stage torque converter; YEC final drive to one axle, outside coupling rods
TRACTIVE EFFORT: 67kN (15,000lbf)
MAX. OPERATING SPEED: 32km/h (20mph)
WEIGHT: 29t (62,720lb)
OVERALL LENGTH: 6.7m (22ft) approx.
GAUGE: 1435mm (4ft 8.5in)

Sometimes known as 'rail tractors', these small four-wheelers had a variety of uses where single units or short sets of stock, or 'dead' locomotives, had to be moved about.

CLASS 37 CO-CO BRITISH RAILWAYS (BR) GREAT BRITAIN 1960

English Electric provided the diesel engine and the electrical parts for this solidly reliable and long-lived mixed traffic locomotive. Living up to its intended versatility, it began on

express trains to East Anglia before being distributed more widely and being placed mainly on heavy freight duties.

In the 1970s, pairs of 37s were drafted to work Britain's heaviest

freight duty, 2140-tonne (2000-ton) iron ore trains from Immingham Docks to Scunthorpe steelworks. Others were later modified with train heating alternators and used on passenger work on the Scottish

West Highland lines. After over 40 years of work, only a handful of the class remain in action in Britain. A few have been sold to private freight operators and some work for the nuclear industry. They have also been used in France and Spain on construction trains for new high-speed railways.

TYPE: mixed-traffic main-line diesel-electric
WHEEL ARRANGEMENT: Co-Co
POWER: English Electric 12CSVT 12-cylinder V-form diesel, 1305kW (1750bhp); DC generator; six axle-hung DC traction motors
TRACTIVE EFFORT: 245kN (55,500lbf) to 280kN (62,680lbf)
MAX. OPERATING SPEED: 130km/h (80mph)
WEIGHT: 104t (228,480lb) to 122t (268,880lb)
OVERALL LENGTH: 18.745m (61ft 6in)
GAUGE: 1435mm (4ft 8.5in)

English Welsh & Scottish Railways' No. 37667 heads a train of oil tanks from Milford Haven through South Wales.

CLASS 124 'TRANS-PENNINE' BRITISH RAILWAYS (BR) GREAT BRITAIN 1960

The Pennine hills separate the major conurbations of Yorkshire and Lancashire, and steam services had been slow and smoky in the long tunnels. Steam trains were replaced by powerful six-car diesel multiple units (DMUs) formed of four power cars and two trailers,

working Hull–Liverpool via Leeds and Manchester. Five carriages were second class and the buffet car had first-class compartments. Later the buffet cars were removed, and the sets reduced to four cars. 'Sprinter' DMUs replaced the 124s in the early 1980s.

TYPE: express diesel multiple-unit six-car (later five-car) set
POWER: Leyland Albion horizontal six-cylinder diesel (two per power car), 170kW (230bhp); fluid flywheel; four-speed epicyclic gearbox; cardan shaft to reversing gearbox on nearest axle

MAX. OPERATING SPEED: 110km/h (70mph)
WEIGHT: 41t (89,600lb) power cars; 33t (71,680lb) trailers
OVERALL LENGTH: 19.66m (64ft 6in)
GAUGE: 1435mm (4ft 8.5in)

CLASS E.321/E.322 C STATE RAILWAYS (FS)

Modelled on short diesel 'hood' types, with a box pantograph mounted on the single end cab, these were carriage shunters. E.321s were simple electric shunting locomotives with rod drive. A single traction motor under the low bonnet drove a jackshaft to supply torque to the coupling rods that turned the three coupled axles. FS used them singly for lighter duties such as attaching

TYPE: shunting electric locomotive (class E.321) and slave unit (class E.322)
WHEEL ARRANGEMENT: C+C (0-6-0 + 0-6-0) when in multiple with one slave
POWER PER UNIT: 3000V DC overhead

and detaching coaches at passenger terminals and junctions. For heavier loads, some were coupled in multiple with cabless slave units of Class E.322. These

line collection; 190kW (255bhp); one body-mounted DC traction motor, jackshaft drive to side coupling rods
TRACTIVE EFFORT: not known
MAX. OPERATING SPEED: 50km/h (31mph)

were basically the same locomotives as the master E.321, but with control and traction current from the E.321. Some E.321s worked in multiple with

WEIGHT PER UNIT: 36t (79,060lb)
OVERALL LENGTH: 9.28m (30ft 5in) per unit
GAUGE: 1435mm (4ft 8.5in)

two Class E.322 slaves, when greater tractive effort was needed. All are now withdrawn.

CLASS TEM2 CO-CO SOVIET RAILWAYS (SZD)

With a production history spanning almost 30 years, the TEM2 six-axle heavy shunter and transfer locomotive was a useful design, replacing the huge, obsolete fleet of Class E10 0-10-0 steam locomotives. Many thousands were built, and the SZD also imported the ChME3 design of similar layout and power from Czechoslovakia (see 1964). Both TEM2 and ChME3 were deployed on similar duties across the entire Soviet SZD and successor networks. Several improved and revised versions of TEM2 appeared, and were also produced for export. The direct ancestor of the class was the Alco RS1 imported from the United States under Lend-Lease, and the 746kW (1000hp) TEM1 model produced between 1958 and 1968 was the first Soviet switcher design, of which nearly 2000 were built.

TEM stands for *teplovoz elecktroperedachei manevrovyi* literally 'diesel electric shunter', while the '1' simply represents the original version. TEM2 is an uprated form with an 883kW (1200hp) power unit and the same

maximum tractive effort but increased line service speed from 90 to 100km/h (56–62mph), and reduced weight. The first three prototypes appeared from the Bryansk factory in 1960, followed by several pilot batches, and mass production went on from 1967 to 1987 at both Bryansk and Lugansk works. The basic TEM2 has spawned a number of different sub-types with typical Russian suffix letters including M (*modernizirovannyi*), U (*uluchshchennyi*) and T (*tormozhenie*) indicating modernized, improved and electric dynamic braking respectively. Many TEM2 locomotives worked on the building of the BAM line (*Baikalo Amurskaya Magistrale*) – the second trans-Siberia route. Model TEM2U, dating from a 1978 prototype and in production from 1984, has a revised body design of more angular styling as well as technical revisions of the TEM2, while TEM2UT and TEM2T are electric braking versions of both. TEM2M experimented with a Kolomna 6D49 vee-eight configuration power unit in place of the standard

in-line Penza six-cylinder engine; and TEM2US version were built as experiments with electromagnetic adhesion equipment. TEM2UM appeared in prototype form in 1988 and entered series building in the following year with 994kW (1350hp) engines. TEM2s are still found at work in Russia, and also Poland and Cuba and the Baltic States.

TYPE: Co-Co diesel-electric heavy shunter
POWER: 883kW (1200hp) from Penza PD1 series engine
TRACTIVE EFFORT: 206kN (46,350lbf) at 11km/h (6.9mph)
MAX. OPERATING SPEED: 100km/h (62mph)
WEIGHT: 120t (264,600lb)
OVERALL LENGTH: 16.97m (55ft 4in)
GAUGE: 1524mm (5ft)

The American ancestry of the omnipresent Russian TEM-2 is evident – see the Alco Rs 1 (1941).

TEP-60 CO-CO SOVIET RAILWAYS (SZD)

It was not until 1960 that the hard-pressed Soviet locomotive industry got round to producing a

'pure' passenger diesel-electric rather than an adapted freight locomotive, as with the higher

geared TE7 variant of the TE3, and TEP10 based on TE10.

Up to 1985, over 1200 TEP-60s were built, many surviving today in some areas, others held in reserve or stored out of use. They were double-ended cab units, but two prototype examples of a twin-unit version, type 2TEP-60, appeared in 1964, and 116 of these were built between 1966 and 1987, along with some rebuilds from pairs of single units. Kolomna Works built them all, using its own 11D45 two-stroke V16 engines, reputed to be the most fuel-efficient in the Soviet Union. With the advent of the TEP-60, many passenger services could be speeded up, and the numbers of Class S 2-6-2 steam locomotives began to fall rapidly. Despite the TEP-60s being dedicated passenger

units, as was the convention in Russia, no provision was made for any train heating supply. Coaches were self-heated – at this time still from coal-fired stoves or boilers – and the typical long-distance coach still had a lady at one end presiding over a *samovar* from which hot tea could be dispensed.

TYPE: Co-Co diesel electric passenger
POWER: 2208kW (3000hp) from Kolomna 11D45 series engine
TRACTIVE EFFORT: 124kN (27,900lbf) at 47km/h (29.4mph)
MAX. OPERATING SPEED: 160km/h (100mph)
WEIGHT: 129t (284,445lb)
OVERALL LENGTH: 19.25m (62ft 10in)
GAUGE: 1524mm (5ft)

The advent of the TEP-60 passenger units brought about a rapid reduction in the numbers of S-class 2-6-2 steam passenger locomotives.

GE U25B BO-BO VARIOUS RAILROADS

USA 1960

Since 1952, General Electric (GE) had been going it alone in the locomotive market, though still supplying components to Alco. GE had long been a producer of straight electric locomotives, a supplier of electrical components for diesel-electric locomotives, and a builder of small diesel locomotives for switching and industrial service. Now with the U25B road-switcher, it was competing head-to-head with Electro-Motive Division (EMD) in the most lucrative section of the market. 'U' was for 'universal', though the irreverent called the

TYPE: Bo-Bo, diesel-electric
POWER AND OUTPUT: General Electric 7FDL-16 producing 1863kW (2500hp)
TRACTIVE EFFORT: Various
MAX. OPERATING SPEED: Various
WEIGHT: 118 tonnes (260,000lb)
OVERALL LENGTH: 18.339m (60ft 2in)
GAUGE: 1435mm (4ft 8.5in)

locomotives 'U-boats'. The U25B, a four-motor heavy freight locomotive, was to be the first of a long line of such types. It was powered by a 7FDL-16 diesel engine, a design GE licensed from Cooper-Bessemer. With the U25B, GE established its place in the American market, and in 1963 it introduced a bigger six-motor road

Maine Central RR's U25B No. 238 runs in a multi-locomotive set at the head of a long freight train, in August 1987.

diesel, the U25C. One of the largest users of U25Bs was Southern Pacific, which had been looking for more powerful diesel locomotives. The launch of the 'U-boat' sparked off a race between

GE and EMD, in which each sought to be market-leader. By now, Baldwin had given up locomotive building altogether, and Alco was busy diversifying into other industries.

CLASS 212 BO-BO BELGIAN RAILWAYS (SNCB)

BELGIUM 1961

Off the main lines, the SNCB had many unelectrified secondary lines and branches, and a general-purpose diesel-electric locomotive was essential. The

Class 212 (later Class 62) answered this need so well that a total of 231 were built. Conventional Bo-Bo diesel-electrics, they had General Motors

two-stroke diesel engines, suitable for mid-range mixed-traffic duties. They were built in Belgium by Brugeoise et Nivelles and used in multiples on heavy freight trains,

but mostly ran singly on lighter freight and local passenger trains, including push-pull workings from Antwerp and Charleroi. Now mostly withdrawn, several have been sold to private operators in Holland and elsewhere.

TYPE: mixed-traffic main-line diesel-electric
WHEEL ARRANGEMENT: Bo-Bo
POWER: GM 12-567C 12-cylinder V-form diesel, 1050kW (1405bhp), DC generator, four traction motors
TRACTIVE EFFORT: 212kN (47,660lbf)
MAX. OPERATING SPEED: 120km/h (75mph)
WEIGHT: 79t (172,610lb)
OVERALL LENGTH: 16.79m (55ft 1in)
GAUGE: not known

In the 1971 renumbering of SNCB motive power, this became Class 62. They have since been superseded by Class 77.

CLASS 55 'DELTIC' CO-CO BRITISH RAILWAYS (BR)

GREAT BRITAIN 1961

The Type 5 'Deltics' succeeded in winning the British public's admiration, and did so both by performance and appearance, despite supplanting the great steam A4 'Pacifics' on the London–Edinburgh main line. These were British Railways' first diesel locomotives designed to operate at 161kph (100mph). Twenty-two of them replaced 55 Pacific steam locomotives on the

East Coast main line. Unusually at the time, they were bought with service contracts, with English Electric responsible for maintenance. Their lofty streamlined appearance, with high noses and set-back cabs, and deep exhaust roar when accelerating, combined with high speed to gain them popularity. At 2462kW (3300bhp), they were also BR's most powerful diesels, not being

outclassed in power throughout the life of BR, and only equalled over 20 years later by the classes 58 and 59 freight locomotives.
Technically the Napier 'Deltic' diesel engine, of which each locomotive had two, was a complex device, designed to produce high power from a compact size and low specific weight. Its three crankshafts arranged in triangular, delta

formation gave rise to the 'Deltic' nickname. Between each pair of crankshafts were six pairs of opposed pistons operating in six cylinders, 18 in all. They were two-stroke engines, originally designed for high-speed marine application in motor torpedo boats. In other respects, the locomotives were of conventional Co-Co type with six axle-hung traction motors on two three-axle bogies with compensation beams in their primary suspensions. Bogie design and traction motors were shared with the Class 37 locomotives, also designed by English Electric. The class was modified to operate both air- and vacuum-braked trains in the 1970s, ready for allocation of air-braked passenger coaches to the East Coast main line trains. At about the same time, they were fitted with generators for electric train heating (ETH) supply – a quirk of this equipment as fitted was that it provided ETH only when the engine was idling or working full out, since at intermediate speeds the voltage regulator cut off the ETH, causing

TYPE: express passenger main-line diesel-electric
WHEEL ARRANGEMENT: Co-Co
POWER: two Napier 'Deltic' D18.25 diesels with DC generators, totalling 2462kW (3300hp); six EE DC axle-hung traction motors
TRACTIVE EFFORT: 225kN (50,000lbf)
MAX. OPERATING SPEED: 160km/h (100mph)
WEIGHT: 100t (221,760lb)
OVERALL LENGTH: 21.185m (69ft 6in)
GAUGE: 1435mm (4ft 8.5in)

A 'Deltic' locomotive of original appearance, in Brunswick green and yellow, and with a large train identifier screen mounted in front.

some problems in supposedly air-conditioned coaches.

All the Deltics were named, those on the Eastern Region after racehorses, the North Eastern and Scottish Region locomotives less imaginatively after army regiments. The locomotives originally appeared in Brunswick

green livery with a lighter green strip along the base of the body. The complete change to BR corporate blue with yellow nose ends came from 1965, a style that made the locomotives appear heavy. In fact, at 100 tonnes (98 tons) they were actually lightweight mechanical racehorses

compared with many other contemporary British diesel-electric classes.

Throughout their working lives, the Deltics performed magnificently on the fastest trains between London and Newcastle, Edinburgh and Aberdeen, and London to Leeds and Hull, and several 'Deltics' exceeded 4,828,000km (3 million miles) in service. They were the only power rostered regularly for the *Flying Scotsman* from their introduction in 1961 until the High Speed Trains took over from them in 1979. When the last scheduled run came in 1982, there were emotional scenes at London's King's Cross station.

A number of '55s' have been preserved privately and one is in the national collection; three preserved 'Deltics' are permitted to operate on the public network and thus appear on special trains from time to time, with running up to 145km/h (90mph) allowed.

GT3 2C (4-6-0) ENGLISH ELECTRIC

Looking like a modernistic steam locomotive design, this demonstration locomotive was built by English Electric in the hope of convincing the British Railways management of the gas turbine's fuel-saving and performance qualities. Engine construction, on a 4-6-0 locomotive frame, was done in 1953, and was then tested on the Rugby static testing plant, but it was not fully built until 1961. GT3 had a top speed of 145km/h (90mph) and was a powerful performer during road trials over Shap incline.

This one-off experimental engine by no means solved all the problems associated with gas turbine drive, including its noise

and heavy fuel consumption at low speed. But in any case, British Railways had decided for electrification and dieselization, and there was to be no place for turbine drive on UK railways.

TYPE: experimental mixed-traffic gas turbine
WHEEL ARRANGEMENT: 2-C (4-6-0)
POWER: EE EM27L 2014kW (2700hp) gas turbine; mechanical drive
COUPLED WHEEL DIAMETER: 1752mm (5ft 9in)
TRACTIVE EFFORT: 160kN (36,000lbf)
MAX. OPERATING SPEED: 145km/h (90mph)
WEIGHT: 126t (276,640lb)
OVERALL LENGTH: 20.74m (68ft 1in)
GAUGE: 1435mm (4ft 8.5in)

English Electric's experimental GT3 on one of its test runs in 1961. Despite a promising performance, it remained a one-off.

CLASS 35 'HYMEK' B-B BRITISH RAILWAYS (BR)

BR's Western Region, managing to secure some autonomy in locomotive matters, pursued an interest in diesel-hydraulic transmission. Beyer Peacock built 101 of this 'Hymek' (hydro-mechanical) Type 3 design of B-B locomotive, with Maybach engines that delivered 1270kW (1700bhp), giving the class a very favourable weight-to-power ratio. Initially liveried in standard Brunswick

green with a light-green lower bodyside band, and with off-white cab window surrounds, they looked less attractive when painted overall BR blue with yellow ends, from 1965.

Capable of handling fast and heavy South Wales–London expresses, they lasted only until the mid-1970s. By then, the decline in freight traffic was releasing surplus diesel-electric

capacity and the Hymeks, being non-standard, were withdrawn

TYPE: mixed-traffic main-line diesel-hydraulic
WHEEL ARRANGEMENT: B-B
POWER: Bristol-Siddeley/Maybach MD870 16-cylinder V-form diesel, 1270kW (1700bhp), Mekydro K184U torque converter and gearbox unit

despite their good performance. A small number are preserved.

TRACTIVE EFFORT: 205kN (46,600lbf)
MAX. OPERATING SPEED: 145km/h (90mph)
WEIGHT: 75t (165,760lb)
OVERALL LENGTH: 15.76m (51ft 9in)
GAUGE: 1435mm (4ft 8.5in)

CLASS V41 BO-BO HUNGARIAN STATE RAILWAYS (MÁV)

HUNGARY 1961

In order to enable them to run on either 25kV or 15kV current, rather complex Ward Leonard (WL) equipment was installed in this small class of lightweight freight engines. The control system fed two synchronous motors, each driving a DC generator that powered the traction motors.

TYPE: Bo-Bo light duty and shunting
POWER: 1214kW (1649hp)
SUPPLY: 16 or 25kV 50Hz AC
TRACTIVE EFFORT: 152kN (34,200lbf)

MAX. OPERATING SPEED: 80km/h (50mph)
WEIGHT: 74 tonnes (163,170lb)
MAX. AXLE LOAD: 18.5t (40,793lb)

OVERALL LENGTH: 12.29m (40ft 1in)
GAUGE: 1435mm (4ft 8.5in)

Common in industrial applications, the WL apparatus did not adapt well to use in locomotives. This was a pioneer effort, however, as successful multi-current locomotives did not otherwise appear for another three decades. All the class have been withdrawn.

CLASS 121 BO-BO CÓRAS IOMPAIR ÉIREANN (CIE)

IRELAND 1961

CIE looked to America for these main-line diesels in 1960. Ordered from EMD, 15 121s entered service in 1961 and continued in service for more than 40 years, running Dublin–Belfast and Dublin–Cork trains until upgrading of the infrastructure enabled new motive power to be effectively used. The Irish engines were closely based on EMD's SW9 road switcher. Among the differences was a low-profile cab to accommodate the lower clearances in Ireland, and a different bogie type. In modern times, a surviving 121 has been assigned to the Limerick–Limerick Junction push-pull shuttle. Others are used in freight services, including cement trains and seasonal sugar-beet trains.

TYPE: Bo-Bo, diesel-electric
POWER AND OUTPUT: EMD 8-567CR producing 652kW (875hp) for traction
TRACTIVE EFFORT: 156kN (35,000lbf) starting TE; 135kN (30,400lbf) continuous TE at 12.8km/h (8mph)
MAX. OPERATING SPEED: 123km/h (77mph)
WEIGHT: 65t (143,325lbs)
OVERALL LENGTH: 12.141m (39ft 10in)
GAUGE: 1600mm (5ft 3in)

In CIE livery, No. 124 hauls a matching set of passenger coaches on a local working.

CLASS D235 C STATE RAILWAYS (FS)

ITALY 1961

The 'C' wheel formation, equivalent to the steam-powered 0-6-0, was standard for small diesel-engined yard shunters on virtually all European railways. In Italy in 1961, the bulk of shunting in non-electrified yards was still carried out by steam tank engines, but these were being withdrawn as new diesel types came into service. Among these were two 'C' classes, D234 and 235, both with hydraulic transmission, supplied in the case of D235 by Voith of Heidenheim, Germany, with a single torque converter and two fluid couplers.

The final reduction gearing provided two possible ratios, to be engaged while the locomotive was stationary: a lower one for shunting, and a higher one for road work. D235, though with a lower power rating than D234, had lower gearing, smaller coupled wheels – 1070mm (42.2in) compared to 1310mm

(51.5 in) – and a consequently higher tractive effort. D234, with its higher gearing, could manage a higher speed on open track, with a maximum of 60km/h (37mph). These minor differences were significant in operation, depending on requirements and conditions in the large freight yards. Trip workings between

yards were more effectively operated by D234. Forty-five D235s and 37 D234s were brought into service between 1961–71, with engines and mechanical parts supplied by a range of mostly Italian companies, including Breda, Officine Meccanice, and Badoni. All have been replaced by similar but later classes.

TYPE: Diesel-hydraulic shunting locomotive
POWER: Diesel engine rated at 261.2kN (350hp) driving all axles via hydraulic

transmission and coupling rods.
TRACTIVE EFFORT: 143.2kN (32,200lbf)
MAXIMUM OPERATING SPEED: 60km/h (37mph)

TOTAL WEIGHT: 39 tonnes (85,995lb)
MAXIMUM AXLE LOAD: 13t (28,665lb)
OVERALL LENGTH: 9.54m (31ft 4in)
GAUGE: not known

CLASS 1200 BO-BO PORTUGUESE RAILWAYS (CP)

Lightweight diesel-electrics, this single-cab hood unit class was deployed on stopping trains along the Algarve coast and other medium-type passenger workings centred on Lisbon and Porto. Built by Brissonneau & Lotz in France, and relatively low-powered, they were similar to more than 800 built for the French railways. For Portugal, they were fitted to haul vacuum-braked stock. Multiple-working links were not installed. Now displaced by more powerful English Electric locomotives and diesel railcars, the remaining 1200s are scattered throughout Portugal on shunting duties, painted in CP's 'shunting yellow'. When delivered, they were liveried in blue, but spent most of their lives in the standard CP orange with white diagonal stripes across the ends.

TYPE: mixed-traffic main-line diesel-electric
WHEEL ARRANGEMENT: Bo-Bo
POWER UNIT: MGO V 12ASHR 12-cylinder V-form diesel, 615kW (825bhp), DC generator, four traction motors
TRACTIVE EFFORT: 157kN (35,200lbf)
MAX. OPERATING SPEED: 80km/h (50mph)
WEIGHT: 61t (134,180lb)
OVERALL LENGTH: 14.68m (48ft 2in)
GAUGE: 1668mm (5ft 6in)

Portugal's 1668mm (5ft 6in) gauge is a generous one, but, as in Spain, locomotives and rolling stock are built to a European rather than a Russian or American scale.

CLASS K CO-CO SOVIET RAILWAYS (SZD)

Despite the size of their home building programme, the Russian railways were chronically short of up-to-date motive power in the 1960s, particularly for efficient high-power electric traction at 25kV. This was the reason for placing an order with Krupps of Essen, Germany, for 20 locomotives capable of moving 5000-tonne (4921-ton) loads on level track and 3000-tonne (2953-ton) on 1 in 50 grades, in temperatures that could range from -50 to +30°C depending on operating region and season.

Class K stayed in traffic until the late 1970s, as did similarly imported Class Fs from France.

TYPE: Co-Co
POWER: 4965kW (6734hp)
SUPPLY: 25kV 50Hz AC
TRACTIVE EFFORT: 357kN (80,300lbf)
at 48.4km/h (30.2mph)
MAX. OPERATING SPEED: 100km/h (62.1mph)
WEIGHT: 138t (304,290lb)
MAX. AXLE LOAD: 24t (52,920lb)
OVERALL LENGTH: 21.02m (68ft 7in)
GAUGE: 1524mm (5ft)

SERIES 282 2-8-2+2-8-2 SPANISH NATIONAL RAILWAYS (RENFE)

Rather strangely, Europe's last new main-line steam locomotives were not an ultra-modern steam design but a virtually complete replica of a design going back to 1930. In that year, Garratt types had been acquired for passenger and freight work on the Central Aragón Railway from Valencia through Teruel to Calatayud. They must have been considered effective, as these 10 new oil-burners, built under licence by Babcock & Wilcox's Bilbao works, were effectively a re-order of the 282 freight class that had been supplied by the same builders in 1930. With none of the refinements of shape and detail that characterized the post-war Garratts built in England for Africa and Australia, they were employed on the same section of line as their predecessors, and on the same duty, hauling heavy freight.

BOILER PRESSURE: 15kg/cm² (213psi)
CYLINDERS: 440x610mm (17.3x24in)
DRIVING WHEELS: 1200mm (47.2in)
GRATE AREA: 4.2m² (45.2sq ft)
HEATING SURFACE: 197m² (2121sq ft)
SUPERHEATER: 69.4m² (747sq ft)
TRACTIVE EFFORT: 22,226kg (49,000lb)
TOTAL WEIGHT: 170.25t (375,401lb)

KRAUSS-MAFFEI CO-CO SOUTHERN PACIFIC (SP)

Diesel-electric transmission had taken such a hold in the United States that the alternative of diesel-hydraulic was rarely considered and not available except by import from Europe. Southern Pacific, always looking for maximum power whether steam or diesel-engined, decided to explore this option in the early 1960s. For heavy freights over its rugged mountain grades, it wanted engines of more power than US builders were currently offering, and in 1961 SP and mountainous western carrier Denver & Rio Grande Western each imported three diesel-hydraulic locomotives from German manufacturer Krauss-Maffei. These had an engine output of 2984kW (4000hp), with 2570kW (3450hp) available for traction. Two years later, SP imported a second batch of locomotives, in a road-switcher form rather than the earlier carbody design. It also bought some experimental diesel-hydraulic units from Alco. But by the late 1960s, SP dropped its interest in diesel-hydraulic traction technology and turned instead to new high-output diesel-electric designs.

TYPE: Co-Co, diesel-hydraulic
POWER AND OUTPUT: a pair of Maybach 16-cylinder MD870 engines producing 2570kW (3450hp)
TRACTIVE EFFORT: 400kN (90,000lbf)
MAX. OPERATING SPEED: 112km/h (70mph)
WEIGHT: 150t (330,600lb)
OVERALL LENGTH: 20.1m (66ft)
GAUGE: 1435mm (4ft 8.5in)

CHAPTER SIX

TECHNOLOGICAL CHANGES

1962–1981

Up to the 1960s, diesel-electric engines produced Direct Current (DC) electricity by driving a generator. Between the 1960s and 1980s, however, production switched to Alternating Current (AC), as an alternator was smaller and lighter than a generator, and the technology was available to reconvert to DC in the drive motors. Diesel-mechanical and diesel-hydraulic transmissions are still used in some cases, but diesel-electric power dominates non-electrified lines throughout the world. The spread of electrification was stalled by the lack of standardization between national systems or even between companies within a single country. The decision of the engineers, based on particular needs, enthusiasms or prejudices, was supreme. This had made little difference when trains changed engines at the frontier, and may even have been useful in showing the characteristics and effectiveness of different systems. But by the 1970s, trains began to cross frontiers, especially within the European Union rail systems, and the changes of voltage on electrified lines became a challenge to designers. A generation of versatile electric motors appeared, which could adapt to three or four voltage changes in the course of a single journey. During this same period, the manufacture of locomotives and trains became a multinational industry, dominated by a small number of large corporations that had factories in many countries, sometimes combining on major projects, building a range of modular machines that run with only minor variations in different countries.

Against the breathtaking background of the Rocky Mountains, a set of Amtrak F40PH diesel-electric locomotives, dating from1976, hauls the eastbound 'Empire Builder' express at Grizzly, Montana.

CLASS AM9 ELECTRIC MULTIPLE UNITS BRITISH RAILWAYS (BR)

For the overhead-wire electrification of lines from London (Liverpool Street) to Clacton and Walton-on-the-Naze,

BR bought 19 GEC-powered four-car, and four two-car express units. End-gangwayed for through-corridor multiple

working, they were mounted on American-designed Commonwealth-type bogies. Geared for 160km/h (100mph)

working, they were the only UK express electric multiple units (as opposed to outer suburban types) on the 25kV routes. Their status was rewarded by being painted in the lined maroon livery carried by express locomotive hauled stock. Later the class was known as 309. They have been replaced by units with automatic sliding doors.

A four-car set of Class 309 on a London–East Anglia service. This set was painted in a special advertising livery – a practice often used by train operating companies both for promoting their own services and for other products.

TYPE: four-car electric multiple unit express trains (also two-car)
POWER: 25,000V 50Hz AC overhead line collection, one power car, four GEC 210kW (280hp) axle-mounted DC traction motors, tap changer control
MAX. OPERATING SPEED: 160km/h (100mph)
WEIGHT PER VEHICLE: 35 to 60t (78,400 to 134,400lb)
MAX AXLE LOAD: not known
OVERALL LENGTH: 19.76m (64ft 10in) outer cars; 19.66m (64ft 6in) inner cars

CLASS 17 'CLAYTON' BO-BO BRITISH RAILWAYS (BR)

Though classified as a mixed-traffic type, this locomotive was used almost wholly on freight trains. It had two diesel engines under low bonnets, with a central cab providing two driving positions, depending on the direction of travel. Electrical equipment was from Clayton (88 locomotives) and Crompton

Parkinson. In all, 117 were built, and allocated to southern Scotland and north-east England, working

mostly on coal trains from colliery sidings to local marshalling yards, but the type quickly gained a

reputation for unreliability. All were withdrawn by 1971 after very short lives. One is preserved.

TYPE: mixed-traffic main-line diesel-electric
WHEEL ARRANGEMENT: Bo-Bo
POWER UNITS (2): Paxman 6ZHXL

diesel, 670kW (900bhp), DC generator, four traction motors
TRACTIVE EFFORT: 178kN (40,000lbf)
MAX. OPERATING SPEED: 95km/h (60mph)

WEIGHT: 69t (152,320lb)
OVERALL LENGTH: 15.24m (50ft 7in)
GAUGE: 1435mm (4ft 8.5in)

CLASS 47 CO-CO BRITISH RAILWAYS (BR)

For most of the later twentieth century, the Class 47 was the backbone of British railway diesel operations. Designed by the Brush company of Loughborough, and with Brush traction equipment, it was by far the largest class numerically of non-steam main-line locomotives ever to operate in the UK, with a total of 512 built. Equally at home on 145km/h (90mph) express trains and on bulk freights, the Class 47 could be seen anywhere between Penzance and Inverness. Their Brush traction equipment enabled them to exert high tractive effort, thus improving the acceleration performance of express trains as well as enabling the haulage of heavy freights. They took over the top link passenger work on the Western Region (shared with Class 52), on cross-country routes and in Scotland. On the East Coast main line, they backed up the 'Deltic' fleet, and performed reliably on overnight sleeping car trains. Other 47s worked 'merry-go-round' coal trains between collieries and

power stations, for which they were modified with slow-speed control for automated loading and unloading of wagons. Staple power for the growing oil train network across the UK, they also became the regular traction for container trains, part of the burgeoning network of Freightliner Limited.

Inside a Class 47 was a Sulzer twin-crankshaft 12-cylinder diesel engine driving Brush main and auxiliary generators, a steam heating boiler (in the original version), and a copious radiator bank. The six direct-current traction motors were axle-hung, nose-suspended. Five locomotives were delivered in the mid-1960s with Sulzer V-form engines of type 12LVA24 engines of 1975kW (2650hp). These non-standard engines were subsequently replaced by standard ones. Original maximum speed of 150kph (95mph) was exceeded only when 16 locomotives were equipped for the Scottish Region's InterCity push-pull services between Glasgow and Edinburgh. Classed as 47/7, they

were uprated for 160km/h (100mph) running. Many locomotives on InterCity services were fitted with larger fuel tanks, thus extending their operating range – a modification made possible by the removal of redundant water tanks for steam train heating.

When built, the locomotives were liveried in overall Brunswick green with a mid-green band around the centre of the bodysides. They later received the standard rail blue. In the 1980s and 1990s, the different BR businesses painted them in their own colours, and after privatization many were painted in Virgin red with white stripes. A small fleet of locomotives is operated now by Fragonset Limited on a spot hire basis. These are black with smart maroon lining edged in gold.

Withdrawals of 47s are proceeding apace. In the 2000s, the class has dwindled drastically in numbers, but remaining 47s were still being occasionally called on to haul First Great Western's London–Penzance sleeper service

in 2006, and in late 2006 some 69 were still operational. However, 33 of the class were re-engined from 1998 with re-conditioned General Motors 645-series engines and Brush alternators extracted from withdrawn Class 56s, the new engines being reclassified Class 57, thus extending their lives by up to 15 years. They work Freightliner trains; others are kept as high-speed train rescue units, nicknamed 'Thunderbirds'.

TYPE: mixed-traffic main-line diesel-electric
WHEEL ARRANGEMENT: Co-Co
POWER UNIT: Sulzer 12LDA28C 12-cylinder twin-bank diesel, 2050kW (2750bhp) reduced to 1925kW (2580bhp); Brush DC generator and six axle-hung DC traction motors
TRACTIVE EFFORT: 265kN (60,000lbf)
MAX. OPERATING SPEED: 160km/h (100mph)
WEIGHT: 111 to 125t (243,765 to 274,510lb)
OVERALL LENGTH: 19.355m (63ft 6in)
GAUGE: 1435mm (4ft 8.5in)

WDM2 CLASS CO-CO INDIAN RAILWAYS (IR)

In 1961, the Diesel Locomotive Works (DLW) at Varanasi was established, and very soon became extremely busy in producing the many members of this class, which was eventually to reach a total of some 2700. The spread of diesels on the Indian broad gauge began in 1958–59, with the import of 100 locomotives from Alco, classed as WDM1. Class WDM2 units were also first imported as complete model RSD29 locomotives from Alco, the original order being for 40, followed by an order for 212, 12 of which were supplied to DLW in completely knocked-down kit form for local assembly. Having thus gained experience with the type, DLW went on to produce WDM2 in volume, resulting in a number of different versions for Indian Railways, and also export units. Earlier units have 298kW (405hp) GE 752 traction motors, later superseded by locally supplied motors of 320kW (435hp). Prime mover was a 16-cylinder Alco 251-series engine, turbo-charged, four-stroke with open combustion chambers and solid-fuel injection, supplying power to a DC shunt-wound, 12-pole main generator, which transmitted current to the six axle-hung, nose-suspended

traction motors. They ran on well-tried Alco 'trimount' bogies. Cooling equipment, at the hood-end, incorporated an eddy current clutch drive to the vertical-spindle roof-mounted fan; the clutch was driven by a thermostatically controlled extension of the engine crankshaft.

Class WDM2A were modified with air train-braking equipment (instead of vacuum) after entry into service, while CLass WDM2B had this from new. WDM2C was a modification carried out by DCW Patiala with a General Electric turbocharger, Woodward governor, and roller-bearing suspension, the last-mentioned change being made to overcome one of the weakest points of the design. Under the most recent locomotive classification system, new WDM2C conversions are now WDM3A. (Confusingly, there is another, newer series of WDM2C with 2281kW/3100hp engines. These are numbered in the 14000 series.) DCW Patiala is also modernizing some units with alternating current traction alternators replacing the direct-current main generator. Class WDM2s modified for push-pull passenger work are described as Class WDM2D. A number of Class WDM2s constructed in the

late 1970s have a different body style, with the short hood extended laterally to full width, and they were known to train crews as 'Jumbos'. Another local modification is a repositioned cab, right forward at one end, involving relocating items of equipment such as the dynamic brake resistor grid, behind the new cab. Such alterations apart, the majority of Class WDM2s have both short and long high-hood sections on either side of the driving cab in traditional early North American road switcher styling.

On 11 March 1969, the 'Rajdhani Express' from New Delhi to Howrah was inaugurated. This fully air-conditioned train, which was booked to run at a top speed of 120 km/h (75mph), broke the old 100km/h (62mph) limit of the Indian Railways and heralded a new era of speed and comfort. Initially, the train was formed of nine coaches with two generator cars cum brake vans, an air-conditioned pantry car and six air-conditioned chair cars. Hauled by a WDM4 diesel-electric locomotive, it took 17hrs, 10 mins to complete the 1441km (895-mile) journey with one immediate stoppage at Kanpur and a crew-changing stop at Mughalsarai. Later, the

formation was increased to 18 coaches by introducing sleeper and first-class coaches along with the original cars. To pull this formation, paired WDM2 were employed, an arrangement that continued till the mid-1980s, when the WAP1 electric class could be used on the Rajdhani service.

Class WDM7 is a lighter, lower-power version designed for branch-line operation. Only 15 were built in the late 1980s and are 1492kW (2000hp) with the 12-cylinder Alco 12-251 rather than the 16-cylinder 1914kW (2600hp) 16-251 of Class WDM2, and are limited to 100km/h (62mph) maximum speed instead of 120km/h (75mph). The last five WDM7s were built new with traction alternators, and 105km/h (65.6mph) maximum speed. All class WDM7 are now generally used on shunting duties.

With such a large quantity built and in service, Class WDM2s may be found throughout the subcontinent as the default motive power for freight, and they also handle many passenger workings. The DLW factory and India Railways main depots seem likely to continue to improve, modify and alter the basic type, which is still very much the work-horse of Indian railway operations.

TYPE: Co-Co diesel-electric
POWER: 1914kW (2600hp) from Alco 16-251 series engine
TRACTIVE EFFORT: 241kN (54,120lbf) at 18km/h (11.3mph)
MAX. OPERATING SPEED: 120km/h (75mph)
WEIGHT: 113t (249,165lb)
OVERALL LENGTH: 17.120m (55ft 10in)
GAUGE: 1676mm (5ft 6in)

Coupled nose to nose, two high-hood WDM-2 engines on express passenger service with one of Indian Railways' immensely long inter-regional trains.

TG400 AND TG300 C-C SOVIET RAILWAYS (SZD)

In an experiment with diesel-hydraulic traction, the Russian railways acquired two high-power hydraulic-transmission prototypes from Germany. The larger and more powerful was the TG400

from Henschel with two 16-cylinder Maybach MD870 engines and Mekydro transmissions. This machine, TG400-01, can be considered as technically equivalent to the Krauss-Maffei

TG300
TYPE: C-C diesel-hydraulic prototype
POWER: 2208kW (3000hp) from two Maybach MD655 series engines
TRACTIVE EFFORT: 187kN (42,020lbf) at 22.8km/h (14.3mph)

MAX. OPERATING SPEED: 140km/h (87mph)
WEIGHT: 109t (24,030lb)
OVERALL LENGTH: 22.06m (72ft 0in)
GAUGE: 1524mm (5ft 0in)

TG400
TYPE: C-C diesel-hydraulic prototype
POWER: 2944kW (4000hp)
TRACTIVE EFFORT: 303kN (68,200lbf) at 20kmh

MAX. OPERATING SPEED: 160km/h (100mph)
WEIGHT: 112t (246,960lb)
OVERALL LENGTH: 22.98m (75ft)
GAUGE: 1524mm (5ft)

units delivered in 1961 to Southern Pacific and Denver & Rio Grande in the United States (although these had Voith transmissions). TG300 was built by MaK to a Deutz design with two

Maybach MD655 12-cylinder engines, and Voith hydraulic transmissions. Little was heard of either type after arrival in Russia, although both appear to have remained in existence until 1967.

CLASS 352 B-B SPANISH RAILWAYS (RENFE)

This year saw the introduction of the Talgo train concept, for which this locomotive was specially built. *Tren Articulado Ligero Goicoechea Oriol* (Talgo) was a Spanish company formed to design and build lightweight articulated passenger cars, developed by Goicoechea and backed by Oriol from 1942. The new train-sets, known as 2000T trains, were low-profile vehicles with a unique articulation system. The Class 352s were lightweight, single-cab, low-profile machines to match the passengers cars. German-designed, they were built in two batches by Krauss-Maffei of Germany and Babcock & Wilcox in Spain. The 10 locomotives had Maybach engines and Mekydro hydraulic transmissions. The 2000T cars were each 11.1m (36ft 3in) long, operated in 10- or 15-car sets.

Initial services were between Madrid and Irun/Hendaye,

Barcelona, Bilbao and Seville. Services further expanded in 1968, joined by T3000 sets and double-ended locomotives of Class 353, which had 1650kW (2242hp) engines and were capable of 180km/h (112.5mph). Electrification and high-speed (AVE) routes gradually eroded the need for Talgo diesels, and it was expected to eliminate them altogether by 2001. But into 2002 three 352s and two 353s were still in use on daily services from Madrid.

TYPE: B-B diesel-hydraulic Talgo
POWER: 2200kW (2990hp) from two Maybach MD655 engines
TRACTIVE EFFORT: 173kN (39,000lbf)
MAX. OPERATING SPEED: 140km/h (87mph)
WEIGHT: 74t (163,170lb)
OVERALL LENGTH: 17.45m (56ft 11in)
GAUGE: 1676mm (5ft 6in)

The wide 1676mm (5ft 6in) Spanish conventional gauge accentuates the squat appearance of the diesel-hydraulic 'Talgo' train.

EMD GP30 BO-BO VARIOUS US RAILWAYS

By the early 1960s, locomotive manufacture in the United States was a two-horse race between General Motors' Electro-Motive Division (EMD) and General Electric (GE). Each was continually upping the horsepower output of

In the yards at Denver, Colorado, a pair of Rio Grande GP30 locos are ready to pick up their train.

their top-performing diesels in the struggle to keep or grow market share. Also by now, many railroads were looking to replace diesels acquired in the 1940s. In 1959, EMD's 1492kW (2000hp) GP20 superseded the 306kW

(1750hp) GP9; then in 1961, the 1676kW (2250hp) GP30 in turn replaced the GP20, spurred no doubt by by the arrival of the GE U25B, with its 1679kW (2500hp) engine. For the GP30, an additional 186kW (250hp) was coaxed out of the 567-series engine. The GP30's distinctive appearance set it apart from other road switchers, featuring a semi-streamlined cab with a hood extension reaching over the top. The hood was airtight with a single inertial intake for electrical cooling. GP30s were ordered in both high-nose and low-nose variations, as well as a cabless, GP30B 'slave' type used only by Union Pacific. Although built for fast freight, as with most types, new models displaced them on to local and short-haul services. The GP30 was something of a stop-gap offering, in production for just two years before the 1865kW (2500hp) GP35, with a new

engine, was introduced. But 948 units were sold, outselling the U25B by almost two to one. As with many other diesel-electric types of the 1960s, a large number of the GP30s have been rebuilt or reconditioned, either at the EMD shops or by other workshops like Morrison Knudsen (now part of Motive Power Industries), or, like the Santa Fe at Cleburne, Texas, doing the job for themselves. In renewed form, a number of GP30s still work.

TYPE: Bo-Bo, diesel-electric
POWER AND OUTPUT: EMD 16-567D3 producing 1676kW (2250hp)
TRACTIVE EFFORT: 227 kN (51,000 lbf) at 19.2km/h (12 mph)
MAX. OPERATION SPEED: 105km/h (65mph)
WEIGHT: 118t (260,000 lb)
OVERALL LENGTH: 17.12m (56ft 2in)
GAUGE: 1435mm (4ft 8.5in)

SERIES 2 2-10-2 RIO TURBIO INDUSTRIAL RAILWAY (RFIRT)

After public railways had gone over wholly to building and using diesel and electric motive power, some industrial railways continued to build steam locomotives. A striking example comes from one of the world's most southerly railways, a 750mm (29.5in) gauge line, 255km (158 miles) long, completed in 1951 and linking a coal mine to the Atlantic coast. It was the unlikely scene of a new

leap in steam technology when, in 1957, L.D. Porta became manager, and applied his own gas producer firebox and exhaust system to three out of ten 2-10-2 Mitsubishi locomotives supplied in 1956. He left the RFIRT in 1960, but the remaining engines, plus 10 new ones delivered by Mitsubishi in 1963, were fitted with his improvements. The nominal tractive effort was increased by 30 per cent, fuel consumption was

greatly reduced and reliability increased. Porta's work was to be fundamental to the rebuilt Class 25 of the South African Railways in 1981. Fifteen of the 2-10-2s were

still in service in 1992, but diesels took over soon afterwards. One of the 2-10-2s was restored to running order by 2006, and plans are in hand to reinstate others.

BOILER PRESSURE: 15.7kg/cm² (224psi)
CYLINDERS: 420x440mm (16.5x17.3in)
DRIVING WHEELS: 850mm (33.5in)
GRATE AREA: 2.4m² (25.8sq ft)
HEATING SURFACE: 91.9m² (989.4sq ft)

SUPERHEATER: 30.3m² (326.2sq ft)
TRACTIVE EFFORT: 12,441kg (27,433lb)
TOTAL WEIGHT: 48.5t (106,942lb)
(engine only)

CLASS 04 BO-BO BULGARIAN STATE RAILWAYS (BDZ)

These Austrian-built diesel-hydraulics were BDZ's first main-line diesels in service and were used throughout the system on freight and passenger duties. A single prototype was delivered in 1959,

(ÖBB number 2020.01 – preserved today outside Wien Sud station after withdrawal in 1980) and from 1963, 50 units were delivered to Bulgaria. The BDZ units were gradually withdrawn through the 1990s.

TYPE: B-B diesel-hydraulic
POWER: 1620kW (2200hp) from two SGP T12 series engines
TRACTIVE EFFORT: 187kN (42,000lbf)
MAX. OPERATING SPEED: 120kmh (75mph)

WEIGHT: 82 or 83.5 tonnes (180,810lb or 184,118lb)
OVERALL LENGTH: 18.24m (59ft 6in)
GAUGE: 1435mm (4ft 8.5in)

CLASSES 68000 AND 68500 A1A-A1A FRENCH NATIONAL RAILWAYS (SNCF)

In the early 1960s, the SNCF began to appreciate that its range of diesel power was inadequate for the work required on non-electrified lines where steam power was being phased out. This resulted in orders for the Sulzer-engined Class 68000 and the very similar but more powerful 68500, with AGO engines. Over 100, of which four-fifths were Class 68000, were supplied by five different manufacturers – CAFL, CEM, Sulzer, SACM and Fives-Lille-Cail. Unlike later French diesel-electrics, which are of the *monomoteur* type with one traction motor on each bogie, these locomotives have traction motors on the outer axles on each bogie, producing the A1A-A1A

TYPE: mixed-traffic main-line diesel-electric
WHEEL ARRANGEMENT: A1A-A1A
POWER: Sulzer 12LVA24 12-cylinder V-form diesel, 1950kW (2615bhp) Class 68000; AGO 12DSHR 12-cylinder V-form diesel, 1985kW (2660bhp) Class 68500;

DC generator; four DC traction motors
TRACTIVE EFFORT: 298kN (66,995lbf)
MAX. OPERATING SPEED: 130km/h (80mph)
WEIGHT: to 104t (228,400lb)
OVERALL LENGTH: 17.91m (58ft 9in)
GAUGE: 1435mm (4ft 8.5in)

wheel arrangement. They were first intended for mixed-traffic duties and were fitted with train-heating boilers, but with the spread of electrification and electric train heating these were later removed.

The locomotives were then restricted to heavy freight work in areas of operation extending from Normandy and Brittany to central France on the Rouen–

Le Mans–Tours route and across the eastern part of the country between Paris, Troyes and Belfort, with some duties in the Vosges mountains. In appearance, the classes 68000 and 68500 are heavily stylized at the front ends, and with bodyside equipment room grilles styled into an arrow formation. Lining out is with two white lines at one end and one at

the other, which gives the end views different aspects when seen approaching. Although SNCF trains used to run with two headlamps, these locomotives came with the 'triangle of lights' arrangement of head lamps, a development now standard across Europe. It enables an approaching train to be easily distinguished at night from any adjacent road traffic.

The French diesel locomotive fleet had remained relatively stable since the 1960s construction phase. Indeed, nothing new had appeared between 1975 and the end of the century. Large-scale renewal of the stock is now in hand, and all of Class 68000 were withdrawn by 2006.

Six axles, four driving motors – No. 68043 on a cross-country passenger service, in its original blue-and-silver paintwork.

CLASS X4300 DIESEL MULTIPLE UNITS FRENCH NATIONAL RAILWAYS (SNCF)

Familiar throughout France, these diesel units comprising power car and driver-trailer were the standard trains for local services on non-electrified routes. Each power car has one underfloor diesel engine driving a six-speed mechanical gearbox linked to the axles on one bogie. The time taken for each gear

TYPE: diesel multiple unit 2-car set
POWER: Poyaud or Saurer horizontal diesel engine, 320kW (430hp); fluid flywheel; six-speed epicyclic gearbox;

cardan shaft to gearbox on axle
MAX. OPERATING SPEED: 120km/h (75mph)
WEIGHT: 35 to 36t (76,850 to 79,060lb)

power cars; 23t (50,510lb) trailers
OVERALL LENGTH: 21.24m (69ft 8in)
GAUGE: 1435mm (4ft 8.5in)

change, particularly while in the lower gears, makes for slow acceleration. Nonetheless, nearly 900 of these and later

derivatives were built. Many of the old branches they worked have been closed, and elsewhere they are rapidly

being replaced by more modern diesel-electric units capable of greater acceleration and road speed.

CLASS V43 BO-BO HUNGARIAN STATE RAILWAYS (MÁV)

HUNGARY 1963

The Western European consortium known as the 50Hz Group designed this class, whose first seven locomotives were built by Krupp in Germany with French monomotor bogies. The rest of what was quite a large class of 379 were built under licence in Hungary by Ganz MÁVAG. V43 may be found everywhere as the default motive power for all but the heaviest passenger and freight traffic on the Heygeshalom route. The class also operates for the GYSEV railways with 15 locos, all acquired from MÁV. From 1999 onwards, a modification programme adapted some engines as Class V43.2 for push-pull suburban work. Some V43s are still at work.

TYPE: Bo-Bo multipurpose
POWER: 2290kW (3111hp)
SUPPLY: 25kV 50Hz AC
TRACTIVE EFFORT: 265kN (59,625lbf)
MAX. OPERATING SPEED: 130km/h (81.3mph)

WEIGHT: 80t (176,400lb)
MAX. AXLE LOAD: 20t (44,100lb)
OVERALL LENGTH: 15.7m (51ft 2in)
GAUGE: 1435mm (4ft 8.5in)

Versatile V43 mixed-traffic locomotive No. 322 of the GYSEV Railway system leaves the marshalling yard at Csorna, Hungary, with a freight train, on 20 August 2003.

CLASS M61 CO-CO HUNGARIAN STATE RAILWAYS (MÁV)

HUNGARY 1963

Another manifestation of the six-axle locomotive running in Denmark as the MX (see 1960) appeared in Hungary during a MÁV modernization drive. Unable to obtain main-line diesel locomotives in Hungary, MÁV obtained permission to order 20 Co-Co diesel-electrics with EMD engines from Nohab in Sweden. They worked express trains to the south out of Budapest Deli station. Displaced by electrification, they spent their last years based at Tapolca depot working passenger trains in the area to the west of

TYPE: Mixed-traffic main-line diesel-electric
WHEEL ARRANGEMENT: Co-Co
POWER: GM 16-567D1 16-cylinder V-form two-stroke diesel, 1435kW (1925bhp); DC generator; six axle-hung DC traction motors

TRACTIVE EFFORT: 198kN (44,510lbf)
MAX. OPERATING SPEED: 105km/h (65mph)
WEIGHT: 106 tonnes (232,785lb)
OVERALL LENGTH: 18.9m (62ft)
GAUGE: 1435mm (4ft 8.5in)

Lake Balaton on trains to and from Székesfehérvár. The last scheduled service run by a locomotive of this much-appreciated class was in December 2000. Two are still in working order and others are under restoration.

Only four M61 locomotives were equipped for electric train heating. One was No. 020, seen here on a passenger service.

CLASS VL80 BO-BO+BO-BO SOVIET RAILWAYS (SZD)

With heavy trains and long-distance workings, the Soviet locomotive designers clung to the twin-unit with a cab at each end, already familiar from other mass-produced classes. Well over 4000 of VL80 and its derivatives were built at the Novocherkassk factory, with production continuing into the 1990s. This was the first mass-produced twin-unit AC rectifier design for 25kV operation, and the locomotive bodies were of similar external design to the single-unit six-axle Class VL60. Only 25 of the the basic Class VL80 were built, with mercury arc rectifiers, but the bulk of production were Class VL80K locomotives, provided with more up-to-date silicon (*kremnievyi*) rectifiers, and Class VL80T with electric resistance (*tormozhenie reostatnoe*) braking (of which 718 and 1073, respectively, were constructed). Sub-class VL80R followed with electric regenerative (*tormozhenie rekuperativnoe*) braking. Series building of type VL80S started in 1980, equipped for multiple-unit operation, and these accounted for around 3000 of the total.

Several other experimental versions appeared over time. The various main versions (VL80K, VL80T, VL80R, VL80S) remain in active freight service today throughout the Russian AC electrified network.

TYPE: Bo-Bo+Bo-Bo twin unit freight
POWER: 3160kW (4293hp)
SUPPLY: 25kV 50Hz AC
TRACTIVE EFFORT: 220kN (49,500lbf) at 52km/h (32.5mph)
MAX. OPERATING SPEED: 110km/h (68.3mph)
WEIGHT: 92t (202,860lb)
MAX. AXLE LOAD: 23t (50,715lb)
OVERALL LENGTH: 16.42m (53ft 7in)
GAUGE: 1524mm (5ft)

Message on a stick – instructions are passed up to a VL 80 driver before departure. With more than 4000 built, locomotives of this type are seen all over Russia.

CLASS DM3 1-DO-DO-DO-1 SWEDISH RAILWAYS (SJ)

By 1963, the original electric locomotives of the Lapland line had been doing heavy haulage for more than 40 years in some cases. (The line was the Kiruna–Luleå and Kiruna–Narvik iron-ore railway across the far north of Sweden and penetrating a few miles into Norway, pulling iron-ore trains east and west from Kiruna.) This line has always required special heavy motive power, and new locomotives were badly needed. Even in 1963,

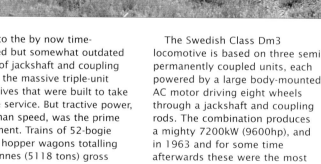

TYPE: heavy freight triple-unit electric locomotive
POWER: 15,000V 16.67Hz AC overhead line collection; 7200kW (9600hp); body-mounted AC traction motor on each unit driving jackshaft and eight coupled wheelsets
WHEEL ARRANGEMENT: 1D+D+D1
TRACTIVE EFFORT: 940kN (211,320lbf)
MAX. OPERATING SPEED: 75km/h (47mph)
WEIGHT: 270t (592,940lb)
MAX AXLE LOAD: not known
OVERALL LENGTH: 35.25m (105ft 10in)
GAUGE: 1435mm (4ft 8.5in)

SJ kept to the by now time-honoured but somewhat outdated system of jackshaft and coupling rods for the massive triple-unit locomotives that were built to take over the service. But tractive power, rather than speed, was the prime requirement. Trains of 52-bogie iron-ore hopper wagons totalling 5200 tonnes (5118 tons) gross operate on both single-track routes several times each day.

The Swedish Class Dm3 locomotive is based on three semi-permanently coupled units, each powered by a large body-mounted AC motor driving eight wheels through a jackshaft and coupling rods. The combination produces a mighty 7200kW (9600hp), and in 1963 and for some time afterwards these were the most powerful locomotives in the world. The Dm3s are now owned by the

Beside Kiruna's lake, a Dm3 passes with an ore train in 2002. Traffic management systems ensure maximum use of the single track line.

mining company LKAB, through its subsidiary MTAB. New ADtranz-built IORE 101 Co-Co+Co-Co locomotives are now on stream, these being rated at 10,800kW (14,675hp) (see 2000).

ALCO C-420 CO-CO VARIOUS RAILROADS

Alco as a company was already diversifying away from locomotive building by the 1960s, but in 1963 it was still competing, though well behind the market leaders, and brought out its new 'Century' line as rivals to the new locomotives offered by Electro Motive Division and General Electric. In order to win new sales, the builders had to present a compelling argument that new diesels would have a significant advantage over the previous generation of locomotives. They opted for 'unit reduction' as their prime sales angle – the offering of increased power units, powerful enough for three locomotives to do the work of five of the previous generation. Trains were getting heavier, and adding to the numbers of locomotives on a train increases the odds of an on-the-road failure with each unit added. Also, three locomotives require less maintenance than five. For Alco, there was also the reliability factor. Their diesels had done less well than those from General Motors in the first generation; while poorer reliability was not the

One of Long Island Railroad's C-420 locos, No, 225, intended primarily for passenger service but seen here on a track maintenance train.

only cause of lesser sales, Alco considered it critical to future success to improve reliability substantially. The Century series featured numerous features aimed at this aspect. Much work was done on the 251-series engine to improve its reliability and reduce internal stresses. A major innovation, though shared with other builders, was the use of a pressurized hood cover; all the access doors were sealed, and air could enter the engine compartment only through filters. Filtered air was ducted to the traction motors to cool them; another duct led to the generator compartment to cool the main and auxiliary generators. The waste air

from this was directed into the engine compartment, pressurizing it and preventing outside air and dirt from entering, before exiting through vents in the far end.

At the time of the Century line launch, there were three locomotives in the range. These were the 1492kW (2000hp), four-axle Century 420; the 1765kW (2400hp), four-axle Century 424; and the 1765kW (2400hp) six-axle Century 624. The latter was never built, and the initial six-axle unit was the Century 628 with 2022kW (2750hp) of output.

Later additions to the Century range included the four-axle Century 425 (with uprated generator), the 2238kW (3000hp)

Century 630 and a large switcher, the Century 415. The six-axle range added a 2238kW (3000hp) Century 630 (see 1965), and the 2686kW (3600hp) Century 636. Still using the 251-series engine, the 'C' improvements were largely a matter of styling and minor technological aspects. The C-420 was a road switcher designed for freight or passenger service, similar to the 1492kW (2000hp) RS-32 that it effectively replaced. A longer low hood than other Century types quickly identifies most C-420s. Long Island Rail Road had a fleet of high-nose C-420s, which closely resembled the Alco RS-11 save for minor styling attributes and air-intake

placement. One of the last users of C-420s is Arkansas & Missouri, which continues to employ its Alco fleet in daily freight service, but few others remain in use. The Century range was a strong claimant in the locomotive market, but it failed to command enough share to be sustainable.

TYPE: Co-Co, diesel-electric
POWER AND OUTPUT: Alco 12-cylinder 251C producing 1492kW (2000hp)
TRACTIVE EFFORT: N/A
MAX. OPERATING SPEED: N/A
WEIGHT: N/A
OVERALL LENGTH: N/A
GAUGE: 1435mm (4ft 8.5in)

GE U50C CO-CO+CO-CO UNION PACIFIC RAILROAD (UP)   USA 1963

Like Southern Pacific and other long-distance haulers, UP was searching for higher-power locomotives in the early 1960s. Double-unit diesels were far more common in Russia than in the United States, but General Electric (GE) supplied two varieties for the railroad to try out. The first were U50s (sometime described as U50Ds), which rode on four sets of Bo trucks in a Bo-Bo+Bo-Bo

TYPE: Co-Co, diesel-electric
POWER AND OUTPUT: A pair of 7FDL-12 diesel engines producing 3730kW (5000hp)
TRACTIVE EFFORT: N/A
MAX. OPERATING SPEED: N/A
WEIGHT: N/A
OVERALL LENGTH: 24.079m (79 ft)
GAUGE: 1435mm (4ft 8.5in)

arrangement like that of UP's early gas-electric turbines. These were built between 1963 and 1965. The later kind used a more common Co-Co wheel arrangement and were built between 1969 and 1971. Both delivered 3730kW (5000hp), but while the earlier locomotives used a

Ready for handover at the manufacturer's works in 1964, a new U50C unit with two 16-cylinder engines. Ten were built in this unusual form.

pair of 7FDL-16 diesels, the U50Cs had smaller 7FDL-12 engines. All of these big GE's had unusually tall cabs with almost no nose section.

Availability of more power in a single frame, and of more efficient multiple-working, made it unnecessary to pursue the concept.

CLASS 2043 AND 2143 B-B AUSTRIAN STATE RAILWAYS (ÖBB)

German enthusiasm for diesel-hydraulic transmission extended into Austria, and one result was this very successful class of mixed-traffic locomotives. Single-engined diesel-hydraulics with Voith transmission, they were until the arrival of Class 2016 the most powerful diesels in Austria. Jenbach were builders of Class 2043, and SGP of 2143. In configuration, they are full-body-width twin-cab locomotives. They

are liveried in the standard ÖBB red with a cream band around the base of the bodysides and ends, and with dark grey surrounds to the cab windows. Until quite recently, about 160 of these useful if modestly sized mixed-traffic locomotives were employed on non-electrified secondary routes. They had one international duty, on the route from Innsbruck via Brennero to San Candido and Lienz, entailing

a section of travel in Italy. Four of the Class 2043s were modified with magnetic track brakes for

the now-closed Leoben to Hieflau route. Withdrawals of both classes are under way.

TYPE: mixed-traffic main-line diesel-hydraulic
WHEEL ARRANGEMENT: B-B
POWER: Jenbach LM1500 (class 2043) or SGP T12c (2143) V-form diesel, 1100kW (1475bhp); Voith L830 rU2 torque co-nvert-er; cardan shafts to gearboxes on axles

TRACTIVE EFFORT: 197kN (44,285lbf)
MAX. OPERATING SPEED: 100 to 110km/h (63 to 69 mph)
WEIGHT: 68t (149,335lb)
OVERALL LENGTH: 14.76 to 15.8m (48ft 5in to 51ft 10in)
GAUGE: 1435mm (4ft 8.5in)

CLASS 42 BO-BO BULGARIAN RAILWAYS (BDZ)

Widely used on both passenger and freight duties, the 90 locomotives of this class were built by Skoda of Plzen, Czechoslovakia, with modern electrical equipment that included silicon current rectifiers and tap changer control. Their rather startling cab design marked one of the earliest applications of glass-reinforced plastic to locomotive construction. Skoda built essentially similar machines for domestic use by CSD, and some are still in in fleet service on both Czech and Slovakian railways as classes 230 and 240.

TYPE: Bo-Bo mixed-traffic
POWER: 3200kW (4348hp)
SUPPLY: 25kV 50Hz AC
TRACTIVE EFFORT: 250kN (56250lbf)
MAX. OPERATING SPEED: 110km/h (68.3mph)
WEIGHT: 85t (187,425lb)
MAX. AXLE LOAD: 21.5t (47,408lb)
OVERALL LENGTH: 16.44m (53ft 8in)
GAUGE: 1435mm (4ft 8.5in)

By 2005, only 7 of the Class 42 remained in service, based at Varna and Kaspichan, and used on freight trains. All had remodelled bodywork replacing the original 'plastic' end design.

CLASS 749 BO-BO CZECHOSLOVAK RAILWAYS (CSD)

Between 1964 and 1970, 312 of these Bo-Bo diesel-electrics were built by CKD of Plzen. Specified to equal the performance of Class 475.1 and 477.0 steam locomotives, the design was successful and effective. Originally they were designated T478.1, which had steam heating boilers

for mixed-traffic work, and T478.2 without heating, for freight. On the break-up of CSD, Czech Railways (CD) took 145 and 81 respectively of these two classes, and Slovak Railways (ZSR) took a total of 43 and 27. The ZSR machines are unaltered, but from 1992 CD equipped 60 locomotives with

electric train heating and classified them as 749.
Class 749s have passenger duties over some highly scenic routes north of Olomouc over the Jesenick mountains, in the Liberec and Karlovy Vary areas, and around Ceske Budejovice. On both systems, the type is outliving

newer 753s as the latter are less reliable with rather higher fuel consumption. Two prototypes are already preserved as 'museum locomotives'.

TYPE: Bo-Bo diesel-electric
POWER: 1102kW (1500hp) from CKD K6S310DR series engine
TRACTIVE EFFORT: 185kN (41,624lbf)
MAX. OPERATING SPEED: 100km/h (62mph)
WEIGHT: 75t (165,375lb)
OVERALL LENGTH: 16.5m (54ft 2in)
GAUGE: 1435mm (4ft 8.5in)

As part of the Trans-Europ Express network, a Class CC40100 hauls a Paris–Amsterdam express in pre-'Thalys' days.

CO-CO DJIBOUTI–ADDIS ABABA RAILWAY (CFE)

ETHIOPIA 1964

In 1964, this line was in a relatively thriving state, already operating 12 twin-unit A1A-A1A diesels bought from SLM in 1951 to supplement its stock of around 65 steam locomotives. By the time these two Alsthom Co-Cos were delivered in 1964 and 65, CFE had 25 main-line diesels, and all remaining steam locomotives were in store. The Alsthom locomotives were the most powerful to run on this metre-gauge line, and when fully loaded with fuel they stretched the maximum axle-

TYPE: diesel-electric freight locomotive
POWER: 16-cylinder PA 4 Chantiers de l'Atlantique diesel engine, rated at 1343.3kW (1800hp) and delivering 189.3kN (42,560lb) at 17km/h (10.6mph)
TRACTIVE EFFORT: 259kN (58,240lb)
MAXIMUM OPERATING SPEED: 70km/h (43mph)

TOTAL WEIGHT: 86.3t (190,320lb)
MAXIMUM AXLE LOAD: 14.4t (31,752lb)
OVERALL LENGTH: 17.398m (56ft 9in)
BUILDER: Alsthom, France
GAUGE: not known

loading almost to the limit. The CFE posed difficulties for diesel operation, rising to 2470m (8105ft) at Addis Ababa from sea level at Djibouti, through a possible temperature range from 0–43°C (0–109°F), and from a maximum humidity of 96 per cent

on the coast to the aridity and dust-storms of the interior. Alsthom had considerable experience of building locomotives for hot conditions, having supplied CC diesels for Mauritania with special anti-sandstorm protection, and built Bo-Bo and Bo-Bo-Bo types for Burma. Warfare hit the railway hard in the last decade of the twentieth century, and it is currently being refurbished with French aid. The wheelless frame of one of the Co-Cos is still to be seen at Addis Ababa.

DV12 B-B FINNISH STATE RAILWAYS (VR)

FINLAND 1964

The Dv12, in three different series numbering 12 locomotives and built between 1964 and 1984, is the VR's most numerous diesel class. Production was split between two Finnish companies, Lokomo and Valmet. Differences between the three series are relatively minor. All use a Tampella 16-cylinder diesel

TYPE: mixed-traffic diesel-hydraulic
POWER AND OUTPUT: Tampella-MGO V16 BSHR producing 1000kW (1360hp)
TRACTIVE EFFORT: N/A

MAX. OPERATING SPEED: 85km/h (53mph) in freight service; 125km/h (78mph) in passenger service
WEIGHT: 60.8t (134,064lb)

OVERALL LENGTH: 14m (45ft 11in)
GAUGE: 1524mm (5 ft)
(Specifications based on 2501 series)

engine (of French design built in Finland under licence), with a Voith L216rs hydraulic transmission. Originally known as Sv12, the

class designation was changed to Dv12 in 1976. With two alternative gear ratios, they can be and are used in both passenger service

and freight service (often in multiples up to three).

CLASS CC-40100 CC FRENCH NATIONAL RAILWAYS (SNCF)

FRANCE 1964

No universal standard was worked out before Europe's railways began electrification, and the subsequent mix of voltages and cycles has always been a problem for engineers responsible for planning inter-system electric traction. France has both 1500V DC and 25,000V AC 50 Hz; Belgium has 3000V DC; Luxembourg also uses 25,000V AC; the Netherlands use 1500V DC; and the German railways use 15,000V AC at 16.667 cycles/sec. Class CC-40100, 10 strong, was a pioneer design to operate passenger trains under all these current collection voltages. Four pantographs were mounted, to meet the design differences of each country. Monomotor locomotives, they were striking in appearance with sharply-raked cab

TYPE: C-C quadri-voltage mainline passenger electric locomotive
POWER: 25,000V 50Hz AC, 1500V DC, 3000V DC and 15,000V AC 16.67Hz overhead line collection; 3710kW (4985bhp) first four locomotives and 4480kW (6020bhp) last six locomotives; two DC frame-mounted traction motors
TRACTIVE EFFORT: 196kN (44,060lbf)
MAX. OPERATING SPEED: 160km/h (100mph)
WEIGHT: 109t (239,375lb)
MAX AXLE LOAD: not known
OVERALL LENGTH: 22.03m (72ft 3in)
GAUGE: 1435mm (4ft 8.5in)

windows and ribbed stainless steel bodywork. Once the Thalys network of jointly owned TGVs

serving Paris, Brussels, Amsterdam and Köln came into service, they were no longer needed.

As part of the Trans-Europ Express network, a Class CC40100 hauls a Paris–Amsterdam express.

CLASS 290 B-B GERMAN FEDERAL RAILWAYS (DB)

Based in most respects on the prototype diesel-hydraulic V80 shunter of 1952, this was a heavy-duty yard engine intended for work in marshalling yards with hump sorters, of which there were many more in the mid-1960s than today. German freight trains were often split and re-marshalled at key points on the network. The Class 290 diesel hydraulics propelled the trains slowly over the humps, from where the wagons were distributed among the sidings to form trains for different destinations.

TYPE: diesel-hydraulic shunting locomotive
WHEEL ARRANGEMENT: B-B
POWER: MTU MB 16V 6652 TA 10, 16-cylinder V-form medium speed, 820kW (1100hp); Voith L206rs hydraulic transmission
TRACTIVE EFFORT: 241kN (54,180lbf)
MAX. OPERATING SPEED: 70 to 80km/h (45 to 50mph)
WEIGHT: 77 to 79t (169,100 to 173,050lb)
OVERALL LENGTH: 14 to 14.32m (45ft 11in to 47ft)
GAUGE: 1435mm (4ft 8.5in)

A surviving Class 290 in the livery of the German Railion freight group. All the class members still in use have been fitted with new low-emission engines.

CLASS D9500 C BRITISH RAILWAYS (BR)

Swindon Works on BR's western region was Britain's main producer of diesel-hydraulic types. However, this six-wheeled shunter, similar to the DB Class V60, appeared at a time when freight business was falling and freight yards closing, and though 57 were built, they lasted for only a few years in service. Even the western region could not find work for them, and all had disappeared from BR by 1971. Several are preserved.

TYPE: freight main-line diesel-hydraulic
WHEEL ARRANGEMENT: C (0-6-0)
POWER: Paxman Ventura 6YJX six-cylinder diesel 485kW (650bhp), Voith L217U torque converter, jackshaft, external coupling rods
TRACTIVE EFFORT: 137kN (30,910lbf)
MAX. OPERATING SPEED: 65km/h (40mph)
WEIGHT: 51t (112,000lb)
OVERALL LENGTH: approx. 11m (36ft)
GAUGE: 1435mm (4ft 8.5in)

SHINKANSEN ELECTRIC HIGH-SPEED TRAINS JAPANESE NATIONAL RAILWAYS (JNR)

The future of high-speed train development was revealed in Japan with the inauguration of the *Shinkansen* ('new trunk line') in 1964. Superbly engineered, with heavy rails and deep ballast, many viaduct stretches, and laid with 1435mm (4ft 8.5in) gauge tracks, the completely new 320km (200-mile) line linked Tokyo and Osaka, with 10 intermediate stations. Running more or less parallel to the old 1067mm (3ft 6in) gauge Tokaido main line, which continued in use for stopping trains and freight services, it was known as the 'New Tokaido' line. Initially, 12-car double-ended *Shinkansen* electric multiple-unit trains were used, their high-speed operation and characteristic streamlined front ends earning the nick-name 'Bullet Trains'. The coach-class cars featured 3-2 seating – comfortable but simple. First-class cars, known in Japan as 'Green Cars', offered larger, more comfortable seats in a 2-2 arrangement. Each intermediate car measured 24.5m (80ft 5in) in length, 3.38m (11ft 1in) width and 3.98m (13ft 1in) height. In JNR parlance, the original trains are known as Series 0 to distinguish them from later ones. Although some trains had been operated at faster speeds in specialized test runs, maximum running speed for the Series 0 trains was set at 208km/h (130mph). In operation, many runs regularly averaged 160km/h (100mph) or more between terminals, making them by far the world's fastest regularly scheduled trains for the better part of two decades. Stopping trains were designated *Kodama*, picking up on the pioneer 'fast' trains of 1958, while express services were known as *Hikari*.

The *Shinkansen* was immensely successful and the 12-car trains were expanded to 16-car configurations. Since each car had its own traction motors, extension did not present a power problem. More than 3200 Series 0 cars were produced between 1963 and 1986. These were typically painted in a blue and white livery. JNR also began to widen its *Shinkansen* network. The original line was extended south-east, and a separate network of new lines was built north and west of Tokyo, engineered to an even higher standard than the original New Tokaido route, to allow for faster running. South and east of Osaka the mountainous terrain required many long tunnels. North and west of Tokyo, the electrification standard is different as a result of differences in Japan's national electric grid. Instead of 25kV at 60Hz, which is used by the original lines and those to the south and west, the lines north and west use 25kV at 50Hz. This electrification variance is often cited as one of the reasons why the *Shinkansen* networks do not offer a through service. All Tokyo-bound trains terminate at Tokyo's Central Station, despite the fact that the *Shinkansen* terminal platforms are adjacent to one another.

New trains were developed for the new lines, using the latest technologies to obtain significantly higher speeds. Series 0 used a traditional propulsion system that powered every axle on the train using DC traction motors, but later trains have fewer power axles and give greater efficiency. In 1982, Series 200 trains were built for service north and west of Tokyo. Aluminium-bodied and with thyristor-controlled motors, their top speed was first set at 240km/h (149mph). Later 200-series trains are capable of 275km/h (170 mph). The 100 Series entered service in 1985, on services south and west of Tokyo. They were given a sharper, more

A series 200 *Shinkansen* train streaks along its dedicated tracks at Fukushima.

angular styling than seen on the previous sets.

After the privatization of JR in 1987, three different companies took over *Shinkansen* routes, and many new trains have appeared. The Series 300 is a futuristic train with a sleek wedgelike front end and a lower profile than the earlier trains, designed for 269km/h (168mph) in regular service on lines south and west of Tokyo, with its fastest regular running on lines south of Osaka. This train was among the first in the world to employ a modern three-phase AC traction system that uses asynchronous motors with forced air ventilation. For services north

and west of Tokyo, six-car Series 400 and various 'E Series' trains made their debuts in the 1990s, with the E1 and E4 types using double-deck design, as with some French TGVs, to increase capacity. E1 uses just 12-car sets, while the E4 features eight-car sets, which are fitted to run in multiple, allowing for a 16-car train.

JR West's Series 500 trains, introduced in 1997 to work the *Nozomi* 500 service between Osaka and the southern city of Hagata, were the first to be built for a top speed of 300km/h (186mph), and claimed the word's fastest station-to-station timing, but FASTECH 360 trains on the new Tohoku

Shinkansen will take the maximum speed up to 360km/h (223mph). *Shinkansen* services are of proverbial reliability and punctuality: in 2003, average arrivals on all services were within six seconds of advertised time. JR's original Series 0 remains one of the most readily recognized high-speed trains in the world, although the last of them were withdrawn from high-speed services on the New Tokaido route at the end of 1999. They are now museum pieces for the most part.

Portions of Series 0 trains are displayed at museums in Tokyo and Osaka, and also at the National Railway Museum in York, England.

Shinkansen train technology is also in use in Taiwan, Korea, China and on the new Channel Tunnel rail link in Britain.

TYPE: 'Series-0' high-speed electric passenger train
POWER: 25kV 60Hz via overhead
OUTPUT: 11,846kW (15,900hp)
TRACTIVE EFFORT: N/A
MAX. OPERATING SPEED: 208km/h (130mph) in regular operation
WEIGHT: N/A
OVERALL LENGTH: intermediate cars 24.5m (80ft 5in)
MAX. AXLE LOAD: 16t (35,280lb)
GAUGE: 1435mm (4ft 8.5in)

MAT '64 ELECTRIC MULTIPLE UNITS NETHERLANDS RAILWAYS (NS)

NETHERLANDS 1964

Now quite elderly, the MAT '64 units are being replaced by higher-capacity and more energy-efficient two-deck trains.

The nickname 'dog-nose' was given to the preceding class of electric multiple unit (EMU), but in this class the snouty effect favoured by NS for multiple unit sets was toned down somewhat. Designed to work on both all-station and inter-city services, 214 two-car and 32 four-car sets were supplied; the four-car units being known as 'ELD4' sets. All were fitted with heavy Scharfenberg automatic couplers to facilitate joining and splitting operations, enabling trains to merge and demerge in quick time. Internally, their fittings were basic by modern standards, but considered adequate for the stopping-train duties to which all of them have since been relegated. The 1964

group of EMUs has always been liveried in the overall bright yellow colour characteristic of NS passenger trains.

TYPE: two-car and four-car electric multiple-unit stopping trains
POWER: 1500V DC overhead line collection, two power cars per unit, four GEC 210kW (280hp) axle-mounted DC traction motors (eight on four-car sets)
MAX. OPERATING SPEED: 140km/h (87mph)
WEIGHT PER VEHICLE: 35 to 47t (76,860 to 103,215lb)
MAX AXLE LOAD: not known
OVERALL LENGTH: outer cars – 26.07m (85ft 6in); inner cars – 24.93m (81ft 9in)
GAUGE: 1435mm (4ft 8.5in)

PLAN MP PARCELS VAN NETHERLANDS RAILWAYS (NS)

NETHERLANDS 1964

Postal and parcel services were run by these self-propelling electric vans, based on passenger-unit designs, with a 'dog-nose' cab at each end. The units were powerful enough to pull two or three four-wheeled vans at peak periods, and they were fitted with standard side buffers and hooked drawbars. The Werkspoor company built 34 of these vehicles for Netherlands Railways, but all were taken out of service by the late 1990s. A few remain in use with infrastructure companies as stores vans and personnel carriers.

TYPE: single-car electric parcels vans
POWER: 1500V DC overhead line collection, four Heemaf 145kW (195hp) axle-mounted DC traction motors
MAX. OPERATING SPEED: 140km/h (87mph)
WEIGHT: 54t (118,590lb) per vehicle
MAX. AXLE LOAD: not known
OVERALL LENGTH: 26.4m (86ft 7in)
GAUGE: 1435mm (4ft 8.5in)

Two MP units working multiple. The Netherlands Railways and Post Office established a central depot at Utrecht, from which these units carried mail to major distribution centres round the country.

CLASS EU07 BO-BO POLISH STATE RAILWAYS (PKP)

Twenty express passenger electrics were built by English Electric at its Vulcan Foundry works, based on the newly designed British Railways Class 83, and with the same forward-sloping end design. They were delivered to Poland in 1963–65, thus maintaining a tradition of using

TYPE: Bo-Bo, electric
POWER: 3000V DC from overhead wire
OUTPUT: 2000kW (2685hp)

TRACTIVE EFFORT: N/A
MAX. OPERATING SPEED: 125km/h (78mph)
WEIGHT: 83.5t (184,123lb)

OVERALL LENGTH: N/A
MAX. AXLE LOAD: N/A
GAUGE: 1435mm (4ft 8.5in)

British electric technology that began in the 1930s. In Poland, they were Class EU06. In the mid-1960s, Poland's Pafawag works licensed

the type and built 240 additional locomotives to the same basic pattern at its Wroclaw facilities, from 1964 to 1974. The Polish-built

machines were designated as Class EU07 and used interchangeably with EU06 on passenger services.

CLASS 060-EA CO-CO ROMANIAN RAILWAYS (CFR)

The 060-EA and 060-EA1 classes (later CFR classes 40 and 41) form Europe's largest class numerically of standard-gauge electric locomotives.

An enlarged version of Sweden's ASEA-designed Rc2 Co-Co electric locomotive, this was CFR's basic general-purpose engine for heavy duties. More than 900 were built under licence at the Electroputere works at Craiova. They were later redesignated as Class 40. For passenger-only operation a variant, Class 060-EA1 (later 41), was developed with higher gearing. Liveried in the standard CFR grey with metallic stripes, the locomotives were seen all over the country, the 41s working on international and internal passenger trains, and the Class 40s, often in tandem, on heavy freight trains.

This type has also been exported by Electroputere to Yugoslav and Bulgarian railways, by agreement with ASEA.

TYPE: Co-Co mixed-traffic mainline electric locomotive
POWER: 27,000V 50Hz AC overhead line collection; 5100kW (6835hp); six DC traction motors
TRACTIVE EFFORT: 412kN (92,620lbf)
MAX. OPERATING SPEED: Class 40 120km/h (75mph); class 41 160km/h (100mph)
WEIGHT: approx. 120t (263,530lb)
MAX AXLE LOAD: not known
OVERALL LENGTH: 19.8m (65ft)
GAUGE: 1435 (4ft 8.5in)

CLASS CHME3 CO-CO SOVIET RAILWAYS (SZD)

This prolific class is the world's most numerous single unit diesel-electric. Heavy-duty shunting is its task, in marshalling and transfer yards. Since the Czech and the Soviet railways both required a similar locomotive at the same time, the project became a joint one, and three prototypes were built in 1963 by CKD in Praha, Czechoslovakia, one as standard-gauge CSD T669.001 (preserved by the Czech Railways), and two as Russian gauge (1524mm/5ft) SZD ChME3 001 and 002, of which the first is preserved in St Petersburg. Class production followed in 1964 and continued to 1993, by which time a total of 7454 units were built for the Soviet Railways. Further machines were built for industry and export to Poland, Albania, Iraq, Syria and India. The SMZ Works at Dubnica nad Vahom – in present-

The Russian loading gauge gives ample room for a wide cab and foot-walk on the ChME3, seen here moving freight in an electrified marshalling yard.

TYPE: Co-Co diesel-electric heavy shunter
POWER: 993kW (1350hp) from CKD K6S310DR series engine
TRACTIVE EFFORT: 226kN (50850lbf) at 11.4kmh (7.1mph)
MAX. OPERATING SPEED: 95km/h (59.4mph)
WEIGHT: 123t (271,215lb)
OVERALL LENGTH: 17.22m (56ft 2in)
GAUGE: 1524mm (5ft)

day Slovakia – participated in the early years of production.

Designed as hood units, with an off-centre cab and railings round the foot-plates, the ChME3 locomotives were powered by the robust and reliable CKD 310mm (12.2in) bore six-cylinder engine, of the same 993kW (1350hp) power rating as the TEM2 locomotives being built in parallel at the Bryansk

Works in Russia. (The Czech engine, more reliable than Soviet ones, has been used to re-power some TEM1 units). On the ChME3, the engine unit is fitted beneath the long hood and the accumulators beneath the short one.

Sub-classes of ChME3 are numerous, with local variants, and include ChME3T with electric braking, and the ChME3E modernized but without electric brake. ChME3B is a switcher-slave set for slow-speed shunting. More recently, twin ChME3 switcher sets have been created. A twin-unit Bo-Bo+Bo-Bo, of Class ChME5, was

due to replace ChME3, but after prototypes and pre-series testing, the Soviet Union collapsed and quantity production was cancelled. Within the Czech Republic and Slovakia, the design is designated Class 770 and Class 771. In Czech and Slovak, the classes are nicknamed *Cmelak* and *Cmeliak* respectively, both meaning 'bumble-bee'. Large numbers have been withdrawn but some have been sold on, including one consignment to the Guinea Railways in Africa. Some have been re-engined and modernized in other ways.

CLASS 73 BO-BO BRITISH RAILWAYS (BR)

Known as 'electro-diesels', these locomotives were not powered by some early version of a hybrid engine but could use either electric or diesel propulsion. For use in goods yards and on non-electrified track, they were essentially DC electric locomotives using components common to the BR Southern Region electric multiple units (EMUs), but also provided with a modest diesel power unit like that in their diesel multiple units (DMUs). Away from the third rail, it could operate in a yard as a low-speed diesel-electric, and on reaching the main line the diesel engine could be turned off and it became a more powerful straight electric locomotive. Six prototypes were tried out, followed by 43 as a production batch for the electrification of the Bournemouth line, and to complete the elimination of steam from the Southern Region. Several still operate, including some on back-up 'Gatwick Express' duties, and moving 'Eurostar' stock in the London depot.

TYPE: mixed-traffic main-line electro-diesel
WHEEL ARRANGEMENT: Bo-Bo
POWER: English Electric 750V DC camshaft control electric traction equipment, four traction motors, 1195kW (1600hp); 4SRKT four-cylinder in-line vertical diesel engine, 450kW (600bhp); DC generator
TRACTIVE EFFORT: 180kN (40,000lbf) electric mode; 160kN (36,000lbf) diesel mode
MAX. OPERATING SPEED: 145km/h (90mph); some reduced since to 95km/h (60mph)
WEIGHT: 77t (170,240lb)
OVERALL LENGTH: 16.36m (53ft 8in)
GAUGE: 1435mm (4ft 8.5in)

Class 73 locomotives worked the 'Gatwick Express' with one at each end. This one is at the pushing end of the train as it leaves Victoria Station, in July 2000.

CLASS M62 CO-CO HUNGARIAN STATE RAILWAYS (MÁV)

One of the world's most numerous diesel types, seen here as MÁV Class M62. Most of the type still running are of recent manufacture or have reconditioned engines.

Built at the Ukrainian Lugansk Works, the total numbers of this type approach 4000, and by no means all of them went to Hungary. More than half of the output was supplied as exports from the Soviet Union, and over 2000 went to Eastern European countries, where they acquired various nicknames, like *Sergei*, *Gagarin*, *Iwan*, *Taiga trommel*, *Wummen* or *Mashka*. Power came from the Kolomna 14D40 engine, a two-stroke 12-cylinder vee-type of 230mm (9in) bore driving a DC generator supplying six motors in permanent parallel. Control is by 15 notches increasing engine speed from 400rpm at idle to 750rpm in even steps. Outside temperature operating range is -30˚ to +35˚C (-22 to 95˚F). Early production did not include silencing apparatus, the resultant noise giving rise to the *taiga trommel* ('drum of the taiga')

nickname. Standard-gauge M62s are fitted with European screw couplings and side buffers. On the Russian gauge, they are are fitted with Soviet SA3 centre couplers.

A total of 2484 were exported between 1965 and 1979: Hungary had 288 for MÁV (270 standard-gauge, 18 broad-gauge) and six for the GySEV lines; CSD in Czechoslovakia had 601 (574 standard-gauge, 25 broad-gauge) and two for industry; PKP in Poland had 1182 (1114 standard and 68 broad), plus nine for industrial use; the GDR had 378 and 18 for industry. Despite these very large numbers, the class had a reputation for high consumption of fuel and lubricating oil, and the number still in operation fell dramatically during the 1990s, though the Lugansk works were still producing an updated version. German Railways (DB) had none by 1994, but in 2000 there were over

50 M62s in service with private operators. MÁV retains the highest number, although declining – a life extension programme will see many survive past 2010. Few, if any, remain in the Czech Republic (CD), while Slovakia (ZSR) retains some only as snowplough pushers. Poland had none after 2002. In Russia, M62 locomotives of more recent construction than the export units are still running. Low axle weight relative to other Soviet domestic types made the design attractive for SZD's use on secondary routes with a lighter permanent way, carrying ever-increasing freight traffic. An updated M62U series was devised to extend working ranges with bigger fuel tanks and increased sand supplies. Temperature operating ranges were extended to -50 to +45˚C (-58 to 113˚F) to meet the extremes of Soviet conditions. Production for SZD was at least

723 M62, 1261 2M62, 389 2M62U and 104 3M62U, computation of the totals being complicated by industrial batches. Military locomotives include 41 M62UP and nine 3M62UP.

The class has had many specialist functions. M62UP was the motive power for rail-launched SS-24 'Scalpel' intercontinental ballistic missiles deployed from 1989. Locomotives of Class 3M62UP are used for hauling the Russian space shuttle starting towers at the Baikonur space port (now in Kazakhstan). M62s also went to other countries under Soviet influence, including the Baltic states, North Korea, Mongolia and Cuba. Even today, the factory still offers new M62s, produced most recently for Iran. The prototype M62-01 is in the St Petersburg museum collection.

TYPE: Co-Co diesel-electric freight
POWER: 1492kW (2000hp) from Kolomna 14D40 series engine
TRACTIVE EFFORT: 196kN (44100lbf) at 20.0kmh (12.5mph)
MAX. OPERATING SPEED: 100km/h (62mph)
WEIGHT: 118 to 126t (260,190lb to 277830lb)
OVERALL LENGTH: 17.56m (57ft 4in)
GAUGE: 1435mm (4ft 8.5in) or 1524mm (5ft)

EMD SD45 CO-CO VARIOUS US RAILROADS

USA 1965

Responding to the demands of railroads for increased power, Electro-Motive Division (EMD) introduced its new 645-series engine in 1965, and it proved to be very successful. Unusually, it was launched with a maximum-size version, of 20 cylinders, with the six-axled SD45. When this locomotive came on stream in 1965, it quickly gained acceptance. In fact, with 2686kW (3600hp) available from its turbocharged 20-cylinder engine, it became a 'must have' locomotive for many motive power chiefs under pressure to run fast freight. Western railroads like the Southern Pacific and Santa Fe were especially keen on the SD45 and subsequent 20-cylinder types and ordered many hundreds. Enthusiasm for the 20-cylinder engine gradually diminished because of its higher maintenance costs and greater thirst for fuel as compared with the 16-cylinder 645E, though EMD maintained it with the SD45-2, introduced from 1972. Some railroads continued to operate SD45s down to 2002. When the big lines discarded it, from the mid-1980s, the type was popular among regional railroads looking for second-hand 'bargain' power.

TYPE: Co-Co, diesel-electric
POWER: EMD 20-645E producing 2686kW (3600hp)
TRACTIVE EFFORT: 330kN (74,200 lbf) at 14.4km/h (9 mph) continuous TE
MAX. OPERATING SPEED: 125km/h (77mph)
WEIGHT: 185t (407,000 lb)
OVERALL LENGTH: 20.053m (65ft 9.5in) or 20.015m (65ft 8in)
GAUGE: 1435m (4ft 8.5in)

The leader of two SD45 locomotives with a freight train of the Wisconsin Central Railroad, at Milwaukee, May 1996.

ALCO C-630 CO-CO VARIOUS US RAILROADS

USA 1965

Though scoring a first by employing North America's first AC/DC transmission system (soon followed by its rivals), Alco's Century-630 was not a success. A six-motor, 2238kW (3000hp) diesel, it was designed to compete with EMD's SD40 and GE's U30C types. Unfortunately, it had the worst reputation in service, and less than 100 were built for American railroads during its two years of availability. It was superseded by the more powerful C-636, a design that sold even less well, and soon afterwards Alco withdrew from locomotive building altogether. Among C-630 users were Atlantic Coast Line, Reading Company, Southern Pacific, and Norfolk & Western (N&W). N&W had a high-hood version, purchased in two groups. The first five were delivered in 1966 and rode on standard Alco Tri-mount trucks. In 1967, the second group was delivered using trucks salvaged from dismantled Fairbanks-Morse Train Masters. Around 50 were constructed in Canada by Montreal Locomotive Works for Canadian lines. Two are preserved, one in operational condition.

TYPE: Co-Co, diesel-electric
POWER: Alco 16-cylinder 251E diesel producing 2238kW (3000hp)
TRACTIVE EFFORT: 458 kN (103,000lbf) starting TE
MAX. OPERATING SPEED: 105km/h (65mph)
WEIGHT: N/A
OVERALL LENGTH: 21.184m (69ft 6in)
GAUGE: 1435mm (4ft 8.5in)

CLASS K CO-CO WESTERN AUSTRALIAN GOVERNMENT RAILWAYS (WAGR)

AUSTRALIA 1966

Smoother in line and finish than North American road-switcher types, but of similar hood design, WAGR classes K and R were built in Australia by the English Electric Rocklea plant. Both were powered by the EE 12CSVT engine. The 10 K class, 201–210, were built for standard-gauge operation, and five similar R class, numbered 1901–1905, for narrow-gauge work. K and R class engines were set at a power rating of 1455kW (1950hp), but a second narrow-gauge batch of 13 class RA were rated lower, at 1339kW (1795hp). Three Class RA were re-gauged in 1974 as Class KA. Class K was first used for construction works in the completion of the last stage of the standard-gauge trans-continental route between Perth and Kalgoorlie; then it moved to grain and passenger work. Iron ore from Koolyanobbing mines was hauled by four Class Ks in multiple formation. Several Class Ks were passed on to industrial use or small users for shunting work. On lines in the south and west of the state, Class R were used on bauxite, salt, grain and general freight.

TYPE: Co-Co diesel-electric
POWER: K/R 1455kW (1950hp), KA/RA1339kW (1795hp) from EE 12CSVT series engine
TRACTIVE EFFORT: 225 to 264kN (50,625 to 59,400lbf) at 18/19kmh (11.3/11.9mph)
MAX. OPERATING SPEED: K/KA: 128km/h (80mph); R/RA 96km/h (60mph)
WEIGHT: (K) 110t (242,550lb)
OVERALL LENGTH: 15.24 to 16.76m (49ft 7in to 54ft 8in)
GAUGE: K/KA 1435mm (4ft 8.5in); R/RA 1067mm (3ft 6in)

GMD GP40TC GO-TRANSIT

CANADA 1966

With the drastic decline of North American passenger services in the late 1950s and 1960s, almost nobody was ordering new passenger diesels. But in the mid-1960s, Toronto's suburban passenger operator, GO (Government of Ontario) Transit, ordered eight specialized GP40 diesel-electrics from General Motors Diesel in Canada, for use on heavy trains. The GP40TC was an adaptation of the Electro-Motive Division GP40 freight locomotive, with a frame 1.981m (6ft 6in) longer than a conventional GP40, and consequently a greater distance between the truck (bogie) centres. This resulted from the requirement for an auxiliary head-end power generator, used for 'hotel power' – passenger car heating and lighting – in place of a conventional steam generator. GO Transit sold its GP40TC fleet to Amtrak in the late 1980s.

TYPE: Bo-Bo, diesel-electric
POWER: EMD 16-643E3 producing 2235kW (3000hp)
TRACTIVE EFFORT: N/A
MAX. OPERATING SPEED: N/A
WEIGHT: N/A
OVERALL LENGTH: 20.015m (65ft 8in)
GAUGE: 1435mm (4ft 8.5in)

CLASS 120 CO-CO GERMAN STATE RAILWAYS (DR)

Built at the Soviet Union's Voroshilovgrad plant for mixed-traffic work, this Co-Co was imported to East Germany as Class 120 and used primarily on passenger services. It was heavy on fuel and slow in speed, and all have been withdrawn from German operation.

Many more of the same type were built for use across the Soviet Union and exported also to Hungary, Poland and Czechoslovakia. Some of the class have returned to work on German lines, bought by open access train operators.

A pair of Class 120s against an industrial backdrop. Up to the reunification of Germany, a centralized transport policy kept much freight on rail in the former East Germany.

TYPE: mixed-traffic main-line diesel-electric
WHEEL ARRANGEMENT: Co-Co
POWER: Kolomna V-form diesel, 1470kW (1970hp); DC generator; six axle-hung DC traction motors
TRACTIVE EFFORT: 373kN (83,855lbf)
MAX. OPERATING SPEED: 100km/h (62mph)
WEIGHT: 116t (254,745lb)
OVERALL LENGTH: 17.55m (57ft 7in)
GAUGE: not known

CLASS DE10 AAA-B JAPANESE NATIONAL RAILWAYS (JNR)

The 475 DE10 locomotives were the broom that finally swept steam locomotives off the JnR's tracks. This diesel-hydraulic design has an unusual asymmetric five-axle arrangement. Intended for light-to-medium freight work on secondary routes, DE10s were also used for heavy shunting and trip and transfer work at freight marshalling yards. Class DE15 is a DE10 equipped for winter snow-plough operation. Many of the class were made redundant in the 1970s and 1980s by the drastic decline in freight carried by Japanese railways and by the privatization and restructuring of the state system. But JNR Freight, the new cargo operator resulting from the division of JNR into business units, continues to operate around 150. JNR East uses a fleet of around eight class DE10 and DE15, while JNR Central, JNR West, JNR Hokkaido, JNR Kyushu and JNR Shikoku each retain a few.

TYPE: AAA-B diesel-hydraulic lightweight
POWER: 1000kW (1359hp) from DML6ZB series engine
TRACTIVE EFFORT: 191kN (42,900lbf)
MAX. OPERATING SPEED: 85km/h (53.1mph)
WEIGHT: 65t (143,325lb)
OVERALL LENGTH: 14. 15m (46ft 2in)
GAUGE: 1067mm (3ft 6in)

On a non-electrified siding, a DE10 shunts freight vans under the elevated tracks near Tokyo Central station, in April 1997.

CLASS 3100 BO-BO KOREAN NATIONAL RAILWAYS (KNR)

Forty-nine Alco/MLW model RS8 road switchers form this KNR class. Used mainly on freight traffic, mostly in the northern region of the country, they had the Alco 251 series engine of 746kW (1000hp). KNR has re-powered some of the class, replacing the original engine with EMD 645 units, and also renumbered the locomotives as Class 3200 (but not in order of the original class). For the dedicated locomotive historian, the re-classing and re-numbering of locomotives is often a challenge in seeking to establish the life history of a particular locomotive or class. In the case of Class 3100, the hood shape had to be altered and partly raised to accommodate the EMD prime mover, making a visible difference compared with the original Schenectady-built examples. All are painted in KNR orange and black freight livery.

TYPE: Bo-Bo diesel-electric freight
POWER: 709kW (950hp) from EMD 8-645 series engine
TRACTIVE EFFORT: 160 kN (36,000lbf)

MAX. OPERATING SPEED: 105km/h (66mph)
WEIGHT: 72t (158,760lb)
OVERALL LENGTH: 14.65m (47ft 10in)
GAUGE: 1435mm (4ft 8.5in)

EMD GP38 BO-BO VARIOUS US RAILROADS

Headlines in the US locomotive world were grabbed in the mid-1960s by the arrival of high-power, turbo-charged engines, typified by the SD45. But not all railroads required 2608W (3500hp) or more, with the attendant extra fuel consumption, and steady

Scene at New London, CT, in September 1998.

demand for more moderately powered machines was still present. One of the new 645-engine diesel models introduced by Electro-Motive Division (EMD) at this time, the GP38 was effectively an improved version of the popular 'General Purpose' models that had dominated EMD's locomotive production through the 1950s. It used a normally-aspirated 16-cylinder 645 diesel to produce 1470kW (2000hp). With its successor-type GP38-2, it was a standard medium-power workhorse locomotive that could handle a variety of freight services from local switching work to heavy-unit coal trains, and most most American railroads used it.

TYPE: Bo-Bo, diesel-electric
POWER: EMD 16-645E producing 1492kW (2000hp)
TRACTIVE EFFORT: 245kW (55,000lbf) at 17.2 kmh (10.7 mph)
MAX. OPERATING SPEED: 104 km/h (65mph)
WEIGHT: 119t (262,000lb)
OVERALL LENGTH: 18.034m (59ft 2in)
GAUGE: 1435mm (4ft 8.5in)

EMD GP40 BO-BO VARIOUS US RAILROADS

Another new item in EMD's shop window was the GP40, also using the new 645 engine introduced in 1965. Basically an expansion of the successful 567 design, this engine had nevertheless been rigorously tested before going into production. The new generation of 645-powered locomotives also featured improved electrical components and an AC/DC transmission system (yet still used conventional direct-current traction motors). A high-output four-motor locomotive, the GP40 was designed for fast freight service, for which its 16-cylinder 645 engine delivered 2235kW (3000hp). New York Central was first to order the type, and it became popular with users of EMD's earlier high-output four-motor types. Variations of the GP40, such as the GP40P, were designed for passenger service. In 1972, the model was succeeded by the GP40-2, which offered no significant variations but maintained the sense of being the latest thing.

TYPE: Bo-Bo, diesel-electric
POWER: EMD 16-645E3 producing 2235kW (3000hp)
TRACTIVE EFFORT: 213kN (48,000lbf) at 21km/h (13mph)
MAX. OPERATING SPEED: 104km/h (65mph) to 123km/h (77mph)
WEIGHT: 126t (277,500 lbs) (based on CSX units)
OVERALL LENGTH: 18,034m (59ft 2in)
GAUGE: 1435mm (4ft 8.5in)

The Wisconsin Central's was not the first livery of this GP40, seen here with shining paintwork in May 1996. It was a Baltimore & Ohio locomotive until August 1991.

EMD SD40 VARIOUS US RAILROADS

Here was yet a further EMD model using the new 645 engine – in this case, a 16-cylinder version, 645E3. EMD were covering all the bases, and this was the heavy freight locomotive. As such, it quickly became a standard model on many American railroads, with a formidable combination of high horsepower, reliability and versatility. With a 60:17 gear ratio, the SD40 could operate at a maximum speed of 113km/h (70 mph) – the absolute maximum allowable speed for freight operations by most American railroads. It had an AR10 main generator and D77 traction motors. Until the Dash-2 model came along in 1972, it was the market leader in its class. The SD

TYPE: Co-Co, diesel-electric
POWER: 16-cylinder 645 producing 2235kW (3000hp)
TRACTIVE EFFORT: depends on gear ratio
MAX. OPERATING SPEED: 104–141km/h (65–88mph) depending on gear ratio
WEIGHT: 173t (382,000 lb)
OVERALL LENGTH: 20.015m (65ft 8in) – based on earlier models
GAUGE: 1435mm (4ft 8.5in)

40-2 was even more successful: 3945 were built; if the SD40 class locomotives are also included, a total of 5752 were produced. The vast majority are still in service on American railroads.

EMD SW1500 VARIOUS US RAILROADS

USA 1966

This 645-engined switcher type was fitted with a 12-cylinder version of the engine, producing 1118kW (1500hp), and was built from 1966 to 1974. It effectively supplanted the older SW1200 model, but by the mid-1960s the demand for new switching diesels had declined dramatically. Most lines found older models still did the job. Some used SW1500s in road freight service, combining them in pairs, or with other diesels. Southern Pacific had one of the largest fleets and used them as switchers in yards and industrial parks around its vast system. Other switcher types using the 645

engine were the smaller eight-cylinder SW1000 and SW1001, the latter type featuring a low-profile cab to allow it to work on sites with restricted height clearances.

TYPE: Bo-Bo, diesel-electric
POWER: EMD 12-645 producing 1118kW (1500hp)
TRACTIVE EFFORT: 200kW (45,000lbf) at 19.3km/h (12 mph)
MAX. OPERATING SPEED: 104km/h (65mph)
WEIGHT: 118t (260,000lb)
OVERALL LENGTH: 13.614m (44ft 8in)
GAUGE: 1435mm (4ft 8.5in)

The SW1500 was a useful compact switcher. This Conrail No. 9576, at Buffalo NY in 1988, has a traditional bell mounted on the hood.

GE U30B BO-BO VARIOUS US RAILROADS

USA 1966

Faced with an entire new range from EMD, General Electric (GE) relied on the solid virtues of its U-range but did boost the output of its Bo-Bo Universal Line road-switcher models. In 1966, it introduced the U28B, more powerful than its pioneering U25B. Later in the year, GE introduced the U30B, which

TYPE: Bo-Bo, diesel-electric
POWER: GE 7FDL-16 producing 2235kW (3000hp)

TRACTIVE EFFORT: 229kN (51,500lbf) continuous TE at 20.8km/h (13mph)
MAX. OPERATING SPEED: 127km/h (79mph)

WEIGHT: 123.5t (272,000 lbs)
OVERALL LENGTH: 18.339m (60ft 2in)
GAUGE: 1435mm (4ft 8.5in)

remained in production for the better part of the next decade. Intended to compete with EMD's GP40/GP40-2, the U30B did not, however, enjoy the robust sales of

the EMD types. Both high-nose and low-nose U30Bs were built according to customer specifications. Burlington, Frisco, New York Central, Norfolk &

Western, Seaboard Coast Line and Western Pacific were among the lines to order them. In 1977, the model was finally replaced by the B30-7.

CLASS L CO-CO WEST AUSTRALIAN GOVERNMENT RAILWAYS (WAGR)

AUSTRALIA 1967

Based on the American EMD's SD40 type, but reduced to the WAGR loading gauge, the Class L

TYPE: Co-Co diesel-electric
POWER: 2460kW (3300hp) from EMD 16-645 series engine
TRACTIVE EFFORT: 298kN (67050lbf) at 21kmh (13.1mph)

locomotives were both the highest-powered (at the time) and first turbocharged diesels to run

MAX. OPERATING SPEED: 134km/h (83.8mph)
WEIGHT: 137t (302,085lb)
OVERALL LENGTH: 19.36m (63ft 2in)
GAUGE: 1435mm (4ft 8.5in)

on state railways in Australia. Twenty-five were supplied by Clyde Engineering, of Granville, New South Wales, and they were initially used on Koolyanobbing iron ore, displacing Class K locomotives. Later, Class Q took over this duty, and in the 1990s several of the Class L were passed to Australian Transport Network (ATN Access) to work on export

Recently overhauled Class L No. 260 in Forrestfield Yard, NSW, on 7 December 2001. Many of these powerful units have seen long service on different Australian lines.

grain flows in New South Wales and Victoria. Four were used on construction trains on the Alice Springs to Darwin extension.

CLASS CC-72000 C-C FRENCH NATIONAL RAILWAYS (SNCF)

Maintaining the raked-back windscreen and front-end design that were by now almost an Alsthom trademark, this turbocharged class was for a long time France's most powerful diesel locomotive, and the pride of the SNCF diesel fleet. They had the characteristic whistling sound of a turbo engine, being fitted with two Hispano-Suiza HS419B turbo blowers. In the now standard manner for SNCF, they had only two traction motors, fitted in *monomoteur* bogies, but these

delivered ample tractive effort and the CC-72000 locomotives were reputed to have very good adhesion on starting off with heavy trains. Their principal use was on express passenger trains on non-electrified routes out to the extremities of Brittany; displacing 4-8-2 steam locomotives of Class 241P, they also worked long-distance trains on the main line through the Massif Central via Clermont Ferrand until they were themselves displaced by electrification to the Amiens–Calais and Paris–Trouville lines. In May 1973, CC-72075 was experimentally fitted with a SEMT Pielstick engine of 3530kW (4740hp), making it the most powerful single-engined diesel locomotive in the world at the time. They ended their careers in the east, working on the Paris–Basle line. Once they had been the only French diesel class allowed to run at a maximum service speed of 160km/h (100mph). Now this speed merely showed their age; all were withdrawn by 2004–5.

TYPE: mixed-traffic main-line diesel-electric
WHEEL ARRANGEMENT: C-C
POWER: SACM 16-cylinder V-form diesel, 2648kW (3550hp); DC generator; two monomoteur frame-mounted DC traction motors
TRACTIVE EFFORT: 189kN (42,490lbf) passenger; 362kN (81,380lbf) freight
MAX. OPERATING SPEED: 140 to 160km/h (88 to 100mph)
WEIGHT: 114t (250,355lb)
OVERALL LENGTH: 20.19m (66ft 3in)
GAUGE: 1435mm (4ft 8.5in)

Unmistakably French and Alsthom-built with its 'broken nose' – but the CC72000 class were the only diesels with this feature. 72076's home depot was Chalindrey, outside Paris.

CLASS 50 CO-CO BRITISH RAILWAYS (BR)

Named for famous admirals, a few of this class were still running passenger trains between Fishguard Harbour and Cardiff in 2006. Nicknamed 'Hoovers' because of their characteristic noise, they were of a generally conventional diesel-electric design, but BR had insisted on the use of 'modern'

Conference of admirals – three Class 50 locomotives at the Penzance terminus, in the 1970s.

electronics in the power circuits, and these became unreliable. Electrification of the Crewe–Glasgow sector displaced them to BR's Western Region (WR), where the

TYPE: mixed-traffic main-line diesel-electric
WHEEL ARRANGEMENT: Co-Co
POWER: English Electric 16CSVT 16-cylinder V-form diesel, 2014kW (2700hp); DC generator; six axle-hung DC traction motors
TRACTIVE EFFORT: 215kN (48,500lbf)
MAX. OPERATING SPEED: 160km/h (100mph)
WEIGHT: 117t (256,940lb)
OVERALL LENGTH: 20.88m (68ft 6in)
GAUGE: 1435mm (4ft 8.5in)

control systems were modified to improve reliability. The '50s' and the high-speed trains displaced the WR diesel-hydraulics from the main

lines to Bristol, South Wales and the West Country. Most have been scrapped; a few are preserved, apart from those still in public service.

CLASSES 279 AND 289 BO-BO SPANISH RAILWAYS (RENFE)

Six of this dual-voltage class were still operative in 2007, plus 18 converted into permanently coupled double units as Class 289.1.

Virtually identical both in externals and in mechanical and electrical design, both of these classes are dual-voltage machines, designed to work on the Spanish 3000V system and at border stations (on Spanish gauge) on the

French 1500 V system. The Class 279, which was built first, is slightly less powerful than Class 289, which followed in 1971. Surviving locomotives of both classes belong to the RENFE Cargas freight business.

TYPE: Bo-Bo mixed-voltage electric
POWER: 279 - 2700kW (3621hp); 289 - 3100kW (4157hp)
SUPPLY: 1500V or 3000V DC
TRACTIVE EFFORT: low gear – 263kN (59,175lbf); high gear – 164kN (36,900lbf)
MAX. OPERATING SPEED: low gear –

80km/h (50mph); high gear – 130km/h (81.3mph)
WEIGHT: 279 – 80t (176,400lb); 289 – 84t (185,220lb)
MAX. AXLE LOAD: 21t (46,305lb)
OVERALL LENGTH: 17.27m (56ft 4in)
GAUGE: 1668mm (5ft 3in)

GE U30C CO-CO VARIOUS US RAILROADS   USA 1967

The six-motor U30C, in direct competition with EMD's SD40/SD40-2 as a heavy freight locomotive, was the best selling of General Electric's 'U-boats' (as the Universal line locomotives came to be known), helping GE to the position of America's No. 2 diesel-electric manufacturer and pushing its one-time partner Alco into a

distant third position. Between 1967 and 1977, GE sold nearly 600 U30Cs in the United States. It also offered the more powerful U33C, and U36-C versions. All three used the same 7FDL-16 diesel engine.
   In 1977, GE's improved DASH-7 line superseded the Universal line. The biggest users of the U30C

TYPE: Co-Co, diesel-electric
POWER: GE 7FDL-16 producing 2235kW (3000hp)
TRACTIVE EFFORT: 329kN (74,000lbf) at 18.3km/h (11.4mph) (varied – these figures based on some Burlington Northern U30Cs)

MAX. OPERATING SPEED: 113km/h (70mph)
WEIGHT: 176t (388,000lb)
OVERALL LENGTH: 20.498m (67ft 3in)
GAUGE: 1435mm (4ft 8.5in)

were Burlington Northern, with 180, Union Pacific with 150, and

the Louisville & Nashville Railroad, which had 79.

CLASS SS1 CO-CO CHINESE STATE RAILWAYS   CHINA 1968

Electrification of public railways began in China in 1958 on the 600km (375-mile) Qinling mountain route between Chengdu and Baoji, with the first section opened in 1960 and worked by ignitron rectifier locomotives of Class 6Y2 supplied from Alsthom in France.
   Current supply at 25kV 50Hz AC, by then the international

TYPE: Co-Co
POWER: 3780kW (5136hp)
SUPPLY: 25kV 50Hz AC
TRACTIVE EFFORT: 301kN (67725lbf)
MAX. OPERATING SPEED: 95km/h (59.4mph)

WEIGHT: 138t (304,290lb)
MAX. AXLE LOAD: 23t (50,175lb)
OVERALL LENGTH: 20.368m (66ft 6in)
GAUGE: 1435mm (4ft 8.5in)

standard, enabled China to utilize very up-to-date forms of motive power. The first mass-produced

electric locomotive built within China, the SS1 (classed 6Y1 at first) from the Zhuzhou works,

had silicon rectifier and transformer tap changer technology, but was otherwise based on 6Y2 and retained a distinctly French appearance. It was equipped with a 3600kW (4891hp) rheostat brake, being designed for a mountain route. Zhuzou built 810 before the class was superseded by the higher-powered SS3 from 1979.

CLASS 753/754 BO-BO CZECHOSLOVAK STATE RAILWAYS (CSD)   CZECHOSLOVAKIA 1968

Despite efforts to give this diesel-electric class a futuristic look – the cab window styling earned the design the nickname *brejlovec* ('goggles') – the mechanics of CSD Class 753/754 were conventional. Originating as Class T478.3 (later 753), 408 were built up to 1977. Class 753 had train steam heating boilers while the

later T478.4 (class 754) have electric supply only. Prototypes of the latter were built in 1975, and 84 were built between 1978 and 1980. From 1989, Class 750s were converted to electric train heating and reclassed as 753s. On the division of Czechoslovakia into the Czech Republic and Slovakia in 1993, the two railway systems

TYPE: Bo-Bo diesel-electric general purpose
POWER: (753) 1325kW (1800hp); (754) 1492kW (2000hp) from CKD K12V230DR series engines
TRACTIVE EFFORT: 185kN (41,625lbf)

MAX. OPERATING SPEED: 100km/h (62mph)
WEIGHT: 753 – 76.8t (169,344lb); 754 – 74.4t (164,052lb)
OVERALL LENGTH: 16.5m (53ft 10in)
GAUGE: 1435mm (4ft 8.5in)

No. 754. 078-4 at Ostrava, Czech Republic, on 27 April 2003.

respectively acquired 41 and 18 of Class 750; 275 and 53 of Class 753; and 60 and 26 of Class 754. On both systems all were being

withdrawn as fast as possible in the early 2000s due to poor engine reliability and high fuel consumption.

CLASS 218 B-B GERMAN FEDERAL RAILWAYS (DB)

German locomotives usually belong to locomotive families, or build-groups – *Baureihe* in German – and Class 218 forms the major element in *Baureihe* 216. What typified it was a single diesel engine. Previous DB diesels, like the V200 (see 1953), had two engines, and were expensive to build and maintain. From 1960, work went on in the development of a range of diesel locomotives with a single, more powerful prime mover. The DB engineers were happy with hydraulic transmission, and this was retained. Various protoypes were built between

1960 and 1963, when the Class 216 was produced. It was a mixed-traffic locomotive, and 214 were constructed up to 1969. As the first of its kind, its number was attached to the *Baureihe* that also embraced classes 210, 215, 217, and 218. Class 215, of which 150 were built, was a passenger train engine, of greater maximum speed; 217 was a small class of 15, like 215 but equipped with an auxiliary engine to provide power for train heating. By 1968, it was decided to develop the concept with a more powerful engine than the 1320kW (1795hp) engine used

in classes 216 and 215, and the outcome of this was the Class 218.

Progress in engine design made it possible for a single-engined Class 218 to exceed the power output of the earlier twin-engined V200. Variously engined with MTU or Pielstick diesel engines, all with Voith hydraulic transmission, this mixed-traffic type became and long remained a prime resource of the DB's diesel fleet. Eight were provided with gas turbines as boosters for a time and were denoted Class 210 until the turbines were removed. Said to

have been nicknamed 'rabbits' because of sticking-up exhaust vents, 410 of Class 218 were built up to 1979, and they operated all over western Germany, hauling express passenger trains off the electrified routes and also working general freight, in multiple formation when required. In latter years, their employment has chiefly been on push-pull local trains. Class 216 locomotives are now withdrawn, but many Class 218s are still at work, and some have been reconditioned and re-classed as Class 218.8.

TYPE: mixed-traffic main-line diesel-hydraulic
POWER: MTU MA 12V 956 TB 10, 12-cylinder V-form diesel, 1840kW (2465hp), or MTU MA 12V 956 TB 11 or Pielstick 16 PA 4V 200, 2060kW (2760hp); Voith L820rs hydraulic transmission
TRACTIVE EFFORT: 245kN (55,080lbf)
MAX. OPERATING SPEED: 140km/h (87mph)
WEIGHT: 76.5 to 78.5t (168,000 to 172,390lb)
OVERALL LENGTH: 16.4m (53ft 10in)
GAUGE: 1435mm (4ft 8.5in)

The distinctive 'rabbit ears' stick up from this Class 218, in DB red livery, working a regional passenger service.

CLASS 581 ELECTRIC MULTIPLE UNIT SLEEPER SET JAPANESE NATIONAL RAILWAYS (JNR) JAPAN 1968

An *Ariake* sleeper set of the 1970s, when they were very popular; today Japanese sleepers are under-used.

TYPE: 12-car multiple-unit sleeping car train
POWER: 24 100kW (160hp) electric motors drawing current from an overhead catenary geared to the axles of two power cars and four other cars in a 12-car set
TRACTIVE EFFORT: 142.9kN (32,140lb)
MAX. OPERATING SPEED: 72km/h (45mph)
TOTAL WEIGHT: 553t (1,218,812lb)
MAX. AXLE LOAD: 12t (26,460lb)
OVERALL LENGTH: 249m (816ft 11in)
BUILDER: Nippon Sharyo, Kisha Seizo Kaisha, Kawasaki, Hitachi, Kinki Sharyo

Sleeping cars have generally been considered to be specialized vehicles requiring locomotive haulage, but Japan has had a fleet of electric multiple-unit sleeper trains since 1968. Particularly during the 1960s, and earlier, the length of the country,

especially on the main island of Honshu, made overnight trains a useful means of travel between north and south. The Class 581 was a 12-car set, and apart from a dining car and guard's compartment all the space was given over to sleeping

compartments. The sleeping berths, arranged longitudinally, and set in triple tiers, were all of the same standard, and a premium price was paid for the lowest bunk. The total number of berths was 444. With the upper-level berths folded away, the cars could

also be used for daytime services, with seating accommodation for a maximum of 656 passengers. Air conditioning equipment, water tanks, etc., were fitted in the roof spaces. The driving cars at each end were not powered. The power cars were the second vehicles, whose axles, and those of four other cars, were motor-driven, giving traction from half the axles of the train, and the motors' hourly output was rated at 2800kW (3860hp). The trains were built to the standard Japanese 1065mm (3ft 6in) gauge. Because of the different supply systems in Japan, the motors were equipped to use different kinds of current: alternating current at 25,000V

50 or 60Hz, or direct current at 150V. An updated Class 583 sleeper train was also produced, but numbers of this and the Class 581 sleepers have been converted into commuter cars for suburban traffic.

The building of the 53.85km (33.5-mile) Seikan Tunnel, the longest in the world, links Honshu to the northern island of Hokkaido, by 1067mm (3ft 6in) gauge rail, as

used by sleeping car stock. Despite this, overnight sleeper services in Japan have been in a state of decline. But though the effect of high-speed trains has been to reduce the sleeping-car network, the Japanese railways still operate sleeper trains in the twenty-first century, including the Tokyo-Sapporo Hokutosei (via the Honshu-Hokkaido tunnel); the seasonal 'Twilight Express'

between Osaka and Sapporo; the 'Sunrise Izumu' between Tokyo and Izumoshi; the 'Sunrise Seto' between Tokyo and Takamatsu; the Akatsuki, Kyoto–Osaka–Nagasaki; and the Suisei, Shin Osaka–Kokura–Miyazaki. But numbers of the Class 581 and 583 sleeper sets have been converted into commuter cars which are designated for suburban traffic.

CLASS EF66 B-B-B JAPANESE NATIONAL RAILWAYS (JNR)   JAPAN 1968

A light maximum axle load of 17 tonnes (16.7 tons) was the reason for the triple bogies of this electric class, which totalled 71 locomotives by 1989, with the final 16 having various modifications. All were built by Kawasaki. The middle bogie had

mechanical levers and air suspension allowing side movements. Today, most EF66s operate for JR Freight on fast cargo over the Tokaido and San'yo main lines while 13 units remain with JR West on passenger duties between Tokyo and cities in Kyushu.

TYPE: B-B-B heavy freight
POWER: 3900kW (5230hp)
TRACTIVE EFFORT: 192kN (43200lbf) at 72km/h (45mph)
MAX. OPERATING SPEED: 120km/h (75mph)

WEIGHT: 101t (222,705lb)
MAX. AXLE LOAD: 17t (37,385lb)
OVERALL LENGTH: 18.2m (59ft 8in)
GAUGE: 1067mm (3ft 6in)

An EF-66 passes a gradient marker with a train of flat cars, in April 1997.

CLASS EA BO-BO NEW ZEALAND RAILWAYS (NZR)   NEW ZEALAND 1968

Lighter weight in body construction and mechanical parts enabled NZR to use the Bo-Bo format on these five electric locomotives, which replaced the 1923-built Class EO on the steep Otira to Arthur's Pass section. Later redesignated EO, the Toshiba-built locomotives operated in a multiple

of three, maintaining a 508-tonne (500-ton) load at 27km/h (17mph) going up the 1 in 33 gradient.

Coming down, they used rheostatic braking to hold a 610-tonne (600-ton) load at

32–40km/h (20–25mph). Electric working of the section finally ceased in 1998.

TYPE: Bo-Bo
POWER: 960kW (1285hp)
SUPPLY: 1500V DC

TRACTIVE EFFORT: 103kN (23,175lbf)
MAX. OPERATING SPEED: 72km/h (45mph)
WEIGHT: 55t (121,275lb)

MAX. AXLE LOAD: 18t (39,690lb)
OVERALL LENGTH: 11.6m (37ft 10in)
GAUGE: 1067mm (3ft 6in)

CLASS DJ BO-BO-BO NEW ZEALAND RAILWAYS (NZR)

As with NZR locomotives from steam days on, concern about heavy axle loads on lightly laid and light-weight track ensured that more wheels rather than less were fitted to spread the load. In the case of this Mitsubishi-supplied mixed-traffic class, there was also the advantage of powering all three bogies for maximum adhesion on starting and on wet rails, though the Bo-Bo-Bo arrangement is more common on electrics than on diesels (other than units supplied to various African countries by Alsthom). The Class DJs were also among some of the earliest diesels in the world to be fitted with a traction alternator producing alternating current rectified for direct-current traction motors. Unfortunately, these advanced technical features were offset by operational difficulties, and the over-rated, unreliable engines of the original locomotives, at 773kW (1050hp), were later modified to 671kW (900hp). With the arrival of the 64 DJ class, steam was eliminated in South Island, but they themselves began to be withdrawn quite early from service, starting in 1986, despite the engine downrating. The last DJ was taken out of use by NZR in 1991.

TYPE: Bo-Bo-Bo diesel-electric
POWER: 671kW (900hp) from Caterpillar D398 V12 series engine
TRACTIVE EFFORT: 128kN (28,800lbf)
MAX. OPERATING SPEED: 96km/h (60mph)
WEIGHT: 64t (141,120lb)
OVERALL LENGTH: 14.1m (46ft)
GAUGE: 1067mm (3ft 6in)

DJ 3424 at the once-busy station in Dunedin, South Island, 2002. DJs are used to haul tourist trains on the scenic Taieri Gorge Railway.

CLASS EL 14 CO-CO NORWEGIAN STATE RAILWAYS (NSB)

Abundant hydro-electric power made it natural for NSB to pursue a major electrification programme through the 1950s and 1960s. The main lines from Oslo to Bergen, Trondheim and Stavanger have all been worked by the powerful Class El 14 locomotives, successors to Norway's heavy-duty steam locomotives.

They, in turn, have been displaced from front-line duties by successive deliveries of faster and more modern locomotives, but can still be seen on freight workings. Screen grilles (for protection against tunnel icicles rather than railside vandals) and low-level snowploughs are typical NSB fixtures.

TYPE: Co-Co mixed-traffic mainline electric locomotive
POWER: 15,000V 16.667Hz AC overhead line collection; 5080kW (6930hp); rheostatic brakes; six DC traction motors
TRACTIVE EFFORT: 350kN (78,685lbf)
MAX. OPERATING SPEED: 120km/h (75mph)
WEIGHT: 105t (230,590lb)
MAX. AXLE LOAD: not known
OVERALL LENGTH: 17.74m (58ft 2in)
GAUGE: 1435mm (4ft 8.5in)

EL14 No. 2173, without window grilles. Thirty-one were built by Thune in Norway between 1968 and 1973.

'METROLINER' ELECTRIC MULTIPLE-UNITS PENNSYLVANIA RAILROAD (PRR) USA 1968

Though it was in no position to build a dedicated track, the PRR was said to have been prompted by the success of the Japanese *Shinkansen* train when it set out to develop a high-speed service on its already-electrified Northeast Corridor route between New York, Philadelphia, and Washington DC. Post-war US governments had done little to support the railroad network but, in recognition of the pressing need to improve surface transport in this heavily congested region, federal funding (in place from 1965) assisted in the development

TYPE: high-speed electric multiple-unit train
POWER: 11.5kV AC at 25Hz
TRACTIVE EFFORT: N/A
MAX. OPERATING SPEED: 177km/h (110mph) in revenue service; 257km/h (160mph) potential

WEIGHT: 149t (328,400lb)
OVERALL LENGTH: 51.816m (170ft) for two-car set
MAX. AXLE LOAD: 19t (41,887lb)
GAUGE: 1435mm (4ft 8.5in)

of an electric multiple unit set capable of 257km/h (160mph). However, by the time the new train was ready to run, the PRR had become part of Penn Central, and the first 'Metroliner' service started on 16 January 1969 rather than in 1967 as had been originally planned. In regular service, the

trains were limited to a 177km/h (110mph) maximum, but still cut half an hour off the previous New York–Washington DC schedule. Following the collapse of Penn Central, Amtrak inherited the 'Metroliner' units in 1971. The service was very popular and the trains' main disadvantage was lack

of space to accommodate all those who wanted to use them. By the early 1980s, they had been assigned to other services, in which their potential high speed was less in evidence, and the Metroliner name was assigned to locomotive-hauled services. Many Metroliner cars were scrapped in the 1990s or converted into Amfleet coaches for locomotive-hauled services. 'Acela Express' trains later worked the old Metroliner route, and some Metroliners were recalled to service when the Acela trains were temporarily taken out of service.

EMD FP45 CO-CO SANTA FE RAILROAD (SF) USA 1968

New passenger train locomotives were rarities in the United States, but in 1967 Santa Fe placed orders for locomotives to pull its highly acclaimed, streamlined, stainless-steel passenger trains, including the *Super Chief*. Semi-streamlined diesels were ordered from both Electro-Motive Division (EMD) and General Electric (GE). They were not carbody units as the early streamlined diesels,

like the EMD F units had been, with the outer carbody being integral to the locomotive structure. Based on a road-switcher design, these second-generation passenger locomotives were built on road-switcher frames with full-width, non-structural metal 'cowl' bodywork protecting the works. Initially, Santa Fe ordered nine FP45s, with the 20-645E3 engine. They were fitted with a large steam generator,

since passenger cars of the time were still steam-heated. Later, SF ordered a freight-only version, designated F45. These were similar in most respects, but they did not require the steam generator and were several feet shorter. Burlington Northern and Milwaukee Road also ordered F45s.

TYPE: Co-Co, diesel-electric
POWER AND OUTPUT: not known
TRACTIVE EFFORT: 316kN (171,000lbf) at 21km/h (13.2mph)
MAX. OPERATING SPEED: 123km/h (77mph)
WEIGHT: 175t (386,000 lb)
OVERALL LENGTH: 20.561m (67ft 5.5in)
GAUGE: 1435mm (4ft 8.5in)

No. 5972, in Santa Fe paintwork, is lead unit on a Wisconsin Central freight, near Fond du Lac, Wisconsin, in March 1995.

EMD SD39 CO-CO VARIOUS US RAILROADS

USA 1968

Among US railroads, purchasing interest was mostly in the higher-powered new road-switcher types, and this medium-powered, six-motored locomotive, though it filled an apparent market gap, found few buyers, and was built only between 1968 and 1970. In externals, the SD39 closely

resembled the more powerful SD40, but inside it was a 12-cylinder version of the 645 engine, producing a more modest 1714kW (2300hp). A variant was the lightweight SDL39 that rode on different trucks and was intended for branch lines needing low axle loadings. Milwaukee Road was the

only line to buy the SDL39, ordering 10 of them. In later years,

these locomotives were acquired by Wisconsin Central.

TYPE: Co-Co, diesel-electric
POWER: EMD 12-645E3 at 1714kW (2300hp)
TRACTIVE EFFORT: 365kN (82,200lbf) at 12.9km/h (8mph)

MAX. OPERATING SPEED: 115km/h (71mph)
WEIGHT: 161t (356,000 lb)
OVERALL LENGTH: 20.1m (65ft 10in)
GAUGE: 1435mm (4ft 8.5in)

CLASS 342 BO-BO YUGOSLAVIAN RAILWAYS (JDZ)

YUGOSLAVIA/SLOVENIA 1968

A Class 342 entering Hrostnik, Slovenia, with a freight train, on 19 August 2003.

The Italian Ansaldo company built these mixed-traffic locomotives for the JDZ, and they have been inherited by the Slovenian Railways. Though reaching the end of their effective lives, they were still active in 2003.

With increasing freight from Koper sea port and no decision on new motive power, Class 342s seem likely to remain at work all over the system on secondary passenger and freight duties, including some double-headed freight to Koper.

TYPE: Bo-Bo mixed-traffic
POWER: 2280kW (3098hp)
SUPPLY: 3000V DC
TRACTIVE EFFORT: 177kN (39,825lbf)
MAX. OPERATING SPEED: 120km/h (75mph)

WEIGHT: 76t (167,580lb)
MAX. AXLE LOAD: 19t (41,895lb)
OVERALL LENGTH: 17.25m (56ft 8in)
GAUGE: 1435mm (4ft 8.5in)

AB CLASS CO-CO WESTRAIL

Electro-Motive Division's Australian subsidiary Clyde Engineering built 26 locomotives for Westrail's iron and aluminium ore freight traffic, classed A, AA, and AB. Class A used the EMD 567 series engine; the others had the newer 645 series. Some of the Class A were transferred to TasRail in Tasmania and all the others were sold to Chile in 1998.

TYPE: Co-Co diesel-electric
POWER: 1231kW (1650hp)
TRACTIVE EFFORT: 226kN (50,850lbf) at 14kmh (8.8mph)
MAX. OPERATING SPEED: 100km/h (62mph)
WEIGHT: 99t (218,295lb)
OVERALL LENGTH: 15.04 to 15.49m (49ft to 50ft 5in)
GAUGE: 1067mm (3ft 6in)

Class AB was slightly longer than AA. Photographed while still in the Western Australian Government Railway fleet, No. 1535 was the penultimate member of the class.

CLASS 422 CO-CO VICTORIAN RAILWAYS (VR)

Another Clyde product, flat-ended and flat-sided, the box-like Class 422 took the local name of 'flying bricks'. Engined with the EMD 16-cylinder 645-series, they were quite powerful locomotives, but designated for mixed-traffic duties. Originally deployed in the Melbourne area, they indeed ran mixed-traffic services, including some passenger duties on Sydney trains. Class 422 was withdrawn in the late 1990s, but 16 were passed on to the Australia Southern Railroad, who are progressively returning them to operational service. Four worked on Alice Springs to Darwin construction traffic. Two others are operated by Interail and three by Freightcorp.

Seen here around 1999 in Freightcorp blue livery, this former VR loco was sold on to Australian Railroad Group in 2000, and when overhauled at Port Augusta in 2006 was renumbered 2209.

TYPE: Co-Co diesel-electric
POWER: 1641kW (2200hp) from EMD 16-645 series engine
TRACTIVE EFFORT: 271kN (60,975lbf) at 12km/h (7.5mph)
MAX. OPERATING SPEED: 124km/h (77.5mph)
WEIGHT: 110t (242,550lb)
OVERALL LENGTH: 18.44m (60ft 2in)
GAUGE: 1435mm (4ft 8.5in)

MLU-14 CO-CO BANGLADESH RAILWAYS (BR)

In 1965, Bangladesh Railways had bought Alco units for its 1676mm (5ft 6in) gauge, and four years later bought some of DL535 for the 1m (3ft 3.4in) gauge network. Montreal Locomotive Works, who continued the Alco tradition after Alco ceased to build

TYPE: Co-Co narrow-gauge
POWER: 1030kW (1400hp) from Alco 6-251 series engine

TRACTIVE EFFORT: 178kN (40,000lbf) at 11.6kmh (7.3mph)
MAX. OPERATING SPEED: 96km/h (60mph)

WEIGHT: 70.5t (155,453lb)
OVERALL LENGTH: 13.818m (45ft 1in)
GAUGE: 1000mm (3ft 3.4in)

locomotives in 1969, supplied 24 (numbers 2301 to 2324) in 1969 and a further 12 (2401 to 2412) in

1978, forming class MLU14. These engines work on freight and passenger services across

the whole of the Bangladesh metre-gauge system.

MLW M-630 CO-CO CANADIAN PACIFIC RAILWAY (CPR)

Alco's Canadian affiliate, Montreal Locomotive Works (MLW), continued to build locomotives based largely on its Century-series for several years after Alco itself abandoned locomotive building in 1969. MLW's primary six-motor designs were the M-630 and M-636, models that closely resembled

the Alco C-630 and C-636 respectively. The M-630 was a 2238kW (3000hp) locomotive powered by a 16-cylinder Alco 251 diesel. It used a different style of bogie from the C-630, and had a slightly different hood configuration.

Canadian Pacific was the largest buyer of the M-630 type, owning

TYPE: Co-Co, diesel-electric
POWER: Alco 16-cylinder 251E diesel producing 2238kW (3000hp) for traction
TRACTIVE EFFORT: 329kN (74,000lbf) continuous TE

MAX. OPERATING SPEED: 120km/h (75mph)
WEIGHT: 177t (390,000 lb)
OVERALL LENGTH: 21.184m (69ft 6in)
GAUGE: 1435mm (4ft 8.5in)

most of the 60-plus locomotives built for service in North America in the three-year production run

that began in 1969. Some remained in service on CPR into the late 1990s.

CLASS SY 'AIM HIGH' 2-8-2 CHINESE STATE RAILWAYS

More than 1800 of this class were built up to 1999, the last of the standard Chinese steam classes to enter production, and the last steam locomotives in volume production anywhere. A light freight type, with two cylinders and outside valve gear, its general design appears to go back to the JF6 2-8-2 introduced in Japanese-occupied Manchuria in 1934. Two

BOILER PRESSURE: 14kg/cm² (199psi)
CYLINDERS: 530x710mm (20.8x28in)
DRIVING WHEELS: 1370mm (54in)
GRATE AREA: 4.57m² (49.2sq ft)
HEATING SURFACE: 171.9m² (1850.7sq ft)

SUPERHEATER: 42.8m² (460.8sq ft)
TRACTIVE EFFORT: 17,209kg (37,945lb)
TOTAL WEIGHT: 88.2t (194,481lb) (engine only)

prototypes were built at the Sifang (Qingdao) works, but most of the production run has come from Tangshan, though Tongling, Jinan

and Changchung works have also built some. The railed bogie tender with its down-sloping back (not on the prototypes, which had

conventional tenders) suggests shunting or backwards-running work, and the SY class was extensively used on industrial lines and was an unusual sight on main lines. A considerable number are believed to still exist, and in 2006 some are still in regular or occasional service on industrial lines, chiefly on steelworks and coal-mining sites.

CLASS DF4 CO-CO CHINESE STATE RAILWAYS

Produced in very large numbers, this became the 'standard' big diesel on Chinese Railways. Variations were added over a long period from the 1960s into the 1990s. The original Class DF4 were passenger units first built at the Dalian locomotive works in 1969 and capable of 120km/h

(75mph). From 1974, they were also produced as DF4A freight locomotives, to run at 100km/h (62mph), and with 2430kW (3302hp) engines. Up to 1984, 390 of Class DF4 and 360 of Class DF4A had appeared. Production then switched to the uprated class DF4B, with the tractive effort of

the freight units significantly increased. Four factories – Dalian, Datong, Sifang and Ziyang – were involved, and 4250 higher-power units were built. Class DF4C swere introduced in 1975, with 2650kW (3600hp) engines, but lower performance characteristics, and 920 of these were built. Further

Class DF4 designations appearing through the 1990s included a high-speed 132km/h (82.5mph) freight, a higher-powered 2940kW (3995hp) passenger type, asynchronous motor versions, and single-cab hood units for switching. In terms of overall numbers, it is China's largest diesel class (see 2003).

TYPE: Co-Co diesel-electric
POWER: 2430kW to 2940kW (3295 or 3995hp) from 16V240ZJ series engines
TRACTIVE EFFORT: 215 to 302kN (48,375 to 67,950lbf) continuous; 303kN to 440kN (68,175 to 99,000lbf) maximum
MAX. OPERATING SPEED: 100 or 120km/h (62 or 75mph)
WEIGHT: 138t (304,290lb)
OVERALL LENGTH: 20.5m (66ft 11in)
GAUGE: 1435mm (4ft 8.5in)

A scene that could be reproduced anywhere in China – a well-maintained DF4B waits in the centre road to take over an incoming train. DF4 locos are normally geared either for passenger or for freight work.

CLASS 103.1 CO-CO GERMAN FEDERAL RAILWAYS (DB)

With a characteristic DB rounded-end design, this electric class initiated locomotive-hauled express services with long trains at speeds of up to 200km/h (125mph). After testing of four prototypes, a total of 145 were constructed. The class 103s became favourites with crews and travellers as a result of highly competent and quiet performance in service. Painted red-and-cream to match the first-class carriages in their intercity rakes, later versions of DB red followed. A handful were still working in 2002, but almost all had gone by 2006, except for 103.245, which is to be preserved, and was still occasionally in service.

TYPE: express passenger electric
POWER: 15,000V 16.67 Hz AC overhead line collection; 7440kW (9975hp); thyristor control; rheostatic braking; six frame-mounted DC traction motors.
WHEEL ARRANGEMENT: Co-Co
TRACTIVE EFFORT: 314kN (70,590lbf)

MAX. OPERATING SPEED: 200km/h (125mph)
WEIGHT: 114t (250,350lb)
MAX AXLE LOAD: not known
OVERALL LENGTH: 19.5m (63ft 8in) up to No. 103 215, and 20.2m (66ft 3in)
GAUGE: 1435mm (4ft 8.5in)

Under the platform awnings at Köln (Cologne), DB No. 103.159-0 was photographed in August 1998.

EMD DDA40X DO-DO UNION PACIFIC RAILROAD (UP)

Running on two four-axle bogies, these locomotives put the power of two GP40s on to a single frame. Forty-seven were constructed, the largest and last of Union Pacific's 'double-diesel' units, which for so long had been familiar in pictures of long trains snaking through the Western landscape. Its carbody with single cab was of the 'wide nose' cowl-style first introduced on Santa Fe's FP45 locomotives in 1967, predating the now common North American 'Safety Cab' by more than two decades.

The DDA40X was powered by a pair of turbocharged 16-645E engines that generated 4923kW (6600hp). DDA40Xs were the world's largest single-frame diesel locomotives – known as 'Centennials' and introduced in the centenary year of completion of the first transcontinental railroad and accordingly numbered as the 6900 series. By 1985, most were out of service, but one locomotive, No. 6936, remains in Union Pacific's heritage fleet.

TYPE: Do-Do, diesel-electric
POWER: two 16-645E3 diesel engines producing 4923kW (6600hp)
TRACTIVE EFFORT: 596kN (133,766 lbf) starting TE
MAX. OPERATING SPEED: N/A
WEIGHT: 247t (545,400lb)
OVERALL LENGTH: 30m (98ft 5in)
GAUGE: 1435m (4ft 8.5in)

CLASS CL CO-CO AUSTRALIAN NATIONAL RAILWAYS (ANR)

Of streamlined carbody design – by now very unusual on a new freight locomotive – and with a single set-back nose cab, the 17 Cl class were built by Clyde Engineering to work on the Broken Hill to Port Pirie freight service, and were also used on Leigh Creek coal and Broken Hill ore workings. In 1992–93, they were rebuilt by Morrison Knudsen and emerged as seven Class CLF freight haulers, and 10 Class CLP for passenger service, with respective maximum speeds of 130 and 140km/h (80.7 and 87mph). Class CLP was subsequently redeployed on freight duties.

Both classes are operated by Australian Southern Railroad, the successors as freight operator to Australian National in South Australia.

TYPE: Co-Co diesel-electric
POWER: 2460kW (3300hp) from EMD 16-645 series engine
TRACTIVE EFFORT: 270kN (60,750lb) at 24km/h (15mph)
MAX. OPERATING SPEED: 155km/h (97mph)
WEIGHT: 129t (284,445lb)
OVERALL LENGTH: 19.58m (63ft 10in)
GAUGE: 1435mm (4ft 8.5in)

One of the rebuilt CL class locomotives, Australian National Railways CLP No. 15, refuels at Cook, in June 1994.

CLASS 32 ELECTRIC MULTIPLE UNIT BULGARIAN STATE RAILWAYS (BDZ)

Bulgarian main-line electrification began in 1962, with the heavily used Sofia–Plovdiv main line. This was followed by the lines from the capital to Karlova and to Ruse on the Romanian border. The schemes were all built to the by then international standard supply system of 25kV AC at 50 cycles.

The 79 four-car sets of Class 32 were built by RVZ-Riga in Latvia. They were single-class trains with seating capacity for 316 passengers, and they went into use on inter-city services between Sofia, Plovdiv and Karlova.

TYPE: four-car train set
POWER: 660kW (884.4hp)
TRACTIVE EFFORT: not known
MAX. OPERATING SPEED: 130km/h (80mph)
TOTAL WEIGHT: not known
OVERALL LENGTH: not known
BUILDER: RVZ-Riga, Latvia

A Class 32 set on a local service. Some have been scrapped but many still run, in some cases re-painted from the original red livery.

CC-21000 C-CO FRENCH NATIONAL RAILWAYS (SNCF)

This small but celebrated class pulled such high-speed expresses as the Paris–Marseille *Mistral* and the Paris–Toulouse *Le Capitole* in the years immediately before the construction of the *Lignes Grand Vitesse* put these great trains out of business. It was a dual-current class, in most respects very similar to the much more numerous 15kV Class CC-6500 with which it shared very many parts, and the two were not easily distinguishable from each other, apart from the CC-21000's large centrally placed transformer

under the body. It also had separate pantographs for each current type. The six-wheel monomotor bogies were driven by TTB 655A1 motors. Two prototype machines were ordered in January 1966 and delivered in July 1969, and were tested at very high speeds, up to 280km/h (174mph). In regular service from May 1970, they were stationed at Perrigny depot, Dijon, to work on the Jura grades, where they hauled fast freights, replacing double-headed BB-25500 units, as well as the principal expresses. Two more

TYPE: express passenger electric Co-Co locomotive
POWER: 5900kW (8100hp)
SUPPLY: 15000V and 25kV 50HzAC
TRACTIVE EFFORT: not known

MAX. OPERATING SPEED: 220km/h (137mph)
WEIGHT: 123t (271,168lb)
OVERALL LENGTH: 20.19m (66ft 2in)
GAUGE: 1435mm (4ft 8.5in)

locomotives completed the class in July 1974; one of these was sent to the United States for testing against the Swedish Rc4 in 1977 (temporarily becoming Amtrak's X996), but its bogies did not appear to suit American tracks. It was returned to the SNCF and the Swedish engine became the basis

of Amtrak's AEM-7 class. With the arrival of TGV services, the CC-21000 locomotives found little employment except as test-units on the newly built high-speed lines, and eventually in 1994–95 all four were converted to Class 6500, with maximum speed reduced to 160km/h (100mph).

CLASS CF7 BO-BO SANTA FE RAILROAD (SF)

Rail operators had forecast relatively short lives for individual diesel-electric classes in the 1940s, but many showed a longevity comparable with steam locomotives. The major Class A railroads were most likely to buy in new types, but they normally sold on older classes, or traded them in against new purchases, rather than scrap them. In the later 1960s, many railroads were disposing of 1950s locomotives in

this way. Electro-Motive Division ran a substantial reconditioning operation quite apart from building new locomotives. Santa Fe, however, adopted its own policy of conversion and rebuilding, and between 1970 and 1978 more than 230 of its fleet of F7s were rebuilt as road switchers, designated CF7. The carbody, which had been an integral part of the load-bearing structure, was replaced by a frame, hood and

cab. Primary mechanical and electrical components from the F7 were retained and incorporated in the converted locomotives. All the rebuilding was done in SF's own shops. Early CF7s featured a contoured cab that matched the profile of the F7 carbody, while later rebuilds featured a taller, boxy cab. In the early 1980s, Santa Fe began selling off its CF7 fleet and many were acquired by shortlines, though Amtrak

acquired a few in exchange for its SDP40Fs and assigned them to maintenance trains.

TYPE: re-manufactured Bo-Bo diesel-electric
POWER: EMD 16-567BC producing 1119kW (1500hp)
TRACTIVE EFFORT: N/A
MAX. OPERATING SPEED: N/A
WEIGHT: N/A
OVERALL LENGTH: 17.043m (55ft 11in)
GAUGE: 1435mm (4ft 8.5in)

M-640 CO-CO CANADIAN PACIFIC RAILWAY (CPR)

CPR's No. 4744 was a one-off. Built by Montreal Locomotive Works (MLW), with a power output of 2948kW (4000hp), it was the most powerful single-engine Alco diesel. The power unit was an Alco 18-cylinder 251 series. Generally similar similar in appearance to MLW's M-630 and M-636 types, the

locomotive had large 'bat-wing' radiators at the rear of the unit. At the time, 4744 was significantly more powerful than production single-engine diesel-electrics, which topped out at 2686kW (3600hp). The M-640 worked in the railroad's road freight fleet, assigned to trains with CPR's other

TYPE: Co-Co, diesel-electric
POWER: Alco 18-cylinder 251 diesel, producing 2984kW (4000hp)
TRACTIVE EFFORT: 354kN (79,590lbf) continuous TE

MAX. OPERATING SPEED: N/A
WEIGHT: 177t (390,000lb)
OVERALL LENGTH: 21.298m (69ft 11in)
GAUGE: 1435mm (4ft 8.5in)

large MLW diesels, but in 1985 it was substantially rebuilt for use as

a test-bed for alternating current traction.

CLASS BJ B-B CHINESE STATE RAILWAYS

CHINA 1971

A diesel-hydraulic type, the only one to be volume-produced in China, this class was a small one in Chinese terms, eventually running to 340 locomotives. Prototypes were built in 1971, but series production did not start until 1975. The BJ class locomotives were intended originally for passenger work, but were dislodged from this role by the far more numerous Class DF4 (see 1969), and they were either cascaded to freight duties or withdrawn.

A freight version with slightly lower-powered 1840kW (2500hp) engines was geared for 90km/h (145mph) maximum speed, and a single-ended version for working back-to-back in pairs also appeared in small numbers. A few run on 1524mm (5ft) gauge wheelsets, to work in border exchange yards.

The diesel-hydraulic BJ (for Beijing) Class was the main type of passenger locomotive on the Beijing–Shanghai and Beijing–Guangzhou lines in the 1970s. One is preserved at the Beijing Railway Museum.

TYPE: B-B diesel-hydraulic passenger and freight
POWER: 1990kW (2700hp) from 12V240ZJ series engine
TRACTIVE EFFORT: 163kN (36,675lbf) continuous; 227kN (51,075lbf) maximum
MAX. OPERATING SPEED: 120km/h (75mph)
WEIGHT: 92t (202,860lb)
OVERALL LENGTH: 16.505m (53ft 10in)
GAUGE: 1435mm (4ft 8.5in)

CLASS BB-15000 B-B FRENCH NATIONAL RAILWAYS (SNCF)

FRANCE 1971

For 30 years, the 65 members of class BB-15000 were the principal 25kV AC express passenger locomotives on main lines in eastern France. Built by Alsthom-MTE between 1971 and 1976, they are of monomotor bogie design, with a single motor to each bogie: the same as the BB-7200 type but designed for the AC electrification system. A dual-voltage version also exists, Class BB-22200. The end-design is the typical *nez-cassé* ('broken nose') designed by Paul Arzens and first applied to the CC-40100 class.

TYPE: B-B mainline mixed-traffic electric locomotive
POWER: 25,000V 50Hz AC overhead line collection; 4400kW (5900hp); AC thyristor control; two DC frame-mounted traction motors
TRACTIVE EFFORT: 294kN (66,095lbf)
MAX. OPERATING SPEED: 160km/h (100mph)
WEIGHT: 90t (197,645lb)
MAX AXLE LOAD: not known
OVERALL LENGTH: 17.48m (57ft 4in)
GAUGE: 1435mm (4ft 8.5in)

The BB 15000 class hauled French and German rolling stock on international expresses. There were several different liveries, of which the 'Multiservice' version, as shown by No. 15013, was the most common.

CLASS M41 B-B HUNGARIAN STATE RAILWAYS (MÁV)

Its locomotives known as 'Rattlers', this is a general-purpose diesel-hydraulic class. MÁV acquired 107 from Ganz-MÁVAG and the GYSEV railway system took seven (later transferred to MÁV). It was originally conceived as a centre-cab locomotive, and two prototypes, M41-2001 and 2002, were built in this form in 1967, but the production units had neat end cabs. For a long time, Ganz-MÁVAG had been using a Ganz-Jendrassik diesel engine, but this had been taken to the end of its capacity, and a licence was obtained to use the French SEMT-Pielstick PA4-185 series engine. Railways at the time were changing over from steam to electric heating in the coaching stock, and the class was MÁV's first to be equipped for electric train heating, allowing it to dispense with the separate heating

cars previously used. These locomotives are distributed throughout Hungary and are found on passenger work on the majority of non-electrified secondary routes. MÁV intends keeping up to 100 beyond 2010 and is evaluating new engines for these. In 2001/2002, M41-2207 (now M41-2301) was rebuilt with a MTU 16V4000 engine and M41-2115 (now M41-2302) with CAT 3516. The hydraulic transmission was unchanged.

TYPE: B-B diesel-hydraulic mixed-traffic
POWER: 1325kW (1800hp) from Pielstick 12PA4-185 series engine
TRACTIVE EFFORT: 151kN (34,000lbf)
MAX. OPERATING SPEED: 100km/h (62mph)
WEIGHT: 66t (145,530lb)
OVERALL LENGTH: 15.5m (50ft 7in)
GAUGE: 1435mm (4ft 8.5in)

An old class being revamped for service into the 2010s – MÁV's Class M41 'Rattlers' have proved their reliability and durability.

CLASS WAM-4 CO-CO INDIAN RAILWAYS (IR)

No. 21259 on a long-distance train in 2004. The paintwork of the WAM-4s varies, depending on their home shed and, in some cases, the service.

Though its oldest members date back more than 30 years, Class WAM-4 can still be seen on many prime Indian passenger services. After numerous imports, this was the first wholly Indian-designed and built electric locomotive, with all of them constructed at Chittaranjan Works. India's first AC electric locomotive was the WAM-1, introduced in 1959 and built by the European 50Hz consortium to a French design. Working in Indian

conditions, a variety of problems developed, and Indian Railways set about the design of a 'home-grown' AC electric locomotive that would suit its own requirements.

TYPE: Co-Co multipurpose
POWER: 2715kW (3689hp)
SUPPLY: 25kV 50Hz AC
TRACTIVE EFFORT: 332kN (74700lbf)
MAX. OPERATING SPEED: 120km/h (75mph)

In 1971, this resulted in the WAM-4, and with on-going modifications the class was built until about 1997. Alco 'trimount' bogies, which had been fitted to

WEIGHT: 113t (249,165lb)
MAX. AXLE LOAD: 19t (41,895lb)
OVERALL LENGTH: 18.974m (61ft 10in)
GAUGE: 1676mm (5ft 6in)

the successful WDM-2 diesel class, were used, as also in the following WAG-5A, WCG-2 and WCAM-1 classes. Class WAM-4s employed silicon current rectifiers and a high-tension traction control system, but reverted to axle-hung nose-suspended traction motors because of the high maintenance costs of spring-borne motors. Multiple-unit operation of up to four units was possible. Air brakes for the locomotive and vacuum train brakes were fitted as original equipment, and rheostatic braking was also provided. Speed control was by three series-parallel motor combinations and weak field operation. Auxiliary equipment came from Westinghouse and Kirloskar (compressors), SF India (blowers), and Northey (exhauster), among other suppliers.

This class proved highly successful, its rugged design and simplicity of maintenance making it entirely suitable for Indian conditions, and IR went on to use the basic design for a number of variant types (WCAM-1, WAG-5A, WCG-2, and some WAP models). WAM-4Bs were re-geared versions for freight use with a maximum speed of 50km/h (31.3mph), and many were later modified and converted to other classes. WAM-4Ps are intended for passenger operations, with some re-gearing

and usually allowing all-parallel operation of some or all of the traction motors, and a top working speed of 140km/h (87.5mph) A single WAM-4 can generally haul up to a 24-coach passenger rake, if at relatively low speed. The WAM-4P loco is still among the most heavily used electric locomotive classes on the IR. Nearly 500 of the class were built, including the variants from the basic design. Many depot-specific

local modifications have been made to individual locomotives or sub-groups over the years. With the introduction of the 'super-fast' Shatabdi express trains from July 1988, some of the class were fitted with dual braking system and suffixed DB, HS or both. Although their WAM code meant 'wide gauge, AC, mixed traffic', the WAM-4 locomotives were and still are primarily used in passenger service.

CLASS 92 1-CO-CO-1 EAST AFRICAN RAILWAYS (EAR) KENYA 1971

Montreal Locomotive Works (MLW) supplied this 15-strong class, fitted with Alco 12-cylinder 251-series engines and intended for freight haulage. To reduce axle loading on the lighter permanent way, it follows the wheel-layout adopted by English Electric on several British-use and export models. Similar machines were supplied to Nigerian Railways –

a batch of 54 MLW MX615 locomotives. Though they were hood units, the EAR locomotives had a so-called 'Africa cab', with full width and low nose styling not used on other MLW export models. In 1976, when EAR was divided into separate Kenyan, Tanzanian and Ugandan systems, all the Class 92s passed to Kenya Railways. In 1980, MLW supplied

TYPE: Co-Co mainline mixed-traffic dual-voltage electric locomotives
POWER: 25,000V 50Hz AC overhead line collection and 750V DC conductor rail collection; 5040kW (6755hp) on AC, 4000kW (5360hp) on DC; three-phase asynchronous control; six traction motors

TRACTIVE EFFORT: 400kN (89,925lbf)
MAX. OPERATING SPEED: 140km/h (87mph)
WEIGHT: 126t (348,650lb)
MAX AXLE LOAD: not known
OVERALL LENGTH: 21.34m (70ft 1in)
GAUGE: 1435mm (4ft 8.5in)

Malawi with similar but smaller Co-Co units, fitted with Alco eight-

cylinder 251 series engines, developing 1120kW (1522hp).

CLASS ET22 CO-CO POLISH STATE RAILWAYS (PKP) POLAND 1971

Departing from PKP's previous use of British electric designs, this class was constructed by Pafawag using Dolmel electrical gear. Almost 1200 were built, making them the most numerous electrics on the Polish State Railways. Each machine has six direct current series-wound traction motors that can produce up to 3000kW (4020hp) of pulling power. Though designed primarily for heavy freight service, some of the class have been regularly assigned to passenger trains as well. Notably, heavy sleeping car trains, like those that continue to points in Russia and the Ukraine, are sometimes assigned ET22 haulage. More typical tasks would be coal and iron-ore trains and other heavy freight traffic on PKP's busy electrified routes. A small number of the class were also exported to Morocco.

TYPE: Co-Co mixed-traffic (primarily freight) electric
POWER: 3000V DC from overhead
OUTPUT: 3000kW (4020hp)
TRACTIVE EFFORT: 212kN (47,600lbf) continuous TE at 50km/h (31mph)
MAX. OPERATING SPEED: 125km/h (78mph)
WEIGHT: 120t (264,480lb)
OVERALL LENGTH: 19.24m (63ft 2in)
MAX. AXLE LOAD: 20t (44,080lb)
GAUGE: 1435mm (4ft 8.5in)

ET 22 No. 337 stands with a long-distance passenger train in Poznan, Poland, on 24 May 2000.

CLASS 6CE CO-CO ALGERIAN NATIONAL RAILWAYS (SNCFA)

Phosphate traffic from the interior deposits at Djebel Onka and Tebessa to the sea at Annaba port was the prime reason for the introduction of this heavy freight electric. In a joint construction programme between Eastern Bloc manufacturers LEW of East Germany and Skoda of Czechoslovakia, 32 were built, numbered 6CE 1 to 32. A more powerful type, Class 6FE, was introduced in 1992, but up to half of the 6E class remain in service.

TYPE: Co-Co multipurpose
POWER: 2715kW (3689hp)
SUPPLY: 25kV 50Hz AC
TRACTIVE EFFORT: 332kN (74700lbf)
MAX. OPERATING SPEED: 120km/h (75mph)

WEIGHT: 113t (249,165lb)
MAX. AXLE LOAD: 19t (41,895lb)
OVERALL LENGTH: 18.974m (61ft 10in)
GAUGE: 1676mm (5ft 6in)

CLASS Z CO-CO TASMANIAN RAILWAYS

Freight operations are by far the prime activity on Tasmanian railways and these Co-Cos, designed for freight haulage, were closely related to other freight types used in Australia, and also built by GEC of Australia, new owners of the English Electric Rocklea plant. Class Z was based on WAGR Classes K and R, while the later Class ZA was similar to Queensland Railways' Class 2350, but with revised body and lower nose instead of the high, short-nose hoods of the original design. Both batches were built for a new traffic flow of logs and wood chips on the northern section of the main Tasmania line and on the Bell Bat, Fingal and Western routes. Classes Z and ZA operate side by side and may be found on other parts of the network. In 1987–88, the ZA's 'parent' type also arrived in Tasmania, having been displaced by electrification in Queensland, and it was re-classed as ZB. In 2003, a total of six were in current use alongside classes Z and ZA.

TYPE: Co-Co diesel-electric freight
POWER: Z – 1502kW (2025hp); ZA – 1900kW (2580hp)
TRACTIVE EFFORT: Z – 221kN (49750 lbf); ZA – 289kN (65000lbf)

MAX. OPERATING SPEED: 37.3km/h (60mph)
WEIGHT: 96t (211,642lb)
OVERALL LENGTH: 16.31m (53ft 3in)
GAUGE: 1067mm (3ft 6in)

RTG GAS TURBINE TRAINS FRENCH NATIONAL RAILWAYS (SNCF)

The steep rises in oil prices of the 1970s helped to spur French engineers to develop gas turbine motors, which burn low-grade oil fuel. At the same time as they worked on the original TGV gas turbine prototype (later abandoned), they were also bringing out the RTG (*Rame à turbine à gaz*) train. The first was a prototype three-car unit, officially numbered as T1000. The T2000, with five cars, became the production model. The producers installed two 775kW (1054hp) Turmo III turbines for main drive and two auxiliary 300kW (408hp) Astazou turbines to power air-conditioning and lighting. The power cars were at each end, the

TYPE: Express passenger gas-turbine electric five-car unit (1979 re-engined version)
GAS TURBINE ENGINE: Turboméca Turmo XII 1200kW (1610hp) at one end of unit; Turmo IIIF1 820kW (1100hp) at other end; hydraulic transmission
MAX. OPERATING SPEED: 160km/h (100mph)

WEIGHT: Power cars (2) 54 tonnes (118,590lb); trailers (3) 37 to 42 tonnes (81,255 to 92,235lb)
OVERALL LENGTH: Power cars 26.22m (86ft); trailers 25.5m (83ft 8in)
GAUGE: not known

turbines driving the end wheelsets through hydraulic transmission. Electro-pneumatic braking was fitted. In 1979, one of the original main turbines in each set was replaced by a Turmo XII model, which was both more powerful and more economical on fuel.

The trains were provided with large fuel tanks for long-distance express work on cross-country routes. Forty-one sets were built by *Ateliers du Nord de la France* (ANF) between 1972 and 1976, numbered from T2001-2 to T2081-2 and forming much the largest fleet of gas-turbine trains in the world. Two were sold to the United States, Nos. T2017-8, and T2019-20. The distinctive orange-liveried RTGs worked fast services from Paris to Cherbourg and Caen in Normandy, and also east–west between Lyon and Nantes and Bordeaux, providing swift and comfortable travel. Each was equipped with a 'grill-bar' to cater for passengers. By the mid-1990s, locomotive-hauled trains were taking over their routes. They were retired in 2005, but the last five were promptly sold to the Iranian Railways, and made the long rail journey through Switzerland, Austria, the Balkans and Turkey to their new home. One power car is preserved at Mulhouse.

Note the sidewall air intakes on the power car of this T2000 five-car set. The demise of the RTGs was regretted.

DX CLASS CO-CO NEW ZEALAND RAILWAYS (NZR)

First used on coal traffic in North Island, this class of 49 diesel-electrics, all built by General Electric, represented a large investment by NZR in freight haulage. Following electrification of some routes, a number were transferred to South Island in the 1980s. In 1997, 15 of the class were modified as 'since 1968ctunnel motors' with increased air ducting to work through the Otira Pass tunnel, and the electric catenary on that route was dismantled. Two DX models were substantially rebuilt as DXR, one with a new cab – the second retained the original layout.

TYPE: Co-Co diesel-electric
POWER: 2050kW (2750hp) from GE 7FDL12 series engine
TRACTIVE EFFORT: 207kN (46,575lb)
MAX. OPERATING SPEED: 120km/h (75mph)
WEIGHT: 97.5t (214,988lb)
OVERALL LENGTH: 17.9m (58ft 5in)
GAUGE: 1067mm (3ft 6in)

The large windscreens replaced double front glasses when single manning was introduced.

CLASS RM A1A-2+2-BO 'SILVER FERN' NEW ZEALAND RAILWAYS (NZR)

In body-work rather resembling US Budd railcars, New Zealand's first diesel-electric railcars had an unusual asymmetric wheel arrangement between the two vehicles. Three sets were built in Japan by Nissho-Iwai. They featured air-conditioning and aircraft-style seating for 96 passengers. Apart from some special excursion services, for which they were ferried across to South Island, the 'Silver Ferns' worked only in North Island. Each

car was powered on the end bogie, and each had a driving compartment. The main driving car, however, was the A1A-2 vehicle, which housed the main engine, with the three-axle bogie to spread the weight. They replaced older British-built Drewery-Fiat powered 'Blue Streak' units on the Auckland-Wellington services. From December 1991, they inaugurated a 'Geyserland Express' twice-daily between Auckland and Rotorua, replacing

TYPE: two-car diesel-electric express set
POWER: 670kW (898hp) Caterpillar D398TA engine, V12, bore 159mm (6.25in), stroke 203mm (8in) driving four traction motors. Auxiliary Caterpillar D330T generator engine
TRACTIVE EFFORT: not known

MAXIMUM OPERATING SPEED: 120km/h (75mph)
TOTAL WEIGHT: 107t (235,935lb)
MAXIMUM AXLE LOAD: not known
OVERALL LENGTH: 47.2m (155ft)
BUILDER: Nissho-Iwai, Japan
GAUGE: not known

locomotive-hauled trains, and also the Auckland–Tauranga 'Kaimai Express'. These services lasted until 1999. Since NZR's abandonment of long-distance

passenger services, the 'Silver Fern' units run Veolia Auckland's Auckland–Pukekohe commuter services and are used for charters and special tours.

CLASS 8000 BO-BO-BO KOREAN RAILWAYS (KNR)

The French origin of this class is immediately apparent from the 'broken-nose' cab-front with its back-raked, glare-proof windscreens. Alsthom built these 90 AC supply, DC-rectifier, thyristor-controlled, rheostat-braked locomotives to a demanding traction specification. Following the electrification of the

449km (279-mile) line between Seoul and Bugpyeong across the Taebaeg mountains, the Class 8000s were required to haul heavy freight loads over 1 in 40 gradients through relatively sharp curvature (for that purpose, the centre bogie was permitted a maximum of 4.57cm/1.8in of lateral movement).

Geared for heavy freight haulage over steeply graded routes, the Class 8000 has been a valuable locomotive type for KNR's increasing traffic on electrified lines.

TYPE: Bo-Bo-Bo heavy freight
POWER: 3990kW (5350hp)
SUPPLY: 25kV 50Hz AC
TRACTIVE EFFORT: 426kN (95850lbf)

MAX.OPERATING SPEED: 85km/h (53mph)
WEIGHT: 128t (282,240lb)
MAX. AXLE LOAD: 21t (46,305lb)
OVERALL LENGTH: 20.73m (68ft)
GAUGE: 1435mm (4ft 8.5in)

RE 6/6 BO-BO-BO SWISS FEDERAL RAILWAYS (SBB)

On its introduction, this was the most powerful non-articulated electric locomotive in the world, and it remains among the prime heavy haulers. For almost two decades, the Ae 6/6 Co-Co locomotives (see 1952) had handled almost all heavy traffic over the Gotthard route, and the more powerful Re 6/6, with greater speed and tractive effort on grades and curves, was planned to maintain the high levels of service on this intensively used international trunk route. Among the four prototypes built in 1969–72, Nos. 11601 and 11602 had a two-section body pivoting on a hinge that gave up-and-down movement only. Nos. 11603 and 11604 had the single-body design that was used for the production machines. Intensive testing of the prototypes, in all aspects of performance and suitability, was carried out before 85 were ordered from SLM of Winterthur and Brown Boveri, as usual with specifically spelled-out performance parameters. These were formidable, including the capacity to accelerate an 800-tonne (787-ton) train on a gradient of 1 in 38 to 80km/h (50mph) and maintain that speed. Series construction began in 1975 and went on until 1980. In the SBB renumbering scheme, they were designated Re 620 and numbered 620.005 to 620.089.

The body is constructed of welded steel sheet, with four big side windows and a single driver's door on each side, in a style basically similar to that of the preceding Co-Co types. A new drive motor, Type 12 FHW 7659, was developed for the class, in order to provide the required tractive effort of 195kN (43,837lbf) at 140km/h (87mph). The triple-bogie Bo-Bo-Bo layout with all axles powered gives it excellent adhesion on starting heavy trains. Despite its length and maximum 20-tonne (19.6-ton) axle-load, a weight transfer reduction system in the bogies, as developed for the Re4/4 type, helps to take it comfortably round curves.

These were the first Swiss locomotives to provide air-conditioning in the driver's compartments, and ergonomics were applied to make the drive controls and gauges as effectively placed as possible: in this period before micro-processor controls, the task of the driver of a large electric locomotive was not an easy one. Electric brakes were fitted, with a regenerative system to return current to the catenary, effective enough for three downhill-running freight trains to supply power for one going up, and the mechanical braking system was used primarily to hold trains at a standstill once they had stopped.

Allocated to the depots at Lausanne, Erstfeld and Bellinzona, the Re6/6s dominated passenger and freight traffic over the St Gotthard and Simplon routes from their introduction until partially displaced by Class 460 in the late 1990s. They also worked from Lausanne on the Lötschberg line. Re6/6s are expected to remain in freight traffic well into the twenty-first century.

TYPE: Bo-Bo-Bo for freight and passenger mountain traffic
POWER: 7856kW (10,665hp)
SUPPLY: 15kV 16.2/3Hz AC
TRACTIVE EFFORT: 11601–11604 – 394kN (88650lbf); 11605–11689 – 398kN (89550lbf)
MAX. OPERATING SPEED: 140km/h (87.5mph)
WEIGHT: 120t (264,600lb)
MAX. AXLE LOAD: 20t (44,100lb)
OVERALL LENGTH: 19.31m (63ft)

An Re 6/6 emerges into the snow from the northern portal of the Gotthard Tunnel at Göschenen, in the winter of 2000–2001.

EMD SD45T-2 CO-CO SOUTHERN PACIFIC RAILROAD (SP)

The theoretical high power output of Electro-Motive Division's 20-cylinder 645-series engine, installed in the SD45 type and useful for pulling or pushing on long uphill grades, was adversely affected by high-altitude working (as with other diesel-engined locomotives). SP's line over Donner Pass through the Californian Sierra had unventilated tunnels and many snow-sheds as well as high altitude, and engine overheating and power reduction caused problems in operation. Alterations to the SD45T-2 included a change of air-flow pattern, lowering the air intakes from the top of the hood to the level of the running boards (footwalks), allowing the locomotive to take in cooler and cleaner air in tunnels. Between 1972 and 1975, some 247 SD45T-2s were built, all of them for Southern Pacific and its Cotton Belt subsidiary line.

These specialized design changes were implemented, along with the many new Dash-2 components introduced in 1972. To distinguish improved locomotives from earlier models, a '-2' was added to the model designation. Previous EMD new models had had increased power or new body styling, but the Dash-2 changes – some 40 altogether – did not affect these aspects. The still-recent 645-series engine continued in use. The most significant developments were the introduction of solid-state electronic modules in the place of conventional relay control, and a new high-adhesion truck design intended to increase tractive effort. Externally the '-2' models appeared much like their respective predecessors, but the convenience in operation and maintenance provided by the modifications were very popular, and the full range of five GP and six SD types all appeared in Dash-2 form; in addition, many earlier versions were rebuilt to Dash-2 standard either by EMD or other workshops.

TYPE: Co-Co, diesel-electric
POWER: 20-cylinder 645 producing 2686kW (3600hp)
TRACTIVE EFFORT: 408.9 kN (92,000 lbf)
MAX. OPERATING SPEED: 114km/h (70.8mph)
WEIGHT: 176t (388,000 lb)
OVERALL LENGTH: 21.539m (70ft 8in)
GAUGE: 1435mm (4ft 8.5in)

GP40-2L BO-BO CANADIAN NATIONAL RAILWAYS (CN)

CANADA 1973

A non-standard, full-width cab design marked this passenger diesel-electric, a variation of Electro-Motive Division's GP40-2 built by EMD's Canadian subsidiary, General Motors Diesel. Canadian National and Ontario Province's GO Transit both used it; sometimes described as GP40-2W, GP40-2L, or

TYPE: Bo-Bo, diesel-electric
POWER: EMD 16-643E3 producing 2235kW (3000hp)

TRACTIVE EFFORT: N/A
MAX. OPERATING SPEED: N/A
WEIGHT: N/A

OVERALL LENGTH: 20.015m (65ft 8in)
GAUGE: 1435mm (4ft 8.5in)

even just as GP40-2 with no suffix to distinguish it from standard-cab models, which Canadian National also possessed. In addition to

operating in Canada, some were cleared for international service and were regularly assigned to run on Central Vermont and other

American subsidiaries of CN. In 2000, Guilford Rail System picked up a small fleet of GP40-2Ls for work on its New England lines.

CLASS 810 RAILBUS CZECHOSLOVAK STATE RAILWAYS (CSD)

CZECHOSLOVAKIA 1973

Curtailment of branch-line services, and old age, have reduced the numbers of this once-prolific four-wheel railcar class, but many still remain active. A total of 680 class 810 were built by Vagonka Studenka. Today CD operates around 530 in the Czech Republic, and ZSR has 130 in Slovakia. CD is rebuilding some of

TYPE: four-wheel diesel railbus
POWER: 155kW (208hp)
TRACTIVE EFFORT: N/A

MAX. OPERATING SPEED: 80km/h (50mph)
WEIGHT: 20t (40,500lb)

OVERALL LENGTH: 13.97m (45ft 6in)
GAUGE: 1435mm (4ft 8.5in)

the 810 units as a new class designated 812, for work with Class 912 driving trailers. The relatively low 80km/h (50mph) speed is not a problem on many lines, which often

have a 40km/h (25mph) speed limit. Hungary took 205 Class Bzmot railbuses of the same type, many now rebuilt with various Raba MAN and Volvo engines and

hydraulic transmissions. Some have have been upgraded with 2+2 seating and air conditioning for inter-city feeder services, marketed as *inter picy* (inter-tiny).

CLASS SR1 BO-BO FINNISH STATE RAILWAYS (VR)

FINLAND 1973

With the same gauge of 1524mm (5ft), and direct rail connection with its large neighbour, Finland's largest

railway interchange partner has always been the Russian railways. The VR's first all-electric locomotives, the Class Sr1 came

from Russia, with mechanical and most electric components built by Novocherkassk Electric Locomotive Works, with some

parts produced in Finland by Oy Strömberg Ab. All are mixed-traffic locomotives for use on any service, paired if necessary.

With three decades of service behind them, the Sr1 class has seen its territory greatly expanded as VR has gradually extended the range of electrification, which uses the European standard of 25kV AC at 50Hz.

TYPE: Bo-Bo mixed-traffic electric
POWER: 25kV AC at 50Hz
TRACTIVE EFFORT: 176.5kN (39,700lbf) at 73km/h (44mph)

MAX. OPERATING SPEED: 140km/h (87mph)
WEIGHT: 84t (186,000lb)
OVERALL LENGTH: 18.96m (63ft 3in)

MAX. AXLE LOAD: 21t (46,500lb)
GAUGE: 1524mm (5ft)

The roof-mounted equipment typical of a 1970s electric locomotive is displayed in this view of a VR Class SR1 taken in September 2001.

CLASSES 130 TO 132 CO-CO GERMAN STATE RAILWAYS (DR)

GERMANY 1973

In new DB red livery, a pair of Russian-built Class 232 locomotives stand at the *Hauptbahnhof* in Dresden, in the summer of 2001.

Russian-built locomotives were not always popular with operators in Eastern Europe, who usually had little choice in matters of supply, but this class of over 700 mixed-traffic diesel-electric locomotives, built at Voroshilovgrad with Kolomna vee-form diesel engines, was well received both by the *Deutsche*

Reichsbahn (DR) and later by *Deutsche Bundesbahn* (DB). Reclassed in the 1990s as DB Class 230 to 232 following amalgamation of DR and DB as *Die Bahn*, they have penetrated as far west as Aachen and Rotterdam. The class differences relate to the provision of electric train heat supply and different

maximum speeds, depending on the traffic mode. The type also

works in Bulgaria and in some former Soviet countries.

TYPE: Mixed-traffic main-line diesel-electric
WHEEL arrangement: Co-Co
POWER: Kolumna V-form diesel, 2200kW (2950hp); DC generator; six axle-hung DC traction motors
TRACTIVE EFFORT: 340kN (76,435lbf)

MAX. OPERATING SPEED: 120km/h (75mph)
WEIGHT: 123 tonnes (270,120lb)
OVERALL LENGTH: 20.62m (67ft 8in)
GAUGE: 1435mm (4ft 8.5in)
Specifications for Class 232.

CLASS 87 BO-BO BRITISH RAIL (BR)

GREAT BRITAIN 1973

Thirty-five electric locomotives of this class were built from 1973, when the more severely graded northern section of Britain's West Coast Main Line underwent electrification in the early 1970s. The locomotives were a direct development of the

Class 86 fleet, but with more power and a maximum speed of 160km/h (100mph). They were later adapted for push-pull working on express trains. 'Voyager' and 'Pendolino' trains have displaced them and most are not in use.

TYPE: Bo-Bo mainline mixed-traffic electric locomotive
POWER: 25,000V 50Hz AC overhead line collection; 3730kW (5000hp); tap-changer control; four DC frame-mounted traction motors with quill drives to the axles
TRACTIVE EFFORT: 258kN (58,000lbf)

MAX. OPERATING SPEED: 160km/h (100mph)
WEIGHT: 85t (187,040lb)
MAX. AXLE LOAD: not known
OVERALL LENGTH: 17.83m (58ft 6in)
GAUGE: 1435mm (4ft 8.5in)

CLASS 381 ELECTRIC MULTIPLE UNIT JAPAN NATIONAL RAILWAYS (JNR)

JAPAN 1973

Japan's thousands of miles of curving main lines encouraged an early experimentation with tilting train technology, even while also developing the *Shinkansen* project. A tilting design of the 'pendulum' type was tried out on a prototype EMU three-car set, Series 591, in 1970, and was sufficiently successful to be incorporated in the Class 381 nine-car units. Their body design was based on that of the Class 581, but narrower to allow for the tilting effect within the overall loading gauge.

The Class 381 units ran from Kyoto and Osaka on 'Ocean Arrow'

services to the Pacific coast resorts of Shirahama and Shingu, until they were eventually displaced in the 1990s by Series 283 EMU trains.

TYPE: express 'tilting' train set
POWER: six motor cars, each with four 100kw (160hp) traction motors
TRACTIVE EFFORT: N/A
MAX. OPERATING SPEED: 120km/h (75mph)
TOTAL WEIGHT: 342t (753,802lb)
MAX. AXLE LOAD: 9.75t (21,490lb)
OVERALL LENGTH: 191.70m (628ft 11in)

The inward curve of the sides is the most distinctive feature of this pioneering tilting design, seen on the Hanwa line in November 1978.

CLASS 6E BO-BO SOUTH AFRICAN RAILWAYS (SAR)

This mixed-traffic class marked a significant step forward in SAR's electric fleet. Technical improvements in motor design gave the Class 6E a 75 per cent higher tractive effort over the preceding Class 5E. Many improvements and adaptations were made, from insulating materials to redesigned bogies, with axle-hung nose-suspended motors, and an air suspension between bogies and body. Eighty of the class were built, all fully compatible and operating freely in multiple with the older classes 5E, 5E1 and 6E1.

TYPE: Bo-Bo universal traffic
POWER: 2252kW (3020hp)
SUPPLY: 3000V DC
TRACTIVE EFFORT: 193kN (43400lbf) at 41km/h (25.5mph)
MAX. OPERATING SPEED: 112km/h (70mph)
WEIGHT: 89 tonnes (196,245lb)
MAX. AXLE LOAD: 22.5 tonnes (49,613lb)
OVERALL LENGTH: 15.495m (50ft 6in)
GAUGE: 1067mm (3ft 6in)

Over the years, the front-end details of the class varied as locomotives were refitted, as did the paintwork. Compared to the exuberance of some European designs, Spoornet locomotives have an austere appearance.

CLASS 1044 BO-BO AUSTRIAN FEDERAL RAILWAYS (ÖBB)

Based on the Swedish Rc concept (see 1975) with minor external design differences and single-arm pantographs, these Austrian-built locomotives were rated to deliver considerably more power. Totalling 140, they were intended to haul both passenger and freight trains on main-line service, and can be seen all over the country. Always liveried in ÖBB red, their distinctive outline is also familiar in southern Germany, where they work through to Munich and even as far as Frankfurt am Main.

TYPE: Bo-Bo mainline mixed-traffic electric
POWER: 15,000V 16.67Hz AC overhead line collection; 5300kW (7105hp); thyristor control; rheostatic braking; four frame-mounted DC traction motors
TRACTIVE EFFORT: 314kN (70,590lbf)
MAX. OPERATING SPEED: 160km/h (100mph)
WEIGHT: 83t (182,275lb)
MAX. AXLE LOAD: not known
OVERALL LENGTH: 16m (52ft 6in)
GAUGE: 1435mm (4ft 8.5in)

This versatile class can still be seen on freight trains as well as inter-city expresses. 'Taurus' locomotives are replacing them now.

CLASS 350 BO-BO CZECHOSLOVAK STATE RAILWAYS (CSD)

Now running on the Slovakian Railways following the break-up of Czechoslovakia, the Class 350 are dual-voltage locomotives. Something about their body-styling earned them the nickname of 'gorillas'. Two prototypes in 1974 were followed by 18 more in 1976. Today Class 350 is responsible for running EuroCity and international trains on the Budapest and Vienna to Dresden and Berlin corridor south of Praha to Brno and Bratislava, although most of the route is in the Czech Republic. Locomotive 350.01 has been modified for 160km/h (100mph) operation. The rest of the class are likely to be treated similarly.

TYPE: Bo-Bo express passenger
POWER: 4000kW (5435hp)
SUPPLY: 25kV 50Hz AC or 3000V DC
TRACTIVE EFFORT: 210kN (47250lbf)

MAX. OPERATING SPEED: 140 or 160km/h (87.5 or 100mph)
WEIGHT: 89t (196,245lb)
MAX. AXLE LOAD: 22.5t (49,613lb)

OVERALL LENGTH: 16.74m (54ft 8in)
GAUGE: 1435mm (4ft 8.5in)

CLASS 181.2 BO-BO GERMAN FEDERAL RAILWAYS (DB)

This was DB's first dual-voltage electric locomotive, intended for cross-border work into Luxembourg and eastern France. Twenty-five strong, they were built by Krupps of Essen, with AEG electrical parts. Capable of working under either 15,000V or 25,000V wires, the class 181.2 operates on both passenger and freight services from locations such as Frankfurt-am-Main, Saarbrücken and Koblenz to Strasbourg and Metz in France and also to Basel. All are based in Frankfurt, though not all are in service and two are held for spare part provision.

TYPE: Bo-Bo mainline mixed-traffic dual-voltage electric
POWER: 15,000V 16.667Hz AC and 25,000V AC 50Hz AC overhead line collection; 3200kW (4290hp); rheostatic braking; four DC traction motors
TRACTIVE EFFORT: 285kN (64,070lbf)
MAX. OPERATING SPEED: 160km/h (100mph)
WEIGHT: 83t (182,275lb)
MAX. AXLE LOAD: not known
OVERALL LENGTH: 17.94m (58ft 10in)
GAUGE: 1435mm (4ft 8.5in)

A Class 181 on an inter-city service. Newer electric multiple-unit trains have reduced the range of services for these locomotives.

CLASS 250 CO-CO GERMAN STATE RAILWAYS (DR)

East Germany (the DDR) built some very effective electric locomotives in the post-war years, and this heavy freight class was a prime example. Prior to German unification, the Class 250s worked all over East Germany on electrified main lines, their high tractive effort enabling them to handle heavy freight loads with confidence. They were among the DR's first types to use thyristor electronic traction control.

After reunification, they were very well received by engine crews in the former Federal Republic. Now classified as '155' – in line with the electric freight Class 150 on the former *Deutsche Bundesbahn* (DB), which it began to displace – these somewhat austere-looking locomotives are liveried in DB Cargo red. After the collapse of heavy freight traffic in the former DDR, surplus Class 155s have found useful work in western Germany and can be seen in the Ruhr and Rhein areas, and also work in the south around Nürnberg and Munich.

TYPE: Co-Co mainline heavy freight electric
POWER: 15,000V 16.67Hz AC overhead line collection; 5400kW (7240hp); thyristor control; six axle-hung traction motors

TRACTIVE EFFORT: 465kN (104,535lbf)
MAX. OPERATING SPEED: 125km/h (78mph)
WEIGHT: 123t (270,120lb)

MAX. AXLE LOAD: not known
OVERALL LENGTH: 19.6m (64ft 1in)

CLASS WCAM-1 CO-CO INDIAN RAILWAYS

INDIA 1974

Built at Chittaranjan Locomotive Works (CLW), and sharing mechanical parts with Class WAM-4, the 53 engines of this class were the first Indian locomotives able to run under dual voltage, and are fitted with separate AC and DC pantographs. On the Bombay (Mumbai) to Ahmedabad line, the direct current and alternating current networks meet

at Virar, and until the arrival of WCAM-1 a change of locomotive was necessary. Although built to use either AC or DC supply, the WCAM-1 has had some problems with both. To take the direct current 1500V supply, it uses series-parallel resistance control, which in practice has been limited just to series connections, holding maximum speed down to 75km/h

(46.8mph). The 25,000V supply is transformed and rectified to 1500V, but here again the control

system limits practical running to the top notch of each series, series parallel and parallel connections.

TYPE: Co-Co multi purpose dual voltage
POWER: AC 2715kW (3689hp); DC 2185kW (2969hp)
SUPPLY: 25kV 50Hz AC and 1500V DC
TRACTIVE EFFORT: AC 332kN (74,700lbf) DC 277kN (62,325lbf)

MAX. OPERATING SPEED: AC 110km/h (68.8mph) DC 75km/h (46.8mph)
WEIGHT: 113t (249,165lb)
MAX. AXLE LOAD: 19t (41,895lb)
OVERALL LENGTH: 20.95m (68ft 4in)
GAUGE: 1676mm (5ft 6in)

CLASS 2601 B-B PORTUGUESE RAILWAYS (CFP)

PORTUGAL 1974

Class 2601 is a clone of the France's SNCF Class BB-15000, also designed and built by Alsthom. They have the same

monomotor layout – in CP's case with changeable gear ratios for passenger and freight working, implemented with the engine

stationary. Twelve were built in France, before the Portuguese Sorefame works took over. The locomotives operate express

passenger trains throughout the electrified network in Portugal, including international services from Spain. They see some freight service, though this tends to be the preserve of the more modern Class 5600 Bo-Bos that do not require gear re-setting.

TYPE: B-B mainline mixed-traffic electric
POWER: 25,000V 50Hz AC overhead line collection; 2940kW (3940hp); tap-changer control; two frame-mounted monomotor DC traction motors
TRACTIVE EFFORT: 205kN (64,200lbf) passenger gearing; 245kN (55,000lbf) freight gearing
MAX. OPERATING SPEED: 160km/h (100mph) passenger gearing; 100km/h (62mph) freight gearing
WEIGHT: 78t (171,295lb)
MAX. AXLE LOAD: not known
OVERALL LENGTH: 17.5m (57ft 5in)
GAUGE: 1668mm (5ft 6in)

Though designated as mixed-traffic types, the Class 2601 often work on express services, such as Madrid–Lisbon.

ER200 14-CAR SET SOVIET RAILWAYS (SZD)

RUSSIA 1974

Moscow to Leningrad (St Petersburg) was always Russia's prime express route, and, with express electric multiple unit sets successfully employed in other countries, SZD had embarked on planning the ER200 as long ago as 1965. The prototype set was built from 1972 – 14 cars were to form the full consist of two driving trailers and twelve motor coaches. In 1990, it was split into two shorter sets, with two new driving cars. Neither these nor the full set ever went into production, and services between the cities remained locomotive-hauled.

The ER 200 still runs a 'super-fast' service between Moscow and St Petersburg in the summer months.

TYPE: express EMU
POWER: 960kW (1304hp) per motor coach
SUPPLY: 3000V DC
TRACTIVE EFFORT: not applicable

MAX. OPERATING SPEED: 200km/h (125mph)
WEIGHT: 58t (127,890lb) motor; 48t (105,840lb) trailer

MAX. AXLE LOAD: 14.5t (31,973lb) motor
OVERALL LENGTH: 26.5m (86ft 6in) per car
GAUGE: 1524mm (5ft)

GE CLASS E60 CO-CO AMTRAK

At a time of crisis for the American railways, with most of them losing money heavily on passenger services, National Rail Passenger Corporation, better known as Amtrak, was established by the US Congress in May 1971 to run all the nation's inter-city passenger services. Initially it was wholly dependent on existing passenger locomotives and rolling stock, but in 1972, Amtrak ordered the first of 26 new electrics from General Electric, intended as replacements for its inherited and now elderly ex-PRR GG1 fleet. The new locomotives were designed for passenger service at a maximum 192km/h (120mph) operation. In 1974–5, two varieties were delivered; seven E60CPs that featured a steam generator to provide heat for older passenger stock, and 19 E60CHs that used head-end electric power for modern passenger stock such as Amtrak's Budd-built Amfleet cars. The six-wheel power bogies proved unsuitable for running at the maximum speeds, and after the derailing of a test train at 169km/h (105mph) the maximum operating speed was reduced to just 137km/h (85mph), and Amtrak had to look to Europe for a really effective high-speed electric locomotive. In the 1980s, Amtrak sold many of its E60s, but some were still used up to 2003 on heavy long-distance trains. One is preserved.

TYPE: Co-Co passenger electric
POWER: Alternating current: 12.5 at 25Hz; and 25kV at 60Hz
TRACTIVE EFFORT: 334kN (75,000lbf) to 364.4kN (82,000lbf)
MAX. OPERATING SPEED: 137km/h (85mph)
WEIGHT: 176t (387,900lb)
OVERALL LENGTH: 21.717m (71ft 3in)
MAX. AXLE LOAD: 29t (64,650lb)
GAUGE: 1435mm (4ft 8in)

Between 1986 and 1988, those E60s that remained with Amtrak were rebuilt, fitted for electric train heating and reclassified as E60MA (Motor Alternating) in the 600 series.

CLASS 20 CO-CO BELGIAN NATIONAL RAILWAYS (SNCB)

For more than 20 years, this was the SNCB's most powerful electric class, though in service it was not always reliable. Twenty-five were built in Belgium between 1975 and 1977 and worked – always in dark-green SNCB colours – as mixed-traffic engines, hauling passenger trains on the Brussels–Luxembourg axis, and container and bulk freights on southbound lines from the port of Antwerpen. Following the arrival of the SNCB's Class 13 in 1997, survivors have been relegated to carriage shunting and other tasks.

TYPE: Co-Co mainline mixed-traffic electric
POWER: 3000V DC overhead line collection; 5200kW (6970hp); thyristor control; rheostatic braking; six frame-mounted DC traction motors
TRACTIVE EFFORT: 314kN (70,590lbf)
MAX. OPERATING SPEED: 160km/h (100mph)
WEIGHT: 110t (241,570lb)
MAX. AXLE LOAD: not known
OVERALL LENGTH: 19.5m (63ft 8in)
GAUGE: 1435mm (4ft 6in)

No. 20007 outside Brussels Midi. In 1975, these were among the first DC supply locomotives to be equipped with thyristor technology.

CLASS V63 CO-CO HUNGARIAN STATE RAILWAYS (MÁV)

The sidewall design of these long engines earned them the irreverent nickname of 'hi-fi', but these were MÁV's most powerful locomotives until 'Taurus' types were introduced in 2002. Although prototypes existed in 1975, line production did not start until 1980, and a total of 56 were built by Ganz MÁVAG. Thyristor controls developed by Ganz were installed, and the powerful 2575kW (3500hp) rheostatic brake is also under thyristor control. Eleven units have been upgraded to 160km/h (100mph) working as Class V63.1. In 2003, 60 were in current traffic, most of them deployed east of Budapest and working on international freight and passenger traffic, with some workings taking them to Bratislava in Slovakia.

TYPE: Co-Co express passenger and heavy freight
POWER: 3680kW (5000hp)
SUPPLY: 25kV 50Hz AC
TRACTIVE EFFORT: 442kN (99,450lbf)
MAX. OPERATING SPEED: 120 to 160km/h (75 or 100mph)
WEIGHT: 116t (255,780lb)
MAX. AXLE LOAD: 19.5t (42,998lb)
OVERALL LENGTH: 19.54m (63ft 9in)
GAUGE: 1435mm (4ft 8.5in)

CLASS E656 BO-BO-BO STATE RAILWAYS (FS)

Three bogies supporting an articulated double body unit have long been an Italian speciality, a mechanical arrangement going back to the E625 prototypes of 1927 introduced with the very first Italian 3000V DC electrified route between Foggia and Benevento. But by 1975, the power that an AC electric locomotive could pack into a single body and two four wheel bogies was such that the articulated type, for anything but the heaviest freight duties, was no longer necessary. The Class E656, known as *caimano,* or 'alligator', was to be the last of its kind: the FS' final development of direct-current motored articulated-body electric locomotives, and the last three-bogie design. The direct-current Bo-Bo-Bo layout was built in large numbers, from the E626 production batch derived from the

E625 prototypes through E636, E645, E646 to E656, of which 458 were built, bringing the total for the type to well over a thousand. The direct-current electrification system of FS did not need the bulky transformer required by the alternating-current system in Switzerland, where (because of its weight) the transformer had to occupy a central position in the locomotive body. Italian engineers had no such restrictions in their machines, hence the attraction of the articulated design in a country with many curving, hilly railway lines. Class E656's six fully-suspended, direct-current, series-wound traction motors are double-armature machines geared to a common hollow-axle drive arrangement. Double-armature traction motors were relatively outdated technology, but their use

allowed more flexible permutations of traction motor connections and economical running notches. Caseralta, Casertane, Reggianne, Sofer and TIBB all built locomotives of this class, with electrical equipment from Ansaldo, Asgen, Ercole, Marelli, Italtrafo and TIBB. Some design changes were introduced in later production batches, including modern electronics such as static inverters, which replaced rotating motor generator sets for auxiliary functions.

The division of FS into business sectors saw the E6546 class split among express passenger operations (154 locomotives), regional passenger (77), regional passenger equipped for push-pull working (58) and freight (169). In recent years, E656 has been reduced to 150km/h (93.8mph)

Class E656 No. 469 waits for a freight train at Domodossola station, 11 April 1996.

maximum speed and is no longer used on fast inter-city passenger trains. Withdrawals have been frequent, though some are still used on heavier slower duties.

TYPE: Bo-Bo-Bo heavy freight and express passenger
POWER: 4800kW (6522hp)
SUPPLY: 3000V DC
TRACTIVE EFFORT: 131kN (29500lbf) at 103km/h (64mph)
MAX. OPERATING SPEED: 160km/h (100mph)
WEIGHT: 120t (264,600lb)
MAX. AXLE LOAD: 20t (44,100lb)
OVERALL LENGTH: 18.29m (59ft 8in)
GAUGE: 1435mm (4ft 8.5in)

PLAN Y0 'SPRINTER' ELECTRIC MULTIPLE UNIT NETHERLANDS RAILWAYS (NS)

Rapid acceleration gave this two-car electric multiple unit (EMU) set its appropriate 'Sprinter' name. A high-performance EMU for high-density traffic, it was first deployed by Netherlands Railways on the *Zoetermeer Stadslijn* in Den Haag. It was Talbot-built with Oerlikon electrics, and all the axles were powered in the eight Class Y0 and 15 Y1 sets.

From 1994, they were modified as *Spitspendel* ('peak shuttle'), with fewer seats but increased standing room. Later they were further adapted for short distance work, and marketed under the name *Citypendel.* These names were a

sign of a new era, of train 'marketing' to a public educated to follow brand names; previously, type designations had been mostly for railway use.

TYPE: high-density suburban EMU
POWER: 1280kW (1739hp) all axles motored
SUPPLY: 1500V DC
TRACTIVE EFFORT: N/A
MAX. OPERATING SPEED: 125km/h (78.1mph)
WEIGHT: 105t (231,525lb) two cars
MAX. AXLE LOAD: 13.2t (29,106lb)
OVERALL LENGTH: 52.22m (170ft 5in)
GAUGE: 1435mm (4ft 8.5in)

In standard NS yellow livery, a Plan Y0 'Sprinter' runs along an embankment in the Dutch polder-lands.

CLASS RC4 BO-BO STATE RAILWAYS (SJ)

Taking over from the long-established (and still-running) D range, the Rc range brought modern electric operation to the SJ and dominated its locomotive stock, with a total of 366 units delivered between 1967 and 1988. It formed a group of six classifications of basically identical locomotives, with different traffic characteristics. Class Rc3 was introduced from 1967, and over 360 of classes Rc1 to Rc6 were built, of which 130 are currently Class Rc4.

Straightforward Bo-Bo machines, they work almost all passenger and freight trains throughout Sweden. Rc4 was the first thyristor-controlled

locomotive in quantity production: a mixed-traffic type, but largely used for main-line freight work. It was the last locomotive type built by the Swedish firm of NOHAB before it finally abandoned railway work in 1979.

Built for Swedish 15,000V 16,67Hz AC current, and visually distinctive with their horizontally-ribbed bodysides, these classes have an involved history, with various conversions from one to another. Class Rc6, introduced in 1985, consisted of 40 new locomotives and 60 conversions of Rc5, which had been introduced only three years earlier. Class Rc7 (now withdrawn) was a small

number of Rc6s re-geared to run at 180km/h (112mph) to substitute for high-speed electric multiple unit trains.

The versatility and reliability of the Rc locomotives have made them an export success for Sweden, running in other countries mostly under the 25,000V catenary. Ten were ordered by ÖBB in Austria (these were later sold back to a Swedish railway) and others were built under licence; a large number were built under licence in the former Yugoslavia, some of which are running on the railways of Serbia, Croatia and Macedonia. Romania has 130, and a group of Croatian locos have

been sent on loan to Turkish State Railways. An Rc4 sent to the United States in late 1976 became the basis of Amtrak's high-speed AEM-7 locomotive.

TYPE: Bo-Bo mainline mixed-traffic electric
POWER: 15,000V 16.67Hz AC overhead line collection; 3600kW (4825hp); thyristor control; four DC traction motors
TRACTIVE EFFORT: 290kN (65,200lbf)
MAX. OPERATING SPEED: 135km/h (84mph)
WEIGHT: 78t (171,295lb)
MAX AXLE LOAD: not known
OVERALL LENGTH: 15.52m (50ft 11in)
GAUGE: 1435mm (4ft 8.5in)

CLASS 363 C-C YUGOSLAVIAN RAILWAYS (JDZ)

Now Slovenian Railways Class 363, these were acquired by the former JDZ from France and are appropriately known as

Brigittes. Typical Alsthom designs of a kind seen on railways of many countries, with negative-raked cab windscreens, they had two-speed

monomotor bogies provided with separate gearing for freight or passenger duties. Significant freight from the Adriatic seaport of

Koper is shifted by Class 363 with most trains requiring additional power up the heavy gradients from sea level. The class also hauls inter-city passenger services centred on Ljubljana.

TYPE: C-C electric
POWER: 2750kW (3736hp)
SUPPLY: 3000V DC
TRACTIVE EFFORT: 131kN (29475lbf)
MAX. OPERATING SPEED: 125km/h (75mph)
WEIGHT: 114t (251,370lb)
MAX. AXLE LOAD: 19t (41,895lb)
OVERALL LENGTH: 20.19m (65ft 11in)
GAUGE: 1435mm (4ft 8.5in)

Now ageing but still in harness – here with the Slovenian Railways – the Class 363 resembles the SNCF CC72000 but is less powerful.

CLASS BB-22200 B-B FRENCH NATIONAL RAILWAYS (SNCF)

With electrified networks at 1500V and 25kV in France, trains passing from one to the other have either to change locomotives or use dual-voltage machines. Class BB-22200 is a dual-voltage version of classes BB-7200 and BB-15000 (add the series numbers together). Of

typical French appearance with monomotor bogies, it is a chopper-controlled DC locomotive in effect, also carrying a transformer and solid-state rectifiers that are switched into use when the locomotive passes under 25kV AC wires. The class as complete totalled 205 locomotives.

TYPE: B-B mixed-traffic dual-voltage electric locomotive
POWER: 1500V DC and 25,000V 50Hz AC overhead line collection; 4360kW (5845bhp); AC transformer/rectification; DC chopper control; two DC frame-mounted monomotor traction motors
TRACTIVE EFFORT: 294kN (66,095lbf)
MAX. OPERATING SPEED: 160km/h (100mph)
WEIGHT: 90t (197,645lb)
MAX AXLE LOAD: not known
OVERALL LENGTH: 17.48m (57ft 4in)
GAUGE: 1435mm (4ft 8.5in)

This class includes the only SNCF locomotives ever to work on British tracks, if only in the Channel Tunnel freight yard.

CLASS BB-7200 B-B FRENCH NATIONAL RAILWAYS (SNCF) FRANCE 1976

Running on DC electrified lines, particularly in the south-east of France, these are modern mixed traffic electrics. Although they are of monomotor type, they do not have a gear-change mechanism. Instead, the electronically controlled traction system automatically sets up the requested characteristics for fast

TYPE: B-B mainline mixed-traffic electric locomotive
POWER: 1500V DC overhead line collection; 4040kW (5415hp); DC chopper

control; two DC frame-mounted traction motors
TRACTIVE EFFORT: 288kN (64,745lbf)
MAX. OPERATING SPEED: 160 or

200km/h (100 or 125mph)
WEIGHT: 84t (184,470lb)
MAX AXLE LOAD: not known
OVERALL LENGTH: 17.48m (57ft 4in)

passenger or heavy freight work – an early sign of the application of electronics and, later, microprocessors that would

revolutionize the management of locomotive engines and control systems. Apart from the 240 BB-7200, there is an AC version (Class

BB-15000) and a dual-voltage version (Class BB-22200) of this highly successful class.

'INTERCITY 125' HIGH-SPEED TRAINS BRITISH RAIL (BR) GREAT BRITAIN 1976

In 'Midland Mainline' livery, three Class 43 IC-125 trains at St Pancras in September 1999.

New standards of speed, efficiency and punctuality established by the '125' trains on Britain's many non-electrified main lines changed travellers' perceptions and generated much new traffic. For some time, British Rail engineers had been working on a high-speed train (HST) project – the Advanced Passenger Train (APT) – and had developed tilting technology that would enable it to travel faster on existing tracks with their many curves, but progress was slow. In 1972, with work still in hand on the tilting train, some criticized the decision to invest in a conventional diesel-electric train with a top speed of 200km/h (125mph). Two power cars that were basically simple, single-ended, streamlined, lightweight Bo-Bo diesel-electric locomotives, were positioned at each end of a rake of BR standard Mark 3 coaches using a new design of air sprung bogie with a swing bolster, with bodies longer than any before in the UK, at 23m (75ft). The extra length did not increase the vehicle weights because of the intelligent design of the steel body structures, which at 37 tonnes (36.4 tons) are models of engineering efficiency. A high-speed Paxman Valenta engine was installed in the power cars, coupled to a brushless alternator feeding four fully suspended DC

traction motors. The combined power of the two engines totalled 3357kW (4500hp). The carriages were fully air-conditioned and used standard body layouts for both first and standard classes. Inside, they were fitted out with airline-type seat rails on the floors and bodysides that enabled different seating layouts to be installed easily without disturbing the wall-to-wall carpets.

After extensive prototype running, 98 HST production sets were built from 1976, either as seven-car or eight-car sets. All were initially liveried in BR's standard blue-and-grey colours, the power cars having a striking layout of blue and warning yellow. In the years that followed, they took over many routes, particularly after electrification displaced them from the London–Glasgow route. For the first time, a daytime service was established on Britain's longest single-train haul, the 912.5km (567-mile) run from London to Inverness. An unusual change was made to a small number of power cars to assist in the introduction of fast electric push-pull trains when the London–Newcastle–Edinburgh East Coast main line was being electrified. In the absence of driving trailer cars, eight HST power cars were equipped with side buffers at the streamlined cab ends and used as powered driving

trailers (if that is not a contradiction in terms) for the Class 91 electric locomotives temporarily working rakes of Mark 3 stock taken from HSTs that would soon be moved elsewhere. After the arrival of IC225 Mark 4 carriages and driving trailers, the HST sets were reformed and sent to cross-country services. The side buffers remain an anomaly on the few cars that have them.

The establishment by BR of the InterCity business resulted in a new livery for the HSTs. This used dark grey across the window band`with light beige below the side windows and a dark grey roof. Each coach was lined out in white and red just below the window line.

The HST was originally designed for long stretches of running at up to 200km/h (125mph). Cross-country services introduced them to more stop-start working, which caused some stress to the Paxman Valenta engines. In warm weather, the heat of an engine that has been running hard in stop-start conditions has to be dissipated even when the engine is shut down to idling speed as the train slows down and calls at the next stop. The radiator system on the HSTs had not been designed for such treatment, and began to suffer from coolant leaks and a build-up of sludge or scale inside. Paxman supplied for trial five of

their VP185s, a more modern engine rated at the same output and with the same 'footprint' (allowing it to fit the power cars), but with stronger components, better wear rates and a more capacious cooling system. This became the standard replacement for the HST power cars as the older Valenta engines wore out. The VP185 reliability is good, and they need overhauling only after running at least twice the engine hours of the older engines.

Privatization of BR into separate regional companies and franchises brought many changes to HST services and many new livery styles. Great North Eastern Railway (GNER) painted them dark blue with a red stripe. The Midland Mainline (MML) company painted its eight-coach sets green with tangerine stripes. Virgin has replaced most of its HSTs with 'Voyager' DMUs. First Great Western (FGW) is still largely dependent on its HST fleet.

Though now 30 years old, the '125' trains are still in intensive use, and remain popular with passengers, and their presence on the railways of Great Britain is assured for some years yet. When finally withdrawn, they are likely to be among the highest-mileage trains in the world.

Details below are for the production power cars (two per train):

TYPE: 'InterCity 125', diesel-electric power cars
WHEEL ARRANGEMENT: Bo-Bo
POWER EQUIPMENT: Paxman Valenta 12RP200L, high speed V-form diesel, 1680kW (2250bhp); Brush alternator with rotating diodes; four Brush or GEC traction motors, fully suspended with flexible drives to each axle
MAX. OPERATING SPEED: 200km/h (125mph)
WEIGHT: 70t (153,725lb)
OVERALL LENGTH: 17.805m (58ft 5in)
GAUGE: 1435mm (4ft 8.5in)

CLASS 56 CO-CO BRITISH RAIL (BR)

GREAT BRITAIN 1976

In a purchase surprising to many people, the first 30 of this bulk freight diesel-electric were supplied by Electroputere of communist Romania, as sub-contractors to the Brush company of Loughborough, but quick delivery had been requested, and Electroputere could do it. The other 90 of Class 56 were built by British Rail Engineering at Crewe and Doncaster works. The bogie design was based on the Romanian CFR Class 060-DA, while the body was based on the BR Class 47. Ruston supplied a development of the EE 16-cylinder diesel engine. All were deployed on coal haulage, and many of the class had slow speed

TYPE: freight main-line diesel-electric
WHEEL ARRANGEMENT: Co-Co
POWER: Ruston 16RK3CT 16-cylinder V-form diesel, 2425kW (3250hp); Brush alternator; six axle-hung DC traction motors
TRACTIVE EFFORT: 275kN (61,800lbf)

MAX. OPERATING SPEED: 130km/h (80mph)
WEIGHT: 126t (276,705lb)
OVERALL LENGTH: 19.355m (63ft 6in)
GAUGE: 1435mm (4ft 8.5in)

control for automatic loading and unloading of wagons on the 'merry-go-round' system. Some are now withdrawn.

CLASS 071 CO-CO IRISH TRANSPORT COMPANY (CIE)

IRELAND 1976

For nearly 20 years, until the arrival of the Class 201 in 1994, these were the largest and most powerful locomotives ever to operate in Ireland. Of impressive length at 17.3m (56ft 10in), they had full-width cabs at each end but a hood-type superstructure between them, with railed side walkways. Eighteen were delivered for main-line use from Electro-Motive Division, and the six-axle JT22CW locomotives were known as 'the big engines'. The 071 class worked Dublin–Belfast expresses, and still appear on intercity passenger trains and through freights, and they are preferred power on the Dublin–Rosslare

TYPE: Co-Co, diesel-electric
POWER: EMD 12-645 producing 1679kW (2250hp) for traction
TRACTIVE EFFORT: 209kN (48,850lbf) continuous TE at 24.2km/h (15.1mph)

MAX. OPERATING SPEED: 144km/h (90mph)
WEIGHT: 100.5t (221,606lb)
OVERALL LENGTH: 17.3m (56ft 10in)
GAUGE: 1600mm (5ft 3in)

Europort and Dublin–Sligo runs, where 201s are presently prohibited because of weight restrictions. Three similar locomotives are also operated by NIR in Northern Ireland.

Irish Rail Class 071.087 at the renovated Victorian station of Dundalk, on 3 August 2003.

ETR 401 PROTOTYPE TILTING TRAIN STATE RAILWAYS (FS)

ITALY 1976

Japan's bold construction of dedicated high-speed lines, though followed by France, was not considered a viable option by other countries, which nevertheless sought ways of speeding up services on existing tracks. On many lines, curves gave rise to local speed restrictions, which reduced the average speed of trains even when they were capable of high speeds. The solution was to incorporate a tilting mechanism in the bogies, so that as the train entered a curve, the carriage bodies were automatically tilted inwards, enabling the train to run 35–45 per cent faster in safety and with no discomfort to passengers. The concept of the tilting train began in the late 1960s, with design work in Great Britain, Canada, Italy, Japan and Sweden. In 1973, Japan built a tilting electric multiple unit set. The APT, 'Advanced Passenger Train', was extensively tested in Britain during the 1980s, but design problems persisted and in the end, through lack of capital to invest in the project, it was abandoned. In Italy, the prototype of a tilting train, Y 0160-71-99, a single-unit vehicle, was tested on the twisting Trofarello–Asti line in Piedmont and also on the fast Rome–Naples main line, and the construction of ETR 401, a four-car set, followed. After many tests, this train was acquired by the FS, and from 1976 was put into revenue-earning service on the Rome–Naples route as a luxury high-speed express.

First-class only, it seated 120 passengers and the third car was fitted out as a bar-restaurant. Despite the success of this unit, it remained a one-off, and

development of the concept did not really get under way until 1985. Britain, having abandoned the APT, sold its tilting technology to Italy, and the traction

equipment used on ETR 401 was now wholly redesigned. A new train, ETR 450, was put into service in 1988, incorporating the work of both Italian and British

designers. While ETR 401 had required a gyroscope and accelerometer to be fitted to every bogie, with consequent expense and risk of individual units failing to function, ETR 450 had these fitted only on the end bogies of the train. On all other bogies, the tilt mechanism operated automatically, in simultaneous conjunction with the master units. ETR technology, now owned and developed by Alstom-Ferroviaria, is incorporated in the very successful 'Pendolino' trains, now used by several countries including Britain and Finland.

The prototype ETR 401 train has recently been refurbished, and work is also going ahead in Britain to restore the APT-P train.

TYPE: four-car tilting electric train
POWER: N/A
TRACTIVE EFFORT: 250kN (56,215lbf)
MAX. OPERATING SPEED: 171km/h (106mph)
TOTAL WEIGHT: not known
MAX. AXLE LOAD: N/A
OVERALL LENGTH: 26.9m (88ft 4in)
BUILDER: FIAT, Turin

Doing the tilt – the ETR 401's lead vehicle reacts to the track's curve as it passes through a wayside station.

CLASS E1100 CO-CO MOROCCAN RAILWAYS (ONCF)   MOROCCO 1976

Moroccan freight traffic is dominated by the phosphate extraction industry and each year millions of tons are moved by rail, forming over 75 per cent of all freight traffic, and with a consequent need for heavy haulage power. Hitachi's, and Japan's, first locomotive sales to Africa were the 22 members of

this powerful class. Essentially derived from domestic Japanese designs, and similar mechanically to JNR Class EF81, the E10 class, with electric braking in the form of rheostats, and low 100km/h (62.5mph) speed with correspondingly high tractive effort, is entirely appropriate for heavy mineral workings.

E 1115 heads with a long rake of self-unloading phosphate wagons to the coast, where the contents will be transferred to a cargo ship.

TYPE: Co-Co heavy mineral traffic
POWER: 3000kW (4020hp)
SUPPLY: 3000V DC
TRACTIVE EFFORT: 314kN (70650lbf)
MAX. OPERATING SPEED: 100km/h (62.1mph)

WEIGHT: 120t (264,600lb)
MAX. AXLE LOAD: 20t (40,500lb)
OVERALL LENGTH: 19.7m (64 ft 7in)
GAUGE: 1435mm (4ft 8.5in)

F40PH CO-CO AMTRAK

USA 1976

Amtrak selected Electro-Motive Division's F40PH as a standard diesel-electric express passenger locomotive, and was, inevitably, the largest operator of the type. It is essentially a 'cowl' version of the GP40 road-switcher type, with full-width but unstressed carbody, mounted on the locomotive frame. Amtrak assigned F40PHs across all its network. On the as-yet unelectrified section of the North-East Corridor between Boston, Massachusetts, and New Haven, Connecticut, F40PHs were permitted to operate at their highest speed, though by the standards of many other countries it was an undistinguished pace, at 103km/h (64mph). By 2002, Amtrak had retired most of its F40PHs, having largely replaced them with General Electric GENESIS types. Some F40PHs are still operated by commuter agencies, and Canada's VIA Rail, and a few have been modified for freight.

TYPE: diesel-electric
POWER: 16-cylinder 645 engine producing 2235kW (3000hp).
TRACTIVE EFFORT: 304kN (68,440lbf)

MAX. OPERATING SPEED: 103km/h (64mph)
WEIGHT: 117t (257,985 lb)
OVERALL LENGTH: 17.12m (56ft 2in)
GAUGE: 1435mm (4ft 8.5in)

No. 403 heads a pair of F40PH locomotives on Amtrak's 'Empire Builder' train past Duplainville, Wisconsin, in May 1996.

CLASS C30-7 CO-CO VARIOUS US RAILROADS

USA 1976

A class that became very popular with railroad companies, the C30-7 was built by General Electric (GE) from 1976 up to 1986, when the Dash-8 line was introduced. More than 1100 were sold in the United States during that decade. Three gear ratios were offered: 83:20 for 43.5km/h (70mph) service; 81:22 for 49km/h (79mph); and 79:24 for 52km/h (84mph), depending on whether fast or slower freight was intended. Most C30-7s were used on bulk coal and ore trains, using the lowest ratio. The standard C30-7 used GE's turbocharged 7FDL-16 engine, while a variation designated C30-7A used a 12-cylinder GE 7FDL for better fuel economy. Burlington Northern, Conrail, CSX, Santa Fe, and Union Pacific, as well as railways in Mexico, operated C30-7s.

TYPE: Co-Co, diesel-electric
POWER: GE 7FDL-16 producing 2238kW (3000hp)
TRACTIVE EFFORT: 402kN (90,500lb) at 13.6km/h (8.5mph)

MAX. OPERATING SPEED: 112km/h (70mph) with 83:20 gear ratio
WEIGHT: 189t (420,000lb)
OVERALL LENGTH: 20.5m (67ft 3in)
GAUGE: 1435mm (4ft 8.5in)

B23-7 BO-BO VARIOUS US RAILROADS

The 'Dash' designation that had done so well for Electro-Motive Division (EMD) was also taken up by General Electric (GE) to indicate classes equipped with new electronics. On its middle-horsepower UB23 Bo-Bo road switcher, GE dropped the 'Universal' tag to replace it with the B23-7 when the Dash-7 line supplanted GE's older line in 1977. Using a 12-cylinder 7FDL diesel engine operating at 1050rpm to produce 1676kW (2250hp), the B23-7 was well suited for moderately heavy freight service, switching and

TYPE: Bo-Bo, diesel-electric
POWER AND OUTPUT: GE 7FDL-12 producing 1676kW (2250hp)
TRACTIVE EFFORT: 271kN (61,000lbf) at 6.2km/h (10mph) with 83:20 gear ratio

MAX. OPERATING SPEED: 112km/h (70mph)
WEIGHT: 127t (280,000lb)
OVERALL LENGTH: 18.948m (62ft 2in)
GAUGE: 1435mm (4ft 8.5in)

branch-line work. It was a worthy rival to EMD's GP38-2. Conrail was the first line to order B23-7s, and used them in a variety of secondary freight services, as well as on

switching work in yards and on track ballast trains. CSX, NS, Santa Fe and Union Pacific were also among large railroads that employed fleets of B23-7s.

A Conrail track geometry train is headed by a B23-7 as it runs through autumn woodlands past Becket, Massachusetts, on 7 October 1997.

CLASS E499.2 BO-BO CZECHOSLOVAK STATE RAILWAYS (CSD)

Identical in appearance to the dual-voltage Class 350 of 1974, and sharing the affectionate nickname of 'gorilla', all 27 locomotives of this DC electric class became an integral part of the Czech Republic (CD) fleet, as Class 150. Built by Skoda and designated as CSD Class E499.2,

TYPE: Bo-Bo express passenger
POWER: 4000kW (5435hp)
SUPPLY: 3000V DC
TRACTIVE EFFORT: 150 – 138kN

(31050lbf) at 101.2km/h (63.3mph); 151 – 123kN (27675lbf) at 113.9km/h (71.2mph)
MAX. OPERATING SPEED: 150 – 140km/h (87mph); 151 – 160km/h (100mph)

WEIGHT: 82t (180,810lb)
MAX. AXLE LOAD: 20.5t (45,203lb)
OVERALL LENGTH: 16.74m (54ft 8in)
GAUGE: 1435mm (4ft 8.5in)

it was used on heavier daytime and overnight passenger and mail trains east of Praha on the Praha–

Olomouc–Bohumin route, plus a variety of other main lines. A total of 13 members of the class were

also uprated to run at 160km/h (100mph), between 1996 and 2002.

CLASS 7E CO-CO SOUTH AFRICAN RAILWAYS (SAR)

The Union Carriage Works (UCW) of South Africa constructed these rather austere-looking units, using thyristor technology and other electrical equipment produced in South Africa by Brown Boveri and Siemens subsidiaries. Ordered for the newly electrified 25kV route from Ermelo to Richards Bay, linking the Transvaal coalfields to the sea, they were designed as heavy freight haulers, though they have been known to pull heavy passenger trains also. Traction rods, rheostatic braking, multiple unit control, and air and vacuum train braking equipment are fitted. Sixty-seven locomotives form Class 7E, with a further 64 designated 7E2, all of them assigned to Spoornet's 'CoalLink' traffic division.

TYPE: Co-Co heavy freight
POWER: 3000kW (4020hp)
SUPPLY: 25kV 50Hz AC

TRACTIVE EFFORT: 300kN (67400lbf) at 35km/h (21.8mph)
MAX. OPERATING SPEED: 100km/h (62.1mph)

WEIGHT: 124t (273,420lb)
MAX. AXLE LOAD: 21t (46,305lb)
OVERALL LENGTH: 18.465m (60 ft 7in)
GAUGE: 1067mm (3ft 6in)

CLASS 9E CO-CO SOUTH AFRICAN RAILWAYS (SAR)

A specialized electric type for an ore line, the 9E was not exceptionally powerful, but was intended to operate in multiples of three, which provided enough traction to keep 20,200-tonne (19,882-ton) ore trains on the move. The route, between Sishen and Saldanha, 864km (540 miles) long, was run by the South African Iron & Steel Industrial Corporation (ISCOR). Electrification is at 50kV, which reduces installation capital costs.

To fit the catenary, the locomotive body height is reduced to about two-thirds height at one end to give clearances for the pantograph and equipment. The DC traction motors are axle-hung, nose suspended, separately excited. Originally, 31 were ordered, followed by an additional six class 9E1 with certain differences of detail. Operation of the route was transferred from ISCOR to South African Railways (now renamed as Spoornet).

TYPE: Co-Co heavy freight
POWER: 3696kW (5021hp)
SUPPLY: 50kV 50Hz AC
TRACTIVE EFFORT: 382kN (85,900lbf)
MAX. OPERATING SPEED: 90km/h (56.2mph)

WEIGHT: 168t (370,440lb)
MAX. AXLE LOAD: 28t (61,740lb)
OVERALL LENGTH: 20.12m (65ft 8in)
GAUGE: 1067mm (3ft 6in)

GE C36-7 CO-CO VARIOUS US RAILROADS

As with other Dash-7 models, the C36-7 featured a number of detail improvements and modernizations over earlier General Electric (GE) designs, aimed at improving locomotive efficiency and reliability. The high-horsepower C36-7 diesel-electric succeeded the earlier six-motor U36-C, of the same power rating. Early C36-7s were nearly identical to GE's 2208kW (3000hp) C30-7, and the primary difference was an increase in the output of the 7FDL-16 diesel-engine. From 1983, GE supplied an improved C36-7 that incorporated some of the micro-processor controls featured on the Dash-8 types, and a new adhesion system. The last C36-7 featured a higher output and had a pronounced hump behind the cab that housed dynamic brake grids. In 2002, a fleet of former Union Pacific C36-7s were rebuilt by GE and shipped to the Estonian Railways.

TYPE: Co-Co, diesel-electric
POWER AND OUTPUT: GE 7FDL-16 producing 2686kW (3600hp)
TRACTIVE EFFORT: 431kN (96,900lbf) at 17.6km/h (11mph) with 83:20 gear ratio

MAX. OPERATING SPEED: 112km/h (70mph)
WEIGHT: 189t (420,000lb)
OVERALL LENGTH: 20.5m (67ft 3in)
GAUGE: 1435mm (4ft 8.5in)

CLASS AEM-7 BO-BO AMTRAK

Following dissatisfaction with the performance of the GE E60 electric locomotives on its New Haven–New York–Washington DC route, Amtrak turned to European suppliers for an effective high-speed design. Having tested French and Swedish electrics, it decided upon a variation of the versatile Swedish Rc-4 built by Nohab and ASEA. This became the AEM-7, built from 1979 by General Motors' Electro-Motive Division (EMD) at La Grange under license from ASEA. Though similar in looks to its Swedish antecedent, the AEM-7 is both heavier and designed to be much faster than the Rc-4. The required top speed on the North East Corridor was 200km/h (125mph). Several suburban commuter railways also bought AEM-7s and its successor class, the ALP44. Three have been scrapped but most are still in service, wearing Acela colours.

TYPE: Bo-Bo, high-speed electric locomotive
POWER: AC – 12.5V at 25Hz; 25kV at 60Hz
TRACTIVE EFFORT: 237kW (53,300lbf)
MAX. OPERATING SPEED: 200km/h (125mph)
WEIGHT: 90.47t (199,500lb)
OVERALL LENGTH: 15.583m (51ft 2in)
MAX. AXLE LOAD: 22.6t (49,875lb)
GAUGE: 1435mm (4ft 8.5in)

No. 928 on an East Coast Corridor train, its boxy shape at variance with the US-designed coaches. Note the single-arm pantograph.

TRAINS À GRANDE VITESSE (TGV) FRENCH NATIONAL RAILWAYS (SNCF) FRANCE 1980

Japan's incredible *Shinkansen* locomotive was undoubtedly the model, but being French, the planners and engineers of the SNCF did it their own way. In both the Japanese and French cases, the track was simply a high-quality version of classic railway track: the trains were what made the concept into a super-speed reality. With a top operating speed of around 300km/h (187mph), the first *Ligne à Grande Vitesse* (LGV *Sud-Est*) would run from Paris through to Lyon with very few intermediate stations, on a completely new line with wide curves but some quite severe gradients. Originally gas-turbine drive was planned for the trains and a prototype was built (France had already developed a gas-turbine multiple-unit train: see 1972), but rising oil prices in the early 1970s prompted a change to electric drive.

The first generation of production trains for the Paris–Lyon LGV, delivered in April 1980, were eight-coach articulated electric trains with a power car at each end. The power cars were streamlined, single-ended Bo-Bo electric locomotives with body-mounted electric motors driving

the axles of the bogies through cardan shafts. The outer end bogies of each carriage rake were also driven, each by two motors. The trains were liveried in a striking bright-orange colour that has only recently been supplanted by the grey-and-blue colours of later TGVs. On 27 September 1981, public services began between Paris and Lyon. Centre to centre, the TGV was the fastest transport available, beating air transport, and though the premium business market was the first to be targeted, they became immediately popular with a much wider public.

The runaway success of the Paris–Lyon TGV service led to a rapid expansion of TGV routes across the country. The *Atlantique* scheme took TGVs westwards from Paris towards Le Mans and Nantes (1989) with TGVs running on conventional railways as far as Brittany, Bordeaux and the Spanish border. These trains were 10-car sets with no motors on the carriages themselves, the milder gradients enabling two power cars to cope. TGV *Atlantiques* have a top operating speed of 300km/h (187mph). The Paris–Sud-Est sets

TGV power car No. 115 at Dijon, on the *Sud-Est* route between Paris and Lyon. The advent of the TGV brought a new appreciation of rail travel and the early 8-car units were filled to capacity and two-deck trains have since been introduced (see 1995).

were built for 280km/h (175mph) running, but are being upgraded now for the higher speed. The northern route links Paris with Lille and Calais, and with Brussels in Belgium (1993). For the Lille services and for trains using the new links around Paris that join up the *Nord*, *Sud-Est* and *Atlantique* lines, the TGV *Réseau* (Network) series was produced, formed of eight-car sets with two power cars. Some *Réseau* sets have the ability to run not only under the SNCF electrification voltages of 1500V DC and 25kV AC but also Italy's 3000V DC. Others have an additional voltage of 15kV AC, enabling them to operate into Switzerland. The *Sud-Est* line was extended to Valence by 1992 and TGVs were running from Paris to Marseille by 2001. An eastbound LGV to Strasbourg, to link with high-speed lines in Germany, is under construction. Expansion of traffic on the *Sud-Est* route prompted SNCF to order a fleet of double-deck TGVs, the first

double-deck high-speed trains in the world (see 1995).

The world rail speed record of 515km/h (322mph) was held by TGV *Atlantique* set No. 325 until beaten by the experimental Japanese Maglev train (see 2001). The following specifications refer to TGV *Sud-Est* sets.

TYPE: high-speed articulated electric trains
POWER (PER TRAIN): 1500V DC and 25,000V 50Hz AC overhead line collection; 6300kW (8445hp); AC transformer/rectification; 12 DC body-mounted traction motors
WHEEL ARRANGEMENT: Bo-Bo + Bo-2-2-2-2-2-2-Bo + Bo-Bo
MAX. OPERATING SPEED: 300km/h (187mph)
WEIGHT: 65t (142,745lb) power car; 44t (96,625lb) end carriage; 28t (61,490lb) intermediate carriage
OVERALL LENGTH: 22.15m (72ft 8in) power car; 21.845m (71ft 8in) end carriage; 18.7m (61ft 4in) intermediate carriages
GAUGE: 1435mm (4ft 8.5in)

U20C CO-CO JORDANIAN AQABA RAILWAY

JORDAN 1980

Phosphate haulage from the mines at El Abyad and El Hasa to the Red Sea port of Aqaba was the reason for existence of this 1050mm (3ft 4in) gauge railway – unusually, neither the more common 'narrow' 1m (3ft 3in) gauge nor the 'colonial' 1067mm (3ft 6in) version was used. To run

its bulk trains, the Jordanian Aqaba Railway bought 18 GE model U20C machines built in Brazil. The U20C was a standard single-cab road switcher produced by General Electric for export, and supplied to several countries, with many detailed variations to its basic hood unit design and GE 12-cylinder

TYPE: Co-Co diesel-electric
POWER: 1583kW (2150hp) from GE 7FDL-12 series engine
TRACTIVE EFFORT: 251kN (55,000lbf)

MAX. OPERATING SPEED: 100km/h (62mph)
WEIGHT: 112t (246,960lb)
OVERALL LENGTH: 17.2m (56ft 1in)
GAUGE: 1050mm (3ft 4in)

7FDL series engine, normally rated in this model at 1583kW (2150hp).

Eleven of the Jordanian units were operational in 2002.

CLASS DI4 CO-CO NORWEGIAN STATE RAILWAYS (NSB)

NORWAY 1980

After 25 years of successful operation of their Nohab/General Motors (GM) Class Di3 locomotives, NSB returned to GM for the power units of their next main-line diesel-electric purchase. Five powerful locomotives were required for the non-electrified routes leading out of Trondheim, the long line to Bodø in the north

and the mountainous Røros route south to Oslo. The locomotives were constructed by the Henschel works of Kassel, Germany (for some time an Electro-Motive Division affiliate), with EMD 16-cylinder 645E3B engines, and were for mixed-traffic use, with a maximum speed set at 140km/h (87.5mph). The angle-fronted cab

TYPE: mixed-traffic diesel-electric
WHEEL ARRANGEMENT: Co-Co
POWER: General Motors 16-645E3B 2451kW (3285hp); NEBB electric traction equipment

TRACTIVE EFFORT: 360kN (80,930lbf)
MAX. OPERATING SPEED: 140km/h (87.5mph)
WEIGHT: 114t (249,475lb)
OVERALL LENGTH: 20.8m (68ft 3in)
GAUGE: 1435mm (4ft 8.5in)

design was said to be effective in snow dispersal, and the typical

Norwegian snow deflectors were also fitted below the buffer beam.

CLASS 269 B-B SPANISH RAILWAYS (RENFE)

SPAIN 1980

Spanish builders CAF constructed this Japanese-designed class under Mitsubishi licence, using Westinghouse electrical parts. Class 269 had monomotor bogies with two gear options: fast-passenger and slow-freight. The initial Class 269.0 were set for 80/140km/h (50/87.5mph), but in order to provide different permutations, Class 269.2 was geared for 100/160km/h (62.5/100mph); and Class 269.5 for 90/160km/h (56.2/100mph). They were

deployed on freight, passenger and intermodal, and freight and intermodal duties respectively. A later variant, Class 269.9, was geared solely for intermodal traffic at 120km/h (75mph). These variations indicate the efforts of separate RENFE business divisions trying to optimize the performance of their locomotive stock. Class 269 seems likely to remain the default motive power for passenger and freight on most of the RENFE system.

A class 269.5 locomotive with a train of low-height 'Talgo' coaches. This was a common sight in Spanish express services in the pre-AVE era (see 2005). Class 269s still operate overnight passenger services between principal Spanish cities.

TYPE: B-B multipurpose
POWER: 3100kW (4155hp)
SUPPLY: 3000V DC
TRACTIVE EFFORT: varies from highest gear 143kN (32175lbf) to lowest gear 263kN (59175lbf)

MAX. OPERATING SPEED: varies from 80km/h (50mph) low gear to 160km/h (100mph) high gear
WEIGHT: 88t (194,040lb)
MAX. AXLE LOAD: 22t (48,510lb)
OVERALL LENGTH: 17.27m (56 ft 8in)
GAUGE: 1676mm (5ft 6in)

040 DL/DO B-B TUNISIAN NATIONAL RAILWAYS (SNCFT)

Engines from the SEMT-Pielstick works (which became part of the MAN group from 1988) were often chosen to work with hydraulic transmissions, and the results were normally good. Being four-axled Pielstick-engined diesel hydraulic locomotives, classes 040 DL and DO were identical in external appearance but differed in power rating. Ganz-MÁVAG of Hungary were the suppliers, and they were based on the Hungarian Class M41, the DL being of the same 1325kW (1800hp) power rating, and the DO of 1764kW (2400hp). Ten 040 DLs were built in 1980, and 20 040 DOs in 1984. Both types, however, proved to be unreliable in service and were withdrawn early. The last remaining operational DLs worked in the Tunis area on empty passenger stock trains.

TYPE: B-B diesel-hydraulic
POWER: DL 1325kW (1800hp);
DO 1764kW (2400hp) fromPielstick
PA4-185 series engines
TRACTIVE EFFORT: 143kN (33,000lbf)
MAX. OPERATING SPEED: DL –
110km/h (68.3mph); DO – 130km/h
(81.3mph)
WEIGHT: DL – 62 tonnes (136,710lb);
DO – 64 tonnes (141,120lb)
OVERALL LENGTH: 15.5m (50ft 7in)
GAUGE: DL – 1000mm (3ft 3in); DO –
1000 or 1435mm (3ft 3in or 4ft 8.5in)

Near the end of a short career, a smoke-stained DO moves stock on a wet day in Tunisia.

CLASS GP50 BO-BO VARIOUS US RAILROADS

TYPE: Bo-Bo diesel-electric	based on 70:17 gear ratio	**WEIGHT:** 117.9t (260,000lb)
POWER: 2611kW (3500hp)	**MAX. OPERATING SPEED:** 112km/h	**OVERALL LENGTH:** 18.211m (59 ft 9in)
TRACTIVE EFFORT: 285kN (64,200 lbf)	(70mph)	**GAUGE:** 1435mm (4ft 8.5in)

Amid the travails of the US railroad system, as companies collapsed, merged and collapsed again, they continued to move vast tonnages of freight, and freight operations were growing much more sophisticated with computerized control. Locomotives were modified or developed to match demand. Among the features on the GP50, new this year, was Electro-Motive Division's new Super-Series wheel slip control, using micro-processor control and ground-speed radar inputs to improve tractive effort. Like other high-horsepower Bo-Bo locomotives, the GP50 was intended for fast intermodal container services. In the late 1970s, EMD had pushed its 645 engine design almost to the limit, but the GP50, like its Co-Co counterpart the SD50, was powered by a 16-645F engine. Chicago & North Western was the first purchaser. Southern Railway ordered a high-hood version. Reported flaws in the 645F engine and the railroad industry's troubles limited sales of the GP50. In 1985, EMD replaced the GP50 with the new GP60 model.

B36-7 BO-BO VARIOUS US RAILROADS

Bo-Bo locomotives were now working at power rates that only six-axle locomotives would have achieved a few years previously, reflecting the speeding-up of many US freight services as well as the diesel-engine and electric motor improvements by the manufacturers which made it possible. General Electric's B36-7 was a high-horsepower four-motor diesel-electric locomotive intended for fast freight service and typically used in multiples on priority intermodal trains. Externally, it was very like the lower-output Dash-7 four-motor

CSX No. 5835 at Palmer, Massachusetts, in 2001, does not look like a locomotive 20 years old. It was originally part of the Seaboard Air Line fleet.

GE diesel electrics. It usually ran on GE's FB-style bogie, a type often known as the floating bolster truck. Santa Fe, Seaboard System (a component of CSX), Southern Pacific and Conrail were primary users of

the B36-7 type. Conrail would typically use B36-7s in sets of three (or mixed with EMD GP40-2s) on its fast 'Trail-Van' intermodal trains, which regularly operated at speeds up to 112km/h (70mph).

TYPE: Bo-Bo, diesel-electric
POWER: GE FDL-12 producing 2686kW (3600hp)
TRACTIVE EFFORT: 287kN (64,600lbf) with 83:20 gear ratio

MAX. OPERATING SPEED: 112km/h (70mph)
WEIGHT: 127t (280,000lb)
OVERALL LENGTH: 18.948m (62ft 2in)
GAUGE: 1435mm (4ft 8.5in)

CLASS 21 AND 27 BO-BO BELGIAN NATIONAL RAILWAYS (SNCB)

BELGIUM 1981

Introduced to replace or supplement older electric classes now up to to 30 years in service, these classes, identical both in external appearance and interior layout, went into general-purpose main-line service. Class 27 appeared first, from 1981. At this time, Belgium's rail speed limit was being raised from 140km/h (87mph) to 160km/h (100mph), and the new locomotives were geared for this speed. The 4150kW (5650hp) Class 27 Bo-Bos were assigned to express-train haulage on the Ostend–Brussels–Liege–Aachen axis, but were also designed to haul heavy freights trains on the Antwerp–Montzen–Aachen line. Hitherto these trains had been hauled by 1800kW (2560hp) units of Class 22 and 23, which were both underpowered for these duties and also constrained by a 130km/h maximum speed. The Class 27's specification set out a requirement for the locomotive to

maintain a speed of 160km/h (100mph) with a load of 600 tonnes (590.5 tons), the equivalent of about 13 international passenger coaches. For freight, the requirement was to haul 800 tonnes (787 tons) at a sustained speed of 80km/h (50mph) on the Luxembourg trunk route, where there is an average gradient of 1 in 83 for approximately 20km (12.4 miles), with some stretches worsening to 1 in 62.5. On level track, the Class 27 was expected to cope with 2000-tonne (1968.5-ton) freights without strain.

Chopper technology, first used on Belgian National Railways in 1969, was used on the Class 27 and 21 engines. Besides the improvement in traction characteristics, it produced lower maintenance costs and reduced catenary wear. On Belgium's compact network with numerous and fairly frequent stops, thyristor control reduced the demands on the system from

repeated stops and starts. The Class 27 was the first Belgian electric locomotive to be fitted with rheostatic brakes, which can be applied separately, or be blended in with air braking. It was also the first SNCB electric locomotive to be fitted for MU operation. Another new feature for the SNCB was automatic couplers. The 60 Class 27's are SNCB-designed and Belgian-built with mechanical parts from Brugeois-Nivelles and electrical equipment from ACEC. External finish is in peacock blue with horizontal yellow bands over body ends and sides, and set off by a lighter blue finish to the roof.

Class 21, also 60 in number and produced from 1984, is a lower-powered version of Class 27. Whereas Class 27s are used mainly on express passenger and heavy

freight, Class 21 tends towards more secondary passenger work, including push-pull local services, and freights. Both classes are still in service.

TYPE: Bo-Bo mainline mixed-traffic electric locomotive
POWER: 3000V DC overhead line collection; 4380kW (5870bhp) class 27, 3310kW (4435bhp) class 21; chopper control; four frame-mounted DC traction motors
TRACTIVE EFFORT: 234kN (52,600lbf)
MAX. OPERATING SPEED: 160km/h (100mph)
WEIGHT: 85t (186,665lb) Class 27; 84 t (184,470lb) Class 21
MAX AXLE LOAD: not known
OVERALL LENGTH: 18.65m (61ft 2in)
GAUGE: 1435mm (4ft 6in)

SNCB No. 2713 about to leave with an express. When new, this class was replete with new technology that has since become standard and sometimes obsolescent over the course of 25 years.

CLASS ME CO-CO DANISH RAILWAYS (DSB)

DENMARK 1981

In appearance and equipment, these were highly up-to-date locomotives in 1981, supplementing or replacing the 20-year old MX and MY diesels. Principally for express passenger trains on the island of Zeeland, they were also the last main-line

diesel locomotives purchased by Danish Railways. Initially all the 'MEs' were painted in DSB corporate red livery, but a programme of repainting some in dark-blue livery began around 2003. Using the well-tried GM 645E3B engine, with 16 cylinders,

TYPE: mixed-traffic diesel-electric
WHEEL ARRANGEMENT: Co-Co
POWER UNIT: General Motors 16-645E3B 16-cylinder V-form two-stroke diesel, 2450kW (3285hp); alternator; six axle-hung AC traction motors

TRACTIVE EFFORT: N/A
MAX. OPERATING SPEED: 175km/h (110mph)
WEIGHT: 115t (252,550lb)
OVERALL LENGTH: 21m (68ft 11in)
GAUGE: 1435mm (4ft 8.5in)

Class ME on a local train at Copenhagen. Thirty-six were built up to 1987, and all remain in service apart from one destroyed by fire.

the Class ME locomotives introduced DSB to the use of alternating current traction

equipment in a diesel-electric design, with particularly lightweight traction motors.

CLASS 1600 B-B NETHERLANDS RAILWAYS (NS)

NETHERLANDS 1981

Operating under 1500V DC wires, this is a Dutch adaptation of the French BB-7200 class of 1976, which explains its very French looks. The 58 Class 1600s are general-purpose types, hauling intercity trains from Amsterdam to Heerlen and

Maastricht as well as general freight, and working local and commuter trains around the Randstad cities. The recent creation of operating company NS Reizigers has caused the last 25 of the fleet to be renumbered as Class 1800.

TYPE: B-B mainline mixed-traffic electric locomotive
POWER: 1500V DC overhead line collection; 4400kW (5900hp); DC chopper control; two DC frame-mounted traction motors
TRACTIVE EFFORT: 294kN (66,095lbf)

MAX. OPERATING SPEED: 160km/h (100mph)
WEIGHT: 83t (182,275lb)
MAX AXLE LOAD: not known
OVERALL LENGTH: 17.48m (57ft 4in)
GAUGE: 1435mm (4ft 8.5in)

CLASS 26 'RED DEVIL' 4-8-4 SOUTH AFRICAN RAILWAYS (SAR)

SOUTH AFRICA 1981

Apart from China, no country was building main-line steam locomotives in 1981, but several systems still had quite substantial fleets of steam locomotives at work, including South Africa. Among some engineers, there was serious interest in how steam traction could be modernized and maintained in effective service, rather than be simply run down as new diesel and electric units were

acquired. With the converted Rio Turbio Railway Mitsubishi 2-10-2s of 1963, the Argentinian engineer L.D. Porta, a specialist in thermodynamics who had also qualified as a locomotive driver, had shown how a modern steam locomotive's performance could be dramatically improved. Porta developed a new firebox and method for burning low-quality coal, the Gas Producer Combustion

System (GPCS). It required a thick but relatively cool bed of burning coal, with the greatest heat, around 1400°C (2552°F), generated above it. Air inlets and steam jets into the firebox to aid combustion had been used before, as long ago as the 1850s, but this was the first scientifically worked-out method. Exhaust steam was piped to the ashpan and mixed with air, keeping the temperature down

and preventing the formation of clinker. Live steam jets and air intakes from above helped in the gasification process by creating a controlled turbulence that kept coal particles in suspension rather than blasting them almost instantaneously through the tubes. Although reduction of coal and water consumption was the main aim, it also resulted in less soot and smoke being produced.

The 'Red Devil' in its final form, on one of many test runs made between Pretoria and Witbank in the course of 1983. Behind it is a SAR 4-8-4.

Porta also made substantial improvements in draughting and lubrication systems.

Porta's ideas were taken up in South Africa by David Wardale, an Assistant Mechanical Engineer (Steam) on the SAR system. In 1979, he successfully modified a 1938-built 19D 4-8-2. In 1981, he was allowed to tackle a non-condensing Class 25 4-8-4 dating from 1953, No. 3450. The Class 25NC was still considered to be the last word in steam design, with virtually every modern feature from Timken roller bearings to a self-cleaning smokebox. At the SAR Salt River workshops in Cape Town, 34 significant modifications were implemented, among them

the fitting of a Porta gas producer firebox, a Lempor (Lemaître-Porta) double-exhaust system, a longer and internally aerodynamic smokebox, and an enlarged superheater with a superheat booster, achieving temperatures of around 440°C (824°F). New steam pipes, an enlarged steam chest, and a feedwater heating system (never before used on SAR locomotives) were fitted, the cylinders were insulated, and many improvements were made to the valves and pistons.

Wardale's aim was to show what a modern technological approach to steam power design could achieve. He named the engine *L.D. Porta*, after his mentor, but its

bright red paint coat earned it the popular nickname of 'Red Devil'. Tests in service revealed a 28 per cent reduction in coal consumption and a 30 per cent drop in water consumption, compared to the Class 25s. But in addition, the maximum recorded power output of No. 3450 was 2823kW (3784hp) at 74km/h (46mph) – a 43 per cent improvement on the Class 25's performance. The transformation was such that the locomotive was reclassed 26.

Like all prototypes, it had weaknesses and problems, though technically resolvable and minor compared with the levels of economy and performance promised. But SAR policy was already firmly committed to the phasing-out of steam. Wardale's hopes of starting a line of 'second-generation' steam locomotives

were not to be realized in South Africa, and he left in 1983. The 'Red Devil', though remaining in service, suffered from the effects of unspecialized maintenance, but in 1991 it was still rostered for the 'Trans Orange' express along with some 25NC locomotives. In 1992, steam locomotives were finally taken off main-line work in South Africa. But No. 3450 was saved from scrapping and restored to running order.

BOILER PRESSURE: 15.5kg/cm² (220psi)
CYLINDERS: 610x711mm (24x28in)
DRIVING WHEELS: 1524mm (60in)
GRATE AREA: 6.4m² (68.9sq ft)
HEATING SURFACE: 288.3m² (3104sq ft)
SUPERHEATER: 171.2m² (1843.2sq ft)
TRACTIVE EFFORT: 22,914kg (50,526lb)
TOTAL WEIGHT: 136.1t (300,120lb)

CLASS 441 BO-BO YUGOSLAVIAN RAILWAYS (JDZ)

Yet another variant of the Swedish Rc basic electric locomotive, this large class now serves on the Croatian Railways (HZ) as Class 1141, and also on other now-independent systems. Several sub-classes evolved, but the design is based on ASEA prototype Rb1, broadly similar to SJ Class Rc1. Ordered from the 50Hz Group, a consortium of European manufacturers, the first 80 units were constructed by SGP

in Austria, followed by 35 kits assembled in Yugoslavia by Rade Koncar. From 1990, production moved wholly to Zagreb. Variations to the original Class 441 were sub-classes 441.0 as the basic 120km/h (75mph) type; 441.3 with rheostatic braking and multiple-unit working (26 built); 441.4 identical to Class 441.3 but with flange lubrication (34 built); 441.5 identical to Class 441.0 but with flange lubrication (32 built);

441.6 geared for running at 140km/h (87.5mph) – 24 were built but some were converted to Class 441.7; and finally 441.7, as 441.6 but capable of multiple-unit working (55 built). Following the disintegration of Yugoslavia, Class 441 was distributed among the new republics. Croatia Railways (HZ) have 94; Bosnia (ZBH) have 29, Macedonia (MZ) have eight, and 96 are running on the remnant JZ in Serbia.

TYPE: Bo-Bo mixed-traffic
POWER: 4080kW (5471hp)
SUPPLY: 25kV 50Hz AC
TRACTIVE EFFORT: 132kN (29700lbf) at 103km/h (64.4mph)
MAX. OPERATING SPEED: 120 or 140km/h (75 or 87.4mph)
WEIGHT: 78 to 82t (171,990lb to 180,810lb)
MAX. AXLE LOAD: 20.5t (45,203lb)
OVERALL LENGTH: 15.47m (50ft 5in)
GAUGE: 1435mm (4ft 8.5in)

CHAPTER SEVEN

THE MODERN ERA

1982–PRESENT

New railways continue to be built, notably the extension of Australia's 'Ghan railway from Alice Springs to Darwin, and the rail link from China to Lhasa in Tibet, as well as specialized lines for ore and coal transport. In India too, the rail infrastructure is receiving enormous investment, seen as vital for maintaining economic development and ease of movement in a vast and densely populated country. Nowadays, though diesel-hydraulic traction holds a respectable place, especially in multiple-unit trains, electric traction is predominant by a long way, whether the power is provided by a diesel-engined prime mover or drawn from a wire. The merits of the all-electric system include the fact that all the locomotive's capacity can be used for the electric drive and its

associated equipment, without having to give space and weight to a diesel engine: this gives it greater power. It can be independent of fossil fuels, running on hydro- or nuclear-generated power. It emits no smoke and makes very little noise. For certain types of train, including immensely heavy ore and coal trains, often loading to 5000 tonnes and more, and very fast long-distance passenger trains of the Shinkansen or TGV type, the 'pure' electric is the only possibility, and the same applies on lines, like the new Bologna–Florence line in Italy, which are built almost entirely in tunnels. For the new magnetically levitated trains now being developed, electricity is, of course, the essential source of power. The future of railways is definitely an electric one.

Prior to the completion of the new overhead-catenary railway track between London and the Channel Tunnel, in November 2007, a 'Eurostar' train draws current from the third rail as it heads from London to Paris.

CLASS 2180 SNOW CLEARING MACHINE AUSTRIAN STATE RAILWAYS (ÖBB)

AUSTRIA 1982

In further northern and southern latitudes, and in mountain areas, snow-clearing equipment is essential to maintain regular services, and while ploughs are often fitted on locomotive fronts there are also specialist self-propelling ploughs or fans to deal with bigger snow-blocks. The ÖBB Class 2180 is produced by

Beilhack: a simple, self-propelled, two-axle vehicle with a full-width cab at the rear. At the front is mounted an array of rotating blades and screws for breaking up and slicing loose or packed snow, and for blowing it through directed shutes to the lineside. The Class 2180 machine has three 370kW (495hp) diesel engines,

one for forward movement and two for working the snow-clearing blades and screws. It is a

development of a similar but smaller machine bought by ÖBB in 1975.

TYPE: rail-mounted snow-clearing machine
WHEEL ARRANGEMENT: B
POWER UNIT: three 370kW (495bhp) diesel engines, one for traction and two for snow-clearing equipment

MAX. OPERATING SPEED: 80km/h (50mph)
WEIGHT: 43t (94,430lb)
OVERALL LENGTH: 12.35m (40ft 6in)
GAUGE: 1435mm (4ft 8.5in)

LRC BO-BO VIA RAIL

CANADA 1982

Keeping a low profile, one of the first LRC power cars brings its train into Montréal, Quebec, in August 1984. The cars remain, but the locomotive has gone.

LRC stands for 'Light, Rapid, Comfortable' – applying to the newly introduced VIA Rail trains rather than to the locomotives specially built to haul them. They were tilting trains, though the locomotives did not tilt, and could also be used to haul conventional passenger services. Diesel-electrics built for high speed by Bombardier, they had wedge-shaped, low-profile carbodies to fit the Talgo-type coaches, and were powered by 16-cylinder Alco 251 engines.

In origin, the LRC was a joint project begun in the late 1960s by a consortium of Montreal Locomotive Works (MLW), Alcan and Dofasco. A demonstration train (one locomotive and coach) was sent on tour in Canada and the United States in 1973 and 1974. The LRC was the first train to incorporate successfully a tilting system to maintain speed and passenger

comfort as the train ran round curves on conventional track. Bombardier acquired MLW in 1975 and pressed on with the LRC production model. Amtrak ordered 10 coaches and two locomotives, and these worked up and down the Northeast Corridor in the early 1980s. Pulled by conventional-technology diesel-electric locomotives designed for 200km/h (124mph) normal operating speed, the LRC entered full-scale service in 1981 for VIA Rail, linking cities in the busy Quebec–Windsor corridor, but at speeds limited to a 170km/h (105mph) maximum by the constraints of the signalling system.

Until the late 1990s, the Amtrak LRC coaches (in VIA livery) worked the Chicago–Toronto 'International' service. In Canada, the LRC had a

tremendous public impact, and became the hallmark of VIA Rail Canada's improved Corridor services. Today almost all of VIA's original 100 LRC coaches are still in service, and the LRC is the oldest tilt-train that is still operational. The Bombardier Bo-Bo locomotives were not satisfactory performers, however, and were all retired by 2000, and replaced by more conventional diesel-electric locomotives manufactured by General Motors (GM) and General Electric (GE).

In 2000, new GE GENESIS types arrived. However, ambitious proposals are still being made for high-speed rail operation in eastern Canada. In 1998, the 'Lynx' consortium, including Bombardier and SNC-Lavalin, proposed a

300km/h (186mph) high-speed line from Toronto to Quebec City via Montreal based on French TGV technology, and later a high-speed service along the Quebec–Windsor corridor, using Bombardier's experimental JetTrain tilting trains. This unproven technology involves the use of a jet engine rather than overhead-fed electric motors.

TYPE: Bo-Bo, diesel-electric
POWER AND OUTPUT: 16-cylinder 251 producing 2760kW (3700hp)
TRACTIVE EFFORT: N/A
MAX. OPERATING SPEED: 200km/h (125mph)
WEIGHT: 113.4t (250,000 lb)
OVERALL LENGTH: 19.406m (63ft 8in)
GAUGE: 1435mm (4ft 8.5in)

CLASS 143 BO-BO GERMAN STATE RAILWAYS (DR)

Built as general mixed-traffic locomotives, these thyristor-controlled engines were found to be extremely efficent and reliable, and have been called the *Deutsche Reichsbahn*'s most successful electric locomotive. Total build of the class was 647, and since reunification they have been in action all over Germany, designated as DB Class 143. They are still common on express passenger trains as well as lighter freights and on local suburban push-pull workings.

Following the huge reduction of rail freight traffic that occurred in eastern Germany after the events of reunification, large numbers of this class were reallocated to passenger workings in the western part of

Germany, particularly on *S-Bahn* push-pull services in the Rhein-Ruhr region and around other major conurbations. Many locomotives of classes 140 and 141 have been withdrawn in favour of Class 143.

TYPE: Bo-Bo mixed-traffic electric
POWER: 15,000V 16.67Hz AC overhead line collection; 3540kW (4745hp); thyristor control; rheostatic braking; four DC traction motors with direct drive to axles
TRACTIVE EFFORT: 248kN (55,755lbf)
MAX. OPERATING SPEED: 120km/h (75mph)
WEIGHT: 82t (180,080lb)
MAX. AXLE LOAD: not known
OVERALL LENGTH: 16.64m (54ft 7in)
GAUGE: 1435mm (4ft 8.5in)

One of the many Class 143 locomotives, No. 003.2 on the outskirts of Düsseldorf with an express in August 1998.

CLASS EM MULTIPLE UNIT SET NEW ZEALAND RAILWAYS (NZR)

Suburban trains round the two main cities of New Zealand were the only thriving passenger services on NZR, and the need to maintain an efficient service brought about the purchase of these 43 two-car units 1982–83. Ganz MÁVAG of Budapest were the builders, with British GEC electrical equipment.

The new stock displaced locomotive haulage and older English Electric Dm-class units, which from then on were only used to supplement peak-hour services around Wellington. The Em class was used on all lines except the Johnsonville branch. A new blue livery has been applied to the stock in recent years.

TYPE: suburban multiple-unit two-car set
POWER: four 400kW (535hp) traction motors, driving each axle in the power car, supplied with 1500V DC via overhead catenary
TRACTIVE EFFORT: not known
MAX. OPERATING SPEED: 100km/h (62mph)

TOTAL WEIGHT: 35.9t (79,159lb)
MAX. AXLE LOAD: not known
OVERALL LENGTH: 20.7m (67ft 11in)
BUILDER: Ganz MÁVAG, Budapest, Hungary. Electrical equipment by GEC, England

---

CLASS 250 C-C SPANISH RAILWAYS (RENFE)

Rather as was the case with many Spanish steam types, this electric class combines French and German elements in a Spanish synthesis. German-designed, apart

from French-type monomotor bogies, some were constructed by Krauss-Maffei in Munich and some by CAF in Spain, all with Brown Boveri electrical parts. The final

five make up Class 250.6, with DC chopper controls, reflecting the heavy weight of early power electronics systems. In common with most European railway

administrations, RENFE has divided its motive power between different business sectors. All Class 250s are assigned to the two freight businesses, with Transporte Combinado (intermodal) operating all Class 250.6s and 16 class 250.0s, while the remaining 19 are with Cargas (freight).

TYPE: C-C electric
POWER: 4600kW (6169hp)
SUPPLY: 3000V DC
TRACTIVE EFFORT: Low gear 316kN (71,100lbf); high gear 197kN (44,325lbf)
MAX. OPERATING SPEED: low gear 100km/h (62mph); high gear 160km/h (100mph)
WEIGHT: 124 or 130t (273,420lb or 286,650lb)
MAX. AXLE LOAD: 22t (48,510lb)
OVERALL LENGTH: 20m (65ft 3in)
GAUGE: 1668mm (5ft 6in)

No. 250.010 6 on a typical duty with a container train. All the Class 250 locomotives are geared for freight haulage.

CLASS 251 B-B-B SPANISH RAILWAYS (RENFE)

Parent class of this Spanish six-axle, three-bogie locomotive was the Japanese Railways EF66, designed by Mitsubishi. A consortium of Mitsubishi, Westinghouse and the Spanish builders CAF and Macosa built the 30 Class 251. Initially they worked on express passenger trains, and some were painted in the AVE high-speed livery.

All the Class 251s are now assigned to cargo and operate permanently in the lower speed, 100km/h (62mph), higher tractive effort gearing mode.

TYPE: B-B-B freight
POWER: 4650kW (6236hp)
SUPPLY: 3000V DC
TRACTIVE EFFORT: Low gear 349kN (78,525lbf); high gear 216kN (48,600lbf)
MAX. OPERATING SPEED: low gear 100km/h (62mph); high gear 160km/h (100mph)
WEIGHT: 138t (304,290lb)
MAX. AXLE LOAD: 23t (50,715lb)
OVERALL LENGTH: 20.7m (67ft 6in)
GAUGE: 1668mm (5ft 6in)

CLASS A CO-CO VICTORIAN RAILWAYS

In an act of virtual resurrection, the 11 Class A locomotives were rebuilt from already 30-year-old Class B locomotives, General Motors export models that first appeared from Clyde Engineering in 1952. Retaining their 1950s-style nosed carbodies, they were re-engined with General Motors' 12-cylinder 645-series engines, and put into use as freight rather than express passenger locomotives. In the early twenty-first century, V/Line was still using four Class A trains, now 50 years old, while Freight Australia operated seven.

TYPE: Co-Co diesel-electric
POWER: 1846kW (2475hp) from EMD 12-645 series engine
TRACTIVE EFFORT: 212kN (47700lbf) at 24km/h (15mph) continuous
MAX. OPERATING SPEED: 133km/h (83mph)
WEIGHT: 118t (260,190lb)
OVERALL LENGTH: 18.542m (60ft 6in)
GAUGE: 1435mm and 1600mm (4ft 8.5in and 5ft 3in)

Two Class A locomotives hard at work on a V/Line passenger train in Victoria, Australia. V/Line has four of these locomotives and Freight Australia has seven.

CLASS 58 CO-CO BRITISH RAIL (BR)

Unusually for British double-cab locomotives, the Class 58 had a narrow body between the full-width end-cabs, similar to the Irish Class 071 of 1976. There were 50 in the class, all with a modern Ruston engine developed from the much older English Electric 12 CS type. The engine drove an alternator, current from which was rectified and fed to six axle-mounted DC traction motors. In service, they operated coal trains in the English Midlands, and later gravitated to general freight, finishing in the south of England. They were underpowered for bulk freight and have been displaced by later types. All are out of service, and held in storage pending a possible sale.

TYPE: freight main-line diesel-electric
WHEEL ARRANGEMENT: Co-Co
POWER UNIT: Ruston 12RK3ACT 12-cylinder V-form diesel, 2462kW (3300hp); Brush alternator; six axle-hung DC traction motors
TRACTIVE EFFORT: 275kN (61,800lbf)
MAX. OPERATING SPEED: 130km/h (80mph)
WEIGHT: 130t (285,490lb)
OVERALL LENGTH: 19.140m (62ft 9in)
GAUGE: 1435mm (4ft 8.5in)

Photographed at Didcot Parkway station in June 2001, a Class 58 from the English, Welsh & Scottish Railways fleet is still on active duty.

CLASS V46 BO-BO HUNGARIAN STATE RAILWAYS (MÁV)

MÁV's V46 No. 023 on station pilot duty. Steps and handrails for the carriage shunter are provided at each corner.

Low hoods on each side afford a good look-out to this centre-cab machine, with a single pantograph mounted on the cab roof. Sixty were constructed in Budapest by Ganz MÁVAG between 1983 and 1992. Shunting of passenger and freight stock is the main purpose, but their 80km/h (50mph) road speed is sufficient for light freight work also.

TYPE: Bo-Bo
POWER: 820kW (1114hp)
SUPPLY: 25kV 50Hz AC
TRACTIVE EFFORT: 153kN (34425lbf) at 71km/h (44.4mph)
MAX. OPERATING SPEED: 80km/h (50mph)
WEIGHT: 80t (176,400lb)
MAX. AXLE LOAD: 20t (44,100lb)
OVERALL LENGTH: 14.4m (47ft)
GAUGE: 1435mm (4ft 8.5in)

CLASS X10 ELECTRIC MULTIPLE UNITS STATE RAILWAYS (SJ)

Similar to hundreds of *S-Bahn* and similar electric multiple-unit trains that work around European cities, Class X10 trains are run both by SJ and by private operators on certain lines around Stockholm and Malmö, operating about 80 units. SJ is the largest owner, with over 100 of these modern two-car sets. As elsewhere, they are basic short-distance commuter trains with minimal facilities, but better-equipped versions exist as classes X11 to X14 for longer-distance routes. These have more spacious seating, toilets and end doors only.

TYPE: two-car electric multiple unit suburban trains
POWER: 15,000V 16.67Hz AC overhead line collection; 1280kW (1715hp); axle-mounted traction motors
MAX. OPERATING SPEED: 140km/h (87mph)
WEIGHT PER VEHICLE: not known
OVERALL LENGTH: not known
GAUGE: 1435mm (4ft 8.5in)

SKODA 27E BO-BO-BO

Special-purpose locomotives are comparative rarities in Europe, but this three-section articulated locomotive type, Skoda 27E, was designed and built specially to work on open-cast mining operations in the huge Czech brown-coal workings in north-west Bohemia. The city of Most was physically relocated in the 1970s to make way for these extensive mines on which the economy once depended for coal-fired power generation. The 27E is no light-weight, though it runs on temporary rails that are moved and re-laid as mining progresses. Equipped with slow-speed controls for 0.5 to 3km/h (0.25 to 1.9mph) loading operations directly from giant dragline excavators, the locomotives have four side-mounted current collectors so that wagons can be top-loaded.

Conventional pantographs are carried for normal running. Water spray gear and large intake air filters are standard in the dusty environment. Ninety units dating from 1984 to 1989 are used by mining concerns *Mostecká uhelná spolecnost* and *Sokolovská uhelná* around the cities of Most and Sokolov. They are designated Class 127 under the Czech computer number system.

TYPE: Bo+Bo+Bo special purpose mines
POWER: 2520kW (3424hp)
SUPPLY: 1500V DC
TRACTIVE EFFORT: 314kN (70650lbf) at 28.7km/h (17.9mph)
MAX. OPERATING SPEED: 65km/h (40.6mph)
WEIGHT: 180t (396,900lb)
MAX. AXLE LOAD: 30t (66,150lb)
OVERALL LENGTH: 21.56m (70ft 4in)
GAUGE: 1435mm (4ft 8.5in)

CLASS 163 BO-BO CZECHOSLOVAK STATE RAILWAYS (CSD)

These locomotives, universally used in their respective power supply regions, had a short life under CSD before the splitting of the Czech Republic and Slovakia created two railway systems, CD and ZSR, and required division of the stock. Known collectively as *persching* (i.e. missile), Czech and Slovak classes 162, 163, 263, 362

In the livery of the Slovakian ZSR, a Class 163 heads a passenger train on 24 April 2005.

and 363, all from Skoda, share interchangeable components. Classes 163/263/363 are geared for 120km/h (75mph) maximum speed, while 162 and 362 are geared for 140km/h (87.5mph). Class 162 and 163 run on 3000V DC supply; 263 runs on 25kV

50Hz AC; and 362 and 363 are both dual-voltage. Production of the 120km/h (75mph) versions ran to 179 of the 363s, 12 263s, and 120 163s. A second set of 60 163s were the victim of politics – ordered by CSD and built by Skoda, neither CD nor ZSR were

able to take them for financial reasons. Eventually CD took 40 and ZSR 11, and nine went to *Ferrovie Nord Milano* (FNM) in Italy. The 140km/h (87.5mph) 362001 appeared in 1990 while 60 Class 162s were built the same year.

Both CD and ZSR have

collaborated in various permutations among these class versions. Initially CD required more 140km/h (87.5mph) machines for the Praha–Brno corridor when EuroCity services started in 1993/94, and so a bogie exchange was made between seven of Classes 363 and 162 respectively, to produce 140km/h (87.5mph) 362s and 120km/h (75mph) 163.2s. ZSR followed suit in 1999/2000 with a similar exchange creating 15 'new' 362s and 163s.

TYPE: Bo-Bo universal traffic
POWER: 3060kW (4158hp)
SUPPLY: 3000V DC or 25kV 50Hz AC
TRACTIVE EFFORT: 209kN (47025lbf)

MAX. OPERATING SPEED: 120 or 140km/h (75 or 87.5mph)
WEIGHT: 85 to 87t (187,425lb)
MAX. AXLE LOAD: 22t (48,510lb)

OVERALL LENGTH: 16.8m (55ft 2in)
GAUGE: 1435mm (4ft 8.5in)

CLASS 141 DIESEL MULTIPLE UNITS BRITISH RAIL (BR)   GREAT BRITAIN 1984

These lightweight diesel-hydraulic railbuses were two-car sets, each car having one underfloor diesel engine driving through a hydraulic transmission to one axle. With road bus-style bodies on what in effect was a

modern wagon underframe, they gave a rather vibrant ride and were not popular with passengers. The 20 '141' units were withdrawn in 1999 after only 15 years service. Later-built classes 142 to 144 survive.

TYPE: local passenger diesel multiple unit
DIESEL ENGINE (PER CAR): Leyland TL11 149kW (200hp) six-cylinder
TRANSMISSION: Voith T211r hydraulic

MAX. OPERATING SPEED: 120km/h (75mph)
WEIGHT: 25+2 t (54,880+56,000lb)
OVERALL LENGTH: 15.25m (50ft)
GAUGE: 1435mm (4ft 8.5in)

Too much like a bus on rails to win passenger approval, a Class 141 Metro unit calls at Meadowhall station, South Yorkshire, in the 1990s.

CLASS 150 'SPRINTER' DIESEL MULTIPLE UNIT BRITISH RAIL (BR)   GREAT BRITAIN 1984

Volume production of these units began to accelerate the decline of locomotive-hauled passenger trains in Britain, already started by the '125' high-speed trains. In 1983, two prototype units came from British Rail Engineering Limited (BREL). The first was powered by a Cummins NT855R5 engine rated at 213kW

(285hp) at 2100rpm, driving a Voith 211 hydraulic transmission via a cardan shaft. The second unit originally featured a Rolls Royce Eagle C6280HR engine. This had mechanical transmission via an R500 fully automatic gearbox via a cardan shaft. The first Class 150 was delivered to BR on 8 June 1984, with the second following

shortly afterwards. Maximum speed for the prototype units was 120km/h (75mph). The prototypes ran extensive trials on regular passenger services on the Derby–Matlock branch, clipping up to 10 minutes off the normal journey time.

So impressive were these prototypes that an order was placed

in November 1984 with BREL, York, for further two-car Sprinter sets, fitted with the Cummins/Voith power equipment. Eventually, 225 units were delivered, Nos. 150 010–150 150 (some as three-car sets operate with Class 150/2 centre cars). The subsequent Class 150/2 two-car sets, Nos. 150 201–150 285, appeared with cab-end corridor connections, making them visually less attractive than their predecessors but operationally more flexible when working in multiple.

TYPE: general-purpose passenger diesel multiple unit
POWER: 1 x Cummins NT855R5 of 213kW (285hp)
TRACTIVE EFFORT: N/A
MAX. OPERATING SPEED: 121km/h (75mph)
WEIGHT: 38.45t (84,782lb)
OVERALL LENGTH (AVERAGE VEHICLE): 19.964m (65ft 6in)
GAUGE: 1435mm (4ft 8.5in)

A 'Sprinter' set stands at Great Malvern's picturesque station with a Hereford–Birmingham service.

RBDE 560 NPZ TRAIN SWISS FEDERAL RAILWAYS (SBB)

Even-interval operation was the concept behind the *Pendelzug,* or shuttle train – a conventional three- or four-car unit with power car and driving trailer at opposite ends –

first used in intensive services in Switzerland and Germany. NPZ stood for *Neue Pendelzug,* an up-to-the-minute version. Testing began in 1981 with four prototype trains

on the Thun–Berne and Fribourg–Biel lines. Between 1984 and 1996, 132 sets were built and they now run on all divisions of the SBB. In order to run cross-border 'Regio'

services, six sets were adapted to dual voltage, running under the French 25kV catenary as well as on the Swiss system. Classed RBDe 562, they operate between Basel and Mulhouse.

TYPE: interurban multiple-unit train
POWER: 1650kW (2211hp) 15kV 16.67Hz
TRACTIVE EFFORT: 166kN (37,326lb)
MAX. OPERATING SPEED: 140km/h (87mph)
TOTAL WEIGHT: 70t (154,350lb)
MAX. AXLE LOAD: not known
OVERALL LENGTH: not known
BUILDER: not known

As on many other modern systems, the doors on the SBB's RBDe 560 and 562 units are distinctively painted for the benefit of sight-impaired travellers.

B39-8 BO-BO 'DASH-8' VARIOUS US RAILROADS

The US locomotive builders were quick to adapt micro-processor control systems to improve the performance and efficiency of diesel-electric locomotives. General Electric's Dash-8 line marked the inception of its micro-processor control systems in the early 1980s. Prior to regular production of Dach-8 locomotives, GE built a number of 'pre-production' models for service on North American railways. Santa Fe operated three B39-8s numbered 7400 to 7402.

TYPE: Bo-Bo, diesel-electric
POWER: GE 7FDL-16 producing 2909kW (3900hp)
TRACTIVE EFFORT: 303kN (68,100 lbf) continuous TE at 29.3km/h (18.3 mph) with the 112km/h (70mph) gear option
MAX. OPERATING SPEED: 112km/h (70mph); 120km/h (75mph) using optional gearing
WEIGHT: 127t (280,000 lbs)
OVERALL LENGTH: 20.218m (66ft 4in)
GAUGE: 1435mm (4ft 8.5in)

These locomotives produced 2909kW (3900hp) and like other high-horsepower Bo-Bo types were primarily used on fast intermodal trains. Later, GE built production B39-8s (sometimes designated B39-8E) for Southern Pacific and LMX, the latter being a lease fleet originally assigned to Burlington Northern. The B39-8 was superseded by the Dash-840B in the late 1980s. The prime mover of the Dash-8 locomotives is the GE 7FDL turbocharged diesel engine, in 12- or 16-cylinder versions, and providing power for six DC traction motors. The Dash-8 delivered fuel savings over earlier models as a result of efficiencies and parasitic load controls.

In later models, engine power has been uprated by 2006 to 3200kW (4,100ghp). Auxiliary systems are computer-controlled, eliminating belts and pulleys or shafts in the drive arrangements. An interactive diagnostics panel reports faults automatically and

gives the locomotive operator performance data on command. Electronic fuel-injection packages

offer further fuel economy as well as reduction of emissions, and lower maintenance costs.

No. 8565 leads two of Connecticut Southern Railroad's fleet of B39-8 locomotives, used on general freight and mineral trains.

CLASS 11 BO-BO BELGIAN NATIONAL RAILWAYS (SNCB)

Very similar to SNCB's Class 21 electrics of 1981, but equipped to run under either 3000V or 1500V DC, this class was introduced to haul Belgian-Dutch joint-venture hourly push-pull intercity trains between Amsterdam and Brussels via Antwerpen. Rolling stock came from NS while SNCB provided the locomotives, all in the same maroon-and-yellow livery.

TYPE: Bo-Bo express passenger push-pull electric locomotive
POWER: 1500V and 3000V DC overhead line collection; 3310kW (4435hp); chopper control; four frame mounted DC traction motors
TRACTIVE EFFORT: 234kN (52,600lbf)
MAX. OP. SPEED: 140km/h (87mph)
WEIGHT: 85 tonnes (186,665lb)
MAX. AXLE LOAD: Not known
OVERALL LENGTH: 18.65m (61ft 2in)
GAUGE: 1435 (4ft 8.5in)

No. 1189 on a Brussels–Antwerp–Amsterdam push-pull service.

'CASTLE' CLASS DIESEL-ELECTRIC MULTIPLE UNITS NORTHERN IRELAND RAILWAYS (NIR)   GREAT BRITAIN 1985

This class represented an ingenious use of old stock to provide new trains. British Rail Engineering Limited in England supplied a three-car design using underframes from withdrawn BR Mark 1 carriages, and new bogies and bodies (modelled on the BR Class 455 suburban EMUs) were

TYPE: passenger DEMU
POWER: English Electric 4SRKT 410kW (550bhp) four-cylinder upright diesel (one per three-car unit); EE DC generator; two EE

DC traction motors on power car's inner bogie
MAX. OPERATING SPEED: 120km/h (75mph)
WEIGHT: 62.0+30.4+32.4 tonnes

(138,880+68,095+72,575lb)
OVERALL LENGTH: 20.28m (66ft 6in) end cars; 20.38m (66ft 10in) centre cars
GAUGE: 1600mm (5ft 3in)

added, along with redundant NIR power units and electric traction equipment from older units. Nine

of these half-price units were shipped to Northern Ireland, where they operate over the whole NIR

system. Refurbishing in 2006 is intended to prolong their use by another five or six years.

CLASS EP09 BO-BO POLISH STATE RAILWAYS (PKP)   POLAND 1985

Polish-built, by Pafawag, these electrics were capable of 160km/h (100mph) running, for use on express passenger trains, particularly on the lines southwest from Warsaw to Katowice and Kraków, and eastwards to the German border. For the 1980s, their appearance was distinctly angular and uncompromising, with no effort to suggest they were built for speed, though they had their own brown and yellow livery. They are used on trains such as the *Berolina* and *Varsovia* that run between Berlin and Warsaw via Poznan.

TYPE: Bo-Bo electric, 3000V DC overhead
POWER: 2920kW (3914hp)
TRACTIVE EFFORT: N/A
MAX. OPERATING SPEED: 160km/h (100mph)
WEIGHT: N/A
OVERALL LENGTH: N/A
MAX. AXLE LOAD: N/A
GAUGE: 1435mm (4ft 8.5in)

Big headlights stand out on the front of this EP09 locomotive, seen at Krakow on 18 April 2002.

CLASS 6E1 BO-BO SOUTH AFRICAN RAILWAYS (SAR)   SOUTH AFRICA 1985

Designed for general purpose use, with 859 built, this is a very large class, especially in SAR terms, representing a huge investment, and it is currently being rebuilt in updated form under Spoornet as Class 18E. Like the 7E freight class, it was provided with a suspension system of low-level inclined rods

that took buffing and drawbar loads between body and wheels. The rods are clearly visible in pairs, appearing as a low vee shape upwards from the bogie centres. The rebuilds have single end driving positions, with the second cab space for additional equipment and crew facilities.

TYPE: Bo-Bo universal traffic
POWER: 2252kW (3020hp) continuous
SUPPLY: 3000V DC
TRACTIVE EFFORT: 193kN (43400lbf) at 41km/h (25.5mph)

MAX. OPERATING SPEED: 113km/h (70.6mph)
WEIGHT: 89t (196,245lb)
MAX. AXLE LOAD: 22t (48,510lb)
OVERALL LENGTH: 15.495m (50ft 6in)
GAUGE: 1067mm (3ft 6in)

Workmanlike rather than handsome, the 6E1 is audibly recognizable from a distance by the whine of the high-speed fans used to cool the four traction motors.

DE 11000 DIESEL-ELECTRIC RAILCAR TURKISH STATE RAILWAYS (TCDD)

TURKEY 1985

Most of the TCDD's railcars were supplied from German builders, or were German-designed. This diesel-electric class, totalling 85 two-car units, was the product of a joint venture between Krauss-Maffei of Munich and the Tülomsas works of Turkey. Intended for use

TYPE: diesel-electric railcar
POWER: 780kW (1045.2hp)
TRACTIVE EFFORT: 225kN (50,593lbf)

MAX. OPERATING SPEED: 80km/h (50mph)
TOTAL WEIGHT: not known

OVERALL LENGTH: 13.25m (43ft 6in)
GAUGE: not known

on branch-line work, they were built between 1985 and 1990. TCDD made extensive use of diesel

railcars, mostly power cars with trailers for branch-line use, but others were long-distance express

units running such trains as the Bogaziçi Express between Haydarpasa (Istanbul) and Ankara.

GP60 CO-CO VARIOUS RAILROADS

USA 1985

Electro-Motive Division (EMD) regarded this locomotive as inaugurating its 'third-generation' of diesel-electrics. Apart from possessing new 710-type engines, replacing the over-stressed 645 series, it was equipped with a set of electronic micro-processors that monitored and managed a host of engine, cooling system and control functions. On-board micro-processors were the defining feature of third-generation locomotives,

TYPE: Co-Co diesel-electric
POWER: EMD 16 710G engine producing 2835kW (3800hp)
TRACTIVE EFFORT: not known

MAX. OPERATING SPEED: 112km/h (70mph)
WEIGHT: 118t (216,000lb)
OVERALL LENGTH: 18.2m (59ft 9in)
GAUGE: 1435mm (4ft 8.5in)

replacing hundreds of wiring circuts, dozens of relays and all but one module card in one of the most significant technological advances since the first lightweight diesel engines. The new 16-cylinder EMD

710G3 diesel engine, which could produce 2835kW (3800hp), proved to be a winner. Cabless units of this locomotive model were also built, purchased exclusively by the Santa Fe Railroad and known as GP60B. A

version with 'safety cab' cab and a wide nose were designated GP60M (see 1990). Southern Pacific (SP) purchased the first, last and largest fleet of GP60s, ordering 195 units between December 1987 and February 1994, when the type went out of production. Nearly half of the SP Fleet was lettered for its Cotton Belt subsidiary, with the others in Southern Pacific paintwork. A total of 294 GP60, 23 GP60B and 63 GP60M units were built.

CLASS 3500 BO-BO-BO QUEENSLAND RAILWAYS (QR)

AUSTRALIA 1986

Australian-built by Clyde and Walkers, fitted with Swedish electrical parts from ASEA, this was the third of three classes of Bo-Bo-Bo electric locomotives for heavy freight on the QR system, following

the 3100 and 3300 classes. Fifty were constructed. Some members of all three classes are fitted with GE Harris 'Locotrol' equipment, enabling their drivers to operate additional locomotives, interposed

TYPE: Bo-Bo-Bo freight
POWER: 2900kW (3870hp)
SUPPLY: 25kV 50Hz AC
TRACTIVE EFFORT: 260kN (58500lbf) at 40km/h (25mph)

WEIGHT: 110t (242,550lb)
MAX. AXLE LOAD: 18.5t (41,625lb)
OVERALL LENGTH: 20.02m (65ft 4in)
GAUGE: 1067mm (3ft 6in)

Queensland Railways No. 3546 leads a double-header on a coal train bound for Gladstone, south of Rockhampton, on 16 March 1997.

between the wagons of very long trains, by remote control; and

these were re-classed as 3200, 3400 and 3600 respectively.

CLASS 46 CO-CO BULGARIAN STATE RAILWAYS (BDZ)

BULGARIA 1986

Electroputere of Craiova, Romania, built the 45 locomotives forming this class. Designed for heavy-duty freight and passenger work, its origins go back to 1965, when the 060EA class, a Swedish design from ASEA, was licensed to Electroputere

and became the basis also of Romanian Railways' Class 46. In fact, 46 machines were built for BDZ, as the original 46.001 was severely damaged in an accident and its number given to a replacement locomotive.

TYPE: Co-Co heavy freight and passenger
POWER: 5100kW (7000hp)
SUPPLY: 25kV 50Hz AC
TRACTIVE EFFORT: 280kN (63000lbf)
MAX. OPERATING SPEED: 130km/h (81.3mph)

WEIGHT: 126t (277,830lb)
MAX. AXLE LOAD: 21t (46,305lb)
OVERALL LENGTH: 19.8m (64ft 8in)
GAUGE: 1435mm (4ft 8.5in)

CLASS 59 CO-CO FOSTER YEOMAN (MENDIP RAIL)

Powered by 16-cylinder GM 645E3C diesel engines, and built specifically to haul bulk stone trains for quarry contractors Foster Yeoman, these were the first privately owned main-line diesel locomotives to work on British Rail tracks. Working between the Mendip Hills and London yards with trains of up to 3000 tonnes (2953 tons) with one locomotive, the Class 59s have electronic wheel creep control enabling the wheels to slip very slightly when starting heavy loads and thus maximize wheel/rail adhesion. No. 59005 set a European record for single-locomotive haulage by pulling a stone train of 11,982 tonnes (11,790 tons) and 5415ft (1650m) in length. ARC and Northern Power also purchased small numbers of these locomotives, bringing the total production to 15.

TYPE: freight main-line diesel-electric
WHEEL ARRANGEMENT: Co-Co
POWER UNIT: GM 16-645E3C 16-cylinder V-form two-stroke diesel, 2460kW (3300bhp); GM alternator; six axle-hung DC traction motors
TRACTIVE EFFORT: 542kN (122,000lbf)
MAX. operating speed: 95 to 120km/h (60 to 75mph)
WEIGHT: 126t (276,705lb)
OVERALL LENGTH: 21.35m (70ft 1in)
GAUGE: 1435mm (4ft 8.5in)

The Foster Yeoman company owns eight Class 59 locomotives, mostly engaged in hauling trains of tippler wagons between the Mendip Hills quarries and London depots.

CLASS 5047 DIESEL RAILCAR AUSTRIAN STATE RAILWAYS (ÖBB)

Built for one-man operation with a driver-conductor, by Jenbacher Werke, this one-class railcar was intended to serve lightly used routes. A conventional single car design, it has a cab at each end and swing plug entrance doors at each end of each bodyside. The driving cabs have a door through which the driver can walk to inspect tickets, and he has a passenger communication microphone in the cab for travel information (not as common then as now). These vehicles are used particularly in the lowlands and hills in a radius of about 200km (125 miles) around Vienna, and also cross into Hungary at Sopron and further south. The joint Austro-Hungarian GYSEV railway company has also taken delivery of some of this class. ÖBB has over 30. Some of the cars have trailer units for peak services.

An ÖBB Class 5047 unit. Sixty-two passengers can be seated in the railcar. Its use is primarily on branch lines, making connections with inter-city services.

TYPE: secondary and branch-line passenger diesel multiple unit
POWER: Daimler Benz OM 444A 420kW (560bhp) six-cylinder diesel (one car only)
TRANSMISSION: Hydraulic
MAX. OPERATING SPEED: 120km/h (75mph)
WEIGHT: not known
OVERALL LENGTH EACH CAR: 25.42m (83ft 5in)
GAUGE: 1435mm (4ft 8.5in)

CLASS 120.1 BO-BO GERMAN FEDERAL RAILWAYS (DB)

Capable of 200km/h (125mph) operation with heavy trains, the Class 120 electrics number 60 locomotives, principally concerned with express passenger workings, though some fast freights are also handled. They are fitted with control and response systems, enabling them to work over DB's new high-speed lines (*Neubaustrecken*), and are also fitted for push-pull working of IC and EC (EuroCity) trains, enabling quick turn-rounds at intermediate terminal-form stations at Frankfurt-am-Main, Stuttgart and Leipzig, where trains leave in the reverse direction.

TYPE: Bo-Bo mainline mixed-traffic electric
POWER: 15,000V 16.67Hz AC overhead line collection; 5600kW (7500hp); thyristor control; four DC traction motors
TRACTIVE EFFORT: 347kN (78,010lbf)
MAX. OPERATING SPEED: 200km/h (125mph)
WEIGHT: 84t (184,470lb)
MAX. AXLE LOAD: not known
OVERALL LENGTH: 19.4m (63ft 8in)
GAUGE: 1435mm (4ft 8.5in)

The class prototypes were the first electric locomotives to be equipped with three-phase motors. All are run by DB Fernverkehr (long-distance).

CLASS 628.2 DIESEL MULTIPLE UNITS GERMAN FEDERAL RAILWAYS (DB)

GERMANY 1987

Representing a new generation of small diesel-hydraulic multiple units, these have been produced in large numbers to replace older Uerdingen diesel railbuses and battery electric railcars on suburban networks and country and connecting lines. Two basic classes exist: 628.2, of which 150 were

built; and 628.4, of higher power, and numbering 310. Mechanical and internal layout of these vehicles is modelled on a successful small fleet of prototypes that entered service from 1974. Underneath one car of each two-car unit is a horizontally mounted diesel engine driving through a hydraulic torque

converter gearbox and cardan shafts to the wheels of one bogie. Each side of a unit has three passenger entrance doors – single leaf and of

the swing plug type. The units are designed for one-man operation. They can be seen throughout the country on non-electrified lines.

A Class 628.2 unit enters Eutin, in Holstein, north Germany, with a service from Lübeck. Some 150 of these units, with improved ventilation, were built in 1986–89.

TYPE: secondary and branch line passenger diesel multiple unit
POWER: Daimler Benz OM 444A 410kW (550bhp) 6-cylinder diesel (one car only)
TRANSMISSION: Voith T320rz hydraulic

MAX. OPERATING SPEED: 120km/h (75mph)
WEIGHT: 40+28t (87,845+61,490lb)
OVERALL LENGTH EACH CAR: 23.2m (76ft 1in)
GAUGE: 1435mm (4ft 8.5in)

CLASS E492 STATE RAILWAYS (FS)

ITALY 1987

A project to electrify the railways of Sardinia at 25kV 50Hz AC was started in the 1980s, and the E492 class was designed in anticipation of this. The scheme was halted, but six passenger-train E492 locomotives had been built,

as well as 19 of a mixed-traffic version, Class E491.
 Unable to work on mainland Italy's network of 3000V direct current lines, all the Class E492s were put in store, and have yet to find buyers.

POWER: E491 3130kW (4197hp); E492 – 3510kW
SUPPLY: 25kV 50Hz AC
TRACTIVE EFFORT: E491 – 228kN (51300lbf); E492 – 199kN (44775lbf)
MAX. OPERATING SPEED: E491 – 140km/h

(87.8mph); E492 – 160km/h (100mph)
WEIGHT: 86t (189,630lb)
MAX. AXLE LOAD: 21.5t (47,408lb)
OVERALL LENGTH: 17m (55ft 6in)
GAUGE: 1435mm (4ft 8.5in)

CLASS RE4/4, LATER 456 BO-BO SCHWEIZERISCHE SÜDOSTBAHN (SOB)

SWITZERLAND 1987

Six locomotives of this class were constructed for the former *Schweizerische Südostbahn* by SLM in Winterthur with Brown Boveri electrical equipment, conforming with SBB Type Re4/4. In 2001, the SOB merged with the *Bodensee Toggenburg Bahn* (BT), whose tracks made up the eastern section of the

Romanshorn–Rapperswil–Lucerne route; the new company owns 120km (75 miles) of standard-

gauge track electrified at 15kV 16.67Hz AC. The six locomotives, now re-classed 456, are used on

through services and also run on SBB tracks as well as their 'own' dedicated route.

TYPE: Bo-Bo universal electric
POWER: 3200kW (4348hp)
SUPPLY: 15kV 16.67Hz AC

TRACTIVE EFFORT: 255kN (57,375lbf)
MAX. OPERATING SPEED: 130km/h (81.3mph)
WEIGHT: 68 tonnes (149,940lb)

MAX. AXLE LOAD: 17 tonnes (37,485lb)
OVERALL LENGTH: 14.8m (48ft 4in)
GAUGE: 1435mm (4ft 8.5in)

CLASS RBDE4/4 ELECTRIC MULTIPLE UNITS SWISS FEDERAL RAILWAYS (SBB)

SWITZERLAND 1987

Designed as single-unit power cars, these cars are gangwayed at the inner ends to work in pairs or with intermediate trailers. Their colourful and attractive paint-scheme earned them the nickname *Kolibri*

('humming birds'). Officially termed *Neue Pendelzug*, or NPZ (new shuttle train), they today operate local and regional services between Geneva and Berne and can also be found on several other busy routes.

TYPE: stopping train electric multiple-unit power car
POWER: 15,000V 16.67Hz AC overhead line collection; 1650kW (2210hp); electronic traction control; four bogie-mounted traction motors

TRACTIVE EFFORT: 166kN (37,318lbf)
MAX. OPERATING SPEED: 140km/h (75mph)
WEIGHT: 70t (153,725lb)
MAX. AXLE LOAD: not known
OVERALL LENGTH: 25m (82ft)

E43000 BO-BO-BO TURKISH STATE RAILWAYS (TCDD)

TURKEY 1987

In a Turkish–Japanese collaboration, the 45 E43000 locomotives were built by Tülomsas and Toshiba, for the electrification between Istanbul (Haydarpasa) and Ankara, which was finally completed in 1994. These three-bogie machines are derived from standard Japanese designs and are equipped with two alternative drive gear ratios permitting 120km/h

(75mph) for passenger trains, or a lower 90km/h (56.3mph) speed – but correspondingly higher tractive effort – for freight work. They require two different pantographs for through operation along the whole length of the route, due to two different electrical gauge clearances. In the early days of the 25kV electrification around Istanbul, a wide 1950mm (76.8in)

pantograph head was adopted, as it was thought cross-winds in the coastal region could deflect the

contact wire. Later inland stages used a smaller clearance, allowing a narrower 1600mm (63in) head.

TYPE: Bo-Bo-Bo
POWER: 3180kW (4320hp)
SUPPLY: 25kV 50Hz AC
TRACTIVE EFFORT: 275kN (61875lbf) maximum

MAX. OPERATING SPEED: 120km/h (75mph)
WEIGHT: 120t (264,600lb)
MAX. AXLE LOAD: 20t (44,100lb)
OVERALL LENGTH: 18.2m (59ft 8in)
GAUGE: 1435mm (4ft 8.5in)

DASH 8-40B BO-BO VARIOUS US RAILROADS

USA 1987

It was only three years before General Electric (GE) brought in the Dash 8-40B, to supplant the B39-8, which had very similar specifications and characteristics, on paper at least. Confusingly, GE moved its designations around at this time: under the earlier system, this would have been listed as B40-8 (and sometimes was). Like other GE high-horsepower

four-motor models, the Dash 8-40B was designed for high-horsepower applications, particularly fast intermodal work.

As might be expected, the principal intermodal carriers (Conrail, Southern Pacific and Santa Fe) were the primary customers. New York,

Susquehanna & Western (a regional railroad competing with Conrail for intermodal traffic) also operated a fleet of Dash 8-40Bs. Standard Dash 8-40Bs have a somewhat boxier cab than early Dash-8 types. Santa Fe ordered the class with North American Safety Cabs.

TYPE: Bo-Bo, diesel-electric
POWER: GE 7FDL-16 producing 2984kW (4000hp)
TRACTIVE EFFORT: N/A
MAX. OPERATING SPEED: N/A
WEIGHT: 130.1t (287,000lb)
OVERALL LENGTH: 20.218m (66ft 4in)
GAUGE: 1435mm (4ft 8.5in)

No. 4026 of the New York, Susquehanna & Western Railroad heads up three other DASH 8-40B diesels of the same line as they pass Swain, NY, in January 1990.

DASH 8-40C CO-CO VARIOUS US RAILROADS

USA 1987

Big brother to the 8-40B, Dash 8-40C was a six-motor model introduced in the same year, for the heaviest freight duties. With 2984kW (4000hp) each, linked up in multiple, they provided enormous power. The Dash 8-40C had a cab of very similar appearance to that of the 8-40B. One of General Electrics's most successful designs, this locomotive helped the company overtake Electro-Motive Division (EMD) to become America's foremost locomotive builder. Union Pacific was the first to order the Dash

8-40C and amassed a roster of 256 of them, numbered in the 9100–9300 series. It acquired more Dash 8-40Cs (which Union Pacific designates C40-8) with the purchase of Chicago & North Western in 1995. Conrail and CSX also bought the type, and it is still in use with freight operators today.

Even Class One railroads did not simply buy brand-new locomotives totally 'off the peg', as it were. Contracts often specified the use of reconditioned or second-hand parts. Union Pacific's purchases of 8-40C locomotives in the late 1980s were

not untypical: they were complex deals involving the trade-ins of older types and the re-use of certain parts. The railroad took delivery of 75 units, with road numbers 9100–9174 between December 1987 and February 1988. The first 50 were built with remanufactured trucks from traded-in U30C locomotives. These trucks came in two variations, General Steel Industries castings and Adirondack castings, both of which were rebuilt to match the new standard high brake-cylinder mounts. Parts contributed in 1987 by the U30C trade-in units (39 from

Union Pacific and 11 from Missouri Pacific) included not only truck frame components, but also traction motor frames, along with other parts used on the new Dash-8s. Along with the 50 trade-in U30C units, UP shipped five carloads of various locomotive parts to GE for use as credit against the new locomotives. Many U30C trucks lived on underneath Union Pacific's new Dash 8-40Cs.

Before delivery of the first order was completed, UP signed the contract for a second group of 75 8-40Cs, road numbers 9175–9249, with delivery taking place between July and October 1988. As in the first order, a portion, 9175–9233, used the trucks from trade-in U30Cs. Incidentally, the 75 units of this order were the first UP locomotives from GE to be equipped with flange lubricators, which spray a small amount of grease on the wheel flange of the lead axle of the rear truck, reducing friction. Flange lubricators increase fuel efficiency by five to seven percent, as well as increasing wheel and rail life. The main visible evidence of this equipment are the grease reservoirs, which are located behind the 5000gal (6005 US gal) fuel tank.

TYPE: Co-Co, diesel-electric
POWER: GE 7FDL-16 producing 2984kW (4000hp)
TRACTIVE EFFORT: N/A
MAX. OPERATING SPEED: N/A
WEIGHT: 176.6t (389,500lb)
OVERALL LENGTH: 21.539m (70ft 8in)
GAUGE: 1435mm (4ft 8.5in)

A pair of DASH 8-40C locomotives traverse the Iowa farmlands with a long Chicago & North Western freight train in April 1995.

CLASS AM86 ELECTRIC MULTIPLE UNITS BELGIAN NATIONAL RAILWAYS (SNCB) BELGIUM 1988

New materials were being brought into locomotive and train construction by this time, and the cab-front and bodyside cladding of these units were made of plastic. The prominent oblong frame in which the windscreen is set (reminiscent of the Czech diesel-electric Class 753 of 1968) earned them the nickname of 'snorkels'. Fifty-two two-car sets were built, and they work a range of services between Brussels, Antwerp, Charleroi, Hasselt and Leuven.

TYPE: two-car electric multiple-unit stopping trains
POWER: 3000V DC overhead line collection; four axle-mounted 172kW (230bhp)
traction motors under one power car
MAX. OPERATING SPEED: 120km/h (75mph)
WEIGHT: 59 and 48t (129,570 and 105,410lb) per vehicle
MAX. AXLE LOAD: not known
OVERALL LENGTH: 26.4m (86ft 7in) per vehicle
GAUGE: 1435mm (4ft 8.5in)

Under a brilliant blue sky Class AM86 No. 938 awaits departure. The quick-connection automatic coupler-buffer can be noted.

CLASS BB-26000 B-B FRENCH NATIONAL RAILWAYS (SNCF) FRANCE 1988

Later Class 426, these dual-voltage locomotives were the first to be equipped with 'Sybic' design. In this three-phase traction system, the single-phase alternating current received via the pantograph is transformed as usual and then rectified to direct current; it is then split electronically into three phases enabling much simpler design, construction and maintenance of the traction motors. Under 1500V DC catenary, the current is used as supplied. This use of traction electronics gives the class a versatile range of outputs, making them as efficient on 200km/h (125mph) passenger expresses as on heavy slower-speed freight trains. The 234 BB-26000s are used for mixed-traffic services on most French main lines.

TYPE: B-B mixed-traffic dual-voltage electric locomotive
POWER: 1500V DC and 25,000V 50Hz AC overhead line collection; 5600kW (7500bhp); AC transformer/rectification to DC; three-phase conversion from DC; two AC synchronous frame-mounted monomotor traction motors
TRACTIVE EFFORT: 320kN (71,940lbf)
MAX. OPERATING SPEED: 200km/h (125mph)
WEIGHT: 91t (199,845lb)
MAX. AXLE LOAD: not known
OVERALL LENGTH: 17.48m (57ft 4in)
GAUGE: 1435mm (4ft 8.5in)

The 'Sybic' locomotives, built by Alsthom, were precursors of the manufacturer's 'Prima' range (see 1998).

CLASS 91 BO-BO BRITISH RAIL (BR)

GREAT BRITAIN 1988

Unlike all previous main-line British electric locomotives, the Class 91s were built with single-end main cabs, of a new forward-sloping design (a small secondary driving position was installed at the 'blunt' end). This design followed a decision to operate express services from London King's Cross to Edinburgh and Leeds in a push-pull formation. These trains were designated as 'InterCity 225', denoting both their 225km/h (140mph) top operating speed and their upgrading of the 'InterCity 125' concept (see 1976). Thirty-one locomotives were built between 1988 and 1991, at British Rail Engineering's Crewe workshops, with General Electric

Two Class 91 locomotives pause at York with an East Coast Main Line express for Newcastle and Edinburgh Waverley.

electrical parts. Much of the design work on the abandoned 'Advanced Passenger Train' was adapted for the Class 91, apart from the tilting mechanism. The trains were formed of nine new BR standard Mark 4 coaches, in fixed set formations with a driving position in the end car, a DVT or 'driving van trailer'. These coaches were designed with the possibility of a tilting mechanism being installed, but with rebuilding this has been removed.

During a test run, locomotive 91010 reached 260.7km/h (162mph), the highest speed

achieved by a British locomotive, but the Class 91 locomotives suffered from a number of mechanical problems that reduced their reliability. Between 2000 and 2003, the entire class was given a full refit and since then reliability has been greatly improved. Although they were designed for a maximum of 225km/h (140mph) operation, the necessary resignalling of the East Coast Main line, to allow for increased stopping distance, did not take place, and 200km/h (125mph) remained the limit. They are still at work on the East Coast Main Line

expresses, under lease from HSBC Rail to Great North Eastern Railway (GNER), owners of the line franchise.

TYPE: Bo-Bo high-speed passenger electric
POWER: 25,000V 50Hz AC overhead line collection; 4540kW (6085bhp); thyristor control; four DC underframe mounted traction motors driving through cardan shafts
TRACTIVE EFFORT: not known
MAX. OPERATING SPEED: 200km/h (125mph)
WEIGHT: 80t (184,470lb)
MAX. AXLE LOAD: not known
OVERALL LENGTH: 19.405m (63ft 8in)
GAUGE: 1435mm (4ft 8.5in)

CLASS 442 ELECTRIC MULTIPLE UNITS BRITISH RAIL (BR)

GREAT BRITAIN 1988

Replacing older electric traction on the London–Bournemouth and Weymouth route with a new 160km/h (100mph) service, the Class 442 'Wessex Express' units are five-car buffet sets with BR Mark 3 carriage bodies riding on air-sprung bogies. Although in all other respects completely new, the 24 trains used electric traction equipment salvaged from the older

TYPE: five-car electric multiple unit express trains
POWER: 750V DC conductor rail collection, camshaft motor control; four axle-mounted 300kW (400bhp) traction motors under one centrally located power car

TRACTIVE EFFORT: not known
MAX. OPERATING SPEED: 160km/h (100mph)
WEIGHT PER VEHICLE: 35 to 54t (76,860 to 118,590lb)

OVERALL LENGTH: 23.15m (75ft 9in) outer cars; 23m (75ft 6in) inner cars
GAUGE: 1435mm (4ft 8.5in)

Bournemouth sets, as it was capable of decades of further use. Internally the Class 442s are

comfortable if somewhat high-density in their second-class seat layout. In the late 1990s, they were

refurbished to a higher standard and painted in the colours of South West Trains, the operating company.

CLASS 6400 BO-BO NETHERLANDS RAILWAYS (NS)

NETHERLANDS 1988

With a single 'off-centre' two-way cab, these are general-purpose diesel-electric locomotives for light freight assignments, equally capable of hauling trains on the open road and shunting stock in yards. Built

NS No. 6410 on a typical duty, shunting mineral wagons. Like American 'road switchers', they do both yard and main-line workings.

in Germany by MaK, with Brown Boveri electrical equipment, and three-phase AC traction, they were intended to take over from the NS' Class 2200 and 2400 diesels. There are 120 of them, fitted for working in multiples of one, two

or three as required by the weight of trains, and some are equipped to work into Germany or Belgium. The 6400s began life in NS grey-and-yellow livery, but are now being repainted in NS Cargo (Railion) red.

TYPE: freight main line diesel-electric
WHEEL ARRANGEMENT: Bo-Bo
POWER: MTU 12V396 TC 13 12-cylinder V-form diesel, 1180kW (1580hp); Brown Boveri alternator; four axle-hung AC traction motors

TRACTIVE EFFORT: 290kN (65,195lbf)
MAX. OPERATING SPEED: 120km/h (75mph)
WEIGHT: 80t (175,685lb)
OVERALL LENGTH: 14.4m (47ft 3in)
GAUGE: 1435mm (4ft 8.5in)

CLASS EF30 BO-BO-BO NEW ZEALAND RAILWAYS (NZR)

NEW ZEALAND 1988

Electrification of the 1066mm (3ft 6in) gauge 'Main Trunk' route between Auckland and Wellington to 25kV AC was completed in 1980. The 22 EF30 class were supplied by Brush of Loughborough, England, in 1988–89, using the triple bogie format popular on lines that required a combination of power, flexibility, and low maximum axle load. With a power output of 2984kW (4000hp), they are also

TYPE: heavy mixed-traffic locomotive
POWER: six traction motors developing 2984kW (4000hp), supplied with current at 25kV AC, 50Hz, via overhead catenary

TRACTIVE EFFORT: not known
MAX. OPERATING SPEED: 105km/h (65mph)
TOTAL WEIGHT: 107t (235,935lb)

MAX. AXLE LOAD: 18t (39,690lb)
OVERALL LENGTH: 19.6m (64ft 4in)
BUILDER: Brush, Loughborough, Great Britain

the most powerful locomotives ever to have operated on New Zealand Railways. They were originally intended as mixed-traffic types, hauling the 'Overlander' express between the two cities, but more often –

and now exclusively – they are employed on freight trains. As New Zealand's only remaining electric locomotives in service, they they are nowadays usually known simply as Class EF. After the privatization of New Zealand

Railways, the EFs continue to run under the new dispensation on freight operations. Eighteen of the class remain in action; No. 30036 was written off following an accident at Oio, and three others are currently in store.

CLASS IC3 DIESEL-HYDRAULIC MULTIPLE UNITS DANISH RAILWAYS (DSB)

DENMARK 1989

With their 'rubber ring' connecting ends, these are unusual but highly successful trains. The cab fronts have a novel style of gangway end. The driver sits in a central position with a wide-view windscreen. Surrounding the vehicle front is a deep and flexible rubber-type ring. When units are coupled together, the driver's cab swings inwards into the side of the vehicle interior to open

up a gangway, and the rubber rings compress to seal the join between the adjacent carriages. Ninety-two sets were originally supplied, and the three-car articulated DMUs can couple in multiples of up to 12 vehicles. Externally they have white-painted ribbed bodysides in a curved profile. The sound insulation is very good, and even outside the trains the running of the diesel engine under each car is not

obtrusive. Internally the IC3s are spacious and comfortably upholstered. Newer IR4 electric

multiple units, to the same body design, can be worked in multiple with the IC3.

TYPE: express three-car articulated diesel multiple unit
POWER: four Deutz BF8L eight-cylinder diesel engines, each of 294kW (395hp); hydraulic drive
TRACTIVE EFFORT: N/A

MAX. OPERATING SPEED: 180km/h (112mph)
WEIGHT PER UNIT: 97t (213,020lb)
OVERALL LENGTH PER UNIT: 58.8m (192ft 11in)
GAUGE: 1435mm (4ft 8.5in)

CLASS 240 CO-CO GERMAN FEDERAL RAILWAYS (DB)

GERMANY 1989

This might have become a substantial class but for the reunification of Germany and the amalgamation of its two state railway systems. In the late 1980s, DB needed some large diesel locomotives capable of hauling intercity express passenger trains and heavy freights. Three prototypes were built by Krupp,

with three-phase electric traction equipment. After testing, they worked on express trains running north from Hamburg. But with the availability of DR Class 232 locomotives, the need for the Class 240 evaporated. DB has sold them to the Dutch company Short Lines who use them on freights from Rotterdam.

One of the the three prototypes, all built by Krupp-MaK at the former Maschinenbau Kiel works in Kiel, north Germany.

TYPE: mixed-traffic main-line diesel-electric
WHEEL ARRANGEMENT: Co-Co
POWER: MaK 12M282 12-cylinder V-form diesel, 2650kW (3550hp); alternator; six AC traction motors
TRACTIVE EFFORT: 400kN (89,925lbf)

MAX. OPERATING SPEED: 160km/h (100mph)
WEIGHT: 120t (263,530lb)
OVERALL LENGTH: 20.96m (68ft 9in)
GAUGE: 1435mm (4ft 8.5in)

CLASS 60 CO-CO BRITISH RAIL (BR)

Transformation of British rail freight to bulk minerals, tank trains, fast container trains and single-customer services created a new demand for freight locomotives of high power. The Brush company of Loughborough supplied 100 of the Class 60 locomotives, which for a time were Britain's most powerful diesel-electrics. Provided with six separately excited DC traction motors for high adhesion, they worked on coal, oil, steel and aggregate trains as well as general freight. BR's Railfreight business painted the locomotives in three shades of grey with decals for particular product groups. Owned after privatization by EWS, they received that company's maroon-and-gold colours.

TYPE: freight main-line diesel-electric
WHEEL ARRANGEMENT: Co-Co
POWER: Mirrlees 8MB275T eight-cylinder diesel, 2313kW (3100hp); Brush alternator; six axle-hung DC traction motors
TRACTIVE EFFORT: 475kN (106,500lbf)
MAX. OPERATING SPEED: 100km/h (62mph)
WEIGHT: 129t (283,295lb)
OVERALL LENGTH: 21.335m (70ft)
GAUGE: 1435mm (4ft 8.5in)

Before UK railway privatization, a Class 60 in Railfreight's oil haulage division heads a train of tank wagons.

CLASS 158 DIESEL MULTIPLE UNITS BRITISH RAIL (BR)

Five years into their life, the Class 150 'Sprinters' were developed into an express design with full air-conditioning, double-glazing and carpeting throughout, and with a top speed of 145km/h (90mph). The Class 158s are formed as 17 three-car sets and 155 twin units. They work cross-country routes between major provincial centres in England and Scotland, including the trans-Pennine axis and routes between East Anglia and the Midlands, and in Wales and the southwest. The three-car Class 159s of South West Trains (a further stage away from the 150s) have set even higher standards of comfort for diesel multiple unit passengers.

TYPE: express passenger diesel multiple unit
POWER: Cummins NTA855R 260 to 300kW (350 to 400bhp) or Perkins 2006-TWH 260kW (350bhp) horizontal diesel (one per car)
TRANSMISSION: hydraulic
MAX. OPERATING SPEED: 145km/h (90mph)
WEIGHT: 38 to 39t (84,670 to 86,240lb)
OVERALL LENGTH EACH CAR: 22.57m (74ft 1in)
GAUGE: not known

On a Shrewsbury–Aberystwyth service, a 158 unit stops at the attractive and well-maintained junction station of Machynlleth, in Wales, built by the former Cambrian Railway.

CLASS 601/651 DIESEL-ELECTRIC TRAINS HELLENIC RAILWAYS (OSE)

Beginning in 1989, Hellenic Railways have been upgrading the quality of main-line services, based on the provision of comfortable if not exceptionally fast services operated by well-appointed diesel-electric trains. Twelve four-car sets were built in 1989, and a further eight five-car units were delivered from LEW in Germany from 1995. The two power cars, one at each end of a unit, are each fitted with a 1343kW (1800hp) diesel power unit supplying current for the electric traction motors.

Internally the trains have comfortable, spacious seating, air-conditioning and buffet facilities. They are used on the Athens–Thessaloniki trunk line, and also on the long, single-track main line that links the Bulgarian and Turkish borders with Thessaloniki.

TYPE: intercity express diesel-electric four-car (class 601) and five-car (651) multiple units
POWER: 1343kW (1800hp) diesels (2), electric transmission to bogie mounted traction motors

TRACTIVE EFFORT: N/A
MAX. OPERATING SPEED: 160km/h (100mph)
WEIGHT: not known
OVERALL LENGTH: not known
GAUGE: 1435mm (4ft 8.5in)

The units are able to operate in multiple as eight-, nine- or 10-car trains, and have a potential top speed of 160km/h (100mph), which will be achieved when the infrastructure and signalling improvements are completed.

CLASS X2000 TILTING TRAINS STATE RAILWAYS (SJ)

Contrasting with the period architecture of central Stockholm, an X2000 of Swedish Railways threads the tracks in June 1998.

Tilting-train technology was of particular interest to SJ, with its long and often twisting main lines threading their way through mountain and forest.

Originally designated as Class X2, later given a 'millennium' label as 'X2000', the trains are seven-car units with a power car at one end and a passenger-carrying driving trailer at the other end. The power car, effectively a locomotive, unlike the rest of the train does not tilt on curves. Thus the driver and other train crew in this vehicle experience the full lateral forces of higher speed curving. They are, of course, comfortably seated and well used to the experience. All the trailer cars tilt, however, and on Swedish main-line tracks this is a more or less continuous feature of the journey. The well-controlled tilting of these trains is not intrusive, and passengers experience a generally smooth and comfortable ride.

One disadvantage of tilting trains is that, because the train body tilts about its centre of gravity, the upper corners would foul the loading gauge if the train were built to normal dimensions. Thus tilting trains have bodies that slope in more sharply towards the roof line. This leaves less room inside for useful luggage racks, and headroom can be restrictive. Also, some passengers may find the aircraft-style interior somewhat claustrophobic, though interior design is intended to counteract this impression.

The body tilt is achieved by hydraulic rams acting on a swing cradle between the body underframe and the bogie frame, reacting to impulses from sensing mechanisms on the leading bogie of the vehicle or on the carriage in front of it. A tilt angle of up to

8º from the vertical permits the train to run through a curve at a maximum speed 20–30 per cent faster than conventional trains without passenger discomfort. Tilting on the X2000s does not compensate for all lateral forces, since it is accepted that passengers expect to feel some lateral force as a train rounds a bend; so only 60–70 per cent of the lateral imbalance is compensated for by the body tilt angle at any time. Nonetheless, journey time reductions of 10–20 per cent are possible, depending on the route.

Locomotive and trailer units have streamlined ends, and the traditional Swedish ribbed style is employed on the carriage sides. The trains have a maximum operating speed of 200km/h (125mph). Later batches include a

number of four- or five-car units nominated as InterRegio units. The main lines on which the class X2000 series can be seen include Stockholm to Göteborg, Stockholm to Sundsvall, Göteborg to Malmö, Stockholm to Oslo (Norway); and over the new Øresund link joining Sweden and Denmark to Copenhagen.

TYPE: seven-car tilting express passenger electric trains

POWER: 15,000V 16.67Hz AC overhead line collection, thyristor control; four body mounted traction motors in power car only delivering 3260kW (4370hp) in total

TRACTIVE EFFORT: not known

MAX. OPERATING SPEED: 200km/h (125mph)

WEIGHT PER VEHICLE: not known

MAX. AXLE LOAD: not known

OVERALL LENGTH: not known

GAUGE: 1435mm (4ft 8.5in)

SD60M CO-CO VARIOUS US RAILROADS

USA 1989

In 1984, Electro-Motive Division (EMD) finally replaced the now-venerable 645F engine with its new 710G, which became the standard power unit in the company's domestic locomotive line. It was fitted in the SD60 model, and this, rated at 2831kW (3800hp), was both more powerful than the SD5, and much more reliable mechanically. The first of the production line went to Union

More than 15,000 horsepower at work, as UP's SD60M No. 6122 leads a long eastbound freight through Nebraska in September 1989.

Pacific, fitted with the North American Safety Cab, the so-called 'wide nose' cab, designed to national anti-collision standards, and which has since become the predominant crew accommodation on new US locomotives. The 'M' prefix in EMD's class designation

indicates the Safety Cab option. Some later locomotives were equipped with an 'Isolated Cab' (with better sound-proofing), and these locomotives are designated SD60I. Union Pacific, Conrail, Burlington Northern and Soo Line were among SD60M operators.

TYPE: diesel-electric
POWER: 16-cylinder 710G producing 2831kW (3800hp)
TRACTIVE EFFORT: 445kN (100,000lbf) continuous TE; 664kN (149,500lbf) starting TE with 70:17 gear ratio and 25 per cent adhesion
MAX. OPERATING SPEED: N/A
WEIGHT: N/A
OVERALL LENGTH: 21.819m (71ft 7in)
GAUGE: 1435mm (4ft 8.5in)

DASH 8-40CW CO-CO VARIOUS US RAILROADS

USA 1989

General Electric (GE) also supplied the North American Safety Cab – in its case using the

designation letter W. Union Pacific bought the first GE wide-nose cabs in 1990, with an order of DASH 8-

40CWs. Other than the cab design, and the additional weight brought about by its greater structural

strength, which adds a few thousand pounds to the total weight, the Dash 8-40CW is exactly the same locomotive as the Dash 8-40C. By the mid-1990s, nearly all new freight locomotives were being built with wide-nose cabs. Conrail, CSX and Santa Fe also bought Dash 8-40CWs, assigning them to general road freight service.

TYPE: Co-Co, diesel-electric
POWER: GE 7FDL-16 producing 2984kW (4000hp)
TRACTIVE EFFORT: N/A
MAX. OPERATING SPEED: N/A
WEIGHT: 180t (398,000lb)
OVERALL LENGTH: 21.539m (70ft 8in)
GAUGE: 1435mm (4ft 8.5in)

Safety-first – Dash 8-40CW locomotives work in multiple on a long-haul freight. Ownership of many of these locomotives had been transferred to secondary lines by 2007.

CLASS EL CO-CO AUSTRALIAN NATIONAL RAILWAYS (ANR)

Built by the Australian General Electric (GE) licensee Goninan, and based on GE model C30-8, the 14 members of Australian National diesel-electric Class EL had not been very long in action when all were taken out of traffic on the privatization of Australian National. As mileage and engine hours of the locomotives were both low, all but one of the class were eventually sold to Chicago Freight Car Leasing for contract leasing to other operators within Australia. All may be found today working on the eastern side of Australia with companies such as Freight Australia, Austrac and Lachlan Valley Railfreight.

Behind the EL, its freight train shows the undulating terrain as it comes down to cross a creek bridge.

TYPE: Co-Co diesel-electric
POWER: 2462kW (3300hp) from GE 7FDL-12 series engine
TRACTIVE EFFORT: 197kN (44,325lbf) at 34km/h (21.3mph)
MAX. OPERATING SPEED: 140km/h (87mph)
WEIGHT: 114t (251,370lb)
OVERALL LENGTH: 19.6m (64ft)
GAUGE: 1435mm (4ft 8.5in)

CLASS 1700 B-B NETHERLANDS RAILWAYS (NS)

Based on the Alstom-built Class 1600 of 1981, but equipped with thyristor controls and with typical Alstom end-design, the Class 1700s run push-pull trains, often with double-deck stock, in the densely populated Amsterdam–Rotterdam–Utrecht 'Randstad' region. Eighty-one were supplied by Alstom, and they are painted in NS passenger-train bright yellow.

TYPE: B-B mainline passenger electric locomotive
POWER: 1500V DC overhead line collection; 4400kW (5900hp); DC thyristor control; two DC frame-mounted traction motors
TRACTIVE EFFORT: 294kN (66,095lbf)
MAX. OPERATING SPEED: 160km/h (100mph)
WEIGHT: 83t (182,275lb)
MAX. AXLE LOAD: not known
OVERALL LENGTH: 17.48m (57ft 4in)
GAUGE: 1435mm (4ft 8.5in)

CLASS RE 450 BO-BO SWISS FEDERAL RAILWAYS (SBB)

Like the Dutch Class 1700, these locomotives are designed for push-pull passenger working, but the Swiss engines have a more modern external design with single-piece windscreens and sides extending into skirts that almost completely hide the wheels. In accordance with push-pull working, they are single-cab units, and can be controlled from a driving cab in the end passenger car. The 115-strong class works local *S-Bahn* services in the Zürich area. Drive is by three-phase asynchronous motors from ASEA Brown Boveri, mounted in SLM-designed shifting axles.

TYPE: Bo-Bo push-pull suburban passenger
POWER: 3200kW (4348hp)
SUPPLY: 15kV 16.67Hz AC
TRACTIVE EFFORT: 240kN (54000lbf)
MAX. OPERATING SPEED: 130km/h (81.2mph)
WEIGHT: 78t (171,990lb)
MAX. AXLE LOAD: 19.5t (42,998lb)
OVERALL LENGTH: 18.4m (60ft)
GAUGE: 1435mm (4ft 8.5in)

With a double-deck *S-Bahn* train, Class Re450 No. 067 stands in Zurich's central station on 6 May 1994.

GP60M C0-CO SANTA FE RAILROAD

USA 1990

The long-haul railroads, with their many vulnerable level-crossing sites, led in developing the North American Safety Cab in the late 1980s, in order to provide crews with a better and safer working environment. The first Santa Fe locomotives to use the new cab were this variant of the Electro-Motive Division's GP60 (see 1985), delivered in 1990. These were also the first new locomotives since the 1960s to be delivered in the railroad's famous 'Warbonnet' livery. Designated as 'Super Series' machines, the GP60Ms were primarily assigned to priority intermodal freight. Santa Fe was the only line to order it. With the locomotives of EMD and GE able to operate interchangeably or in multiple, railroads often deliberately split their locomotive purchases in order to avoid becoming dependent on a single monopoly supplier.

TYPE: diesel-electric
POWER AND OUTPUT: EMD 16-710G producing 2835kW (3800hp)
TRACTIVE EFFORT: N/A
MAX. OPERATING SPEED: N/A
WEIGHT: 118t (260,000lb)
OVERALL LENGTH: 18.212m (59ft 9in)
GAUGE: 1435mm (4ft 8.5in)

A set of Santa Fe's GP60M diesels, with 'Safety Cabs', haul a freight train through Franklin Canyon, California, in October 1990.

CLASS 470 ELECTRIC MULTIPLE UNIT CZECHOSLOVAK STATE RAILWAYS (CSD)   CZECHOSLOVAKIA 1991

Ordered by CSD, political and technical events prevented this prototype from going into production. Only two five-car sets were built, of three double-deck cars set between two single-deck power cars of Bo-Bo formation. The project was begun by CSD and put in abeyance by the splitting of the organization into

TYPE: five-car double-deck prototype EMU
POWER: 2208kW (300hp)
SUPPLY: 3000V DC
TRACTIVE EFFORT: N/A

MAX. OPERATING SPEED: 120km/h (75mph)
WEIGHT: 317t (698,985lb)
MAX. AXLE LOAD: 16t (35,280lb)

OVERALL LENGTH: 132m (430ft 8in)
GAUGE: 1435mm (4ft 8.5in)

the new state railways of the Czech Republic and Slovakia.

New developments in electronic traction control made the design of the Class 470 outmoded, and it was replaced by Class 471, of similar concept and purpose but incorporating the new technology. The prototypes are in service with Czech Railways (CD).

CLASS 401 ICE HIGH-SPEED ELECTRIC TRAIN GERMAN RAILWAYS (DB)

1991

Inaugurated in 1991, Germany's electric ICE service is now using 'third-generation' trains (see ICE-3 in 2000). Germany chose a different way to Japan or France in developing a high-speed train system, and it it is only recently that some new long high-speed lines have been built. In the 1980s and 1990s, DB was upgrading its existing main-line infrastructure to obtain maximum possible speed from these routes, which gave many stretches suitable for 200km/h (125mph) running. Class 103 and 120 locomotives could

The smooth but rather austere lines of the Class 401 train are here seen to advantage, at Frankfurt am Main *Hauptbahnhof,* June 2001.

operate at this speed. The next move was to build by-pass lines to avoid sharply curved or exceptionally busy sections of track, and some of these

Neubaustrecken (new-build sections) are quite long. On these, and on other new lines, speeds of 300km/h (187mph) are possible. To work on the upgraded and new lines, new trains were built and a brand-name borrowed from Britain: 'InterCity Express' or ICE.

These were the Class 401 – long trains of 12 passenger cars with a power car at each end. The power cars were effectively Bo-Bo locomotive units, and their engines were derived from the then-new Class 120 electric locomotives,

given a more aerodynamic lining. The cars are not articulated like the French TGV, but are independent bogie vehicles. The Class 401 ICEs could run at speeds up to 280km/h (175mph) wherever the track allowed. Internal layout was spacious and comfortable from the first, with a restaurant car incorporated in the consist. A

distinctive off-white livery with a broad red stripe below window-level easily identified the stock, along with the streamlined but rather understated design of the power-car ends.

Second-generation ICEs are basically the same as the original sets, but the trains are only half as long as the first generation, and

may be coupled together if greater capacity is needed. Unlike the French TGV Paris-centred network, the ICE network has multiple hubs, working in complement with the system of intercity fast trains, with which they have always shared the main-line tracks. The main difference is the higher speed: the ICE trains travel at the maximum line speed, while IC trains are limited to 200 km/h (125mph).

All ICE first-generation units are involved in a refurbishing programme, to be completed by 2008, which will extend their working lives well into the second decade of the century.

TYPE: high-speed passenger electric trains
POWER: 15,000V 16.67Hz AC overhead line collection; 4800kW (6430hp) per power car; four body-mounted traction motors in each power car

TRACTIVE EFFORT: not known
MAX. OPERATING SPEED: 280km/h (175mph)
WEIGHT PER VEHICLE: 80t (175,685lb) power cars; 52 to 56t (114,195 to

122,980lb) trailer cars
MAX. AXLE LOAD: not known
OVERALL LENGTH: 20.56m (67ft 5in) power cars; 26.40m (86ft 7in) trailer cars
GAUGE: 1435mm (4ft 8.5in)

CLASS 252 BO-BO SPANISH RAILWAYS (RENFE)

Siemens employed the modular concept in their 'Eurosprinter' range, offering a standard design package with a range of options for power rating and able to be adapted to the requirements of different operating systems. The Spanish RENFE network had 75 delivered between 1991 and 1994, classed 252, 15 of them wheeled for standard-gauge work

on the new Madrid–Seville AVE high-speed line, with Talgo trains; others ran on the traditional Spanish 1676mm (5ft 6in) gauge. The AVE group had a maximum service speed of 220km/h (137.5mph), making them among the fastest locomotives in the world; the others ran up to 160km/h (100mph). Thirty-one of the class were dual-voltage and

TYPE: Bo-Bo universal electric
POWER: 5600kW (7609hp)
SUPPLY: 3000V DC and 25kV 50Hz AC
TRACTIVE EFFORT: 300kN (67500lbf)
MAX. OPERATING SPEED: 220km/h (137.5mph)

gauge-adaptable locomotives; the others were DC and wide-gauge only. With new units on the AVE

WEIGHT: 90t (198,450lb)
MAX. AXLE LOAD: 22.5t (49,613lb)
OVERALL LENGTH: 20.38m (66ft 6in)
GAUGE: 1435 or 1676mm (4ft 8.5in or 5ft 6in)

lines, all the 252s are normally now employed on broad-gauge services.

CLASS X12 ELECTRIC MULTIPLE UNITS STATE RAILWAYS (SJ)

The X12 is a development of the extremely successful X10 electric multiple units of 1983 – a fast two-car unit for intercity work, with higher standards of

passenger comfort than the X10, and fewer access doors. The Swedish SJ runs 18 X12s, and others are in use with private operators.

TYPE: two-car intercity electric multiple units
POWER: 15,000V 16.67Hz AC overhead line collection; 1280kW (1715bhp); axle-mounted traction motors
TRACTIVE EFFORT: not known

MAX. OPERATING SPEED: 160km/h (100mph)
WEIGHT PER VEHICLE: not known
MAX AXLE LOAD: not known
OVERALL LENGTH: not known
GAUGE: 1435mm (4ft 8.5in)

CLASS RE 460 BO-BO SWISS FEDERAL RAILWAYS (SBB)

First planned in 1987, with 119 delivered by 1996, this is a 'universal locomotive' designed for all purposes, whether singly operating a push-pull passenger service, or working in multiples using remote control on massive freight loads. Ownership is divided between the SBB's passenger business and SBB Cargo. The class has played a valuable part in SBB's *Bahn 2000* strategy for improving the capacity and operating speeds of its services, and is sometimes referred to as the *Lok-2000* type. One of its prime routes is the ever-testing St Gotthard line, a vital European freight corridor, but with 2.6 to 2.8 grades on the northern climb, and 2.1 to 2.6 on the southbound ascent, it represents a constraint – not so much on

Lok 2000 – an SBB Re 460 stands at Brig with a train of single-deck coaches from Zürich, in the late 1990s.

hauling power, which the latest electric types have in plenty, as on maximum drawbar loads. These conditions resulted in a maximum permitted train weight of 1300 tonnes (1280 tons), the train hauled by two Re 460 locomotives, with an additional 300 tonnes (295 tons) if a banking engine was added at the rear. This weight limit was increased to 2000 tonnes (1968 tons) with the inclusion of a 'helper' locomotive in the middle of the train, which became possible from 1998 using the American GE-developed Harris Locotrol system of radio control.

Not only climbing benefited; downhill running could also be made faster by utilizing the full electric brake capacity of the helper as well as the head locomotives, enabling a steady 75km/h (48.8mph) rather than the former combination of 75km/h plus periods at 40km/h (25mph). This performance has resulted in much-improved line capacity, and at least half the SBB Cargo fleet of Re 460s is now equipped for remote control working, along with Re 4/4 and Re 6/6 locomotives. In 1994, eight locomotives of a higher-powered

version, Class Re 465, was delivered for use on the BLS Lötschberg route, with a further ten in 2000.

In lowland areas, Re 460s can work in multiples of up to four on freight trains, but they are very often seen on push-pull passenger services. SBB took delivery of 60 IC-Bt driving trailers from Schindler in 1994, with driving cabs of the same design as the Re 460, and the resulting trains work high-intensity regular-interval services in the SBB core area between Geneva, St Gallen, Lucerne and Brig, with Zürich as the pivotal

point. More recently, the trains have been supplemented by double deck IC2000 carriage sets from Schindler.

TYPE: Bo-Bo universal locomotive
POWER: 4800kW (6522hp)
SUPPLY: 15kV 16.2/3Hz AC
TRACTIVE EFFORT: 275kN (61875lbf)
MAX. OPERATING SPEED: 230km/h (143.8mph)
WEIGHT: 81t (178,605lb)
MAX. AXLE LOAD: 20t (44,100lb)
OVERALL LENGTH: 18.5m (60ft 4in)
GAUGE: 1435mm (4ft 8.5in)

F40PHM-2 BO-BO METRA, CHICAGO   USA 1991

The emergence of large urban transit authorities like METRA re-established a modest US market for passenger locomotives, and Electro-Motive Division (EMD) developed the F40PHM-2 between 1991 and 1992 for use on Chicago's METRA suburban passenger system. In most respects, it is the same basic locomotive as model F40PH-2.

Most obviously different is its raked-front cab style, more European than American in appearance. The roof line of the F40PHM was extended forward, and instead of a traditional nose, the windshield dropped down at an angle to join the front end of the locomotive. This cab style was first used on EMD's experimental F69PH-AC – a model used in the

late 1990s to forward AC traction technology and assigned to Amtrak. As with METRA F40PH models, the F40PHM-2 has two sets of headlights, the top set being of the oscillating variety. The F40PHM-2s were largely used to replace ageing Burlington Northern E9s on the Chicago Union Station to Aurora route. From this year, EMD decided to consolidate all its locomotive production at the General Motors Diesel plant in London, Ontario, a development that ended locomotive construction

at the which is commonly called after its postal address, in 1991, although the Illinois facility still produces large diesel motors.

TYPE: Bo-Bo passenger diesel-electric
POWER: EMD 16-645E producing 2384kW (3200hp)
TRACTIVE EFFORT: N/A
MAX. OPERATING SPEED: N/A
WEIGHT: N/A
OVERALL LENGTH: 17.2m (56ft 2in)
GAUGE: 1435mm (4ft 8.5in)

At Stone Avenue, La Grange, Illinois (still then the centre of EMD loco building), a Metra express hauled by an F40PHM-2 crosses a local service, on 4 September 1995.

CLASS 6FE CO-CO ALGERIAN NATIONAL RAILWAYS (SNTF)

In the 1990s, Algeria's 1972-vintage Class 6CE electrics were showing their age and reaching the end of their useful careers, and this class of 14 was ordered from GEC-Alsthom and ACEC to replace them on bulk phosphates and ore transport from Djebel Onka and Tebessa to Annaba port on the Mediterranean Sea. The maximum operating speed was still 80km/h (50mph), but the 6FEs increased the overall power and the tractive effort.

TYPE: Co-Co
POWER: 2400kW (3261hp)
SUPPLY: 3000V DC
TRACTIVE EFFORT: 266kN (59,850lbf)
MAX. OPERATING SPEED: 80km/h (50mph)

WEIGHT: 132t (291,060lb)
MAX. AXLE LOAD: 22t (48,510lb)
OVERALL LENGTH: 17.48m (57ft)
GAUGE: 1435mm (4ft 8.5in)

CLASS 127 BO-BO GERMAN RAILWAYS (DB)

Built by Krauss-Maffei with Siemens electrical equipment, this was one of a number of prototype locomotives constructed around this time to explore and show the working and potential of modern three-phase electronics in traction systems. Using these, input of either AC or DC can be converted to three phases of DC at variable frequencies and voltages. This prototype did not go into line production but was the basis of DB's Class 101 and played a part in the development of Siemens' 'Eurosprinter' concept.

TYPE: Bo-Bo mainline mixed-traffic electric prototype
POWER: 15,000V 16.67Hz AC overhead line collection; 5600kW (7500bhp); three-phase control; four body-mounted traction motors
TRACTIVE EFFORT: not known
MAX. OPERATING SPEED: 220km/h (137mph)
WEIGHT: 84t (184,470lb)
MAX AXLE LOAD: not known
OVERALL LENGTH: 20.38m (66ft 10in)

On August 6 1993, this locomotive attained a speed of 310 km/h (193 mph) on a test run between Würzburg and Fulda. No modifications were made. This is a world record for locomotives running on three-phase current.

CLASS 323 ELECTRIC MULTIPLE UNIT BRITISH RAIL (BR)

Greater passenger capacity on inner suburban traffic was helped by the use of longer carriages than before. Modelled on intercity stock, these three-car sets were also of lighter weight, using aluminium alloy for the body construction. Each end car was driven by four DC motors, power coming through a gated thyristor control system that feeds variable voltage rectified current to the motors. These units have run in a variety of liveries in the shifting pattern of ownership and stock exchange and transfer of Britain's privatized rail system, and they serve mostly on routes around Birmingham and Manchester.

TYPE: three-car suburban electric multiple units
POWER PER THREE-CAR SET: 25,000V 50Hz AC overhead line collection; 1168kW (1565hp); eight axle-mounted traction motors
TRACTIVE EFFORT: not known
MAX. OPERATING SPEED: 145km/h (90mph)
WEIGHT: 39 and 41t (86,525 and 90,040lb) per vehicle
OVERALL LENGTH: 23.4m (76ft 9in)
GAUGE: 1435mm (4ft 8.5in)

The paint game: new franchise holders Northern have blanked out the logo of First North-Western on the livery of class 323 units in their Manchester-centred franchise area.

CLASS 165 DIESEL MULTIPLE UNITS BRITISH RAIL (BR)

GREAT BRITAIN 1992

Modernization of British passenger trains speeded up in the 1990s, and these two and three-car turbo-diesel-hydraulic sets gave new standards of comfort for passengers. Running on former Great Western routes, they are wider than previous types, taking advantage of the old GWR's slightly more generous loading gauge. The 'Networker' Turbos provide comfortable seating with a quiet ambience compared to earlier diesel multiple units. Chiltern Trains refurbished their stock, with air cooling, between 2003 and 2005.

TYPE: outer suburban diesel multiple unit
POWER: Perkins 2006-TWH 260kW (350bhp) horizontal (one per car)
TRACTIVE EFFORT: N/A
TRANSMISSION: Hydraulic

MAX. OPERATING SPEED: 145km/h (90mph)
WEIGHT: 38t (82,880lb)
OVERALL LENGTH EACH CAR: 23m (77ft 1in)
GAUGE: 1435mm (4ft 8.5in)

Chiltern Railways, Thames Trains and First GreatWestern all run two- or three-car Class 165 DMU trains on lines running west from London.

CLASS 787 SEVEN-CAR ELECTRIC TRAIN KYUSHU RAILWAY

JAPAN 1992

Seen as technically innovative on its appearance, with thyristor phase-controlled DC motors in its two power cars, this train ran express services on the separate rail system of Japan's southernmost main island. Using the old main lines between the principal cities of Fukuoka, Kumamoto, and Kagoshima, it was, however, in no position to rival the high-performance speed being attained on *Shinkansen* tracks on Honshu.

TYPE: long-distance express train set
POWER: not known
TRACTIVE EFFORT: not known
MAX. OPERATING SPEED: 130km/h (81mph)

TOTAL WEIGHT: not known
MAX. AXLE LOAD: not known
OVERALL LENGTH: not known
BUILDER: not known

CLASS E1300 B-B MOROCCO STATE RAILWAYS (ONCFM)

MOROCCO 1992

Closely related to SNCF's excellent Class 7200, 27 of this class were delivered, in small batches, by GEC-Alsthom to Morocco through the 1990s. The first 18 were intended for passenger work, and were geared for a maximum speed of 160km/h (100mph). Nine arrived in 1999, geared for freight haulage at

TYPE: B-B electric
POWER: 4000kW (5435hp)
SUPPLY: 3000V DC
TRACTIVE EFFORT: E1300 – 275kN

(61875lbf); E1350 – 330kN (74250lbf)
MAX. OPERATING SPEED: E1300 – 120km/h (75mph); E1350 – 160km/h (100mph)

WEIGHT: 85.5t (188,528lb)
MAX. AXLE LOAD: 21.5t (47,408lb)
OVERALL LENGTH: 17.48m (57ft)
GAUGE: 1435mm (4ft 8.5in)

100km/h (62mph) maximum, and classed as E1350. This gearing arrangement was different from most French monomotor

locomotives (though the same as the Class 7200), which were provided with alternative gear settings. The E1350 variant

replaced the old E900 on phosphates traffic, working trainloads of 4680 tonnes (4606 tons).

CLASS 100 AND 252 AVE ELECTRIC TRAIN SPANISH RAILWAYS (RENFE)

AVE stands for *Alta Velocita Español* ('Spanish High Speed'), and for its first dedicated high-speed line, built to standard 1435mm (4ft 8.5in) gauge, RENFE ordered 18 TGV-style eight-car trains from Alstom as Class 100. These have worked with exemplary reliability on this excellently engineered line. In addition, 11 'Eurosprinter' Bo-Bo locomotives were supplied by Siemens to work 'Talgo' trains on the same tracks and at the same speed level. The Talgo coaches are lightweight articulated vehicles, fitted with variable-gauge bogies (see 2006) enabling them to run from the Spanish 1676mm (5ft 6in) gauge on to standard-gauge track, and vice versa.

TYPE: high-speed electric passenger train
TRACK GAUGE: 1435mm (4ft 8.5in) AVE, and 1668mm (5ft 6in)
POWER PER TRAIN: 25,000V 50Hz AC and 3000V DC overhead line collection; 8800kW (11,795hp); body mounted traction motors, cardan shafts to driven axles
TRACTIVE EFFORT: not known
MAX. OPERATING SPEED: 300km/h (187mph)
WEIGHT: 65t (142,745lb) per power car
MAX AXLE LOAD: not known
OVERALL LENGTH PER UNIT: 22.15m (72ft 8in) power car; 21.845m (71ft 8in) end carriage; 18.7m (61ft 4in) intermediate carriages

RENFE Class 252 No. 061 brings an express train of 'Talgo' stock into Tarragona station. The AVE concept has revolutionized rail travel in Spain.

CLASS DK5600 DIESEL-HYDRAULIC RAILCAR TURKISH STATE RAILWAYS (TCDD)

The collapse of the Soviet bloc suddenly opened up a host of new perspectives between Eastern and Western Europe, in railway engineering as in other ways. International collaboration, with body-work by the Turkish Tüvasas works and the mechanical parts supplied by the Budapest-based

TYPE: diesel-hydraulic railcar
POWER: 300kW (402hp)
TRACTIVE EFFORT: Not known

MAX. OPERATING SPEED: 120km/h (75mph)
TOTAL WEIGHT: not known

MAXIMUM AXLE LOAD: not known
OVERALL LENGTH: not known
GAUGE: not known

British-Hungarian joint venture of Ganz-Hunslet, lay behind this small class of 10 railcars. Diesel-hydraulic railcars were not new to

the TCDD, which had been operating MAN-engined express units with Voith transmission since the 1960s. Holding 68

passengers, these are relatively high-speed units intended to operate between major centres on main lines.

CLASS 373 'EUROSTAR' HIGH-SPEED TRAIN

The opening of the Channel Tunnel and introduction of direct train services from London to Paris and Brussels from November 1994 inaugurated a new era in transport between Britain and the European mainland. The 'Eurostar' trains designed to operate the service were perhaps the most complex in the world. The British link-line from the Tunnel to London had not yet been started on (due for final completion in 2007), and trains had to be able to run on the British 750V DC third-rail system, and the

25kV AC overhead wire system of the Tunnel and the French and Belgian high-speed lines, as well as 3000V DC in Belgium and 1500V AC in France. The conventional British loading gauge could not be exceeded. GEC-Alsthom, with experience of building France's TGVs, led the design consortium, and an articulated 20-car set was decided on, with an axle loading of 17 tonnes (16.7 tons) maximum. Each train is effectively a back-to-back set of locomotive unit and nine passenger cars, with a total capacity of 794 passengers.

Assembly of the cars was at Belfort in France and Birmingham in England and test-running began in January 1993. Maintenance depots were established in London (North Pole), Brussels (Forest) and Paris (Landy). Thirty-eight sets were constructed, of which Eurostar UK owns 18, SNCF 16, and SNCB four. The initial journey time from London to Paris was 3hrs, reduced when the first section of the British-side link line was opened in 2003 and to be reduced to 2hrs, 15min when the CTRL (Channel Tunnel Rail Link) is

completed in 2007. By the end of 1995, Eurostar had already carried more than three million passengers. Now it carries more than double that number each year, and commands almost 70 per cent of London–Paris traffic.

Many observers feel that that the full potential of the Channel Tunnel link has yet to be exploited. Apart from the shuttle trains and freight services, the only passenger services are between the three capitals, and no attempt has yet been made to link major provincial cities on both sides of the Channel, or to extend the Eurostar's range beyond Brussels and Paris. Sleeping cars built for an overnight Britain–Continental Europe service have never been utilized.

Refurbishing of the trains began in 2004. Service life for the Eurostars has been estimated at 15 years, but it is a fair guess that this will be extended.

TYPE: Anglo-Belgian-French Channel Tunnel express passenger train
POWER: 25kV AC overhead; 750V DC third rail; 3000V DC overhead (some sets also equipped for 1500V overhead DC use)
TRACTIVE EFFORT: not known
WEIGHT: 829.2t (1,828,064lb)

MAX. AXLE LOAD: not known
MAX. OPERATING SPEED: 300km/h (186mph)
OVERALL TRAIN LENGTH: 381m (1250ft)
GAUGE: 1435mm (4ft 8.5in)

Eurostars at London's Waterloo International, terminus of the Paris and Brussels service until inception of St Pancras station in 2007.

CLASS 9000 BO-BO-BO

FRANCE AND GREAT BRITAIN 1993

Thirty-eight electric locomotives were built in 1992–93 by Brush Traction of Loughborough, England, to handle freight services and the shuttle service of car and lorry trains through the Channel Tunnel between Britain and France. Electrical equipment was supplied by ASEA Brown Boveri. Too large to operate within the normal British loading gauge, these locomotives are 22m (72ft 2in) long, 4.2m (13ft

9in) high above the rail, and 2.97m (9ft 9in) wide. The car-transporter vehicles are even higher and wider. Although two are always employed on each shuttle train (in case of failure), one locomotive has sufficient power to push or pull a fully loaded 2400-tonne (2362-ton) train plus a 'dead' partner. Both locomotives are manned, by a driver and 'train captain' respectively. The triple bogie

formation was selected to give maximum adhesion, with all six axles under power, and also to improve the flexibility of the long locomotive (the central bogie has a degree of possible lateral movement). Normal operating speed through the tunnel is 140km/h (87mph), with a possible maximum of 160km/h (100mph). Power supply is 25kV AC from overhead catenary. Though they

appear as single-cab units, a small rear driving cab is fitted, for yard movements only, in the first set. A later 9100 series of 12 locomotives dispensed with the rear cab, and a further six, of higher power output but same body style as the 9100s, appeared in 1999 as the 9700 series.

The locomotives are maintained at Coquelles depot, outside Calais. They carry the 'Eurotunnel' grey and white livery. The tunnel fire destroyed one locomotive in November 1996, but it was replaced by a new one.

The 'Tourist Shuttle' train-set comprises 24 carriages, two loading carriages and two unloading carriages, together capable of holding 120 cars and 12 coaches, and the 'Freight Shuttle' carries 28 heavy goods vehicles at up to 44 tonnes (43.2 tons) weight each.

TYPE: Shuttle Channel Tunnel locomotives
POWER: 25kV AC overhead, asynchronous three-phase, ABB 6PH, 5595kW (7500hp)
TRACTIVE EFFORT: 400kN (90,000lbf)
MAX. OPERATING SPEED: 160km/h (100mph)
WEIGHT: 132t (291,060lb)
MAX. AXLE LOAD: not known
OVERALL LENGTH: 21.996m (72ft 2in)
GAUGE: 1435mm (4 ft 8.5in)

The height of the shuttle wagons demonstrates the high loading gauge of the Channel Tunnel; the locomotives have severe route restrictions in Britain.

CLASS 92 CO-CO BRITISH RAIL (BR)

A Class 92 of the freight-hauling English Welsh & Scottish Railways company on a container train – the most frequent task of these locomotives.

Built by ADtranz at Crewe, with traction equipment by the Brush company, the 46 dual-voltage electric locomotives of Class 92 were designed to pick up 750V DC current from the British third rail, and from 25kV AC overhead wire, so that they could work trains from Britain through the Channel tunnel and into France. Though international freight was the prime consideration, they were also expected to haul sleeping-car trains, a service that has yet to materialize. These are Britain's most powerful electric locomotives.

TYPE: Co-Co mainline mixed-traffic dual-voltage electric locomotives
POWER: 25,000V 50Hz AC overhead line collection and 750V DC conductor rail collection; 5040kW (6755hp) on AC, 4000kW (5360hp) on DC; three-phase asynchronous control; six traction motors
TRACTIVE EFFORT: 400kN (89,925lbf)
MAX. OPERATING SPEED: 140km/h (87mph)
WEIGHT: 126t (348,650lb)
MAX AXLE LOAD: not known
OVERALL LENGTH: 21.34m (70ft 1in)
GAUGE: 1435mm (4ft 8.5in)

CLASS 5601 BO-BO PORTUGUESE RAILWAYS (CP)

CP's choice for a new main-line mixed-traffic locomotive on its growing electrified network was the 'Eurosprinter' type also used in Spain, and built by Krauss-Maffei, with Siemens electrics. Running under standard 25kV 50Hz AC wire supply, they share both freight and passenger services with CP's Alsthom Class 2601.

TYPE: Bo-Bo mainline mixed-traffic electric
TRACK GAUGE: 1668mm (5ft 6in)
POWER: 25,000V 50Hz AC overhead LINE COLLECTION; 5600kW (7500bhp); three-phase control; four body-mounted traction motors
TRACTIVE EFFORT: not known
MAX. OPERATING SPEED: 200km/h (125mph)
WEIGHT: 88t (193,255lb)
MAX AXLE LOAD: not known
OVERALL LENGTH: 20.38m (66ft 10in)

SD70MAC CO-CO BURLINGTON NORTHERN RAILROAD

This locomotive type marks a significant technical milestone. During the late 1980s and early 1990s, EMD worked with Siemens to develop a practical alternating current (AC) traction system for heavy North American diesel-electrics. Up until the SD70MAC, all American commercial mass-produced diesel-electric locomotives used conventional direct-current (DC) traction motors. The advantages of AC traction include significantly greater tractive effort through superior motor control, more effective dynamic braking (especially at slow speeds) and longer motor life. Burlington Northern supported the development of the SD70MAC by ordering hundreds of the type for use on its Powder River Coal

trains, and found it could use three SD70MACs in place of five SD40-2s in coal service as a result of the significantly higher tractive effort produced by AC traction. CSX and Conrail also ordered small fleets of SD70MACs for heavy service.

TYPE: Co-Co, AC traction, diesel-electric
POWER: EMD 16-710G3C-T1 producing 2980kW (4000hp)
TRACTIVE EFFORT: 609kN (137,000lbf) continuous TE; 778kN (175,000lbf) starting TE with 85:16 gear ratio and 33 per cent adhesion.
MAX. OPERATING SPEED: N/A
WEIGHT: N/A
OVERALL LENGTH: 22.555m (74 ft)
GAUGE: 1435mm (4ft 8.5in)

SD70MAC No. 4795 of CSX, on the snowy morning of 3 March 2006, at Middlefield, Massachusetts.

DASH 9-44CW CO-CO VARIOUS US RAILWAYS

USA 1993

Dash-9 was General Electric's initiative in 1993, bringing together a new range of technological modifications in its domestic locomotive line – improvements that resulted in greater fuel efficiency, tighter emission control and better adhesion. A new bogie design, GE's 'Hi-AD' truck was also

introduced, making the most obvious difference between the Dash-9 line and Dash-8 models. The Dash-9 line became GE's standard direct-current traction model line. The Dash 9-44CW should not be confused with the outwardly similar AC4400CW, which was fitted with AC traction motors.

Initially, the line of Dash-9 locomotives consisted only of the Dash 9-44CW, which was ordered by Chicago & North Western, Southern Pacific and Santa Fe among other carriers. Later, other models were also ordered, such as the Dash 9-40C, by Norfolk Southern.

TYPE: Co-Co, diesel-electric
POWER: GE 7FDL-16 producing 3278kW (4400hp)
TRACTIVE EFFORT: varies with options
MAX. OPERATING SPEED: not known
WEIGHT: varies with options; 181.6t (400,000lb)
OVERALL LENGTH: 22.403m (73ft 6in)
GAUGE: 1435mm (4ft 8.5in)

DASH 8-40BP 'GENESIS' BO-BO AMTRAK

USA 1993

Amtrak No. 823 offers a detailed side view as it crosses Millers Falls, Massachusetts, in October 2002.

The imperatives of marketing had an effect on the naming of locomotive types. This smooth-lined diesel-electric, with cab at one end only, was first known as AMD-103 ('AMtrak Diesel, 103mph') when GE Transportation Systems and Amtrak worked together on the planning of a successor to Amtrak's ageing fleet of Electro-Motive Division (EMD) F40PH diesel-electrics, which had been the mainstay of its long-distance passenger fleet for almost two decades. Also known technically as model Dash 8-40BP, and as the P40DC, it was called the Genesis type by GE's marketing department. Unlike the F40PH, the structure of this new design started from scratch, not as an adaptation of an existing freight locomotive, and it had a variety of new features, including a newly designed monocoque body, whose shell, including the fuel tank, is integral to the structure of the locomotive. The first Genesis locomotives were built in 1993 and numbered in the 800 series. There are now three types of

Genesis, and it is Amtrak's standard diesel-electric passenger locomotive for long hauls, often used in tandem. The electrical components came from GE's then current line of four-axle freight locomotives, the 2984kW (4000hp) B40-8 series. After thoroughly testing the P40s for several years, Amtrak went back to GE in 1997 for more Genesis units. The new locomotives, known as known as P42DC, produced 3100kW (4200hp) and had a higher top speed of 177km/h (110mph). Amtrak eventually owned 44 P40s and 207 P42s. Canada's VIA Rail also purchased several P42s.

Amtrak also required replacements for its elderly dual-power FL9 class (see 1956), still in use on the Hudson River line from Albany, NY, to New York City. These locomotives could operate either off their diesel prime movers, or off the 600V DC third rail extending from New York to Croton-Harmon, 53km (33 miles) to the north. At first, Amtrak wanted a 'tri-power' unit that could use diesel, third-rail DC, or overhead

16kV AC power, but this proved impracticable, and it opted for a modified Genesis type unit, with the same diesel/third-rail capabilities as the FL9s. These were P32AC-DM, or Genesis II, locomotives, and though similar to the Genesis Is the dual-power Genesis IIs incorporated several major changes, apart from the ability to run under their own power. The prime mover was a 12-cylinder unit of 2386kW (3200hp), and the transmission included DC/AC inverters and AC traction motors. Eighteen Genesis IIs were built for Amtrak, and several more were built for Metro North Commuter Railroad. The Genesis locomotives run almost all of Amtrak's long-distance passenger services on non-electrified tracks, running in pairs or triple-headed on the heaviest consists.

In Canada, the GE P42DC displaced VIA Rail's Bombardier LRC locomotives from service in 2000. VIA Rail's P42DC fleet is primarily used on the Quebec–Windsor rail corridor, where train

consists are typically short and light, formed of three to six cars, which allows the powerful locomotives to quickly bring the train to full speed. Between Montreal and Toronto, some track sections allow the P42 to pull the trains at its maximum sustained speed of 177km/h (110mph). Longer trains of eight to 10 cars may have a second P42 at the trailing end to maintain the high-speed schedule. The 177km/h (110mph) trains operating on the Quebec–Windsor corridor use LRC aluminium tilting cars, the predecessors of Amtrak's tilting stainless-steel 'Acela Express'.

TYPE: Bo-Bo, passenger diesel-electric
POWER: GE 7FDL-16 producing 2984kW (4000hp)
TRACTIVE EFFORT: 171kN (38,500lbf) at 53km/h (33mph) with 74:20 gear ratio
MAX. OPERATING SPEED: 165km/h (103mph)
WEIGHT: 121.8t (268,240lb)
OVERALL LENGTH: 21.031m (69 ft)
GAUGE: 1435mm (4ft 8.5in)

CLASS 3000 BO-BO-BO QUEENSLAND RAILWAYS (QR)

Three six-axle electrics were acquired by QR to add to the heavy freight types used in the North Queensland coalfield behind Rockhampton. As has become usual on heavy mineral freights, especially on dedicated lines, trains of vast tonnage are moved by several locomotives, up to five in the case of this line,

TYPE: Bo-Bo-Bo electric freight
POWER: 3000kW (4020hp)
SUPPLY: 25kV 50Hz AC

TRACTIVE EFFORT: 260kN (58,500lbf) at 40km/h (25mph)
MAX. OPERATING SPEED: 80km/h (50mph)

WEIGHT: 113t (249,165lb)
MAX. AXLE LOAD: 19t (41,895lb)
OVERALL LENGTH: 20.55m (67ft)
GAUGE: 1067mm (3ft 6in)

with two or three as mid-train helpers, controlled via the Locotrol system by a single driver in the lead locomotive. The reason for the mid-train position is that it shares the drawbar pull with the lead engines: without this, the pull exerted by three or more 5600kW (7500hp) locomotives coupled in line would be such as to pull the wagon couplings out.

CLASS 61 BO-BO BULGARIAN RAILWAYS (BDZ)

Despite its four-axle configuration, this is a modestly powered centre-cab electric switcher designed for the usual range of shunting tasks around main termini, junctions and freight yards. Built by Skoda in Plzen, Czech Republic, it uses thyristor control technology developed by Czechoslovak Railways (CSD) in the early 1990s.

TYPE: Bo-Bo electric switcher
POWER: 960kW (1304hp)
SUPPLY: 25kV 50Hz AC
TRACTIVE EFFORT: 122kN (27,450lbf)
MAX. OPERATING SPEED: 80km/h (50mph)
WEIGHT: 74t (163,170lb)
MAX. AXLE LOAD: 18.5t (40,793lb)
OVERALL LENGTH: 14.4m (47ft)
GAUGE: 1435mm (4ft 8.5in)

These distinctive locomotives do shunting work with both freight and passenger stock at Sofia and a number of larger stations, including Plovdiv, Burgas, Dupnica and Karnobat.

CLASS S699 CO-CO CZECH RAILWAYS (CD)

This was to have been one of the main locomotive classes of the CSD. Unfortunately, it was planned before the break-up of Czechoslovakia and neither of the resulting national systems wanted to pursue the type, which would have been a long-distance main-line locomotive for both passenger and freight. The prototypes remain with the Czech Republic Railways (CD), working on freight in the brown-coal region of Bohemia.

TYPE: Co-Co prototype
POWER: 5220kW (7092hp)
SUPPLY: 3000V DC
TRACTIVE EFFORT: 575kN (129,375lbf)
MAX. OPERATING SPEED: 95km/h (59.4mph)

WEIGHT: 120t (264,600lb)
MAX. AXLE LOAD: 20t (44,100lb)
OVERALL LENGTH: 20.346m (66ft 4in)
GAUGE: 1435mm (4ft 8.5in)

CLASS SR2 BO-BO FINNISH STATE RAILWAYS (VR)

Based on the Swiss Re 460 class and very similar in looks, though without the low-level skirting of the Swiss type, VR's Class Sr2 is also intended as a 'universal engine' capable of all main-line duties. Finnish electrified railways are powered from 25kV

50Hz Ac, and this engine has a slightly higher continuous power rating than the Re460. The class numbers 46 in total. With the extension of 'Pendolino' services on VR, the Class Sr2 locomotives are increasingly concentrated on freight train duties.

TYPE: Bo-Bo mixed-traffic electric
POWER: Maximum output for 1 hour 6000kW (8054hp); continuous output 5000kW (3725hp)
TRACTIVE EFFORT: 300kN (67,500 lbf) starting TE; 240kN (54,000lbf) continuous TE

MAX. OPERATING SPEED: N/A
WEIGHT: 83t (183,015lb)
OVERALL LENGTH: 13m (45ft 3in)
MAX. AXLE LOAD: 20.75t (45,754lb)
GAUGE: 1524mm (5 ft)

CLASS CLASS 201 CO-CO IRISH RAIL (IR)

Capable of 160km/h (100mph), a speed not attained in Ireland since the probably mythical achievements of the '800' steam class of 1939, the 35 Class 201 diesel-electrics became IR's prime motive power for passenger and freight. Built by

Electro-Motive Divsion, they confirmed a 30-year relationship between builder and user. The first locomotive, No. 201, was flown in on an Antonov 124 Aircraft. The 201s have a cab at each end, and are equipped with head-end power for use on the

A new look and higher speeds on Irish Railways – an EMD Class 201 on a Dublin-bound train, at Kildare station in 1999.

TYPE: Co-Co, diesel-electric
POWER: EMD 12-710G3B producing 2253kW (3000hp) for traction.
TRACTIVE EFFORT: 194kN (43,611lbf) continuous TE

MAX. OPERATING SPEED: 161km/h (100mph)
WEIGHT: 112t (230,000 lbs)
OVERALL LENGTH: 20.949m (68ft 9in)
GAUGE: 1600mm (5ft 3in)

Dublin–Belfast *Enterprise* service. Two are owned by Northern Ireland Railways. As of 2002, five of IR's Class 201s were painted

for the *Enterprise* service; the remainder were in the Irish Rail orange, black and yellow livery.

CLASS IRM DOUBLE-DECK ELECTRIC MULTIPLE UNITS

Some of the most striking-looking and effective multiple unit designs in the world are to be found on NS. The IRM units were designed and built with remarkable speed to cater for ever-increasing passenger numbers, and are a very familiar sight on NS tracks. Double-decked to provide maximum capacity, they were NS' first air-conditioned cars. Another amenity was a dumb-waiter lift for catering supplies to be brought easily to the upper deck by the steward. Named 'Regio Runners' in

TYPE: double-deck express electric multiple units
POWER: 1500V DC overhead line collection (25kV to be added); 604kW (810hp); two traction motors in one bogie
TRACTIVE EFFORT: not known

MAX. OPERATING SPEED: 160km/h (100mph)
WEIGHT PER VEHICLE: 50 to 62t (110,680 to 136,595lb)
MAX. AXLE LOAD: not known
OVERALL LENGTH: 27.28m (89ft 6in) driving cars; 26.5m (86ft 11in) intermediate cars

Euro-English marketing jargon, they were built for inter-region services, but are mostly used on city-to-city routes like Amsterdam–The Hague, Amsterdam–

Dordrecht–Vlissingen, and Utrecht–Eindhoven. Capable of 160km/h (100mph) and of acceleration from 0 to 140km/h (87mph) in 65 seconds, they are

fitted electrically for NS' eventual conversion to universal 25kV 50Hz AC current supply. Each driving car has a power bogie at the non-driving end, driving both axles. Initially 80 were supplied by Talbot and De Dietrich, in three and four-car formations, but 252 new coaches were ordered in 2000 to expand the four-car to six-car sets, plus 12 new six-car sets. Bombardier were the suppliers, with the last of the new units appearing in May 2005.

MK5000C CO-CO SOUTHERN PACIFIC RAILROAD (SP)

In the mid-1990s, locomotive re-manufacturer and railroad equipment supplier MK Rail made a vigorous effort to capture a share of the highly competitive road diesel market, dominated since 1970 by the giants of General Motors' Electro-Motive Division (EMD) and General Electric (GE). For heavy freight service, MK Rail brought out its

six-axle MK5000C, a locomotive designed to rival similar products by EMD and GE. It was powered by a turbocharged 12-cylinder Caterpillar 3612 diesel engine and used electrical components supplied by KATO Engineering. For a short time, the MK5000C was the most powerful diesel-electric in the United States. Three prototypes were painted

TYPE: Co-Co diesel-electric
POWER: 3612 Caterpillar diesel producing 3725kW (5000hp)
TRACTIVE EFFORT: 506kN (113,800lbf) with 83:20 gear ratio

MAX. OPERATING SPEED: 112km/h (70mph)
WEIGHT: 177 to 190t (390,000 to 420,000lb) depending on options
OVERALL LENGTH: 22.352m (73ft 4in)
GAUGE: 1435mm (4ft 8.5in)

for Southern Pacific, operating on its lines for a few years. But the locomotive did not offer anything

that the established companies did not provide, and sales were very few.

F59PHI VARIOUS US RAILROADS

Undeterred, or spurred on, by General Electric's 'Genesis', Electro-Motive Division (EMD) brought out its new passenger locomotive in the following year. Designated as F59PHI and capable of 176km/h (110mph), and so marginally faster than the GE rival, it featured a streamlined design with a distinctive rounded cab, at one end only. EMD promotional literature described the new image as 'Swoopy'. Amtrak was the first customer, and assigns its F59PHIs for medium-distance trains on the West Coast. Some city transit passenger operators, such as Los Angeles' Metrolink, also acquired small fleets of F59PHIs. Perhaps the most unusual owner of the type was cigarette manufacturer Marlboro, which acquired two for use on a deluxe passenger train as part of a promotional scheme. However, the scheme was scrapped before the locomotives were used.

TYPE: Co-Co diesel-electric
POWER: 3612 Caterpillar diesel producing 3725kW (5000hp)
TRACTIVE EFFORT: 506kN (113,800lbf) with 83:20 gear ratio
MAX. OPERATING SPEED: 112km/h (70mph)
WEIGHT: 177 to 190t (390,000 to 420,000lb) depending on options
OVERALL LENGTH: 22.352m (73ft 4in)
GAUGE: 1435mm (4ft 8.5in)

A North Carolina F59PHI speeds along at Spencer, NC, with the three-car 'Piedmont' train, on 14 February 2004.

TGV THIRD GENERATION 'DUPLEX' FRENCH NATIONAL RAILWAYS (SNCF)

France's first TGV line, the *Sud-Est* from Paris to Lyon, is also the busiest in the country, and from its opening in 1981 it had reached its full traffic capacity by the early 1990s. The solution to the overcrowding problem was the world's first high-speed two-deck train, TGV Duplex, with passenger seating on two levels and 45 per cent more passenger capacity (545 seats) than an equivalent single level TGV. In anticipation of the need, a Duplex feasibility study was completed in 1987, and in 1988 a full-scale mockup was built to gauge customer reaction to a concept traditionally associated with commuter rail rather than with fast luxury trains. A TGV *Sud-Est* trailer was tested in revenue service with the inside furnished to simulate the lower floor of a bi-level arrangement, and later that year another TGV *Sud-Est* was modified to study the dynamic behaviour of a train with a higher centre of gravity. In July 1990, GEC-Alsthom won the contract to build the 'TGV-2N', as it was then known. The first tests of a two-deck trainset were in November 1994. Soon after their first run, the first rake of eight trailers was tested at 290 m/h (180 mph) on the *Sud-Est* line. The trainset was powered by TGV *Réseau* power cars as the Duplex power cars were still undergoing development. The first Duplex power car appeared in June 1995, and the 30 complete sets of eight passenger cars and two power cars were built in 1995–97.

In several key respects, the third-generation TGVs represent significant advances over the first trains built for the *Sud-Est* line. Power to weight ratio is 23kW

In February 2000, a TGV 'Duplex' glides into the Gare de Lyon, Paris, at the end of its journey from Lyon.

per tonne (31.28hp per 2205lb), compared to 17; weight per passenger seat is 0.7 tonnes (0.68 tons) compared to 1.1 tonnes (1.08 tons); and power per seat is 16.15kW (22hp) per seat, compared with 18.34kW (25hp). The Duplex trains have now been running for more than 10 years and are an accepted aspect of the TGV service. As of 2006, they run from Marseille to Paris and will be seen on other TGV services as traffic continues to expand.

Research and development is a major aspect of TGV management, with particular attention focused on brakes, traction, construction materials and noise. As these considerations apply equally to all very high-speed trains, it is worth looking at them in some detail. At present, TGVs use two sets of brakes: disc brakes on the wheels and dynamic brakes on the powered axles; some also have tread brakes for emergency application. At speeds in excess of 350km/h (218mph), these standard braking systems are not sufficient to enable a safe emergency stop, and though the 'Duplex' trains have improved brakes, with dynamic braking performance enhanced from 24kN (5400lb) to 30kN (6800lb) for each powered axle, something different will be needed for higher-speed trains. Work is in progress on magnetic induction brakes, which dissipate kinetic energy as heat in the rail by means of eddy currents, with no metal-on-metal contact. Traction for the TGV NG is by asychronous three-phase AC induction motors, which offer simplicity of maintenance and very high power to weight ratio (around 1kW/kg). The 2 x 6000kW (8046hp) traction package, 40 per cent more powerful than second-generation units, requires that a total of six powered axles be used instead of the previous four, so that sufficient tractive effort can be put to the rail despite the low (17 tonnes/16.7 tons) axle load.

The additional powered axles are located under the first and last trailer, immediately adjacent to the power cars. The trainset is designed to be capable of starting on a 4 per cent (4 in 100) grade with two traction motors shut down. Cooling of the traction equipment must work at ambient temperatures up to 45°C (113°F), using an environmentally friendly liquid coolant for the semiconductors, rather than freon. Traction motors are individually controlled, whereas they were previously controlled in pairs using one inverter. There is nothing radically new in the traction equipment, but the challenge lies in satisfying a very large power and tractive effort requirement, within severe axle load constraints.

The current axle load limit is 17 tonnes (16.7 tons), and there is a possibility that this will be reduced to 16 tonnes (15.7 tons) for the faster TGV NG. Meanwhile, it is desirable to retain an articulated design (with two axles per trailer), a bilevel seating arrangement, and a host of other requirements that would tend to increase the axle load of a trainset. Keeping weight down is one of the biggest challenges in the design of a 350km/h (218mph) train. The first approach to reduction is new materials. French LGV tracks have the strict weight limit of 17 tonnes (16.7 tons) per axle; to keep the 'Duplex' cars within it, extruded aluminum construction, as used on the German ICE trains, made possible a 20 per cent reduction in weight. At the same time, aerodynamics were also improved over the original TGV profile. The trailers are a monocoque design assembled from extrusions, yielding a weight reduction of 20 per cent over an equivalent steel structure. The frame of the power cars is of high-tensile strength steel, as in the TGV *Atlantique* units, with a weight reduction of 10 per cent over lower-grade steel. Stainless steel

could also make an entry into the new trainsets, as well as composites. Composite materials are not used on the Duplex's main structural components partly for reasons of cost, partly because the technology was not considered sufficiently mature. Future generation trains, however, may be built with a composite main structure assembled with glue. Other weight reductions are achieved by using better paints, electrical wires with thinner insulation, and many other small measures that become significant when added together. The second way to cut weight is by using the least possible material to fulfill structural requirements, or optimization. This has become a worthwile pursuit with the advent of extensive computer finite-element analysis. The connection between trailers has been completely redesigned, and is now attached to the trailer bodies rather than the truck and suspension assembly. This allows a substantial reduction in the weight of the secondary suspension, with a 400kg (880 lb) saving. The Y237B bogie used on the *Atlantique* has been redesigned, saving 200kg (440lb) on each. The interior, as with commercial aviation, is designed for maximum lightness. Seats have been entirely redesigned for the Duplex, with each one reduced from 26kg (57lb) to 14kg (31lb).

Noise is another major concern, not only for the passengers but for those living near the tracks. Research focuses on identifying the sources of noise at speeds in excess of 350km/h (218mph) and finding ways to combat them. Interior noise level of the new TGVs, in particular, suffers from the weight-reducing measures described above. In the new bi-level trailers, new methods are needed to reduce noise, especially on the lower level, which sits much closer to the track than before. The solution is to isolate the interior from the outer

structure, using flexible blocks as well as a sound-deadening composite laminate. Outside the train, aerodynamic noise exceeds wheel noise at high speeds. Better aerodynamics not only reduce the noise, but also moderate the energy consumption of the train. Much attention centres around the nose profile, and shrouding of the trucks; data is being shared with Japanese researchers working on the same problem. The fifth-generation TGV, currently in the form of the MX100 research project, will have a streamlined nose profile, because at the speeds envisioned aerodynamic drag dwarfs every other source of resistance to motion.

Other points of interest are the study of the interaction of the train with nearby obstacles, such as tunnel sides. Special shapes reduce the strength of pressure waves generated by the train, improving passenger comfort. An early result of this research was the profile of Eurostar's nose, optimized for running in the Channel tunnel. Pressure-sealing of the trainsets began with the TGV *Réseau*, and active pressure compensation (not full pressurization) is being considered. Trackside noise reduction has also been a focus, with passive and active solutions. Acoustic walls have been built in many places to shield noise-sensitive areas, yielding reductions of overall train noise of the order of 10 to 15dB. Active systems using loudspeakers embedded in the walls are also under consideration.

TYPE: high-speed two-deck electric train
POWER: 25kV 50Hz AC, 1.5kV DC; 8 3-phase synchronous AC traction motors, developing 8800kW (12,000hp) under 25kV supply
MAX. OPERATING SPEED: 300km/h (186mph)
OVERALL LENGTH: 200m (656ft)
WEIGHT: 380t (837,756lb)
MAX. AXLE LOAD: 17t (37,478lb)
GAUGE: 1435mm (4ft 8.5ins)

CLASS 325 POSTAL ELECTRIC MULTIPLE UNITS ROYAL MAIL   GREAT BRITAIN 1995

These dedicated four-car sets lasted in regular postal service for only a few years until the Royal Mail decided to use road and air for all but Christmas peak mail transport. Sixteen sets were built by ABB at Derby, to run both under overhead wire and with third-rail supply, and fitted internally to hold wheeled postal containers. They were based on the Class 319 electric multiple units operated by Thameslink, which were similarly dual-voltage fitted. Now they are largely redundant.

TYPE: four-car postal electric multiple units
POWER PER UNIT: 25,000V 50Hz AC overhead line collection and 750V DC conductor rail collection; 980kW (1315hp); four axle-mounted traction motors
TRACTIVE EFFORT: not known
MAX. OPERATING SPEED: 160km/h (100mph)
WEIGHT PER VEHICLE: 29 to 50t (65,185 to 112,000lb)
MAX. AXLE LOAD: not known
OVERALL LENGTH: 20.35m (66ft 9in)
GAUGE: 1435mm (4ft 8.5in)

A four-car Royal Mail set speeds along the West Coast Main Line in evening light, with the equivalent of four road-truck loads on board.

BVMOT ELECTRIC MULTIPLE UNIT HUNGARIAN STATE RAILWAYS (MÁV)

Performance problems have dogged the three prototypes of what was intended to be a substantial class running intercity

One of MÀV's BV MOT power cars, in the system's bright Inter-City livery. They are named after celebrated Hungarians, though their performance has been dogged by problems.

services in and from Hungary. Unusually for an EMU, they are formed of a combined power-passenger car and three trailers, the end one with a driving cab. The power car is a Bo-Bo with all axles driven. Another feature is a 1845kW (2505hp) electric dynamic braking system. Design and construction was by Ganz-Hunslet in Budapest. In the early

2002s, they have been mostly in use on the route from Budapest

to Kaposvar and Nagykanisza. Series production seems unlikely.

TYPE: four-car prototype express EMU
POWER: 1755kW (2385hp) per unit
SUPPLY: 25kV 50Hz AC
TRACTIVE EFFORT: N/A
MAX. OPERATING SPEED: 160km/h (100mph)

WEIGHT: 68t (149,940lb) motor coach; 206t (454,230lb) complete unit
MAX. AXLE LOAD: 17t (37,485lb)
OVERALL LENGTH: 103.2m (336ft 8in) complete unit
GAUGE: 1435mm (4ft 8.5in)

WDG2 CO-CO INDIAN RAILWAYS (IR)

Designed for freight service, this is a modern Indian diesel-electric design based around the well-tried Alco 251-series engine, with 16 cylinders, a GE or ABB turbo-charger, and driving an alternator in place of a generator. It runs on the same type of high adhesion bogie design as fitted to

electric locomotives of classes WCAM3 and WAG7. Class WDG2 can be identified from the cab,

which is set further back than on its WDM2 predecessor, giving a longer hood compared to a class

WDM2. In 1995, it was a powerful and up-to-date type, and will give good service beyond 2010.

TYPE: Co-Co diesel-electric freight
POWER: 2282kW (3100hp) from Alco 16-251 series engine

TRACTIVE EFFORT: 258kN (58,080lbf) at 19km/h (11.9mph)
MAX. OPERATING SPEED: 100km/h (62mph)

WEIGHT: 123t (271,215lb)
OVERALL LENGTH: 17.12m (55ft 10in)
GAUGE: 1676mm (5ft 6in)

SD70I CO-CO CANADIAN NATIONAL RAILWAYS (CN)

SD70, as a basic locomotive type, was Electro-Motive Division's modern direct-current alternative to its successful alternating current motor SD70MAC. Both used a 16-cylinder version of the 710G3 diesel engine to generate 2980kW (4000hp). SD70 was built in several variations depending on the crew cab specifications made by the purchasing railroad. The SD70I uses a wide-nose safety cab of similar appearance to that found on other modern EMD locomotives. In fact, it is physically isolated from the rest of the locomotive to provide a significantly quieter and more comfortable ride for crews – an arrangement called the

'WhisperCab' by EMD. The WhisperCab can be identified by the vertical breaks on the cab-nose of the locomotive.

Canadian National has been the only purchaser of the SD70I version.

TYPE: Co-Co, diesel-electric
POWER: EMD 16-710G3C-T1 producing 2980kW (4000hp)
TRACTIVE EFFORT: 484kN (109,000lbf) continuous TE; 707kN (159,000lbf) starting TE
MAX. OPERATING SPEED: N/A
WEIGHT: N/A
OVERALL LENGTH: 22.047m (72ft 4in)
GAUGE: 1435mm (4ft 8.5in)

A good impression of the front of the 'Whisper Cab' is given in this shot of a C SD 701 as it rounds a bend with a freight train in June 1996.

WAP-5 CO-CO INDIAN RAILWAYS (IR)

INDIA 1995

The first 10 members of this class, India's first three-phase electric locomotive, were imported from ABB (now Bombardier Transportation) in Switzerland in 1995. Chittaranjan Works (CLW) took up production from 2000. It is designed to haul 26-coach passenger trains at 160km/h (100mph). Other notable features of the class are the provision of taps from the main transformers for hotel and pantry loads; flexible gear coupling; wheel-mounted disc brakes, and a potential for speed enhancement to 200km/h (124mph). ABB's 6FXA 7059 three-phase squirrel-cage induction motors (1150kW/1542hp, 2180V), with forced-air ventilation and fully suspended, provide the traction. Gear Ratio (three stage) is 67:35:17. Braking systems include regenerative braking (160kN/35,969lbf), locomotive disc

brakes, automatic train air brakes and a charged spring parking brake. Bo-Bo Henschel Flexifloat bogies are fitted. Multiple-unit operation is possible with one other locomotive.

The utilization of WAP-5 engines began to justify the claim of 'superfast' that had been successfully though somewhat inaccurately attached to IR's 'Shatabdi Expresses' since these trains were introduced in July 1988. New Delhi–Jhansi was the route of the first one, extended to Bhopal in February 1989. The name 'Shatabdi' means centenary in Hindi, and the first service was a celebration of the birth centenary of Jawaharlal Nehru, the first Prime Minister of India. Intended to serve as connections between major cities that are relatively close to each other, they are typically operated in such a way that they

depart from their respective originating stations early in the morning, reach their destinations by noon or early afternoon and return after a stopover of 30 minutes to 1 hour, arriving back at the originating station by late evening. Shatabdi Expresses offer fast connectivity with very few stops in between. They are fully air-conditioned and are very luxurious and comfortable. In the interest of less wealthy travellers, Indian Railways later introduced a lower-priced version called Jan-Shatabdi Expresses, which had mostly non-air-conditioned stock and have lower fares.

While Shatabdi Express series of trains run over a short distance, Rajdhani Expresses are long-distance trains connecting the national capital of Delhi to various state capitals. Both series of trains

are the fastest in India, with an operating speed, wherever possible, of 130km/h (81mph). The fastest operational speed in India is that of the New Delhi–Bhopal Shatabdi Express, which on the New Delhi–Agra section of the route runs at a speed of 150km/h (93mph). The WAP-5 locomotives haul such premier 'superfast' services, as this one, as well as the Mumbai Rajdhani Express, the Lucknow Shatabdi Express, and many others.

TYPE: Co-Co express passenger locomotive
POWER: 4007kW (5450 hp)
TRACTIVE EFFORT: not known
MAX. OPERATING SPEED: 160km/h (100mph)
WEIGHT: 78t (171,960lb)
MAX. AXLE LOAD: 19.5t (42,990lb)
OVERALL LENGTH: 18162mm (59ft 5in)
GAUGE: 1676mm (5ft 6in)

SD80MAC CO-CO CONRAIL

USA 1995

In its latter years, Conrail bought 30 very powerful AC traction diesel electrics from Electro-Motive Division (EMD), the SD80MAC type. Externally these locomotives were very similar to the SD90MAC, but used a 20-cylinder 710G engine to

Two 20-cylinder SD80MACs head an intermodal freight past Milepost 129, west of Chester, Massachusetts, on 1 July 1997.

develop 3730kW (5000hp) for traction. This made them the most

---

TYPE: Co-Co, AC traction diesel-electric
POWER: EMD 20-710G3B producing 3730kW (5000hp)
TRACTIVE EFFORT: 653kN (147,000lbf) continuous TE ; 822kN (185,000lbf) starting TE with 83:16 gear ratio and 35 per cent adhesion

---

powerful single-engine diesel-electrics until the first 4476kW

MAX. OPERATING SPEED: 120km/h (75mph)
WEIGHT: 192.7t (425,000lb)
OVERALL LENGTH: 24.435m (80ft 2in)
GAUGE: 1435mm (4ft 8.5in)

(6000hp) locomotives came into service in the late 1990s. Initially Conrail bought 28, numbering them in the 4100 series, and later added two SD80MAC demonstrators. All were painted in a handsome blue-and-white livery to distinguish them from Conrail's DC fleet. When Norfolk Southern and CSX divided Conrail operations between them in 1999, each took 15 of the SD80MACs.

AC4400CW CO-CO VARIOUS RAILROADS

Though Electro-Motive Division (EMD) were first in North America with alternating-current traction on its diesel-electrics, General Electric (GE) caught up with a vengeance with the AC4400CW. General Electric's first commercial AC traction diesel has proven to be one of the best-selling and best-performing modern locomotives since it was introduced in 1994. Micro-processor controlled, they use GE's single inverter per-axle system of AC motor control.

While similar in appearance to other modern GE 'wide nose' or safety cab diesels, the AC4400CW can be distinguished from its DC traction counterparts by the large inverter cabinets behind the cab on the left-hand or 'fireman's'

side of the locomotive. The AC4400CW is typically used in very heavy freight services. Some are fitted to run as remote-controlled helpers at the rear of heavy trains, or are cut into the consist.

By the late 1990s, Union Pacific, Canadian Pacific and CSX were all operating large numbers of AC4400CWs.

TYPE: Co-Co, AC traction diesel-electric
POWER: GE 7FDL-16 rated at 3267kW (4380hp)
TRACTIVE EFFORT: various
MAX. OPERATING SPEED: 120km/h (75mph)
WEIGHT: 188t (415,000lb) – varied with options
OVERALL LENGTH: 22.301m (73ft 2in)
GAUGE: 1435mm (4ft 8.5in)

GE AC6000CW CO-CO UNION PACIFIC RAILROAD (UP)

General Electric's market position was further consolidated when it introduced the first 4476kW (6000hp) single-engined diesel-electric in 1995. A single locomotive of this power appealed to many railroad managers because it would allow a one-for-two replacement of older 2238kW (3000hp) locomotives. This degree of power, combined with an awesome tractive effort, was made practicable by the successful development of three-phase AC traction, via GE 5GEB13 AC traction motors, and the introduction of a new diesel engine. Instead of the standard Cooper-Bessemer inspired 7FDL diesel, the AC6000CW uses the

new 7HDL engine, with 15.7l (958ci) cylinders, developed jointly with Deutz MWM in Germany.

A collection of teething problems first had to be dealt with – engine block walls were not thick enough, leading to significant vibration problems and turbocharger faults. The engine built in Germany had been too large and would not fit the locomotive. Having already redesigned the engine once, GE were forced into further work to increase block wall thickness. With additional turbocharger supports, this removed the vibrations.

Union Pacific, eagerly awaiting the new 'super power' machine, took some 'advance' locomotives

with 7FDL engines, temporarily rated at 3282kW (4400hp). The AC6000CW is almost 90cm (3ft) longer than the AC4400CW, and is also distinguished by a large radiator section at the rear of the locomotive.

The world record for both the heaviest and longest train is held by Australian ore-carrying railway BHP, using all eight of its AC6000CW units, under the control of a single driver. Distributed to work as three pairs and two solo, all the locomotives were linked by the GE Locotrol radio remote-control system. On 21 June 2001, the 7.3km (4.5 mile) long 682-wagon train, weighing 99,734 tonnes (98,158 tons), worked over

the 275km (172 miles) between Yandi and Port Hedland on the BHP's Mount Newman line. BHP acquired its AC6000CWs to permit a reduction in both total quantity of locomotives and number of units per train.

TYPE: Co-Co, diesel-electric, AC traction
POWER: GE 7HDL-16 producing 4476kW (6000hp)
TRACTIVE EFFORT: 738kN (166,000lbf) at 18.8km/h (11.6mph)
MAX. OPERATING SPEED: 120km/h (75mph)
WEIGHT: 192.7t (425,000lb)
OVERALL LENGTH: 23.165m (76ft)
GAUGE: 1435mm (4ft 8.5in)

CLASS 471 ELECTRIC MULTIPLE UNIT CZECH RAILWAYS (CD)

The standard 'Berne' European loading gauge makes double-deck electric vehicles quite feasible and they are in use in many urban regions, where traffic is greatest. This class, operating between Praha and Pardubice, has low-set lower-deck floors between the wheels. It is formed from a Class 971 power car and Class 071 trailer vehicles. Six in three-car formation and four two-car sets were built by Moravskoslezská Vagonka a.s. under licence from Switzerland but using Czech-made electric components from Skoda.

TYPE: double-decker suburban EMU
POWER: 2000kW (2717hp) per motor coach
SUPPLY: 3000V DC
TRACTIVE EFFORT: N/A
MAX. OPERATING SPEED: 140km/h (87.5mph)
WEIGHT: 66t (145,530lb) motor coach
MAX. AXLE LOAD: 17t (37,485lb)
OVERALL LENGTH: 26.4m (86ft 2in) per coach
GAUGE: 1435mm (4ft 8.5in)

The carbody of 'City Elefant' is made of aluminium sheets for lightness.

CLASS SA ELECTRIC MULTIPLE UNIT DANISH RAILWAYS (DSB)

DENMARK 1996

Designed to replace older suburban stock, these were built to a novel formation as single-axle articulated vehicles, with three axles shared by two cars, so that an eight-car set runs on only nine axles, though each car is only half the length of a normal bogie vehicle. They operate in the Copenhagen area.

TYPE: suburban eight-car articulated electric multiple unit
POWER: 1500V DC overhead line collection; 1720kW (2305bhp) per unit
TRACTIVE EFFORT: not known
MAX. OPERATING SPEED: 120km/h (75mph)
WEIGHT: not known
MAX. AXLE LOAD: not known
OVERALL LENGTH: not known

Marking the fourth generation of DSB's S-trains, the SA class will total 105 units when delivery is complete.

CLASS DE2550 CO-CO EGYPTIAN NATIONAL RAILWAYS (ENR)

EGYPT 1996

Engined by Electro-Motive Diesel (EMD), this is a class of diesel-electric freight units built by the former Henschel factory in Kassel, Germany, by then ABB Thyssen. A first group of 45, with single cabs, were shipped in 1996 to handle phosphates traffic on a

TYPE: Co-Co diesel-electric
POWER: 1877kW (2550hp) from EMD 12-645 series engine

TRACTIVE EFFORT: 282kN (63,500lbf)
MAX. OPERATING SPEED: 80 or 160km/h (50 or 100mph)

WEIGHT: 126t (277,830lb)
OVERALL LENGTH: not known
GAUGE: 1435mm (4ft 8.5in)

new line between Abu Tartour and the Red Sea port of Safarga, inaugurated that year. A second batch of 23, all fitted with cabs at each end, followed for general traffic in the Nile Delta region.

Both batches are designated DE2550 by the makers, and JT22CW by EMD.

'THALYS' HIGH-SPEED ELECTRIC TRAIN

FRANCE/BELGIUM/GERMANY/NETHERLANDS 1996

Inaugurated in June 1996 and first known as PBA after the initials of the cities it served, 'Thalys' was initially a high-speed service operated from Paris to Brussels and Amsterdam. With the completion of Belgium's first high-speed lines in December 1997 by arrangement with the various national railway authorities (who participate in its ownership and management), its service now extends to Köln in Germany. Originally a single type of trainset, known as PBKA, was ordered from a consortium formed by GEC-Alsthom, De Dietrich, ACEC Transport and Bombardier Eurorail (Belgium). The traction motors came from Holec in the Netherlands. These trains were similar but not identical to TGVs, and amounted to 27 10-car sets. Delays and problems with the design led to a change of order, for 10 'PBA' sets, a multi-voltage

version of the SNCF's second-generation *Réseau* TGV, to be followed by 17 of the PBKA design. This enabled the 'Thalys' service to start on its planned date. Both sets are formed of eight intermediate cars between two power cars, and look the same except that PBA power cars have a double windscreen and PBKA a single one.

Travel time from Brussels Midi to Paris Nord is normally 1hr, 25mins, for a distance of approximately 300km (186.4 miles). Peak speed is 300km/h (186mph) on a dedicated high-speed track. Beyond Brussels, the main cities Thalys trains reach are Antwerp, The Hague, Rotterdam, Amsterdam, Liège, Aachen and Köln.

Trains to these destinations run partly on dedicated high-speed tracks and partly on older tracks shared with normal-speed trains.

In its inaugural month and year, a new 'Thalys' train waits at the Gare du Nord, Paris, with an evening service to Lille and Brussels, on 17 June 1996.

Plans to continue the service between Köln and Frankfurt had to be abandoned because the power generated by the Thalys trains when operating under the 15kV voltage system used in Germany is insufficient for operation on this steeply graded high-speed line.

The LGV link-line to Paris Charles de Gaulle airport allowed Air France to withdraw its air service between Paris and Brussels; instead, Air France books seats on Thalys. Uniquely for a railway train, Thalys has been given the IATA designator 2H.

TYPE: high-speed intercity train set
POWER: 8800kW (11956hp)
SUPPLY: 25kV 50Hz AC or 1500V DC or 3000V DC or 15kV 16.7Hz AC
TRACTIVE EFFORT: N/A
MAX. OPERATING SPEED: 300km/h (187.5mph)

WEIGHT: 388t (855,540lb) 10-car set
MAX. AXLE LOAD: 17t (37,485lb)
OVERALL LENGTH: 200.19m (653ft 2in) 10-car set; 22.15m (72ft 3in) motor coaches; 18.7m (61ft) trailers
GAUGE: 1435mm (4ft 8.5in)

CLASS 670 RAILCAR GERMAN RAILWAYS (DB)

GERMANY 1996

The small railcar has a long and respectable history in Germany, and even in 1996 the *Deutsche Bundebahn* (DB) was looking at protoypes of new models. One of

them was this compact double-deck four-wheeler. It was assigned a classification, but only five were produced, and in 2002 only one was still operative.

TYPE: two-axle double-deck diesel railcar
POWER: 250kW (335bhp) underfloor diesel engine
TRACTIVE EFFORT: not known

MAX. OPERATING SPEED: 100km/h (63mph)
WEIGHT PER VEHICLE: not known
OVERALL LENGTH: not known
GAUGE: not known

CLASS WCAM-3 CO-CO INDIAN RAILWAYS (IR)

INDIA 1996

Made for the IR 1676mm (5ft 6in) gauge and Indian-designed and built, though with Japanese Hitachi force-ventilated, nose-suspended, axle-hung traction motors, this dual-voltage DC- or AC-using class was developed by Bharat Heavy

Electrical Ltd (BHEL) as a mixed-traffic locomotive for main-line duties. Many of the WCAM-3's components are shared with other recent IR types. It represents a considerable advance in efficiency when compared with the earlier WCAM-1 of 1974.

TYPE: Co-Co mixed-traffic
POWER: 3432kW (4600hp) DC; 3730kW (5000hp) AC
SYSTEM: 1500V DC and 25 kV 50Hz AC
TRACTIVE EFFORT: 254kN (57200lbf) DC; 327kN (73480lbf) AC

MAX. OPERATING SPEED: 105km/h (65.6mph)
WEIGHT: 113t (249,165lb)
MAX. AXLE LOAD: 19t (41,895lb)
OVERALL LENGTH: not known
GAUGE: 1676mm (5ft 6in)

CLASS EL 18 BO-BO NORWEGIAN STATE RAILWAYS (NSB)

NORWAY 1996

Here is another manifestation of the Swiss Re 460, complete with its low skirting but with the addition of Norwegian-type snowploughs beneath the buffers fore and aft. Twenty-two were bought by NSB and, as elsewhere, they perform with almost silent efficiency on passenger and freight assignments. With a power rating slightly higher than the Swiss engines, they work chiefly on the Oslo–Bergen, Oslo–Stavanger and Oslo–Trondheim lines.

TYPE: Bo-Bo mainline mixed-traffic electric prototype
POWER: 15,000V 16.67Hz AC overhead line collection; 5400kW (7240hp); three-phase control; four body-mounted traction motors
TRACTIVE EFFORT: 275kN (61,820lbf)
MAX. OPERATING SPEED: 200km/h (125mph)
WEIGHT: 80t (175,685lb)
MAX. AXLE LOAD: not known
OVERALL LENGTH: 18.5m (60ft 8in)
GAUGE: 1435mm (4ft 8.5in)

With the separation of NSB into passenger service and Cargo Net divisions, the EL 18 class has been dedicated exclusively to passenger train working.

CLASS DI8 BO-BO NORWEGIAN STATE RAILWAYS (NSB)

NORWAY 1996

Looking also to expand their main-line diesel-electric fleet, with something more up-to-date than the Class Di4 of 1980, NSB first acquired Co-Co locomotives of similar appearance to the Di4s, as Class Di6. These proved unsatisfactory and were returned to the manufacturers. After trying out some Dutch Class 6400 Bo-Bos in order to see if a three-phase AC drive design could meet their requirements, NSB opted for this smaller, lighter locomotive type, ordering 20 Bo-Bo

Cargo Net Di8 loco 8.709 has been requisitioned to help out a failed Nohab Di3 Co-Co on a passenger train.

hood-unit locomotives from Krupp/Siemens in Germany, classed Di8. These have proved perfectly satisfactory on the freight duties for which they were bought.

TYPE: freight main-line diesel-electric
WHEEL ARRANGEMENT: Bo-Bo
POWER: 1570kW (2105hp) diesel; Siemens alternator; four axle-hung three-

phase AC traction motors
TRACTIVE EFFORT: 270kN (60,700lbf)
MAX. OPERATING SPEED: 120km/h (75mph)

WEIGHT: 82t (180,080lb)
OVERALL LENGTH: 17.38m (57ft 3in)
GAUGE: not known

CLASS 13 BO-BO BELGIAN NATIONAL RAILWAYS (SNCB)

BELGIUM 1997

Sixty of these mixed-traffic electric locomotives were ordered by SNCB in 1997, to replace some ageing types going back to the 1950s (though some of these, like the Class 122 of 1953, have proved remarkably durable). With dual-voltage capability, they run under either 3000V DC or 25,000V AC supply systems for their three-phase AC traction motors. They work push-pull services from Oostende through Ghent to Brussels, and can work beyond Belgium as far as Aachen, just over the border in Germany. Freight haulage is their main activity, however.

TYPE: Bo-Bo mainline mixed-traffic electric
POWER: 3000V DC and 25,000V 50cHz AC overhead line collection; 5000kW (6700bhp); three-phase AC control; four frame-hung traction motors
TRACTIVE EFFORT: 288kN (64,745lbf)
MAX. OPERATING SPEED: 200km/h (125mph)
WEIGHT: 90t (197,650lb)
MAX AXLE LOAD: not known

Class 13 locomotives sometimes work passenger services on certain lines like Charleroi–Couvin, but mostly haul freight on the Antwerp–Leuven–Luxembourg main line.

CLASS SS8 BO-BO CHINESE RAILWAYS

CHINA 1997

SS stands for Shaoshan, the town where Mao Tse Tung was born. Originating from two prototypes built and tested in 1994, and in production at the Zhuzhou Works from 1997, this fast passenger unit was conceived initially for the Guangshen high-speed line, and is still mostly employed there, hauling trains of double-deck air-conditioned coaches. SS8 001 is

TYPE: Bo-Bo
POWER: 3600kW (4891hp)
SUPPLY: 25kV 50Hz AC
TRACTIVE EFFORT: 126kN (28350lbf)
MAX. OPERATING SPEED (IN SERVICE): 170km/h (106.3mph)

WEIGHT: 88t (194,040lb)
MAX. AXLE LOAD: 22t (48,510lb)
OVERALL LENGTH: 17.516m (57ft 2in)
GAUGE: 1435mm (4ft 8.5in)

China's fastest locomotive, with a record of 240km/h (149.1mph) established on 24 June 1998. By

2006, approximately 250 had been built. A six-axle Co-Co development, the SS9, appeared

in 1998, and worked on the Shenyang–Harbin line. With the same type of traction motors but two more, it is 50 per cent more powerful, and has a slightly lower maximum axle loading, of 21 tonnes (20.6 tons). A modified form of this, SS9G, also exists, with a more 'modern' front end design reminiscent of the Swiss Re locomotives.

CLASS 101 BO-BO GERMAN RAILWAYS (DB)

GERMANY 1997

The Class 103 of 1969 and the Class 120 of 1987 have been responsible for locomotive haulage on virtually all of Western Germany's InterCity and EuroCity express services. By this time, however, the entire German network was reintegrated, with such major cities as Leipzig and

Dresden needing to be served – not to mention Berlin, which acquired a vast new through-line Central Station in 2006 in order to improve the convenience and management of the intercity services. Furthermore, the Class 103, magnificent machines though they were, were beginning to wear

out after three decades of intensive running. New generation haulage was required, and, conveniently, ADtranz was demonstrating its prototype three-phase express Bo-Bo type, No. 128.001. This machine was thoroughly tested before the unified DB (*Deutsche Bahn*) decided

to make it the basis of the new Class 101, and ordered 145 locomotives of the new class to replace the same number of Class 103. The four-axle layout of the new locomotives and their weight, only two-thirds of that of the six-axle Class 103, showed how far electric drive technology had

advanced over the 30-year gap. ADtranz were the builders and delivery commenced in 1997.

The Class 101 have three-phase control and the four traction motors are body-mounted, each fed power from its own three-phase converter, which enables the input to be adjusted to adhesion and load conditions. The axles are driven through cardan shafts. All the class are fitted for push-pull operation, an essential in the InterCity system because a number of big city central stations, including Frankfurt, Stuttgart, Munich and Leipzig, are built as termini and quick entry and exit would otherwise be impossible. Normally painted in the DB's 'traffic red', the Class 101 shares regular

Aerodynamic considerations determined the shape of the Class 101 even to such details as the inwards-hinged pantographs. This loco is the basis for New Jersey Transit's ALP-46 type.

InterCity and Eurocity services with the Class 120. These services form an impressive pattern of coverage, speed and punctuality.

TYPE: Bo-Bo mainline express passenger electric
POWER: 15,000V 16.67Hz AC overhead line collection; 6400kW (8780hp); three-phase control; four body-mounted traction motors
TRACTIVE EFFORT: 300kN (67,440lbf)

MAX. OPERATING SPEED: 220km/h (137mph)
WEIGHT: 87t (191,060lb)
MAX. AXLE LOAD: not known
OVERALL LENGTH: 19.1m (62ft 8in)
GAUGE: 1435mm (4ft 8.5in)

CARGO SPRINTER/MULTI-PURPOSE VEHICLES DB/RAILTRACK GERMANY AND GREAT BRITAIN 1997

The *Deutsche Bahn* (DB) was interested in testing an idea for a freight 'multiple unit' train. This was developed experimentally with a pair of 'multi-purpose vehicles' (known in the UK as MPVs), each with a cab at one end, a flat topped underframe suitable for carrying containers, and an under-frame diesel engine and transmission driving the wheels of an adjacent axle. Between each pair of MPVs would be coupled semi-permanently a number of

Semi-permanently coupled to its partner unit, this Windhoff-built Railtrack MPV is fitted with locks for standard ISO container-size modules.

container-carrying wagons. End-to-end wiring enabled the MPVs to operate as linked power cars.

The project envisaged that short freight multiple-unit trains would load at small yards and set off to couple with similar trains from other yards to form a long train for the trunk haul, and then split up again to reach their various

destinations. In practice, the concept failed to attract business or to work effectively, and DB withdrew its prototype freight

DMU in 2000. In the UK, the MPV concept is not used commercially but is applied for infrastructure and renewal services, such as

track maintenance, weed-spraying and overhead wiring work. The details above are for a Windhoff multi-purpose single-cab vehicle.

TYPE: general-purpose diesel freight vehicle	
WHEEL ARRANGEMENT: 1A-A1	
POWER: Two Volvo horizontal diesels	

265kW (355bhp)
TRACTIVE EFFORT: not known
MAX. OPERATING SPEED: 95 and 120km/h (60 and 75mph)

MAXIMUM GROSS LADEN WEIGHT: 78t (171,295lb)
OVERALL LENGTH: 20.5m (67ft 3in)
GAUGE: not known

CLASS 332 HEATHROW EXPRESS ELECTRIC MULTIPLE UNIT

GREAT BRITAIN 1997

Partly on a new line tunneled under the airport, partly sharing the old Great Western main line out of London Paddington, these trains provide a fast service from central London to two stations serving Heathrow Airport's four terminals. Journey time and train frequency are both 15 minutes, with maximum speed reaching 160km/h (100mph).

Fourteen four-car sets are used, built by CAF at Zaragoza in Spain, and with electric equipment from Siemens. Air-conditioned and designed to accommodate passengers' luggage, they have two-class seating. Monitors in the carriages provide flight information, and passengers can 'check in' at Paddington before boarding the train.

TYPE: airport express four-car electric multiple unit
POWER PER UNIT: 25,000V 50Hz AC overhead line collection; 1400kW (1875bhp); four traction motors
TRACTIVE EFFORT: not known

MAX. OPERATING SPEED: 160km/h (100mph)
WEIGHT: 36 to 49t (78,620 to 107,200lb)
OVERALL LENGTH: 23.74m (77ft 11in) end cars; 23.15m (75ft 11in)
GAUGE: 1435mm (4ft 8.5in)

Coming in under Isambard Brunel's 150-year old iron roof, a Heathrow express electric multiple unit set enters Paddington Station, London, in 1997.

CLASS WDP-4 BO1-1BO INDIAN RAILWAYS (IR)

INDIA 1997

This class, with its unusual wheel configuration, was one of the results of a joint technical agreement made between Electro-Motive Division (EMD) and Diesel Locomotive Works (DLW) of Varanasi in 1995. It allowed for the initial import, then local production, of asynchronous-motor diesel-electric locomotives based on EMD models, and 710-series engines. India Railways' freight Class WDG-4 is EMD model

GT46MAC and its passenger version, Class WDP-4, corresponds to model GT46PAC.

The first 13 WDG-4 units were completed in the United States from 1997, and the next eight were delivered in 1998 as kits for assembly. Components for the next 80 for local build by DLW were ready, with the first 10 built in 2002. While the freight units had conventional Co-Co wheel arrangements, Class WDP-4 has a

TYPE: WDG4 Co-Co heavy freight; WDP-4 Bo11Bo passenger
POWER: 2944kW (4000hp) from EMD 16-710 series engine
TRACTIVE EFFORT: WDG-4 539kN (121,220lbf); WDP4 269kN (60,500lbf)
MAX. OPERATING SSPEED: WDG-4

120km/h (75mph); WDP-4 160km/h (100mph)
WEIGHT: WDG4 – 126t (277,830lb); WDP4 – 119t (262,395lb)
OVERALL LENGTH: not known
GAUGE: 1676mm (5ft 6in)

Bo1-1Bo configuration, by the omission of one traction motor from the inner end of each bogie. Otherwise the same design of

high-adhesion truck is used on both. The first 10 WDP-4s were built by EMD in 2001 with DLW now involved in series production.

CLASS ALN DAP RAILCAR STATE RAILWAYS (FS)

ITALY 1997

This is a highly specialized unit for the transportation of prisoners and therefore lacks the usual amenities of a passenger vehicle. The interior is divided into benched cells, and 'passengers' are locked in for the duration of the journey. Five DAP units were built to move convicts to provincial jails. They are based on the Class Aln 663, which was introduced in 1983 and was itself a development of Class Aln 668, dating back to 1959. Over 400 of the Aln diesel cars are in operation on the FS.

TYPE: diesel-mechanical special unit
POWER: 340kW (455.6hp)
TRACTIVE EFFORT: not known

MAX. OPERATING SPEED: 120km/h (75mph)
TOTAL WEIGHT: not known

OVERALL LENGTH: not known
GAUGE: not known

CLASS DD-AR (7800) ELECTRIC MULTIPLE-UNIT NETHERLANDS RAILWAYS (NS)

NETHERLANDS 1997

While growing city populations have meant the construction of new urban lines in many places, the problem for NS, operating in one of the most densely populated areas of the world, is how to provide sufficient services on its existing lines while maintaining quality. Though track capacity has been added wherever possible, train capacity is the key.

Since 1985, NS has used double-deck carriages to cope with its steadily increasing passenger load, much of which is concentrated into peak commuting periods. Actually, the NS lines are well suited to the use of these vehicles, as the overall loading gauge is quite generous in European terms, and its double-deck units are among the tallest and widest passenger vehicles on the European standard gauge. Early sets were formed as push-pull trains with Class 1700 locomotives, and used chiefly for outer suburban traffic served from Amsterdam. Expansion of the concept came in 1992, when 79 three and four-car sets of double-deck cars were acquired for use in the 'Randstad' city region embracing Amsterdam, Rotterdam and Utrecht. Able to carry 576 seated passengers in just four cars, these also were powered by Class 1700 locomotives. Layout of the two-deck coaches is as developed in France and now in general use, with stairways at each end, a low-level central section, and doors above the bogies, opening on to circulating spaces.

From 1997, the locomotives began to be replaced by powered driving cars. These have passenger accommodation on the upper floor, adding to the train's overall passenger capacity, with the lower level being packed with operating equipment, all accessible through side-opening hatches. The power cars have triple bogies, giving them a Bo-Bo-Bo arrangement and powerful traction supplied by six motors.

Though less powerful than the Class 1700s, they appear to have adequate power to move their p-p sets along at speeds up to 140km/h (87mph) on tracks that are usually dead level.

TYPE: Bo-Bo-Bo suburban electric multiple-unit power car
POWER: 1500V DC overhead line collection; 2400kW (3215hp); six traction motors
TRACTIVE EFFORT: not known
MAX. OPERATING SPEED: 140km/h (87mph)
WEIGHT: not known
MAX. AXLE LOAD: not known
OVERALL LENGTH: 26.4m (86ft 7in)

Classified as type mDDm, the motor unit of a DD-AR train, with its three bogies, at Amsterdam Central.

WL86 2XBO-BO RUSSIAN RAILWAYS (RZD)

RUSSIA 1997

In the post-communist system of competition and restored private enterprise, the numerous Russian locomotive works have had to adapt to customers who can pick and choose their purchases, and to railway systems that are looking for economy, efficiency, increased speed and freedom from harmful emissions. The monolithic Soviet days of huge production runs and assured state purchase are over. The Kolomna Works, *Kolomensky*

TYPE: Bo-Bo-Bo-Bo
POWER: EP100/101 – 9600kW (13133hp)
EP200/201 – 8000kW (10870hp)
SUPPLY: 3000V DC or 25kV 50Hz AC

TRACTIVE EFFORT: 235kN or 284.5kN (52875lbf or 63900lbf)
MAX. OPERATING SPEED: 160 or 200km/h (100 or 125mph)

WEIGHT: 180t (396,900lb)
MAX. AXLE LOAD: 22.5t (49,616lb)
OVERALL LENGTH: 25m (81ft 6in)
GAUGE: 1524mm (5ft)

Zavod, developed a range of models for large electric express passenger engines based on prototypes that, uniquely, run on two four-axle double-Bo bogies. Broadly classified as WL86, there are two DC versions, for operation at 200 and 160km/h (125 and 100mph) respectively; and two corresponding AC versions. Substantial power is also available for rheostatic braking, of 8000kW (10,807hp), and for 'hotel' supply to heat and air-condition the carriages (a new concept for the Russian locomotive builders). Eight of the lower-speed DC models have been supplied to Russian Railways, and the others have been around for some years as prototypes.

CLASS 1016/1116 'TAURUS' BO-BO AUSTRIAN FEDERAL RAILWAYS (ÖBB)

AUSTRIA 1998

The successful 'Eurosprinter' electric locomotive concept, which Siemens began in association with Krauss-Maffei and which resulted in such locomotives as the RENFE Class 252 of 1991, was developed into this: another 'universal' design whose high power and sophisticated electronic controls enable it to be an express passenger or a heavy freight locomotive depending on the requirements of the daily roster. Class 1016 of the ÖBB was for 15kV working; Class 1116 was a dual-voltage 15kV/25kV locomotive. It has high power output and maximum speed. 'Taurus' was a name bestowed by the ÖBB, which owns large numbers. On other national systems, Hungary (both MÁV and GYSEV) uses dual-voltage versions, and 25 of the German 'Eurosprinter' type Class 152 were converted into Taurus types as Class 182, with bogies applying less track force than the 152. Other Taurus locomotives are in leasor and private-owner fleets, and the type is still in production.

In ÖBB red livery, a 'Taurus' locomotive climbs towards the Semmering Pass, on the Vienna–Trieste line, with bi-level stock on 21 August 2003.

TYPE: Bo-Bo universal
POWER: 6400kW (8696hp)
SUPPLY: 15kV 16.7Hz or 25 kV 50Hz AC (1500V and 3000V DC planned)
TRACTIVE EFFORT: 300kN (67500lbf)
MAX. OPERATING SPEED: 230km/h (143.8mph)
WEIGHT: 85t (187,425lb)
MAX. AXLE LOAD: 21.5t (47,408lb)
OVERALL LENGTH: not known
GAUGE: 1435mm (4ft 8.5in)

TEM18 CO-CO RUSSIAN RAILWAYS

The most recent derivative of the TEM1 model is this TEM18 heavy-duty shunting locomotive. Produced by Bryansk Works (BMZ) in the city of that name in central Russia, it is available in various weight, power, gauge and environmental options.

Approximately 150 have been built, all for Russian railways and industry. A gas-powered TEM18G is available, being recognizable by roof-mounted gas cylinders.

TYPE: Co-Co diesel-electric heavy shunter
POWER: 757 to 993kW (1030 to 350hp) from PD4A series engine
TRACTIVE EFFORT: up to 283kN (63675lbf) maximum
MAX. OPERATING SPEED: 100k/mh (62.1mph)

WEIGHT: 108 to 124t (238,140 to 273,420lb)
OVERALL LENGTH: 16.9m (55ft 2in
GAUGE: Adaptable 1435 to 1676mm (4ft 8.5in to 5ft 6in)

DE30AC BO-BO LONG ISLAND RAIL ROAD (LIRR)

Like an up-to-date version of the British Class 73 of 1965, this is a dual-mode locomotive whose electric motors can be run from a electrified third rail or by its own diesel-powered prime mover. With lines crossing Long Island, bringing passengers to and from New York City, New York's Long Island Rail Road is one of the most

intensively used suburban railways in North America. Until the 1950s, LIRR was a subsidiary of the Pennsylvania Railroad, which began electrifying its lines, and today most LIRR routes are electrified with a third rail. To provide through services on non-electrified lines, it operates the dual-mode DE30AC.

Assembled by Super Steel Products, these locomotives use an Electro-Motive Diesel 12-710G3B engine in a monocoque body with stainless steel sides. Like EMD's FL9, the DE30AC can operate from the third rail in electrified territory. LIRR also operates a straight diesel-electric version, designated DM30AC.

TYPE: diesel-electric/electric
POWER: dual mode-EMD 12-710G3B producing 2235kW (3000hp); and third-rail electric pick-up
TRACTIVE EFFORT: N/A
MAX. OPERATING SPEED: N/A
WEIGHT: N/A
OVERALL LENGTH: 22.86m (75 ft)
GAUGE: 1435mm (4ft 8.5in)

CLASS DDJ1 ELECTRIC HIGH-SPEED TRAIN GUANGZHOU RAILWAY

China's first home-developed high-speed trains, brought out in prototype form in 1998, went into service in 2000. With a maximum running speed of 200km/h (125mph), they are intended to run on traditional tracks rather than on the super-high speed tracks being built for TGV-

TYPE: high-speed EMU
POWER: 3600kW (4892hp)
SUPPLY: 25kV 50Hz AC
TRACTIVE EFFORT: N/A

MAX. OPERATING SPEED: 220km/h (137.5mph)
WEIGHT: 440t (970,200lb)
MAX. AXLE LOAD: 20t (44,100lb)

OVERALL LENGTH: 176m (574ft 3in) per unit
GAUGE: 1435mm (4ft 8.5in)

type trains. The standard formation is a six-car one, with Bo-Bo power car, five intermediate cars, of which

one is double-deck, and a driving trailer. Accommodation for 438 passengers is provided.

DDJ1 sets operate the 'Blue Arrow' service between Guangzhou and Shenzhen.

CLASS BB-27000 BO-BO FRENCH NATIONAL RAILWAYS (SNCF)

Alstom (as it called itself from 1997) latched onto the modular concept with its trademarked PRIMA range, covering electric and diesel models. As with the other manufacturers, who already had, or would soon have, a similar approach, the aim was to cater to a changing and changeable world market. So it offered a set of designs that could be configured in various ways and adapted to use either as 'universal' or more specialist locomotives, and local or long-distance multiple-unit trains, while retaining as many basic parts as possible and – ever more important – able to run with little or no special adaptation on systems with different kinds of signalling and warning systems and varying overhead supply currents.

The PRIMA electric range was unveiled with the Bo-Bo EL4200B, configured either for general freight haulage at a speed of

Illustrated is a BB37000, the triple-voltage version of the BB27000, identical in appearance. SNCF has 29 of these locomotives.

140km/h (87.5mph) or for passenger service at 220km/h (137.5mph); the more powerful EL6000B for heavy passenger express work, and the Co-Co EL6300C for heavy freight. In addition to the above, a double unit Bo-Bo type, rated at 9600kW (13,043hp), to run at a geared-down speed of 100km/h (62mph), was also on offer for the heaviest trains on the steeply graded routes. Since micro-electronic technology was changing very

rapidly, the initial range and specification of PRIMA did not remain static, and modifications followed.

France was the initial customer, with SNCF looking to the PRIMA concept for replacements of large numbers of ageing electric locomotives, and with a particular need for freight types. In 2001, Alstom began the delivery of BB-27000 units – 90 locomotives fitted for dual-voltage use under 1500V DC and 25kV 50HzAC

wires. Following these came 29 of Class BB-37000, which could also run under 15kV 16.67Hz AC. These were the SNCF's first freight locomotives for some time, as previous policy had been to use displaced passenger engines on

freight haulage, and their performance was correspondingly better. Locomotives of these classes are still being produced, including five identical to Class BB-37000 for Veolia Transport (formerly Connex) in 2006.

TYPE: Bo-Bo electric locomotive
POWER: 4200kW (5706hp) continuous output from 57 to 140kph
SUPPLY: 1500V DC or 25kV 50Hz AC

TRACTIVE EFFORT: 250kN (56,250lbf) at 57kph (35.6mph)
WEIGHT: 90t (198,450lb)
MAX. AXLE LOAD: 22.5t (49,613lb)
GAUGE: 1435mm (4ft 8.5in)

CLASS 66 CO-CO ENGLISH, WELSH & SCOTTISH RAILWAY (EWS) GREAT BRITAIN 1998

No. 66222 of EWS Railways, a subsidiary of Wisconsin Central. Toton Depot is the main centre for the entire class.

English, Welsh & Scottish Railway (EWS), the largest freight operators in Britain after the privatization and fragmentation of British Rail, bought 250 large General Motors diesel-electrics from North America to replace older, less powerful and less reliable freight classes. In some ways, the Class 66 was a development of the heavy haul Class 59, but designed as a general freight machine. Powered by a 12-

cylinder version of EMD's 710G3 engine driving six axle-hung DC traction motors, the Class 66s are reliable and competent, and work all over the British railway system. Other British freight operators also use this class. Freightliner Limited, the container haulage company, has a fleet of 77 Class 66s, of which six are geared for heavy

freight haulage. GB Rail Freight has a new fleet of 12. Around 30 more are now in use in Europe, mainly in the Netherlands, Germany and Scandinavia, having proved popular among smaller 'open access' freight companies there. Low-emission versions were in production in 2005–06 for GB Railfreight and Freightliner.

TYPE: freight main-line diesel-electric
WHEEL ARRANGEMENT: Co-Co
POWER: GM 12N-710G3B-EC 12-cylinder V-form two-stroke diesel, 2385kW (3200hp); GM alternator; six axle-hung DC traction motors
TRACTIVE EFFORT: 409kN (91,945lbf)
MAX. OPERATING SPEED: 120km/h (75mph)
WEIGHT: 126t (276,705lb)
OVERALL LENGTH: 21.35m (70ft 1in)
GAUGE: 1435mm (4ft 8.5in)

CLASS 170 'TURBOSTAR' DMUS VARIOUS OPERATORS

Working on a limited-term franchise basis after privatization, British train operating companies wanted as much as possible to buy or lease modern trains 'off the shelf' to manufacturers' standard designs. ADtranz (later purchased by Bombardier) developed a modular vehicle body for its 'Turbostar' range of diesel-hydraulic multiple-unit sets, which could be adapted

Central Trains has 53 of these Derby-built units, used for its longer-distance trains like Norwich–Liverpool, and Birmingham–Stansted Airport.

for different routes or traffics. With a 160km/h (100mph) top speed, they were the fastest diesel multiple units (DMUs) in the UK when first put in service. Available as two- or three-car sets, they employ powerful underfloor engines driving through hydraulic transmissions, and are fully air-

conditioned, but retain the suburban layout of two pairs of double-leaf doors in the bodysides. They have proved popular on such services as Anglia's London–Norwich, and ScotRail's express services. Central Trains use them on cross-country work, for which they are also well suited.

TYPE: express and local passenger two-car and three-car diesel multiple unit
POWER: MTU 6R183TD13H six-cylinder horizontal diesel, 315kW (422bhp)
TRANSMISSION: Voith T211rzze hydraulic torque converter/gearbox
MAX. OPERATING SPEED: 160km/h (100mph)
WEIGHT: 45t (98,825lb)
OVERALL LENGTH: 23.62m (77ft 6in)
GAUGE: 1435mm (4ft 8.5in)

CLASS H561 BO-BO HELLENIC RAILWAYS ORGANIZATION (OSE)

Known on OSE as the 'Hellas Sprinter', this, Greece's first main-line electric locomotive class, is the Siemens-Krauss-Maffei 'Eurosprinter' type. Six were delivered in this year to work the first opened sector of electrified

track, under 25kV 50Hz AC wire, between Thessaloniki and the Macedonian border. Options on more, or perhaps more likely an updated version, will be taken up as electrification progresses towards Athens.

TYPE: Co-Co heavy freight and passenger
POWER: 5000kW (6793hp)
SUPPLY: 25kV 50Hz AC
TRACTIVE EFFORT: 300kN (67500lbf)
MAX. OPERATING SPEED: 200km/h (125mph)

WEIGHT: 90t (198,450lb)
MAX. AXLE LOAD: 22.5t (49,613lb)
OVERALL LENGTH: 20.38m (66ft 6in)
GAUGE: 1435mm (4ft 8.5in)

CLASS A 471 BO-BO HELLENIC RAILWAYS ORGANIZATION (OSE)

Swiss-built by ADtranz, these two-engined diesel-electrics are capable of being converted to full electric operation with greatly increased tractive power when electrification of main lines takes place. Their bogies are constructed for 200km/h (125mph) running. Their arrival enabled the Greek

railways to rationalize their locomotive stock, with actual or virtual elimination of classes A551,

A301, A321 and A351. Meanwhile, A471s work passenger services on main lines, including the Athens–

Thessaloniki route now in the course of major upgrading and new alignment.

TYPE: Diesel-electric express passenger
POWER: 2100kW (2853hp) from two MTU 12V386 **SERIES ENGINES**

TRACTIVE EFFORT: 202kN (45,360lbf)
MAX. OPERATING SPEED: 160kmh (100mph)

WEIGHT: 90 tonnes (198,450lb)
OVERALL LENGTH: 18.5m (60ft 4in)
GAUGE: 1435mm (4ft 8.5in)

CLASS 3000 BO-BO LUXEMBOURG RAILWAYS (CFL)

LUXEMBOURG 1998

In keeping its small stock of locomotives and rolling stock up-to-date, CFL has always sought to combine purchasing with its larger neighbours SNCF or SNCB, and this policy has resulted in a very modern fleet. This dual-system AC/DC locomotive is identical to SNCB's Class 13 and

serves the same mixed-traffic purpose. Built by ACEC with Alsthom electrical equipment, the

contours of the cab styling are intended to reduce aerodynamic effects on the front-mounted

pantograph when trains pass each other at high speed.

TYPE: Bo-Bo universal
POWER: 5200kW (7065hp)
SUPPLY: 25kV 50Hz AC or 3000V DC or 1500V DC

TRACTIVE EFFORT: 288kN (64800lbf)
MAX. OPERATING SPEED: 200km/h (125mph)
WEIGHT: 90t (198,450lb)

MAX. AXLE LOAD: 22.5t (49,613lb)
OVERALL LENGTH: 19.11m (62ft 4in)
GAUGE: 1435mm (4ft 8.5in)

CLASS BM71 'FLYTOGET' ELECTRIC MULTIPLE UNIT NORWEGIAN STATE RAILWAYS (NSB)

NORWAY 1998

The branch line to Gardemoen already existed before Oslo's new airport was built there, and 16 new three-car electric multiple units were built in order to provide a fast even-interval service from

city centre to airport. Like most other new airport-line trains, they are well-appointed for a wide variety of customer types, with air-conditioning and the provision of ample luggage space.

TYPE: airport express three-car electric multiple unit
POWER PER UNIT: 15,000V 16.67Hz AC overhead line collection; 1950kW (2615hp); traction motors
TRACTIVE EFFORT: not known

MAX. OPERATING SPEED: 210km/h (130mph)
WEIGHT: not known
MAX AXLE LOAD: not known
OVERALL LENGTH: not known

CLASS EU43 BO-BO POLISH STATE RAILWAYS (PKP)

POLAND 1998

As locomotive and railway engineering became ever more multi-national and more competitive, old-established names

were often swallowed up in, or joined to, rival or new businesses, and many workshops were closed down in the subsequent

'rationalizations'. Poland's Pafawag (National Wagon Factory) works in Wroclaw, builders of the country's first electric locomotives (Class

EP02, in 1953) were taken over by ADtranz, then Daimler-Chrysler, before Bombardier in 2001. In 1998, they supplied this dual-voltage Bo-Bo type for cross-border work into Germany.

TYPE: Bo-Bo dual voltage electric, 3000V DC and 15kV 16 2/3Hz AC
POWER: N/A
TRACTIVE EFFORT: N/A
MAX. OPERATING SPEED: 200km/h (125mph)
WEIGHT: N/A
OVERALL LENGTH: N/A
MAX. AXLE LOAD: N/A
GAUGE: 1435mm (4ft 8.5in)

This is a universal all-purpose locomotive. Because of PKP's financial difficulties the first nine were sold to Rail Traction Co. for working container trains.

HHL BO-BO AMTRAK

USA 1998

Sometimes listed as HHP-8 (HH standing for 'high horsepower'), this high-speed electric locomotive was ordered by Amtrak for first deliveries in 1998 to operate express trains on the completed

electrification between Boston and New York. The builders are a consortium of Alstom and Bombardier, also constructors of the Acela express trains. Double-ended, with steeply raked cab fronts, the

locomotives present a streamlined appearance that is rather at variance with the rolling stock. Not as fast as the Acela express units, the HHLs nevertheless run at speeds up to 200km/h (125mph).

TYPE: Bo-Bo high-speed electric locomotive
POWER: 12kV AC at 25Hz, 12kV AC at 60Hz, 25kV AC at 60Hz
OUTPUT: 5968kW (8000hp)
TRACTIVE EFFORT: N/A
MAX. OPERATING SPEED: 200km/h (125mph)
WEIGHT: 100t (220,500lb)
MAX AXLE LOAD: not known
OVERALL LENGTH: N/A
GAUGE: 1435mm (4ft 8.5in)

The double-wedge outline of an Amtrak HHL locomotive stands out as it rolls across the bridge at Branford, CT, in Ferbruary 2006.

CLASS EG CO-CO DANISH RAILWAYS (DSB)

In 1935, Denmark's *Lyntog* diesel train had been introduced for the opening of the Little Belt Bridge. Engineering works on a much greater scale were necessary to complete the bridge and tunnel links across the Great Belt and the Sound, to provide unbroken road and rail connections from the Jutland peninsula right across the main Danish islands and on to Sweden. Work on the Great Belt, or Størebaelt, was completed in late 1996, and it was opened for rail traffic in April 1997. In July 2000, the opening of the Øresund link completed the route. The new railway link, electrified on the

TYPE: Co-Co heavy freight, dual-voltage
POWER: 6500kW (8832hp)
SUPPLY: 25kV 50 AC or 15kV 16.67Hz AC
TRACTIVE EFFORT: 400kN (90000lbf)
MAX. OPERATING SPEED: 140km/h (87.5mph)

WEIGHT: 129 tonnes (284,445lb)
MAX. AXLE LOAD: 21.5 tonnes (47,408lb)
OVERALL LENGTH: 20.95m (68ft 4in)
GAUGE: 1435mm (4ft 8.5in)

Danish 25kV 50Hz AC system, required new motive power for a substantial increase in traffic, including heavy freight trains, and a new *Gods* (goods) electric class, the EG, was introduced, capable of

working a 2000-tonne (1969-ton) load at 120km/h (75mph) on level track, and also of mastering the 1.6 per cent (1 in 64) gradients of the Størebaelt line as it rose and fell from tunnel to bridge. The EG

is another member of the Siemens/Krauss-Maffei 'Eurosprinter' family, though running on three-axle power bogies as required by the loads and gradients, rather than Bo-Bo like the others, and geared for freight operation with a maximum speed of 140km/h (87.5mph). It was equipped for dual-current work, since Sweden, as with Germany, was electrified on the 15kV supply system, and the EG class has worked over the Øresund link with freight once it was opened, handling all the traffic as SJ has no dual-voltage freight locomotives.

'Gods' No. 3103 shows off its striking livery. DSB has twelve of the Class EG, and keeps them in intensive use.

CLASS ET ELECTRIC MULTIPLE UNIT DANISH (DSB) AND SWEDISH (SJ) RAILWAYS   DENMARK/SWEDEN 1999

The building of the Øresund road and rail link between Denmark and Sweden, which opened in July 2000, was as momentous for these countries as the Channel Tunnel was for France and Britain. For passenger traffic on this bridge-tunnel combination, DSB and SJ combined to order fast, high-performance three-car trains. The original order for 27 sets was divided into 17 for DSB (Class ET) and 10 for SJ (Class X10), with follow-ups taking the respective totals to 20 each. Builders ADtranz (later part of Bombardier)

TYPE: Three-car express EMU	**TRACTIVE EFFORT:** N/A
POWER: 2120kW (2880hp)	**MAX. OPERATING SPEED:** 180km/h
SUPPLY: 25kV 50Hz AC or 15kV	(112.5mph)
16.67Hz AC	**WEIGHT:** 153t (337,365lb)

MAX. AXLE LOAD: 19t (41,895lb)
OVERALL LENGTH: 78.9m (257ft 6in) three-car unit
GAUGE: 1435mm (4ft 8.5in)

used their own AIM modular electric multiple unit concept, but with the 'rubber ring' car ends and connections as used by DSB on electric and diesel MUs since the Class IC3 in 1989. The Class ETs are powerful units rated at 2120kW (2880hp), with dual

supply capacity, since Denmark uses 25kV 50Hz AC and Sweden uses 16kV 67Hz AC. Voltage detection and switching are automatic on entering the altered catenary.

The ET units operate a shuttle service between Copenhagen and

Helsingor, and Helsingborg and Malmö at the other side of the Sound, sharing the tracks with EuroCity services from Hamburg and international freight traffic, which is run by DSB Class EG freight locomotives or DB's Cargo Class 185.

No. 2027's rubber nose is prominent in this picture. Built for international service over the Øresund link, this dual-voltage class is denoted as X31K in Sweden.

CLASS 460 'JUNIPER' ELECTRIC MULTIPLE UNITS GATWICK EXPRESS   GREAT BRITAIN 1999

One of the reasons for the popularity of modular design and build is that ownership of locomotives and trains has become more flexible than before, and often quite temporary. As the great national systems and corporations were privatized or broken down, a new generation of franchise operators came on the scene, anxious to drive down operating costs in relation to revenue. Locomotives and train-

sets were inter-changed and re-branded, and many are now owned by leasing companies that want machines to operate with no or minimal adaptation on different rail systems. The process leads towards a certain 'sameness' or family resemblance across a range of locomotives and multiple units, distinguished mostly by the difference in colour schemes and operator logos, though the demands of national track

authorities can still impose specific characteristics.

The range of electric multiple units grouped under the 'Juniper' brand name, and built by Alstom, are typical of this process. The first to appear were Class 460, eight sets of eight-car trains bought to operate the 'Gatwick Express' service from Gatwick Airport to London Victoria. Five of the cars are powered, each with two traction motors on one bogie.

Regenerative brakes are fitted, enabling them to feed current back into the 750V DC supply rail. Though operating a non-stop 'express' service, they have wide-entrance automatic doors of a type more usually associated with suburban service, though as it happens it is also quite convenient for airline passengers who have bulky luggage. One of the power cars has been adapted as a baggage car.

An eight-car 'Juniper' unit forms a non-stop Gatwick Express service from Gatwick Airport to London Victoria. One of the cars is a baggage van to hold travellers' luggage.

Of the same family, with modified front ends to permit through-connection between units, are the Class 458s, which work many outer suburban and commuter services from London Waterloo. Thirty four-car sets were originally supplied. These are also 750V DC third-rail powered. The Class 334 units based around Glasgow, all three-car sets, run under overhead wire with the standard 25kV 50Hz AC current, and do not have the end-gangway doors that rather spoil

the appearance of Class 458s. The 'Juniper' sets originally suffered from reliability problems and a number of modifications were made at Alstom's Birmingham plant. Now, however, they operate regular high-intensity services, aided by such contemporary devices as CCTV so that the driver can close the automatic doors without having to lean out of a window.

Alstom itself, as it was named from 1997, was the new manifestation of GEC-Alsthom,

which had existed since 1988. For 60 years before that, it had been simply Alsthom, following the 1928 amalgamation of the Société Alsacienne and Thomson-Houston. The Société's history went back to the early years of

steam locomotive construction. The name changes reflected the increasing consolidation, on a world-wide basis, of locomotive building among a small number of very large international companies.

TYPE: eight-car ('460'), four-car ('458') and three-car ('334') electric multiple unit
POWER PER UNIT: 750V DC conductor rail collection classes 458 and 460, and 25,000V 50Hz AC overhead line collection class 334; three-phase AC traction control; four (class 334), six (class 458), or 10 (class 460) 270kW (360bhp) axle-mounted traction motors

TRACTIVE EFFORT: not known
MAX. OPERATING SPEED: 160km/h (100mph)
WEIGHT: 34 to 45t (75,000 to 101,470lb)
MAX AXLE LOAD: not known
OVERALL LENGTH: 21.16m (69ft 5in) end cars, 19.94m(65ft 5in) middle cars
GAUGE: 1435mm (4ft 8.5in)

'ACELA' EXPRESS ELECTRIC TRAIN AMTRAK

USA 1999

In October 1994, Amtrak requested bids from manufacturers for new trains that could negotiate the electrified but crowded 'Northeast Corridor' system at up to 241km/h (150mph). A joint venture by Bombardier and Alstom was selected in March 1996. A tilting design was used to compensate for track curvature and ensure that passengers would remain comfortable at higher speeds than a conventional train could safely achieve on the same tracks. The trainset consists of two power cars, a bistro car, a first-class car, and four business-class cars, semi-permanently coupled together. Seating is spacious and comfortable, especially in the 44-seater first-class car. Business class provides 260 seats. Originally there was a range of amenities for passengers, including an on-board headset entertainment system, but this has been dropped.

Introduction of the service was originally planned for late 1999, but various problems appeared.

The trainsets were about 10cm (4in) too wide to fully tilt, and as a result were unable to achieve the speeds originally intended. After many delays, the first Acela Express service began on 11 December 2000, a year behind schedule. With the completion of electrification between New Haven and Boston, all trains on the line have become faster; Acela Express runs between Boston and New York in just over 3hrs, 30mins – an improvement of half an hour on the previous timing. New York to Washington runs take about 2hrs, 45mins. These schedules, as well as the relative convenience of rail as opposed to air travel, have made the Acela Express highly competitive with the Northeast air shuttles. Its highest speed is 241km/h (150mph) on two sections of track in Rhode Island and Massachusetts, which total 29km (18 miles). There are also many miles of track, especially north of New Haven, on which speeds of 177 and 201km/h (110

or 125mph) are permitted. South of New York, the Acela Express is limited to 217km/h (135mph) with many stretches of 201km/h (125mph). The elderly overhead catenary here does not have the constant-tension features of the new catenary and cannot support running speeds over 217km/h (135mph). The slowest section of the electrified line is owned by Metro-North Railroad and the Connecticut Department of Transportation between New Haven and New Rochelle, where trains are limited to 145km/h (90mph) on a 6km (4 mile) stretch in New York State, and to 121km/h (75mph) between the New York state line and New Haven. Tilting is not allowed on Metro-North or ConnDOT tracks. At its maximum tilt, the wide Acela Express trainset would be just 25cm (10in) from other trains running on parallel tracks.

Although the design of the trains, with identical streamlined 4474kW (6000hp) power cars at

each end, resembles France's TG. In fact, the only component directly derived from the TGV is the four asynchronous AC traction electric motors in each power car. The tilting carriages are based upon Bombardier's earlier LRC trains rather than the TGV's articulated trailers, and the locomotives and cars are much heavier than those of the TGV in order to meet North America's different criteria on crash standards.

Journey time from Washington, DC to Boston's South Station on Acela Express is 6hrs, 36mins, an average speed (excluding the New York stop) of 109km/h (68mph) for the 720km (450-mile) trip. For the 400km (250-mile) journey between Washington, DC and New York's Penn Station, the transit time is 2hrs, 48mins, an average speed of 143km/h (89mph). These speeds are significantly slower than most other high-speed trains, but the majority of those, like *Shinkansen* and Eurostar, run on new dedicated tracks.

In August 2002, Acela Express trainsets were briefly removed from service when the brackets that connected truck dampers (shock absorbers) to the power-unit carbodies ('yaw dampers') were found to be cracking. The damper brackets have since been redesigned and the old brackets replaced. In April 2005, Acela Express trains were again taken off when cracks were found in the disc brakes of most of the passenger coaches. The

Close to Mystic Harbor, CT, a New York-bound Acela Express speeds along on an autumn day in 2001. Power car and coaches make an excellent 'fit' compared with locomotives such as the HHL.

Bombardier-Alstom consortium replaced the discs under warranty, and limited service resumed in July 2005. In the meantime, Metroliner trains of 1968 vintage, which the Acela Express was intended to replace, filled in. Amtrak announced on 21 September 2005 that all 20 trainsets had been returned to full operation.

TYPE: eight-piece/six-car high-speed electric train
POWER: 12kV AC at 25Hz, 12kV AC at 60Hz, 25kV AC at 60Hz
OUTPUT: 9200kW (12,337hp)
TRACTIVE EFFORT: 222kN (50,000lbf) starting TE
MAX. OPERATING SPEED: 240km/h (150mph)

WEIGHT: 566t (1,248,000lb) for whole train set
TRAIN LENGTH: 202.082m (663ft) for whole train set
POWER CAR LENGTH: 21.209m (69ft 7in)
MAX. AXLE LOAD: N/A
GAUGE: 1435mm (4ft 8.5in)

CLASS 67 BO-BO ENGLISH, WELSH & SCOTTISH RAILWAY (EWS) GREAT BRITAIN 1999

Capable of 200km/h (125mph) running, this is Britain's fastest diesel-electric locomotive class. Numbering 30 units, it was built for EWS by Alstom at their Valencia factory in Spain, with GM engine and electrical components. It was ordered partly to haul a speeded-up postal train service, but subsequently the Post Office decided to abandon rail-hauled mail except for the peak Christmas season, leaving the Class 67 short of express work, apart from the non-electrified sections of Scotrail's Aberdeen and Inverness sleeping-car services. Many Class 67s now undertake freight duty, while two are specially painted and maintained to operate Britain's Royal Train.

TYPE: mixed-traffic main-line diesel-electric
WHEEL ARRANGEMENT: Bo-Bo
POWER: GM 12N-710G3B-EC 12-cylinder V-form two-stroke diesel, 2385kW (3200hp); GM alternator; four frame mounted DC traction motors
TRACTIVE EFFORT: 141kN (31,750lbf)
MAX. OPERATING SPEED: 200km/h (125mph)
WEIGHT: 90t (197,645lb)
OVERALL LENGTH: 19.69m (64ft 8in)
GAUGE: 1435mm (4ft 8.5in)

High-speed diesel – a Class 67 with a postal train, around 2000. Trains have carried mail from the opening of the Liverpool & Manchester Railway in 1830.

CLASS 403 ELECTRIC HIGH-SPEED TRAIN ICE 3 GERMAN RAILWAYS (DB)   GERMANY 2000

The 'third generation' of Germany's ICE trains shows many differences to the original Class 401 of nine years earlier. Technological change, operating experience and expansion of the network in unified Germany, all played parts in the new design. An ICE 3 unit consists of eight cars, four of which are powered, while the others carry different electrical equipment, including the pantographs. To assure wide route availability, the profile is slightly narrower than Class 401's. The entire traction equipment is fitted underfloor, with a larger number of motors, but each less powerful than before. This design allows seating in all parts of the train, including 'lounge' seats at both ends, separated from the driver by a glass window. The drive of the eight powered bogies follows the principle used in the Japanese *Shinkansen* trains, in the first application of this kind of drive in Europe. The 1st, 3rd, 6th and 8th cars are each driven by four 500kW traction motors, giving a total power of 8kW in AC systems. Each powered car is supplied by one water-cooled GTO inverter for all four traction motors; two of these are installed in the 3rd and 6th carriages. The bogies have a primary suspension with two coil springs per axle and

a secondary suspension with two pneumatic springs per bogie, with 118l (7200ci) additional air volume. Rubber springs are also fitted as a default suspension if the pneumatic system should go wrong. To reduce train weight, the air-conditioning system uses air as a cooling medium, similar to systems used in aeroplanes. This system also reduces maintenance costs, although it is slightly higher in energy consumption. The *ICE 3* was the first train in series production to be equipped with a magnetic-induction eddy-current brake that provides non-frictional braking. Also, because of the higher number of powered axles, the regenerative electric brake can be used more efficiently. The *ICE 3* is also fitted with disc brakes.

Testing of the first *ICE 3* vehicles started in late 1998. The first 50 *ICE 3* trains were delivered to the DB *Reise&Touristik AG* and NS *Reizigers BV* towards the end of 1999 and started regular service in May 2000. Thirty-seven sets were of Class 403 and 13 of Class 406 (ICE 3M). The latter sets were designed for maximum route availability, including cross-border workings, and are fitted for multi-current supply, carrying pantographs of Germany and Austria's 1950mm (76.7in) width; and of Swiss, French and Belgian

(for 25kV wire) 1450mm (57in) width. Clearance of ICE-3M for working in France was obtained in late 2005, after resolution of problems that including flying gravel and trackside equipment ripped loose by the ICE's eddy current brakes. The *ICE 3* already works into the Netherlands, Belgium and Switzerland.

In September 2001, an *ICE 3* train reached a speed of 369.44km/h (229.5mph) on test, demonstrating that the class has ample power to operate 300km/h (186mph)-plus services on routes that allow such speeds. These are considerably more numerous than they were in 1991, including the new high-speed line between Köln and Frankfurt, the fast line between Berlin and Wolfsburg, in the direction of both Hannover and Braunschweig, and the line from Hannover to Würzburg, along with speeded-up sections between Stuttgart and München, and numerous others.

During the development of the *ICE 3*, DB also requested that new tilting trainsets be developed, to run on conventional tracks that had not been upgraded for higher speeds. Originally these trains

were to be called IC-T *(InterCity-Triebzug)*, but DB decided to bring them into the ICE operation (and charge ICE fares), and renamed them as ICE-T. These trains have distributed traction similar to that of the *ICE 3*. Electric versions form two classes: Class 411 (with seven cars) and Class 415 (with five cars). These trains, equipped with the Fiat tilting-bogie technology of the ETR 460, entered service in 1998, before the Class 403 sets. A second order for additional Class 411 ICE-Ts was delivered in 2004. These units, known as ICE-T2, had a number of cost-cutting features, which to some observers detracted from the high-quality image of the ICE system.

TYPE: high-speed electric train
UIC CLASSIFICATION: Bo Bo+2-2+Bo-Bo+2-2+2-2+Bo-Bo+2-2+Bo-Bo
POWER: multi-voltage
TRACTIVE EFFORT: 300kN (67,500lbf)
MAX. OPERATING SPEED: 330km/h (205mph)
TOTAL WEIGHT: 409t (901,690lb)
MAX. AXLE LOAD: not known
OVERALL LENGTH: 200m (656.2ft)
GAUGE: 1435mm (4ft 8.5in)

The difference in front end design between the ICE-3 and the ICE-1 (see 1991) is striking – showing the application of science as well as fashion.

CLASS 643/644 'TALENT' DIESEL MULTIPLE UNITS GERMAN RAILWAYS (DB)   GERMANY 2000

DB's new-generation DMUs came in two forms, diesel-electric and diesel-hydraulic, all constructed by Talbot (later part of Bombardier). They are streamlined, articulated three-car units with a low floor section between the outer bogies, and power cars at each end. Most have hydraulic transmission, but those on the Köln S-Bahn services are diesel-electrics with more

passenger access doors. The diesel-hydraulics are mostly deployed on regional and local lines, operating even-interval services within the overall timetable. Some smaller rail operators in Germany also use 'Talent' units. An electric version is being delivered to Austria and Slovenia. Specifications here are for a diesel-hydraulic unit (diesel-electric in brackets).

TYPE: local and suburban passenger diesel-hydraulic (electric) multiple units
POWER: two 315kW (420hp) or 550kW (735hp) diesels
TRACTIVE EFFORT: N/A
TRANSMISSION: hydraulic torque converter; or alternator, four traction motors

MAX. OPERATING SPEED: 120km/h (75mph)
WEIGHT: not known
OVERALL LENGTH: not known
GAUGE: 1435mm (4ft 8.5in)

Ranged outside the factory, sleek and shiny 'Talent' DMUs. These units are now running also in Norway and Canada, where they form 3-car units on Ottawa's OC Transpo system.

MAK G2000BB B-B VARIOUS OPERATORS   GERMANY 2000

MaK is the old-established Maschinenbau Kiel company, which became Krupp-MaK in 1964 and since 1998 has been a part of locomotive builders Vossloh, with its headquarters located at Werdohl near Düsseldorf. Vossloh launched the G2000BB at the Berlin Innotrans 2000 exhibition. As a diesel-hydraulic with Voith transmission, it stands in a well-established German tradition. The innovative, asymmetric front-end layout for twenty-first century operations combines near full-width cabs with platforms for shunting personnel on one side at each end. This feature is aimed at 'open access' operations where train locomotives handling contract flows shunt their own payloads. Radio remote control is among the options, with long-

range fuel tanks, alternative power units up to 2500kW (2297hp) and maximum speeds from 100 to 140km/h (62 to 87.5mph). The first 10 were acquired for leasing and a second 10 were speculatively built by Vossloh. G2000BBs started to appear all over Germany on various privately operated freight flows from 2001 onwards.

TYPE: B-B diesel-hydraulic freight
POWER: 2240kW (3043hp) from Caterpillar 3516 series engine
TRACTIVE EFFORT: 283kN (63675lbf)
MAX. OPERATING SPEED: 120km/h (75mph)
WEIGHT: 87.3 tonnes (192,497lb)
OVERALL LENGTH: Not known
GAUGE: 1435mm (4ft 8.5in)

The G2000 has been a very successful design, used by freight operators not only in Germany but also in France and Italy. The locomotive hiring company Angel Trains had 41 in 2007.

CLASS 175 DIESEL MULTIPLE UNITS NORTH-WEST TRAINS (NWT)   GREAT BRITAIN 2000

Built for city-link and cross-country services, with air-conditioning and comfortable seating, these 'Coradia' diesel-hydraulic units were built by Alstom in Birmingham, England. Initially 11 two-car and 16 three-

car sets were supplied. The units are air-conditioned, have sliding plug doors at the ends of each bodyside and can run at 160km/h (100mph). For NWT, they are painted in First Group's blue livery with pink and white lining.

TYPE: express diesel-hydraulic multiple units
POWER: 335kW (450bhp) Cummins N14 underfloor horizontal diesel (one per car)
TRANSMISSION (ONE PER CAR): Voith T211rzze hydraulic torque converter gearbox, cardan shafts to wheelsets on one bogie

MAX. OPERATING SPEED: 161km/h (100mph)
WEIGHT: 51t (112,000lb) driving cars; 48t (104,315lb) intermediate cars
OVERALL LENGTH: 23.71m (77ft 9in) driving cars; 23.03m (75ft 7in) intermediate cars
GAUGE: 1435mm (4ft 8.5in)

CLASSES 220/221 'VOYAGER' DIESEL-ELECTRIC MULTIPLE UNITS VIRGIN TRAINS

Perhaps the most innovative among Britain's new wave of rail franchise holders, Virgin Trains were first in the field with diesel-electric multiple units embodying the most up-to-date design and technology. To replace its locomotive-hauled trains and High Speed Trains (HSTs) on cross-country services, it ordered 34 four-car non-tilting (Class 220) and 44 five-car tilting (Class 221) trains, these having a 200km/h (125mph) top speed.

The two classes operate in multiple on heavily trafficked routes in the UK, and singly elsewhere, at much improved frequencies. Bombardier supplied the sets from their factories at Brugge in Belgium and Wakefield in the UK, and they were placed in service with very few development problems.

Unusually for a UK train, the Class 220 bogie has an inside-frame layout. The bogie of Class 221 has an outside frame to provide the width and strength necessary for the body tilting mechanism. Both classes have the same body and interior design,

TYPE: high-speed diesel-electric four-car (220) and five-car (221) multiple units
POWER: one per car – 560kW (750bhp) Cummins underfloor horizontal diesel; Alstom ONIX three-phase control; rheostatic braking; underframe mounted traction motors; cardan shafts to nearest axle on each bogie

MAX. OPERATING SPEED: 200km/h (125mph)
AVERAGE VEHICLE WEIGHT: 46t (101,020lb) Class 220; 54t (118,590lb) Class 221
OVERALL LENGTH: 23.85m (78ft 3in) driving cars; 22.82m (74ft 10in) intermediate cars
GAUGE: 1435mm (4ft 8.5in)

with air-conditioning, comfortable if close-spaced seating, and a buffet incorporating a shop. The Voyagers attracted some criticism on the grounds of inadequate luggage space and poorly sited seats, but in general they have been appreciated for their ability to provide fast and regular services.

ETR 500 EUROSTAR ITALIA ELECTRIC TRAIN STATE RAILWAYS (FS)

The introduction of the ETR 500 marked a complete re-branding of the country's high-speed network in an effort to reflect its integration into the wider European rail system. On the introduction of 60 new trains, the routes on which they operated were relaunched as 'Eurostar Italia', borrowing the name of the London–Paris/Brussels high-speed train. Italy had been a pioneer of the 'tilting train' in order to avoid the building of new tracks, but by the end of the century it had accepted the need to provide new lines for very fast trains. A key feature of the scheme is the upgrading of the existing high-speed Rome–Florence line, known

as the *Direttissima*. Major expansion will also be undertaken on the Milan–Naples, Turin–Milan–Venice and Genoa–Po Valley via Terzo Valico routes. The 252km (157-mile) Rome–Florence line was the first dedicated high-speed line in Europe when it opened in 1978, but it now requires heavy upgrading to raise speeds to 300km/h (186mph). When complete, it will link with the Florence–Bologna line by means of a new tunnel and subterranean station under Florence. Although the alignment for the new 79km (49-mile) Florence–Bologna line was agreed in 1995, it is taking over a decade to complete. All but 5km (3 miles) is in a tunnel

An ETR 500 at Milan Central on a bright wintry morning. The front end design reflects the Franco-British 'Eurostar' train, but there are already numerous variations of detail and livery among the 60 trains.

through the Apennine mountains. Journey times will be cut by half. High-speed trains were diverted away from the original Rome–Naples route from December 2005 with the opening of an all-new high-speed line, which reduced journey times between the Italian capital and Naples to around 1hr, and is the first line in Italy to be electrified at the European standard 25kV AC 50Hz for high-speed lines. On the 182km (113 mile) Bologna–Milan route, which is one of the most congested in Europe, 6.1 billion

Euros of investment will increase route capacity by 88 per cent and reduce end-to-end journey times to 1hr. Reconstruction of the 127km (79-mile) Turin–Milan line to virtually double its capacity has been controversial because of the route chosen. New works begin at Certosa, 9km (6 miles) from the centre of Milan, and run to Settiimo Torinese. Connections with existing lines were provided to reduce journey times in time for the 2006 Winter Olympics, with phase one of the line running from Turin to Novara and the Novara–

Milan section to open later. The final choice of route from Milan to Venice (212km /132-miles) is still under discussion. It will start at Melzo, 20km (12 miles) from Milano Centrale station, and join the FS system at Verona. The route to Venice was approved in March 2000. Finally, a new line from Milan to Genoa is planned to be open by 2010, requiring a 1.6km (1-mile) tunnel through the mountains to link the port of Genoa to the existing rail system.

The first generation of new rolling stock was the tilting ETR 450 'Pendolino', built by Fiat Ferroviaria, which entered service in May 1988 on routes radiating from Rome. It was followed by the ETR 460 single-voltage electric multiple unit, the tri-voltage ETR 470 for 'Cisalpino' services to Switzerland and Germany and the

dual-voltage (3kV DC/25kV AC) ETR 480. The latter was developed with the new high-speed lines in mind, although its tilting capacity is used to best advantage on classic lines with frequent curves, such as the Genova–Rome coastal main line. The non-tilting ETR 500 variant from Gruppo Ferroviario Breda in Pistoia is designed for operation on the new high-speed lines. This is a 13-vehicle unit seating 671 passengers, with 195 in First Class, and capable of 300km/h (185mph). The 60-strong fleet entered service during 2000. The second batch of 30 ETR 500s has dual-voltage power cars (3kV DC/25kV AC) for operation on 25kV AC high-speed lines. In addition to this, 60 new E404.600 dual-voltage power cars are replacing 3kV DC-only E404.100 power cars on the original 30

trains. The latter will be cascaded to power 30 InterCity push-pull trains formed of Type Z1 locomotive-hauled stock for use on the standard network from 2006–07. Alstom Ferroviaria's next generation of Pendolino tilting train for international Cisalpino and Italian domestic services is more powerful and formed of seven, rather than nine, cars to work in multiple where necessary. Trenitalia's units replace ageing ETR 450 sets on long-haul routes such as Rome to Bari, Lecce and Reggio Calabria, while the Cisalpino replaces locomotive-hauled trains between Italy and Switzerland and runs at up to 250km/h (155mph) through the new Lötschberg base tunnel.

The Italian high-speed network is relatively self-contained, so there is expected to be little

expansion beyond the network currently under development. Nevertheless, the Italian government and railway authorities are keen to integrate with the Trans-European Network System (TENS), which will take through trains to Lyon, Trieste, Ljubljana, Budapest and Kiev, with a western extension linking Marseille and Barcelona.

TYPE: electric high-speed train
POWER: 8800kW (11,968hp)
SUPPLY: 3kVDC or 25kV 50Hz AC
TRACTIVE EFFORT: 400kN (90,000lb)
MAX. OPERATING SPEED: 300km/h (186mph)
WEIGHT: 642t (1,415,367lb)
MAX. AXLE LOAD: not known
OVERALL LENGTH: 354m (1160.5ft)
GAUGE: 1435mm (4ft 8.5in)

CLASS M9 CO-CO SRI LANKA RAILWAYS (SLR)

SRI LANKA 2000

The Sri Lankan Railways were one of the first non-French customers for Alstom's modular range of modern locomotives, known as PRIMA, though many had been built for the SNCF. Ten AD32C diesel-electric locomotives deriving from this range were ordered, in this case as six-axle units with the 12-cylinder Ruston RK215 engine, intended for mixed traffic. Deliveries began from the Alstom Belfort factory in France in autumn 2000.

The two-cab, full-body style, painted blue, yellow and white, is

in contrast to the SLR's other hood-unit locomotives. Thirty similar machines, but of higher power-rating, have been built for Syria.

TYPE: Co-Co diesel-electric
POWER: 1350kW (1834hp) from Ruston 12RK215 series engine
TRACTIVE EFFORT: 240kN (54000lbf)
MAX. OPERATING SPEED: 110kmh (68.3mph)
WEIGHT: 108t (238,140lb)
OVERALL LENGTH: not known
GAUGE: 1676mm (5ft 6in)

Sri Lankan Railways' most powerful locomotive type, the M9 hauls both passenger and freight main-line services between provincial centres and Colombo.

IORE CO-CO LUOSSAVAARA KIRUNAVAARA AB (LKAB)

SWEDEN 2000

In 1963, the Class Dm3 of Swedish Railways (SJ) employed on the Kiruna–Narvik iron ore trains was a triple-unit electric, with a power-rating of 7200kW (9600hp) and a tractive effort of 940kN (211,320lbf). The IORE types now supplementing them, and eventually to take over completely, are single units, though designed to operate as pairs. In tandem, they are rated at 10,800kW (14,675hp) and have a maximum tractive effort of 1350kN (303,750lbf). Built by ADtranz at Kassel, Germany, the first was delivered in 2000. While SJ had built and run the Dm3

One of the most powerful locomotives in current use, an LKAB Co-Co at work at Nattavaara, northern Sweden, in July 2002.

class, deregulation enabled the ore company to take control of its rail logistics from mid-1996 through subsidiary companies MTAB in Sweden and MTAS in Norway. The lines from Kiruna to Narvik on the Norwegian coast and Luleå on Sweden's Baltic coast, and to the concentration and pelletizing plants at Svappavaara, carry some 20 million tonnes (19.7 million tons) of iron ore a year.

The new locomotives haul trains of up to 68 wagons, each of 100-tonne (220,500lb) payload. The wagons are of Uanoo-type, with bogies of South African design, built to exert low track force. Longer and heavier loads have enabled the number of trains to be reduced from about 7000 runs a year to about 4000, with

TYPE: double Co-Co for heavy mineral traffic
POWER: twin unit 10,800kW (14,675hp)
SUPPLY: 15kV 16.67Hz AC
TRACTIVE EFFORT: twin unit unballasted 1200kN (270,000lbf); ballasted 1350kN (303,750lbf)
MAX. OPERATING SPEED: 80km/h (50mph)
WEIGHT: twin unit 300t (661,500lb) (excluding ballast); 360t (793,800lb) (including ballast)
MAX. AXLE LOAD: 25t (55,125lb) (excluding ballast); 30t (66,150lb) (including ballast)
OVERALL LENGTH: twin unit 45.8m (149ft 5in)
GAUGE: 1435mm (4ft 8.5in)

consequent saving on locomotive and wagon miles. At the same time, average train speed has been raised from the DM3s' 50km/h (31.3mph) to 60km/h (37.5mph).

The nine IORE locomotives replace 15 Dm3 types plus six former NSB E115 single units (which had worked as pairs). Each axle is fitted with a single asynchronous traction motor, and each three-axle bogie has a water-cooled GTO inverter. Adhesion

control enables the locomotives to get under way in wet or icy conditions, and they have regenerative braking enabling them to feed current back into the catenary on the long downhill runs. Electric braking systems of 10,800kW (14675hp) deliver a maximum braking effort of 750kN (168,750lb). ADtranz MITRAC diagnostic and information systems are fitted.

The new locomotives and high-capacity wagons have dramatically

lowered the ore company's transport costs, by an estimated 45 per cent per tonne-kilometre, and so not only to maintain the viability of the giant Kiruna mining operation, but also to increase its productivity towards a target of 30 million tonnes of high quality iron ore a year. ADtranz, the builders, formed by the merger in 1996 of ABB Henschel and AEG Transportation. In 2001, they were taken over by the Bombardier Group.

IMU 120 INTERURBAN ELECTRIC TRAIN AIRTRAIN CITYLINK

AUSTRALIA 2001

Linking Brisbane with its main airport and the holiday resorts of the Gold Coast, this line, opened in 2001, is laid to the same 1067mm (3ft 6in) gauge as Queensland Railways (QR). Its trains operate an even-interval integrated service with QR Cityrail and suburban workings, using four three-car electric multiple unit sets, with an intermediate car between two driver-motor cars. These stainless-steel bodied cars were among the first to be

TYPE: interurban three-car train
POWER: eight three-phase asynchronous traction motors of 180kW (241.2hp), supplied by 25kV 50Hz AC overhead catenary
TRACTIVE EFFORT: not known
MAX. OPERATING SPEED: 140km/h (87mph)
TOTAL WEIGHT: 130t (286,650lb)
MAX. AXLE LOAD: 14t (30,870lb)
OVERALL LENGTH: 72.6m (238ft 4in)

equipped with insulated gate bipolar transistor (IGBT) systems to control their four AC motors. Micro-processors also operate their electropneumatic braking systems.

Airport link services are steadily growing as traffic congestion makes road access ever more difficult. As with the Air Train, special rolling stock is provided.

CLASS 2070 B-B AUSTRIAN STATE RAILWAYS (ÖBB)

AUSTRIA 2001

Updating its non-electric motive power, ÖBB ordered 60 of these medium range diesel-

hydraulic freight locomotives from Vossloh/Siemens, with an option for a further 90. The newcomers

replaced second-hand ex-DB class V100 B-Bs and enabled the removal of all rod-drive shunting

locomotives and some other earlier diesel types. They are low-profile hood units with off-centre cabs. Two-speed gearing makes them versatile in service, able to take fast light freights and parcel trains as well as passenger trains, through shunting, for which they have railed platforms.

TYPE: mixed-traffic light diesel-hydraulic
WHEEL ARRANGEMENT: B-B
POWER: medium-speed diesel, 500kW (670hp); hydraulic transmission with cardan shaft drives
TRACTIVE EFFORT: 233kN (52,380lbf) freight gearing; 151kN (33,945lbf) passenger gearing
MAX. OPERATING SPEED: 45km/h (28mph) freight gearing; 100km/h (62mph) passenger gearing
WEIGHT: 80t (176,368lb)
OVERALL LENGTH: not known
GAUGE: 1435mm (4ft 8.5in)

Known as 'Hectors' on the ÖBB, these Kiel-built locos can be remote-controlled by radio. They are currently based at Vienna, Wels and St Pölten.

CLASS 2106 BO-BO AUSTRIAN STATE RAILWAYS (ÖBB)

AUSTRIA 2001

These advanced Siemens 'Hercules' diesel-electrics were ordered to replace the Austrian State Railways' classes 2050, 2043 and 2143. Originally 70 firm and 80 options were ordered, with so far 30 options taken up. Of modular construction, Class 2016 is longer than ÖBB required, but

the format allows for larger engine options and a 22.5-tonne (21.8-ton) axle loading for other potential users. 'Hercules' has 1000kW (1341hp) electric braking power available, and is fitted with full multiple-unit and push-pull capability for ÖBB's passenger train sets. Its signalling and safety systems

TYPE: Bo-Bo diesel-electric universal
POWER: 2000kW (2717hp) from MTU 16V4000 series engine
TRACTIVE EFFORT: 235kN (61,875lbf)

MAX. OPERATING SPEED: 140km/h (88.5mph)
WEIGHT: 80t (176,400lb)
OVERALL LENGTH: 19.275m (62ft 10in)
GAUGE: 1435mm (4ft 8.5in)

allow for operations into neighbouring Slovenia and Germany. Complementing its

'Eurosprinter' electric locomotive, Siemens markets the diesel-elctric as 'EuroRunner'.

CLASS 146 BO-BO GERMAN RAILWAYS (DB)

GERMANY 2001

AEG and Henschel built a prototype three-phase locomotive in 1994, given the class number 128.001, and at the same time Krauss-Maffei built a similar Class 127.001 – both based on the DB's Class 120 of 1987 but incorporating later technology. In 1996, ABB-Henschel merged with AEG Transportation as ADtranz, and in turn this was acquired by Bombardier in 2001. From the work begun on 128.001 emerged Bombardier's 'TRAXX' family of locomotives, a range covering all

forms of electric traction, AC, DC and multi-voltage, as well as diesel-electric locomotives. A first derivative was the DB's Class 145 Bo-Bo, of which 80 were built by ADtranz from 1997. From 2000, a multi-system version was produced, Class 185, which DB liked even better, cancelling the uncompleted order for Class 145 in favour of an order for 400 of Class 185, still being fulfilled by the Kassel factory in 2006.

Class 146 is a development of Class 145, in which the direct axle

drive is replaced by quill drive, enabling it to work heavy double-deck trains at 160km/h (100mph). In 2003, a similar adaptation of Class 185 was produced, and classed 146.1. Significant redesign of both classes was undertaken in 2005, with the installation of insulated gate bipolar transistor (IGBT) controls, resulting in their reclassification as 185.2 and 146.2. Class 185 locomotives have also been ordered by SBB Cargo and BLS Cargo, for freight work on Swiss mountain routes.

TYPE: Bo-Bo regional passenger push-pull electric
POWER: 15,000V 16.6Hz AC overhead line collection; 4200kW (5630hp) continuous rating; electronic control; rheostatic braking; four traction motors with direct drive to axles
TRACTIVE EFFORT: 260kN (58,450lbf)
MAX. OPERATING SPEED: 160km/h (100mph)
WEIGHT: 86t (188,860lb)
MAX AXLE LOAD: not known
OVERALL LENGTH: 18.9m (62ft)

CLASS 605 DIESEL-ELECTRIC TILTING TRAIN ICE-TD GERMAN RAILWAYS (DB)

GERMANY 2001

Intended to be a four-car, non-electrified equivalent of the very successful ICE trains, with tilting bogies for high maintained speeds, these trains have been less successful. Problems with braking systems delayed their arrival from 2000 to 2001. The tilting technology was not the same as in the ICE-T sets, but was developed independently by Siemens, and

difficulties with this, and with software in the computer systems, compromised their reliability in the first year of service. In December 2002, after these problems were solved, a train derailed due to a broken axle. All the diesel sets trains were temporarily ordered out of service by the Federal Rail Authority, but after resolution of the problem DB declined to take the

TYPE: InterCity Express diesel-electric tilting four-car multiple units
POWER UNITS (FOUR): 425kW (570hp) diesel, AC alternator, body-mounted traction motors with cardan shafts to bogie wheelsets

TRACTIVE EFFORT: N/A
MAX. OPERATING SPEED: 200km/h (125mph)
WEIGHT: 220t
OVERALL LENGTH: 105m (345ft)
GAUGE: 1435mm (4ft 8.5in)

trains back from Siemens, claiming they did not meet specifications. Although not in routine services,

some of the trains were used for special services during the FIFA World Cup in the summer of 2006.

CLASS 390 'PENDOLINO' ELECTRIC TRAIN VIRGIN TRAINS

GREAT BRITAIN 2001

In September 2006, a 'Pendolino' ran from Glasgow to London, 645.3km (401 miles), in 235 minutes, setting an average speed of 164.75km/h (102.38mph), and breaking a record set over 20 years earlier by British Railways' experimental (and later abandoned) Advanced Passenger Train (APT). Like the APT, the Pendolino was applying tilting technology in order to maintain high speeds on a curving track that otherwise would require frequent speed limitations. Virgin operates 53 of these trains on its West Coast Main Line routes to Birmingham, Glasgow, Manchester

A 'Pendolino' on the West Coast route. Its tilting ability enables it to travel round curves at up to 25 per cent higher speeds than conventional trains.

and Liverpool. They are formed of nine cars, with a caterpillar-nosed driving car at each end carrying pantographs and transformer equipment; the seven intermediate cars all have powered bogies with cardan shaft drive, evening out both overall train weight and the axle load of individual wheelsets. Rheostatic regenerative braking is fitted as well as the full range of diagnostics and information systems available on modern trains and locomotives. All bogies are fitted with the electrically activated tilt mechanism developed on the Italian FIAT-SIG

TYPE: high-speed electric nine-car tilting trains
POWER: 25,000V 50Hz AC overhead line collection; two Alsthom ONIX 800 power packs each on seven power cars, totalling 5950kW (7975bhp) continuous rating; rheostatic and regenerative braking; two underfloor traction motors on each power car, each with cardan shaft drive to nearest axle.

bogie. Like other tilting trains, it does not compensate for the full lateral pressure exerted on curves, but enough to avoid any passenger discomfort. The

TRACTIVE EFFORT: not known
MAX. OPERATING SPEED: 225km/h (140mph)
WEIGHT PER VEHICLE: 50 to 62t (109,805 to 136,155lb)
OVERALL LENGTH: 23.05m (75ft 7in) driving cars; 23.9m (78ft 5in) intermediate cars
GAUGE: 1435mm (4ft 8.5in)

maximum speed, where allowed, is 225km/h (140mph), making them the fastest trains in service in the United Kingdom, apart from Eurostar. In other respects, the

British Pendolinos are laid out as long-distance trains, with air conditioning, buffet facilities and the inevitable shop. In-train headphone-based entertainment systems are also available, and power points for laptop computers are fitted. The Pendolinos have reduced journey times and would also make a more intensive service possible, but current route volume is restricted by the capacity of signalling and information systems, which are unable to handle a high-density, high-speed service level.

CLASS M62.3 CO-CO HUNGARIAN RAILWAYS (MÁV) HUNGARY 2001

New locomotives, with a range of equipment and accessories almost unimaginable only a few decades ago, are expensive, and many railways are extending the life-spans of older types by extensive refurbishments and adaptations that are still much cheaper than acquiring a completely new machine. New pollution-control requirements

enforced by the EU and the United States also require alterations to existing diesel engines in thousands of locomotives. MÁV sub-class M62.3 is typical of this exercise. Hungarian Railways plan to retain about 40 refurbished M62 freight locomotives, with a life expectancy running past 2010. In parallel with similar re-engining of the M41, both MTU and CAT

TYPE: Co-Co diesel-electric freight
POWER: 1500kW (2038hp) from MTU 12V4000 or CAT 3512 series engine
TRACTIVE EFFORT: 196kN (441,00lbf) at 20km/h (12.5mph)

engines are fitted, selected for compliance with future EU emission-control regulations. The original DC generator is replaced

MAX. OPERATING SPEED: 100km/h (62mph)
WEIGHT: 120t (264,600lb)
OVERALL LENGTH: 17.56m (57ft 4in)
GAUGE: 1435mm (4ft 8.5in)

by an alternator. The on-going work is carried out by MÁV at its Eszaki works in Budapest.

AD43C CO-CO IRANIAN ISLAMIC REPUBLIC RAILWAYS (RAI) IRAN 2001

From Alstom's PRIMA 'family', on the diesel-electric side, locomotives of this type were produced also for Sri Lanka and Syria. The prime mover is the Ruston RK215 four-stroke diesel engine, with a 215mm (8.42in) bore and 275mm (10.77in) stroke – it is the first Ruston engine to have an underslung crankshaft (Ruston is now part of MAN). The

RK215s for Iran are 16-cylinder, driving a traction alternator and three-phase asynchronous electric motors through Alstom's Onix insulated gate bipolar transistor (IGBT) system.
Twenty AD43Cs were built at Alstom's Belfort factory in France, with the first delivered in 2002. Five were sent to Iran in kit form, and subsequent locomotives have

TYPE: Co-Co diesel-electric
POWER: 3160kW (4240hp) from Ruston 16RK215 series engine
TRACTIVE EFFORT: 542kN (121,950lbf) unballasted to 662kN (148,950lbf) ballasted

been built there. Thirty are geared for passenger work, at 150km/h (93.8mph) maximum, and the

MAX. OPERATING SPEED: 150km/h (93.8mph)
WEIGHT: 123t (271205lb) – ballasted up to 150t (330,750lb)
OVERALL LENGTH: 22.33m (64ft 3in)
GAUGE: 1435mm (4ft 8.5in)

other 60 are freight locomotives, operating at speeds up to 110km/h (68.9mph).

8500 SERIES ELECTRIC MULTIPLE UNIT DUBLIN AREA RAPID TRANSPORT (DART) IRELAND 2001

The steady growth of metropolitan Dublin has been matched by an increase in the coverage of its DART rapid transit system, first established in 1984. Extensions of the network in 2000 and 2001 brought additional stock in the form of the 8500 series. These are two-car sets, with a power car (8500) and a driving

TYPE: suburban passenger electric multiple-unit train
POWER: 1500V DC from overhead wire
TRACTIVE EFFORT: N/A

trailer (classed as 8600) seating 80 passengers between them but with standing room for many more. These units were built by

MAX. OPERATING SPEED: 100km/h (62mph)
WEIGHT: 39t (85,995lb) – powered car

Mitsui in Japan. At the same time, a further class, Series 8200/400 of similar design, came from Alstom in Spain. The DART system

OVERALL LENGTH: 20m (65ft 7in)
MAX. AXLE LOAD: 9.75t (21,499lb)
GAUGE: 1600mm (5ft 3in)

uses overhead electrification at 15000V DC.

MLX01 'MAGLEV' PROTOTYPE TRAIN JAPANESE NATIONAL RAILWAYS (JNR) JAPAN 2001

The first trains to be worked by magnetic levitation principles linked Birmingham Airport, in England, with its rail station, a slow service over a 600m (1968ft) track that ran from 1984 to 1995. The service proved too unreliable, however, and was replaced by more conventional wheeled vehicles.

Since then, considerable advances have been made with 'Maglev technology' and a new airport link has been opened at Shanghai (see 2003). The countries that have done most to pursue the principle in recent years are Japan, Germany, China and South Korea. Japan's aim is to run a 1hr passenger service

between Tokyo and Osaka, as compared with the 2hrs, 30mins taken by the *Shinkansen* train – requiring a speed of 450km/h (310mph). A test-track has been established in Yamanashi Prefecture since 1996, replacing an earlier one built in Miyazaki Prefecture in 1977, in order to develop the necessary

technology and techniques of operation. On its 18.4km (11.4-mile) track, incorporating over-bridges and a tunnel, speeds well in excess of this have been recorded, the first being 552km/h (324mph) on 14 April 1999, surpassed on 2 December 2003 by 581km/h (361mph).

The Japanese test track is run by the Railway Technical Institute. The prototype train is a five-car set of wheel-less vehicles, using the EMS electromagnetic system in which two types of ground coil fitted in the track sides provide power both for levitation and forward propulsion.

A public Maglev line finally opened in March 2005 at Aichi, consisting of the Tobo–Kyushu line of 8.9km (5.5 miles). This is an 'urban Maglev', with nine intermediate stations and a maximum operating speed of 100km/h (62mph), showing the concept at work on short-distance local service. The 'urban Maglev' is also being pursued in South

Korea's *rotem* project, which is due to be unveiled in 2007.

TYPE: magnetic levitation train	**MAX. OPERATING SPEED:** 500km/h (310mph)
POWER: not known	**TOTAL WEIGHT:** not known
MAGNETOMOTIVE FORCE: 700kA	**MAXIMUM AXLE LOAD:** N/A
TRACTIVE EFFORT: N/A	**OVERALL LENGTH:** not known

CLASSES 4023/4 'TALENT' ELECTRIC MULTIPLE UNIT AUSTRIAN FEDERAL RAILWAYS (ÖBB) AUSTRIA 2002

The 'Talent' trains are a modular range of both electric and diesel articulated multiple units developed by Bombardier and its affiliate ELIN of Vienna. Fifty-one electric units were ordered by ÖBB for delivery in 2002, of three cars (Class 4023) and four cars (Class 4024). Use on local services around Salzburg for the 4023s, and Vienna for the 4024s, was intended.

As often on modern suburban sets, these trains have low floors between the bogies, with tram-style low-level access doors. Streamlined in appearance, they are capable of 160km/h (100mph) operation. In 2003, ÖBB ordered a

further 60 of Class 4024, to come from Bombardier's plant at Aachen, Germany.

TYPE: local (three-car) and suburban (four-car) articulated electric multiple units	
POWER (PER UNIT): 15,000V 16.67Hz AC overhead line collection; 2000kW (2700hp); traction motors with direct drive to axles	
TRACTIVE EFFORT: not known	
MAX. OPERATING SPEED: 160km/h (100mph)	
WEIGHT: not known	
MAX AXLE LOAD: not known	
OVERALL LENGTH: not known	

Away from their normal daily schedules, three three-car 'Talent' units make a special run over the Semmering Pass route on 23 August 2005.

'TRANSRAPID' MAGNETIC LEVITATION TRAIN SHANGHAI AIRPORT CHINA 2003

Final preparations are made to one of the Shanghai Airport 'Transrapid' units in the workshops.

Linking Shanghai's Pudong Airport with the city's urban transit system at Longyang Road, this is the world's first high-speed 'Maglev' line in full public service. Opened in October 2003 but not fully operational until March 2004, it is 30km (18.6 miles) long and the journey duration is 7 minutes 20 seconds, with a maximum speed of 431km/h (268mph). The constructors are the German

'Transrapid' company, a consortium formed by Siemens and ThyssenKrupp. The history of the venture goes back to the 1930s, when patents were first issued in Germany for trains operating on the magnetic levitation principle, but serious practical work got under way in 1971 when the Messerschmitt-Bölkov-Blohm combine demonstrated the 'Transrapid 02'

on a 660m (2125ft) long track near Munich. It used opposing electromagnets to lift the vehicle above its trackway, and an early form of linear motor for propulsion. In 1980, after considerable development work on the motor aspect, a longer test-track, now 31.5km (19.6 miles)

long was constructed at Emsland, between Rheine and Emden. This track was not only the guidance line and levitation source but 'drove' the train through a 'longstator' system in which what would have been the commutator coils of a conventional electric motor were laid out longitudinally along the track. The test track is capable of running trains at speeds of up to 450km/h (280mph), though the potential speeds (as demonstrated in Japan) are a good deal higher.

Maglev is based on the idea that a train having no physical contact with its track will have none of the friction, wheel-slip problems, expensive bogie designs, etc., of a conventional steel-wheel-on-steel-rail train, meeting only air and wind resistance. The 'Transrapid' vehicles are mounted on a track that is overlapped by their lower body construction in a partial 'wrap-round' effect. Electromagnets facing upwards underneath each side of the track are the lift magnets that attract the stator laid out along the under-side of the track beam. When activated, these lift the vehicle towards the track magnets so that it is suspended in

the air, not touching the track. Propulsion is enabled by a reaction rail on each side of the track beam – in effect, a long plate forming the outer faces. Facing this rail on the vehicle structure is a series of superconducting drive magnets, which provide forward movement by means of harmonic waves in the propulsion magnetic field acting on the rail. In this arrangement, the drive magnets are on the train and not in the track, reducing construction cost considerably. The trains are intended to be driverless, monitored and controlled from a central point.

Intensive testing on the Emsland line went on before construction of the Shanghai system, to establish reliability and durability. Many design and operating problems had to be tackled, including the extreme sensitivity of the

superconducting magnets to external disturbances, which can reduce or even eliminate power. Despite vast investment, and a range of proposals for both short and long-distance Maglev lines, there are still question-marks over the future of this technology. Critics point out that the friction resistance of wheeled high-speed trains is only about a quarter of the total, with Maglev also suffering the air-resistance factor. The trains do not run silently, as is often supposed, but have quite a high external noise level. Constructions costs are also extremely high and (unlike high-speed rail lines) difficult to estimate precisely.

In August 2006, a fire broke out on the Shanghai Maglev train. In September 2006, 23 people were killed when a demonstration run on Transrapid's Emsland line

collided with a maintenance vehicle on the track. Although a number of projects, most notably in Germany and China, remain in the planning stage, and a British company, UK Ultraspeed, is proposing a north–south line linking Scotland and England, the wider future of Maglev remains uncertain.

TYPE: magnetic levitation high-speed trains
TRACK: steel or concrete beams carrying levitation stator magnets and longstator propulsion reaction rail
POWER: electromagnetic levitation and longstator propulsion
MAX. OPERATING SPEED: up to 500km/h (310mph)
WEIGHT: 53t (116,400lb) per vehicle
OVERALL LENGTH: 27m (88ft 7in) end cars; 24.8m (81ft 4in) intermediate cars – up to 10 cars per train

---

CLASS DF4B CO-CO CHINESE RAILWAYS   CHINA 2003

Although the Ziyang Works in Sichuan Province have been building this sturdy diesel-electric locomotive type in large numbers, since the 1960s (see 1969), its design has been updated on various occasions, and the specification given here was that current in 2003. The workaday and familiar DF4B gained a degree of fame when one of the class, No. 3225, pulled the first train into Lhasa on the completion of the Qinghai–Tibet line, on 1 July 2006. This 1142km (709.6-mile) line replaces the Central of Peru as the world's highest, at 5072m (16,636ft). Because of the difficulties of operating with

TYPE: Co-Co diesel-electric locomotive
POWER: 16V 240JZB engine, producing 2430kW (3305hp)
TRACTIVE EFFORT: 327.5kN (73,687lbf) on starting (passenger); 435kN (97,875lbf, freight)
MAX. OPERATING SPEED: 120km/h (74.5mph)
WEIGHT: 138t (304,237lb)
MAX. AXLE LOAD: 23t (50,706lb)
OVERALL LENGTH: 21.1m (69.2ft)
GAUGE: 1435mm (4ft 8.5in)

internal combustion at these extreme altitudes, a new locomotive class had been under design. The Qishuyang Works had displayed an engine with two 16V 280JZA engines, named 'Magic Locomotive of the Snow Region', late in 2002, but neither this nor another type under development with General Electric was available, and DF4Bs continue to work the line at present. At lower levels, Class DF4 locomotives of different

The locomotives for regular service on the Lhasa line are DF 8CJ 9000 units, built at Qishuyang Works, and based on the Bombardier-GE 'Blue Tiger' locomotive. They work in triple sets.

versions are employed on a host of passenger and freight duties on China's non-electrified tracks. The prime mover is a 16V 240JZB engine, supplying power to a three-phase synchronous traction alternator. Axle-suspended AC motors drive the wheels through traction gears. Electric resistance

and air brakes are both fitted. Ziyang Works, China's prime diesel-electric manufacturer, along with Zhuzhou as the country's electric locomotive builder, are becoming major contenders in the international locomotive market, making export sales to many countries from Vietnam to Iran.

CLASS 680 ELECTRIC TILTING TRAIN CZECH RAILWAYS (CD)   CZECH REPUBLIC 2003

Commissioned by Czech Railways in 1995, the Class 680 was meant to be a Czech-produced train, through a collaboration between the CKD

A Class 680 set the Czech rail speed record of 237km/h (147.3mph) on 18 November 2004.

works in Prague, Siemens, and Alstom's Ferroviaria subsidiary, developers of the tilting bogie. Rising costs and many production problems resulted in its abandonment, and instead seven seven-car units were obtained from Ferroviaria in 2003. These are based on the Italian 'Pendolino' sets ETR 470 and ETR 480. Equipped for dual-voltage

operation under 25kV 50Hz AC or 15kV 16.67Hz AC, they have a maximum speed of 230km/h (143.8mph). Currently working

within the Czech Republic, between Praha and Pardubice and on other main lines, they are intended to serve on European

Corridor IV, Berlin–Praha–Vienna, and also Berlin–Praha–Bratislava–Budapest.

TYPE: EMU tilting, express passenger, multi-voltage	
POWER: 4000kW (5500hp) projected	
SUPPLY: 3000V DC or 25kV 50Hz AC or 15kV 16.67Hz AC	
TRACTIVE EFFORT: N/A	
MAX. OPERATING SPEED: 230km/h (143.8mph) projected	
WEIGHT: not known	
MAX. AXLE LOAD: 13.5t (29,768lb) projected	
OVERALL LENGTH: not known	
GAUGE: 1435mm (4ft 8.5in)	

CLASS 360 'DESIRO' ELECTRIC MULTIPLE UNIT FIRST GREAT EASTERN (FGE) GREAT BRITAIN 2003

Siemens's 'Desiro' modular multiple units were ordered by several train operating companies in the UK between 2003 and 2006.

Built at Uerdingen, Germany, which had specialized in powered railcar production for almost a century by then, Desiro offers a varied

range of interior plans, door arrangements and traction type with the same basic body shell and frame. The trains for FGE (a

company now replaced in the Eastern region by 'One' Railways) are four-car electric units, seating 266 passengers, and equipped with air-conditioning, audio-visual passenger information system and CCTV. Unlike other Desiros ordered for British lines, they do not have end-gangways between units. Other Desiros ordered for, or operating in, the UK are AC electric Class 350 (2004), and DC electric classes 444 (2004) and 450 (2003). A diesel-hydraulic version, Class 185, also arrived in 2006. Bulgaria, Greece and Romania also operate Desiro units (diesel in the case of Greece), and in the United States, the San Diego North County Transit District ordered the diesel version for its 'Sprinter' line in 2006.

TYPE: electric multiple unit set
POWER: 1550kW (2108hp)
SUPPLY: 25kV 50HzAC
TRACTIVE EFFORT: not known
MAX. OPERATING SPEED: 160km/h (100mph)
TOTAL WEIGHT: 170t (374,785) in four-car set
LENGTH: drive car 23.71m (77.8ft); intermediate car 23.03m (75.5ft)
GAUGE: 1435mm (4ft 8.5in)

Much planning went into the interior arrangements to make the 'Desiro' passenger-friendly, including low door-sills, good vestibule spaces and seat placement related to windows.

CLASS BB-37000 BO-BO FRENCH NATIONAL RAILWAYS (SNCF) FRANCE 2004

In January 2001, Alstom further developed its PRIMA modular concept with what it described as 'the first trans-European locomotive', an engine that was inter-operable over most systems, either in electric or diesel-electric versions. Advanced IGBT (insulated gate bipolar transistor) technology was used to control power to the motors. The prime customer for the PRIMA range was SNCF, whose freight (*Fret*) division was

burdened with a stable of mostly elderly and under-powered diesel-electric and electric locomotives and which badly needed new motive power.

In the early 2000s, SNCF Fret ordered hundreds of locomotives from the PRIMA range, including 180 BB-27000 electric dual-voltage types, delivered between 2001 and 2005. In 2004, 60 of the 37000 class (often found prefixed with a '4' to indicate *Fret*) were ordered.

This is a tri-current machine of Bo-Bo configuration. Alstom unveiled a more powerful electric freight locomotive in 2004, the PRIMA6000, the number referring to its 4411kW (6000hp) power rating, capable of four-voltage working and handling heavy freights at 140km/h (87mph). Though evaluations are going on with SNCF and SNCB, the BB-37000 has not been put into line production.

TYPE: tri-current electric freight locomotive
POWER: 3088kW (4200hp)
SUPPLY: 25kV 50HzAC; 3000DC; 15kV 16.67HzAC
TRACTIVE EFFORT: 320kN (72,000lbf)
MAX. OPERATING SPEED: 140km/h (87mph)
WEIGHT: 72t (158,732lb)
MAX. AXLE LOAD: 18t (39,683lb)
OVERALL LENGTH: 14160mm (46.4ft)
GAUGE: 1435mm (4ft 8.5ins)

KTX HIGH-SPEED ELECTRIC TRAIN KORAIL

SOUTH KOREA 2004

South Korea joined the ranks of countries with a dedicated high-speed rail system from 30 March 2004, when its first such lines opened, the Gyeoungbu line between Seoul and Taegu (eventually on to Pusan), and the Honam line between Seoul, Gwangju and Mokpo. The Seoul–Pusan corridor accounts for two-thirds of the country's passenger rail traffic. French TGV technology was selected as the basis of the new lines, whose construction, as with the Japanese *Shinkansen*, has to take account of earthquake hazards. A novel feature of the power catenary is that the

overhead wire is slightly warmed to prevent the formation of ice. Forty-six trains were built for the initial services, 12 at Alstom's Belfort plant in France, the others in South Korea. They are formed of two power cars, two booster cars and 16 coaches, and both trains and traffic control installations incorporate the safety and efficiency features available in TGV technology. Up to 64 services can be operated daily between Seoul and Pusan, and with completion of the line in 2008, journey time will be reduced to 1hr, 56mins, compared to 4hrs, 20mins in the pre-high speed era. Further

extension of high-speed rail lines is planned in a national strategy that currently extends to 2015.

Having begun operations with French train technology, South Korea has also developed its own high-speed train, the product of nearly 10 years of research and development in a partnership between the train-builders Rotem (part of Hyundai Industries), who are also involved in Maglev train development, and the Korean Railroad Research Institute. From September 2003, trials have been carried out of a prototype known as the G7, or HSR (High-Speed Rail) 350x) train. This is designed

to run faster than the TGV of 2004, at 350km/h (217mph) as opposed to 300km/h (186mph), and like all trains designed to operate at this speed, it is at the forefront of technical development in materials use, braking and noise control. One of its interior features is reversible seating, since (unlike passengers elsewhere) many passengers complained about having to sit facing backwards on the KTX trains. Unlike the original trains, which have a fixed 20-car formation, the set-consist will be adjustable to allow for fluctuations in passenger usage. The G7 project has the disadvantage of lacking the many millions of miles of running experience gained by its Japanese, French, German and Italian rivals over the past 30 years, but it continues to receive government backing.

The specification is for the Alstom-designed KTX train.

TYPE: high-speed electric train
POWER: 13200kW (17,952hp)
SUPPLY: 25kV 50Hz AC from overhead catenary
TRACTIVE EFFORT: not known
MAX. OPERATING SPEED: 300km/h (186mph)
WEIGHT: 700t (689 tons)
MAX. AXLE LOAD: 17t (16.7 tons)
OVERALL LENGTH: 387m (1268ft 10in)
GAUGE: 1435mm ($ft 8.5in)

KTX, the 'Korean Train Express', established a world record by carrying over one million passengers in the first 14 days of service.

CLASS TER 2N NG ELECTRIC TWO-DECK MULTIPLE UNIT LUXEMBOURG RAILWAYS (CFL)

LUXEMBOURG 2004

Luxembourg's CFL are, in fact, very modest purchasers of these units compared to the SNCF. As often before, CFL's order for 12 was 'piggy-backed' with a French order for 85, with consequent cost benefits of volume production. The class designation indicates '*Transport Express Régional,* two-deck, new generation'. The TER concept, developed by SNCF since 1984, has revolutionized local and medium-distance transport in

France's operating regions, with new, comfortable, fast trains operating regular services.

The homogenizing of different signalling and automatic warning systems, and time-tabling collaboration between various national rail authorities, makes it possible for modern multiple-unit trains to move from system to system, to the much greater convenience of passengers, and TER units operate from Gouvy in

Belgium through Luxembourg to Metz in Eastern France.

Alstom and Bombardier shared the 2004 order, with delivery intended for completion by 2006. Three-car sets are classed ZZ4500 by the SNCF, while four and five-car sets are ZZ6500. Among the SNCF regions operating these sleek double-deck units are Nord Pas-de-Calais; Picardie; Provence–Alpes–Côte d'Azur; and Rhin–Rhône–Alpes.

TYPE: electric double-deck multiple unit
POWER: multi-voltage
OUTPUT: 1500kW (2040hp)
TRACTIVE EFFORT: not known
MAX. OPERATING SPEED: 140km/h (87mph)
WEIGHT: 124t (273,373lb)
LENGTH OF 3-CAR SET: 72.75m (238.7ft)
GAUGE: 1435mm (4ft 8.5in)

CLASS ALP 46 BO-BO NEW JERSEY TRANSIT (NJT)

USA 2004

New Jersey Transit operates the biggest state-wide integrated transport system in the United States, and this new electric locomotive class was ordered in

TYPE: Bo-Bo passenger dual-voltage electric locomotive
POWER: 5300kW (7100hp)
SUPPLY: 25kV 50HzAC or 12kV 25HzAC

TRACTIVE EFFORT: 316kN (71,000lb) on starting
MAX. OPERATING SPEED: 160km/h (100mph)

WEIGHT: 83t (182,983lb)
MAX. AXLE LOAD: 24.8t (54,674lb)
OVERALL LENGTH: 19.1m (62.6ft)
GAUGE: 1435mm (4ft 8.5in)

2001 as part of a continuing programme of expansion and service improvement to meet growing usage in this densely populated state. The ALP 46 passenger locomotive is based on the very successful Class 101 built for the German *Deutsche Bahn* (DB) by the same suppliers, Bombardier Group, at the former ADtranz works in Kassel, Germany. Intended to operate at speeds of up to 160km/h (100mph), it can haul trainloads of 12 single-level or 10 bi-level cars, with the rapid acceleration and smooth braking needed by high-intensity commuter services.

No. 4601 was first the of the ALP 46 locomotives, which cost $4.7 million each. They are capable of hauling 12 single-deck or 10 bi-level coaches at full speed.

'COMET' V ELECTRIC RAILCAR NEW JERSEY TRANSIT (NJT)   USA 2004

The 'Comet' series goes back to the 1970s, and it was primarily to replace time-expired 'Comet' I stock that these 200 units were ordered from Alstom in 2001 and delivered through 2003. The carbodies were built in Brazil with final assembly at Alstom's US plant. There are three interior

TYPE: electric railcar and trailer	**MAX. OPERATING SPEED:** 160km/h (100mph)	**MAX. AXLE LOAD:** 11.3t (24,912lb)
POWER: not known	**WEIGHT OF POWER CAR:** 45.3t	**OVERALL LENGTH OF CAR:** 25.9m (85ft)
SUPPLY: 25kV 50HzAC or 12kV 25HzAC	(100,000lb)	**GAUGE:** 1435mm (4ft 8.5in)
TRACTIVE EFFORT: not known		

configurations, with the power car having 109 seats, the trailer 117 and the trailer with 'rest room' 111

seats. Though the ride quality and quietness of these units have been praised, fault has been found with

some aspects of the interior fittings. Future sets for the NJT system will be bi-level.

ES 44 'EVOLUTION' SERIES VARIOUS US AND CANADIAN RAILROADS   USA 2004

The 'Evolution' name is given by General Electric (GE) to a new generation of diesel-electric locomotives, which is being produced after six years of

preliminary work to achieve new standards of efficiency and economy while also conforming to, or exceeding, federal and state requirements on pollution levels.

The response and customer take-up have been very positive, and the 1000th 'ES' locomotive rolled off the assembly lines only 17 months after series building had

A pair of ES 44 locomotives power a two-decked Union Pacific container freight through the Feather River Canyon in California, on 13 July 2005.

begun. At the heart is the new GEVO 12-cylinder diesel engine, which produces the same power level of 3278kW (4400hp) as its larger 16-cylinder predecessor, while using less fuel. Its emission level is 40 per cent lower than those of pre-ES diesel locomotives and conforms to US Environment Protection Agency standards set for 2007 and beyond.

Three different models are currently in production. ES40DC replaces the former Dash 9-40CW, and is supplied to Norfolk

TYPE: diesel-electric Co-Co freight locomotive
POWER: GEVO 12-cylinder diesel engine producing 3278kw (4400hp)
TRACTIVE EFFORT: 737kN (166,000lbf)

MAX OPERATING SPEED: 120km/h (75mph)
WEIGHT: 188t (415,000lb)
OVERALL LENGTH: 22.403m (73ft 6in)
GAUGE: 1435mm (4ft 8.5in)

Southern's specification with a slightly lower power rating of 2980kW (4000hp) compared to the standard ES mode. ES44DC, with direct-current transmission, replaces the former Dash 9-44CW, and is being delivered through 2005 and 2006 to several

railroads, including BNSF, CSX Transportation and Canadian National. ES44AC, with alternating-current transmission, replaces the AC440CW locomotive, and is on order in 2006 from Union Pacific, Canadian Pacific and Kansas City Southern.

All three types are freight locomotives, though a passenger-hauling version is in process of being designed.

Similar in appearance to their predecessors, the ES models feature a few profile changes that relate primarily to the shorter engine space and a larger radiator section forming part of a new and effective cooling system; and detail changes to the outline reflect this, including the 'hump' at the front end to accommodate a larger intercooler.

'PENDOLINO' HIGH-SPEED ELECTRIC TRAIN FINNISH STATE RAILWAYS (VR)   FINLAND 2005

In September 2005, 18 new trainsets began operation on VR, a major development in Finland's high-speed services, which began with its first introduction of 'Pendolino' tilting trains in 1995. As in Sweden, the tilting-train concept has enabled a considerable speeding-up of express services without the requirement to build new lines.

The Finnish Pendolinos have a maximum speed of 220km/h (137mph). Built in Italy by Alstom-Ferroviaria, they use the Ferroviaria tilting bogie. Business travellers especially are being wooed by these trains, which feature a 'meeting-room', enabling small conferences to take place even in transit. Standard features for passengers include an in-train

TYPE: high-speed electric tilting train
SUPPLY: 25kV 50HzAC from overhead wire
POWER: 4000kW (5440hp)
MAX. OPERATING SPEED: 220km/h (137mph)

WEIGHT: 328t (723,116lb)
MAX. AXLE LOAD: 14.3t (31,526lb)
LENGTH: 159m (521.7ft)
GAUGE: 1524mm (5ft)

entertainment system, laptop plugs, and an Italian-style buffet car. Current routes include

Helsinki–Tampere, Helsinki–Oulu, Helsinki–Turku, Helsinki–Joensuu, and in 2007 Helsinki–Kajaani.

CLASS P160DE BO-BO GERMAN RAILWAYS (DB)   GERMANY 2005

Eleven diesel-electrics of Bombardier's TRAXX family, designated as P160DE, have been ordered for 2007 by DB to work push-pull trains on the *Niederelbebahn* (Lower Elbe line) running between Hamburg and Cuxhaven. These locomotives, which share around 75 per cent of

parts with their all-electric sisters of P160AC2 (nine have also been ordered by DB for 2007, as Class 146.19), will operate at speeds of up to 160km/h (100mph). Water-cooled IGBT (insulated gate bipolar transistor) converters transmit drive to asynchronous motors on all four axles.

TYPE: diesel-electric Bo-Bo passenger locomotive
POWER: 2200kW (2992hp)
TRACTIVE EFFORT (STARTING): 270kN (60,750lbf)

MAX. OPERATING SPEED: 160kph (100mph)
WEIGHT: 82t (180,779lb)
MAX. AXLE LOAD: 20.5t (45,194lb)
OVERALL LENGTH: 18.9m (62ft)
GAUGE: 1435mm (4ft 8.5in)

AVE S-103 HIGH-SPEED ELECTRIC TRAIN SPANISH RAILWAYS (RENFE)   SPAIN 2005

Based like Germany's ICE-3 on the 'Velaro' concept elaborated by Siemens, these trains are being built for the new Madrid–Barcelona high-speed line that will form a major new arm in the extension of Spain's growing ultra-fast rail system. This began with the Madrid–Sevilla line in 1992, which has proved very successful. Designated *Velaro E* by the makers, the first trains were

delivered for testing in July 2005. Twenty-six have been ordered. When running on the completed line, they will reach a maximum speed of 350km/h (217mph). All are fitted with inter-operable European Train Control Level 2 equipment, and variable-gauge axles, and the ultimate intention is that these trains will also run from Barcelona northwards into France.

Trains of similar type have been ordered from Siemens by Russia

('Velaro Rus') and China, for the high-speed Beijing–Tinjian line.

TYPE: high-speed electric train
UIC CLASSIFICATION: Bo Bo+2-2+Bo-Bo+2-2+2-2+Bo-Bo+2-2+Bo-Bo
POWER: 25kV 50HzAC, developing 8800kW (11,968hp)
TRACTIVE EFFORT: 283kN (63,675lbf)

MAX. OPERATING SPEED: 350km/h (217mph)
TOTAL WEIGHT: 425t (936,964lb)
MAX. AXLE LOAD: 15t (33,069lb)
OVERALL LENGTH: 200m (656.2ft)
GAUGE: 1435mm (4ft 8.5in)

'GREEN GOAT' BO-BO BURLINGTON NORTHERN & SANTA FE RAILROAD (BNSF)   USA 2005

Railpower Technologies of Vancouver, Canada, are developing a range of 'hybrid' locomotives that use a small diesel engine to charge a set of lead-acid batteries which provide the driving power. The locomotives are technically 'rebuilds', using the reconditioned frame of a GP9 or similar switcher type, but with a lower hood than the conventional diesel-electric.

TYPE: Bo-Bo energy-storage 'hybrid' switching locomotive
POWER: diesel engine of 250-500kW (340-680hp) output range
Electric storage: 310 VRLA lead-battery

cells; 700VDC nominal, 1.200 amp-hour
TRACTIVE EFFORT: 88.8kN (20,000lbf) starting; 219kN (49,300lbf) continuous, at 12.8mph
MAX. OPERATING SPEED: 96.5km/h (60mph)

WEIGHT: approx 125t (275,000lb)
MAX. AXLE LOAD: variable
OVERALL LENGTH: dependent on original frame
GAUGE: 1435mm (4ft 8.5in)

The diesel engine, mounted at the opposite end from the cab, is a six-cylinder Caterpillar C9 8.8l (537ci) in-line, compliant with the US Environment Protection

Agency's Tier II requirements, and operating only when the batteries need re-charging; thus it does not 'idle' as many diesel engines are allowed to do. In fact,

it is estimated to emit 80–90 per cent less NOx and particulate emissions than a diesel engine in a locomotive of comparable power, as well as achieving fuel

savings of the order of 40–60 per cent. The micro-processor controls of the GG are entirely up-to-date. Users so far include the US Army as well as BNSF, who have ordered four cabless units for use in Texas. These are controlled remotely from the lineside by a portable RC system.

Railpower's 'ultra-clean' hybrid loco also offers a capital saving of over 30 per cent compared with a new switcher. Most switchers in the United States are now about 30 years old.

CLASS 3800 BO-BO-BO QUEENSLAND RAIL (QR)

AUSTRALIA 2006

QR's 1067mm (3ft 6in) gauge vies with South Africa's Spoornet in its operation of immensely long and heavy coal trains with powerful electric locomotives. Its coal haulage capacity is planned to increase from 157 million tonnes (154 million tons) in 2005 to 250 million tonnes (246 million tons) by 2010. To achieve this, while at the same time reducing cost-per-tonne, locomotives of exceptional

power and efficiency are required. In 2005, QR began a programme of upgrading the Class 3200 of 1986 vintage as Class 3700. In addition, 20 completely new locomotives of Class 3800 were ordered in 2006 from Siemens, which is also doing the upgrades. These are being built in Munich for delivery in 2008. All Class 3700s and 3800s will be equipped with Locotrol remote management, so that a single driver can control

TYPE: Bo-Bo-Bo heavy haulage electric locomotive
POWER: 4000kW (5440hp)
SUPPLY: 25kV 50HZAC from overhead wire
TRACTIVE EFFORT: 525kN (118,125lbf) starting; 450kN (101,250lbf) continuous

MAX. OPERATING SPEED: 80km/h (50mph)
WEIGHT: 132t (291,010lb)
MAX. AXLE LOAD: 22t (48.501lb)
OVERALL LENGTH: not known
GAUGE: 1067mm (3ft 6in)

helper and banking locomotives. The state-of-the-art bogies are designed and built at Siemens' specialist bogie plant in Graz,

Austria. Regenerating and rheostatic brakes are fitted, each with a maximum braking power of 4000kW (5440hp).

CLASS BB-75000 BO-BO FRENCH NATIONAL RAILWAYS (SNCF)

FRANCE 2006

Four hundred of this diesel-electric type were ordered by SNCF's *Fret* division in 1995, as part of the drive to modernize and speed up its operations. The first two to be delivered appeared in 2006, directed to Longueau depot in the north-east, where they will work on trains of up to 1400

tonnes (1378 tons). One of the Alstom PRIMA range, it is being built at Belfort by Alstom with Siemens electrical equipment.

TYPE: diesel-electric freight locomotive
POWER: 1600kW (2176hp) from MTU16V engine

TRACTIVE EFFORT: 250kN (58,500lbf)
MAX. OPERATING SPEED: 120kmh (75mph)
WEIGHT: 84t (185,188lb)

MAX. AXLE LOAD: 21t (46,297lb)
OVERALL LENGTH: 20.28m (66.3ft)
GAUGE: 1435mm (4ft 8.5in)

Technically up-to-date in every respect, its asynchronous three-phase motors have IGBT controlled drive, and it can

operate cross-border in Belgium's SNCB system.

VOITH MAXIMA 40CC C-C PROTOTYPE FREIGHT LOCOMOTIVE

GERMANY 2006

Much freight still runs on non-electrified lines, and multi-voltage electric locomotives are very expensive. Consequently, the principal European manufacturers have targeted the freight market, especially the heavy haulage end. Voith is a company that has always been associated with hydraulic power transmission, but the 40CC project marks a new departure. The Voith Maxima 40CC is being assembled at the former MaK works in Kiel, though many components originate in the company's factory in Heidenheim. The locomotive is designed to hold a 12- or 16-cylinder diesel engine, with a nominal rating of 3600kW (4896hp), and the power plant in the prototype is a 16V DZC engine from Belgian supplier

TYPE: diesel-hydraulic C-C freight locomotive
POWER: 3600kW (4896hp)
TRACTIVE EFFORT: 408kN (91,800lbf) on starting

MAX. OPERATING SPEED: 120km/h (75mph)
WEIGHT: 135t (297,624lb)
MAX. AXLE LOAD: not known
OVERALL LENGTH: 23.2m (76ft)
GAUGE: 1435mm (4ft 8.5in)

ABC. The engine drives through a Voith LS640reU2 split transmission able to supply each bogie independently; the bogies also have independent wheelspin and wheelslide controls. Derived from the LS620reU2 fitted to the MaK2000 locomotives built by Vossloh, the LS640reU2 transmission is linked through a Küsel universal joint shaft coupling and cardan shafts to the SK-720 final drives. Hydrodynamic brakes provide up

to 2·5MW of continuous braking power through two KBD385 retarders. Multiple-unit controls are fitted, and the cabs are air-conditioned. The prototype is fitted with the German Indusi PZB90 automatic warning system and is equipped to accept the European Train Control System (ETCS). Other features include GSM remote diagnosis, and options include exhaust gas after-treatment and broad gauge bogies. All current TSI emission

requirements are met. The bodyshell is a self-supporting, torsionally stiff structure with crashworthy cabs meeting the requirements of EN15227. Removable roof panels offer good access to equipment for maintenance. Bogies with Flexicoil secondary suspension are designed for low wear and tear on the track and have low-level traction linkages.

The 40CC is designed to haul a 2000-tonne (1968-ton) freight train up a 1 per cent grade at 60km/h (37mph), although eventually there will also be a passenger train version able to provide hotel power for passenger cars and capable of 160km/h (100mph), or more likely a higher speed.

The maker's model indicates the locomotive's home town of Kiel. Its 7000l (1849 US gal) tanks give it a range of 2000km (1240 miles).

VOSSLOH EURO 4000 CO-CO PROTOTYPE FREIGHT LOCOMOTIVE

Having acquired the former Alstom works at Albuixech, near Valencia, Spain, Vossloh set about developing a heavy freight diesel-electric capable of operating on virtually any European or similar system. A partnership established between Vossloh and US locomotive builders Electro-Motive Diesel (the former General Motors Electro-Motive Division, sold by

Prototypes of the Spanish-built 'Euro 4000' have been tested in Spain since 2005. Orders for line production include 18 from Angel Trains.

GM to Greenbriar Equity Corp and Berkshire Partners in May 2005) puts an EMD 16-cylinder 710G3B two-stroke turbocharged engine with electronic fuel injection into the Euro 4000. EMD had previously announced its own plan to build for the booming European freight market. The power plant has a DIN rating of 3165kW (4300hp) and drives an AR20 main generator with AC/DC transmission. The six D43 nose-suspended traction motors give a maximum speed of 120km/h

TYPE: diesel-electric Co-Co freight locomotive	
POWER: 3178kW (4322hp) at 900rpm	

TRACTIVE EFFORT: 400kN (90,000lbf) on starting	
MAX. OPERATING SPEED: 120km/h (75mph)	

WEIGHT: 123t (271,168lb)	
MAX. AXLE LOAD: not known	
OVERALL LENGTH: 23.02m (75.5ft)	
GAUGE: 1435mm (4ft 8.5in)	

(75mph). Bogies have fabricated steel frames with coil-spring primary and rubber-metal secondary suspension. Hollow axles are used and there is one brake disc per axle. Vertical, horizontal and yaw dampers are fitted. The locomotive is TSI-compliant, meeting all norms for

exhaust emissions, noise crashworthiness and fire-resistance. Exhaust emissions remain below the levels stipulated by Directive 97/68/EC Stage 3A, which takes effect for locomotives in January 2009. Air-conditioned cabs were designed to meet DIN5566, EM12663 and

UIC651 standards, and the driver's desk and other equipment are prepared for ETCS. A GSM data transmission system can be fitted, and GPS location equipment is provided. This locomotive is a powerful challenger for a multi-billion euro market.

CLASS 19E BO-BO SPOORNET

SOUTH AFRICA 2006

Spoornet's Coal-Line division has ordered 110 new heavy-haul electrics from Mitsui African Rail Solutions (MARS) for service on the Ermelo–Richards Bay line. Due for delivery in 2008–11, they will enable a large number of older locomotive types to be 'cascaded' to general freight work. The Class 19E will be

assembled at South Africa's Union Carriage Works. They will be dual voltage AC/DC to cope with the voltage change on the line, which previously necessitated a locomotive change. Driven by the Toshiba General Packet Radio System (GPRS) system, they will have touch-screen diagnostics and control, and 'black box'

TYPE: Bo-Bo heavy haulage dual-voltage electric locomotive	
POWER: not known	
SUPPLY: 5000V DC/25,000V 50Hz AC	
TRACTIVE EFFORT: not known	

MAX. OPERATING SPEED: not known	
WEIGHT: 100t (220,462lb)	
MAX. AXLE LOAD: 25t (55,115lb)	
OVERALL LENGTH: not known	
GAUGE: 1067mm (3ft 6in)	

technology will be fitted. Able to pull 300-wagon trains rather than the present 200-wagon maximum,

the Class 19E will have a dramatic impact on the cost and efficiency of the service.

L-9202 VARIABLE-GAUGE BO-BO TALGO-TEAM

SPAIN 2006

Spain's railways were originally built to 1676mm (5ft 6in) gauge, but its new high-speed railways, ultimately to extend to 4500km (2796 miles) or more, have been laid to the European standard of 1435mm (4ft 8.5in). The Spanish railways have used variable-gauge transfer technology

since the 1960s, enabling passenger coaches to move between standard and Spanish gauge by automatic adjustment of axle-widths between the wheels. Two systems are in existence, developed by Talgo and CAF respectively. With the introduction of the high-speed tracks, the need for trains to run from one gauge to the other within Spain, as well as at the border with France, became imperative, and a means had to be found of making powered axles capable of gauge variation. Krauss-Maffei in Germany developed a variable-gauge traction bogie in 1999 to fit the power car of a prototype Class 355 Talgo XXI set, and in 2005 RENFE placed an order with Talgo and Bombardier for 18 high-speed trains equipped

with variable-gauge axles, and 10 power units to pull variable-gauge Talgo coaches, all for delivery in 2007–09. In addition, a prototype high-speed variable-gauge locomotive, using all-Spanish technology, has been developed in a joint venture by Talgo and Grupo Ingeteam, known as TEAM, with support from the Spanish government. Named *Virgen del Bueno Camino*, it is a dual-voltage powered machine, of modular design, with a traction system of two converters, using insulated gate bipolar transistor (IGBT) technology to drive four asynchronous motors. Built in modular style, it is expected by its designers to be the pioneer of a production class able to haul trains on the high-speed lines at 260km/h

(143mph) and to move non-stop onto conventional broad-gauge lines, to run at the allowed speed. It can include sleeping car trains and other non multiple-unit stock. The system clearly has potential for use elsewhere, such as the break-of-gauge that occurs between Eastern Europe and Russia.

TYPE: Bo-Bo variable gauge high-speed electric locomotive	
SUPPLY: 5kVDC or 25kV 50HzAC, from overhead wire	
POWER: 3200kW (4352hp) on 5kVDC; 3600kW (3299hp) on 24kVAC.	
TRACTIVE EFFORT: 160Kn (36,000lbf)	
MAX. OPERATING SPEED: 260km/h (143mph)	
WEIGHT: 72t (158,732lb)	
MAX. AXLE LOAD: 18t (39,683lb)	
OVERALL LENGTH: 19.4m (63.6ft)	
GAUGE: 1676mm (5ft 6in) and 1435mm (4ft 8.5in)	

The first locomotive with automatic gauge variation, it is classed by RENFE as 253.001. Front and side views show it in Talgo paintwork.

The roof equipment is shielded for high-speed running. The dual-voltage traction system consists of two converters, designed to operate at 3000V DC and 25kV AC and based on the latest-generation IGBTs (insulated gate bipolar transistors), controlling four asynchronous motors.

TEP 150 CO-CO LUGANSKTEPLOVOZ

UKRAINE 2006

Lugansk's prototype heavy diesel-electric locomotive, unveiled in 2006, is a descendant of the former Class 132 of the *Deutsche Reichsbahn* in the former GDR, still running as DB Class 232 with Railion. It is a thoroughly up-to-date, two-cab machine, with AC or DC transmission systems available, and gas-turbine supercharging system for its 16-cylinder 4-stroke diesel engine.

As a passenger train locomotive, the TEP 150 has an auxiliary generator, synchronous with the traction generator, for train heating and air-conditioning power. Electro-dynamic and automatic-pneumatic braking systems are fitted.

TYPE: diesel-electric Co-Co locomotive
POWER: 5D49 16-cylinder engine producing 3100kW (4216hp)
TRACTIVE EFFORT: 167kN (37575lbf) continuous
MAX. OPERATING SPEED: 160km/h (100mph)

WEIGHT: not known
MAX. AXLE LOAD: not known
OVERALL LENGTH: not known
GAUGE: 1524mm (5ft) or 1435mm (4ft 8.5in)

EMD SD70 M-2 CO-CO FLORIDA EAST COAST RAILROAD (FEC)

USA 2006

In its first new diesel-electric locomotive purchase for 20 years, FEC opted for four of the SD70 M-2. This new DC-transmission model, introduced in 2005, with its sister-type SD70ACe, represents Electro-Motive Diesel's 'new generation' of locomotives built to meet the EPA's Tier II requirements (which are operative from January 2005), as well as incorporating new standards of efficiency in other respects.

TYPE: Co-Co heavy freight diesel-electric locomotives
POWER: 16-710 G3TC-T2 engine developing 3161kW (4300hp)

TRACTIVE EFFORT: M-2: 724kN (163,000lbf) starting; ACe: 849kN (191,000lbf) starting
MAX. OPERATING SPEED: variable

WEIGHT: 188t (414,469lb)
MAX. AXLE LOAD: 31.3t (47,619lb)
OVERALL LENGTH: 21.6m (74ft)
GAUGE: 1435mm (4ft 8.5in)

Among these are the HTSC bolsterless truck, which is capable of running 1,609,000km (1,000,000 miles) between overhauls. Both types use the 16-cylinder 710G3TC-T2 engine. By EMD's own estimation, three of the M-2s can replace the work-load of four SD40-2 locomotives, and three of the ACe, with its higher tractive effort, can replace five SD40-2 locomotives in high-traction applications. Among other owners of the SD70M-2 are Norfolk Southern and Canadian National, while the SD70ACe can be seen on the tracks of BNSF, CSX, Kansas City Southern and Union Pacific, among others.

A lone youngster admires the Norfolk Southern's latest acquisition, a 'new generation' SD70 M-2, No. 2667, at Cassandra, PA, on 23 June 2006.

GLOSSARY

'A' and 'B' units: A linked pair of diesel or electric locomotives, in which only the first, 'A', has a driving cab. This is sometimes referred to as a 'cow and calf' unit. Some are A-B-A, three units with a driving cab in each 'A' locomotive.

AC: Alternating current; an electric current that reverses its direction flow at regular intervals, known as cycles.

ACFI: Acronym of the Société Auxiliaire des Chemins de Fer et de l'Industrie, a French manufacturer of auxiliary equipment, especially feed-water heaters.

Adhesion: The ability of loco-motive driving wheels to turn without slipping on the rails.

Adhesion factor: The ratio of the locomotive's tractive effort to its adhesive weight.

Adhesive weight: The proportion of a locomotive's or power car's weight resting on the driving wheels.

Adriatic: A name sometimes applied to a 2-6-4 locomotive.

Anti-vacuum valve: Also known as a snifting valve; it introduces air into the steam passages when a locomotive's steam is shut off. The valve prevents a partial vacuum forming, which would otherwise suck ash from the smoke-box into the steam passages.

Atlantic: A 4-4-2 locomotive (see Wheel Arrangement), so called from the Atlantic Coast Line of the United States, which first built them.

AVE: The Spanish high-speed rail link which runs between Madrid and Sevila.

Axle load: The weight placed on the track by a pair of wheels with an axle between them. Maximum axle load is that of the wheels supporting the greatest individual weight.

Backhead: The rear end of a boiler, on which are mounted the controls of a steam locomotive. Also known as Backplate.

Baltic: A locomotive consisting of 4-6-4 wheel arrangement; also known as a Hudson in the United States.

Banker: An additional engine used to help push a train up a gradient, or 'bank'. Also known as a Pusher, or Helper.

Nineteenth-century design: *Lion*, the world's oldest working locomotive (1838).

Bar frame: A structure of joined bars of iron or steel, supporting a locomotive boiler, typical of American and German practice.

Bearing: The point at which a turning axle or other turning part meets the supporting frame or part.

Berkshire: A locomotive of 2-8-4 wheel arrangement, named after the Berkshire Mountains in the United States.

Beyer Garratt: A Garratt articulated locomotive built by the firm of Beyer Peacock.

Bissell truck: A single axle for the leading carrying wheels which could pivot and thus lead the engine into a curve. It was patented by the US inventor Levi Bissell in 1858.

Blinkers: The British name for the smoke deflectors that are fitted to the side of the firebox or the chimney.

Blower: A steam vent which is fitted to the blast-pipe and controlled by the driver, and which creates a draught when the engine is stationary and no exhaust draught is available. The blower's function is to keep the fire hot and to prevent a 'blow-back' of steam into the firebox.

Bogie: A wheeled undercarriage for an engine or railway vehicle. It is attached to a pivot or slide which allows it to turn or move sideways independently.

Boiler: The long metal barrel, filled with tubes for water, steam and fire exhaust, in which steam is generated by means of the firebox situated at one end.

Boiler pressure: The maximum pressure, expressed in pounds per square inch (psi), or kilograms per square centimetre (kg/cm2), of steam within the boiler before the safety valve opens to release excessive pressure.

Bonnet unit: A diesel or electric locomotive which has a bonnet end which protrudes below the level of the windscreen.

Booster: An auxiliary engine fitted to a steam locomotive's trailing wheels (or sometimes to the tender wheels). A booster can be used to provide extra tractive power on starting or on severe grades. It is used only at low speeds.

Boxpok: A type of wheel cast as a solid block with a pattern of holes, rather than spokes.

Brick arch: An arch of fire-resistant brick built across a firebox, deflecting the path of gases and thus securing more adequate heating work, as well as providing the opportunity for the admixture of supplementary air supply.

Twenty-first century design: tilting technology allows trains to maintain high speeds on a curving track.

Brotan boiler: A boiler with a firebox lined with water-tubes; developed by Johann Brotan on the Austrian Imperial Railways.

Büchli drive: A type of electric power transmission developed by Brown Boveri, in Switzerland, providing direct drive to the wheels while enabling them to move vertically and horizontally.

Buffer beam: The metal plate found across the front end of the frame, to which the buffers are fitted.

Buffers: The spring-loaded shock absorbers which are fitted to each end of a locomotive in the United Kingdom and in various other countries.

Cab forward: A locomotive with a cab at the front end only.

Cab unit: A diesel locomotive in which the cab sides extend to the outside of the frame, with no external walkway.

Between 1951 and 1955 Czech Railways built the powerful Class 477 4-8-4T passenger trains.

Camelback: A steam locomotive with the driving cab placed over the boiler.

Caprotti valve gear: A patent valve gear developed by the Italian engineer Arturo Caprotti, driven by a rotating shaft rather than by rods and levers, and normally operating poppet valves.

Cardan shaft: A driving shaft with a universal coupling at one or both ends.

Carrying wheels: The non-coupled or non-powered wheels of a locomotive.

A Danish Railways Class ME Co-Co diesel-electric of 1981. This was the first DSB diesel class to have AC traction.

Catenary: The structure of poles and wires which are used to supply electric power to electrified trains.

Clack valve: A one-way valve, used for admitting water to a locomotive boiler.

Clerestory: A raised central roof section which as small vertical windows or ventilators at the sides.

Compound expansion: The use of steam first in high-pressure, then in low-pressure cylinders before it is ejected through the chimney.

Conjugated valve gear: The operation of a three-cylinder locomotive using only two external sets of valve gear; conjugated levers set ahead of the cylinders actuate the middle piston's valve.

Connecting rod: The rod joining the piston rod to the driving axle crank, via the cross-head.

Consolidation: A locomotive of 2-8-0 wheel arrangement.

Counterpressure brake: A means of supplementing the wheel brakes on a steam locomotive, by bringing the engine into midgear and then reverse, the cylinders then acting as compressors and absorbing power from the driving wheels (the Riggenbach system). The Le Chatelier system allowed for the admission of very hot water to the cylinders, which then vaporized under pressure.

Coupled wheels: Engine wheels which are joined by coupling rods.

Crank: An arm attached at right angles to an axle or rotating spindle, to which a rod may be joined.

Cross-compound: A two-cylinder compound arrangement; high-pressure on one side, low-pressure on the other.

Crosshead: The linking piece between the piston and the connecting rod; it slides backwards and forwards while held in place vertically by a guide bar or bars.

Crown sheet: the top of the firebox in a steam boiler. Although the whole of the back end of the boiler is referred to as the firebox, in fact there is a space between the crown sheet and the boiler top, in which much of the locomotive's steam is generated.

Cut-off: A term used to express the amount of steam admitted to the cylinder, in relation to the position of the piston. Steam supply can be cut off, by adjustment of the valve gear, when the piston has travelled a certain distance. Cut-off is expressed as a proportion of the piston's travel. On starting, maximum cut-off is applied, with steam admitted for around 75 per cent of the piston stroke. In full forward motion, cut-off may be reduced to around 15 per cent. The degree to which cut-off can be altered and the fineness of gradation depend on the type of valves and valve gear utilized.

Cylinder: The part of the engine where the drive is generated: a solidly cast metal unit bored out to a set diameter. Inside the cylinder, the power of steam or combustion is converted into motion by pushing the piston. This power can be measured as indicated horsepower.

Dabeg: A French producer of locomotive components, including feed-water heaters and valve gear.

DC: Direct current; an electric current that flows continuously in a single direction.

Decapod: A locomotive with 10 coupled wheels; the name is usually used for a 2-10-0.

Diesel-electric: A diesel-powered locomotive or power car that transmits its power to electric motors.

Diesel-hydraulic: A diesel-powered locomotive that transmits its power to the wheels by means of a hydraulic system.

Diesel-mechanical: A diesel-powered locomotive that transmits its power to the wheels by a direct mechanical method.

dmu: Diesel multiple unit; a set of carriages of which two or more are motor-driven, with a driving position at each end of the set.

Dome: A feature of most but not all steam locomotives, normally to provide a location for steam collection well above the boiler water-level, and where the steam is admitted through a valve (controlled by the regulator handle in the driving cab) into the main steam pipe.

Double chimney: A locomotive chimney with two exhaust blast-pipes inside.

A pair of *Deutsche Bundesbahn* Class 181 dual-current locomotives.

Gauge: The width between the rails. Standard gauge is 1435mm (56.5in). Narrow-gauge lines are less than this; broad-gauge lines are wider.

GEC: Acronym for General Electric Company, a US manufacturer of electric motors and locomotives.

Double heading: The use of two engines to pull a train.

Down: The direction leading away from the major terminus of a railway, hence 'down line', 'down train', etc.

Drawbar: The part of a locomotive's frame to which the draw-hook is attached. The horsepower exerted at the drawbar is an important means of assessing a locomotive's performance.

Drawgear: Also known as draftgear; the drawhook and the shock-absorbing, load-bearing attachments which prevent it being jerked severely.

Driving car: The front (or rear) car of a multiple-unit set, with a driving position. It is not necessarily a power car.

Driving wheels: Engine wheels driven directly from the cylinders of a steam engine or the motors of diesel and electric engines. Often used to refer to coupled wheels.

Dynamic braking: In a diesel-mechanical or diesel-hydraulic locomotive, the use of the engine compression or torque convertor to slow the train, and so to save subsequent wear on the wheel-brakes.

Eccentric: A mechanism for converting rotary motion into reciprocal motion, widely used on internally fitted valve gears, like Stephenson's link motion.

EMD: The Electromotive Division of General Motors, formed to construct diesel-electric locomotives.

EMU: Electric multiple unit; a set of carriages of which two or more are powered by electric motors taking power from an outside supply, with a driving position at each end.

Feed-water: The water supplied to the boiler for conversion into steam.

Feed-water heater: Preheating the feed-water speeded up the steam-generation process. As a result, there were numerous patent systems used by locomotive builders.

Footplate: The floor level of an engine's driving cab.

Frame: The structural bed of a locomotive, resting on the axles. It may be inside the wheels or outside them, or, in the case of a double frame, with the wheels placed in between.

Franco-Crosti boiler: A boiler with a large drum or drums attached or incorporated, in which exhaust gases, drawn backwards from the cylinders, preheat the feed-water. It was developed by the Italian engineers Attilio Franco and Piero Crosti.

Garratt locomotive: An articulated locomotive in which the boiler is mounted on a frame under which two engine units are pivoted.

Giesl ejector: A form of blast system and chimney which was devised in 1951 by the Austrian engineer Dr A. Giesl-Gieslingen.

Grate area: The surface space of the firebox floor in a steam locomotive.

Hammer blow: The force exerted by the thrust of a connecting rod on the crank; it is transmitted to the rail by the turning of the driving wheel.

Headcode: An arrangement of lamps, discs, letters and numbers, or other items, on the front of a locomotive, normally indicating the type of train or the route to be followed.

Heating surface: The combined surface area of the firebox and the boiler tubes.

Helper engine: See Banker.

Hood unit: A diesel or electric locomotive with walkways alongside the 'hood' covering the power unit, as well as a full-width driving cab.

HST: High Speed Train, the British 200km/h (125mph) set.

Hudson: A locomotive of 4-6-4 wheel arrangement.

ICE: Inter-City Express, a service operated by the *Deutsche Bundesbahn*.

Injector: Invented by the French engineer Henri Giffard in 1859, this device forces water from the tank into a steam boiler; it can be driven by live steam or by exhaust steam that has already passed through the cylinders.

Inside bearings: Wheel bearings fitted on the axle on the inner side of the wheel.

Inside cylinders: Cylinders which are fitted within a locomotive's frame.

Kylchap chimney: A widely used patent steam exhaust system developed by the Finnish engineer Kylälä and the French Chapelon, between 1919 and 1926.

Lap: In steam locomotives, an expression defining the length of a valve face and the extent to which it overlaps the edges of the admission ports when in midposition.

Lead: In steam locomotives, a term defining the extent to which the valve is open to steam admission when the piston has reached the end of its stroke.

Lenz valve gear: A form of valve gear which uses an oscillating cam shaft and poppet valves; it was developed by the Austrian engineer Dr Hugo Lenz.

Marc Seguin's bellows-assisted 1829 locomotive was the second to be fitted with a tubular boiler.

Britain's first 'Pacific' type, the Great Western Railway's *The Great Bear*, built at Swindon Works in 1905.

Limited: Used of trains, it means an express with limited accommodation, which should be booked in advance.

Loading gauge: The limits of height and width imposed by fixtures of a railway track, e.g. platforms, bridges, tunnels.

Mechanical stoker: A power-operated system for feeding coal into a locomotive firebox; a mechanical stoker is usually a revolving spiral within a large-diameter steel tube.

Mikado: A locomotive of 2-8-2 wheel arrangement.

Mixed traffic: Designation of a locomotive designed for both passenger and freight work.

Mixed train: A train with both passenger and goods vehicles.

Mogul: A locomotive of 2-6-0 wheel arrangement.

Monomotor bogie: A bogie which is driven by a single electric motor.

Mother Hubbard: A name for 'Camelback' locomotives.

Motion: The system of rods and cranks that operates the valve gear.

Mountain: A locomotive of 4-8-2 wheel arrangement; these locomotives are known as 'Mohawks' on the New York Central Railroad.

Multiple-unit: Two or more locomotives or power units operated in combination by a single driver.

Non-adhesive weight: The proportion of a locomotive's or power car's weight that is supported by its carrying (non-driving) wheels.

Northern: A locomotive of 4-8-4 wheel arrangement.

Outside bearings: Wheel bearings attached to the frame on the outer side of the wheel.

Outside frame: A locomotive frame whose edges are outside the wheels.

Pacific: A locomotive of 4-6-2 wheel arrangement.

Pannier tank: A tank engine whose tanks are attached to the upper flanks of the boiler side.

Pantograph: The extendable overhead power collector which is mounted on the roof of an electric locomotive or power car.

Pendelzug: A shuttle train, in Germany and Switzerland.

Pilot: American term for the cow-catcher.

Pilot engine: The front engine of a double-headed steam-hauled train.

Piston valve: A device which is used for controlling the admission and exhaust of steam to and from a cylinder. The piston valve is normally formed from two short pistons attached to a rod, the movement of which is operated by the engine's valve gear.

Plate frame: A locomotive frame made of riveted steel plates, typical of British construction.

Pony wheels: A single set of trailing wheels which is set behind the coupled wheels, as in a 4-4-2.

Poppet valves: Spring-mounted valves which are derived from those used in internal combustion engines, often vertically set.

The 'Kolibri' electric multiple unit set, SBB type RBDe 560, introduced in 1987, can be seen on regional services all over Switzerland.

Power car: In a multiple-unit train, the power car is the car, or one of the cars, in which the motors are fitted.

Power classification: A notation system which is used to grade the power of locomotives.

Prairie: A locomotive of 2-6-2 wheel arrangement.

Prime mover: In a diesel-electric locomotive, the prime mover is the diesel engine, which provides the initial source of motive power.

Priming: In a steam locomotive, priming is the siphoning of water into the steam collection pipe, with consequent deleterious effect on steaming capacity and also possible damage. This is often caused by impurities or chemicals which result in the boiler water foaming up.

Pullman: A luxury carriage built for and leased by the Pullman Car Company; often used to refer to a train which is made up of such cars.

Quill drive: A form of traction via sprung members fixed to a driving wheel; the name originates from a misreading of German *Feder* which means both 'quill' and 'spring'.

Rack and pinion: A system to maximize adhesion on steep gradients, with a toothed wheel or wheels on the locomotive or power car engaging with a toothed rail laid between the running rails. There are several different systems.

Railcar: A self-propelling vehicle which is able to carry passengers or light goods items.

Reciprocating motion: A backwards-forwards motion, as in the movement of pistons in a steam locomotive.

Rectifier: A device to convert an AC electric supply to DC current for the traction motors.

Regenerative braking: A form of dynamic braking in electric locomotives, in which the motors can be switched to work as generators, producing current which can be fed back into the power catenary, or dissipated via resistance banks.

Regulator: The device controlling the flow of steam from the boiler to the cylinders; a regulator is one of the chief driving instruments of a steam locomotive.

Reverser: The device that sets the valve gear for forward or reverse motion in a steam locomotive: another of the chief driving instruments. It may be manual or power operated.

Rheostatic braking: A form of dynamic braking in diesel-electric locomotives, in which the traction motors can be switched to work as generators, creating current which is dissipated in resistance banks.

Road engine: A locomotive that hauls trains on the open track.

Road switcher: A locomotive that works both as a road and a yard engine.

Running gear: The framework and wheels of a diesel or electric locomotive.

French-built by Alsthom in the mid-1970s, the class 363 Co-Co electrics of Slovakian Railways are known as the 'Brigittes'.

Running plate: The decking along the sides of some locomotives, accompanied by a handrail.

Saddle tank: A tank engine whose water tank is mounted over the boiler.

Safety valve: An automatic valve which opens to release steam if the boiler pressure reaches the boiler's maximum operating pressure.

Sandwich frame: A type of locomotive frame made of hardwood, often oak or teak, reinforced by thin metal plates on each side.

Santa Fe: A 2-10-2 locomotive which derives its name from the Atchison Topeka & Santa Fe Railroad.

Saturated: A term applied to an engine, or its steam, when there is no superheater fitted and the steam remains in a saturated state.

Selkirk: A 2-10-4 locomotive of the Canadian Pacific Railway.

Shoe: The device for picking up electric current from a third-rail supply system. A brake shoe is the brake block which is applied against the wheel rim.

Shunter: The British term that is used for a switching engine which is used to remarshal trains and move rolling stock in station yards.

Side tank: A tank engine whose water tanks are at the boiler sides, from the running plate upwards.

Simple expansion: Also known as single expansion: this term refers to the use of steam only once, at uniform pressure, in the cylinders, before it is exhausted through the chimney.

Skyline casing: A sheet-metal shrouding found along the boiler top of a steam locomotive; skyline casing provides an air-smoothed covering for the dome, safety valves and other fittings.

Slave unit: A diesel or electric engine with no driving facility; a slave unit is operated as supplementary motive power to another engine.

Slide valve: A device for controlling the admission and exhaust of steam to and from a cylinder: shaped as a flat rectangle and operated by the engine's valve gear.

Smoke deflectors: Side screens fixed to the side of the smoke-box, or to the chimney sides, in order to help lift smoke upwards and keep the driver's view clear.

Steam chest: The steam reservoir immediately adjacent to the cylinders.

Steam drier: A device that is intended to prevent steam from condensing (rather than expanding) in the cylinders. There were several patent forms of the steam drier, all of which were overtaken by the superheater.

Superheater: A set of tubes which reheat steam that has passed through the boiler tubes, raising its temperature to 'superheated' level so that it does not condense when admitted to the cylinders.

Switcher: American term for a shunting engine.

Preserved Class S15 No. 825 of the Southern Railway, built 1920, is usually seen on the North Yorkshire Moors Railway.

Tank engine: A steam locomotive carrying its coal and water supply within its own frame: the tank engine has no tender.

TEE: Acronym for Trans-Europ Express, an international network which was formerly operated by several European countries.

Tender: The coal (or oil) and water-holding vehicle attached to a locomotive. Note that, in German, *Tenderlokomotive* means tank engine.

Texas: A 2-10-4 locomotive (Selkirk on the CPR).

TGV: Acronym for *Train à Grand Vitesse,* French 'High Speed Train' set.

Thalys: A meaningless 'Euro-term' and brand name for the TGV sets which operate between the cities of Paris, Amsterdam and Cologne.

Thermic syphon: A water-tube, usually in the shape of an inverted Y, which passes diagonally upwards through the firebox and helps to circulate and heat water more rapidly.

Thyristor: A semiconductor current rectifier, in which the flow of current between two electrodes is triggered by a signal at a third electrode.

TIA: Acronym for *Traitement Intégrale Armand,* a patent process which purifies locomotive feed-water.

Tractive effort: Usually expressed in pounds/kilos as 'nominal tractive effort', it is worked out by a mathematical formula to establish the theoretical backward push exerted on the rail by the driving wheels with the locomotive in full gear and (in the case of steam) usually with 85 per cent of the maximum boiler pressure, assuming no friction anywhere other than between wheels and rail.

Trailing wheels: Wheels of a locomotive positioned to the rear of the coupled wheels.

Transformer: A device which is used to regulate the voltage of electric current.

Transmission: The means by which the power developed by an engine is passed to the driving wheels.

Travel: In valve gear, travel is the distance moved by the valve as it opens and closes the steam ports.

Truck: American term for a wheeled undercarriage attached to a locomotive or railway vehicle, allowing for pivoted or lateral movement to assist with negotiation of curves and alterations in gradient.

Turbo-charging: In a diesel engine, the use of engine exhaust to increase pressure in the cylinders.

Universal engine: A locomotive adaptable to all forms of freight and passenger train work.

Up: The direction leading towards the major terminus of the line, hence the terms 'up line', 'up train', etc.

Valve gear: The arrangement of rods and cranks by which the driver of a steam engine controls steam flow in and out of the cylinders, and sets the engine in forward or reverse motion. More than a hundred versions were developed, although Stephenson's in the 19th and Walschaerts' in the 20th century were by far the most common.

This diesel-electric type E9A was originally built for Union Pacific in 1955.

Vanderbilt tender: A tender formed from a cylindrical water tank with a coal bunker mounted on its forward end.

Well tank: A tank engine whose water tank is contained within the frame.

Wheel arrangement: There are several standard notations for describing locomotive types, based on the number of driving and carrying wheels, or the number of wheels in motor bogies. That for steam locomotives (developed by F. M. Whyte in the United States in 1900) is based on a sequence of coupled wheels with carrying wheels in front and behind. Thus a 'Pacific' is a 4-6-2. Where there are no carrying wheels, a zero is used, as in 0-10-0. To denote a tank engine, T is added, as in 4-4-2T. For semi-articulated locomotives, such as Mallets, each set of coupled wheels is shown separately, as in 4-8-8-2. Articulated locomotives, such as Garratts, are normally treated as two separate but linked engines, as in 4-6-2+2-6-4. France and some other countries note the number of axles, rather than wheels, and with them a 'Pacific' is a 231, and a 'Mogul' a 130. Both diesel and electric locomotive types, and steam locomotives in Germany and some other countries, are denoted by a letter code based on the number of coupled or combined-drive axles, with 'A' standing for a single driving axle, 'B' for two axles, and so on up to 'F', for six axles.

The majority of modern locomotives have powered bogies of either four or six wheels. Outside the United States, a small 'o' used to be (and sometimes is still) added when the axles have separate rather than combined drive. Thus Bo-Bo denoted a locomotive with two two-axle bogies, each axle driven independently; and B-B implied that one power unit drove both axles. Digits from 1 upwards were used to show the position of non-powered carrying axles. Thus a German 4-4-0 steam locomotive is 2B. A two-axle bogie with one powered axle is denoted A1. A three-axle bogie with a central carrying axle is denoted A1A. A four-axle bogie with a single carrying axle in front, and three combined driving axles, is denoted 1C, and an engine mounted on two such bogies is 1C-C1. The power cars of almost all modern multiple-unit trains run on two four-wheel bogies with independent drive on all axles. Although technically this is Bo-Bo, it is increasingly often referred to simply as B-B.

Rack wheels fitted to locomotives are sometimes denoted as 'z' (from German *Zahn,* 'tooth'). A locomotive with three coupled axles and two rack axles would be C-2z.

Yard engine: Used to indicate an engine that operates only in shunting yards.

An 1840s 'Crampton'. Its wide steam pipes were more influential on later designs than its low-slung boiler and rear-set driving wheels.

INDEX

1-B-1 Gas Turbine Locomotive (Halmstad-Nässjö Ry) 171
1-C-C-1 (Chilean Transandine Ry) 130
1-C+C-1 (SJ) 107
2-B-2 (KPEV) 104
2-Co-2 (NER) 120
4COR (SR) 198–9
5Bel Pullman Electric Multiple Units (SR) 164–5
19-1001 (DRG) 217
040 DL/DO (Tunisian National Ry) 364
'59th' Class (EAR) 284–5
160.A.1 (SNCF) 212
231-132 BT Garratt (PLM) 201–2
240.P1 (PO) 163
262 BD1 (PLM) 198
1400 Class (MOPAC) 124–5
8500 Series (Dublin Area Rapid Transport) 425
10201 to 10203 (BR) 261

A1A-A1A test cars (STES) 68
AA 20-1 (SZD) 177
AB Class (Westrail) 338
AC4400CW (various r/r) 403
AC6000CW (UP) 403
'Acela' Express (Amt) 417–18
AD43C (Iranian Republic Islamic Ry) 425
Adler (Nüremberg-Fürth Ry) 18
Adriatic Network (Ita) 65
AEC Diesel Railcars (GWR) 170–1
Airtrain Citylink (Aus) 423
Algerian National Railways 201–2, 345, 391
AM 4/6 (SBB) 229
Amtrak (USA)
  diesel-electric 312, 359, 396, 399
  electric 353, 361, 414, 417–18
'Andes' Class (Central Railway (Peru)) 187
Argentina
  1885-1924 46, 68, 80, 88, 105
  1923-1963 122, 125, 145, 254, 316
Arica-La Paz Railway (Bol) 102
Árpád Diesel Railcars (MÁV) 176
Articulated Diesel Set (LMS) 202
articulated locomotives see Fairlie; Mallet
Atchison, Topeka & Santa Fe Railroad (USA) 75, 232
Atlantic Coast Line (USA) 56, 327
'Atlantic' No.153 (ACL) 56
Atlas-ASEA Railcar (Södermanland Mainland Ry) 101
Atlas (P&RR) 25
Australia see Airtrain Citylink; Australian National Railways; New South Wales Government Railway; Queensland Railways; South Australia Railways; Tasmanian Railways; Victorian Railways; Western Australian Government Railways
Australian National Railways 340, 387
Austria see Austrian Federal Railways; Imperial & Royal State Railway; Kaiserin Elisabeth Railway; Southern Railway (Aut); Vienna-Gloggnitz Railway
Austrian Federal Railways 158–9, 370, 424
  diesel-hydraulic 321, 378, 423
  electric
  1924-1940 126, 135, 140, 159, 205, 211
  1955-2002 282, 350, 410, 426
AVE S-103 (RENFE) 431

B-AR see Berlin-Anhalt Railway
B23-7 (various r/r) 360
B36-7 (various r/r) 364–5
B39-8 'Dash-8' (various r/r) 375, 380
BAGS see Buenos Aires Great Southern Railway
Baldwin RF16 'Shark Nose' (various r/r) 240
Baltimore & Ohio Railroad (USA) 19, 33, 57, 77, 158, 196
Bangladesh Railways 339
Bayonne-Biarritz Railway (Fra) 40
BDZ see Bulgarian State Railways
Belgian National Railways
  diesel-electric 283, 308
  electric 246, 267, 353, 365, 375, 381, 406

steam 180, 205
Belgian State Railways 33, 69, 89
Belgium see Belgian National Railways; Belgian State Railways; 'Eurostar'; Liège & Namur Railway; 'Thalys'
Bengal-Nagpur Railway (Ind) 79, 106
Benzol-Electric Railcar (EGR) 102
'Berkshire' (Illinois Central RR) 134
Berlin-Anhalt Railway (Ger) 23
Berne-Lötschberg-Simplon Railway (Swi) 95, 231
BESA (Western Ry) 79
Best Friend of Charleston (Charleston & Hamburg RR) 16
Beuth (Berlin-Anhalt) 23
'Big Goods' (Highland Ry) 55
Birmingham & Gloucester Railway (GB) 19
'Bloomer' Class (LNWR) 27
'Blue Pullman' (BR) 305–6
B&O see Baltimore & Ohio Railroad
Bo-Bo (B&O) 57
Bo-Bo (Halmstad-Nässjö Ry) 150
Bo-Bo (Metropolitan Ry) 78, 119
Bo-Bo (NER) 106
Bo electric locomotive (City & South London Ry) 51
Bourbonnais (PLM) 28, 32
BR see British Rail; Burlington Railroad
Brazil 47, 151, 216, 228, 246, 263
Bremen-Thedinghausen Railway (Ger) 164
British Rail (GB)
  diesel 264, 306, 374, 384, 407–8
  diesel-electric
  1951-1961 261, 270, 293, 298, 303, 305–6, 308–9
  1962-1989 314, 331, 356–7, 372, 376, 384
  diesel-hydraulic 306, 309, 323, 374, 392
  electric
  1953-1962 269–70, 297–8, 303, 314
  1973-1993 349, 382, 391, 395
  electro-diesel 326
  gas turbine 248, 309
  steam 219, 242–3, 248, 260–1, 269, 278
  see also Great Britain
Budd Rail Diesel Car (RDC) (various r/r) 251
Buenos Aires & Pacific Railway (Arg) 88, 145
Buenos Aires Great Southern Railway (Arg) 46, 68, 80, 105, 122, 125
Bugatti Railcar (ETAT) 169
Bulgarian State Railways 102, 159, 216, 317, 321, 341, 377, 397
Burlington Northern Railroad (USA) 395, 431–2
Burlington Railroad (USA) 178, 179, 191, 251, 301
Bury locomotive (London & Birmingham Ry) 15, 19, 27
BVMOT (MÁV) 401

C-liner (various r/r) 257
C36-7 (various r/r) 361
C-420 (various r/r) 319–20
C-630 (various r/r) 327
Caledonian Railway (GB) 58, 69, 81–2
Camden & Amboy Railroad (USA) 16–17
'Camelback' (P&RR) 59
Canada 250 see also Canada Northern Railway; Canadian National Railway; Canadian Pacific Railway; Champlain & St Lawrence Railway; GO Transit; VIA Rail
Canada Northern Railway 96
Canadian National Railway 146, 229, 287, 295, 348, 401, 430–1
Canadian Pacific Railway 151, 192, 197, 287, 339, 341, 403
Cape Government Railways (SA) 52, 54, 74
Cardean (Caledonian Ry) 81–2
Cargo Sprinter/multi-purpose vehicles (DB/Railtrack) 407–8
'Castle' Class (GWR) 123–4, 141
'Castle' Class (Northern Ireland Ry) 376
'Cauliflower' Class (LNWR) 43
CD see Czech Railways
Celestial Empire (Shanghai & Woosung Ry) 41

Central Argentine Railway 254
Central of Aragón Railway (Spa) 158, 311
Central Railroad of New Jersey (USA) 135
Central Railway of Uruguay 90, 117
Central Railway (Peru) 187
Central Trains (GB) 413
Ceylon Government Railway 282
CFR see Romanian Railways
'Challenger' Class (UP) 195, 220
Champlain & St Lawrence Railway (Can) 19
Channel Tunnel 393–4
Charleston & Hamburg Railroad (USA) 16
Chesapeake & Ohio Railroad (USA) 189, 225
Chicago, Milwaukee, St Paul & Pacific Railroad (USA) 188–9, 200–1
Chicago, Milwaukee & St Paul Railroad (USA) 108, 115
Chicago, North Shore & Milwaukee Railroad (USA) 221
Chicago & North Western Railroad (USA) 203, 380
Chile 130, 277
China 339, 342, 426–7
  electric 332, 406, 411
  steam 41, 172, 180–1, 192, 288, 296, 339
Chinese Government Railways 172, 192
Chinese State Railways 332, 339, 342, 406, 427
Chugoku Railway (Jap) 85
CIE see Irish Transport Company
City & South London Railway (GB) 51
'City' Class (GWR) 73
Class 01 (DRG) 131–2, 137
Class 1 (SNCB) 180
Class 01.49 (PKP) 262
Class 02 (BR) 306
Class 2.6 (NORD) 63
Class 2D2-9100 (SNCF) 254
Class 2MT (BR) 269
Class 04 (BDZ) 317
Class 4 (BR) 261
Class 04 (BR) 264
Class 4.1200 (NORD) 160
Class 4CEP (BR) 297–8
Class 4E (SAR) 281
Class 4F (LMS) 128, 132
Class 05 (DRG) 172
Class 5E (SAR) 286
Class 5P5F (LMS) 175
Class 6 (Cape Government Ry) 54
Class 6CE (Algerian National Ry) 345
Class 6E (SAR) 350
Class 6E1 (SAR) 376
Class 6FE (Algerian National Ry) 391
Class 7 (BAGS) 46
Class 7 (Cape Government Ry) 52
Class 7B (BAGS) 68
Class 7E (SAR) 361
Class 7MT 'Britannia' (BR) 260, 278
Class 08 (BR) 270
Class 8E (BAGS) 122
Class 8F (LMS) 183
Class 9E (SAR) 361
Class 9F (BR) 278
Class 10 (DB) 289
Class 11 (BDZ) 216
Class 11 (Benguela Ry) 257
Class 11 (SNCB) 375
Class 11B (BAGS) 105
Class 11C (BAGS) 125
Class 12 (Rhodesian Ry) 138
Class 12 (SNCB) 205
Class 12B (BAGS) 80
Class 12L (Central Argentine Ry) 254
Class 12M (State Railways (Arg)) 116
Class 13 (SNCB) 406
Class 15A (Rhodesian Ry) 249
Class 15CA (SAR) 157
Class 15F (SAR) 203
Class 16D (SAR) 133
Class 16E (SAR) 187
Class 17 'Clayton' (BR) 314

Class 18 (EB) 69
Class 19D (SAR) 208
Class 19E (Spoornet) 434
Class 020 (CP) 133
Class 20 (Serbian State Ry) 100
Class 20 (SNCB) 353
Class 21 (NSB) 80
Class 21 (SNCB) 365
Class 22 (MÁV) 148
Class 25 (SAR) 274–5, 316, 367
Class 26 'Red Devil' (SAR) 366–7
Class 27 (NSB) 90
Class 27 (SNCB) 365
Class 30 (EAR) 284
Class 030 (Madrid-Zaragoza Alicante Ry) 29
Class 31 (BR) 293
Class 31B (NSB) 117
Class 32 (BDZ) 341
Class 32A (NSB) 110
Class 34 (Ottoman-Anatolian Ry) 95
Class 35 'Hymek' (BR) 309
Class 37 (BR) 306, 309
Class 40 (BR) 298
Class 40 (NSGWR) 258
Class 42 (BDZ) 321
Class 42.01 (Trans-Iranian Ry) 193
Class 44 (BR) 303, 304
Class 44 (DRG) 137
Class 46 (BDZ) 377
Class 46 (TCDD) 200
Class 46.01 (BDZ) 159
Class 47 (BR) 314, 357
Class 47 (NS) 233
Class 48 (NSWGR) 302
Class 49 'Dovregubben' (NSB) 186
Class 50 (BR) 331
Class 51 (Indonesian State Ry) 10
Class 52 (DRG) 222–3
Class 55 'Deltic' (BR) 184, 308–9
Class 56 (BR) 357
Class 56 (KKSTB) 47
Class 56 (Malayan Ry) 202
Class 56 (TCDD) 113
Class 58 (BR) 372
Class 59 Foster Yeoman (Mendip Rail) 378
Class 60 (BR) 384
Class 060-DA (CFR) 304, 357
Class 060-EA (CFR) 325
Class 61 (BDZ) 397
Class 65 (DB) 260
Class 66 (EWS) 412
Class 67 (EWS) 418
Class 071 (CIE) 357
Class 73 (BR) 326
Class 78 (BBÖ) 158
Class 80 (DRG) 147
Class 85 (DRF) 163
Class 86 (DRG) 148
Class 87 (BR) 349
Class 91 (BR) 382
Class 92 (BR) 395
Class 92 (EAR) 344
Class 97 (Kaiserin Elizabeth Ry) 42
Class 100 AVE (RENFE) 393
Class 100 (DRG) 152, 172
Class 101 (DB) 406–7, 430
Class 101 (SNCB) 246
Class 103.1 (DB) 340
Class 120 (DR) 328
Class 120.1 (DB) 378
Class 121 (CIE) 310
Class 122 (SNCB) 267
Class 124 'Trans-Pennine' (BR) 306
Class 127 (DB) 391
Class 130-132 (DR) 349
Class 131 (CFR) 207
Class 140C (ETAT) 111
Class 141 (BR) 374
Class 141F (RENFE) 275
Class 142 (CFR) 194
Class 143 (DR) 371
Class 146 (DB) 424

Class 150 'Sprinter' (BR) 374, 384
Class 151.3101 (RENFE) 224
Class 161.E (PLM) 131
Class 163 (CSD) 373–4
Class 165 (BR) 392
Class 165 (JNR) 304
Class 170 (KKSTB) 57, 115
Class 170 'Turbostar' (various operators) 413
Class 175 (NWT) 420
Class 180 (KKSTB) 62
Class 181.2 (DB) 351
Class 190 (Southern Ry (Aut)) 96
Class 201 (IR) 398
Class 202/3/4 (SNCB) 283
Class 206 (KKSTB) 72
Class 212 (SNCB) 308
Class 218 (DB) 333
Class 220/221 'Voyager' (VT) 421
Class 220 (MÀV) 45
Class 231C (NORD) 123
Class 231C (PLM) 97
Class 232 (SZD) 203
Class 232.U1 (SNCF) 247
Class 240 (DB) 383
Class 241-A (EST) 131
Class 241.P (SNCF) 241
Class 242 A.1 (SNCF) 242
Class 242.12 (EST) 73
Class 250 (DR) 351
Class 250 (Erie RR) 31
Class 250 (RENFE) 371
Class 251 (RENFE) 372
Class 252 AVE (RENFE) 393
Class 252 (RENFE) 389
Class 269 (RENFE) 363
Class 276 (RENFE) 291
Class 277 (RENFE) 265
Class 279/289 (RENFE) 331
Class 290 (DB) 323
Class 321-4 (DRG) 172
Class 321 (MÀV) 58
Class 323 (BR) 391
Class 324 (MÀV) 66, 87
Class 325 (Royal Mail) 400
Class 328 (MÀV) 113
Class 332 Heathrow Express (GB) 408
Class 335 (MÀV) 36
Class 342 (JDZ) 337
Class 350 (CSD) 351
Class 350 (SAR) 246
Class 352 (RENFE) 316
Class 360 'Desiro' (First Great Eastern) 428
Class 363 (JDZ) 355
Class 373 'Eurostar' (Bel/Fra/GB) 368, 393–4, 417
Class 375 (MÀV) 89
Class 381 (JNR) 349
Class 384 (Egyptian Railway Administration) 60
Class 387 (CSD) 136
Class 390 'Pendolino' (VT) 424–5
Class 401 ICE (DB) 388–9, 419
Class 403 ICE 3 (DB) 9, 419
Class 422 (VR) 338
Class 423/433 (CSD) 241
Class 424 (MÀV) 127
Class 429 'Director' (Great Central Ry) 104
Class 429 (KKSTB) 87
Class 434.2 (CSD) 115
Class 441 (JDZ) 367
Class 442 (BR) 382
Class 460 'Juniper' (GE) 416–17
Class 464 (CSD) 167
Class 464.2 (CSD) 283
Class 470 (CSD) 388
Class 470 (FS) 84
Class 471 (CD) 403
Class 476.0 (CSD) 246
Class 477.0 (CSD) 259
Class 498.1 (CSD) 277
Class 500 (Adriatic Network) 65, 84
Class 500 (Sudan Ry) 286
Class 520 (SAR) 228
Class 534.03 (CSD) 233

Class 551 (Royal Siamese Ry) 162
Class 556 (CSD) 255
Class 581 (JNR) 333–4
Class 601/651 (OSE) 384
Class 601 (MÁV) 106
Class 605 (DB) 424
Class 628.2 (DB) 379
Class 629 (Southern Ry (Aut)) 101
Class 640 (FS) 84
Class 643/644 'Talent' (DB) 420
Class 670 (DB) 405
Class 680 (CD) 427–8
Class 685 (FS) 99
Class 735 (EGR) 102
Class 740 (FS) 114, 121
Class 741 (FS) 121, 252, 284
Class 749 (CSD) 321
Class 753/754 (CSD) 332
Class 787 (Kyushu Ry) 392
Class 800 (Great Southern Ry) 207
Class 810 (CSD) 348
Class 835 (FS) 82
Class 900 (BDZ) 102
Class 940 (FS) 116
Class 1001 (NS) 244
Class 1010 (ÖBB) 282
Class 1016/1116 'Taurus' (ÖBB) 410
Class 1018 (ÖBB) 205
Class 1020 (ÖBB) 211
Class 1044 (ÖBB) 350
Class 1080/1180 E (ÖBB) 126
Class 1099 (Mariazellerbahn) 88
Class 1170 (ÖBB) 135
Class 1200 (CP) 311
Class 1200 (NS) 255
Class 1500 (BR) 219, 242
Class 1500 (Buenos Airea & Pacific) 88
Class 1600 (NS) 366
Class 1700 (NS) 387
Class 1900 'Claud Hamilton' 63
Class 2000/2050 (EFS) 228
Class 2043 (ÖBB) 321
Class 2070 (ÖBB) 423
Class 2090 (ÖBB) 140
Class 2106 (ÖBB) 424
Class 2131 (Northern Ry (Spa)) 42
Class 2143 (ÖBB) 321
Class 2180 (ÖBB) 370
Class 2400 (NS) 279–80
Class 2601 (CP) 352
Class 2900 (ATSF) 232
Class 3000 (Buenos Airea & Pacific) 145
Class 3000 (Luxembourg Ry) 414
Class 3000 (QR) 397
Class 3100 (KNR) 328
Class 3500 (QR) 377
Class 3800 (QR) 432
Class 4000 (UP) 220
Class 4001 (NS) 234
Class 4023/4 'Talent' (ÖBB) 426
Class 4500/3500 (PO) 84, 163
Class 5047 (ÖBB) 378
Class 5400 (ETAT) 198
Class 5601 (CP) 395
Class 6400 (NS) 382–3
Class 8000 (KNR) 346
Class 8310 (DR) 283
Class 9000 (Fra/GB) 394
Class 9000 (UP) 139
Class 68000/68500 (SNCF) 317
Class A (CMSTP&PRR) 188–9
Class A (SJ) 85
Class A (VR) 372
Class A1 (BR) 243
Class A1 (GNR) 118–19
Class A3 (LNER) 118–19, 184
Class A4 (LNER) 118, 184
Class A 471 (OSE) 413
Class Ab (NZR) 109, 165
Class ABmot (MÁV) 143
Class AC-5 'cab-first' (SP) 150
Class AD60 (NSWGR) 262–3

Class AE3/6 (SBB) 116
Class AE4/4 (BLS) 231
Class AE4/7 (SBB) 139
Class AE6/6 (SBB) 266, 347
Class AE8/14 (SBB) 208
Class AEM-7 (Amt) 361
Class AL1 (BR) 303
Class ALn DAP (FS) 409
Class ALP 46 (New Jersey Transit) 429–30
Class AM9 (BR) 314
Class AM86 (SNCB) 381
Class AP (East Indian Ry) 86
Class B (Darjeeling Himalaya Ry) 49
Class B (SJ) 88
Class B2 (Central Mexican Ry) 71
Class B50 (SS) 44
Class B51 (SS) 65
Class BB-7200 (SNCF) 356
Class BB-12000 (SNCF) 267, 296
Class BB-15000 (SNCF) 342
Class BB-16000 (SNCF) 296
Class BB-16500 (SNCF) 297
Class BB-22200 (SNCF) 355
Class BB-26000 (SNCF) 381
Class BB-27000 (SNCF) 411–12
Class BB-37000 (SNCF) 428
Class BB-75000 (SNCF) 432
Class Be 4/6 (SBB) 114
Class BE 5/7 (BLS) 95
Class BJ (CSR) 342
Class BM71 'Flytoget' (NSB) 414
Class C 'Coupe-Vent' (PLM) 61
Class C 5/6 (SBB) 105
Class C12 (SS) 53
Class C27 (SS) 111
Class C30-7 (various r/r) 359
Class C 36 (NSWGR) 130
Class C 38 (NSWGR) 227–8
Class C53 (SS) 112
Class C62 (JR) 244
Class CC (SJ) 52
Class CC (SR) 218
Class CC50 (SS) 147
Class CC200 (Indonesian State Ry) 271
Class CC-7100 (SNCF) 263
Class CC-21000 (SNCF) 341
Class CC-40100 (SNCF) 322
Class CC-72000 (SNCF) 331
Class CF7 (SF) 341
Class ChME3 (SZD) 307, 325
Class CHS2 (SZD) 301
Class CL (Australian National) 340
Class CP 1500 (CP) 244–5
Class D (SJ) 133
Class D1 (DSB) 70
Class D14 (NSB) 363
Class D18 (NSB) 405–6
Class D51 (JR) 193–4
Class D70 (various r/r) 277
Class D235 (FS) 310
Class D9500 (BR) 323
Class DA (NZR) 285
Class DA (SJ) 276
Class DD-AR (7800) (NS) 409
Class DD50 (SS) 111
Class DDJ1 (Guangzhou Ry) 411
Class DE10 (JNR) 328
Class DE2550 (Egyptian National Ry) 404
Class DF4 (CSR) 339
Class DF4B (CSR) 427
Class DG/DH (NZR) 286
Class DIV (Royal Bavarian State Ry) 40
Class DJ (NZR) 335
Class DK5600 (TCDD) 393
Class DL500 (Southern Railway of Peru) 290
Class DM3 (SJ) 319, 422
Class E (CP) 93
Class E (RSR) 100
Class E-4 (Chicago & North Western RR) 203
Class E04 (DRG) 169
Class E6 (PRR) 91
Class E10 (DB) 289

Class E10 (SSS) 120
Class E18 (DRG) 182, 205
Class E19 01/02 (DRG) 183
Class E40 (DB) 293
Class E.321/E.322 (FS) 307
Class E428 (FS) 176
Class E432 (FS) 149
Class E466 (CSD) 146
Class E492 (FS) 379
Class E499.2 (CSD) 360
Class E 503 (PO) 168
Class E550 E (FS) 86
Class E636 (FS) 212–13
Class E656 (FS) 354
Class E1100 (Moroccan State Ry) 358
Class E8000 EMU (TCDD) 287
Class EA (NZR) 334
Class EA-1 (GIPR) 148–9
Class EC (NZR) 153
Class EE 3/3 (SBB) 166
Class EF-1 Boxcab (Chicago, Milwaukee & Saint Paul RR) 108
Class EF-1 (GIPR) 148
Class EF30 (NZR) 383
Class EF66 (JNR) 334
Class EG (DSB) 415
Class EL (Australian National) 387
Class EL 14 (NSB) 335
Class EL 18 (NSB) 405
Class EM (NZR) 371
Class EM2 (BR) 269–70
Class EO (NZR) 124
Class EP-5 (NHR) 287
Class EP5 (DRG) 126
Class EP09 (PKP) 376
Class ET (DSB/SJ) 416
Class ET6 (Chinese Government Ry) 192
Class ET22 (PKP) 344
Class EU07 (PKP) 325
Class EU43 (PKP) 414
Class EW (NZR) 264
Class F (Indian State Ry) 40
Class F (SJ) 107
Class F-2A (CPR) 192
Class F3 (Mexican Ry) 55
Class F7 (CMSTP&PRR) 200–1
Class F10 (SS) 98
Class FD (SZD) 162
Class FEF-2 (UP) 209
Class FL9 (NHR) 292
Class G (SJ) 35
Class G3 (Mexican Ry) 62
Class G8 (KPEV) 70
Class GE6/6 (Rhaetian Ry) 134
Class GMA/GMAM (SAR) 280–1
Class GS-6 (SP) 204
Class GTO3 (NS) 157
Class H (NZR) 41
Class H1C 'Royal Hudson' (CPR) 197
Class H-6-G (Canada Northern Ry) 96
Class H8 (Chesapeake & Ohio RR) 225
Class H561 (OSE) 413
Class HGE4/4 (SBB) 153
Class HR1 (VR) 197, 212
Class HS (Bengal-Nagpur) 106
Class Hv 1 (VR) 109
Class IC3 (DSB) 383
Class IRM (NS) 398
Class J (Norfolk & Western Ry) 219
Class J1 'Hudson' (NYC) 145, 204
Class J3 (Chesapeake & Ohio RR) 189
Class J-3A (NYC) 203–4
Class JF 'Standard' (South Manchurian Ry) 180–1
Class K (DSB) 54
Class K (NZR) 165
Class K (SZD) 311
Class K (Tasmanian Ry) 87
Class K (VR) 117
Class K (WAGR) 52, 327
Class K1 (GNR) 116, 118
Class K4 (PRR) 33, 108, 227
Class K9 (Savannah Florida & Western Ry) 69

Class KF1 (Chinese Government Ry) 172
Class L (SZD) 234
Class L (WAGR) 330
Class L4-A (NYC) 229
Class L-304 (NSWGR) 46
Class LV (SZD) 266
Class M1 (PRR) 125, 134
Class M2 (Ceylon Government Ry) 282
Class M9 (Sri Lanka Ry) 422
Class M41 (MÁV) 343
Class M44 Switcher (MÁV) 290
Class M61 (MÁV) 318
Class M62 (MÁV) 326
Class M62.3 (MÁV) 425
Class MA (SEK) 271
Class MA (SJ) 72
Class ME (DSB) 366
Class MS (Uganda Ry) 105
Class MX (DSB) 305
Class N1 (Central Railway of Uruguay) 90
Class O1 (Serbian, Croatian & Slovenian Ry) 124
Class OK-22 (PKP) 122
Class P (NSWGR) 51
Class P1 (DSB) 83
Class P2 (LNER) 173–4, 180, 184
Class P5 (PRR) 158
Class P8 (KPEV) 81, 88, 122
Class P10 (KPEV) 118
Class P36 (SZD) 273–4
Class P-38 (SZD) 280
Class P160DE (DB) 431
Class PC (Iraq State Ry) 212
Class PM-36 (PKP) 199
Class PO3 (NS) 93
Class PO4 (NS) 152
Class PT-47 (PKP) 239
Class Q (NZR) 68–9
Class Q2 (PRR) 231
Class Q34 (GIPR) 29
Class QJ (Railways of the People's Republic) 288
Class QR-1 (Mexican National Ry) 237
Class R (SAR) 47
Class R (VGR) 257–8
Class RBDE4/4 (SBB) 379
Class RE4/4 (456) (Schweizerische Südostbahn) 379
Class RE 450 (SBB) 387
Class RE 460 (SBB) 389–90, 405
Class RM (Railways of the People's Republic) 296
Class RM 'Silver Fern' (NZR) 346
Class RS-11 (various r/r) 292
Class S (Central Railway of Uruguay) 117
Class S (DSB) 126
Class S (NSWGR) 72
Class S (RSR) 94
Class S (SAR) 153
Class S (VR) 146
Class S 3/6 (Royal Bavarian State Ry) 85
Class S1 'Northern' (GN) 154
Class S1 (PRR) 209–10, 227
Class S3 (KPEV) 53
Class S-3 (New York, Chicago & St Louis RR) 177
Class S699 (CD) 397
Class SA (DSB) 404
Class SR1 (VR) 348
Class SR2 (VR) 397
Class SS1 (CSR) 332
Class SY 'Aim High' (CSR) 339
Class T1 (CPR) 151
Class T9 (London & South Western Ry) 61
Class T18 (KPEV) 97
Class T161 (KPEV) 103
Class T-524 (NSWGR) 56–7
Class TC S118 'MacArthur' (United States Army Transportation Corps) 226–7
Class TC S160 (United States Army Transportation Corps) 225–6
Class TE3 (SZD) 266
Class TE10 (SZD) 300–1
Class TEM2 (SZD) 307
Class TER 2N NG (Luxembourg Ry) 429
Class Tk2 (VR) 73

Class Tk3 (VR) 140
Class TKT 48 (PKP) 256
Class TM11 B (SBB) 256
Class TR1 (VR) 211–12
Class TV1 (VR) 112
Class TY 51 (PKP) 273
Class U (RSR) 74
Class U1-F (CN) 229
Class V2 (LNER) 192–3
Class V4 (LNER) 224
Class V16/V140 (DRG) 183
Class V40 (MÁV) 161
Class V41 (MÁV) 310
Class V43 (MÁV) 318
Class V46 (MÁV) 373
Class V55 (MÁV) 255
Class V63 (MÁV) 363
Class V80 (DB) 264, 323
Class V100 (DB) 297
Class V200 (DB) 268
Class V3201 (DRG) 141
Class VB (VR) 302
Class VL80 (SZD) 319
Class VR1 (VR) 103
Class VT95 Diesel Railbuses (DB) 264
Class W (NZR) 50
Class W (WAGR) 258
Class WAG1 (IR) 304
Class WAM4 (IR) 343–4, 352
Class WCAM-1 (IR) 352
Class WCAM-3 (IR) 405
Class WCM1 (IR) 279
Class WDP-4 (IR) 408
Class WM (East Indian Ry) 206
Class WP (IR) 190, 236
Class WT (IR) 299
Class X (VR) 150–1
Class X (WAGR) 276
Class X10 (SJ) 373
Class X12 (SJ) 389
Class X2000 (SJ) 384
Class X4300 (SNCF) 317
Class XC (IR) 143
Class Y43 (GIPR) 31
Class YA-01 (SZD) 171
Class YE (RSR) 110
Class YP (IR) 248–9
Class Z-5 (Northern Pacific RR) 158
Class Z (Tasmanian Ry) 345
Class Z530 (Piraeus-Athens-Peleponnesus Ry) 92
CMSTP&PRR see Chicago, Milwaukee, St Paul &
  Pacific Railroad (USA)
CN see Canadian National Railway
CNJ-1000 Bo-Bo (Central Railroad of New Jersey)
  135
'Comet' V (New Jersey Transit) 430
Conrail (USA) 360, 380
Consolidation (Lehigh & Manahoy RR) 34–5
Cordova & Huatusco Railway (Mex) 71
County Donegal Railways (Ire) 161
CP see Portuguese Railways
CPR see Canadian Pacific Railway
Crampton locomotive (Liège & Namur) 17, 23
'Cross-Compound' (CFE) 72
CSD see Czechoslovak State Railways
CSR see Chinese State Railways
Czech Railways 388, 397, 403, 427–8
Czechoslovak State Railways
  diesel 348
  diesel-electric 321, 332
  electric 146, 351, 360, 373–4, 388
  steam
    1920-1945 115, 136, 167, 233
    1948-1955 241, 247, 259, 277, 283

Danish State Railways
  diesel-electric 181, 305, 366
  diesel-hydraulic 383
  electric 404, 415–16
  steam 54, 70, 83, 126
Dash 8-40B (various r/r) 380
Dash 8-40BP 'Genesis' (Amt) 396

Dash 8-40C (various r/r) 380–1, 386
Dash 8-40CW (various r/r) 386
Dash 9-44CW (various r/r) 396
DB see German Federal Railways
DD1 (PRR) 91
DD17 Class (QGR) 241
DDA40X (UP) 340
De Arend (Holland Iron Ry) 21
De Witt Clinton (Mohawk & Hudson RR) 17
DEII diesel multiple units (NS) 272
DE30AC (Long Island RR) 411
DE 1100 (TCDD) 377
Decapod (DPSR) 47
Delaware & Hudson Railroad (USA) 16, 82, 171
Derwent (S&D) 24
DF Class (NZR) 280
Diesel Railcar (County Donegal Ry) 161
'Director' Class 429 (Great Central Ry) 104
Djibouti-Addis Ababa Railway (Eth) 322
DL109 V (various r/r) 213
Dom Pedro Segundo Railway (Bra) 47
Donna Teresa Christina Railway (Bra) 216
Dorchester (Champlain & St Lawrence Ry) 19
DR see German State Railways (DR)
DR-12-8-1500/2 (PRR) 236
DRG see German State Railways (DRG)
DSB see Danish State Railways
Dublin Area Rapid Transport (Ire) 425
'Duchess' Class (LMS) 170
'Dunalastair II' (Caledonian Ry) 58, 61, 69
Dutch East Indies 44, 53, 65, 98, 111, 112, 120,
  147
DV12 (VR) 322
DX Class (LNWR) 28
DX Class (NZR) 346
DY Class (IR) 284

E Series E.50 (FS) 99
E Types (B&O) 196
E-Units Model E7 (various r/r) 238
E60 (Amt) 353, 361
E69 (Lokalbahn) 78
E330 (FS) 107
E.401 (PO) 136
E43000 (TCDD) 380
East African Railways (Ken) 284–5, 344
East Indian Railway 86, 206
Eastern Railway (Fra) 73, 85, 131, 160–1
EB see Belgian State Railways
EC 40 (JNR) 93
Egypt 30, 60, 63, 102, 259, 404
EL-3A Boxcab (VR) 135
EL-C/EF-4 (VR) 291–2
Electric Multiple Units (Lancashire & Yorkshire Ry)
  76
Electro-Motive SW1 (various r/r) 210
Elephant (Sacramento Valley RR) 27
English, Welsh & Scottish Railways (GB) 306, 384,
  418
EP-3 (NHR) 162
ER200 14-Car Set (SZD) 352
'Erie Built' (Milwaukee RR) 235–6
Erie Railroad (USA) 31, 35, 107–8
ES 44 'Evolution' Series (various r/r) 430–1
EST see Eastern Railway
ETA515 Battery Railcar (DB) 277
ETAT see State Railways (Fra)
ETR-200 Three-Car Train (FS) 207
ETR-300 'Settebello' Fast Electric Train (FS) 271–2
ETR-400 Prototype Tilting Train 357–8
ETR-500 Eurostar Italia (FS) 421–2
'Eurostar' Class 373 (Bel/Fra/GB) 368, 393–4, 417
Experiment (Mohawk & Hudson RR) 17, 23

F-Units, Model F7 (various r/r) 239
F40PH (Amt) 312, 359
F40PHM-2 (MET) 390
F59PHI (various r/r) 399
FA/FB (various r/r) 237
Fairlie (Ffestiniog Ry) 38
Fairlie Locomotive (Mexican Ry) 93
Fell system 41, 50

Ffestiniog Railway (GB) 38, 87
Finnish State Railways 322, 348, 397, 431
  steam 73, 103, 109, 112, 140, 197, 211–12
First Great Eastern (GB) 428
Five-Car Diesel Train (Egyptian State Ry) 259
Florida East Coast Railroad (USA) 435
Forney's tank locomotive (Manhattan Ry) 46
FP45 (SF) 336
FPA-4 (Canada Northern Ry) 8, 295
France 13–14
  see also Bayonne-Biarritz Railway; Eastern
    Railway; 'Eurostar'; French National Railways;
    Northern Railway (Fra); Paris-Lyon-Mediterranean
    Railway; Paris-Orleans Railway; Paris-Rouen
    Railway; Paris-Strasbourg Railway; State Railways
    (Fra); 'Thalys'
Franco-Ethiopian Djibouti-Addis Ababa Railway
  (Eth) 109
Franco-Ethiopian Railway (Eth) 72
French National Railways
  diesel 254, 317
  diesel-electric 317, 331, 432
  electric
    1950-1971 254, 263, 267, 296–7, 322, 341, 342
    1976-2006 355–6, 362, 381, 399–400, 411–12,
    428
  gas turbine 345
  steam 212, 241–2, 247
FS see Italian State Railways
FT Four-Unit Set (various r/r) 210–11

Garratt Type (Central of Aragón Ry) 158
'Gas Electric' Motor Cars (USA) 82–3
Gatwick Express (GB) 416–17
The General (Western & Atlantic RR) 28–9
German Federal Railways
  battery railcar 277
  diesel 264, 405, 407–8
  diesel-electric 383, 420, 424, 431
  diesel-hydraulic 264, 268, 297, 323, 333, 379,
    420
  electric
    1950-1974 255, 289, 293, 340, 351
    1987-2001 9, 378, 388–9, 391, 406–7, 419, 424
  steam 260, 289
German State Railways (DR) 283, 328, 349, 351,
  371
German State Railways (DRG)
  diesel 141, 152
  diesel-electric 164, 191
  diesel-hydraulic 172, 183
  electric 126, 169, 182–3, 205
  steam
    1925-1932 131–2, 137, 147–8, 163
    1934-1942 172, 206, 215, 222–3
Germany 68, 432–4
  see also Berlin-Anhalt Railway; Bremen-
    Thedinghausen Railway; German Federal
    Railways; German State Railways; Lokalbahn AG
    (München); Lübeck-Büchen Railway; Nüremberg-
    Fürth Railway; Oldenburg State Railways; Royal
    Bavarian State Railways; Royal Prussian Union
    Railways; 'Thalys'
GG1 (PRR) 177–8
GIPR see Great Indian Peninsular Railway
GN see Great Northern Railway (USA)
GNR see Great Northern Railway (GB)
GO Transit (Can) 327
Gowan & Marx (P&RR) 22
GP7/GP9 (various r/r) 249, 305
GP20 (various r/r) 305
GP30 (various r/r) 316
GP40-2L (CN) 348
GP40TC (GT) 327
GP50 (various r/r) 364
GP58 (various r/r) 329
GP60 (various r/r) 377
GP60M (Santa Fe RR) 388
Grand Junction Railway (GB) 22
The Great Bear (GWR) 86, 124
Great Britain
  diesel

1933-1952 170–1, 185–6, 202, 264
1960-1998 306, 374, 384, 407–8
diesel-electric
1948-1959 243, 261, 270, 293, 298, 303
1960-1985 305–6, 308–9, 314, 331, 356–7, 372, 376
1986-2000 378, 384, 412, 418, 421
diesel-hydraulic 306, 309, 323, 374, 392, 413, 420
electric
1884-1932 45, 51, 76, 78, 106, 119–20, 164–5
1937-1959 198–9, 218, 269–70, 297–8, 303
1962-1995 314, 349, 382, 391, 393–5, 400
1997-2003 408, 416–17, 424–5, 428
electro-diesel 326
gas turbine 248, 309
steam
1804-1851 11–13, 14–15, 19, 20, 24, 25, 27
1859-1880 29–30, 32, 34, 36–7, 38–9, 43
1889-1900 48–9, 55, 58, 60, 61, 63, 64
1902-1912 71, 73–4, 81–2, 85, 86, 92, 98
1913-1923 104, 116, 118–19, 123–4
1925-1930 7, 128, 132, 137, 141–2, 152, 155–6
1933-1941 170, 173–5, 183–5, 192–3, 217–18, 219
1942-1954 223–4, 230, 242–3, 248, 260–1, 269, 278
Great Central Railway (GB) 92, 104
Great Eastern Railway (GB) 63
Great Indian Peninsular Railway 29, 31, 79, 148–9
Great Northern Railway (GB) 6, 36–7, 60, 116, 118–19
Great Northern Railway (USA) 31, 154
Great Southern Railway (Ire) 207
Great Western Railway (GB) 7, 25, 63, 71, 73–4, 86, 123–4, 141, 170–1, 174
Greece 92, 271, 384, 413
'Green Goat' (BNSF) 431–2
GS2 Class (SP) 201
GT3 (BR) 309
Guangzhou Railway (Chi) 411
GWR see Great Western Railway

H-Class 'Heavy Harry' (VR) 215
H10-44 (various r/r) 232–3
H-24-66 'Train Master' (various r/r) 276
Halmstad-Nässjö Railway (Swe) 150, 171
Heathrow Express Class 332 (GB) 408
Heisler geared locomotive (USA) 45, 51
Hellenic Railways (Gre) 271, 384, 413
HHL (Amt) 414
Highland Railway (GB) 55
Holland Iron Railway (Ned) 21
Hungarian State Railways
diesel 143, 176
diesel-electric 290, 318, 326
diesel-hydraulic 343
electric 161, 255, 310, 318, 353, 373, 401, 425
steam
1869-1910 36, 45, 58, 66, 87, 89
1912-1928 96, 106, 113, 127, 148

Ichigo (Imperial Japanese Ry) 37
Illinois Central Railroad (USA) 134
Imperial & Royal State Railway (Aut) 47, 57, 62, 72, 87, 91–2
Imperial Japanese Railways 37
IMU 120 (Airtrain Citylink) 423
India see Bengal-Nagpur Railway; Darjeeling Himalayan Railway; East Indian Railway; Great Indian Peninsular Railway; Indian Railways; Indian State Railways; Indus Valley State Railway; Western Railway
Indian Railways
diesel-electric 315, 401, 408
diesel-hydraulic 284
electric 279, 299, 304, 343–4, 352, 402, 405
steam 143, 190, 236, 248–9
Indian State Railways 40
Indonesian State Railways 10, 271
Indus Valley State Railway (Ind) 43
'Intercity 125' High-Speed Trains (BR) 356

IORE (Luossavaara Kirunvaara AB) 319, 422–3
IR see Indian Railways
Iran 193, 345, 425
Iraq State Railways 212
Ireland 48, 161, 207, 295, 310, 357, 398, 425
Irish Rail 398
Irish Transport Company 295, 310, 357
'Iron Duke' Class (GWR) 25
Italian State Railways 310, 409
electric
1908-1928 86, 99, 107, 149
1934-1953 176, 207, 212–13, 271–2
1960-2000 307, 354, 357–8, 379, 421–2
steam 82, 84, 99, 114, 116, 121, 252, 284
Italy see Adriatic Network; Italian State Railways; Upper Italian Railways

Japan see Chugoku Railway; Imperial Japanese Railways; Japanese National Railways; Japanese Railways; Kyushu Railway; Nippon Railways
Japanese National Railways
diesel-hydraulic 328
electric 93, 300, 304, 323–4, 333–4, 349
Maglev 425–6
steam 53
Japanese Railways 55, 104, 193–4, 244
Jaroslav-Vologda-Archangel Railway (Rus) 55
JDZ see Yugoslavian Railways
'Jenny Lind' Type (L&B) 24
JNR see Japanese National Railways
John Bull (Camden & Amboy RR) 16–17
Jordan 261, 363
JR see Japanese Railways

Kaiserin Elisabeth Railway (Aut) 42
'King' Class (GWR) 7, 141
Kitson-Still 'diesel-steam' 208
KKStB see Imperial & Royal State Railway
'Klondyke' (GNR) 60
'Kodama' Train (JNR) 300
Korail 429
Korean Government Railways 114, 176
Korean National Railways 328, 346
KPEV see Royal Prussian Union Railways
Krauss-Maffei diesel-hydraulics (SP) 311, 315
KTX High-Speed Electric Train (Korail) 429
Kyushu Railway (Jap) 392

L-9202 Variable-Gauge (Spa) 434–5
L Class (IVSR) 43
Lake Shore & Michigan Southern Railway (USA) 74–5
Lancashire & Yorkshire Railway (GB) 48, 76
Lancaster (P&C) 18, 19
Landwührden (OSR) 35
Lartigue's monorail (Listowel & Ballybunion Ry) 48
'Leader' (BR) 248, 295
Lehigh & Mahanoy Railroad (USA) 34–5
Liège & Namur Railway (Bel) 23
Limmat (Northern Ry (Swi)) 26
Lion (L&MR) 20
Listowel & Ballybunion Railway (Ire) 48
'Little Joe' (various r/r) 250
Liverpool & Manchester Railway (GB) 11, 14–15, 19, 20
L&MR see Liverpool & Manchester Railway
LMS see London, Midland & Scottish Railway
LNER see London & North Eastern Railway
LNWR see London & North Western Railway
Locomotion No.1 (S&D) 11, 12–13, 16
Lokalbahn AG (München) (Ger) 78
London, Brighton & South Coast Railway (GB) 38, 98
London, Midland & Scottish Railway (GB) 185–6, 202, 243
steam 128, 132, 142, 170, 173, 183, 185
London & Birmingham Railway (GB) 19
London & Brighton Railway 24
London & North Eastern Railway (GB) 118, 156, 184, 192–3, 224
London & North Western Railway (GB) 22, 27, 28, 29–30, 39, 43, 49

London & South Western Railway (GB) 61
Long Island Railroad (USA) 320, 411
'Lord Nelson' Class (SR) 137, 155
Lovett Eames (P&RR) 44
LRC (VIA) 370
Lübeck-Büchen Railway (Ger) 181
Luossavaara Kirunavaara AB (Swe) 319, 422–3
Luxembourg Railways 414, 429
'Lyntog' Train (DSB) 181

M-630 (CPR) 339
M-640 (CPR) 341
M-10000 Train (UP) 178
Madagascar Railways 86, 161
Madrid-Zaragoza-Alicante Railway (Spa) 29, 30
MaK G2000BB (various operators) 420, 432
Malayan Railways 202
Mallet (B&O) 77
Mallet Compound (EST) 85
Mallet (J-V-AR) 55
Mallet (SZE) 51
Mallet Type (Madagascar Ry) 86
Mallet Type R441 (Eritrean Ry) 168
Manhattan Railway (USA) 46
Mariazellerbahn (Aut) 88
MAT '64 (NS) 324
MÀV see Hungarian State Railways
Mendip Rail (GB) 378
'Merchant Navy' Class (SR) 217–18, 223
METRA (USA) 390
'Metroliner' (PRR) 336
Metropolitan Railway (GB) 34, 78, 119
Mexico 55, 62, 71, 93, 237
'Micheline' Railcar (EST) 160–1
Midland Railway (GB) 32, 64, 132
MIKA 1 Class (Korean Government Ry) 114
'Mikado' (Nippon Ry) 59
Milwaukee Railroad (USA) 235–6
Ministry of Supply (GB) 230
Missouri Pacific Railroad (USA) 124–5
MK5000C (SP) 398
MLU-14 (Bangladesh Railways) 339
MLX01 'Maglev' Prototype Train (JNR) 425–6
Mohawk & Hudson Railroad (USA) 17
Morocco 300, 358, 392
Moscow & St Petersburg Railway (Rus) 23
MPS4 (PRR) 109

National Railways Department (Bra) 246
NER see North-East Railway (Swi); North Eastern Railway (GB)
Netherlands Railways
diesel-electric 272, 279–80, 294, 382–3
electric 244, 255, 324, 354, 366, 387, 398, 409
steam 93, 152, 157, 233–4
New Haven Railroad (USA) 162, 213, 287, 292
New Jersey Transit (USA) 429–30
New South Wales Government Railway (Aus) 302
steam 41, 46, 51, 56–7, 72, 130, 227–8, 262–3
New York, Chicago & St Louis Railroad (USA) 177
New York Central & Hudson River Railroad (USA) 54
New York Central Railroad (USA) 76–7, 145, 171, 203–4, 229, 234–5
New Zealand Railways
diesel-electric 280, 285–6, 335, 346
electric 124, 153, 264, 334, 371, 383
steam 41, 50, 68–9, 109, 165
NHR see New Haven Railroad
Nigeria 132, 244
93 Class (NSWGR) 41
Nippon Railways (Jap) 59
No.1 (GN) 31
No.1 (GNR) 36–7
No.101 (Smyrna-Kassaba & Extension Ry) 101
No.148 (R-VR) 34
No.999 (New York Central & Hudson River RR) 54
No.9000 (CN) 146
No.10000 (LMS) 243
No.10000 (LNER) 156
No.18000 (BR) 248
NORD see Northern Railway (Fra)

Norfolk & Western Railway (USA) 189, 219, 327
Norris locomotive (B&O) 19
North-East Railway (Swi) 28
North Eastern Railway (GB) 106, 119, 120
North Shore 'Electro-Liner' (Chicago, North Shore & Milwaukee RR) 221
North-West Trains (GB) 420
'Northern' Class S1 (GN) 154
Northern Ireland Railways (GB) 376, 398
Northern Pacific Railroad (USA) 124, 125, 158, 195
Northern Railway (Fra) 21, 32, 36, 47, 63, 123, 160
Northern Railway (Spa) 42
Northern Railway (Swi) 26
Norwegian State Railways
  diesel-electric 363, 405–6
  electric 335, 405, 414
  steam 80, 90, 110, 117, 186
Nos.153-7 (Donna Teresa Christina Ry) 216
NS see Netherlands Railways
NSB see Norwegian State Railways
NSWGR see New South Wales Government Railway
Nüremberg-Fürth Railway (Ger) 18
NYC see New York Central Railroad
NZR see New Zealand Railways

ÖBB see Austrian Federal Railways
Odin Class (Zealand Ry) 24
Oldenburg State Railways (Ger) 35
Ottoman-Anatolian Railway (Tur) 95
'Outrance' Class 2 (NORD) 36

P1 'Triplex' locomotive (Erie RR) 107–8
PA/PB (various r/r) 240
Paris-Lyon-Mediterranean Railway (Fra) 28, 61, 97, 131, 198
Paris-Orleans Railway (Fra) 39, 69, 84, 136, 163, 168
Paris-Rouen Railway (Fra) 22
Paris-Strasbourg Railway (Fra) 23
'Patentee' Class (L&MR) 15, 18, 21
'Pendolino' Class 390 (VT) 424–5
'Pendolino' (VR) 431
Pennsylvania Railroad (USA) 91, 109, 177–8, 236, 336
  steam
    1876-1914 35, 63, 91, 108
    1923-1944 108, 125, 158, 209, 227, 231
Peru 187, 290
Philadelphia, Germanstown & Norristown Railroad (USA) 20
Philadelphia & Columbia Railroad (USA) 18, 19
Philadelphia & Reading Railroad (USA) 22, 23, 25, 28, 44, 59, 192
Philadelphia (P&RR) 23
Piraeus-Athens-Peleponnesus Railway (Gre) 92
PKP see Polish State Railways
Plan MP (NS) 324
Plan Y0 'Sprinter' (NS) 354
'Planet' Class (L&MR) 15, 16, 19
Plant System (USA) 69
PLM see Paris-Lyon-Mediterranean Railway
PO see Paris-Orleans Railway
Polish State Railways
  electric 325, 344, 376, 414
  steam 122, 199, 239, 256, 262, 273
Portuguese Railways 93, 133, 244–5, 311, 352, 395
'Prairie' Type (Lake Shore & Michigan Southern Ry) 75–6
'Precedent' Class (LNWR) 39
'Princess of Wales' (Midland Ry) 64
'Princess Royal' Class (LMS) 170
'Problem' Class (LNWR) 29–30
PRR see Pennsylvania Railroad
P&RR see Philadelphia & Reading Railroad
"Puffing Billy" (GB) 12

Q1 (SR) 223
Queensland Railways (Aus) 241, 377, 397, 423, 432

RAe 2/4 Railcar 'Rote Pfeil' (SBB) 188
railways, early history 6–7, 11
Railways of the People's Republic (Chi) 288, 296
RBDe 560 NPZ Train (SBB) 375
Re 6/6 (SBB) 347
RENFE see Spanish National Railways
RFIRT see Rio Turbio Industrial Railway
Rhaetian Railway (Swi) 134
Rhodesian Railways 138, 249
Rio Turbio Industrial Railway (Arg) 316, 366
'River' Class (Nigerian Ry) 244
Robert Stephenson & Co. 11, 12, 13, 14, 15, 16, 28
Rock Island Railroad (USA) 221
Rocket (L&MR) 11, 14, 15, 24
Romanian Railways 194, 207, 304, 325
Royal Bavarian State Railways (Ger) 40, 85
Royal George (S&D) 13
Royal Mail (GB) 400
Royal Prussian Union Railways (Ger) 104, 106
  steam 53, 63, 70, 76, 81, 97, 103, 118
'Royal Scot' Class (LMS) 142
Royal Siamese Railways (Thai) 69, 162, 224–5
RS-1 (Rock Island RR) 221
RS-2/RS-3 (various r/r) 237, 238, 244
RS-3 (Estrado de Ferro Central do Brazil) 263
RS-18 (various r/r) 287
RSR see Russian State Railways
RTG Gas Turbine Train (SNCF) 345
Ruse-Varna Railway (Bul) 34
Russia see Jaroslav-Vologda-Archangel Railway; Moscow & St Petersburg Railway; Russian Railways; Russian State Railways; Soviet State Railways
Russian Railways 410, 411
Russian State Railways 74, 94, 100, 110

S-Motor 1-Do-1 (NYC) 76–7
S1 'Niagara' Class (NYC) 234–5
S-2 Type (various r/r) 214
Sacramento Valley Railroad (USA) 27
'Saint' Class (GWR) 71
St Pierre (Paris-Rouen Ry) 22
'Santa Fe' Class (AT&SF) 75, 77
Santa Fe Railroad (USA) 301, 336, 341, 380, 388, 431–2
SAR see South African Railways; South Australia Railways
SATA 1 Class (Korean Government Ry) 176
Savannah Florida & Western Railway (USA) 69
SBB see Swiss Federal Railways
Schienenbus (BTR) 164
'Schools' Class (SR) 155–6
Schweizerische Südostbahn (Swi) 379
S&D see Stockton & Darlington Railway
SD7/SD9 (SP) 267
SD24 (various r/r) 301, 305
SD39 (various r/r) 337
SD40 (various r/r) 329, 330
SD45 (various r/r) 327
SD45T-2 (SP) 347
SD60M (various r/r) 386
SD70 M-2 (Florida East Coast RR) 435
SD70MAC (Burlington Northern) 395
SD80MAC (Con) 402
SD701 (CN) 401
Serbian, Croatian & Slovenian Railways 124
Serbian State Railways 100
Series 2 (Rio Turbio Industrial Ry) 316
Series 60 (Lübeck-Büchen Ry) 181
Series 61 (DRG) 206
Series 282 (RENFE) 311
Series 310 (KKSTB) 91–2
Series 1082 (ÖBB) 159
Series C4/5 (SBB) 76
Series E.10 (DB) 255
Series E.91 (KPEV) 106
Series EB 3/5 (SBB) 94
Seven-Car Train (Moroccan Ry) 300
Shay type locomotive (USA) 45
Shinkansen Electric High-Speed Trains (JNR) 323–4, 362, 417

SJ see Swedish State Railways
Skoda 27E (CSD) 373
Smyrna-Kassaba & Extension Railway (Tur) 101
SNCB see Belgian National Railways
SNCF see French National Railways
Södermanland Mainland Railway (Swe) 101
Sorocabana Railway (Bra) 228
South Africa see Cape Government Railways; South African Railways; Spoornet
South African Railways
  electric 281, 286, 350, 361, 376
  steam
    1925-1938 133, 153, 157, 187, 203
    1939-1981 208, 274–5, 280–1, 316, 366–7
South Australia Railways 47, 228, 246
South Manchuria Railway (Chi) 180–1
Southern Pacific Railroad (USA)
  diesel-electric 267, 327, 347, 380, 398
  diesel-hydraulic 311
  steam 150, 158, 201, 204
Southern Railway (Aut) 96, 101
Southern Railway (GB) 137, 152, 155–6, 164–5, 198–9, 217–18, 218, 223
Southern Railway of Peru 290
Soviet State Railways
  diesel-electric 127, 266, 300–1, 307, 325
  diesel-hydraulic 315
  electric 166, 301, 311, 319, 352
  steam
    1931-1938 162, 171, 177, 203
    1939-1954 208, 234, 266, 273–4, 280
SP see Southern Pacific Railroad
Spain see Central of Aragón Railway; Madrid-Zaragoza-Alicante Railway; Northern Railway (Spa); Spanish National Railways; Tarragona-Barcelona & France Railway
Spanish National Railways
  diesel-hydraulic 316
  electric
    1952-1980 265, 291, 331, 363
    1982-2006 371–2, 389, 393, 431, 434–5
  steam 224, 275, 290–1, 311
Spoornet (SA) 434
SR see Southern Railway (GB)
Sri Lanka 282, 422
SS see State Railways (DEI)
State Belt Railroad of California (USA) 144
State Railways (Arg) 116
State Railways (DEI) 44, 53, 65, 98, 111, 120
State Railways (Fra) 111, 169, 198
Steam-Diesel Locomotive (SZD) 208
Steam Railcar (GWR) 74
Steinbruck (Vienna-Gloggnitz Ry) 26
Stockton & Darlington Railway (GB) 11, 12–13, 24
Susquehanna (P&RR) 28
SVT 877 'Fliegende Hamburger' (DRG) 164, 191
SW1500 (various r/r) 330
Sweden see Luossavaara Kirunavaara AB; Swedish State Railways
Swedish State Railways
  electric
    1914-1975 107, 133, 276, 319, 355
    1984-2000 373, 385, 389, 416
  steam 35, 52, 72, 85, 88, 107
Swiss Central Railway 51
Swiss Federal Railways
  diesel 256
  diesel-electric 294
  electric
    1918-1932 114, 116, 139, 153, 166
    1935-1987 188, 208, 231, 265, 347, 375, 379
    1990-1994 387, 389–90
  gas turbine electric 229
  steam 76, 94, 105
Switzerland see Berne-Lötschberg-Simplon Railway; North-East Railway; Northern Railway (Swi); Rhaetian Railway; Schweizerische Südostbahn; Swiss Central Railway; Swiss Federal Railways
SZD see Soviet State Railways

T 1 Duplex-driver (PRR) 227, 231
Talgo trains (RENFE) 316, 363, 393, 434–5

Tarragona-Barcelona & France Railway (Spa) 30
Tasmanian Railways (Aus) 87, 345
TCDD *see* Turkish State Railways
TEM18 (Russian Ry) 411
TEP-60 (SZD) 307
TEP 150 (Ukr) 435
'Terrier' (London, Brighton & South Coast Ry) 38
Teutonic (LNWR) 49
TG400/TG300 (SZD) 315
TGV (SNCF) 362
TGV Third Generation 'Duplex' (SNCF) 399–400
Thailand 69, 162, 224–5
'Thalys' (Fra/Bel/Ger/Ned) 404–5
'Thatcher Perkins' Class (B&O) 33
Trains à Grande Vitesse see TGV
'Trans Europ Express' (NS/SBB) 294
'Transrapid' Magnetic Levitation Train (Chi) 426–7
Tunisian National Railways 364
Turbomotive (LMS) 185
'Turf Burner' (CIE) 295
Turkey *see* Ottoman-Anatolian Railway; Smyrna-
    Kassaba & Extension Railway; Turkish State
    Railways
Turkish State Railways 113, 200, 276, 287, 377,
    380, 393
Type 1 (EB) 33
Type 2 (BR) 298
Type 10 (EB) 89
Type 36 (EB) 89
Type 97 (DRG) 215
Type 5500 (JR) 55
Type 9600 (JR) 104
Type EP-2 'Bi-Polar' (Chicago, Milwaukee & Saint
    Paul RR) 115
Type S9 (KPEV) 76

U20C (Jordanian Aqaba Ry) 363
U25B (various r/r) 308, 330

U30B (various r/r) 330
U30C (various r/r) 332
U50C (UP) 320
'Union' Class (Union RR) 194
Union Pacific Railroad (USA) 178, 245
    diesel-electric 301, 305, 320, 340, 380–1, 403
    steam 139, 195, 209, 220
Union Railroad (USA) 194
United States 82–3, 178, 245, 431–2
    diesel-electric
    1925-1941 135, 179, 191, 196, 210–11, 213–14,
    221
    1945-1953 235–6, 237–9, 240, 250, 257, 267,
    276
    1956-1965 292, 301, 305, 308, 316, 319–20,
    327
    1966-1972 329–30, 332, 336–7, 340, 341, 347
    1976-1985 312, 359–60, 361, 364–5, 375, 377
    1987-1994 380–1, 386, 388, 390, 395–6, 398–9
    1995-2006 402–3, 411, 430–1, 435
    diesel-hydraulic 251, 311
    electric
    1896-1919 57, 76–7, 91, 108–9, 115
    1925-1949 135, 162, 177–8, 221, 250
    1955-1998 287, 291–2, 336, 353, 361, 414
    1999-2006 417–18, 429–30
    steam
    1812-1850 11, 15–18, 19–20, 22, 23, 25, 27
    1855-1885 28–9, 31, 33, 34–5, 44–5, 46
    1891-1904 51, 54, 56, 59, 69, 75–6, 77
    1910-1925 91, 107–8, 124–5, 134
    1926-1930 139, 144–5, 150, 154, 158
    1933-1937 171, 177, 188–9, 194–5, 200–1
    1938-1941 203–4, 209–10, 219–20
    1942-1945 225–7, 229, 231–2, 234–5
United States Army Transportation Corps 219,
    225–7
UP *see* Union Pacific Railroad

Upper Italian Railways 46
Uruguay 90, 117, 277

VIA Rail (Can) 8, 370, 396
Victorian Railways (Aus) 117, 146, 150–1, 215,
    257–8, 302, 338, 372
Vienna-Gloggnitz Railway (Aut) 26
Virgin Trains (GB) 421, 424–5
Virginian Railway (US) 107, 135, 189, 291–2
'Vittorio-Emanuele' Class (Upper Italian Ry) 46
VL-19 Series (SZD) 166
Voith Maxima (Ger) 432–3
Volk's Electric Railway Railcar 45
Vossloh Euro 4000 (Ger) 433–4
VR *see* Finnish State Railways; Victorian Railways;
    Virginian Railway

WAGR *see* Western Australian Government Railways
WAP-5 (IR) 402
WDG2 (IR) 401
WDM2 Class (IR) 315
Western & Atlantic Railroad (USA) 28–9
Western Australian Government Railways 51, 52,
    258, 276, 327, 330
Western Railway (Ind) 79
Westrail (AUS) 338
WL86 (Russian Ry) 410

X-3800 Diesel Railcars (SNCF) 254

Yugoslavia 62, 69, 113, 124, 213, 337, 355, 367
Yugoslavian Railways 337, 355, 367

Zealand Railway (Den) 24
Zephyr (BR) 178, 179, 191, 251

PICTURE CREDITS

Angel Trains: 433(b); **Art-Tech/MARS**: 68(b), 78, 88(t), 95(t), 130(b), 133(b), 165(b), 176, 181, 207(b), 271, 286(t), 317, 322, 331(t), 333(b), 335(b), 345, 349(b), 354(b), 358(t); **P. Austin**: 193(t); **A. Barnes**: 14(t); **Stephen Baxter**: 269; **Paul Bigland**: 96, 127, 255(t), 279, 290, 304(t), 314, 318(b), 343(both), 346(t), 391(b), 404(t), 412, 422(t); **Tony Bond**: 12(b); **Matthew J. Brown**: 432; **Peter Burgess**: 21(b); **Alan Crotty**: 61(b); **Cody Images**: 16(b), 29(t), 31(b), 34(t), 118, 178, 211(b), 231(b); **E.J. Dyer**: 38(b); **Emap Active**: 14(b), 20, 32, 37(t), 39, 49(b), 50, 55, 58, 69, 71, 74(t), 84(b), 86, 89(t), 98(t), 99, 111(t), 114, 120, 122(t), 125, 131(both), 136, 137(b), 138(b), 147(b), 156(b), 173(b), 174(b), 180(t), 185, 186(t), 187, 202(b), 208(t), 219, 220, 222, 230, 233(t), 243(b), 248(b), 249(t), 259, 260(b), 277, 281, 285(b), 289, 293(b), 303(t), 306(t), 309(t), 366, 382(t), 384(t), 392, 413, 436(b), 438(b), 439(t); **M.J. Fox**: 152(t); **Getty Images**: 423(t) (Per-Anders Petterson), 429 (Chung Sung-Jun); **D. Gillis**: 437(t); **P. Girdlestone**: 157(b); **A. Guppy**: 417; **Mel Holley**: 199; **P. Howard**: 418(b); **N. Huxtable**: 205(b); **J. Hunt**: 116(t); **Ben Jones**: 139(t), 166, 169, 208(b), 268, 296(b), 297(t), 311, 323(t), 333(t), 342(b), 350(b), 353(b), 355(both), 375(b), 378(b), 381(b), 389, 438(t), 439(b); **Trevor Jones**: 273(t); **Miaow Miaow**: 427(t); **Milepost 92½**: 6, 7, 10, 13, 16(t), 17(b), 21(t), 22(both), 23, 24(all), 25(t), 26, 27(b), 29(m), 29(b), 30, 33(b), 34(b), 36, 37(b), 38(t), 40, 41, 42(both), 43, 44(t), 45, 46, 47, 48(both), 49(t), 51, 52, 53, 54(both), 56(both), 57, 59(b), 60, 61(t), 62, 63(both), 64(both), 65, 66, 67(t), 70, 72(both), 74(m), 74(b), 75, 76, 79, 80, 81(both), 82, 84(t), 85, 87(both), 88(b), 89(b), 90, 91, 92, 93, 95(b), 97(both), 98(b), 100(both), 101(both), 102, 103(both), 104(both), 105(both), 106, 107, 108, 109(b), 110, 111(b), 112(both), 113, 117, 119, 121, 122(b), 123, 124, 126, 128, 130(t), 132, 133(t), 134(b), 135(both), 138(t), 140(both), 141, 142(both), 143(both), 144(both), 145(both), 146, 147(t), 149(t), 150, 151, 152(b), 153, 155, 156(t), 159, 160(t), 162(t), 163(both), 164, 167, 168, 170, 171, 172, 173(t), 174(t), 175, 180(b), 182, 183, 184, 186(b), 188(both), 190, 195, 200(t), 201(t), 202(t), 203, 204(both), 205(t), 206, 207(t), 209(both), 211(t), 213(t), 214(b), 215, 216, 217, 223, 224, 225, 226(both), 228(t), 229(b), 231(t), 234, 235, 236(b), 237(t), 238(b), 240(t), 241(all), 242, 243(t), 244, 245(t), 246, 247(t), 249(t), 249(m), 252, 254(b), 255(b), 256, 257(b), 258(both), 260(t), 261(m), 261(b), 262(b), 264, 265, 266, 267, 270(both), 272, 274, 275, 276, 278, 280, 283, 284, 285(b), 286(b), 288, 291(t), 293(t), 296(t), 297(m), 297(b), 298, 299(both), 302(both), 303(b), 304(b), 305(b), 308(b), 309(b), 310, 315, 316(t), 320(t), 324(both), 326(t), 328(b), 330(b), 335(t), 338(both), 340(b), 344, 346(b), 350(t), 352(t), 353(t), 354(t), 358(b), 367, 368, 372(t), 373(t), 374(both), 375(t), 376(b), 377, 378(t), 378(m), 379, 381(m), 382(b), 383, 387(b), 391(t), 393, 394(t), 395(t), 399(t), 400, 401(t), 403, 404(b), 405(both), 406, 407(b), 408, 409, 411, 415, 416, 420(t), 421, 424, 426(b), 427(t), 441(both); **Millbrook House**: 139(b), 149(b), 157(t), 160(b), 161, 165(t), 198(both), 200(b), 201(b), 218, 228(b), 229(t), 232(t), 233(b), 236(t), 240(b), 247(b), 248(t), 254(t), 394(b); **G.W. Morrison**: 15; **New Jersey Transit**: 430(t) (Michael Rosenthal); **Les Nixon**: 436(t); **Robin Patrull**: 59(t); **Popperfoto**: 12(t); **P.J. Robinson**: 194; **David Ross**: 18(t), 27(t), 31(t), 33(t), 44(b), 77(b), 137(t), 154, 257(t), 291(b), 320(b); **E.H. Sawford**: 261(t); **R. Shenton**: 197(t); **Siemens**: 428; **Peter J.C. Skelton**: 73; **Brian Solomon**: 8, 9, 17(t), 25(b), 35, 77(t), 83, 109(t), 115, 134(t), 162(b), 177, 179, 189, 192, 193(b), 196, 197(t), 210(both), 213(b), 214(t), 221, 227, 232(b), 238(t), 239(all), 245(b), 250(all), 262(t), 282, 287(both), 292(both), 295, 300, 301(b), 304(m), 305(t), 306(b), 308(t), 312, 316(b), 318(t), 319(b), 321(b), 323(b), 327, 328(b), 329(both), 330(t), 332, 334, 336, 337, 340(t), 347, 348, 349(t), 356, 357, 359, 360, 362, 363, 364(b), 370, 371(t), 372(b), 373(b), 376(t), 380, 381(t), 384(b), 385, 386(both), 388(both), 390, 395(b), 396, 398, 399(b), 401(b), 402, 410, 414(b), 418(t), 419, 422(b), 426(t), 430(t), 435(b); **Richard Jay Solomon**: 237(b), 251, 294; **J.P. Storer**: 440(b); **Talco**: 434(both), 435(t); **Gordon Thomas**: 18(b), 158; **Mervyn Turvey**: 19; **Voith**: 433(t); **S. Widdowson**: 331(m); **P. Wormald**: 273(b), 301(t), 305(t), 307(both), 319(t), 321(t), 324(both), 326(b), 331(b), 339, 341, 342(t), 351, 352(b), 361, 364(t), 365, 371(b), 375(m), 387(t), 397, 407(t), 414(t), 420(b), 423(b), 437(b), 440(t); **Ian Wright**: 94